SOCIAL WORK

An introduction to contemporary practice

SECOND EDITION

Professor Kate Wilson
University of Nottingham

Dr Gillian Ruch
University of Southampton

Mark Lymbery, Associate Professor
University of Nottingham

Professor Andrew Cooper
University of East London and the Tavistock Clinic, London

Longman
is an imprint of

Harlow, England • London • New York • Boston • San Francisco • Toronto
Sydney • Tokyo • Singapore • Hong Kong • Seoul • Taipei • New Delhi
Cape Town • Madrid • Mexico City • Amsterdam • Munich • Paris • Milan

Pearson Education Limited

Edinburgh Gate
Harlow
Essex CM20 2JE
England

and Associated Companies throughout the world

Visit us on the World Wide Web at:
www.pearsoned.co.uk

First published 2008
Second edition 2011

© Pearson Education Limited 2008, 2011

ISBN: 978-1-4082-4470-8

British Library Cataloguing-in-Publication Data
A catalogue record for this book is available from the British Library

Library of Congress Cataloging-in-Publication Data
Social work : an introduction to contemporary practice / Kate Wilson . . . [et al.]. --
2nd ed.
    p. cm.
Includes bibliographical references and index.
ISBN 978-1-4082-4470-8 (pbk.)
1. Social service.   2. Social case work.   I. Wilson, Kate, 1943-
HV40.S6175 2011
361.3--dc22

2011008490

10 9 8 7 6 5 4 3
15 14 13 12 11

Typeset in 9.5/12pt Minion by 35
Printed by Ashford Colour Press Ltd., Gosport

Brief contents

Contents

Contents

Contents

Contents

Contributors to this book

Contributory chapters to this book are written by:

Alison Brammer, Senior Lecturer, Keele University (Chapter 8, Law and social work)

Professor Saul Becker, University of Nottingham (Chapter 15, Informal family carers)

Professor Brian Littlechild, University of Hertfordshire, and **Professor Roger Smith**, De Montfort University (Chapter 18, Social work with young offenders)

Rachael Clawson, Development Manager, Centre for Social Work, University of Nottingham (Chapter 19, Social work with disabled children and adults)

Dr Ian Paylor, University of Lancaster (Chapter 21, Social work and drug use)

Dr Margaret Bell, University of York (section on domestic violence in Chapter 17, Social Work with Adults: policy and practice)

In addition, the publishers gratefully acknowledge the work of Gary Clapton from the University of Edinburgh for his considerable and generous input of a Scottish perspective across all chapters in the book, except for Chapter 8, Law and social work, where for this edition we particularly thank Janice West, previously of Glasgow Caledonian University, who kindly built on the work of Kathryn Cameron from the first edition. We would also like to thank Mary McColgan, of the University of Ulster, for providing a Northern Irish perspective across selected chapters.

Preface

Social work is a professional activity which takes place at the boundary of many different spheres of society: private and public life, the civil and judicial spheres, and the personal and political arenas. However, it is above all about relationships. We see at the heart of social work the provision of a relationship to help people (children, young people and adults) negotiate complex and painful transitions and decisions in their lives. Students will have been selected to train as social workers because they are seen to be people who are capable of making these relationships and who have the potential to develop the qualities which research and practice wisdom suggest people want from social workers – warmth, reliability, respect for other people, a straight and well-informed approach to difficult issues, and an ability to get things done. Our purpose in writing this book is to introduce students to the knowledge and skills which will enable them to develop and use these qualities effectively.

Our book, then, is based on the belief that relationships are at the heart of effective social work and that the essential and distinctive characteristic of social work is its focus on the individual *and* the social setting and context. By this we mean not only individual service users in their social settings but also social work practitioners in their practice contexts. So we have written this textbook with a particular emphasis both on the personal qualities and capacities which social workers need to bring to their practice and on the centrality of social work methods – the practical and sophisticated tools with which social workers can help bring about change and improvements in the lives of service users.

More specifically, the book is intended to provide students, practitioners (both newly qualified and experienced), managers and trainers with a clear and comprehensive introduction to contemporary social work in the UK. It provides a logical path through the range of activities which social workers undertake and also explores the key areas of knowledge, themes and critical debates which make up the complex, challenging but, as we hope to show, endlessly absorbing experience of professional social work practice. So our text aims to be:

Comprehensive in its coverage of key areas of theories, knowledge and understanding which underpin contemporary practice (incorporating national differences)

Conceptual in the way in which it helps readers make sense of modern social work

Critical and academically rigorous in how it draws on theories, concepts and research evidence to make sense of social work practice

Practical in guiding readers in developing their skills in undertaking key social work roles and activities, and in working with different user groups

Companionable in the way in which ideas are presented and practice issues and dilemmas which face the qualifying social worker are described and related to day-to-day practice.

Who should use this book?

The book is intended to provide an introduction to social work for all students on social work qualifying training programmes in the UK, whether they be following undergraduate or postgraduate courses of study. Although it is specifically organised to address the learning needs outlined in the Department of Health's prescribed curriculum for trainee social workers, it will also be useful for newly qualified practitioners and practice assessors, and will appeal to students undertaking a range of social and health care courses in further education, people considering a career in social work or care, and health and other professionals seeking to understand the nuances, dilemmas and requirements of the social work role. Experienced and qualified social workers, especially those contributing to practice learning, will also find the book useful as a source book for consultation, teaching, revision and, we hope, general interest.

How to use the book

The book begins with three key 'scene-setting' chapters which describe the distinctive characteristics of relationship based social work, the ways in which policy and the organisational context in which social workers operate impact on the professional social worker's day-to-day experiences and key challenges for social work in the twenty-first century. The remainder of the book is divided into three sections:

The first, **Understanding social work**, focuses on the history of social work, and on the subject areas which form key parts of the knowledge base of social work, namely theoretical approaches, law, human development through the lifespan and research evidence and methods.

The second, **Practice skills and practice theories**, focuses on the key practice roles and tasks of social work, namely assessment, communication, intervention, and working with service users, with carers and with other professionals.

The third, **Social work in relationship-based practice with user groups**, focuses on the more specialist knowledge and practice skills required for social work practice with a range of different service users.

How you will use the book is, however, very much a matter for you personally. It seems to us highly unlikely that you will read the book from cover to cover: in thinking how to guide you through the book we liked the advice given by Martin Davies in the introduction to his *Companion to Social Work* (which we refer to from time to time in our book), quoting a teacher of his, that he should remember that an academic book 'isn't a detective novel. There is no rule that says you must start at the beginning and read all the way through to the end'. Indeed, he adds, 'there is a great deal to be said for reading the last few pages first. That way you can often save yourself a lot of unnecessary time and effort' (2002: 2).

We probably would not, in fact, recommend reading the last chapter of our book first, as it might not make a great deal of sense without the earlier parts, but we do recognise that you may want to skim through the contents list and go directly to those chapters which particularly interest you or which are on topics which you are studying at any given moment. However, your pathway through the book will, we hope, be helped by certain distinctive and consistent features in the way in which it is organised:

Chapter structure
All the chapters are structured along the same lines, beginning with an introduction, learning objectives, an identification of the National Occupational Standards addressed in the chapter, a case study with a question for you as the reader, followed by the main body of the chapter and concluding with key learning points, useful websites, further reading and an activity.

Case examples
Every chapter includes a case example suitable for class discussion, and a number of shorter case examples and/or vignettes are used throughout each chapter to illustrate the text and to help you think through how the concepts and theories are imbedded in practice.

Features to help your learning
Boxed examples are introduced throughout the chapters, which invite you to reflect on the implications for you personally of what is being discussed, or which highlight particular points or dilemmas which may warrant further exploration, or summarise specific pieces of research or relevant discussion material.

Study activities
These are activities which support the learning objectives of the chapter. They can be done individually or in groups.

Selected further reading
Every chapter ends with a short list of further reading which takes further the topics discussed in the chapter, or highlights some important related issues or topics which for reasons of space have not been addressed in the chapter itself. A note as to the content of the further reading is also given.

Useful websites
A short list of relevant websites is given at the end of each chapter.

Glossary
A selective glossary is included at the end of the book, which gives brief definitions or summaries of key terms from each of the chapters.

Companion website
For additional chapter-by-chapter cases and topic-organised, clickable links into additional media resources, including those produced by IRISS, visit **www.pearsoned.co.uk/wilsonruch**

Guided tour

Navigation and setting the scene

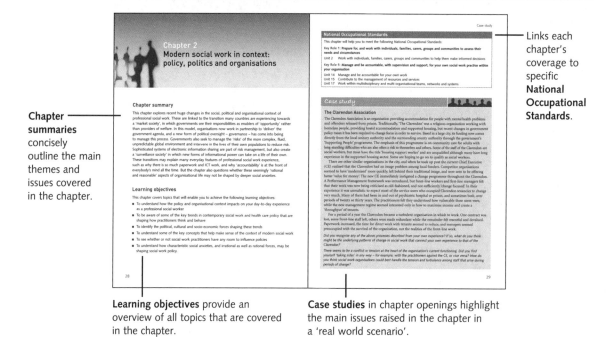

Chapter summaries concisely outline the main themes and issues covered in the chapter.

Links each chapter's coverage to specific **National Occupational Standards**.

Learning objectives provide an overview of all topics that are covered in the chapter.

Case studies in chapter openings highlight the main issues raised in the chapter in a 'real world scenario'.

Aiding your understanding

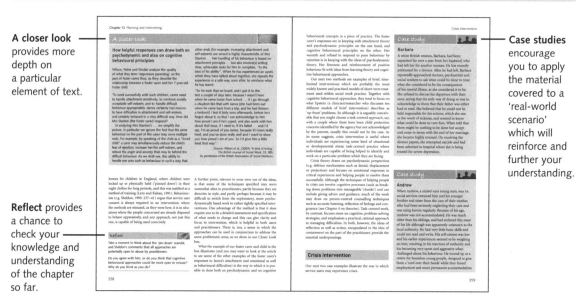

A closer look provides more depth on a particular element of text.

Reflect provides a chance to check your knowledge and understanding of the chapter so far.

Case studies encourage you to apply the material covered to a 'real-world scenario' which will reinforce and further your understanding.

xvi

Professional tips provide practical guidance and advice for social work practice.

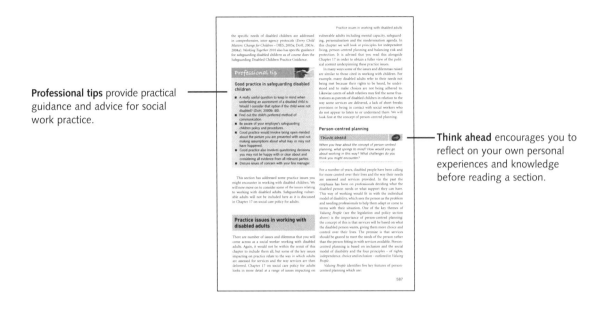

Think ahead encourages you to reflect on your own personal experiences and knowledge before reading a section.

End of chapter

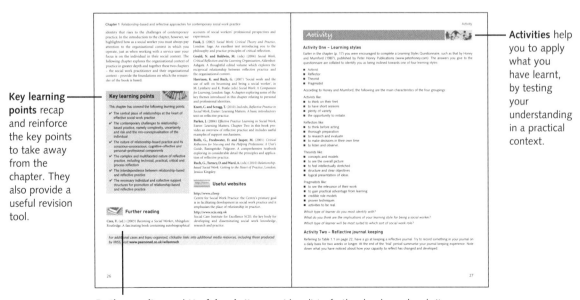

Key learning points recap and reinforce the key points to take away from the chapter. They also provide a useful revision tool.

Activities help you to apply what you have learnt, by testing your understanding in a practical context.

Further reading and **Useful websites** provide a list of other books and websites you may wish to explore to find out more about the areas discussed in the chapter.

Acknowledgements

This book draws on the experience and inspiration provided by many years of work with students, service users and colleagues in a wide range of institutions. We have written this book with the aim of better establishing relationship-based work at the heart of our profession. Over the years it is our own relationships with people which have nourished our commitment to this project, and we thank everyone who played a part in this.

We owe also a great deal to the sustaining enthusiasm and wisdom of our editor at Pearson Education, Andrew Taylor, who originally commissioned the book and has since its inception been unflagging in his support and encouragement. To him, our development editor, Steven Jackson, desk editor Christina Venditti and Professor Adrian James, who worked with us on the planning stages of the book and subsequently proved an invaluable critical friend in commenting on drafts, our grateful thanks.

Publisher's acknowledgements

The publishers and authors would like to thank the panel of academic reviewers whose constructive comments on the first edition helped shape this second. We would also like to thank all the students, whose enthusiastic response to the first edition helped motivate the team to tackle this revision.

We would also like to thank all contributors and authors, who again delivered an excellent manuscript. To the principal authors we again extend our gratitude for their commitment, enthusiasm and hard work towards the second edition. Special thanks once more to Kate Wilson, who has led the project admirably, despite more important calls upon her time and energies.

The Publisher would like to thank Kevin Smith (Kes) for his cartoons (Website – www.kescartoons.com) and Neil Ballantyne (freelance researcher and consultant, and visiting senior research fellow at the Glasgow School of Social Work) for his work developing the companion website for this second edition.

We are grateful to the following for permission to reproduce copyright material:

Cartoons

Cartoon 5.1 from Clare in the Community cartoon *The Guardian*, 01/01/2000 (Harry Venning); Cartoons 8.1, 9.1, 10.1, 10.2, 12.1, 14.1 from Cartoonist: Kevin Smith (Kes) www.kescartoons.com. The publisher would like to thank Kevin Smith (Kes) for the cartoons he drew for this edition. Website – www.kescartoons.com; Cartoon 11.1 from Clare in the Community cartoon *The Guardian*, 01/01/2000 (Harry Venning); Cartoons 21.1.1, 21.2.2 from Cartoonist: Kevin Smith (Kes) www.kescartoons.com

Figures

Figure 1.2 adapted from *Experiential Learning: Experience as the Source of Learning and Development* Prentice Hall (Kolb, D. A. 1987); Figure 1.5 adapted from 'Broken and twisted' – fig on p. 145, *Journal of Social Work Practice* 17(2), pp. 143–52 (Bower, M. 2003); Figure 2.1 from *Cleared by Andrew Cooper*; Figure 3.1 from *Rethinking Social Work* Addison Wesley Longman (Ife, J. 1997) p. 47; Figure 5.1 from *TOPSS (2002)The National Occupational Standards for Social Work*, p. 12; Figure 7.4 redrawn from illustration designed by Dr. Pam Zinkin; Figure 7.6 adapted from *A child's journey through placement*. BAAF (Fahlberg, V. 1994); Figure 7.7 adapted from *Child Development for Child Care and Protection Workers* Jessica Kingsley Publishers (Daniel, B., Wassell, S. and Gilligan, R. 2000); Figure 9.1 adapted from Decision making in child protection: The use of theoretical, empirical and procedural knowledge by novices and experts and implications for fieldwork placement, *British Journal of Social Work* Vol. 29, No. 1, pp. 142–69 (Drury-Hudson, J. 1999); Figure 9.2 adapted from *Understanding Research for Social Policy and Practice*, The Policy Press (Becker, S. and Bryman, A. (eds) 2004); Figure 10.1 from *The Assessment Framework: critique and reformulation'* in Calder, M.C. *Assessment in Child Care: Using and Developing Frameworks for Practice* (Calder, M. and Hackett, S. 2003) Figure 11, page 35, reproduced by permission from Calder, M. C. and Hackett, S. eds, *Assessment in Child Care*, Lyme Regis, Russell House Publishing; Figure 10.2 adapted from *The Process of Social Work: Assessment Planning, Intervention and Review'*, in *Social Work: A Companion to Learning* Sage (Lymbery, M. and Postle, K. (eds) 2007); Figure 10.3 from *'Ecological perspectives in assessing children and families'* *The Child's World Assessing Children in Need* Jessica Kingsley (Jack, G. – Howarth, J. (ed.) 2000) p. 54; Figure 11.1 from a presentation by Keith Williamson; Figure 12.2 from *A child's journey through placement*, BAAF (Fahlberg, V. 1994) p. 331; Figure 15.1 from *Framework for the Assessment of Children in Need and Their Families* Department of Health (2000); Figure 20.0 from Appendix B, http://www.bis.gov.uk/assets/biscore/corporate/migratedD/ec_group/116-08-FO_b

Tables

Table 5.1 adapted from *Social Policy: A Critical Introduction*, Polity Press (Williams, F. 1989) pp. 16–17; Table 2.1; Table 5.4 adapted from *'An introduction to Social Work Theory'* Ashgate (Howe, D. 1987) p. 47; Table 5.5 adapted from *Critical Reflection for Nursing and the Helping Professions: A Users Guide* Figure 1.3 p. 11, Palgrave (Rolfe, G., Freshwater, D. and Jasper, M. 2001); Table 7.2 adapted from *'Chart Illustrating the developmental progress of infants and young children'* HMSO (Sheridan, M. 1975) No. 102; Table 8.1 adapted from *Social Work Law* 2nd (Brammer, A. 2006); Table 8.3 from *Social Work Law*, 3rd edition, Pearson Education (Brammer, A. 2010); Table 8.4 adapted from *Social Work Law* 3rd edition, Pearson Education (Brammer, A. 2010); Table 14.1 from *Census 2001 data, London: ONS*, compiled by Carers UK in Carers UK (2003) *'Census 2001 and carers – Results from around the UK'*, Carers UK (2003); Table 14.2 from Global perspectives on children as caregivers: Research and policy on 'young carers' in the UK, Australia, the United States and sub-Saharan Afric, *Global Social Policy*, 7 (1): 23–50 (Becker, S. 2007); Table 14.3 calculated from data in ONS (2003) Census 2001, London: ONS, Crown Copyright material is reproduced with the permission of the Controller, Office of Public Sector Information (OPSI); Table 15.1 from *Figures taken from Department for Education and Skills (2006) Statistics of education: referrals, assessments and children and young people on child protection registers: year ending 31 March 2006*, London: The Stationery Office, Crown Copyright material is reproduced with permission under the terms of the Click-Use License; Tables 15.1, 15.2, 15.3 from www.nspcc.org.uk/inform, all figures credited to NSPCC are Government Statistics. For the latest figures please see the NSPCC website; Table 20.1 from *Mental Health Social Work: Evidence Based Practice, Abingdon* Routledge (Pritchard, C. 2006) 112–113

Text

Example 1. from *Extract from TOPPS (2002) The National Occupational Standards for Social Work*; Example 1.1 from *Extract from TOPPS (2002) The National Occupational Standards for Social Work, Unit titles – Key Role 1, 2 and 3* (2002), Skills for Care & Development have kindly given permission for reproduction of the National Occupational Standards for Social Work within this publication. See: www.skillsforcare.org.uk, www.cwdcouncil.org.uk, www.sssc.uk.com, www.ccwales.org.uk, www.niscc.info; Example 2 extract from *TOPSS (2002) The National Occupational Standards for Social Work, Unit titles – Key Role 1 and Key Role 5*; Article 2 extract from: 'We can have any child in the world in this house, except our son' *Daily Telegraph*, 03/08/2004, copyright © Telegraph Media Group Limited; Quote 5 extract from Cabinet Office (2006) Reaching Out: An Action Plan on Social Exclusion, p. 3; Extract 5 from 'Black students' experience on social work courses: accentuating the positives *British Journal of Social Work*, 26 (1), 1–16 (Aymer, C. and Bryan, A. 1996); Example 6 extracts from *The National Occupational Standards for Social Work – Key Role 5, Unit 14 and Unit 15, Key Role 6 Unit 18–Unit 21*; Extract 6 from 'The personal–professional interface in learning: Towards reflective education', *Journal of Interprofessional Care*, 6 (3), 261–71 (Ash, E. 1992), Original source of publication and 'Taylor & Francis Ltd., http://www.informaworld.com'; Example 7 extracts from *The National Occupational Standards for Social Work – Key Role 1, Unit 1–Unit 3, Key Role 2 Units 5, 6, 9, Key Role 5 Unit 14, Key Role 6 Unit 18*; Poetry 7 from *Hot Earth Cold Earth*, Bloodaxe (1995), James Berry, Hot Earth, Cold Earth (Bloodaxe Books, 1995); Extract 7 from *Consequences and indicators of child abuse in The Child Protection Handbook* 3rd, Elsevier (Hankes, H. and Stratton, P.; Wilson, K. and James, A. (eds) 2007) 91; General Displayed Text 7 extract from 'The social readjustment rating scale', (First ten items from list of 43) *Journal of Psychosomatic Research*, 11, 2, pp. 213–18 (Holmes, T. H. & Rahe, R. H. 1967); Poetry 7 from *Collected Poems*, Carcanet Press Ltd (Anne Ridler 1994), Anne Ridler, Collected Poems, Carcanet Press Ltd.,

1994; Example 8 from *The National Occupational Standards for Social Work – Key Role 1 – Key Role 6*; Box 8 from *Social Work Law* 3rd, Pearson Education (Brammer, A. 2010) p. 274; Example 9 from *The National Occupational Standards for Social Work – Key Role 6, Unit 18–Unit 21*; Extract 9 from *University of York Social Work Student Dissertation Handbook*, adapted from the University of York Social Work student dissertation handbook and acknowledged with gratitude; Example 10 from *The National Occupational Standards for Social Work – Key Role 1, Units 1–3, Key Role 2, Units 4, 5, 6, 7, 9, Key Role 3, Units 10 and 11, Key Role 4 Units 12 and 13*; Quote 10 from Professor Olive Stevenson Launch of Center for Social Work Practice. Held at the Tavistock Clinic, 28/04/2006; Box 10 from *(2000) Social Work and Social Problems: Working towards Social inclusion and Social Change – Summary of the Key Characteristics of the Exchange Model'* p. 152. Macmillan (Smale, G., Tuson, G. and Stratham, D. 2000) p. 152; Example 11 from *The National Occupational Standards for Social Work – Key Role 1, Units 1–3, Key Role 2, Units 4, 5, 6, 9, Key Role 3, Unit 10*; Example 12 from *The National Occupational Standards for Social Work – Key Role 1, Units 1–3, Key Role 2, Units 4, 5, 6, 7, 8, 9, Key Role 3, Units 10 and 11, Key Role 4 Units 12 and 13, Key Role 5 Units 14 and 17, Key Role 6 Units 18, 19, 20, 21*; Extract 12 Abridged extract from 'A kind of loving: a model of effective foster care', *British Journal of Social Work, January*, p. 995 33, 991–1003 (Wilson, K., Petrie, S. and Sinclair, I. 2004); Extract 12 from Unpublished Handout by John Corden; Extract 13 from *The National Occupational Standards for Social Work – Key Role 2, Unit 6, Key Role 3, Unit 11, Key Role 5, Units 14 and 17, Key Role 6 Units 18, 19, 20, 21* Skills for Care & Development; Extract 14 from *The National Occupational Standards for Social Work – Key Role 1, Unit 1, Key Role 2, Unit 8, Key Role 3, Units 10 and 11, and 17, Key Role 6 Units 18, 19, 20, 21*; Extract 14 from Advocacy in Action/ Suresearch Collective, *'Editorial', Social Work Education* 25 (4), 315–18 (Cairney, J. et al. 2006); Extract 14 from 'Partnership Working: Service Users and Social Workers Learning and Working Together', in *Social Work: A Companion for Learning* Sage (Beresford, P., Branfield, F., Lalani, M., Maslen, B., Sartori, A., Jenny, Maggie and Manny M. Lymbery and K. Postle (eds) 2007) p. 217; Extract 14 from 'Partnership Working: Service Users and Social Workers Learning and Working Together', in *Social Work: A Companion for Learning*, Sage (Beresford, P., Branfield, F., Lalani, M., Maslen, B., Sartori, A., – M. Lymbery and K. Postle (eds) 2007) pp. 218–19; Extract 14 from 'Partnership Working: Service Users and Social Workers Learning and Working Together', in *Social Work: A Companion for Learning*, Sage (Beresford, P., Branfield, F., Lalani, M., Maslen, B., Sartori, A. – M. Lymbery and K. Postle (eds) 2007) p. 223; Example 15 from *The National Occupational Standards for Social Work – Key Role 1, Units 1, 2, 3, Key Role 2, Units 4, 5, 6, 7, Key Role 3, Units 10 and 11, and 17, Key Role 4 Unit 12, Key Role 6 Units 18, 19, 20, 21*; Extract 15 from Verbatim account given by young carers, extract from Bibby, A. and Becker, S. (2000) Young Carers in Their Own Words. London: Calouste Gulbenkian Foundation, Young Carers in Their Own Words edited by Andrew Bibby and Saul Becker, published by The Calouste Gulbenkian Foundation; Example 16 from *The National Occupational Standards for Social Work – Key Role 1, Units 1, 2, 3, Key Role 2, Units 5, 6, 7, 9, Key Role 3 Unit 10, Key Role 4, Unit 12, Key Role 5 Units 16 and 17, Key Role 6 Units 18, 19, 20, 21*; Examples 17, 19 from *The National Occupational Standards for Social Work – Key Role 1, Units 1, 2, 3, Key Role 2, Units 5, 6, 7, 9, Key Role 3 Unit 10, Key Role 6 Units 18, 19, 20, 21*; Extract 18 from *The National Occupational Standards for Social Work – Key Role 1, Units 1, 2, 3, Key Role 2, Units 5, 6, 7, 9, Key Role 3 Unit 10, Key Role 4, Unit 12, Key Role 5 Units 16 and 17, Key Role 6 Units 18, 19, 20, 21*; Example 20 from *The National Occupational Standards for Social Work – Key Role 1, Key Role 2, Key Role 4*; Extract 20 Extract from article 'Paul Jenkins: Changing minds' *The Guardian, Society*, 14/03/2007, p. 5 (Mary O'Hara'); Extract 21 from *The National Occupational Standards for Social Work – Key Role 1, Units 1, 2, 3, Key Role 2, Units 4, 5, 6, 7, 8, 9, Key Role 3 Units 10 and 11, Key Role 4, Units 12 and 13, Key Role 5 Units 14, 15, 16, 17, Key Role 6 Units 18, 19, 20, 21*; Box 22 adapted and abridged from *SCODA Guidelines* DrugScope; Example 22 from *The National Occupational Standards for Social Work – Key Role 1, Units 1, 2, 3, Key Role 2, Units 4, 5, 6, 7, 8, 9, Key Role 3 Units 10 and 11, Key Role 4, Units 12 and 13, Key Role 5 Units 14, 15, 16, 17, Key Role 6 Units 18, 19, 20, 21*

In some instances we have been unable to trace the owners of copyright material, and we would appreciate any information that would enable us to do so.

Picture Research by: Alison Prior

Every effort has been made to trace the copyright holders and we apologise in advance for any unintentional omissions. We would be pleased to insert the appropriate acknowledgement in any subsequent edition of this publication.

National Occupational Standards

As noted above, Skills for Care & Development have kindly given permission for reproduction of the National Occupational Standards for Social Work within this publication. Since National Occupational Standards (NOS) are regularly reviewed, Skills for Care & Development recommend that reference should also be made to the NOS website or partners' websites, which contain the most up-to-date version. See:

www.skillsforcare.org.uk
www.cwdcouncil.org.uk
www.sssc.uk.com
www.ccwales.org.uk
www.niscc.info

INTRODUCTION

Chapter 1
Relationship-based and reflective approaches for contemporary social work practice

Chapter summary

This chapter introduces you to the two fundamental conceptual frameworks that underpin this book: relationship-based approaches to social work and reflective practice. The first half of the chapter concentrates on explaining the place and nature of relationship-based practice. Consideration is given to why relationship-based practice is 'making a comeback' and what it means to practise in a relationship-based way. In the second half of the chapter attention is turned to understandings of reflective practice: what it is, why it matters and how it connects with relationship-based practice. In the final part of the chapter support structures are outlined that help to develop and sustain relationship-based and reflective practice.

Learning objectives

This chapter covers topics that will enable you to achieve the following learning objectives:

- To identify characteristics of relationship-based and reflective practice
- To understand the role of relationship-based and reflective practice in helping to make sense of the diverse forces that impact on social work
- To recognise your personal learning styles and their compatibility with relational and reflective approaches to social work practice
- To understand the interrelationship between relationship-based and reflective practice
- To be familiar with the range of reflective tools and their usefulness for your practice
- To understand how specific organisational conditions can facilitate the development of reflective practice.

Case study

The service user perspective on professional relationships

In a workshop about the design and content of a new post-qualification (PQ) childcare social work programme, service users made some powerful statements to the social work educators facilitating the meeting. The overarching message of the service users was that what mattered to them most was having a good relationship with their social worker. For them this meant having a social worker who was available and reliable. The service users wanted the PQ programme to equip social workers with the professional capacity to be able to sustain working in challenging situations and not to be off long-term sick or only able to stay in the job for a short period.

Secondly, the service users wanted the PQ programme to help social workers to challenge the tendency of organisations to respond to service shortcomings by major restructuring initiatives. This was experienced by service users as detrimental to them. It invariably meant the relationship they had established with a social worker was prematurely terminated as the social worker's role, remit and location within the new organisational structure were redefined.

What do you think social workers would find helpful to meet the expectations of these service users?

The vignette above, based on a true experience, strikes to the core of social work practice. In this consultation forum, service users succinctly captured what mattered to them in terms of social work interventions: the social worker and service user relationship. And before any simplistic misconceptions arise, it is important to state that the type of professional relationship these service users were referring to was not a naive notion of social workers being their friend, although being a friendly professional is part of the social work role. Nor were they portraying social workers as simply being 'street-wise grannies' (Martyn, 2000), someone with maturity and common sense but without professional training. No doubt if asked they would be clear they want social workers attending a PQ programme to be familiar with up-to-date research, clear about their statutory responsibilities and familiar with local services that could support the service user. But what they chose to articulate over and above any of these qualities was the centrality for them of having the experience of a sustained social worker and service user relationship. And this is our starting point.

Introduction

This book is premised on the belief that relationships are at the heart of effective social work. This is easy to write about but not so easy to achieve for a whole host of reasons, which this chapter and the following chapter on the organisational context of social work seek to address. The essential and distinctive characteristic of social work is its focus on the individual and the social, by which we mean not only the individual service user in their social setting but also social work practitioners in their socio-political practice contexts. As a social worker you have to be capable of thinking simultaneously about:

- the uniqueness of each individual service user;
- the relationship of service users to their social circumstances;
- your relationship with individual service users;
- your relationship with the socio-political context in which you practise (see Figure 1.1).

In order to understand the relationship-based stance we are adopting, it is necessary to briefly outline recent trends in practice that have led to the current state of affairs. Several ideas and concepts introduced briefly in this first chapter will be developed in later chapters and where this is the case it is signposted. Having 'set the scene', the concept of relationship-based practice is introduced as a way of helping you to begin to negotiate the complex web of relationships of which social work is composed. The second half of the chapter focuses on reflective practice as a way of enabling social workers to sustain relationship-based practice even when the wider socio-political context in which they are located is not conducive to it. A number of the themes and issues that are necessary to contextualise the place of relationship-based practice in contemporary social work are complicated and you will have the opportunity to revisit them in later chapters (Chapter 4 on the history of social work, Chapter 6 on social work knowledge/theories). We start by examining two contemporary trends that have had a significant influence on the renewed interest in relationship-based practice.

Contemporary trends in social work practice

Placing the relationship at the heart of social work practice is not a new phenomenon. Historically, social work had strong connections with psychosocial approaches to practice (see Chapter 4 on the history of social work and Chapter 12 on social work interventions) which had the professional relationship at their core. The psychosocial casework model associated with Florence Hollis (1964), an early social work theorist and practitioner, was one of the foundational approaches to social work practice at its inception. The relatively recent (since the late 1990s) resurgence of interest in relationship-based practice, however, can be understood with reference to two prominent trends within social work specifically and in society more generally:

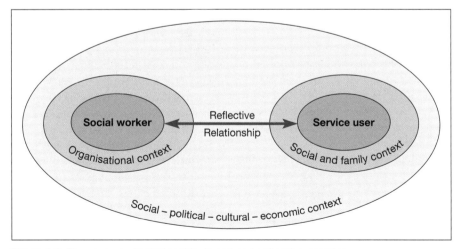

Figure 1.1 The context of relationship-based and reflective practice

- challenges arising from complexity, uncertainty and risk;
- contemporary understandings of the individual.

Responding to uncertainty, complexity and risk

Think ahead

One of the main challenges you will face as a social worker is to be able to acknowledge and work with complexity, uncertainty and risk. What this means is that you will need to be able to deal with complex situations concerning individuals and their social circumstances which have no clear answers and where there is often an element of risk to the individual, e.g. the risk of an elderly person falling while living independently; the risk to a child living with neglectful parents.

What do you think and feel about working in situations of uncertainty, complexity and risk?

In answering the question in the Think Ahead box it is important you recognise your own responses to social trends, as social work does not happen in a vacuum but is shaped by wider social and political forces. To understand the contemporary context of social work, we need to look a little more broadly at some sociological and philosophical shifts that have been taking place in recent years.

Over approximately the past twenty years there has been an active and ongoing debate within society generally and within social work specifically about whether society is moving from a modern to a post-modern state of development and the implications for social work (Howe, 1994; Parton, 1994a and b; and discussed in more detail in Chapter 6 on knowledge and practice). Modern societies are characterised by:

- a reliance on a few large-scale theoretical perspectives – psychoanalysis, behaviourism, humanism – as the way of understanding how the world – culture, society, human agency – works;
- belief in one 'truth' as an explanation for phenomena;
- an understanding of knowledge as being absolute, fixed, neutral and objective;
- scientific explanations and objective perspectives being regarded as the only acceptable ways of understanding.

The core characteristics of post-modern societies are:

- their refusal to accept overarching explanations, or what are called grand narratives, as the dominant way of understanding the world;
- recognition that there is no 'one truth' about phenomena but rather there are 'multiple truths' and an infinitely variable number of responses to human situations;
- the belief that 'truth' is a relative and dynamic concept and knowledge is a socially constructed phenomenon;
- a commitment to subjectivity as an inevitable, unavoidable and necessary component of understanding.

Accompanying these characteristics of a post-modern society is an increasing recognition of the inherently complex, unpredictable and risky nature of social phenomena. The notion of the 'risk society' (Giddens, 1990; Parton, 2006) has become increasingly recognised in recent years and reflects the acknowledgement that progress and the evolution of knowledge is not the linear process associated with modern societies. In contrast to this linear model, post-modern thinking requires social workers to recognise the unpredictable nature of social situations, which by implication are risk-laden, as responses to incidents or events cannot be predicted. Consequently, as the case study below highlights, social workers need to develop skills in working with the uniqueness of each individual's circumstances and to recognise that service users and professionals will have diverse views about and responses to specific situations.

Case study

Alison

As a social worker working in a hospice that cares for people with life-limiting conditions, Alison is familiar with the different theoretical models that explain the bereavement process and has had substantial experience of supporting bereaved relatives. Several of these models suggest that a bereaved person will go through a number of stages in the bereavement process. However, Alison's experience over the years in working in this practice context has helped her understand that individual responses to the death of a relative do not necessarily conform to theoretical models and that post-modern perspectives that emphasise the socially constructed nature of the world are more in keeping with her experiences. Theoretical models offer a broad framework for understanding people's experiences, but in terms of human behaviour each response is different and the models cannot entirely predict how someone will react.

In response to the complexities, uncertainties and risks inherent in post-modern societies, there have been a number of noticeable trends that have become evident within contemporary society generally and within social work contexts in particular. One of the key trends has been the rise of bureaucratically driven models of social work practice and managerialism (see Chapter 2 on organisational contexts for a fuller discussion of these issues).

Managerialist perspectives on social work emphasise 'meeting administrative requirements at the expense of time spent looking at casework' (Hafford-Letchfield, 2006). Within the social work profession, managerialism is apparent in the growing emphasis on paperwork, procedures, 'quick fix' solutions and approaches that will eradicate 'risk', whether it relates to child abuse, mental health difficulties or vulnerable older people. Such practices are all strategies for coping with the key features of post-modernity (Blaug, 1995). In recent times procedures and bureaucratic practices have become the main framework around which social work practice is structured, at the expense of the professional relationship (Gupta and Blewitt, 2007). What seems to have happened is that rather than face the realities of the socio-political landscape of social work practice, policy makers and senior managers generate increasingly restrictive procedures and practices in an attempt to simplify or eliminate the complexities, uncertainties and risks that have been identified. While they have their place, managerialist practice approaches are incomplete responses to the conditions they are seeking to address.

One explanation for these trends and the emergence of bureaucratic and procedurally dominated practice lies in its role as a defence against the anxiety inherent in emotionally charged professional practice (Menzies-Lyth, 1988b) (see Chapter 2 for more discussion of the place of anxiety in social work practice). What Menzies-Lyth meant by this is that rather than facing and working with the challenging realities of people's social circumstances – poverty, disadvantage, disability, illness, abusive relationships – they are denied or minimised. By adopting procedural responses to social work practice, it is possible to practise in a depersonalised manner that ignores the unpredictability and complexity of people's lives. The danger of such proceduralised practice is that it runs the risk of being insensitive to and inappropriate for an individual's circumstances and becomes 'a substitute for human contact and exploration, denying the necessity for professional judgement in assessing high risk situations' (Hughes and Pengelly, 1997: 140).

One of the strengths of post-modern understandings of the world is their recognition of the complexity of human behaviour and their refusal to accept simplistic causal relationships – A + B = C – that are central to modern understandings. In the following section we explore in more detail how human behaviour is understood and conceptualised.

Understanding the individual

Alongside the post-modern developments referred to above, a second significant influence on British society has been the emergence in all aspects of society of economic models that emphasise individual rights and responsibilities and the role of market principles. The combined impact of these prevailing socio-political and economic contexts for social work practice has been an altered perception of human beings and their behaviours. These perceptions reduce people to straightforward, rational beings and dismiss understandings of 'the individual' that acknowledge the irrational and emotional aspects of human behaviour. One way that the complexity, risk and uncertainty that are inherent in social work have been bypassed is by the re-conceptualisation of people from 'individuals with difficulties' to 'service users' (Adams, 1998; Munro, 2000; Parton, 1998a). When referred to as 'service users', individuals are treated as rational consumers, able to choose which services they want, and no consideration is given to how their personal and social circumstances impact on their capacity to make rational choices. Accompanying these restrictive and reductionist understandings of human behaviour has been a shift in understanding of human behaviour, from seeing it as complex and unique to each individual to one which engages only superficially with the presenting problem and does not explore its roots, what Howe refers to as surface not depth interventions (Howe, 1994). As a consequence of these developments the emphasis in practice, as the Closer Look box illustrates, is on the legal and administrative requirements and tasks and outcomes, as opposed to the professional relationship and emotional aspects of an individual's circumstances.

When this conceptualisation of individuals is placed alongside the socio-political context that emphasises managerial, risk-avoidant models of practice, it is easy to see how the relational dimensions of social work have become marginalised. The persistence of childcare and mental health tragedies, the recurrent care scandals in residential homes for children, and the public concerns about the care afforded to adults with disabilities and the

A closer look

'Surface not depth' social work

Two social work academics in the United Kingdom, David Howe and Nigel Parton, identified the shift towards managerialist social work practice as far back as the early 1990s and their writing around this time charts these developing trends which persist today. Howe (1994: 529) describes how in managerialist contexts

'professional discretion disappears under a growing mountain of departmentally generated policy and formulae.'

and how the managerialist approach to practice

'is antithetical to depth explanations, professional discretion, creative practice and tolerance of complexity and uncertainty.'   (Howe, 1996: 92)

Similarly, Parton (1998a: 6) sees how in contexts where practice is bureaucratically driven

'the essential focus for policy and practice no longer takes the form of a direct face-to-face relationship between the professional and the client but resides in managing and monitoring a range of abstract factors deemed liable to produce risk for children.'

Aymer and Okitikpi (2000: 69), social work academics writing more recently, similarly recognise that

'what it [managerialism] achieved was to change the ethos of the professional intervention from one of trust to that of contract culture where everyone involved from providers and purchasers to customers (people) only related to each other through contractual obligations that had been agreed . . . guidelines, procedures, manuals act as a defence against the anxiety of "not knowing".'

---

elderly (Stanley and Manthorpe, 2004), however, suggest that the managerialist, market-driven, rational perspectives on practice that have come to dominate social work practice in recent years are not proving to be as efficient and effective as hoped. The shortcomings of these perspectives are, in part, attributable to the model of human behaviour on which it is based, being both inadequate and inappropriate for the nature of social work. Practising in ways that minimise the relational and interpersonal dimensions of social work, according to research undertaken with service users, is clearly part of the problem. Several research studies endorse the message of the service users that opened this chapter, that it is the quality of the relationship with the social worker that is the key to effective social work interventions (de Boer and Coady, 2007; Quinton, 2004).

From the above discussions you can see how contemporary social work practice is founded on and dominated by two interdependent assumptions: that human beings are rational and operate outside of their personal social contexts and that human behaviour can be rationalised and rendered predictable and managed through bureaucratic means. As a consequence of this legacy, practice has been described as 'an emotionally-distanced way of managing people in need' (Woodhouse and Pengelly, 1991: 187). What then do we mean by relationship-based work and how can we restore relationships to their central place at the heart of social work?

Relationship-based practice – some fundamental principles

Think ahead

Think about your motivation for wanting to become a social worker. What is it about social work that attracts you to the profession? Which aspects of your life have influenced your decision to become a social worker?

How do you think your personal perceptions of social work and life experiences will shape the relationships you establish with service users?

The Think Ahead box above encourages you to consider how you perceive social work and understand your own personal experiences and functioning. Your responses to these questions will inevitably have a bearing on the relationships you establish in practice. Social work is essentially about relationships: first and foremost with service users, but also with social work colleagues and colleagues from other professional backgrounds – health, education, police, to name a few; with the organisational context and wider policy context of practice; and finally with 'the self', or oneself. These relationships do not exist in isolation from each other and are interrelated and exert influences on each other.

What do we mean by relationship-based practice?

As already stated, relationship-based practice is not a new phenomenon (Ruch, 2010). Relationships are central to social work practice but are shaped by the nature and purpose of the intervention, whether the relationship is the primary means of intervention, i.e. 'the end in itself' or, as it is more commonly utilised, as a 'means to an end' (Network for PsychoSocial Policy and Practice, 2002), and the timescales involved (Ruch, 2005). Definitions of relationship-based practice are hard to come by but it is closely related to and builds on psychosocial approaches to practice and the psychodynamically informed case-work tradition (Hollis, 1964). The central characteristic of relationship-based practice is the emphasis it places on the professional relationship as the medium through which the practitioner can engage with and intervene in the complexity of an individual's internal and external worlds. The social worker and service user relationship is recognised to be an important source of information for the worker to understand how best to help, and simultaneously this relationship is the means by which any help or intervention is offered.

The model of relationship-based practice we are proposing has several core characteristics:

- It recognises that each social work encounter is unique.
- It understands that human behaviour is complex and multifaceted, i.e. people are not simply rational beings but have affective – conscious and unconscious – dimensions that enrich but simultaneously complicate human relationships.
- It focuses on the inseparable nature of the internal and external worlds of individuals and the importance of integrated – psychosocial – as opposed to polarised responses to social problems.
- It accepts that human behaviours and the professional relationship are an integral component of any professional intervention.
- It places particular emphasis on 'the use of self' and the relationship as the means through which interventions are channelled.

What these characteristics imply is that relationship-based practice involves practitioners developing and sustaining supportive professional relationships in unique, complex and challenging situations. An important but not necessarily explicit implication arising from this model is the need to reconceptualise not only the nature and behaviour of service users but also of professionals. This model places equal importance, therefore, on the unique and complex nature of professionals and the rational and emotional dimensions of their behaviours. This is often referred to in social work literature as the professional 'use of self'. As a social worker one of the biggest challenges you will face is being able to simultaneously focus in professional encounters on what is happening for the service user and what is happening to you. By developing this ability to understand holistically the service user's and your own responses to a specific situation, you will ensure you are acting in the service user's best interests. Chapter 14 on the perspectives of service users and carers along with the chapters in Part Three on work with specific service user groups will encourage you to think further about these issues. Below we explore three dimensions of this holistic understanding.

Complex human behaviours and the 'use of self'

Understanding the complexity of human behaviours and its implications for the professional 'use of self' is not as straightforward as it might at first seem. Considerable attention has been paid within the discipline of philosophy to how human behaviours develop and what is meant by the 'self' (Colton et al., 2001 and see Chapter 7 on human growth and development). In social work a crucial feature of the 'use of self' is its capacity to hold together aspects of the functioning of individuals that could become polarised (Harrison and Ruch, 2007). Three aspects in particular are worth highlighting:

1. conscious and unconscious behaviours
2. cognitive and affective responses
3. personal and professional selves.

Conscious and unconscious behaviours

The references above to the complex nature of human behaviour and its rational and irrational or affective components are related to psychological understandings of how the mind functions, and the distinction between that which is understood at a conscious level and known to be influencing behaviours and that which is unconscious and unknowingly affecting how an individual behaves. Being aware of how unconscious processes and material can influence the behaviour of service users and you as a social worker is crucial information that contributes to the establishment of an effective professional relationship. Current trends discussed in the previous section, which reduce social work to a rational, bureaucratic exercise, are less inclined to recognise the unconscious dimensions of behaviour, but in marginalising the contribution they make to human behaviour, professionals engaging with people in distressing and dysfunctional personal and social circumstances are ill-equipped to understand what is happening, as the case study on Marcus highlights.

Marcus

Marcus is a 12-year-old black boy living in a small residential unit, as his mother, a registered drug misuser, is unable to care for him. Marcus has had a very disrupted childhood with brief periods of time spent living with his mother but these have always ended in dramatic incidents when Marcus, against his will, has been removed from the family home. Marcus has a history of offending behaviours and attends, erratically, an exclusion unit having been expelled from four local schools. Most weeks the social worker is contacted by the residential unit following incidents involving Marcus in disruptive, or at times, violent behaviour within the unit or in the local community. Sarah, the social worker, has attempted on several occasions to meet with Marcus to help him think about his behaviour but Marcus either fails to attend the sessions or, when he does, cannot manage to attend for the duration and leaves part-way through a session, often in a disruptive manner.

It is not difficult to see from reading the case example on the left that for Marcus thinking about what has happened in his life is too painful for him to face. By continuously behaving disruptively and creating crises Marcus prevents himself, and those around him, from really focusing on the sources of his emotional distress. One of Sarah's tasks as Marcus's social worker is to try to help Marcus recognise his behaviour and to think about why coming to the sessions is so difficult. By offering an explanation to Marcus that demonstrates some understanding of how his behaviour deflects from the emotionally painful realities of his circumstances, it is possible for Sarah to build a relationship which might, at least, enable Marcus to stay in the room for longer.

There has been a long, ongoing debate about whether qualifying social workers, like trainee therapists, should undergo intensive psychotherapy themselves. We do not regard it as an absolute prerequisite for social work training but do advocate for social workers to have an understanding of the role of the unconscious on behaviours and to be open to its significance for the professional relationships they establish. Chapter 7 on human growth and development, Chapter 20 on mental health and the section in Chapter 11 on communicating with people with mental health problems explore these issues in more detail.

Cognitive and affective responses

Closely connected to the roles of the conscious and unconscious is the emphasis on cognitive and affective behaviours. As the Closer Look box highlights, there is a tendency in contemporary culture to value cognitive understanding and behaviours over affective responses.

The challenge for you as a social worker is to hold the two ways of functioning – rationally and affectively – in a creative tension. This means you need to be able to recognise how service users' behaviours can go to one

Keeping 'the self' whole

'Two central aspects of human behaviour are the capacity to think – intellectual or cognitive development – and the capacity to feel – emotional or affective development. The danger underpinning any polarised ideas . . . is that one of the identities is forced to adopt an inferior position to the other. All too often in relation to the thinking and feeling binary the "head" activities of thinking are valued more highly than the "heart" activities of feeling. A duality of superior and inferior "ways of being" is constructed that privileges rational, cognitive behaviours over emotional, affective behaviours. Phrases such as "I think therefore I am" and "mind over matter" illustrate this point. Healthy and holistic understandings of the "self" require individuals to integrate their affective and cognitive capabilities.' (Harrison and Ruch, 2007)

extreme or the other. In response to difficult situations service users' behaviours can become emotionally charged: for example, violent and aggressive, depressed and withdrawn or distraught and upset. In these situations service users often have little or no ability to think or talk about what their behaviour means. Alternatively service users can resort to cognitive responses, which minimise the emotional significance of their situation. In such cases service users can talk about what is happening at a rational, verbal level but cannot allow themselves to get in touch with what it feels like. For many service users, talking about their feelings rather than 'acting them out' or rationalising them does not come easily. This is particularly the case for those people with experiences of deprived or abusive early relationships, who can find it difficult to recognise and articulate their feelings and can experience being given the opportunity to 'get in touch with' and better understand their feelings as unfamiliar and potentially frightening, as the case example about Marcus illustrates.

What Marcus's circumstances also highlight is how as a social worker an important aspect of the professional 'use of self' is your ability to recognise when you are inclined to become overly cognitive and rational in your own responses to distressing circumstances or, conversely, when your own emotional reactions prevent you from being able to respond in a thoughtful way to the situation you are facing. In Marcus's case, Sarah, if inclined towards more rational responses, might have been tempted to stop offering Marcus appointments on the basis of her understanding that his behaviour was due to his being disorganised and not able to keep to the times she had arranged. For Marcus this would simply fuel his low self-esteem, rather than help him think about what made it difficult to attend. A more helpful response would be to offer a number of sessions and for Sarah to turn up and stay for the duration of the session, regardless of whether Marcus did or not, to demonstrate her commitment to wanting to meet with him and help him address his feelings about his situation. In numerous research studies one of the qualities in social workers that children most valued was continuity, consistency and reliability (Bell, 2002; Munro, 2001; Prior et al., 1999, all cited in Luckock et al., 2006). Understanding and effectively utilising 'the self' enables social workers to intervene professionally in a balanced and integrated way that recognises the emotional impact of experiences on service users and allows the service users to 'make sense' of their emotional reactions in order to develop more balanced and integrated responses of their own.

Professional and personal responses

The third dimension of the 'use of self' that deserves consideration is the distinction between the personal and professional self. Once again there is a tendency to polarise the two and to place greater importance on the professional as opposed to the personal self, despite the well-recognised phenomenon of social workers entering the profession because of their personal experiences (Cree, 2003). If you recall the Think Ahead box that opened this section you can remind yourself of the personal motivations that contributed to your decision to train as a social worker. It can be tempting, however, to try to separate off the personal from the professional elements of the social work role, but it is a false dichotomy. It is more helpful to endeavour to integrate both dimensions into the role. Maintaining a personally professional or professionally personal relationship is not easy (Ash, 1992, 1995). The temptation to become a 'friend' of a service user is unhelpful and unethical as it denies the statutory roles that you carry as a social worker. The skill lies in behaving in ways that draw on your personal experiences, motivations and qualities within a professional context. Recent research (de Boer and Coady, 2007: 35), exploring what contributes to an effective social work relationship, highlighted the importance for service users of the 'soft, mindful and judicious use of power and a humanistic attitude and style that stretches traditional professional ways-of-being'.

In practice a relationship-based approach must acknowledge that the professional encounter is unique to the professional and service user concerned and the relational dynamics are the combined result of their individual characteristics. You may consider this to be stating the obvious but in the current climate it is all too easy for the centrality of this relationship to be marginalised. The Reflect feature below will help you to think about where you fit into the model of a relationship-based social worker.

Reflect

With reference to the preceding discussion about the features of relationship-based practice, if each of the three pairs of characteristics were placed on a continuum, where would you position yourself?

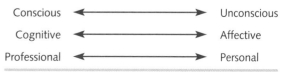

Conscious ⟷ Unconscious

Cognitive ⟷ Affective

Professional ⟷ Personal

A closer look

Good helping relationships in child welfare

According to research undertaken with families involved with child protection services in Canada (de Boer and Coady, 2007), the two key characteristics of 'good helping relationships' are:

'The soft, mindful and judicious use of power which included:

Being aware of one's own power and the normalcy of client fear, defensiveness and anger

Responding to client negativity with understanding and support instead of counter hostility and coercion

Conveying a respectful and non-judgemental attitude

Providing clear and honest explanations about reasons for involvement

Addressing fears of child apprehension and allaying unrealistic fears

Not pre-judging the veracity of intake, referral or file information

Listening to and empathising with the client's story

Pointing out strengths and conveying respect

Constantly clarifying information to ensure mutual understanding

Exploring and discussing concerns before jumping to conclusions

Responding in a supportive manner to new disclosures, relapses and new problems

Following through on one's responsibilities and promises.

A humanistic attitude and style that stretches traditional professional ways-of-being which include:

Using a person-to-person, down-to-earth manner (vs donning the professional mask)

Engaging in small talk to establish comfort and rapport

Getting to know the client as a whole person – in social and life history context

Seeing and relating to the client as an ordinary person with understandable problems

Recognising and valuing the client's strengths and successes in coping

Being realistic about goals and patient about progress

Having a genuinely hopeful/optimistic outlook on possibilities for change

Using judicious self-disclosure towards developing personal connection

Being real in terms of feeling the client's pain and displaying emotions

Going the extra mile in fulfilling mandated responsibilities, stretching professional mandates and boundaries.'

(*Source*: de Boer and Coady, 2007: 35, Table 2)

Having outlined why we think relationship-based practice matters and what we understand it to be, attention now turns to what it looks like in practice. To do this, however, we need to consider a related concept – reflective practice – which is an integral part of relationship-based practice.

Understanding reflective practice

Think ahead

In a practice learning agreement drawn up by a student with their practice teacher and tutor at the beginning of their first practice learning experience, a practice learning aim was identified that read, 'the student will become a reflective practitioner'. Nothing further was stated about what this might mean or how it might be achieved.

What is your understanding of the term 'reflective practice'? What do you think might help you become a reflective practitioner?

As the Think Ahead box indicates, there is a tendency for assumptions to be made about what is understood by reflective practice. Most, if not all, social work students and qualified practitioners will be familiar with the term 'reflective practice'. It is embedded in the National Occupational Standards (TOPSS, 2002 and see the Closer Look box opposite) and the Social Work Degree Benchmarking statements (QAA, 2000), both of which inform social work education and practice. The Benchmarking statement expects degree programmes to 'help students learn to become accountable, reflective and self-critical' and have 'the ability to collect, analyse and interpret relevant information and to use research and enquiry techniques with reflective awareness'. In assessing students, degree programmes are required to 'contain elements that test students' "reflective analysis"', their capacity to draw on diverse knowledge sources as part of an academic or practice-related assignment. It is not uncommon to find reflective practice referred to alongside reflexivity. Reflexivity shares characteristics with reflective practice, but to simplify matters for the purposes of this book we have chosen to refer to reflective practice as the activity associated with professional practice, while reflexivity is associated with research activities. While the concept of reflective practice may be well recognised and considered to be an integral component of competent practice, it is important to recognise that it is a contested, problematic concept and that debate is ongoing as to what exactly it is and how it can be identified and developed (Ixer, 1999, 2000; Quinn, 2000; Ruch, 2004, 2005).

 A closer look

National Occupational Standards' definition of reflective practice

'Reflective practice is grounded in the social worker's repertoire of values, knowledge, theories and practice, which influence the judgements made about a particular situation. The characteristics of reflective judgements indicate that the practitioner has developed the ability to view situations from multiple perspectives, the ability to search for alternative explanations, and the ability to use evidence in supporting or evaluating a decision or position.'   (*Source*: TOPSS, 2002)

What is reflective practice?

Reflective practice is, in essence, about thinking. This may seem to be a ridiculous definition of a professional activity, as all social workers would claim to think about what they do. The distinction lies in the quality and content of the thinking. Reflective practice involves holistic thinking, which embraces facts and feelings, artistic and scientific understanding, and subjective and objective perspectives. All sources of knowledge need to be recognised and drawn on, as Fook's definition emphasises. The diverse types of knowledge that are explored in Chapter 6 provide the essential ingredients for reflective practice.

Reflective practice, associated particularly with the work of Donald Schön (1987, 1991), an American social scientist, involves the recognition that for professions working with people there is never a straightforward solution to a problem, as each individual experiences their circumstances and their problems differently. From this perspective 'scientific' solutions, or what Schön refers to as technical–rational responses, are insufficient in

 A closer look

Definition of a reflective practitioner

'[R]eflective practitioners are those who can situate themselves in the context of the situation and can factor this understanding into the ways in which they practise. This on-going process of reflection allows for practitioners to develop their theory directly from their own experience. It also allows for them to practise in ways which are "situated" in the specific context. It allows them to take an holistic perspective, because they must take into account all factors which impinge on the situation at any given time, so that they might accurately interpret their practice relative to its context. In this holistic sense the practitioner uses a range of skills and perspectives to respond to the particular situation as a whole.'   (Fook, 2002: 40)

interpersonal professional contexts. More complex and fluid understandings are required that acknowledge the uniqueness of the individual and the inter-subjective dimensions of social work interventions. For Schön the development of such understanding requires practitioners to embrace the breadth of knowledge that can inform professional practice and to reflect both *on* practice, i.e. after the event, and *in* practice, i.e. during the event. You might like to think about your own experiences of reflecting on and in action as the Think Ahead box outlines.

Think ahead

Schön (1987: xi) sought to

'stand the question of professional knowledge on its head by taking as its departure the competence and artistry already embedded in skilful practice – especially the reflection-in-action (the thinking what they are doing while they are doing it) – that practitioners sometimes bring to situations of uncertainty, uniqueness and conflict.'

Can you think of an occasion in your personal or professional life, such as a challenging family situation or a difficult meeting with someone, where you were aware of reflecting-on-action and/or reflecting-in-action?

What sorts of things informed your reflections, e.g. your prior knowledge of the situation, your feelings?

Schön's reflection-on-action and reflection-in-action can be likened to the 'conversations in our heads' that happen when social workers engage in practice. Often, while relating to service users, social workers are thinking or feeling things that are pertinent to the encounter but they fail to articulate them. It is only afterwards while reflecting on the encounter that they are able to make explicit this internal conversation. As a social worker becomes more skilled in their practice the capacity to reflect-in-action becomes greater. With heightened awareness of the processes and dynamics at work in an encounter, reflective practitioners can make them explicit in the course of the interaction and use them to inform subsequent actions, as the case study of Edna illustrates.

Case study

Edna

Sheila, a white, 54-year-old social worker in an older person's team has been asked to visit and assess Edna, an 81-year-old white woman, who has recently been bereaved following the death of her husband. Edna is partially sighted and registered disabled. Up until the death of her husband the couple had managed to live independently. When Sheila arrives Edna spends a long time explaining her personal circumstances. During this conversation Sheila realises that, despite gathering a lot of information, she is having difficulty getting an accurate picture of the extent of Edna's care needs and level of independence. However, the more Sheila attempts to clarify Edna's circumstances the more confused Sheila becomes. Sheila is aware of the theories of bereavement and the grieving process and knows from her own personal and professional experiences of grief how it could be affecting Edna's abilities and judgements. It is only when Sheila acknowledges her sense of confusion to Edna, that Edna is able to express her own uncertainty and confusion about her dependency needs. At this point Sheila and Edna can engage in a 'real' conversation focusing on Edna's fears about needing external input to enable her to retain her independence.

It is not uncommon for practitioners in their relationships with service users to feel confused by the service user's 'story' and unsure of what it is exactly that is being communicated. Other commonly experienced feelings are ones of anxiety, anger, fear, frustration, guilt, uselessness. These feelings, and in this case the sense of confusion and uncertainty, can be experienced by the social worker as an internal conversation that keeps on cutting across the external conversation that is 'focusing on the task', i.e. in this case trying to find out more factual information and assess Edna's circumstances. A potentially more informative, relationship-based and reflective response would be to articulate the feelings – the confusion and uncertainty, for example – being experienced. It is often the case that in so doing, the service user can acknowledge their own affective responses – their confusion and uncertainty, perhaps – and a more real and productive conversation and relationship can develop.

Since the late 1980s, numerous academics have taken up Schön's ideas and devised models of reflective practice. The work of Boud et al. (1985), Gibbs (1988) and Kolb (1984, cited in Quinn, 2000) are the most commonly cited as they encapsulate the core elements of reflective practice, illustrated in an adapted four-stage model of reflective practice (Figure 1.2).

The four stages of the reflective cycle involve: specific and unique practice encounters; holistic reflection; hypothesising, synthesising and conceptualising; and active collaborative exploration.

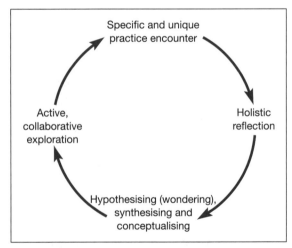

Figure 1.2 The reflective practice cycle

(*Source*: Kolb, David A., *Experiential Learning: Experience as the Source of Learning and Development*, 1st edn © 1984, pg. 21. Adapted with the permission of Pearson Education, Inc., Upper Saddle River, NJ.)

Specific and unique practice encounters

While most explanations of the reflective cycle encourage the practitioner to identify a situation that has troubled or perplexed them, the essence of reflective practice implies that all encounters and interventions can be reflected on and attention should not be solely focused on problematic scenarios. The concrete experience, therefore, that is reflected on can be any piece of practice undertaken.

Holistic reflection

This stage in the cycle involves differing degrees of reflection. Drawing on the work of Ruch (2001, 2002, 2005) it is possible to identify different types or levels of reflection, which may exist together or separately: technical, practical, critical and process.

Technical reflection

This form or level of reflection focuses on explanation and problem-solving. Technical reflection involves asking 'what did I do, and how can I do it better?' The question 'why', i.e. 'why did I?' or 'why didn't I do something?' is not asked at this level of reflection. To inform how a 'better' response might be offered in a similar situation, external sources of knowledge, e.g. formal theory and research, are drawn on. These knowledge sources are the sole components of reflection at the technical level and have as their aim efficient, effective, measurable outcomes. Technical levels of reflection tend to focus more on reflection-on-action, i.e. after the event, and pay less attention to the affective, process dimensions of the work and its impact on the practitioner. In certain professions, for example, engineering, there may only be one way of resolving a problem related to building a structure based on mathematical formulae, and technical reflection based on theory and research is sufficient to ensure an appropriate and effective outcome. Within social work and other people-based professions, formal theory and research are important sources of information for effective practice but cannot be relied upon in isolation. The appropriate choice of intervention, for example, in the case of an adult with depression, will be informed by current research and theoretical perspectives but this is mediated by the individual's own perception of their difficulties and their unique combination of personal and social conditions plus the professional experience and perspectives of the practitioner. While research might suggest that cognitive behavioural approaches work well for people with depressive conditions, it is not a foolproof solution that can be adopted in an indiscriminate way for all service users.

Practical reflection

In comparison with technical reflection, practical reflection is more inclusive in its understanding of what constitutes knowledge. Practical reflection understands knowledge to be relative, constructed, contextual and inter-subjective. Practical reflection, therefore, allows both the formal, theoretical influences on knowledge construction and the informal sources of understanding, such as personal experience, practice wisdom, self-awareness and intuition (see Chapter 6 on social work knowledge and practice), to be acknowledged. By analysing professional performance, practical reflection identifies and modifies personal and professional assumptions underpinning practice, enhances professional understanding and seeks alternative responses. In subscribing to this approach professionals demonstrate their openness to new ways of thinking, their eclectic view of knowledge and their wish to encourage reflection with the 'self' and with others. Reflection at this level can help a social worker engaging with an adult experiencing depression, for example, to identify relevant theoretical and research-based approaches, such as cognitive behavioural therapy, but simultaneously to acknowledge their own scepticism about this approach, which they believe insufficiently addresses the causes of the depression and overemphasises the search for a 'cure'. Recognising their 'professional prejudices' ensures that practitioners keep an open mind and do not preclude the service user taking up this option if they wish to.

Critical reflection

Critical reflection comprises the previous two levels of reflection but in addition it seeks to challenge the prevailing social, political and structural conditions that promote the interests of some and oppress others. As Stepney (2000) acknowledges, a critical stance on the reflective cycle requires practitioners to be both conceptually and morally informed and alert and is closely aligned with an anti-oppressive stance. In the case of an adult with depression the social stigma associated with mental health difficulties is one that can influence how they are responded to by a wide range of health, social care and other professionals. Challenging these entrenched views and powerful professional discourses is the central component of critical reflective practice.

A closer look

Questions to prompt your reflective practice

Technical reflection
What did you do and how? What informed your behaviour/intervention? What would you do differently next time?

Practical reflection
What did you feel while engaged in this encounter? Why did you behave in the ways that you identified? What were you thinking and feeling while relating to the service user(s)? What would help you respond differently next time?

Critical reflection
What was focused on, by whom and why, and what was not addressed? Who was included and who was not? What decisions were reached, actions taken, by whom and why?

Process reflection
How did you make sense of the way in which the service users related to you? How did you make sense of your professional behaviours? Was there evidence of your behaviours mirroring those of the service users?

Reflect

'Being reflective and being critically reflective share important similarities. Both involve recognition of how, as knowers, we participate in creating and generating the knowledge we use and an appreciation of how knowledge is therefore contingent upon the holistic context in which it is created. A reflective stance points up the many and diverse perspectives which can be taken on knowledge itself, and the shaping of knowledge. The important difference is that critical reflection places emphasis and importance on an understanding of how a reflective stance uncovers power relations and how structures of domination are created and maintained.'

(Fook, 2002: 41)

In the light of Fook's comments consider how a critical stance can help you have an enhanced understanding of the experiences of service users. For example, how might the dominant views on mental health problems and old age affect Edna?

Who is responsible for these views and how are they perpetuated? How can social workers challenge them?

Process reflection

The distinctive feature of process reflection is the importance it attributes to the unconscious aspects of reflection. Drawing on psychodynamic understandings of 'knowing' and the unconscious and conscious processes at work in interpersonal encounters, it suggests that mirroring and transference dynamics are a key component in social work knowledge construction (Mattinson,

1992). The opportunity to reflect, to think about and feel, as well as act on, the relationship dynamics and associated thoughts and feelings, enables professionals to gain insight into the experiences of those with whom they work and their own responses to situations. In comparison with the three other types of reflection, process reflection emphasises the affective dimensions of the reflection process as much as the cognitive ones. Later in this book the case study at the heart of the section on psychodynamic methods in social work (see Chapter 12) develops this idea in much more detail.

Reflect

Identify a recent activity/incident you were involved in that you are interested in thinking about. Allow yourself fifteen minutes to record the incident. Complete your recording in as much factual detail as you can, including not only what was said and done but also what you felt and what you thought the other people involved were feeling. When you have completed your recording, try to relate what you recorded to the different types of reflection above using the questions below as prompts:

Which type of reflection do you find easiest to identify in your practice? Do you know why this is?

Which type of reflection do you find hardest to identify in your practice? Do you know why this is?

When thinking about how our professional identities and reflective capabilities develop, it is helpful to consider how we learn and our preferred learning styles. One way of becoming more familiar with your learning styles is to complete a questionnaire such as Honey and Mumford's (1987) Learning Styles Questionnaire, published by Peter Honey Publications.

Hypothesising (wondering), synthesising and conceptualising

The third stage of the reflective cycle requires practitioners to try to 'make sense' of their experiences holistically and conceptually rather than in compartmentalised and concrete ways. All the knowledge sources identified as contributing to professional practice need to be accounted for and drawn on to inform future interventions. At this stage it is important that practitioners feel comfortable in wondering about and speculating on alternative explanations and action plans. It is important to retain a professional curiosity about practice issues and to feel confident about 'not knowing' rather than grasping for premature, often ineffective, inadequate or inappropriate solutions. It is at this stage in the reflective cycle when well-developed support systems are important. It is also at this stage in the reflective process when practitioners are most likely to draw on different social work interventions and practice models they are familiar with (see Chapter 12 on interventions) and adapt them to accommodate the unique dimension of the situation being reflected on.

Active collaborative exploration

The fourth and final stage of the reflective cycle is crucial as it ensures reflection does not remain a navel-gazing activity that produces no action, a fear voiced in critiques of reflective practice (Payne, 1998; Quinn, 2000). In Kolb's model this stage is referred to as 'active experimentation'. In the context of social work practice, the use of the term 'experimentation' has unhelpful scientific connotations. In the proposed model the term 'active collaborative exploration' is used which conveys an ongoing, interpersonal activity. What is vital for reflective practitioners to grasp, however, is that they can never feel they have 'arrived', as the reflective cycle is a never-ending spiral to improve practice. Consequently the fourth stage inevitably leads back into the 'real world' experiences of practice and generates further 'food for thought' and reflection.

The holistic reflective practitioner

It is not uncommon for social workers to regard themselves as reflective practitioners. Unfortunately in many cases the extent of their reflective understanding means

they do not move beyond the technical level of reflection. As Figure 1.3 illustrates, the reflective cycle aims to promote holistically reflective practitioners, who draw on all four levels of reflection – technical, practical, critical and process. Part of the explanation for the truncated nature of reflective practice in many social work settings is the non-existence of appropriate structures and systems that encourage and promote such practice. This issue is discussed further below, but before doing so it is important to ask the question why reflective practice is considered to be such an important ingredient in contemporary social work practice. In so doing, the close connections between relationship-based and reflective practice are crystallised.

Reflective practice and relationship-based practice – why are they so important?

Think ahead

Think back over what you have read about the key characteristics of relationship-based and reflective practice. In what ways do you think they are complementary?

From the preceding discussion you will have perhaps noticed how relationship-based and reflective practice overlap with each other and share perspectives on, for example, human behaviour. The underpinning shared perspective held by both approaches is their commitment to holistic understandings of human behaviour – both the service users and social workers. We would go so far as to say that by adopting one of these two conceptual frameworks you, by implication, engage with the other (Ruch, 2005). For example, by developing your reflective capabilities in your social work role, it requires you to adopt a relational stance. Conversely, social workers operating in relationship-based ways implicitly pay attention to the unique and specific needs of the individual, which, in turn, requires social workers to adopt a reflective approach. Relationship-based practice has, at its centre, the professional relationship and the practitioner's endeavours to understand the service user's circumstances and behaviours. Implementing relationship-based approaches in practice means, therefore, being prepared to work in uncertain, unpredictable,

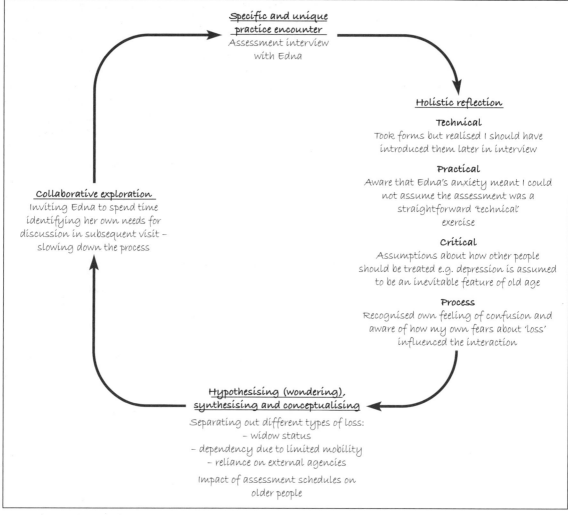

Figure 1.3 The reflective practice cycle 'in action'

messy and unique situations (Yelloly and Henkel, 1995). It means being open to change, to vulnerability and to the possibility of making mistakes. In order to develop and enhance their professional understanding and capacity to practise in relationship-based ways, practitioners need the opportunity to make sense of what they are experiencing professionally and personally. Reflective practice is the means by which this goal can be realised.

Having made the connections between relationship-based and reflective practice it seems appropriate to review how they together provide a robust professional framework for practice that responds to and creatively challenges the social, political and economic trends identified at the outset of this chapter by:

- promoting thoughtful, risk-tolerant practice;
- recognising the uniqueness and complexity of the service user;
- utilising the role of the 'self' as a social work resource.

Promoting thoughtful, risk-tolerant practice

Earlier in the chapter we noted the reluctance to think about the complex and risky nature of social work practice and emphasised that social work encounters must be recognised for their specific and unique nature, which requires personalised relational responses that are intrinsically risky and unpredictable. A further defining trait of social work practice that contributes to its risky and unpredictable character is the unavoidable emotional content of service users' circumstances. The fact that service users are involved with a social worker implies that there is a difficulty that requires professional assistance. Therefore, whether the difficulty being addressed arises from a disability, old age, poverty, abusive experiences or bereavement, to name but a few examples, the professional encounter will have substantial emotional content. Social workers need to be equipped to think about and respond to the challenging emotions they encounter – anger, violence, grief, depression, disinterest, fear and hopelessness. The seminal study, mentioned earlier in the chapter, by Menzies-Lyth highlighted how the role of professionals in organisations contributes to the creation of social defences as a way of coping with the anxiety generated by their work. One of the most common defences is the depersonalising of the practitioner and service user relationship through procedurally dominated practice (Hughes and Pengelly, 1997; Waterhouse and McGhee, 2009). Many of the inquiries into the deaths of children known to social services departments have emphasised the apparently 'thoughtless' professional behaviours that have contributed to the tragedies. One way of understanding these 'thoughtless' behaviours is to regard them as social defences against anxiety (Rustin, 2005).

Relationship-based approaches recognise the complex emotional dynamics of interventions and combined with a reflective stance are able to constructively engage with them. Reflective practice allows practitioners to remain thoughtful, flexible and alert to the risk of 'thoughtless' personal and organisational defence mechanisms that are characteristic of individuals and organisations, which are unable to face the emotional implications and unconscious aspects of the work with which they are engaged. The prevailing adversarial and bureaucratic climate, in which social workers find themselves, is not conducive to reflective practices and has been described as being 'antagonistic towards thoughtful practice' (Pietroni 1995: 35), as it stifles emotionally informed, sensitive practice and creative and reflective practitioners. Furthermore, it marginalises the 'thinking and feeling' aspects of practice, while privileging the 'doing' dimensions (Morrison, 1997: 23). For example, by paying more attention to procedures and bureaucratic requirements, such as completed assessment forms and reviews, practitioners avoid having to engage with the emotionally uncomfortable dynamics of people's lives. Procedures clearly have their place in ensuring that effective and accountable practice is maintained but the danger is when they become

the end in themselves and not the means to an end, i.e. effective social work interventions.

As the frameworks for relationship-based and reflective practice outlined above illustrate, holistically reflective practitioners will be aware of the affective content of their professional encounters and through meaningful professional relationships will be better equipped to resist the bureaucratisation of their practice. This relational and reflective awareness will ensure their practice is holistically informed, thereby averting the need to resort to defensive professional behaviours in order to cope. Practitioners also need to know that their organisational context supports reflective practitioners, particularly with regard to the issue of mistake making. Fish et al.'s (2008) work on systemic as opposed to individualised understandings of error is an important development for reflective practitioners as it does not collude with ideas of professional omnipotence and its corollary individual blame.

Reflect

Remind yourself of how you responded to the earlier Think Ahead box (p. 6) that asked you to think about how you responded to situations of complexity, uncertainty and risk and what you have discovered about your preferred learning style.

How does what you have thought about and identified about yourself contribute to your capacity to be a thoughtful, risk-tolerant social worker?

Recognising the uniqueness and complexity of the service user

Case study

Yvonne

Yvonne is a 30-year-old, single, black woman with a long history of clinical depression. Yvonne lives on her own in a small housing association flat, which she struggles to maintain. On numerous occasions there have been complaints from neighbours about the health and safety risks associated with Yvonne's flat. Yvonne has few friends and spends most of her time on her own.

As a child Yvonne was a victim of physical and sexual abuse and spent time living in foster placements and residential care. She has no contact

▶

with her birth family. Despite numerous attempts by social workers and health professionals to engage with Yvonne, there has been little success, with Yvonne finding it difficult to trust any professional support.

The circumstances of most individuals in contact with social work agencies, such as Yvonne above and Edna earlier in the chapter are by definition, problematic, complex and emotionally charged. Consequently simplistic, rational explanations of human behaviour and solutions are inappropriate. It is not helpful to pare down explanations of Yvonne's depression, for example, to a purely physiological problem, which if treated with the correct medication will disappear. A more realistic and holistic explanation of Yvonne's circumstances would recognise both the medical and the social factors contributing to her depressed state, which include current and past experiences. In a similar vein, Edna's adjustment to the death of her husband is unlikely to happen in an entirely rational manner as the significance for Edna of her relationship with her husband and her widowed status will provoke a range of affective, potentially irrational, responses that need to be understood in order to intervene appropriately.

The prevailing tendency to reduce understandings of human behaviour to a purely rational level and to dismiss the emotional and irrational aspects of people's lives is unhelpful. It assumes that any two individuals faced with similar difficulties will react in the same way. Similar reactions may be noted and form the basis for theorising from practice, but they are never identical. Relationship-based practice respects the individuality of each person and reflective practice encourages practitioners to pay detailed attention to the specific ingredients of an individual's circumstances and ensures blanket responses are avoided. In the midst of the wealth of legislative and procedural guidelines and the expectations placed on practitioners to ascertain service users' perceptions and participation, the need for practitioners to 'make sense' of service users' circumstances has never been greater (Parton, 1998a; Schofield, 1998).

Utilising the role of the 'self' as a social work resource

The use of self and its corollary, self-awareness, is a fundamental component of relationship-based practice, which is developed and sustained by reflective practice through its emphasis on diverse knowledge sources. By ensuring that personal knowledge, such as self-awareness, is valued and not marginalised in practice, relationship-based and reflective practice help safeguard the professional well-being of practitioners. Social workers who understand their affective and irrational responses to anxiety-provoking and emotionally charged situations do not need to resort to defensive strategies in order to survive professionally. In addition, this awareness ensures that practitioners remain emotionally available to service users whose own self-awareness may be underdeveloped.

The significance of this professional trait is heightened in resource-depleted contexts where social workers are unable to provide appropriate services such as therapeutic interventions or additional care packages because of financial constraints. The quality of the professional relationship and how social workers in these circumstances relate and help service users manage their situation, in spite of inadequate financial or material resources, is central to an effective outcome. The service user and practitioner relationship becomes a professional resource and self-awareness is a vital ingredient in this relationship, as the Closer Look box highlights.

A closer look

Use of self

'An authentic and personal response cannot be achieved . . . without thought and without pondering upon the way the world without is inextricably bound up with the world within. We carry with us throughout our life structures of meaning, assumptive worlds which frame our experience and enable us to interpret and articulate it and act . . . Effective learning is, therefore, dependent, at least in part, on access to that world of feeling and phantasy, which allows structures of meaning to be recognised and to be open to change, in a way which facilitates a different and perhaps more constructive professional response.'

(Yelloly and Henkel, 1995: 9)

For Yelloly and Henkel the acknowledgement of the inner and outer worlds of both service users and practitioners is a central feature of 'good' practice, and, through reflective practice, practitioners can hold these two worlds in a healthy and informative tension. The development of self-awareness through reflective practice enables practitioners to disentangle the dynamics of practice and to ensure that their actions are determined by the needs of the service user and not their own needs (Lishman, 1998; Ward and McMahon, 1998). Without well-developed self-awareness, social workers are at risk of getting caught up in unhelpful 'rescuing' or over-dependent professional relationships (Ward, 2010).

Reflect

The use of self

'Doubts, for example, about not being good enough or not getting it right; feeling liable to be blamed; not knowing, not understanding, feeling helpless, feeling intrusive or perhaps in reverse, feeling intruded upon, feeling lost and confused, are liable to beset most of us at times when attempting new endeavours or in difficult situations. Such feelings can be burdensome when there is the double task of relating to our own anxieties, and distinguishing them from feelings evoked in us by the service user.'   (Copley and Corryan, 1997: 21)

The above quote refers to professionals involved in therapeutic work with children but it is not difficult to relate it to your own personal experiences.

How many of these feelings can you identify from your own experience? How did you address them? What would you like to help you address them?

From the preceding discussion you will be aware of the inextricably interlinked nature of relationship-based and reflective practice (see Figure 1.4). What is important to highlight is how it does not matter where you

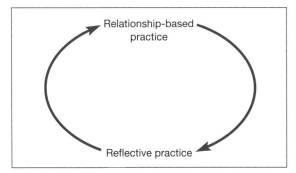

Figure 1.4 The inextricably interlinked nature of the relationship-based and reflective practice

start on the cycle, whether from a relational or a reflective perspective, because, by implication, the other practice perspective will be embraced.

Having highlighted the considerable potential of a relationship-based and reflective model of social work practice to address contemporary challenges, it is necessary now to consider what is needed to ensure it is promoted and sustained.

How can relationship-based and reflective practice be promoted?

To maximise the likelihood of social workers becoming relationship-based and reflective in their practice, it is vital that appropriate support structures exist: first, social workers need to develop individual, internal support structures that help to nurture and sustain their relationship-based and reflective identity and secondly, but simultaneously, they need to ensure there are external support systems in place to assist them to promote their practice.

Internal, individual support systems

Within the existing literature on reflective literature, there are numerous references to a range of 'tools' that can assist individual practitioners in developing their reflective capabilities (see Table 1.1).

Fook (2002), Johns (2004), Parker (2004) and Rolfe et al. (2001) are all social and health care academics who have written extensively around reflective practice, and in their work you can find more detailed accounts of these different tools. The common feature, however, of all these reflective techniques is their recognition of the complex and multifaceted nature of practice. Bower (2003) has conceptualised this reflective learning process and developed what she refers to as an internal professional support structure (Figure 1.5). The different types of knowledge referred to in this model are explored in more detail in Chapter 6 on social work knowledge and practice.

Bower's model provides a helpful way of illustrating how, by integrating the different knowledge sources, an internal reflective space is created which enables the practitioner to adopt a different position/perspective on the situation being addressed. What the model does not indicate, however, is the need for external support systems

Table 1.1 Tools for facilitating reflective practice

Technique	Features
Reflective journal (see Parker, 2004; Rolfe et al., 2001)	Focuses on a practice experience and encourages expression of affective and cognitive dimensions of intervention.
Critical incident analysis (see Fook, 2002)	Focuses on a critical incident, as defined by the practitioner, and seeks to understand what aspects were experienced as difficult and why.
Narrative (see Fook, 2002; Parker, 2004)	Form of 'storytelling' that invites practitioner to reflect in depth on 'their story': what happened, what was said, what was felt and its connections with earlier experiences. Involves making connections with the affective, cognitive, spiritual and moral dimensions of practice.
Guided reflection (see Johns, 2004; Rolfe et al., 2001)	A framework of 'cue' questions that help the practitioner reflect on an incident by answering structured questions that seek to address all facets of the incident and the diverse knowledges informing practice.
Inquiry and action learning (see Taylor, 1996)	Unlike the previous three practice-based techniques, this is a pedagogic approach that involves hypothetical practice scenarios and invites the practitioner to try to understand and suggest interventions based on an holistic reflective assessment of the problem. Helps practitioners engage with specific situations outside of the practice context.
Reflective recording	As a way of making case recording more than an administrative exercise, it is possible to develop reflective recording strategies that address the 'process' dimensions of an encounter. These recordings need to be understood to be a learning tool that provides information which complements the official case recordings of factual information but is retained separately from the case notes.

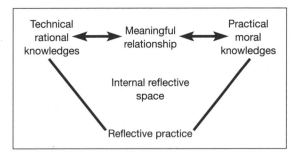

Figure 1.5 Bower's internal reflective space

(*Source*: Adapted from Bower, 2003:145. Taylor and Francis Ltd., http://www.informaworld.com)

to provide the initial experiences of developing reflective strategies, which over time can be internalised. While nurturing practice settings provide reflective spaces for all practitioners regardless of their competence or level of expertise, many work settings do not offer such conditions. Although this state of affairs is not to

be condoned, there is some reassurance to be gained from knowing that once an individual has internalised reflective strategies they are capable of surviving professionally in less supportive and less reflective work contexts.

Reflect

Developing reflective practice – individual reflective tools

Choose two of the tools identified in Table 1.1. Read up on what they involve and then apply them to a recent piece of practice you have engaged in.

Which approaches did you choose and why? What were the differences in the process of using the two tools and the learning derived from them? Which did you prefer and why?

Can you think of an approach that would be better?

External, collective support systems

It is not uncommon for the idea of reflection to conjure up images of an individual sitting absorbed in their own thoughts. As a consequence, within the literature on reflective practice, considerable time and attention has been given to debating what exactly reflective practice is and to how it might be developed at an individual level. This preoccupation with the individual and internal nature of the reflective process has detracted attention from the external and collective support systems, which also play an important part in the development of reflective practice, particularly in professional contexts. To redress this balance this section considers the contribution to reflective practice of a number of types of supervision, co-working, team practices and the learning organisation.

Before looking at each of these external support systems it is also important to note that their existence (or absence) is an indicator of the extent to which the organisational context is sympathetic towards reflective practice. No doubt if you talk to practitioners from different organisations their experiences of reflective forums will differ considerably both between different organisations and even within different sections of the same organisation. Ruch (2004), in her research into reflective practice childcare teams, discovered that the organisational context and, in particular, the front-line manager were crucial to the existence of reflective forums that supported childcare practitioners engaged in challenging, complex and risky practice situations.

Supervision

Supervision has historically been the backbone of professional support for practitioners engaged in complex and demanding work. The original tripartite structure of supervision ensured that attention was paid to the management, professional development and support needs of practitioners. This model was referred to as 'casework supervision' and focused on the details of a particular case and its impact on the social worker concerned.

The changing climate of contemporary practice has impacted, however, on the supervisory process, with most practitioners receiving what is referred to as 'case management supervision'. This model of supervision places less emphasis on the support and developmental needs of practitioners and prioritises the managerial objectives of performance-driven organisations. This shift in emphasis is unfortunate given that the altered focus of the work is not mirrored in changes in the social problems being confronted. Practitioners increasingly find themselves dealing with complex and challenging situations with insufficient support. There are some causes for optimism. In 2009 following the death of the toddler Peter Connelly in Haringey, Lord Laming was commissioned by the Government to produce a Progress report (2009) on developments in Children's Services since his report into the death of Victoria Climbié. In his report Lord Laming emphasised that 'Staff supervision and the assurance of good practice must become elementary requirements' (p. 4) in Children's Services. The report of the Social Work Task Force (2009), established in the wake of Lord Laming's report, reinforces this message by underlining the importance of the quality and frequency of supervision, and initiatives are being instigated to ensure supervisors have the appropriate skills to offer reflective, case-oriented supervision to practitioners.

A closer look

Reflective practice

'There is concern that the tradition of deliberate, reflective social work practice is being put in danger because of an over emphasis on process and targets, resulting in a loss of confidence amongst social workers. It is vitally important that social work is carried out in a supportive learning environment that actively encourages the continuous development of professional judgement and skills. Regular high quality organised supervision is critical, as are routine opportunities for peer learning and discussion ... Supervision should be open and supportive focussing on the quality of decisions, good risk analysis and improving the outcomes for children rather than meeting targets.' (Laming, 2009:32)

A closer look

The role of supervision

The classic text on supervision by Kadushin (1976) identifies three components of good supervisory practice:

1. Administrative/managerial/normative – ensuring good standards are maintained
2. Educative/formative – developing workers' skills, understanding and abilities
3. Supportive/restorative – enabling workers to reflect on their reactions to the work.

(after Inskip and Proctor, 1995 and Kadushin, 1976)

Where existing supervision does address the casework issues and developmental and support needs of practitioners, it has the potential to offer practitioners an important reflective space. This experience can be internalised and become the framework for Bower's internal professional structure. It is important to acknowledge that there have also been modifications to the orthodox one-to-one supervision model that complement it when it does still exist and partially compensate for it when it is absent (see Table 1.2).

Co-working

Research into the conditions that facilitate reflective practice (Ruch, 2004) found that social workers who demonstrated holistic reflective capabilities valued the existence of communicative and collaborative working practice. One such practice is co-working, the benefits of which are considerable. By implication, a co-worked case is considered and reflected on from more diverse perspectives. Simply sharing responsibility for a case requires workers to engage in more conversation than might otherwise happen. The differing views – theoretical perspectives, practice wisdom, personal and professional prejudices and values – of the practitioners involved have to be considered and integrated into the action plan. As a consequence the likelihood of more accurate and appropriate interventions is enhanced. In addition, the experience of co-working can be enormously supportive, particularly in anxiety-provoking and high-risk situations. The blame culture that pervades social work can become professionally paralysing, and co-working is one way of minimising its impact. Inevitably there is always risk, when co-working, of disagreements arising between co-workers, some of which can be as a result of dynamics in the case being dealt with. 'Conflict by proxy' (Furniss, 1991) is a term used to describe how professionals involved with a family can, unwittingly, play out a family's dynamics within their own professional system. It is not uncommon, for example, where co-workers are engaged with a two-parent family to discover one worker feeling more drawn towards one parent's point of view and the other worker to the other parent. The risk of such conflicts arising underlines the importance of co-workers talking after visits to or meetings with a family but, equally, it emphasises the need for joint supervision. Co-working should not be seen as a replacement for supervision.

It is unfortunate that current working practice appears to militate against co-working, with the emphasis particularly in care management settings on individualised practice, involving practitioners carrying

Table 1.2 Reflective supervisory forums

Supervision forum	Characteristics
Casework and case management supervision	In some organisations the demise and reduction in scope of supervision has been recognised and addressed by devolving casework-related supervision to senior practitioners, with managers retaining responsibility through case management supervision.
Peer supervision	Practitioners offering each other casework supervision outside of the hierarchical manager–worker supervisory structure.
Group supervision	Forums where teams or groups of like-minded professionals meet together to engage in casework supervision.
Consultation	A form of 'clinical' supervision, involving a consultant (often with therapeutic skills) who is external to the team/organisation and holds no managerial responsibility. Provides a space for practitioners to reflect on the details of their casework.

extensive caseloads which require considerable amounts of time spent on computers, compiling electronic records and reports.

Teamwork

In tandem with co-work the potential of teamwork is similarly under-realised in contemporary practice. While practitioners may be based in teams this is no guarantee that team-working is taking place. The complexities and the associated potential and pitfalls of teamwork have intensified in recent years with the emergence of increasingly multi-professional teams associated with the implementation of the *Every Child Matters* agenda (2004) and integration of children's services.

Think ahead

Team-working

The effectiveness of teamwork, according to Ward (1998: 50), like good practice, depends on positive relationships and good communication, but he recognises this is not easily achieved:

'Such (i.e. clear) communication does not happen by accident and by and large, it cannot happen through solely bureaucratic channels such as memos and noticeboards; nor can it rely on simply having a schedule of staff meetings. It requires people to give of themselves in communication, to receive awkward feedback at times and to take risks in talking about things which may feel confusing and uncertain at first.'

Consider Ward's comment above and your own experience of working in a team/group. What did you like/not like about the team/group?

Would you describe it as a work environment that encouraged communicative and collaborative practices? If it did, how did it achieve this? If it did not, what stopped it and what would need to happen for such practices to be introduced?

Effective teams appear to value both informal and formal communicative and collaborative practices. Hence reflective teams will encourage informal work-related conversations in team rooms, akin to informal peer supervision. In addition a range of formal forums for discussion and reflection will also exist. Opportunities for reflective discussions in the context of team meetings or allocation meetings are defining features of reflective team contexts (Ruch, 2004) and are environments that encourage the development of holistically reflective practitioners.

Learning organisations

The term 'the learning organisation' is relatively new in social work circles but is becoming increasingly popular and is often associated with ideas related to developing reflective practice. Gould and Baldwin (2004) have written a detailed account of the ideas underpinning learning organisations and suggest that for organisations to be deemed to be 'learning', it is imperative systems are in place, such as those outlined above, that encourage the development of reflective practitioners. It is vital, therefore, when considering how reflective practice might best be facilitated, that attention is spread across the whole individual and collective spectrum to ensure the potential reflective resources that reside in practitioners, teams and organisations are harnessed.

This brief overview of the necessary conditions for the promotion of relationship-based and reflective practice shows there is no shortage of models to support practice. The challenge is for the individual to identify and access the approaches most compatible with their styles of learning and professional development and for organisations to recognise their collective responsibility of making a range of reflective forums available to maximise the potential of the social workers they employ.

Conclusion

This chapter has introduced you to what we believe is the bedrock of effective and ethical social work practice: sound professional relationships and a reflective professional stance. Any suggestions that social work relationships are straightforward are immediately countered by the complex dynamics involved in any social work encounter and the need to be open to understanding both the service user and yourself. Equally any suggestions that reflection is a self-indulgent, navel-gazing activity can be challenged with the statement that without reflection – good quality thinking – social work practitioners run the risk of engaging in value-laden and ill-informed practice that does not respond to the specific needs of individual service users. This chapter has highlighted how it is the responsibility of all social workers to develop their relationship-based and reflective capabilities and of all social work related agencies to provide the facilities to ensure that the reflective potential of their workforce is realised.

This chapter has focused primarily on how you as an individual social worker can develop a professional identity that rises to the challenges of contemporary practice. In the introduction to the chapter, however, we highlighted how as a social worker you must always pay attention to the organisational context in which you operate, just as when working with a service user your focus is on the individual in their social context. The following chapter explores the organisational context of practice in greater depth and together these two chapters – the social work practitioner and their organisational context – provide the foundations on which the remainder of the book is based.

Key learning points

This chapter has covered the following learning points:

✔ The central place of relationships at the heart of effective social work practice

✔ The contemporary challenges to relationship-based practice, namely complexity, uncertainty and risk and the mis-conceptualisation of the individual

✔ The nature of relationship-based practice and its conscious–unconscious, cognitive–affective and personal–professional components

✔ The complex and multifaceted nature of reflective practice, including technical, practical, critical and process reflection

✔ The interdependence between relationship-based and reflective practice

✔ The necessary individual and collective support structures for promotion of relationship-based and reflective practice.

Further reading

Cree, V. (ed.) (2003) *Becoming a Social Worker*, Abingdon: Routledge. A fascinating book containing autobiographical accounts of social workers' professional perspectives and experiences.

Fook, J. (2002) *Social Work: Critical Theory and Practice*, London: Sage. An excellent text introducing you to the philosophy and practice principles of critical reflection.

Gould, N. and Baldwin, M. (eds) (2004) *Social Work, Critical Reflection and the Learning Organisation*, Aldershot: Ashgate. A thoughtful edited volume which explores the reciprocal relationship between reflective practice and the organisational context.

Harrison, K. and Ruch, G. (2007) 'Social work and the use of self: on becoming and being a social worker', in M. Lymbery and K. Postle (eds) *Social Work: A Companion for Learning*, London: Sage. A chapter exploring some of the key themes introduced in this chapter relating to personal and professional identities.

Knott, C. and Scragg, T. (2010) 2nd edn, *Reflective Practice in Social Work*, Exeter: Learning Matters. A basic introductory text on reflective practice.

Parker, J. (2004) *Effective Practice Learning in Social Work*, Exeter: Learning Matters. Chapter Two in this book provides an overview of reflective practice and includes useful examples of support mechanisms.

Rolfe, G., Freshwater, D. and Jasper, M. (2001) *Critical Reflection for Nursing and the Helping Professions: A User's Guide*, Basingstoke: Palgrave. A comprehensive textbook exploring in considerable detail the principles and application of reflective practice.

Ruch, G., Turney, D. and Ward, A. (eds) (2010) *Relationship-based Social Work: Getting to the Heart of Practice*, London: Jessica Kingsley.

Useful websites

http://www.cfswp
Centre for Social Work Practice: the Centre's primary goal is in facilitating development in social work practice and it emphasises the place of relationship in practice.

http://www.scie.org.uk
Social Care Institute for Excellence SCIE: the key body for developing and disseminating social work knowledge, research and practice.

For additional cases and topic-organised, clickable links into additional media resources, including those produced by IRISS, visit **www.pearsoned.co.uk/wilsonruch**

Activity

Activity One – Learning styles

Earlier in the chapter (p. 17) you were encouraged to complete a Learning Styles Questionnaire, such as that by Honey and Mumford (1987), published by Peter Honey Publications (www.peterhoney.com). The answers you give to the questionnaire are collated to identify you as being inclined towards one of four learning styles:

- Activist
- Reflector
- Theorist
- Pragmatist

According to Honey and Mumford, the following are the main characteristics of the four groupings:

Activists like:
- to think on their feet
- to have short sessions
- plenty of variety
- the opportunity to initiate.

Reflectors like:
- to think before acting
- thorough preparation
- to research and evaluate
- to make decisions in their own time
- to listen and observe.

Theorists like:
- concepts and models
- to see the overall picture
- to feel intellectually stretched
- structure and clear objectives
- logical presentation of ideas.

Pragmatists like:
- to see the relevance of their work
- to gain practical advantage from learning
- credible role models
- proven techniques
- activities to be real.

Which type of learner do you most identify with?

What do you think are the implications of your learning style for being a social worker?

Which type of learner will be most suited to which sort of social work role?

Activity Two – Reflective journal keeping

Referring to Table 1.1 on page 22, have a go at keeping a reflective journal. Try to record something in your journal on a daily basis for two weeks or longer. At the end of the 'trial' period summarise your journal keeping experience. Note down what you have noticed about how your capacity to reflect has changed and developed.

Chapter 2
Modern social work in context: policy, politics and organisations

Chapter summary

This chapter explores recent huge changes in the social, political and organisational context of professional social work. These are linked to the transition many countries are experiencing towards a 'market society', in which governments see their responsibilities as enablers of 'opportunity' rather than providers of welfare. In this model, organisations now work in partnership to 'deliver' the government agenda, and a new form of political oversight – governance – has come into being to manage this process. Governments also seek to manage the 'risks' of the more complex, fluid, unpredictable global environment and intervene in the lives of their own populations to reduce risk. Sophisticated systems of electronic information sharing are part of risk management, but also create a 'surveillance society' in which new forms of informational power can take on a life of their own. These transitions may explain many everyday features of professional social work experience, such as why there is so much paperwork and ICT work, and why 'accountability' is at the front of everybody's mind all the time. But the chapter also questions whether these seemingly 'rational and reasonable' aspects of organisational life may not be shaped by deeper social anxieties.

Learning objectives

This chapter covers topics that will enable you to achieve the following learning objectives:

- To understand how the policy and organisational context impacts on your day-to-day experience as a professional social worker
- To be aware of some of the key trends in contemporary social work and health care policy that are shaping how practitioners think and behave
- To identify the political, cultural and socio-economic forces shaping these trends
- To understand some of the key concepts that help make sense of the context of modern social work
- To see whether or not social work practitioners have any room to influence policies
- To understand how characteristic social anxieties, and irrational as well as rational forces, may be shaping social work policy.

National Occupational Standards

This chapter will help you to meet the following National Occupational Standards:

Key Role 1: Prepare for, and work with individuals, families, carers, groups and communities to assess their needs and circumstances

Unit 2   Work with individuals, families, carers, groups and communities to help them make informed decisions

Key Role 5: Manage and be accountable, with supervision and support, for your own social work practice within your organisation

Unit 14   Manage and be accountable for your own work
Unit 15   Contribute to the management of resources and services
Unit 17   Work within multidisciplinary and multi-organisational teams, networks and systems

Case study

The Clarendon Association

The Clarendon Association is an organisation providing accommodation for people with mental health problems and offenders released from prison. Traditionally, 'The Clarendon' was a religious organisation working with homeless people, providing hostel accommodation and supported housing, but recent changes in government policy mean it has been required to change focus in order to survive. Based in a large city, its funding now comes directly from the local unitary authority and the surrounding county authority through the government's 'Supporting People' programme. The emphasis of this programme is on community care for adults with long-standing difficulties who are also often a risk to themselves and others. Some of the staff of the Clarendon are social workers, but most have the title 'housing support worker' and are unqualified although many have long experience in the supported housing sector. Some are hoping to go on to qualify as social workers.

There are other similar organisations in the city, and when he took up post the current Chief Executive (CE) realised that the Clarendon had an image problem among local funders. Competitor organisations seemed to have 'modernised' more quickly, left behind their traditional image, and were seen to be offering better 'value for money'. The new CE immediately instigated a change programme throughout the Clarendon. A Performance Management framework was introduced, but front-line workers and first-line managers felt that their work was now being criticised as old-fashioned, and not sufficiently 'change focused'. In their experience it was unrealistic to expect most of the service users who occupied Clarendon tenancies to change very much. Many of them had been in and out of psychiatric hospital or prison, and sometimes both, over periods of twenty or thirty years. The practitioners felt they understood how vulnerable these users were, while the new management regime seemed interested only in how to maximise income and create a 'throughput' of tenants.

For a period of a year the Clarendon became a turbulent organisation in which to work. One contract was lost, some front-line staff left, others were made redundant while the remainder felt resentful and devalued. Paperwork increased, the time for direct work with tenants seemed to reduce, and managers seemed preoccupied with the survival of the organisation, not the realities of the front-line work.

Did you recognise any of the above processes described from your own experience? If so, what do you think might be the underlying patterns of change in social work that connect your own experience to that of the Clarendon?

There seems to be a conflict or tension at the heart of the organisation's current functioning. Did you find yourself 'taking sides' in any way – for example, with the practitioners against the CE, or vice versa? How do you think social work organisations could best handle the tension and turbulence among staff that arise during periods of change?

Some of the features of organisational change described in the case study above will probably be familiar to you, even if you have only limited experience of social work or social care work. They may even be recognisable from other aspects of your experience of modern social life, for example from contact with your children's school or from using your family doctor or other NHS services. This is because the whole 'public sector' project in British society has been undergoing a radical transformation since at least the late 1980s, and social work is no exception. In fact, some of the earliest attempts to reform and 'modernise' the public sector were in social work. This chapter maps out some of the most important features of the new organisational and social policy cultures that now affect all social workers.

Introduction: navigating change as a social worker in modern society

It is important for several reasons to understand the wider processes of social change that have impacted on social work in recent years. First, they lead to new and sometimes puzzling or sudden changes in expectations of the professional role of social workers, just as the front-line staff of the Clarendon Association found. Secondly, these changes are often presented as inevitable and necessary – as though they are the 'new natural order of things' – when they are always a matter of political decisions, and policy choices. This does not mean they can easily be questioned or opposed if people do not agree with them, but just as we take the view in this book that social workers need to be aware of *themselves*, we also think that you need to be critically aware of the wider organisational and policy context in which you work. If you are critically aware in this way then the question will probably arise for you, 'What position should I take?' but also 'Can I do anything about it?' There was a time when social workers in Britain had a much stronger trade union identity than is usual now, and were sometimes openly engaged in strikes and political struggles about the nature and extent of service provision. Such conflicts have all but disappeared from the public sector in general, but this may not mean that the underlying issues have been resolved. Awareness of the political and social policy forces affecting social work organisations leads to an understanding that there are real and complex debates to be had about the way social services are organised, funded and provided, as well as

about the values informing the thinking of policy makers. The nature of these debates has also changed in recent years, and this chapter will reflect on and examine these changes.

However, the key message of this chapter is consistent with the rest of the book – as an individual practitioner, but also as a member of a team, an organisation and of the profession of social work, you cannot avoid being a part of such debates. You have a *relationship* with the wider processes affecting you and the service users with whom you work; these processes have direct and indirect emotional and relational consequences, as well as 'material' ones, for everyone who is a part of them. Being aware of this context means deciding how to behave within this context. For example, the exercise above asked you to think whether you 'took sides' in the dilemma about 'old' and 'new' ways of doing things in the Clarendon Association. If you did, then it might mean you would be inclined to take up a particular position in a similar process in your own organisation, and this would have consequences. Because dilemmas like this one are ever present in modern social work life, you are probably always 'navigating change' – partly in relation to yourself and partly in the external environment.

So, what are the key features of the modern organisational and policy environment that might help make sense of these levels of practice experience?

A new culture of social work?

In this section of the chapter we review a wide range of interconnected themes that taken together provide an account of the contemporary cultural context of social work. We use the idea of a 'culture' because, as we suggested above, it can often seem as though this way of conceiving how to run social work services just 'is' the way it must be done. But a short study tour of any other country, or a careful comparison with how things were done since the late 1980s in Britain, quickly dispels this myth. Social workers in France, South Africa, New Zealand, Nigeria or the USA each live in a professional and organisational world that works on very different assumptions from any other country. Many readers of this book will know this from direct experience, having grown up in or been professionally trained in a different country. While there are some trends in public policy which seem to be international, these interact with local historical and political forces in any nation state to produce distinctively different conditions (see e.g. Hetherington et al., 1997, for a cross-national comparison of different European cultures of child protection work).

Across the industrialised world, organisations of all kinds, in both the private and public sectors, have changed in recent years. They now tend to be less hierarchical than they were, less well 'bounded' and stable, more open to interaction with other organisations, and less likely to provide a 'job for life'. The sociologist Manuel Castells (2000) links these developments in organisational forms to what he calls the emergence of the 'network society' in which looser, more fluid and changing relationships are found than was the case when organisations were more 'stand alone' entities, linked to a particular time and place and a local workforce. Today, it can seem hard to know where the 'centre' of an organisation is, or who exactly owns or manages its operations. You probably have direct experience of this. For example, you may have taken out vehicle breakdown insurance with a well-known traditional company, but when you actually need a service from them it is likely that they have 'outsourced' (contracted out) the service to a local garage who are the people who turn up at the roadside to help you. Sometimes the local garage has further outsourced a part of the service they provide to another company. The person who fixes your car or tows it away will obtain your signature, confirming that they have done the work they were supposed to do. Why? Because without this confirmation they will not be paid for their work by the company to which you originally paid your insurance premium.

How does this example relate to social work practice? Organisations responsible for planning and delivering social care services, such as local authorities, now operate in much the same way, outsourcing much direct 'provision' to other organisations which are often located in a different 'sector' – for example, the independent or private sectors. This creates a distinction between the commissioners and the providers of care. This means that it can be hard to see not only where an organisation begins and ends, but also where the boundaries are of the different 'sectors' – public, private and independent. This way of organising the provision of human services is often described as a mixed economy of care, to distinguish it from a previous model in which one sector – the public sector – was almost exclusively responsible for the planning, provision, evaluation and development of care services. Some of the anxieties and uncertainties of working in 'unbounded' organisations are discussed in

more detail in Cooper and Dartington (2004) who refer to these conditions as 'the vanishing organisation'.

Think ahead

Social work and social care now seem to be a 'business activity', in which managers and organisations are as concerned about budgets, financial survival and the costs of care as they are about the people they are supposed to be helping.

When you came into social work did you expect this to be the case? Does it affect the way you feel about the job, or do you find you can just 'get on with it' despite all the worry about finances?

How can we explain the apparently growing similarities between organisations providing services as disparate as vehicle breakdown cover and the care of elderly people? The clearest answer is marketisation, the political and socio-economic process whereby whole areas of social life that were once kept beyond the reach of the market by governments have been opened up to market forces. In health and social care the resulting socio-economic model of activity is often called a quasi-market, or an internal market, to distinguish it from what economists think of as a pure market in which there are fewer constraints on competition. In their aptly titled book, *A Revolution in Social Policy: Quasi-market reforms in the 1990s*, Bartlett et al. say, 'Quasi-markets are highly regulated by overall budget allocations, charter standards, and sundry government legislation and regulations that constrain professionals' (1998: 277). But, so pervasive is the tendency of modern societies to embrace market principles in all spheres of activity that one influential political theorist refers to a new historical period defined by the emergence of the 'market state' (Bobbitt, 2003).

Philip Bobbitt argues that in market societies governments no longer pursue the traditional 'universalist' aims that inspired the founders of organised welfare states in the period after the Second World War: redistribution of wealth, equality, provision of a reliable economic 'safety net' for those afflicted by poverty or unemployment, social housing and so on. Instead of 'making provision', governments seek to provide structures that promote *opportunity*, or remove barriers to opportunity that hold people back from achievements in education and employment. Now and in future, citizens will increasingly be provided with the *means* for self-advancement, but will be left to pursue the *ends* for themselves. Structures of *choice* in how to make use of

A closer look

Managerialism and markets

'A key feature of the new managerialism (in the private as well as the public sector) is the stress that it places on the "heroic" and "bold" role of senior managers in inspiring and enthusing workforces with a broader understanding of and commitment to the "missions" of the organisations for which they work. The second, equally important aspect of management is the operational emphasis on the devolution of responsibility, which implies an increased importance for local management in "downsized" organisational settings and requires a closeness to and interaction with customers ... Consequently we would argue that managerialism is the connecting thread linking markets, partnerships, and emphasis on customers and the recomposition of the labour force. In certain respects, "management" is what the public sector learns from the business world, but it also perhaps more significantly, increasingly links the two worlds by offering solutions to comparable problems faced.'

(Clarke et al. (eds), 1994: 3)

opportunity replace direct material, educational and health provision. Within this important shift of orientation, party political differences may still be significant. For example, British 'new' Labour governments' emphasis on introducing 'choice' into the NHS in the years up to 2010 can be seen as a way of countering the preference of the Conservative party or the new 'Coalition' government that came to power in 2010 for promoting choice between the NHS and private medicine.

All over Western Europe and in other developed economies the same political methods can be seen at work in this respect: cut direct taxation, reduce direct welfare state provision, put more money directly into people's pockets, expand choice and opportunity by promoting a 'mixed economy' of welfare in which the public, private and voluntary sectors all play their part. All of this means that the experience of working in and managing social work and social care has a particular 'flavour' to it these days. Apparently very different developments in society are in fact linked by a common underlying trend towards the promotion of individual responsibility for accessing and using opportunity. Students entering higher education in England (but not Scotland) are now responsible for their own tuition fees and for supporting themselves financially during their studies. Interest-free loans 'place' opportunity in their hands. The apparently unconnected development of direct payments to service users, or independent budgets through which they have control of the purchase of care, represents the same principle at work – the 'reconstruction' of the once 'dependent' client of social services or patient of the health service into an autonomous customer who can make choices in the health and care marketplace.

Does this model, which seems to borrow so heavily from a private sector business or commercial ethos, work when it is applied to social care? This is a subject of continuing controversy. For example, *Care Matters*, the government's (2007) Green Paper on 'looked after children' (which happens to recommend that we now revert to the term 'children in care'!) argues strongly for a new policy approach that removes the supposed barriers to opportunity that prevent children in care from achieving to the best of their potential. But many of those who work most closely with children in the care system – foster parents, adoptive parents, social workers, child psychotherapists, family therapists – have argued in response that the reason why children in care often do not 'achieve' is much more complex than this. Many children and young people enter the public care system in such a psychologically vulnerable and 'damaged' state that they cannot make use of opportunities in the way that most children can. A placement is an opportunity in itself, and there are many reasons why so many children in care move placements so often; but one reason is that they need to test the resilience of their carers because of the deep insecurities they carry about whether 'care' is a good and reliable thing or not. This can place foster carers, children's home staff and even adoptive parents under great strain. Children in care are just one group for whom the idea of the 'rational consumer' does not seem to work as a welfare principle. Lyn Froggett's vivid evocation of this dilemma in the Closer Look box captures this very well.

The development of marketised welfare is associated with a range of other practices and principles that directly affect everyone's experience of both providing and receiving social care. As we have just seen, while we

A closer look

Service users go missing?

'Up until the restructuring of social services under the 1990 NHS and Community Care Act, a very substantial part of many social workers' caseloads was made up of people who were effectively being maintained at a just about adequate level of functioning by the intermittent low or medium level support from a social worker, health visitor, or one of the many small scale voluntary projects that had emerged to fill in the gaps left by official services. These people's problems were by no means trivial and always had the potential to spiral into crisis . . . Working with such people yielded few spectacular rewards and outcomes were barely discernible if conceived in terms of measurable change . . . It is not clear to me what now happens to such people. This kind of work came to be frowned on as the "what works" movement gained momentum and time-limited interventions became synonymous with effective practice . . . I could go on but the point is that these groups who formerly received support have been a casualty of the idealisation of a narrowly conceived culture of "efficiency" demanded of public institutions by government and the Exchequer.'

(Froggett, 2002: 126–7)

often refer to 'service users', it is also common to talk of the 'customers' of social work services, reflecting the fact that the dominant model and language in play is a commercial one. In line with this model, recent years have also seen the emergence of managerialist practices in social work. Managerialism involves more than just an increased emphasis on the importance of management and the skills and techniques associated with being a good manager. Arguably, it is also an 'ideology', a complete way of seeing the world, incorporating values, attitudes and beliefs about the best way to run organisations, or even whole sectors of society, such as health and social care. Sometimes this new ideology about the centrality of management in public sector life has been called the New Public Management (NPM). Researchers have identified four main strands driving the practices associated with NPM, each of them a response to the perceived failure of 'traditionally organised' public sector services and management (see Dawson and Dargie, 2002):

- The control of costs through the introduction of competition
- The effective improvement of quality, again through competition among providers
- Setting and meeting the standards of service expected by citizens, through providing a charter of rights and measuring performance against standards
- Reducing the power and influence of 'special interest groups' such as professional associations and trade unions that may place their own interests above those of the consumer.

Reflect

The 'commodification of care' may be in tension with other values and principles shaping social work practice. For example, commercial principles in social work play a part in encouraging a culture of service user involvement by emphasising 'customer focus'.

Do you think service user perspectives should always come first, or only sometimes, or should they be just one perspective among several?

Can you think of examples where you were faced with competing value systems in your practice?

Professional groups and associations in health and social care once prided themselves on being 'self-regulating', and on their capacity to exercise independent judgement in their work. But as the final bullet point above suggests, their influence in policy-making and in how they directly deliver services has been curtailed. In the new 'culture of care' that has become established in social work (and the whole of the public sector), there are both new forms of regulation governing the activities of professionals and new forms of monitoring of everyday activity and decision-making. Reliance on 'professional judgement' has been replaced by new principles such as 'accountability', self-regulation by the requirement to be registered with national government approved regulatory bodies (such as the General Social Care Council or GSCC), and reflective supervision by 'managerial supervision' in which, arguably, the anxieties of managers about performance have tended to override practitioners' need to think carefully and systematically about their direct work with service users.

Much of the influence of this culture on day-to-day professional social work experience is captured by writers who have discussed the 'audit explosion' in public life (Power, 1994) and the impact of audit on social work practice (Munro, 2004). Audit is a practice originating in accountancy, and so its link with the modern emphasis on 'accountability' is not accidental. Essentially, the auditor asks, 'Are people doing what they say, or are supposed to be doing?' and implements a system of measures and checks to find out. Today, any public authority such as a local authority or an NHS Trust is subject to numerous audits of performance in a single year. Because overall 'performance' by an organisation is in part the aggregate outcome of the behaviour of each individual practitioner and manager, the effects of the audit culture are felt by everyone. Much of the increase in 'bureaucracy' and paperwork that has afflicted social care organisations (so much so that in 2006 *Community Care* journal sponsored a conference called 'People not Paperwork') derives from the demands of audit measures and performance management. But perhaps more important is the way in which organisational performance has become linked to performance target-setting. Setting performance targets is a way of securing change and improvement in service outputs and service outcomes (see Activity box at the end of the chapter) at an organisational and national level. But in pursuing this aim, they often directly alter individual professional decision-making, sometimes in ways which seem to practitioners to conflict with other important principles that guide their conduct as practitioners.

The New Labour government's drive to increase adoptions, a policy initiative that was personally sponsored by the Prime Minister Tony Blair, is an example of this. In August 2004 the *Daily Telegraph* newspaper published a two-part investigation into the impact of this policy initiative, under the heading 'We can have any child in the world in our house, except our son'. In essence the article claimed that in meeting adoption targets, local authorities may have succumbed to the pressure of these targets and compromised 'good practice principles'.

Reflect

All statutory organisations (those which are a part of the local authority or the health service) have a huge range of 'targets' they must meet each year.

As a practitioner, are you aware of any targets that directly influence your practice? Or do targets seem to be something that people at a different level from you are managing?

The journalist who wrote this article refers to possible 'unfortunate repercussions' of target-setting in this instance (see the Closer Look box). Policy analysts have a more technical language for this, and talk about the 'intended and unintended consequences' of policy, or sometimes 'perverse consequences', meaning that policies can have exactly the opposite effects to those intended.

At their most critical, some policy analysts hold that the entire machinery of contemporary social policy is faulty because it inevitably generates as many unintended consequences as intended ones. This happens in their view because policy makers have mistaken the nature of the social and organisational processes they are attempting to influence, treating society as though it were a machine that needs fixing rather than a complex system which is more like a living being in which the sum of the parts is greater than the whole because the parts interact in subtle ways that have produced their own independent effects. Such systems cannot be controlled in any straightforward way, but control nevertheless

A closer look

Social work in the news

'Within social services there are fears that the increase in the speed and numbers of adoptions might lead to more breakdowns if adopters are not properly prepared to cope with difficult children. Funds are being made available to prevent that. Among parents and extended families, there is concern that "letterbox contact" between birth families and adopters is available in theory but not so often in practice, because many adopters fear that contact will disrupt their newly forged family.

But the most serious concern is that the well-intentioned setting of targets in relation to time and numbers may be having unfortunate repercussions. "Targets are a two-edged sword," says Earl Howe. "Some may be over-zealous in meeting those targets."'

(Source: Daily Telegraph, 3 August 2004)

Global and local – governance is the means of managing interdependence in the modern world.

(*Source*: Alamy Images/Imagebroker; Alamy Images/Photolibrary, Wales)

seems to be what governments and policy makers remain intent upon. This view (see for example, Chapman, 2002) might be thought to chime with some of the experience of practitioners and managers who feel that modern practitioners have lost a vital degree of autonomy within 'the new culture of social work'.

What is 'governance'?

In a society where government no longer just directly provides services funded through taxation, but 'enables' a complex system of delivery and opportunity in which a range of commissioners and provider 'sectors' compete and collaborate, how is the whole system made to hang together? The idea of 'governance' is an important part of the answer. It is a strange word that seems to evoke the idea of 'government' while simultaneously making it clear that something different is being named. The word is now used to describe how processes of decision-making, negotiation and political responsibility are handled at the level of international relations (such as the United Nations) right down to local neighbourhood renewal schemes.

Thus, as we have tried to show in this chapter, understanding 'governance' is part of understanding the new context of social work in a world where nation-states and their leaders now think of themselves as globally 'interdependent' rather than autonomous, and within their borders think of their responsibilities in terms of enabling partnership (another form of interdependence) among various sectors of society (private and commercial, public and statutory, independent and

voluntary) to work for the public and the national good. But who, or what institution, oversees the behaviour and ethical conduct of the private or charitable sector when they are contributing to a 'public sector' service like social care? How are the very different and possibly competing interests of children's services, the police, leisure services, primary health care, private fostering agencies and so on that make up a modern children's service sector to be managed and reconciled? That is where governance comes in.

In this new way of doing things, traditional government takes its place *alongside* other institutions and social actors in a partnership arrangement, but must continue to accept responsibility for creating the systems whereby these lateral, non-hierarchical arrangements for providing services are managed, evaluated, inspected, regulated, and so on. This creates a potential tension – are partnerships a way of releasing resources on behalf of society and facilitating creativity and autonomy among the various partners, or are they a way of getting 'more for less' while retaining centralised control and *using* the mechanisms of 'governance' for this purpose? In a very interesting qualitative research study of one health partnership in Northern Ireland, Leslie Boydell (2007) has revealed the complex tensions at work inside such arrangements. She makes the following general comment:

'The government may in fact be using governance to strengthen its power over local politics in that local stakeholders, including community groups and business organisations, are drawn into a more direct relationship with government to carry out government's agenda. Rummery (2002) concludes that strong central control, in the form of targets to increase vertical accountability, is inimical to the horizontal sharing of goals which would enable local partnerships to work effectively. She suggests that an over-prescriptive encouragement of partnership working by government can undermine the kind of reflexive, adaptive working methods necessary for effective partnerships.'　　　　(2007: 12)

This tension between the creative possibilities of organisational partnership, and the tendency for government, and by extension partnerships themselves, to want to control what partnerships do (or deliver) is something practitioners and managers *experience* every day. It often emerges in a sense that practitioners are not able to be autonomous, to make flexible and creative choices about how to work, even though more resources and possibilities for creativity *seem* to be at their disposal. The demands of accountability, efficiency, targets, standards, audit, seem to many to override and to undermine the potential for creative practice in the interests of service users. Under these circumstances, it is not surprising that sometimes we have heard senior and experienced managers say that they resort to 'cheating' the system. They decide to ignore what feels like the anxiety-driven instructions being passed down the 'governance pipeline' in favour of courses of action that they believe to be professionally and ethically appropriate. But they also feel bad about this, because they want to work in a system that supports rather than undermines their integrity.

In the next two sections we explore more deeply how the forces acting on organisations produce such 'subjective effects', before moving on to consider how the individual practitioner can sustain a sense of autonomy and choice in the complex organisational conditions in which social work is now carried out.

Walking the jagged line – a different perspective on contemporary policy

Tony McCaffrey is a social worker who went on to train as a psychotherapist and then used his understanding of relationships and psychological processes to inform his work as an organisational consultant. Since the late 1990s, much of his work has been with social care organisations, although he also consults to private sector companies, using his experience of each to inform the other – another example of how the boundary between private and public sector work is no longer fixed. Over

time, as he witnessed the emergence of many of the features of contemporary social work organisational culture, McCaffrey developed a theory about how these processes were affecting staff at all levels in organisations. Like many social workers trained in the 1970s and 1980s, he learned about the role that anxiety arising from contact with service users can play in shaping how practitioners think and behave.

According to this way of seeing things, social workers are frequently asked to support and help people who have chronic and acute personal and social difficulties, and who are often themselves very anxious, depressed or emotionally burdened and conflicted. These states of mind communicate themselves to practitioners, who may then become emotionally stirred up themselves. In this book we assume that this is an ordinary, everyday part of the job. However, in a classic paper a psychotherapist called Isabel Menzies Lyth (1988b), who had been asked to investigate the high staff turnover among nurses in general hospitals, suggested that the everyday anxieties of the job might have more far-reaching effects than just their impact on individuals. She proposed that the organisation itself can develop a system of defences against the anxiety carried by its staff. Her research suggested that although nurses want to develop close working relationships with patients, these relationships also entail emotional contact with profound feelings of loss, fears about dying, acute anxieties about pain and illness and so on. In turn this creates anxiety in nurses, and also in their managers, that should they become 'too involved' with patients, they might be less able to perform their core tasks. The solution, developed at an unconscious level by the organisation as a whole, is to create a range of *organisational* defences against the painful nature of the 'primary task'. Menzies Lyth describes many of these defensive strategies, such as depersonalising patients through the use of language, rotating nurses constantly so they are never in contact with the same patient too long, or focusing on technical rather than human aspects of the job.

Social work organisations which understood how detrimental it could be to develop rigid defences against the everyday demands of the job developed strategies, including regular reflective supervision, that could help staff process the emotional impact of the work rather than defend against it. This entailed reflecting openly on difficult feelings arising from the work, in the context of a trusting supervisory relationship, rather than pushing this dimension of the job 'under the carpet' – or into a defensive organisational structure. Where these coping

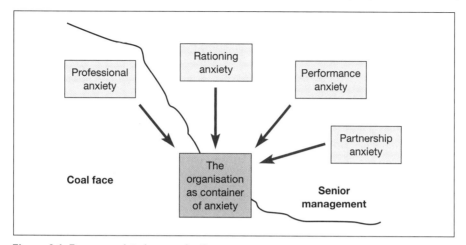

Figure 2.1 Excess anxiety in organisations

(*Source*: with permission from Tony McCaffrey, 2007)

strategies were successful, then we could say that social work organisations 'contained' the anxiety arising from the job 'well enough'. For many social workers in the 1970s and 1980s (including some of the authors of this book) this was their experience. The relationship between 'professional anxiety' and the organisation as 'container of anxiety' is represented by the two boxes, on the left hand side and at the bottom of Figure 2.1.

However, what Tony McCaffrey observed through the 1990s and into the present century was how a host of new and different kinds of anxieties began to impact on social work organisations. These are directly associated with many of the features of the 'new culture' we have discussed above. First, in the 1980s doubts about the sustainability of the funding base of the post-war welfare state enter the picture. Allied to the 'neo-liberal' policies of the Conservative governments of the time, this leads to a period of marked economic restraint in the funding of health and welfare. Suddenly organisations experienced themselves as subject to 'rationing anxiety', no longer able to assume that they would be bailed out of financial difficulty and often subject to cuts in funding. Managing this became a central preoccupation of senior staff. Then as the culture of targets, performance management and audit becomes established, organisations must cope with the anxiety of 'failing', of being publicly 'named and shamed'. Directors and chief executives no longer feel their jobs are safe – 'You're only as good as your last inspection report'. Performance anxiety has arrived. Finally, as organisations are exhorted to work 'in partnership' with one another, to develop 'joined up' multi-agency and multi-professional working

practices, new forms of complex interdependence arise in the new working 'sectors' that are created. Mental health social workers are seconded into NHS care trusts and feel their traditional identity is threatened, and children's social workers become part of a sector dominated by education services and managers. Partnership anxiety is added to the growing list of organisational pressures.

This narrative is not intended to be a commentary upon the wisdom or otherwise of the policy initiatives with which it is associated – who could be against the aim of more integrated or joined-up working, for example? Rather it draws our attention to the *experiential* dimension of policy processes, a dimension which may, however, serve to undermine or obstruct the potential of the policy initiatives themselves if the associated anxieties (now working at all levels of social work organisations) cannot be processed. Tony McCaffrey suggests that as *organisational survival* comes to preoccupy managers more and more, their attention is increasingly turned outwards towards the external forces acting on the organisation, and away from the anxieties arising from the primary task – the task of providing services and care for vulnerable people. This leads to a kind of fracture in organisational functioning, represented by the jagged line in the diagram, with front-line workers increasingly left alone to manage their professional anxieties, while managers are preoccupied with the range of other pressures facing them. This representation of affairs often seems to resonate with first-line managers and practitioners. After a presentation of this story and the diagram, one first-line manager in a Child and

Adolescent Mental Health service said, 'I feel I walk along that jagged line the whole time'.

Why is there so much paperwork?

There is no doubt that the quantity of routine adminis-tration, record-keeping, and general form-filling required of the front-line social worker and of social care man-agers has vastly increased in recent years. There have even been professional social work conferences devoted to examining the problem! Much of this work is now elec-tronically managed, and the image of the modern social worker is often of an office-bound, bug-eyed individual suffering from repetitive strain injury as a result of too much typing. Is this just 'bureaucracy gone mad', or is it something more explicable and understandable? In other words is there 'method in the madness'? Perhaps you can begin to see an answer to this question on the basis of the arguments presented in this chapter.

We now live in an era of 'accountability' that is linked to but much more widespread than the 'audit' society referred to above. Where society once placed faith in the idea of professional *responsibility* to ensure good practice, ethical conduct, effective delivery of services and so on, this has been replaced by the notion of accountability,

which is quite different. In a sense, modern political ideology tries to ensure 'responsible' conduct, by empha-sising that we are 'accountable' for what we have done, or what those working under our management have done. So accountability becomes linked to the idea of 'micro-management', in which organisational and political leaders introduce systems of reporting, information analysis, and continual performance monitoring in an attempt to 'know' what is happening in their organisations on a day-by-day basis. The somewhat hidden force driv-ing this way of doing things may be as much fear of things 'going wrong' – for which the chief executive or service manager can be 'held to account' even if they were not in any sense directly responsible by their actions – as it is a wish to improve or assure quality of service.

Think ahead

There is some evidence that requirements for more paperwork – common assessments, risk assessments, reviews and so on – are often quietly ignored by many workers in social care organisations, or only attended to when there is an audit or inspection.

What seems to be the reality in the organisations you have worked in? How do you, and other staff, cope with the tension between getting the direct work done, and the form-filling?

A modern social work office . . . or is it?
(*Source*: Alamy Images/Imagestate)

Thus, 'risk management' procedures have become a major source of additional paperwork – but one can ask, 'What is the risk being managed: the risk to the service user or to the organisation if a serious incident occurred, or both?'

Arguably, of course, this aspect of the new culture of social work and public services is a complex mixture of forces and motives, but an accountability culture inevitably produces a need for comprehensive record-keeping. If one case can 'go wrong' with disastrous consequences, *any* case can go wrong – we cannot predict which ones will and which will not; and in an era of partnership working there is a pressing need to keep track of exactly who, on behalf of which agency, did what in each 'care episode', both for reasons of retrospective quality assurance and also for reasons of more conventional 'accounting'; who did what is a measure of who is paying for what.

Again the consequences of this shift in culture may be double-edged. Everyone may be better at keeping up to date with their case records, but the quality of these records may have changed, and possibly suffered, as records become more a means of registering information than of offering assessments or subtler qualitative perspectives.

Below we extend the exploration of possible 'non-rational' sources of modern policy and practice with a case study of the evolution of child protection work in Britain. The proliferation of paperwork in social work can almost be traced back to these events, and the shocking impact that 'failure' to protect children in public care had on our society and profession.

Paperwork? How old fashioned! You mean electronic record-keeping . . .

No book about social work that emphasises the importance of face-to-face relationships can sidestep a look at the place of computer-based work and electronic systems in the life of the modern practitioner. We all know that attending to our emails can easily dominate our time (and our minds), at work and home. Electronic modes of communication have mushroomed in all our lives, although some people make more use of more varieties than do others.

Social workers in training are now often required to complete their European Computer Driving Licence – basic familiarity with the use of information technology is a competence every practitioner needs. On the other hand, in the period of turmoil following the Baby Peter case in England in 2009, it was regularly reported that

children's service social workers were spending up to 80 per cent of their time on computer-based work. Anecdotally, there have been stories of social workers during power cuts, or 'systems crashes' sitting in their offices believing they were unable to do any work without access to computers. Is it true that the most important relationship a social worker now has is with her or his PC? Or can there be a happy medium? And why has such heavy reliance on electronic systems of record-keeping evolved in social work?

In 1990 people were just becoming accustomed to owning a personal computer, or having regular use of one at work. Within a few years the dilemmas for social workers were recognised and anticipated:

'unless social workers do become involved in the ways in which new technologies are used within organisations, they will fail to influence its impact on their clients and may further fail to control the way in which computers affect the nature of social work itself in the future.' (Sapey, 1997: 803)

The 'electronic turn' in social work is not simply a consequence of the availability of more and more sophisticated technology. It is an inherent part of the developments, described above, in how governments, organisations and, in particular, public services have evolved in recent years. Technology is a resource. All resources can be deployed in different ways, for better or worse, and with greater or lesser attunement and adaptation to the primary tasks they are designed to facilitate. Information technology is a means to an end, and not an end in itself, although when computer-based activity increases to the extent described above then, arguably, means have become confused with ends.

Social work is a 'public service'. All public services have become a focus of political concern in relation to:

- consistency of standards, delivery, and performance within and *between* organisations and sectors;
- quality of information-sharing among professionals, agencies, and sectors, as a dimension of both efficiency and risk management;
- thus, public service 'systems' are increasingly deployed as a part of the 'surveillance society', while being themselves an object of surveillance with respect to their performance.

Electronic systems are therefore part of a wider trend towards 'bureaucratisation' in social work and other services. With the election of a new government in Britain in 2010, and the need to make enormous savings in public expenditure after the global financial crisis of

2008–9, we can anticipate a phase of 'bureaucracy busting' in social work. Shortly before the 2010 election, the Conservative Party appointed Professor Eileen Munro of the London School of Economics as a bureaucracy-busting champion for social work. Here are some of her published views about social work bureaucratisation and its impact, in the context of a discussion about whether Britain has introduced a system of 'mandatory reporting' of concerns about children:

'A fundamental expectation in the safeguarding agenda is that better agency communication will increase co-operative working. However, the experience from mandatory reporting systems is that increased sharing of information may have the opposite effect. Instead of increasing responsibility, it can reduce it, with practitioners believing that they have done their duty by making a report.

Moreover, the risk of no-one taking responsibility is particularly great in the English system because the report is not made to an agency with a clear responsibility to respond but to a database where the information may or may not be noticed and acted on by other agencies. Practitioners will also face the difficult judgment of when information about a cause for concern is serious enough to warrant entering an indication but not serious enough to warrant immediate action. Concern that a child is suffering significant harm, for instance, should be immediately communicated directly to the child protection agency, not merely noted on a database.

The government believe that improved communication between agencies will lead to improved collaboration and, in turn, this will lead to improved outcomes for children. They cite no empirical research to support this claim and, indeed, such research in other countries tells *against* their claim.'
(Munro and Parton, 2007: 12–13)

Dependence on IT-based systems for recording, monitoring, information-sharing, assessment and so on have had the greatest impact in the areas of social work perceived to involve the most 'risk'. Thus, it is children's service workers who have experienced the really sharp end of this trend. The Common Assessment Framework (CAF), contact point (scrapped immediately following the 2010 election), initial assessment (IA), processes, core assessment (CA), child protection plans (CPP) and the integration of a number of these into what has become known as the Integrated Children's System (ICS) are some of the main features of this electronic landscape. In a Channel 4 *Dispatches* documentary of June 2010, an 'undercover social worker' in a front-line child-care team was shown estimating the number of pages of forms he would be required to fill out at a certain point in one routine child protection investigation. The total was about 100.

In an important research project Broadhurst et al. (2010) studied the working life experience of a number of local authority children's service teams and found that management of 'workflow', the demands of assessment deadlines, and the constraints imposed by electronic record-keeping had a major impact on the nature and quality of direct social work practice, so that 'data input demands seriously eroded valuable face-to-face time with children and their parents/carers' (2010: 365) and 'Workers consistently claimed that it was easy to lose sight of the primary activities of supporting families and safeguarding children, to the second-order activities of performance and audit' (2010: 359).

So, modern social work is not just suffering from 'bureaucracy gone mad' but is caught up in a complex process affecting the whole of modern society. Sophisticated information management systems are often seen as part

---

A closer look

Social workers under 'electronic pressure'

'Team leader: Being a bit cheeky . . . we contacted the health visitor and said when did you last see the child and lucky enough the health visitor had seen the baby recently and it wasn't as bad as the grandmother had alleged . . . so we didn't take it any further, no further action.

Workers widely reported that the timescales created undue pressure. One senior practitioner observed: "I personally worry about sometimes the time scales that you've, you've got to do it in . . . I've been sort of worrying about work for, for a while really."

The tempo and volume of work, together with the seven-day target for IA completion, were widely reported as making cases at this second stage equally susceptible to partial analysis and rapid disposal.

Social worker: If it's not looking that serious . . . sometimes you don't get all the information and the temptation is then to take a short-cut and maybe not contact the school, or because the school are on holidays you say I think I've got sufficient information to make a decision – NFA.'

(Broadhurst et al. 2010)

of the answer to 'complexity' and 'risk' in social life. In truth they seem to *add* to it. Currently we live in an age when we

'substitute *confidence in systems* for *trust in individual professionals* so that the introduction of the most up-to-date technology becomes a major priority, the processing and manipulation of information becomes the key element for judging and managing change.'   (Parton, 2006: 177)

And for social workers committed to 'relationship based' practice:

'Crucially, the gathering, inputting, sharing and manipulation of information becomes a key activity and the relationship between the user/client/parent/child and the professional becomes very different.'   (Parton, 2006: 174)

Experiencing social policy

The story of 'modern organisational anxieties' above, and the case study of the Clarendon Association both show how 'policy' and 'the organisation' are not abstract or remote features of our working lives. If we open ourselves to thinking about them in the ways described, we quickly come to see that policy, organisational processes and our daily working experience are quite intimately tied together. The impact of excess anxiety on organisations and the individuals working in them may be another example of the 'unintended consequences' of social policy discussed earlier. There is even some evidence from research by government agencies of this. Eileen Munro reports that the Audit Commission has conducted a study of why staff leave social work and concluded that most are leaving because of 'push not pull' factors, all of which can be linked to the managerial and audit culture of recent years. The key factors include 'a lack of autonomy', a change agenda that 'feels imposed and irrelevant' and a sense of being 'overwhelmed by paperwork and targets' (Munro, 2004: 1091).

Our main aim in this chapter is to encourage you to think of your experience of organisational and policy processes as valid experience, and to offer some tools with which to render that experience generalisable and relevant to policy analysis and even action in relation to policy. Therefore in this section and the final one we turn to two more aspects of this general topic. First, we want to consider the possibility that the social forces shaping and informing social work policy may often be less rational than they seem to be. If this is true, it is important

because a critical perspective on policy needs to be capable of grasping as many of the factors driving policy processes as possible and to articulate them. Perhaps social workers, with their sensitivity to the whole range of material, relational, emotional and ethical dimensions of social life could be especially adept at this kind of policy analysis? To suggest that policy may have non-rational aspects is not to criticise these, or necessarily to suggest they should be eliminated. Rather, we take the view that it is inevitable that complex social processes will be a blend of rational, emotive and value-laden elements. The point is to understand this, and so put us in a better position to interrogate policy as a 'holistic' phenomenon, and not the exclusively 'rational–instrumental' one it often presents itself to be. Looked at this way, we think that policy makers and policy analysts often misunderstand and misrepresent the enterprise they are themselves engaged in. Jake Chapman (2002) whom we mentioned above is another policy analyst who thinks this is the case. Thus his pamphlet about policy system failure is subtitled 'Why governments must learn to think differently'.

The final theme of the chapter concerns whether, and how, in a professional and organisational context that often feels 'depoliticised' by comparison with some earlier decades, it is possible to think in terms of influencing policy processes. The two themes are connected in some respects because if, as we are suggesting, policy processes are more complex in character than they are usually presented to be (both in their causes and their effects) then 'unmasking' this might lead to an idea of 'doing policy differently' and of gaining greater purchase on processes of policy influence. The case study below contains a summary of just one central area of social work policy-making, including some thoughts about why and how the processes involved might be more complex than they seem at first sight. The box is an invitation to further your own thinking by first reflecting on your own experience of similar processes, and then asking the question, 'Are there other ways to tell the story of this policy process, and what would be my evidence for this alternative story?'

Finding space for thought and action

If the findings of the Audit Commission's research into why so many public sector staff leave their jobs are accurate, so that feeling 'undervalued by government, managers and the public', and 'lack of autonomy' within the target-driven, audit culture are real factors in this trend, then we must ask whether this is a situation social workers must just accept. Or is there space for influence, assertiveness, and advocacy within the contemporary policy culture? Most practitioners want, correctly, to work responsibly and accountably on behalf of the service users to whom they have responsibilities. Yet the system within which they do this often seems to work against the interests of *both* professionals and users. Perhaps then there is a good ethical case for advocating that social workers do find ways to speak out about their experience of the system. In line with the whole empha-sis of this book, we suggest that such action must be grounded in good analytical reflection on circumstances – in this case reflection upon the practitioner's wider organisational and policy context. This is about under-standing the nature of the particular psychosocial or organisational 'space' which bounds your day-to-day experience. In the continuation of the case study of the Clarendon Association, the staff are helped to find this space through reflective group supervision that gives them time to think in depth about their work with service users, but also about the pressures and conflicts of their working context.

Case study

Child protection policy in Britain: irrational responses to irrational fears?

Social policy in relation to child welfare and child safety in Britain has been shaped by many factors and forces over the past few decades. One of the underlying factors is the relationship that is assumed to exist between the state, family life and children in *all* spheres of policy. In Britain, the state is taken to be a 'residual' entity that enters the picture when private arrangements and the sphere of 'civil society' can no longer manage. In other countries, including many other European ones, the state is assumed to be much more all-embracing, and to have definite obligations to citizens, while citizens have defined responsibilities towards the state. This can mean that children of all ages are thought of as citizens whom the state has a duty and a right to protect at all times, not just when things 'go wrong'.

Perhaps this helps to explain one of the peculiarities of child protection policy in Britain, namely that policy is often dictated by practice 'failures' rather than success. Particularly since the mid-1980s, major policy changes have often followed in the wake of one of the prominent cases of child death which have then been the subject of a full-scale public inquiry. The cases of Jasmine Beckford on whose death the panel of inquiry reported in 1985, Kimberley Carlile (1987) and Tyra Henry (1987) are among those that most influenced public policy, although a series of cases in the 1970s beginning with Maria Colwell (1974) are also very significant. The Cleveland Report (1988) also had a huge impact on policy, as well as public and professional awareness of child sexual abuse. In the 1990s the stream of inquiries abated until the case of Victoria Climbié (2003) which resulted in important new adjustments to the organisational and policy framework for child 'safeguarding'. Then in 2008 the case of 'Baby P' provoked massive political, media and professional concern resulting in a further review of child protection services by Lord Laming who conducted the Victoria Climbié Inquiry, but also the establishment of the Social Work Task Force and the national College of Social Work.

On the one hand, it can be argued that the wider public have a right to know about the worst cases of tragedy and 'failure' in our systems of public care for vulnerable children (just as we should know about safety problems on the railways or airlines), and that government has a political duty not to shield society from this awareness. On the other hand, it is highly questionable whether the intense emotions and public anxieties aroused by months of media exposure to the details of the suffering endured by these children, the climate of blame that accompanies the inquiry process, and the detailed scrutiny of professional practices in one particular case, create a climate in which rational policy-making is possible.

As Michael Rustin (2004) argues in a paper about the Climbié inquiry, 'How can valid recommendations for improvements in service be made without evidence not only of what happened in this instance, but concerning the standard of practice which prevails more generally? No such broader evidence is adduced by the report.' However, this is exactly the methodology for child protection policy-making which has repeatedly been chosen in Britain, and which is more or less unknown in other countries. Despite the fact that the emotive climate of the public inquiry probably does not lend itself to generating thoughtful and emotionally intelligent policy recommendations, it is notable how our society repeatedly chooses to commission these inquiries. Reder and Duncan (2004a) note that successive inquiries produce the same kinds of conclusions about the same kinds of problems leading up to the various tragedies, and remark that they therefore cannot be regarded as very successful processes of learning. So, is it possible that these inquiries fulfil deeper, less visible, functions for our society, and that social policy is, at least in this instance, being shaped by powerful 'unconscious' forces operating in society such as our collective fear of torture and death – the tragic fate of so many of the children whose short lives become headline news?

Cooper and Lousada (2005) have suggested that perhaps the inquiries are forms of public mourning which provide an 'overdetermined' focus for public feeling and emotion extending far beyond the particular event in question, rather as the death of Diana Princess of Wales may have done. Others have noted how the inquiries offer opportunity for a drama of scapegoating and blame to be played out on a national stage, creating a moral panic with attendant 'folk devils', a kind of reality soap opera. Or perhaps, as Cooper and Lousada (2005) suggest, such inquiries have played a useful part in 'softening up' various professional groups when government wishes to intervene in the autonomy of professions for policy purposes.

Whatever the possible explanations, child protection policy-making is an interesting entry point to the idea that policy-making may not be the wholly rational–instrumental activity it often purports to be.

Case study

The Clarendon Association contd . . .

The CE of the Clarendon recognised that not all the problems of the organisation lay with the front-line staff, and they needed support to negotiate the complex transition they were experiencing, so he brought in group supervision for the different teams. In one team, discussions would focus for a period of a few weeks on practitioners' work with individual tenants, and then on their thoughts and feelings about the organisation and the network of other organisations in which they functioned.

One team member's experience with a service user seemed also to capture something of the quality of the team's wider experience of being 'hemmed in'. The service user had a diagnosis of schizophrenia, and had been in and out of hospital over many years. She had managed her tenancy with the Clarendon erratically, often upsetting neighbours because she believed they were talking about her or conspiring against her. However, she seemed to also feel anxious and guilty about the impact she may have had on these neighbours and this made her reluctant to return to her flat. The most hopeful sign in the situation was her relationship with the Clarendon worker whom she appeared to trust, and with whom she could at least share her thoughts about the above situation, although this did not necessarily lead to much change in her ability to use the tenancy.

Indeed, while the Clarendon's funders were now requiring that 'measures of change' be recorded so that tenants could be seen to be progressing towards 'resettlement' (where exactly, the practitioners often asked themselves), the team doubted that many of their tenants were capable of much change. This did not mean they could not be helped and supported, however. In addition, the community mental health teams and probation officers who referred cases and also worked with their tenants usually wanted Clarendon staff to act as 'monitors' for their clients, assisting in the task of 'managing risk'. With funders and Clarendon management both now undertaking spot-check audits on practitioners' record-keeping, the team often felt beleaguered. As one team member put it, 'The funders, the tenants, the referrers and our management all seem to want different things from us'.

The group supervisor tried to help the team see that these *were* the boundary conditions of their work, and that while he could empathise with their sense of being hemmed in, they were also articulate and very intelligent about their situation. From this basis, perhaps they could *both* continue to work responsibly within the organisation, *and* advocate on behalf of their tenants' needs for longer-term housing support that suited their potential. After all they were the people who really *knew* their tenants.

These outline suggestions about how to conceptualise everyday experience in terms of both a relationship to policy and to service user experience, but mediated by organisational understanding, has much in common with ideas about 'street-level bureaucrats' developed by Michael Lipsky in the 1970s (Lipsky, 1979), ideas that are perhaps more relevant today than when they were originated, given that they are critical of 'top down' models of policy-making. More recently Paul Hoggett (2006) has articulated a similar thesis, arguing that welfare state workers continually negotiate and mediate the conflicts, tensions and contradictions of policy through the use of individual discretion and creativity. There are two kinds of lesson to be drawn from these analyses. The first is that if we study how social workers and others actually behave on the front line then we will find that they are not automatons, passively 'implementing' policy according to a set of protocols or procedures, but are always interpreting, mediating and negotiating complex realities. They are inevitably creative in their work, and this sets limits to the degree of control that any policy can achieve. The second kind of lesson is to propose that policy and organisational processes work better if exactly this kind of behaviour (based in first-hand knowledge of the realities of people's lives) is taken as a starting point for formulating policy, rather than the abstractions of the traditional policy makers' aims and objectives. But these perspectives are mostly at odds with the dominant ethos of contemporary policy-making. We would conclude that social workers need to understand the ethos of the times they live and work in, and make their own decisions and choices about what stance they adopt to the realities of whatever 'context' they find themselves working within.

Conclusion

In this chapter we have described how social policy processes directly affect the everyday experience and functioning of the social worker and the organisation in which they are situated. In recent years, however, the nature of organisations has changed, reflecting developments in the way governments approach the whole project of social welfare. Partnerships and networks between agencies located in different sectors are now the dominant organisational form, and 'governance' arrangements are the means of ordering and regulating how these networks function. In some respects policy has become much more directly 'prescriptive' of individual practice, and again this reflects a wish on the part of governments to influence how individual citizens and professionals behave, and to manage risks in their populations. However, some social policy analysts have suggested that there are new kinds of possibilities for influence in the revised 'settlement' between government and the various groups that make up the rest of society. In this chapter we have begun to 'map' some of these spaces, and suggested that individually, and in the context of your organisation, you need to 'navigate change', which means finding your own space for critical reflection, activity and influence.

Key learning points

This chapter has covered the following learning points:

✔ The social policy process directly affects the daily life of modern social workers in new and rapidly changing ways. There are some major policy trends and 'forces' acting on social care organisations, and social workers need skills in understanding and exerting positive influence on this web of influences.

✔ There are a number of critical perspectives on modern policy processes, including some that suggest policy is not always a rational process and that policies can have unintended consequences as well as intended ones.

✔ Modern social policy is shaped by the way in which governments have withdrawn from direct provision of welfare, and moved towards 'enabling' different sectors in society to collaborate in both funding and providing services. Social workers need to understand, be able to work with, and also critique the new 'governance' arrangements that manage these 'networks'.

✔ The prevalence of computer-based form-filling and 'paperwork' is an aspect of the development of an 'information society' and a 'surveillance society' aimed at managing risks, but arguably also manufactures risk and greater social complexity – the very things these practices are designed to limit and control.

✔ A number of features of modern social welfare – managerialism, markets, audit and inspection – have formed a coherent new 'ideology of welfare' in the early part of the twenty-first century.

 ## Further reading

Broadhurst K. et al. (2010) 'Performing 'initial assessment': identifying the latent conditions for error at the front door of local authority children's services', *British Journal of Social Work,* 40: 352–70. This paper explores the working lives of social workers in the context of 'modernised' services struggling with resource constraints on the one hand, and the demands of audit and electronic data-recording and assessment systems on the other. The authors identify various 'strategies' evolved by staff to manage the resulting 'workflow' and argue that the overall end result erodes possibilities for direct practice engagements with service users.

Chapman, J. (2004) *System Failure: Why Governments Must Learn to Think Differently,* London: DEMOS. This short pamphlet (obtainable free online at the web address opposite) is a critique of the assumptions underlying most policy initiatives, and suggests that many policies fail to make an impact because governments think about influencing society in 'linear' rather than complex terms.

Cooper, A. and Lousada, J. (2005) *Borderline Welfare: Feeling and Fear of Feeling in Modern Welfare,* London: Karnac. This book is a critical analysis of the culture of modern health and welfare, and contains chapters which explore the 'audit society', life in modern organisations, the organisational tensions of adult mental health work, and a critique of the Victoria Climbié inquiry report.

Huffington, C., Armstrong, D., Halton, W., Hoyle, L. and Pooley, J. (eds) (2004) *Working Below the Surface: The Emotional Life of Organisations,* London: Karnac. This edited collection provides an interesting and challenging view of how emotions are central to organisations and the experience of working in them. Cooper and Dartington's chapter may be especially useful for social workers.

Newman, J. (2005) *Remaking Governance Peoples, Politics and the Public Sphere,* Bristol: The Policy Press. Janet Newman is one of the leading theorists of the evolution of governance and social policy in recent years. This book contains chapters that look at the wider European context of changing welfare states, as well as a valuable introduction explaining and summarising the trends in social policy explored above.

Stanley, N. and Manthorpe, J. (2004) *The Age of the Inquiry: Learning and Blaming in Health and Social Care,* London: Routledge. This edited collection provides a comprehensive range of perspectives on the part played by public inquiries in shaping social policy in modern British health and welfare. The various chapters contain very useful summaries and analyses of inquiries, and well-argued discussions of their meaning and impact.

Useful websites

www.socialpolicy.net
Social policy net – the internet guide to social policy links on the web.

http://csp.sagepub.comhttp://csp.sagepub.com
Critical Social Policy journal.

www.users.globalnet.co.uk/~opusuk
OPUS – 'an organisation for promoting understanding of society' promotes activities and events that link developments in work and society with citizenship and personal experience. OPUS also publishes a valuable journal, *Organisational and Social Dynamics*.

www.grubb.org.uk
The Grubb Institute promotes experiential understanding of social life through 'group relations conferences' and other activities, focusing especially on 'pressure points' in modern social life.

www.demos.co.uk
DEMOS is a 'think tank' that commissions a wide range of innovative and 'cutting edge' pamphlets on contemporary social policy issues. All their publications are free online.

For additional cases and topic-organised, clickable links into additional media resources, including those produced by IRISS, visit **www.pearsoned.co.uk/wilsonruch**

Activity

Audit and social work

Read Eileen Munro's (2004) article 'The impact of audit on social work practice', in *British Journal of Social Work*, 34: 1075–95. Munro argues that the difference between service outputs and service-user outcomes is crucial if audit practices are to make a meaningful difference to social work. Study her arguments and decide whether you think she is right.

Investigating 'governance'

Find out how the 'governance' arrangements in your organisation work by talking to a middle or senior manager about this. How are partnerships with other organisations managed? Is one organisation in the partnership arrangements more influential than others? Who 'really' holds power and influence in the view of people you talk to?

Chapter 3
Contemporary challenges: social work in the twenty-first century

Chapter summary

In this chapter we reflect on some of the key social and professional trends which are shaping the future of social work. We do not attempt to predict the future, but through analysing current patterns of development we set out some likely alternative scenarios, and some probable lines of development in twenty-first century social work. However, we begin the chapter by suggesting that the central challenge facing social work is about professional confidence: whether the profession can establish a greater degree of self-confidence in a period of rapid change, uncertainty, and no little competition between professional groups, competition which is sharpened by a context of funding pressures.

Introduction: looking ahead to the shape of twenty-first century social work

In the second decade of the twenty-first century British social work will be defined and shaped by a number of key trends and social forces. These include:

- Political responses to the consequences of the global financial crises of 2008–9. What strategies will governments and national assemblies (in Britain, Scotland, Wales and Northern Ireland) adopt to address massive national debt and 'structural deficit', while attempting to protect public services? What new models of funding and development for social services involving direct state provision, and the private and independent sectors will emerge?
- Whatever the answer to the above questions, it is likely that new and unfamiliar contexts or 'social spaces' will evolve in which social work can play a role. These might include new forms of voluntary and community-based organisation funded from a variety of sources – 'social enterprises'. Society as a whole is bigger, more complex and more encompassing than governments or public policy, and increasingly the trend towards 'post-modern' social dynamics creates these new social spaces and possibilities for innovation and diversity.
- The privatisation and 'outsourcing' of local authority and state-run services is almost certain to gather pace. The desire to free social work agencies from excessive regulation and bureaucracy may be entwined with this trend, but this may oscillate according to the differing philosophies of governments with respect to the centralisation or decentralisation, regulation or deregulation of service provision. It has been remarked that in times of financial plenty governments like to control as much as possible in order to gain credit for achievements, while in periods of austerity they prefer to 'devolve' responsibility for social development in order to evade or 'share' its costs!
- Devolution of power and control over the purchasing and organisation of services via policies of 'personalisation' will be widespread. This trend will aim to integrate philosophies of service-user empowerment and choice, marketisation (service providers survive

according to success in meeting demand), value for money, and decentralisation of social care planning to local social care 'markets'.

- Trust in professionals to 'get on with the job' and trust in citizens to 'get on with their lives' will be in continuing tension with anxiety about how to manage and reduce risks in society. Faith in sophisticated 'systems' (electronic, organisational, legal) to manage information, risk and social complexity is likely to recede somewhat because they are expensive, cumbersome and fallible. But crises of 'risk' are certain to continue, and an important question is whether we will see the emergence of greater tolerance towards risk and 'failure', or perhaps new social and political attitudes towards the uncertainties and dangers inherent in social life.

The key to social work's future: professional confidence and identity

As you will have discovered reading Chapters 2, 3 and 4, social work is a part of society and, during its evolution as a profession, has reflected political processes and debates in the wider society. The process of political and value debate within social work and struggles over what kind of activity social work is, or should be, have often been a source of conflict and tension within the profession, as well as providing opportunities for growth in response to challenge. This chapter tries to anticipate some of the key trends, challenges and dilemmas that will affect social work in coming years.

In part, we believe we are helped to 'see into the future' of social work by a careful analysis of what is happening now, because to some degree the social and political trends affecting social work are predictable. But also, social work has always occupied a distinctive place within the range of professions which make up the health and welfare systems of modern economies and their welfare states. This has meant that social work has been afflicted by certain 'core contradictions' or characteristic 'tensions' about its role and contribution in society. In turn these tensions have been reflected in debates, arguments, controversies and differences of perspective *within* the profession.

As we discussed in Chapter 2, at times these internal professional debates have been very destructive to social work; equally from time to time social work comes under

fire from outside, most famously in a book by Brewer and Lait published in 1980, entitled *Can Social Work Survive?*, whose criticisms we touched on in Chapter 8. Sometimes, then, it can seem as though social workers are an occupational group afflicted by chronic, and at times acute self-doubt. If this book has an underlying ambition, it is to promote the *confidence* of social workers.

Social work – safe in their hands?

Confidence emerged as a key theme in the aftermath of the 'Baby P' crisis in Britain in 2008–9. At the height of the crisis it seemed that social work, and the government, were almost to be shaped by a kind of 'mob rule' stemming from the *Sun* newspaper's campaign for the sacking of several named social workers who had been involved with Peter Connelly (Baby P) and his carers. No established profession has ever been the object of such widespread hostility or, when the Secretary of State responsible for children and families at the time appeared momentarily to endorse the *Sun* campaign, come so close to losing the confidence of government (Cooper, 2010a). As the government of the day collected its wits, it set in train a reform process for social work – The Social Work Task Force (whose membership included the *Sun's* 'agony aunt') and whose final report was called 'A safe, confident future for social work' (DCSF, 2009), then a Social Work Reform Board, followed by the establishment of a national College of Social Work. The stress on 'confidence' can be gauged from the following short passage:

Good social work . . . depends on confident, effective front-line professionals. These professionals depend, in turn, on a system of high quality training, regulation and leadership behind them. This system should provide them with the resources and conditions they need to do their job well. When social workers have confidence in their own skills, purpose and identity, and in the system in place to back them up, they have a huge amount to offer.

(DCSF, 2009: 5)

Similar concerns about professional competence have emerged in Northern Ireland in the wake of a review of child protection services (SSI overview report 2007) and several high-profile public inquiry reports of child deaths perpetrated by close family members. (McElhill, 2007 (DHSSPSS 2008) and O'Neill 2007 (WHSSB and EHSSB 2008). Both reports were critical of multidisciplinary working citing concerns about the lack of effective professional communication and the inadequacy of risk assessments. In establishing review mechanisms through The Regulation and Quality Improvement Authority (RQIA), local Health and Social Care Trusts have engaged in implementing quality improvements to child protection services. Although monitoring the impact of progress achieved has gone some way to reestablishing public confidence, the impact on staff morale and professional confidence in childcare is less evident.

Confidence – a question of identity

The debates and controversies noted above, and the sense of a crisis of confidence, are about the *identity* of social work – what kind of profession is it, and what are its defining methods and values? Without a strong and clear identity any professional group will struggle to maintain direction in its development, will be vulnerable to the competing interests of 'neighbouring' professions, and open to the charge that it cannot articulate its distinctive contribution. Professionals are expensive, so why should anyone – taxpayers, employers, commissioners – agree to fund a profession that doesn't seem to know what it is all about?

One way in which this tension may have an immediate impact stems from the organisational separation of services to adults from those for children and families, which took place in relation to statutory services in 2006, discussed in Chapter 3. Social work has held on to a generic identity for several decades, despite the loss of training for the probation service in the late 1990s which represented a substantial challenge to this (see Chapter 16 and Aldridge and Eadie, 1997). However, the recent organisational division of social work services could have grave consequences for the identity of social work. There are many areas of practice where it could be argued that there is no need for a continued social work presence, particularly in relation to social work with adults where care management models of practice have markedly altered the professional social work role. It means that the ability of social workers to be able to justify their existence takes on a particular importance.

Social work methods – the missing key to identity

We have written this textbook with a particular emphasis on the centrality of social work *methods* – the practical and sophisticated tools with which social workers can help create change and improvement in the lives of service users – because we are convinced that a strong social work identity depends upon each worker having a really good grasp of *how* to facilitate effective interventions – not just complete routine 'assessments'. Without this, there will always be a serious gulf between our professional aims and the service outcomes we aspire to achieve. Social work in recent decades has been strong on values, but relatively weak on methods, and this has seriously negatively affected its professional identity – and the confidence of practitioners.

Thus, among the range of themes, issues and trends we anticipate will influence social work in coming years (see below) there will almost certainly be continuing pressure to provide an 'evidence base' for social work. In the UK one of the official leadership bodies for social work, the Social Care Institute for Excellence (SCIE), has taken an interesting strategic line in relation to this question. Rather than promote the 'evidence and outcomes game' in social care, it has focused energy on building the 'knowledge base' for the profession – a number of SCIE's Knowledge Reviews are referred to in the course of this book (see Chapters 5, 8 and 15, for example). One argument for the good sense of this strategy is that as we discuss in some detail in Chapter 8, the kinds of situations with which social work is concerned are generally too complex to be researched according to the 'gold standard' Randomised Controlled Trial models underpinning the 'evidence informed practice' movement in the health service and which may be ethically unacceptable in a social welfare context. However, where interventions typically used by social workers can be researched in these ways, there is a good argument for doing so. Whatever anyone's view, the tension between values, methods, knowledge and evidence as defining underpinning aspects of social work identity is likely to persist.

Finding our 'fight'

However, there are other dimensions to the project of restoring social work's self-confidence, some of them addressed by the Social Work Task Force, and some not:

■ A need not just for stronger collective professional identity, which the College of Social Work may or may not provide, but for social workers individually and collectively to develop a capacity for 'fight', to be able to publicly and articulately contest negative stereotypes, scapegoating and misinformation. A stronger sense of what social work's *unique* contribution to society amounts to is a prerequisite for this.

- A need to find and cultivate influential 'champions' of the profession – in government, the media and among other professions.
- The importance of resolving our collective ambivalence about whether we wish to be 'professionalised'. The fear that if we seek a stronger professional identity then we will become distanced from the lives and struggles of service users and disadvantaged communities is at the root of this uncertainty. There are some grounds for this fear because many established professions have indeed become closed self-protective systems, but equally medicine and law, for example, retain significant progressive, critical and radical elements. Arguably, these are more effective for being a legitimate part of a strong profession – 'in and against the establishment'.

With this understanding of the tensions pervading contemporary social work, it is possible to consider some more detailed themes that will shape its practices in the coming decade.

Themes in twenty-first century social work

Below we unpack the very broad trends for the future set out in the introduction, and then focus on some central areas of debate and tension that these involve. Some of the specific trends we can anticipate are:

- The continued development of 'marketised' solutions to welfare needs and problems that are based on the purchaser and provider models of practice, introduced to you in Chapter 2, and the extension of an ideology of welfare as a set of opportunities which 'responsibilised' citizens are enabled to access via the brokering function of social work, social care and other welfare professionals.

  Associated with the above is the continuing tension about whether the core tasks of social work practice concern maximising **choice and responsibility** or whether they concern the provision of **professional relationships** as a response to human needs and enforced dependency.
- The growth of new and perhaps creative models of care based on principles of **personalisation**. To date, developments flowing from this idea have been mostly confined to the introduction of individual budgets. But some writers and reformers have a wider and

more radical vision of **'self-directed support'** incorporating a principle of individual 'resource allocation' (Duffy, 2010). This entails much more than a 'cash transfer' and would extend to negotiated agreements between service users and professionals about the quality and quantity of provision offered and transacted.

- However, developments like this may highlight a complex boundary between the realms of social *care* and social *work*. Arguably, many of the core or 'reserved' functions of social work concern situations of actual or potential **conflict** – between vulnerable children and carers (neglect, abuse, exploitation), within families or between couples (domestic violence, family breakdown), between the individual or family and the state (crime, serious mental illness, school refusal, child maltreatment) and it is harder to see how a pure model of personalisation can be effective or meaningful in many of these situations. This is not to say that the (practical and ethical) principles of negotiation and reciprocal respect cannot be much further extended in practice areas where compulsion and statutory intervention prevail (See, for example, Cooper et al., 2003). Not all social and personal difficulties are, or ever can be, resolvable within a policy and ideological framework of 'reciprocity', 'rights', or 'empowerment'. Conflict is at the heart of human social life, and it may be that we should and will arrive at a clearer understanding of social work's central concern with this.
- A continuing emphasis, discussed in Chapter 13, on multi-professional, multi-agency and inter-organisational **partnerships** in the provision of human services – a trend that will mean that tensions around the professional identity of social work and social workers will remain at the forefront of debate.
- The trend towards an ageing population and the consequent declining tax base will mean that social work and **social care with older people**, explored in Chapter 22, will be an expanding and increasingly controversial area of practice and policy.
- Changing patterns of **international migration** associated with global economic inequalities, post-conflict dispersion of ethnic groups, and the shifting balance of socio-economic power among nations and continents, are likely to result in social work with asylum seekers, immigrants, people who have been trafficked, and people who are part of the 'grey economy' becoming an increasing focus of need and intervention.

- The development of political and social strategies for the management of **social 'risk'**, which include sophisticated **information-sharing and surveillance** systems will continue to impact on social work despite trends towards **bureaucracy-busting** (see Chapters 2 and 15).

- In the context of a widening **inequality gap** between a smaller number of poor, marginalised and socially excluded communities and groups on the one hand, and an economically secure and affluent majority on the other, questions about the **political contribution** of social work as a function that either maintains inequality or functions to challenge it, as outlined in Chapter 2, are likely to sharpen.

- The role of **service users and carers** in planning, commissioning and delivering social care services and training, explored in Chapters 14 and 15, is likely to consolidate, but whether service user movements can advance beyond a limited and ultimately rather token contribution to the overall social care project is uncertain and likely to be a focus of controversy, although in a context of restricted state funding 'personalisation' may deliver more influence into the hands of citizens.

- A continued process of 'discovery', or disclosure, of hitherto unrecognised or **hidden forms of abuse and exploitation**; at the time of writing it seems that vulnerable adults and 'adult protection', referred to in Chapters 19 and 22, may achieve a more widespread level of public and professional recognition, and consequently could be another area in which the practice of social workers becomes particularly exposed. Events in Ireland during 2009-10 exposed an unprecedented degree of collusion between the Catholic Church, the police and the Irish State in suppressing evidence of systematic child abuse inside religious organisations.

- In the context of a trend towards 'small government' and a declining, or at best stable, tax base for social care provision, tensions around **resource allocation** and the new mechanisms via which governments regulate professional behaviour – performance management, targets, regulation and inspection – are likely to continue (see Chapter 2). Thus, whether social work is defined in terms in terms of a commitment to respond to **human needs**, human rights, interpersonal stress and conflict, and mental pain on the one hand, or in terms of **effective service delivery** and the targeting of limited resources towards 'problem populations' on the other, will be a continuing source of debate.

Below, we expand on these themes and link some of them together.

Social work and the 'new welfare': cry freedom or cry foul?

In Chapter 2 of this book we presented a perspective on the development of modern welfare that stressed the impact of 'market' mechanisms and managerialism in 'market societies' in shaping our everyday experience as both professionals and users of social and health care services. The authors of this book all entered social work at a time when the underpinning principles of social work were rather different, as discussed in Chapter 4, and seemed to reflect organised political and social concern for disadvantaged, oppressed and disempowered sections of the population, as well as 'state' responsibility for funding and delivering services.

The professional mood of those times was also very different, and much less bound up with questions of effectiveness, efficiency, evidence, performance and outcome. Do we expect this shift in thinking and practice to continue, and if so what does this mean for social workers entering the profession in the first decades of the twenty-first century?

One of the ways in which 'market philosophy' tempts us into pursuing its solutions is by seeming to offer new 'freedoms'. Often these are freedoms *from* the supposedly obstructive or constraining influence of state and local authority regulation, bureaucracy, funding limits and so on. This is one way in which, for example, 'Foundation Trust Status' has been promoted to hospitals and mental health trusts in Britain in recent years. The positive freedoms on offer are the possibility of relative financial independence, the opportunity to earn and invest a financial surplus and thus have organisational autonomy over professional and service development. In effect, the proposal to establish independent social work agencies to work with children in care (DfES, 2007a) is promoting similar trends in social work, as a solution to the same kinds of perceived problem. At an individual level the introduction of the direct payments schemes for adults in receipt of 'care packages', outlined in Chapter 17 in relation to adults with disabilities, offers service users similar 'freedoms'.

In Britain, the 'third way' programme of the Labour Government which came to power in 1997 was developed in the hope that it would combine the best that a tradition of state-funded services and the best that market freedoms and a 'mixed economy' of provision could offer. How well it has worked so far, and how this trend will evolve are key questions facing social work. One way of searching out possible answers is to look at social work in societies that have already travelled further down this road, and compare these with societies that have preserved or opted for very different principles as they seek to maintain their welfare states in an era of declining tax revenues and declining support for the idea of direct state intervention in personal life.

In their cross-national studies of child protection systems and practices Hetherington et al. (1997) compared the professional and political cultures of childcare work in European societies with diverging philosophies of welfare and its relationship to the rest of society. On many criteria, England and Wales emerge in these studies as more 'different' from any of the comparator countries than are any of these countries from one another. Even Scotland emerges as closer to the more 'solidaristic' continental welfare systems than it is to England.

On a recent trip to the United States one of us heard about a senior professional in an independent social work agency who had been diagnosed with cancer. 'But the prognosis is looking good, and we held some fundraisers and got $10,000 towards her hospital bills', said one of her colleagues. What do we learn from this, admittedly anecdotal, story about the meaning of welfare in a very rich society in which a senior professional in her mid-50s must raise funds to pay for treatment for a very serious but also very common medical condition? In the same American state, we met families with several children adopted from the state care system or from abroad as well as several 'birth' children. All these children were 'home schooled' – the mothers and in their time the older girls taking the role of teachers – and the families were members of a church which they had formed themselves, meeting in one another's houses. These families were functioning in effect outside any mainstream state educational or welfare system, and formed a networked 'community' of their own funded by the fathers' and older boys' work in 'regular' jobs. On the one hand, there was something deeply impressive and substantial in this manifestation of 'family values'; on the other hand, one could see such patterns of behaviour as an inevitable and 'natural' outcome in a society that makes only minimal commitment to creating and sustaining a network or culture of state provision. Arguably, it can work very well – for those families and communities which have the financial and cultural resources to generate their own 'self-help'. But what of those who do not?

England has always been positioned somewhere between the 'two cultures' of welfare represented by the United States and continental Europe, but where is it now heading? This is one of the great questions of our time, and the answer will profoundly affect the future of social work in the approaching decades. A central feature of the debates relating to the new models of welfare is the increasing tendency to replace professional relationships as the central component in social work interventions with resource packages, a trend, we would argue, that gives cause for concern.

Relationships or resource packages?

The relationship–resource packages tension referred to above and discussed in Chapters 1, 2 and 10 relates to the different perspectives on the social work role and remit. On the one hand, the social work role is understood as one of developing and sustaining therapeutic (in its broadest sense) relationships with preventative dimensions. On the other hand, it is understood to be a reactive role, focusing on the management of scarce resources. As with all tensions, it is often more helpful to resist polarising the potentially conflicting dimensions of the tension in order to understand how they can both be effectively addressed. It is naive to assume that there would ever be a world of limitless resources for social work activities and management of scarce resources is integral to the social work role. Conversely, it is equally naive and, we would argue, ineffective and inefficient to endeavour to practise in ways which assume people are always or only rational beings who can identify what services they need, and whose circumstances will automatically improve with the provision of the necessary resources.

A partial explanation for shortcomings in social work in general, and in the care management approaches in particular, has been the underestimation of the emotional dimensions of social problems. In this book (see Chapters 14 and 15) and other recent publications (Cree, 2007) the voices of service users and carers have clearly articulated this perspective by emphasising that relationships and emotional understanding and support are central to effective social work interventions. Effective care packages need to be both sensitively constructed and delivered, but it is through the medium of the social work relationships that change is effected.

What does this mean, then, for you as a social worker? Firstly, it means that regardless of your role, how you develop and sustain relationships should be a top priority in your professional activities. This attention to relationships is not simply about the service user–social worker relationship. Equally important, as Chapter 13 emphasises, are the professional relationships established within and across organisations, as inevitably these impact on service users. Secondly, it means that your effectiveness is closely connected to your own professional well-being. To ensure this is nurtured and sustained, it is essential that appropriate support systems exist, as discussed in Chapter 1. Such provision will enable you to keep thinking about what you are doing, in order to avoid you becoming engaged in random activity in response to the demands of others – service users, carers, other professionals, employers.

However, as we stressed in Chapter 2, the immediate future will manifest a continued tension between a concept of social work rooted in responding to actual human psychological and social needs, and one rooted in maintaining a population fit for labour market needs at least economic cost. Such a tension has serious implications when it is put alongside the increasingly ageing demographic profile in the United Kingdom.

An ageing population and the development of policy for social care and social work

As we have indicated in Chapter 22, changes in the balance of the population will create further challenges for social work. Both the numbers and proportion of older people will increase, with the fastest-growing sector of society being those aged over 85 years. Although there are major implications of this as far as social policy decisions are concerned, we are interested here in the implications of this development for social work, particularly given the fact that working with older people has been so dominated by forms of practice that emphasise the need to process work swiftly, and which have downplayed the importance both of 'traditional' approaches to social work as well as more 'radical' approaches (see Chapter 4 and Lymbery et al., 2007).

This poses a number of challenges for social work, particularly in relation to the development of social policy. It is argued in Chapter 22 that financial imperatives have been dominant in the development of community care, a possibility first noted by Huxley (1993) and central to the thesis of Jane Lewis and Howard Glennerster in their seminal text (1996). The ongoing challenges posed by this are critical: certainly, there appears to be a direct conflict between the preventive focus that suffuses both the 2005 Green Paper (DoH, 2005b) and the 2006 White Paper (DoH, 2006a), and the continuing focus on the need to control costs (Holloway and Lymbery, 2007). If the preventive dimension is to dominate, social workers

are likely to be involved at an earlier stage of people's problems, and their roles will also expand from the circumscribed and humdrum reality of much adult social work – assessing needs against the eligibility criteria of the agency; establishing packages of care; closing the case. In his *Managing Vulnerability* Dartington (2010) has explored the power of the hidden and unconscious dynamics of social care for vulnerable and dependent adults and there is no doubt that these represent a significant practice challenge – should the resourcing of *potentially* adequate care systems ever become available. Institutionalised ageism in our society represents a major barrier to the prospect that they will. Thus, positive development of the forms of practice advocated in this book is by no means certain, potentially leading to problems for the role of social work with older people. More importantly, this could also lead to the continuation of a second-class service for the increasing numbers of older people that will characterise British society.

In general terms, the next few years will be of particular importance in the development of social care for adults, and the specific role that social workers play within the wider range of services. While government documents have outlined the general direction that health and social care services should take, there is relatively little discussion within such documents of the professional social work role. Indeed, it was significant that neither of the terms 'social work' and 'social workers' actually appears in the White Paper outlining the development of health and social care (DoH, 2006a), despite being a major element of the preceding Green Paper (DoH, 2005b). Therefore, there is great uncertainty about what the impact of any future developments might have on the social work profession. The voice of service users and carers could play a crucial role in how these developments unfold.

The voice of service users and carers

We referred earlier in this chapter to the importance in contemporary social work of relationships with service users. One of the most significant and influential developments in the delivery of social work in recent years – and particularly in the education of its practitioners – has been the recognition that as far as possible social care services need to be planned and organised in accordance with the views of service users. There is little doubt that a failure to respond effectively to the demands of service users and carers has characterised much social work, as well as other similar occupations.

However, as we have noted in Chapter 14, the knowledge and insights that service users bring are not the only source of evidence that should concern social workers (see Pawson et al., 2003). A critical skill for social workers will be their ability to manage the tensions that this recognition may generate in practice. Although somewhat limited in scope at this stage, some writing is beginning to emerge that questions the orthodoxy of social work's current preoccupation with service user perspectives (see, for example, Cowden and Singh, 2007). As our knowledge of the complexities involved in engaging user and carer increases, new ways of conceptualising the relationship between services, professionals, users and carers will be considered and established.

While it is impossible to be precise about where future areas of conflict might be located, an obvious source of tension derives from the split loyalties of social workers, particularly those employed in the statutory sector. Alongside the overriding professional obligation to users and carers, practitioners also have to balance their responsibilities to employers; there is no necessary fit between these different requirements, even though potential conflicts are glossed over in key governmental publications (see DoH, 2005b). Governments are rarely transparent about the effect of, for example, budgetary restrictions on the opportunities that may be available for service users and carers, yet these become a critical backdrop to practitioners' work. For example, it has long been recognised that the active involvement of informal carers is both a reality of care and generally the most cost-effective form of response. For social care services, there exists a fine line between recognising and supporting the desire of carers to look after needy people within their families and the exploitation of such people. As is often the case, the complexities that such conflicts produce have to be managed by professional social workers, acting on the boundaries between individuals and the wider society. Such conflicts cannot be resolved simply by a rhetorical commitment to the involvement of users and carers, important though such a commitment undoubtedly is. Social workers will continually have to work such issues out on an individual basis: the apparently simple injunction to involve users and carers will therefore be the location for a number of complex and difficult debates. Adding to the challenges that service user involvement generates are the increasingly diverse personal needs and social contexts which service users encompass. It is to this final challenge of diversity and difference we now turn.

Disclosing new forms of need and conflict

We tend to think of social work services as providing a response to known and identifiable needs and problems. Of course this is accurate, but there is another less recognised role that organised social welfare plays in society – one of uncovering or disclosing previously hidden and unrecognised forms of need, abuse and conflict. Major developments of this kind do not occur very often, but when they do, then sometimes our whole picture of ourselves as human beings can alter.

In recent decades the most important and dramatic of such shifts in perception concerns child sexual abuse, discussed in Chapter 16. Before the 1987 'Cleveland crisis' during which more than two hundred children from one local authority were taken into care in the space of a few weeks, child sexual abuse was widely assumed (in both public and professional circles) to be a fairly rare phenomenon. In the space of a few months, events in Cleveland altered the landscape of British and international thinking about child abuse forever. In turn it became widely accepted that many adult mental health problems had their roots in a history of childhood sexual abuse. How could such a widespread and damaging feature of personal and social life have remained so effectively hidden for so many centuries? And are there other, similarly important dimensions of private and public experience 'waiting' to be disclosed in future?

A proper answer to these questions is beyond the scope of this short chapter (for a fuller discussion see Cooper and Lousada (2005), chapter 6), but we believe it is important to accept that it *could* be true that in years to come our societies will undergo comparable transformations of understanding. Social work played a central role in bringing child sexual abuse to light. In earlier generations it made a huge contribution to the public recognition of the physical abuse and neglect of children, child and family poverty, conditions in psychiatric hospitals, and so on. In the current social context the growing awareness of vulnerable adults mentioned earlier (see Chapters 19 and 22 for fuller discussions) is an example of a contemporary preoccupation for social workers which is altering our perception of the care needs of adults. Another relatively new but increasingly high-profile issue with which social workers are actively engaged is that of asylum seekers, where, for example, their professional duty to protect unaccompanied minors may be brought into sharp conflict with the demands for surveillance and controls of the immigration services. The social, cultural and ethical dilemmas generated by the issues of difference and diversity represented by these groups of people are likely to prove a major challenge for social work over the next decade. These examples reflect something about how social work practice straddles the line between 'private troubles and public issues' (Wright Mills, 1959) in a unique way in our societies. In terms of key challenges for the twenty-first century, our question is 'Can social work continue to perform this discomforting "critical" role in society, or will it be rendered more conformist and less independently minded?'

In Northern Ireland, the significance of post-conflict context for social work provides an important backdrop to professional practice. As the region emerges from over thirty years of political conflict and violence, increased emphasis has been given to the needs of victims and survivors of the 'Troubles' and communities which have experienced trauma and economic deprivation. Effecting change in society which has embraced a peace process also involves reconciliation and restorative justice approaches but social work has been slow to mainstream such interventions. Critically future economic growth and prosperity may well depend on the extent to which such initiatives are incorporated into professional practice.

Making space: the struggle to reclaim social work

'Reclaiming social work' was the proud and optimistic title of the initiative taken by the London Borough of Hackney children's services in 2008. Small, therapeutically skilled, multidisciplinary teams with dedicated administration to help 'bust' the bureaucratic burden, replaced the over-stretched, 'workflow' dominated, target-led and demoralised services found in other parts of the country by Broadhurst et al.'s (2010) study and exposed to public view by the Channel 4 Dispatches programme *Undercover Social Worker* in June 2010 (Channel 4, 2010). The evidence of early evaluations was that the strategy 'worked' with fewer child protection plans and less statutory intervention ensuing. *Reclaiming Social Work* was cited as a possible model for reform of the child protection system nationally by Eileen Munro when she was appointed to lead the latest review of this area of work in June 2010.

However, the problem of 'recovering the space' in which the possibility of direct, face-to-face, relationship-based social work might flourish once again is profound, and probably beyond the reach of localised bureaucracy-busting initiatives. Why? The answer lies in themes explored more fully in Chapter 2, and above in this chapter, which extend far beyond the direct control of social work itself. This is not to propose a counsel of despair, but to suggest that professional social work must engage with some complex political realities in pursuit of its own survival and integrity. In summary:

- Despite their immense relative prosperity, modern Western societies are anxious about their own survival in a changing world economic order, and following the financial crisis that swept through their economies in 2008–9. Preparing and educating citizens, and children as 'future citizens', for demanding and unpredictable labour market conditions is a political priority. 'Performance' and 'competence' in children (from birth) and adults become central political preoccupations. Human 'growth and development', the traditional intellectual foundations of relationship-based and therapeutic social work practice, is too open-ended a notion allowing too much scope for the autonomous realisation of personal desires and trajectories, to be consistent with the more 'instrumental' social objectives of modern governments.

- Modern social and psychological sciences have delivered real advances in understanding the origins and development of a wide range of social and personal 'troubles'. But science is always about averages in 'populations', not about individuals and their biographies or emotional life-worlds. The science is deployed in favour of policy strategies that are targeted on vulnerable groups and communities with accumulated 'risk factors' rather than via (paradoxically) 'personalised' face-to-face interventions.

- Thus, prevention becomes a form of control of potential 'problem populations' as opposed to being primarily a humane intervention in relation to suffering and disadvantage, although much good work fulfilling these latter aspirations may still occur within a framework whose primary objective is control.

- In order to *engage* individuals and families in this project, rather than just subject them to policy-led strategies, ideologies of 'responsibilisation' and, to some extent, 'personalisation' are developed. But what these give with one hand (autonomy over resources and management of care) they often take back with the other as the state monitors, inspects, audits and evaluates their 'impact' on terms it controls.

- In summary, modern social life and personal identities are increasingly complex and uncertain, risks abound, while advances in research aided by sophisticated information storing and sharing systems offer the hope of controlling, managing and preventing risk; but in a context where professionals are mistrusted, the result is a world in which faith in the power of systems to manage abstract bundles of risk factors replaces faith in 'relationships', while the systems of control and surveillance subordinate professional autonomy, and themselves generate additional complexity and uncertainty (Parton 2006).

Yet despite this gloomy picture, well-managed organisations and creative teams and individuals are often still in evidence, sustaining the conditions in which authentic relationship-based practice flourishes. Foster (2009) studied a number of front-line teams at close hand and identified a range of variables that differentiated those which managed to preserve space for reflective thought and practice and those which struggled to do so. Coherence or incoherence of the policy framework, dedicated regular reflective time for the team, autonomy over decision-making and practice planning, and support for continuing professional development were key factors in keeping hope and a sense of the *meaningfulness* of practice alive.

It took a national crisis of distressing and turbulent proportions to kick-start an effort to revive the fortunes of professional social work in Britain. In future, we suggest that social workers will need to be more continuously proactive in diagnosing and challenging the complex sources of malaise that so often seem to afflict our profession. This is a political and cultural project, and we believe that social workers in training need to be educated about its challenges.

Conclusion

Social work is a professional activity that takes place on the boundary of many different spheres of society: private and public life, the civil and judicial spheres, the personal and political, and so on. The lines demarcating these spheres are not constant, and as they shift, the question of what social work is all about becomes contested, and sometimes confused. Above, we have summarised our view of some of these boundary movements that will affect social work in coming years, for example the fundamental question of 'Who is responsible for welfare?' – the state as a provider, or the individual as consumer of a range of opportunities offered by the state in partnership with other sectors of society?

Associated with this perspective, social work is shaped by political and social ideologies but these are not fixed either. As a profession, social work has been rather prone to being 'pushed around' by the conflicting and shifting forces acting upon it and arising from the inherent tensions it contains. This has affected its capacity to establish and preserve a strong professional identity. We have suggested that social work's confidence in its own identity will be the key factor in its capacity to survive and flourish in future.

Key learning points

This chapter covers the following learning points:

✔ Social work's ability to develop and preserve a strong professional identity will be a key factor in the profession, successfully negotiating the many changes it inevitably faces in the coming years.

✔ These changes arise from wider changes in society, as well as the process of internal professional development.

✔ Some of the central tensions with which social work must engage in future include: pressures arising from the fact of an ageing population; changing patterns of international migration; contested views about social work's role in society and how far it can preserve its 'critical' function.

✔ 'Creating space' for reflective and relationship-based practice is a political and professional challenge to social workers, not something they can be passive about.

Activity

Read Chapter 9, 'Towards "the preventative state"', in Nigel Parton's book *Safeguarding Childhood*. It provides an excellent analytical account of the contradictions of modern politics, social life and policy that shape the experience of children and families and the professionals who work with them, as well other groups in society. Ask yourself:

Do you agree with his analysis?

Which experiences of your own support the picture he paints, and which suggest a different view?

Do you think life has changed in Britain since new Labour lost power at the 2010 election?

How would you like to see your team or organisation create more 'space' for autonomy in its work? Do you think this is possible?

Part One
UNDERSTANDING SOCIAL WORK

Chapter 4
The development of social work: key themes and critical debates

Chapter summary

In this chapter we trace a number of key debates in social work back to their historical roots. We suggest that an understanding of social work's historical development is important in placing current policy and practice in perspective. It serves as a reminder that the organisation of social work in British society is the product of argument and debate since (at least) the late nineteenth century; as a result, its focus and priorities in the early years of the twenty-first century should not be accepted as inevitable, but representative of one strand of thought about social work's possibilities.

Learning objectives

This chapter covers topics that will enable you to achieve the following learning objectives:

- To understand the development of social work in the British context
- To appreciate the debates and controversies that informed the direction of social work at specific points in its history, from its origins to the present day
- To identify key themes that have featured in these debates and chart their impact on present-day practice
- To ascertain the nature and form of contemporary social work within the context of British society.

National Occupational Standards

This chapter will help you to meet the following National Occupational Standards:

Key Role 1: Prepare for and work with individuals, families, carers, groups and communities to assess their needs and circumstances.

Unit 1   Prepare for social work contact and involvement

Key Role 5: Manage and be accountable, with supervision and support, for your own social work practice within your organisation

Unit 14   Manage and be accountable for your own work

Key Role 6: Demonstrate professional competence in social work practice.

Unit 18   Research, analyse, evaluate, and use current knowledge of best social work practice
Unit 19   Work within agreed standards of social work practice and ensure own professional development
Unit 20   Manage complex ethical issues, dilemmas and conflicts
Unit 21   Contribute to the promotion of best social work practice

Case study

The international definition of social work

In 2001 the International Federation of Social Workers adopted the following definition of social work to be applied on an international basis. Because it is meant to apply within a global context, the definition is pitched in broad terms.

'The social work profession promotes social change, problem solving in human relationships and the empowerment and liberation of people to enhance well-being. Utilising theories of human behaviour and social systems, social work intervenes at the points where people interact with their environments. Principles of human rights and social justice are fundamental to social work.'   (IFSW, 2001)

Does this definition hold good within the British context, when considering the roles that social workers have to adopt within society (for example, the controlling powers that social workers have in relation to child protection or mental health)?

It is clear that the scope of social work practice in many countries is much broader than that which is common in Britain (Shardlow, 2007). For example, in many parts of Europe, a developmental role – that of social pedagogue (Cameron, 2004) – has been established alongside more traditional social work activities. Elsewhere in the world, social work practice equates much more closely to forms of community development or social action, with the function of individual casework much less apparent than in this country. Why is it that social work practice in Britain has tended to focus more on individual responses to social need, and has – in some areas of practice at least – a much more clearly defined statutory responsibility?

Introduction

The key purpose of this chapter is to provide ways of understanding the advance of social work in Britain, identifying key moments when its direction was uncertain (an approach that is very similar to that deployed by Harris (2008)). It suggests that its development has not been inevitable, but has resulted from choices that have been made along the way. To illustrate the nature of some of these choices, the chapter will focus on five key moments in the growth of social work, where clear alternatives for its future direction were particularly apparent. These are as follows:

1. The disputes of the late nineteenth and early twentieth centuries regarding the causes of poverty and the role of social work in contributing to its resolution.
2. The difference in view in the 1950s between those who advocated the promotion of 'social casework' and those who suggested a more modest role for social workers.
3. The competing principles of genericism and specialisation in social work that resulted from the implementation of the Seebohm Report (1968) in England and Wales and the Kilbrandon Report (1964) in Scotland.
4. The emergence of 'radical social work' in the 1970s, and its particular opposition to individually oriented practice; it also addresses the re-emergence of similar 'radical' energies in the early years of the twenty-first century.
5. The disputes that fragmented the efforts of the committee that sought to define the 'role and tasks' of social workers (Barclay Report, 1982).

The chapter will suggest that many continuing conflicts about the nature and function of social work have their origins within these various disputes: it is therefore vital to understand the choices that faced social work at key points in its history, and to comprehend the impact of decisions that were made at these points on its future direction. It should be noted at this stage that this chapter does not pretend to offer a detailed summary of the history and development of social work in Britain – for such a work see Seed (1973), Jordan (1984) or Payne (2005) – but represents a thematic analysis of particular issues that have affected its direction.

The purpose of this chapter is to analyse key moments in the history of social work, and through this to identify points at which genuine debates were held about its future direction. The themes that are highlighted through these debates have had continued significance in social work, affecting its development to the present day. Drawing on the work of the Australian social work thinker Jim Ife (1997) we offer our understanding of how social work should best be perceived in the context of British society. We hope that our analysis will also have relevance for areas outside Britain. While this is necessarily a complex area of debate, we have sought to convey it in terms that can be readily understood, using a range of pedagogical features to underscore our argument.

The early years

The Charity Organisation Society

Many historical accounts identify the Charity Organisation Society (COS) as a key element in the formation of the occupation of social work (see, for example, Seed, 1973), giving 1869 as the date from which the occupation of social work originated. It is important to understand that the conception of social work developed by the COS was a direct extension of a social theory concerning the causes of social disadvantage and unrest. As a result, it is important first to consider the elements of this social theory, and its consequences for the subsequent development of social work.

The critical element of this is the clarity with which the COS viewed the cause of social problems in Victorian Britain, graphically expressed by Helen Bosanquet (1914). It recognised that the Industrial Revolution had created a range of major social problems, particularly in rapidly expanding urban areas – a perception shared with writers associated with the Fabian Society, such as Beatrice Webb (1971). Where the views of the COS diverged from the Fabians was in their conviction that the genuine hardship of many in society was accompanied by a 'mass of chronic pauperism, beggary and crime' (Bosanquet, 1914: 5) that resulted not from economic but moral problems. In the view of the COS, there were two main causes of this:

1. The Poor Law (the main legal basis that supported the relief of poverty, originally enacted in the reign of Elizabeth I!) was regarded as deficient, as the assistance provided under its framework was both indiscriminate and inadequate. It made no distinction between those people who were in poverty through

misfortune and those who were deemed to have brought their troubles on themselves. In the view of the COS, therefore, all available forms of Poor Law relief tended to maintain appalling social conditions rather than alter them (Bosanquet, 1914).

2. The second aspect of the problem was the rapid and disorganised proliferation of charitable giving in Victorian times. It was recognised that many organisations for the relief of the poor had been developed as a consequence of the failings of the Poor Law; however, the relief that they offered was held to be equally indiscriminate, and also provided an incentive for people to throw themselves onto charity rather than maintain their independence.

Writing an historical summary of the development of the COS, Rooff (1969) summarised their position in the following way:

'The declared aim of the C.O.S. was so to organise charity that the condition of the poor would be permanently improved; worthy families in temporary distress would be assisted to become independent, self-respecting citizens. The Society firmly believed, and frequently asserted, that their methods of enquiry and assistance went to the root of the problem: they were dealing with *causes* not symptoms.'
(Rooff, 1969: 27: italics in original)

In a remarkably even-handed summary of the role of the COS in combating poverty, Beatrice Webb (1971) – who represented a very different view of the causes of poverty and how it should therefore be addressed – confirmed this view of its response to the problems of the time:

'The immediate purpose of the Society was to organise all forms of charitable assistance so as to prevent overlapping and competition between the innumerable and heterogeneous agencies. And from the standpoint of the mid-Victorian time-spirit, there was no gainsaying the worth of the three principles on which this much-praised and much-abused organisation was avowedly based; patient and persistent service on behalf of the well-to-do; an acceptance of personal responsibility for the ulterior consequences, alike to the individual recipient and to others who might be indirectly affected, of charitable assistance; and finally, as the only way of carrying out this service and fulfilling this responsibility, the application of the scientific method to each separate case of a damaged body or a lost soul; so that the assistance given should be based on a correct forecast of what would actually happen, as a result of the gift, to the character and circumstances of the individual recipient and to the destitute class to which he belonged.'
(Webb, 1971: 207–8)

There are key concepts and themes which underpin the thought of the COS and which reappear in the development of social work since. For example, it believed that destitution was caused primarily by moral flaws in people's characters. Unlike Webb and other Fabian writers, the COS did not believe that the Victorian capitalist system was responsible for the many ills that people experienced, preferring to construct its philosophy and practice on the basis of the notion of 'individual responsibility' (Mowat, 1961). As Rooff (1969) has it, a strong moral purpose defined the leadership of the COS, who had no interest in addressing the nature and organisation of the class structure.

Reflect

Bringing this discussion up to date, do you believe that the problems of individuals and families are largely their own responsibility, or do you think that they primarily result from economic circumstances over which individuals have no control?

Organisations such as the COS emerged from a sense of the inadequacies of the institutions of the Poor Law, which was increasingly viewed as perpetuating rather than alleviating poverty.
(*Source:* Getty Images/Hulton Archive)

The practical development of social work within the context of the COS is of particular interest in relation to contemporary concerns. Because the COS was concerned about the relationship between charitable giving and the statutory functions of the Poor Law, an understanding needed to be reached about the respective roles and purposes of these two arms of welfare. It was therefore agreed that charity should be the first port of call for people in need, with the Poor Law and its institutions functioning as a general safety net (Lewis, 1995). This gave the role of charity a position of huge importance in the context of welfare of the time. As a result, an obvious priority was to establish an organisational structure that could assist people in need, and then to form systems by which decisions could be reached to determine the appropriate nature and type of response. In ensuring that charity was appropriately directed to those who both 'needed' and 'merited' assistance, the COS employed a number of workers – the majority of whom were unpaid – to make these judgements following a thorough assessment of their needs. It is here that Webb's attribution to the COS of a 'scientific' approach to their methods (see above) particularly applies, and it is also in this process where the origins of social work practice are clearly visible.

Indeed, the basic techniques of 'casework' that the COS instigated have continued applicability. For example, then as now, judgements were based on a detailed assessment of the applicant's circumstances, requiring home visits; workers operated within the context of guidance about their practice, which is broadly analogous to the contemporary operational guidance provided by government and/or employers of social workers. Following assessment, two sequential judgements were made: first, whether or not an individual should receive a service, and second, what service would most contribute to enabling the recipient to re-create a productive role in the community (the core aim of all of the work of the COS).

Before considering the way in which the COS made a particular contribution to the development of social work, a few words are indicated that clarify why its legacy has been mixed. The main problem is that it was an unpopular organisation, even at the height of its influence in the late nineteenth/early twentieth century. As Rooff (1969: 32) puts it: 'The C.O.S. certainly aroused considerable hostility in some quarters, both on account of its methods of investigation and of its social theory.' Regarding the social theory on which the COS was based, its analysis of the causes of poverty was both partial and limited, and took no account of the external factors that affected poverty and the quality of life – for example, unemployment, low wages and appalling housing. It is here that the differences between the COS and other social reformers – notably Beatrice and Sydney Webb and Canon Barnett (of whom more below) become evident. They believed that external social and economic factors had a major impact on people's lives. This represented a more structural approach to understanding society,

and the different perceptions of the nature of poverty and distress led – in Barnett's case – to an alternative course of social work action. In addition, as Webb (1971) observed, there was dissatisfaction that the government took little direct interest in social welfare, with the primary responsibility for the relief of poverty being placed with private charity. The Poor Law had become a residual and woefully inadequate source of support for those who had exhausted all other avenues.

The methods of investigation developed by the COS, who prided itself in its rigorous processes (Bosanquet, 1914), appeared harsh in the extreme, as indicated in the quotation by Madeleine Rooff cited above. For example, it has been pointed out that barely 33 per cent of people who came to the COS for assistance were actually granted any (Woodroofe, 1962). Largely as a result of this the public perception of charitable institutions became very poor: the cry of 'Curse your charity' was evident at workers' meetings and protests (see Barnett and Barnett, 1915; Webb, 1971). It is evident that having to turn to the COS for assistance was regarded as both demeaning and stigmatising, therefore.

In addition, the COS was markedly hostile to other perceptions of the causes of poverty (as is evident throughout Bosanquet (1914)). For example, when Canon Barnett accepted an invitation to debate the most appropriate response to poverty, he observed that – in his view – the council of the COS was composed of people who did not fully appreciate the lives of the poor and who were wedded to inappropriate and misguided dogmas in their response. It was later observed that Barnett failed in his mission to persuade his audience to amend their approach, and that C.S. Loch – the director of the COS – was able to give a 'full reply' justifying its operations (Bosanquet, 1914: 143). When considering the contribution of the Socialist parties to an understanding of the causes of poverty and an appropriate response to this, Bosanquet (1914: 401) is yet more damning, observing that they 'contributed little towards the serious study of social problems and less towards their resolution'. With the benefit of hindsight we can see that the COS was never able to escape from a paradox that it had itself created: 'The fact remained that the "unassisted" might be those who most needed help but least deserved it . . . while those helped, the respectable and provident, ought least to have needed help' (Mowat, 1961: 37).

For the development of social work, it is significant that particular primacy was given to individual decision-making, where each case 'should be regarded as unique and in need of thorough investigation' (Vincent, 1999: 73).

The main focus of the COS was therefore on the individual and the family; in this, there was an automatic difference between their approach to resolving the problems of poverty and disadvantage and the method contemporaneously developed by Canon Barnett. The basic process of assessment was later transformed by Mary Richmond (1917) into an even more rigorous and 'scientific' method. The preference for individually focused practice within British social work – which is certainly in the ascendant in the early years of the twenty-first century – can clearly be traced back to the significant influence of the COS on its development.

Think ahead

What alternative strategy for responding to people's needs and difficulties can you think of?

The Settlement Movement

The approach to social reform and social work developed by Canon Barnett was markedly different, although stemming from the parallel sense of obligation that the upper-middle classes had towards those less fortunate than themselves. Barnett founded what became known as the Settlement Movement, with the first settlement (Toynbee Hall in Whitechapel, London) established in 1884. He based his perceptions on his direct experience of living and working among the poor as a clergyman in the East End of London. While he was a strong early supporter of the COS, he gradually developed a different view of how to respond to the existence of poverty, which stemmed from an alternative conception of its causes. While he agreed with the COS that there were defects in the character of the poor, he viewed these as deriving directly from inequalities in the organisation of society:

'Custom is perhaps as powerful as law in putting obstacles in the way of life's wayfarers. It is by custom that the poor are treated as belonging to a lower, and the rich to a higher, class: that employees expect servility as well as work for the wages they pay: that property is more highly regarded than a man's life: that competition is held in a sort of way sacred . . . Many of our customs, which survive from feudalism, prevent the growth of *a sense of self-respect and of human dignity.*'

(Barnett and Barnett, 1915: 148–9; emphasis added*)

The final phrase of the above quote is critical. As a deeply religious man, Barnett's ambitious vision was to enable all people to live in accordance with their full potential. The development of an awareness of their spiritual needs was a core component of this – in his own words, he desired to raise 'all men to the level of Christ' (Barnett and Barnett, 1915: 144). He came to believe that people neither wanted nor needed the gifts of charity, and that the only lasting way to secure change in their circumstances was through more effective education. This recognition caused Barnett to withdraw his support for the COS, while developing an alternative vision for the form of action that should follow from his beliefs. He proposed that universities should establish settlements in deprived parts of cities, framing his ideas as follows:

'In East London large houses are often to be found . . . Such a house, affording sufficient sleeping rooms and large reception rooms, might be taken by a college, fitted with furniture and . . . associated with its name. As director or head, some graduate might be appointed, a *man of the right spirit*, trusted by all parties; qualified by character to guide men and by education to teach . . . Others engaged elsewhere would come to spend some weeks or months of the vacation, taking up such work as was possible, touching with their lives the lives of the poor, and learning for themselves facts which would revolutionize their minds.'

(Barnett and Barnett, 1915: 99; emphasis added)

Barnett was convinced that such people would provide a vital service in poor communities by their example, and that through living among poor people they would also understand much more about the circumstances of the poor: 'A Settlement in the original idea was not a mission but a means by which University men and women might by natural intercourse get to understand one other and co-operate in social reform' (Barnett and Barnett, 1915: 127). Through this they could jointly create a society 'in which every human being shall enjoy the fullness of his being' (125). The moral underpinning of this shift can be seen in the need to appoint a *man of the right spirit*: much of Barnett's thinking depended upon the ability of such an individual to provide moral leadership within the community. His was an idealistic vision, which was attractive to many educated men and women – including Clement Attlee, who became the Labour Prime Minister between 1945 and 1951, but who spent many of his early years working as a social worker within the Settlement Movement, writing a book about social work (Attlee, 1920) and becoming a university lecturer.

---

* Where direct quotations are used, the language deployed is that of the original author; we will invite you to consider the implications of this towards the end of the chapter.

Although Barnett did not discuss the Settlement Movement as a form of social work – he viewed it as a form of 'practicable socialism', the primary purpose of which was to help create a better society (Barnett and Barnett, 1915) – the rapid growth of Settlements was swiftly followed by the establishment of forms of training that would help equip the settlers for their role. (In this respect, the COS was engaged upon a similar process: see Jordan, 1984). However, the practice that Barnett brought into being differed in key respects from the work of the COS. For example, it sought to work through the community to improve general social conditions, and had as its goal a much wider process of social reform. It eschewed individual casework, and did not have as its outcome the dispensation of charity. Through a combination of guidance and moral instruction, it sought to improve the ability of the community to realise its potential. In addition, although Barnett believed that many of the ills of poorer communities within the city were visited on them by the capitalist system – a perspective shared by Beatrice Webb and others – the work of the settlers was not directed towards changing that system. In reality, the 'practicable' aspect of his approach of 'practicable socialism' indicated a preparedness to work within existing structures and systems. In this he differed from the Fabians, although Webb clearly held him in the highest regard (see Webb, 1971).

In conclusion, the COS and Settlement Movement represent two different possibilities for social work, based respectively on individual and collective response to problems. However, as Webb (2007) observes, both were characteristic of a 'modern' concept of society in that they believed that their work represented a rational response to its circumstances. In addition, both were expressions of a combination of Christian convictions allied to a humanist concern for others (Bowpitt, 1998).

Social work in the 1950s

While both the COS and the Settlement Movement were hugely influential in the origins and early development of social work, their influence waned in the middle years of the twentieth century. Two key reasons can be advanced for this:

1. Both arose from strong convictions about the nature of social problems and the most appropriate and effective way of addressing them. In the case of the COS at least, it clung to its social theory beyond a point when it had any relevance to the actual problems of the poor (Rooff, 1969). As a result, it ceased to have such a powerful impact on the development of social policy.

2. Since the work of the COS and the Settlement Movement stemmed largely from the characters and charisma of its leading lights – Loch and Barnett in particular – a problem occurred once they both died. In both cases, the innovation and creativity that had characterised the early years waned as a need for consolidation increased. (A contrast with the growth of the Settlement Movement in the USA is instructive here, as Jane Adams assumed the role of dynamic and creative leadership that was absent in the UK.)

As part of this process of consolidation, the methods used in assessment became much more 'scientifically' developed. The principal focus of this was the codification of methods to be used in the process of 'social diagnosis' (Richmond, 1917). The assessment of needs was the central activity, taking account of information derived from numerous sources: individuals and their families, and external bodies such as schools, doctors, employers, etc. In addition, social work practice became increasingly influenced by theories of the mind, much of them deriving directly from psychology and psychiatry (McLaughlin, 2008). In part, the attraction of such a theoretical approach for social work was linked to its search for a governing purpose, lost since the fall of the COS from authority and influence. As Cooper (1983) has it, the early part of the twentieth century saw social work fragmenting into a range of specialist areas; the development of what became known as 'social casework' represented an opportunity for the disparate areas of social work to coalesce around a unified approach to practice.

Summarising the development of social work in post-war Britain, Younghusband (1955) noted that social workers required knowledge of community resources and a deep understanding of people. The emphasis was clearly on the latter, however, as Younghusband (1955: 197) advocated the development of a 'consciously understood and guided relationship' through which the 'client' may be 'helped to free themselves from those nets of their own and others weaving in which they are enmeshed'.

The increased ambition and burgeoning self-confidence of social work as a discipline can be clearly seen: indeed, in 1954 Younghusband was instrumental in setting up the first social work training course that built on these generic principles (Seed, 1973). However, at a point

A closer look

Younghusband and social work

The primacy of the need for detailed understanding of each individual is made particularly clear in the following illustration of what Younghusband (1955) suggested was required of social workers:

'It is now demanded of her that she shall seek to understand the person in needs, not only at that particular moment in time, but also the pattern of personality, the major experiences and relationships which make him the person he now is: with conflicts of whose origin he may be unaware; with problems whose solutions may be less in external circumstances than in his own attitudes; with tensions, faulty relationships, inabilities to face reality, hardened into forms that he cannot alter without help. Instead of seeing his situation through her own eyes and producing a ready-made solution, the social worker must be able to understand him and his needs and his relationships as they appear to the person in need himself. She must enter into his problems as he sees them, his relationships as he experiences them, with their frustrations, their deprivations, their satisfactions, and see him, or his different selves, as they appear to him himself. Yet at the same time she must also be clearly aware of the realities of the situation and through her professional skill in relationships enable him to come to a better understanding of himself and others.' (Younghusband, 1955: 199)

This passage could be held to represent orthodox academic thinking about social work at this time, and is certainly ambitiously framed. It also represents an optimistic perspective, in that the capacity of each individual to change is accepted, with the social worker promoted as a key facilitator of such change.

where the therapeutic dimensions of social work appeared pronounced, the above passage directly featured in a critique of the social work orthodoxy by Barbara Wootton, a prominent social scientist. In her critique (1959) she also focused on a wealth of other thera-peutically derived writing on social work, much of it of American origin. Wootton was concerned about the direction social work was taking, particularly its move away from the impulses which (as we have seen) first contributed to its creation.

A closer look

Wootton's refutation of Younghusband's position

Wootton fundamentally disagreed with the nature of social work as outlined in much of the literature of the 1950s, arguing for a very different sort of practice:

'The contemporary social worker no longer regards the relief of poverty as her primary function; still less does she concentrate upon the detection of fraud or upon discriminating between the "deserving" and the "undeserving". To-day the "maladjusted", or the social misfits, have taken the place formerly reserved for the poor in the ideology of social work.' (Wootton, 1959: 269)

While she acknowledged that this had led to some advances in the quality of practice, Wootton was convinced that there had been worrying consequences:

'But the price of these advances has been the creation of a fantastically pretentious façade, and a tendency to emphasise certain aspects of social work out of all proportion to their real significance, while playing down others that are potentially at least as valuable . . . modern definitions of "social casework", if taken at their face value, involve claims to powers which verge upon omniscience and omnipotence; one can only suppose that those who perpetuate such claims in cold print must, for some as yet unexplained reason, have been totally deserted by their sense of humour.' (Wootton, 1959: 271)

This quotation neatly encapsulates both the essence of Wootton's critique, and its witty expression. Indeed, the clarity, humour and dexterity of Wootton's language are precisely the reason why her critique is so devastating. Take, for example, her response to the words of Younghusband, cited above:

'It might be said that the social worker's best, indeed perhaps her only chance of achieving aims at once so intimate and so ambitious, would be to marry her client'! (Wootton, 1959: 273)

Wootton did make important points about the development of social work practice. For example, she highlighted the absurdity of some of social work's wilder claims: 'The idea that complex problems of personal unhappiness or of defiance of social standards can be resolved by a young woman with an academic training in social work is difficult to take seriously' (Wootton, 1959: 274). She was particularly scathing about what she perceived as social work's failure to engage with the actual problems presented by the 'client':

'A favourite theme of contemporary casework literature is the social worker's capacity, and indeed her duty, to penetrate behind what is called the "presenting problem" to the "something deeper" that is supposed to lie beneath . . . In some cases this emphasis upon the hidden psychological issues . . . has gone so far as to lead to almost deliberate disregard of the practical problems which were the immediate occasion of the relationship being developed.'

(Wootton, 1959: 277)

Here, Wootton's position carries echoes of the vision of Canon Barnett when envisaging the first settlements: a recognition that many of the difficulties faced by people are not of their own making, but created by the social circumstances which they inhabit. In the light of later critiques of social work from the political left (see the *Case Con* manifesto, discussed later), it is notable that Wootton's analysis did not extend to the recommendation for social workers to work in such a way as to change the nature and structure of society. Rather, her remedy for social work practice was that it should develop a more modest focus on helping people by acting as what she termed a 'middleman': mobilising, organising and coordinating the services of other professional colleagues, and by guiding people through the mass of legislation and policy that could affect them. In this way, Wootton suggested that the social worker could once again be essential to the effective functioning of the welfare state 'as is lubrication to the running of an engine' (Wootton, 1959: 297), an image that recurs in the influential text by the distinguished British social work academic Martin Davies (Davies, 1981) discussed in a later section.

It is interesting to reflect on the extent to which the writings of either Younghusband or Wootton engaged with the daily reality of practice. For example, despite its representation of academic orthodoxy, there was an element of unreality in Younghusband's analysis: relatively few people actually received the sort of service she identified (Lewis, 1995). Indeed, looking at an account of statutory social work practice of the 1950s, it is clear that the bulk of a social worker's practice was more attuned to the modest aspirations identified by Wootton (Rodgers and Dixon, 1960). Even in voluntary organisations, working with a more selective clientele, the ideals of individual casework were difficult to put into practice. (They could also, as we shall see, create divisions between worker and client: see Mayer and Timms, 1970.) Similarly, Wootton's analysis did not engage fully with the reality that confronted social workers. If the social work role was to be limited to a 'middleman' role, what service could the practitioner offer those people whose problems were of much more serious and enduring a nature – an abused child or a person with a mental health problem, for example (Lewis, 1995)?

From the perspective of the twenty-first century, it appears that this debate was conducted in abstract terms, and was more about the rhetoric that characterised much social work literature of the time than it was related to the majority of practice. As Wootton herself noted:

'Happily, it can be presumed that the lamentable arrogance of the language in which contemporary social workers describe their activities is not generally matched by the work they actually do; otherwise it is hardly credible that they would not constantly get their faces slapped. Without doubt the majority of those who engage in social work are sensible, practical people who conduct their business on a reasonably matter-of-fact basis. The pity is that they have to write such nonsense about it . . . Indeed, the very fact that social workers *are* sensible, practical people makes it the more surprising that they should continue unblushingly to perpetrate such fantastic claims; and that they should so blandly ignore the ethical questions raised by their own practices which suggest that they take advantage of other people's poverty, sickness, unemployment or homelessness in order to pry into what is not their business.'

(Wootton, 1959: 279)

It is in this quote that a key problem in Wootton's own analysis become clear; in praising social workers who practise in a 'matter-of-fact' way, she appears to suggest that social workers need little more than common sense and a good heart (an oft-repeated sentiment in more recent years: see Perrott, 2002). In attacking what she saw as the pretensions of much academic writing on social work, she failed to identify alternative visions that could harness some of the gains from this work. For example, unless one assumes that all problems encountered by individuals, families and communities are the product of the nature of society – characteristic of the later radical social work movement – there are understandings to be drawn from a range of disciplines, including psychology and psychiatry, that can be of assistance to people in managing their lives. The development of social casework represented an attempt to identify the ways in which such knowledge could be deployed. That it failed to take full account of people's social circumstances and the administrative character of much social work practice of the time are clear weaknesses, which Wootton acerbically identified. However, Wootton's own solutions are also flawed, as we have seen. As a result, a form of practice that was simultaneously socially aware and attuned to individual psychological needs still seemed distant.

Reflect

Where do you position yourself in the debate between Younghusband and Wootton?

Genericism and specialisation: the Seebohm Report and after

The debate concerning the opposing principles of genericism and specialisation within social work practice has been a significant issue within social work organisation, education and practice in the past 40 years. Although the current dimensions of the debate were formed by the responses to the Seebohm and Kilbrandon Reports of the 1960s, which presaged the formation of unified social services organisations, its origins can be historically traced. From the very start of social work's development, it was assumed that practice in different settings required a specialised form of preparation and training. The originators of social work in the British context – the COS and the Settlement Movement – both had strong but separate links with universities, and the first education for social work was specifically linked to the roles and tasks carried out in these settings. Subsequently, the areas of social work that developed – probation and aftercare, psychiatric social work, hospital almoners, etc. – all had their own individual forms of education and training. As we have previously noted, the first generic social work training course did not emerge until the 1950s. In the early days, therefore, it was assumed that each separate area of social work required a specialised

preparation; the argument that there was a generic foundation of social work was of much later origin – with its major political support only arriving in the 1960s.

When parallel committees were established for England/Wales and Scotland to examine the organisation of social services and the role of social work – which both published their reports in the 1960s (the Seebohm Report for England and Wales and the Kilbrandon Report for Scotland) – a number of influences came to the fore. For example, numerous social policy theorists had argued that there needed to be a unified approach to the delivery of social welfare (Hill, 1993). This commitment was based on three connected contentions:

- The first was practical in its nature: the belief was that there were major problems with the existing arrangements – included among which was poor coordination and quality of services, with a limited capability to respond quickly to changing needs.
- The second more philosophical point was related to the belief that a single unified point of contact for families in need was to be preferred to the fragmented systems that prevailed at that time.
- The third important belief was that social services should be freely available to the entire community, and that the creation of a universalist approach with a single point of contact would help to combat the stigma that was associated with seeking social work support.

As the Seebohm Report stated, the unified departments that would be created should 'provide a more co-ordinated and comprehensive approach to the problems of individuals, families and communities' (Seebohm Report, 1968, para. 9). At this point, the principles of genericism seemed to be firmly in the ascendant, as the aspiration for a unified, comprehensive service for families presupposed that generic principles would underpin practice (Stevenson, 2005). Indeed, since social work interests had been powerful in the work of the two committees (Cooper, 1983; Hill, 1993) it is reasonable to assume that the pursuit of a generic approach to social work was representative of the orthodoxy of social work thinking in Britain at the time; a number of subsequent developments reinforce this perspective.

Alongside the creation of unified Social Services Departments in England and Wales – Social Work Departments in Scotland – was a change to a unified and generic form of education for social work, with the advent of the Certificate of Qualification in Social Work (CQSW); significantly in the light of subsequent developments, this included education for probation officers, who were also located within Social Work Departments in Scotland (although separate organisations for the probation service existed within England and Wales). In the early 1970s there was a massive expansion in the numbers of qualified social workers being produced from educational establishments and employed in the new organisations. In 1970 the British Association of Social Workers was formed from the individual and separate professional associations that had previously represented practitioners in different parts of the social work world (Cooper, 1983). The launch of the *British Journal of Social Work* as the unified academic face of social work occurred simultaneously. Indeed, at this time there was generally a confident, optimistic perception of social work and its possibilities (Bamford, 1990).

However, tensions between the principles of genericism and specialisation were soon to emerge (Stevenson, 1981), and the process of forming the new social services organisations also was found to be problematic (Satyamurti, 1981). There was a conflict between those staff trained before and after 1970, with the existing members of the social work profession slow to adopt a more generic role in their practice (Stevenson, 2005). In addition, in seeking to retain a sense of control over their practice, many staff adopted an informal specialist role within the supposedly generic structures (Satyamurti, 1981). It could be argued that at no time was a genuinely generic service offered in the way that had been intended, despite the avowedly generic principles that applied.

Some areas of practice (for example, work with children and families) were given priority: others (for example, work with older people) were much less well developed (Lymbery, 2005). As the financial situation of social services worsened through the 1970s, the universalist aspirations of the reforms receded even further. In an attempt to manage the pressures on available resources, the unified departments had to consider mechanisms that could be used to make their services more efficient to deliver – the implications of this will be discussed in a future section.

A particular source of weakness at this time was that there was no single agreed conception of the social work role on which the generic organisations could be firmly based. Although there were periodic attempts to construct such a role (see, for example, Bartlett, 1970; Butrym, 1976) they were not markedly successful in attracting the support of the majority of practitioners. As we shall explore in the following two sections, there remained considerable disagreement about what should legitimately be the approach of social work to public problems. The tension between the conceptions of genericism and specialisation was one way in which this has been played out.

The 18 years of the Conservative administration (1979–97) were a pivotal period in the development of contemporary social work. Although there were problems in the establishment of a generic vision for practice (Stevenson, 2005), the relationship between government and social work was the source of many future problems (Lymbery, 2001). There were two key aspects of this:

A closer look

Effects of the pre-eminence of child protection

In reflecting on the effects of the dominance of child protection, the eminent social work academic Olive Stevenson – the first editor of the *British Journal of Social Work*, and a major figure in the development of social work for several decades – has suggested that there are three linked areas to consider (Stevenson, 2005):

1. A major blow to the confidence of social work. While the quality of social work practice highlighted by the enquiries was often poor, many of these enquiries failed to take proper account of the context within which the abuse occurred, nor did

they adequately analyse failures in management. The cumulative impact on morale, Stevenson suggests, has been considerable.

2. The distortion of patterns of specialisation. Here, Stevenson notes that child protection concerns have tended to dominate not only more general childcare issues but also other areas of social work practice; the priority given to this area of work for post-qualifying training she takes as token of this shift.

3. A drive to improve partnership working across disciplines and agencies. This has led to the effective replacement of the integrated Social Services Department in England and Wales with organisations that focus on the separate needs of children and adults.

1. antipathy towards the core purposes of the occupation;
2. fundamental dislike and distrust of the large public authorities that employed the majority of social work practitioners.

At the same time, social work has been beset by a preoccupation with issues relating to child protection, which has further weakened its sense of self-confidence, while appearing to confirm the more critical views taken by it opponents (Stevenson, 2005). This has had serious consequences.

The enactment of these changes took effect in April 2006 with the creation of separate Children's Trusts and Adult Social Care Departments. By contrast, there has not been the same pressure to change the structure of Social Work Departments in Scotland, although the desire to improve partnership and inter-agency working still exists within that country. A return to the separate organisational forms that existed prior to the enactment of the Seebohm recommendations has a number of serious implications for social work, many of which bear on the critical themes within this section.

In particular, it calls into question the principle of genericism in social work. If the work settings for social workers are to be clearly differentiated between adults and children (let alone the greater degrees of separation between different categories within these broad groupings), will there continue to be a need for a single, unified form of education preparing practitioners for their tasks? (However, the report of the Social Work Task Force in 2009 was – perhaps surprisingly – committed to the continuation of social work as a unified, generic profession: DH/DCSF, 2009.) In this respect, the way in which preparation for probation work was separated from social work in the late 1990s represents a significant potential threat. Here, despite probation training being considered to be the jewel in the crown of social work education (Marsh and Triseliotis, 1996) a separate form of training was established for it in England and Wales, based largely on a rhetorical insistence on the differences between probation and social work. (At the same time, the integration between probation and social work was maintained in Scotland, which retains a unified form of both training and organisational location.) There were strong political forces at work, ignoring – or denying – the continuity between social work and probation, even though there are strong arguments to suggest that much of what probation officers actually do derives substantially from social work theory and research (Smith, 2005).

The potential for a similar shift to take place in relation to other areas of social work is clear. Although the principle of genericism seems to have been restated in both the *Requirements for Social Work Training* (DoH, 2002) and in the report of the Social Work Task Force (DH/DCSF, 2009), it would take little to change this position. The construction of a post-qualification framework for social work already is based on a substantially specialised model (GSCC, 2005). In practice, there are few tasks that only social workers can deliver and a number of other occupations can lay claim to at least some of the knowledge, values and skills of social work. Given that many people do not hold that social workers possess either unique or detailed knowledge or skills, it would not be far-fetched for a number of the activities that make up social work practice to be redefined as requiring a different (lower) level or type of qualification.

In order to defend itself against such developments, social work has to undertake two critical activities.

- Firstly, it needs to establish clarity about what constitutes the social work task. This has always been a difficult task, as the controversies highlighted in the following two sections – and which have characterised much of the development of social work – make clear. If there is no clearly outlined foundation for social work it will be impossible to argue for its continued existence against the pressures that seem to point towards fragmentation as a likely characteristic of policy.

- Secondly, social work needs to demonstrate that it can achieve important goals that aid the development of social policy. If it is to thrive, social work has to be perceived as playing a significant part in the operation of society. This was not at all characteristic of the 18 years of Conservative rule that ended in 1997; indeed, there has been a lack of clarity about the role that social work should play in society since that time (Butler and Drakeford, 2001), arguing that uncertainty continued to surround social work throughout the 13 years of the 'new' Labour government. Important decisions that affect this are, of course, not taken by social work itself – the ability to impress decision makers with the potential for social work to contribute towards a vision for the development of society therefore becomes critical. This may be particularly challenging, given the financial priorities of the Conservative–Liberal Democrat coalition government formed in 2010.

Having read the entire section, do you believe that social work should be delivered on a generic or a specialist basis? If the latter, do you believe that qualifying-level education and training for social workers should remain on a generic basis?

What are the factors that particularly influence your judgement?

The emergence of radical social work

In a historical context, the most significant element in the development of social work literature of the 1960s was the fact that it followed a model where the dominant form of practice was assumed to be individual casework. The debates of the past, to which this chapter has alluded, had led to forms of practice that sought to respond to the immediate needs of individuals and families, rather than seek a transformation of their social conditions. As Bailey and Brake (1975b: 1) put it: 'The influence in particular of psychology has led to an over-emphasis on pathological and clinical orientations to the detriment

of structural and political implications.' However, as we have noted, the reality of social work practice within a statutory setting did not equate to this claim (Rodgers and Dixon, 1960), although it accurately reflected the tenor of much writing on social work. Certainly, however, if we trace a line back to the origins of social work, the individual orientation of practice first defined by the COS was in the ascendant.

Despite this, the actual state of social work was somewhat complex and divided at this point. By 1970, a group of disaffected social workers produced a magazine entitled *Case Con* (its name being a mischievous adaptation of the title of the long-standing journal *Case Conference*) which was explicitly intended as a critique of established ways of thinking within social work. Within a few years a new movement had grown in its wake; this was given the title of 'radical social work', after the book that first brought the term to wider attention (Bailey and Brake, 1975a). This represented a key attempt to develop a theory of social work practice that was based on a desire to change the social circumstances within which social workers and their 'clients' interacted.

It is worth outlining some of the key points of the *Case Con Manifesto*, as this identifies both the presumed cause of the problems experienced by people in society, and the actions that social workers should take in response to these problems.

A closer look

The *Case Con Manifesto*

The following are some of the key elements from the *Case Con Manifesto*:

- The problems faced by social workers derive from the capitalist structure of society and the place of welfare within it: effective practice must stem from an understanding of how the welfare state has developed, and the pressures to which it is subject.
- The welfare state should be seen as an administrative arm of capitalism.
- The principle of universal entitlement to welfare services had been gradually eroded in the post-war period.
- The establishment of generic social work was part of a shift whereby responsibility for welfare was transferred from the state to the family.
- One of the principal functions of generic workers is to persuade clients that their problems are of their own making, and that they need to be changed in order to fit within society.
- One of the functions of individual casework is to divert attention from the real causes of poverty, which are primarily economic in their origin.
- Many social work methods are in reality mechanisms of social control.
- The move towards professionalisation in social work does not resolve the basic contradiction in social work – that it cannot, in itself, resolve the basic inadequacies and inequalities of society.
- Social workers need to organise and unionise independently of the state and in the interest of the working class, and seek to join the struggle for a workers' state to replace capitalist structures.

(Adapted from the Case Con Manifesto, 1975)

In a number of ways, this serves more as a historical document than one that has contemporary relevance. For example, the notion that social workers can legitimately join the struggle to forge a 'workers' state' is very much of its time. Similarly, the notion (expressed in another part of the manifesto) that trade union activism could help to promote the aims of the radical social work movement is clearly no longer (if it ever was) likely. In addition, the idea that the state is simply an administrative arm of capitalism analyses the complexity of the welfare state's formation and existence in a crudely reductive fashion. Finally, the manifesto is weak on detailed solutions to the problems that it diagnoses.

However, in other ways aspects of the manifesto still resonate. After several decades where the welfare state has been further eroded, the effect of cuts and the consequent need to ration services has become more explicit. The critique of an individualised response to problems that do not actually lie within the individual carries echoes of the earlier perspectives of Canon Barnett and Barbara Wootton. *Case Con*'s analysis of the causes of social problems highlighted structural, economic and political factors rather than locating them within individuals, and argued that since the individualist focus of social work left the fabric of society essentially unchanged it was therefore an inadequate response. As a consequence, the 'proper' role for social work was to seek a change to the status quo, rather than to address the problems of individuals in isolation. These remain important perspectives to be debated – indeed, they are still energetically propounded within parts of the social work world (see, for example, Ferguson, 2008; Ferguson and Woodward, 2009).

Reflect

Are the arguments of the radical social work movement consistent with the international definition of social work, included at the start of this chapter?

Although radical social work became popular within the academic community and spawned a considerable body of literature, as a 'movement' it foundered on a number of contradictions. In particular, it was much more effective at pointing out the failings of the system than it was in defining what should be done in response to them. For example, the radical social work agenda appeared to assume that social workers had more or less unlimited capacity to challenge and change policy: this was never a

realistic possibility. Employers are no more likely now to encourage their staff to foment revolutionary approaches to practice than they were in the past. Further enduring criticisms derive from what Stanley Cohen (the eminent sociologist) observed in one of the more sophisticated contributions to the radical literature: that the emphasis on structural causes of disadvantage did not enable individuals to address the specific problems that they encountered. Indeed, Cohen suggested that the most radical work undertaken by social workers would be outside their daily jobs. The *Case Con Manifesto* exhorts practitioners to hold fast to their principles in practice, but says little about how this could be done. As Cohen (1975: 88) puts it: 'On the practical level it must be said that . . . there is very little in Case Con circles of how the revolutionary social worker would operate very differently from his non-revolutionary colleagues.' Cohen (1975) agreed that radical social workers needed to work towards a longer-term goal, but suggested that they should also be motivated to respond to people's immediate, short-term needs. (Even here, there is a lack of detail about precisely how workers might be able to maintain this balance.)

In large measure, the inability of the radical social work movement to alter the direction of policy and practice was predictable: if its goals were global and unattainable, how could practitioners maintain their belief in them? However, it did focus attention to various issues – the role of the state, the impact of poverty, the potential of community – that had been long neglected. And, as we shall see, the insights which the movement provided have had continued relevance on the development of social work since. For example, the emphasis on race, gender and disability – all of which became significant issues in social work from the 1980s – clearly has its origins in the radical literature of the 1970s. And, as the publication of a revised manifesto focusing on social work and social justice makes clear (Jones et al., 2004), the radical impulse still exists in relation to the development of critical thinking for social work. The first section of the new manifesto goes under the heading of 'Social Work Today', both the title of a defunct weekly journal and a paper jointly written by one of the authors (Jones and Novak, 1993).

The manifesto's authors suggest that, as a result, there is a need to develop a form of social work 'that has prevention at its heart and recognises the value of collective action' (Jones et al., 2004). While appreciating that there is a need for individual work – to a much greater extent than is true in the *Case Con Manifesto* – the full focus of

A closer look

The Social Work Manifesto

The manifesto starts with a statement that social work remains in crisis, a conclusion that represents a clear continuity with the *Case Con Manifesto*:

'Social work in Britain today has lost direction. This is not new. Many have talked about social work being in crisis for over thirty years now. The starting point for this Manifesto, however, is that the "crisis of social work" can no longer be tolerated. We need to find more effective ways of resisting the dominant trends within social work and map ways forward for a new engaged practice.

Many of us entered social work – and many still do – out of a commitment to social justice or, at the very least, to bring about positive change in people's lives. Yet increasingly the scope for doing so is curtailed.'   (Jones et al., 2004)

Many practitioners will find that the manifesto's depiction of the organisational and managerial pressures on social workers resonates with their own experience, giving weight to the relevance of the critique on which it is based. As a result, the authors claim that:

'the need for a social work committed to social justice and challenging poverty and discrimination is greater than ever. In our view, this remains a project that is worth defending. More than any other welfare state profession, social work seeks to understand the links between "public issues" and "private troubles", and seeks to address both. It is for this reason that many who hold power and influence in our society would be delighted to see a demoralised and defeated social work, a social work that is incapable of drawing attention to the miseries and difficulties which beset so many in our society. This alone makes social work worth fighting for.'   (Jones et al., 2004)

---

the manifesto's attention remains on the development of an essentially different form of practice:

'We are looking to a social work that can contribute to shaping a different kind of social policy agenda, based on our understanding of the struggles experienced by clients in addressing a range of emotional, social and material problems and the strengths they bring to these struggles.'
(Jones et al., 2004)

While the call for a different type of social organisation is less obvious here, the key role of social work is defined as its contribution to wider social change (emphasising the sense of continuity with the *Case Con Manifesto*). There are a number of mechanisms through which social work can aspire to such a goal, some of which grow out of the direct connections that practitioners have with disadvantaged people and groups, and others where social workers are invited to align themselves with broader protest movements and the debates that such movements can help engender. It is suggested that such debates 'can help us think about the shape of a modern engaged social work based around such core "anti-capitalist" values as democracy, solidarity, accountability, participation, justice, equality, liberty and diversity' (Jones et al., 2004).

While there are many aspects of this vision with which we concur – notably the suggestion that positive changes

in the nature of social work practice can be started by establishing relationships with service users of a different nature and kind (see Chapter 14) – we regard other aspects with more suspicion. Once again, the vision of social work that is conveyed does not convey the breadth of practice: for example, where does child protection or statutory mental health work fit within this vision? Similarly, the broad injunction that social work could ally itself with anti-capitalist movements to discover a new paradigm for practice seems impossibly utopian. The development of social work in a British context has taken place alongside the welfare state, as part of it: while there have been oppositional voices, the occupation has always fulfilled a role for society as part of the complex apparatus of welfare. While it is potentially possible to devise a form of social work that would be in accordance with more radical and collective visions, to suggest that this can be grafted onto the continued functions of practitioners in the current system seems implausible. However, the existence of radical alternatives to the prevailing climate of much practice does serve as a reminder that there are other ways of thinking about welfare and social work's place within it, even if the practical prescriptions for change that are proposed appear unlikely in the current social and political context.

Even among writers sympathetic to the radical cause within social work there are clear differences of view about the most appropriate way forward. One of the most interesting debates in the pages of the *British Journal of Social Work* in recent years was between two academics who would position themselves at the forefront of modified, 'radical' thinking (Ferguson, 2001 and 2003; Garrett, 2003 and 2004). In his contributions to the debate Ferguson – drawing on ideas associated with post-modernist thought – suggested that social workers should appropriately focus less on its potential to transform society (what is labelled as 'emancipatory politics'), and instead concentrate on ensuring that their services enable people to maximise their abilities to enhance their lives at the more individual level ('life politics'). Garrett takes exception to this focus, arguing that this perspective underestimates the extent to which people's life chances are limited by social structures and consequently overestimates the ability of people to exercise personal agency in the ways envisaged. As a result he suggests that – particularly in a troubled political and social climate – social work needs particularly to focus on the enhancement of emancipatory politics (see Activity One).

Perhaps the most important reminder for contemporary social work practice from this debate is that social work exists as both an example of a social project, devoted to emancipatory goals, and as a human encounter, in which the ability of the practitioner to maximise the opportunities and independence of the service user is critical (Butler and Drakeford, 2005). The nature of what constitutes valid emancipatory goals for social work changes with the historical times, as an examination of the two manifestos for social work confirms: the preoccupations of two different social and political worlds are clearly evident. Perhaps the most important contribution of the radical tradition in social work has been to draw attention to an aspect of social work's history that can too easily be forgotten – its origins as a movement committed to social justice. This perspective has continued relevance, even if it is difficult to construct forms of practice that directly contribute towards an increase of social justice. In addition, there are now some who write within the radical tradition who also articulate the values of relationship-based practice (Ferguson and Woodward, 2009).

The (forgotten?) Barclay Report

The publication of the Barclay Report (1982) was intended to clarify the purpose and function of social workers, whether or not these workers were employed by the statutory sector or within voluntary agencies. It was the product of a committee chaired by Sir Peter Barclay, which worked to the following terms of reference: 'To review the role and tasks of social workers in local authority social services departments and related voluntary agencies in England and Wales and to make recommendations.' These broad terms of reference were interpreted by the committee as requiring it 'to provide an account and clarification of what social workers do, appraised against an explicit view of what they are needed to do' (Barclay Report, 1982: vii–viii). It is the second part of this interpretation that created particular difficulties for the committee, which failed to agree on its final conclusions and recommendations. As we shall demonstrate, the main body of the Barclay Report has had little impact on the development of practice other than in the most general terms, but the dissenting note by Robert Pinker does resonate with the development of practice since. For that reason, we pay particular attention to his disagreement with the remainder of the committee.

The general conclusions of the Barclay Report

However, the majority of the report did contain some elements that have continued relevance to the development of social work. First, there was an interesting discussion about the distinction between 'formal' social work and a more general, less specialised use of the term. The Report states that 'We have no wish, and certainly have no power, to stop people using the term "social work" in this wide sense' (Barclay Report, 1982: xvi), reflecting the uncertain status of social work as a distinctive, professional occupation. It is a symbol of how times have changed that the Care Standards Act 2000 has achieved precisely this end: social work is now a reserved title, and only those people who are eligible to join the social care register as qualified social workers are able to use it.

Secondly, it contained an explicit acknowledgement that social work encompassed two distinctive elements. These are:

1. 'Counselling': this was defined in the following way: 'the process (which has often been known as "social casework") of direct communication and interaction between clients and social workers, through which clients are helped to change, or to tolerate, some aspects of themselves or of their environments'

(Barclay Report, 1982: xiv). The continuity between this approach and the perception prevalent in the early post-war period (exemplified in the quotations from Younghusband, on p. 68 above) is obvious.

2. 'Social care planning': this was defined as including 'plans designed to solve or alleviate existing problems and plans which aim to prevent the development of social problems in the future or to create or strengthen resources to respond to those which do arise' (Barclay Report, 1982: xiv–xv). In the report's view, social care planning could occur in relation to individuals, groups and communities, involving statutory and voluntary groups, as well as the training, development and support of other social services staff. Here, the conception is closely connected to the idea of a social worker as 'middleman', espoused by Wootton (1959); it can also be argued that the idea espouses some of the import of radical social work.

The most potentially far-reaching recommendation of the majority report was its promotion of 'community social work'. The broad definition of this is as follows:

'formal social work which, starting from problems affecting an individual or groups and the responsibilities and resources of social services departments and voluntary organisations, seeks to tap into, support, enable and underpin the local networks of formal and informal relationships which constitute our basic definition of community, and also the strengths of a client's communities of interest. It implies, we suggest, a change of attitude on the part of social workers and their employing agencies. The detailed activities in which community social workers engage may include an increased measure of activities of the kind carried out by community workers but they will continue to have statutory duties and other responsibilities to individual, families or groups which do not fall within the remit of community workers.'   (Barclay Report, 1982: xvii)

This conception significantly widened the role of a social worker, reflecting the growth of community development through the 1970s. However, not all of the committee were able to agree the vision thus articulated. One group of three members – the key driving force among whom was the distinguished social policy academic, Professor Roger Hadley – welcomed the general thrust of the report, but argued that the notion of community social work should be extended, with social workers operating within a system where they were located in neighbourhoods, more closely integrated with other professional and community networks. From this base neighbourhood social workers would carry out

a much broader range of roles and tasks and would necessarily have a greater level of autonomy (Barclay Report, 1982, Appendix A: 219–35). While the advocacy of 'neighbourhood social work' went further than the main recommendation of 'community social work', the difference was substantially a matter of degree: both saw social work travelling in the same general direction.

The Barclay Report: a dissenting voice

The conception of both 'community social work' and 'neighbourhood social work' was challenged by a single member of the committee, another renowned social policy academic, Professor Robert Pinker; he argued that social workers had no mandate for the sorts of activity that could be grouped under the banners either of 'community social work' or 'neighbourhood social work'. As a result, he claimed that both the majority report and the minority appendix of Hadley and colleagues were fundamentally flawed. There were a number of aspects of this analysis:

- The concept of 'community' was not clearly defined.
- There were ambiguities in the nature of a social worker's accountability: was it to the employer, to the community/neighbourhood, or to a broader conception of social work principles?
- There were unresolved tensions between the principles of 'specialism' and 'genericism' within social work practice. (As we have discussed, these have been significant themes in the development of social work.)

Pinker believed that what was most needed was not a radical change in the direction of social work, but a refinement in the way in which it was organised. A summary of his position is contained in the concluding comments of his appendix to the main report. Here, he expressed his disagreement with the proponents of both 'community' and 'neighbourhood' social work on the basis that both models were intellectually incoherent, and potentially created alarming conflicts between social workers and those who employ them. He reserved particular scorn for the concept of 'neighbourhood social work', claiming that:

'It conjures up the vision of a captainless crew under a patchwork ensign stitched together from remnants of the Red Flag and the Jolly Roger – all with a licence and some with a disposition to mutiny – heading in the gusty winds of populist rhetoric, with presumption as their figurehead and inexperience as their compass, straight for the reefs of public incredulity.'   (Pinker, 1982: 262)

A closer look

Pinker's appendix to the Barclay Report

In opposing the recommendation of 'community social work' Pinker's alternative started from a more restricted perspective:

'Our present model of so-called client centred social work is basically sound, but in need of a better defined and less ambitious mandate. Social work should be explicitly selective rather than universalist in focus, reactive rather than preventive in approach and modest in its objectives. Social work ought to be preventive with respect to the needs which come to its attention; it has neither the resources nor the mandate to go looking for needs in the community at large.'

(Barclay Report, 1982: 237)

Pinker goes on to suggest that the role and tasks of social work are better defined in relation to what he terms 'institutional imperatives':

■ The range and variety of needs with which social workers are confronted
■ The legislation that defines their mandatory local authority functions and that indicates what discretionary activities are permitted
■ The responsibilities of the employers of social workers
■ The professional standards and values of social work.

He argues for the close relationship between historic notions of social casework and social work, but broadens the definition to a range of practical tasks. In this he draws to some degree on the preceding work of both Younghusband and Wootton, cited above. Pinker's thinking owes a particular debt to the work of Martin Davies (1981), in what became an influential social work text. Davies rejected the opposing notions that social workers were either agents of social change or of social control, arguing that 'a far more satisfactory model to employ in describing the role of social work in society is to regard it as a form of *maintenance*. Social workers are the maintenance mechanics oiling the inter-personal wheels of the community' (Davies, 1981: 137 – italics in original). Davies suggested that the role of maintenance had two elements:

1. Curbing some of the excesses of people's deviant behaviour.
2. Helping to improve the living conditions of people who find themselves unable to cope.

Depending on circumstances, a social worker would focus on either controlling or caring functions, but in both cases is primarily seeking to contribute towards the maintenance of society.

By contrast he suggested that a more cautious approach to the reform of social work was indicated, and that there was a solid framework on which to build. In reality, he suggested, the suggestions for change created more difficulties than they resolved:

'there is nothing fundamentally wrong with the ship in which we sail today, and certainly nothing that cannot be put right with common sense and cautious reform. It is not the present state of social work that gives cause for alarm, but the proposals for radical change in its nature and direction.' (Pinker, 1982: 262)

With the benefit of hindsight, the most important effect of the Barclay Report was not in the future direction of practice: there were few moves in the direction of community social work – let alone neighbourhood social work – in the years following, dominated as they were by retrenchments in the personal social services brought about by the Thatcher-led Conservative government. However, it did encapsulate – and bring up to

date – the ongoing debate within social work between those who argued for a wider involvement of the occupation in social action and community development and those who took a more limited view of its role and functions. Although framed in different terms and language, the nature of this dispute reflected tensions that we have observed in earlier stages of social work's history. For example, the broader conception of the need for community-based approaches to social problems echoed the perceptions of Canon Barnett and the Settlement Movement; it differed from the radical social work movement in that there was no professed intention to challenge state authority – although Pinker highlighted this as a genuine and unresolved tension. By contrast, the notion of social work as a form of social casework derived from the work of COS and the psychologically oriented practice of Younghusband and others.

Given the political climate that has been the backdrop for social work since the publication of the Barclay Report, it is hardly surprising that restricted and limited visions of the potential of social work have dominated. Increasingly, as the laments of numerous commentators bear witness (see, for example, Jones, 2001), the conditions within which social work is carried out are characterised by tight managerial controls, limited budgets, increased bureaucracy and proceduralism, centrally driven targets and ever-increasing fragmentation of practice and despondency of practitioners.

However, we do not align ourselves with those who insist that the task of social workers in British society is impossible: often thankless and unrewarded, yes, but still remaining vital for the needs of society. In the following section we discuss how we believe the condition of social work can best be understood, and put forward our belief in a socially aware, relational form of practice that can help produce a better quality of life for those people most in need. This remains, as it has been throughout the existence of social work, a critical task.

Social work today

Following the historical analysis of the preceding sections, this part of the chapter seeks to identify how we perceive the nature of social work in Britain in the twenty-first century. It draws on the preceding historical summary of key points in the development of social work, and reflects our contention, expressed earlier in this chapter, that the essence of social work (in the British context, at least) lies in the establishment of trusting and productive relationships between social work practitioners and those who require their services – whether individuals, groups or communities. This does not mean that we are unaware, or deny the impact, of problems that people encounter which have their origins beyond their direct control. We make no statement that the structure and organisation of society should be amended, preferring instead to focus on the tasks that society defines as appropriate for social workers. As a result, social work students and practitioners need to understand how positive and productive relationships can be fostered within the context of the social and organisational problems and constraints that confront them. We acknowledge that this will carry potential difficulties for practitioners, and contend that these difficulties cannot be airbrushed out of existence through a retreat into theoretical abstractions. Fundamentally, social work is a practical activity and must be both understood and theorised as such. A book that does not provide

practitioners with the capacity to act in relation to the problems with which they will be encountered is in danger of being perceived as an irrelevance to precisely those people who are its intended readership.

We articulate our position in relation to the model for understanding social work developed by the Australian social work academic, Jim Ife (1997). We use this framework not to echo his conclusions, but rather because it functions as a clear way of understanding the contested place of social work within society. Ife argues that social work can be located within a matrix formed from the intersection of two dimensions of analysis – a power dimension (represented by the vertical axis), and a knowledge dimension (represented by the horizontal axis).

He suggests that the power dimension 'represents a fundamental dichotomy in thinking about human services (Ife, 1997: 42), with the hierarchical (top–down) approach assuming that power, authority (and wisdom) rest at the top of an organisation, and that a social worker's primary responsibility lies in implementing the policies that come from above. In relation to people who use services, Ife contends that the power dimension is played out in a different way. He suggests that the social worker exercises power over the service user through a combination of status, knowledge and skill. This is contrasted with what he terms an anarchist (or bottom–up) position, where the knowledge and expertise are reversed. In this perspective, a front-line social worker would be presumed to have more knowledge and expertise than her/his managers, simply through the day-to-day carrying out of social work activities. In respect of service users, a bottom–up approach would particularly value the wisdom that comes from their lived experience. Ife contrasts the patterns of accountability that would arise from either a top–down or a bottom–up position, suggesting that the former emphasises accountability to the organisation, whereas the latter focuses on accountability to the service user or the community. It is clear that Ife favours such an approach, although he does acknowledge that this is 'directly contradictory to many of the assumptions behind the structures of the welfare state' (Ife, 1997: 44).

At the poles of the knowledge dimension Ife locates what he terms positivist and humanist forms of knowledge. He sees positivist knowledge as deriving primarily from the physical sciences, where the social world can be studied in such a way as to generate known 'facts' and where the social worker can apply known techniques to address these in order to bring about a desired social change. In his view, the humanist form

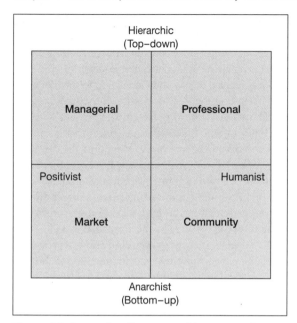

Figure 4.1 Competing discourses of human services

(*Source*: Ife, J. *Rethinking Social Work*, p. 47, Addison Wesley Longman (1997). Reproduced with permission from Pearson Education Australia.)

of knowledge 'emphasises a practice based on the centrality of human values and the need to understand another's subjective reality' (Ife, 1997: 46). He characterises the contrast between the two positions as being between scientific rationality and the recognition of difference and diversity. The continued salience of this opposition between the two can be seen in the debate between Webb (2001) and Sheldon (2001), conducted in the pages of the *British Journal of Social Work* (see Activity Two).

In putting these dimensions together Ife argues that there are four key discourses that characterise human service delivery – managerial (hierarchic positivist), market (anarchist positivist), professional (hierarchical humanist) and community (anarchist humanist). These are illustrated in Figure 4.1.

If practice is located within the 'managerial' discourse (in the top left quadrant) it would be based within a framework whereby expertise and authority is seen to lie with managers, who dictate forms of practice that are based on scientific positivist principles. If practice is located within the 'market' discourse (in the bottom left quadrant) the presumption is that welfare services are essentially commodities and that it is appropriate to apply the rules and structures of commerce, focusing

on the extent to which individuals have the capacity for free choice between competing options. There are many examples of policy development in the late twentieth century that applied either the 'managerial' or the 'market' discourse, as these have become dominant in the development of the personal social services. Indeed, for some commentators (see the various chapters in Harris and White, 2009, for example) the various elements of policy development that made up 'new' Labour's 'modernisation' strategy come into this category.

The establishment of the New Public Management within public services since the 1980s (Hood, 1991) can be seen as an example of the power of the 'managerial' discourse. A number of salient factors that relate to this can be identified. For example, there has been a sharp increase in the involvement of the independent sector in the provision of welfare services, which derives from a belief in the improved efficiency that can be generated by increasing competition in the delivery of services.

Over the years, there has already been substantial public services reform in relation to the delivery of social care. In residential and home care services for adults, for example, the near-monopoly provision of local authorities has been superseded by the development of a mixed economy of welfare (McDonald, 2006), with a substantial majority of both services now provided on a for-profit basis. (Of course, this is also an illustration of the application of a 'market' discourse to the development of services.)

Another feature of a 'managerial' approach to service delivery can be seen in the increased prominence of performance measurement in the entirety of social care and health services (Harris and Unwin, 2009). This has been trailed as a means to improve the efficiency of public services, although there is little recognition that performance measurement might have unintended consequences (de Bruin, 2002); critically, it can also be seen as a managerialist attempt to control the practice of social workers. The hallmarks of managerial control can be discerned in the hardening of specialisation within social work. While the organisational separation of children's from adult services is an exemplar of this, the separation of service categories is apparent even within these broad groups. For example, most social workers operating with adults would work either with older people, with people with learning disabilities, in mental health services or with people with physical disabilities. The categorisation represents a quest for managerial efficiency rather than a response to the fluid problems of individuals and their families.

Similarly, the increased focus on the management of risk, largely derived from the intense scrutiny given to all matters connected with child protection, is another symptom of managerial control (Webb, 2006). It appears intolerable that any level of risk can be supported, and the reality of social work practice – that it is inevitably uncertain and ambiguous, containing elements of risk that are largely managed through the judgement of practitioners (Parton, 1998b) – is profoundly at odds with the apparent attempt to define risk out of existence. From the 'market' perspective, it has been suggested that 'personalisation' of services (Leadbeater, 2004) – which in the provision of social services entails the extension of concepts such as individual budgets – can be interpreted as a further encroachment of market thinking into social work's territory (Ferguson, 2007). In addition, in recent decades there has been a revival of support for the role of the voluntary sector in responding to social problems, with a consequent reduction in the role of the state. While this has been most marked in the case of adult services, it also holds good for other service areas. While this could be interpreted as a preference for a 'community'-based approach to social problems, the fact that favoured voluntary organisations function much more akin to businesses (a situation forced on them by the demands of the contractual arrangements through which many are funded (Badham and Eadie, 2004)) means that their promotion is much more related to a market discourse. In addition, as Ferguson and Woodward (2009) have observed, many voluntary sector organisations share the same sets of bureaucratic and managerialist characteristics as local authorities.

Discussion of a 'big society' by the incoming Prime Minister David Cameron has changed the basis by which we can understand policy change, however. In his words (Cameron, 2010) 'The Big Society is about a huge culture change where people, in their everyday lives, in their homes, in their neighbourhoods, in their workplace don't always turn to officials, local authorities or central government for answers to the problems they face but instead feel both free and powerful enough to help themselves and their own communities.' To bring about the Big Society Cameron emphasises the need for more active engagement with the community, and the development of grass-roots organisations that can deliver public services. It also implies a substantial reduction in the role and scope of the public sector, the argument being that there is a compelling need to cut public services to reduce the budget deficit.

For Cameron, three things are needed to bring the Big Society into being – social action, public service reform and community empowerment (Cameron, 2010). (It is important to note the elasticity of language that can allow concepts such as community empowerment and social action to be used by both the political right and left!) All three potentially have the capacity to bring about fundamental change in the nature of social work practice. Certainly, a reduction in public expenditure challenges the position of social work which has been a largely public sector based profession since the 1970s. In addition, the rhetoric of social action and community empowerment also implies a substantial challenge to social work. In Cameron's words, 'We've got to give professionals much more freedom, and open up public services to new providers like charities, social enterprises and private companies so we get more innovation, diversity and responsiveness to public need.' It remains to be seen what the precise dimensions of the phrase 'give professionals more freedom' will mean for social work among other professions.

This change of emphasis heightens the need for social work to be proactive in establishing a clear basis for its work. If practice were to be found within the 'professional' discourse (in the top right quadrant) the governing principle would be of service, with the social worker presumed to possess the skill and expertise that can determine what would be the most appropriate outcome for the service user; however, it is humanist in that the governing principle is that the services provided should be tailored to meet the defined needs of the individual. If practice is within the 'community' discourse (the bottom right quadrant) the emphasis switches to be on 'the relationships and transactions that occur between people within the context of human communities' (Ife, 1997: 50). Both could potentially fit within the vision of the Big Society.

Of course, a schema such as this is very much an ideal type, and there are a number of practical and theoretical difficulties with such apparently clear distinctions. For example, in making his points, Ife could be accused of blurring the overlaps between the different discourses; for example, in community care policy in the early 1990s there were clear connections between managerial and market discourses, as our examples indicate. Similarly, he presents the discourses and the practice that derives from them in absolutist terms, when the reality is that there are often connections between those forms of practice – for example, much community care practice in the late 1990s and beyond links both managerial and professional discourses (Lymbery, 2005). While Ife favours the community discourse, he is relatively silent about some of its difficulties and constraints. Social workers in British society operate within tight time limits and to restricted budgets, carrying out duties that are often statutorily defined (for example, work in child protection, with young offenders and much mental health work) or administratively focused (the establishment of care packages for older people). A community-based orientation simply could not be put into practice in such circumstances. Finally, and this is critical for our argument, his contention about what constitutes practice within the 'professional' discourse bears little relation to thinking about the nature of professions that developed towards the end of the century.

In historical terms, the concept of 'profession' received relatively little critical sociological attention until around 1970. Professions were presumed to be good for the development of society, providing a service based on the superior knowledge and skill of its practitioners. Classic theories of what professions were, and hence how professionals should act, derived from a consideration of the presumed characteristics that those professions had in common. One of the key problems with such an analysis is that it takes the professions' descriptions of their purpose and actions at face value, not subjecting the claims that were made by and on behalf of professions to critical analysis. When such a critique was developed, professions were castigated for seeking to maximise the power of professionals over those who required their service (Johnson, 1972), for attempting primarily to secure their own interests rather than those of the people they were supposed to serve (Wilding, 1982), for trying to secure their own power relative to other professions (Abbott, 1988) and for engaging in a process whereby they sought to maximise their occupational control over the work that their members undertook (Larson, 1977). The impact of such critiques suffuses the radical literature of the 1970s and beyond (see *Case Con Manifesto*, 1975; Simpkin, 1983), which vigorously deny both that social work is a profession, and that it would be a legitimate enterprise for social work to become such.

This debate has particular salience in the early years of the twenty-first century, as there remains lack of clarity about the defining characteristics of social work. In this respect, the decision of the government to create Social Care Councils throughout the United Kingdom and the fact that social work now has many of the accepted features of a profession – graduate-level education as a prerequisite to join, legal protection of title, a professional association, a body of knowledge and theory on which

to draw – is at odds with the tightly drawn and prescriptive role that it sees for qualified social workers within its social policy (Jordan and Jordan, 2000). There is also a fundamental uncertainty within public policy about the distinction between social work and social care. Often the terms appear to be used interchangeably, as if there is no distinction between the two. The fact that there is no mention of social work in the title of the Social Care Councils is indicative of this ambivalence. At governmental level there seems to be a continued level of uncertainty about the distinctions between a qualified social worker and the remainder of the social care workforce, all of whom are overseen by Social Care Councils. This lack of clarity is evident throughout a document that purports to represent a statement of what ought to characterise good social work practice (GSCC, 2008).

Reflect

What do you understand the difference to be between **social work** *and* **social care**? *What are the possible consequences of a lack of clarity between the two terms?*

We do not believe that the traditional criticisms of professions should inevitably apply to social work. The emphasis, in all of the critiques, is of the distance between the professional and the lay person, enabling one (the professional) to define matters on behalf of the other (the service user). Given the relational nature of social work, and the importance we give to the service user voice, such a distanced approach could not possibly be effective. Rather, we believe that it is possible to develop a form of 'new professionalism', drawing on the work of Larson (1977). She suggested that the traditional distance between professional and the lay person is amenable to change, and that it is therefore possible to break down the barriers between professionals and others. For social work, its practitioners must therefore recognise that the trust of service users must be earned and cannot be assumed; as a result, they must work in ways to build up the confidence and self-respect of those with whom they work (whose experience of life has often involved the stripping away of such self-respect). Hugman (1998: 191) has suggested that it is possible to develop a renewed form of professionalism where the social worker bases her/his practice on the principles of 'responsiveness, openness and service', and argues that putting such principles into practice would ensure that the occupation would not develop in ways that augmented its status and hence excluded the people with whom social workers practise. (The implications of this as far as the development of relationships with service users is concerned are explored in Chapter 14.)

The means by which this is managed are a combination of the personal qualities of the social worker and her/his ability to establish productive relationships. This principle holds whether or not s/he is engaged in therapeutic work with an individual, processes of community development, patterns of service brokerage, or practice which is heavily circumscribed by legislative and administrative restrictions. It also applies to all groups of people with whom social workers function, whether people with physical or learning disabilities, children, families, young offenders, older people, mentally ill people, etc. If a social worker is unable to carry out this aspect of the work effectively, the values, skills and knowledge that s/he possesses become irrelevant, as the opportunity to put them into practice would simply not be available. Social work is, in our view, an activity carried out on a relational basis, and the first priority for a practitioner must be to establish a quality of relationship that can enable effective practice to take place. The details of how this can be achieved are outlined in later chapters, examining the role of social workers with specific groups.

Returning to Ife's (1997) model, it is clear from the foregoing that our orientation lies more within the professional discourse, although what we propose is a modified form of professionalism that should avoid the pitfalls of more traditional models. We recognise that a combination of principle and pragmatism informs this position. At the level of principle, we believe in the person-focused nature of social work, requiring of social workers well-developed interpersonal skills to maximise benefits for service users. Pragmatically, we accept the constraints that legislative, organisational and bureaucratic requirements place on practitioners, ensuring that much practice is reactive in nature. Given that a social worker functions at the intersection of people and their social environments (as in the IFSW definition of social work), her/his role is necessarily that of an intermediary, representing the needs and requirements of those people to society (and vice versa). There is, as Ife (1997) acknowledges, a tension between the two that social work practitioners have to mediate. This cannot be managed without a level of authenticity in the way in which the social worker engages with the service user, and the quality of relationship that is developed is key to this.

As we shall encounter in future chapters, there are a range of factors that might obstruct the development of this relationship (organisational, resource-driven, legislative, etc.) and these will be examined in relation to the separate chapters that explore the roles, functions and tasks of social workers with separate service user groups. In addition, we recognise that the 'community' orientation advocated by Ife does have value, although we contend that it does not equate to the work carried out by social workers within British society on a day-to-day basis; as such it plays a lesser role in this book. In addition, we recognise that good management is a precondition of effective practice; however, we take issue with the managerial forms of practice (as defined by Ife) that have become ingrained within many areas of social work practice. We fail to understand how forms of practice that are not predicated on a detailed understanding of an individual's needs could be deemed to be effective. (Chapter 2 discussed some of the organisational problems that social workers can expect to encounter, many of which are derived from these managerial roots.) Similarly, we do not believe that social work services can be effectively organised on a market basis, with the manifest forms of inhumanity that have accompanied such developments in other aspects of life.

Think ahead

From the examples, given in this chapter, it is worth considering how and why the nature of language has changed during social work's existence. For example, most writers until the contemporary period use the male pronoun to be all-inclusive.

How do you respond to this? Similarly, Younghusband specifically writes of the social worker as 'she' but the client as 'he'. *What might have caused such a linguistic construction?*

Conclusion

In this chapter, we have summarised key debates about social work from five key points in its history and development. In so doing, we have sought to explain how particular forms of practice have assumed dominance at points in its history, while articulating several voices of dissent from the prevailing orthodoxy, as these can provide insight into the contribution of social work within society. There are many aspects of social work's history and development that have a continued impact on the delivery of social work and social care today, and which are therefore important for contemporary practitioners to understand:

- *The legacy of stigma.* There was a profound sense of stigma associated with the need to seek social work support in the nineteenth century. This has never fully been resolved. In large measure, that fact that social work services are selective, rather than universal, reinforces the sense of stigma experienced by those people who require them.
- *The role of the state as against the role of the independent sector.* In the nineteenth century, social work was largely located in the charitable sector, transferring to the state through the twentieth century. The relationship between the two remains critical – its importance has been forcibly restated by the policies of the coalition government.
- *The role of the state in determining the role and functions of social work.* Since the transfer of the bulk of British social work into the statutory arena during the twentieth century, the state has played a major role in defining what social work is in policy and practice.
- *Dispute about the purposes and methods of social work.* From the early days of social work there has been a vigorous debate about the purpose of social work within society, and the most appropriate methods that would allow it to fulfil that purpose. As the chapter has demonstrated, this debate is unresolved and ongoing.
- *The continuing debate between specialisation and genericism in social work.* As we have noted, most social workers now operate in specialised roles within their organisations, indicating that a de facto form of specialisation has overtaken the principle of genericism. However, despite this change in the organisation of practice, social work education at qualifying level remains organised on generic principles.

We have sought to clarify our own position in relation to Ife's (1997) conception of competing discourses of human services, suggesting that what social workers require in British society is the development of a modified version of professionalism, whereby the skills and knowledge that social workers possess can be placed at the disposal of service users, breaking down the barriers of status that have traditionally separated the two. The practical expressions of what we mean by such forms of practice will be developed further in subsequent chapters.

Key learning points

This chapter has covered the following learning points:

✔ The core of social work is 'relational', in that the quality of relationship that can be developed with service users materially affects both the quality of service they receive and also how this is perceived.

✔ The COS and the Settlement Movement were important to the development of social work in the late nineteenth and early twentieth century; the forms of practice developed in both were an extension of the social theories and visions of their founders.

✔ In the 1950s, the rhetoric surrounding social work emphasised psychologically derived forms of practice, and we discussed the extended critique of this by Barbara Wootton.

✔ By contrast, the 'radical social work' movement of the 1970s proposed a form of practice that was oriented more towards a change in social circumstances than changes within the individual (*Case Con Manifesto*, 1975); the broad aims of this movement have been revived in an updated manifesto for change (Jones et al., 2004). Although this drew attention to the structural nature of many social problems, the radical perspective struggled to provide practitioners with a detailed sense of how their practice should change on a daily basis as a result of this understanding.

✔ The Barclay Report (1982), although it was intended to clarify the purpose and direction of social work practice, has had relatively little impact on the direction of British social work, which has followed more in the direction signposted by Pinker (1982) who, in his appendix to the report, argued for a more narrowly defined set of responsibilities for social workers, and focused particularly on the requirement for a mandate for any action that they undertook.

✔ In the final section, we have drawn on an analysis of social work developed by Ife (1997), who suggests that there are four basic orientations: market, managerial, professional and community. We have argued that a modified form of professional ideology is the appropriate position for British social work.

Further reading

Harris, J. and White, V. (eds) (2009) *Modernising Social Work: Critical Considerations*, Bristol: Policy Press. This text provides a challenging appraisal of the 'new' Labour government's modernisation programme for social work.

Ife, J. (1997) *Rethinking Social Work*, Melbourne: Addison Wesley Longman. A stimulating analysis of the relationship between social work and society.

Lewis, J. (1995) *The Voluntary Sector, the State and Social Work in Britain*, Aldershot: Edward Elgar. A text analysing the history of the Family Welfare Association (formerly the COS), drawing on fascinating historical data.

Lymbery, M. and Butler, S. (eds) (2004) *Social Work Ideals and Practice Realities*, Basingstoke: Palgrave Macmillan. This book seeks to analyse contemporary social work, using an approach that brings together policy, organisational constraints and social work practice.

McLaughlin, K. (2008) *Social Work, Politics and Society: From Radicalism to Orthodoxy*, Bristol: Policy Press. A challenging text that develops the consequences of the politicisation of social work from the 1970s onwards.

Payne, M. (2005) *The Origins of Social Work*, Basingstoke: Palgrave. A book that analyses the development and growth of social work, drawing on international as well as national sources.

Payne, M. (2006) *What is Professional Social Work* (2nd edn), Bristol: Policy Press. A particularly interesting read, focusing on how to define the essential nature of professional social work.

Useful websites

www.basw.co.uk

The British Association of Social Workers (BASW) is the largest association representing social work and social workers in the UK. BASW campaigns on all social work issues and is recognised throughout the UK as the voice of social workers, contributing to social policy development nationally and internationally. BASW is consulted by civil servants, ministers, elected representatives, regulatory councils, service users and other key social services organisations.

www.ccwales.org.uk

The Care Council for Wales is the first ever regulatory body for the social care profession in Wales. Through the Care Standards Act 2000 it has powers to set standards for people working in the sector in Wales, to register them against those standards for the first time ever, and also to remove them from the register for not adhering to those standards.

www.gscc.org.uk

The General Social Care Council (GSCC) is the workforce regulator and guardian of standards for the social care workforce in England. It was established in October 2001 under the Care Standards Act 2000. It is responsible for the codes of practice, Social Care Register and social work education and training.

www.iassw-aiets.org

The International Association of Schools of Social Work (IASSW) is an international association of institutions of social work education, organisations supporting social work education and social work educators. Its mission is:

- to develop and promote excellence in social work education, research and scholarship globally in order to enhance human well-being;

- to create and maintain a dynamic community of social work educators and their programmes;

- to support and facilitate participation in mutual exchanges of information and expertise;

- to represent social work education at the international level.

www.ifsw.org

The International Federation of Social Workers (IFSW) exists to promote social work as a profession through international cooperation, to promote the establishment of national organisations of social workers and to support the participation of social workers in social planning and the formulation of social policies, the enhancement of social work training and the values and professional standards of social work.

www.niscc.info

Northern Ireland Social Care Council (NISCC) is the new regulatory body for the social care workforce in Northern Ireland. Its aim is to increase the protection of those using social care services, their carers and the public. The NISCC was legally established on 1 October 2001 by the Health and Personal Social Services Act (Northern Ireland) 2001.

www.scie.org.uk

Social Care Institute for Excellence (SCIE) aims to improve the experience of people who use social care by developing and promoting knowledge about good practice in the sector. Through the use of knowledge gathered from diverse sources and a broad range of people and organisations, SCIE develops resources which are shared freely, in order to both support those working in social care and empower service users.

www.sssc.uk.com

The Scottish Social Services Council (SSSC) is responsible for raising standards in the Scottish social service workforce. It registers key social service workers involved in providing or delivering social work, social care services and early education and childcare. These workers will be expected to meet agreed standards of conduct, practice, education and training.

For additional cases and topic-organised, clickable links into additional media resources, including those produced by IRISS, visit **www.pearsoned.co.uk/wilsonruch**

Activity

Activity One

Read the articles by Ferguson and Garrett, noted in the text. Where do you position yourself in this debate?

Activity Two

Read the articles by Sheldon and Webb, noted in the text, and ask yourself the following questions: Do you believe that either author is correct about the nature of evidence? What factors influence your judgement?

(As an indicator of where we stand on the issue, consider the earlier chapter discussing what we believe to be the nature of social work. There is an interesting debate in the 1970s, also conducted through the pages of the *British Journal of Social Work*, which you might like to consider (see Jordan, 1978; Sheldon, 1978) as it bears on similar themes.)

Chapter 5
The values and politics of social work practice

Chapter summary

Values in social work have been a subject of heated debate and even conflict over the decades, and this has sometimes been divisive for the profession. In this chapter you will be introduced to various ways of 'mapping' the value positions that have shaped social work practice. However, the chapter proposes that while it is important to have real and meaningful debate about values in the profession, it is not helpful to use value positions as weapons in a war. These 'maps' of values and political positions in social work show that there is no one 'politically correct' stance for a social worker to adopt. There are undoubtedly wrong and inappropriate stances and value positions, but there are also many ways of being 'right'. You have to negotiate your way through the value 'maze' in social work, including the pressure under which others may sometimes place you to adopt 'their' position.

Changes in the value principles informing social work tend to reflect changes in the wider society, and the decline of 'universalist' frameworks and the rise of 'pluralist' ones is an important instance of this. But a good understanding of inequalities in society, and how they are produced and reproduced, is central to being a competent social worker. The psychosocial mechanisms through which inequalities have been created and maintained cannot be 'split off' from our value positions. Tackling inequalities through social work is a practical matter, as well as a political one, and the chapter focuses on some particular examples of how inequalities are reproduced at both the social and interpersonal levels.

Learning objectives

This chapter covers topics that will enable you to achieve the following learning objectives:

- To know the range of basic value frameworks that have informed social work practice, and which of these are most current

- To understand how various ideologies and theories of power relationships, oppression and domination have informed social work practice

- To see some different views about 'political correctness' and how to relate to it when you think you encounter it

- To understand some theories of how 'external' factors such as gender relations and racism shape people's experience and relationships and get 'inside' them as individuals; and how the individual is more than the sum of these external forces which are in turn influenced by people's creativity or 'agency'

- To appreciate the way in which social work values and political commitments have evolved through time, in response to wider changes in society

- To know how to integrate your thinking about values and politics with your skills in working with service users

- To know how to think about and negotiate value conflicts in yourself, between yourself and service users, and with your colleagues.

National Occupational Standards

The national occupational standards document makes it clear that values and ethics are at the centre of social work practice, and underpin all 6 key roles – below we reproduce the diagram from the NOS document illustrating this:

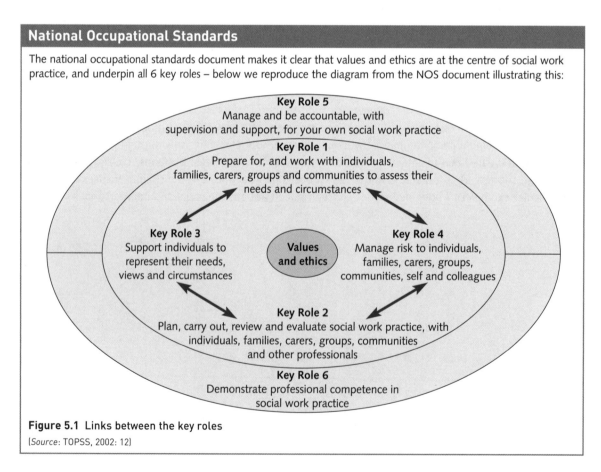

Figure 5.1 Links between the key roles
(*Source*: TOPSS, 2002: 12)

Case study

Bridget

Dionne has been a qualified social worker for a year. She now works in a local authority children in need team, although some of the cases she handles are complex and involve possible neglect or abuse of children. Dionne grew up in a working-class family in an industrial town in Yorkshire with large ethnic minority communities of Asian and Afro-Caribbean people. She is white, but at school many of her friends were black and Asian, and after her father died (when she was 13), her mother had relationships with two black men, one of whom is her long-term partner now. For a time, in the year after her father's death she was bullied at school, but she remembers that a particular teacher saw what was happening and intervened effectively to help her. Dionne has always thought of herself as a strong woman, a feminist, and particularly admires her mother for the way she coped after her father died. However, she knows she can have powerful irrational negative feelings about black and Asian men sometimes, and she thinks this is to do with her jealousy and anger about the men who replaced her father. When she was 18 she had a massive row with her mother about her partner at that time, and was shocked to find herself calling him racist names. Afterwards she realised what lay behind these feelings, but it took nearly two years for her relationship with her mother to heal and she still doesn't feel close to her mother's partner.

Recently Dionne took on a difficult case at work, and soon found herself very confused, at the centre of powerful team dynamics that challenged her sense of her own values, and also her sense of competence. The case concerned Bridget and her two children Ruth (3) and Tom (6 months) and a referral from the health visitor which suggested that Ruth was depressed, arguing constantly with her partner Dave who does not live with the family, and that she might be neglecting the two children. Dave is a mixed-race man, and is the father of Tom but not Ruth. Dionne visited the family, and came away feeling worried but also very frustrated with Bridget. The house was dirty and Bridget did seem emotionally disconnected from both children, responding to them in a mechanical way, but she also seemed very passive in relation to Dionne. Bridget agreed with everything Dionne said, but in a way that left her with the feeling that she was being 'fobbed off', and not taken seriously. Dionne left unconvinced that Bridget would be able to actually do any of the things they had discussed that might be helpful for her and the children.

When she discussed the case and her visit at a weekly team meeting, she expressed her worries about Bridget's apparent state of mind, and her care of the children. But team members seemed to adopt accusing positions towards Dionne, and towards each other. Joan, a senior social worker, suggested that Bridget's problems might all stem from post-natal depression, and that intervening to protect the children would 'victimise' her and them for something that wasn't their fault. Another colleague suggested that Dionne 'must' engage Dave – if he was creating arguments with Bridget then maybe he was 'the problem'; but this immediately drew an accusation from another colleague that this would be racist – making Dave the scapegoat for the whole situation. Ignoring this, Joan insisted that an 'empowering' approach was needed with Bridget, and that depression was mostly just 'feeling disempowered'.

None of this really felt helpful to Dionne, who herself now felt overpowered by her colleagues. She agreed with bits of what everyone had said, but felt angry that no one seemed able to also listen to her worries about the children and about Bridget. The team meeting broke up with a bad atmosphere among everyone. Dionne certainly didn't want to do anything unethical, and felt she had been as encouraging and supportive to Bridget as she could have been. But something in Bridget – at the moment at any rate – seemed to stand in the way of Dionne being able to implement any of these fine 'value' principles which her colleagues were so keen to insist she should take account of.

You have probably had heated discussions with colleagues about some aspect of politics or values in social work. Some discussions may have felt helpful to you, and some perhaps left you feeling hurt, manipulated, or attacked. What do you think made the difference in these discussions?

Values and political perspectives on society have always been at the heart of social work theory and practice. Like Dionne in the case study above, many social workers are motivated to enter the profession because they want to work for social justice, and they want to work directly with people. These two aspirations often fit together well, but sometimes they do not. Each of us has a personal 'story' or biography that concerns our relationship to injustice, disadvantage and discrimination, and each of us has some kind of story of psychological struggle. As practitioners we need to know ourselves well as social and political 'subjects', as well as psychological 'subjects' in order to be able to balance our passion and commitment with the right degree of objectivity, based in a political analysis of the circumstances of service users. This chapter explores these interconnecting themes in more detail.

Introduction

This is how the British Association of Social Workers (BASW) defined social work in a recent publication:

'A profession which promotes social change, problem solving in human relationships and the empowerment and liberation of people to enhance well being. Utilising theories of human behaviour and social systems, social work intervenes at the point where people interact with their environments. Principles of human rights and social justice are fundamental to social work.'   (BASW, 2003)

From this definition it is clear that values play a central role in what social work is all about. In this chapter you will be introduced to a range of debates, ideas and research about the political and ideological aspects of social work practice, but also to discussion about how values and ethics interact with questions about 'problem-solving' and 'social change' and the theories of human behaviour referred to above. The discussion will focus on how different fundamental value positions have informed social work, and how these have intertwined with political debates about the impact of social class, race and ethnicity, and sex and gender upon the lives and the 'life chances' of service users; and also on how social work as a profession has tried over time to incorporate attention to these dimensions of service users' experience, as well as address their impact and meaning for social workers and their organisations. This process of political and value debate within social work and struggle over what kind of political activity social

work is, or should be, has often been a source of conflict and tension within the profession. At times it has brought social work into conflict with government, and sometimes divided the profession itself sharply.

We argue that as an individual practitioner you cannot avoid becoming engaged with these tensions and debates, and the message of the chapter is very much that you need to come to 'know yourself' as a political and ethical 'subject', someone who has been shaped by social and political circumstances and who is confronted with political and value choices all the time in practice situations. The feminist slogan 'the personal is political' and its inverse 'the political is personal' are central to how we want to discuss these questions.

Think ahead

What family and life experiences do you think have influenced your values? Can you identify any areas where personal experience might interfere with your ability to work ethically rather than help this?

On the one hand, debate and argument about different values and political perspectives in social work is healthy and necessary; on the other hand, complete breakdown in communication and dialogue between different 'factions' or groups is ultimately destructive for the profession and to the interests of service users. So, in this book we take the view that it is not just important to 'know where you stand' with respect to values and politics in social work, but equally important that you develop skills in staying in dialogue and communication about values if arguments and debates threaten to get out of hand (as they seem to have done in Dionne's team), or lead to a breakdown of relationships with colleagues, service users or professionals from a different discipline. This reflects a view of politics and value questions that is, like everything in this book, ultimately relationship-based. We hold that it is important as well as inevitable to have differences among ourselves because it is through the continual discussion and resolution of differences that change, progress and growth occur, at both the individual and social levels. The development of value positions and political perspectives is always a social or interpersonal process as well as an intellectual or academic one. If we were to place an ultimate value on anything, it might be on the capacity of professional social workers to find a way to 'stay engaged' with one another even when conflicts are 'hot' and threaten to become destructive.

When the case study is continued later in the chapter, we will see that it may be possible to negotiate a way through such value conflicts. This is similar to the perspective we present in Chapter 2 about policy and organisations in social work, where we suggested that practitioners are always called upon to actively negotiate their way through complex organisational and policy terrain in which it is easy to feel trapped – rather as, maybe, Dionne felt trapped in the crossfire of competing value perspectives among her colleagues. Part of the strength of social work, but also perhaps a weakness, is that it has turned to many different value positions and ideological perspectives over the course of its history in its search for ways to respond to the complexity of its social task. These value positions are an essential resource if people are able to use them well, but they are also a rather dangerous armoury if people do not. In the experience of the authors of this book, there is nothing easier than to pick up one or other 'value position' and use it as a weapon in an argument, rather than as a way of being thoughtful about the ethics of social work practice. We have all done it at times, and we have all also found ourselves in positions a bit like that of Dionne.

The political pendulum: politics in twenty-first century Britain

On 11 May 2010, five days after the general election, an important shift occurred in British politics that will almost certainly affect social work for at least a decade. The outcome of the election was inconclusive, and after frantic and sometimes secret negotiations a full coalition government was formed by the Conservative and Liberal Democrat Parties. New Labour had been in power for thirteen years, altering the landscape of Britain's health service, social care provision and public sector with a massive programme of reforms and 'modernisation' (see Chapter 2). The election was fought against the background of the world economic crisis of 2007–9 which both deepened and exposed the level of national debt. The big decision facing any incoming government concerned the means by which to reduce this financial deficit, and in particular the extent to which public sector services like social work and social care should be protected – or not. These decisions would have slightly different consequences in England, Scotland, Wales and Northern Ireland because of the devolved powers for organising services and raising taxes invested in the governments and regional assemblies of the latter three.

By the summer of 2010 it was clear that huge spending cuts would hit all public services – education, health, housing, social care – although sometimes the effects would be indirect and gradual rather than immediate. Just as important, it had become clear that the new coalition government had a completely different vision of how to organise society than the outgoing Labour administration. The coalition Prime Minister David Cameron promoted his idea of a 'Big Society' of locally organised voluntary effort and social entrepreneurship; at the same time many of the regulatory bodies and strategic organisations that had shaped health and social care provision over the previous decade were abolished or merged with other organisations. In July 2010 it was announced that the General Social Care Council which had registered and regulated the social work profession in England would be disbanded and its functions incorporated by the Health Professions Council. English Primary Care Trusts and Strategic Health Authorities were also abolished and General Practices (family doctors) asked to assume new health commissioning responsibilities.

The changes are important for the politics of social work because:

- They announced a vision of society in which strategic planning and central control of policy-making would be largely 'devolved' to local level, opening the way for more private and independent sector interests to flourish. However, a central function of strategic planning lies in its ability to redistribute resources and services to disadvantaged regions and localities, offsetting some of the 'structural' causes and effects of poverty (see below).

- With fewer social work and social care 'support' services which are easy targets for savings, less strategic social care, education and health planning, and the likelihood of higher unemployment as the public sector contracts, localised poverty and disadvantage is certain to increase. Pressure on core, statutory social work services will mount as a result.

- The vision of a 'deregulated' society has other implications. The coalition spoke often of the need to 'return power to professionals', and putting health planning in the hands of family doctors rather than 'bureaucrats' was one expression of this. Likewise, the government's support for the emerging College of Social Work signalled their willingness to invest more autonomy and trust in the profession's own organisations. But the granting of greater 'autonomy' in a context of far more restricted opportunities and resources is a double-edged gift. Governments seem to find it hard to strike a balance between centralised state planning and resourcing and devolved professional responsibility for innovation and creative local delivery.

In 2009 Richard Wilkinson and Kate Pickett published an important book called *The Spirit Level: Why more equal societies almost always do better*. They show that above a certain level of minimum social prosperity what really makes a difference is not how wealthy a society is overall, but how equal or unequal its population groups are relative to one another. The wider the gap between prosperity of the 'top' and the 'bottom' groups, the more the whole society will suffer from all kinds of social, psychological, and psychosocial problems. Under New Labour Britain became more unequal, and this may explain why some of their positive social and health programmes had less impact than expected. But the signs are that in the new political era ushered in by the economic crisis and the coalition government, inequality is set to accelerate – those in relatively comfortable financial circumstances will suffer less than the poor from the overall impact of recession. Because these trends seem to have effects on the rates of mental ill health, violent crime, child maltreatment, educational performance and so on, the consequences for front-line social work are clear. The political pendulum may swing, but what lies at each end of the arc has different consequences for those with fewer economic and cultural resources. If you came into social work motivated by concerns about social justice, the implications are clear.

Reflect

What do you think of the idea of a 'Big Society'? Is it just a political sound bite with little substance, or a positive effort to revitalise 'civil society' by supporting cooperative effort, citizen power, diversity and responsiveness in service design and provision?

Can 'voluntary' organisations start up and thrive without state-funded support – especially in poorer communities?

Is the Big Society a cover story for 'cuts' or a radical new way of generating self-help and local autonomy?

Mapping the language of values in social work

In this section we introduce a wide range of basic terminology that you are likely to encounter in the social work literature and in debates and teaching about values, politics and social work practice. As we have suggested already, over time social work has favoured a variety of ways of conceptualising its own political dimensions. Occasionally there have been sharp divisions about these questions, but overall we have witnessed a complex evolution of ideas, and it is the resulting 'map' or network of values and political concepts informing social work that we now want to describe.

It is has sometimes been suggested that people may have two fundamental motives for entering the profession of social work – a commitment to furthering the aims of social justice on the one hand, and a desire to engage in therapeutic or helping relationships with people on the other. For social work, one great question has always been how (and whether) it is possible to combine or integrate these two purposes or motivations, and the theories of social work associated with them. Wilkinson and Pickett (2009, see above) are clear about this:

'the quality of social relations in a society is built on material foundations. The scale of income differences has a powerful effect on how we relate to each other. Rather than blaming parents, religion, values, education or the penal system, we will show that the scale of inequality provides a powerful policy lever on the psychological wellbeing of all of us.'
(2009: 4–5)

So, at first sight it might seem there should not be any particular problem about this, but in practice the distinction between 'social justice' and 'relationship-based practice' has frequently been a source of significant tension. Why might this be? In so far as social work has always been about engaging with socially disadvantaged groups – people afflicted by poverty, poor housing, lack of formal education, societal racism or sexism, employment difficulties, compounded perhaps by disabilities that mean they find it very difficult to combat these circumstances – then social workers have often wanted to emphasise the structural origins of these conditions of life. This means that in some real sense it is not the individual that is directly responsible for their difficulties, but rather the conditions of life into which they are born, which are inscribed in the social and familial environment that shapes them. Overall, in many societies, despite huge efforts to combat social inequality and poverty, for example, the proportion of people living in poverty remains the same. There seems to be something about social structures that is constantly replicated.

When sociological analysis of particular service user groups – the socio-economic and ethnic origins of children in public care, for instance – reveals that they are disproportionately drawn from the lower socio-economic classes, or from particular ethnic minority communities, then the contribution of social work to producing these outcomes – rather than countering such trends – can be thrown into sharp ethical, political and professional relief. As you can see, this line of argument is strongly associated with the 'social justice' dimension of social work practice and values.

Values and explanations

However, this short introduction illustrates an important distinction when it comes to thinking about values and social work practice. Debates about the 'value base' of social work tend to reflect wider arguments about the principles informing 'welfare' in general, and this is part of the area of study we usually call social policy. In her valuable book *Social Policy: A critical introduction* Fiona Williams presents a schema for understanding the range of ideas that have informed modern social policy, and still do today. She makes the fundamental point that

'Some writers have examined the philosophies or *values* which different perspectives have and the implication of these for their goals or objectives for welfare provision, other writers have included an analysis and evaluation of how different perspectives *explain* the existence of social problems, or the nature of social change. These are often referred to as the *normative* and *explanatory* approaches, respectively.'
(Williams, 1989: 14)

While it is valuable to keep this distinction in mind, it is also true that a particular normative approach will be associated with a particular explanatory one, and vice versa. But in debates about social work values, you will often hear people slipping almost unnoticed between normative and explanatory arguments for their position, and this can be confusing unless the distinction is kept in mind. So, in the opening paragraph of this section, notice how easily we passed from discussing a commitment to social justice (a value position) to a particular explanation for the persistence of inequalities in society.

Williams then describes seven perspectives on welfare and their associated attitudes to the welfare state, all of which have informed social work practice and policy, and in most cases continue to do so. These are:

1. Anti-collectivism
2. Social reformism
3. Fabian socialism
4. Radical social administration
5. Political economy of welfare
6. Feminist critique
7. Anti-racist critique.

Perhaps Fiona Williams's table (Table 5.1) can be extended in two ways to make it fully relevant to the particular case of modern social work. First, much of this chapter concerns the very specific role that social work occupies within the much broader range of services and initiatives that make up 'welfare'. Social work has always straddled the divide between the 'public' and the 'private' aspects of people's lives, and this is reflected in the idea of 'personal social services' which seems to acknowledge that the 'personal' is also 'social'. In her book Williams gives much attention to the emergence of feminist and anti-racist perspectives in social policy, and these perspectives have often emphasised what we might call 'social *experience*'; this involves the idea that it is the experience, arising from the nature of everyday relationships in a patriarchal or racist society, of being a woman or a black person that can be oppressive. These relationships are *both* personal and political. We discuss such perspectives in more depth towards the end of the chapter. For example, the feminist psychotherapists Orbach and Eichenbaum, whose work we focus on there, are concerned with women's experience of themselves in the context of their 'reproductive' role as mothers and carers. From the perspective of social policy, this role is a vital economic and social one, as well as being personal and subjective.

Reflect

Do you 'identify' clearly as holding a particular strong value position – as a feminist, or socialist, or perhaps a religious value position? How important is this personal commitment in your work? What might be any positive or negative influences of your values in being a professional, social worker?

Secondly, as we discussed in Chapter 2, social policy in the past few years has been organised around a complex interplay between 'social reformist' perspectives and 'anti-collectivist' ones to produce a new kind of category that could be added to Williams's table. We

Table 5.1 Different perspectives of welfare: a simple account

Type	Attitude to the welfare state
Anti-collectivism	State welfare limits individual freedom, initiative and choice, and leads to excessive demands. Provision to come from private/voluntary sector as well as through family and self-help
Social reformism (three types) *Non-socialist welfare collectivism*	State welfare provision necessary for national efficiency and alleviation of worst deprivation, but can also come from private/voluntary sectors ('mixed economy of welfare' or 'welfare pluralism')
Fabian socialism	The welfare state is central to the transformation of society through redistribution of wealth and the creation of a more equal, just and harmonious society to counter the inequalities of the private market
Radical social administration	Welfare state to be central to a socially planned society which consists of radical redistribution of wealth and resources and the pursuit of equality
Political economy of welfare	Welfare state as outcome of fundamental conflict between capitalism and working class, but unable to meet need under capitalism
Feminist critique	State welfare provision important for amelioration of women's lives but also reinforces female dependency and the sexual division of labour
'Anti-racist critique'	State policy reflects shifting relations between imperialism, capitalism and patriarchy. Welfare state is part of institutionalized racism of society, by denial of access, second-class provision, reproduction of racial divisions and maintenance of immigration controls

(*Source*: Williams, 1989: 16–17, Table 2.1)

might call it 'social reformist-capitalist', given its emphasis on the provision of services via 'socially managed market mechanisms'. So, many of the most recent value positions that have emerged in social care – advocacy, service user involvement, empowerment – reflect, or partly reflect, this development because they are concerned with people's relative power or powerlessness as 'consumers' of services.

Since the late 1990s, the value base of social work has been strongly shaped by the idea of anti-discriminatory or anti-oppressive practice. These notions are broad enough to encompass both a considerable number of the welfare perspectives outlined above, as well as interventions aimed at tackling discrimination at the interpersonal, organisational, and community levels. Increasingly, though, in the more market dominated context of modern social work, it is the concepts of choice and empowerment that assume prominence in the struggle to extend rights, resources, and autonomy to service users, for example, in campaigns to develop direct payments and individual budgets to new groups of users. In turn this reflects the more individualised political culture we how inhabit (see Chapter 2) and the notion that welfare is a question of promoting 'opportunity'. Nevertheless, social work remains alive with political debates that have roots in many other traditions of critique and radicalism. We now review a range of these.

Empowerment, identity politics, individualism – the waning of 'universalist' politics?

An important normative principle of social work, which also represents a form of continuity between old and new visions of welfare, is the principle of service user self-determination. This principle involves a fundamental commitment to the idea that people are their own agents, meaning that they have not only the right, but also the capacity (under most circumstances), to exercise choice and make decisions about their own lives. It is not the job of social work or social workers to supplant these rights or capacities, but rather to encourage, support, liberate, and help develop such agency. The principle and practice of advocacy is closely connected with this value position, although advocacy as a defined occupational role rather than an aspect of general practice is a recent development in social care. Advocacy involves the assumption that some people may need support in managing their relationships with the organisations, institutions and personnel they encounter in their dealings with welfare, health or legal services. In turn, this recognition is tied to an analysis of the inevitability of unequal power relationships in service user encounters with welfare organisations. For this reason empowerment principles have become an important part of how many practitioners think and behave. But as Beresford and Croft (2000) stress, (see the Closer Look box) empowerment, like all the value positions outlined in this section, is itself a much contested concept.

If it is true that a view of social work as inherently a political project, concerned with supporting and enabling disadvantaged communities and individuals, can find 'common cause' with a view of social work as primarily about the psychological difficulties or deficits which make 'self-realisation' difficult for people, making such 'common cause' has often been much more difficult than it appears it should be. Why is this? And have we made any progress with this central problem of social work practice and theory?

One allegation often levelled by proponents of structural social work, empowerment philosophy or radical social work against practitioners who wish to emphasise the importance of the individual helping relationship is that the latter are psychologising the social or political. This critique intends to point out that problems, difficulties and disadvantages are being attributed to, or constructed as caused by, the psychological functioning of individuals or families, when the 'true' cause or explanation is to be found in the social structural or socio-economic conditions of life of the individual.

Conversely, those theorists and practitioners who want to lay stress on the relationship with the individual have often complained that too much focus on the social and political context of people's lives obscures or even denies other truths or realities: first, the fact that individuals do retain their 'agency' – their capacity to act, make choices, respond helpfully or unhelpfully to their own circumstances – irrespective of how these came about and even in the most dire and adverse of circumstances; and secondly that it is impossible to 'read off' the situation or understanding of an individual, or a particular family or community from an analysis based on generalisations about class, ethnic, gender or other social divisions and categories. The particular, unique experience, conditions of life, and explanation for an individual's predicament cannot be known until and unless you have got to know that individual and understood the particularities as well as the generalities of their situation. Sometimes then, psychologically and 'therapeutically' minded social work practitioners have wanted to 'hit back' at their more 'politically' minded critics, saying that a failure to take account of the reality and particularity of an individual's life (especially if the person is disadvantaged or socially excluded) is itself a form of oppression. This may seem a fair point, but we can also sense how this important discussion might be degenerating into a slanging match – or even a serious civil war within social work. In fact, this is what happened in the 1970s and 1980s (see also Chapter 4 of this book) in Britain. We will consider some ideas about why 'war breaks out' in social work, and some thoughts about how to avoid this happening, in the next section. But first, there are a few more central concepts which it is important to introduce.

A closer look

Models of empowerment

'Many different strands can be identified in the development of the idea and usage of empowerment. There are self-help, liberational, professional, managerialist and market models of empowerment. They are in complex relationship with each other. While there are overlaps between them, there are also important differences. Empowerment has become the site of key struggles over the nature and purpose of politics, policy, services and professional intervention. That is why its meanings are heavily contested and it is important to recognize its *regulatory* as well as its *liberatory* potential.

The two approaches to empowerment most in evidence in social work and social policy are the *professional* and the *liberational* ones. Professional interest in empowerment developed in response to the new demands of the consumerist care market. The idea offers human service professionals like social work, facing uncertainty and insecurity, new arguments for their own autonomy and consolidation by emphasizing the prior need for *their* empowerment if they are to empower service users. The concept has been embraced enthusiastically as providing a new paradigm for practice, giving it vitality, legitimacy and credibility.'

(Beresford and Croft, 2000: 117)

A closer look

Radical social work, structural social work and socialism

As with all the value frameworks discussed in this chapter, there is no single text or statement that is absolutely definitive of 'structural social work' or 'radical social work', but in the following passage taken from his book *Structural Social Work: Ideology, theory and practice*, Robert Mullaly summarises the central theoretical position of radical and structural thinkers, and the implications of this stance for practice.

'Based on socialist ideology and located within the radical social work camp, structural social work views social problems as arising from a specific societal context – liberal/neo-conservative capitalism – rather than from the failings of individuals. The essence of socialist ideology and of the radical social work perspective is that inequality: (1) is a natural, inherent (i.e. structural) part of capitalism; (2) falls along the lines of class, gender, race, sexual orientation, age, disability, and geographical region; (3) excludes these groups from opportunities, meaningful participation in society, and a satisfactory quality of life; and (4) is self-perpetuating . . . Given this view of social problems, structural social workers seek to change the social system and not the individuals who receive, through no fault of their own, the negative results of social arrangements.'   (Mullaly, 1993: 124)

In the 1980s in Britain the nature of politics in society as a whole began to change very significantly, and this affected social work as well as many other professions and sectors of society. With hindsight we can see that the defeat of the Labour government in 1979 and the election of Ronald Reagan in the USA were the beginning of the end of a long period in which a particular brand of left wing thinking and politics shaped how we thought about ourselves. With its roots in the Trade Union movement, or in one or another variety of socialism, communism, or Marxist thinking and practice, this kind of politics had emphasised the importance of social class above all else in determining people's life chances, opportunities, health, income and so on. But the defeat of 'old' Labour in Britain coincided with the emergence of wider cultural and social developments that were challenging the dominance of long-accepted intellectual frameworks like Marxism. Post-modernism proposed an end to 'grand narratives' (theories that try to explain a whole area of life within a single universalist or modernist framework of ideas), and this helped liberate a plethora of new, but also competing, frameworks of thought and practice, giving rise to a much more pluralist political culture. Thus, although modern feminism is a movement with roots in the nineteenth century at least, in late twentieth century social work it joins anti-racism, anti-ageism, and campaigns around the politics of disability in a broad 'coalition' of perspectives on practice known variously as anti-discriminatory practice (ADP) or anti-oppressive practice. Sometimes these definitions have acquired 'official' status within social work, and ADP, for example, has been written into the national social work curriculum.

Think ahead

People who came into social work in the 1970s or 1980s (some of your managers perhaps) will have grown up in a world where the idea of 'universal' political values were the norm. Since then, politics has changed in the direction of 'single issue' and 'identity politics'.

What do you think are the relative strengths and weaknesses of either approach?

Political thinkers as well as social work theorists in the late twentieth and early twenty-first centuries have sometimes welcomed this new political landscape, and sometimes bemoaned the loss of the old universalist frameworks. Identity politics, or a preoccupation with single issue political campaigns, have been criticised precisely because they seem to detract from a fully 'structural' analysis, and focus attention on just one dimension of the production of oppression, marginalisation and discrimination. How can negative aspects of the situation of black women in Britain, for example, be adequately grasped through theories or movements that concern themselves only with gender, or only with race? But if the obvious answer is to link or integrate theories of race and gender to deal with this objection, then what of the possible connections and the potential for solidarity between black men, and white and black women, in an analysis that seems to exclude the former? One can replicate this dilemma many times over, once all the categories of possible oppression are added into the mix – sexual identity, race, gender, class, disability, age . . .

Thus the problem of hierarchies of oppression – questions about who is more oppressed than whom, and according to what criteria – have often dogged this new political culture. Universalists point to this fragmentation and say that the whole strength of an inclusive, single framework of political analysis is that it promotes solidarity; pluralists, on the other hand, and proponents of the value of identity politics have stressed how personal experience and the subjective dimensions of political life are more easily linked and assimilated to one another within an approach to politics that makes more room for subjectivity and is thus less 'totalising' or 'objectifying' of the very people that political and value-driven movements are claiming to emancipate.

Reflect

Think about your own 'social identity'. For example, everyone has a race, class, gender, sexual identity, and is of a particular age.

Are some descriptions of yourself much more important to you than others? Do you think about, or are you more sensitive about some of these than others? If so, what might this mean?

In modern Britain it is the concept of social exclusion that has become established in political left-of-centre discourse as one of the most accepted frameworks for tackling problems of social and structural marginality.

Social exclusion was originally a French notion that in some ways served to resolve the various tensions about hierarchy and competition between different political discourses and practices which we have discussed above. Social exclusion is itself a highly 'inclusive' concept, allowing 'traditional' political categories, like class and gender, to be brought into fluid relationship with less traditional ones, like mental illness or homelessness, to explain and provide a basis for action in relation to groups of all kinds which find themselves unable to compete, participate or achieve status and recognition within the mainstream of society. After the new Labour government came to power in 1987, a government social exclusion unit was quickly set up, and in 2006 the unit published a new action plan, *Reaching Out: An action plan on social exclusion* that restated the government's commitment to tackling the problems faced by the most deprived and marginalised communities, groups and individuals. As the Prime Minister's foreword says:

'This Action Plan examines the reasons why, despite the huge progress we have made, there are still individuals and families who are cut off. About 2.5 per cent of every generation seem to be stuck in a lifetime of disadvantage. Their problems are multiple, entrenched and often passed down through generations.' (Cabinet Office, 2006: 3)

Why is this important to social work? Many, if not most, of the service users with whom you will work are part of this '2.5 per cent'. This reinforces the inherent connection between social work as a job, and the political and value-related meaning of the fact that, as Tony Blair's comments imply, the 'socially excluded are always with us'.

A closer look

The diversity of social work values

'There is no dependable consensus about what type of concept, principle or precept merits the implied high status of a social work "value", and there are different views about the specific character of social work values. These are sufficient reasons to explain why there is no universally accepted, definitive set of social work values. Overlaid on the conceptual ambiguity lies the diverse range of substantive beliefs and theories, religious outlooks, moral values, political principles and the general world-views to be found amongst social workers just as amongst any comparable section of society. There is no evidence for a stronger consensus on moral, social and political questions amongst social workers than among any other comparable group in modern pluralist and multicultural societies. Moreover, most versions of social work values strongly recommend the acceptance and positive evaluation of diverse ways of life, making the identification of essential values even more elusive, for example, social workers usually claim to value both ethnic and cultural diversity, and equal rights for women. Their cultural standards deny gender equality, the issue cannot be resolved by appealing to social work values.'

(Clark, 2000b: 360)

Outside in . . . inside out – how values and politics in social work are about more than just language and 'taking positions'

One of the strengths of the idea of social exclusion is that it creates the space to think about politics and values as questions of both public and private concern, as relating to *both* the personal *and* the political. We think this is very important, since one of the dynamics surrounding arguments over values in social work is, as we have tried to show already, the way in which everyone very quickly can take up fixed positions in relation to everyone else. Part of how this happens concerns what is called 'binary thinking', which is another word for 'either/or' forms of discussion and argument, as opposed to 'both/and' forms of debate. In other words, it is easy for people to defend a position on one or other side of the list of 'connected opposites' (and there are many more!) in the Activity box below.

In this section we want to review briefly a number of theories, and also some research, that has tried to bridge the gap between these 'opposites' and keep them in connection. *Outside in . . . Inside out* is the name of a famous feminist book about women's (and men's) mental health (Eichenbaum and Orbach, 1982) and how what's 'inside people' or part of what we think of as their 'psychology' may be traced to what was once 'outside them' in their family relationships, but also in the way these relationships were and are organised by 'political factors', such as gender in society. Similar work has been done on questions of race – both about how people with racist inclinations become like that, and also how the experience of living in a racist society can be 'internalised' by people who are its victims in very complicated ways, so that they do not always think, feel and behave in ways that make obvious sense. This way of thinking that tries to connect psychology and sociology, the 'inside' and the 'outside', and agency and structure (see above) in people's lives we call 'psychosocial'.

But first, it is important to say something about another kind of thinking that could also be said to attempt this 'connecting task', but which we think has definite limits (although it is very useful) because it tends to concentrate too exclusively on the role of language in performing this bridging function. 'Social constructivism' is the name for a whole range of theories and research perspectives that stress how social processes and social institutions systematically create (or 'construct') the range of positions in society it is possible for anyone to occupy at any one point in time. Constructivism often lays great emphasis on the interconnected role of language and everyday social practices in this process of creating 'subject positions' which people then have little choice but to take up; thus, the social roles of 'wife', 'mother', 'criminal', 'patient', 'welfare client' and so on are constructed through systems of language or discourses that work powerfully to shape the possibilities and the limits of what people in any one 'subject position' can think, say, do, suggest, or act upon. The importance of this set of perspectives is that it has shown us how power relations in society are created and sustained through a whole variety of means other than direct 'down the barrel of a gun' oppression. Rather it is these discourses – reproduced every day through social and linguistic exchange – that function to maintain groups of people in both powerful and less powerful positions with respect to one another. One consequence of this way of understanding things is that challenging language, and the fixed way that certain groups are labelled, named, discussed becomes a form of political activity in itself. You are certain to be familiar with this to some extent. To take a stark example, when black people (supported by others) began to challenge the use of words like 'nigger' or 'darkie', and to insist that they wanted to be known as 'black people', they were not just opposing the use of words that were deeply offensive to them, but a whole system of domination that was held in place by the systematic positioning of black people through names, descriptions and theories that all insisted on their inferiority. To challenge the language was to take up arms against a structure of oppression.

This stance has a lot to do with the range of political practices that became known as 'political correctness'. Sometimes this expression has been used to decry and ridicule a set of political attitudes and practices that is alleged to pivot around the 'correct' or 'incorrect' use of words. Often then, the idea of political correctness is used to attack those who hold important value positions by suggesting that they lack real substance and that they are more interested in controlling others than they are in any authentic political programme. Unfortunately, challenging people directly about their use of words can sometimes degenerate into a game of 'control', while at other times it can *feel* like someone is trying to control your use of language when they may be authentically asking you to think twice about the offensive or politically thoughtless implications of the words you use.

On the one hand, to accuse someone of being politically correct can be a very 'cheap shot', a way of dismissing their stance; on the other hand, the term does capture something about the way in which people do take up rigid ('correct') positions in political exchange and eliminate the possibility of thoughtful debate or argument. Looked at this way, 'Political correctness depends upon a reduction of complexity and has the consequence of freezing thinking. The tendency then is to search for someone who has infringed the rules, and this person becomes a site of projection for "crimes" that belong elsewhere' (Cooper and Lousada, 2005: 100). However, the debate about what political correctness is, and whether it is a helpful or unhelpful phenomenon, is itself very complex, and very much a part of our times in so far as the nature of language and how it helps construct the social world has moved centre stage.

So, this view of people and their relationship to society does have a 'psychosocial' slant to it, because language (and ideas about the self and identity) are both public phenomena and private or individual – each of us 'thinks' with the language available to us, and much of that thinking is undertaken privately or silently as well as through dialogue and interaction with others. But this view of how people and their identities are formed also seems to ignore and downplay many other dimensions of our experience of ourselves – our feelings and the way in which our emotionally significant relationships seem to have shaped us as people. The great strength of how certain feminist and anti-racist thinkers, influenced by *both* their politics *and* their practice as therapists, have moved this debate on is that they have taken full account of these dimensions that seem to get rather lost in the social constructionist view of things. We believe their thinking is important, and of great value for social workers who after all, in their day-to-day practice, are always dealing with live 'people-in-their-social-situations'.

Women, mothering and the reproduction of caring

Susie Orbach and Louise Eichenbaum set up the Women's Therapy Centre in London, and wrote a series of books based on this experience. They wanted to make sense of their observations as therapists – of their clients as well as of themselves – that there was something distinctive about the way many of the distressed women they met seemed to think, feel and behave that had something to do with them 'being women'. But they did not want to perpetuate the idea that women's problems

or identities were therefore something 'biological' or 'genetic' – a way of thinking that is sometimes called 'essentialist', meaning that there is a core 'essence' of womanhood, or 'manhood', or anything else, that we carry in us in some mysterious way and which explains us. But if that is not the case, how does a woman *psychologically* 'become a woman' and would the answer to this question provide a link to the observation that women have particular experiences of personal distress and mental health difficulties? Orbach and Eichenbaum came to the conclusion that an important part of the process of becoming a woman lies in a girl's relationship to her own mother; in turn of course each mother was also once a daughter, and so on down the generations. 'In our practice' they write, 'we often hear women describe how startling it is to hear themselves speaking to their daughters just as their mothers spoke to them. As one woman put it "I couldn't believe it came out of my mouth . . ."' (1985: 38).

In most societies, mothers are the people primarily responsible for the provision of emotional care in infancy and childhood. In understanding that this emotional care is not always perfect, and that in this way mothers may transmit emotional difficulties to their daughters in particular ways, Orbach and Eichenbaum are not wanting to 'blame mothers', but to *understand a complex process of inter-generational development*. Moreover, their view is that this process of transmission must be understood by reference to the politics of gender relationships in society, and that men are of course also implicated in this. As a mother, a woman in our society may often have 'split off' or 'repressed' the part of herself that needs and craves emotional care, because she got the message from her own mother that this aspect of herself was unacceptable, or distressing to mother, or frightening; thus when a woman's infant daughter expresses her 'baby', 'needy' self – crying, distressed, clinging – this can be painful and create anxiety since it may resonate with mother's own 'baby self' which she has kept mostly out of consciousness – 'split off' in herself. So she subtly gives her infant and growing child the message that it is better not to show this side of herself, and not to depend on other women, or men, to get these emotional needs met. Of course this is often only half the picture. Mothers identify closely with their daughters, and vice versa. But the combination of intimacy and fear of intimacy can create a difficult, ambivalent, 'push–pull' dynamic between these women. At worst then, 'She must hide *her self*. She comes to feel that there must be something wrong with who she really is'

(1985: 48). Could this 'feminine psychology' (an inter-personal psychology) have something to say about why, for example, women are at least twice as likely as men to be diagnosed with clinical depression at some time in their lives?

Think ahead

Men are from Mars and Women are from Venus, so the saying goes. 'Gender wars' have played a big part in the politics of the past fifty years. Do you think men and women have different strengths and capacities in relation to social work, or do you think this is a myth? Do you think men are typically 'oppressive' to women in the workplace, or does it work both ways?

If so, what of men in all this? These writers develop their theory in an interesting way to take account of men and masculinity. One consequence of having a 'hidden' emotionally needy self can be that a person becomes highly attuned to the presence of emotional needs in others. Other people's distress 'resonates' powerfully and immediately; we 'pick up on it' as the saying goes. Or as Eichenbaum and Orbach put it: 'She develops the radar to pick up the needs of others; *she learns to give what others need; and she gives to others out of the well of her own unmet needs*' (1985: 56). So, we see that perhaps women can become very good at providing care, while being much less good at receiving care, and that this is at a cost to themselves. To whom do they typically 'give care' then? Perhaps most readers will have caught the drift of this argument now! We know that professions like social work, nursing, psychotherapy and even the 'childhood' specialities in medicine are heavily female-dominated. Is it possible then that the *whole structure of caring in society* is shaped by this quite complex psychosocial process described above? And is it possible that the part men play in all this is to be better at receiving care than at giving it?

Again, these thinkers do not want to blame men for their part in reproducing gender dynamics in society, but to show us how we may all be caught up in processes that do nonetheless lead to inequalities in society. In their view, mothers may often give different emotional messages to their sons. A mother's fear of encountering her own 'neediness' in her daughter may not be replicated with a son; after all, as we have seen above, one solution to the problem of what to do with unmet emotional needs is to get them met vicariously: in other words, by meeting another's needs, and in part

experiencing that person as 'oneself'. Sons, as men of the future, are not encouraged in our culture to be *openly* emotionally dependent. But it is possible that men become adjusted to simply having their needs met, and that women (first mothers and later wives or partners) fall in with this. In this way a kind of false or defensive solution to the problem which emotional need poses for women coincides neatly with men's perfectly ordinary need for emotional care, *but in a manner that may distort the identities and experience of both sexes, and contribute significantly to the reproduction of gender inequalities in society.*

This way of understanding gender relations seems to integrate a concern for values and political analysis with attention to the complex social and psychological processes that are actually involved in creating and sustaining 'unequal and persisting patterns of relationship in society', which could be another way of defining 'social structures'. In our view, this kind of integration is necessary for successful, competent social work. The battle against inequality, discrimination and injustice cannot be fought just on the ground of 'value positions' and language games. Real relationships and interpersonal struggle are involved in doing such work because the production and reproduction of inequality in society is itself an interpersonal process, driven as much by group and individual feelings as it is by cognitive stances in relation to ethics and morals, or our positioning within systems of ideology, important as these things are.

The pain and complexity of racism – in social work training

Such an approach to thinking about ethnicity and racism in social work has also been developed. We may all understand the idea that racism, whether personal, institutional or societal, is oppressive, unjust and damaging to our humanity. But the idea that it is a site of complex personal, emotional pain for those who have been its objects is perhaps less common; and that there may be different but corresponding psychosocial complexities for white people or other 'perpetrators' of racism – guilt, anxiety, confusion about responsibility – that are also less familiar. Cathy Aymer is a black social work academic and teacher who has written about the complex personal and professional experience of being both black and in a senior position in the social work profession. Here she is musing on an everyday experience in the life of a social work teacher (and in the life of a social work student!):

'I am at a three-way placement meeting with a black social work student and a black practice teacher. There is a possibility that if we were to tell our migration stories, that this might bring the type of hurt into the room that might threaten to overwhelm us when we discuss the black client with whom my student is working. How are these feelings to be managed? It is my belief that whether they are spoken or not they play a part in our professional understanding and in our professional development.'   (Aymer, 2002: 20)

Aymer says in another part of her paper that the experience of migration to Britain among Afro-Caribbean people, combined with the unexpected force of racism and rejection they encountered when they arrived, made it hard for this community to be good citizens, good professionals – or good clients. It is a striking thought, the possibility of being a 'better' or 'worse' client or service user, but perhaps it addresses something important but often felt to be too sensitive to articulate – that people, including 'clients', can be difficult, but that maybe a history of pain, trauma, disadvantage, rejection and so on is what usually lies behind this 'difficult' presentation.

However, what might also strike the reader is the echo in Cathy Aymer's story of the analysis of gender relations presented in the last section. Can the practice teacher, the tutor, and the student *bear* to know about and share their possibly mutual painful experiences of migration and racism? And if not, what might be the implications for the student's capacity to work effectively with the black service user? Is the pain of these experiences something black people can help each other with, or are 'wounds' of racism passed on down through the 'generations' as well as being constantly reinforced by continuing racism in white society?

Most of the pioneering texts about anti-racist practice in social work were rooted in the assumption that a campaigning social justice perspective was needed in order to place the question of institutional and societal racism firmly on the agenda of British social work training and leadership. This was undoubtedly necessary in the climate of British politics and professional life of the 1980s when the 'universalist' paradigm of politics was still a force, and the power of the new 'social movements' and of 'identity politics' was still uncertain. Even among 'supportive' and progressive groupings, black people were still wary in case the distinctive experience and politics of racism became subsumed back into a general

politics of 'class' or 'oppression'. When racism and the need to combat it did surface at an official and governmental level in Britain, as with the Scarman Report (1981) following the Brixton riots in London, the doubts of ethnic minority communities over whether white society really understood the issues tended to be confirmed. Well-meaning and bold in certain respects, this report was also much criticised for seeming to perpetuate a 'bad apple' theory of racism in the police force, attributing the difficulties to a few deviant, malicious, or misguided individuals rather than developing an analysis in terms of institutional racism. This latter approach was taken up much more confidently and with considerable impact in the MacPherson Report (1999), the inquiry report into the murder of Stephen Lawrence in South London. However, this also showed how long the process had been of our society really being able to accept, and register, the fact of racism at the level of government and political leadership.

Against this background, many of the classic 'anti-racist' social work texts seem to be written in a rather exhortatory, preaching, 'hectoring' style which can leave the reader feeling guilty if they find themselves questioning anything, and unable to engage thoughtfully with the debates, because few genuine arguments are presented, but rather a series of 'positions' are asserted. Arguably, this way of promoting the struggle against racism does more harm than good, subtly suggesting that the arguments cannot be won through open engagement, but must be imposed. No self-respecting academic, scholarly or research text makes pronouncements of this sort, however controversial or radical its thesis might be, because the author probably assumes that an intelligent, discerning readership will expect to have their mind engaged in a critical and thoughtful way.

Reflect

On your social work training, or in your workplace, do you feel that 'race relations' can be openly discussed and 'worked through', or is there a lot of tension under the surface of the group about these matters? If so, what could help relieve this tension?

As many more black people entered social work, and through the 1990s began to achieve positions of seniority and responsibility – although undoubtedly the forces of institutional racism continue to prevent some ethnic minorities achieving proper representation in all walks of public life – there was a sense that the terms on which

Professional tip

Handling value conflicts with confidence

Values are central to social work practice, but can also be a source of tension and conflict. We suggest:

- If you see something happening in your agency or in a colleague's work that bothers you in value terms then take time to think about how you will tackle this openly. Do not rush in before you have a clear plan, and have looked at the situation from as many angles as possible.

- Read about the important 'value questions' from different angles, not just through the social work literature. There are many excellent, moving, insightful novels and autobiographical accounts by people who have experienced oppression and discrimination, have mental health problems or who are disabled.

- If you find yourself in the middle of a 'values' war with colleagues, take some 'time out' with yourself, stand back a moment and try to understand what is happening and why you might be getting so heated. Are your personal experiences being touched on in some important way?

the debate about racism and anti-racist practice in social work in the twenty-first century should be conducted were changing. Many more young people had now grown up in more fully multiracial communities, schools and families; particularly in cities, a much increased proportion of black and Asian young people had successfully entered higher education. By 2006, the proportion of ethnic minority social work students entering MA-level trainings as graduates, as distinct from undergraduate BA trainings, was as high as 70 per cent in some places; in addition, many more students from African rather than Afro-Caribbean backgrounds are now entering the profession, bringing with them a very different cultural experience, and experience of racism in relation to white British society.

Partly responding to these shifts, and partly helping to create them, social work theorists of race and racism such as Agnes Bryan and Cathy Aymer (see above) have tried to extend and deepen the terms of the debate around social work, black people and racism. In their (1996) paper 'Black students experience on social work courses: accentuating the positives', Aymer and Bryan, without for one moment retreating from a determined anti-racist stance, issue a kind of challenge to us all to move beyond simple 'for' or 'against' positions. They believe that in some respects this kind of thinking has been damaging to black professionals trying to establish their self-belief in a difficult environment. They describe their experience as black social work tutors thus:

'Black students in "public" arenas either openly or tacitly condemn the course for being racist, whereas "privately", these same students assure us the course was the best thing

that ever happened to them . . . Why are they unable to tell their stories in public? . . . It is important that black students' positive experiences are made public for several reasons. They serve to challenge mythologies that describe black intelligence as inferior. We need to celebrate our triumphs and successes and make public the skills that are in the black community, so that our communities can be valued for their achievements.' (1996: 3)

These authors are keen that black students and teachers in social work engage with the complex, and sometimes contradictory, realities of their situation, rather than maintain defensive positions or postures. They are clear that their 'agency' as people functioning in adverse circumstances (see the section above on mapping the language of values) is undermined if they cannot embrace their own total situation openly and honestly.

'We know that racism is a destructive force which is kept alive by acts of commission and omission within all institutions . . . As black professionals we are placed in a paradoxical position. On one level we have high aspirations for education, seeing it as a liberating force. On another level, we experience it as a depressing and oppressive force. At times, we contribute to that depressing experience and we need to examine that . . . We wish to affirm that black people are active agents who can make choices. They can take action to ensure that they have control over what happens to them even within the context of a racist institution or a racist society. Black students therefore have some control over what happens to them on social work courses.' (1996: 7)

In a different but related way to the approach of the feminist therapists discussed above, these writers are espousing an integration between values, politics and psychosocial analysis. Their value position is deeply connected to their day-to-day experience, with all its ups and downs, contradictions, imperfections, uncertainty and difficulty. It is not a politics of certainty, even if it is a politics of determination in the struggle against oppression and the part social work can play in that struggle.

Case study

Bridget cont . . .

When Dionne went back to visit Bridget two days later, she had done a lot thinking about her and the children, as well as her uncomfortable experience in the team meeting. She felt convinced that if she could find a way to *relate* better to Bridget, rather than worry only about 'child protection issues' or how to 'empower' Bridget, then she might see some progress. She also felt when all her colleagues poured out their ideas and started arguments with each other that this had something to do with how 'absent' or passive Bridget had been – it was as though everyone tried to fill up the space this left with their own thoughts and agendas, making it even more difficult for Bridget (or Dionne herself) to be listened to.

Dionne decided that she would need to take some risks when she met Bridget again. She tried first of all just to 'name' what she felt Bridget's feelings were, to try to show that she understood this. Bridget did seem just as hopeless in the way she felt as last time, and Dionne spoke about this, then mused a bit further about whether Bridget felt she was getting any support from her own mother. Was her own mother, or father, in the picture at all, she asked? Dionne thought that Bridget might be feeling more openly distressed at the mention of this and she asked her if she wanted to talk further about her mother. It soon emerged that Bridget had a very uncertain connection to her mother, but that underneath she desperately wanted her to come closer and help her with the children. She admitted that she had always imagined her mother 'being there' when she became a mother herself, but everything had gone wrong between them in the last few years. Her mother did not like Dave, the father of Tom and

Ruth, and Bridget suspected she despised her for being with a 'black man'. At the same time Bridget acknowledged something she found very hard – that ever since she had been a teenager she had tended to have black boyfriends partly as a way of provoking her parents, and of getting her own sense of identity as different from theirs.

As Bridget was talking about these feelings, she was crying, and seemed racked by uncertainty about who she was or what she should do. Dionne was struggling to concentrate on Bridget because inside her the interview was bringing up memories and painful feelings about her own conflicts with her mother – feelings she thought had 'gone away' and been dealt with. On the one hand, she now felt excited and hopeful because she had perhaps made a real connection to Bridget, who seemed much more alive even if she was distressed – this felt like a connection based on her capacity as a woman to identify with another woman. On the other hand, she felt a weight of responsibility, because she could feel that it was likely Bridget might come to trust and depend on her quite easily, and although Dionne was more hopeful she didn't know whether or not Bridget would be able to begin caring adequately for her children . . .

Conclusion

In this chapter we have not tried to propose a definite answer to the question of what value positions practitioners should adopt in their day-to-day work. There are many perspectives on inequality which we have not touched upon. However, we have taken some positions *about* the nature of values and politics in social work at a more general level. We have assumed that there are certain facts about the society we live and work in that seem to make it impossible, inescapable, that we engage with these questions. We live in a society still ruptured by social inequalities, and nobody can 'step outside' this situation. You cannot renounce your class, gender, sexual or ethnic identity and this identity is formed and reproduced all the time in relation to that of others – some probably more advantaged and some almost certainly less so than you. This situation is made more complicated by the fact that you are training to become a 'professional' and professionals inevitably hold power in relation to others. So, this requires you to think deeply about the ethics of your engagement with service users – that is the one message which we would preach to you! Because social inequality is *not only* a problem of social justice *but also* of social relationships, social experience and 'life chances' that radically affect how people's lives unfold, we have taken a 'psychosocial' stance on the nature and meaning of values in social work. Language and discourse are important to this way of seeing things, but so are the psychological, social and interpersonal mechanisms involving feelings, conflict, love, hatred, and so on, through which inequality is produced and reproduced everyday. It is in relation to these forces that you, as a practitioner, have to find and negotiate your own sense of political agency in social work.

Key learning points

This chapter has covered the following learning points:

✔ Values in social work have been a subject of heated conflict over the decades, and this has sometimes been divisive. It is important to have real debates about values in the profession, but not to use value positions as weapons in a war.

✔ Changes in the value principles informing social work tend to reflect changes in the wider society, and the decline of 'universalist' frameworks and the rise of 'pluralist' ones is an important instance of this.

✔ Understanding of inequalities in society, and how they are produced and reproduced, is central to being a competent social worker.

✔ The psychosocial mechanisms through which inequalities have been created and maintained cannot be 'split off' from our value positions. Tackling inequalities through social work is a practical matter, as well as a political one.

✔ The 'map' of values and political positions in social work shows that there is no one 'politically correct' stance for a social worker to adopt. There are undoubtedly wrong and inappropriate stances and value positions, but there are also many ways of being 'right'. You have to negotiate your way through the value 'maze' in social work.

Further reading

Adams, R., Dominelli, L. and Payne, M. (2005) (eds) (2nd edition) *Social Work, Themes, Issues and Critical Debates*, London: Macmillan. A comprehensive collection that looks at questions of power, empowerment and taking up a critical stance as a practising social worker across the whole range of service user groups.

Froggett, L. (2002) *Love, Hate and Welfare: Psychosocial Approaches to Policy and Practice*, Bristol: The Policy Press. This wide-ranging account of the political and social development of welfare in Britain, written by a social work teacher and researcher, offers a range of interesting and thought-provoking arguments and analyses that link the 'personal and the political'. Many of the case studies are drawn from direct experience of social work practice.

Hoggett, P. (2000) *Emotional Life and the Politics of Welfare*, Houndmills: Macmillan. This book takes an explicitly 'therapeutic' look at the foundations of social welfare in society and in each of us. It succeeds in moving our thinking beyond a purely 'materialist', structural, or resource-based view of social work and welfare services to consider the emotional and imaginative dimensions that are an essential basis for the 'idea of a welfare state'.

Parton, N. (1996) *Social Theory, Social Change and Social Work*, London: Routledge. This edited collection contains a number of powerful papers that remain key contributions to the understanding of social work in a complex, or 'postmodern', political world. A number of leading social work academics are among the contributors.

Thompson, N. (2006) *Anti-Discriminatory Practice*, Houndmills: Palgrave Macmillan. Recently revised and updated, Thompson's book is a valuable introduction to the key debates, language and arguments relevant to anti-discriminatory social work practice. This book offers a good way of expanding your understanding of the 'map' of values and value positions sketched out in this chapter.

Useful websites

www.scie.org.uk
The 'social care online' website contains a huge range of resources, references and links relevant to contemporary social work practice and its value and legislative base.

www.cabinbet-office.gov.uk/social_exclusion_task_force
The Social Exclusion Task Force.

www.jrf.org.uk
The Joseph Rowntree Foundation – research into social policy and the causes of poverty.

http://www.runnymedetrust.org
The Runnymede Trust – policy and research for justice in a multi-ethnic society.

For additional cases and topic-organised, clickable links into additional media resources, including those produced by IRISS, visit **www.pearsoned.co.uk/wilsonruch**

Activity

Monitoring value positions

With colleagues, monitor the way your team or agency functions in relation to values and politics in social work. Do managers really hold these questions in mind? What are the forces acting on them and everyone else to deprioritise such questions in favour of resource acquisition or organisational survival?

Values – finding your position

Find a colleague and set aside 20 minutes for a discussion based on the statements below. As you talk, note whether you start to agree or disagree, put the alternatives into a priority order, always end up saying 'both are important', and so on . . .

Discuss the conversation you had, and the dynamics of it, with other colleagues who have done the same exercise.

People's problems should be thought about in terms of:

- their psychology – their position in society
- their responsibility for themselves – the difficulties they have suffered
- a sociological analysis – a psychological analysis
- understanding behaviour so they can change – doing something about their behaviour
- their suffering and history – the effect they have on other people (whom they make suffer)
- their individual functioning – their place within a human system that influences their individual functioning
- their 'developmental needs' and the things they have lacked in life – their responsibility to 'get over it' and move on.

Chapter 6
Social work knowledge and practice

Chapter summary

This chapter introduces you to the nature of social work and the knowledge that informs it. The chapter begins by outlining the long-standing and ongoing debate about whether social work is a science or an art, which is explored alongside the diverse sources of knowledge that inform and underpin social work practice. Particular attention is paid to those sources of knowledge, often referred to as informal or personal knowledge, which are pertinent to relationship-based approaches to practice. This chapter relates closely to Chapter 1 on relationship-based and reflective practice.

Learning objectives

This chapter covers topics that will enable you to achieve the following learning objectives:

- To explore the different types of knowledge that inform social work practice
- To consider the art–science debate that underpins how social work is understood and practised
- To enable you to identify knowledge sources informing practice interventions
- To recognise the importance of attributing equal value to all sources and types of knowledge
- To introduce you to a model of knowledge acquisition and application.

National Occupational Standards

This chapter will help you to meet the following National Occupational Standards:

Key Role 5: Manage and be accountable, with supervision and support, for your own social work practice within your organisation

Unit 14   Manage and be accountable for your own work
Unit 15   Contribute to the management of resources and services

Key Role 6: Demonstrate professional competence in social work practice

Unit 18   Research, analyse, evaluate and use current knowledge of best social work practice
Unit 19   Work within agreed standards of social work practice and ensure own professional development
Unit 20   Manage complex ethical issues, dilemmas and conflicts
Unit 21   Contribute to the promotion of best social work practice

Case study

Jim

Jim is a white, British, 55-year-old man who was diagnosed with schizophrenia at the age of 25. He lives with his 78-year-old mother in a small two-bedroom flat on the fourteenth floor of an inner-city tower block. Jim regularly sees his GP and a Community Mental Health Team social worker who monitor and review his medical and social circumstances. Jim hears voices and on numerous occasions has stopped taking his medication and disappeared for weeks at a time.

What do you already know which might be helpful in understanding Jim's situation? What further knowledge would help you respond appropriately?

Reading Jim's case study may leave you feeling concerned that you have very limited, possibly no, understanding of mental health issues. Alternatively you may have studied models of mental health or have personal experience of someone with mental health difficulties and feel able to draw on these theoretically or personally informed understandings. All of these responses are appropriate. As you will discover in this chapter the first response of 'not knowing' about a particular condition or situation is a legitimate form of knowledge and one social workers need to recognise and integrate into their practice in ways which allow the service user to share their knowledge of their experiences and circumstances. In addition the chapter emphasises the equal importance that needs to be attributed to theoretically informed and personally informed knowledge.

Introduction

As the case study introducing this chapter highlights, the different sources of knowledge informing social work practice are numerous and diverse. Historically, within professional contexts a certain type of knowledge, notably what is referred to as 'scientific' knowledge, has been privileged over other forms of knowledge. Social work students are no exception and along with other professional groupings they tend to undervalue what can be called the informal, non-scientific or personal sources of knowing, such as personal experiences and professional wisdom accumulated over years of practice. This chapter introduces a number of fundamental issues related to the nature of social work knowledge and practice. A long-standing and ongoing source of debate in social work education that is connected to the question of what sort of knowledge 'counts' in professional practice focuses on whether social work is an art or a science. Accompanying this debate is a parallel

A closer look

What do I know? A social work educator's story

Throughout my time as a social work educator it has continued to surprise me how difficult social work students find it to articulate why they had chosen the social work profession. By way of encouraging them to think about their motivation to take up social work as a career, I invite them in a tutorial early in the first term of their programme to firstly record what they are *feeling* as they embark on the course and secondly to construct a life map that captures key events in their life and to consider how these may (or may not) have influenced their choice of career and what they understood social work to be about. As the students engage in these two exercises they begin to get in touch with vital sources of knowledge that will become important resources as they travel along the road towards professional qualification and registered practice.

Firstly, they become aware of their affective or emotional selves and how feelings are as important as facts in social work practice. Secondly, the students begin to make sense of their own personal experiences – for example, of having parents who separated acrimoniously, of coping with a close relative with mental health problems, of knowing someone with a learning difficulty or of coping with the death of a grandparent – and begin to recognise how these experiences have been significant in their motivation to train as a social worker and how they might inform and influence their responses to similar situations in social work practice.

When asked to identify the knowledge required for effective and ethical social work practice, however, the responses given generally focus primarily on 'academic' knowledge, such as psychology and sociology. Experiential or practice-based knowledge, of the sort identified above, does not appear to get recognised or enter into their thinking.

unresolved issue concerning the knowledge base underpinning social work practice: is it dominated by other disciplines, e.g. psychology, sociology, social policy, medicine? Is it discrete to social work? Should it be? Are all the different sources of knowledge of equal value? The Closer Look box above illustrates a social work educator's experience of helping students think about which types of knowledge underpin their practice. Throughout this chapter you are invited to consider the different sources of knowledge informing your approach to social work.

The chapter falls broadly into three sections: it starts with an exploration of the nature of knowledge, and in particular the art–science debate, before moving on to explore the two main groupings of knowledge – informal, reflective knowledge and formal, theoretical knowledge – that inform social work practice. Most chapters exploring the knowledge base of social work begin with an exploration of the formal understandings of knowledge and the contribution to social work, for example, of research evidence and orthodox theoretical perspectives from different disciplines. This chapter challenges this orthodoxy and starts by addressing what are often the undervalued or most critiqued sources of social work knowledge – informal, reflective, 'soft' knowledge – before considering the formal, theoretical, 'hard' knowledge. The content of this chapter is closely related to Chapter 1

on relationship-based and reflective practice and to Chapter 12 on social work interventions and you are encouraged to refer to these chapters throughout.

The nature of knowledge and the art–science dichotomy and debate

Before we move on to examine the different types of knowledge informing social work practice in more detail, it is imperative to address the contested issue of the status of social work and nature of knowledge. The position adopted, whether social work is an art or a science, depends on the understandings held about the nature of knowledge and the types of knowledge that are prioritised and privileged.

The art–science dichotomy is defined by how knowledge is understood. In Chapter 1 you were briefly introduced to the nature of knowledge and how scientific perspectives on knowledge are associated with modernism and positivism (see the glossary for definitions of these terms). For those adopting a scientific approach, knowledge is understood to be definitive and capable of representing 'the truth' of the situation, an example of this being the knowledge that the earth goes around the sun. Thompson (1995: 38) identifies the key characteristics of positivism as:

- The belief that universal laws can be discovered by scientific investigation;
- A commitment to 'objective', observable and measurable factors and mistrust, or even total rejection, of subjective factors;
- A view of science as a neutral or value-free enterprise;
- A commitment to empirical research as the most appropriate form of scientific investigation.

From this perspective, knowledge is of a technical–rational nature i.e. there is a certain explanation for why something happens and a particular response that will address it. In relation to the natural sciences this perspective on knowledge can be understood but in the social sciences it is more problematic. In social work contexts this perspective would provide causal relationships between phenomena and explanations for a phenomenon, such as schizophrenia, and offer an intervention that is deemed to tackle it. Another example of scientific knowledge would be attachment theory, which suggests that children display different types of attachment behaviour depending on their early experiences of care. Knowing about attachment theory would enable social workers to assess a child's behaviour and devise an intervention that would endeavour to provide more constructive experiences of attachment. Positivist understandings of knowledge have dominated thinking in modern times. Priority has been placed on scientific testing to 'prove' that something is 'true'. You might like to refer to Chapter 9 on research to read about how positivist perspectives have shaped research agendas in recent years.

The challenge for the social work profession and discipline is to assert the limitations of scientific perspectives on knowledge, given social work's roots in the social sciences and its focus of attention on human beings and behaviours. Social work is more compatible with artistic and post-modern understandings of knowledge that promote the belief that there is not a 'single objective truth' to be discovered but rather an infinitely variable number of responses to human situations. Post-modern perspectives challenge understandings of knowledge that support grand theories and 'meta-narratives' i.e. overarching explanations for phenomena. Instead a post-modernist stance would suggest that truth is a relative and dynamic concept and knowledge is a socially constructed phenomenon. Post-modern, social constructivist understandings of knowledge when compared with Thompson's characteristics of scientific knowledge would be characterised by:

- The belief that everything is unique and that phenomena are socially constructed;
- A commitment to subjectivity as an inevitable, unavoidable and necessary component of understanding; a disbelief in objectivity;
- A view of knowledge generation as a value-laden enterprise;
- A commitment to diverse forms of empirical research, particularly qualitative methods, as the most appropriate ways of gaining understanding.

Social work as an art form requires practitioners to recognise the uniqueness and complexity of each professional encounter and to seek interventions pertinent to the specific circumstances. In this case, knowing about attachment theory, from an artistic perspective, is helpful, but not the exclusive source of knowledge shaping our intervention in practice. Central to an artistic perspective is what has been called practical-moral knowledge (Schön, 1991), knowledge that derives from subjective experiences. Artistic or practical–moral perspectives on schizophrenia, for example, would seek to understand what this diagnosis meant for an individual, such as Jim, and would seek to understand its significance in a specific context. The search for *understanding* is the driving force of 'artistic practice', as opposed to the search for *explanations* that underpins scientific perspectives.

Which perspective, the artistic or the scientific, is championed depends on the knowledge sources that individual practitioners most value. These arguments link closely with the contemporary challenges and dilemmas associated with the concepts of research-informed and evidence-based practice, discussed in more detail in Chapter 9. Social work academics who ally themselves with the evidence-based practice movement would consider themselves closely allied with scientific approaches

Table 6.1 Key characteristics of scientific and artistic knowledge perspectives

Characteristics of artistic knowledge	Characteristics of scientific knowledge
Subjective	Objective
Value-laden	Value-free
Qualitative, narrative evidence-based	Quantitative, experimental evidence-based (randomised-controlled trials)
Seeks understanding	Seeks explanation

to social work practice. For them the effectiveness of social work practice is dependent on being able to implement objective and scientifically rigorous ways of measuring outcomes.

Reflect

Consider the features of scientific and artistic perspectives of social work. Which are you more drawn towards? Do you know why?

In answering the above question you may have found you came down in favour of one or other perspective more strongly, or that you found aspects of both helpful to your understanding of social work. A major shortcoming of dichotomising social work as either an art or a science is that it implies one perspective is more valid and valuable than another. A more helpful and inclusive response to this dichotomy is one which recognises that artistic knowledge sources are different from scientific ones but neither inferior nor superior – simply different (Cooper, 2005). It is also possible to build a model of knowledge that considers different knowledge sources as complementary rather than conflictual. This chapter upholds this position by recognising the contribution of scientific forms of knowledge but equally valuing artistic understandings of knowledge that emphasise the importance of the professional relationship and the narrative as a way of understanding the meaning of experiences for individuals. From a shared understanding of what an experience has meant can come a negotiated assessment and plan of intervention. Some of the debates surrounding this issue are covered in an exchange in the *British Journal of Social Work* (Sheldon, 2001; Webb, 2001).

Tangles in terminology

The nature of knowledge

The sociology of knowledge is a complex phenomenon and confusion can arise when exploring the terminology used to describe the knowledge that informs social work practice. For the purposes of this chapter the different sources of knowledge are divided into 'formal' knowledge – theory, research, legislation, policies and procedures, service user and carer perspectives – and informal knowledge – practice wisdom, personal experiences, intuiton, tacit knowledge. The formal knowledge types are more closely aligned with scientific understandings of knowledge, in that they are derived from contexts external to an individual practitioner and to a greater or lesser extent have the characteristics associated with scientific knowledge: objective, testable, etc. (see Figure 6.1). In contrast the informal types of knowledge are predominantly artistic in orientation as they derive from the personal and professional experiences and understanding of the individual.

While the above classification of knowledge sources into two broad categories is helpful, it is not unproblematic. One danger of referring to knowledge as informal is that it can be deemed to be less significant compared with its formal counterpart. This splitting of knowledge into superior and inferior categories must be resisted on all counts. In most textbooks on knowledge and theory for social work, formal sources of theoretical knowledge would be the first type of knowledge to be focused on. Alongside this focus it is likely there would be reference to the recurrent debate within academic circles about whether social work can claim its own knowledge base

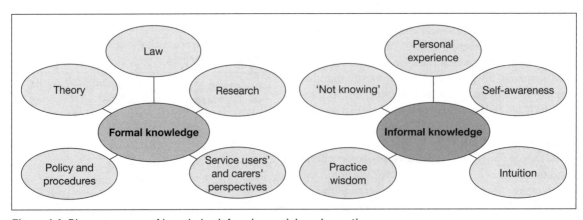

Figure 6.1 Diverse sources of knowledge informing social work practice

(Webb, 2001). The significance of this claim lies in it having been considered a key criteria for professional status (see Chapter 4 for a fuller discussion of this aspect of social work). While not wishing to underplay the importance of the knowledge derived from formal sources, this chapter has challenged the existing orthodoxy relating to different knowledge sources. Given the increasing importance attributed to informal sources of knowledge within social work, it is debatable whether the orthodox requirements for professional status that privilege formal, scientific knowledge remain relevant.

One way of addressing this issue is to emphasise that formal theoretical perspectives are of equal, but not greater, importance for social work practice compared with informal knowledge sources. Interestingly, given the higher profile usually afforded to the formal knowledge sources, Table 6.2 highlights the equal number of informal knowledge sources that exist. Up until recently the number of informal knowledge sources that exist has not been reflected in the amount of attention paid to them in the literature on social work knowledge, a point made in the Social Care Institute for Excellence (SCIE) review of the types of knowledge informing social work practice. Pawson et al. (2003: viii), authors of the review, urged practitioners to adopt an inclusive attitude to knowledge and emphasised that when devising a knowledge classification system 'it is important not to neglect sources of knowledge that are tacit, that currently lack prestige and seem less compelling'.

Another shortcoming of this two-fold knowledge classification is the implication that formal and informal knowledge sources and the subcategories within them are separate **entities**, whereas what exists in practice is a tangled web of knowledge. Firstly, the subcategories of knowledge within the formal and informal knowledge categories interrelate and inform each other. An example

of these interrelationships is the creation of laws, policies and procedures that reflect research findings. The Children Act 1989, for example, was informed by substantial research evidence about poor planning of admission of children into local authority care and concerns about children 'drifting' within the care system once admitted (DHSS, 1985). Within the informal sphere it is not difficult to see how personal experience can be a contributory factor in the development of practice wisdom. Secondly, there are significant interconnections between the formal and informal groupings. The formal types of knowledge that social workers draw on to inform their practice are invariably influenced by their personal experiences, perspectives and preferences, i.e. the informal sources of knowledge influence which formal sources of knowledge are valued. A student social worker, who has had a positive experience of counselling, might be drawn to the psychological explanations for behaviour and to models of social work practice that focus on the individual. Students with community work experience may be more interested in the collectivist perspectives on the social work role and the influence of sociological thinking on social work practice. As Clare (2000) acknowledges, we do not find ourselves drawn to particular theoretical or practice perspectives 'by chance' and 'there is more of oneself in every interaction than meets the eye' (Ash, 1995: 26).

Reflect

Refer back to the case of Jim introduced earlier in the chapter and try to identify the different scientific and artistic perspectives on Jim's circumstances and the formal and informal sources of knowledge that would inform your practice.

Which types of knowledge did you identify first? Consider how you arrived at your conclusions.

Table 6.2 Knowledge classification system

Formal 'scientific' knowledge	Informal 'artistic' knowledge
Orthodox theories	Practice theories
Organisational knowledge	Practice wisdom
Policy and procedure	Personal experience
Research evidence	Self-awareness
Service user and carer perspectives	Intuition/tacit knowledge

Your response to the above question will have highlighted that both informal and formal knowledge inform your practice and are interrelated. Usually, if we allow the time to reflect on our 'formal' theoretical choices and practices, they can be accounted for in relation to previous personal, academic and professional experiences, i.e. our 'informal' perspectives, as illustrated by the examples in the previous paragraph. If this holds true, it is appropriate to use these informal sources of knowledge as the baseline from which other formal knowledge sources are explored and incorporated into our professional practice.

A shortcoming of this apparently neat and straight-forward 'informal to formal' model of knowledge acquisition is that it does not accord with reality. Informal knowledge does not determine formal knowledge choices in a linear one-directional fashion. Nor does it happen straightforwardly in reverse, i.e. formal knowledge influencing informal responses. What this chapter seeks to promote is a spiralling model of knowledge acquisition, with informal and formal knowledge sources informing and being informed by the other in a complex, 'messy but real', cyclical fashion. You are encouraged, however, not to see the informal and formal sources of knowledge as competing or mutually exclusive but as complementary and inclusive of each other. Fook (2002), a social work academic, whose work is informed by post-modern thinking, refers to such knowledge as being contextual and interrelated. The best professional practice will be informed by a wide range of knowledge sources that can be identified and accounted for and will be responsive to individual circumstances. In the final section of this chapter a model of knowledge acquisition and application for social work practice that incorporates these diverse sources of knowledge is outlined.

Theories, theoretically informed practice and theorised practice

Trevithick (2000) in her exploration of the terrain of social work practice refers to a plethora of terms, often used interchangeably, which she suggests mean slightly different things but broadly relate to how social work practice is understood and made sense of. The list includes: theories, methods, models, practice orientations, hypotheses, perspectives and approaches. A student new to the field could, quite understandably, be perplexed by the diversity of terms.

Theory is one of the most widely used terms and it is worth clarifying how it is being used in this chapter. In its orthodox application, theory refers to

'a way of ordering knowledge in a descriptive, explanatory or predictive framework; it enables us to employ knowledge in order to describe some aspect of the world, to explain it and to make predictions about it.'   (Rolfe et al., 2001: 3)

The Closer Look box below identifies the key features of a theory. In this chapter, theory is used to refer to knowledge which broadly fits with the characteristics in the box below. The section on formal knowledge sources

later in this chapter considers the sub-groupings of theory that are relevant for social work.

The application of theory to practice is referred to as theoretically informed practice. In a similar vein to formal knowledge being valued more highly than informal knowledge, there is a risk of theoretically informed knowledge being given greater recognition and status than the practically informed knowledge associated with informal knowledge sources. For example, practice with people with a disability that is informed by the outcomes of a research project may be more readily drawn on to inform organisational procedures than recommendations based on the practice wisdom of an experienced practitioner who has worked for many years with this service user group.

One way of overcoming this imbalance is to recognise the importance of both formal, theoretically informed practice and informal, *theorised* knowledge, which is derived from the theorisation of knowledge emerging from practice. For the practitioner, what is important is their ability to recognise the original roots, informal and formal, of the approaches they are implementing. This inclusive perspective on knowledge endeavours to reduce the commonly recognised theory–practice gap. This gap arises from social workers either being able to articulate a theoretical perspective but unable to illustrate how it is put into practice, or conversely, practising in a particular way but being unable to identify the theoretical underpinnings of their actions.

A closer look

Characteristics of orthodox theory

Trevithick (2005: 15), drawing on the work of Sheldon (1995: 10), lists the key characteristics of orthodox theories as:

- Potential refutability – ability to disprove the theory
- Riskiness of prediction – strength of evidence
- Testability – ability to check it out
- Logical consistency – does it 'make sense'?
- Clarity of expression – can it be understood?
- Applicability – is it relevant?
- Simplicity – is it straightforward?
- Potential – can it address 'important things not yet known' or those circumstances in which there is no convincing explanation available?

In the following section we explore in more detail the different types of informal knowledge before moving on to consider the range of formal knowledge sources.

Informal knowledge sources

Practice wisdom

Practitioners who have worked with people like Jim who suffer from mental health difficulties will have developed over time ways of working that are helpful to individuals at the point of crisis. This accumulation of knowledge and expertise over time is referred to as 'practice wisdom'. Practice wisdom or 'practitioner knowledge' (Pawson et al., 2003) is derived from

'social workers' or probation officers' experience of dealing, over and over again with clients from similar backgrounds, facing similar problems. Practitioner knowledge tends to be personal and context-specific and, therefore, difficult to surface, articulate and aggregate.'

(Pawson et al. 2003: 25–6)

As Pawson et al. (2003) recognise, the difficulty associated with practice wisdom is that often it is not made explicit. It requires practitioners to articulate 'the unspoken'. The cumulative manner in which practice wisdom evolves necessitates practitioners being reflective about their practice to ensure they can articulate why they do what they do, thereby ensuring the quality and effectiveness of their work (Nathan, 2002). Munro (2000) in her work looking at child protection practice argues strongly for practitioners to improve their understanding of the contribution of informal knowledge sources to their practice.

In the case of Jim it might be that the social worker has developed strategies that seem to be helpful to Jim. The social worker's formal knowledge derived from medical models of schizophrenia recognises the importance of ensuring Jim is taking his medication. From her experience of working with Jim, however, she has also learnt that Jim is more receptive to help if he is seen at home with his mother. If the social worker arranges to visit Jim at home later that day, it is more likely she can accurately assess his social and medical state and plan any further interventions.

Case study

Sadie

Sheila, an experienced, white social worker in her mid-fifties, who has worked in the field of childcare social work for ten years, has just taken over working with an eight-year-old dual-heritage girl, Sadie, who is waiting to move to a long-term foster family. Sheila always starts her work with a new child by sharing a home-made booklet called 'All about me . . .'. In the booklet, which has hand-drawn illustrations, Sheila talks about herself and her professional role and describes how she will work with Sadie. There are spaces where Sadie can fill in bits of information about herself too.

Over the years Sheila has discovered that her knowledge of attachment theory and her professional experience have helped her recognise how the issues of separation and loss that arise for children, such as Sadie, when they move, can cause them to display emotionally disturbed behaviour. For Sheila this booklet is an important tool as it enables Sadie to have a clear understanding of who Sheila is and what she will do. The unexpected and unfamiliar is outlined and the booklet can be returned to at different stages of Sheila's involvement with Sadie, offering some continuity when lots of aspects of Sadie's life will be changing.

In the above example, Sheila, the social worker, has developed a way of engaging children based on her practice wisdom. It could be argued that the formal theoretical frameworks of attachment, separation and loss that inform Sheila's practice, what Rolfe et al. (2001) refer to as 'knowing that' i.e. knowing that insecure attachments are associated with specific behaviours, are added to by her practical knowledge of what helps children. Rolfe et al. refer to this practical knowledge as 'knowing how', in this case knowing how to relate to children experiencing disruptions as opposed to scientific theoretical understanding of 'knowing that' i.e. 'knowing that' the theories of attachment, separation and loss are relevant for children who experience disrupted placements.

Personal experience

Identify what you consider to be the three main personal influences on your decision to train as a social worker. How do these influences contribute to your understanding of the role of the social worker?

The Think Ahead box above invites you to consider and recognise the influence of your own biography on your understanding of the professional role of a social worker, which is a crucial aspect of your professional development. As the 'story' told at the outset of this chapter highlights, social work practitioners and students do not recognise, as readily as they might, the potential value of their own experiences of situations they encounter in their professional lives. This state of affairs is of concern for two reasons. Firstly, failing to recognise and draw on personal experiences dismisses a valuable source of knowledge and understanding derived from *within* a person's life. Students who have a sibling with a disability, for example, will have had experience of social workers relating to their family and will have formed views both about what might be most helpful to their sibling, alongside opinions on how well a practitioner related to their sibling and supported their family in general, and to them as someone with a disabled sibling, in particular. These experiences offer invaluable insights into service user views on social work involvement and inevitably, but not always as explicitly as is desirable, shape the way a student will subsequently practise.

The second reason for being concerned about the lack of attention paid to personal experience as a know-ledge source informing practice is the risk associated with the failure to acknowledge the significance of personal experiences on practice. Omitting to consider personal experiences as part of the knowledge base informing practice can impact on the quality of professional relationship that is established and intervention that is agreed on. In the case of the student with a disabled sibling, for example, there is a risk of bad personal experiences of social work intervention fuelling unhelpful attitudes in a student or practitioner – perhaps feeling militant, aggrieved or cynical about poor practice or inadequate resources – that will not necessarily be of benefit to service users. It is vital, therefore, that personal experience is accompanied by well-informed self-awareness, the next type of informal knowledge, explored below.

Drawing on personal experiences to inform professional practice, however, must be managed carefully. As with any of the informal knowledge sources it is crucial that social work students and practitioners utilise the knowledge knowingly and thoughtfully.

The issue of self-disclosure – when is it appropriate to share with service users personal experiences of similar experiences to theirs and when is it better to remain silent – is an ethical dilemma for all practitioners. And as with all such dilemmas, there is no prescriptive answer. A guiding principle in such situations is always to ask whose interest self-disclosure is serving: is it helpful to the practitioner or to the service user (Trevithick, 2005)? Practitioners need to be able to clearly justify why they shared personal experiences with a service user to ensure they do not abuse their professional position and use contact with service users to address their own unresolved personal issues.

(Copyright Harry Venning 2000)

Self-awareness

Self-awareness relates to and comprises all the other sources of informal knowledge but specifically refers to one's own understanding of what 'makes you tick', and influences how you act and respond in particular situations. While the cartoon above makes light of the notion of 'emotional baggage', in social work knowing what you are bringing into the profession is crucial to your identity as a social worker and to the quality of your social work practice.

On a scale of 1 to 10 (1 = little self-awareness, 10 = very self-aware) where would you locate yourself?

What has contributed to your developing the level of self-awareness that you selected?

What strategies do you have in place to help you develop and sustain your self-awareness?

What support systems would you find helpful?

Think ahead

'New recruits to social work often struggle with questions about how they should relate with service users – for example, "Am I supposed to be their friend?", "How much should I reveal about myself?" and "Should I get involved with them?" These are all very significant questions which are not to be dealt with lightly . . . It is questions such as these that open the way into thinking about the use of self in practice, because they draw our attention to the inevitability that social work practice will always make demands on the self of the worker, and will therefore require the worker to think about how to handle their *use* of self. Novices soon discover that too much self-disclosure may weaken their perceived authority, although too little "give" on their part may mean that they are perceived as remote and uninterested, and therefore less likely to establish a working rapport. However, it is much more complicated than this: beyond the questions of conscious decisions about levels of involvement or self-disclosure, there are much more elusive questions about, for example, how to handle "resonance" or similarities between a service user's situation and some issue in our own past or present concerns, how to remain focused on difficult judgements despite emotional pulls one way or the other, and how to cope with the unconscious communications which may leave us feeling confused or angry after a difficult exchange. The key terms here are "how to handle" or "how to cope", because they suggest that the social worker has to be continually aware of the ways in which these sorts of personal or emotional undercurrents are operating and may be influencing him, and actively working out how to respond. In other words, in the midst of the encounter he needs to be monitoring his own emotional and cognitive reactions to what is happening and working out how to modify his input accordingly.'

(Ward, 2010: 46ff)

Your answers to the questions in the Think Ahead box opposite will help you begin to think about your level of self-awareness, but what is considered 'sufficient' is open to question. There has been a long-standing debate about whether social work students should engage in personal therapy (Winnicott, 1964b cited in Kanter, 2004; Bower, 2005) as a means of ensuring heightened levels of self-awareness. In an ideal world with sufficient resources to support social work students to engage in therapy, there is considerable merit in this argument. No doubt this debate will run and run but what is beyond dispute is the importance of students and practitioners not only having a well-developed level of self-awareness but, as importantly, having the willingness to continue to develop and sustain this awareness throughout their professional career. Self-awareness is not a static discrete commodity that is acquired and needs no further work. For all of us, as we grow and mature, the issues that affect us change and we can never rest in the knowledge that we are immune to all practice realities. The extract below captures the importance of practitioners being self-aware and the challenges of managing the boundary between our personal and professional identities:

'What is personal and what is professional? What is the difference between "personal" and "professional"? What do we mean when we say "personally speaking . . ." and "professionally speaking . . . ?." Trying to answer these questions leads us into murky waters; the more one sees clarity of definition, the more confused become the boundaries. Yet, in common parlance, reference to "professional" implies elements of specific knowledge, expertise, experience, training and a certain reliable objectivity in action. Professions vary in their prescriptiveness to practitioners. Codes of practice and ethics commonly exhort professionals to ideals of attitude and behaviour towards clients and colleagues, implying that "personal" and "professional" matters are usually quite separate. Being professional seems to mean monitoring and restraining expression of feeling, and, in particular, suppressing the subjective experiences, which may be part of the current moment or be triggered by it. This can result, from the client's viewpoint, in behaviour which emphasises the head rather than the heart. Being "personal", on the other hand, suggests the possibility of expressing (perhaps spontaneously) a whole range of feelings, which the present or any previous situation arouses, and emphasising heart rather than head.'

(*Source*: Ash, 1992: 262. Taylor and Francis Ltd, www.informaworld.com)

Reflect

Referring to the quote above from Ash's article how do you distinguish between your 'personal' and 'professional' identities? Should you?

Intuition or tacit knowledge

Intuition, according to the *Oxford English Dictionary* (2002), means 'immediate apprehension by the mind without reasoning'. To be intuitive means to be unconsciously aware of something. Hugh England (1986: 43), in what many regard as a defining social work text, *Social Work as Art*, has a chapter entitled 'The persistent mystery of the intuitive use of self' in which he states:

'The intuitive use of self in social work seems neither to go away nor to become clear; like those grand social work objectives – with which it is inevitably and inextricably linked – it haunts the institutions of social work as an embarrassment or puzzle rather than the necessary source of creative energy. It is an inevitable presence, but social workers do not know how to deal with it. Its development is too often half-hearted or reluctant, yet for some unseen reason it seems difficult to abandon.'

Although written two decades ago the ambivalence England refers to remains. The idea of 'gut feelings', a colloquial term for intuitive or tacit responses, being a source of knowledge for practice generates sceptical responses in some quarters and these responses are a direct reflection of the disproportionate amount of attention paid to rational cognitive responses, at the expense of the irrational, affective ones. McMahon and Ward (1998), writing in an insightful and thought-provoking book entitled *Intuition is not Enough*, provide a balanced account of the significance of intuition, recognising its potential and its shortcomings. They quote Dockar-Drysdale, an eminent child psychotherapist, who states:

'Intuition informed is an essential tool; intuition uninformed can be a dangerous weapon.'

(Dockar-Drysdale, 1968, cited in McMahon and Ward, 1998)

While most of the writing on intuition in the social work literature refers to it as a 'non-conscious reasoning process' and one that involves 'an apparent bypassing of the linear reasoning process' (Nash, 2000), they do not suggest how we can gain greater understanding of the intuitive to ensure that it is informed. Within the literature an important distinction is drawn between reflective practice and intuition (Trevithick, 2005; Watson and Burrows, 2002). Whereas reflective capabilities and reflective practice can be taught, intuition is considered to be an innate 'gift' with some individuals being more intuitive than others. This view can appear to suggest that a person is more or is less intuitive and there is nothing further to be said. This gives cause for concern as other writers (Munro, 2000, 1996; Trevithick, 2005) support Dockar-Drysdale and McMahon and Ward's position and emphasise the need for practitioners to be able to gain understanding of their intuitive responses. In contrast to most of the literature addressing intuition, McMahon and Ward (1998) offer ideas that help us understand what influences the original development of intuition and its subsequent existence. In so doing they provide a potentially safe and effective model of intuitive practice that challenges the views of those sceptical about the appropriateness of intuitive responses or the benefits of intuition. According to McMahon and Ward, intuition is informed by conscious and unconscious early childhood responses that determine the capacity of an individual to be sensitive to the emotional state and needs of another. These early experiences have a bearing on the 'natural' intuitive capacities of an individual. In order to ensure that practitioners, in the context of their intuitive responses, are able to differentiate between their own personal responses and those aroused by the service user, understanding of unconscious processes and features of psychodynamic theoretical frameworks, such as transference and counter-transference dynamics, can be very helpful (see the glossary and Chapter 12 for a fuller discussion of these terms and perspectives). Intuitive responses should never be allowed to inform practice in isolation but are in turn informed by theoretical frameworks. This state of affairs is wholly consistent with the integrated model of knowledge acquisition and application outlined later in this chapter.

Reflect

One worker wrote:

'Intuition is individual and precarious and is not enough for me. I need to be self-aware, informed and closely supported within a suitable environment if I am to make good use of the intuition I have.'

(McMahon and Ward, 1998: 39)

How do you respond to this statement?

Can you think of examples of how the development of intuition can be facilitated? What would be the characteristics of a 'suitable environment'?

One way of encouraging a 'suitable environment', referred to above in the Think Ahead box, that supports the development of intuitive capabilities, is by enabling practitioners to acquire the skill of meta-reflection: the ability to think about the 'thinking about doing' (Rolfe et al., 2001). Developing these reflective skills ensures that the potential usefulness of intuitive responses is responsibly maximised.

'Not knowing'

A feature of the informal knowledge base of social work which receives scant attention is the extent to which social workers do not know about specific issues. The myriad of circumstances which any individual or family can present to social workers means that it is impossible to have comprehensive knowledge of every situation that will be encountered. The idea of admitting to 'not knowing' presents student social workers with a curious paradox. Student social workers and practitioners encounter complex situations of service users where they might have little or no knowledge of a particular social circumstance such as domestic violence, mental health problem such as schizophrenia or disability such as cerebral palsy. Acknowledging you 'don't know', which, put bluntly, is the reality for most students and often for many practitioners a lot of the time, is anathema to social work students in learning situations. Appearing knowledgeable and competent are important qualities for qualifying practitioners. Equally, however, they can become 'defences' to honest practice and it is well recognised that service users prefer honest and authentic responses from the social workers they are involved with. Paradoxically, therefore, the most authentic, honest and, it could be argued, professional response would be to acknowledge what you do not know. This transparent response is respectful and enables the practitioner to draw on the service user's expertise on their circumstances. In addition, it ensures practitioners demonstrate their willingness to 'fill the gaps' in their knowledge and to identify sources of information, as well as emphasising their ability to collate the relevant factual knowledge that will inform their intervention.

A closer look

Not knowing . . .

'The knowledge base that is potentially relevant (in social work) is endless . . . the key to coping with this lies not in knowing it all, but in knowing enough to know whom to ask and where to look.'

(Hillman and Mackenzie, 1993: 42 cited in Shardlow and Nelson, 2005: 17)

Another 'take' on the concept of 'not knowing' is derived from systemic models of practice (Dallos and Draper, 2000). In this context maintaining an attitude of 'not knowing' enables practitioners to retain an open-mind attitude about what is happening in a particular situation. It avoids reaching premature conclusions in a false search for certainty. Such behaviour can be attributed, in part, to the drive of scientific ways of knowing which are unable to tolerate positions of uncertainty and 'not knowing'. Within the field of child observation (see Chapter 16 on working with children and families for an account of the child observation model) the 'not knowing' way of practising is actively encouraged. As the Closer Look box illustrates, practitioners who have been involved with child observation identify how the experience of learning to suspend 'knowing' and tolerating uncertainty facilitated enhanced self-awareness.

The findings of the Laming Inquiry into the tragic death of Victoria Climbié similarly endorse the importance of practitioners developing their reflective capabilities and a 'healthy scepticism' about 'right' responses (DoH, 2003; Reder and Duncan, 2004b). Laming refers to the need for practitioners to retain a 'respectful uncertainty' in their practice:

'This urges practitioners at all times to maintain a sceptical outlook and to be prepared to routinely challenge information they are given – both by parents/carers and by other professionals'.

(Ferguson, 2005: 793)

A closer look

Not knowing and understanding

'The process of giving emotional attention to what is observed and the deliberate delaying of "knowing" facilitates in practice the kind of measured assessment that is blocked if stereotypes and prejudices are unthinkingly adopted . . . The qualitatively different level of involvement that observation demands creates "learning from experience" and its concomitant emotional experience and change. This contrasts with "learning about" in which there is merely an addition to the stock of knowledge without emotional engagement and therefore without change.'

(Briggs, 1992: 60)

Having explored the different types of informal knowledge that can inform practice, the next section considers the other main knowledge grouping – formal knowledge.

Formal knowledge sources

As you are aware from the discussion earlier in this chapter, what is meant by theory is complex. In social work contexts, orthodox theories are primarily derived from other disciplines and are widely referred to as 'grand theories'. Grand theories originate from outside of the social work discipline and are superimposed on to it. Trevithick (2005) refers to 'borrowed knowledge', which includes psychology, sociology, law, medicine, social policy, political science, philosophy, organisational theory and economics. Examples of grand theories include Marxism, derived from the disciplines of sociology and politics, and social learning theory and psychoanalysis, derived from psychology. In the context of social work practice,

Table 6.3 Grand theories, social work theories and practice methods

Grand theory	Social work theory	Practice method
Psychoanalytic theory	Psychodynamic theory Ego-psychology Object relations theory Attachment theory Crisis intervention theory	Psychosocial casework Relationship-based practice Therapeutic communities Direct work with children Crisis intervention
Behaviourism	Social learning theory Task-centred theory Cognitive behavioural theory	Behavioural social work Behaviour modification Task-centred casework Cognitive behavioural therapy
Systems theory	General systems theory Ecological theory	Systemic work Family therapy Solution-focused therapy Brief-focused therapy
Marxism Feminism	Social constructionist theory Collectivism Empowerment Anti-oppressive theory Critical theory	Radical social work Community development Radical casework Welfare rights Advocacy User involvement Anti-oppressive practice
Humanism	Rogerian theory Maslow's Hierarchy	Client-centred counselling Person-centred therapy Transactional analysis

however, it is the practice-related theories derived from these grand theories that are of more relevance for social work practice.

Practice theories

Practice theories are referred to as 'middle range theories' and are the result of the influences of 'grand theoretical perspectives' combined with practice experience. They provide an excellent example of how the formal and informal knowledge sources are interrelated and overlap. Practice theories can also embrace what are referred to as social work methods, e.g. task-centred practice and crisis intervention with their roots in social learning theory, family therapy or systemic work associated with systems theory and direct work with children, informed by psychoanalytic principles. Table 6.3 illustrates the relationships between grand theories, social work theories and practice methods. And in Chapter 12 on social work interventions, several of the most commonly used theoretical frameworks for social work are explored in detail.

One way of conceptualising the different formal theories is offered in Table 6.4 adapted from Howe (1987: 47) who subdivides social work theory into four broad categories and identifies which theoretical perspectives belong to which category.

While Howe's grid provides a helpful framework for thinking about the theories that inform social work practice, two notes of caution need to be heeded. Firstly, the theoretical frameworks that are considered to be more sympathetic to relationship-based ways of practising – e.g. psychodynamic approaches, systemic work – occupy positions in Howe's grid that favour more regulatory understandings of the social work role. The use of the word 'regulatory', however, is in danger of having dero-

gatory connotations and implies that social work controls how people live and behave. A more accurate and acceptable description of the impact of these approaches might be emancipatory – approaches that enhance the life opportunities for individuals. The defining characteristic of the theoretical frameworks in the two lower quadrants of the grid is their focus on individual/families as opposed to collective community contexts of practice.

Secondly, it is crucial to emphasise, in relation to Howe's model, the dynamic nature of theory and knowledge. It does not remain static but develops and evolves. Advocates of systemic ways of working and models of family therapy, for example, would be the first to recognise how the contemporary systemic perspectives are engaging with socially constructed understandings of knowledge and no longer favour the expert professional connotations of objective knowledge and 'fixer' professional identities. This shift in thinking would place family therapy, for example, more firmly in the subjective quadrant of the grid.

Reflect

Take a close look at the four theoretical perspectives in Howe's grid on p. 120.

Where would you position yourself and why?

Do you feel 'comfortable' in this position or would you like to be moving towards a different position? What would you need to help you make this move?

After reading the Closer Look box above it is worth thinking about how your own perspective on this debate influences the knowledge you draw on to inform your practice.

A closer look

Finding a theoretical perspective

'The pragmatist will seek knowledge sources that fit their internal concept of what social work should be about. If you believe that the problems of clients are caused by an unjust economic system that distributes wealth unfairly then a radical perspective combined with a client-centred approach might appeal to you. On the other hand if you felt that a client's problems stem from an emotionally deprived childhood you may be drawn to offering an individual psychodynamic

intervention. With experience you will begin to see the limited value of these dichotomies and understand the complexities of people's lives cannot be simply ascribed to a particular experience. More likely they are a combination of socio-economic factors, ntra-familial experiences and a unique pre-disposition to dealing with stress. The important point is that you are aware that you are more or less acting consciously within an intellectual framework that you can defend to justify your activity.'

(Walker and Beckett, 2003: 24)

Table 6.4 Characteristics of theoretical perspectives

RADICAL CHANGE		
	Radical humanists	**Radical structuralists**
	Image: 'Raisers of consciousness'	*Image:* Revolutionaries
	Theory: Humanism and politics	*Theory:* Structural analysis; Marxism
	Practice: Radical practice, feminist social work	*Practice:* Marxist social work
	Perspective: Political causes of personal problems; personal problems in political context	*Perspective:* Problem people and people with problems under capitalism
S U B J E C T I V E	*Aim:* To become aware and to take control	*Aim:* Redistribution of wealth and power
	Method: Consciousness raising and taking control	*Method:* Socialist welfare work
	Interpretivists	**Functionalists**
	Image: 'Seekers after meaning'	*Image:* 'Fixers'
	Theory: Interpretivism, social constructionism, humanism	*Theory:* Psychoanalytic theory, behaviourism, systems theory
	Practice: Client-centred approaches, counselling	*Practice:* Psychodynamic approaches, CBT, family therapy
	Perspective: A problem for you or for me?	*Perspective:* People with problems, people as problems
	Aim: To understand experiences and create new meanings	*Aim:* Mend and maintain
	Method: Via communication of understanding	*Method:* Treatment, support and maintenance
REGULATION		

(*Source*: Adapted from Howe, 1987: 47)

(Right side column: **O B J E C T I V E**)

A closer look

Knowledge types

'*Organisational knowledge* – all modern organisations engage in governance and regulation, and these activities provide the broad framework that shapes social care. Such materials furnish an overview of the operation of social services in the wider contexts of government agencies, local and regional authorities, and local communities.

Policy community knowledge – this category sets social care in its wider policy context. Despite its diversity social care can be thought of as one set of provisions among dozens of others made available by the public and voluntary sectors. Vital knowledge about the organisations and implementation of services thus exists in the broader policy community of ministries, civil service, think tanks and agencies.

Research knowledge – among the most palpable sources of social care knowledge is that derived from empirical inquiries based on pre-determined research strategies. These provide the reports, evaluations, assessments, measures and so forth which are the most orthodox item in any evidence base. The social care database needs to respond, however, to the particularly broad church of perspectives and paradigms that make up its research base.'

(from Pawson et al., 2003: 25–6)

'Other' knowledge sources

In addition to theories which are a substantial component in the formal knowledges informing social work, there are a number of other categories of knowledge that play an important role in informing social work interventions. Pawson et al. (see Closer Look box above) categorise them as organisational knowledge, policy community knowledge and research knowledge. What these types of knowledge have in common, which enables them to conform to the characteristics of the formal knowledges classification, is that they are externally created and do not arise from personal practice-related experiences. Although, as we have already acknowledged, there can be overlaps with informal knowledge, for example when practice wisdom informs procedures or research into practitioner experiences informs policy/procedure creation.

With the prevailing trends towards increasingly bureaucratised practice contexts, social workers out of necessity need to be aware of the political and organisational context of practice and current trends in policy and procedures. Against this pervasive socio-political backdrop it is vital that practitioners maintain a critical stance on policy and procedural developments, and feel able to challenge new initiatives if they appear to serve the interests of the organisation more than those of the people it exists to serve.

The other category identified by Pawson et al. is research knowledge which is recognised to be a core characteristic of the competent practitioner. This area of knowledge is explored further in Chapter 9 on research in and for social work.

Another separate and substantial 'formal' knowledge source is service user and carer perspectives.

Think ahead

'User and Carer knowledge – users of social care services are not passive recipients of "treatment" but active participants in their own "care". They possess vital knowledge gained from first-hand usage of, and reflection on interventions. This knowledge, once again, also tends to be unspoken and undervalued.'

(Pawson et al., 2003: 26)

Referring back to the case study of Jim how would you go about obtaining Jim's views?

How would you use this information to inform your practice?

What are the challenges inherent in completing this task?

To ascertain Jim's views you might simply have a conversation with him about his experience of your involvement and how it could improve. If Jim's experiences are negative, however, he may feel unable to express them for fear of offending you or having a service withdrawn. To overcome this problem many organisations have standardised systems for obtaining service user and carer perspectives, such as questionnaires or feedback sheets. Answers can then be given anonymously. Chapter 14 explores these issues in more detail and examines how the various models of service user and carer involvement that have evolved differentiate between different levels of participation and involvement (Braye, 2000).

One service user perspective, noted by Howe (1987: 2) in his work on social work theories (see Table 6.4 on p. 000), was the importance service users placed on practitioners knowing why they did what they did and being able to articulate the knowledge that underpinned their practice.

The increasing importance attached to the feedback provided by service users and carers means this source of knowledge should not be overlooked when devising intervention plans. Within the new qualifying awards, programme providers and students are required to engage with service users in a range of ways. Qualifying degree programme providers are required to involve service users and carers in the design and delivery of the course and in assessing students' competence (DoH, 2002). Service users and carers, for example, deliver lectures that provide the opportunity for them to share with students their experiences as recipients of social work interventions. They also take on assessing responsibilities and participate in 'fitness for practice' assessment panels. The principle of thinking inclusively about service user and carer perspectives is becoming firmly established from the outset of the professional development process, and maintaining an inclusive approach to knowledge that embraces service user and carer perspectives is essential for ethical practice.

While service user and carer perspectives is the last knowledge source to be discussed in this chapter, this in no way suggests it is the least important. In the same way as formal knowledge sources should not be privileged over informal knowledge sources, different types of formal knowledge should not be privileged over each other.

Having outlined the range of knowledge available for you as a social worker to draw on, we now propose a model for knowledge acquisition and application.

Developing a model of knowledge acquisition and application for relationship-based social work practice

Having surveyed, albeit briefly, the diverse and wide-ranging sources of knowledge informing social work

practice, it is possible, in this final section of the chapter, to develop a model of knowledge acquisition and application. The model, outlined below, encourages practitioners to adopt a flexible and holistic approach that considers all sources of knowledge as potentially helpful in making sense of and facilitating their professional practice. Fisher and Somerton (2000) emphasise the importance of adopting such a position as it ensures that practitioners not only practise in theoretically informed ways (i.e. formal, orthodox theories are applied to practice) but also learn to theorise their practice (i.e. practice informs the creation of practice theories). What we hope you are becoming increasingly aware of is the overlap between the need to develop an holistic and inclusive approach to knowledge acquisition and the requirements of reflective and relationship-based practice. If you are beginning to identify and weigh up different sources of knowledge for different practice situations, you are developing the qualities associated with reflective and relationally orientated practitioners.

Table 6.5 illustrates one way of conceptualising the different knowledge sources practitioners can draw on (Rolfe et al., 2001). You will notice that in this conceptualisation of knowledge both formal (scientific) and informal (experiential) knowledge is referred to as theoretical or theorised.

As Rolfe et al. (2001) acknowledge, the experiential sources of knowledge can be more difficult to identify and articulate as they are embedded in who we are and how we practise. Munro (2000) and Nathan (2002) caution practitioners in this regard and urge social workers to pay attention to these experiential, informal knowledge sources that can be unconscious or tacit in nature. Making them explicit and transparent is a professional responsibility. In essence what is required is for practitioners to integrate their theoretical understandings with their practice experience.

Table 6.5 Diverse sources of knowledge

	Scientific knowledge	Experiential knowledge
Theoretical 'knowing that'	Scientific theoretical knowledge	Experiential theorised knowledge
Practical 'knowing how'	Scientific practical knowledge	Experiential practical knowledge

(*Source*: Adapted from Rolfe et al., 2001: 11, Fig. 1.3)

Case study

Karen

A newly qualified, white, male social worker, Patrick, is involved in working with a white, single mother, Karen, who has a 3-year-old white son, Jake. The social worker has become involved because the mother has had difficulties caring for her son who has had three short placements with a foster carer to give Karen a break.

Scientific theoretical knowledge – attachment theory and understanding of how different types of attachment affect the mother–child relationship.

Scientific practical knowledge – Patrick tries to identify the type of attachment being exhibited by Jake and work with Karen to help her understand what Jake needs to feel secure.

Experiential practical knowledge – drawing on personal experience as a man and father with three sons and his previous experience of working with mothers and sons, Patrick encourages Karen to engage in physical play activities with Jake to encourage more positive attachment behaviours.

Experiential theoretical knowledge – Patrick's ability to articulate what he did based on his practice wisdom and personal experiences that can subsequently inform scientific theorising and become a practice theory.

Reflect

Following Rolfe's model of knowledge types, think about how the four different types of knowledge might be understood in relation to the case study of Jim's circumstances and experiences.

One way of standardising the quality of knowledge informing practice and as a way of assisting practitioners in making explicit the knowledge they do have and use, is to apply the list of criteria that Pawson et al. (2003, cited in Parker, 2004) devised as part of their review of the type and quality of knowledge informing social work practice. They invite practitioners to scrutinise their practice by asking the TAPUPA question, i.e. applying the criteria below to the knowledge under review:

- *Transparency* – is it scrutinisable? Do you know what is informing your practice?
- *Accuracy* – is it grounded in an identifiable 'theoretical' framework?
- *Purposive* – is it suited to the specific situation?
- *Utility* – is it fit to be used?
- *Propriety* – is it legal and ethical?
- *Accessibility* – can it be easily understood?

While the benchmarks against which formal theory is assessed are well recognised (see the earlier section on the nature of knowledge and Chapter 9 on research), the informal more personal knowledge sources tend to be less explicit. By implication, subjecting different knowledge sources to this test ensures that practitioners are not acting exploitatively or oppressively, for example by relying overly heavily on personal preferences or applying less commonly used theoretical perspectives. The TAPUPA approach, however, has one obvious shortcoming related to its use of the term 'theoretical' to describe the accuracy of the knowledge used. Referring back to the discussion on terminology earlier in this chapter, it is important that you remember that, if an inclusive approach to knowledge is adopted, then theoretical knowledge refers not only to formal theories but also to the theorising – thinking theoretically – about informal knowledge sources. We would suggest that under the criteria of accuracy it should refer to 'theorised' as well as 'theoretical' frameworks to ensure it encompasses informal knowledge sources.

The model of knowledge acquisition and application proposed requires you to adopt an inclusive approach to relevant knowledge, to be able to scrutinise their relevance and to nurture a relationship between these knowledge sources which allows for a developmental spiral of knowledge applied to practice to emerge. In essence it requires you to be a reflective practitioner.

Conclusion

This chapter has introduced you to some challenging ideas about the nature of knowledge which are closely related to Chapter 1 on reflective and relationship-based practice. Social workers need to be able to identify and access a wide range of knowledge if, in the context of partnership working, they are to promote the best interests of the service users with whom they work. To ensure this can be achieved, practitioners need to be aware of the breadth of knowledge they can draw on, know which sources of knowledge they tend to readily access and why, and which they are less familiar with or find harder to access. This is the starting point for a developmental process that will enable practitioners to identify what forms of professional support they might need to realise their potential as informed and reflective practitioners.

Key learning points

This chapter has covered the following learning points:

✔ Knowledge for social work practice is a contested and contentious issue that requires practitioners to embrace formal and informal knowledge sources.

✔ The art–science dichotomy needs to be reconstructed to recognise the contribution of artistic and scientific knowledge to social work practice.

✔ Social work practice is underpinned by a diverse range of knowledge – self-awareness, personal experience, intuition, practice wisdom, service user perspectives, formal theory, research and organisational issues.

✔ Each source and type of knowledge should be afforded equal weight and its contribution to understanding the uniqueness of an individual's situation should be recognised.

✔ Ethical, effective and reflective practice requires social work interventions to be informed by a model of knowledge acquisition and application that embraces both informal and formal knowledge sources.

Further reading

Munro, E. (2000) 'Defending professional social work practice', in Harris, J., Froggett, L. and Paylor, I. (eds) *Reclaiming Social Work: The Southport Papers Volume One*, Birmingham, Venture Press. A short but thought-provoking chapter which encourages social workers to identify and to articulate the different types of knowledge that inform their practice.

Payne, M. (2005) *ModernSocial Work Theory*, 3rd edn, Basingstoke: Palgrave Macmillan. A thorough consideration of the principles of theoretical frameworks and coverage of a number of key perspectives.

Ward, A. and McMahon, L. (eds) (1998) *Intuition is not Enough: Matching Learning with Practice in Therapeutic Child Care*, London: Routledge. A fascinating book exploring alternative ways of understanding and the place of intuition alongside other knowledge sources.

Watson, F. and Burrows, H. (2002) *Integrating Theory and Practice in Social Work Education*, London: Jessica Kingsley. A useful and accessible book that provides practical approaches to the thorny issue of integrating theory and practice.

Useful websites

www.scie.org.uk
The Social Care Institute for Excellence website includes invaluable up-to-date research on all aspects of social work and social care.

www.swap.ac.uk
The Social Work and Policy website promotes learning and practice in social work and social policy, and provides an excellent gateway to resources.

www.elsc.org.uk
The Electronic Library of Social Care website enables you to access a wide range of social work literature.

www.scie-socialcareonline.org.uk
A website under the auspices of the Social Care Institute for Excellence full of up-to-date research, government guidance and training and learning resources.

For additional cases and topic-organised, clickable links into additional media resources, including those produced by IRISS, visit **www.pearsoned.co.uk/wilsonruch**

Refer back to Figure 6.1, the diagram of different sources of knowledge. Find an article on a social work related issue in a newspaper, such as *Society Guardian* on Wednesdays which is always full of relevant articles, or a professional journal such as *Community Care*, and try to work out which of the different types of knowledge identified in Figure 6.1 apply to your understanding of the subject matter in the article. Think about which type of knowledge you identified first and why that might be. For example, if you were reading about the social circumstances of asylum seekers and economic migrants you might have read/heard about well publicised research by the Joseph Rowntree Foundation about this group of people which informs your engagement with the topic. Alternatively you might have closer to hand personal experience of someone who is an asylum seeker.

Chapter 7
Human development through the lifespan

Chapter summary

This chapter of our textbook is about how we as human beings grow and develop throughout our lives – from babyhood and infancy, through childhood and adolescence, to young and middle adulthood into older age. Although we cannot in one chapter hope to offer a comprehensive coverage of the topic – it would take many books to do so – we shall introduce you to some of the key themes and perspectives which will help you to understand how people develop physically, emotionally, psychologically and intellectually, and enable you to begin to think through the implication of these ideas for your practice as social workers. The way in which the chapter is organised corresponds more or less to the stages in human life. It begins, as we shall see, with a birth and we conclude the chapter with a poem about old age. In Section I, we consider some general ideas and dilemmas about development (for example the 'nature nurture' debates) and the range of theoretical perspectives you need to know about. Section II explores infancy and childhood, adolescence, adulthood and older age. In addressing each stage, as well as considering what we know about its major challenges and changes, we shall usually focus on a specific theory (or theories), particularly if it contributes importantly to our understanding of the developmental stage (such as attachment theory in relation to infancy). One further point to make is that, as you may yourselves notice, the sections on adulthood and older age are a good deal shorter than those on childhood and adolescence. We discuss the possible reasons for this later, suggesting that it may in part reflect the fact that in adulthood we follow more divergent paths rather than the kinds of 'normal' trajectories followed at earlier life stages and which are therefore easier to document. Another reason is that developmental changes are extensive and rapid in earlier years, and psychological theorising and writings have therefore tended to reflect this.

Learning objectives

This chapter covers topics that will enable you to achieve the following learning objectives:

- To give a brief overview of patterns of development through the lifespan, with particular emphasis on childhood development

- To provide a grounding in some of the basic concepts and theories which form the framework for understanding these patterns

- To understand some key psychological ideas relating to the life stages of early years, adolescence, adulthood and older age

- To consider the application of these to situations encountered in social work practice

- To develop a critical awareness of theories of human development and how such theories may be applied in social work practice.

National Occupational Standards

This chapter will help you to meet the following National Occupational Standards:

Key Role 1: Prepare for, and work with individuals, families, carers, groups and communities to assess their needs and circumstances

Unit 1   Prepare for social work contact and involvement
Unit 2   Work with individuals, families, carers, groups and communities to help them make informed decisions
Unit 3   Assess needs and options to recommend a course of action for individuals, families, carers, groups and communities

Key Role 2: Plan, carry out, review and evaluate social work practice, with individuals, families, carers, groups and communities and other professionals

Unit 5   Interact with individuals, families, carers, groups and communities to achieve change and to improve life opportunities
Unit 6   Prepare, produce, implement and evaluate plans with individuals, families, carers, groups, communities and professional colleagues
Unit 9   Address behaviour which presents a risk to individuals, families, carers, groups and communities

Key Role 5: Manage and be accountable, with supervision and support, for your own social work practice within the organisation

Unit 14   Manage and be accountable for your own work

Key Role 6: Demonstrate professional competence in social work practice

Unit 18   Research, analyse, evaluate, and use current knowledge of best social work practice

Because we think you are more likely to approach this chapter by reading sections of it at a time rather than taking it all at one go, we have provided summaries of learning at the end of each life stage to help you.

Before beginning our discussion, we want you to read and reflect on, rather than our usual case study, the following poem by the poet James Berry, about when he was born. He comments that his grandmother, his mother's mother, was at his birth: 'she gave me my name, after her husband who had recently died in a sudden accident.'

Of course there are all sorts of ways in which you may respond to the poem. But some of the questions which it might raise in your mind – and which we shall explore in the pages to follow – are to think about this new baby, what we know about him and can deduce about the culture he was born into. Was his future personality already determined at his birth, or will it be affected by, say, the special significance he has in his grandmother's eyes? In some cultures, sons are preferred to daughters, but in other circumstances, a third son instead of, say, a longed-for daughter might give

Case study

My arrival

Showing the creature I landed,
I slipped from my mother's womb
Flesh connected, laced in a blood spatter.

My father waited with a bottle of rum
The moon floated somewhere
The sea drummed and drummed our coastline
Mullets darted in wooded streams.

A good night end to our labour – Saturday.
The country-midwife held me up
'Look is yu third boy child!'
My mother asked, 'Him all right?'
'Yes – all eyes, all ears
Yes – all hands, all feet.'
My mother whispered, 'Thank God'.
My granny said, 'My Jim, Jim
My husband. You come back?'
I slept
Roosters crowed
All around the village.

(*Source*: James Berry, *Hot Earth, Cold Earth*, Bloodaxe Books, 1995)

rise to ambivalent feelings – did this happen here? What difference would it have made to how his parents felt if he had not been, in his mother's words, 'all right'? Did you reflect, too, on how only females were involved in the birth, and how it felt to be Jim's (now James's) father – perhaps you wondered whether giving birth was so 'gendered' when you yourself were born, and what implications in general men's involvement (or not) has for family relationships as children grow and develop?

But first, before exploring some of these questions, we consider why, apart from its intrinsic fascination, social workers need to study human development. As you may be aware, it is one of the key knowledge requirements at both qualifying and post-qualifying levels for UK social workers.

Section I
THE STUDY OF HUMAN DEVELOPMENT

Five key theorists on human development (from left to right): Jean Piaget, Lev Vygotsky, Sigmund Freud, Erik Erikson and John Bowlby.

(*Sources*: J. Piaget from Science Photo Library Ltd/Bill Anderson; L. Vygotsky from TopFoto; S. Freud from Alamy Images/Mary Evans Picture Library; E. Erikson from TopFoto/Topham Picturepoint; J. Bowlby, by kind permission of Sir Richard Bowlby)

Why study human development?

First, many, if not most, children and adolescents show behavioural problems or difficulties at some point in their lives. A key issue for anyone beginning to assess, as you will have to, what kind of help if any may be needed, is how much a particular child's overall development is a departure from the norm for children of that age, as well as how normal or abnormal it is for that particular child. A common question, for example, might be whether a child's emotional development is normal for her or him, or shows an impairment because of a difficult experience or other factors. This is illustrated by the following case study of Julie whose child, Susan, was developing normally until she was involved in an accident.

Case study

Julie and Susan

During a routine home visit by a health visitor, a young mother, Julie, said that Susan, her 3-year-old daughter, had become for the last two months extremely distressed whenever Julie goes out of her sight. Susan refuses to play outside, follows Julie from room to room and insists on sleeping in her parents' bed (and then only when they've gone to

bed). She is easily frightened and seems to be getting worse, including insisting on accompanying her mother to the toilet, and screaming if she is not allowed to do so.

On questioning, Julie informs the health visitor that two months ago, Susan was out in the car with her father when they were sideswiped by another car, forced off the road and overturned. Neither was injured but they were both shaken and frightened, as was Susan's mother when she went to the scene of the accident.

Secondly, we know that many of you will have worked, or will go on to work when you qualify, with children, families, adults and older people whose experiences fall outside the normal range of developmental issues and problems. It is important to ground ourselves in the varieties of typical children's, adolescents' and adults' experiences in order to keep a sense of perspective and to make more precise judgements of atypical functioning. Two of the child abuse inquiries conducted in the 1980s following two tragic deaths of children in the care system, the Jasmine Beckford Inquiry and the Kimberley Carlile Inquiry, illustrate among other things failures to observe children's impaired development (Department of Health, 1991).

Thirdly, at the centre of social work practice is the ability to make relationships and communicate sensitively with the people you are working with. A knowledge of developmental stages is an important prerequisite in being able to communicate with them. For example, knowing about a child's likely stage of cognitive understanding will help you get attuned to understanding what they are communicating and how best to respond. Understanding the changes which take place as we enter old age can help us become attuned to the possible experiences and needs of the older person with whom we are working. (We discuss the skills involved in more detail in the chapter on communicating with children and adults later in the book, but this chapter will help you develop the foundations for this.)

And finally, working with other professionals is an important part of most social work practice. Knowledge of human development is an essential component of finding a common language and helping you to communicate effectively and professionally across professional boundaries.

It is also important to remember that you already know a good deal about development, not least from your own experiences of growing up in a particular culture and family, and from engaging in some form of higher education. These experiences form a vital part of your knowledge, and another objective of this section of the textbook is to enable you to become more aware of how your own experiences may influence the judgements you

make about others and to encourage you to draw on your own knowledge to help others learn too. We hope this will help you to become aware of how you already use theories *implicitly* and to understand how psychologists attempt to make these theories *explicit*.

Thinking about your own experiences

So before introducing you to some of the key concepts and research relating to human development, we would like you first to consider your own history and life events. We ask you to do this at this point, because it will help you to understand the way in which important events have influenced how you have developed as a person and by extension begin to understand this process for others too. Throughout the book, too, we emphasise the importance of being aware of the impact of your own perceptions, capacities and feelings on how you interact with others whom you are helping, and this is as much true here as later in the book. (For example, experiencing your parents' divorce while you were at primary school might make you particularly attuned to the impact of loss on young children: it *could* also make you less inclined to understand that it might affect others in ways which differ from your own experience.) Doing your own life map will also be a way of bringing alive some of the points which we go on to discuss next.

Think ahead

Think about your own life, your childhood and adolescence, and what has happened to you since you left school. Draw a 'road' to illustrate what has happened to you, noting down on one side of the road the 'event' (e.g. moved to secondary school) and on the other, any feelings you have or had about the 'event'. If you wish, you can show the ups and downs in your experiences by drawing the road as a series of plateaus, peaks and troughs – we have drawn an example to give you an idea of what a life map could look like.

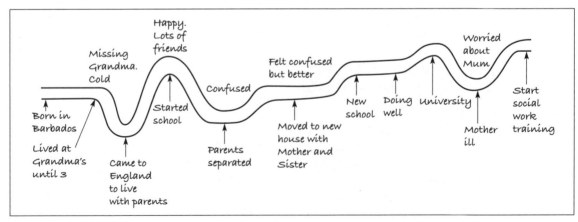

Figure 7.1 Road map

Now if possible find someone else, ideally a fellow social work student, with whom to compare your 'road map'. You will see from this that there are certain points in your development which are broadly similar: for example, in infancy and childhood, we will all of us have been dependent on others; you may remember or have been told about reaching certain milestones such as learning to talk or walk. There will be differences though, which may seem to reflect such things as your race and culture, class, gender, and other factors such as your own temperament, the impact of family events (such as parental divorce, unemployment) and so on.

Understanding these similarities and differences may help you to recognise the personal and social impact which life events have on those people you work with as a social worker, and to become attuned to different cultural and familial and social experiences. It may also guide you in considering the next part of our discussion, which addresses some of the important issues in learning about human development.

Some key debates in studying human development

In introducing you to some of the concepts and theories which form the framework for understanding patterns of development, we shall also explore some of the critical questions which arise for social workers in applying them.

Nature versus nurture

The first of these key debates is the question of whether the people we are or become is mainly determined by our biological inheritance, or whether we are shaped by the environment in which we grow up. As well as being a scientific and indeed a philosophical question, it is also a highly political one: for example, the extent to which the environment is emphasised may have an impact on how society responds to a particular issue. Thus, policies designed to lift children out of poverty stem at least in part from the recognition that children from poorer backgrounds fail to realise their full potential not because of their innate qualities ('nature') but because they have not had access to the opportunities (e.g. health and education) available to the better off. An example, however, of the way in which the 'nurture' perspective can be used oppressively was the idea promulgated in the 1960s that

certain kinds of families (termed 'schizophrenogenic') could drive their children to madness by the way they communicated with them, giving them conflicting messages which placed them in what is called a 'double bind'. The term was coined by Gregory Bateson, a clinician who hypothesised that the underlying cause of autism and schizophrenia is the mixed messages given by a parent who has difficulty with close relationships but cannot admit to these feelings. The parent communicates withdrawal, the child reacts to this coldness, the parent then reaches out to the child with simulated love, and the child is thus caught in a situation where no course of action is satisfactory – the double bind. (See Bateson et al., 1956.)

It is likely, if you reflect for a moment on your own personal or professional experiences, that you will conclude that a whole range of factors, some of which could be classified as inherited and some environmental and some probably both, go to make up who we are. (We began to touch on some of these in considering your possible responses to the poem at the beginning of the chapter.) Such factors may include genetic inheritance; sex/gender; other physical dimensions such as health, disability, physical good looks and so on; cultural factors such as class, ethnicity, living environment; family factors such as upbringing, position in the family, positive or difficult experiences there, and a range of random events such as accidents, illness, winning the lottery and so on. As we go through the stages of lifespan development, we need to bear in mind the way in which these factors, including our own perspectives on them, interact – an obvious illustration of this is contained in the percentile chart of Tracey (page 147), but you may like to consider, in relation to the example of Jim in Chapter 6, where you would stand on the question of the relative impact of his early experiences on his later behaviour. If, as seems likely, you would attribute at least some of his predicament to traumatic events in his childhood, do you think there were also predisposing factors, for example, to do with his temperament, which contributed to the downward spiral we describe?

One influential theorist who has explored the complex interplay of factors and traced the way in which the experience of inequality (being at the 'bottom of the heap') has negative consequences for health, poverty, unemployment, etc. is the social epidemiologist, Richard Wilkinson. Put briefly, he argues that it is not the experience of, for example, poverty or disadvantage per se which has this impact, but the experience of inferiority in relation to others – so feeling that everyone is 'in the same boat' is not as bad (and has less serious consequences for your health, among other things) as feeling that you are worse off than others in your network (Wilkinson, 2005).

Historical, cultural and ethnic views of development

Implicit in much of the discussion about the impact of environmental factors on development is the recognition that how we view child-rearing, our expectations of what is appropriate and inappropriate behaviour for ourselves and other people, our views of physical beauty and so on are all influenced by the culture and time in history in which we live. Theories, too, are permeated, as we shall see later in our case studies, with historical and cultural influences. Many of these are not easily teased out from our own experiences and may be a largely unconscious basis for our spontaneous behaviours and thinking. These inevitable biases may limit our professional understanding of and interventions with those we work with. It has been said that formal theories of development, such as Freud's, are as much about the theorists themselves as they are about the world in a broader sense. For example, is Freud's emphasis on psychosexual development heavily the result of the concerns of his time and place (late nineteenth century Vienna) and traumas from his own infancy and childhood, as one of his biographers, Breger (2000), suggests?

Think ahead

The article on child abuse in Hong Kong which we suggest you read links together cultural and historical issues, as well as emphasising psychopathology (through considering pathological experiences of child abuse in Hong Kong society). It considers traditional and modern Chinese culture, but also prompts other relevant questions:

How can these ideas be applied to British ethnic-Chinese groups?

How are they different from other ethnic groups in Britain today? How are they different from other mainstream British culture?

More general theoretical questions are also triggered, e.g. Are there universals of development and needs across cultures and historical eras? Can we – should we and do we – assign value judgements to child-rearing practices?

Read O'Brian and Lau (1995) *Child Abuse Review*, 4, 38–46 (see Activity at end of chapter).

Two other case studies from our recent past in the United Kingdom show how cultural assumptions and stereotypes have contributed to poor practice (see Case study box).

Case study

Tyra Henry and Christopher Clunis

Tyra Henry
In 1984, 21-month-old Tyra Henry was murdered by her father Andrew Neil after white social workers from Lambeth Council in south London were found to lack the confidence to challenge the family, in part at least, because the latter were black. Neil had already been convicted of cruelty to his son Tyrone whose injuries had left the boy blind and with a learning difficulty. Following his release from prison in 1983, the Inquiry found that professionals were too ready to believe Tyra's mother, Claudette, that she had finished with him, which she had not, and overestimated, because of stereotyping, the way in which black extended families function and the ability of her wider family to intervene and protect the little girl (London Borough of Lambeth, 1987).

Christopher Clunis
On 17 December 1992, Christopher Clunis, a young man who had come to this country from Jamaica, attacked a stranger, Jonathan Zito, on the London Underground and killed him. In the Inquiry report which followed the killing, it emerged that Clunis had been diagnosed as suffering from paranoid schizophrenia when he was living in Jamaica and was well known to psychiatric services in this country. The report commented that the fact that he was black may have contributed to the diffident manner in which he was treated by some professionals, and led to them deferring to his wishes against his own best interests. The report also recommended that professionals should be cautious in concluding that disturbed behaviour was the result of drugs rather than mental illness (Ritchie et al., 1994).

Normative and individual development

One of the reasons which we gave above for studying development is that in order to be alert to the possible impact of difficult experiences on people's lives, you need to be familiar with what would usually be seen as typical for any given stage of development. This of course raises the question of the extent to which we can view certain events as common to all human beings, and the extent to which there are variations or divergences because of our inherited characteristics, cultural experiences and so on. Developmental theorists generally distinguish between 'normative' development and individual development.

Normative or *typical* development refers to general changes and reorganisations in behaviour which virtually all children share as they grow older. The summary chart adapted from Sheridan given later in the chapter is an example of descriptors of normative or typical development which are rooted in Western perspectives but can be generalised to a greater or lesser extent to all cultures.

Individual development by contrast refers to the way in which individuals may vary around the typical course of development. If you were to follow the progress of a hundred children from birth through adolescence, you would find much the same sequence in achieving developmental milestones, such as sitting, walking, talking, playing cooperatively with another child. However, as you may have recognised, if you compared, say, the age at which you started to walk/talk with that of other student(s) in your group, there is some variation in the ages at which children reach these milestones. For example, on average, children begin to sit unsupported at six months, but this ability may emerge later even in normal infants, or can emerge as much as six weeks earlier. The point at which children with a range of disabilities reach certain milestones is also likely to diverge from what is typical for their age. Children with Down's syndrome, for example, do not smile at a game of peep-bo with a cloth (Bee, 1995) until their second year, and do not recognise themselves in a mirror until about 2.5 years – in other words, they progress towards these achievements in the same way as other children, but at a slower pace.

Individual development refers also to continuity within each individual child's pathway over time. That is why we said at the outset that you need to know not only what is 'typical' for that age group, but also how the particular child has developed. A confident, sociable three-year-old is more likely to be the same at six: so if there has been dramatic change in personality, such as we saw in the example of Susan above, it is much more likely than not that there will be a specific reason for it, such as illness or a move to a more nurturing family

Professional tip

Two important elements of a child's development

Practitioners must hold in mind the two aspects which are important for the individual child in her/his development:

1. How is this child developing in the light of age norms, that is, essentially, compared with other children of the same age?
2. How is this child progressing in comparison, say, to how s/he was a year or six months ago? As we have just suggested, this has special relevance for children with disabilities, with any assessment being within the 'norm' framework but also reflecting the progress of the individual child.

environment. The key message here is that individual development is, as a general rule, coherent and predictable, just as normative development is.

Individual psychology rather than structural and environmental issues

Another ongoing debate in social work which you need to be aware of has been the concern that by using psychological insights into assessments and interventions, we approach social problems in a way which inevitably is focused on changing individuals rather than in addressing structural and environmental issues, such as ameliorating poverty. It is important to maintain awareness of the individualistic tendency of much developmental psychology and we shall return to this and other caveats later.

(Read further on this in an article by Carolyn Taylor, 2004. See end of chapter Further Reading on page 194.)

Case study

Ken

Ken is a physically large and overweight 4-year-old who attends a playgroup on a daily basis. He is an only child of a white British couple who are now approaching their mid-forties. Playgroup staff report that he is clumsy and inattentive in interactions with adults and in carrying out instructions and seems to have very little speech or, at least, speaks little at the playgroup. He is always at the edge of groups of children, but not playing with them. The staff are concerned about the interactions which they have witnessed between Ken and his mother. In particular, recently Ken's mother lost her temper, hit Ken and dragged him out of the building. The staff's intervention seemed to increase Ken's mother's anger.

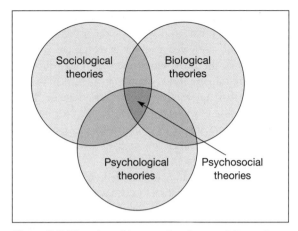

Figure 7.2 Theories of human development through the lifespan

In the above case study, what are your own assumptions about Ken's development and the factors which contribute to it? How would an understanding about human development and theories of human development be helpful for social workers and others in the caring professions working with Ken and his family?

To conclude this section of the chapter, you might like to read the trenchant views of two professionals (a family therapist and child psychologist) with much experience of working with maltreated children (see the next Closer Look box).

We now consider different explanations of human development, and what each contributes to our understanding of this. Although we encourage you to make use of informal theory (as discussed in our previous chapter), here we're emphasising formal knowledge and theories. As you will remember from that chapter, any scientific theory is an organised set of ideas about how things operate, which attempts to explain and to provide a framework for understanding the past and present experiences and events and predicting future ones.

Theories of development

Our knowledge of how we develop as we do draws, broadly speaking, on three disciplines: biology, sociology and psychology. Each of these disciplines tends to emphasise different factors in explaining how we develop. All these perspectives will be drawn upon as we consider changes through the different life stages. As we shall see, there is a considerable overlap between the perspectives, some (such as Erikson's) being called psychosocial to indicate this (see Figure 7.2).

Biological perspectives

Biological theories focus, as you might expect, on physical development, genetic influences and instinctual behaviours. A key early figure whom you will have heard of here is Charles Darwin, who argued that human behaviour is genetically determined. Biological theories tend to explore younger children's growth and development, while biological explanations of adolescence and adulthood and older age focus on physiological changes. We consider these changes at each stage of the life course. Recent significant studies of brain development have also contributed considerably to our understanding of the interrelationship of psychological and physiological factors (a point we shall illustrate in our discussion later of infants' percentile charts) and suggest that this is an area of research where technological advances are likely to yield greater knowledge in the future. In the next Closer Look box, we refer to research on the impact of early experiences on brain development which you may wish to explore further in your reading. Although the research review referred to here focuses on the impact of trauma, it also tells us a lot about the impact of positive experiences on brain development in non-traumatised children.

Sociological perspectives

Sociological disciplines emphasise the importance of social and economic factors in influencing our development. Social relationships and the individual's position in society and community are key in this perspective. Development is explained by examining the interactions between people and the society in which they live.

A closer look

Hanks and Stratton on the nature–nurture issue and the 'spoilt child'

During the twentieth century Western society gave considerable thought and discussion to the issue of how children should be brought up. We entered the so-called 'child centred' era. With hindsight we can easily detect deficiencies in earlier views, and with insight we may even criticise our current beliefs. Two themes that apply both to the past and the present relate to the idea that if children get their way they will become too powerful, and the rather contradictory image of the child as a helpless recipient of influence. What seems to unite the two positions is an assumption of conflict between what children want and what parents want. Giving children what they want is assumed to be at the expense of parents and, indeed, many parents place themselves under financial and other stresses in order to provide material goods or an endless stream of events for their children. With such a limited and materialistic definition of the duties of good parents, it is not surprising that children are first seen as passive consumers of parental resources, and then become resented for having such power to demand what they do not appreciate.

The 4-hour feeding schedule is an example of a demand for compliance, sameness and the teaching of obedience. Here the rules are that the child that cries at night must not be picked up and comforted; the child who has not eaten their dinner must not have a pudding; there must be no talking during mealtimes, etc. These are just a few examples of what people generally think might spoil a child.

Though it is not an original idea, we would like to draw attention to what we consider to be the true meaning of a 'spoilt' child. Something being spoilt is defined in the dictionary as being damaged or injured, something made useless, valueless – destroyed. The paradoxical juxtaposition of the meaning of 'the spoilt child' in the English language alerts us to a fundamental ambivalence about the rights of children. When attempting to help maltreated children, professionals and parents alike have to take into consideration that these are the children that someone has tried to spoil, in the 'real' (dictionary) sense. The abused, maltreated children are the children that are at risk of being spoilt.

The other myth, which can damage professional attempts to care for maltreated children, is of the child as passive recipient of influence. Our whole approach to child-rearing, and to education, reflects this assumption. We are very ready to talk of the effects of education, of childcare practices and of maltreatment on the child. It is much more difficult to recognise that children are active participants in creating their worlds. Perhaps we are afraid of blaming the victim; perhaps it is just easier to see things from an adult's point of view. But damage is not primarily something that can be put into a child to be carried around, invisible inside them. Damaging environments are places in which children nevertheless have to function and grow. The ways they function and the form of their growth will be affected and that is what we need to understand. It may be helpful to think in terms of the child adapting to the environment. The important effects of abuse are at least as likely to be in the kinds of adaptations the child comes to make as in simple direct consequences.

(*Source*: Hanks and Stratton, 2007: 91)

One approach here, which has been prominent in recent social work thinking, is the ecological approach, first put forward by Bronfenbrenner (1979). This approach takes a holistic view of the person in her or his environment, and is capable of incorporating other theories or approaches. It is generally seen as helpful in providing an organising framework for theories which might be seen otherwise to be competing, by allowing the immediate familial experiences of the individual child and family (the microsystem in Bronfenbrenner's terms), the school and neighbourhood influences (the exosystem) and the wider societal factors of culture and economic circumstances (the macrosystem) to be considered.

Using Bronfenbrenner's model of development enables us to break down the many factors which influence development. As we can see in the example of Ken above, he would be at the centre of the circle, bringing to development his particular biological make-up. Surrounding him is the second circle, consisting of his immediate environment, which in Ken's case we know includes his mother and his playgroup teachers and the other children in the playgroup. So here we can consider the influences of his parents and immediate family and school. Exploration of his exosystem (the third circle) allows us to look at the impact of the social and economic context in which he and his family live: for example, the local neighbourhood,

A closer look

Research on brain development

Danya Glaser (2000), a psychiatrist who has worked as a clinician and researcher for many years in the field of child maltreatment, has reviewed research studies which look at child abuse and neglect and how this impacts on brain development. She points out that the physical, behavioural, cognitive and emotional consequences of abuse now have counterparts to the psychological consequences known so far and recognised in how these children's brain structure, chemistry and brain function are affected. Research into the neurobiological effects of child abuse shows how particularly early abuse has consequences on the brain which are profound in their effects on abused children's later adjustment. Although the sequence of development

within the brain is genetically determined, the nature of this development is determined to a considerable extent by the infant and young child's experiences. Negative behaviours and actions will affect the brain's 'connectivity'. The important message this kind of research seems to highlight is that although we can add new learning and experiences throughout life into our brain structures and functioning, previous patterns cannot be erased, only added onto and more slowly. Glaser concluded that 'A further aspect of child maltreatment which has a profound effect on brain development is the significant neurobiological stress which the young child experiences' (pp. 99–100). She points out that it is the experience of a secure attachment which can protect the brain 'from the worst effects of stress'.

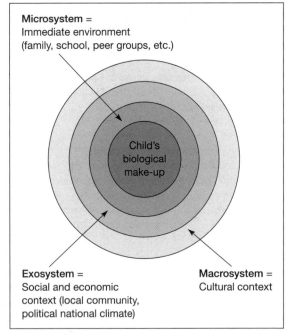

Microsystem =
Immediate environment
(family, school, peer groups, etc.)

Child's biological make-up

Exosystem =
Social and economic
context (local community,
political national climate)

Macrosystem =
Cultural context

Figure 7.3

Reflect

Taking the example of Ken at the beginning of this section, what would be the influences on Ken's life at the different levels described by Bronfenbrenner?

How did you get on? Perhaps you thought about Ken's physical make-up (the inner circle), even wondering if he might have a hearing impairment, or if earlier experiences at his birth may have made relationships more difficult for him and his mother and father. You will probably have had questions about parental relationships, and also thought about his lack of sociability, and if this reflected isolation of his family (the next, microsystem circle). His teachers are clearly expressing the influence of wider expectations, both on their responsibilities and on how children should be reared, and how families should be supported in doing this (the exosystem).

Psychological perspectives

Psychological theories emphasise people's personalities, emotions, relationships and behaviours, often although not always from the point of view of how these develop and change as individuals progress through their lives.

Over the years, psychologists have put forward a number of theories to explain human development. Modern theories both influence and themselves are influenced by certain views, particularly of childhood and adolescence. Some theories focus on universal processes

policies about children's pre-school education and so on. At another level, the macrosystem draws into the frame wider cultural issues, such as class or economic factors and the beliefs, values and attitudes and guidelines for behaviour which people in his particular society tend to share. Part of this will include the influences of how children should be reared and nurtured in our society.

in development and usually view children as progressing through predetermined stages to maturity (e.g. Freud, Piaget, Erikson). Some focus on all aspects of development, others concentrate on specific areas or, as they're sometimes called, domains of development, e.g. Bowlby's attachment theory has as its primary focus how children form social and emotional relationships; cognitive behavioural theories focus more on how children perceive and understand the world around them and so on.

At the end of the section we show through a case study how theories lead to different explanations of children's (and adults') behaviour, and also how they mostly tell you more about one aspect of development than others.

At this point, however, we give you an overview of some major theories which have been used in studying human development. Some of these you may be familiar with and some may be theories which you encounter here for the first time. In the latter case, it is useful not only to memorise the key terms, but also to play around with the ideas themselves, using exercises to help you gain confidence in using the ideas (we give you some suggestions at the end of the chapter).

Theories which emphasise cognitive development

Our first three theories focus on cognitive development, i.e. children's thinking, language and other mental skills. The next two focus on social and emotional development – the development of children's feelings and relationships with others.

The central figure in cognitive-developmental theory is the Swiss psychologist Jean Piaget (1932, 1936; Piaget and Inhelder, 1969). Along with other cognitive theorists, Piaget was struck by the way in which children's thinking seems often to differ from how adults think, and also by what he discerned as the regularity and consistency in the development of children's thinking. He noticed that children seemed to go through the same kinds of discoveries about their world, in roughly the same order, making the same mistakes and arriving at the same solutions. An example of this is the way in which infants acquire the idea of 'object permanence', that is, the understanding that objects continue to exist even if they are out of your sight. This is clearly important for our understanding of reality, including our knowledge that we are distinct from other people. Before they reach a certain age – around 12 months – studies suggest that infants have

still an incomplete understanding of object permanence. If you repeatedly hide a rattle under a cushion, an 8- to 10-month-old will find it each time. If you, with the infant watching, then put the rattle under a different cushion, he or she will continue to look for it under the original cushion, where it has always been before.

Think ahead

Can you think of any examples from your own experience or reading of ways in which children's thinking is different from yours as an adult?

Perhaps you remember as a child at the beginning of a long journey asking whether you were soon going to arrive? Perhaps you have seen a small child hiding their eyes and thinking they were invisible? Or you remember being puzzled at the answer to the question – which weighs more, a pound of feathers or half a pound of lead? All these would be examples of how children interpret events and information, and in ways which are different from ours as adults.

Piaget's observations of children's thinking led him to several key assumptions, the most important of which is that human organisms *adapt* to their environment in an active process. He proposed that infants are born with basic cognitive structures, which he called schemas (sometimes referred to as schemes). These mental structures become increasingly complex as we grow older. Piaget proposes that these changes involve three basic processes: assimilation, accommodation and equilibration. These processes bring about alterations in the child's internal mental structures or schemas. He also considered that changes occur which involve reorganisation at three significant stages or points in the child's development: the first roughly at 18 months, the second at roughly 5–7 years and the third at adolescence. The following are the main major developmental periods as Piaget envisaged them.

Piaget's theory of how children's thinking develops

- Children actively construct systems for understanding the world, i.e. they engage with their surroundings with every means they have, practising skills and encountering problems beyond their current capacities. On the basis of feedback from these encounters and continuing brain maturation, they develop more advanced abilities.

- Children's understanding is limited by their current cognitive structures (schemas).
- Major shifts in thinking occur at approximately 2 years, 7 years and 12 years.

Piaget's developmental stages

0–2   Sensori-motor – understand world through senses

2–6   Pre-operational – egocentricism

7–11 Concrete – logical operations operational on concrete objects

12+   Formal – abstract, logical operational thinking

A closer look

Key terms of Piaget's theory

- Schemas – basic building blocks
- Assimilation – absorb experiences to existing schema
- Accommodation – modify existing schemas or create new ones to fit
- Equilibration – strive for coherence
- Theory of mind – ability to understand that people may see world differently

We'll discuss these stages in more detail in the appropriate age-based section. For now, it is worth noting the following points about Piaget's ideas:

- Each stage grows out of the preceding one, and involves a major restructuring (alteration) in thinking.
- All children make cognitive progress in this order.
- Not all children move at the same speed or achieve the same end point; virtually all achieve pre-operational stage, the large majority concrete operations, but not all necessarily achieve formal operations.

In our next Closer Look feature, we take the discussion of Piaget's terms further, and suggest how you might find examples of them from your own experience.

Sociocultural theory

In recent years, there has been much more interest in studying children's cognitive development in its social and cultural context. This theory emphasises the part played by social interaction and cultural practices on cognitive development. A key figure who has influenced research done from a sociocultural perspective is a Russian psychologist called Vygotsky.

Vygotsky's socialcultural theory

Vygotsky's thinking is similar to Piaget's in that he argues that children actively participate in their own development (an apparently simple act on the part of a baby of reaching out to a ball and then putting the ball in the mouth can be seen as an example of the infant actively acquiring knowledge). Unlike Piaget, however, who as we have seen focuses on the content of children's thought, Vygotsky emphasises the role of other people in children's learning: children acquire the means of learning and understanding, including language, from the social interactions with other more knowledgeable adults and older children. He argues that children learn to plan and to regulate their own behaviour by gradually absorbing (internalising) 'messages' which they originally receive in interactions with others. For example, a child who has regularly been reminded by a parent not to touch something because it may break, or to wait their turn in a game, gradually learns to reproduce these behaviours in other settings and without the adult's instruction. One other way in which he differs from Piaget is that whereas Piaget argues that children need to be ready before they are able to learn, Vygotsky proposes that adults should provide activities and learning which take them slightly beyond what they are currently capable of – enough to challenge them but not to demoralise them. This idea in his theory is called the 'zone of proximal development' and is seen as the point where learning and cognitive development take place, as children gradually internalise skills which they could initially only do in a social setting or with adult help, and thus expand their repertoire of cognitive abilities. It is important to remember that the zone of proximal development does not extend indefinitely – at any point in development there will be skills which extend beyond the child's current abilities. (For example, a 2-year-old will usually be able to put on pants and top with an adult's help, but tying shoe laces will be beyond them.)

The following are the key points to remember from Vygotsky's theory:

- Children first learn cognitive skills in social settings and only later internalise them.
- Children develop inner speech to regulate their behaviour – self-direction becomes internal rather than external.

A closer look

Adaptation: assimilation and accommodation

Biologically oriented theories such as those of Piaget and Bowlby assume that all the activities of children – and of other living organisms – during their development further their environmental adaptation. Adaptation is viewed as consisting invariably of two functions: accommodation and assimilation. That is, children continuously take in or *assimilate* their surrounding environment to their own ongoing activities; they also adjust themselves, or *accommodate* their activities, to their environment. From birth onwards therefore children are assumed actively to take part in the process of assimilating every external person and object they interact with along with assimilating their internal activities (bodily and mental activities) into their past experiences.

This active internalisation of experience, or *assimilation*, is seen as the most basic mental activity, and one that is more elemental than accommodation.

An example of an assimilative process during imaginative play is the interaction of a young child with a play object, say, a policeman's hat. The child can choose to assimilate the hat to ongoing play by pretending that it is a bucket, filling it with bricks and carrying it by its strap as a bucket, or pretend that the hat is a tortoise's shell and hiding something under it, or that it is a hill and having a toy car climb over it. All of these play actions show the child performing highly assimilative activities; the hat is used to serve the child's internal motivations; most – but not all – of the hat's usual characteristics and functions are disregarded. Therefore the hat is said to be used by the child symbolically in play to represent something else the child has in mind. Turning to the function of accommodation in this example, playing symbolically with the hat is not a purely assimilative activity. The child must still accommodate to the object's characteristics to a certain extent by taking the shape of the hat and/or its function into account when using the hat imaginatively (see Wilson and Ryan, 2005).

Can you think of an example which you have observed of this process of assimilation and accommodation? You may have observed children in make-believe play, as in the example. Or perhaps you might have watched a baby learning to drink from a cup – the baby's innate sucking reflex patterns no longer work, so she/he has to modify (accommodate) the existing strategy of sucking so that the drink will not spill. Having learnt to do this, s/he has adapted to drinking from a cup.

- The one of proximal development is where learning takes place – this represents the gap between child's current performance and potential performance if guided by someone more skilled.
- The theory focuses on social interaction and cultural practices in development of child's understanding of the situation.

Social learning theory

This is a development of earlier learning theory which proposes that all behaviours are learned through associations with different kinds of consequences. In learning theory, it is argued that humans tend to repeat behaviours which have resulted in them getting positive or rewarding experiences, or have allowed them to avoid unpleasant consequences, and to discontinue behaviours which do not bring these consequences. Social learning theory emphasises in addition the process of modelling, where people imitate behaviours which they have seen others do (we explore this theory in more detail in our chapter on interventions in the next section). Possibly the most influential theorist here is Albert Bandura whose early work focused on the role of imitation in children's aggressive behaviour, while later theorists have been interested in identifying what factors make it likely that children will imitate behaviour, and in explaining the development of aggression and what is called prosocial behaviour (i.e. behaviour which is socially acceptable and advances the interests of the self and others). For example, he found, perhaps unsurprisingly, that children were more likely to copy models identified in some way as high status, and/or who were like themselves in some way, and/or they had seen being rewarded for their actions. You can probably think of examples in your own experience which make these ideas seem plausible (for example, a sibling copying an older brother, the influence of a gang leader on the behaviour of the group). The following are key points to remember:

- Focus is on social behaviour rather than thinking.
- Focus is on explaining specific social and emotional responses rather than universal patterns.
- Helps explain differences in same-age children.
- Identifies factors which make it more likely that children will imitate a model, and helps explain prosocial or aggressive behaviour.

Our remaining theoretical perspectives emphasise social and emotional development.

Psychoanalytic approaches

Psychoanalytic theories are perspectives which attempt to describe normal development and also to explain individual pathways and variations from the norm. A large and influential grouping of theorists, including Freud, Carl Jung, Alfred Adler and Erik Erikson, have sought to explain human behaviour by understanding the underlying processes of the psyche, a Greek term meaning 'soul', mind or 'spirit'. Freud is usually credited with creating the psychoanalytic approach, and we explore many ideas derived from his thinking in our section on psychodynamic approaches (in our later chapter on interventions); Freud viewed early experiences as being vital to understanding development. He proposed that the human mind is divided into three systems: the id, the ego and the superego. The id strives for immediate gratification by any possible means and is the source of all motivation. The super ego is the guide to morals and ethics. The ego is a more conscious element which serves as a kind of executive of the personality and has the function of mediating between the demands of the id, the demands of the external world (such as social experiences, demands and expectations) and the demands of the superego, and being responsible for the appropriate expression of emotions, delay in gratification and so on.

Although some of Freud's explicit influence on developmental psychology has diminished, his ideas have contributed greatly to our understanding of human functioning and the nature of helping relationships more generally, as the discussion in our interventions chapter also suggests. One of Freud's most significant theoretical contributions is that all behaviour is governed by both conscious and unconscious processes. And ideas derived from this have become very much part of our culture and passed into our general language, even if we are unaware of where they derive from. For example, you are

likely already to have come across the phrase 'defence mechanisms', and perhaps thought of them as an abnormal or deviant kind of behaviour. Freud, however, conceived of them as entirely normal, and that their primary purpose is to help protect us from unmanageable anxiety. Helen Bee (1995) in a useful passage discusses the way in which different defence mechanisms (such as denial, intellectualisation, distortion, displacement, suppression) may operate. We give an extract from this in our Closer Look box, in which she describes possible ways of dealing with receiving a letter rejecting a hypothetical journal article.

A closer look

We all use defence mechanisms in daily life: illustrated by responses to the experience of having a journal article rejected

'All defense [sic] mechanisms distort reality to some extent, but they vary in the amount of distortion involved. At one extreme end is *denial*. I might deny that I had ever submitted the paper or that it had ever been rejected. Or I could use *distortion*, such as by persuading myself that the journal really loved the paper but there hadn't been enough space. A notch less distorting are mechanisms such as *projection*, in which I push my feelings on to someone else. "Those people who rejected this paper are really stupid! They don't know what they're doing."'

(Bee, 1995: 27)

Reflect

Can you think of equivalent examples in your own life?

Think of the last time something difficult happened to you or you observed someone else experience something upsetting. *How did you, or they, handle it*?

Perhaps you, metaphorically or actually, 'kicked the cat' or took your disappointment out on someone else, i.e. you showed the defence mechanism of *displacement*, putting your anger not on the object which had caused it – say, in Bee's case, the journal editors – but on to another innocent object. Remember, these defences are, mostly, entirely normal.

Modern thinkers (and indeed Freud in his later work) put more emphasis on the ego but Freud's legacy is important in stressing:

- Emotions have critical impact on thinking.
- Early relationships are vitally important.
- Past conflicts can be pushed out of conscious awareness but still affect a person's life.
- The same events can have different meanings for different people, depending on their developmental histories.

Of the other psychoanalytic writers, Eric Erikson has probably had the greatest influence on the study of development. Like Freud, from whom many of his ideas derive, Erikson assigned an important role to feelings and social relationships, and the importance of early experiences. However, he differs in some crucial aspects. He proposed a series of qualitatively distinct stages which occur in a certain order. Each stage involves a certain issue or task which everyone resolves in some way, although some people do so more satisfactorily than others. His issues are broader than Freud's (e.g. the quality of care a baby receives entails more than feeding or oral gratification which Freud describes, since it gives opportunities to develop basic trust or mistrust). He focuses on the emergence of a sense of identity. Common cultural demands are seen as very important, so his stages are called psychosocial rather than psychosexual. The issues which characterise Erikson's stages have provided an important organising framework for describing human development. Unlike other theorists, he considers later developmental stage in detail. Indeed, his imagination and interest seem most engaged by the fifth, adolescent phase. We shall return to consider his ideas in later sections. Erikson's eight psychosocial stages and Freud's psychosexual stages are summarised in Table 7.1.

Attachment theory

Attachment theory, of which the first exponent was John Bowlby, brings together social emotional and cognitive aspects of development. Bowlby derived his ideas significantly from Darwin, but was also influenced by Freud. In developing his thinking he sought to explain why just being separated from a parental figure should cause so much anxiety; why distress following separation did not cease immediately contact was restored; why prolonged separation from a parent figure should have a lasting effect; and the similarities between adult and child mourning.

He considered that the tendency to form early attachments is inbuilt, and for virtually all children it unfolds through a sequence of stages. The tendency to form attachments and the stages in their development are universal, but security of attachments varies greatly. Attachment theory includes an important role for cognition and learning. We shall consider these theories in more detail in our next section on infancy.

The basic premises of John Bowlby's attachment theory are:

- Intimate emotional bonds between individuals have a primary status and biological function.
- The way a child is treated has a powerful influence on a child's development and later personality functioning.
- Attachment behaviour is to be viewed as part of an organisational system which utilises 'internal working model(s)' of self and other to guide expectation and the planning of behaviour.
- While attachment behaviour is resistant to change, there is a continuing potential for change, which means that at no time of life is a person impermeable to adversity or to favourable influence.

Why so many theories rather than just one?

We have so far presented you with a brief overview of a few theories of human development. We have selected these – for there are many others – because they have been central to developing our Western understanding of development, and/or because they offer fruitful ways of understanding both normal development, challenges to development and the risk factors which are involved in the development of psychopathology.

A limitation (or is it?) of all these current theories is that we do not have a complete theory of development but only views from a variety of perspectives. In other words, different theories focus on different aspects of development. For example, as we have seen, Piaget focuses on cognitive development, Vygotsky on the social aspects of learning. Each theorist concentrates on different factors, even within the same area of development. It is important to:

- understand the different perspectives being offered;
- recognise that different theories (explanations) may suggest different forms of intervening;
- recognise the limitations of the theory and also its potential 'range of convenience'.

Finally, as you become more familiar with the concepts you will begin to see ways in which the different theories are addressing the same phenomena, in ways which can be seen to have some things in common. In our discussion of the case with which we conclude this section we show briefly how you might apply the theories we have encountered so far.

Table 7.1 Erikson's psychosocial and Freud's psychosexual stages of development

Stage	A Psychosocial crises	B Radius of significant relations	C Approximate age	D Psychosocial modalities	E Psychosexual stages
I	Trust vs. Mistrust	Maternal person	About 1st year	To get To give in return	Oral–Respiratory, Sensory–Kinesthetic (Incorporative modes)
II	Autonomy vs. Shame, Doubt	Parental persons	2nd–3rd years	To hold (on) To let (go)	Anal–Urethral Muscular (Retentive–Eliminative)
III	Initiative vs. Guilt	Basic family	4th–7th years	To make (= going after) To 'make like' (= playing)	Infantile–Genital, Locomotor (Intrusive, Inclusive)
IV	Industry vs. Inferiority	'Neighborhood', School	7th–11th years	To make things (= completing) To make things together	'Latency'
V	Identity and Repudiation vs. Identity diffusion	Peer groups and Outgroups; Models of leadership	Adolescence 12th–19th years	To be oneself (or not to be) To share being oneself	Puberty
VI	Intimacy and Solidarity vs. Isolation	Partners in friendship, sex, competition, cooperation	Early adulthood Age 20/25–40/45	To lose and find oneself in another	Genitality
VII	Generativity vs. Stagnation	Divided labor and shared household	Middle adulthood Age 40/45–60/65	To make, be To take care of	
VIII	Integrity vs. Despair	'Mankind' 'My Kind'	Late adulthood/ older age Age 60–65 plus	To be, through having been To face not being	

Case study

The Smith family

Dave Smith – age 35, father to Katy, Tracey and Leo – white British

Christine Smith – age 23, mother to all four children – white British

Lennie Clarke – father to Hareton – whereabouts unknown – black British

Hareton Clarke – age 6½ – black British

Katy Smith – age 4 – white British

Tracey Smith – age 3 – white British

Leon Smith – age 20 months – white British

Telephone call to duty social worker, children's services, from Mrs Dean, St Mary's primary school. Mrs Dean is concerned that Hareton Smith has been missing a lot of school recently, and when he does come to school, he looks unhappy and unkempt, and the other children tend to avoid him as he gets into a lot of playground fights. A social worker, Paula, who is herself white British, later visits the home at midday to find Mr and Mrs Smith (Christine and Dave) in bed. The door was answered by Hareton who was clearly not at school. The children appeared to have made their own arrangements for breakfast and the house is dirty and untidy. Christine Smith says that she has called on a bad day as she had been up very late arguing with Dave who had woken her up on his return from the club. Christine is now looking after her father (who is registered disabled and is now living with the family) and Paula wonders if this is putting an extra strain on her.

Hareton appears small for his age, and the younger children, according to Christine, still wet the bed and have a lot of minor infections.

In considering what is happening to Hareton, developmental psychology would be likely to focus on Hareton's own perspective and in particular his early relationship with his mother. It would involve speculating on the quality of the attachment he formed to her, in what was likely to have been a turbulent time in her life (given her age when she became pregnant and the fact that his father must have disappeared from the scene at some point during Hareton's early years), and his experience of being displaced by younger half-siblings. So Bowlby's theory would consider the quality of the attachment relationship, while Freud might question the extent to which he successfully negotiated separation from his mother and possible rivalrous feelings towards his step-father. A biological perspective would consider Hareton's physical development, wondering whether his small stature is to do with his genetic inheritance, or reflects emotional factors, or undernourishment, or all of these factors. A social learning or behavioural approach will consider how Hareton has been responded to by others, including his stepfather, school and peers, looking at, for example, how he has been rewarded or punished for behaviour, and the kinds of behaviours which he may have witnessed or experienced at home. The task which Erikson ascribes to this period (industry versus inferiority) might help us further focus on and understand Hareton's sense of himself and his identity, possibly feelings of failure or of being socially isolated, as the one black child in his family and perhaps his school. And drawing on Piaget's or Vygotsky's theories of cognitive development might help us to reflect on his ability to reason and understand his experience: for example, it is possible that he might feel himself to blame (inferior) for being racially different from his siblings, or for his own father's absence.

As we have said earlier, the theoretical perspective chosen will influence the approach taken to intervention. What is also important to remember is that the perspective will only suggest the 'direction of travel' and the hypothesis which you need to test. For example, if attachment theory suggests a focus on Hareton's relationships with his caregivers, and that he may be missing school because he is too anxious and preoccupied about his relationships with them to settle and complete tasks at school or find pleasure in engaging in play with peers, then this would need to be explored further. Equally, it is unlikely that this perspective alone will explain all that is going on for Hareton; taking one approach in isolation would lead to other aspects of his life being ignored (such as his peer relationships at school) so that a range of theories will always need to be drawn upon.

Reflect

Turn to the case of Ken earlier in this chapter, or that of Jim (in Chapter 6) and consider how you might apply the theories we have discussed so far to their situations.

We now turn to consider the different stages of human life course development in more detail.

Section II
DIFFERENT STAGES IN DEVELOPMENT THROUGH THE LIFE COURSE

Infancy and early childhood

(*Source*: Photofusion Picture Library/Debbie Humphrey)

If you think about your own childhood, or your observations of infants and children you have had the chance to watch closely, you will see that children's development occurs across a number of different dimensions: biological, social, emotional and cognitive. They grow physically. They learn to use language. They learn emotional and social skills which help them in making relationships with family, friends, adults such as teachers and others in the wider community. While theorists may compartmentalise these changes, and while we may need to separate them in order to be able to make sense of what is happening, in reality development progresses across all these different fronts at the same time. And as we shall see, development is the product of many different processes or systems: what happens in one system influences and is influenced by another. It may be more obvious that environmental factors such as poverty will influence a child's physical growth, but it is also true that cultural factors (e.g.

expectations or the necessity of gaining independence from adults) will also do so. It may be less obvious although equally true that factors within the family, such as emotional cruelty, can have an effect on a child's physical growth (as we show later in this section).

In the next sections, we consider the development of infants and young children from the point of view of their physical, social and emotional and cognitive development. But as social workers you will need to keep this interrelatedness in mind, even though we consider these dimensions separately here.

It may help you as you read to bear in mind the primary tasks of the developmental stage which we are considering. So in relation to infancy and early childhood, these are:

- Developing trust and a sense of security and forming attachments to caregivers
- Differentiating self from others
- Developing gross and fine motor skills
- Learning to communicate and to use language to do so
- Learning self-control and compliance.

Pre-natal development and birth

We shall not spend long on this topic but it is important to remember that, from a social worker's point of view, there is a whole range of factors which can affect the baby's physical state before she/he is born. Factors which can influence prenatal development include genetic 'errors' (e.g. chromosomal or hormonal differences), the mother's general health, diseases, smoking, drug-taking and excessive drinking. Social workers who may have to assess the risks to an unborn child will need to familiarise themselves with the literature on fetal alcohol syndrome, or the effects on growth and development of being born to mothers who are addicted.

Motor and physical development in infancy and early childhood

Babies come equipped with a number of innate reflexes and a surprisingly mature set of perceptual skills: for example, the newborn can focus both eyes on the same spot; easily hear sounds and locate objects by their sounds, and discriminate some individual voices; taste the four basic tastes – sweet, sour, bitter and salty. In contrast, the motor skills of a newborn are limited to such survival reflexes as sucking and breathing. Gross motor skills such as sitting up and walking develop from about six months onwards, while fine motor skills such as picking up small objects take longer to build up. The stages of development (up to 12 months) are illustrated in picture form in Figure 7.4. Try to familiarise yourself with these by observing babies and infants you see in your daily lives.

Between the ages of two and about six, significant development occurs in children's growth. They change from toddlers who move with a characteristic lolloping gait to taller, thinner 6-year-olds who can run, skip and jump. However, there are considerable variations in children's weight and height which are caused in part by genetic inheritance (including gender) but also in part by temperament, and worldwide by cultural and racial variations.

The following are key points to remember:

- Knowledge of a newborn's innate capacities and in the case of some reflexes, their normal time of disappearance, can be used in the diagnosis of neurological and physical disorders because these capacities are so predictable.
- Infants are social beings from birth, able to make social connections to their carers immediately.
- Differences between newborns' temperaments on measures such as activity level, irritability and other basic biological functions (e.g. sleeping/feeding) are measurable, but there is as yet no discovered link between these and later personality traits.
- The infant's biological needs are dominant: social relationships are embedded in these biological imperatives (for example, the rhythmical sucking burst–pause sequence which you may have witnessed very probably lays the foundations for later turn-taking in carer–child interactions).
- For assessment purposes, it is important to remember that motor development follows a predictable sequence.
- Motor development has an important interactive role in overall development – for example, by crawling around the room, the infant develops an understanding of space.

An important way to monitor growth which is used regularly by health practitioners is by using percentile charts. These are ways for mapping individuals' physical growth by measuring height and weight against a series of average standards or norms. The percentile chart (Figure 7.5) is used to record head size, weight, and height, with boys and girls having different 'average' charts because of their slightly different pattern of development. The thick vertical line which goes across the page depicts the average growth rate. The individual baby's weight is plotted on a line (which can be either above or below the average) and as the baby grows older dots show where age and weight come together. Most babies double their birth weight by 4 or 5 months and at 12 months will have roughly trebled it.

It is important to recognise familial characteristics (some families are smaller than others) and racial variations, e.g. Asian babies are usually lighter and shorter, Afro-Caribbean taller and heavier. However, what is most important is that a baby should have a fairly steady growth line. Variations from this may suggest significant changes in the child's circumstances. In Tracey's chart, illustrated, it is noticeable that her weight increased when she was away from her father and stepmother's care and plateaued when she was returned. This would form vital evidence in any assessment of her care. It also provides graphic illustration of our earlier point about the interrelatedness of physical and emotional factors, underlined, too, in the report into the death of Jasmine Beckford (see the Closer Look box).

Perceptual and cognitive development in infancy and early childhood

We now consider how the infant and young child's understanding of the world develops: the mental processes or thinking skills by which they acquire and process knowledge. These include such things as memory and language, facts and concepts and so on. It may be helpful to think of this development in terms of building blocks, with each stage a necessary step towards the next, until the child reaches an adult understanding of the world. Thus children need, for example, to be able to understand about the existence of objects (as in our earlier discussion of 'object permanence'), including people, *before* they can understand that other people see things differently to the way they do (called a 'theory of mind').

We introduced you in the first section to Jean Piaget's theories of cognitive development and these are a good starting point for your study of this aspect of development. Piaget called infancy the sensori-motor period

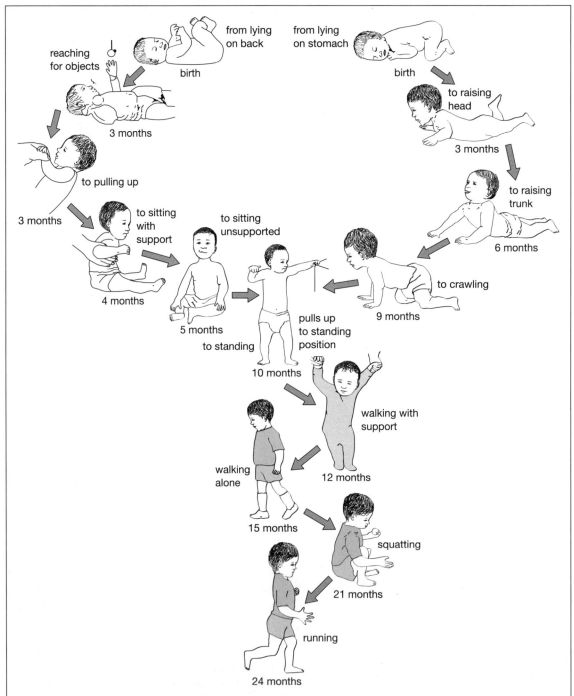

Notice that (i) the process is one of continuous development, not steps and stages; (ii) the sequence is the same for all children (for example, head control always comes before sitting, sitting before crawling, etc.) but there may be many individual variations (for example, some babies do not crawl but progress straight to walking); and (iii) the age at which a particular motor skill is achieved varies within certain limits.

Figure 7.4 Motor development of a child from birth to 2 years

(*Source*: Illustration designed by Dr Pam Zinkin)

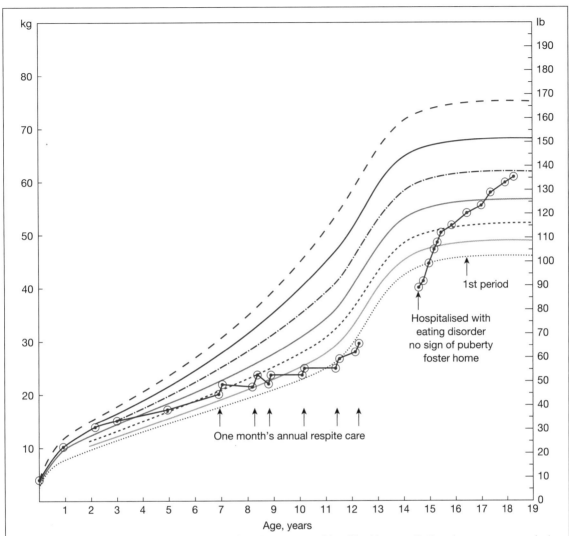

Tracey's weight was above average for the first three years of her life. Her growth then became progressively poorer and her curve crossed the centile lines downwards. During this time, the relationship between her father and mother deteriorated: her mother left home acrimoniously when Tracey was five and her father's new partner moved into the home. Tracey's teachers and social workers were concerned that she was being emotionally abused, but the decision was taken for her to remain in her father's care. She was, however, given a month's respite care each year, where she was weighed and measured and was shown to gain weight rapidly. Her growth was not charted at other times, so the degree of downward progression was not recognised. In her early teens her home situation worsened, and she developed anorexia and was hospitalised. A short period in hospital, followed by placement in foster care, restored her growth, and her puberty rapidly advanced to normal. It is likely, sadly, that the psychological damage of her early experiences will remain with her.

Figure 7.5 Tracey's chart: birth to late adolescence (weight)

because he considered that infants' knowledge of the world is limited to what they know through sensory, physical awareness and motor acts. Their learning at this stage is primarily through immediate perception and physical experiences. Piaget believed that motor activity is essential to development and that children actively put together a rudimentary understanding of how things work. At first, babies seem to make discoveries almost by

A closer look

The importance of physical measures in assessing and monitoring children's development

The report into the death of Jasmine Beckford describes in detail the percentile charts which recorded her growth up until she reached the age of 2 years and 3 months. Although she was a full-term and normal delivery and gained weight satisfactorily during the first four months of her life (when her weight was close to the 50th percentile), by the time when she was admitted to hospital at the age of 20 months with a broken femur, her weight had dropped to below the 3rd percentile. During the following seven months which she spent in foster care, her weight showed a dramatic improvement, so that at 27 months she was nearly at the 25th percentile. The report comments: 'This development strongly indicated a period of "catch up" growth, highly suggestive of a dramatic change in her well-being and of something radically wrong with her early development . . . when the decision to return the children to the Beckford home was taken, [someone] should have called for a medical examination which would have unearthed the tell-tale of the percentile chart.'

(London Borough of Brent, 1985: 73)

accident and only later become more intentional as they try out actions and investigate consequences. So babies start with basic physical reflexes and gradually through the process of *adaptation* (assimilation and accommodation) extend what they can accomplish. Thus as infants interact with their environments, their early schemas become adapted to more and more situations, so that by the end of this phase (around 18 months) they can hold representations of things in their minds and begin to think in advance about what to do. (An example of this ability to hold a representation in mind might be when a seventeen-month-old, whose mother goes out of the room leaving him with a stranger, repeats her name, 'Mama', hesitates and then returns to his play.) Another vital process which is occurring over this period (and reflects the growing ability to make one thing stand for or represent another) is the development of symbolic thought, which Piaget traced through stages in the development of children's play.

- Sensori-motor play: 12 months
- Constructive play: 12–24 months onwards
- First pretend play: 15–21 months onwards
- Substitute pretend play: 24–36 months
- Socio-dramatic play: preschool – may include an 'imaginary friend'

At around the age of eighteen months, the toddler moves to what Piaget termed the stage of pre-operational thought. During this period (which lasts until about 6 or 7 years of age), children acquire an increasing understanding of the world and increasing sophistication in their ability to think and reason. But although their thinking differs from that of smaller children, they have some fundamental *limitations* in comparison to older children and adults.

A closer look

Understanding others' perceptions of the world

Two psychology researchers (Jeremy Avis and Paul Harris) carried out a test with the Baka, a hunter–gatherer people who live in Cameroon. Each child on their own watched an adult, Mopfana, put some mango kernels into a bowl. Mopfana left the hut, and another adult told the child they were going to play a game with Mopfana, by hiding the kernels in a cooking pot. Then he asked the child where Mopfana would look for the kernels when he returned to the hut, and whether he would feel good or bad before he lifted the lid of the bowl and after he lifted the lid. Younger children, 2, 3 and early 4 year olds were much more likely to say that Mopfana would look for the kernels in the pan, or say that he would be sad before he looked in the bowl, while older children (4 and 5 year olds) were nearly always right on all three questions.

(Avis and Harris, 1991)

They have difficulty in seeing things from a point of view of someone else. Piaget describes this as the child being *egocentric*, by which he did not mean that children are selfish but that they find it difficult to understand that other people's perspectives may differ from their own. In other words, children are said to lack a *theory of mind*, that is, that other people may see, feel and experience things differently from how they do. So a small child, speaking on the telephone, pointing out something in the room, cannot grasp that the other person cannot see it. Or a small boy, seeing an older sister hurt, might try to comfort her by giving her his favourite truck, in the expectation that what would please him would also appeal to her. In the Closer Look box, we tell you about an interesting test which illustrates the way in which this 'theory of mind' develops.

Other differences in children's thinking include what is called *centration*, which refers to the way in which children tend to fix their attention on one aspect of a situation and ignore other aspects. They have difficulty in recognising that a situation may have a number of different dimensions, and in integrating multiple pieces of information. So, for example, if you ask a 3–4-year-old which of two cars is going faster, the child is likely to say that the one in front is, even if the car behind is rapidly catching it up. A third limitation lies in managing what are called attentional and memory processes, so that although pre-school children show growing ability to remember everyday occurrences they often have trouble with tasks which require memory strategies (such as remembering to pass on a message or a note). And a fourth is that children in this period are only beginning to distinguish between appearance and reality. An example of this (which also shows children's early difficulties with reversability) is in Piaget's classic conservation experiments, in which he showed, for example, that when liquid is poured from a tall thin glass into a short fat one, pre-school children focus on the feature of the glass's height, miss the other features such as width, and think there is more liquid in the taller glass.

To sum up, children's thinking during this period advances so that they show:

- steadily increasing understanding of others' thoughts and perspectives;
- emerging understanding of causation, especially of simple or familiar things;
- ability to distinguish between appearance and reality;
- expanding attention and memory skills.

Language

Piaget tended not to focus overmuch on the development of language, but clearly throughout this period children make enormous progress, from the first babbling sounds (proto-language) to the earliest ability to understand the meaning of individual words (receptive language) to the first words which may appear typically at around 12 months. In this early period children tend to learn words quite slowly, and can take 6 months to acquire 30 words. Somewhere between 16 months and the end of the second year the pattern usually shifts, and they may move from a speaking vocabulary of around 50 words to over 300 words by 24 months. By 5 years, many children are fluent speakers, although practitioners need to remember that even older children may use words which they do not fully understand. (The poet and novelist, Laurie Lee, in his autobiography *Cider with Rosie*, describes how on his first day at school, the teacher told him to wait there 'for the present', and how cross he was to discover, having waited all day in the expectation of receiving a present, that all she had meant was 'for the time being' or 'for now'.) As Crawford and Walker (2003) and others discuss, young children tend to grasp and use concrete rather than abstract terms, and have difficulties with metaphor, for example. They also have difficulties with categorisation (as you might predict from the discussion above about centration, for example) and may not understand more abstract concepts such as before and after, above and below and so on.

Proto-language skills seem to progress in a regular sequence across different cultures. Down's syndrome children develop in a similar but slower fashion to normal children in their language acquisition. Deaf children, as Pettito (1988) and others are examining, seem able to keep pace with hearing children if they have the opportunity to learn signing as a 'language' from their parents, and they use sign babbling, pointing and first words at the normal time for their development.

Although there are wide variations in the patterns and speed of language acquisition, in general, the fact that language capacities in children follow a regular sequence means that speech delays can be 'early and subtle pointers' to a child's atypical development.

In our Closer Look box, we refer you briefly to some of the studies of how blind babies develop language and motor skills, studies which are both useful for those of you who will work with children with disabilities, but also give us insights into the processes involved in typical development.

Reflect

Perhaps you have been wondering why these theories are important for professionals to know about. Take a few moments to consider situations in working with children where these ideas might be relevant. Here are some suggestions to start you off:

■ *Children seeing themselves as responsible for parental breakup, or blaming themselves for a parent or sibling going into hospital.*

■ *Assessing developmental delays.*

■ *Anticipating how to explain to a small child that s/he is going to a new family.*

Can you think of any other examples?

Social and emotional development

We now consider the social and emotional development of infants and young children and the emergence of infants' attachment relationships with their caregivers, usually their parents. (The term 'caregiver' rather than 'parent' is used to make it clear that the attachment relationship is not necessarily formed with the birth parent, although of course it frequently is.) The development of secure relationships with caregivers is a vital aspect of children's development. It is also now recognised as laying the foundations for the capacity for the individual to participate in cooperative, reciprocal, meaningful and intimate adult relationships later in life.

Think ahead

The word 'attachment' when used by social workers and developmental psychologists and other professionals has very precise meanings. Before we look at what these are, spend a few moments thinking about what they mean when they use this term.

Possibly you concluded that the word 'attachment' means something about the relationships people form with important people in their lives. As you read on, though, you will learn that the term is rather more specific and precise than this. The essence of attachment is captured by the phrase 'the tie that binds' or 'affectional bonds', to use Bowlby's description. A useful working (although, as we shall see, incomplete) definition is provided by Aldgate: 'Attachment is a protective mechanism which enables young children to explore their environment knowing that they can return to the safety of significant adults' (1993: 13).

These infant–caregiver relationships are the culmination of all cognitive, social and emotional development in the first months of life. We have already seen that infants from birth have perceptual and proto-language capacities; these tie in with the emotional life of the infant in promoting social interactions with carers in particular. In the second six months of life, infants acquire specific attachments to caregivers. These close relationships evolve over the first year of life and continue to develop during early childhood and beyond.

Anyone who looks after young children cannot fail to notice their protest and distress at being separated from the adults they know. A small child's protest at being

A closer look

Development in children who are born blind

In an early study of these children, Selma Fraiberg, a psychologist who worked closely with and studied the development of blind children concludes:

'We were able to facilitate the blind infant's development in every sphere of development, but the impediment of blindness could be discerned at every point . . . at which representational intelligence would

lead the sighted child into the organisation of an object world . . . We facilitated locomotion but we could still discern the impediment to locomotion, the absence of the distant lure usually provided by vision, the "reach for something out there". We saw that blindness was not a major impediment to the acquisition of language when we were able to maximize . . . [the] language environment. But the impediment . . . revealed itself most cruelly in the protracted delay in the constitution of a stable concept of "I".'

(Fraiberg, 1977: 282–3)

separated from their carer is the best evidence you can get that they have an attachment relationship with that person. Becoming an attachment figure for a child is the result of direct and sustained physical and emotional care for the child. This relationship is known as the 'attachment relationship', the key part of attachment theory which was first most fully expounded by John Bowlby and which is currently for a variety of reasons highly influential.

As we have seen in our first section, other theorists such as Eric Erikson also considered the social and emotional development of infants and young children, and his ideas about the progressive achieving of developmental tasks are ones which you may find fruitful to consider alongside our discussion of attachment theory. Erikson also stresses the importance of parental responses which are responsive to the child's need for trust (his 'task' for this stage) and 'firmly reassuring' to their children's striving for autonomy. So his framework is compatible with attachment theory.

Attachment is defined as an emotional tie which children develop with a preferred adult (usually a parent who has main responsibility for looking after them) which endures over time, whether or not the caregiver is present. It is distinguished from attachment *behaviour*, which is the outward manifestation of this tie, defined by Bowlby (1979) as 'seeking and maintaining proximity to another individual'. It has special emotional qualities, which are evident not only in the infant's distress at being separated from the caregiver, and joy when reunited, but also in the security which the infant seems to experience just from being in the caregiver's presence. By age 12 months, infants want to be picked up specifically by the caregiver, they seek her or him out when distressed, and are happier exploring new surroundings if the caregiver is nearby. Attachment behaviour is less obvious in the older child, when attachment is felt to be secure. The need for attachment remains throughout life, but although attachment behaviour continues to be heightened during crises, it continues normally at low levels during adulthood (see section on adult development).

Although the exact way attachment happens varies, the basic process is the same across diverse cultures in all parts of the world. One sign that attachment is emerging is separation protest. At about the same time that infants show negative reactions to strangers, they also cry (protest) when their caregivers temporarily leave them. These reactions are seen by the end of the first year in all cultures which have been studied, although they may appear a little earlier in cultures where carers (usually but not always mothers) remain in close physical contact with their infants. Greeting reactions also emerge at about the same time. A further significant mark of attachment is secure-base behaviour: at 12 months old, children explore more confidently when the caregiver is present, monitor accessibility (checking that the caregiver is within reach) and retreat to their safe base – that is, the attachment figure – when threatened.

The purpose of the small child's protest is to ensure that the attachment figure stays in close physical and emotional contact with the child when the child feels anxious or under threat. Small children do not have the physical or emotional resources to protect themselves or meet their needs. Attachment relationships therefore have a primary objective of ensuring the child's survival.

If the observable physical evidence of attachment behaviour is closeness to the attachment figure, the felt experience for the child is security, comfort and emotional warmth. The physical care of and interaction with the child is the most observable aspect of the attachment process, but the psychological processes are crucial and they are now known to have a direct impact on the developing brain. Attachment experiences can be thought of as core learning about the nature of relationships. From the myriad experiences of being cared for, the child builds up a sense of what an attachment relationship involves, which is called in the theory an *internal working model*, but is very similar to Piaget's ideas of basic scaffolding or schemas.

Some aspects of this are largely unconscious and are very resistant to change (we give you an illustration of this resistance in the case study of Katie at the end of this section on attachment). This may in part explain a commonly observed occurrence of individuals as adults repeatedly seeking out and making damaging partnerships. As you read further you will see that there is ample evidence for the long-term impact of these early emotional experiences (e.g. Helfer, 1990; Hobbes, Hanks and Wynne, 1993).

However, numerous studies have failed to demonstrate a critical need for immediate contact between caregivers (usually parents) and the newborn infant. And since attachment is the product of repeated interactions with a caregiver, it does not have to be the biological parent to whom a baby becomes attached (as the largely successful outcomes for babies adopted as infants attest to). Infants will often form attachments to more than one caregiver; it seems likely that they develop hierarchies of attachments; and if someone other than the biological mother (or indeed father) is the principal caregiver in terms of both time and emotional commitment, then that person is likely to become the child's main attachment figure.

Patterns of attachment

Much of what is discussed is readily observable in any family with small children. However, it has also become apparent that the quality of the attachment relationship may vary. A method of measuring early attachment relationships in a controlled setting, developed by Mary Ainsworth (an American who spent some time working with John Bowlby at the Tavistock Clinic in London in the 1940s), has helped to classify different patterns of attachment (Ainsworth et al., 1978). The method, which evolved originally from Ainsworth's observations of mothers and children in their home setting in Uganda, involves exposing a small child to a number of 3-minute episodes of separation from an attachment figure (see the Closer Look box). Observations are then recorded of the child's response to the separation and reunion, and the interaction with a stranger who comes into the room. If the pattern described below was observed in the laboratory setting, this would be the basis for what is termed a 'secure' pattern of attachment:

- Protest and distress at separation from the caregiver/attachment figure, leading to;
- Seeking out the attachment figure on reunion, leading to;

- Direct and appropriate levels of comfort and reassurance from the attachment figure, which has the effect of;
- Comforting the child so that they can;
- Resume playing with the toys in the room.

However, observation with some children and their attachment figures indicates a pattern which does not conform to this. Different responses may be observed in any of the five sequences described above, although behaviour at the second reunion is usually seen to be the most significant:

- The child may not protest or show distress.
- The child may show highly contradictory kinds of behaviour, both distress and turning away.
- The child may not seek out the attachment figure on reunion or may actively turn away from them.
- The caregiver may not comfort or reassure the child.
- The child may not be comforted.
- The child may not resume playing with toys.

Careful observation and analysis of these sequences across large numbers of children have enabled researchers to classify patterns of attachment relationships. The research evidence suggests also that the distribution will be similar across any given population (the percentages are given in brackets in the relevant Closer Look box).

A closer look

Ainsworth's Strange Situation Test

Purpose of 'test'

- Activate the child's attachment system via separation from caregiver
- Activate the exploration system via unfamiliar playroom

Observation of the child's strategy upon reunion suggests the following proportions showing different attachment styles:

- Secure (65 per cent)
- Avoidant (20 per cent)
- Resistant/Ambivalent (10 per cent)
- Disorganised (5–10 per cent in non-clinical populations *but* up to 80 per cent of maltreated infants)

The Test

(Unfamiliar room with toys)
- Infant and mother enter room
- Infant put down and left to play, mother present (1 minute)
- Stranger enters
- Mother leaves room, stranger stays (3 minutes)
- Mother returns, stranger leaves (3 minutes)
- Mother leaves child alone (3 minutes)
- Stranger enters (3 minutes)
- Mother returns (3 minutes)

Findings: when the caregiver returns, there are marked individual differences in infant response to reunion.

The *secure-pattern B* child explores freely when the caregiver is present, using caregiver as secure base. The child may be distressed at separation. She/He greets caregiver on reunion, accepts comforting and settles to play. The child's behaviour and emotions are organised to communicate the need for comfort and reassurance because she/he has experienced secure caregiving and expects the caregiver to act responsively and sensitively.

Three other patterns, considered to be different manifestations of insecure attachment, have also been discerned. We give all four patterns here together with brief behavioural descriptions.

- **Insecure-avoidant attachment** – Group A
  Infants actively ignore and avoid parent, turning or moving away
- **Secure attachment** – Group B
  Infants may be distressed at separation, greet and accept comforting on reunion, settle to play
- **Insecure-ambivalent attachment** – Group C
  Infants show anger and resistance: a desire for proximity, and inability to be comforted
- **Insecure-disorganised/disoriented attachment** – Group D
  Infants show 'dazed' behaviour on reunion with parent; stoppage of movement and postures suggestive of depression, confusion, fear; strong avoidance following strong proximity seeking; attachment behaviours in confused sequence; undirected expressions of affection.

To associate these patterns with normal or abnormal development is unhelpful. Instead, think of them as children adapting to the relationship with their attachment figure and the circumstances they are in. Their behaviours are organised to get the best out of their attachment figure, given the circumstances. However, the best predictor of whether or not a child will be securely attached is the behaviour, responsiveness and sensitivity (sometimes called 'attunement') of the caregiver. Observation of caregivers with their children, particularly at times when they are tired or distressed, can be helpful to you in assessing the quality of the attachment relationship. (Schofield and Beek, 2006, social work academic and practitioner respectively, explore this helpfully in Chapter One of their attachment handbook for adopters and foster carers.)

Caregiver and child interactions

Child	Caregiver responses
Secure	Caregiver remains accessible and available to child, tunes in to child's needs and expressions of feelings, responds to child's vocalisations, usually holds and cuddles child as part of normal interaction, follows child's lead rather than intruding, say, in play
Avoidant	Caregiver finds it difficult to respond to child, and rebuffs or appears indifferent. More controlling than cooperative in interaction
Ambivalent	Caregiver is inconsistent, insensitive and tends to fail to respond accurately to child
Disorganised	Caregiver shows little or no sensitivity to child's needs, is rejecting, unpredictable and frightening or frightened, representing themselves as hostile or helpless in protecting the child

Fahlberg's *A Child's Journey through Placement* also provides a helpful checklist for assessing attachment which you may want to look at. We reproduce below one of the two models which she developed, the 'arousal and relaxation' cycle, which shows in detail how caregiver responses to their children's arousal may work to help the child 'settle'. Again, understanding these detailed interactions can be helpful to you in your practice with families and children and can be usefully adapted to working with caregivers and helping them to develop sensitivity and responsiveness to their children's needs.

Reflect

Imagine you hear a social work colleague say of an 8-year-old child who is being taken to a different foster home after a number of moves: 'She's so good about it all. She never complains. I think she's progressing really well because she used to scream and yell.'

In the light of what you have been learning about attachment theory, what might you want to point out to your colleague?

Because it is grounded in actual observed behaviours and the immediacy of lived experiences and relationships, attachment theory also provides a useful framework for helping children and their carers with problems of attachment. In the following example, the social worker working with Katie and her foster carers might have suggested a number of different strategies for helping them to develop a secure pattern of attachment.

Drawing on what you have learnt and read so far, perhaps you concluded that Katie's attachment pattern

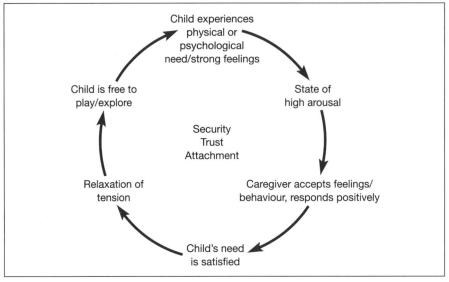

Figure 7.6 Working with problems of attachment: the arousal–relaxation cycle

(*Source*: Adapted from Vera Fahlberg, 1994)

was one of avoidance, and that because she anticipated that her caregivers' behaviour would be rejecting or damaging to her (her internal working model) she adopted this as a defensive strategy, minimising attachment behaviour and affect (feelings) in order not to elicit rejection or physical/emotional harm. Although earlier damaging experiences such as Katie's are hard to integrate, so that a compensatory placement on its own may not be enough – hence the need for therapy – this case shows also that faulty early attachments are not irreversible (although studies would suggest that she may remain vulnerable to rejection/loss and so on).

Case study

Katie

Katie aged 2½ years had been removed from her home at 18 months, following severe abuse, physical and possibly sexual, by her birth parents. She was placed with her current foster carers a year ago. She was referred for therapy when she failed to develop close relationships with her foster carers, despite their sensitive and loving care of her. For example, she refused help in small things such as cutting up food, resisted expressions of affection towards her, and became very still and 'frozen' when her nappy was changed. She was offered eight sessions of play therapy, conducted at her foster carers' home because she was so anxious, and going to an unfamiliar place would have been too stressful for her. Following the sixth session, she awoke her foster carers during the night, and described some of her birth parents' abusive treatment of her. After this she became affectionate and settled in her foster home.

If possible answer the following questions with a colleague:

What kind of pattern of attachment was Katie showing towards her foster carers?

How would attachment theory explain the fact that during the first twelve months of her placement, she remained fearful and did not respond to her foster carers' affection towards her despite their sensitive care for her?

From Katie's experiences described here, do you think that difficult early attachment and caregiving experiences can be overcome?

Professional tip

Some suggestions for working with problems of attachment

- Help the carers recognise the arousal/relaxation cycle (see above: Fahlberg, 1991)
- Help them to encourage, accept and respond to intense feelings and/or to
- Accept that behaviours (whether aggressive or unresponsive) may go on for some time
- If appropriate, respond as if to a younger child

- Talk about feelings
- Help create feelings of security at critical times, e.g. bedtime, through consistent routines, pleasurable physical experiences such as bathtimes, familiar stories, etc.
- Help child develop self-awareness, e.g. identify reason for physical discomfort
- Help child develop conscience, acknowledge, accept, address behaviour such as stealing
- Set up manageable short separations
- Initiate positive experiences.

Now, again using the framework of attachment, what advice would you give to Katie's foster parents in order to promote her feelings of security? We have given you some suggestions below.

Reflect

Now we have reached the end of the section, we suggest you take a few moments to ask yourself: Why is attachment theory important for professionals?

Here are some suggestions to start you off:

- *Provides a means (model) of assessing quality of key relationships in child's life*
- *Provides a way of understanding impact of difficult experiences on child's ongoing behaviour*
- *Critical to thinking about placement choices*
- *Provides a framework for guiding interventions to promote child's secure relationships.*

The different stages of development up to the age of 5 are shown by Mary Sheridan (Table 7.2 below).

Before we go on to our next section, we shall summarise the key points for this life stage.

Key points for infancy and early childhood

This phase is highly significant for later development into older childhood and adulthood. Some of the major changes and developments include:

Cognitive development

- Children begin to understand objects and object permanence and gradually distinguish themselves from other people.
- They begin to be able to remember objects (things and people) when they are not present.
- They have a beginning understanding of differences between appearance and reality, and other people's perception of events.
- However, their thinking still differs from those of older children and adults, e.g. in egocentricity, centration, reversibility.

Language development

- Language acquisition is a critical part of development during this period.
- There is a wide range of ages at which language skills begin, and some children may not begin to speak until 18 months to 2 years.
- However, failure to acquire language skills may be an indication of developmental difficulties, or reflect a lack of a stimulating language environment.

Emotional and social development

- Social and emotional development in the first year of life culminates in the formation of attachments between infants and their caregivers.
- The quality of attachment varies, depending on the quality of care received.
- How children relate to their attachment figures is critical for their emotional well-being, how they feel about themselves (self-esteem), how secure they feel and how ready they are to explore the world around them.
- Children develop the ability to play during this period, which is important for the development of emotional, cognitive and social skills.

Table 7.2 The developmental progress of infants and young children

	1 Month	3 Months
Posture and large movements	Lies back with head on one side; arm and leg on same side outstretched, or both arms flexed; knees apart, soles of feet turned inwards. Large jerky movements of limbs, arms more active than legs. At rest, hands closed and thumbs turned in. Fingers and toes fan out during extensor movements of limbs. When cheek touched, turns to same side; when ear gently rubbed, turns head away. When lifted or pulled to sit, head falls loosely backwards. Held sitting, head falls forward, with back in one complete curve. Placed downwards on face, head immediately turns to side; arms and legs flexed under body, buttocks humped up. Held standing on hard surface, presses down feet. Straightens body and often makes reflex 'stepping' movements.	Now prefers to lie on back with head in mid-line. Limbs more pliable, movements smoother and more continuous. Waves arms symmetrically. Hands now loosely open. Brings hands together from side into midline over chest or chin. Kicks vigorously, legs alternating or occasionally together. Held sitting, holds back straight, except in lumbar region, with head erect and steady for several seconds before bobbing forwards. Placed downwards on face, lifts head and upper chest well up in midline, using forearms as support, and often scratching at table surface; legs straight, buttocks flat. Held standing with feet on hard surface, sags at knees.
Vision and fine movements	Turns head and eyes towards light. Stares expressionlessly at brightness of window or blank wall. Follows pencil flash-lamp briefly with eyes at 1 foot. Shuts eyes tightly when pencil light shone directly into them at 1–2 inches. Notices silent dangling toy shaken in line of vision at 6–8 inches and follows its slow movement with eyes from side towards midline on level with face through approximately quarter circle, before head falls back to side. Gazes at mother's nearby face when she feeds or talks to him with increasingly alert facial expression.	Visually very alert, particularly interested in nearby human faces. Moves head deliberately to look around him. Follows adult's movements near cot. Follows dangling toy at 6–10 inches above face through half circle from side to side, and usually also vertically from chest to brow. Watches movements of own hands before face and beginning to clasp and unclasp hands together in finger play. Recognises feeding bottle and makes eager welcoming movements as it approaches his face. Regards still objects within 6 to 10 inches for more than a second or two, but seldom fixates continuously. Converges eyes as dangling toy is moved towards face. Defensive blink shown.
Hearing and speech	Startled by sudden loud noises, stiffens, quivers, blinks, screws eyes up, extends limbs, fans out fingers and toes, and may cry. Movements momentarily 'frozen', when small bell rung gently 3–5 inches from ear for 3–5 seconds, with 5 second pauses: may *come* (eyes towards sound). Stops whimpering to sound of nearby soothing human voice, but not when screaming or feeding. Cries lustily when hungry or uncomfortable. Utters little guttural noises when content. (Note, deaf babies also cry and vocalise in this reflex way, but if very deaf do not usually show startle reflex to sudden noise. Blind babies may also move eyes towards a sound-making toy. *Vision* should always be checked separately.)	Sudden loud noises still distress, provoking blinking, screwing up of eyes, crying and turning away. Definite quietening or smiling to sound of mother's voice before she touches him, but not when screaming. Vocalises freely when spoken to or pleased. Cries when uncomfortable or annoyed. Quietens to tinkle of spoon in cup or to bell rung gently out of sight for 3–5 seconds at 6–12 inches from ear. May turn eyes and head towards sound: brows may wrinkle and eyes dilate. Often licks lips in response to sounds of preparation for feeding. Shows excitement at sound of approaching footsteps, running bath water, voices, etc. (Note, deaf baby, instead, may be obviously startled by mother's sudden appearance beside cot.)

Table 7.2 (*continued*)

	1 Month	3 Months
Social behaviour and play	Sucks well. Sleeps much of the time when not being fed or handled. Expression still vague, but becoming more alert, progressing to social smiling about 5–6 weeks. Hands normally closed, but if opened, grasps examiner's finger when palm is touched. Stops crying when picked up and spoken to. Mother supports head when carrying, dressing and bathing.	Fixes eyes unblinkingly on mother's face when feeding. Beginning to react to familiar situations – showing by smiles, coos, and excited movements that he recognises preparation for feeds, baths, etc. Responds with obvious pleasure to friendly handling, especially when accompanied by playful tickling and vocal sounds. Holds rattle for few moments when placed in hand, but seldom capable of regarding it at same time. Mother supports at shoulders when dressing and bathing.

	6 Months	9 Months
Posture and large movements	Lying on back, raises head from pillow. Lifts legs into vertical and grasps foot. Sits with support in cot or pram and turns head from side to side to look around him. Moves arms in brisk and purposeful fashion and holds them up to be lifted. When hands grasped, braces shoulders and pulls himself up. Kicks strongly, legs alternating. Can roll over, front to back. Held sitting, head is firmly erect, and back straight. May sit alone momentarily. Placed downwards on face, lifts head and chest well up, supporting himself on extended arms. Held standing with feet touching hard surface, bears weight on feet and bounces up and down actively.	Sits alone for 10–15 minutes on floor. Can turn body to look sideways while stretching out to grasp dangling toy or to pick up toy from floor. Arms and legs very active in cot, pram and bath. Progresses on floor by rolling or squirming. Attempts to crawl on all fours. Pulls self to stand with support. Can stand holding on to support for a few moments, but cannot lower himself. Held standing, steps purposefully on alternate feet.
Vision and fine movements	Visually insatiable: moves head and eyes eagerly in every direction. Eyes move in unison: squint now abnormal. Follows adult's movements across room. Immediately fixates interesting small objects within 6–12 inches (e.g. toy, bell, wooden cube, spoon, sweet) and stretches out both hands to grasp them. Uses whole hand in palm grasp. When toys fall from hand over edge of cot, forgets them. (Watches rolling balls of 2 to ¼ inch diameter at 10 feet.)	Very observant. Stretches out, one hand leading, to grasp small objects immediately on catching sight of them. Manipulates objects with lively interest, passing from hand to hand, turning over, etc. Pokes at small sweet with index finger. Grasps sweets, string, etc., between finger and thumb in scissor fashion. Can release toy by pressing against firm surface, but cannot yet put down precisely. Searches in correct place for toys dropped within reach of hands. Looks after toys falling over edge of pram or table. Watches activities of adults, children and animals within 10 to 12 feet with eager interest for several seconds at a time. (Watches rolling balls 2–5 inches at 10 feet.)

Table 7.2 (*continued*)

	6 Months	9 Months
Hearing and speech	Turns immediately to mother's voice across room. Vocalises tunefully and often, using single and double syllables, e.g. ka, muh, goo, der, adah, er-lah. Laughs, chuckles and squeals aloud in play. Screams with annoyance. Shows evidence of response to different emotional tones of mother's voice. Responds to baby hearing tests at 1½ feet from each ear by correct visual localisation, but may show slightly brisker response on one side. (Tests employed – voice, rattle, cup and spoons, paper, bell; 2 seconds with 2-seconds pause.)	Vocalises deliberately as means of interpersonal communication. Shouts to attract attention, listens, then shouts again. Babbles tunefully, repeating syllables in long strings (mam-mam, bab-bab, dad-ad, etc.). Understands 'No-No' and 'Bye-Bye'. Tries to imitate adults' playful vocal sounds, e.g. smacking lips, cough, brr, etc. (Immediate localising response to baby hearing tests at 3 feet from ear and above and below ear level.)
Social behaviour and play	Hands competent to reach for and grasp small toys. Most often uses a two-handed, scooping-in approach, but occasionally a single hand. Takes everything to mouth. Beginning to find feet interesting and even useful in grasping. Puts hands to bottle and pats it when feeding. Shakes rattle deliberately to make it sound, often regarding it closely at same time. Still friendly with strangers but occasionally shows some shyness or even slight anxiety, especially if mother is out of sight.	Holds, bites and chews biscuits. Puts hands round bottle or cup when feeding. Tries to grasp spoon when being fed. Throws body back and stiffens in annoyance or resistance. Clearly distinguishes strangers from familiars, and requires reassurance before accepting their advances. Clings to known adult and hides face. Still takes everything to mouth. Seizes bell in one hand. Imitates ringing action, waving or banging it on table, pokes, dapper or 'drinks' from bowl. Plays peek-a-boo. Holds out toy held in hand to adult, but cannot yet give. Finds partially hidden toy. May find toy hidden under cup. Mother supports at lower spine when dressing.
	1 Year	**15 Months**
Posture and large movements	Sits well and for indefinite time. Can rise to sitting position from lying down. Crawls rapidly, usually on all fours. Pulls to standing and lets himself down again holding on to furniture. Walks round furniture, stepping sideways. Walks with one or both hands held. May stand alone for a few moments. May walk alone.	Walks unevenly with feet wide apart, arms slightly flexed and held above head or at shoulder level to balance. Starts alone, but frequently stopped by falling or bumping into furniture. Lets himself down from standing to sitting by collapsing backwards with bump, or occasionally by falling forward on hands and then back to sitting. Can get to feet alone. Crawls upstairs. Kneels unaided or with slight support on floor and in pram, cot and bath. May be able to stoop to pick up toys from floor.

Table 7.2 (*continued*)

	1 Year	15 Months
Vision and fine movements	Picks up small objects. e.g. blocks, string, sweets and crumbs, with precise pincer grasp of thumb and index finger. Throws toys deliberately and watches them fall to ground. Looks in correct place for toys which roll out of sight. Points with index finger at objects he wants to handle or which interest him. Watches small toy pulled along floor across room 10 feet away. Out of doors, watches movements of people, animals, motor cars, etc., with prolonged intent regard. Recognises familiars approaching from 20 feet or more away. Uses both hands freely, but may show preference for one. Clicks two bricks together in imitation. (Watches rolling balls 2–5 inches at 10 feet.)	Picks up string, small sweets and crumbs neatly between thumb and finger. Builds tower of two cubes after demonstration. Grasps crayon and imitates scribble after demonstration. Looks with interest at pictures in book and pats page. Follows with eyes, path of cube or small toy swept vigorously from table. Watches small toy pulled across floor up to 12 feet. Points imperiously to objects he wishes to be given. Stands at window and watches events outside intently for several minutes. (Watches and retrieves rolling balls of 2$^1/_8$ inches at 10 feet.)
Hearing and speech	Knows and immediately turns to own name. Babbles loudly, tunefully and incessantly. Shows by suitable movements and behaviour that he understands several words in usual context (e.g. own and family names, walk, dinner, pussy, cup, spoon, ball, car). Comprehends simple commands associated with gesture (give it to daddy, come to mummy, say bye-bye, clap hands, etc.). Imitates adults' playful vocalisations with gleeful enthusiasm. May hand-examine common objects on request, e.g. spoon, cup, ball, shoe. (Immediate response to baby tests at 3–4$^1/_2$ feet but rapidly habituates.)	Jabbers loudly and freely, using wide range of inflections and phonetic units. Speaks 2–6 recognisable words and understands many more. Vocalises wishes and needs at table. Points to familiar persons, animals, toys, etc. when requested. Understands and obeys simple commands (e.g. shut the door, give me the ball, get your shoes). (Baby test 4$^1/_2$–6 feet.)
Social behaviour and play	Drinks from cup with little assistance. Chews. Holds spoon but usually cannot use it alone. Helps with dressing by holding out arm for sleeve and foot for shoe. Takes objects to mouth less often. Puts wooden cubes in and out of cup or box. Rattles spoon in cup in imitation. Seizes bell by handle and rings briskly in imitation, etc. Listens with obvious pleasure to percussion sounds. Repeats activities to reproduce effects. Gives toys to adult on request and sometimes spontaneously. Finds hidden toy quickly. Likes to be constantly within sight and hearing of adult. Demonstrates affection to familiars. Waves 'bye-bye' and claps hands in imitation or spontaneously. Child sits, or sometimes stands without support, while mother dresses.	Holds cup when adult gives and takes back. Holds spoon, brings it to mouth and licks it, but cannot prevent its turning over. Chews well. Helps more constructively with dressing. Indicates when he has wet pants. Pushes large wheeled toy with handle on level ground. Seldom takes toy to mouth. Repeatedly casts objects to floor in play or rejection, usually without watching fall. Physically restless and intensely curious. Handles everything within reach. Emotionally labile. Closely dependent upon adult's reassuring presence. Needs constant supervision to protect child from dangers of extended exploration and exploitation of environment.

Table 7.2 (*continued*)

	18 Months	2 Years
Posture and large movements	Walks well with feet only slightly apart, starts and stops safely. Runs stiffly upright, eyes fixed on ground 1–2 yards ahead, but cannot continue to run round obstacles. Pushes and pulls large toys, boxes, etc., round floor. Can carry large doll or teddy-bear while walking and sometimes two. Backs into small chair or slides in sideways. Climbs forward into adult's chair then turns round and sits. Walks upstairs with helping hand. Creeps backwards downstairs. Occasionally bumps down a few steps on buttocks facing forwards. Picks up toy from floor without falling.	Runs safely on whole foot, stopping and starting with ease and avoiding obstacles. Squats to rest or to play with object on ground and rises to feet without using hands. Walks backwards pulling large toy. Pulls wheeled toy by cord. Climbs on furniture to look out of window or open doors, etc., and can get down again. Walks upstairs and down holding on to rail and wall, two feet to a step. Throws small ball without falling. Walks into large ball when trying to kick it. Sits astride large wheeled toy and propels forward with feet on ground.
Vision and fine movements	Picks up small sweets, beads, pins, threads, etc. immediately on sight, with delicate pincer grasp. Spontaneous scribble when given crayon and paper, using preferred hand. Builds tower of three cubes after demonstration. Enjoys simple picture book, often recognising and putting finger on coloured items on page. Turns pages 2 or 3 at a time. Fixes eyes on small dangling toy up to 10 feet. (May tolerate this test with each eye separately.) Points to distant interesting objects out of doors. (Watches and retrieves rolling balls 2⅛ inches at 10 feet.) (Possibly recognises special miniature toys at 10 feet.)	Picks up pins and thread, etc., neatly and quickly. Removes paper wrapping from small sweet. Builds tower of six cubes (or 6+). Spontaneous circular scribble and dots when given paper and pencil. Imitates vertical line (and sometimes V). Enjoys picture books, recognising fine details in favourite pictures. Tums pages singly. Recognises familiar adults in photograph after once shown. Hand preference becoming evident. (Immediately catches sight of and names special miniature toys at 10 feet distance. Will now usually tolerate this test with each eye separately.) (Watches and retrieves rolling balls 2⅛ inches at 10 feet.)
Hearing and speech	Continues to jabber tunefully to himself at play. Uses 6–20 recognisable words and understands many more. Echoes prominent or last word addressed to him. Demands desired objects by pointing, accompanied by loud, urgent vocalisation or single words. Enjoys nursery rhymes and tries to join in. Attempts to sing. Shows his own or doll's hair, shoe, nose. (Possibly special 5 toy test. Possibly 4 animals picture test.)	Uses 50 or more recognisable words and understands many more. Puts 2 or more words together to form simple sentences. Refers to himself by name. Talks to himself continually as he plays. Echolalia almost constant, with one or more stressed words repeated. Constantly asking names of objects. Joins in nursery rhymes and songs. Shows correctly and repeats words for hair, hand, feet, nose, eyes, mouth, shoe, on request. (6 toy test, 4 animals picture test.)

Table 7.2 (*continued*)

	18 Months	2 Years
Social behaviour and play	Lifts and holds cup between both hands. Drinks without spilling. Hands cup back to adult. Chews well. Holds spoon and gets food to mouth. Takes off shoes, socks, hat. Indicates toilet needs by restlessness and vocalisation. Bowel control usually attained. Explores environment energetically. No longer takes toys to mouth. Remembers where objects belong. Casts objects to floor in play or anger less often. Briefly imitates simple activities, e.g. reading book, kissing doll, brushing floor. Plays contentedly alone, but likes to be near adult. Emotionally still very dependent upon familiar adult, especially mother. Alternates between clinging and resistance.	Lifts and drinks from cup and replaces on table. Spoon-feeds without spilling. Asks for food and drink. Chews competently. Puts on hat and shoes. Verbalises toilet needs in reasonable time. Dry during day. Turns door handles. Often runs outside to explore. Follows mother round house and copies domestic activities in simultaneous play. Engages in simple make-believe activities. Constantly demanding mother's attention. Clings tightly in affection, fatigue or fear. Tantrums when frustrated but attention readily distracted. Defends own possessions with determination. As yet no idea of sharing. Plays near other children but not with them. Resentful of attention shown to other children.
	2½ Years	**3 Years**
Posture and large movements	Walks upstairs alone but downstairs holding rail, two feet to a step. Runs well straight forward and climbs easy nursery apparatus. Pushes and pulls large toys skilfully, but has difficulty in steering them round obstacles. Jumps with two feet together. Can stand on tiptoe if shown. Kicks large ball. Sits on tricycle and steers with hands, but still usually propels with feet on ground.	Walks alone upstairs with alternating feet and downstairs with two feet to step. Usually jumps from bottom step. Climbs nursery apparatus with agility. Can turn round obstacles and corners while running and also while pushing and pulling large toys. Rides tricycle and can turn wide corners on it. Can walk on tiptoe. Stands momentarily on one foot when shown. Sits with feet crossed at ankles.
Vision and fine movements	Picks up pins, threads, etc., with each eye covered separately. Builds tower of seven (or 7+) cubes and lines blocks to form 'train'. Recognises minute details in picture books. Imitates horizontal line and circle (also usually T and V). Paints strokes, dots and circular shapes on easel. Recognises himself in photographs when once shown. Recognises miniature toys and retrieves balls 2⅛ inches at 10 feet, each eye separately. (May also match special single letter-cards V, O, T, H at 10 feet.)	Picks up pins, threads, etc., with each eye covered separately. Builds tower of nine cubes, also (3½) bridge of three from model. Can close fist and wiggle thumb in imitation. R and L. Copies circle (also V, H, T). Imitates cross. Draws man with head and usually indication of features or one other part. Matches two or three primary colours (usually red and yellow correct, but may confuse blue and green). Paints 'pictures' with large brush on easel. Cuts with scissors. (Recognises special miniature toys at 10 feet. Performs single-letter vision test at 10 feet. Five letters.)

Table 7.2 (*continued*)

	2½ Years	**3 Years**
Hearing and speech	Uses 200 or more recognisable words but speech shows numerous infantilisms. Knows full name. Talks intelligibly to himself at play concerning events happening here and now. Echolalia persists. Continually asking questions beginning 'What?', 'Where?'. Uses pronouns, I, me and you. Stuttering in eagerness common. Says a few nursery rhymes. Enjoys simple familiar stories read from picture book. (6 toy test, 4 animals picture test, 1st cube test. Full doll vocabulary.)	Large intelligible vocabulary but speech still shows many infantile phonetic substitutions. Gives full name and sex, and (sometimes) age. Uses plurals and pronouns. Still talks to himself in long monologues mostly concerned with the immediate present, including make-believe activities. Carries on simple conversations, and verbalises past experiences. Asks many questions beginning 'What?' 'Where?' 'Who?' Listens eagerly to stories and demands favourites over and over again. Knows several nursery rhymes. (7 toy test, 4 animals picture test. 1st or 2nd cube test, 6 'high frequency' word pictures.)
Social behaviour and play	Eats skilfully with spoon and may use fork. Pulls down pants or knickers at toilet, but seldom able to replace. Dry through night if lifted. Very active, restless and rebellious. Throws violent tantrums and when thwarted or unable to express urgent needs and less easily distracted. Emotionally still very dependent upon adults. Prolonged domestic make-believe play (putting dolls to bed, washing clothes, driving motor cars, etc.) but with frequent reference to friendly adult. Watches other children at play interestedly and occasionally joins in for a few minutes, but little notion of sharing playthings or adult's attention.	Eats with fork and spoon. Washes hands, but needs supervision in drying. Can pull pants and knickers down and up, but needs help with buttons. Dry through night. General behaviour more amenable. Affectionate and confiding. Likes to help with adult's activities in house and garden. Makes effort to keep his surroundings tidy. Vividly realised make-believe play including invented people and objects. Enjoys floor play with bricks, boxes, toy trains and cars, alone or with siblings. Joins in play with other children in and outdoors. Understands sharing playthings, sweets, etc. Shows affection for younger siblings. Shows some appreciation of past and present.
	4 Years	**5 Years**
Posture and large movements	Turns sharp corners running, pushing and pulling. Walks alone up and downstairs, one foot per step. Climbs ladders and trees. Can run on tiptoe. Expert rider of tricycle. Hops on one foot. Stands on one foot 3–5 seconds. Arranges or picks up objects from floor by bending from waist with knees extended.	Runs lightly on toes. Active and skilful in climbing, sliding, swinging, digging and various 'stunts'. Skips on alternative feet. Dances to music. Can stand on one foot 8–10 seconds. Can hop 2–3 yards forwards on each foot separately. Grips strongly with either hand.

Table 7.2 (*continued*)

	4 Years	5 Years
Vision and fine movements	Picks up pins, thread, crumbs, etc., with each eye covered separately. Builds tower of 10 or more cubes and several 'bridges' of three on request. Builds three steps with six cubes after demonstration. Imitates spreading of hand and bringing thumb into opposition with each finger in turn. R and L. Copies cross (also V, H, T and O). Draws man with head, legs, features, trunk and (often) arms. Draws very simple house. Matches and names four primary colours correctly. (Single-letter vision test at 10 feet, seven letters: also near chart to bottom).	Picks up minute objects when each eye is covered separately. Builds three steps with six cubes from model. Copies square and triangle (also letters: V, T, H, O, X, L, A, C, U, Y). Writes a few letters spontaneously. Draws recognisable man with head, trunk, legs arms and features. Draws simple house with door, windows, roof and chimney. Counts fingers on one hand with index finger of other. Names four primary colours and matches 10 or 12 colours. (Full nine-letter vision chart at 20 feet and near test to bottom.)
Hearing and speech	Speech completely intelligible. Shows only a few infantile substitutions usually k/t/th/f/s and r/l/w/y groups). Gives connected account of recent events and experiences. Gives name, sex, home address and (usually) age. Eternally asking questions 'Why?' 'When?' 'How?' and meanings of words. Listens to and tells long stories sometimes confusing fact and fantasy. (7 toy test, 1st picture vocabulary test, 2nd cube test; 6 'high frequency' word pictures.)	Speech fluent and grammatical. Articulation correct except for residual confusions of s/f/th and r/l/w/y groups. Loves stories and acts them out in detail later. Gives full name, age and home address. Gives age and (usually) birthday. Defines concrete nouns by use. Asks meaning of abstract words. (12 'high frequency' picture vocabulary or word lists; 3rd cube test, 6 sentences.)
Social behaviour and play	Eats skilfully with spoon and fork. Washes and dries hands. Brushes teeth. Can undress and dress except for back buttons, laces and ties. General behaviour markedly self-willed. Inclined to verbal impertinence when wishes crossed but can be affectionate and compliant. Strongly dramatic play and dressing-up favoured. Constructive out-of-doors building with any large material to hand. Needs other children to play with and is alternately cooperative and aggressive with them as with adults. Understands taking turns. Shows concern for younger siblings and sympathy for playmates in distress. Appreciates past, present and future.	Uses knife and fork. Washes and dries face and hands, but needs help and supervision for rest. Undresses and dresses alone. General behaviour more sensible, controlled and responsibly independent. Domestic and dramatic play continued from day to day. Plans and builds constructively. Floor games very complicated. Chooses own friends. Cooperative with companions and understands need for rules and fair play. Appreciates meaning of clocktime in relation to daily programme. Tender and protective towards younger children and pets. Comforts playmates in distress.

(*Source*: Adapted from Sheridan's Charts from *Reports on Public Health and Medical Subjects* No. 102. HMSO 1960, revised 1975.)

Middle childhood

(*Source*: Alamy Images/Janine Wiedel)

In this section, we move on to considering children's development in middle childhood, usually defined as the period between roughly 7 and 12 years old. As we have done in the previous section, we shall explore psychosocial theories which describe cognitive and emotional development, and we shall also look at children's physical growth over this period.

This tends to be a period of relative stability, and perhaps for this reason, there is a noticeable change in the amount of psychological knowledge available to us about middle childhood. It has been argued, for example, by Helen Bee (an American developmental psychologist, in one of two useful texts which she has written about development), that this period of development is under-researched because no dramatic changes normally occur. As she points out, even Freud referred to this as the 'latency' period, 'as if development had gone underground' (Bee, 1994: 207). Physical growth and development, so markedly rapid during infancy and young childhood, are less noticeable, and the noticeable physical and emotional changes of puberty and adolescence are still to come. However, important changes do occur during these years, as we shall see.

As one useful book about social work with children suggests, too, this can be both a challenging and a rewarding age group for social workers to engage with. It can be challenging because children may be more cautious about revealing their thoughts and fears to adults whom they do not know, and gauging children's level of understanding and language

abilities at this age takes skill, too. In addition it is said that:

'It can often be the case that children in this age group who have been struggling to make sense of difficult experiences, perhaps of separation and loss or of maltreatment, are very much in need of someone to help them . . . we also know that children whose parents have mental health problems or learning difficulties may have taken on a great deal of responsibility for their parents even during their primary school years and may not have had their concerns listened to.'   (Brandon, Schofield, and Trinder, 1998: 51)

With these thoughts in mind, as in the previous section, we summarise the key tasks before exploring them in more detail. The key tasks for this period include the following:

- achieving increasingly complex physical capabilities and coordination;
- developing a sense of self in relation to the outside world;
- learning to get on with other children and making friends;
- establishing literacy and numeracy skills;
- establishing social skills such as turn-taking and delayed gratification.

Physical development

Children grow steadily during this period, with gross and fine motor skills continuing to develop (see the Sheridan chart, Table 7.2). The growth patterns of the pre-school years continue: most significant motor skills are developed by about the age of 6 or 7, so that what is now being developed is increasing speed, better coordination and greater skill at specific physical tasks. Boys and girls are very similar at this stage in strength and speed, although girls are still slightly ahead of boys in their rate of maturation. However, researchers (and others, including perhaps you!) have also observed differences in physical levels of activity between boys and girls, with boys tending to play more boisterous games while girls form smaller more intimate groups (e.g. Macoby, 1990). It seems likely that many of these differences are culturally determined (i.e. arising from what is generally expected in the wider society – 'boys will be boys', for example).

What also begins during this period is the set of changes which eventually lead to puberty. There is some evidence that these are occurring at earlier ages in affluent Western societies, and pubertal hormonal changes may begin as early as 8 for girls (slightly later for boys). Early onset may lead to some embarrassment, from a sense of being different from peers. (These changes are discussed in more detail in DeHart et al., 2004, for those of you who wish to follow this up in more detail.)

The effects of acute or chronic disease, severe accidents or atypical bodily images developed in childhood (see Bee's discussion of obesity as a major health hazard, 1994: 208) can persist for some children throughout childhood and adolescence, and unless compensated by other achievements, attributes and/or good social relationships, a child can develop a negative self-image, leading again to pervasive feelings of inferiority. Racial and ethnic stereotypes and prejudices will also become more understandable and hurtful, because with a developing cognitive sense of what other people are thinking comes greater awareness by individuals of how they compare physically as well as socially and emotionally to other children.

Cognitive development

As we have seen, Piaget considered that one of the major shifts in children's thinking occurs during the period, and that children by the end of this developmental period will have grasped for themselves (*internalised* is the psychological word for it) and be able to use rules about objects and their relationships to one another. He labelled these processes *operations*, by which he meant that children at this age discover a set of powerful, abstract, general rules or strategies for examining and engaging with the world around them. Children now can grasp the principle of addition, subtraction, reversibility (reversing an action so that the original state is reproduced) and serial ordering (putting things in order of size or some other feature). Of all the operations, Piaget considered the most critical was reversibility: the understanding that both physical actions and mental operations can be reversed. Piaget uses the example of a clay sausage being reshaped into a ball, where a child at this age can usually work out that the quantity of each is the same; similarly they can successfully master the 'puzzle' of water in different shaped glasses which we described in the previous section. He also argued that the 'concrete operations' child is good at dealing with things which s/he knows or can see or manipulate, but does much less well with contemplating ideas or possibilities – what can be called *deductive logic*.

Reflect

Possibly, although you may easily understand how this would be significant information for primary schoolteachers, you are wondering what particular relevance knowledge of this cognitive stage has for you as a social worker. Take a few moments, however, to think through the implications of this 'concreteness' for how you might explain to a child that there is to be a court hearing about her/him, or that s/he is to go to hospital for an operation. You may make the link to some of the suggestions for communicating with children (given in Chapter 11).

Although Piaget considered that children only move on to the next stage of thinking when they are ready, Vygotsy, whose ideas we introduced you to in the first section, took a rather different view of how children develop their thinking, considering that children acquire the means of learning and thinking from their interactions with others around them, usually adults with greater knowledge. In our case study, next, we give an illustration of how these principles might influence your approach to work with children of this age group.

Case study

Anthony and Kayleigh

Anthony aged 6, and Kayleigh age 7 have been in foster care for just over a year, following their parents' severe neglect of them. After one attempt to return them to live with their parents failed, a decision has been made to place them for adoption. Neither child seems concerned about this, and their social worker, Mark, feels that they do not as yet understand what this move to a 'forever' family means, and that their ideas about a family and family relationships are limited by their early experiences. Mark spends time with them building up their trust in him, and then with the foster carers prepare life-story books about their early experiences, and using drawings, pictures, play materials and stories help them begin to understand what a new permanent family involves. (See Chapter 11 on communications and Chapter 16 on working with children and families for illustrations of this 'direct work'.)

As we can see from this, Mark does not assume that the children will be able to conceive of these new experiences by themselves but, as a trusted adult, helps them to build up the necessary frameworks for understanding them.

Children's memory

Another area of relevance to social workers is children's memory skills and information-processing strategies. Although we shall not spend much time on them here, issues of memory development feature in a developing body of research on everyday or autobiographical memory (i.e. memories of personal events). There are some interesting findings about children's memory for earlier events which have been correlated with their parents'. In general, young children's memories are found to be accurate, but are dependent upon environmental triggers more strongly than older children's memories and are less elaborate.

One type of memory, which researchers variously call 'procedural' or 'emotional' or 'behavioural' memories, seems to be the memory of experiences which are inaccessible to verbal recall. They are encoded as memories of behavioural interactive patterns rather than verbally. 'Declarative' memories, as the name implies, are accessible verbally. Both types of memories may run parallel to one another. Research on the enactments and drawings of traumatised children documents this type of procedural memory which seems to be fully functional from early infancy onwards.

Again this body of work has implications for your work as social workers, particularly those of you who are working with traumatised or maltreated children, whose early memories may be inaccessible to conscious, verbal recall. For those of you interested in reading further, Moore's (1994) study of children's drawings shows how the evidence of early traumatic events is visible in their figure drawings, while Terr (1988) and Ryan and Wilson (2000) discuss the emergence of consciously accessible and 'unremembered' earlier traumatic experiences in childhood. Ryan and Wilson explore the way an abused child re-enacted early experiences of physical maltreatment through her drawings and play, drawing for example physical scars, which seemed to derive from early memories of trauma (2000: 100).

Social and emotional development during middle childhood

A growing proportion of Western children will have experienced being away from home in day care or pre-school settings, so the beginning of formal schooling may not constitute the same major transition which it once did. Nonetheless, the beginning of formal education is still a significant change, representing the point where children are expected to develop specific competencies at the same time as learning appropriate social skills with peers. Erikson's theory of identity formation seems a useful way of organising thinking about emotional and cognitive developments in middle childhood. He focuses on this specific aspect of development, seeing a child's major task in middle childhood as the development of a healthy sense of industry (or, as we might now describe it, a basic belief in one's own competence and ability to accomplish tasks successfully) without a preponderance of feelings of inferiority about the self. Children seek approval and gain enjoyment in mastering intellectual and social skills such as reading, writing and the formation of friendships (and, as we have seen, are developing the commensurate cognitive structures for doing so). If children are unable to develop these skills, or become isolated from friendship groups, then they are at risk of developing a sense of inferiority and inadequacy which

---

A closer look

The implications of children's memory capacity for working with children placed away from their birth families

Understanding how children remember has implications for social work with children of this age group, who, for a variety of reasons, may not be brought up in their own families. Such children have a range of early experiences which they do not share with the adults (say, foster carers or adoptive parents) with whom they are now living and which they may not be able to retrieve from memory or understand by themselves. Young children usually need help from adults who have shared in their experiences in order meaningfully to process and retrieve their early memories. This is a normal part of family life which may be a largely unfamiliar experience for this group of children. For these reasons looked-after children and children who are adopted after early childhood need relationships with adults who are able to imagine what these earlier experiences may have been like for them from very little concrete information from the children themselves or their written histories.

can be pervasive and may persist into adolescence and adulthood.

What Erikson describes is part of a broader developmental task at this stage which is the emerging feelings about oneself, one's abilities and feelings of being accepted and valued by others, all of which are consolidated in middle childhood as a coherent self-concept or sense of identity. As well as these new ways of thinking about themselves, middle childhood is also marked by major developments in peer relationships, and a growing understanding of emotions (mirroring the greater cognitive capacity of this age group which we have been discussing above).

The inner world of the self

The more mature way of thinking about oneself, including mental abilities and customary ways of thinking and feeling which emerge during this period, has been described as the *psychological self*. Pre-schoolers tend to think of themselves as concrete entities, and when they describe themselves usually do so in terms of physical activities or traits. 'I'm a big boy. I've got red hair'. In contrast, in middle childhood, children increasingly describe themselves in terms of inner thoughts, feelings, abilities and attributes (for example, children may begin to think of and describe themselves as shy or kind. One 7-year-old told his teacher solemnly, 'I do not like drawing but I am very good with words.').

Alongside this emergence of a child's sense of an inner, multifaceted self is a growing awareness that all people have internal thoughts and feelings which are often hidden from others and sometimes even from themselves. We saw this capacity beginning to develop in younger children and as children progress through this stage it becomes more firmly established. One child, Dan, aged $6\frac{1}{2}$, for example, reported to his mother that his teacher had said to Simon (another boy in the class who was clearly struggling with his reading), ' "You're a good reader, Simon." But she said it in a weary sort of voice.' Dan was clearly aware of some sense of dissonance between his teacher's statement and her inner feelings, although doubtless could not have articulated this.

Another advance is the development of the *social self*: in this the inclination to define the self in terms of relationships with others (e.g. membership of cubs/teams at school) is closely linked to using others as a source of information in evaluating the self – i.e. social comparison. (An example of how this develops is to be found in a study by Ruble, in 1987. He compared the performance of 5- to 10-year-olds on given tasks and found that children of up to 7 to 8 years old did not routinely compare their own performance with others, and that they did not systematically use social comparisons in making self-assessments until age 9 or 10.) Children of course differ in the importance they attach to friendship groups, but for many children the wish to belong and be part of a group is very powerful. Researchers have also shown that popular children are more skilled at reading the intentions and feelings of others, and therefore can adapt and respond more appropriately (Asendorpf, 1993). (We discussed this developing capacity earlier, and in thinking about a 'theory of mind'.) The converse of this seems also to be true: that many children who have been neglected or abused by their families have not been able to develop this capacity, tending to respond inflexibly in social situations, and indeed frequently to misjudge them and perhaps most seriously to read hostility where none was intended.

Reflect

What implications do you think that neglected and rejected children's difficulties in 'reading minds' might have for their ability to get on with their peers, and for you in helping them to do so?

Other aspects of the self-concept which continue to develop are the *sense of gender*, the *sense of personal effectiveness* and *sense of competence*. Susan Harter (1999), for example, discusses the way in which children's beliefs that they can master and prevail in challenging circumstances (or not) develops in middle childhood. They also develop capacities to cope with stress and emotionally challenging situations, tolerate aversive situations, and delay gratification in order to achieve a greater reward later on. As you will be able to see, all these developing capacities (or self-doubts) will contribute to how confident and successful a child feels. Harter identifies six domains which children view as important to their feelings of competence, and suggests that their self-esteem is based on a balance between what they would like to be and what they actually think they are. The domains are as follows:

- Athletic competence
- Physical appearance
- Scholastic competence
- Acceptance by peers
- Behavioural conduct
- General feelings of self-worth.

You may want to consider these in our case studies below. However, at this point, as we assess the factors which make the children you will encounter in your practice vulnerable to, or able to cope better with, adversity, it is helpful to draw on the framework of resilience. This framework has gained currency in recent years, because it seems to offer a way of helping us understand why some children are able to overcome or rise above adverse experiences while others are deeply adversely affected by them. It also provides a positive and hopeful way of reframing difficulties, and is useful in guiding assessments and identifying strategies for helping children cope with stressful experiences.

Defining resilience

Resilience has been defined by Fonagy (who first developed the concept as a psychological idea) as 'Normal development under difficult conditions' (Fonagy et al., 1994). Resilience can be seen to consist of qualities which can cushion a vulnerable child from the worst effects of adversity and may help the child cope, survive and even flourish in the face of great hurt and disadvantages. Emmy Werner, writing in 1990, explored from a review of international research key factors in the child, the family and community which have been found to promote resilience. Some of these qualities, which we reproduce below (cited in Daniel, Wassell and Gilligan, 1999: 64–5, three psychology and social work academics and practitioners), you may have been able to guess at from our earlier discussions. For example, you might judge the capacity to be reflective rather than impulsive to be associated with the ability to make friends, which in turn will influence self-confidence and esteem, and hence the capacity to overcome difficulties. Others, such as gender differences, we have not really touched on but you may wish to follow up in your reading.

In middle childhood, resilient children are:

- Well-liked by peers and adults;
- Reflective rather than impulsive in thinking style;
- Feel that they can influence their environments positively;
- Are able to use flexible coping strategies, including humour;
- Are adept at recruiting surrogate parents, even if not blood relatives;
- Resilient boys are emotionally expressive, socially perceptive and nurturant;
- Resilient girls are autonomous and independent;

- Resilient children display flexible coping strategies which promote mastery over adversity rather than reactions in a rigidly sex-stereotyped manner;
- Overall, girls are generally more resilient to stress and trauma than boys.

The research also suggests that there are factors in the child's family life and in the community (such as schools or youth groups) which are also associated with or can promote resilience. Many of these are in line with what we have already learned about attachments to caregivers: for example, a close stable bond with a caregiver, affectionate ties with alternative caregivers (such as grandparents) and even involvement in sibling caregiving can be protective factors against stressful events.

Daniel, Wassell and Gilligan suggest that these different factors can be presented in diagrammatic form, as we show in Figure 7.7. (The domains identified may also remind you of Bronfenbrenner's ecological perspective from the first section.) These can be a useful way of assessing a child's vulnerability, identifying potential adversity and stress factors, and also importantly harnessing strengths and protective factors.

Think ahead

Take a moment or two to consider the diagram. Now, ideally with a fellow student or colleague, read the following cases, and write down, as in the diagram, the different factors relating to the four domains for each child.

Case study

Neil and Sally

Neil is an 8-year-old white British boy. His parents are planning to divorce and there is considerable acrimony between them. His father, to whom he was close, has now moved out of the home and lives nearby. He has been doing reasonably well at school, and is reported by his teachers to be good at sport and quite popular, but recently has been getting into playground scraps and on several occasions has had to stay after school. Last week he overheard a violent argument between his parents, and went upstairs to his bedroom and refused to come down, and now is refusing to see his father.

Sally is a 9-year-old of mixed race, with a mild learning disability, who lives in a predominantly white neighbourhood and is one of few mixed-race

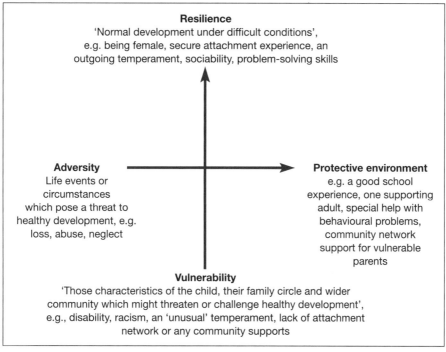

Figure 7.7 Framework for assessing the vulnerability of an individual child, elements of adversity and focusing on supporting resilience and harnessing protective factors

(*Source*: Adapted from Daniel et al., 1999)

or black children in her school. She has a sunny disposition and comes from a large, affectionate family, who together with the extended family are very supportive of the children and want them to do well.

Perhaps in both cases you could identify strengths (for example, Neil is good at sport and seems able to make friends), vulnerabilities (Sally's ethnicity and mild disability may make her vulnerable) and also protective factors in their respective environments (for example, Sally's family may help her with potential learning problems; Neil's relationship with his father has provided him in the past with a warm attachment relationship, and with care may be harnessed in the future).

Now ask yourselves: in the light of what you know about resilience, what interventions would you propose for Neil and his parents, and for Sally and hers?

Contexts of development in middle childhood

One of the key factors which you are likely to have highlighted in the cases of Neil and Sally is the importance of their relationships with their parents, and the way these can provide a buttress against stresses which they experience. You will, we hope, also have reflected at this point on your earlier reading about attachment relationships. In other words, parents (or caregivers and other family members, including siblings) are powerful influences on children's development. At this point, we want to introduce you to ideas about how different styles of parenting are said to be significant in developing resilience and promoting children's sense of well-being and self-efficacy.

Certain parental characteristics have been found by researchers to be closely related to differences in children's behaviour. Thus, parenting which is characterised by warmth, support and a reasoning approach to discipline is consistently associated with positive child characteristics such as:

■ cooperativeness;
■ effective coping;
■ low levels of behaviour problems;
■ strongly internalised norms and values;
■ a sense of personal responsibility and
■ high levels of moral reasoning.

Such correlations do not *prove* parental behaviours cause the children's characteristics. There may be an influence

A closer look

Parenting characteristics associated with particular outcomes for children

Diana Baumrind, an American researcher, identifies three major patterns of parenting styles towards pre-school children, which she describes as:

- *Authoritative* – parents who are nurturant and responsive, set firm limits and demand maturity of their children, rely on discipline techniques based on reasoning and take care to respect child's point of view.
- *Authoritarian* – parents who are harsh in discipline, rigid in enforcing rules and seldom try to understand the child's point of view.
- *Permissive* – parents who are somewhat nurturant but fail to maintain firm and consistent limits and standards.

A follow-up of the children in her original research when they reached middle childhood (8–9 years old) showed that authoritative parenting continued to be associated with positive outcomes. There were some interesting gender differences between boys and girls in this research. School-age children raised in authoritative homes tended to score high in *agency* – i.e. the ability to rise to challenges, take initiative and so on. Girls who scored high on agency tended to have argumentative interactions with their parents, especially their fathers, whereas this was not found with boys with comparable increased agency.

Two other researchers, Eleanor Macoby and John Martin, offer a framework which emphasises two further but related factors:

- Frequency of parent–child conflict over goals – they found that children had the best development outcomes when these conflicts are relatively infrequent.
- Degree of balance in how parents and children resolve disagreements – they found the best developmental outcomes were in those relationships where neither parent nor child always prevails.

So this suggests that, as with Baumrind's parents, parents who are responsive and willing to negotiate, but also require children to respect their views, are most likely to nurture children who have positive outcomes.

from child to parent as well as vice versa. However, there is some evidence that parenting styles before the child is old enough to display stable behavioural characteristics are generally related to how children behave at later ages.

In our next Closer Look box, we describe research which identified three styles of parenting, and show the findings linked to parenting styles when the children were followed up at ages 8/9.

Reflect

What are the implications of Baumrind's research on parenting styles/behaviour, discussed below, for your work as a social worker with families?

Siblings

One phenomenon which you may have wondered about, and which will be relevant to you in your practice, is that children in the same family don't always develop in the same way – children growing up with the same parents can turn out quite differently. One reason for this seems to lie in differences in parental behaviour. Parents may treat their children differently for many reasons, including the child's age (think back to the article you read on child-rearing in Hong Kong), temperament, gender, skills and talents. They may also change their parenting styles as they themselves grow older, possibly becoming more relaxed or, conversely, more stressed. Some of the best evidence for such differences comes from studies by an English researcher, Judy Dunn, and her colleagues, of family interactions, which show also how children are highly sensitive to variations in treatment by their parents.

A closer look

The impact on children of differences in how their parents treat them

Research note: Children who receive less affection and warmth from their mothers are likely to be more depressed, worried or anxious than their siblings. The greater the differences in the way siblings are treated by their parents, the more likely are the brothers and sisters to show rivalry and hostility towards each other (Dunn and McGuire, 1994).

Reflect

If you have siblings, are you alike or are you different in temperament, interests and so on?

Think of another family you know well. How do the children differ from one another? What do you think the reasons for this are? Do their parents treat them differently? If so, why do you think this is?

To summarise this discussion, the role of parents and the way in which they carry out parenting tasks is of great importance in thinking about children's development, and there are aspects of parenting which have been shown to be more helpful than others in supporting the development of children's potential. The relationship is also unique, in that it requires parents to adapt and respond to their children's developing capacities. An ongoing issue in parenting, for example, is the appropriate amount of freedom to allow a child at a given age, and how to take into account the child's individual temperament in judging this. Some of the characteristics identified, for example, in the research by Baumrind have been criticised as 'a cosy ad-man's dream' by Meadows (1986), suggesting that the researchers emphasise qualities valued in Western societies, and fail among other things to take account of gender differences valued in certain other groups and societies. This much acknowledged, there are certain consistencies in the parenting qualities seen as most likely to be helpful. Research summarised by the Department of Health (1995) suggests that environments which are low in warmth and high in criticism are likely to have the most damaging effect on children. And while it is important not to be too prescriptive about parenting, most studies would stress the importance of warmth, sensitivity, encouragement and consistent discipline.

Think ahead

In relation to the following dimensions or tasks of parenting, identify and describe the kind of behaviours on the part of parents which might be an appropriate response to their child's needs in middle childhood. We have given you a couple of suggestions to start you off. And of course, you may want to identify parenting tasks which we haven't included. (The ones we have selected are suggested by Christine Cooper, 1985.)

Physical needs: *e.g. providing a nourishing breakfast before school*

Sense of safety and security: *e.g. reliably meeting off school bus or ensuring familiar figure is there at school gate*

Affection: *e.g. physical expressions such as hugs and cuddles*

Stimulation of innate potential: *e.g. now you are on your own*

Guidance and control:

Age-appropriate responsibility:

Age-appropriate independence:

How did you get on? You might find it interesting to compare your ideas with a fellow student or colleague. You might also, rightly, say that some of the suggestions (e.g. whether or not to allow a 6- or 7-year-old to go to the shops on their own) might depend on your child's temperament and her/his environment.

Before we go on to the next section we shall summarise the key points about middle childhood.

Key points for middle childhood

This is no longer seen as an uneventful time as important social and emotional development occurs during these years. This includes:

Developing a sense of industry and competence

Forming a coherent sense of identity (self-concept) including:

- Psychological self, with growing awareness of own inner thoughts, feelings, etc. and of others' internal thoughts and feelings as being different from the child's own (theory of mind).
- Social self, defined in terms of groups they belong to, and in part through social comparison.
- Sense of gender and gender stereotypes.
- Sense of personal effectiveness and ability to manage own behaviour.

Peer relationships become important developmental setting, helping children to:

- Understand perspectives, needs and feelings of others.
- Develop interaction skills.

Family remains important developmental context:

- Relationships with parents change.
- Parenting styles have considerable impact on children's behaviour and development.

Cognitive development

- Ability to see underlying reality despite superficial appearance.
- Information-processing capacity and control over attention and memory, individual differences becoming more apparent in these years.
- Maturer understanding of conservation and performance on classification tasks.

Adolescence

(*Source*: Photofusion Picture Library/Maggie Murray)

Adolescence, the period from roughly age 12 through to the late teens, is a time of dramatic and far-reaching changes. It is characterised by an especially close connection between physical and psychological development. During this period, new cognitive skills, for example the ability to reason about hypothetical situations, emerge, which in turn contribute to many aspects of social development, such as the concepts of self and others, relationships with family and peers and moral reasoning. Adolescence is often seen as a period of transition and some see it as the most challenging and difficult in terms of development. While the search for identity and the changing nature of relationships with friends and families are critical features of the period, it is important too to remember that researchers suggest that 'adolescent turmoil' is not evident in about two-thirds of the population and that psychiatric disorders in this age group are in a minority (Barker, 1990). So although it may be a time of considerable change, for many, the transitions will be accomplished without major difficulty. (Indeed, for those going on to higher education, and whose path to this point has been fairly smooth, the period following this may produce as much, if not more, challenge.)

Because adolescence covers a number of years and involves major social, emotional, cognitive and physical changes, it makes sense to divide it into different sub-stages. These are commonly given as:

Early adolescence: (12–14) – i.e. the years from the beginning of puberty to about 13–14, which include most of the major physical changes and are accompanied by changes in relationships with peers and parents.

Middle adolescence: (14–16) – i.e. a time of increasing independence and preparation for adult occupations and further education. Some experience physical changes now rather than earlier (e.g. growth spurt, voice breaking.) Some young people enter adult roles directly from middle adolescence.

Late adolescence: (17–19) – i.e. a time of continued preparation for adulthood.

Think ahead

How do these sub-stages reflect your own experience and that of others you know? What about physical changes? Relationships with your family? Intimate relationships with the opposite sex, or growing awareness of sexual identity/difference? Choosing a career or further education?

How did your adolescence compare to that of your own parents/carers? Did you form any significant relationships with other adults, for example teachers, family friends?

How would you guess your adolescence would compare to those of young people in different cultures? In many cultures, the transition from childhood to adulthood is marked by some ritual or ceremony – did you experience anything at all to resemble these rites of passage?

If possible, having explored your own experiences and reflected on those of people around you, find someone from another culture to discuss this with. We stress this because psychological theorising on adolescence as a whole can sometimes suffer from being time bound and linked too closely to a particular culture or group.

As before, we consider different aspects of development, while needing to keep in mind, again as before, how closely these are interlinked. As you read you will see that the key tasks for adolescents are usually seen to be:

- establishing a secure sense of who they are as they prepare for adult roles;
- establishing more interdependent relationships with families;
- achieving physical adult maturity;
- establishing relationships with peers.

Biological changes

The dramatic changes which occur in adolescence are apparent to everyone. Puberty produces a transformation of physical appearance and reorganisation of functioning: that is, it is an example of a qualitative change (referred to in our introduction to this chapter). Carson McCullers, an American writer, describes a young adolescent's anxieties about this growth spurt in her novel *Member of the Wedding*:

'This August she was twelve and five-sixths years old. She was five feet five and three quarter inches tall, and she wore a size seven shoe. In the past year she had grown four inches, or at least that was what she judged . . . If she reached her height on her eighteenth birthday, she had five and one-sixth growing years ahead of her. Therefore, according to mathematics and unless she could somehow stop herself, she would grow to be over nine feet tall. And what would be a lady who is over nine feet high? She would be a freak. (And Frankie has seen the House of Freaks in the local annual fair.)'   (McCullers, 1952: 259)

Think ahead

Perhaps you can recall similar anxieties yourself about the physical changes you were experiencing during adolescence, or are aware of others having these worries.

Accompanying the growth spurt which occurs at some point during this period are changes in body shape and proportions, such as the wider hips of girls and the broadening shoulders of boys. At the same time, important changes occur in the structure and function of the brain, which may have implications for cognitive development. As suggested above, these physical changes undoubtedly influence social relationships, with adolescents and parents/carers having changing expectations of one another.

Some key points to note in relation to physical developments are:

- Puberty usually begins about two years earlier in girls than boys.
- Timing is influenced by heredity, nutrition, stress and exercise.
- Average age of puberty has been decreasing since at least the early 1900s, probably due to improvements in health and nutrition, but the average age of menarche does not appear to have changed much since the late 1970s and the time taken to complete pubertal development appears to be increasing (Kaplowitz et al., 2001).
- In addition to physical changes relating to sexual development, there is mounting evidence that the brain changes substantially during adolescence, resulting in

decreased plasticity and increased efficiency in brain functioning.

- Physical changes of puberty have both direct and indirect impacts on other areas of adolescents' lives (body image, social relationships and problem behaviours). But note for girls in particular, sexual activity is heavily influenced by peers rather than biological changes.
- Attainment of physical maturity in girls can be met with an ambivalence that is not so evident for boys (Simmonds et al., 1987; Stattin and Magnusson, 1990). Early maturing girls remain dissatisfied with height and weight mainly because they differ from peers' in ways which are a disadvantage at every age. Family attitudes have an important effect on young persons' security with their body.
- Physical changes such as acne, increased muscularity in boys and increased fatty deposits in girls can influence adolescents' self-image, since they tend to be highly sensitive to their own and others' opinions of their physical changes.
- Reactions to puberty are not universal but depend on the context in which physical changes occur (e.g. the elongated, slender body type which results from late maturation may be seen as particularly advantageous for some occupations and in some communities).

We suggest you turn to Bee (1994), Chapter 16 for a fuller discussion of physical developments in adolescence. (Our Closer Look box cites research on the effects of early puberty on behaviour and emotional well-being.)

A closer look

Links between physical changes and self-confidence and well-being

Some researchers have considered the impact which the timing of pubertal changes may have on the adolescent's sense of well-being and behaviour. Girls who are early developers (i.e. before 11 or 12 for major physical changes) consistently show more negative body images, such as thinking they are overweight, are more likely to get into trouble at home and at school and are more vulnerable to depression. Conversely, the earlier the boy's development, the more positive his body image, the better his school performance and general popularity.

(Tobin-Richards et al., 1983: 137; Rierdan and Koff, 1991)

Cognitive changes

Adolescence is a time when young people acquire significant new changes in their thinking capacities. Although theorists differ in whether these changes represent a qualitative difference in development (Piaget) or emphasise continuity with the past (Siegler et al., 2003), all agree that greater maturity occurs in reasoning and problem-solving abilities. There does seem to be a qualitative shift in adolescents' thinking towards being able to maintain different perspectives simultaneously, viewing knowledge and values as more relative than during childhood, and considering more options and possibilities in their decision-making. One of the consequences of these shifts is that adolescents are more able to reflect on their relationships with others, including their parents/carers, and begin to differentiate what they can offer and to consider how they are treated. However, whether or not these more advanced capacities are used depends a good deal on experience, expertise and environmental demands.

- Logical thinking now applied to the possible and hypothetical as well as to the real. This means in effect that instead of thinking only about actual things or events which have been experienced first-hand, the older child/adolescent begins to be able to explore possible occurrences and options systematically.
- Ability to think about relationships emerges more strongly. For example, in their book of case studies of play therapy with children and adolescents, Ryan and Wilson describe how Patricia, a thirteen-year-old who had been placed in foster care following sexual abuse by her uncle, struggled with the recognition that her own family, to whom she was still very attached, had refused to believe her, while outsiders such as her social worker and foster carers had known she was speaking the truth (Ryan and Wilson, 2000).
- Adolescents' thinking becomes even more logical and systematic than it was in childhood. An important feature of formal operations is the ability to search for a solution systematically and logically.

These changes in reasoning capacities also tend to be accompanied by continuing improvement in attention and memory skills.

Recent work on cognitive development has tended to support the description of 'formal operations' as accurate, but Piaget's explanation of new skills has been criticised on a number of counts. These emphasise the fact that this kind of thinking develops rather more gradually than Piaget proposed; that it may be more culturally bound than was first thought – perhaps, for example, because the need for formal operational thinking is greater in industrialised societies. Finally, there is evidence that training in some circumstances in formal thinking can be effective: that it is possible to improve young people's problem-solving abilities with practice, which would suggest that Piaget's view of how these mental changes occur requires some modification.

One other paradox may occur to you in relation to Piaget's ideas, which is that his descriptions of changes in children's and adolescents' thinking suggest that egocentrism, which characterised younger children's thinking, should decrease as they move into adolescence: yet most of us associate this period with a greater preoccupation with the self, and often a lack of consideration of the needs of others. One theorist, Elkind (1967), suggests that in fact the adolescents are *capable* of recognising the thoughts and feelings of others, and are therefore not strictly egocentric in the way a younger child is, but nonetheless give undue weight to their own.

To summarise, there does seem to be a qualitative shift in adolescents' thinking towards being able to maintain different perspectives simultaneously, viewing knowledge and values as more relative than they did in childhood, and considering more options and possibilities in their decision-making.

These ideas may seem rather remote from the kinds of situations you will encounter as social workers. However, changes in *thinking* have direct links with social and moral development, as we shall see. It also has immediate and obvious relevance to the kinds of struggles which young people begin to experience as they move on to secondary school, where downward spirals in achievement can quickly lead to loss of confidence, demoralisation and general disaffection with school. Some of the research findings about the possibilities of improvements through training and practice are also important. An example of this is Delroy, below, but you may be able to think of similar examples from your own experience.

Case study

Delroy

Delroy, aged 16, now in foster care, described to his social worker vivid memories of his first week in school in Britain when he had arrived here aged 12 to join his parents. Back home in Jamaica he had enjoyed school and done well there. Here he couldn't understand what the teacher was talking about, and gradually stopped paying attention or trying to complete class and homework. He thought that was when his troubles at home had started, because his parents were very disappointed and disapproving of his failures to 'make the grade' at school.

Moral development

Another aspect of development which interested Piaget is the way in which children and young people think and reason about moral questions, and the development of values about the way in which we treat and behave towards other people, and how we ourselves are treated. Piaget, as one might expect, emphasised the cognitive aspect of moral development, believing that it is closely linked with children's cognitive development. As we shall see, others have argued that there are other influences, for example those of culture and gender, on moral development.

You may perhaps wonder why we are considering moral development here. Of course, children too are very concerned with issues of fairness, justice and punishment. But because several key changes in moral reasoning appear to occur during adolescence, or with the emergence of formal thinking, it seems an appropriate time to introduce these ideas. Issues concerning morality, too, have particular relevance to social work practice with adolescents because the focus of much work is on youth offending and substance abuse.

Piaget was the first to describe the stages in the development of moral reasoning, concluding that there are two broad stages of moral development.

Stage one, that of 'moral realism', emerges during the period of concrete operations, around the age of six or seven. Children see rules as strictly to be obeyed, and treat morality as absolute and moral constraints as unalterable. When a toddler is told not to do something (go near water, touch stove, ornament) they tend to see that adults will disapprove, rather than understand the moral judgement involved. When asked to judge whether an action is right or wrong, they are likely to base their answers on the consequences of the action rather than the intentions of the perpetrator. (For example, 3-year-old Jane observed a child being punished for deliberately throwing his mug of milk on the floor. When she herself later accidentally knocked over her milk she burst into tears, saying 'Janey not go to my cot.')

Stage two, that of 'autonomous morality', Piaget considered to be attained around late childhood or early adolescence. Rules are established and maintained through negotiation, intentions as well as consequences are considered, and moral rules are no longer seen as absolute (Piaget, 1932). Piaget considered moral development to be the direct consequence of cognitive development and increased social experience. In later childhood and adolescence, the ability to consider the viewpoint of others as well as one's own systematically makes it possible to recognise different moral viewpoints and the idea that moral rules are based on social agreement.

These ideas have been taken further particularly by Lawrence Kohlberg, who similarly proposed a stage model of moral development, but concluded from his research that there were three levels of moral development, and two stages in each level. One of the well-known tests on which Kohlberg based his subsequent theorising is known as the 'Heinz dilemma'. In this individuals of different ages are given a vignette (i.e. a brief story to illustrate a point) about a man who cannot pay for a drug for his dying wife, and when his request to be given it and pay for it later is refused, breaks into the store to steal it. Kohlberg argues that the reasoning given for their responses reflects individuals' differing developmental stages in relation to morality and moral judgements. (See Kohlberg, 1969: 379.)

Criticisms and dilemmas

One of the most trenchant criticisms of both Piaget and Kohlberg has been that measures of moral reasoning are only weakly if at all linked to actual moral behaviour ('do as I say, not as I do' may reflect this). There are other criticisms you may wish to follow up in your reading.

- Kohlberg's research is based on male values, and may have overlooked gender differences. Gilligan, for example, argues that there are two distinct orientations towards morality: a morality of care and a morality of justice. (Morality of care: women tend to respond to moral dilemmas on the basis of concepts such as caring, personal relationships and interpersonal obligations which are likely to be scored at the stage 3 level. Morality of justice: the tendency of men to appeal to abstract concepts such as justice and equity, which are likely to be scored at stage 5 or 6.) In response to Gilligan's criticism, the recent version of Kohlberg's scoring system has been revised to reduce bias against responses based on caring for others. (However, the issue is probably more complex. Some researchers, for example, found no consistent gender-based differences. Wark and Krebs, 1996; Walker, 1989.)

- Kohlberg's research and stages/levels are very culture specific. Some critics argue that level 3 reasoning in particular reflects liberal Western intellectual values. Other cultures may place more emphasis on cultural and community values.

Social and emotional development in adolescence

At the beginning of this section, we asked you to reflect on your own experiences of adolescence. As well as physical changes and changes in what you were doing, you may also have remembered it as an exciting time of new feelings and a sense of widening horizons and increased self-awareness, but also feelings of frustrations, disappointments and emotional upheaval. Although as we have said, conflicts and difficulties are not inevitable, there will be few adolescents who do not at some point during this period experience feelings of self-doubt, uncertainty and anxiety. These are likely to reflect stresses around one or more of the key developmental tasks of this period.

As they go through adolescence, individuals are faced with similar issues to those experienced at an earlier developmental stage, issues, for example, of trust, autonomy, competence and a sense of self. However, although similar, the ways in which these are experienced may be more conscious, challenging and disturbing, since they have to be worked through not only in relation to carers and parents, but also increasingly with peers, who themselves are in the throes of adolescence too. It is a period of increasing independence and impending separation from parents and siblings. The wider cognitive resources which we just been exploring also, however, provide new ways of thinking about who they are, relationships, problems, values and where they stand on important issues. In working through these issues, adolescents may be seen to face four important tasks:

- establishing a personal identity;
- achieving a new level of closeness and trust with peers;
- acquiring a new status in the family;
- moving towards a more autonomous stance toward the wider world.

These tasks are clearly all interlinked: for example, the sense of personal identity will include the values, principles and roles which you as an individual adopt in relation to peers, family and the wider world.

The challenge of establishing a secure sense of identity, or self-concept as it is sometimes called, is seen as a process which continues throughout adolescence, and is of course closely bound up with the pressures to succeed at school, to make intimate relationships outside the family and to find sexual partners. Forming an identity requires integrating into a coherent whole past experiences, ongoing personal changes, and society's demands and expectations for the future. Erikson, in his eight stages of development, encapsulated the key challenge of this period as the establishment of identity versus role confusion. As Chris Beckett points out in a useful chapter about adolescent development, Erikson's is only one of several models of adolescence which see identity as the central theme of this stage of development (2002: 117). However, his theory of identity formation has been one of the most influential in studying adolescent personal and social development. He considered that the key to establishing a secure personal identity lies in the successful interactions that the individual has with family, peers, school and the wider community: in other words, forming a secure sense of self involves social interactions and processes as well as internal mental activity. It is an ongoing task, involving the ability to reflect on success and disappointment (requiring the cognitive abilities discussed above) and to process both kinds of experiences without losing a sense of self. Successfully resolving difficult experiences, developing new skills and finding new accomplishments become a source of additional strength and contribute to a deepening sense of personal identity.

As with other stages in his theory, Erikson believed that successful resolution of this process depends in part on how well the individual has resolved the earlier tasks of infancy and childhood. This is consistent with perspectives drawing on attachment theory, where the tasks of forming an identity are seen as being more straightforward for young people who have in early and middle childhood developed a secure internal working model.

However, Erikson and other theorists who have developed his thinking such as James Marcia, as well as those writing from an attachment perspective, also stress that adolescents vary in how easily they establish a personal identity. Attachment theorists, for example, stress that being secure at age 11 is no guarantee of being secure at 18, although continuity is, as we have seen, much more likely. A child of average intelligence, for example, who has been managing successfully at primary school, may find themselves struggling at a more demanding secondary school, with consequent knocks to confidence and self-esteem.

Marcia and colleagues have described four categories of what they call identity status, based on whether or not adolescents have passed through a period of exploring their identity, and whether or not they have committed to an adult identity.

1. *Identity diffusion* – adolescents are not engaged in active exploration of roles and values, have no long-range goals and live for immediate pleasures. This is considered normal in early adolescence, but some young people have difficulty moving beyond this phase. So the 15-year-old who stays in bed and stays up late, spends hours playing computer games and refuses to take part in activities or think about the future could be said to be in a state of identity diffusion.

2. *Foreclosure* – involves a commitment to a set of roles and values without going through a period of crisis or exploration or questioning of parental values. For all of us, some parts of our identity reflect those of our parents and family networks. The argument here is that without some critical questioning, and challenge, the individual is failing to establish her or his own identity, having acquiesced in accepting others' values and ideas too readily.

3. *Moratorium* – adolescents are actively exploring options for a personal identity, but have not yet committed to any of them. Marcia considered this to be the least stable identity status. It is appropriate developmentally for middle adolescence, in that in most Western cultures at least it is appropriate to think through different options, for example, about going into further education, but it can become problematic if continued into adulthood.

4. *Identity achievement* – occurs when an individual commits to values and roles after a period of active exploration. Adolescents in this group are confident about the consistency and continuity of self and equally confident about how they are seen by others (Marcia, 1980).

Bear in mind that a person's identity status is not always consistent in all the aspects of their development. Students in higher education, for example, are more likely to have attained identity achievement in career roles, but may still be in a state of diffusion or foreclosure regarding religious beliefs or sexual identity.

According to Erikson, two sets of factors are necessary to consolidate an optimal sense of personal identity. First, adolescents must carry forward an innate sense of confidence from their middle childhood. Second, they should have during adolescence ample opportunity to experiment with new roles, both in fantasy and in practice, coupled with support in this effort by carers and other adults. There is some research evidence that warm supportive parents who encourage resolution of differences and communication foster self-development and identity formation during this period. (You can read further on this in Baumrind, 1989.)

Researchers have also found plausible correlations between identity status and other characteristics. Identity *achievers* are more likely to be goal-oriented, show greater cognitive sophistication and take more responsibility for their actions. They report low levels of anxiety, but self-reported anxiety levels are highest for those in *moratorium* and lowest in *foreclosure*.

Many features of Erikson's theory have generated interesting hypotheses and research but the question remains whether many of his ideas were specific to the culture and historical period in the USA during which he developed them. We have come full circle then, seeing that cultural and historical questions posed in your early reading (the article about child abuse in Hong Kong) are raised again very strongly in adolescent theorising and research. Individual and sub-group experiences, such as ethnic identity formation, or the complications of a homosexual identity, or identity development which is less accessible owing to adoption, fostering (as we alluded to in the previous section on middle childhood), migration and, for some young people, displacement, all lend added stress to this period of development. We introduce you to some of these variations in experience in what follows.

Group differences in identity formation

Ethnicity

For those belonging to minority ethnic groups, there is another aspect of forming a sense of self which means facing distinctive challenges. Minority ethnic adolescents are often confronted with two sometimes conflicting sets of cultural values – those of their ethnic community and those of wider society. Phinney (1989) suggests that there are three stages in the development of ethnic identity:

1. *Unexamined ethnic identity* – although this is common in pre-adolescence, it can be seen as the equivalent of what Marcia describes as 'foreclosed' identity.

2. *Ethnic identity search* – equivalent to Marcia's moratorium, where previous attitudes are questioned and there is heightened awareness of specific ethnic

traditions or practices, political beliefs and positive (and negative) attitudes towards the cultural group.

3. *Ethnic identity achievement* – the exploration stage is followed by a resolution of conflicts and contradictions, analogous to Marcia's identity achievement (Phinney, 1989).

In one of the child development texts which give you more detail on this issue, Bee (1995: 285) comments:

'This stage model may be a decent beginning description of the process of ethnic identity formation. But let us not lose sight of the fact that the details and the content of the ethnic identity will differ markedly from one subgroup to another. Those groups that encounter more overt prejudice will have a different road to follow than those who may be more easily assimilated; those whose own ethnic culture espouses values that are close to those of the dominant culture will have less difficulty resolving the contradictions than will those whose family culture is at greater variance with the majority.'

Reflect

What might these cultural differences include? Can you give examples from your own experience of where customs/behaviours/values have seemed to be at variance with those of the dominant culture? What kinds of difficulties might these differences create for adolescents?

Gender

Identity development is seen by some researchers and theorists as proceeding differently in males and females. Kroger, for example, argues that the interpersonal domain, especially that relating to future partnerships, marriage and family roles, is more prominent in girls' identity exploration than boys'. Erikson believed that identity issues have to be resolved before the intimacy issues of early adulthood, but there is some evidence (e.g. Marcia et al., 1993) that young women deal with identity and intimacy simultaneously rather than sequentially. Because of this, Kroger argues that identity formation is more complex for females than males (Kroger, 2000; Marcia, 1980; Marcia et al. 1993).

Gay and lesbian youth

Negative attitudes pose a challenge to these young people's identity formation and acceptance of self. Researchers who have studied these groups in depth suggests that gay and lesbian adolescents who express their sexual orientation openly, even in the face of social stigma, go through the stages of forming an identity at appropriate ages and show greater self-esteem than those who maintain secrecy (Dube and Savin-Williams, 1999).

Think ahead

In order to test for yourselves the plausibility of the idea that identity is formed in adolescence, we suggest now that you undertake the following exercise.

Stage One: Write on a piece of paper a list of six characteristics which you consider best describe you as you are now – it is probably best to choose a mix of physical and psychological attributes, but really it is what springs to your mind in thinking about who you are. DO THIS without reading on!

Stage 2: Having written this list, see how many of these characteristics were things which you would have thought about yourself in adolescence.

How did you get on?

Of course, we cannot guess what characteristics you used to identify and describe yourself with. But we hope this will help you reflect on the question of how accurate is it is to see adolescence as a period of identity formation. Sometimes, too, people find that some of these characteristics are ideas which they did once have about themselves, but which may in fact no longer be so true now of their older selves (shyness, a quick temper, for example).

Possibly this is true for you too?

Peer relationships in adolescents

'This was the summer when for a long time she had not been a member. She belonged to no club and was a member of nothing in the world. Frankie had become an unjoined person who hung about in doorways and she was afraid' (McCullers, 1952: 241). The kinds of processes described in identity formation, and changes in adolescents' ability to think systematically and in more abstract terms about social issues and values are critical to the establishment of secure relationships with peers, which, as our quotation from the American novel cited earlier suggests, is seen as the second challenge of adolescence. Clearly this is an interactive process, with friendships growing deeper as individuals acquire the cognitive potential for mutual exploration and discovery. And the experience of friendships and membership of friendship groups contribute to the development of personal identity; as the quotation suggests, belonging to a group is an important part of knowing who you are, and NOT belonging can create a sense of anxiety and longing. Relationships with friends are likely to be more personal, expressive and closer than those formed in middle childhood. A critical feature will be the development of more intimate relationships, most commonly with the opposite sex. How adolescents respond to and negotiate these new experiences depends in part on their developmental history. Longitudinal research shows that those who successfully negotiated the task of forming peer relationships in middle childhood are more effective in mixed-sex groups and in general better able to meet the more complex challenges of peer relationships.

One American theorist, Harry Stack Sullivan, emphasised the role of friendship in identity formation, and concluded that there are three stages during this period which he describes as:

- *Pre-adolescence* – the need for validation and same-sex friendships.
- *Early adolescence* – the need for sexual contact and the beginnings of intimacy, generally with the opposite sex.
- *Late adolescence* – older adolescents are able to coordinate a broader range of friends, and friendships need not be so exclusive.

Sullivan also identifies one of the key challenges as the need to integrate the need for intimacy with that for sexual contact. Differences in the way males and females form friendships have also been identified, as you may have guessed, by a number of researchers. Becket gives a helpful summary of the arguments, pointing out that 'stage models of development (at adolescence and other stages) are sometimes guilty of offering male development as the "norm" and either ignoring female development or tagging it on as an afterthought.' The author goes on to quote other researchers who have proposed that girls follow different paths, suggesting that those who adopt a more traditional feminine route do tend to fuse identity and intimacy in the way which Erikson describes, while those who adopt a more stereotypically 'masculine' route (more oriented to careers, for example) work on identity before intimacy, which is seen as the male pattern (Beckett, 2002).

Think ahead

Think about your own experience of friendships during middle childhood and adolescence.

In what way were they different or the same? Did your friendships change during your teenage years?

Do you think your own friendship patterns differed from those of your peers of different gender?

Acquiring a new status in the family

Finally in this section we consider the issue of family relationships in adolescence. Despite the increasing importance of peer relationships, the family remains a critical arena for development during the period. For parents, the challenge may be to support development by allowing adolescents to explore new roles and values, by tolerating self-expression and by discussing different opinions, while still providing firm guidelines, support and encouragement.

Adolescents have two apparently contradictory tasks in their relationships with their parents: to establish autonomy and independence while at the same time maintaining an emotional connectedness to them. The cognitive skills which allow hypothetical thinking also allow teenagers to counter their parents' arguments, be more critical of their behaviour, appearance and opinions, and to conceive of other ways in which the family might function. The underlying push for autonomy gives rise to an increase in conflict which has been documented by many researchers. However, as we said at the beginning of this section, it is important not to assume that this indicates a major disruption of the parent–child relationship. In the great majority of families, conflict takes the form of mild bickering and arguments over rules, housekeeping, homework and so on. If this is not to be seen as too serious (although it is certainly stressful, perhaps more for the parents than their offspring), what are the underlying reasons for it?

A number of researchers and theorists have suggested that far from being a negative occurrence, this rise in parent–child conflict may in fact be developmentally healthy – a necessary part of the process of separation and individuation. Steinberg, for example, demonstrated the process whereby more symmetrical parent–child relationships (i.e. one where power was more equally distributed) develop during adolescence. (See the Closer Look box.) After a period of what could be seen as jockeying for position, in later adolescence, family relationships became more flexible again. However, this realignment often involves stress and conflict.

One reason for this may be that especially during early adolescence, the parents' appraisal of the teenagers' abilities may lag behind the advances in their cognitive abilities and capacity for autonomy. The mismatches in parent and child expectations, however, gradually decline as the relationship goes through a series of realignments.

Parenting patterns and adolescent development

One important area of study which is highly relevant for social workers is that of the impact of parenting styles on

A closer look

Family relationships in adolescence

In Steinberg's 1988 study, researchers visited families with sons several times as the boys passed from middle childhood through puberty. As they entered puberty the parent–child interactions during certain problem-solving discussions changed considerably. Mothers and sons interrupted each other more, responded less to each others' opinions and interacted more rigidly. Fathers typically stepped in and asserted their views strongly and boys continued to defer to them. After the peak of puberty, interactions became less stressful and more flexible.

Other studies show differences in mother–child and father–child relationships: that teenagers spend more time with their mothers than their fathers, confide in them more, and that they feel more accepted by them. Mothers encourage more closeness and are more self-disclosing towards their teenagers.

Other studies also found that adolescents accept parental authority, e.g. in relation to moral, legal and social issues but want increasing autonomy over dress, activities and other personal issues (Collins et al., 1997). This holds true across ethnic groups. Most recent studies of teenagers reflect desire for redefinition of the parent–child relationship away from unilateral parental authority towards cooperative negotiation. Most parents make shifts in response to pressures from their offspring (Bumpus et al., 2001).

development. We shall return to this later in our text (in Chapter 16 on children and families) but a brief summary is useful here.

Many of the parenting qualities which were important in earlier periods remain important here too. Warmth, support, authoritativeness and continued supervision have been found by researchers to be linked to positive outcomes. Parenting changes during the period ideally involve giving more responsibility and autonomy to the emerging young adult, while at the same time staying involved and concerned, and offering guidance and feedback. Pointers from research include the following:

- Adolescent development proceeds best when parents stay involved with their children and continue to offer directions and guidance (Baumrind, 1989; Collins et al., 1997).
- Adolescents who receive authoritative parenting tend to be more psychologically mature, have a stronger orientation towards achievement and do better at school than those from non-authoritarian or permissive homes (Baumrind, 1989; Steinberg and Levine, 1990).
- Positive development including higher self-esteem is associated with consistency between parents in discipline measures and their responsiveness to their offspring (Johnson et al., 1991).
- Erratic and harsh parental treatment by parents strongly correlates with aggressive behaviour and delinquency in their adolescent children (Sampson and Laub, 1994).

Non-conventional paths through adolescence

A range of difficulties of greater or lesser severity may emerge during adolescence for the first time, and as social workers you are likely to become very aware of those adolescents for whom the period throws up significant difficulties. In some individuals, these may be best seen and understood as part and parcel of the tasks of adolescence – i.e. of the process of identity formation, participating in different peer groups, and testing autonomy by oppositional behaviour. Drug and alcohol use increases markedly at this age (see Chapters 18 and 21 on youth offending and substance abuse). The incidence of depression and eating disorders increases in adolescence and in your work you will come into contact with young people who are involved in a range of antisocial behaviour and those who present with emotional issues such as depression and anxiety. Some of these are transitional problems, which may be resolved without too much longer-term difficulty, but for others they may be the precursors of ongoing and more serious difficulties. A distinction therefore needs to be made between those behaviours for the individual which might be associated with developmental issues and those which may be more serious. A small proportion of adolescents do present with psychiatric disorders such as schizophrenia, eating disorders such as anorexia and bulimia, or severe depression and suicide attempts.

As with other serious difficulties, certain behaviours which have occurred in earlier periods do appear to be precursors of adolescent mental illness – for example, schizophrenia. These include behaviours which seem to have a neurological component: for example, a child's clumsiness, attentional or verbal difficulties. The child may also experience difficulties in maintaining interpersonal relationships. However, these behavioural dispositions do not seem automatically to lead to schizophrenia, despite having in part a genetic basis. Various explanations are proposed to explain this, including the idea that individuals who have this predisposition are particularly susceptible to the effect of stressful experiences once their neural development has reached sufficient maturity. Environmental factors also may contribute to this condition. Rutter and Rutter, two eminent British researchers and theoreticians, state: 'High levels of intrusive family criticism make schizophrenia more likely to remain manifest once it develops and possibly they might have a role in its initial precipitation' (1993: 256). So although we might be hesitant in following this line of argument (which links back to our reference to schizophregenic families, earlier), since it might seem to be apportioning responsibility for the development of mental illness to parental behaviour, it is important to keep in mind that there is some evidence that a supportive environment can ameliorate, and an unsupportive one exacerbate, the experience of some mental illnesses. As social workers, therefore, encountering these problems of mental illness, as with other problems such as delinquency or conduct disorders, you will need to establish the psychosocial context of the behaviours, as well as the meaning of them to the young person concerned.

Before moving on to the next section, we shall summarise the key issues we have covered in relation to adolescence.

Key points for adolescence

Major developmental tasks of this period include the following:

- Establishing a personal identity.
- Achieving a new level of closeness and trust with peers.
- Acquiring a new status in the family.
- Moving towards a more autonomous stance toward the wider world.
- Adolescence is characterised by a particularly close connection between physical and psychological development and between cognitive and social development.
- Adolescence is often considered to be a turbulent period but although marked by some conflicts, for the majority these are relatively minor and transitional. The amount of actual conflict and turmoil depends on:

  - the period of adolescence being considered – early adolescence is more conflicted than late;
  - which domain of life is being considered (e.g. emotional or cognitive development);
  - individual differences, including differences in how the individual is being parented.

- Between middle childhood and late adolescence, the sense of personal identity becomes increasingly coherent, reflective and differentiated. This involves both emotional and cognitive changes.
- Changes in cognition involve a qualitative shift in adolescents' thinking towards being able to maintain different perspectives simultaneously, viewing knowledge and values as more relative than they did in childhood, and considering more options and possibilities in their decision-making. This is also marked by changes in moral reasoning.

Adulthood

(*Source*: Getty Images/Photonica)

In this and the following section we shall be considering the kinds of changes which occur to adults from the point at which they leave adolescence until death. In some respects, the study of adults differs from that of children and adolescence which we have been considering up till now. One way in which it is different is that it is no longer possible, as it was at earlier stages, to consider development as entirely, as it were, being on an upward trajectory. When we study the physical, cognitive and, to some extent, emotional processes in adults, we at some point begin to have to talk about decline and loss of function rather than progression. Secondly, our involvement as social workers with adult individuals is likely to arise because they are encountering problems between themselves and the wider society, in managing the roles and expectations of society of them as adults, rather than because they are not meeting developmental milestones. And thirdly, it is different because physical and cognitive change in adulthood is more gradual and more variable from one individual to another than it is in childhood and, to a lesser extent, between one group in society and another. So as one theorist suggests, 'developmental trajectories are socially and historically situated . . . it becomes inappropriate to place great emphasis on searching for a developmental theory with predictive capacity across generations' (Sugarman, 1986: 3).

Nonetheless, there are changes in physical and cognitive functioning which it is possible to set out as reasonably consistent baselines. There are also certain ways of conceptualising the experience of stresses and the overcoming of difficulties which can provide a useful starting point in understanding life in adulthood.

First we need to consider what we mean by adulthood. Then we shall look briefly at physical changes, how theorists conceptualise the processes and tasks of adulthood, and look in detail at the application of attachment theory to adulthood.

Defining adulthood

Theorists and researchers have tended to divide the span of years from leaving the transitional phase of adolescence into early, middle and older age. Most of us will have our own definitions of these, which may alter as we get older – one of the authors of this textbook for example is over 60, and very surprised to find herself considered now to be one of the elderly population, since this outward description does not fit her inner experience or sense of self. Before we consider the demarcation points commonly used, we suggest you undertake the following activity.

Think ahead

At what point did you consider that you had become an adult? (We assume that you will have by now left school and either are or have been engaged in higher education.) *When do you consider middle age to begin? And what about older age?*

Then ask yourself on what basis you defined the breaks. *Were they reflecting legal status such as voting ages, social roles, physical changes, work patterns and so on?*

Now turn to the diagrams on pages 142 and 184 and see if you agree with the lifespan demarcation set out there.

By convention, most lifespan researchers set one division at 60 or 65, the age when most people in Western society retire from work. A second division, between early and middle adulthood, is commonly set at about 40 or 45, reflecting the fact that the optimal physical and cognitive functioning, present in the twenties and thirties, begins very gradually to wane, and that there are role changes, often although certainly not always, which occur around this time, as children leave home and careers begin to peak. Building on this point, we may say that the key tasks of this period are to establish a firm sense of adult identity, through negotiating a secure position in relation to three key areas: work, intimate adult relationships and parenting.

What the above makes clear is that there is no straightforward agreement about certain aspects of adulthood. What does seem to be a common theme, however, is that, having reached adulthood, individuals are expected to take responsibility for themselves and at some point others around them. So perhaps, as Beckett argues, what marks out adulthood is this expectation of responsibility (Beckett, 2002).

As an illustration of these contradictions, however, it is estimated that there are in the United Kingdom 50,000 or more teenagers and children acting as carers for adults with mental and physical disabilities. It is also the case that some adults with physical or learning difficulties struggle to get society to allow them to take responsibility for their own lives.

Reflect

What does this say to you about the idea of responsibility as the defining characteristic of being an adult?

It is important to bear in mind this lack of clear and agreed definitions, however, as social workers, because:

- We need to be sensitive to how the individuals we are working with view themselves and locate themselves along the life course. Many older people, for example, comment on the difference between how they look and how they feel as they get older.

- We need to remember how laws, policies and agency remits affect how people are responded to.

- There is some evidence that being 'off-time' in how you reach particular life tasks exacts some psychological price, perhaps because it operates through the individual's internal model of their expected life history (Hagestad, 1986; Troll, 1985). Another possibility is that the social supports are less likely to be there: for example for a mother who has her first child in her late thirties, when her contemporaries may be facing the challenges of their adolescents' behaviour.

A closer look

Further evidence of difficulties arising in being 'out of sync'

This lies in research by Burton and Vern Bengston (1985) of black grandmothers: those who were 'early' rather than 'on-time' (defined as between 43 and 57) found the experience, including having to help care for the baby, more stressful and disturbing.

Physical and cognitive changes in early and middle adulthood

We shall not spend much time on these, noting, however, that at the end of adolescence, physical growth is complete, and the body remains at its peak until the decline in powers which sets in very gradually during the fourth decade. There are certain issues relating to physical/cognitive development where social workers may need to become involved: for example, the issue of reproductive capacity, the fact that fertility is at its height in the late teens and early twenties and declines thereafter, with the risk of miscarriage and other complications of pregnancy becoming greater in the later thirties, will require a more detailed knowledge of physical development than we can offer here.

Also worth noting is that you will remember that Piaget's stages of cognitive development ended with that of 'formal operations', supposedly reached in adolescence. Some psychologists, however, have suggested that there may be further changes in adulthood. In general, however, these may relate to the development of specific areas of expertise, necessary for work or parenting roles. (For further reading on this see Sugarman, 1986.)

Finally worth noting here is that there is now abundant evidence that adults with adequate social supports have lower risk of illness, earlier death and depression than do adults with weaker social networks or less supportive relationships, reflecting again the interconnectedness of the different domains of development which we have observed at earlier stages. It is to the area of socio-emotional development that we now turn.

Social and emotional development in early and middle adulthood

There are a number of features of adulthood which although certainly not universal are commonly experienced by adults in industrialised societies. The key tasks involved have been conceptualised as those of *acquiring, learning and performing* three roles central to adult life, namely those of:

- Worker – work patterns and careers tend to be established in this period.
- Partner – most people leave the parental home and marry or establish a living-together relationship.
- Parent – many people have children during this period.

There have been a number of attempts to conceptualise adult development through describing its stages which you might want to follow up. A well-known one is that of Daniel Levinson (1978). Levinson proposed that adult life for men typically evolved through a series of stable (structure building) stages and transitional (structure changing) phases, as in the diagram shown. His original model only involved men – and only 40 of them, interviewed over a number of years and drawn from different walks of life – although he subsequently undertook a follow-up study of women (1978, 1996). Transitional phases in his model refer to the process of passing from one stage to another, and require adaptation and planning for the change. Stable stages are those of stability and consolidation: for example, establishing an adult partnership, committing to a work career. Havinghurst's staged approach has similarities to that of Erikson, in seeing life stages and developmental tasks.

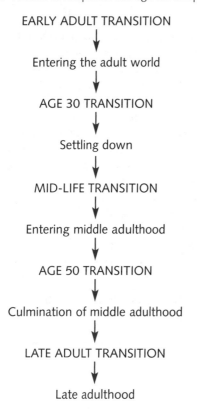

EARLY ADULT TRANSITION

↓

Entering the adult world

↓

AGE 30 TRANSITION

↓

Settling down

↓

MID-LIFE TRANSITION

↓

Entering middle adulthood

↓

AGE 50 TRANSITION

↓

Culmination of middle adulthood

↓

LATE ADULT TRANSITION

↓

Late adulthood

(*Source*: Levinson, 1978)

Research on adult attachments is relevant to understanding the transition from home to independent living; to the choice of partner; and to parenting.

A closer look

Erikson's (1959) view of early and middle adulthood

Intimacy v isolation

The challenge here is to experience intimacy yet retain a secure sense of your identity. Successful negotiation of this will allow individuals to establish close relationships with others, while unsuccessful negotiation will lead to isolation and/or superficiality of relationships with others.

Generativity v stagnation

This stage is linked with parenting, employment and contributing to the community and wider society. Successful outcomes involve the ability to be concerned and to take care and responsibility for others in the community, while unsuccessful negotiations lead to boredom, a sense of lack of fulfilment and over-preoccupation with self.

Erikson saw the two challenges of early and middle adulthood as the achievement of *intimacy over isolation*, and the achievement of *generativity over stagnation*. As before, it is important to see Erikson's conceptualisation as suggestive rather than wholly factual, since it is a model rather than something which he had tested empirically. Nonetheless it is useful in encapsulating what most would agree to be important themes in early and middle adulthood. Within our Closer Look box we give you Erikson's commentary on these two stages.

Erikson described the establishment of intimacy as 'the ability to fuse your identity with someone else's without fear that you're going to lose something yourself'. Successful negotiation of this task allows the individual to experience love and commitment to others, probably importantly, one other person, while failure successfully to manage this risk is seen as leading to feelings of isolation and forming superficial relationships with others.

Some empirical support for this can be found in some psychological studies, such as those by Kahn et al. (1985). However, perhaps one of the most fruitful ways of exploring this theme is through the application of attachment theory to adult development and it is to this we now turn.

Our earlier discussions proposed that there were certain characteristics of attachment relationships which distinguished them from other relational bonds (i.e. not all relationships are classified as *attachment relationships*. The relationship which a young child has with a baby sitter, for example, can be friendly without necessarily having the properties which would characterise attachment). You will remember from our earlier section and we hope also from your further reading (!) that these characteristics are commonly seen to be:

- Proximity-seeking
- Secure base effect
- Separation process
- Elicitation by threat
- Specificity of attachment figure (i.e., once an *internal working model* of an attachment is formed, only that figure provides a secure base, and separation from that figure gives rise to protest. Other figures may provide companionship)
- Inaccessibility to conscious control (attachment feelings persist even when the attachment figure is no longer available, possibly through death, and adequate alternative figures are available)

- Persistence (attachment does not lessen through habituation or in long-lasting relationships. Attachment seems to persist even in the absence of reinforcement, and prolonged absence produces pining and longing which only abate slowly and imperfectly)
- Insensitivity to experience with the attachment figure (i.e. attachments are formed and can persist even if the attachment figure is neglectful or abusing).

In the light of these characteristics, a first question in considering the close relationships which adults form is whether *any* of these relationships should be considered as attachment relationships. Some theorists, for example Robert Weiss, who has studied adult attachments and relationships extensively, argue that they should be.

'Studies of individuals whose marriages are ending in divorce, for example, show that even though each of the partners is apt to feel misused by the other, each continues to feel linked emotionally to the other . . . In other ways too the pair-bonds of adults display the properties of childhood attachment. So too do . . . the relationships with parents maintained by some adults in which the parents continue to be seen as guarantors of security, and the relationships of patients with counsellors or therapists. Not all pair-bonds, relationships of adults and their parents, relationships of patients to therapists, and parental relationships are attachments, nor is it impossible for friendships, work relationships, or kin ties to be attachments. However, some of these relationships are likely to be attachments, others unlikely. The question is whether the relationship displays attachment properties.'

(Weiss, 1991: 67)

We are not going to resolve this question here, but this gives you a flavour of the kinds of ideas he puts forward and may help you to understand issues such as the difficulty which people experience commonly in, for example, separating from their marital partners through divorce, or times when you may have felt an adult to be over-dependent on her/his own parent. Some of you may be interested in reading more of Weiss's arguments. But the question of adult attachments is also relevant to our next point, which is that the relinquishing of attachment to parental figures appears to be of central importance among the processes of achieving individuality in late adolescence and early adulthood. Thus leaving home is 'more than just setting up a separate residence. It involves a highly significant psychological emancipation process in which the young person distances himself [sic] emotionally from his parents to at least some degree' (Bee, 1994: 334).

This is not of course to say that attachment to the parent is fully given up in adult life; merely that some pulling back from this relationship is necessary if an intimate relationship with an adult partner is to be formed. This withdrawal may be quite a gradual process. Bee cites evidence that of the various properties of attachment, the first to shift is that of proximity-seeking: late adolescents commonly wish to spend more time with their peers, while still thinking of their parents as a secure base. In adulthood, most of us shift this safe-base aspect of attachment to a partner or spouse (see Hazan et al., 1991, cited in Bee, 1994). Work colleagues and friendship groups provide alternative sources of support and confirmation of self, while romantic partners potentially provide these in addition to a secure base and sense of belonging. There is some evidence that securely attached young people make the transition from home into independence more easily than do those who are anxious and ambivalently attached. In one study, researchers Zirkel and Cantor (1990) found that college students who were still absorbed by their relationship with parents and with their need to become independent showed more stress and anxiety and physical symptoms than those who were securely attached.

Reflect

What are the similarities between this behaviour pattern and that of a small child described as anxiously attached?

What might be the explanations, psychologically, for the difficulties which such students have in settling in a new environment?

Choosing a partner

You will remember that Erikson saw establishing intimacy as the key theme of this life stage. There has been a large amount of sociological research about the basis on which we choose partners, why some pairs break up and some remain committed and stable. You may wish to follow these themes up in your own reading. Here we again draw on attachment theory, which draws attention to the importance of internal working models of attachment and the influence of these on partner selection. There is some evidence that the patterns of internal working models of attachment which are carried into adult life have an impact on the kinds of adult partnerships which we form, along such dimensions as trustfulness, openness, closeness and anxiety. Adults with secure attachment models are said to be more likely to trust others, see their partners as friends as well as lovers, and show less anxiety and jealousy towards their partners. Adults with an anxious attachment model are uncertain about themselves in relationships, more anxious about their feelings being reciprocated and are jealous and preoccupied with their involvement. Those with avoidant internal models are less happy, less trusting in their relationships, avoid closeness, disclose little, are more intolerant, provide less reassurance to their partners and find it harder to commit themselves. In research conducted by two American researchers, Hazan and Shaver (1987, 1990), adult attachment patterns were found to reflect those in children, and to be remarkably similar in incidence to those in childhood (see the Closer Look box).

Two important points to note here are that, first, attachment histories are not the only ingredient in the forming of adult partnerships. However, it is plausible that the more difficult the attachment history, the less free and flexible the adult will be in selecting a partner. (Mattinson and Sinclair in their classic book *Mate and Stalemate* (1979) about working with very damaged couples in local authority social service departments explore the reasons for this more fully.)

Secondly, changes in internal working models of attachments can occur; importantly, adults with insecure earlier childhood attachments do seem to be able to create new models. There is some evidence that some adults who have experienced loss, neglect, traumatic experiences and/or abuse in childhood (and therefore most probably experienced insecure attachment to their caregivers), but who have been able to reflect on and accept their earlier experiences, can create new internal working models. One method of establishing evidence of this, used in research and highly influential in developing thinking about attachment relationships, is the Adult Attachment Interview, first developed by an American researcher Mary Main, principally as a way of trying to develop understanding about inter-generational links (i.e. why adults with difficult early histories tended to replicate these difficulties in their own parenting and with their own children).

This is a semi-structured interview which, although asking apparently simple questions about childhood and earlier and current significant relationships, has the effect of 'surprising the unconscious', by getting under the skin as it were of the adult being interviewed, to reveal the way in which s/he uses thoughts, feelings and 'different strategies and rules to access, process and express attachment-related material' (Main, 1995: 420, quoted in Schofield and Beek, 2006). Adults are asked, for example, to give five adjectives to describe their relationships with their mother and then their father, and to give examples of each word (see A Closer Look opposite, Adult Attachment Interview, Hesse, 1999).

The interviews are analysed and coded from the point of view less of the content of the transcript than of the coherence and fluidity of the account. From this it is possible to classify individuals according to the different secure and insecure patterns. (This is a complex process, but one example would be an individual who while

---

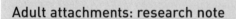

A closer look

Adult attachments: research note

Hazan and Shaver measured types of internal models by asking each of their subjects to choose one of three descriptions of relationships. They found adults of the three types differed, as expected, in the way they described their most important relationship and in their expectations about intimate relationships.

Attachment question/descriptions used by Hazan and Shaver in their research:
Which of the following best describes your feelings?

1. I find it relatively easy to get close to others and am comfortable depending on them and having them depend on me. I don't often worry about being abandoned or about someone getting too close to me (seen as equivalent to secure – 56 per cent of sample of over 600 adults of varying ages).

2. I am somewhat uncomfortable being close to others. I find it difficult to trust them completely, difficult to allow myself to depend on them. I am nervous when anyone gets too close and, often, love partners want me to be more intimate than I feel comfortable with (avoidant – 25 per cent).

3. I find others are reluctant to get as close as I would like. I often worry that my partner doesn't really love me or won't want to stay with me. I want to merge completely with another person and this desire sometimes scares people away (anxious/ambivalent – 19 per cent).

describing her childhood in an idealised way as a perfect childhood cannot recall experiences in any detail or give examples of a 'wonderful' mother.) Although Schofield and Beek (2006) rightly caution against the use of the interview by social work practitioners as a means of formally classifying adults, some agencies use the core questions in their assessment interviews, and they can be helpful in providing a guiding framework in other interventions. As can be seen from the summary below, adult attachment patterns are classified into four groups, each of them reflecting the four patterns of childhood attachments.

A closer look

The adult attachment interview

Individuals are asked to describe their childhood, e.g.

- What happened?
- Were you emotionally upset?
- Separated from parents? Rejected?
- Did you experience abuse? Or loss?
- Give 5 adjectives for early relationship with mother and with father.
- What do you make of it?
- Why do you think your parents behaved the way they did?
- Has childhood influenced the kind of person you are today?

Adult attachment patterns
- Secure autonomous – the adult equivalent of Type B
- Insecure dismissing
- Insecure preoccupied
- Unresolved.

Adult attachment interviews
Parents who were rated secure:

- value attachment relationships in abstract sense;
- regard as influential on personality;
- realistic in describing particular relationship;
- many had had unfavourable attachment-related experiences;
- readiness of recall;
- ease in discussion;
- lack of idealisation;
- coherent, internally consistent accounts;
- mother's security strongly correlated with infant's.

Characteristics of 'free' or 'autonomous-secure' interviews
- Narrative shows coherence, fluidity.
- Personal history indicates either a secure base in childhood or coherence in relation to adverse experiences.

Characteristics of dismissing interviews
- Narrative suggests significance of negative experiences is denied; lack of coherence re truth, economy and manner.
- Personal history suggests rejection and neglect.
- Excessive valuation of self-reliance, undervaluation of closeness/attachment.

Characteristics of preoccupied interviews
- Narrative suggests lack of coherence through e.g. manner.
- Personal history points to rejection, neglect and role reversal.
- Speaker appears highly confused, given to involving anger or passive speech, including incomplete sentences and a child-like voice.

Characteristics of unresolved interviews
- Narrative suggests lack of coherence through e.g. lapses in the monitoring of speech or reasoning around loss or trauma, possibly including excessive attention to detail.
- Personal history points to significant loss and/or abuse during childhood or adulthood.
- Speaker appears absorbed, prone to dissociation, guilt and fear.

Parenting

Adult attachment patterns have also been valuable in establishing evidence of a correlation between the adult attachment patterns of caregivers and the attachment patterns of their infants. Fonagy et al. (1994) found that a mother's attachment pattern, as measured by the AAI during pregnancy, predicted their infant's attachment pattern at 12 months in 75 per cent of cases.

Reflect

This is clearly not a hundred-per-cent correlation, and, if you accept the basic premise of this research, you might want to ask yourself also what other factors might have intervened.

What kinds of experiences might you hypothesise could occur, so that her attachment patterns are NOT passed from mother to infant?

A closer look

Adulthood and parenthood for those with resistant-preoccupied patterns of attachment

'As adults, the preoccupying anger with childhood attachment figures who let you down continues, as does the search for unconditional love and for the perfect relationship. Neighbours, friends, partners and social workers come into the frame as people who might be "the one". Adulthood can be an emotional roller coaster rather as childhood has been, as the playground is replaced with the workplace or the neighbourhood, but the feelings of anxiety and the expectations of being let down by those around you interferes in establishing relaxed rewarding relationships. As with ambivalent patterns in children, preoccupied adults may present very brightly and openly, chatting at length about themselves and their past. This is very appealing to social workers, as is the message you might get on a first or second visit, "You are the perfect social worker, you really listen and understand me – not like the last one, she was very unsympathetic and never came to see me or answered the phone." Inevitably, there are times when you too cannot get to the phone or make the visit when asked – especially if phone calls from the parent are coming in ten times a day – at which point you too will be added to the list of social workers who are not to be trusted. This pattern is a genuine marker for anxious distress in the adult, but engenders irritation and may be a cause of a great deal of difficulty in multidisciplinary networks when the health visitor is "wonderful" but the doctor "doesn't care" or vice versa. As parents, the legacy of all that need, anger, hope and disappointment can lead to high expectations, initially, of what the baby will bring into their lives. This may lead to a great deal of anticipation, buying of expensive clothes and so on. But this cannot be matched by any consistent sensitivity to the child or commitment of emotion, energy and interest. The child makes demands and inevitably disappoints too. Without intervention with caregiver and child, the cycle is likely to continue.'

(Schofield and Beek, 2006: 114–5)

What is important about the research is that the way in which the mother *talks* about her life and early relationships (even if these have been difficult) seems likely to predict her child's secure or insecure behaviour in the strange-situation procedure. See A Closer Look for one account of how adult attachments impact on care-seeking behaviour. The book from which this is taken gives detailed descriptions of adult patterns of attachment, discussing the implications of these for children who are placed for adoption, which you may wish to follow up in further reading.

Erikson's description of the stage of middle adulthood as 'generativity versus stagnation' may be a good way of drawing this section together. We cannot cover in detail all the myriad ways in which people's lives as adults develop. As Bee (1994: 390) comments:

'When I look at social and personality development in these middle years of adult life, what is most striking is how much less tightly the garment of social roles now fits. . . . Many of the same roles that dominate early adult life continue, of course . . . But by age 40 or 50, these roles have changed in important ways. Children begin to leave home . . . job promotions have usually topped out . . . and because parenting and working are less demanding, there is more time for a marriage or partnership relationship.'

So the theories which suggest fixed life-cycle stages common to the experience of all adults may not be all that helpful, particularly to social workers who will mostly be involved with adults who are experiencing one or more stressful events, who may find, and indeed feel themselves to be, at odds with the experiences of wider society. The Holmes and Rahe Social Readjustment Scale, for example, lists 43 stressful events in adulthood, which the researchers scored to measure the increased risk of stress and ill health if experienced over a twelve-month period:

Death of spouse	100
Divorce	73
Marital separation	65
Jail term	63
Death of close family member	63
Personal injury	52
Marriage	50
Sacked from job	47
Marital reconciliation	45
Retirement	45

(*Source*: Holmes and Rahe, 1967: 213–18)

Erikson's approach would see these as challenges which require the individual to cope and adapt to changes, drawing on personal, psychological or inner strength, and also having recourse to physical and external resources, such as support networks, family and friends, or professional and voluntary support. Although his concept of generativity is slightly elusive (in part because he links it to parenthood, which is almost invariably an experience which one might associate equally readily with early adulthood), one of the cornerstones of his approach is the idea that stress or crisis can be transforming rather than overwhelming. Such ideas reflect those in crisis theory, already discussed in Chapter 6 (on theories), and will be picked up again in our chapters on interventions with different user groups and different problems.

(*Source*: Photofusion Picture Library/Paul Doyle)

Key points for adulthood

- Adulthood is 'constructed' in different ways (legal, social, emotional), with different demarcation points possible, depending on what aspect of development is being considered and from what perspective.
- No longer follows so clearly common developmental paths – indeed 'development' may no longer be appropriate descriptor.
- Stage theorists set out sequence of tasks or challenges which they suggest confront all adults. Erikson's key themes in his eight stages of development, although they cannot be applied too rigidly, may provide a helpful framework for thinking about adulthood.
- Common tasks of adulthood in early and middle years are seen as centring around three roles of work, partnerships and parenting.
- Attachment theory, and the adult attachment interview, are fruitful ways of helping us to understand some of the core issues in emotional development in adult life.

Older age

In this final section, we turn to older age, the seventh age in Shakespeare's seven ages of man, described rather pessimistically by his character Jacques as 'second childishness, and mere oblivion, sans teeth, sans eyes, sans taste, sans everything' (*As You Like It*). Erikson, however, for whom late adulthood is the final and eighth stage, is more positive, and we shall consider his view of the key theme of older age when we look in a moment at social and emotional development.

As in earlier sections of this chapter, it is important to recognise this life stage as involving the complex interaction of physical, cognitive and psychosocial factors, all of which affect how the individual experiences older age. Many of the issues which we have already considered are important here, too, so that although we shall not repeat them here we hope you will draw on ideas and theories in earlier sections to help you make sense of the experience of older people. For example, ideas about resilience which we introduced in our discussion of middle childhood may be a fruitful way of understanding and conceptualising how an older person addresses some of the painful experiences of loss which are almost invariably a hallmark of these years: loss of a loved partner, loss of work roles, and lessening of health being common and obvious examples.

It would, however, be a mistake to think about people in older adulthood as a single group. Some researchers (e.g. Neugarten, 1975; Kroger, 2000) have suggested that we should look at two distinct phases in older age and distinguish between the young old and the old old, the latter group beginning perhaps around 80. But it could in fact be more helpful to distinguish between the healthy and unhealthy elderly, since some adults are already frail and in decline by 65, while others are full of energy and active well into their 80s. As we observed in relation to adulthood, the process of ageing is highly individual, and grouping people together into a category of 'old age' fails to acknowledge the wide differences, not just between someone of 65 and someone 20 or 30 years older, but also between people's experiences at the same age. So we should keep in mind that ageing is not something which happens rapidly at 65 and that the social and physical needs and abilities of older people vary enormously.

We shall pause here to ask you to reflect on your own attitudes to and experiences of older age. This is important because it helps us to demonstrate the above point, that older adults are diverse individuals rather than a homogenous group; it may also be a starting point for ideas about the way in which older age is a cultural construction – i.e. that the meanings, interpretations and images of age in any society affect the way in which we, as members of that society, view older people. These ideas, including those of ageism and cultural differences in responses to older age, are developed more fully in the third section of this book (Lymbery's chapter (22) on working with older people) so we shall not explore them in detail here.

Reflect

Think of the older people whom you have known or worked with. *Do you find the distinctions (between the 'young old' and the 'old old') helpful?*

Perhaps you have had (or observed) a close relationship with a grandparent or older neighbour or relative, which may have enriched your life and given you insight into the feelings of older people, and how they can contribute to younger lives, too. *What are the qualities which the older person was able to share?*

Physical and cognitive changes in late adulthood

Although one study of American older people found that a good proportion of their respondents described their health as good or excellent (Suzman et al., 1992), the likelihood of experiencing ill health or disability particularly in older age (over 75) does increase. There are also a number of physical changes which if not leading immediately if at all to illness or disability may produce feelings of frustration, loss of confidence and even loss of a secure sense of self. For someone who has prided themselves on having an excellent memory, independence of mind and being physically active, decline in these powers can be experienced as emotionally humiliating/ difficult as well as practically inconvenient. Physical changes which are more or less inevitable, although they may occur at different ages, include:

- *Changes in the structure of the brain* – dendritic loss and loss of neurons, which initially may have little impact because of 'over-supply' but which gradually accumulate to the point where everyday activities become noticeably more difficult.

- *Changes in the senses* – hearing loss, which may include high-frequency sounds, ability to discriminate words and tinnitus (a persistent ringing in the ears). Changes in sense of smell and taste are also apparent, markedly in the case of the former.
- *Sleep changes* – sleep patterns change, with older adults waking more frequently during the night and dozing during the day to compensate for loss of sleep.
- *Memory loss* – there is some deterioration in memory in old age, which seems to lie particularly in the area of retrieving items from the memory (obvious examples are in remembering names, dates and so on).
- *Decline in cognitive processes* – this includes loss of 'fluid intelligence' – i.e. involving the ability to find solutions to problems not previously encountered. However, although there is a physiological basis for some deterioration, external circumstances also have a major effect on functioning. For example, older people may become dramatically more confused on admission to residential care or as a result of other changes in their routines.

Other serious physical and mental challenges which occur in older age much more frequently than for younger adults include the onset of dementia (Alzheimer's and multi-infarct dementia being the two most common), functional disability arising from arthritis, cardiovascular problems and Parkinson's disease and hypertension. Older adults seem also at higher risk of depression, particularly after the age of about 75, for reasons which you may readily be able to deduce. (See Chapter 22 on working with older-aged adults for fuller discussion of implications for social work and social care.)

Social and emotional development

Erikson thought that the central theme of this period involves that of 'integrity over despair'. As with his earlier stages, he sees this period too as one in which its challenges or tasks can be successfully or unsuccessfully met, suggesting that it is a time when individuals look back over their lives and experiences, and ideally reach some kind of self-acceptance, or as Erikson describes it 'ego integration'. Although this task, according to Erikson, begins in middle adulthood, it is most central to later adulthood, and to achieve it successfully involves accepting one's life for what it has been, responsibility for choices made, acceptance of opportunities gained or lost. There is, it seems to us, some risk of smugness or even intolerance creeping into this account: successful ageing after all depends to some extent on external factors, the opportunities and encouragement in one's environment, and the good or ill fortune which may arise from physical health or ill health, cognitive functioning, and the well-being of family and friends. Inevitably, with waning powers and capacities, it is less easy to remain resilient, recover from bereavement and to take active steps to deal with the feelings of loneliness which can come as partners and old friends die. Nor has there has been much research on the accuracy or otherwise of Erikson's account. See, however, the Closer Look box.

A closer Look

Research note on identity in older age

Walaskay et al. (1983) classified the older adults whom they interviewed into one of four identity states:

- *Integrity achieved* – the individual is aware of her/his own ageing, able to accept uniqueness of life and able to adjust to change.
- *Despair* – individual has come to a negative evaluation of life and personal achievements.
- *Foreclosed* – individual is content with current life but resists any self-exploration or assessment of the whole lifetime.
- *Dissonant* – the individual is just beginning to attempt resolution of dilemmas around identity and is full of ambivalence.

Those in the achieved and foreclosed states were most satisfied with their lives and least anxious about death.

Reflect

Do the four categories of identity states in our Closer Look box remind you of any used by other theorists we have studied?

Do you yourself feel that acceptance of the past is a necessary ingredient for contentment or adaptation to old age?

Do you think that Erikson's theme for this life stage 'fits the bill'?

One way of coping with such experiences of loss across different domains may be that of gradually feeling less involved in the world around you. This process has been described as *disengagement*: a theory which has been formulated to describe what some see as the central

psychological process of old age, and as a more positive way of thinking about the 'letting go' which is typical of many older people. As restated by Cumming (1975) the process has three aspects:

- *Shrinkage of life space* – interacting with fewer and fewer other people, and filling fewer and fewer roles.
- *Increased individuality* – in the roles and relationships which remain, the individual is less and less governed by strict rules and expectations and obligations.
- *Acceptance of these changes* – in this Eriksonian idea, the healthy adult actively disengages from roles and relationships, turning more and more inward and away from interactions with others.

While the first two characteristics may be fairly readily agreed on, the third seems more doubtful and the research evidence for it is too. You might like to reflect on what you think is likely to be true.

Reflect

From your own personal experience, reading and observations, would you say that those who remain involved and active and least disengaged are MORE or LESS likely to be happy, have high morale and to live longer than their opposites?

Again drawing on your personal views/experiences, do you think older adults are MORE or LESS likely to be content with solitude and being on their own for longer periods of time?

(For example, Helen Bee (1994), in Chapter 14 of her *Lifespan Development* book, suggests that older adults are least likely to describe themselves as lonely.)

Control

Another theme in the gerontology literature is that of control, and the idea that the sense of retaining or losing control of one's life is an important contributing factor in successful ageing. As Bee comments: 'Even life events that seem objectively highly stressful may have little negative effect if the individual feels he [sic] has some choice' (1994: 472).

The predictors of life satisfaction in older adults are given in the Closer Look box below. Finally, it is worth noting that it is, above all, the individual's perception of her or his situation which is most important in almost all cases: perceived adequacy of income, health and support are all better predictors of life satisfaction and morale than any objective measures. Although this may mean a lowering of expectation (for example, in regard to acceptable health), what seems critical for emotional balance is the degree of discrepancy between what one has and what one expects.

Key points for older age

- Older adulthood can be divided into the young old (65–75) and the old old (75 plus)
- Although physical decline is inevitable, there is great variation in how and when this occurs and how it is experienced.
- Physical changes occur in the brain, in the senses and in physical capability, leading to general slowing down of all responses.
- Rates of arthritis, hypertension and heart disease increase. Dementia is rare before late adulthood, becoming more common with advancing age.
- Erikson's view of this life stage, although plausible, has not been supported by research. Nor has disengagement theory been empirically supported.
- Adequacy of perceived support, a sense of control, and match between what one expects and what one actually has seem to be crucial for successful ageing.

Conclusion

We conclude this chapter, as we started it, with a poem, this time one in which the poet at the end of her life reflects on the qualities of old age, and in particular, her present happiness enhanced by memories of contentment and fulfilment. As you read the poem, you may ask yourself whether the positive experiences described here seem to fit with Erikson's description of the task of older age as that of integrity versus despair. You may also notice that the earlier themes of adulthood – intimacy and generativity – are still reflected here.

> Old age has its particular season
> Not quite to be compared with autumn or winter:
> Not to the luxuriance of autumn,
> Not to the austerity of winter.
> Passion it has, compounded of present joy
> And memory of past fulfilment;
> Precarious, being timebound,
> With pleasure the more poignant, so,
> Its durable fire burns a lifelong day.
> I might choose, for an emblem of its happiness,

A closer look

Predictions of life satisfaction in older adults

Demographic factors

- *Income/social class* – those with higher income are more likely to be satisfied with their lives, even when you hold constant other factors such as health.
- *Education* – more highly educated adults are slightly more satisfied, but the difference is small.
- *Gender* – there is essentially no difference, despite the higher levels of aches and pains in older age and the larger number of widows among older women.
- *Marital status* – married adults consistently report higher life satisfaction.
- *Race/ethnicity* – there appears to be no general tendency for black, Hispanic, or other minority groups to have lower (or higher) life satisfaction beyond the effect of social class and income. For this outcome at least, there appears to be no 'double jeopardy' among ageing minorities. Those who are poor and black, for example, are not more dissatisfied than any other group.

Personal qualities

- *Personality* – extroverted adults, and those low in neuroticism, are consistently more satisfied with their lives.
- *Sense of control* – the greater the sense of personal control, the greater the life satisfaction. This may be especially significant in late adulthood, when the objective amount of control may decline.
- *Social interaction* – those with more contact with others, especially more intimate and supportive contact, are more satisfied.
- *Health* – those with better self-perceived health are more satisfied. Note, though, that self-perceived health is not at all perfectly correlated with health as a physician might rate it.
- *Religion* – those who describe themselves as more religious also describe themselves as more satisfied.
- *Negative life changes* – the more negative life changes older people have recently had to deal with, the lower their life satisfaction is likely to be.

From Helen Bee, *Lifespan Development*, Published by Allyn and Bacon, Boston, MA. Copyright © 1994 by Pearson Education. Reprinted by permission of the publisher.

The surprising glass-blue berry,
  held in a magenta star,
Of the fruiting clerodendron.

(*Source*: Anne Ridler, *Collected Poems*,
Carcanet Press Ltd., 1994)

In the chapter, we have taken a lifespan approach to human development. In other words, having identified the key psychological theorists, and also looked briefly at the growing importance of studies of brain development, we then explored sequentially the key changes, achievements and challenges which confront us as we move from infancy into older age. We have highlighted ideas and concepts which seem of particular relevance to social workers – for example attachment and resilience. We hope that what is inevitably a brief introduction will encourage you to read in more depth about this fascinating subject as you, as a practitoner, begin to apply the ideas which we have looked at here.

Key learning points

This chapter has covered the following learning points:

✔ Social workers need to ground themselves in the varieties of typical children's, adolescents' and adults' experiences in order to keep a sense of perspective, to make more precise judgements of atypical functioning and to communicate more effectively both with users and other professionals.

✔ Developmental theories help in understanding normal development, challenges to development and risk factors in the development of psychopathology.

✔ Different theories focus on different aspects of development and each has limitations and a potential 'range of convenience'.

✔ Changes which occur at key phases of development, i.e. infancy, early and middle childhood, adolescence, early and middle adulthood and older age, encompass physical and motor, cognitive, perceptual and emotional aspects of development.

✔ Each phase of development may be seen as posing certain tasks, such as, for example, in infancy, forming attachments to caregivers, learning to communicate and to use language, developing gross and fine motor skills and learning self-control and compliance.

✔ Issues of gender, race, class and culture are relevant to developmental change.

✔ Some of the common challenges to development include physical and learning disabilities and mental ill health.

Further reading

The following are a small selection of texts which you will find useful to follow up. Throughout the chapter, we make reference to other key books on such topics as attachment theory and cognitive theories, and references to key relevant theorists are contained in the bibliography.

Beckett, C. (2002) *Human Growth and Development*. London: Sage.

Crawford, K. and Walker, J. (2003) *Social Work and Human Development*. Exeter: Learning Matters (3rd edition 2010, Walker, J. and Crawford, K.). Both of the above provide useful, accessible introductions to understanding human development written for social workers. They include excellent illustrative case material and, unlike some of the other texts available, discuss all stages of development rather than only addressing childhood and adolescence.

Bee, H. (1994) *Lifespan Development*. New York: Harper Collins.

Bee, H. (1995) *The Developing Child*. New York: Harper Collins. Both of these are comprehensive American-style student texts which provide useful discussion, and explication of relevant theories, illustrated by examples largely drawn from the USA. They have been updated, but earlier editions can be bought quite cheaply on Amazon and most of their content still has currency.

Cabinet Office/Social Exclusion Task Force (2009) *Understanding the risks of social exclusion across the lifecycle*. London Cabinet Office. Available from www.cabinetoffice. gov.uk. Provides quantitative data about the complex relationship between the different risk markers as indicators of social exclusion across the lifespan, and how they vary among the British population.

Daniel, B., Wassell, S. and Gilligan, R. (1999) *Child Development for Child Care and Protection Workers*. London: Jessica Kingsley. The focus of the book is clear from its title. It offers in particular a good introduction to the theory and application of resilience.

DeHart, G., Stroufe, A. and Cooper, R. (2004) *Child Development: Its Nature and Course*. New York: McGraw-Hill. An American text which addresses childhood and adolescent development at a greater level of sophistication, appropriate to specialist practitioners and post-qualifying students.

Fraiberg, S. (1977) *Insights from the Blind*. London: Souvenir Press. Fraiberg is an American psychologist and therapist who pioneered work with children blind from birth and infancy. This very readable account of her early work with these children illuminates the processes of normal development through its focus on the challenges facing unsighted children.

Hockey, J. and James, A. (2003) *Social Identities across the Lifespan*. Basingstoke: Macmillan. This text by two UK academics explores issues of growing older using a lifecourse perspective, and includes a discussion of a life-history approach to human development research.

Ingelby, E. (2010) *Applied Psychology for Social Work*, 2nd edn. Exeter: Learning Matters. The author shows how in social work it is important that psychology is studied in the contexts of social care, since these offer potential explanations of complex aspects of human development.

Lindon, J. (2010) *Understanding Child Development: Linking theory and practice*. London: Hodder Arnold. As the title suggests, this book examines the links between theories, learning and practice in relation to child development.

Robinson, L. (1995) *Psychology for Social Workers: Black Perspectives*. London: Routledge. Lena Robinson explores psychological theories from a black perspective, and urges that this should form part of core learning.

Schofield, G. and Beek, M. (2006) *The Adoption Handbook*. London: BAAF. There are numerous texts on attachment and loss, of which the best-known for social workers are those by David Howe and colleagues (see Bibliography). However, Schofield and Beek's recent book is extremely helpful in showing the detailed ways in which particular attachment experiences inform children's, adolescents' and adults' lives, and in suggesting how these may show themselves in contact with social workers, and the implications for working with them.

Sugarman, L. (1986) *Lifespan Development: Concepts, Theories and Interventions*. London: Methuen. Although written some time ago, this is particularly useful for its approach to understanding development in adulthood.

Taylor, C. (2004) 'Underpinning knowledge for child care practice: reconsidering child development theory', *Child and Family Social Work*, 9: 225–35.

Waddell M. (1998) *Inside Lives*. London: Duckworth (Tavistock Clinic Series). This is a highly accessible and insightful account of human development from birth to death using a psychoanalytic perspective, with excellent discussion of key contemporary concepts and many case illustrations. The author is a child psychotherapist and psychoanalyst with a strong understanding of social work and the impact of the social world on individual development.

http://www. Useful websites

www.bbc.co.uk/child in our time/
The BBC website, especially the 'Child in our time' series following children from birth onwards provides excellent learning material.

home.cc.umanitoba.ca/-mdlee/Teaching/links
Website of the American Psychological Association which offers further resources and reading on lifespan development.

www.marybold.com/CogFunc.htm
One of a number of websites which are useful as sources for each life stage.

www.wiley.com/go/care
Tools used in A Community Health Approach to the Assessment of Infants and their Parents.

www.statistics.gov.uk
A useful resource for government statistics.

www.everychildmatters.gov.uk
The public website gives a range of news, advice and guidance for parents, children and young people.

If you are interested in following up specific theories, models or theorists, you will be able to find information on the relevant webpage – e.g. Erikson, attachment theory, etc.

www.richardatkins.co.uk/atws/index for information on attachment theory.

www.attachmentnetwork.org/links for information on the attachment network.

www.piaget.org/search.html for more information on Piagetian cognitive theories.

A useful video on attachment theory made by John Bowlby's son Richard is available at no cost if you send a blank video tape to Sir Richard Bowlby, Boundary House, Wyldes Close, London, NW11 7JB.

For additional cases and topic-organised, clickable links into additional media resources, including those produced by IRISS, visit **www.pearsoned.co.uk/wilsonruch**

Activity

There are a number of activities in the chapter which you might want to undertake as you read, or revisit when you have reached the concluding section. The article on child abuse in Hong Kong, for example, O'Brian and Lau, (1995) *Child Abuse Review*, 4, 38–46, is a useful way of starting to think about cultural differences and their impact on development. Depending on whether you are working on your own or in a group, you might consider also doing the following:

Activity One

On your own: Write down Erikson's 'task' for each life stage, then jot down next to it what you would consider to be an example (behaviourally) of successful mastery or failure (relatively speaking) to accomplish this.

Activity Two

Or: Take one or more of the life stages, and consider what concepts and ideas psychoanalytic/cognitive/attachment theories say about each. Are these ideas compatible or incompatible with each other – e.g. do they seem to be addressing the same issues? (For example, an 'internal working model' (Bowlby) and 'schema' (Piaget).)

Activity Three

As a class-based exercise: Working in small groups, give a presentation to your fellow students or colleagues to show how one or more theories/concepts/models for practice can help social workers in their understanding of a particular developmental stage, and in their day-to-day practice in connection with this.

Chapter 8
Law and social work

Alison Brammer*

Chapter summary

This chapter will examine the nature of the relationship between social work and law. Initially discussion focuses on general principles of law and social work, examining key legal concepts for social work practice, sources of law, the structure of the legal system within which social workers operate, the way law shapes social work practice through powers and duties which shape the boundaries of practice. The place of law within social work education and practice has been debated over the years. It is now clear from the qualifying frameworks that it is a central component of social work education and practice. The chapter encourages critical engagement with the law, through understanding of its development, the forces that influence new laws and also its limitations. Law provides a framework for resolution of disputes relating to social work practice and for endorsement of good practice, providing a range of responses to issues affecting all client groups.

The second part of the chapter outlines the legal framework for professional social work practice with children and families and with adults. Unless otherwise stated the law referred to is that which applies in England and Wales. The legal system in Scotland differs from that of the rest of the United Kingdom, as does much of the legislation which underpins social work practice. Although many of the principles are the same, there are some significant differences and throughout the text the reader will be directed to where these differences occur.

Learning objectives

This chapter covers topics that will enable you to achieve the following learning objectives:

- To understand how law defines the social work role
- To be familiar with relevant legal terminology
- To understand key sources of law
- To be introduced to the framework of relevant social work law for working with adults and children
- To appreciate the significance of the Human Rights Act 1998 for social work practice.

* The publishers gratefully acknowledge Janice West, formerly of the School of Health, Glasgow Caledonian University, Kathryn Cameron, formerly of the Glasgow School of Social work, and Mary McColgan of the University of Ulster for their significant contribution of material relating to Scotland and Ireland to this chapter.

National Occupational Standards

This chapter will help you to meet the following National Occupational Standards:

Key Role 1: **Prepare for, and work with individuals, families, carers, groups and communities to assess their needs and circumstances**

Key Role 2: **Plan, carry out, review and evaluate social work practice, with individuals, families, carers, groups, communities and other professionals**

Key Role 3: **Support individuals to represent their needs, views and circumstances**

Key Role 4: **Manage risk to individuals, families, carers, groups, communities, self and colleagues**

Key Role 5: **Manage and be accountable, with supervision and support, for your own social work practice within your organisation**

Key Role 6: **Demonstrate professional competence in social work practice**

Case study

Albert and Mary

Albert and Mary are aged 55 and 45. Albert has never enjoyed good health and for several years he has been almost housebound. He has kidney dialysis every day in a converted bedroom at home. Mary was a nursery teacher but has given up work to care for Albert. She is finding it increasingly difficult to care for Albert and they often argue. She would like to get out some evenings with friends and even return to work part-time but Albert wants her to stay with him.

Albert and Mary have a daughter, Denise, who has a mild learning disability and lives at home. She works part-time in the local supermarket but has few friends of her own age. Recently she has become very withdrawn and while she has always been very affectionate she will no longer let anyone touch her. A friend of Mary calls round to tell her that she has heard that John, who lives in the same village, has been bragging that he had sex with 'the nutter'. John has been in trouble with the police for drug-related crimes and is subject to an ASBO. When Mary tries to talk to Denise about this she becomes hysterical and attacks Mary. The next day Mary persuades Denise to take a pregnancy test and it is positive. Denise is adamant that she wants to have the baby but Mary fears she will be unable to look after a child, doesn't really understand what is involved and isn't able to make that decision for herself.

The following evening Mary is woken by shouting coming from next door. She has had concerns for some time about how her neighbour, Julie, is coping with her three children. It appears that her husband, David, had moved out a few weeks previously but returned in a drunken state demanding that Julie let him take their son Robert (5), claiming, 'It's my human right'. Julie has suspected for some time that David has been having an affair and has not let him see the children since he left. When Julie asked him to leave, Robert and both his sisters (Lucy, aged 10 and Sarah, aged 3) witnessed David push and slap Julie.

Lucy has ADHD and has been having problems at school. The headteacher has written to Julie and David several times, inviting them to come in and discuss Lucy's progress but they have not responded. Since David left, Julie has been drinking heavily and has not taken Sarah to play group or Robert to school.

Mary is at the end of her tether and the next day she contacts the duty social worker, explaining that she has concerns for the children next door and asking whether she is entitled to any help with caring for Albert.

Consider how the law guides social work practice in this case. What action must be taken and what action could be taken? Does the law support social work values and good practice?

The case study introduces some of the key issues for social workers working with the law. Within the scenario there are a number of competing interests and assertion of rights. Individuals present a range of needs and might be described variously as vulnerable, in need of support and in need of protection. At all times the social worker has to work within the law, complying with and not exceeding duties and powers.

Introduction

Social workers engage with law on a daily basis. At times this is explicitly clear – when working in the courts or relying on a statutory duty. In other situations it is through exercise of powers and duties, conceptualised as routine social work tasks, which have their foundation in law. The case study above provided examples of duties: to investigate suspicion of harm to the child, and to carry out an assessment of carer needs as well as powers: to provide services to vulnerable adults, children in need and their families.

The study of law and use of law can be the cause of some anxiety among students and practitioners. In part, this may be due to the ever-increasing complexity and volume of law being produced that is of relevance to social work. Clearly the study of law by non-lawyers may be a challenge. It is a challenge, however, that must be met, as it is a requirement of the qualifying framework. Key roles within social work practice have been identified in the National Occupational Standards. For each of the key roles, there is a requirement to 'understand, critically analyse, evaluate, and apply . . . knowledge' of '[t]he legal, social, economic and ecological context of social work practice, country, UK, EU legislation, statutory codes, standards, frameworks and guidance relevant to social work practice and related fields, including multi-disciplinary and multi-organisational practice, data protection and confidentiality of information'. In Scotland, there are six standards which underpin the degree and which are outlined in the *Framework for Social Work Education in Scotland* (2003). Similarly, in Northern Ireland, the Framework Specification for the Degree in Social Work (2003) is underpinned by six key roles. Looking beyond that stipulation, a good grasp of the law can enhance practice and be empowering for both social work professionals and their clients.

This chapter aims to outline an introduction to the key elements of legal understanding required by anyone contemplating a career in social work. It commences with a consideration of the relationship between law and social work practice and a discussion of values. Ongoing study of law as a student and practitioner is an inevitable requirement and the chapter provides coverage of existing sources of law to be explored, as well as guidance for future legal research. An explanation of the various types of law – legislation (statute), case law and the operation of the doctrine of precedent in the court structure – is provided.

Law does not simply exist on paper: it is a dynamic feature of social work practice. The chapter continues by looking at ways in which a social worker may be actively involved in the machinery of law: through exercise of powers and duties and through involvement in the courts where legal decisions are made. As professionals, social workers are accountable and their actions may on occasions be subject to challenge. Sometimes this will be within the court structure itself but other avenues of available challenge are also outlined. Recognition and promotion of 'rights' is a central feature of social work. Whether the law recognises rights in a comparable fashion may be questioned, but important inroads have been made through the introduction of the Human Rights Act 1998. The next section of the chapter considers the impact of this important legislation on social work practice.

Finally, an outline of the key features of the substantive law relating to adults and children completes the chapter.

The relationship between law and social work

The role of law in social work practice today is significant. Over recent years a substantial volume of legislation has been passed, which has impacted on social work practice. Important examples include the Children Acts of 1989 and 2004, the National Health Service and Community Care Act 1990, the Mental Capacity Act 2005, Mental Health Act 2007 and the Adoption and Children Act 2002. Recent legislation in Scotland includes the Adoption and Children (Scotland) Act 2007, Sexual Offences (Scotland) Act 2009 and Criminal Justice and Licensing (Scotland) Act 2010. Law is often described as providing a mandate to practice. It clearly underpins much of social work practice and provides duties and powers to be exercised by social services. An understanding of legal requirements is essential for effective and fair social work practice. Despite the position of legal understanding as key to effective social work practice, a degree of anxiety is associated with its study and practice:

'What appears clear . . . is that social work students and practitioners experience contact with the law and legal system as stressful. They are concerned about their lack of familiarity with legal settings, languages and procedures, and about the frequency with which the legal rules change. They express uncertainty about how the law interfaces with social work values and organizational procedures. Furthermore, legal accountability, which might benefit service users, can be unsettling for social work practitioners. They conceptualise the law as intimidating, conflictual, and more likely to be obstructive than empowering.'

(Braye and Preston-Shoot, 2006)

Anxiety about law may be exacerbated if it is seen as 'separate' or additional to other aspects of social work. More effective understanding and learning may be achieved where law is positioned in the context of contemporary social work practice and the incorporation of social work values relating to oppression, service user's rights and discrimination. Good social work practice is of much greater complexity than simply executing prescribed duties under legislation.

In relation to social work practice, law is relevant as a setting in which decisions are made and a structure within which social workers practise. The courts and institutions of law can become an extension of the workplace. To work effectively within those structures an understanding of the hierarchy of the courts, procedures and roles of other professionals working in that setting is essential. This knowledge can also benefit clients who may be supported when facing court proceedings.

Law constructs some aspects of social work practice through its direction in the form of duties, powers and limitations. There are instances where the law clearly directs action to be taken, e.g. the duty to investigate suspicion of significant harm to a child. It also places limits on what actions can be taken, e.g. through designation of a required mental health diagnosis as a prerequisite for long-term detention. In other areas the law allows exercise of a measure of professional discretion, e.g. in determining whether an individual is eligible for support services that the authority has a power rather than a duty to provide. It is also becoming increasingly important for social workers to have an understanding of legal issues which service users may face even though there may not be a direct social work responsibility involved in the issue, e.g. legal remedies for domestic violence between adults; welfare benefits and housing issues.

Critical understanding of law

To practise effectively it is necessary to have a critical understanding of law and to recognise its limitations alongside its strengths. A common misconception about law is that it is clear-cut and provides unambiguous answers to solutions. In fact some provisions of the law lack that clarity and may be open to interpretation. When new legislation is introduced it is sometimes necessary to wait for clarification on meaning of certain provisions from the courts. In other situations law may appear to lack clear direction because it allows discretion for practice within broad boundaries.

Law tends to develop in a piecemeal fashion in response to particular issues in society and this can result in an overall provision that lacks cohesion. As an example, anti-discrimination legislation has been introduced over a 40-year period alongside formal recognition of the need to respond to different forms of discrimination. First, legislation to tackle race and sex discrimination was introduced in the form of the Equal Pay Act 1970, Sex Discrimination Act 1975 and Race Relations Act 1976. The Disability Discrimination Act 1995 followed and, most recently, as well as further reforms to race, sex and disability legislation, it has become unlawful to discriminate on grounds of religion or belief, age and sexual orientation. The Equality Act 2010 aims to harmonise discrimination law and introduces a single approach to discrimination in one statute as well as strengthening the duty on public bodies (including social services authorities) to advance equality of opportunity.

While there has been a huge volume of legislative activity over recent years, the pace of legal development may still not keep up with practice developments. As a consequence some provisions that appear outdated may remain in place and legal language may not be updated to reflect terms adopted in practice. Practice may develop ahead of a legal framework. As an example, the practice of greater openness in adoption and development of contact was not envisaged in the Adoption Act 1976, developed in the 1980s and 1990s, but the need to consider contact has been incorporated into the Adoption and Children Act 2002 and the Adoption and Children (Scotland) Act 2007.

Law may appear to be discriminatory itself, e.g. restriction on voting rights for detained patients under the Mental Health Act 1983 (in Scotland these restrictions have been repealed), or may be applied in a discriminatory fashion, e.g. police discretion to stop and search exercised disproportionately to include high numbers of young black men. English and Scottish law tends to be reactive rather than proactive, reacting to situations that have occurred, by punishing or providing a remedy, rather than setting out codes of behaviour or entitlements.

The law can seem to be a bureaucratic machine, concerned more with processing forms accurately and following procedures than dealing with the central issue in a case. This approach is partly due to the need to follow principles of natural justice and for justice to be seen to be done.

The study of law within the qualifying framework

The role of law in social work practice is specifically addressed within the framework for social work qualification. The Department of Health *Requirements for Social Work Training* (DoH, 2002e) stipulate that students of social work degrees must have experience in at least two practice settings: of statutory social work tasks involving legal interventions; of providing services to at least two user groups (e.g. childcare and mental health). Programme providers are also required to demonstrate that students undertake specific learning and assessment in key areas, such as 'assessment planning intervention and review; partnership working and information sharing across professional disciplines and agencies, and Law'.

National occupational standards for social work are organised around areas of competence, or key roles of social workers. For each of the key roles, there is a requirement to 'understand, critically analyse, evaluate, and apply . . . knowledge' of '[t]he legal, social, economic and ecological context of social work practice, country, UK, EU legislation, statutory codes, standards, frameworks and guidance relevant to social work practice and related fields, including multidisciplinary and multi-organisational practice, data protection and confidentiality of information'.

In addition, before award of a degree, QAA benchmarks require students to demonstrate knowledge, which is to include:

'The significance of legislative and legal frameworks and service delivery statements (including the nature of legal authority, the application of legislation in practice, statu-

tory accountability and tensions between statute, policy and practice). The current range and appropriateness of statutory, voluntary and private agencies providing community-based, day-care, residential and other services and the organizational systems inherent within these. The significance of interrelationships with other social services, especially education, housing, health, income maintenance and criminal justice. The complex relationships between justice, care and control in social welfare and the practical and ethical implications of these, including roles as statutory agents and in upholding the law in respect of discrimination.'

The objective of each element of the new framework is that understanding of law is integrated with other aspects of social work knowledge for effective application of legal knowledge to practice situations.

Structure of social work

Law provides the operational structure for social work. Social services departments are established within certain local authorities as part of a legal structure provided by the Local Authority and Social Services Act 1970, supplemented by additions from the Children Act 2004. There is now a requirement to appoint a Director of Children's Services for each children's services authority, and a Director of Adult Social Services (replacing the previous duty to appoint an overall Director of Social Services under the 1970 Act). The Director of Children's Services is appointed for the purpose of prescribed functions including those exercisable by the LEA; social services that relate to children; children leaving local authority care; the Children's Services authority for cooperation, safeguarding and promoting the welfare of children and information databases; any health services for children that are transferred to the local authority. The role of the Director of Adult Services includes accountability for assessing needs, ensuring availability and delivery of adult social services, promoting social inclusion and well-being and transition planning for disabled children approaching adulthood.

The 1970 Act also makes provision for the Secretary of State to produce directions for the exercise of social services functions (s. 7); establishes complaints procedures and contains the power for the Secretary of State to require an inquiry into social services functions. In case of doubt the LASSA 1970 also contains a list in Schedule 1 of the Act (updated regularly) of the permitted actions or functions of social services authorities. While the 1970 Act provided for the organisational structure of social services, the law has only responded

A closer look

The Framework for Social Work Education in Scotland (2003)

The Framework is made up of the *Scottish Requirements for Social Work Training*, the introduction to the *Standards in Social Work Education* (SiSWE) and the Standards themselves. The SiSWE set out the knowledge, understanding and skills that social workers need and act as a basis for their continuing professional development. The guiding principles of social work education in Scotland state that social workers must maintain and promote the dignity, safety, choice, privacy and potential of people who use services and balance these with consideration of the needs of others for protection; treat everyone equally, and value their distinctiveness and diversity and maintain public trust and confidence in social services. The SiSWE are made up of 6 key roles taken from the National Occupational Standards. Each key role is broken down into a number of learning foci with related underpinning knowledge, transferable skills and assessed outcomes.

The N. Ireland Framework Specification for the Degree in Social Work (2003)

The framework was developed jointly by the Department of Health and Social Services and Personal Safety (DHSSPSS) and the Northern Ireland Social Care Council (NISCC). Like Scotland the Framework Specification incorporates National Occupational Standards, QAA benchmark statements and the NISCC Code of Practice for Social Care Workers which defines the standards for professional conduct and practice and the Code of Practice for Employers which outlines their responsibilities in regulating social care workers. Uniquely, in N. Ireland, the generic Degree in Social Work qualification is designed to prepare social workers to work in a range of settings, including Health and Social Services, criminal justice and probation, education welfare and the voluntary sector. Following attainment of the Degree in Social Work, graduates have to complete an Assessed Year in Employment (AYE) before they can register as a social worker with NISCC.

recently to the need to regulate staff employed by social services and in other social care posts.

The structure of social work in Scotland

Social work is one of the devolved powers of the Scottish Parliament, and social work provision in Scotland encompasses children and families, community care and criminal justice. The fact that the Scottish Executive has a number of ministerial offices covering Education and Young People, Health and Community Care and Justice means that there may be a number of bodies which are responsible for decision-making in respect of social work in relation to policy directions and service delivery. The report of the 21st Century Review of Social Work, *Changing Lives* (2006), has said quite clearly that social work services need to work with other service providers from across the public, private and voluntary sectors in a joined-up effort to deliver services across the public sector. The Social Work Inspection Agency monitors standards of social work services, and although the Agency acts independently it is directly accountable to Scottish ministers. Following the Crerar Review, however, a new inspection structure will be introduced in 2011 – Social Care and Social Work Improvement Scotland (SCSWIS) which will integrate functions of

SWIA, Care Commission and Her Majesty's Inspectorate of Education. Statutory service provision is carried out at a local level by local authorities. Each local authority is required to have a chief social work officer (s. 3(1) of the Social Work (S) Act 1968) and the qualifications of these officers are set out in the *Qualifications of Chief Social Work Officers (Scotland) Regulations 1996*. In practice, many local authorities now combine departments such as housing, education and social work, a trend which reflects the 'joined up' nature of service delivery. The ongoing implementation of the Community Health Partnerships (Scotland) Regulations 2004, has led to the development of an increasing number of Community Health and Care Partnerships (CHCP) across Scotland.

Regulation of social work

The Care Standards Act 2000 (CSA) vested responsibility for training and regulation of social workers in the General Social Care Council (GSCC). Codes of practice for social care workers and their employers have been developed by the Council. The CSA 2000 provides a registration requirement for social workers (included in the term 'social care workers' under the Act) to register with the GSCC (s. 56). The ultimate aim of the Council is for all individuals engaged in social care work (currently approximately 1 million) to be registered, of which social workers make up around 14 per cent. The requirement for registration under the CSA 2000 applies to: anyone engaged in relevant social work; a person who is employed in or manages a children's home, care home or residential family centre; a domiciliary care agency; fostering agency or voluntary adoption agency; a person from a domiciliary care agency who provides personal care in an individual's own home (s. 55). It is an offence for a person to use the title 'social worker' or imply that s/he is a qualified social worker if s/he is not registered with the General Social Care Council (s. 61 CSA).

It is possible for a person to be removed from the register under s. 59, and there is a right of appeal against removal to the Care Standards Tribunal. This process and its relation to the Protection of Children Act list was considered by the Care Standards Tribunal in the case of *Arthurworrey* v. *Secretary of State for Education and Skills* [2004] EWCST 268 PC.

This case study provides an example of individual accountability. Other social workers have been removed from the register for misconduct such as inappropriate use of restraint and forming relationships with a service user.

On a larger scale, performance of public services, including social services, has increasingly been monitored through inspection and audit systems as a means of ensuring greater accountability. Star ratings were given to authorities, based on their compliance with the performance assessment framework measured according to targets, e.g. the number of adults with learning disabilities helped to live at home, and acceptable waiting times for care packages. This system was replaced in 2009 by 'comprehensive area assessments' but the new coalition government abolished this framework in June 2010. While some inspections will continue, such as Ofsted inspection of children's services, the new government has indicated that it wishes to move away from bureaucratic systems of performance data collection, towards greater transparency in the way councils operate.

A closer look

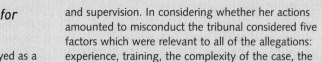

Arthurworrey v. *Secretary of State for Education and Skills* [2004]

The applicant, Lisa Arthurworrey, was employed as a social worker by Haringey Council and was allocated the case of Victoria Climbié in 1999. She gave evidence at the public inquiry into Victoria's death. Following an internal inquiry at Haringey, she was suspended from duty and the Council referred her to the Protection of Children Act list. She successfully appealed against inclusion on the list and her name was removed from the list. The tribunal had to consider whether, under the Protection of Children Act 1999, she was guilty of misconduct that harmed a child or placed a child at risk of harm, and unsuitable to work with children (s. 4(3) PCA 1999). Misconduct can include omissions. The 11 particulars of misconduct presented to the tribunal included: failure to conduct a proper interview with Ms Kouao (Victoria's aunt), failure to complete all the tasks required of her and identified at a strategy meeting, and failure to make contact or to take adequate steps to make contact with Victoria.

The tribunal considered the definition of misconduct and noted the need to consider the context in which the individual was working, including levels of support and supervision. In considering whether her actions amounted to misconduct the tribunal considered five factors which were relevant to all of the allegations: experience, training, the complexity of the case, the question of supervision, and the office environment.

The tribunal found no misconduct and while as a result it did not have to decide on suitability to work with children, it commented that Ms Arthurworrey was a suitable person to work with children, describing her as a 'straightforward and caring individual who has fully acknowledged the mistakes she made in connection with this case'.

As to the use of POCA the tribunal made it clear that to list an individual for 'professional mistakes should be an unusual occurrence, to be used only in the most clear cut cases'. It suggested that the procedure to remove an individual from the General Social Care Council register is the preferable route in cases of mistakes and poor professional practice. The concluding comments of the tribunal were, 'The message that we wish to make beyond the particular case that we have been considering is that Government must ensure that social workers are better trained, better resourced, and better supervised. In this way, it is hoped that the tragedy of Victoria will not be repeated'.

The Care Standards Act 2000, which established the GSCC, also provides for an independent regulation and inspection body. The Care Quality Commission (CQC) has assumed this role from the previous body, the Commission for Social Care Inspection (CSCI). As a single inspection body the CQC took over the functions of CSCI, the Commission for Healthcare Audit and Inspection and the Mental Health Act Commission. Anyone who provides care services must be registered by the new Commission.

The regulation of social work in Scotland

In Scotland, the regulatory framework mirrors that of the rest of the United Kingdom but like Wales and Northern Ireland, it has its own institutions and enabling legislation. The Scottish Social Services Council (SSSC) was set up by the Regulation of Care (S) Act 2001. It has three objectives which are:

1. to strengthen and support the workforce;
2. to raise standards of practice;
3. to protect those who use the services.

In order to fulfil these objectives to protect service users and their carers, the SSSC has responsibility to establish registers of key groups of social services staff, to publish codes of practice for workers and for employers and to regulate training and education for the workforce.

GSCC and SSSC Codes of Practice

It is clear that as well as providing powers and duties to social workers to practise, the law also provides for social workers themselves to be monitored and held accountable, in part through processes established by the Care Standards Act 2000. It is useful to return to consider the GSCC, the body created by the CSA, and consider how its Code of Practice for social work fits with the law.

Law relevant to social work practice does not exist in isolation and in many instances, where there are choices to be made about the exercise of powers, value perspectives are influential. Most obviously, perhaps, wherever possible the law should not be employed in a way that is discriminatory or oppressive. The GSCC and SSSC set out core values for social work in their Codes of Practice.

A closer look

GSCC core values for social work practice

These are the following:

- Protect the rights and promote the interests of service users and carers
- Strive to establish and maintain the trust and confidence of service users and carers
- Respect the rights of service users whilst seeking to ensure that their behaviour does not harm themselves or other people
- Uphold public trust and confidence in social care services
- Be accountable for the quality of their work and take responsibility for maintaining and improving their knowledge and skills.   (GSCC)

Values

It may be argued, however, that some social work values directly conflict with the objectives of available law. For example, it is difficult to reconcile the values of anti-discriminatory and anti-oppressive practice with some of the powers under the Mental Health Act 1983 and its tendency to define and categorise individuals by reference to one characteristic, their medical diagnosis of mental health. Conversely, there will be cases where the law can be used directly to support values. For example, it may be empowering for an individual who has been abused to have direct recourse to the Family Law Act 1996 (or in Scotland, the Protection from Abuse (Scotland) Act 2001), and to obtain an injunction removing the abuser from the household. It may also be argued that certain values that are often closely associated with social work are actually enshrined within legislation. For example, article 14 of the European Convention on Human Rights, the right not to be discriminated against, supports the social work value encapsulated in the Code of Ethics, i.e. recognising 'the value and dignity of every human being irrespective of origin, race, status, sex, sexual orientation, age, disability, belief or contribution to society'.

The relationship between the law and some social work values deserves more detailed consideration. Working in partnership is an integral aspect of good social work practice which may operate at a number of levels, including partnership with service users and partnership with professionals.

Partnership

Partnership with service users may include working to involve them fully in decision-making processes, whether by provision of appropriate literature and information, advocacy services, etc., or active involvement in, e.g., conferences and reviews. The concept of partnership is integral to the philosophy and practice of the Children Act 1989 and the Children (Scotland) Act 1995. There is no specific mention of partnership within the 1989 Act but it may be read in to certain provisions, notably, under s. 17, the duty to promote the upbringing of children in need by their families so far as that is consistent with promoting welfare. A similar duty is contained in s. 22 of the Scottish Act. Whether true meaningful partnership can exist between a professional social worker and a service user has been questioned in view of the obvious power imbalance. It may be an objective which is easier to realise in a case where social services are providing support to a child in need than in a contested child protection scenario. In the latter case, where the views of the social worker and the parents may be in direct conflict, it is still important that the social worker applies elements of a partnership approach, particularly by keeping lines of communication open, sharing and explaining information and any decisions that have been taken and not adopting an inflexible or adversarial stance. Aldgate (2001) suggests further that some of the key features of partnership with parents are:

■ A shared commitment to negotiation and actions concerning how best to safeguard and promote children's welfare
■ A mutual respect for the other's point of view
■ Recognising the unequal nature of power between parents and professionals
■ Recognising that parents have their own needs that should be addressed
■ Good communication skills on the part of professionals
■ The establishment of trust between all parties
■ Integrity and accountability on the part of both parents and professionals
■ Shared decision-making
■ A joint recognition of constraints on the services offered
■ A recognition that partnership is not an end in itself.

Commitment to partnership is also important in working relations between different professional groups in an interdisciplinary framework. The need to work together gained explicit recognition in guidance such as *Working Together to Safeguard Children* (DoH, 1999e, 2006c, 2010) and *No Secrets* (DoH, 2000f) and the consequences of failure to work together and share information is well documented in a number of Child Abuse Inquiry Reports. The Children Act 2004 develops partnership between professionals further. A statutory duty to cooperate with a view to improving children's well-being is imposed on children's services authorities and their relevant partners, which include district councils, police, probation boards, Youth Offending Teams, health authorities and Connexions. Similarly in Scotland, The Adult Protection and Support Act (Scotland) 2007 places a statutory duty on all public bodies to work together to protect the interests of 'adults at risk'.

Anti-discriminatory, anti-oppressive practice

The legal context to anti-discriminatory and anti-oppressive practice can be found in anti-discrimination legislation together with references in other pieces of legislation. Good practice in social work has, however, developed beyond these legal minimum standards. Anti-discriminatory, anti-oppressive practice is integral to social work, and the GSCC Code of Practice stresses the importance of 'Promoting equal opportunities for service users and carers' (1.4) and 'Respecting diversity and different cultures and values' (1.5). This is an area where the role of law has been questioned, in particular that although the aim of early anti-discriminatory legislation was to alter entrenched attitudes and promote change, is it possible for the law, with its focus on dealing with individual problems, and which itself has been charged with discriminatory practice, to be an instrument of social change? While legislation has broken down some barriers, much systematic discrimination still continues. It is important, however, for social workers to have a basic understanding of anti-discrimination legislation as there will be circumstances where clients suffer discrimination. In addition, social workers have a legal obligation to comply with the law and social work actions themselves may be covered by anti-discriminatory legislation. The Race Relations (Amendment) Act 2000 includes a positive duty on local authorities to promote race equality and includes within the remit of the Act certain previously excluded bodies, such as the police. The Act requires local authorities in carrying out its functions to have due regard to the need to eliminate unlawful discrimination and to promote equality of opportunity and good relations between persons of different racial groups.

The 2000 Act also makes it unlawful for a public authority, in carrying out any of its functions, to do any act that constitutes discrimination. A similar duty applies under the most recent Disability Discrimination legislation and extends to all forms of discrimination under the Equality Act 2010.

Other specific provisions in legislation direct anti-discriminatory practice. For example, s. 22(5) of the Children Act 1989 requires that, in making placement decisions, due consideration be given to a child's religious persuasion, racial origin, and cultural and linguistic background. Similar provisions exist in s. 17 of the Children (Scotland) Act 1995.

Reflect

In their consideration of teaching, learning and assessment of law in social work education, Braye and Preston Shoot (2006) noted:

'One problem, however, is the commonly held view of law as being contrary to social work values. Negative images of law pervade social work literature. Law is seen as contributing to the commodification of care and to managerialist-technicist practice that undermines professional judgement (Harlow, 2003), and as compromising social work's value and professional autonomy (Manktelow and Lewis, 2005). While social work programmes indicate a strong values component to law teaching, it is not uncommon for law and social work to be presented as somehow oppositional, with more attention to its role in restricting autonomy than in promoting rights or social justice.'

Do you agree with this comment. Can law be an empowering tool for social workers?

What is law?

Having gained an initial understanding of how law shapes social work practice, it is also important to have a grasp of what law is and where it comes from. Law is actually a broad term which encompasses a number of different sources. The most important are legislation and case law and these are considered in some detail below. An appreciation of other legal sources, including secondary legislation, practice directions and formal guidance, completes the picture. Textbooks and course lectures should provide much of the law relevant to social work practice, e.g. the Children Act 1989, the

National Health Service and Community Care Act 1990. It is unlikely, however, that every aspect of social work law can be addressed in sufficient detail. It must also be recognised that law develops at a rapid pace, and knowledge gained as a student needs to be updated and reviewed as a practitioner. Skills in understanding and accessing law are therefore essential. Legal research skills include being able to identify and use appropriate resources to locate new law and to develop a more specialised in-depth knowledge of particular aspects of law, as dictated by area of practice.

One of the exciting aspects of the study of social work law is the speed at which it changes and develops. Much of the law which is relevant for social work practice is fairly recent and can be linked to government initiatives, such as the 'modernisation' agenda and efforts to tackle social exclusion. Keeping track of those developments and further likely areas of reform is also one of its most challenging demands.

The key sources of law are legislation and case law.

A closer look

Law in Scotland

Students who are particularly interested in the Scottish legal system and Scottish legislation should look at the sections which relate to them, as there are significant differences between the legal system in Scotland and that of the other jurisdictions within the United Kingdom. The distinctions which are made between civil and criminal law are applicable in Scotland, as is the advice given in respect of appearing in court. However, the court structures are different as are some of the remedies and the terminology which is used.

Legislation

Legislation applicable in England and Wales is introduced by Parliament and the process involves scrutiny and amendment by both the House of Commons and the House of Lords. Up to the stage where final approval is given by Royal Assent, draft legislation is referred to as a Bill. During the parliamentary process, where the Bill goes through a series of 'readings' in each house, the content of the legislation may be altered significantly, as a result of debate and amendments, e.g. the Children Act 1989 almost doubled in size.

Most new legislation is introduced by the government, and is preceded by a White Paper that outlines the proposals and background to the need for reform. Elements of new laws may be traced back to election manifestos or reflect particular events or circumstances prevailing in society, e.g. greater fear of crime. There may have been a detailed consultation period prior to this, in some cases coordinated by the Law Commission, or other bodies such as the Department of Health or Home Office. As part of the consultation process a Green Paper may have been published which puts forward proposals for consultation. A recent example is the *Every Child Matters* Green Paper published in September 2003 which (followed by a further White Paper) preceded the Children Act 2004. Most government proposals for legislation in the forthcoming year of office are announced in the Queen's Speech at the state opening of Parliament in November each year. The final stage where a Bill becomes an Act is receipt of Royal Assent.

Legislation is not automatically implemented on receipt of the Royal Assent. Often the Act will be brought into force at a later date by a commencement order. Implementation may be delayed for a number of reasons. A delay of two years took place before the Human Rights Act 1998 came into force on 2 October 2000. One reason for this delay was the need for a major training programme to be conducted at all levels of the judiciary. Acts may come into force in sections over a period of time and some parts of legislation are never implemented. A significant example of this is the Family Law Act 1996. The provisions in the Act which would have completely reformed the basis for divorce have never been implemented.

Legislation may continue to be amended after it receives Royal Assent and has been implemented. Amendments are introduced by new legislation in related areas. This provides an opportunity to fine-tune the earlier legislation, update it and ensure consistency without having to repeal the Act and replace it in full. The Children Act 1989 has been amended on a number of occasions, most recently by the Adoption and Children Act 2002. Among other things amended, the definition of 'harm' as part of the threshold criteria for care proceedings was amended to include 'impairment suffered from seeing or hearing the ill-treatment of another'. This reflects growing understanding of the impact of domestic violence on children.

An Act of Parliament, or statute, contains headed sections, subsections and paragraphs which may be organised into parts (e.g. Mental Capacity Act 2005,

Part 1 'Persons who lack capacity', Part 2 'The Court of Protection and the Public Guardian'). The provisions in an Act are cited according to convention. Section 4(1)(a) of the Mental Capacity Act 2005 refers to section 4, subsection (1), paragraph (a) of the Act and states that in determining what is in a person's best interests, the person making the determination must not make it merely on the basis of age or appearance. Schedules at the end of an Act carry the same force of law as the main body of the Act, but often include more detailed or supplemental matters, such as procedural requirements or formalities, transitional arrangements, repeal of earlier legislation and minor amendments.

Delegated legislation, sometimes referred to as secondary legislation, has the same force of law as Acts of Parliament or primary legislation, e.g. Children (Leaving Care) (England) Regulations 2001 (SI 2000/2874). Most delegated legislation is made by Ministers by statutory instrument (SI) and is in the form of regulations, orders, rules and byelaws. A vast body of law is produced this way and often serves to provide the detail to an associated Act of Parliament. Since devolution, the National Assembly for Wales can make delegated legislation and guidance where the power to do so is provided by Act of Parliament. This provides the opportunity to more closely reflect priorities set by the Assembly, but it will often share similarities with equivalent provision in England. Regulations, known as subordinate or secondary legislation, are also a feature of Scottish law. They provide more detail about how legislation should be acted on, and carry the full force of law. Examples include the Children's Hearings (S) Rules 1996 and the Community Care (Direct payments) (S) Regulations 2003 (SSI 2003/243).

Legislation in Scotland

The Scottish Parliament was established by the Scotland Act 1998. Prior to that, legislation for Scotland was passed by the UK Parliament at Westminster. Some Acts were applicable to the United Kingdom as a whole, while others dealt with only Scottish matters. While these Scottish Bills went through the usual decision-making processes applicable to all legislation, they were additionally debated by the Scottish Grand Committee. Such Acts had the word 'Scottish' in the title, but to make life more difficult, many provisions which applied to Scotland could be found in other UK-wide statutes as well. Since devolution, apart from those matters which are reserved to the Parliament at Westminster, all other legislative measures concerning Scotland will be dealt with in Edinburgh. The Scottish Parliament makes laws which are known as Acts of the Scottish Parliament. Scottish statutes begin their lives as Bills of which there are four main types, namely Executive Bills (introduced by the Scottish Executive), Members Bills (introduced by any MSP), Committee Bills (which may arise following the deliberations of one of the Parliamentary Committees) and Private Bills (introduced by an individual or by an organisation).

Duties and powers

Most social work areas of responsibility defined by legislation may be categorised as either duties or powers.

Duties

Where a duty is imposed by law, social services are obliged to carry it out; it is a mandatory obligation to carry out a particular function. There is no discretion or allowance for shortfall of resources. Breach of a duty could found an action for judicial review. An example is the duty to carry out an assessment for community care services under s. 47 of the National Health Service and Community Care Act 1990 or s. 12A of the Social Work (Scotland) Act where the wording is the same. The section reads:

s. 47

(1) where it appears to a local authority that any person for whom they may provide or arrange for the provision of community care services may be in need of any such services, the authority –

    (a) shall carry out an assessment of his needs for those services; . . .   (DoH, 1990b)

The important word is *shall*, which suggests an imperative. As a general rule, where 'shall' appears, a duty is imposed.

Powers

Where a power is provided, there is an element of discretion. Power provides the authority to act in a particular way but there is scope to decide how to act. An example is the power in para. s. 4. (2) of the Adoption and Children Act 2002 in respect of adoption support services:

s. 4. (2) A local authority may, at the request of any person, carry out an assessment of that person's needs for adoption support services.

The important word is *may*. The authority may act in a particular way; they have a discretion but are not under

an obligation. Guidance may be issued, which assists the interpretation of powers.

S. 12 of the Social Work (Scotland) Act 1968 provides a neat example of the inclusion of both duties and powers within the one section. S. 12 states that

'It shall be the duty of every local authority to promote social welfare by making available advice, guidance and assistance on such a scale as may be appropriate for their area and in that behalf to make arrangements and to provide or secure the provision of such facilities (including the provision or arranging for the provision of residential and other establishments) as they may consider suitable and adequate . . .'

Guidance documents

There are a variety of types of guidance documents, which provide guidance on putting legislation into practice. Guidance relating to social services matters is frequently contained in a circular, issued by the Department of Health or other departments, such as the DfES. Within the general term 'guidance', documents are issued of differing status, commonly referred to as formal policy guidance and general practice guidance. Local authorities are under a stronger obligation to follow the former.

It is often clear that guidance is in fact formal policy guidance because it will be identified as issued under the Local Authority Social Services Act 1970, s. 7(1), which states that local authorities shall 'act under the general guidance of the Secretary of State'. Examples of this type of policy guidance include *No Secrets: Guidance on developing and implementing multiagency policies and procedures to protect vulnerable adults from abuse* (Department of Health, 2000f) and *Working Together to Safeguard Children* (Department of Health, 2006c, 2010). The status of this type of guidance was explained in the case of *R. v. Islington, ex parte Rixon* [1997] 1 ELR 477 High Court:

'If this statutory guidance is to be departed from it must be with good reason, articulated in the course of some identifiable decision-making process . . . In the absence of any such considered decision, the deviation from statutory guidance is in my judgement a breach of law.'

Guidance that is not issued under LASSA 1970, s. 7(1) can be regarded as general guidance and of a lower legal status. It can be described as advice rather than as a directive. Practice guidance can be quite detailed and give particular examples of ways in which a local authority might demonstrate good practice in implementing its responsibilities. For example, the Department of Health published Practice Guidance on *Assessing Children in Need and their Families* (2000a).

Guidance is issued in a similar way in Scotland. For example, the Guidance documents for the Children (S) Act 1995 explain how the legislation is intended to work, discuss its implications for policy and practice and identify areas where particular attention may need to be paid.

Codes of practice

Sometimes legislation is supported by a Code of Practice. Recent examples include Codes of Practice issued alongside the Mental Capacity Act 2005 and the Mental Health Act 2007. The legal status of Codes of Practice is different to guidance. Neither of the Acts mentioned impose a legal duty to comply with its Code but in each case certain professionals must have regard to the Code in carrying out duties under the Act. The Codes are also intended to be helpful to others such as family members who are supporting people affected by provisions of the legislation.

Additional documents

In addition to regulations and guidance above, local authorities and voluntary agencies may have their own policy and procedures which staff are required to follow. These may be based on statute, regulations and guidance and must fall within what has been laid down by law. They may reflect the particular ethos and practices of the agency and while they do not have the force of law employees of the agency would ignore such procedures at their peril! In addition to the above, there are an increasing number of policy initiatives in Scotland which cover all service user groups. Examples of these in Scotland include the *Youth Justice Strategy* (Scottish Executive, 2002) and *Better Outcomes for Older People: Framework for Joint Services* (Scottish Executive, 2005). In England and Wales, National Service Frameworks apply to various service user groups and set quality requirements for care in the context of long-term strategy e.g. the NSF for Older People and the NSF for Child Health and Maternity.

Case law

Decisions of the courts on matters brought before them are known collectively as case law and 'weighted' according to the doctrine of precedent. To understand precedent it is necessary to appreciate that there is a hierarchy of courts. The doctrine of precedent is the principle that decisions of cases made at the higher level of the court hierarchy are binding on other (lower) courts contemplating a decision, e.g. decisions made in the High Court, Family Division, should be followed by magistrates in the Family Proceedings Court. The highest UK court is the Supreme Court (formerly the House of Lords) and its decisions are binding on lower courts. Application of the doctrine of precedent promotes certainty and consistency. It provides an opportunity for the courts to develop, interpret and expand the law,

---

A closer look

Law in Northern Ireland

The political history of N. Ireland has played an important part in the development of primary and secondary legislation. Uniquely, post 1921 Acts of the Westminster Parliament were extended to Northern Ireland and until 1972 N. Ireland had the responsibility to enact its own legislation. As there was no legislative body in Northern Ireland in 1972 and between 1974 and 1999, primary legislation was enacted in the form of Orders in Council under arrangements for government by 'direct rule' by the Secretary of State. In 1999, the Northern Ireland Act 1998 created a new Northern Ireland Assembly which assumed power to enact primary legislation and introduce 'Acts'.

However, during periods of suspension of the N. Ireland assembly, notably in 2000 between February and June and again in October 2002, primary legislation for N. Ireland was once again made under the control and direction of the Secretary of State for Northern Ireland. Like England and Scotland, there are regulations accompanying primary legislation which set out the detail of how the law will work in practice. Such 'subordinate or secondary legislation' has the full force of the law. In addition, there are also volumes of guidance associated with legislation which define how statutory duties will be carried out by social work staff. The N. Ireland Children Order 1995 which comprises primary legislation of 200 Articles and 10 schedules plus 24 subordinate regulations is an example of this.

adding detail that would not be practical to include in legislation. Disadvantages of precedent are that it can seem unnecessarily restrictive and inflexible and that a 'poor' decision can stand for a long time. The courts are also limited to determination of the issues that people choose to litigate.

Case law decisions are published in law reports which contain the full text of a legal judgment and further details about the case.

Law reports are collected together according to the court that decided the case, e.g. Appeal Cases (**AC**) for cases in the Court of Appeal and Supreme Court, and Family Division (**Fam**) for cases heard in the Family division of the High Court. There are also two 'general' series, which include major cases covering a wide range of issues, known as the All England Law Reports (**All ER**) and the Weekly Law Reports (**WLR**).

Where a short summary of a case is required, it is useful to look in *The Times* newspaper, which provides up-to-date reports of cases decided, sometimes as recently as the previous day. A further option is to look at case-note sections in certain journals, which have the advantage of incorporating some commentary on the implications of a decision as well as a summary of the facts and judgment, e.g. *Family Law*. Major cases will also be reported more widely and may be subject to media scrutiny on television and in broadsheet and tabloid press.

Case names are written according to convention and follow a logical pattern. For example, in the case *X (Minors)* v. *Bedfordshire County Council* [1995] 3 All ER 353, an action is brought by X (the letter is used to anonymise the party and 'Minors' tells us it is a case concerning children); 'v.' means 'against', followed by the name of the other party, Bedfordshire County Council. The date in square brackets refers to the year in which the case is reported, '3' refers to the volume of the law report for that year, 'All ER' is an abbreviation for the series of law reports, here the All England Law Reports, and '353' is the page. Sometimes the title of the case will also include a reference to the level of court where it was heard, e.g. SC refers to the House of Lords.

It is now possible to access many case reports on the internet. The system for accessing cases this way is known as 'neutral citation', because it is not linked to any particular law report. The citation begins with the year then follows with UKSC, EWCA Civ or Crim or EWHC Admin or Fam and refers respectively to a decision made by the Supreme Court or in England and Wales made by the Court of Appeal Civil or Criminal Division or the High Court Administrative or Family court. The number

following gives the case position for that court, i.e. whether it was the first or thirty-first case heard by the court in that year.

A closer look

An example of neutral citation

Re MJ (A Child) (Adoption Order or Special Guardianship Order) [2007] EWCA Civ 55.

[2007] – This case was heard in 2007

EWCA Civ – a decision of the Court of Appeal, civil division

55 – the 55th case heard by the Court of Appeal in that year

Re MJ (A Child) – the case has been anonymised as it concerned a child

(Adoption Order or Special Guardianship Order) – the substantial issue for the court to consider

As well as giving judgments in decided cases, the courts also issue Practice Directions from time to time intended to give guidance on how to conduct particular cases, e.g. *Practice direction (Crown Court: trial of children and young persons)* (2000) 2 All ER 285 was issued following the trial in the Jamie Bulger case and stated, among other things, that young defendants should be able to sit next to their family in court.

Civil and criminal law

There are two principal categories of law: civil and criminal. There are a number of ways in which the distinction between civil and criminal law can be drawn.

In a criminal case the dispute is between the state and an individual or 'body'. The parties are referred to as the prosecution and the defence or the accused. The substance of the case is an allegation of behaviour, which falls within the definition of a criminal offence (in statute or common law, e.g. theft or rape). It will be a matter over which society as a whole is taken to have an interest in expressing at least its disapproval and ultimately, if proved, may consider it necessary to sentence the perpetrator of the offence.

In a civil case the dispute is between individuals, referred to as the claimant or applicant and the defendant, or in divorce cases, the petitioner and the respondent.

Civil disputes may be further classified as private or public matters. In a public matter a body may act on behalf of the state in a civil case. An obvious example of this is where a local authority issues care proceedings in respect of a child in its area. This is a civil matter, but could also be described as an aspect of public rather than private law because it involves a public body exercising a public function. A civil matter, which is 'private' as opposed to 'public', would include a divorce between two individuals, or could be a contract dispute between an individual and a company or public body.

Remedies

The outcome or remedy in a case will differ according to whether it is a civil or criminal matter. In a criminal case the object is to determine the question of guilt and then to make an appropriate disposal, which includes imprisonment, community orders, fines and compensation orders.

In civil cases an order will be made giving judgment to either party (crudely speaking, the winner). The most frequent order in civil cases is for compensation or damages to be paid by one party to the other to compensate for loss or damage but could also include an injunction, e.g. non-molestation injunction in a domestic violence case.

The standard of proof is different in civil and criminal cases. In a civil case the standard of proof is known as 'balance of probabilities'. This means that the point to be proven has to be more probable than not. In percentage terms this might be understood as a 49:51 per cent balance, i.e. the scales only just have to tip. In a criminal case the standard of proof is higher and is known as 'beyond reasonable doubt'. Again, to conceptualise this in percentage terms, it might equate to approximately 97 per cent, a high level but still allowing for a slight degree of doubt.

The court structure also reflects the civil and criminal divide. Civil cases may be heard in the Supreme Court, the Court of Appeal (Civil Division), and the High Court. These are known as the superior courts. The inferior courts dealing with civil cases are the county court, which deals with the majority of civil cases, including cases concerning family and child issues and personal injury cases, and the magistrates' court, which, although dealing mainly with criminal matters, hears civil claims relating to family and child matters in its Family Proceedings court. The majority of civil disputes fall into three categories: personal-injury action seeking compensation following an injury; actions for breach of contract; and debt. Some civil cases also involve circumstances where the permission of the courts is required before a particular action can be taken, e.g. a High Court

---

A closer look

Criminal and civil law

The same circumstances may lead to criminal and civil cases and illustrate the application of the different standards of proof, for example harm caused to a child may constitute a criminal offence and may give rise to care proceedings. In the criminal case the evidence focuses on whether the court is satisfied 'beyond reasonable doubt' that the defendant caused the harm and should be convicted. In care proceedings the court must be satisfied on a balance of probabilities that the threshold of 'significant harm' is reached and that the child should be made subject of a care order. It is less concerned with precisely attributing blame for injuries caused. A statement from *Re U (A Child) (Serious Injury: Standard of Proof)* [2004] EWCA Civ 567 reminds us that, 'it by no means follows that an acquittal on a criminal charge or a successful appeal would lead to

the absolution of the parent or carer in family or civil proceedings'.

The criminal law has been amended recently following a number of cases where injuries to children have been caused, care proceedings have been taken, but it has not been possible to convict the perpetrator because of evidential difficulties and the higher standard of proof, e.g. *Re O and N (Children) (Non-accidental Injury: Burden of Proof)*, *Re B (Children)* [2003] UKHL 18. The new criminal law is contained in the Domestic Violence, Crime and Victims Act 2004 which introduced the new offence of 'familial homicide' in section 5. The offence applies where a child (or vulnerable adult) dies as a result of an unlawful act of a person of the same household, who either caused the death, or, aware of the risk, failed to protect the child. In such a case more than one adult can be charged with the offence and it is not necessary to precisely establish who caused the death and who failed to protect.

declaration authorising sterilisation of a woman with a learning disability, or approval to remove a child from the jurisdiction. Tribunals also exercise civil jurisdiction.

Courts that deal with criminal cases are: the magistrates' court, which has both an adult and a youth crime jurisdiction; the Crown Court; the Queen's Bench Division of the High Court; the Criminal Division of the Court of Appeal; and the Supreme Court. The starting point in a consideration of a criminal case is the classification of the crime. There are three groups of offences recognised by the criminal law:

1. *Summary offences*: the less serious criminal offences, including numerous motoring and traffic offences, and drunkenness offences, which are tried by magistrates.
2. *Indictable offences*: the most serious offences, which are tried 'on indictment' in the Crown Court, including murder, rape, arson and robbery.
3. *Either way offences*: as the name suggests, may be tried in the magistrates' court or the Crown Court depending on the seriousness of the offence and the preference of the defendant. Either way offences include criminal acts where there is a possible range of seriousness, such as theft, which may be charged in a petty shoplifting case or a major theft of property worth millions of pounds.

Offences may also be classified according to the type of harm done. This is often reflected in the legislation which establishes particular offences, e.g. the Theft Act 1968 or the Sexual Offences Act 2003. Crimes may be committed: against property, e.g. burglary; physical integrity of the person, e.g. rape or assaults; or general public rights of citizenship, e.g. public order offences.

The court structure has been supplemented by a system of tribunals commonly associated with the rise of the welfare state and exercising administrative and judicial functions. Some of the more important tribunals in social work terms were: the Care Standards Tribunal; Employment Tribunal; Mental Health Review Tribunal; Asylum and Immigration Tribunal; Criminal Injuries Compensation Appeals Panel; and Social Security Tribunal. A new statutory framework for tribunals is provided by the Tribunals, Courts and Enforcement Act 2007. There are now two tribunals, First Tier and Upper Tier, the Upper Tier dealing with appeals from the First Tier. Within the First Tier, areas of tribunal jurisdiction are grouped into Chambers. Of particular relevance to social work, the Health, Education and Social Care Chamber includes care standards; mental health reviews, special educational needs and disability.

As a general principle, court (and tribunal) proceedings should normally be held in public, in open court. In a number of circumstances, however, the public and the press will be excluded and a case will be heard privately or *in camera*. The majority of cases relating to children are heard in camera; however, recent reforms to provide greater transparency in the court system are likely to result in increased media access to family proceedings.

Working in the law

Alongside social workers, various professionals work in the court system. Some of the most significant are: the advocates or lawyers, who may be barristers or solicitors; the Crown Prosecution Service deals with prosecution of criminal cases and lawyers may be provided to defend individuals charged with an offence by the Criminal Defence Service; cases are heard by magistrates (unpaid volunteers) or judges; in the magistrates' court a justices' clerk provides advice to the magistrates on points of law and procedure.

There is the potential for social workers to be involved professionally with cases at all levels of the court structure. Involvement may be as applicant to the court or witness or in giving support to a service user. Table 8.1 outlines key areas of social work involvement.

Key social work roles in court include appearing as an applicant, a witness and a report writer.

As representative of the local authority, a social worker may be the applicant in court in a range of proceedings. Usually a solicitor or barrister will conduct the case and the social worker then becomes the key witness in the application. Where a social worker appears as a witness she owes a duty to the court to tell the truth, even if in exceptional circumstances this may mean expressing a personal view which conflicts with the agency stance. Examples of such cases include: Emergency Protection Orders; Care and Supervision Orders; application to displace the nearest relative under the Mental Health Act 1983; placement orders in adoption cases. A report from the social worker will often be required by the court. The type of report varies according to the case. Sometimes the content is prescribed by regulations or national standards, e.g. pre-sentence reports, permanence reports in adoption cases. Reports may be requested by the court exercising a general discretion or by a specific

Table 8.1 Areas of social work involvement at each level in the court structure

Magistrates' Court Civil	Family proceedings	Emergency Protection Orders, Child Assessment Orders, Care and Supervision Orders, Exclusion Orders, ASBO, Curfew Orders, Provision of reports
Magistrates' Court Criminal	Youth	Crime and Disorder Act Cases Provision of reports
	Adult	Reports to court [Probation Officer's role]
County court	Adoption and Placement Orders Special Guardianship Contact and residence Section 37 Investigation Children Act 1989 Exclusion Order – Family Law Act 1996 Race, sex, disability discrimination cases Displacement of nearest relative – Mental Health Act 1983	
Crown Court	Provision of reports in adult criminal cases for juveniles charged with adults	
High Court Family Division	Family proceedings jurisdiction as for magistrates' and county court – more complex cases Wardship Declaratory relief	
Queen's Bench	Judicial review	
Court of Protection	New orders under the Mental Capacity Act 2005	
Court of Appeal	Appeals on point of law	
Supreme Court	Appeals on point of law	
At each level the social work involvement may vary between applicant, report writer, witness, litigation friend, or may be general support to client.		

(*Source*: Brammer, 2010:66)

power such as under section 7 of the Children Act 1989, in which case a children and family reporter (from CAFCASS, Children and Family Court Advisory and Support Service) would normally provide the report.

In most circumstances, there are some general principles that can be followed in preparing a report for court (see Professional Tip, opposite).

Going to court

Taking a case to court may be the final stage in a lengthy process of work on a case, and the opportunity to achieve a desired outcome. The outcome of a case, where evidence is 'tested', depends not only on the relative merits of a case, and the skills of the advocates, but also on the 'performance' of witnesses. The study and develop-

ment of appropriate skills in court is known as 'court-craft'. Training and practice to improve skills in this area is useful and it is helpful to remember that most people feel nervous before entering court.

The key to a good court experience is preparation. This starts long before a court hearing is anticipated. In the majority of cases, evidence will be required relating to circumstances some time before the actual hearing. It is vital, therefore, that accurate records are kept from first involvement and are sufficiently detailed. Records should be dated and recording should take place contemporaneously with events, or as soon as possible afterwards. Always distinguish between fact and opinion. Records should also include details of notifications to other agencies, their involvement, and any information that has been shared. Rules about sharing evidence

Professional tip

Report writing

- Basic information should be included on the front page, including the name of the court and the case number; the name and date of birth of the subject; the type of application; and the author's name and professional address.
- Clarity and concision of language will always help the reader.
- Avoid dense pages of text, and use bullet points.
- Remember who the report is for, and make appropriate adjustments to style and vocabulary.
- Consider the structure and length of the report – there may be guidance to follow.
- Include a chronology of events.
- A genogram may be useful in family cases if there is a complex family make-up.
- Avoid jargon (ask a non-interested person to check this out and you may be surprised by how much jargon slips in!).

- Be non-discriminatory in the language used.
- Distinguish between facts and opinion.
- Avoid unnecessary repetition within the report of material available to the court in other documents.
- Conclusions should flow logically from the body of the report.
- Where more than one option is available to the court, set out and discuss each in turn, and make a realistic recommendation.
- Objectivity is all; avoid over-personalising your report, although it is inevitable that you will be drawing upon your experience.

Increasingly there are strict timetables for filing of evidence, including reports, e.g. as provided by the *Public Law Outline: Guide to case management in public law proceedings* (2008). Failure to adhere to timetables invites criticism: if unavoidable it is important to seek court approval.

---

in civil and criminal cases should mean that there are very few surprises during court hearings, and new documentary evidence will not normally be produced at such a late stage.

Part of the preparation stage may include having a pre-court conference with the lawyer presenting the case, to make sure that there have been no sudden last-minute changes to the case. This may be the local authority solicitor but may also include a 'conference with counsel' if a barrister is presenting the case. The professional relationship between the lawyer presenting the case, and the social worker who instructs the lawyer, should be seen as another aspect of multidisciplinary working together where communication is essential. Early contact between social workers and solicitors can lead to better final outcomes in the legal process. Studies of the social worker and lawyer relationship have found that unclear boundaries between the two roles can be a major source of tension and the simplified delineation of roles, such as the lawyer advising and the social worker instructing, is difficult to maintain in practice. Dickens (2004) concluded that improved communication and understanding of respective roles is essential here as for all inter-professional relationships. Sometimes, the solicitor will instruct a barrister for the court hearing. The solicitor will then liaise with the barrister and retain

responsibility for day-to-day management of the case and provision of information and materials to the barrister. It is not possible for a social worker to instruct a barrister directly.

Preparation also involves being aware of the various legal options available to the court. An integral part of the evidence is being able to show that all relevant alternatives have been considered and that the case has been considered on an individual basis rather than within a rigid policy framework.

At the actual hearing, there are further steps that can be taken to reduce stress: basic points like checking up on transport arrangements, getting to court in plenty of time, finding which court the case will be heard in if the court building has more than one room, and if possible having a look inside the court and becoming familiar with the layout. Before entering the courtroom any mobile phones or pagers should be switched off. Dress should be sufficiently formal to demonstrate respect for the occasion without being uncomfortable.

Giving evidence

When a witness enters the court and is directed to the witness box, he is required to take the oath or affirmation before giving oral evidence to the court. This is a

When appearing as a witness, it is the duty of the social worker to the court to tell the truth.

(Kevin Smith (Kes): www.kescartoons.com)

useful opportunity to test voice level, start to focus the mind and find a position where eye contact with the judge or magistrates is possible. Although the majority of questions will come from the solicitors or barristers, answers should be addressed to the bench or judge. Evidence normally begins with introductions and this is an opportunity to establish expertise as a prerequisite to giving opinion evidence. The case of *F* v. *Suffolk County Council* (1981) 2 FLR 208 stated that the courts will presume that a qualified social worker is an expert for general issues of childcare.

The process of giving evidence is divided into three parts. First, the solicitor representing your case conducts examination-in-chief. In many civil proceedings where a witness statement has been submitted, the witness will simply be asked to confirm the contents of their statement, or may go straight to cross-examination. Where examination-in-chief does take place, evidence should normally be presented as a logical narrative and is the opportunity to present your arguments (persuasively). During examination-in-chief, the solicitor cannot ask leading questions, i.e. a question that suggests the answer.

Examination-in-chief is followed by cross-examination. At this stage the most important advice is to keep calm.

The objective of the opposing solicitor is to discredit and challenge evidence and elicit evidence favourable to the opposition. It is necessary to remain assertive and convincing to counter this attack. This includes being aware of body language as well as oral answers and remembering to address answers to the bench. Taking a moment to turn away from the advocate and towards the bench can provide a vital few seconds of thinking time. It is acceptable to request that a question be repeated or clarified if it was not heard or understood.

Thirdly, in some cases, the witness may be re-examined by his own solicitor on any new points that have arisen in cross-examination. This is the final opportunity to argue the case. Finally, the magistrates or judge may also ask some questions, after which the witness is released.

Being accountable: challenging social work practice

Accountability in social work practice is an increasingly significant yet complex area. A social worker may be accountable on a number of levels. At the very least, accountability lies with the Social Services Authority in its role as employer and also as holder of the social services functions that are delegated to social workers acting as agents of the authority. Correspondingly, the local authority is liable for the actions of its employees. Only when acting as an Approved Mental Health Professional (Mental Health Officer in Scotland) does a social worker acquire individual liability for action. In addition, a social worker must be accountable to the service user, in that it is possible to explain and justify why particular decisions are made. This accountability may be tested via the Local Authority Complaints System if a service user is dissatisfied, by complaint to the Local Government Ombudsman (or Scottish Public Services Ombudsman) and ultimately by invoking judicial review procedures or action against a public authority under the Human Rights Act 1998. Other formal processes, including the functions of registration and inspection, support the notion of accountability, and in specified areas there is a duty to consult with service users. In cases involving statutory responsibilities toward children, accountability is to the child who is the subject of the case. There are circumstances where the social worker effectively works as an officer of the court and is accountable to the court, e.g. when directed to prepare and present a report or to comply with an undertaking or to follow the court's directions as to supervision of contact. Beyond those clear instances, accountability may also be to team managers, section heads, practice teachers, the university or other institution during pre-qualification placements.

In practical terms the most important means of challenging social work decisions are use of the local authority's complaints procedure, complaints to the Local Government Ombudsman, and judicial review. The Human Rights Act 1998, discussed below, provides a further avenue.

Local authority's complaints procedure

Local authorities are required to have procedures for representations, including complaints, in place. These procedures are contained in the Children Act 1989, Representations Procedure (England) Regulations 2006 and the Local Authority Social Services and NHS Complaints (England) Regulations 2009. The procedures include provision for an element of independence. Complaints and representations may relate to any functions of the local authority affecting the individual, such as the quality of a service or the application of assessment criteria. The Court of Appeal has confirmed in *R (on the application of Ireneschild)* v. *Lambeth LBC* [2007] EWCA Civ 234, that disputes about assessments of community care needs should normally be dealt with through the local authority complaints procedure rather than the courts.

Each local authority has a duty to make information available to the public about its arrangements for dealing with complaints. Complaints should normally be made within a year of the concern arising. Children and young people are entitled to independent and confidential advocacy support if they make a complaint.

Local Government Ombudsman

The Local Government Ombudsman can investigate a complaint against a local authority where there has been maladministration, which causes an injustice to the complainant. Maladministration includes: unreasonable delay; bias; disregard of procedures; and incompetence. The complaint should normally have arisen no more than 12 months before the Local Government Ombudsman is contacted. In practice, because the ombudsman will normally expect a complaint to have been first considered by the complaints procedure outlined above, this time may be exceeded. A significant number of investigations by the ombudsman have concerned delays in processing assessments for services.

Complaints to the ombudsman should be made in writing and the ombudsman is entitled to access relevant information held by the local authority. The ombudsman will prepare a report and can make recommendations, including compensation awards, and, while the

A closer look

An example of a case in which the Ombudsman found maladministration causing injustice: *Oldham Metropolitan Borough Council* (2006)

'Ms Johnston' (not her real name) complained that the Council failed to give appropriate support to her sister during her residency in a social services care home. Her sister had a mild learning disability and was registered blind.

This report focused on the impact of a new resident – who had learning difficulties and bipolar mood disorder – on the quality of life of Ms Johnston's sister and the two other residents of the home, and the time taken for the Council to address the ensuing issues.

The new resident displayed unpredictable and aggressive behaviour that was frightening and intimidating to the complainant's sister and the other residents, and was assessed as likely to result in injury to herself and others. The Council was aware of the difficulties soon after the new resident moved in. Despite this, it took the Council 18 months to resolve the issue.

In investigating the complaint and reaching her conclusions, the Ombudsman recognised and acknowledged the difficulties the Council faced in this case. Nevertheless, she found maladministration by the Council leading to injustice to Ms Johnston's sister. Specifically, the time taken by the Council to address the impact of the new resident's behaviour was unreasonable, given the severity of that impact on the quality of life of the other residents. The new resident was eventually moved to other accommodation.

The Ombudsman recommended the Council to make a payment of £2,000 to be held in trust for Ms Johnston's sister, and the Council agreed.

local authority is not strictly bound to follow these recommendations, in practice they usually do. Advantages of complaining to the ombudsman include the following: the process is free, there is a possibility of informal settlement, compensation may result and the investigation is independent.

Maladministration complaints in respect of the National Health Service, including social work in hospital settings, are dealt with by the Parliamentary and Health Service Ombudsman.

Judicial review

Judicial review is a legal process that allows the High Court (the Court of Session in Scotland) to supervise decision-making of public bodies. Judicial review cases are focused on the process of decision-making rather than the merit of the ultimate decision. Judicial review has proved to be a useful tool for checking the actions of local authorities, as illustrated by a series of cases that related to the relevance of resources of a local authority when carrying out community care assessments. Some of the advantages of using judicial review to challenge decisions are that groups and organisations can bring cases or support individuals to bring a case, provided they have a sufficient interest in the matter. An obvious disadvantage to judicial review is expense if the complainant does not qualify for legal assistance. Proceedings are generally lengthy although it is sometimes possible to deal with cases on an urgency basis and also to make interim injunctions prior to the final hearing. In addition, it is normally necessary first to have exhausted alternative remedies, including the local authority complaints procedure, and there are fairly strict time limits for bringing an action.

The Scottish legal system

Scotland retained its own legal system following the Act of Union in 1707. Since 1998 it again has its own parliament. Because it was a separate country prior to 1707, Scotland had developed its own system of law which had more to do with the legal systems of continental Europe than with its neighbour south of the border. Scots Law is a mixed system of law and contains aspects of Roman law and common law. Since the union, aspects of English (or common law) have crept in and obviously Acts of

the UK parliament have shaped its practices. The law of Scotland was written down by jurists in such works as Stair's *Institutions of the Law of Scotland* (1681) which still have relevance today. The doctrine of case law or judicial precedent has developed in Scotland and, as the House of Lords since 1707 has become the final court of appeal in civil matters, its influence is persuasive in judicial decision-making even in cases which have emanated from Scotland.

Scottish court structure

There are two branches of law, criminal and civil, and the court structure which administers these is as follows:

1. Criminal. There are two divisions within criminal procedure, namely summary and solemn procedure. Summary procedure deals with less serious offences which are heard by a judge sitting alone; solemn cases are heard by a judge and a jury of 15.

The District Court deals only with less serious cases and these proceed by way of summary procedure. Cases can be heard by stipendiary (paid) magistrates who sit alone and who have the same sentencing powers as sheriffs in summary cases. Lay magistrates, accompanied by a legal assessor, can also hear cases in these courts but they have more limited sentencing powers.

Sheriff Courts can deal with both summary and solemn cases. There are sentencing restrictions which apply to each procedure and so this may influence the choice of court for a particular offence. Summary cases proceed by way of a complaint, and solemn cases proceed by way of indictment.

The High Court of Justiciary hears the most serious criminal offences and is the only court which can deal with certain crimes, such as murder. A judge in the High Court has wide sentencing powers which will reflect the gravity of the offence before him/her.

Appeals in criminal cases. The High Court of Justiciary also acts as an Appeal Court and is the final court of appeal for criminal cases in Scotland. Appeals can be heard from the district and sheriff courts as well as from the High Court itself.

2. Civil. Civil matters would include actions for divorce, issues of child welfare, including arrangements for residence and contact with children, adoption, appeals from children's hearings and breaches of the Human Rights

Act 1998. Civil cases are heard in the sheriff court and in the Court of Session. They have almost concurrent jurisdiction, but cases which involve particular complexity or deal with arcane points of law will be raised in the Court of Session.

Sheriff Court. The procedure is started off by an initial writ which is raised by the pursuer and which may be challenged by the defender. The case will be heard by a sheriff sitting alone.

Court of Session. This has two divisions, the Inner and Outer Houses. The Outer House is a court of first instance, i.e. it hears cases for the first time. The procedure, although more complex, is essentially the same as that for civil cases in the sheriff court and cases are for the most part heard by a judge sitting alone. There is also the provision for a civil jury trial where the jury numbers seven, but this is rarely used.

Appeals in civil cases. Appeals can be made from the sheriff court to the Sheriff Principal and also to the Inner House of the Court of Session. Appeals from decisions in the Outer House can be taken to the Inner House and the final court of appeal in civil matters is the House of Lords.

Who's who in the Scottish courts

The following is a list of the personnel in the legal system with whom a social worker may come into contact:

1. Judges

Judges in the supreme courts. Although social workers probably will not have much contact with these members of the legal profession it is, nevertheless, important to know about them because you could find yourself having to write a report for one of their courts, or you might have to give evidence before one of them at some time in your career. Judges preside over our highest courts and in Scotland these are the Court of Session (in civil matters) and the High Court of Justiciary (in criminal matters). The Court of Session always sits in Edinburgh whereas the High Court (as it is commonly known) goes on circuit around Scotland. Judges can hear either civil or criminal matters and can hear appeals. They can adjudicate on appeals both from the lower courts in the systems and from the Court of Session and the High Court.

Sheriffs. Social workers are more likely to have contact with sheriffs who preside over both civil and criminal proceedings in the sheriff court. Most of the cases going to court in Scotland will go to their local sheriff court and social workers will build up a knowledge of their local sheriffs. The Sheriff Principal in each sheriffdom can hear appeals in civil matters, but all criminal appeals have to go to the Court of Criminal Appeal in Edinburgh.

Magistrates. Magistrates are found in the District Courts which deal with the less serious criminal offences. They are not legally qualified but sit with a legal assessor who can advise them on matters of law and procedure.

2. Solicitors
Solicitors must be members of the Law Society of Scotland before they can practise law. They have direct contact with clients and can appear in all the lower courts. Solicitor–Advocates are those members of the profession who have chosen to do some additional studying which allows them to appear in the higher courts.

3. Advocates
Advocates may appear in the higher courts or they may be asked for opinions on complex matters of law. They differ from solicitors in that they do not have direct contact with clients and all their interactions with clients are managed through the client's solicitor.

4. Procurators fiscal
They are solicitors employed by the Crown Office who are responsible for the investigation and prosecution of crime as well as for the conduct of the case in court. Procurators fiscal are attached to local sheriff courts. Social workers could find themselves giving statements, called precognitions, to procurators fiscal who are undertaking the investigation of a crime, e.g. an allegation of sexual abuse made by a child against an adult.

5. Advocates depute
Advocate deputes are advocates who are appointed for a period of time to the Crown Office and who are responsible for the conduct of the more serious criminal trials, i.e. those taking place in the High Court.

6. Clerks of Court
They are responsible for, among other things, the running of the courts, the timetabling and recording of proceedings, the collection of fines and the organisation and distribution of social inquiry reports. They are not legally qualified. In court you will recognise them because they sit at the table directly below the judge's bench facing out towards the court. In the Sheriff Court, sheriff clerks will wear gowns, and in the Supreme Courts they wear both wigs and gowns.

Table 8.2 Main areas of social work involvement in the Scottish courts and tribunals

District Court	Criminal cases	Less serious offences but may require reports and/or advice to the Court
Sheriff Court Civil	Cases involving children and families	Child Protection Orders; Child Assessment Orders; Exclusion Orders; Matrimonial Interdicts; ASBOs; Curfew Orders; Cases referred from children's hearings; Provision of reports in adoption and child welfare cases; Cases dealing with discrimination or breaches of Human Rights Act 1998
Sheriff Court Criminal	All	Provision of reports – probation, Community service, breach of these orders
Court of Session Civil	All cases which can be heard in Sheriff Court, but there may be special reasons for them being heard in this court, e.g. the cases are more complex. Judicial Review	
High Court of Justiciary Criminal	Provision of reports, both pre- and post-sentencing	
Appeals	See Court structure	
Children's hearings	Provision of reports to hearings and to courts when there are court hearings to establish grounds of referral or appeals against decisions of hearings	
Mental Health Tribunals	Provision of reports in relation to compulsory measures under the Mental Health (Care and Treatment (S) Act 2003)	
At each level the social work involvement may vary between applicant, report writer, witness, litigation friend, or may be general support to client.		

The Human Rights Act 1998 and social work practice

The Human Rights Act 1998 (HRA 1998) is having a real influence on the development of law in the United Kingdom. Areas of social work law and practice have already been subject to challenge via the Act and it provides an additional scrutiny of practice. It is therefore essential to have a working knowledge of the principles under the Act that are likely to be asserted. Human rights will permeate all aspects of social work practice and provide a further opportunity to promote best practice.

The HRA 1998 incorporates the Convention for the Protection of Human Rights and Fundamental Freedoms (usually referred to as the European Convention on Human Rights (ECHR)) into UK domestic law. The Convention was ratified in 1951, British lawyers having made a major contribution to its drafting. It contains rights, prohibitions and freedoms arranged in sections referred to as articles. Since 1966 it has been possible for an individual to petition the European Court of Human Rights in Strasbourg directly, bringing a claim against the United Kingdom for violation of one of the articles, e.g. in *Association X* v. *UK* (1978) 14 DR 31, provision of a vaccination programme was tested against Article 2 the right to life. Disadvantages of this process included financial cost and delay. The emphasis in the Act is on making the Convention more accessible, so that remedies which would be available in Strasbourg can be ordered by the domestic courts. To bring a claim under the HRA 1998, the individual must be a 'victim'. This means that they are directly affected by the measure or at least at risk of being affected, or are closely or personally related to one affected. It is not possible to complain in abstract about behaviour.

The rights are incorporated into domestic law in three ways: consideration of European case law, reading legislation compatibly with the Convention, and a new duty on public authorities.

Consideration of case law

A court or tribunal which determines a question which has arisen in connection with a Convention right must take into account any judgment, decision or opinion of the

European Court of Human Rights. This requirement will impact on the doctrine of precedent. The Supreme Court as the superior court will no longer simply be bound by its own decisions but must also consider European decisions as binding and not simply of persuasive authority.

Compatibility of legislation

Secondly, as far as possible, legislation must be interpreted in a way that is compatible with the Convention rights. Where a provision has a range of possible meanings, the court must give effect to the meaning that is compatible with the Convention. This principle applies to past and future legislation. If it is not possible to construe legislation to give effect to the Convention, the High Court may issue a 'Declaration of incompatibility'. The courts cannot quash primary legislation which in their view is not compatible; that remains the responsibility of Parliament. If a declaration is made, the government can use a fast-track process to introduce amending legislation. A declaration of incompatibility has been made in relation to the failure of the law to recognise transsexuals' acquired sex for the purposes of marriage, *Bellinger* v. *Bellinger* [2003] UKHL 21. The Gender Recognition Act 2004 gives effect to the required change in the law.

Public authorities

Thirdly, and of most significance for social work, a new responsibility is imposed on public authorities. It is unlawful for a public authority to act in a way that is incompatible with a Convention right (unless as a result of primary legislation the authority could not have acted differently). A 'public authority' includes any court or tribunal, and any person whose functions are functions of a public nature (s. 6(3)). This is likely to include local government, social services, the police, health authorities, probation, public utilities, inspection bodies and certain private bodies where they are exercising functions of a public nature, e.g. a professional regulatory body. It is possible for a person or body to have both private and public functions. For example, a General Practitioner when undertaking NHS work will be a public authority but not when treating a private patient. The impact of the Human Rights Act 1998 will depend considerably on how widely the courts interpret the concept of a public function and it is an area where further litigation is likely. So far it appears that the courts have interpreted the term rather more restrictively than Parliament may have intended. The Court of Appeal in *R (on the*

application of Heather) v. *Leonard Cheshire Foundation* [2002] UKHRR 883 decided that a private charitable organisation managing a care home was not a 'public authority'. This was a disappointing decision, given that the home was receiving public funding and was providing care which would otherwise have been provided by the State. This position was confirmed in *YL (by her litigation friend, the Official Solicitor)* v. *Birmingham City Council and Others* [2007] UKHL 27. Subsequently legislation has been introduced to make all care homes public authorities under the Act. The Health and Social Care Act 2008 defines a person providing care in a care home as exercising a function of a public nature, and thus required to act compatibly with the Convention, closing this loophole.

It is significant that courts themselves are public authorities. This means that courts are obliged to decide *all* cases before them – whether they arise in connection with a statutory or common law principle, and whether they involve public authorities or private individuals – compatibly with Convention rights. Wall LJ confirmed in *Re V (a child) (Care proceedings: Human Rights Claims)* (2004) EWCA Civ 54, 'Every court hearing proceedings under Part IV of the 1989 Act (that is the family proceedings court (FPC), the county court and the High Court) has a duty under s. 3(1) of the 1998 Act to give effect to the provisions of the 1989 Act in a way which is compatible with convention rights'. (The 1989 Act referred to is the Children Act 1989.)

Section 7 makes clear the significance of section 6. Failure to comply with Convention rights will be a new ground for judicial review of a public authority. A new cause of action against public authorities is created, and Convention rights are available as a defence to actions brought by public authorities against individuals.

A separate action under s. 7 is not necessary where there are ongoing proceedings. For example, in care cases where parents might wish to challenge the action of the local authority, relying on the Convention, the human rights arguments should be dealt with by the court hearing the care proceedings. The arguments should be brought to the court's attention as early as possible to avoid delay and it would only be necessary in exceptional cases to transfer the case to the High Court to address the human rights arguments: *Re L (Care Proceedings: Human Rights Claims)* [2003] EWHC 665 (Fam).

It is also important to note that an individual does not have to wait until the public authority has actually acted unlawfully before bringing a claim under s. 7, as proceedings may be brought where the public authority

A closer look

The Human Rights Act 1998: articles most relevant to social work practice

Article 2
Everyone's right to life shall be protected by law.

Article 3
No one shall be subjected to torture or to inhuman or degrading treatment or punishment.

Article 5
1. Everyone has the right to liberty and security of person. No-one shall be deprived of his liberty save in the following cases and in accordance with a procedure prescribed by law:
   (a) lawful detention of a person after conviction
   (b) lawful arrest or detention of a person
   (c) detention of a minor . . . for the purpose of educational supervision . . .
   (d) lawful detention of persons for the prevention of the spreading of infectious diseases, of persons of unsound mind, alcoholics or drug addicts or vagrants.
4. Everyone who is deprived of his liberty by arrest or detention shall be entitled to take proceedings by which the lawfulness of his detention shall be decided speedily by a court and his release ordered if the detention is not lawful.

Article 6
In the determination of his civil rights and obligations . . . everyone is entitled to a fair and public hearing within a reasonable time by an independent and impartial tribunal established by law.

Article 8
1. Everyone has the right to respect for his private and family life, his home and his correspondence.
2. (2) There shall be no interference by a public authority with the exercise of this right except such as is in accordance with the law and is necessary in a democratic society in the interests of national security, public safety or the economic well being of the country, for the prevention of disorder or crime, for the protection of health or morals, or for the protection of the rights and freedoms of others.

Article 9
Everyone has the right to freedom of thought, conscience and religion; this right includes freedom . . . to manifest his religion or belief, in worship, teaching, practice and observance.

Article 10
Everyone has the right to freedom of expression. This right shall include freedom to hold opinions and to receive and impart information and ideas without interference by public authority . . .

Article 12
Men and women of marriageable age have the right to marry and to found a family, according to the national laws governing the exercise of this right.

Article 14
The enjoyment of the rights and freedoms set forth in this Convention shall be secured without discrimination on any ground such as sex, race, colour, language, religion, political or other opinion, national or social origin, association with a national minority, property, birth or other status.

'proposes to act'. This could apply, for example, to claims in respect of the content of a care plan before it is implemented, or a proposed change to policy or procedures.

Application

Some of the articles, considered below, are of more obvious relevance to social work than others and have already produced some case law. In some cases a number of articles may be argued and the decisions would shed some light on the interrelationship of the articles. The articles are written in quite general terms and apply universally to all. There are no articles that apply specifically to particular groups, e.g. children. The articles provide for basic rights,

and some areas that might seem significant and where individuals would wish to assert a 'right' are not addressed, for example there is no 'right to employment'.

Article 3

Article 3 is an absolute prohibition. It follows that it will be unlawful for any public authority to treat an individual in a way that violates the article. Challenges may be brought based on various circumstances, e.g. use of ECT, restraint, seclusion or force-feeding. An early decision, *Ireland* v. *United Kingdom*, ruled that 'ill treatment' must attain a minimum level of severity to fall within article 3. That minimum level is relative and will depend on all the circumstances of the case, including duration of the treatment, its physical and mental effects, the age, sex and state of health of the victim.

In *Z and Others* v. *United Kingdom* [2001] 2 FLR 612, the European Court found the United Kingdom in breach of Article 3 where a local authority had failed to act to protect children who had suffered 'horrific ill treatment and neglect' by their parents. The court awarded substantial damages and stressed the positive obligation on local authorities to protect individuals from the actions of others.

Article 5

This is not an absolute right as deprivation of liberty is permissible in certain cases (those most relevant to social work are also set out in the box), provided a procedure prescribed by law is followed. It is concerned with *deprivation* of liberty, rather than *restriction* of liberty; the distinction between deprivation of and restriction upon liberty is one of intensity or degree (*Ashingdane Case* (1985) 7 EHRR 528). This distinction is reflected in the Mental Capacity Act 2005. Under the Act it may be permissible for a person who is caring for another who lacks capacity to restrain that person in their best interests, e.g. preventing an individual with dementia from stepping out into the traffic. Deprivation of liberty, however, can never be sanctioned by the Act.

Article 5 could apply to restraint practices, lock-door policies, sedation, etc., in residential establishments, to the use of detention under the scheme of the Mental Health Act 1983 and has been argued (unsuccessfully) in relation to the use of secure accommodation under s. 25 of the Children Act 1989: see the case of *Re K (Secure Accommodation Order: Right to Liberty)* [2001] Fam Law 99. The article was found to have been breached in the case of *HL* v. *UK (2004)*, the European Court judgment of the appeal of *R* v. *Bournewood Community and Mental Health Trust, ex parte L* [1998] 1 CCLR 390, HL. The case concerned informal detention of mental health patients who are mentally incapable of consenting to detention but are compliant. Under the Mental Health Act 1983 such patients are not entitled to the safeguards provided for formally detained patients such as the right of appeal to the Mental Health Review Tribunal. To remedy this deficiency in the law new 'Deprivation of Liberty Safeguards' (DOLS) were introduced in the Mental Capacity Act 2005.

Article 6

Article 6 focuses on procedure or fairness within the legal system. A high proportion of cases before the European Court have been based on this article, and it will often be employed in connection with another article, e.g. where someone is a victim of restraint practices and has no means of challenge. The article would apply to conduct of case conferences and adoption panels.

In *B* v. *United Kingdom, P* v. *United Kingdom* (2001) *The Times*, 15 May, it was found that to hear a custody case and pronounce judgment in public would frustrate the aim of protecting the privacy of children, and the practice of hearing children's cases 'in camera' did not breach Article 6.

Recognition of the detrimental effect of delay on proceedings has led to a number of initiatives to ensure speediness in resolving disputes; however, there still needs to be a proper examination of the facts. In *Re D (A Child)* [2005] EWCA Civ 743, the Court of Appeal found that there had been a breach of the right to a fair trial in a contested contact and residence order case. Limited court time meant that issues were not fully explored and key individuals including the child's paternal grandmother, whom it was proposed would offer daily care, did not give evidence. There was, as a result, an 'impression of overall unfairness within Art 6 terms' (Wall LJ).

Article 8

There is potential for this article to be relied on in various cases, e.g. in the context of vulnerable adults, moving from independent living in the community to residential accommodation – sharing rooms, being offered only communal meals, no provision for couples to be together, lack of after-care services, covert surveillance, physical integrity, e.g. tagging, and violations which relate to a person's dignity as an aspect of private life.

It may be used as a defence against unwanted interference, including overzealous investigations, because any interference by the state with a person's private and family life, home or correspondence must be justified by one of the exceptions. The Act applies to all; it may also therefore be argued by an alleged abuser that his or her removal from home may constitute a violation of his or her rights. It will be increasingly important to recognise the existence of rights conflicts within a family, whether between a child and his parents or between adults.

Family life is interpreted broadly under the Convention, beyond the boundaries of married couples and immediate relatives. In *B* v. *United Kingdom* (1988) 10 EHRR 87, a contested contact case, the court stated that 'the mutual enjoyment by parent and child of each other's company constitutes a fundamental element of family life'. Article 8 includes protection of physical integrity and protection from sexual abuse: *X and Y* v.

Netherlands (1985) 8 EHRR 235. The right to privacy has applied to enjoyment of homosexual sexual relations (*Dudgeon* v. *United Kingdom* (1981) 4 EHRR 149) and in *Pretty* v. *UK* [2002] 35 EHRR 1, it was described as

'a broad term not susceptible to exhaustive definition. It covers the integrity of the person. Elements such as, gender identification, name and sexual orientation and sexual life fall within the personal sphere protected by Article 8. Article 8 also protects a right to personal development and to establish and develop relationships with other human beings and the outside world.'

The second part of article 8 qualifies the right. In doing so the Act seeks to balance rights of individuals with other public interests. This is known as proportionality, as any limitations must be proportionate to the end achieved. The question to be posed will be whether the interference is prescribed by law, serves a legitimate objective and is necessary in a democratic society.

This principle of proportionality was clearly applied in *Re O (A Child) (Supervision Order)* (2001) EWCA Civ 16, where the Court of Appeal decided that a supervision order rather than a care order provided a proportionate response. In the case Hale LJ found that a care order would be severe in three respects: power to the local authority to remove the child from her parents; power to the local authority to have parental control and responsibility; and a long period of time for its discharge. Any intervention of the court needed to be proportionate to the aim for protection of family life in the European Convention. The article is relevant in situations of failure to act as well as where actions cause the violation. In *R (on the application of Bernard)* v. *London Borough of Enfield* High Court October 2002, the court found that human rights were violated by failure to provide adequate community care services. Damages were awarded.

Reflect

Look back at the articles set out in 'A Closer Look' on p. 220. *Can you think of any practices within social work settings where an individual's human rights might be violated?*

For example:

- a care home for elderly people
- a residential home for children and young people
- the work of an Adoption Panel
- a child protection investigation
- detention of a person under the Mental Health Act 1983 or Mental Health (Care and Treatment) (Scotland) Act 2003.

SUBSTANTIVE LAW

The final part of this chapter will outline key aspects of the substantive law relating to social work practice. The text is divided into work with two major client groups: children and families; and adults, although it must be recognised that there are substantial areas of overlapping responsibilities. Significant areas of law and social work practice which are beyond the scope of this chapter include youth and criminal justice; housing, homelessness and welfare; asylum and immigration, and education. The substantive law in relation to social work practice in Scotland is addressed at the end of the chapter.

Law and children and families

Law provides the structure for social work with children and families, through a framework of duties and powers to support children and families and to take protective measures where necessary. Major pieces of legislation include the Children Act 1989, Children Act 2004, and Adoption and Children Act 2002. Each is supplemented by case law decisions which interpret and elaborate on aspects of each Act. Regulations and guidance provide further detail and support the central provisions of the legislation. Social work practice with children attracts a high profile in the media, particularly where inquiry reports have suggested failures in individual practice or systems. One of the responses to such inquiries has been the introduction of new laws. Aspects of each of the major pieces of legislation have their origins in recommendations of such reports. For example the duration of an emergency protection order is significantly shorter than its predecessor, the Place of Safety Order, following recommendations of the Cleveland Report (where children were removed from home following concerns of sexual abuse).

The Children Act 2004 was preceded by the Laming Report into the death of Victoria Climbié, a case where a number of agencies had had contact with but failed to protect Victoria. The new legislation was introduced to strengthen existing practices for sharing information and multi-agency working, although it must be noted that Laming stated,

'I recognise the fact that over the years, successive governments have refined both legislation and policy, no doubt informed in part by earlier Inquiries of this kind, so that in general, the legislative framework for protecting children is basically sound. I conclude that the gap is not a matter of law but in its implementation'.

This part of the chapter will include sections summarising principles applicable to law and practice with children, support for children and families, including orders within the private law, measures for child protection, and options for long-term planning for children unable to remain with their birth parents.

Principles

The Children Act 1989, part 1, starts with key principles that are to apply throughout the Act: welfare, delay, and non-intervention. It also sets out a new concept: parental responsibility.

Welfare

The welfare principle states that where a court determines a question about a child's upbringing (or child's property), the child's welfare shall be the court's paramount consideration. While 'welfare' is a difficult concept to define, the use of the word 'paramount' clearly stresses the importance of decisions being made that meet the child's welfare. This principle is supported by a 'checklist' of factors to be taken into account when determining welfare.

Think ahead

This is the 'welfare checklist' as set out in the Children Act 1989.

(a) The ascertainable wishes and feelings of the child concerned (considered in the light of his age and understanding)
(b) His physical, emotional and educational needs
(c) The likely effect on him of any change in his circumstances
(d) His age, sex, background and any characteristics of his which the court considers relevant
(e) Any harm which he has suffered or is at risk of suffering
(f) How capable each of his parents, and any other person in relation to whom the court considers the question to be relevant, is of meeting his needs
(g) The range of powers available to the court under this Act in the proceedings in question.

Can you think of any omissions from the checklist? Do you think any elements of the checklist should be given more priority than others?

A similarly worded welfare principle and checklist has been included in the Adoption and Children Act 2002.

Delay

The delay principle makes a clear statement that delay in proceedings is assumed to be harmful to the interests of children. It states:

'in any proceedings in which any question with respect to the upbringing of a child arises, the court shall have regard to the general principle that any delay in determining the question is likely to prejudice the welfare of the child'.

(Section 1 (2))

To support this principle courts will draw up timetables to be followed for completion of reports etc. and early exchange of evidence is encouraged. In public law proceedings the Public Law Outline has formalised this process and outlines a timetable for completion of care proceedings. National Standards support the Adoption and Children Act 2002 and suggest timescales for matching and placement, as well as including a similar delay principle in the Act. Some cases will require more time than others and the case of *C* v. *Solihull MBC* [1993] 1 FLR 290 suggests that delay may be justified if it is 'planned and purposeful'.

Non-intervention

The Children Act 1989 included a principle which aims to discourage courts from making unnecessary court orders, where they are unlikely to bring any real benefit to the child. This is most obviously the case where there is agreement between the parties. The actual provision provides an example of rather convoluted legal language!

'Where a court is considering whether or not to make one or more orders under this Act with respect to a child, it shall not make the order unless it considers that doing so would be better for the child than making no order at all'.

(Section 1(5))

In private law proceedings it may be argued that as both parents will retain parental responsibility following divorce, the actual orders are less significant than would have been the case under the previous law.

Parental responsibility

Parental responsibility (PR) is defined in s. 3(1) of the Children Act 1989 as, 'All the rights, duties, powers, responsibilities and authority which by law a parent of a child has in relation to the child and his property'. In practical terms for a person holding parental responsibility this includes being able to make decisions in relation to a range of issues, such as: choosing the child's name, religion, maintaining the child and consenting to medical treatment. Greater clarity is provided by the Children (Scotland) Act 1995 which contains a list of parental responsibilities in s. 1(1), namely: to safeguard and promote health, development and welfare; to provide direction and guidance in a manner appropriate to the stage of development of the child; to maintain personal relations and direct contact with the child on a regular basis, if the child is not living with the parent; and to act as the child's legal representative.

More than one person may hold parental responsibility for a particular child. The rules on acquisition of parental responsibility are quite complex. The child's birth mother will automatically have PR. The child's father will have PR if he is married to (or subsequently marries) the child's mother. If the child's father is not married to the mother he may acquire PR by jointly registering the birth with the mother, by making a PR agreement with the mother or by application to court for a PR order. PR will also be acquired by any person who is granted a residence order; a step-parent by agreement or court order; by a special guardian; prospective adopters when a child is placed for adoption; the local authority under a care order or emergency protection order. Disputes about the exercise of PR may sometimes reach the courts and can be resolved by the use of section 8 orders, as explained below.

The scheme of section 8 orders is intended to provide flexibility to the court to make the best 'package' of orders to suit the needs of each family, or, applying the no-order principle, to make no order. Many families will work out their own arrangements following divorce or separation, without any social work intervention. In other cases families may be known to social services, possibly receiving support or as a result of other concerns, such as domestic violence. If, during family proceedings questions about the child's welfare arise and the court considers a care or supervision order may be required, it can direct the local authority to investigate the circumstances and report back to the court (s. 37). This is in addition to the court's power to seek a report on any particular issue, e.g. contact (s. 7). In those instances a children and family reporter (within CAFCASS) is likely to prepare the report.

Supporting children and families

One of the key themes introduced by the Children Act 1989 was that the usual preference is for children to be cared for by their own families. In support of this the Act requires local authorities to provide a range of services and facilities to children and their families, working in partnership with parents. Some duties are owed to all children living in the local authority area, e.g. to take

---

A closer look

Controlling the exercise of parental responsibility

The Children Act 1989 introduced four new orders in section 8. Referred to as 'section 8 orders', they are: residence, contact, specific issue and prohibited steps. Residence and contact roughly replace the previous custody and access orders and are likely to apply to a medium- to long-term arrangement. In contrast specific issue and prohibited steps orders are likely to apply to 'one off' decisions about the exercise of parental responsibility and are modelled on aspects of the court's wardship jurisdiction.

- A residence order settles the arrangements as to whom the child lives with. It may be split between two or more people who do not live together.
- A contact order requires the person the child lives with to allow the child to have contact (visits, stays or otherwise) with a named person.
- A specific issue order gives direction on a specific question which has arisen (or may arise) of exercise of parental responsibility.
- A prohibited steps order prevents a specified step in the exercise of parental responsibility from being taken without the consent of the court.

Consider the advantages and disadvantages of 'shared care arrangements' where, for example, separated parents each have a residence order for their child so that the child lives alternate weeks with each parent.

reasonable steps to prevent children from suffering ill-treatment and neglect and to encourage children not to commit criminal offences. The key duty in s. 17 is targeted at children in need:

(a) to safeguard and promote the welfare of children within their area who are in need; and

(b) so far as is consistent with that duty, to promote the upbringing of such children by their families, by providing a range and level of services appropriate to those children's needs.

The definition of a child in need is:

(a) he is unlikely to achieve or maintain, or have the opportunity of achieving or maintaining, a reasonable standard of health or development without appropriate provision for him of services by a local authority under this Part;

(b) his health or development is likely to be significantly impaired, without the provision for him or her of services by a local authority under this Part; or

(c) he is disabled.

Practice in this area is supported by the *Framework for the Assessment of Children in Need and their Families* (DoH, 2000c). The *Every Child Matters* strategy and Children Act 2004 develop this area through introduction of the Common Assessment Framework which provides a common approach to assessment for use by the whole of the children's workforce to enable holistic assessment to be undertaken at an earlier stage by a range of professionals. In addition the Act requires children's services authorities to make arrangements for multi-agency cooperation with a view to improving the well-being of children related to the five outcomes of *Every Child Matters*. The Children Act 2004 also requires local authorities to ascertain children's wishes and feelings regarding provision of services and give them due consideration (having regard to age and understanding) before providing any services.

Safeguarding and promoting the welfare of children is defined in *Working Together* (DoH, 2010) as,

'protecting children from maltreatment; preventing impairment of children's health or development; ensuring that children are growing up in circumstances consistent with the provision of safe and effective care; and undertaking that role so as to enable those children to have optimum life chances and to enter adulthood successfully.'   (para 1.20)

For some children this will entail more than support services, and focused child protection work will be appropriate, incorporating investigation of possible abuse, which may lead to court orders for short- and longer-term protection.

Child protection

The legal framework for child protection starts with a duty to investigate in section 47 of the Children Act 1989. This will be triggered where a child in the area is subject to an emergency protection order or is in police protection, or more commonly where the authority 'have reasonable cause to suspect that a child who lives, or is found, in their area is suffering, or is likely to suffer, significant harm.' The duty imposed is then that, 'the authority shall make, or cause to be made, such inquiries as they consider necessary to enable them to decide whether they should take any action to safeguard or promote the child's welfare.'

If there is reasonable cause to suspect the child is suffering significant harm but an assessment is required to determine this and is unlikely to be achieved with cooperation, the authority may apply for a Child Assessment Order (s. 43) which requires the child to be produced for an assessment. This order has been relatively little used.

Following any referral of concerns and subsequent investigation a child protection conference would normally be held within 15 days of the strategy discussion. At that conference, a child's name will be placed on the Child Protection Register, if considered to be at continuing risk of significant harm. If it is decided that the child is likely to suffer significant harm in the future a child protection plan will be formulated outlining further action.

Where it is necessary to secure immediate protection for a child, an Emergency Protection Order may be obtained from the family proceedings court (s. 44). The criteria are that there is reasonable cause to believe that the child is likely to suffer significant harm if he is not removed to accommodation, or does not remain in the place where he is accommodated, or enquiries under s. 47 are being frustrated by access to the child being refused. The applicant acquires parental responsibility for the child for the duration of the order, initially 8 days with a possible extension for a further 7 days. Conditions may be attached to the order regarding contact, medical, psychiatric or other assessment of the child. A power of exclusion, which enables the court to exclude an alleged abuser from the home, rather than removing a child, may be attached to an EPO or an interim care order. Another person living in the household and able to care for the child must consent to the exclusion. In practice this may require one parent to consent to the exclusion of the other.

If longer-term protection is required the local authority may apply for a care or supervision order. Once an application is lodged, during the investigation period the child may be protected by an interim care (or supervision) order. Grounds to be satisfied before an order can be made are commonly referred to as the threshold criteria, contained in s. 31 and based on 'significant harm'. This is a broad term and case law has provided interpretation of its meaning (e.g. *Re G (Children) (Care Order: Evidence)* [2001] EWCA Civ 968, *Re L (Care: Threshold Criteria)* [2007] 1 FLR 2050). The stages of the threshold criteria are set out in the Closer Look box. They can be broken down into the question of significant harm, attribution of that harm, and need for an order. Even if it is proven that significant harm has been caused by failure of the parent to provide adequate care, for example, there may still be cases where an order is not required, owing perhaps to changed circumstances, or alternative orders, such as where a child is placed with a relative under a residence order. In reality the vast majority of care order applications are successful.

Before making an order the court must have considered a care plan for the child which will outline the authority's plans for the child if a care order is granted, e.g. phased rehabilitation to parents' care or adoption, and arrangements for contact. It is possible for the case to return to court after a care order has been made if the care plan is not complied with and this is not in the best interests of the child. An Independent Reviewing Officer will monitor and review the plan.

Looked-after children

Children who are subjects of care orders or otherwise provided with accommodation by a local authority are known as looked-after children. A range of duties are owed to looked-after children, principally the duty to safeguard and promote welfare (s. 22(3)). Before making decisions regarding a looked-after child the authority should ascertain and give due consideration to the views of the child, their parents and any others whose views are relevant. The most significant decision to be made for a looked-after child is where they are to be accommodated and the legal basis of the placement. Options include residential accommodation (sometimes secure), fostering, placement with family members, special guardianship and adoption. On leaving care, the Children (Leaving Care) Act 2000 provides that all care leavers should have a personal adviser and be supported through the use of pathways planning, mapping out a clear route to independence.

A closer look

Stages of the threshold criteria

Stage 1: Is the child suffering or likely to suffer significant harm?

Is the harm:
- *ill-treatment?*
- *impairment of health or development (compared with similar child)?*

Is it significant:
- *in the seriousness of the harm or the implication of it?*

Stage 2: Cause of harm

Is the harm attributable to:
- *care given or likely to be given – not what it would be reasonable to expect a parent to give to him?*
- *child beyond parental control?*

Stage 3: Should an order be made?
Application of:
- *welfare principle*
- *no order*
- *menu – care, supervision, residence, contact*

In the context of:
- *the care plan*
- *proportionality under the Human Rights Act 1998*

(*Source*: Brammer, 2010: 259)

A closer look

Permanency options – special guardianship

Some children are unable to remain with their birth parents and plans to provide permanent alternatives need to be made. This is consistent with the United Nations Convention on the Rights of the Child which states that every child has the right to belong to a family. In addition to adoption, some children may be cared for in long-term fostering arrangements and others will be the subject of residence orders. The Adoption and Children Act 2002 introduced a new order known as 'special guardianship', intended to provide a high level of legal security to a placement but without the complete legal severance that adoption entails. Parental responsibility is acquired by the special guardian and may be exercised to the exclusion of all others, including birth parents. The order is revocable but the court must give permission for any applications

and will do so only if there has been a significant change in circumstances.

Before an order can be made, the local authority must prepare a report considering the applicant's suitability and the wishes and feelings of the child.

The Prime Minister's Review of Adoption suggested that the new order might be appropriate for

'Local authority foster parents, relatives, older children who do not wish to be legally separated from their birth family, children cared for on a permanent basis by their wider family, and certain minority ethnic communities with religious and cultural objections to adoption.'

Case law decisions such as *Re AJ (A Child) (2007)* [2007] EWCA Civ 55 have indicated that these are 'illustrative' examples of possible application of special guardianship and stressed that each case needs to be considered on its own facts in line with the welfare principle.

Think ahead

In the Prime Minister's Review of Adoption Law (DoH, 2000g) Tony Blair made the following statement:

'[I]t is hard to overstate the importance of a stable and loving family life for children. That is why I want more children to benefit from adoption. We know that adoption works for children. Over the years many thousands of children in the care of local authorities have benefited from the generosity and commitment of adoptive families, prepared to offer them the security and wellbeing that comes from being accepted as members of new families. But we also know that many children wait in care for far too long. Some of the reasons are well known. Too often in the past adoption has been seen as a last resort. Too many local authorities have performed poorly in helping children out of care and into adoption.'

Do you agree with the Prime Minister's apparent preference for adoption of looked-after children?

Law and adults

The legal framework for social work practice with adults shares similarities with but also has differences from the framework for work with children and families. Law

provides a structure for the provision of support to adults, based on a range of characteristics. It is also increasingly being recognised that the law has a role to play in responding to the need to offer protection to some adults. This has long been the case in relation to mental health but is also evident in work with other adults who may suffer abuse. Whereas the Children Act 1989 provides a clear and accessible piece of legislation which addresses support and protection, there is no comparable central Act for adult work. A fairly complex raft of legislation must be navigated to achieve a similar end. Contrasts in work with children and adults is often loosely based on the issue of autonomy and decision-making. At its most extreme adults are assumed to have capacity and be able to make their own decisions whereas children are not. This over-simplifies the true picture and it is notable that there is now legislation that addresses the needs of adults whose capacity to make decisions is impaired. As stated previously it is also important to remember that social work cases do not always present with a clear demarcation between adults and children. An obvious example is where there are child protection concerns for a child whose parents have mental health problems. This part of the chapter is divided into sections which consider the groups of adults for which the law provides social work duties and powers; provision for support, adult protection, mental health and mental capacity.

Law and adult service users

Adult service users include older people, people with mental disorder, and people with a physical or learning disability. The law has responded to each of these groups with a range of powers primarily focusing on support. It is arguable that other adults might equally be included in a discussion of the law and social work practice, such as adult asylum seekers, those who are homeless, those involved in the criminal justice system as victims or perpetrators of offences and victims of domestic violence; however, for the most part, discussion in this chapter of the text is confined to the named groups.

A series of pieces of legislation from 1948 to the present day provide a range of duties and powers based on various definitions or criteria. The starting point is the National Assistance Act 1948, s. 29, which provides the power for local authorities to promote the welfare of people

'aged 18 or over who are blind, deaf or dumb or who suffer from mental disorder of any description and other persons who are substantially and permanently handicapped by illness, injury or congenital deformity or other such disabilities as may be prescribed.'

This presents perhaps the first attempt at a definition of a vulnerable adult. The same Act provides the duty of local authorities to provide residential accommodation for persons who, by reason of age, illness, disability or any other circumstances, are in need of care and attention which are not otherwise available to them (s. 21). In practice many authorities fulfil this duty in whole or part by contracted arrangements with the private and voluntary sector as actual providers of the accommodation. Such accommodation is regulated and inspected by CQC, under the Care Standards Act 2000, supported by National Minimum Standards.

Other legislation containing duties and powers is set out in Table 8.3.

Support – community care

Table 8.3 sets out the range of legislation providing powers and duties for social work support to adult service users. Accessing any of these services is dependent on a community care assessment under the National Health Service and Community Care Act 1990. The Act did not introduce a new service; it refers to existing duties and powers to provide services, within an umbrella definition of 'community care services'. It did, however, make significant changes to assessment for service entitlement and introduced the concept of 'care management' to include the whole process of assessment, provision of services and review or reassessment. The key assessment provision is s. 47 (1):

'where it appears to a local authority that any person for whom they may provide or arrange for the provision of community care services may be in need of any such services, the authority
(a) shall carry out an assessment of his needs for those services; and
(b) having regard to the results of that assessment, shall then decide whether his needs call for the provision by them of any such services'.

A closer look

Fair Access to Care Services

Fair Access to Care Services identifies four eligibility bands based on a critical, substantial, moderate and low risk to independence. For example:

Critical risk to independence. Significant health problems have developed/will develop or Serious abuse or neglect has occurred/will occur

Substantial risk to independence. There is/will be only partial choice and control over the immediate environment, or There is/will be an inability to carry out the majority of personal care or domestic routines

Moderate risk to independence. Involvement in several aspects of work, education or learning cannot/will not be sustained or Several support systems and relationships cannot/will not be sustained

Low risk to independence. There is/will be an inability to carry out one or two personal care or domestic routines or One or two family and other social roles and responsibilities cannot/will not be undertaken

The bands tend to be differentiated by degree of risk to independence, e.g. majority, several, one or two family roles cannot be sustained.

Many authorities will only provide services to those whose needs fall into the critical and substantial band.

Table 8.3 Summary of provisions relating to adult service users

Legislation	Section	Summary
National Assistance Act 1948	29	Local authority power to promote the welfare of people aged 18 and over who are blind, deaf or dumb or who suffer from mental disorder of any description and other persons who are substantially and permanently handicapped by illness, injury or congenital deformity
	21	Duty to provide residential accommodation for persons who by reason of age, illness, disability or other circumstances are in need of care or attention which is not otherwise available to them
	47	Power of removal from home
Health Service and Public Health Act 1968	45	Local authority may make arrangements for promotion of welfare of old people
Chronically Sick and Disabled Persons Act 1970	1	Local authorities to inform themselves of number of people within NAA 1948, s. 29
	2	Duty to assess needs and provide services to disabled people
National Health Service Act 1977	Schedule 8	Duty to provide home helps for households where help is required owing to the presence of a person who is suffering from illness, lying in, an expectant mother, aged, handicapped as a result of having suffered from illness or by congenital deformity
Mental Health Act 1983	117	Aftercare services
Health and Social Services and Social Security Adjudications Act 1983	17	Local authority power to make reasonable charges for non-residential community services
Disabled Persons (Services, Consultation and Representations) Act 1986	4	Right to an assessment
	9	Provide information about services
National Health Service and Community Care Act 1990	46	Community care plans
	46(3)	Definition of community care services
	47	Assessment of need for community care services
	47(5)	Services pending assessment
	48	Inspection of premises where community care services provided
	50	Complaints procedure
Disability Discrimination Act 1995 (and 2005)	1 and 19	Unlawful to discriminate on the grounds of disability in the provision of goods and services
Carers (Recognition and Services) Act 1995	1	Assessment of a carer's ability to provide and continue to provide care for a person
Community Care (Direct Payments) Act 1996	1	Power to make direct payments
Carers and Disabled Children Act 2000	1	Carer entitlement to assessment independent of assessment of person cared for
	2	Definition of care services
Carers (Equal Opportunities) Act 2004	1	Obligation to inform carer of right to an assessment
	2	Assessment to include carer's wishes as to work, education, training and leisure
	3	Cooperation between local authority and other bodies

(*Source*: Brammer, 2010: 430–1)

This provision combines a wide initial gateway in the words 'person for whom they may provide', followed by a duty to assess (shall carry out), followed by a discretion to provide services (decide).

Entitlement to services within the local authorities' exercise of discretion has been a contentious area, particularly given limited resources. The decision of *R* v. *Gloucestershire County Council, ex parte Barry* [1997] 2 All ER 1 ruled that local authorities were entitled to take resources into account in setting eligibility criteria, but not on an individual basis. Eligibility criteria operate to allocate finite resources to the most needy cases, but regional variation in criteria inevitably existed. In 2003 the Department of Health published criteria intended to lead to greater consistency, namely, Fair Access to Care Services. Revised guidance was published in 2010 (DoH, 2010). The eligibility bands remain but the guidance aims to reflect policy changes and situate application of the criteria within the wider context of personalisation.

It is apparent from Table 8.3 that a wide and complex range of law applies to adult social care. The Law Commission are currently engaged in a full review of adult social care law. Their initial report recommends a single statute for adult social care law to replace the current law which it describes as, 'a confusing patchwork of conflicting statutes enacted over a period of 60 years' which is 'inadequate, often incomprehensible and outdated' (Law Commission, 2009). As noted earlier, law reform takes time and it is unlikely that any new statute would be in place for several years; however, the commitment to reform and simplification of the law, with guiding principles for practice is encouraging.

Adult protection

Adult protection (also referred to as 'safeguarding adults') is a developing area of social work practice. Most authorities now have Adult Protection Coordinators and since the publication of *No Secrets* (DoH, 2000f) have been required to have multi-agency policies in place to protect vulnerable adults from abuse. There is no statutory definition of abuse, but *No Secrets* suggests that '[a]buse is a violation of an individual's human and civil rights by any other person or persons.' Categories of abuse which are recognised in *No Secrets* are: physical, sexual, psychological, financial, neglect and discriminatory abuse.

In England and Wales there is no statutory duty to investigate abuse, although *No Secrets* clearly places a responsibility on social services as the key agency responsible for adult protection. This position is strengthened by the Human Rights Act 1998 in its requirement that social services (as a public authority) should not act incompatibly with the articles e.g. by failing to take action if a person is subject to degrading treatment (Article 3). Without this precise duty and a focused piece of legislation providing public powers of investigation and intervention, it is necessary to draw on existing law to respond to individual cases of abuse. The law may be used to prevent abuse, through support provisions, good management of finances, regulation of settings and screening out unsuitable people (initially through use of the Protection of Vulnerable Adults index, now replaced by a scheme established under the Safeguarding Vulnerable Groups Act 2006). In some instances individuals who have suffered abuse may engage with the law directly and take action in contract or through use of domestic violence injunctions provided by the Family Law Act 1996. Formal action may be taken in some cases by the police in criminal proceedings, use of the Mental Health Act 1983, interventions by the Court of Protection, e.g. to order that a person (who lacks capacity) and has been abused should move to an alternative setting.

The position in Scotland is different. New legislation, the Adult Support and Protection (Scotland) Act 2006, has been introduced and there is some increasing pressure, led by groups such as Action on Elder Abuse and with some support from the Law commission, to follow this approach in England and Wales. The Act applies to 'adults at risk' as those who, because they are affected by disability, mental disorder, illness, infirmity or ageing are unable to protect themselves from abuse, or are more vulnerable to being abused than persons who are not so affected. The Act includes the principle that any intervention should provide a benefit to the adult and that it is the least restrictive of the adult's freedom. There is a duty to investigate abuse, powers to carry out assessments of the person and their circumstances, power to intervene to remove the adult, to exclude the perpetrator and, if necessary, to force entry.

Mental health

Current law on mental health is contained in the Mental Health Act 1983. This area has been subject to proposals for reform over recent years and amendments have been introduced by the Mental Health Act 2007. Mental health is a significant area of social work practice and many of the existing duties and powers are invested in a

A closer look

Adult protection and the criminal law

No Secrets recognises that the type of intervention (if any) in an adult protection case will be dependent on many factors, including the setting and the relationship of the perpetrator to the victim. One option is to recognise that the abusive behaviour may constitute a criminal offence and a criminal investigation and prosecution might proceed. *No Secrets* states,

'Action should be primarily supportive or therapeutic or it might involve the application of sanctions, suspension, regulatory activity or criminal prosecution, disciplinary action or de-registration from a professional body. Remember vulnerable adults who are victims like any other victims have a right to see justice.'   (6.4)

'Some instances of abuse will constitute a criminal offence. In this respect vulnerable adults are entitled to the protection of law in the same way as any other member of the public.'   (2.8)

The Mental Capacity Act 2005 introduces a new criminal offence which may apply to certain adult protection situations. It is limited to cases where the victim lacks capacity. The maximum penalty for the offence is five years' imprisonment.

Under s. 44, if a person (D)

(a) has the care of a person (P) who lacks, or D reasonably believes to lack, capacity
(b) is the donee of a lasting power of attorney, or
(c) is a deputy appointed by the court for P

D is guilty of an offence if he ill-treats or wilfully neglects P.

---

specialist practitioner, the Approved Mental Health Professional (AMHP), formerly known as the Approved Social Worker. Each social services authority must provide approved training and ensure it has sufficient AMHPs. The AMHP has a duty to 'make an application for admission to hospital or reception into guardianship in respect of any patient if he is not satisfied that such an application should be made'. A Code of Practice accompanies the legislation.

The Act provides a central definition: 'Mental disorder' means 'any disorder or disability of the mind'. The previous further categories: mental impairment, severe mental impairment, mental illness and psychopathic disorder, have been removed under the new legislation.

Compulsory powers of detention are contained in ss 2–5 as set out in Table 8.4.

In addition there are short-term powers which may be used for an AMHP to gain access to a patient (s. 115); to remove a patient (with police support if necessary) who is not being cared for properly or is living alone and unable to care for themselves (s. 135); and for a police officer to remove a person from a public place who appears to be suffering from a mental disorder and removal is necessary in their interest or for the protection of others (s. 136).

A mental health review tribunal (within the Health Education and Social Care Chamber of the First Tier framework for tribunals) operates to review discharge of patients from hospital detention. Following discharge from a section 3 detention or guardianship it is the joint duty of the Health Authority and Social Services to provide aftercare services to the individual. The Mental Health Act 2007 also introduced a new order for supervised community treatment. It is intended to provide support for patients who have been subject to s. 3 detention, to live in the community subject to certain conditions to ensure treatment is received and liable to recall if necessary.

Mental capacity

The Mental Capacity Act 2005 provides a framework to support individual decision-making, allow choice in appointing substitute decision makers and promote decision-making in a person's best interests should they lack capacity. It follows earlier legislation introduced in Scotland – the Adults with Incapacity (Scotland) Act 2000.

Prior to this legislation there was a lack of clarity about how decisions were to be made for a person lacking capacity (i.e. being unable to make the particular decision at the particular time) except in major medical cases and for finance and property matters. The Act provides a test of capacity, based on inability to make a decision because of an impairment or disturbance of the

Table 8.4 Compulsory powers under the Mental Health Act, 1983

	Mental health category	Other criteria	Medical support	Duration	Applicant
s. 2	Mental disorder	Warrants detention for assessment In interests of own health or safety, or protection of other persons	2 doctors	28 days	NR (Nearest Relative) or AMHP
s. 3	Mental disorder – nature or degree makes it appropriate to receive medical treatment in hospital	Necessary for health or safety of the patient or protection of others Cannot be treated unless detained and appropriate treatment is available	2 doctors	6 months	NR or AMHP
s. 4	Mental disorder	urgent necessity	1 doctor	72 hours	NR or AMHP
s. 5	Mental disorder	urgent necessity	Doctor or nurse	72 hours (doctor) 6 hours (nurse)	Doctor or nurse

(*Source*: Brammer, 2010: 452)

mind or brain. Protection from liability is given to those (including carers) who act or make decisions for a person they believe lacks capacity, provided the actions are in the person's best interests and not negligent. The Code of Practice which supports the Act advises that this would include routine acts such as washing and dressing, shopping and domiciliary help. The Act encourages forward planning. Individuals who have capacity but envisage possible lack of capacity in the future can nominate others to act under a Lasting Power of Attorney to make decisions about welfare, health and finance matters. It is also possible to make an advance decision to refuse medical treatment, if at the time treatment is proposed, the individual has lost capacity. A new Court of Protection has jurisdiction over all aspects of the Act and can make single orders to resolve disputes, e.g. as to where a person lives, or in adult protection cases. The court can also appoint a deputy to act on behalf of an individual where longer-term support with decision-making is required, e.g. to manage a trust fund. Where decisions have to be made as to serious medical treatment or long-term accommodation moves, or where there is an adult protection investigation, an Independent Mental Capacity Advocate may be appointed to support and represent the individual.

The Mental Capacity starts with a range of principles.

Reflect

- A person must be assumed to have capacity unless it is established that he does not (s. 1(2))
- A person is not to be treated as unable to make a decision unless all practicable steps to help him to do so have been taken without success (s. 1(3))
- A person is not to be treated as unable to make a decision merely because he makes an unwise decision (s. 1(4))
- An act done, or decision made for or on behalf of a person who lacks capacity must be in his best interests (s. 1(5))
- Before the act is done, or the decision made, regard must be had to whether the purpose for which it is needed can be as effectively achieved in a way that is less restrictive of the person's rights and freedom of action (s. 1(6))

Are these principles consistent with good social work practice as enunciated in the GSCC Code of Practice?

Law in relation to social work in Scotland

Children and families

The key statute in Scotland which relates to children and their families is the Children (Scotland) Act 1995. This is not a consolidating statute, and many significant provisions are contained in other Acts, but it does bring together both private and public law. There are three overarching principles. The welfare of the child is paramount; no court or children's hearing should make an order if there is another way to deal with the case (the no-order principle) and the child should have a voice in proceedings which affect him/her. There are, in addition, themes which run through the legislation such as:

- Partnership: partnership between parents in regard to their parenting role and partnership between parents and local authorities in terms of decision-making about children.
- Parents should normally be responsible for the upbringing of their children and so long as this is consistent with the welfare of the children, local authorities should promote this.
- Account should be taken, as far as is practicable, of a child's religious persuasion, racial origin, cultural and linguistic background when decisions are being made about his/her future.

Private law

The private law provisions of the Act relate to parental rights and responsibilities, what they are, who has them, who can apply for them and how they can do this. It is the first piece of legislation which has tried to set out a statement of what parental rights and responsibilities might be. Up until this Act, the only right which children had in respect of their parents was the right of aliment. Now that parental responsibilities are outlined in s. 2, children could take action against their parents if they fail in their responsibilities towards them. Parents are only given rights (in s. 1) to allow them to fulfil their responsibilities. The people who have parental rights are defined in s. 3, which has now been amended by the Family Law (S) Act 2006. Mothers have parental rights whether or not they have been married to the father of the child. Fathers have parental rights only if they have been married to the mother at the time of conception or thereafter, they have been registered as the father on the birth certificate or if the mother has signed an s. 4 agree-

ment (Children (S) Act 1995) by which she agrees to share parental rights and responsibilities with the father. It is only since the 2006 Act that joint registration of the birth has given a father rights, and this measure is not retrospective. In the absence of any of these factors applying, an unmarried father would have to raise an action under s. 11 for parental rights and responsibilities. This is the section of the Children (S) Act which anyone who wishes to acquire or to regulate the parental rights in respect of a child (e.g. rights to have a child living with you or to maintain contact with a child) would use.

Welfare provisions

Part 2 of the Act sets out the public law provisions. Local authorities have duties to children in need in terms of s. 22 and a child is defined as being in need if he/she is unlikely to achieve or 'maintain . . . a reasonable standard of health or development or his/her health or development are likely to be significantly impaired . . . unless services are provided by the local authority' (s. 93). In addition, local authorities have duties to children with a disability or who are affected by the disability of someone in their family (s. 24). Local authority duties under the Act extend to the provision of accommodation for abandoned children or children whose parents are unable to care for them either permanently or temporarily (s. 25) and duties to those children who are, or have been, looked after and accommodated (s. 17 and s. 29).

Children's hearings

Uniquely in the United Kingdom, Scotland has a system for dealing with children called the Children's Hearing System. This was set up following the report by the Kilbrandon Committee which had been set up to inquire into juvenile delinquency in Scotland but whose proposals went far beyond their remit. The enabling legislation was the Social Work (Scotland) Act 1968 although the provisions are now to be found in the Children (S) Act 1995 and the Children's Hearings (Scotland) Rules 1996. The Kilbrandon Committee recommended the setting-up of a Children's Panel to be composed of three lay people. This panel would not deal with the establishment of facts, so it does not deal with evidence. Grounds of referral to the hearing have to be either accepted by the child and his/her parents (or relevant persons) or established by the court before the hearing can proceed. Grounds are to be found in s. 52(2) of the Children (S) Act and the ground that a child has committed an offence is merely one ground among others. The pivotal person in the system is the Reporter to the Children's Hearing. Referrals are made to the reporter by the police, social workers, the child's parents, the school or anyone else who has reasonable cause to believe that a child may require compulsory measures of supervision (s. 53(2)). Social workers will be asked to provide a report and this will help the reporter to make a decision as to how to proceed. The reporter can decide to take no further action, refer the case to the local authority for help in terms of s. 22 or take the case to a hearing (s. 56). There is no right of appeal against this first stage of decision-making by the reporter. The child, his parents and/or relevant persons attend the hearing. A relevant person is a parent or someone with parental rights and responsibilities, or someone who ordinarily has charge or control over the child. Representatives are allowed to accompany all these individuals to hearings, should they wish to have them. As this is not a court, the proceedings are not adversarial and lawyers attending as representatives are there to support and advise their clients in challenging or pleading their case, apart from cases where the young person may go into secure care. In terms of s. 69, the Panel itself can decide to discharge the case, continue for further reports or impose compulsory measures of supervision. This latter disposal could mean that the child remains at home or they could be placed in foster or residential care. The decision of the hearing can be appealed to the sheriff court where a full hearing of evidence (known as a proof hearing) will take place. At the end of this process, the sheriff may decide to grant the appeal, uphold the decision of the hearing or substitute another decision (s. 73). A discussion of the issues around the effectiveness of the hearing in dealing with persistent offenders is outside the scope of this chapter.

Child protection

New measures to protect children were introduced by the Children (S) Act 1995. If there is reasonable cause to believe that a child is at risk of significant harm (though there is no definition of what is meant by this in the Act), then a local authority may do one of three things. It may apply to the court for an assessment order (s. 55) where it is unlikely that the person caring for the child would allow this to happen. Such an order will last for seven days to allow whatever investigations are necessary to happen. A child protection order (s. 57) (CPO) may be sought by any person where there are reasonable grounds to believe that a child is suffering significant harm or that they will suffer such harm if they are not removed to a place of safety. If the sheriff grants an order, the

reporter will be informed and a hearing will be scheduled to take place on the second working day after the order is granted (s. 59(3)). If the hearing is satisfied that grounds exist for making a CPO, they can continue the order until a second hearing is arranged to decide if compulsory measures of supervision will be required. This hearing must take place on the eighth working day after the order was implemented (s. 65(2)). There are opportunities to challenge all of these decisions after they are made. Obviously, the granting of a CPO is a very drastic measure, and all of those involved will have to take account of the 'no order' principle in exploring alternative courses of action. The third measure which could be taken to protect children is an exclusion order (s. 76). Again, application is made by the local authority to the sheriff and the purpose of the order is to exclude a named person from the home. This provision is very similar to exclusion orders which can be sought in situations of domestic violence.

Permanency and adoption

The legislation in relation to adoption has recently undergone a significant transformation with the passing of the Adoption and Children (S) Act 2007. Similar reforms were introduced in England and Wales with the Adoption and Children Act 2002. This Act has repealed most of the Adoption (S) Act 1978 with the exception of part IV and amended the Children (S) Act 1995. The new legislation was introduced to modernise the adoption system to make it reflect more accurately the realities of modern society. The restrictions which were in place in relation to those categories of people who could adopt have been lifted. Now, as in England and Wales both partners in an unmarried relationship can apply to adopt jointly, and this includes same-sex couples whether or not they are in a civil partnership. Local authorities have a duty to provide a range of adoption services and people who are affected by adoption have a right to pre- and post-adoption services. Parents are required to consent to adoption or, if they do not consent, the court can be asked to dispense with it (s. 31). One of the ways of achieving permanence for children whose parents were unable to care for them, and for whom adoption was not felt to be a reasonable option, was for the local authority to seek a Parental Responsibilities Order from the court by virtue of the Children (S) Act 1995 (s. 86). These orders have now been replaced by Permanence Orders within the Adoption (Scotland) Act 2007. The local authority will still seek these orders and the result of the order will be that the parental rights will pass to the local authority or other specified person. As in adoption, parental consent will be sought, but if it is not forthcoming it may be dispensed with using the same grounds as for adoption. The local authority may, in the application for a Permanence Order, request that the order includes provision to grant authority for the child to be adopted, but this can only be done if the parent consents or the consent is dispensed with. For many children and their families, the interface with the Children's Hearings System is important and the decision to seek any form of permanency planning for a child who is the subject of a supervision requirement must be discussed by a Children's Hearing. Much of the detail of these arrangements is to be found in the Guidance on Looked After Children (Scotland) Regulations 2009 and the Adoption and Children (Scotland) Act 2007 issued in June 2010.

Adults who are vulnerable and at risk

There is a raft of legislation to help and support people who are vulnerable and/or at risk. A broad definition of a 'vulnerable adult' is given in *Who Decides?* (Irvine, 1997) as a person:

'who is or may be in need of community care services by reason of mental or other disability, age or illness; and who is or may be unable to take care of him or herself, or unable to protect him or herself against significant harm or exploitation'.

The relevant legislation encompasses the following:

- Social Work (Scotland) Act 1968
- Chronically Sick and Disabled Persons Act 1970
- Chronically Sick and Disabled Persons (S) Act 1972 (adopted the 1970 Act for Scotland)
- Disabled Persons (Services, Consolidation and Representation) Act 1986
- NHS and Community Care Act 1990
- Carers (Recognition and Services) Act 1995
- Disability Discrimination Act 1995
- Community Care (Direct Payments) Act 1996
- Mental Health (Public Safety & Appeals) (S) Act 1999
- Adults with Incapacity (S) Act 2000
- Regulation of Care (S) Act 2001
- Community Care and Health (S) Act 2002
- Mental Health (Care and Treatment) (S) Act 2003
- Adult Support and Protection (S) Act 2007

Although, as can be seen, there are a significant number of statutes which inform the social work role

and task, and an even larger number of Codes of Practice, Regulations and Guidance, there are a number of shared principles which underpin all practice regardless of the legislation being used. Some of these are now enshrined in legislation such as the Adults with Incapacity (S) Act 2000 and the Mental Health (Care and Treatment) (S) Act 2003. However, even where the law is silent, good practice would demand adherence to these same values. Partnership with, and participation of, service users and their carers in all decision-making should be present. The principle of the minimum intervention necessary to safeguard and promote the welfare of the service user should be at the heart of practice. The wishes of service users should be taken into account and in so far as they can be ascertained, a variety of forms of communication should be used to clarify them. The views of service users and their carers should be taken into account where it is practical and reasonable to do so.

Community care

The NHS and Community Care Act 1990 contains only relatively few sections which apply in Scotland in terms of the provision of community care services. Those sections which do apply have been inserted into the Social Work (Scotland) Act 1968 which remains the primary legislation in terms of community care service provision by local authorities. This legislation requires social work departments to undertake assessments on any person whom they consider to be in need of community care services. S. 12A of the Social Work (S) Act 1968, which was inserted by s. 55 of the NHS and Community Care Act 1990, states that:

'Where it appears to a local authority that any person for whom they are under a duty or have a power to provide, or to secure the provision of community care services, the authority shall make an assessment of the needs of that person for those services'.

The Act covers the following: people with physical disabilities; learning disabilities; mental health problems; HIV/AIDS; addiction problems; dementia; older people with physical and other needs.

One of the key objectives of the legislation is to provide a range of services to sustain people in their own homes. These services might include domiciliary and day care as well as respite. One of the underpinning principles is that assessment should be needs-led rather than resources-led. In all situations where assessments of need are made, the local authority *duty* is to assess need. The *power* exists to provide services but these may not be available because of organisational constraints and financial pressures.

One of the ways to support people in their homes is through the use of direct payments. Direct payments are cash payments made in lieu of social service provisions to individuals who have been assessed as needing services (Community Care (Direct Payments) (S) Act 1996). They can be made to disabled people aged 16 or over, to people with parental responsibility for disabled children, and to carers aged 16 or over in respect of carer services. The aim of direct payment is to give more flexibility in how services are provided to many individuals who are assessed as eligible for social services support. By giving individuals money in lieu of social care services, people have greater choice and control over their lives, and are able to make their own decisions about how their care is delivered. There are, however, problems in casting the service user in the role of the employer with the issues that may arise as a consequence of an employer/employee relationship. In Scotland, free personal care was introduced by the Community Care and Health (S) Act 2002. Personal care will be provided free for people over 65 provided they are assessed as needing it. The care includes help with personal assistance, personal hygiene, food and diet, behaviour management and psychological support.

Mental capacity

The long title of the Adults with Incapacity (S) Act 2000 says that the Act will 'make provision as to the property, financial affairs and personal welfare of adults who are incapable by reason of mental disorder or inability to communicate'. There are four main principles in the Act: any intervention should provide a benefit to the adult concerned, a benefit which cannot reasonably be achieved without the intervention; the intervention is one which is the least restrictive to the adult; any guardian, carer or manager of an establishment managing an adult's finances should be required to encourage the adult to use existing financial and welfare skills and acquire new skills in so far as it is reasonable and practicable to do so; a person proposing to do anything under the legislation must take account of present and past wishes and feelings of the adult with incapacity as far as these can be ascertained as well as the views of the nearest relative and primary carer of the adult in so far as is reasonable and practicable. Incapacity is defined in s. 1(6) as being incapable of acting or making decisions or communicating or understanding decisions or retaining memory of decisions by reason of mental disorder or

inability to communicate because of physical disability. The main provisions of the Act include the establishment of Office of Public Guardian and the availability of intervention orders, guardianship and powers of attorney. It also governs medical treatment and research.

Mental health

The Mental Health (Care and Treatment) (S) Act 2003 repealed the Mental Health (S) Act 1984 (informed by the Millan Report) and made wide changes to the law in this area. It is informed by principles which replicate those of the Adults with Incapacity (S) Act 2000 with the additions that the least restrictive intervention should be used, and in relation to a child, the intervention must be one which best secures the welfare of the child. Some of the specific provisions of the Act include the introduction of mental health tribunals to replace the sheriff court, compulsory treatment orders (including care plans), patient representation and named person, advocacy, advance statements.

Mental disorder is defined in s. 227 of the Act: it means any mental illness, personality disorder or learning disability however caused or manifested. The Act has also excluded a number of conditions from the definition. A person is not mentally disordered by reason only of any of the following: sexual orientation or deviancy; transsexualism; transvestism; dependence on or use of alcohol or drugs; behaviour that is likely to cause harassment, alarm or distress to any other person; acting as no prudent person would.

A number of duties are placed on local authorities in terms of provision of services. Local authorities have a *duty* to provide or secure services which offer care and support to those who are not in hospital but have or have had a mental disorder and there is a *power* to do this in relation to those who are in hospital (s. 25). The services are provided in order to minimise the effect of mental disorder and give people the opportunity to lead lives which are as normal as possible. Care and support will include residential accommodation and personal care and support, though not nursing care (s. 20). In addition, there are local authority duties to provide services which are designed to promote the well-being and social development of people who have, or have had, a mental disorder and who are not in hospital, as well as a power to provide the same for those in hospital (s. 26). Such services might include social, cultural and recreational activities, training for those over school age and assistance in obtaining and undertaking employment. There is also a duty to cooperate with Health Boards and others in the provision of services. There is a duty placed on local authorities to inquire if someone has a mental disorder and it appears that they have been subjected to ill-treatment or neglect, or are living alone without care and unable to look after themselves or their affairs, or, because of the disorder, someone else may be at risk (s. 33). Local authorities have a duty to appoint mental health officers (s. 32). The following paragraphs explain some terminologies used.

Detention. People can only be detained if they have a mental disorder and their ability to make decisions about medical treatment is significantly impaired. There are provisions for emergency detention in hospital for up to 72 hours where there is an element of risk to the patient and others (s. 36); short-term detention for up to 28 days (s. 44) and also Compulsory Treatment Orders. Applications for compulsory treatment orders can only be made by Mental Health Officers (MHO) and they are made to Mental Health Tribunals (s. 63). The tribunals will be required to have regard to the guiding principles of the Act and have regard to the patient, the patient's named person, their guardian or welfare attorney and their primary carer before making a decision. The tribunal can specify detention, place of residence, medical treatment, community care services or other treatment or care for a period of six months. The MHO will produce a report and a care plan for the tribunal.

Named person. This replaces the provisions which relate to 'the nearest relative' in the 1984 Act. The patient can nominate someone to act on his/her behalf as the 'named person'. If they do not do this then the primary carer will take on this role, and in their absence the 'nearest relative'.

Advocacy. In terms of s. 259, every person with a mental disorder shall have the right of access to independent advocacy and there is a duty on local authorities and health boards to collaborate in securing the availability of such services.

Advance statements. These allow people to make statements when they are well about the way in which they wish to be treated (or not treated) if they become mentally disordered. They have to be in writing and signed by the person and also someone authorised to act as a witness. However, designated medical practitioners, while having regard to the wishes of the patient, may give treatment if the patient's ability to make a decision about medical treatment is regarded as being significantly impaired. The tribunal may also override the wishes of the person. However, if such treatment is given, then the reasons for the decision must be put in writing and copies given to the person who made the statement, that person's named person, the welfare attorney or guardian and the Mental Welfare Commission.

Criminal justice

In Scotland, social workers involved in criminal justice are employed by local authorities and must have a relevant social work qualification. This differs from the situation in other parts of the United Kingdom and so this area of practice is not covered elsewhere in this chapter. In brief, social work practice in criminal justice settings in Scotland is informed and shaped by the National Objectives and Standards for Social Work which were first published in 1991 and have been revised and augmented since then. They now cover areas such as services to courts, throughcare and risk. Social work services are provided in terms of s. 27 of the Social Work (S) Act 1968. This legislation places a duty on local authorities to provide reports for the courts as well as advice, guidance and assistance for people who are on probation and other orders, and for those who, following release from custody, are required to be under supervision. Local authorities are also required to provide schemes for probation, community service and supervised attendance orders.

Conclusion

This chapter had attempted to outline some of the essential features of law that social work students will need to grasp. Further, more detailed consideration of discrete areas of law relating to regulation of social work practice, the legal system of the country in which you will practise and the law applicable to practice situations involving a range of services to service users will be required. Beyond qualification, throughout a career in social work it will be necessary to keep up to date with changes in the law as they impact on social work practice. It is likely that substantive law will continue to develop at a rapid pace, with the influence of the Human Rights Act 1998 becoming more apparent in court judgments. It is hoped that this chapter has provided the foundations upon which to develop understanding of the role of law in social work practice and to embrace both the challenge and the mandate to practice which law delivers.

Key learning points

This chapter has covered the following learning points:

✔ The relationship between law and social work practice is complex and evolving.

✔ Law prescribes many aspects of social work practice through statutory duties and powers.

✔ For effective practice it is necessary to have an understanding of how law applies to practice situations.

✔ As law is constantly developing it is helpful to have an understanding of the sources of law and some legal research skills.

✔ Relevant sources of law include legislation, case law and secondary legislation, such as rules and regulations. Formal and practice guidance and codes of practice also add detail to many areas of law relevant to social work practice.

✔ The Human Rights Act 1998 provides further opportunities to promote good practice and uphold rights.

✔ The substantive law relating to children and families is contained primarily in the Children Acts 1989 and 2004 and the Adoption and Children Act 2002, and centres on safeguarding and promoting the welfare of children. Scottish legislation includes the Children (Scotland) Act 1995 and the Adoption and Children (Scotland) Act 2007.

✔ The substantive law relating to adults is contained in a raft of legislation; key Acts are the National Health Service and Community Care Act 1990, the Mental Health Act 1983 and the Mental Capacity Act 2005. (In Scotland this would include amendments to the Social Work (Scotland) Act 1968, Mental Health (Care and Treatment) (Scotland) Act 2003, and Adult Support and Protection Act 2007.

Further reading

Allen, N. (2005) *Making Sense of the Children Act 1989: And Related Legislation for the Social and Welfare Services*, London: John Wiley and Sons Ltd. A useful guide to children's law.

Brammer, A. (2010) *Social Work Law* (3rd edn), Harlow: Pearson Education.

Braye, S. and Preston-Shoot, M. (2010) *Practising Social Work Law* (3rd edn), Basingstoke: Palgrave Macmillan.

Clements, L. (2007) *Community Care and the Law* (4th edn), London: Legal Action Group. A detailed text including guidance and case law.

Dickens, J. (2004) 'Risks and responsibilities: the role of the local authority lawyer in child care cases', *Child and Family Law Quarterly* 16 (1): 17. Presents findings from a study of how local authority social workers and their solicitors work together in childcare cases.

Gibbons Wood, L. (2008) *Social Work Law in Scotland* (2nd edn), Edinburgh: W. Green, Sweet and Maxwell. The most comprehensive coverage of the Scottish social work legislative context.

Golightley, M. (2006) *Social Work and Mental Health* (2nd edn), Exeter: Learning Matters. Excellent coverage of this complex area.

Hothersall S. et al. (2008) *Social Work and Mental Health in Scotland*, Exeter: Learning Matters. Similar text to the above but related to Scottish legislative context.

Long, L. A., Roche, J. and Stringer, D. (eds) (2010) *The Law and Social Work: Contemporary Issues for Practice* (2nd edn), Basingstoke: Palgrave Macmillan.

Partington, M. (2006) *Introduction to the English Legal System* (3rd edn), Oxford: Oxford University Press. Provides a clear overview of the legal system.

Watson, J. and Woolf, M. (2003) *Human Rights Act Toolkit*, London: Legal Action Group Books. A useful practical guide to the Act designed for non-lawyers working in relevant organisations such as health and social services. Includes checklists which can be applied in order to test and demonstrate compliance with the Act.

The *Encyclopaedia of Social Services and Child Care Law*, London: Sweet & Maxwell. A looseleaf encyclopaedia which is updated regularly and contains legislation, regulations and rules, relevant circulars alongside explanatory text.

Useful websites

www.justice.gov.uk
The website of the new Ministry of Justice which took over responsibilities from the Department for Constitutional Affairs and includes information on the courts.

www.scotcourts.gov.uk
'This website provides a single access point for information relating to the civil and criminal courts within Scotland'. Contains a searchable database for court decisions together with useful general information about the courts system in Scotland.

www.scie.org.uk
The website of the Social Care Institute for Excellence which has interactive e-learning materials on understanding law and social work.

www.everychildmatters.gov.uk
Every Child Matters policy and key documents.

www.uk.online.gov.uk
Directgov – the entry point for government information and services online, this website incorporates an open.gov section, which has an alphabetical listing of central government departments, agencies and bodies, and of local councils.

www.gscc.org.uk
General Social Care Council: this body replaced CCETSW and has responsibility for regulation of the social care workforce, including social workers.

www.sssc.org.uk
Scottish Social Services Council: Equivalent body in Scotland to GSCC.

www.opsi.gov.uk
For legislation and explanatory notes to new legislation.

www.parliament.uk
The official website for Parliament provides information about Parliament, gives access to Hansard – the report of parliamentary debates, judgments of the House of Lords – and tracks progress of Bills before Parliament.

www.doh.gov.uk/publications/index.html
Department of Health site for a complete listing of local authority circulars (LACs) and local authority social services letters (LASSLs).

www.scotland.gov.uk
Website of the devolved Scottish Government. Contains all publications by the Scottish government, including consultations, research and links to all regulations, guidance and circulars issued by the Scottish Parliament.

www.homeoffice.gov.uk
The Home Office site provides information on the progress of law reform in the criminal law arena.

www.yourrights.org.uk
Information on the Human Rights Act is available from Liberty. The site gives an overview of the HRA and also considers the rights of particular groups, e.g. immigrants, travellers, children and young persons and prisoners.

www.lgo.org.uk
Summaries of cases and information about how the Local Government Ombudsman investigates complaints are available here.

For additional cases and topic-organised, clickable links into additional media resources, including those produced by IRISS, visit **www.pearsoned.co.uk/wilsonruch**

Activity

Understanding case law

1. Choose one of the cases listed below, all of which are significant cases in social work law:

   Re O (A Child) (Supervision Order: Future Harm) [2001] EWCA Civ 16

   R (J) v. *Caerphilly County Borough Council* [2005] EWHC 586 (Admin)

   R v. *Gloucestershire County Council, ex parte Barry* [1997] 2 All ER 1

   Re F (Adult: Court's Jurisdiction) [2000] 3 WLR 1740

   S v. *Miller* 2001 SC977 (Inner House Human Rights challenge to Children's Hearing)

   MacGregor v. *South Lanarkshire Council* 2001 SC 502 (Judicial Review of a decision of South Lanarkshire Council to delay providing the Petitioner a place in a nursing home)

2. Locate the case in a law library. Read the case fully, including all the judgments. Identify the following from your case:

   (a) names of parties

   (b) court/venue

   (c) name(s) of judge(s)

   (d) date and length of hearing

   (e) full reference case reported under – which law report

   (f) judgment

   (g) cases referred to in judgment

   (h) points of law

   (i) legal representatives.

3. Search on the internet for an electronic version of the case and note the neutral citation.

What are the implications of the decision for social work practice?

Courtcraft

Spend some time thinking about any court experiences you may have had, or anticipate what you think it would be like to give evidence. Consider the following questions:

What are my most important aims when giving evidence to the court?

What impression would I like to make at court?

Whom am I accountable to when giving evidence?

What anxieties do I have about giving evidence in court?

What strategies can I adopt to ensure I say what I want to say?

How can I translate nerves into confidence?

What happens if we 'lose'?

Chapter 9
Understanding and using research in social work practice

Chapter summary

In this chapter we introduce you to the idea of social work as a research-informed and research-oriented discipline. To do this, we have divided the chapter into two sections. In Section I, we consider empirical research as one of the forms of knowledge on which social work is based, discussing what 'counts' as social work research, the types of writing which can reasonably be considered as 'research' and how to judge good quality research in the social sciences. Next we explore some of the policy developments in social work which have led to 'research' becoming centre stage, what is meant by 'evidence based practice', and describe some of the methodological issues, dilemmas and purposes of social work research. In Section II, we introduce you to some of the stages and methods in undertaking research, both as a means of helping you understand the research process more generally, and more specifically, giving you guidance in conducting your own research, whether involving an original investigation or a library-based study. This is intended to help those of you writing dissertations for your professional training, and to give a brief introduction for practitioners who may be considering conducting their own research. We consider here the process of formulating research topics and questions, writing a literature review, different methods of research, structuring a dissertation, data collection, analysis and writing up.

Learning objectives

This chapter covers topics that will enable you to achieve the following learning objectives:

- To give a deeper understanding of the importance of research in social work practice and for social work practitioners
- To give knowledge and understanding of a range of approaches and methods in social work research
- To develop the ability to evaluate critically the appropriateness of a research method to the specific research questions being addressed
- To be able to assess and comment on different forms of research evidence
- To understand some of the key terms and dilemmas in undertaking social work research, including ethical considerations
- To become familiar with the stages involved in undertaking research, including identifying a research topic, structuring a dissertation, writing a literature review, and some of the skills in data collection and analysis.

National Occupational Standards

This chapter will help you to meet the following National Occupational Standards:

Key Role 6: Demonstrate professional competence in social work practice

Unit 18   Research, analyse, evaluate, and use current knowledge of best social work practice
Unit 19   Work within agreed standards of social work practice and ensure own professional development
Unit 20   Manage complex ethical issues, dilemmas and conflicts
Unit 21   Contribute to the promotion of best social work practice

Case study

Anthony

Anthony, a five-year-old black child, had been beaten and sexually abused by his stepfather before he was accommodated and placed with foster carers. He had been too frightened to tell anyone about what was happening at home. Although he has settled well in his new foster home, he is missing his younger half-brothers who are still at home. He also misses and worries about his mum who visits him rather irregularly. His mother is not prepared to leave her husband, who is still in the family home. Since the prospect of safely returning Anthony to his family seems at best uncertain, the social workers are considering a permanent adoptive placement.

Think about the alternative plans for Anthony which the social workers need to consider. What knowledge based on research do you think they might use in order to help the decision?

Are there any other factors, not based on research evidence, which they may need also to draw on and consider?

In the example above, there are a number of dilemmas facing the social workers (and others, including ultimately the courts). Not all of the questions raised will be ones to which social workers might reasonably look to research evidence for answers. For example, one of the dilemmas may prove to be Anthony's wish to live with his birth family, and his reluctance to be adopted because he is fearful of losing touch with his mother and brothers. Addressing this dilemma is likely to raise largely ethical, practice judgements and legal issues: how should Anthony's wishes and feelings be balanced against the risks to his long-term well-being of remaining in an 'impermanent' placement? What does the law say should happen? However, in order to address *these* questions, the social worker needs to know what the implications for Anthony's well-being are of following a particular course of action: is it likely that Anthony would 'do better' in an adoptive placement, than if he stays in foster care? And if he is adopted, would it be better for him to keep in contact with his birth mother, or would it be better to sever the relationship entirely? And is it better for Anthony to be placed with a black adoptive family, even if it means waiting longer for one, rather than be placed with white parents? To answer these questions (which might be called questions about *outcomes*), the social workers might reasonably expect, and be expected to seek, answers from research studies. In the other chapters of our textbook, we explore the kinds of knowledge, including knowledge derived from research, which social workers need to draw on in their reflective practice. Figure 9.1 will remind you of the different forms of knowledge we use, and show how empirical evidence is, as we suggest in the above exploration of the social workers' planning for Anthony, one of these forms. It is with this empirical research – i.e. involving evidence which is based on systematically collected information or data – what it is, how it can be used and how it should itself be judged, that this chapter is concerned.

It may appear self-evident that we should use research evidence in our practice, but social work has had a somewhat shaky history in this respect. In the past, social workers have been severely criticised for their use of untested interventions, the vagueness of the goals they set themselves to achieve, and the ineffectiveness of their interventions. (The more famous of these criticisms were delivered by

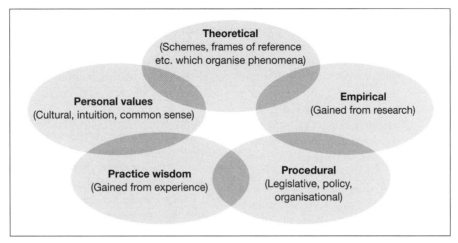

Figure 9.1 Model depicting the interrelationship between different knowledge forms

(*Source*: Adapted from Drury-Hudson, J., 'Decision making in child protection', *The British Journal of Social Work*, 1999, February, Vol. 29, No. 1, pp. 147–69, by permission of the British Association of Social Workers.)

Barbara Wootton, 1959, who accused social workers of grandiosity – i.e. inflating claims about its importance and about what it could achieve – and Brewer and Lait (1980) – who wondered if social work should survive at all.) More recently however, the importance of social workers being up to date and confident about using research has been widely canvassed, with the UK Labour government's 'modernisation' agenda involving a vision of research-driven social services. (See Department of Health, 1998.)

In 2001, the Social Care Institute for Excellence was established by central government in order to promote the use of research in social work and social care, and its ongoing portfolio of research summaries and literature reviews, most of which are available to download from the SCIE website, provide a very useful resource for students, practitioners and policy makers which we encourage you to make use of (see Further Reading at the end of the chapter).

Section I
SOCIAL WORK RESEARCH

What is social work research?

In order to understand the focus of our discussion, and the distinctions being made between research evidence and other forms of knowledge which make up the base of social work as a disciplined activity, we need first to consider what constitutes research knowledge. In our earlier chapter we introduced you to the idea that there are a range of important sources which contribute to the knowledge and practice base of social work: Figure 9.1 will remind you how these interlocking themes include theoretical frames of reference, personal values and experience, practice wisdom and procedural and legal knowledge. However, it is also essential if social work is to be both trustworthy, robust, sensitive and responsive

to the needs of individuals that it bases its activities on evidence which has been generated in a systematic, rigorous and disciplined way. So research in social work (which encompasses research conducted by professionals in related disciplines such as social policy, health and psychology) is concerned with understanding the problems experienced by individuals within societies and the impact of social policies and professional interventions on them. It seeks through this to provide answers and evidence which can contribute to the improvement of policy and practice, to reduce social problems and distress and to promote well-being. To 'count' as research, the evidence produced must have been gathered in an organised way, using methods which are appropriate to the questions being asked, and generating information (data) and conclusions which are capable of being tested, verified or refuted. One definition, then, of social work research is that it involves systematic investigation, which is conducted using the most appropriate research designs and verifiable methods and analysis. It seeks to find answers to questions relevant to social work about which there is disagreement, uncertainty or a lack of knowledge and to contribute to reducing social problems and distress and promoting well-being. It is thus distinct from other ways of knowing, such as knowledge and beliefs founded on personal experience, or perspectives based on values or ideology (although the *impact* of these on social work practice could well be the focus of research enquiry, and personal qualities may, as we discuss below, be found to be at the core of successful professional practice).

A second point which we need to consider in relation to 'relevant' research concerns the issue of which activities or interventions should be covered by 'social work' research. As the example of Anthony at the beginning of the chapter illustrates, a great deal of research relevant to social work will not strictly be measuring or evaluating social work interventions per se, but will influence the way in which they are implemented. So the actual activity on the part of the social worker (in Anthony's case, providing him with an ethnically matched placement, for example) is implicit in the final outcome and therefore harder to measure. For this reason, social work research should on the whole be seen as encompassing more than the measurement of specifically social work concerns, policy and practice, and to include research evidence which is relevant to them: such as the impact of policy, or interventions which are employed by other professionals as well as social workers. This is the approach we take in this chapter. (But see for example, Trevillion, 2000, for a discussion about whether or not it is possible to identify a discrete subject area of social work research.)

Criteria for identifying 'good' social work research

At this point, we introduce you to the idea that in considering research evidence and thinking about what it might mean for you in terms of your practice, you need to acquire the skills to think critically about the characteristics and attributes of any particular piece of research. In other words, you need to begin to evaluate for yourself the quality of the research evidence provided by the research investigation in question. If research is to provide a solid foundation for policy and practice, then

it clearly needs to be of a high standard. What counts as quality in social work research has, as Becker et al. comment, been the subject of some debate, with not all criteria commanding consensus. However, researchers do generally agree that high quality research is characterised by the fact that it

- gives a clear and precise statement of the aims of the research (or the questions or problems to which the investigation seeks to find answers);
- uses methods to answer them which are appropriate to the questions being asked and are clearly described;
- is transparent in explaining how the data has been collected and analysed;
- is based on the informed consent of any participants;
- makes a contribution to knowledge.

We shall return to some of these issues later, in discussing how to choose a method which is appropriate to the questions being explored, and the issue of whether or not there are, as some researchers might argue, 'hierarchies' of evidence: in other words, if research using particular methodologies should be given greater credence and weight than others. At this point, however, you may find it helpful to bear in mind, as you read different accounts of research, ten 'ground rules' for good research which one researcher, based on what researchers themselves consider to be 'good' research, has identified as attributes of such research. Although this refers to research in the social sciences more generally, it has equal relevance for social work research. You will see that the 'rules' include an acknowledgement of the pragmatics of research: for example, research has to be undertaken within realistic time limits (in part at least because of the changing environment it examines), certain questions may be unanswerable at a particular point in time, perhaps because of difficulties of accessing information, and, particularly in social work research and research in the social sciences, close attention has to be paid to conducting research ethically.

According to Denscombe (2002), to qualify as social research, an investigation needs to:

- have clearly stated aims that are
- related to existing knowledge and needs and that are
- investigated within limitations imposed through time, money and opportunity.

Research needs to:

- contribute something new to knowledge, using
- precise and valid data

- collected and used in a justifiable way, to
- produce findings from which generalisations can be made.

The researcher needs to adopt an attitude and approach that is:

- open minded and self-reflective,
- recognises the rights and interests of participants, and is
- cautious about claims based on findings.

(Denscombe, 2002: 2–3)
cited in Alcock (2004: 17–18)

Reflect

Think back to a journal article which reports findings from a research study (if nothing springs to mind, we give you some suggestions at the end of the chapter).

To what extent do you think it met the criteria which Denscombe suggests should characterise good quality research?

What, if anything, does it contribute which is new to knowledge of the subject?

Evidence-informed policy and practice

A further important issue which you need to think about in relation to research is the question of what constitutes *research* evidence, and the related question concerning evidence-based policy and practice. In order to explore this question, we need to make a distinction between evidence from research and other forms of evidence. The *Oxford English Dictionary* gives a number of definitions of evidence, for example, 'that which tends to prove or disprove any conclusion' and 'ground for a belief', but as Davies et al. (2000) comment, the unifying sense of the definitions is that 'the evidence (however construed) can be independently observed and verified and that there is a broad consensus as to its contents (if not its interpretation)' (2002: 2). There are many other kinds of evidence on which social workers and policy makers might need to draw. The relevant literature includes inspection reports, policy documents, the clinical reflections of social workers and therapists, practical advice from voluntary agencies, personal narratives and accounts by service users and much else besides. All these provide ways of 'knowing' about social work policy and practice and can therefore be construed as evidence for the development of policy and for

evaluating the effectiveness of interventions. However, it is only evidence based on empirical investigation, i.e. information that has been gathered and reported systematically and in a way which allows other researchers to check and test conclusions drawn from it, which provides any plausible way of establishing the robustness of a piece of evidence, and verifying the superiority of one claim over another. It is for this reason that evidence from research is given such importance as the basis for rigorous social work policy and practice, and policy makers and professionals alike are expected to draw on research evidence to inform their policy or practice choices, reflected in the now widely adopted term 'evidence-based policy and practice'.

You may well in your reading already have encountered the phrase 'evidence-based practice' (now referred to in government documents as 'evidence-informed'), perhaps being used in discussions about 'what works' in various contexts of social work endeavour: see, for example, books entitled *What Works for Children* (McNeish et al., 2002) or *What Works for Young People Leaving Care?* (Stein, 2004). In the United Kingdom, government policy and, to a varying degree, resources have been increasingly directed towards improving the outcomes for all children, and to minimising the harmful consequences for children and adults who may be at risk of exclusion, disadvantage and other difficulties. This has given added impetus to exploring 'what works?' or in other words the effectiveness of specialist services for adults, children and their families and the impact which service interventions may have on their lives. As a result, a foundation of qualitative and quantitative research studies is gradually being established which is directed towards obtaining the best evidence possible about the likely and actual consequences of a particular intervention, whether it be a particular government-led policy or initiative (for example, that of intermediate care for older people leaving hospital), or an intervention (such as cognitive behavioural therapy for women who are depressed).

The quest for evidence-based policy and practice is not new. Questions about the evidence base began to be asked, for example, trenchantly by a behavioural psychologist called Eysenck, who as long ago as 1952 concluded that the traditional forms of psychodynamically based psychotherapy (which was generally also the approach which underpinned social work casework education at the time and which we describe more fully in Chapter 12 on interventions) led to no greater improvement in adults experiencing certain forms of mental illness than that which occurred as a result of spontaneous remission (i.e. people who got well on their own, without therapy). This supported his general argument in favour of behaviourally based interventions (again see interventions chapter). Carr comments: 'There is little doubt that Eysenck asked the wrong question and that the data he used to answer it were from methodologically flawed studies. He asked *Does psychotherapy work?* when it would be more useful to ask *What works for whom?*' (2000: 1). Nonetheless, his paper sparked considerable debate. This and other movements (for example, the wish by social work as a new profession to establish a recognisable knowledge base) prompted efforts, which continued over the next decades, to conduct more rigorous research into the effectiveness of social psychological interventions by those in the helping professions, including clinicians and social workers.

However, questions concerning the evidence base for effectiveness have received much greater prominence from the 1990s onwards, when they came to be 'badged' as 'evidence-based practice' for the first time. One definition of the approach is as follows:

'Evidence-based practice denotes an approach to decision making which is transparent, accountable and based on a consideration of current evidence about the effects of particular interventions on the welfare of individuals, groups and communities. It relates to the decisions of both individual practitioners and policy makers.'

(Macdonald, 2002: 424)

So ideas about effectiveness are based on the notion of *outcomes*, to which the *Oxford English Dictionary* gives as one meaning 'a visible or practical product, effect or result'. This definition emphasises *causality* – one thing causes another – and *efficacy* – how effective the measure being examined is. Other writers, discussing outcome within a social work context, have expanded the definition somewhat to include intentionality: 'the desired end result and intended improvement after a specified period [in the well-being of children and/or families]. [Outcome] relates to the impact, effect or consequence of a particular service intervention' (Utting et al., 2001).

On the face of it, the underlying principle which we are addressing here seems relatively uncontroversial. You would expect that when social workers and other professionals intervene in people's lives they would do so on the best available evidence about the likely consequences, for good or ill, of that intervention. This will not of course be the only factor in the equation. All activities which involve complex skills have, as Figure 9.1 suggests, knowledge which is not based on research – for

example, the techniques involved for an opera singer in learning to project her top notes, or a tennis player developing a two-handed backhand, are only marginally, if at all, based on research evidence – and social work is no different. The context too of the activity is important: policy makers and practitioners alike will still have to make choices on available resources, including cost-effectiveness, values (for example, an intervention may not be ethically acceptable) and public opinion. Our example in the next section of the combination of research evidence, pressure from the media and public opinion in bringing about new policies for young carers illustrates this point.

However, in any case, using 'evidence-based practice' is rather more complicated than it first appears, so that it has become something of what is sometimes termed a 'contested terrain': i.e. an issue about which there are ongoing debates and disagreements. In addition to the part which other forms of knowledge need to play (again, see Figure 9.1) there are other factors which make it more problematic. Some of these difficulties relate to the nature of the evidence sought (for a variety of reasons which we shall come on to, human exchanges can be more complicated to investigate and evaluate). These difficulties also include a lack of clarity about what is meant by an outcome: for example, deciding the 'cut-off' point in a study of the effects of an intervention may be problematic, a point which we explore in greater detail in our Closer Look box on outcomes. There are disagreements about the relative value of different kinds of research. Debates here tend to mirror wider methodological debates and to focus on the question of *hierarchies* of evidence, with some arguing in principle for the superiority of one design over another, while others point to the need for a variety of approaches to answer different kinds of questions. And there are debates about the extent to which evidence from research can be generalised across different contexts and cultures: for example, can findings from American studies of friends and family foster care be applied to the United Kingdom?

These questions are not ones which we can resolve here, but we introduce them as issues for you to bear in mind in your reading, and which you need to think about in relation to considering the evidence for any particular research study. The more powerful medical and health environments tend to adopt an approach which ranks different research designs and methods in a hierarchy of evidence, with systematic reviews of randomised control trials at the top (i.e. seen as most reliable) and, probably, case studies at the bottom.

However, even here, and more emphatically in research in the social sciences, decisions about *what works* always have to be made on the balance of evidence. This includes not only an assessment of the methodological rigour of the different studies but also considerations of the 'coherence of evidence' and 'prior probability' (i.e. does it seem likely in advance that something will be true or effective?). Where professional opinion, common sense, respectable theory and user views are favourable to an intervention, there is a presumption that it will work. Stronger evidence is required for showing that it does not work than would be the case in other situations. For this reason research that is not strictly comparative – for example, case studies or surveys of professional judgement and consumer views – has a role in building a case for and against interventions (Wilson et al., 2004). So in social work research an acceptable position is likely to be one which acknowledges the varying strengths and weaknesses of different research designs and methods, tries to draw on the most appropriate one to answer the specific question, and when evaluating the evidence considers such factors as the cumulative quality of the evidence (e.g. does the finding occur repeatedly and is it produced regularly and consistently?) and whether the findings seem plausible in their context and have a 'ring of truth'. (See, for example, the researchers' comments on their findings in the article by Sykes et al., 2002.)

The limitations of evidence-informed practice

We should also keep a healthy scepticism about the exhortations to us as professionals about the use of evidence-based practice. These 'health warnings' arise, among other things, because:

- It is important to be alert to the quality of the evidence being cited. (See above discussion and A Closer Look box below.) White et al. (2009), for example, found when they looked at the evidence-based knowledge which was said to have informed decision-making in the integration of the assessment framework and LAC materials that this was 'on close inspection revealed to be somewhat flimsy, comprising four studies without the hall mark of academic peer review' (2009: 407).
- Current fashions and preoccupations affect both whether or not research is commissioned, and whether or not findings are used to shape policy. Thus research evidence may be ignored or used selectively, depending on how receptive the policy

and practice context is. One example of this might be that the increasing preference for custodial sentences contradicts the accumulated research evidence about responses to offending behaviour which are more, or less, effective (these favour community-based interventions).

Reflect

Perhaps you have come across other examples in your reading or from your experience where policies seem to be more driven by political will than research evidence.

- Closely related to the above, there is some evidence that certain kinds of research findings find favour and are followed up while others are not. For example, a meticulous evaluation of the Integrated Children's System carried out by independent researchers at the University of York was highly critical in its conclusions:

'national IT projects such as the Integrated Children's System have often been poorly planned and actually create more difficulties for social workers than they solve, as well as diverting attention away from professional approaches to meeting the needs of children and families . . . ICS is promising and well-intentioned but has not shown it is fit for purpose. Its problems must be addressed.' (Bell et al., 2008)

However, publication of the report which had been completed in 2006 was evidently only published under Freedom of Information rules over two years later, and no action to review or overhaul the ICS has to date been taken by the DCSF.

A further example of the way in which research findings may or may not receive wider currency or be used to affect policy lies in a body of evidence highly relevant to our textbook's core theme of the reflective practitioner. This evidence derives from user research studies which suggest that there are individual differences between practitioners who deliver personal services, and highlight the importance of the individual characteristics of practitioners. (See, for example, Wilson et al. (2004), Cousins (2009).) Sinclair, for example, asks why if this is the case there have been so few studies setting out to identify differences in effectiveness and to explore possible reasons for these (Sinclair, 2002). One answer to his question may lie in the fact that users' wishes are commonly considered in situations where resources or

A closer look

What do we mean by an outcome

One of the dilemmas in measuring 'effectiveness' in researching social work interventions concerns the very nature of outcomes in this context.

First there is the difficulty of deciding the 'cut-off' point for measuring an effect. For example, one French longitudinal study of foster care found that adults who had been in foster care typically experienced difficulties in early adulthood but that the majority by their early thirties were functioning satisfactorily (Dumaret et al., 1997).

Secondly, there is the difficulty in deciding which of a number of variables (i.e. different aspects of an occurrence or experience) have produced the effect or outcome. For example, in the case of a child who has experienced familial abuse, is her poor school performance the result of the abuse itself, or other aspects of her home life, or her experiences at school?

Thirdly, how should we consider effects which are to do with the way in which a service is delivered? These may have only a tenuous impact on final outcomes, but may be important in how people feel about a particular course of action. On the other hand, there is substantial evidence that the manner in which social work is delivered (i.e. the process) can in

fact affect its outcomes and might therefore arguably be perceived as an end in itself. We should therefore distinguish between two kinds of outcomes:

- *Final outcomes* are generally agreed to be significant in their own right. They may occur after being in intermediate care, for example, 'settling down in your own home and managing satisfactorily'. However, they could also be in a sense part of intermediate care and occur at the time – for example, whether or not the individual is happy there, puts on weight and recovers physical capabilities.

- *Process outcomes* (see above) are concerned with the way social work is provided. They would include, for example, the degree to which an elderly individual was consulted over what happened to her or him. They may be valued because of their effect on final outcomes or for other reasons – e.g. because they are seen as rights, or because they are valued by the recipients of social work interventions. (The example from Bell's 1996 study, below, about parents' satisfaction with being invited to case conferences, which can be distinguished from the end result, is an example of a process outcome as opposed to a final one.)

alternatives are lacking and that they are constrained by other pragmatic considerations too (such as the scarcity of a particular form of provision: for example, residential care for the mentally ill, which makes choice by and large irrelevant). Another reason may be that some findings produce a defensive reaction, or are less palatable: for

example, there is some evidence that things go better in children's homes when staff are given more autonomy, rather than being hemmed in by regulations. However, giving staff more autonomy may be seen by managers as exposing them to too much risk of criticism to be countenanced, whatever the research evidence.

A closer look

How to judge the quality of research findings

There are no guarantees, but the following are pointers:

- Was the paper/research subject to peer review?
- What is the reputation of the researchers?
- Was an expert advisory group used?
- Is there consistency between aims, design and specific questions?

- For quantitative research, what is the size and representativeness of the sample, number of missing data, rigour of analysis, appropriateness of statistical tests?
- For qualitative data, what is the depth and authenticity of examples and quotations used? What, if any, computer packages were used in the analysis and did colleagues help identify themes and check selection of examples? Were the researchers careful to check for exceptions to general trends?

(Adapted from Hill, M., 2009, 25–6)

Developing 'practice-near' social work research

A recent development, that of 'practice-near' social work research, has taken place in part out of concern for the effect on children and adult services of what has been called 'practice-distant' research and the culture of managerialism which it reinforces. This is less a distinctive approach, more an underlining of the importance of open-mindedness in research, and the need to be open to the impact of the research on the researcher and participants as well as, hopefully, those using the research. By positioning research close to practice, proponents of the approach argue that it creates opportunities for a greater complexity of experience to be understood by practitioners across a range of fields. Studies which adopt this approach underline the fact that professional judgements cannot simply be condensed into procedures or protocols and allow us to get closer to the emotional experience both for the researcher and potentially the research participants (Cooper, 2009; White et al., 2009). For example, Deacon (2009) records and analyses a variety of long-term consultations and supervisory processes in high security settings with workers who were subject to the kinds of emotional and organisational pressures characteristically encountered by staff on a daily basis with highly disturbed people. As with many of the public inquiries into health and welfare 'failures', the prominent ones from high security settings signally fail to show us how the critical incident occurred or the processes by which a breakdown in professional functioning developed. Deacon's research aims to fill this gap, demonstrating that the processes which explain such incidents are likely to be everyday ones, and not exceptional or aberrant.

Why is using research evidence so important in social work?

In this section, we explore more fully the reasons for drawing on research evidence, as a way also of introducing you to some of the questions which research can usefully address. One leading academic, in an address to a social work audience, summarised the arguments cogently:

'It is ... important [in research in social work] to know whether the effects (or the lack of them) arise because of the singer (the social worker) the song (for example task-centred casework) or the backing orchestra (the agency from which the worker practises).'   (Sinclair, 1992: 67)

We expand these reasons somewhat in the list which follows, which although not exhaustive, may give you a flavour of the kinds of information which research studies can provide and their value variously to professionals, policy makers and ultimately service users.

1. *It can help us evaluate the impact of social policies on individuals, families and groups.* For example, in relation to older people's experiences, research can give us a better understanding of their needs, and the kinds of services they value; these can be central to promoting social inclusion and well-being and may also be important in preventing or delaying their need for statutory support. One study which looked at the experiences of 51 older people in receipt of some form of home care highlighted how much they valued what were described as 'low level' forms of help (a description which the study emphasised should not be read as a judgement about the *quality* of the care offered). These were found to be effective in preventing or delaying their admission to residential settings and the researchers highlight the role of such help in preventing social exclusion and forestalling admission to residential care. However, these forms of care tended not to be considered so important by those planning the delivery of services, and were therefore not given priority in service provision and resourcing (Clark, Dyer and Horwood, 1998).

2. *It can influence the development of policies by providing evidence of the causes of injustice or highlighting the experiences, needs and plight of particular groups.* For example, in the early 1990s, a number of small-scale qualitative studies helped draw attention to the experiences of a small hitherto 'hidden' group of children who were providing significant amounts of unpaid care and support, often of an adult-like nature, to a family member, usually because of the latter's mental illness or disability. The research, which was largely based on interviews with the children and young people concerned, first described and then explained their circumstances and needs, and contributed significantly to the development of policy and law for this group of children and young people. It is also worth noting the way in which research here *contributed* to a growing social or political awareness, rather than being the sole factor in the development of policy or practice in relation to young carers. As Alcock, a social policy professor, comments, the media, campaigning groups and some of the

children themselves also played a significant part in bringing the problem to public attention: 'In this context, policy making combined both rational, top-down, and incremental, bottom-up elements, with research feeding into the process at various stages and being used by various stakeholders for different purposes, as part of a wider process of political negotiations, advocacy and policy development' (Alcock, 2004: 22).

3. *It can help determine the impact of social work, including its explicit and implicit functions, tasks and processes.* Although, as we shall see, there are considerable limitations to and constraints on the evidence available, research can give a sense of what the impact of a particular intervention has been, what its limitations are and what needs to change if more effective work is to be done. For example, in a classic study, Reid and Shyne demonstrated that time-limited interventions, in which clients were actively engaged in selecting the problems to work on, and did so over an agreed, short period, were more effective than the longer-term open-ended approaches favoured on the whole by practitioners. Although the study is methodologically flawed (the follow-up periods used for the two cohorts differed, and thus arguably favoured the short-term interventions), the findings were instrumental in paving the way for greater user involvement in treatment plans, and more structured interventions (which we describe more fully in our later chapter (12)) (Reid and Shyne, 1969).

Another body of research studies examining the impact of social work activities is highly relevant to the approach to social work which we are reflecting throughout this textbook, since the studies consistently highlight the importance that the personal qualities and attributes of individuals have in delivering effective services. Examples of this include, first, a large study of foster care which demonstrated through quantitative and qualitative methods and case studies that some foster carers were more likely to have successful foster placements, and that success was not just dependent on whether or not the foster child was difficult or easy to foster (Wilson, 2006). Secondly, an earlier, rigorous study similarly highlighted the importance of personal attributes and skills in achieving successful outcomes, in this case the reduction of the involvement in delinquent behaviour of young people in probation hostels. (The research study is described in more detail in the Closer Look box.)

4. *Research can also help us see the likelihood or otherwise that a social work intervention will be successful, and therefore help prevent demoralisation, and encourage careful choice of methods.* For example, there is some evidence that motivation or willingness to change plays an important part in the success or otherwise of an intervention, although it may not be the whole story. If it is unlikely, on the basis of the evidence, for example, that the interventions of those involved in trying to alter, say, a teenager's delinquent behaviour from unacceptable to acceptable will have much impact on reconviction rates, then this knowledge may help them to think through more precisely what they are trying to achieve in their activities, and perhaps to set more realistic and achievable goals (e.g. diversion rather than cessation of criminal activity altogether). (See Chapter 18 on youth offending for further discussion.)

5. *Conversely, it can also provide support and encouragement to pursue a course of action in the face of discouragement.* As you will doubtless be aware, social work as a profession comes in for a good deal of public criticism, and it is hard at times not to be demoralised by this. A substantial body of research exists demonstrating, among other things, the appreciation which users feel about the social work service they receive. (It also, as we shall see in Chapter 14, tells us a good deal about what users value in social workers and what they most dislike, which of course is relevant to shaping how social workers interact with those whom they are trying to help.) Studies of all groups of users' views of social workers show that they value those who are warm, non-judgemental, understand the user's perception of the problem, are straight and not two-faced, reliable in keeping appointments and in doing what they say they are going to do, do not fob them off with promises which they cannot keep and are efficient in getting services and benefits. One example of research into what users and carers value in social work is that of Fisher et al. (2000) who, in their study of 596 foster placements, found that foster carers valued social workers who are reliable, easy to get hold of, efficient in chasing payments and complaints, responsive to the family's needs and circumstances, and attend to the individual child's needs and interests and involve the foster carers where appropriate.

6. *It is an important component of our identity as social workers, in that research evidence, and knowledge and understanding of the basis on which social workers act, help provide us with a necessary professional authority.* Hill, in his chapter on the place of research in policy and practice, underlines its contribution and importance to the profession. Although he is referring to child

A closer look

Research example of the impact of professionals' personal qualities and skills

Under different wardens (the hostels were run by husband and wife teams) the proportion of young men leaving prematurely as a result of an absconding or offences varied from 14 to 78 per cent.
The variations were not explained by differences in intake, or by the location, size, physical characteristics or any other aspect associated with the hostel *other than the staff themselves*. The qualitative part of the study which consisted of face-to-face interviews with staff showed fairly clearly why this might be the case. For example, the warden in the least successful hostel said in interview: 'Each boy has his breaking point and I find it.' Statistical evidence in the study showed that the characteristics of the most successful husband and wife teams closely resembled those of the parents of boys on probation (i.e. a kind of control group) who did not reoffend (Davies and Sinclair, 1971).

(Kevin Smith (Kes): www.kescartoons.com)

placement research in particular, his comments are relevant to the wide range of social work activity:

'We live in an era when most politicians and civil servants aspire to make policy evidence based, and when practitioners are exhorted to apply research evidence about the effectiveness of different kinds of intervention. While there is always scope for plenty more research, the UK has built up a substantial empirical base in relation to child placements.'

(2009: 26)

Think ahead

Imagine you are a social worker, talking to a sceptical but not unsympathetic audience about the importance of social work research for improving the lives of users.

What examples might you give? What are the 'good news' messages based on empirical work which you might use?

Section II
STAGES OF THE RESEARCH PROCESS

In the second part of our chapter, we introduce you to some of the stages in the research process, which will help you in understanding and evaluating research more generally, and also more specifically will offer you guidance in conducting your own research, usually for your longer piece of work in your professional training. Many of you will be required to undertake a small piece of empirical investigation for a dissertation as part of your degree work. Others will undertake what is generally called a library-based dissertation, using secondary sources (i.e. not drawing on your own research, but looking at the work of others). And some of you may, as

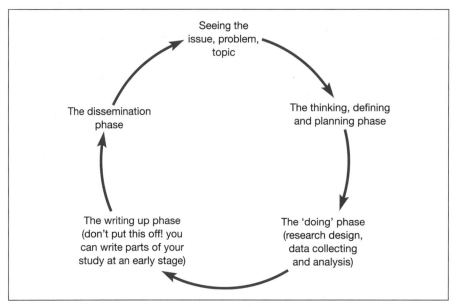

Figure 9.2 The research cycle

(*Source*: Adapted from Becker and Bryman, eds, *Understanding Research for Social Policy and Practice*, The Policy Press, 2004: 61)

practitioners, wish to undertake your own research. We can only give you an outline of the different processes involved, and you will find suggestions for further reading, as always, at the end of the chapter. Since it is relevant to your wider understanding of research evidence, we look at a range of different research methods, although it is unlikely (because of time constraints, the need to get ethical approval which is time-consuming and so on) that you will yourselves use many of these, at least as students. The process of undertaking research can be viewed in the form of a cycle, involving a 'thinking' phase, a 'doing' phase, a writing-up and dissemination phase, and a phase in which the research findings are utilised and implemented. These phases are illustrated in a model adapted from Becker (2004: 61).

The thinking and planning stage

Identifying a research topic

Research studies come into being in different ways – there may be an identified problem which needs addressing and research may be required to tell how best to do this; or an existing policy may be in place and its impact needs to be evaluated; or it may emerge to address a theoretical position or hypothesis, for example about the links between inequality and poor health – to give three situations among many. In selecting the topic for your own study, you may choose a subject about which you have personal experience, or an issue which has intrigued you in your reading, or arises from a problem encountered in your practice. Whatever you choose, it is important to select a subject which will hold your interest and which for you feels worthwhile to invest time in and also which you can demonstrate has relevance to social work. There are following this, usually, three stages in finding the appropriate focus for your study: identifying a research topic, a research issue and a research question.

The *research topic* will reflect a broad area: for example, depression, or eating disorders in adult women, or trans-racial adoption or informal family care. As a focus for research, however, these are too general to provide guidance on how they should be studied and would involve a vast and indigestible literature. So you need to narrow the focus down and decide which aspect of it to follow up. For example, are you interested in how depression affects family members, or whether children suffer from it, or depression in black or minority ethnic adults? In narrowing your focus, you begin to identify a research issue.

A *research issue* is within the broad area which you want to find out more about: for example, in the case of eating disorders, the issue might be something like how far they receive support from the state and its agencies (health and social services). Such a focus narrows down from the general issue to certain aspects of it – probably the experiences of women and possibly the perceptions of those involved in supporting them. You might at this point also decide to break down the broad area to give it a more manageable focus: for example, selecting one eating disorder, such as bulimia, in particular, rather than disorders generally. So at this point we are beginning to see what the research might be about and why it is being done. However, in order to guide us even further in what the research is about, we need to formulate this in the form of a research question.

A *research question* specifies much more precisely what the research is about, and is the essential step in providing a guide and giving direction to the investigation. Unless you formulate your issue in terms of a question, you will have no basis on which to choose who or what the focus of the enquiry should be, what literature you need to examine as the foundation for your investigation, what kinds of questions might usefully be asked of respondents if you are undertaking an empirical piece of research, and so on. So the research *question* in relation to the issue of bulimia in women might be formulated as: What implications do the experiences of women with the eating disorder of bulimia have for social workers and other professionals in helping them? (A research question is rather different from a hypothesis, which speculates that there is some relationship between two aspects, or variables, of the problem, but again, needs to be formulated as a question.)

Think ahead

Working if possible with a fellow student or colleague, provide 20 minutes' consultation to each other on what each wants to do, why they want to do it, and how they propose to do it. (If you are working on your own, try to reflect on and answer these questions for yourself.)

Try to avoid discussing the content of the proposal, but enable the other to bring out why the idea is 'compelling' (i.e. interesting to you, and relevant to social work practice), clear, coherent (i.e. methods should be consistent with aims) and whether or not it can be carried out.

Remember the five C's for research – that it should be

Compelling, Clear, Convincing, Coherent and Capable of being done!

If you are working in a class of students, spend five minutes identifying any problems which you think could be of general interest and discussed in the group.

Writing a literature review

The next stage in conducting your (or indeed any) study is to identify what knowledge already exists about the issue in question. As Becker, in a useful text on conducting social policy research, points out:

'Research in social work is never conducted in a vacuum. Even topics which burst on the scene as apparently unresearched areas still need to be assessed in terms of what we already know because it will almost certainly be the case that there will be cognate topics and issues that have been researched and whose findings will help to illuminate our understanding of our object of inquiry.'   (2004: 68)

So the purpose of a literature review is to give a kind of 'state of the art' view of a particular topic: that is, it provides an assessment of what is known about the issue through a description and analysis of the existing literature on it which you then build on for your study. In giving this 'state of the art' description and analysis, a literature review potentially serves some or all of the following purposes:

- It can be used as a means of helping you identify and further define questions about the issue.
- If you plan to do an empirical study, it can help you identify an area for focus and what approach, perhaps, to adopt.
- It can help you to identify concepts and ideas which have been used to reflect on the issue, and also to appreciate what gaps there are in the existing knowledge of it.
- At a later stage, the literature review will help guide you in analysing your data, by giving you ideas about which aspects of your material you want to emphasise – for example, a particular theme in the literature might be the way in which social work support is made available, and you might then want to identify what your respondents say about the ease of accessing help.

A literature review need not be a precursor to a research study. Many useful social work dissertations are entirely library-based. However, it is important to bear in mind, especially if the latter is your chosen approach, that you do need to identify an issue with a reasonably substantial body of literature. If this is lacking, you may need to abandon the topic, or make sure that there is a body of 'cognate' literature (see below) which will help you locate your focus, and consider using, for example, a case study approach to amplify your discussion. It is best to start by reading widely and letting your imagination flow. In the early stages of moving from your topic to your question, it may seem as if anything is possible and you can envisage yourself taking all sorts of different tacks in relation to your topic. Don't be discouraged if you seem to lack a clear direction during these early stages: the intellectual function of this stage is to 'locate' your subject in a broader framework. But once you have decided which aspect of your area to follow, home in hard on it and do not get sidetracked. The following is a brief outline of the different steps in doing the review.

1. Your next stage is to develop a research strategy, generating a list of search terms, and following guidance for the different search engines available in your library and on the network. (Search terms are key words or concepts which are likely to be central to anything written on your chosen topic. For example, if you were interested in looking at the effects of psychological interventions for children and adolescents, you might use search terms which define anxiety disorders, combined with terms defining psychological interventions, and limit your search to children or adolescents. So your list might include: anxiety, fears, obsessive–compulsive disorders, post-traumatic stress disorder, overanxiety, phobias, and treatment, therapy, intervention, psychodynamic, cognitive behavioural, family therapy, desensitisation, flooding and exposure. There are several valuable sites which provide entry into and guides to the vast resources of social science resources; a useful one, for example, is PsychINFO (see websites at end of chapter).

2. You should also consider using a reference manager (computer applications designed to hold and manipulate details of references and the bibliography) or build a reference database for yourself using an application such as Microsoft Access. Whatever you do, make sure that you keep full and accurate details of all the texts which you read as you go along.

3. Then do your literature search. You can usually begin to identify key texts by seeing which references are frequently used in texts during the early stages of your reading. Remember that books are not always picked up by databases, so do reflect on which books seem to be central to your topic.

4. At some stage, you need to develop inclusion and exclusion criteria. For example, are you going to restrict your search to UK texts, or include the USA, Europe and beyond? Are you only interested in randomised controlled trials (see below – it is doubtful that as a social work student/practitioner you would be)? Do you want to limit your search or your review to a certain period in the development of the literature? And so on. How you choose and why will go into the introduction to the review.

5. Read abstracts (précis which summarise the content of the article) if they are available, and prioritise which you are going to seek out in full text format. Identify which texts and journals (many of them electronically) the library carries, and which you will need to borrow through interlibrary loans. With some issues (topics), there will be the whole range of literature: for example official data (statistics, Inquiries, government reports, White/Green Papers), empirical studies (further divided, e.g. into outcome studies, user perspectives), theoretical approaches, books and book chapters, refereed articles, journal and newspaper articles. Where the whole range is available, you need to rank them, partly to prioritise your reading, but also because a refereed article (i.e. one submitted to a journal which accepts material only after it has been evaluated by others knowledgeable about the area discussed) carries more weight (see our earlier discussion) than, say, an anonymous item off the internet.

6. As you read, you will begin to make judgements about what material to include and exclude. Do not be tempted to include in your review everything which you have read. Be critical, and as you read begin to think what contribution the material is making to your topic, and what its strengths and weaknesses are. Does it overlook important issues? Does it address the questions you want to know about? Do certain themes emerge? Are there gaps in the literature (for example, does the literature leave out major groups of people, e.g. adoption by non-heterosexual couples may discuss lesbian but not gay couples)?

7. If you discover that there are large gaps or limitations in the literature, you then need to decide what implications these have for your chosen area of study. It might mean that you need to abandon or modify your original focus (because at your stage of learning it is difficult to start a topic 'from scratch'), or it may mean that you have to think of a related literature and decide how applicable that is to your topic. For example, one dissertation focused on the support services for young

people who had previously been living with their birth families but were now homeless. Since there was little research into the experiences of this group of young people, the literature review explored studies of looked-after young people leaving care, in order to identify themes, while recognising that their experiences were likely to differ in some significant respects.

8. Adopt a narrative approach when writing the literature review. This means not simply summarising each item, but showing how each contributes to the story which you are constructing about the literature in this area.

9. Read some examples of literature reviews in journal articles or books to get an idea of how they are structured. Most of the chapters in *The Child Protection Handbook* (Wilson and James, 2007) include literature reviews, and they will help you see the different ways in which the material can be organised. If you are going to do a library-based study, then this will clearly have implications for how you organise your work, with two or even three chapters perhaps, each focusing on one theme in the literature.

Selecting your approach

You are now in a position to begin to think about what approach you intend to use to address your research question. You may decide to base your study on library-based research; this also involves data gathering. The difference in these cases is that the 'data gathering' phase is not precisely distinct from the literature search because the function of the search is *both* to 'set the scene' *and* to provide the meat of the study. If you do decide to undertake a piece of empirical work, remember that doing a piece of original enquiry always takes longer than you imagine; it is also important to remember that the kind of work which can be done as part of a taught degree programme is likely to be *illustrative* – for example, you may want to use case studies as examples of some of the themes which you have identified in your literature review.

Different methods of research

Before deciding on your own approach, you need to be familiar with different methodological approaches used in research, and their potential strengths and limitations. These are customarily divided into broad categories of quantitative and qualitative approaches, each of which has a distinctive 'cluster of concerns and preoccupations' (Bryman, 2004).

Quantitative research

This emphasises the measurement of prior concepts, and researchers search for indicators to act as measures which can stand for or point towards the underlying concept. (Goodman's 'strengths and difficulties' questionnaire which you may have encountered in your studies uses measures such as children's characteristics or behaviours and asks adults to rate them: this is a means, among other things, of finding indicators which *measure* the underlying issue/concept of children's overall functioning and well-being.) Central to quantitative research is the idea of a variable (an attribute on which people or things vary) as a means of measuring the dimensions on which people differ from or resemble one another. There is a concern to demonstrate causal relationships between variables: in other words, to show what factors influence people's behaviour, attitudes and beliefs. Quantitative research also seeks to show that findings from the specific study can be generalised to other situations, so that sampling procedures are emphasised in order to show that the sample studied can be generalised to others in similar circumstances. (For example, you might expect people who return questionnaires to be ones who feel most strongly – negatively or positively – about an issue. Because of this, their views may not be typical of the 'non-responders'.) Information may be collected and analysed to test specific hypotheses (for example, that people with depression do better if treated with certain medications and if this is combined with professional support). Methods of research include gathering data through surveys, questionnaires and structured interviews (i.e. interviews which follow a strict, identical set of questions). To summarise, it is generally argued that such research should be:

■ reliable and capable of being replicated;
■ data should be collected systematically and be standardised so that whoever collects it the same findings will emerge;
■ findings should be generalisable, so that principles can be drawn from it.

A common criticism of such research is that although it is good at identifying patterns in phenomena, so-called 'hard data' (for example, at a simple level, information about the ages/circumstances of individuals), it is less good at exploring the nuances of individuals' situations. So quantitative researchers are said to ignore subjective experience and to be interested only in things which can be analysed statistically. However, some writers, such as

Geraldine Macdonald, a social work academic, dispute this limitation, arguing that 'the earliest controlled trials were rich in data' (2002: 426).

Particular forms of quantitative research which you will find frequently referred to in discussions about social work outcomes (e.g. in Cochrane reviews, referred to in Further Reading) are those of *experimental and quasi-experimental approaches*. The former tests the effectiveness of social care programmes using randomised controlled trials (RCTs). This method is regarded by its advocates as providing the most objective data, or knowledge base. The reason for this is that answers to most questions about effectiveness essentially require comparison, and, also, that any comparisons need to be set up at random, without the researcher (or anyone else involved) influencing the process: for example, by failing to identify crucial characteristics in selecting comparable samples (see below).

Ideally we need to be able to compare similar groups who are dealt with in different ways. Such comparisons can be variously achieved. One method might involve randomly allocating women with depression to different 'treatments'. This should ensure comparable groups. Alternatively it may be possible to 'control' for background factors likely to influence outcome. For example, in considering the outcomes of different forms of placement for looked-after children, it seems likely (both for reasons of common sense and because earlier research findings suggest it) that age is strongly related to placement breakdown. If so, any comparison between breakdowns of, say, adoptive and foster care placements must allow in some way for the fact that adoption is primarily available for very young children. Such designs are often called 'quasi-experimental'. In other cases it may be possible to use individuals as *'their own controls'*: in other words, to compare their well-being under some intervention with their previous or subsequent state (for example, before and after they came into foster care.)

Random allocation seems logically likely to yield the most robust results. Where comparisons are made on the basis of controlling for background characteristics it is never possible to be sure that all necessary allowances have been made. (You might, for example, in your sampling procedures fail to take account of a characteristic such as parental age which in fact was crucial.) In studies that use individuals as their own controls, there may be difficulties in distinguishing between effects produced by an intervention and those produced by the passage of time. (There is a good deal of evidence, for example, that adolescents who commit minor acts of delinquency

'grow out' of this with age; so the fact that a young man stops offending may be a reflection of the fact that he is now in young manhood and has a steady girlfriend rather than that a particular social work intervention was successful.) For these reasons, random controlled trials (RCTs) are the preferred method for research measuring, say, the effectiveness of therapeutic drugs.

In social work things tend to be more complicated, for reasons which include the following:

- There are clearly ethical problems in, for example, randomly allocating those suffering from schizophrenia to drug treatment or family therapy, or removing one group of seriously maltreated children from their birth families while leaving others at home, some with and some without support.
- There are practical problems in getting sample sizes which are large enough to have a reasonable chance of showing an effect.
- The allocation to different treatments is rarely made 'blind' (a desirable refinement in medical trials, to avoid influencing the impact on patients – you will probably be familiar with the idea of 'placebos', a related procedure, where one group are given 'pretend' pills and the others the actual ones).
- A particularly fundamental difficulty is that of defining the context of the treatment and the treatment itself. The pills given in medical trials are normally 'known quantities', delivered in reasonably standard conditions to a population whose 'problem' is tightly defined. None of these conditions can easily apply in social work.

A closer look

The merits of RCTs in social work research

Macdonald, arguing for the advantages of RCTs as an approach, puts a slightly different view to the one we have given you here.

'A second concern is that people and social interventions are too complex for what seems, to some, a mechanistic approach. But it is precisely human complexities that make controlled studies in general and RCT's in particular useful. Undoubtedly the implementation of controlled trials in social work is challenging, but it is a technical challenge rather than an epistemological one.' (2002)

Essentially the RCT design is strong in determining how likely it is that there is an effect. The design is less strong in its ability to show why any such effect has taken place, how it has worked and what it is like to be on the receiving end of the intervention. For these reasons it is often difficult to know the conditions under which an effect is likely to be repeated. Ideally therefore RCT designs are complemented by 'observational studies' or qualitative approaches, involving, for example, interviews with participants.

Qualitative research

This is the second broad category of research methods. The focus in this approach is on meanings and experiences, and the research attempts to understand the lives of those being studied, their behaviour, values, beliefs and so on, from the perspectives of the people themselves. Typically, the research is relatively unstructured so that the research is more likely to reveal the individuals' meanings and experiences rather than impose the researchers' perspectives. Typically, too, 'concepts and the development of theories emerge out of the process of data collection rather than appearing at the outset of the investigation' (Becker, 2004: 92), as is more likely to be the case in quantitative research. Data is usually gathered by semi-structured or even unstructured interviews. (See our next Closer Look box for question styles in such interviews.)

Sometimes these standard sets of questions are supplemented by other techniques such as introducing scenarios or vignettes (i.e. brief stories) to help elicit information, for example, about respondents' feelings or attitudes, or to help them explore what may be difficult for them to consider spontaneously. Respondents are asked to 'think aloud' about the same situation, perhaps exploring the kinds of protocols and interventions they would use, or how they would deal with a particular incident or behaviour. (Yang (2005), for example, in her study of attitudes to disciplining children in South Korea, used a series of vignettes about children's behaviour to compare the responses of parents, teachers and professionals.) A common alternative in social work research asks the interviewee to talk through and answer questions on a particular experience. (For example, Nice (2005), interviewed social workers about their understanding of 'child-centred practice' in part by asking them to describe particular interventions when they felt they had worked in this way.) Such research nonetheless involves evidence which is systematically collected and explored to tease out common themes and experiences. Such approaches may provide more detailed information than can be gained from the kinds of quantitative research used in RCTs.

There are a number of other approaches which may be classified broadly as qualitative research, which rely on a detailed exploration of one or a very small number of cases. These include case studies, grounded theory and single case designs.

Case studies do not claim that the case is representative and can therefore be generalised to a wider group of

---

A closer look

Question styles in questionnaires, interviews and semi-structured interviews

- Closed-ended questioning: in a question aiming to build up information about foster placements, social workers were asked to select from a list of possible options (e.g. emergency placement: 'roof over head', to assess the child's needs, give birth parents a break) the purposes for which a foster placement was made.
- In open-ended questioning, social workers might be asked '*Why did you place this teenager in residential care?*'
- Leading questions are not worded neutrally, but either suggest an answer or indicate the questioner's

point of view (and therefore may encourage a particular response). '*When did you stop beating your wife?*' is an example of a leading question, since it assumes that you did beat her, and that you agree you did.

In an interview, the structure of the questions can vary similarly:

- In structured interviews, the order and wording of the questions are predetermined and each respondent is asked the same questions.
- In semi-structured interviews the questions focus on certain predetermined topics, but the interviewer is allowed to choose the words, alter the order of questions, and to follow up specific points, allowing the respondent to answer more freely.

people or events, and raise the question of whether the experiences described are shared by others and thus whether they can be used to influence policy or practice. However, they are often used in social work research to good effect, since they can help capture a process of events, and 'provide a sequence and a structure that is often omitted in surveys or interviews . . . [they] are a useful means by which to chart ideas and develop themes for analysis' (Walters, 2003: 179, quoted in Marsh and Keating, 2006: 123). Thus, they can be used to generate findings which are theoretically interesting, and are capable of being drawn upon by other researchers for further elaboration.

Stake (1995) distinguishes between intrinsic, instrumental and collective case studies. *Intrinsic* case studies are discrete entities in which the interest of the researcher is focused on the specifics, the particularity of the case: for example, researching a childcare team in its entirety with no specific focus. *Instrumental* case studies focus on an issue or process located within a case (or cases) and while the case is explored in detail the purpose of the exploration is to enhance understanding of the external interest. *Collective* case studies involve researching more than one case.

Ruch's (2004) research into practitioners' understandings of reflective practice is an example of case study research. In her study, the research focused on the practices and experiences of social workers located in two childcare teams. Each 'case' was understood to comprise all aspects of family support teams: the individuals in them, contextual factors and their significance for reflective practice. For Ruch, who was undertaking an instrumental, collective case study, the 'external interest' was reflective practice.

Case studies have, as the above suggests, been used in a variety of research traditions. Two examples of these are grounded theory and single case designs.

A **grounded theory** approach derives essentially from a case study approach. It is seen as a means of addressing the limitation of case studies as 'one-offs', by comparing the features of one study with another, in order to identify the critical dimensions or variables which all the examples have in common, exclude those variables which they do not share and thus build a picture of what the essential features of a successful (or unsuccessful) intervention are. Wilson, Petrie and Sinclair, in their study of foster care, adopt this approach in developing a model of 'successful foster care':

'In testing our conclusions we worked "from the bottom up", deriving our model from one case, testing it against the

next, modifying the model according to what we found there, and then continuing to the next case. This procedure of "analytic induction" has, we believe, a respectable logic and led us to a model which, as we saw it, explained both the difference between one successful case and one less so, but also the changes which occurred over time.'

(2003: 993)

Single case designs essentially seek to identify critical features in a particular case by close scrutiny of it, and, by understanding these, collect data which can then be tested out with other cases in order to build a picture about 'what works'. For example, a researcher observes (and describes in detail) an individual's situation or state, intervenes to change it, and then observes the situation again. Of itself, if the person has changed, this design cannot prove 'causation': the person might have changed in any case. However, if change follows sharply and logically after an intervention, and if other contextual factors support it, then cause and effect may plausibly be identified. The approach is compatible with being undertaken with the individual's full agreement (a concern sometimes raised): for example, the detailed account of the process and measures can be agreed and feedback given.

In **action research**, the researchers may themselves participate in delivering a project which they concurrently evaluate. A key characteristic is the 'action reform cycle', whereby findings are systematically incorporated into the project to modify its delivery and practice, changes which are themselves in turn evaluated. Chowns's (2006) research into the experiences of children living with parents with a terminal illness is an excellent account of the intricacies of collaborative action research. The children were co-researchers in an innovative project which involved them forming a group to make a video about their experiences. As part of the action-reform cycle the video was repeatedly honed to reflect the wishes and intentions of the children.

Integrating quantitative and qualitative methods

Research which combines these approaches is arguably more likely to produce evidence which can be relied on and generalised from. Such research is usually described as multi-method, or 'triangulation'. Sinclair et al.'s study of foster care is one such example and also describes how different approaches to collecting data yield different information (see the next Closer Look box).

Other research approaches

Other approaches which you might make use of in your own research involve using groups of people, users of services or documents, such as case records, as sources of information. These do not strictly constitute an approach but rather the focus of the enquiry or source of information, but we include them here for ease of identification.

1. **Focus groups** are discussions which are organised to explore a specific set of issues, in which participants engage in discussion with each other on a specified topic. They are used when the researcher wishes to explore people's experiences, opinions and concerns.

2. **Documentary sources**. Possibly what first occurs to you here, as a social work student or practitioner, is the use of documents such as case records as data by which to explore particular questions. These are indeed a rich source of information on a range of topics: for example, questions about sources of referral, use of assessment protocols, approaches to intervention, to name but a few. However, documents take many forms, and include such sources as government reports and policy papers, or newspaper reports and comments, before and after. (An absorbing account based on parliamentary documents of the lead up to the reforms of childcare law in the 1980s is given in Parton, 1991.) (See also 'Documents in qualitative research', by Jane Lewis (2004: 290–4), in Becker and Bryman for a fuller discussion.)

3. **User or consumer research**. User research has assumed considerable importance in developing the empirical base for social work. It can involve quantitative (e.g.

survey questionnaires) or qualitative (interviews or case studies) approaches and is typically designed to provide information about the needs of individuals and communities and feedback about how a particular service or intervention is experienced by its recipients. The justification for this is clear: services need feedback if they are to improve. There are ethical, practical, therapeutic and legal reasons for consulting the users of services. When asked, most individuals, whether adults or children, are clear they want a chance to speak about their experiences (e.g. Shaw, 1998). User research has, however, been variously criticised:

(a) There may be questions about how representative the service users consulted are of others who have not been – for example, are the group of dissatisfied individuals who are speaking out representative of the 'silent majority', or are the latter silent because they are content with the service?

(b) There may be ethical problems – for example, children may be ambivalent about whether they want to be in foster care; adolescents or older people in residential homes may be reluctant to criticise those caring for them, and the key issues may be sensitive (for example, talking about the experience of domestic violence).

(c) Many larger studies have difficulty in achieving high response rates (a variation on the issue of representativeness).

A closer look

An example of multi-methods, or triangulation in research

Sinclair et al. (2005) in their longitudinal study of foster care used a combination of quantitative, qualitative and case study approaches. They suggest that the three approaches allow different kinds of questions to be answered, as follows.

The *qualitative material*, for example, foster carers' and social workers' extended written comments in answer to open-ended questions, encapsulates in different ways the criteria against which they were evaluating the placement and why they thought a given outcome had occurred. Foster children's written comments on questionnaires, although briefer, also provided vivid insights into their views about being fostered. However, data are seen to lack detail, a history and a context and systematic testing.

Case studies give detailed accounts of what children and their carers did, are grounded in history and context so that it becomes possible to see the connections between changes in one aspect of the placement and in others. They can pick up information which is not easily identified in statistical measures (e.g. the use of 'attachment sensitive times' in working with children).

Quantitative (statistical) measures can show, for example, in a way which qualitative measures cannot, how common a particular phenomenon is or how damaging it is likely to be in particular circumstances. For example, qualitative material showed that contact between birth parents and their fostered children could be very problematic, but could not show, as the statistical evidence did, how frequently, how seriously and in what circumstances this negative impact occurred.

(d) The voices of certain users (for example, very young children, those with severe learning disabilities) are mainly absent.

(e) The user's ability to make a judgement may be questionable – for example, individuals with bipolar disorder at certain phases of their illness are less likely accurately to appraise their need for medication and support. Or, a variant of this –

(f) Users' wishes cannot always be paramount, and in statutory case their 'rights' may conflict with those of others. For example, Bell (1996), a social work academic, examined the effect on parental satisfaction of invitations to attend a case conference about their children's difficulties and possible care proceedings. She found that parents liked to be invited, but that they did not feel that they had influenced the conference decisions (nor was there any evidence that they had done so), and their satisfaction was not related to involvement in the case conference but to whether or not their child had been removed from home.

Despite these caveats, the United Kingdom has a long and honourable tradition of service user research and provided we look at it critically it can give invaluable and enlightening insights into our practice. In the Closer Look box we suggest ways in which you might judge the relative merits of user research evidence.

A closer look

Criteria for judging whether or not you can have confidence in the findings of user research

This will include the following:

- response rates;
- the consistency with which the same themes are repeated in the literature;
- the degree to which they seem 'natural' or have a 'ring of truth' in their context – e.g. we would expect people to prefer to be consulted about how they would like to be cared for rather than the reverse;
- the lack of evidence (on the occasions when this comparison is possible) that respondents differ from non-respondents in ways likely to bias the results.

The 'doing' stage

Structuring your dissertation

In the above, we introduced you to some of the different approaches to empirical research, some of its varieties and complexities and briefly indicated to you where the strengths and limitations of the different methods lie. Now we come to the issue of how you will apply the above discussions (identifying a research question, thinking about methods) in organising your own study.

As we have suggested, you may decide either to undertake a library-based dissertation, or to do some form of original investigation in support of your study. If you do the latter, you will need to bear in mind not only the issues we have highlighted above about the advantages and limitations of different approaches, but also the very real limitations imposed by your time constraints, including the need for ethical approval for your study. For this reason, most social work student dissertations, if they are based on an original piece of research, are likely to use a qualitative or case study approach – involving perhaps four to six interviews, or one or more case studies, designed to give detailed and intensive examination of a person or an experience. (For example, a case study approach could illustrate in detail the experiences of individuals at a particular point in their lives, such as 16–18-year-olds compelled to leave home, or the experiences of social workers in planning respite care for older people.) There are many different types of research projects that could lead to a dissertation. Some ideas might be:

- an extended study of a particular theme, concept or issue in social work using secondary sources;
- an extended study of a particular theme, concept or issue in social work largely using secondary sources, but supported by illustrative material (e.g. case studies, interviews with practitioners/users);
- a small-scale qualitative research project involving data collection, analysis and the drawing of conclusions based on the experiences of a small sample of clients, carers, social workers, managers, students, etc.;
- a small-scale quantitative research project – for example, investigating the response of a small number of social services departments to new developments in social work, such as the new Data Protection Act introduced in 1999;
- an analysis of a particular policy or governmental development in respect of social work.

There are, as this indicates, many different possibilities for a dissertation; you should discuss your ideas with your supervisor. The following is a checklist for you to consider as you formulate your proposal and decide on your methods of addressing the topic. Some points apply particularly to interviews and questionnaires, but most apply more generally.

Checklist for addressing your topic and data collection

1. Is there a clear link between overall aims, detailed sub-purposes/objectives, and plans for doing it?
2. Have the ideas around the project been worked out to the point where it is clear how key ideas (e.g. 'need', 'empowerment', etc.) are defined?
3. Is there a focus for the study (e.g. a particular group, particular documents, certain cases, literature)?
4. Is it clear what methods are to be used in the study (e.g. literature review, analysis of documents, interviews, cases illustrations – if so, how will they be accessed etc.)?
5. Are the details clear: how many interviews, how selected, what kinds of interviews and questions asked, use of vignettes, how will the instruments (e.g. the questionnaires, interview schedule, coding frame) be piloted?
6. Is all this practical: is the focus too wide, is the conceptual task overambitious, will there be time to interview this number, will permission be necessary/granted/granted in time, does the situation exist to study (e.g. are the cases there)?
7. Is it clear how the results could in outline be written up and how will they be relevant to social work?
8. Does any instrument (e.g. questionnaires, questions for semi-structured interviews) have simple clear questions:
   - that relate to the overall aim
   - that do not unwittingly impose presuppositions
   - that flow logically
   - that move from the general to the particular
   - that the person can answer
   - that will get behind a bland answer
   - that are ethical
   - that can be completed in the time available?

Having identified your research question and your approach, you need to think about how you will organise your material. (You may well modify this when you have gone further, but it is useful to have an idea of the structure in advance of doing the work.) There is no single structure which is suitable for all dissertations: however, the following model may give you some useful guidance.

Outline structure for a dissertation

Abstract and research ethics checklist
- A completed abstract and Research Ethics Checklist form (where relevant) must be bound into the dissertation.

Table of contents
- A list of all chapters (ideally all figures and tables should be listed separately).

Acknowledgements
- A chance to thank anyone who has helped you in preparing your dissertation.

Preface
- Any general points (e.g. the use of nongender-specific language and the grammatical implications).

Chapter One: Introduction – the Problem Posed
- Statement of the aims of the dissertation
- Definition of the research question
- The significance of the research question should be highlighted, indicating why the problem is important and why it merits the proposed study
- The expected benefits of the study should be clearly outlined.

Chapter Two: The Context of the Problem – the Literature Reviewed
- Review the previous literature according to a defined schema
- Identify key themes that are evident from reviewing the literature
- Discuss the similarities and the differences between the proposed work and previous studies
- Evaluate how comprehensive your literature review might be
- Include a discussion of how you searched for the literature (this may fit more easily into the next section).

Chapter Three: Methods
- Describe the research methods that have been used
- Explore any conceptual problems highlighted by the use of your particular research methods
- Evaluate the usefulness of the particular methods adopted
- Consider alternative research methods and discuss why these were not used
- Discuss the ethical issues involved in the research project.

Chapter Four: Findings
- A descriptive account of your research findings (use tables and graphs if this will help to explain your findings more clearly).

Chapter Five: Discussion

■ An evaluation of the research findings in the context of the major themes that emerged from the literature review

■ The importance of your findings for current social work policy and practice.

Chapter Six: Conclusion – Implications of the Analysis for Policy and Practice

■ An evaluation of the significance, strengths and weaknesses of the research that you have undertaken

■ To what extent have you been able to answer the questions and issues that were raised at the start of the dissertation

■ Proposals for further work in this area.

Bibliography

■ This should be presented according to departmental guidelines in the handbook.

Appendices

■ Include any questionnaires used, etc.

Note that in this illustrative framework the unqualified use of 'Introduction' and 'Conclusion' has been avoided by specifying the precise purpose of each. In a shorter dissertation, chapters four and five may be combined, so that chapter four encompasses both the main findings, the analysis and discussion, the links with the literature and the implications for social work policy and practice. Or the latter might be included instead in the final conclusions.

The structure and chapter titles will be of course different in the absence of any original empirical research. So an alternative structure, one which uses case examples, perhaps drawn (suitably anonymised) from your practice experience, might look like this:

Chapter One: Introduction – The Problem Posed

Chapter Two: The Context of the Problem – The Literature Reviewed

Chapter Three: The Problem Analysed. The focus of this will vary, but might highlight the different issues which, say, make it difficult for social workers to know how best to proceed in addressing the problem.

Chapter Four: Illustrative Case Examples. These might be used to highlight some of the problematic issues discussed in the previous chapters.

Chapter Five: Conclusions – Implications of the Analysis and Discussion for Policy and Practice

Ethical issues

All social work research needs to be conducted according to social work ethics and values. If you grasp the general principles of social work ethics (and in particular of anti-oppressive practice), you should have little difficulty in thinking your way through the ethical issues which arise in conducting your own research. Overall, you need to be satisfied that in undertaking the inquiry, your conscience is clear about it. You should feel that you have a good reason for undertaking it, that you are not putting others involved to more trouble than you have to, that you are not going to breach anyone's privacy when writing it up, and that you are not going to do harm to anyone. However, the procedures for seeking and obtaining ethical clearance for research in the social sciences, including social work, have been tightened up over the years and you should consult your tutor and university guidelines or your agency about this if you are in any doubt. We give below some particular points where ethical issues commonly arise:

1. *Release of names*. It is commonly accepted that it is wrong for names to be released to an outside researcher or student by a professional without the consent of the person concerned. Usually the professional approaches the potential interviewee and tells them something about the study and asks if they can release their name. Sometimes in order to preserve anonymity, the professional passes on a questionnaire to the individual.

2. *Informed consent*. Before agreeing to become involved in a project, individuals should, as far as possible, understand the purpose of the project and what its implications may be for them. This does not necessarily mean they have to have everything explained. For example, in a study of why some social workers labelled a situation as 'abusive' and some did not, it might be undesirable from a research point of view to tell the social workers what hypotheses underlay the research, for fear of skewing their answers. The reasons for this reticence could, however, be explained and justified.

3. *Confidentiality*. The usual convention is that everything individuals say is confidential in the sense that it is not made public in such a way that it could be identified as coming from them. Salient characteristics (age, ethnicity, gender) may be disguised. However, this is not always straightforward, for example, if a particular identifying characteristic is also significant in the study, and the changed details must be plausible and 'truthful'. The question of whether an agency is identified is usually agreed in advance.

4. *Reasons for breaching confidentiality*. There may be reasons for doing so – for example, if an older vulnerable adult says she/he is being abused. These caveats are usually explained in advance: e.g. 'Everything you say will be confidential unless you tell me that you are being harmed in some way or that someone known to you is being harmed, in which case I may need to tell someone about it. I will discuss this with you, obviously, before I do this'.

5. *Dilemmas*. As with all ethical issues there are dilemmas. For example, you may become concerned about the poor service which a user is getting, or realise that users are entitled to more support than they are receiving, and so on. Or the user's situation may fall short of one which is abusive, but still cause you concern. Taking it further should not breach any assurance which you have given (to the user or the agency, for example) and the reasons for doing so must be explicable and justifiable.

6. *Exchange*. It is important that those involved get realistic rewards for helping with research. This may be no more than the chance to talk through an issue with a concerned and interested outsider (most people greatly appreciate this) or to feel that they have helped you get your professional qualification. If, however, they would benefit from some feedback of the results, this should, wherever possible, be given them.

(*Source*: Adapted from the University of York Social Work student dissertation handbook and acknowledged with gratitude.)

In general, it is worth remembering that many people actually enjoy being able to take part in research and feel that they get something from it. Impressionistically, we think that the satisfactions are greater for those participating in qualitative, interview-based research, provided of course that it is conducted sensitively and non-intrusively.

Data collection and analysis

Your data collection may, as we have said, consist of doing a library-based study, so the data will be just that – what you identify from your reading. If, however, you decide to do a piece of empirical work, you will need to consider further the design of the research instruments, how you will identify and analyse an appropriate example for a case study, and so on. In what follows, we give you some advice about conducting interviews (since, along with case studies, these seem to be the approach most commonly used)

and analysing your data. However, this is necessarily brief, and you will need to read and consult further.

Basic tips for conducting focused interviews or semi-structured interviews

1. You can apply this technique where each of your respondents has experienced an issue which you want to understand more about: for example, paid care via a for-profit agency.

2. Divide your schedule up into very broad main questions which flow in a logical order (e.g. '*I want you to think about the last case you had where a child was referred for play therapy. Could you tell me about it? Do you know how the case came to be considered for therapy?*'

3. For each broad question, think through what is going to count as a satisfactory answer. For example, you ask, '*Why did the child remain at home after the referral?*' Your respondent may reply that '*My manager talked it over and decided that he was not at serious risk and that we could work with the family*'; or '*We decided that as the cohabitee had left home it was safe to do so*'; or '*We decided to put in a package of care to support the family*'. All these answers could apply in the same case, and you will need to decide which areas to probe. Suppose, for example, you are interested in the impact of support services, then you will need to probe the 'package of care' more deeply.

4. In the light of your analysis of each broad question, you will need to associate each one with probes. For example, '*How did the case come to be referred for therapy?*' (probe agency which referred, which professional, referral route – telephone, email, self-referral after discussion, etc., etc.). It is not that you will need to probe all these areas, but you need to have decided in advance what kind of reply will allow you to stop.

5. Develop techniques for dealing with situations where your respondent cannot remember, has never thought about the issue, is uneasy about giving you the information, or has unresolved contradictions in what they think.

Suppose, for example, that you want to explore parents' attitudes to disciplining children. All of the situations may apply. How are you going to enable an open discussion of the issue without conveying disapproval or putting ideas into the respondent's mind?

6. Conduct your interview flexibly, going with the respondent, being clear about what you want to find out, and using your memory. For example, '*I noticed

that you said the child's grandmother lived nearby, but you have not mentioned this as one of the influences on your decision; do you think there was some way in which this played a part?' You will be familiar with using most of these techniques from the interviews you have already conducted with users – for example, for assessment purposes – so you have a head start.

7. The work which you put into structuring the questionnaire and thinking about the probes should make it easier to write up the results. You should be able to show how your experience and the literature led to the questions and probes, and how the responses modified your opinions and led to your conclusions.

Basic tips for analysing qualitative data

1. Analysis of some form should start as soon as data is collected. Do not allow data to accumulate without preliminary analysis.
2. Make sure you keep tabs on what you have collected (literally – get it indexed).
3. Generate themes categories, codes, etc. as you go along. Start by including rather than excluding; you can combine and modify as you go on.
4. Dealing with the data should not be a routine or mechanical task; think, reflect! Use analytical notes (memos to self) to help get from data to a conceptual level.
5. Use some form of filing system to sort your data. Be prepared to re-sort. Play with the data.
6. There is no one 'right' way of analysing this kind of data – which places even more emphasis on your being systematic, organised and persevering. (One more detailed account of doing this through a method called 'content analysis' is given in the appendix to this chapter.)
7. You are seeking to take apart your data in various ways and then trying to put them together again to form some consolidated picture. Your main tool is comparison.

The 'writing up' and dissemination stages

It is hoped that you will have been writing up your dissertation as you go along. For example, you might aim to do a first draft of your introduction and, say, the literature review and methods chapter at quite an early stage. You do not need to wait to do these until you have completed, or even embarked on, your empirical study, if you are doing one, and countless students, before and after you, will attest to the renewed confidence and relief which comes from having written at least part of the dissertation. This is not to say that you should expect to complete a finished draft of the early chapters at this stage; you may need to go back, for example, to the literature review to emphasise certain themes in the light of your further studies. Give yourself a timetable which allows you plenty of time for writing and revising your drafts, remembering that, as with any original study, this too takes longer than you think!

Dissemination is, as Becker makes clear in his research cycle, a vital and integral part of empirical research. Arguably, there is little point in undertaking research unless others are going to hear about it and can make use of your findings. Part of this phase will also involve giving feedback to any users, stakeholders or respondents who have participated in the research, so you will also need to consider how to put it across in a form which is understandable to these different groups and different audiences.

Conclusion

Whether undertaking your own original research, reading secondary sources for a dissertation, or reading research accounts in order to understand better the basis on which to ground your practice, you will be using skills which you have already been developing in your professional training and in your practice. Although we have in this chapter emphasised the importance of such things as weighing evidence, analysing critically what you read, and being mindful of ethical principles when doing your own investigations, these are inherently principles and skills with which you will already be familiar. It is worth also remembering, however, that many of the skills which you will have been learning will give you a head start when it comes to undertaking qualitative research involving interviewing: you know, for example, how to knock on doors, engage with others, formulate questions appropriately, maintain boundaries, and so on. And your practice experiences will give you an invaluable understanding of and sensitivity to the experiences of others, knowledge of relevant case examples, and so on. So in conclusion, we would encourage you, in your practice settings, to recognise and use these skills as reflective, research-minded and, it is hoped, research-active practitioners.

Key learning points

This chapter has covered the following learning points:

✔ Social work research involves systematic investigation, which is conducted using the most appropriate research designs and verifiable methods and analysis in order to find answers to questions relevant to social work about which there is disagreement, uncertainty or a lack of knowledge, and contribute to reducing social problems and distress and promoting well-being.

✔ Emphasis on the importance of evidence to support social work practice is not new, but has been given impetus in recent years by major national initiatives and the (at least nominal) drive to discover whether, and if so in what ways, these are achieving targets and goals.

✔ The idea of 'evidence based practice' is complex, the complexities arising in part because of the difficulties of establishing 'good' reliable evidence in social-work-related activities.

✔ Evidence-based practice aims to help practitioners use the most effective interventions when they are involved in people's lives.

✔ Research in social work can use a variety of methods. The method chosen will be influenced by the nature of the issue (the 'research question') being examined and by ethical and practical considerations. Ideally, research evidence for effectiveness will be built up through the use of a range of methods.

✔ Quantitative research methods aim to measure or quantitatively assess social phenomena; to describe representative samples in quantitative terms and to test or estimate quantitative relationships. Methods include surveys, typically based on a sample of respondents drawn from a specific population. Qualitative research gathers more information from a smaller number of respondents. The focus is on the experiences of people and the meaning given to their experiences, and the aim is to generate rich description from diverse perspectives. Observation, in-depth interviews and case studies are all qualitative methods. This is the research approach most likely to be accessible to social work practitioners undertaking their own empirical study and is one which reflective practitioners may be especially well equipped, from their training, to undertake.

✔ Quantitative approaches involving RCTs are generally seen as more reliable in evaluating the *effects* of a particular intervention. However, in social work they are often difficult and expensive to mount, and there may be ethical issues which curtail their use.

✔ Qualitative approaches enable us to understand why and how something works, and whether it is something which service users find helpful.

✔ Different research questions will merit different approaches – ideally a combination will be used, but such research is time-consuming and demands considerable resources.

✔ Undertaking a piece of empirical research involves key phases, which include a thinking phase, a doing phase, a writing-up and dissemination phase, and are similar to the key stages in planning and writing a dissertation.

✔ All studies for dissertations in social work education, whether using original or secondary sources, must address a clear research question relevant to social work, be conducted according to ethical principles, and use an approach appropriate to the research question and the time available, and other constraints.

 Further reading

There are a range of measures now being taken to support and improve social workers' use of research. One easily accessed starting point is a regular column in *Community Care*, which describes current research findings and asks the authors to raise key points for discussion.

The Joseph Rowntree Foundation produces easily digestible summaries of research findings.

Professional journals such as the *British Journal of Social Work* or *Adoption and Fostering* also now regularly include reports of research which are brief and accessible summaries of projects relevant to social work.

There are a number of organisational developments, which aim at producing systematic reviews of research findings. These include:

■ The Social Care Institute for Excellence, which as part of its brief to encourage the use of research in social work practice commissions and disseminates scoping and systematic reviews of evidence.

Ist floor, Goldings House, 2 Hay's Lane,
London SE1 2HB
www.scie.org.uk

- The Cochrane Collaboration which prepares, maintains and makes accessible systematic reviews of the effects of health care, many of which are relevant to social work and care.

  Summertown Pavilion, Middle Way,
  Oxford OX2 7LG
  www.nelh.nhs.uk

- The Campbell Collaboration which prepares systematic reviews of social interventions.

  University of Pennsylvania,
  6417 Wissahickon Avenue,
  Philadelphia, PA 19119, US
  www.campbell.gse.upenn.edu/intro.html

In addition to this, there are a range of initiatives designed to disseminate research and with the purpose of developing a research-minded culture within the sector. These may be internal strategies within your organisation when you move into practice to support research-informed practice, or external strategies through membership of organisations such as Making Research Count and Research into Practice which are set up to encourage practitioners in developing this.

Making Research Count This is a collaborative research dissemination initiative between a number of English universities which offers staff in local authority adult and children's services and other agencies working jointly with these departments the opportunity to work in partnership with academic colleagues to develop evidence-based social work and social care practice, and to improve the dissemination of research. It aims to ensure that operational staff are involved in setting the research agenda, and that both they and service users benefit from the outcomes. The scheme offers members seminars and workshops to support research literacy and to equip them with evaluation expertise. A subscribing authority is linked to one of the universities, normally the nearest. Authorities within a regional grouping meet to share news and views and plan activities.

  School of Social Work and Psychological Studies,
  Elizabeth Fry Building, University of East Anglia,
  Norwich NR4 7TJ
  www.uea.ac.uk/swk/research/MRC.htm

Research in Practice (RiP) and Research in Practice for adults(Ripfa) The first of these two linked organisations is a partnership between the Dartington Hall Trust, the Association of Directors of Social Services and the University of Sheffield, with approximately 100 participating English local authorities, voluntary childcare organisations, Local Strategic Partnerships (LSPs) and Primary Care Trusts (PCTs). It aims to promote the use of evidence to improve experiences and outcomes for vulnerable children and families, and the capacity of policy, services and professionals to respond to the needs of these. It does so by working closely

with member agencies to test new methods of promoting the use of evidence, and by promoting the use of evidence through professional development and other services. The second, with over 50 participating local authorities, has similar aims in relation to the use of research evidence to improve outcomes for adults.

  Warren House, Dartington, Totnes,
  Devon TQ9 6EG
  www.rip.org.uk

Other useful addresses include:

National Institute for Clinical Excellence

  11 The Strand, London WC2N 5HR

Joseph Rowntree Foundation

  The Homestead, 40 Waterend, York YO30 6WP

NHS Centre for Reviews and Dissemination

  University of York, Heslington, York YO10 5DD

Research Matters

  Community Care, 6th floor, Quadrant House,
  The Quadrant, Sutton, Surrey SM2 5AS

Malcolm Hill's chapter in Schofield and Simmonds' edited book *The Child Placement Handbook* (2009) on child placement research provides a lucid account of key features of research and the limitations and benefits of applying the lessons of empirical studies, which may be generalised to all forms of social welfare research. Iwaniec and Pinkerton's study in the same collection provides a similarly useful account of the processes involved in the application of research findings to policy and practice.

Online publications by the Social Care Institute for Excellence. Research in Practice and Research in Practice for Adults and Making Research Count provide accessible accounts of up-to-date research findings.

There are a number of guides to conducting research, of which Walliman's (2005) and Whittaker's (2009) are useful examples.

The December 2009 volume of *The Journal of Social Work Practice*, 23 (4), is largely devoted to articles on practice-near research. Articles by White et al. (p. 401f), by one of the present authors, Cooper, and three accounts of research conducted as doctoral theses are particularly interesting.

 ## Useful websites

(see also under Further reading)

www.evidencenetwork.org

ESRC Evidence Network

www.nelh.nhs.uk

National Electronic Library for Health

www.scie.org.uk

www.nelh.nhs.uk

www.campbell.gse.upenn.edu/intro.html

www.uea.ac.uk/swk/research/MRC.htm

www.rip.org.uk

Websites of two of the most useful data bases for literature searches are:

www.elsc.org.uk/caredata/caredata.htm

www.psycINFO.com

For additional cases and topic-organised, clickable links into additional media resources, including those produced by IRISS, visit **www.pearsoned.co.uk/wilsonruch**

Activity

Read one or more of the articles listed at the end of the Further Reading section above (we have selected ones which you should be able to access electronically through your library) and then ask yourself the following questions:

What did the researchers aim to accomplish in the research project?

What were the methods used? Would you describe these as qualitative or quantitative approaches or a mixture?

What are the findings drawn from the study?

What application if any do these have for social work policies and/or interventions?

How much weight do you think you and fellow professionals should attach to the findings?

Try to give reasons for your answers.

Appendix to Chapter 9: Content analysis

Some data yielded by interviews is quite straightforward in character while other material is complex and untidy. For all but the most simple, a procedure is needed for moving from the raw material, through a series of rigorous and systematic steps, to plausible summary and interpretation of the data in terms of one's research purposes. How can one move from a number of individual accounts, which are the raw data for a study which uses semi-structured interviews, to conclusions which refer to a class of persons or events? The device employed is some form of content analysis. This usually means taking each interview separately, first extracting and reordering the data, and then making certain judgements about it in a series of steps. When this has been done for each interview separately, you usually need to combine interviews in one or more ways in order to see how the information contained in the interviews relates to the research question in the study. A useful series of steps in doing this manually is as follows; however, as you progress to more complex studies, you may use packages to help you do this.

1. Make a photocopy of each completed interview schedule (your data-unit). This allows you to keep the original interview intact, while using the photocopy to cut (literally, with scissors) and sort out the information in the interview in ways which bear on the aims of your study.
2. Go back to your original research questions, read through the interview, using coloured pencils to mark the photocopied interview in a way which shows you where within the interview the data pertaining to the research question lies. For example, supposing that the overall aim of the research has to do with older people entering residential care, then your first detailed sub-question might have been 'What expectations do older people have when contemplating a move into a residential setting?' You might mark with a green pencil all comments which refer to expectations. Suppose that the second sub-question was 'What do older people think makes the transition to residential care easier or more difficult?' You might mark in red all comments referring to this, and so on.
3. Note that some of the content which is relevant to a particular research question might appear in response to questions which specifically address this. However, additional comments relevant to a particular question might appear anywhere in the interview. It follows that you need to look across the interview in order to collect all the responses together.
4. It is possible that after the content of the interviews has been sorted and categorised in this way, some information is left over and does not relate to any of the sub-questions as initially formulated. Then the researcher has to decide whether these left-over bits of information are either not interesting or outside the scope of the study – in which case they are ignored – or whether they are of interest, representing issues which the researcher would have included as part of the original research question had they been thought of at the time. You may, at this stage, expand the research questions if the data shows that the original set of questions was incomplete.
5. The marked interview can now be reorganised physically, for example, by cutting up the interview into separate slips of paper and putting all the green-marked slips into one envelope or pasting them onto one sheet (or doing this electronically).
6. Usually several more steps are involved in a content analysis procedure. You may, for example, want to further divide the responses to a particular question (for example, in respect of the above illustration, you might divide them into positive and negative expectations, or further subdivide into fear, depression, anger, etc. You will need to decide how to combine the different data-units. For example, if you are interested in the range of expectations represented in the total sample of older people, you would bring together all the sheets of paper, across the subjects, which refer to expectations, perhaps by using a grid or table at this stage, which shows the content analysis along one axis and subjects along the other.
7. Finally, in order to answer certain of the original research questions, you may have to summarise the information contained in all the data-units, or the information contained in certain subsets. You need to look at the original research question carefully to see which summaries or comparisons will be most useful and relevant in your writing up of your findings.

Part Two
PRACTICE SKILLS AND PRACTICE THEORIES

Chapter 10
Assessment in social work practice

Chapter summary

This chapter explores the challenging nature of the assessment process and explores some of the tensions embedded in it. Particular attention is placed on the 'use of self' in the assessment process and the key characteristics – constructed, collaborative, dynamic and holistic – of reflective, relationship-based assessments are outlined. Four dilemmas arising in assessments are explored and the Exchange Model (Smale et al., 2000) is outlined as a way of undertaking relationship-based assessments, and the challenges relating to recognising and drawing on the expertise of service users and social workers are identified. The importance of adopting an ecological approach, which assesses the individual in their wider context and focuses on service users' strengths as well as issues of risk, is discussed. In the concluding section of the chapter, creative techniques – ecomaps, genograms, reflective teams and observation – for implementing reflective, relationship-based assessments are proposed.

Learning objectives

This chapter covers topics that will help you to achieve the following learning objectives:

- To examine the contested and challenging nature of assessment
- To understand the importance of the professional relationship and 'use of self' in assessment activities
- To recognise the constructed nature of the assessment process
- To introduce a collaborative, relational and dynamic model of assessment
- To identify some strategies for implementing collaborative, relational and dynamic assessments
- To understand the importance of adopting a reflective stance throughout the assessment process.

National Occupational Standards

This chapter will help you to meet the following National Occupational Standards:

Key Role 1: Prepare for, and work with individuals, families, carers, groups and communities to assess their needs and circumstances

Unit 1   Prepare for social work contact and involvement
Unit 2   Work with individuals, families, carers, groups and communities to help them make informed decisions
Unit 3   Assess needs and options to recommend a course of action

Key Role 2: Plan, carry out, review and evaluate social work practice, with individuals, families, carers, groups, communities and other professionals

Unit 4   Respond to crisis situations
Unit 5   Interact with individuals, families, carers, groups and communities to achieve change and development and to improve life opportunities
Unit 6   Prepare, produce, implement and evaluate plans with individuals, families, carers, groups, communities and professional colleagues
Unit 7   Support the development of networks to meet assessed needs and planned outcomes
Unit 9   Address behaviour which presents a risk to individuals, families, carers, groups and communities

Key Role 3: Support individuals to represent their needs, views and circumstances. Advocate with and on behalf of people

Unit 10   Advocate with, and on behalf of, individuals, families, carers, groups and communities
Unit 11   Prepare for, and participate in decision making forums

Key Role 4: Manage risk to individuals, families, carers, groups, communities, self and colleagues

Unit 12   Assess and manage risks to individuals, families, carers, groups and communities
Unit 13   Assess, minimise and manage risk to self and colleagues

Case study

Understanding assessment

In the course of undertaking practice learning agreements meetings with social work students, I have been struck by their response to the question 'What have you identified as your learning objectives for this placement?' On several occasions students placed in statutory local authority contexts have indicated that one of their main priorities is to learn how to do the paperwork involved in the assessment process. While this is an appropriate learning objective, presented in this way it suggests that students have developed an understanding of the assessment process as being primarily a paper-based exercise. The implication of this perspective is that, provided you know the correct forms and paperwork that are relevant for that specific practice learning setting, a sound assessment will be conducted.

What do you think are the ingredients of a sound assessment?

'Assessment means steering between the pressures of organisational demands, legislative injunction, limited resources and personal agendas' (Walker and Beckett, 2003).

(Kevin Smith (Kes): www.kescartoons.com)

In thinking about the case study outlined above, you will have needed to consider what the purpose of an assessment is and how, depending on its purpose, the assessment information is best obtained and utilised. In answering this question a number of subsidiary questions also need to be answered: who should be involved, where, when and why? This chapter explores these issues and offers an approach which keeps the relationship with the service user to the fore.

Introduction

Beginnings are frequently unnerving, whether it is starting in a new environment (school, university, workplace), commencing a new task or simply starting a new day! At the beginning of any new experience or task it can feel daunting to know how best to start. Questions abound about what it will be like, what will be required, who will be involved. Assessment, the focus of this chapter, while not solely confined to the beginning phase of a piece of work, is an important aspect of beginnings. The questions raised by practitioners facilitating assessments, and service users participating in them, replicate those already identified associated with beginnings:

- What am I trying to achieve and where do I begin?
- What information is pertinent, why and according to whom?
- Whose views do I incorporate?
- How do I make sense of, interpret and most accurately record and represent the information I have gathered?

The challenge of experiences, such as beginning in a new place with new people, starting a new piece of work or assessing a new referral, is moderated by knowing what is expected by all parties involved, by knowing the boundaries – roles, responsibilities, timescales – associated with the task and by being clear about what is informing your approach to the task. Clear assessments enable both the service user and the practitioner to share a sound understanding of the purpose, nature and extent of professional involvement. Good beginnings are recognised to be an essential component of effective professional practice (see also Chapter 11). They set the tone for future interventions (Parker and Bradley, 2003; Walker and Beckett, 2003).

A fundamental characteristic of sound assessment practice is to be aware of what informs your thinking and actions and how this impacts on the relationship you establish with the service user being assessed. Consequently this chapter pays close attention to the relational aspects of assessment, the constructed nature of the assessment process and the importance of the practitioner adopting and maintaining a reflective stance. The preoccupation of the students referred to above – knowing how to complete the paperwork – is a technical skill subsumed within this relational framework for assessment. More specifically this chapter is informed by the findings and recommendations of a knowledge review, commissioned by the Social Care Institute for Excellence (Crisp et al., 2005), that reviewed the literature relating to the learning and teaching of assessment in social work practice. Three of the review's findings are of particular significance:

- **The policy and practice context of assessment.** In its overarching recommendations the review team cautions readers of texts on assessment, those who write them and those who draw on them in their role as educators, to be aware of and to make explicit the legislative, policy and practice contexts in which the writing is located. In responding to this recommendation the chapter begins with a brief overview of the broad policy context that forms the backdrop for assessment. More detailed contextual material relevant when conducting assessments with specific user groups is included in the specific practice-related chapters in Part Three of this book.
- **Perspectives on assessment.** The knowledge review highlighted the disparate nature of writing on assessment and the tensions between conceptual and theoretically informative texts and more reductionist and prescriptive approaches to the assessment task, as evidenced in, for example, government guidance. This chapter seeks to hold in balance the tension between immersing the reader in academic debates about what constitutes a generic theoretical framework for assessment and simply providing the reader with a 'how to assess' checklist.
- **Understanding assessment.** Within the SCIE review an emphasis is placed on the need for learning and teaching on assessment to take place on both an intellectual and an experiential level. To this end the chapter is interspersed with activity boxes that encourage the reader to engage with aspects of the assessment task that will require them to reflect on what informed their responses and how they experienced completing the activity. In adopting this approach the chapter seeks to model in its format and structure principles

of reflective practice that are integral to effective assessments.

As with all thinking and writing about social work practice there is an unavoidable and inevitable tension between the practice ideals espoused in theoretical frameworks and the realities of practice (Lymbery and Butler, 2004). While seeking to encourage good assessment practice it is imperative that a realistic stance is promoted that acknowledges the complex, contested and challenging contexts in which practitioners are required to undertake assessments. The intention is to make clear for all practitioners that the assessment task in social work practice is challenging but when undertaken in a professional and informed manner is rewarding and sets the foundation for further interventions.

In the first section of the chapter the contested nature of assessment is examined, with attention given to existing definitions of assessment and to the definition of assessment informing this chapter. The following section explores four dilemmas that are associated with the assessment process and considers how they can best be responded to. In the final section we outline a relationship-based, reflective model of assessment along with some specific approaches that can assist you in conducting ethical and effective assessments.

The policy and practice context

Think ahead

'[T]he core social work skill of assessment as an analytical and evaluative tool is being lost or undervalued . . . often case files do not have an assessment section, although many checklists can be found – often inadequately completed . . . it is very difficult to get a holistic view of the person and their unique personality from the case file . . . without this understanding it is difficult to see how social work intervention can be effective.'

(Ford and Ford, 2000, unpublished)

Can you think why assessments might be neglected?

One partial explanation for the demise of holistic assessments is the burgeoning of policy and procedures, assessment checklists and schedules that reconfigure the assessment task into a prescriptive, bureaucratic exercise, as opposed to an interactive, relational process.

A serious source of tension for practitioners is the need to be familiar with local and central government requirements while retaining the service user at the centre of the assessment process. Below we consider the policy and practice context in which assessments are conducted.

Historical overview of assessment

Assessment is not a new phenomenon in social work, as it has always been an integral part of social work practice as evidenced in Chapter 4. In the past two decades, however, contemporary understandings of assessment have been shaped by two key factors: first, the impact of public inquiries into the shortcomings of social work on legislation policy and practice (Trevithick, 2005) and secondly, the emphasis within the Labour government's modernising agenda (DoH, 1998) on what are commonly referred to as the three 'e's – economy, efficiency and effectiveness – as a means of rationing increasingly scarce resources. In the field of adult services, assessment requirements are embedded in the legislation responsible for introducing community care and care management to social work practice: the NHS and Community Care Act 1990, itself a response to concerns about poor risk assessment and decision-making in mental health cases. For Middleton (1997: 8), assessment with a capital 'A' began in the 1990s with the implementation of this legislation. A similar concern about risk and the assessment process has grown out of the public inquiries into the tragic deaths of children known to social services (and social work departments in Scotland) during recent decades, and contributed to the 1989 Children Act (England and Wales) and the Children (Scotland) Act 1995. Most recently the death of Peter Connelly resulted in the creation of the Social Work Task Force (DCFS, 2009) that has identified the need for more robust assessment frameworks following the failings in this case. A third important legislation to impact on approaches to assessment has been the Criminal Justice Act 1991.

You may have noticed that a feature shared by the legislative origins of current assessment practices is their preoccupation with risk. It is important to flag up here that the extent to which risk is the primary focus of the assessment process and task is one of the key dilemmas faced by social workers. The assessment process is not restricted to assessing risk, but the backdrop to contemporary understandings of assessment has played a significant part in risk being a prominent component of any assessment activity. Within the field of childcare, the Framework

A closer look

Key legislative, policy and government guidance

Childcare contexts

Legislation:
The Children Acts 1989 and 2004
Criminal Justice Act 1991
Human Rights Act 1998
Social Work (Scotland) 1968
Children (Scotland) Act 1995
Children (Leaving Care) Act 2000
Criminal Justice (Scotland) Act 2003

Government guidance:
Framework for the Assessment of Children in Need and Their Families (2000)
Every Child Matters (2003)
Working Together To Safeguard Children (2006)
Getting It Right For Every Child (Scotland 2006)
Integrated Assessment Framework (Scotland 2007)

Adults

Legislation:
National Assistance Act 1948
Chronically Sick and Disabled Act 1970
Disabled Persons Act 1986
NHS and Community Care Act 1990
Community Care (Direct Payments) Act 1996
Health and Social Care Act 2001
Community Care and Health Act (Scotland) 2002
Mental Health (Care and Treatment) (Scotland) Act 2003
Disability Discrimination Act 1995 2005
Data Protection Act 1998
Carers and Disabled Children Act 2000

Government publications/guidance:
Guidance for the Protection of Vulnerable Adults (POVA) 2004
Green Paper *Independence, Wellbeing and Choice* 2006
The Same as You? A review of services for people with learning disabilities (2000)
White Paper *Valuing People: A New Strategy for Learning Disability* 2001
Better Outcomes for Older People: A Framework for Older People's Services in Scotland (2004)
Changing Lives: Report of the 21st Century Social Work Review (2006)
Building a Safe, Confident Future: The Final Report of the Social Work Task Force, November 2009.

---

for Assessment, introduced in 2000, does redress the balance to some extent and encourages practitioners to think beyond narrow definitions of risk to consider not only service user needs but also their strengths. Keeping a focus on all three dimensions – risks, needs and strengths – is challenging but fundamental to effective assessments (Crisp et al., 2005).

Contemporary contexts

All assessment activity is bounded by the legislative and policy context in which the practice is located. The recent developments in social work practice that have resulted in more devolved forms of government/organisation make it impossible to talk about universally relevant legislation or policy underpinning assessment procedures. In this chapter the legislation referred to relates primarily to England and in some cases more widely to the United Kingdom (see also Chapter 8 on law).

Several authors writing on assessment acknowledge the lack of a standardised assessment format (Milner and O'Byrne, 2000; Trevithick, 2005). According to Trevithick (2005) this is partly accounted for by the wide range of purposes of assessments. Drawing on the work of Lloyd and Taylor (1995), Trevithick (2005: 130) refers to:

- third party assessments (for example, pre-sentencing reports, case conference reports, social history assessments);
- investigative assessments (for example, risk assessments in relation to child protection and mental health);
- eligibility/needs led assessments (for example, in relation to community care and children in need);
- suitability assessments (for example, in relation to prospective childminders, foster carers, adoptive parents);
- multidisciplinary assessments (for example, in relation to hospital discharge, statementing in education).

It is certainly the case that the reasons for assessments are diverse, as are the individuals with whom assessments are undertaken. It is, however, possible to identify some core principles of sound assessment practice that are appropriate for the different types of assessment and have a generic applicability to all service user groups (Baldwin and Walker, 2005). Having outlined the broader context of assessment we now turn our attention to thinking about what assessment involves.

What is assessment?

Think ahead

What do you understand assessment to mean?

Can you think of an example when you have been assessed? What did it involve?

What did you feel about this experience?

Existing definitions

The SCIE review into the learning and teaching on assessment by Crisp et al., referred to earlier, found that while there were numerous diverse definitions of assessment provided by social work academics, there was no one common definition. Coulshed and Orme (1998: 21) identify the assessment task straightforwardly as

'[a]n on-going process, in which the client participates, the purpose of which is to understand how people relate to their environment; it is a basis for planning what needs to be done to maintain, improve or bring about change in the person, the environment, or both.'

Middleton (1997: 5) concurs with this definition of the assessment task and amplifies what it involves by describing it as

'the analytical process by which decisions are made ... a basis for planning what needs to be done to improve a person's situation, although it is not the plan itself ... involves gathering, and interpreting information in order to understand a person and their circumstances ... it involves making judgements based on information.'

Parker and Bradley (2003: 13) similarly describe assessment as

'a focussed collation, analysis and synthesis of relevant collected data pertaining to the presenting problem and identified needs.'

They go on to define the purpose of assessment:

'to acquire and study information about people in their environment, to decide upon and identify the problem and to plan effective options to resolve that problem.'   (p. 16)

In Lord Laming's *The Protection of Children in England: A Progress Report* (2009) the assessment process is understood to include:

'gathering a full understanding of what is happening to a child in the context of their family circumstances and the wider community, using a variety of sources of information. It must, therefore, be a joint parallel assessment with all professionals concerned for the child's safety and welfare. Time needs to be spent making sense of this information involving the family where appropriate. Assessment processes should build up an increasingly clear understanding of a child's situation over time ...'   (pp. 28–9)

From these definitions it is clear that assessment involves a number of activities that include:

- identifying the area of concern and sources of information;
- collating relevant information;
- assessing the information;
- analysing the information;
- developing a plan of intervention.

Hidden within these seemingly straightforward tasks, however, is a complex web of dilemmas discussed below (Turney, 2009). It is our view that any definition of assessment needs to make explicit the constructed and relational nature of the assessment process. It requires both good organisational and analytical skills and a holistic understanding of the service user, the practitioner and the professional relationship in which they are engaged. Walker and Beckett's (2003: 21) definition comes closest to our own with its acknowledgement of the demanding, personal and affective nature of the task and its broader stance that acknowledges the contested and complex nature of the assessment arena:

'Assessment is a purposeful activity. It is the art of managing competing demands and negotiating the best possible outcome. It means steering between the pressures of organisational demands, legislative injunction, limited resources and personal agendas. It includes having the personal integrity to hold to your core values and ethical base while being buffeted by strong feelings. An assessment should be part of a perceptual/analytic process that involves selecting, categorising, organising and synthesising data.'

Reflect

'Assessment has to partake of scientific, theoretical, artistic, ethical and practical elements – some of which have long been recognised by practitioners and regarded as traditional by social work and all the helping professions.'

(Clifford, 1998 cited in Parker and Bradley, 2003: 4)

Referring back to your responses to the Think Ahead box which asked you to reflect on your own experiences of being assessed, can you think, from your experience, of any examples of the different elements of the assessment process referred to in this quote?

In the following sections we identify four key dilemmas social workers face when undertaking assessments:

1. Assessment: a one-off event or an ongoing process?
2. Objectivity versus subjectivity?
3. Risk-focused versus holistic assessments?
4. Needs or resource led assessments?

Dilemmas in the assessment process

Assessment: a one-off event or an ongoing process?

In the introduction to this chapter assessment was connected with beginnings. Often this is the case with an assessment being undertaken at the commencement of a social work intervention. It was suggested, however, that this is not always the case. One of the key shortcomings of many existing models of assessment is the tendency to present the assessment task as a linear process, with each stage neatly following the previous one, and resulting in a definitive outcome. In reality the assessment process is a convoluted, backwards and forwards activity that produces a dynamic assessment, relevant to the specific time, place and relationship in which it was derived. Unfortunately the linear assessment model has had a significant influence over official assessment guidelines and procedures. Milner and O'Byrne (2000: 2) recognise this tendency to oversimplify the nature of the assessment task:

'There are . . . too many linear, prescriptive and stylised formats that come no where near the complexities, uncertainties and ambiguities of current social work practice.'

Increasingly attempts are being made to shift thinking on assessment from it being a one-off event conducted at the beginning of a new piece of work to an ongoing process, requiring constant evaluation. Assessments should be seen as integral components of social work interventions, from beginning to end. In some cases it is argued that assessment is a never-ending process and an integral part of planning, intervening and reviewing involvement with a service user:

'There should be seamless transition from assessment to intervention in a circular process that includes the crucial elements of planning and reviewing.'

(Walker and Beckett, 2003: 20)

While this chapter concentrates on the assessment stage of involvement with an individual or family, assessment is inseparable from the planning and interventions stages (see Chapter 12 on social work interventions), and all good practice is constantly kept under review. In many ways this could be seen as an ongoing form of assessing (evaluating) how well the intervention is (or is not) working. Assessments need to be understood to be dynamic processes as opposed to one-off events to ensure they remain relevant for the service user concerned. This point is amplified by the following case study in which the service user only shared certain information once a degree of trust had been established with the social worker.

Case study

Parves

A duty social worker is asked to interview Parves, a 25-year-old woman of Pakistani origin, unknown to the office, who has presented herself at the area office as she is having financial difficulties relating to her benefits. In the course of the conversation with Parves, the social worker is told that she is having difficulty managing to feed her children because of recent changes in her benefit status. The social worker agrees to discuss these changes on her behalf with the local benefit office and arranges a further appointment in a few days' time. In the meantime a call is received from the school expressing concern about the well-being of Parves's three children, aged 6, 4 and 2. When the social worker next sees Parves, she informs her of her discussions with the benefits office and the

▶

concerns raised by the school. Having established some trust with the social worker, Parves feels able to tell her that her benefit difficulties are, in part, due to her current boyfriend who takes her money to buy drugs. With this new information the social worker is able to move beyond the 'presenting problem' and begin to think with Parves about the implications of her current relationship for her and her children, something Parves could not face up to on her initial meeting with the social worker.

It is widely recognised that the 'presenting problem', in Parves's case her benefit difficulties, is often not the primary concern of the service user but a 'safe' or socially acceptable way of accessing help, e.g. requests for practical support by a parent/carer that belie more complicated relational difficulties being experienced. This view has been disputed, however, with critics suggesting that social workers should not delve too deep (Brewer and Lait, 1980). Much of this debate resonates with the issues raised in Chapter 4 on the nature of social problems and the purpose and role of social work. In a contemporary context, Olive Stevenson, an eminent, now emeritus, professor of social work has reawakened this debate in her speech given at the launch of the Centre for Social Work Practice (see www.cfswp.org.uk and the recommended further activities at the end of the chapter).

From our point of view 'presenting problem' behaviours endorse the need for assessments not to be confined to 'one-off' visits, nor for a completed assessment to become carved in stone and definitive. Munro's (2002) exploration of decision-making in childcare social work highlights the reluctance of practitioners to review decisions in light of new information and cautions against such behaviour. Milner and O'Byrne (2000) similarly emphasise the importance of practitioners not becoming 'stuck' with one assessment perspective. Assessment is ongoing and integral to all stages of social work involvement. Practitioners need to work alongside service users to ensure an accurate assessment of their circumstances is reached and regularly reviewed and revised.

In recognising this tension between assessment as an event or a process, the model proposed later in this chapter, in keeping with that proposed by Baldwin and Walker (2005), emphasises the constructed and dynamic nature of the assessment process. A crucial component of the non-linear assessment model is reflective practice (see Chapter 1). The Closer Look box outlines the use of observation skills as part of the assessment process. It underlines the importance of assessments taking place over time and not simply at one point in time, and is a means of promoting skills in reflective practice.

The second dilemma associated with assessments in social work practice is closely associated with the experience of observation as it relates to the extent

A closer look

The role and purpose of social work debate

'Although there is a great deal to worry about, I remain as certain today as I was in the Wootton era that social work is needed in complex societies and that it occupies a crucial, possibly unique, position in the space between the individual and his/her environment. The role is essentially one of mediation between the two, needed when individuals are in various states of discomfort within their social milieu. In my mind's eye I see the individual situated in the middle of a series of spiralling circles; the inner circle is usually the close family, moving outwards through complex systems with which interactions are necessary for the physical and psychic survival of the individual. The problems which arise for individuals may derive from tensions or deficits in the material and social environment,

including, of course, the family or *frequently, an interaction between the two*.

Social workers are not psychotherapists, nor, primarily, social reformers (although they acquire crucial information which can be aggregated for this purpose). Nor are they just care managers, important as that role is, because those who have their care managed need a worker who will try to understand how they feel about their position. Without this, the service is incomplete and sometimes ineffective. For example, an elderly person trying to decide whether to give up their own home for residential care needs both information and help about making choices but also, crucially, help in resolving the ambivalence which such decisions engender.'

(*Source*: From speech given by Professor Olive Stevenson at the launch of the Centre for Social Work Practice on 28 April 2006; available online at www.cfswp.org)

A closer look

The assessment event versus assessment process debate

Experienced childcare practitioners undertaking post-qualifying training are required to undertake six child observation sessions. Many of the practitioners are based in childcare assessment teams and all of them are required to undertake different types of assessment, depending on the remit of their job.

The approach is based on the Tavistock Model and involves practitioners observing a pre-school age child in a day-care setting – nursery or playgroup – on six occasions for one hour. As far as possible practitioners are advised to observe at the same time each week. The practitioners are told not to write any notes during the sessions but to simply observe. As soon as possible after the session they are encouraged to write up their observations. Regular seminars are held at which a practitioner will present a written recording of an observation, and the issues it generates are discussed by the group. Two crucial and consistent learning points arising from this experience are:

1. The constructed nature of the assessment process is highlighted by the material included in a practitioner's recording which is understood in diverse ways by the seminar group. This realisation emphasises the importance of practitioners being open-minded and curious, avoiding reaching premature conclusions about a child or their behaviours. No two people see the situation in the same light. In addition it underlines how vital it is for practitioners to engage in a collaborative assessment exercise, in this case with parents/carers and children, in order to check out conclusions being reached.

2. Practitioners were consistent in their view that one-off assessments were inappropriate and inaccurate. Observing a child in a consistent time and place on several occasions enabled the practitioners to establish a much fuller and more accurate picture of the child's functioning. One practitioner commented on how she had concluded after her first observation that the child she was watching was shy and lacking in confidence only to discover this not to be the case in all the subsequent sessions. For many practitioners a crucial point of learning was recognising the impact and importance of having a longer assessment period. This came as a surprise to many of them as they were accustomed to government and departmental assessment requirements that had very tight time constraints built in and precluded more comprehensive and sustained assessment activities.

---

to which assessments are an objective or a subjective activity.

Objectivity versus subjectivity – understanding 'the self' and others

In Chapters 1 and 6 you have been introduced to the debate within the social work profession per se and the assessment process, in particular about the nature of 'knowing', and which sources of knowledge are the most significant for social work practice (England, 1986; Parker and Bradley, 2003). In relation to the assessment task and process, the question relates to whether there is a definitive assessment outcome, 'a truth', or whether assessment should be approached as a negotiated process that involves the practitioner and service user constructing 'a truth' relevant to that unique situation. Connected to the art–science debate is the question of whether it is possible to undertake objective assessments. The more scientifically oriented, checklist-informed approach would

suggest it is, but increasingly acknowledgment is being given to the unavoidable subjectivity built into the assessment process (Milner and O'Byrne, 2002). One clear implication of adopting a relationship-based perspective on assessments is the potential for an assessment to contain subjective bias or error. Providing this is recognised as an integral and unavoidable component of the assessment process, it need not be a problem and can be used to engage more openly and honestly with the individual(s) concerned.

Commencing an assessment relationship requires practitioners to resist assuming that an individual will conform to a service user stereotype or label, e.g. an elderly man with limited mobility, or that an individual's needs can be predetermined by the criteria that have been recorded on the referral form, e.g. looked-after child, single parent on benefits, care leaver, person with mental health problems. Each referral needs to be seen to be unique, as each individual service user will experience their particular difficulty uniquely. This practice principle is of particular importance when referrals are received from service users with whom social work departments are familiar. Previous involvement with service users can, on occasions, unhelpfully influence how new assessments are undertaken. The importance of accurate, non-judgemental recording is central to avoiding such occurrences.

An interesting starting point for thinking about how we engage with others is to reflect on how we understand ourselves.

Think ahead

In this exercise you are invited to think about how your perception of yourself influences your professional responses.

- Identify 10 'I am' statements that might represent interests, activities, affiliations, relationships, likes and dislikes, e.g. 'I am a woman', 'I am Irish' or 'I am keen on sport'.
- Consider how what you have chosen to identify influences your professional practice.

What other aspects of your 'personal self' are significant for your professional self?

The purpose of the exercise is to encourage you to recognise the interconnections between your personal and professional personas. In addition it highlights how selective we can be about what we wish to disclose. On completing the exercise it is possible to reflect on which personal qualities or characteristics were 'selected out'. Making a statement such as, 'I am short-tempered', 'I am a Muslim' or 'I am gay', might leave an individual feeling quite vulnerable and at risk of being judged. Harrison and Ruch (2007) in a chapter entitled 'Social work and the use of self: on becoming and being a social worker' explore these dynamics of professional practice in greater detail. According to Harrison (personal communication, 2006), in her experience of conducting this exercise with students, it is not uncommon for the following to happen:

'People invariably list how old they are, the jobs they do, their national identity, and how they are defined by their primary relationships with others – "I am a mother, sister, wife" etc. This makes it easy to introduce students to the concepts of social categorisation, social identity and social comparison, and draw attention to the way that society is divided on many different bases (age, gender, "race", occupation, religion etc.). The point can also be made that we ourselves belong to a number of different social groups

– some by choice, some by birth and some that are imposed upon us. Importantly, many of the groups we are able to identify have more (or less) power and status than others, and all carry different understandings of social values. This is why it is important for potential social workers to recognise and work with difference and diversity, and that they begin the process of developing a greater sense of self-awareness about the risks of labelling, stereotyping and holding subjective beliefs and values.'

Case study

Jane

Early on in her social work career, Karen was asked to undertake some direct work with a 13-year-old, white girl called Jane who had experienced extensive sexual and physical abuse. Jane was living in a children's home and the plan was for her to be placed for long-term fostering. Karen identified the initial meetings with Jane as assessment sessions that would help determine how best to structure her time with her. Despite introducing a range of different activities, Jane found it difficult to engage with any of them. It soon became apparent that the most regular feature of Karen's sessions with Jane was the struggle she had to stay awake. When Karen raised this issue with her supervisor she was helpfully encouraged to think about Jane's experiences and it was suggested that Karen's drowsiness might mirror Jane's levels of depression. This perspective helped Karen to recognise that what she had interpreted as her own professional inadequacies, i.e. an inability to stay awake in the working day, was in fact part of the professional encounter and relationship dynamics. It provided important information that contributed to her assessment of Jane's circumstances and needs.

Another piece of learning arising from this episode was that Karen had to come to terms with her own need, as a social worker, to 'do' things and gather information when in fact simply 'being' alongside someone was equally informative.

In our view subjectivity is an inevitable, unavoidable and integral component of all assessment processes and relationships, therefore it is essential that there are appropriate support mechanisms in place to enable practitioners to use their self-awareness purposefully (Koprowska, 2007). By developing levels of self-awareness (see Chapter 6 on social work knowledge and practice), acquiring skills in reflective practice (Chapter 1) and accessing appropriate support systems such as supervision (Chapters 1 and 2) you will become increasingly able:

- to engage in more subtle forms of assessment that go beyond checklists and formulaic approaches;
- to build on your subjective knowledge to identify ways of working that promote anti-oppressive practice and partnership working.

The third dilemma facing practitioners engaged in assessment activities relates to the place of risk in the assessment process.

Risk-focused versus holistic assessments

A particular challenge, arising from the wider political influences which shape the nature of the assessment process, is the tension between narrowly defined assessments that focus almost exclusively on risk and those that attempt to retain a broader brief and include risk as one aspect of the assessment process. A comprehensive assessment requires practitioners to weigh up the risks, the needs and the resource implications of a particular situation. As we have identified in Chapter 1, and in Chapter 6 on social work knowledge, difficulties arise from the all-pervasive preoccupation with risk in contemporary society which is responsible for two characteristics of contemporary practice:

1. an unrealistic search for absolute truths and definitive 'right' interventions;
2. a blame culture that constrains creative and effective professional practice.

The fear of being accused of having misjudged or 'mis-assessed' a situation and of 'getting it wrong', causes social workers and other professionals to err on the side of cautious and defensive practice. Practice of this nature fails to consider fully the implications, the risks and benefits, of the decisions reached and actions taken. Deciding, for example, to remove a child from a harmful situation is not a risk-free decision, as research evidence indicates (Sinclair et al., 2005; Taylor et al., 2008; Waterhouse and McGhee, 2009; Wilson et al., 2004). The potential harm that could arise from a child being removed from home and placed in an inappropriate foster placement has to be balanced against the risks of leaving the child with their birth family. Children placed in local authority care often experience unsuitable or unstable placements despite ostensibly needs-led assessments because of resource shortages.

An integral feature of a constructed and collaborative model of assessment is the need to define risk in conjunction with the service user(s) alongside your professional assessment of need and risk, research evidence and available resources. Reductionist definitions of risk equate it with danger and seek its elimination. More helpful understandings of risk relate it to uncertainty (Parton, 2001) and refer to risk management alongside risk assessment and balancing risk factors with safety/ protective factors.

Case study

Lisa

An area team social worker was asked to assess the risks involved in a convicted sex offender being rehabilitated from prison to his family home where his wife and step-daughter, Lisa, lived. Lisa, who had been sexually abused by her stepfather, was 15 at the time of the assessment. An initial assessment had been undertaken that involved the area team social worker drawing up a written agreement on the family that covered issues relating to Lisa's safety. The family described feeling 'ordered' by Social Services to behave in particular ways and felt the written agreement was 'imposed' on them. A full core assessment (Framework for Assessment, 2000) was subsequently completed by two family-centre social workers who operated in a more relationship-based and collaborative way with the family. During the course of the assessment sessions the workers were able to work with the family in ways that enabled the family to hear and understand the social work concerns about the family's circumstances. Through this process the family were able to take responsibility for Lisa's safety and devise a written agreement in conjunction with the social workers that managed the risk factors in an open and creative manner.

As the case study above shows, redefining risk from a broader, shared perspective enhances the likelihood of the assessment being effective and reminds practitioners of the centrality of collaborative approaches in the assessment process.

Collaborative partnerships versus expert professionals

Think ahead

When embarking on a new assessment it is important for practitioners to acknowledge that both they and the service user will hold preconceived ideas about what the assessment process will entail and what the desirable outcome would be. On first meeting it can be helpful for these preformed ideas to be discussed to enable the assessment process to commence from a shared baseline. That is not to say that it will always be easy to agree on what is an acceptable starting point but it will ensure that a transparent approach is being implemented from the outset and that any clearly unrealisable expectations are acknowledged at the outset.

How might you go about implementing this transparent approach?

The Think Ahead feature requires you to think about all the information you will have gathered prior to commencing an assessment and any preconceived ideas/assumptions you might hold or make. This helps you think about one aspect of your power in the relationship. Reflecting on the experience of completing the 'I am . . .' exercise earlier in the chapter highlights how there are parallels between how you might have felt undertaking the exercise and how service users experience the assessment process, and helps you understand how powerless the service user might feel: What should or shouldn't they say? What is or isn't already known about them?

In recent years there has been a significant shift in social work practice towards collaborative and partnership-based practice (Shemmings and Shemmings, 2000). Traditional notions of the 'expert professional' have been challenged (Milner and O'Byrne, 2002). These shifts are attributable to three important developments:

- first, the emergence of post-modern ideas that challenge the confidence placed in grand narratives and theoretical perspectives that suggest there is only 'one truth', and in their place promote social constructivist understandings of reality that encourage 'multiple realities or truths' to be identified and reduce reliance on the 'expert' professional (see Chapter 1 and Milner and O'Byrne, 2002; Baldwin and Walker, 2005);
- secondly, the widespread adoption of anti-oppressive and anti-discriminatory perspectives that emphasise the central role played by power relations in the

construction of social problems and their resolution (Dominelli, 2004; Fook, 2002);
- thirdly, the increasing recognition given to service user perspectives (see Chapter 14).

From a social constructivist perspective, language plays an important part in the definition of social problems. One limitation of the 'traditional' linear assessment model outlined earlier is the language used to describe it that places emphasis on the practitioner being 'in charge' of identifying, gathering, analysing and interpreting the relevant information. It is not immediately apparent that these are shared activities. In contrast the model outlined in this chapter considers the service users' contribution to be fundamental to all assessment activity and we would go so far as to say that, without collaboration with service users, assessments are unethical and likely to be of limited accuracy and effectiveness.

Smale, Tuson and Statham (2000), three social work academics, have drawn on social constructivist ideas and

The exchange model of assessment allows practitioners to 'track rather than lead' in gaining understanding of the service user's perspective.

(Kevin Smith (Kes): www.kescartoons.com)

A closer look

The exchange model of assessment – key characteristics

1. *Enabling people to articulate* and so identify their own needs, clarify what they want, and fed into policy, strategic planning and training.
2. *Adding to, but keeping out of the way of, others exercising their own social problem-solving skills.* Everyone has expertise in these areas, some more than others. Workers do not start with a monopoly; they share what they have with all the other people involved.
3. *Understanding and responding sensitively to differences* in disability, language, culture, ethnicity, age, race, gender and sexuality, and preferences for different forms of communication, in order to work towards an appropriate and relevant solution and identify the necessary resources.
4. *Providing or making accessible information to citizens and sharing expertise* on the workings of social care, health and other systems, and informing people of possible alternative choices. Workers are in a pivotal position in the transfer of information skills and knowledge between the public and the organisation.
5. *Helping people through major transitions involving loss:* assessment and intervention can take place at times of great stress, brought about by the loss of partner or some physical capacity, or some other change that has precipitated referral.
6. *Negotiating and conciliating between people* who have different needs. Situations can be bound up in the conflicting needs of several people whose relationships have formed over many years.
7. *Identifying the relationship between people:* how their behaviour supports current relationships and perpetuates destructive self-fulfilling prophecies, self-defeating strategies and other harmful relationships; how this may be changed to support a different set of behaviours so that the problems can be managed differently, or resolved in the case of people's behaviour being the reason for referral.
8. *Recognising, understanding and intervening in the patterns of relationships* between individuals and between groups and organisations that precipitate and perpetuate social problems.
9. *Recognising, understanding and intervening in the patterns of relationships* that precipitate and perpetuate social problems, and accessing expertise required to contribute to the particular option decided upon.
10. *Providing information for strategic social care planning* and acting as advocates for the ends of citizens. (*Source*: Smale et al., 2000: 152)

identified three models of assessment: the questioning model that places the professional as expert in gathering and analysing information, the procedural model which involves the practitioner in assessing the eligibility of the service user for specific services, and the exchange model that identifies the service user as the expert on their own life and encourages an exchange of information between practitioner and service user. The key feature of the exchange model of assessment is the emphasis it places on terminology that recognises the active role service users should have in the assessment process and on practitioners working in partnership with service users to assess their situation. The strength of this model lies in its ability to promote respect for the individuality of the service user and to empower and encourage the service user's participation in the assessment process and subsequent interventions. The Closer Look box above provides a summary of the key characteristics of this model.

Inviting service users to be 'experts on their own lives' and equal participants in the assessment process,

however, is not entirely straightforward, as our case study about Jane and the discussion about Parves's 'presenting problems' earlier illustrated. Jane's circumstances showed you how as a social worker you need to be aware of the complexity of human behaviours and how unconscious material has the potential, first, to constrain the extent to which an individual is an expert on their situation and secondly to influence professional encounters and your professional response. Parves's circumstances demonstrate how service users are not always comfortable sharing all they know about their situation and certainly do not always feel they 'have the answer', as the service user expertise model can imply.

There can be a tendency when acknowledging the expertise of service users to overestimate service users' ability to identify solutions to their difficulties. Secondly, difficulties can arise when practitioners underestimate or deny their own level of professional expertise. In developing collaborative partnerships it is important that practitioners do not understate their professional perspective and the expertise they bring to the assessment process. Baldwin and Walker (2005: 43) recognise this dilemma but conclude:

'A partnership approach can recognise an individual's rights to autonomy, safety, inclusion and having their voice heard without denying power differentials.'

Perhaps the most challenging contexts for establishing a partnership approach are those which require practitioners to exert their statutory responsibilities, for example in cases where there are child protection or mental health concerns. In these cases power dynamics are to the fore and transparent practice is even more important. As a social worker you are invested with considerable power and how you understand and exercise your power is a critical component of the assessment process. Adopting assessment strategies that are informed by the core principles of collaboration and transparency ensure that the risk of denying, underplaying or abusing the power you carry is minimised. This transparent approach is particularly useful for dispelling anxieties that service users can have about the role of the social worker. While it is well recognised that social workers have both statutory responsibilities and are gatekeepers to resources, it is crucial that these powers and responsibilities are not used to threaten or intimidate service users. Ethical and responsible practitioners will ensure that in establishing an effective assessment relationship with a service user they make explicit the extent of their remit and invite service users to articulate anxieties they might harbour about what could occur.

Managing the power dimension in the assessment process is further complicated by the tension between objectivity and subjectivity in the assessment process that was discussed earlier. While practitioners are responsible for compiling accurate assessments they must acknowledge the subjective nature of the assessment relationship and process. An objective assessment is an unrealisable goal (Milner and O'Byrne, 2002).

At the same time as making visible the power within professional relationships, practising in ways that emphasise the relationship dimension of the work requires practitioners to acknowledge the complexity of human behaviour. Human behaviour extends beyond rational responses to situations and it is precisely because of the emotive nature of the work that practitioners need to be alert in emotionally charged situations *to act* responsibly and *not react* oppressively. Frequently service users' circumstances are sources of considerable distress, anxiety and anger. It is precisely these affective responses to social

circumstances that practitioners need to be aware of and be responsive to. The professional relationship is affected, unavoidably, by both the service user's anxieties (referred to above) about the social worker's role, and by the affective ingredients arising from the service user's circumstances. Experiences of loss, for example, whether of a person through death or relationship breakdowns or other bereavements such as the loss of a physical or mental ability or social status, are common features of service users' circumstances. The impact of such experiences on an individual's emotional functioning is frequently a component of the relationship that is established with the social work practitioner. Practitioners need to be alert to the influence of the service user's conscious and unconscious affective material in the assessment process. Conversely practitioners need to recognise how their own affective responses vary depending on the circumstances of the service user with whom they are engaged. A practitioner's personal experiences of loss, for example, can impact on how the assessment relationship develops.

Equally important is the need for practitioners to be alert to the potential for service users to exhibit aggressive or intimidating behaviours in response to the heightened anxieties that the assessment process can evoke (Ferguson, 2005). In such cases practitioners need to ensure they feel appropriately supported in order to avoid becoming disempowered by such experiences.

Social workers need to be responsive to the distress, anxiety and anger of service users brought about by their circumstances.

(*Source:* Report Digital/Jess Hurd)

Needs or resource led assessments?

On the basis of the above discussions it is clear that practitioners need to be engaging in the assessment process from a dynamic and collaborative perspective. In an ideal world this approach is difficult to criticise. But what happens when the all-prevailing issue of whether assessments are needs-led or resource-led is introduced? This perhaps is where the contested nature of assessment is most evident. How needs are defined and by whom is likely to generate very different outcomes. It is a recognised fact that need will always outstrip resources but perhaps one of the strengths of the assessment model outlined in this chapter is the refusal to believe there is a definitive solution, or what Milner and O'Byrne (2002) refer to as a 'correct' assessment. Social constructivist perspectives that encourage collaborative professional practice conceive assessments as more or less 'helpful'. From this position there is greater likelihood of more accurate and reliable assessments being constructed as they are more holistic and less constrained by preconceived ideas about right and wrong understandings of situations. Additionally these more encompassing understandings of a specific situation are mirrored by a wider range of possible responses. If a sound collaborative relationship has been established, the gap between the identified needs and available resources can be minimised and the scope for creative responses can be maximised.

Managing the ideals and realities of practice is something all practitioners have to come to terms with (Lymbery and Butler, 2004). The harsh reality you may encounter is that working within resource-deficient contexts means that the professional relationship may be the only resource you are able to offer to a service user (see Chapter 1 for definitions of relationship-based practice). How you say 'no' to a service user on the grounds of them not meeting eligibility criteria for services, for example, is a skilled undertaking and will have a significant impact on how the service user experiences your engagement with them. In such circumstances the quality of the professional relationship is crucial.

It is all too common in the current climate of tight timescales and heavy workloads for the relationship dimensions of practice to be marginalised, with priority being given to completing assessment forms in order to close cases as ineligible, or to quickly implement the recommendations in the hope of swiftly resolving the situation (Calder, 2003). What a relationship-based approach to assessment prioritises is the creation of a meaningful professional relationship that will enhance the accuracy and effectiveness of the assessment process and in some cases reduce the need for extensive interventions. It is well recognised in social work (Mattinson, 1992; Rees and Wallace, 1982; Schofield, 1998) and in other related professional fields, such as counselling and therapy, that the professional relationship can be not only the means to an end but also the end in itself. Practitioners who rush the relationship-forming stage of the assessment process do so at their peril, as the likelihood of compiling an accurate assessment is diminished if a sound understanding of the service user perspective is not ascertained. Service users similarly place value and importance on the relationship they establish with the social worker (Doel, 2010) an aspect of practice explored further in Chapter 14.

A closer look

Supporting parents: messages from research

In a compilation of research studies – *Supporting Parents: Messages from Research* (Quinton, 2004) – undertaken into parents' experiences of social work involvement, a number of key themes emerged which parents identified as fundamental to effective support. These included:

- Support is a relationship that requires partnership.
- Support is a dynamic process.
- Emotional support is an important feature of formal and informal sources of support.
- Parents want to feel in control of dealing with parenting problems.
- Families are committed to retaining their independence.
- Parents want to be seen as experts in their parenting problems, even if their views need challenging.

Practitioners working within tight deadlines need to be confident that time spent in the early stages establishing a good rapport and transparent understandings of expectations can be recouped in the later stages of the assessment process. Service users who have developed a trusting relationship with a social worker will have less need to be defensive, to question the purpose of the assessment task or to refuse to engage willingly, thereby making the exercise more protracted.

The dilemmas outlined above serve to demonstrate how challenging assessment activities are. In the following two sections we seek to respond to the challenges and dilemmas discussed above by introducing you to:

- a definition of relationship-based assessment practice;
- a model of relationship-based assessment.

A relationship-based definition of assessment

From a relationship-based perspective, which emphasises the uniqueness and complexity of individuals and the centrality of the professional relationship, as outlined in Chapter 1, and drawing on elements of existing definitions, we understand the assessment process to involve practitioners engaging with service users to develop/construct a shared understanding of the problem(s) being faced. It requires:

- a shared and transparent understanding of professional involvement – identifies the pertinent sources of information;
- a collaborative construction of the concerns – examines and explores the relevant information in a transparent, reflective and cyclical manner;
- a mutually determined analysis – assesses and develops a transparent understanding;
- a collaborative intervention strategy – jointly constructs a plan of action to respond to the difficulties being faced.

It is immediately apparent from reading the above definition of the assessment process that considerable importance is placed on the establishment of an open and transparent relationship between the service user and practitioner, one which encourages shared responsibility throughout the assessment process. It recognises human behaviours and the professional relationship to be an integral but complex component of any assessment. As much importance is attached to the relationship that is established during the assessment process as to the concrete information gathered. This approach values affective, emotional sources of knowledge, i.e. feelings and experiences as well as the technical–rational sources, i.e. facts and concrete evidence. What this definition asserts is that the professional relationship is key to an effective assessment and that assessment is a relational as well as technical activity (Calder, 2003; Parker and Bradley, 2003). This perspective is of even greater importance, given the recognition that needs-led assessments are for the most

part an unrealisable ideal. The relationship formed during the assessment process can be an important component of an effective intervention.

The following sections explore what relational, constructed and reflective assessments might look like and the skills required to realise them.

A relationship-based, reflective and collaborative model of assessment

So how can a relationship-based, reflective, collaborative and constructed assessment process become a practice reality (albeit unique every time it is undertaken)? Figure 10.2 is a proposed model of assessment practice that endeavours to encapsulate all the preceding discussion. Alongside this model some techniques are suggested that facilitate relationship-based and collaborative assessments. As with all techniques or professional tools, practitioners need to select and use them thoughtfully to ensure their appropriateness for any individual situation. Government initiatives such as the *Framework for Assessment in Child Care* (DoH, 2000c) guidelines and the *Single Assessment Framework for Older People* (DoH, 2002c) in adult care are helpful checklists of what to cover in the assessment process. Unfortunately the widespread criticism of them relates to their misuse by practitioners who use them in overly restrictive and prescriptive ways (Calder, 2003; Baldwin and Walker, 2005; Walker and Beckett, 2003). The numerous guidelines in existence are simply that – guides – and should be used to inform assessment practice but not to dictate it.

Below we outline a four-stage model of assessment. Inevitably it simplifies the complex, cyclical nature of the process. It is important to remember that none of these stages are discrete episodes and each one constantly informs and is informed by the other. Before, during and after each stage, whether they are sections of one meeting or spaced over several meetings, practitioners need to reflect back to themselves and to the service user their assessment at that stage. This ongoing, reflective stance ensures practitioners do not prematurely reach a conclusion and that the conclusion that is eventually reached, while not necessarily mutually acceptable to all concerned, is understood. Supervision is a vital reflective resource and needs to be available on a regular formal basis for all practitioners.

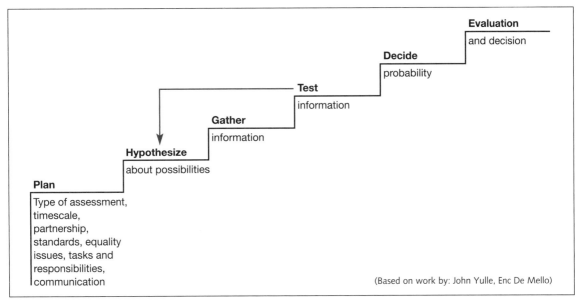

Figure 10.1 Calder's linear model of assessment

(*Source*: Calder, 2003: 35. Reproduced by permission from Calder, M.C. and Hackett, S., eds, *Assessment in Child Care*, Lyme Regis: Russell House Publishing)

Earlier in the chapter when exploring definitions of assessment we identified four key dilemmas associated with the assessment process and the complexities implicit in it. Calder's model of assessment (Figure 10.1) illustrates the process as a linear one, thereby reinforcing the notion of assessment being, literally, a straightforward task.

The model we propose in Figure 10.2 is one which illustrates the complexity of the assessment process. Parker (2007) goes some way to addressing these complexities by designing a cyclical model of the social work process. What the model proposed here adds to Parker's cyclical model is an emphasis in any assessment on the different perspectives that need to be taken into account. Even within one family, there will be differences in how individual family members explain and understand their situation. Social workers and service users are likely to begin the assessment process from different perspectives. Depending on how the relationship evolves, it is the intention of a good assessment for a shared understanding to develop which brings the different perspectives closer. This does not mean the perspectives held will necessarily be the same, although through the assessment process this could happen. The spiralling image is intended to illustrate the dynamic nature of the assessment, with

perspectives shifting backwards and forwards within an overall forward movement.

When thinking about the assessment process from a relational, reflective, constructed and collaborative perspective, it is possible to see how it addresses, and to a large extent overcomes, the key dilemmas identified earlier in the chapter.

Case study

Tamsin

You are allocated a case that involves Mel, the mother of a child, Tamsin, aged 10, who has mild cerebral palsy, and her partner Shane. Mel has a chronic thyroid condition which can leave her feeling very tired. Mel has recently established a relationship with Shane who has moved into Mel's flat. In the past, there has been concern about the quality of care Mel is able to offer to her daughter, Tamsin. The case has been re-referred to the local Children and Families team by the head teacher at Tamsin's school, who is concerned about the physical state in which Tamsin is arriving in the mornings.

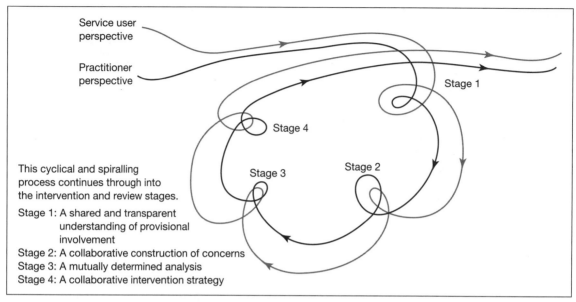

Service user
perspective

Practitioner
perspective

Stage 1

Stage 4

This cyclical and spiralling
process continues through into
the intervention and review stages.

Stage 3

Stage 2

Stage 1: A shared and transparent
          understanding of provisional
          involvement
Stage 2: A collaborative construction of concerns
Stage 3: A mutually determined analysis
Stage 4: A collaborative intervention strategy

Figure 10.2 A relationship-based, reflective model of assessment

(*Source*: Adapted from Parker, 2007)

Stage one: Shared and transparent understanding of professional involvement – identifying, collating and describing the area of concern and sources of information

A clear beginning to the assessment process is crucial. Careful preparation ensures that the practitioner is as fully informed as they can be about the different aspects of the service users' circumstances. As part of your preparations for meeting with Tamsin, Mel and Shane, time needs to be taken to identify what preconceived ideas you and they might have about the nature of your involvement. Unfortunately the time-frames of many of the government-devised assessment frameworks, such as the Framework for Assessment that informs practice in childcare settings, do not encourage attention being paid to the relationship dimensions of the assessment process. This feature of the Framework for Assessment has been a source of recurrent concern and criticism (Calder, 2003). Similar issues arise in the context of social work with adults. The timescales, within which care-management decisions and interventions are expected to be reached and implemented, obstruct the development of a meaningful professional relationship that can enhance the quality of the assessment being undertaken. In addition there are a number of dilemmas that complicate the

development of relationship-based practice – specified in relation to older people in Chapter 22.

It has to be accepted that time is a resource and therefore how it is allocated and used in the assessment process is of importance, particularly for employing bodies (Trevithick, 2005). However, it also has to be recognised that, by allowing time and resource restrictions to determine the type of assessments that take place, there is a greater risk of the depth and analytic quality of practice being compromised and assessments being experienced as oppressive (Walker and Beckett, 2003). A concern identified by Munro (2002) in her review of child protection practice was the failure of social workers to gather, systematically and comprehensively, relevant information.

Practitioners need to be informed but open-minded when embarking on an assessment. Preparatory work can include:

- **Preliminary 'mapping' questions:**
  (a) Who (service user, relatives, friends, professionals) is concerned, about what, why and why now?
  (b) What risks are involved and how quickly is an assessment required?
  (c) Who needs to be involved in addition to the service user(s) – directly, e.g. a carer or indirectly, e.g. other professionals – in the assessment?

(d) Where can I find existing background information on the service user, professional networks and potential resources?

■ **Consulting government/departmental guidelines** – allowing them to inform but not to constrain the use of creativity in the assessment practice.

■ **Explanatory information** – initial involvement with a service user must include clear communication about the nature of the referral and the remit of the practitioner. At this stage it can be helpful to provide a brief written outline of roles and responsibilities. With children, such as Tamsin, and also with adults with learning difficulties this can be done in picture-book format. Similar adaptations can be devised according to the specific service user group. The partnership approach that permeates a relationship-based assessment model must not avoid the challenges of risk-related assessments. Service users need to understand the powers of social work practitioners. Clear understandings of roles and responsibilities and mutual expectations need to be established at this early stage.

Case study

Tamsin cont . . .

In Tamsin's case it would appear that concerns have arisen over time so there is no immediate urgency, but a meeting with her mother, Shane and the school would be an obvious place to start. There may well be an attempt by the school to hand over responsibility for the concern to the social worker and for them to feel they do not need to be involved any further at this stage. To ensure the relationship between the school and the family can be sustained, however, and Tamsin's education is not unduly jeopardised, it is important that the school accept their role in safeguarding Tamsin and that, in the first instance, the social worker and someone from the school meet with Mel and Shane.

It is difficult in the early stages of such a referral to assess the seriousness of the situation and what level of intervention might be required. Explaining the different types of help that might be offered to the family – preventative and compulsory as appropriate – will enable them to feel more confident about engaging in the assessment process. Leaflets and accessible information can help this part of the engagement process.

Stage two: Collaborative construction of the concern – assessing, explaining and predicting the relevant information

Traditional assessment models focus on question-and-answer approaches to gathering information. In contrast a central characteristic of this stage of the assessment process is its collaborative nature. It is important that practitioners can hear the service user's 'story' and can use techniques that ensure a holistic understanding of the service user's perspective views has been obtained. This approach undermines the 'expert professional questioner' and 'needy service user respondent' roles of earlier models. The genograms and ecomaps (detailed below and discussed further in Chapter 16 on working with children and families) help practitioners explore the service user's perspective in less threatening, more inclusive and creative ways. This latter characteristic of the assessment process is an important one, given the difficulties some service users might have with reading and writing. Features of this stage of the assessment process include: the exchange model; the ecological model; visual techniques; co-working, reflective teams and circular questions; and observation.

The exchange model

Use of collaboratively constructed questions/invitations that allows the practitioner to 'track rather than to lead' (Smale et al., 2000: 199) the assessment process in an empathic manner:

■ Inviting the service user to 'tell their story', e.g. 'Can you tell me about your current circumstances and the difficulties you are experiencing?'
■ Paraphrasing and commenting on the service user's 'story' using their language
■ Inviting the service user to identify sources of support or concern in their social and professional networks, e.g. 'Who else is concerned and how do they perceive the situation?'
■ Inviting the service user to identify their own suggested resolutions to the situation, e.g. 'How do you believe your difficulties can be most effectively addressed?'

The ecological model

This model identifies the risks and strengths of the existing situation and potential interventions. Bronfenbrenner's (1979) ecological model (Figure 10.3), which underpins the Framework for Assessment (see Figure 10.4), is a very helpful way of engaging families in thinking about their

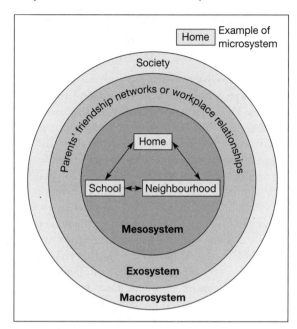

Figure 10.3 Bronfenbrenner's ecological system of human development

(*Source:* Howarth, J., (ed.), 2000, *The Child's World: Assessing Children in Need*, (Jack, G., p. 54), London: Jessica Kingsley.)

strengths. The model has had an important influence in shifting thinking from narrow definitions of need and resources to ensure the wider social contexts of service users' lives are considered as an integral aspect of the assessment process. Assessment with all groups of service users, and not just children and families, can be enhanced by adopting an ecological approach (Baldwin and Walker, 2005).

In talking with Tamsin's mother and Shane at the school, the teacher referred to another family member, Sharon, Mel's sister, who has sometimes dropped Tamsin off at school when Tamsin's mother was unwell. Using the Framework for Assessment's visual aid, Figure 10.4, it was possible for Mel and Shane to think about their wider social context and to identify other family members who could provide regular support. Using this visual aid with service users enables practitioners to explore the ingredients of the different social contexts in which the service user is located. Visual representations can help service users engage more fully in the assessment process as they can 'see' what the practitioner is focusing on and how all the different aspects of their lives do or do not interconnect. It also ensures that the social context is not overlooked as has been the case in the past when assessments have adopted a more

individualistic and pathological stance (Waterhouse and McGhee, 2009). These earlier models of assessment have perceived the service user as the problem, whereas the ecological model sees the service user as a person experiencing a problem that may not necessarily be 'their fault' but the result of structural inequalities. Ecological perspectives allow for equal weight to be placed on internal, personal and external societal causes of difficulty.

Visual techniques – genograms and ecomaps

Genograms involve service users drawing their family tree and exploring the different relationships between family members at that point in time. Ecomaps operate in a similar manner but, informed by Bronfenbrenner's different social contexts, focus on the social networks in which the service user is located and identify the strengths, resources and areas of tension embedded in them. Parker and Bradley (2003) provide a helpful overview of how to incorporate these approaches into the assessment process.

Prompted by the identification of supportive family members in Tamsin's wider family, a genogram was compiled which highlighted the different relationships within the family network. When you look at the family tree (Figure 10.5), it is worth considering what strikes you about it and wondering why this might be and also identifying the questions it makes you want to ask. Genograms are a fascinating way of helping a family explore their relationships, and because they are a visual medium they can trigger unexpected responses. While compiling the genogram it became apparent that a source of tension between Mel and Shane, which made it hard sometimes for them to fully utilise the support available, related to Shane feeling envious of Mel's close relationships with her immediate family. This had meant he had refused to allow Sharon and Mel's mother to be as involved as they would have liked. Exploring this issue allowed the family to come to an agreement about what was in Tamsin's interests, given the stress the family was experiencing.

At this stage in the proceedings, making an opportunity to meet with Tamsin on her own without other family members is important. As the social worker you might want to ask if Tamsin would like her teacher or another member of school staff with her when she meets with you. Compiling an ecomap with Tamsin would help you understand the important people in her life. An example of Tamsin's ecomap is included in Figure 10.6. You can design your own ecomap according to the age

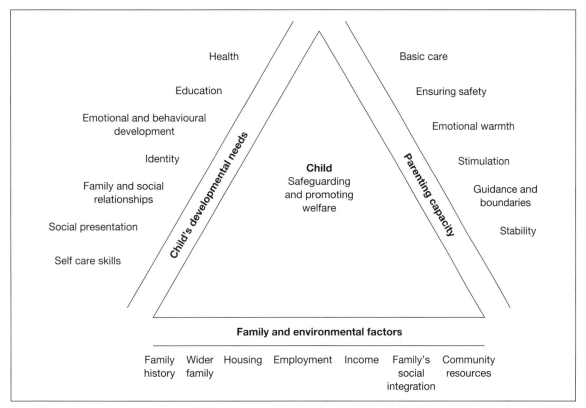

Figure 10.4 Assessment framework triangle

(*Source: The Framework for the Assessment of Children in Need and their Families*, Dept. of Health ISBN 0113223102. © Crown copyright material is reproduced with the permission of the Controller of HMSO and Queen's Printer for Scotland.)

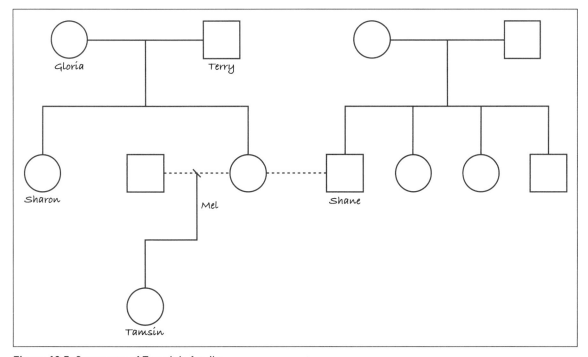

Figure 10.5 Genogram of Tamsin's family

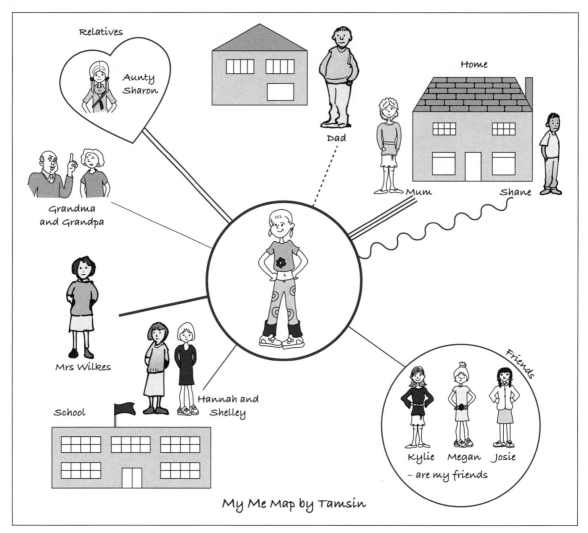

Relatives
Aunty Sharon
Home
Dad
Mum
Shane
Grandma and Grandpa
Mrs Wilkes
Hannah and Shelley
School
Friends
Kylie Megan Josie
– are my friends
My Me Map by Tamsin

Figure 10.6 Tamsin ecomap

of the child but this one highlights the key sources of relationship that a child might have. When completing the ecomap you can discuss with the child how important the relationship is between the different people they, and you, identify and the strength and straightness of the lines can depict this. In Tamsin's case the thick straight line to her mother indicates a strong relationship whereas the jagged line to Shane represents the comments Tamsin has made about not always liking her mother's partner who shouts a lot.

Many of the non-verbal strategies for engaging service users, such as genograms and ecomaps, have their origins in both systemic work with families and in gestalt therapy. Relationship-based assessments need to respond to the individual needs of the service user(s)

involved. In many cases solely verbal or written strategies for gathering information and establishing shared understanding of the situation are insufficient or inadequate. Techniques such as genograms and ecomaps provide accessible and collaborative alternatives to more orthodox verbal/written approaches (Parker and Bradley, 2003). Such strategies also encourage more extensive information-gathering, as the boundaries of the exercises are set by the service user rather than predetermined by the practitioner.

Co-working, reflective teams and circular questions

Systemic family therapy techniques can be very helpful in ascertaining other people's perspectives on the cause

A closer look

Genograms and ecomaps

Assessing the usefulness of visual techniques, Parker and Bradley (2003) conclude that they have numerous benefits:

- they facilitate the disclosure of unanticipated information
- the information gathered is more comprehensive
- the inclusive and non-judgemental approach encourages service users to engage in discussion about their circumstances
- the indirect approach to the assessment task is non-threatening and enables a positive rapport to be established with service users
- the experience of actively participating in the identification of relevant information and the analysis of its significance is empowering for service

users, who can as a result feel more in control of their lives
- the collaborative nature of the exercise minimises the power differentials between practitioner and service user.

Parker and Bradley (2003: 41) do issue a caution, however, emphasising that the effectiveness of these exercises can be diminished if practitioners are not attentive to their emotional impact. Unanticipated reactions can arise, for example, when service users identify patterns in relationships, changes in their social circumstances or reflect on long-buried family events. It is at these points that the quality of the relationship the practitioner has established is put to the test. The capacities to monitor one's own responses and to be self-aware are important professional resources.

---

of concern (see Chapter 12 on interventions for a fuller discussion of systems theory and systemic therapy). Most systemic therapists choose to co-work, in order to help them understand as accurately as possible a family's circumstances. While co-working is less common in social work settings, we would argue there are grounds for it being more widely adopted as an effective and efficient use of resources (see Chapter 1). It can be of particular value in the assessment process as it challenges an individual's subjective assessment and encourages dialogue about constructed understandings.

A creative form of co-working derived from the field of family therapy is the reflective team (Andersen, 1987). In the reflective team model, two or more practitioners engage with the service user(s), with one practitioner taking the lead. Following the initial stages of the assessment meeting, service users are invited to listen to a reflective conversation between the practitioners. In this conversation the practitioners, in front of the service user(s) concerned, reflect on and are curious about the thoughts, ideas, questions, uncertainties and hypotheses that have arisen for them during the meeting. The notion of curiosity is an important one (Cecchin, 1987). The service users are then invited to respond. From this position of curiosity and from the reflective conversation, it is possible to begin to construct new understandings of the situation, and creative responses.

Case study

Tamsin cont . . .

Two social workers met with Tamsin, Mel and Shane as part of the initial assessment process. The meeting focused on how the family managed the care of Tamsin, and who was concerned about what. Each person was invited to explain what they thought worked and did not work in the family. After this section of the meeting was completed, the two social workers had a conversation with each other in front of the family. One of the workers commented on how she had noticed that Shane had lots of thoughts about the family's difficulties and appeared concerned about the school's actions, but she had been aware that whenever Mel voiced her opinion Shane spoke over her. She wondered what Mel felt about this. The other worker similarly commented that when Shane did this she observed that Tamsin looked at her mother and appeared a little worried.

When the family were invited to respond to the workers' reflective conversation, Mel immediately acknowledged how she felt 'silenced' by Shane, and the workers commented that on this occasion Shane kept quiet until he was asked what he thought by a social worker.

A closer look

Using circular questions

Circular questions are invaluable in enabling the therapist to think relationally, and therefore systemically, and enable therapist and client to make new connections. They:

- Broaden the frame from the individual to inter-action
- Shift from linear cause–effect to inter-action
- Demonstrate the importance of relationship
- Bring forth unheard voices
- Make connections between the meaning of important events
- Make links between the present, future hopes, and past stories
- Keep therapist's curiosity alive
- Help the client become more curious about their own life
- Enable both parties to test out and refute hypotheses
- Introduce news of difference
- Open space for new connections
- Enable therapists to respect the client as the expert in their life
- Change the stories.

(Hedges, 2005: 99)

One of the strengths of this practice technique is that it is transparent, inclusive and respectful of everyone's position. Another useful technique that fosters inclusive practice but which simultaneously opens up new perspectives for families on their circumstances are circular questions (see the Closer Look box).

In Tamsin's case, a circular question that might be posed to Tamsin's mother is: '*What do you think most concerns Shane about the situation at home?*' The question to Tamsin might be: '*When your mum gets upset who is most worried in your family?*' And to Shane: '*What do you think Mel would most like to change about the current situation?*'

As the Closer Look box illustrates, the power of this approach lies in its ability to emphasise the connections between people and how small shifts in perception can elicit significant change. Tamsin's mother's response to the question she was asked acknowledged that she recognised that Shane was jealous of her close relationship with her sister, whom she trusted more to take Tamsin to school. This admission enabled them to discuss openly how Shane

could be more actively involved in caring for Tamsin, and shifted the power relations within the family.

Observation

An earlier Think Ahead box highlighted the value practitioners place on opportunities to observe, in this instance children, and the impact such experiences can have on assessment skills. Observation is widely recognised to be an invaluable source of learning (Le Riche and Tanner, 1998). All too often social work practitioners feel compelled to problem-solve and act without allowing sufficient time for observing a situation, digesting the information and ideas generated by the encounter and formulating a thoughtful plan. Practitioners who have had experience of following the Tavistock model of observation are confronted by the tension between 'being' and 'doing', and come to recognise that simply 'being' and observing are not passive or self-indulgent activities. Exposure to observation experiences helps equip practitioners with skills for the assessment process that include:

- an ability to stand back from a natural inclination or perceived expectation to intervene;
- heightened self-awareness;
- recognising the subjective nature of assessments and the importance of giving thoughtful consideration to the reasons for the hypotheses and speculations they have about an individual/situation;
- understanding of the importance of assessment over time;
- enhanced ability to tolerate uncertainty and 'not knowing', for as Milner and O'Byrne (2002: 4) acknowledge, 'Uncertainty is the beginning of hopefulness.'

Evaluative studies of the educational and professional benefits of child observation provide evidence which suggests that practitioners find the observational experience worthwhile and of benefit for their professional practice (Miles, 2002). We would argue that these findings have wider applicability to observation with all service user groups. Practitioners identified the experience of learning to suspend 'knowing' and tolerating uncertainty, enhanced-self awareness and greater understanding of the emotional development of children to be particularly valuable discoveries:

'The process of giving emotional attention to what is observed and the deliberate delaying of "knowing" facilitates in practice the kind of measured assessment that is blocked if stereotypes and prejudices are unthinkingly adopted . . . The qualitatively different level of involvement that observation demands creates "learning from experience" and its concomitant emotional experience and change. This contrasts with "learning about" in which there is merely an addition to the stock of knowledge without emotional engagement and therefore without change.'   (Briggs, 1992: 60)

Stage three: Mutually determined analysis – developing and prescribing a plan of intervention

Developing a shared understanding of the difficulty being addressed is challenging but crucial to an effective assessment outcome. At this stage of the assessment process it is of fundamental importance that consideration is given, not simply to the risk elements presented by the situation but that equal attention is paid to the needs of the individuals concerned and the availability and suitability of resources. Emphasising the partnership component of the assessment process and drawing on strengths-based perspectives help to overcome the challenging nature of this stage of the process. Realistic assessments, however, have to recognise that in cases where the assessment of risk is to the fore, such as in child protection or mental health cases, mutually determined and agreed analyses of the situation can be difficult to reach. In such cases, transparent disagreements can prove equally effective in establishing honest and open relationships that underpin further interventions. Collaborative strategies must not override the place of the social worker's professional judgement. What they must do is incorporate into the assessment process the professional perspective alongside the service user's views and judgements.

Inevitably the dynamic and spiralling nature of the assessment process can mean the circumstances under consideration alter in the course of the assessment and also are altered by the assessment process. The interaction between assessment and service user experience needs to be retained as a central component of the process and not overlooked. Features of this stage of the assessment process can include:

- Risk–benefit analysis: collaboratively drawing up with the service user a table of the anticipated risks, safety factors and benefits of different courses of action.
- Reflective conversations between practitioners in front of service users and with service users: ensuring attention is paid to the process of assessment as well as to its content. This approach enables unasked questions

to be posed hypothetically, for speculations to be mooted and areas where there is a lack of clarity to be identified.

- Research evidence: consideration of existing evidence that can inform actions.
- Critical review of respective roles to ensure oppressive or discriminatory positions have been addressed and that an inclusive, ecological approach has informed the process.

Case study

Tamsin cont . . .

In discussing the school's concerns Mel and Shane recognise that Mel does not trust Shane to understand Tamsin's specific needs, and so has not been willing to allow him to take care of Tamsin as much as he feels able to do. The assessment process enabled Mel and Shane to come to an agreement about which aspects of Tamsin's care Mel felt Shane could manage. It was agreed Shane would take Tamsin to school on a regular basis which meant Sharon, Mel's sister, would only be required in emergencies.

Tamsin's concerns about Shane shouting at her were also discussed. Shane felt his lack of understanding of Tamsin's condition meant he got frustrated by her slow responses to his requests. Mel accepted she had not really talked to Shane about Tamsin's abilities and said she would take the time to do this. The school also offered to talk with Shane and had some helpful suggestions of activities that would help the family learn together about what was in Tamsin's best interests.

Stage four: Collaborative intervention strategy

Endings always relate to beginnings: they are influenced by them and are influences on them. If a clear remit for the assessment process has been identified at the outset it enhances the likelihood of a more effective and accurate outcome being reached. The cyclical nature of the assessment process (Figure 10.2) necessitates practitioners referring back to the initial definition of the situation to assess how accurately, or not, it has been identified and responded to. It is hoped that if this cyclical and reflexive behaviour has permeated the assessment process then the recommended course of action should come as no surprise and should have evolved out of the discussions that have taken place.

In the face of the chronic shortage of resources, creative responses to the circumstances service users experience are important. By encouraging identification of service user strengths and more positive approaches to 'problem definition', there is greater scope for creative proposals to be generated. Suggestions derived from the service user, as opposed to the professional, stand a greater chance of being effective and sustainable. This is where it is essential that an ecological and holistic assessment has been undertaken, as often hidden resources/solutions are located in the wider social setting of the service user. Clearly in cases where the levels of risk are higher, balancing what service users are suggesting should be done and what practitioners assess to be appropriate is challenging and the concept of partnership working is stretched.

Written records of what has been agreed and how it will be reviewed are an integral part of ending an assessment. As has been highlighted earlier, the divide between assessment, planning and interventions is essentially artificial and subject to continual review through the reflective cycle.

Features at this stage of the assessment process include:

- review of initial concerns to check they have all been addressed in the assessment process;
- clear and succinct written agreements with action plans, timetables for review and explicit statements about what will happen if the agreement is breached by any participant;
- inclusive communication with all relevant people to maximise effectiveness of proposed plans.

Case study

Tamsin cont . . .

At this stage the social worker felt the family were taking on board the school's concerns and did not feel any further help was needed. It was agreed that the situation would be reviewed after six weeks in a meeting with the family and the school.

Supervision

At the outset of this chapter the centrality of reflective practice to sound assessments was emphasised. Chapter 1 examines the nature of reflective practice and the forums facilitating it and discusses the role of supervision in greater detail. Suffice to say here that relationship-based approaches to assessment require practitioners to draw on all their cognitive and affective faculties and to engage in a holistic and dynamic process. Supervision is a vital forum where practitioners should be able to reflect on their practice and the collaborative, but nonetheless professional, judgements they are required to make. The extent to which the social worker feels able to be open and honest about their thoughts and feeling in supervision is likely to be mirrored in their assessment practices.

Conclusion

Collaborative and creative assessments are appropriate and ethical professional approaches that recognise the expertise and experiences of the people with whom the assessment is compiled. Simultaneously it can be argued that such approaches to assessment are necessary and efficient within the resource-deficient contexts that social work is located. Without abandoning their professional identity, practitioners are required to work in partnership with service users and to engage in mutually agreed and understood conversations that can effectively and realistically identify and tackle the difficulties being encountered. The complexity of the task must not be underestimated, nor the need for well-developed interpersonal and organisational social work skills. The challenges of undertaking 'good' assessments are currently being addressed by the imperative to develop common assessment processes that encapsulate the different multi-professional perspectives of contemporary practice. For social work practitioners it is crucial that they can promote the centrality of the relationship in the assessment process and the different but equally important expertise that resides in those individuals being assessed and those responsible for undertaking the assessment.

Key learning points

This chapter has covered the following learning points:

- ✔ Assessments in social work are challenging and their nature is contested.

- ✔ Relationship-based perspectives on assessment distinguish between tools for undertaking assessment and the process or relationship through which the assessment is mediated. Assessment guidance and checklists should not become the end in themselves as has been the case in the past, but a means to an end.

- ✔ Effective relationship-based models of assessment are dynamic and require social workers to practise in a collaborative and relational manner.

- ✔ Sound assessments require skilled practitioners who are able to draw on specific theoretical perspectives and assessment tools: for example, the exchange and ecological models, reflective conversations, circular questions and observation skills.

- ✔ Relationship-based assessments require social workers to maintain a reflective stance throughout the process.

 ## Further reading

Baldwin, N. and Walker, L. (2005) 'Assessment', in Adams, R., Dominelli, L. and Payne, M. (eds), *Social Work Futures: Crossing Boundaries, Transforming Practice*, Basingstoke: Palgrave Macmillan. A readable and relevant chapter that introduces an ecologically based, reflective model of assessment.

Martin, R. (2010) *Social Work Assessment*, Exeter: Learning Matters. A basic introductory book on generic assessment practices.

Milner, J. and O'Byrne, P. (2002) 'Assessment and planning', in Adams, R., Dominelli, L. and Payne, M. (eds), *Critical Practice in Social Work*, Basingstoke: Palgrave Macmillan. A condensed version of the ideas presented in the textbook by the same authors, which provides an accessible account of social constructivist approaches to assessment.

Parker, J. (2007) 'The process of social work: assessment, planning, intervention and review', in Lymbery, M. and Postle, K. (eds) *Social Work : A Companion to Learning*, London: Sage. An accessible and up-to-date overview of assessment within a broader framework of social work intervention.

Smale, G., Tuson, G. and Stratham, D. (2000) *Social Work and Social Problems: Working towards Social inclusion and Social Change*, Basingstoke: Macmillan. Provides a detailed account of the Exchange Model of practice (chapters 7 and 10 particularly relevant).

Statham, D. and Kearney, P. (2007) 'Models of assessment', in Lishman, J. (ed.) *Handbook for Practice Learning in Social Work and Social Care: Knowledge and Theory*, London: Jessica Kingsley.

Useful websites

www.dh.gov.uk and **www.dfes.gov.uk**
Government websites containing up-to-date publications that inform and influence assessment processes.

www.cfswp
The website of the Centre for Social Work Practice that promotes relationship-based approaches to social work.

www.rip.org.uk/publications
Includes a comprehensive literature review in the field of children and families on Analysis and Critical Thinking in Assessment.

For additional cases and topic-organised, clickable links into additional media resources, including those produced by IRISS, visit **www.pearsoned.co.uk/wilsonruch**

Activity

Food for thought

Go to the Centre for Social Work Practice website and read the speech given by Olive Stevenson at the launch of the Centre in April 2006. Think about how her comments on the purpose and role of social work fit with the emphasis in this chapter on relationship-based assessment.

Ecomaps

With another student or friend:

- first, take it in turns to compile your own ecomaps. When facilitating the construction of the other person's ecomap, note which aspects of their ecomap you are more curious about. Ask the other student which bits of your ecomap they were curious about.
- secondly, related to the issue that made you curious, see if you can identify a circular question that you could pose to your partner in this exercise.

Chapter 11
Communication skills

Chapter summary

Communication is central to all relationships and this chapter focuses on the characteristics of effective interpersonal communication in professional contexts. In this chapter we shall look at three core characteristics of effective communication: empathy, authenticity and respect. The chapter emphasises how for communication to be effective these characteristics must be integral components of communication in all the different stages of professional relationships – beginnings, middles and endings – regardless of whether the relationship is in the context of a one-off encounter or a more sustained professional intervention. Three specific challenges arising from communicating with service users are explored: dealing with aggressive behaviours, dealing with silence and dealing with emotional pain. Four sections on communication with specific service-user groups – children and young people, people with mental health difficulties, people with disabilities and older people – bring the chapter to a close.

Learning objectives

This chapter covers topics that will enable you to achieve the following learning objectives:

- To understand the ingredients of effective communication
- To understand the importance of demonstrating empathy, authenticity and respect when communicating with service users
- To recognise the key features of communication at different stages of the professional relationship and in different contexts
- To be introduced to some of the most common challenges in communicating with service users: responding to emotional pain, aggression and silence
- To be able to identify strategies for addressing these challenges
- To be familiar with the specific issues arising from communicating with different service user groups.

We are grateful to Rachael Clawson's contribution of material relating to communications with disabled adults and children to this chapter.

National Occupational Standards

This chapter will help you to meet the following National Occupational Standards:

Key Role 1: Prepare for, and work with individuals, families, carers, groups and communities to assess their needs and circumstances

Unit 1   Prepare for social work contact and involvement

Unit 2   Work with individuals, families, carers, groups and communities to help them make informed decisions

Unit 3   Assess needs and options to recommend a course of action

Key Role 2: Plan, carry out, review and evaluate social work practice, with individuals, families, carers, groups, communities and other professionals

Unit 4   Respond to crisis situations

Unit 5   Interact with individuals, families, carers, groups and communities to achieve change and development and to improve life opportunities

Unit 6   Prepare, produce, implement and evaluate plans with individuals, families, carers, groups, communities and professional colleagues

Unit 9   Address behaviour which presents a risk to individuals, families, carers, groups and communities

Key Role 3: Support individuals to represent their needs, views and circumstances. Advocate with and on behalf of people

Unit 10   Advocate with, and on behalf of, individuals, families, carers, groups and communities

Case study

Marianne

Jo, a white, newly qualified social worker based at a day centre for people with physical disabilities, is visiting a service user for the first time. Marianne, a 30-year-old, white British woman who has cerebral palsy has been referred to the day centre and Jo needs to make an assessment of Marianne's needs. On arrival at Marianne's home, Jo is greeted by Marianne's mother who talks to Jo in the hall for the first ten minutes of the visit and tells her about Marianne. Jo is taken into Marianne's downstairs bedroom and introduced to Marianne who is in a wheelchair. Marianne has limited mobility in her lower body, limited coordination in her upper body and a speech impediment. Jo notices that shortly after she arrived Marianne became tearful. Neither Jo nor Marianne's mother comments on this. While Jo is with Marianne, she stands next to Marianne's mother, who has remained in the room and answers the questions Jo raises. When she is about to leave Jo spends a further ten minutes talking with Marianne's mother in the hall.

Think about your response to this scenario. How do you think Marianne felt about this encounter? Do you think Jo could have improved her communication with Marianne and, if yes, in what way?

If you were the social worker involved with Marianne and her mother, your role would require you to provide a clear assessment report of Marianne's circumstances and her eligibility for daycare services. To achieve this goal requires you to be able to communicate effectively with Marianne. By demonstrating an understanding of Marianne's emotional as well as her physical circumstances you can begin to communicate empathically, authentically and respectfully with Marianne. Achieving empathic, respectful and authentic communication, however, is not easy, as is illustrated above by the behaviour of Marianne's mother. This chapter explores how effective communication skills can be developed and the challenges that can be encountered in the emotionally demanding world of social work practice.

Introduction

The requirements determining the curriculum content of social work degrees, often referred to as 'the benchmark statement' (QAA, 2000), and the National Occupational Standards (TOPSS, 2002) that are identified by employers and define professional practice, stipulate that qualifying social workers must be able to demonstrate sound communication skills. This requirement appears to be self-evident as, by definition, relationships, professional or personal, are built on communication. However, there is a big gap between being able to communicate and being able to communicate effectively. Effective professional relationships with service users, and for that matter other professionals, are dependent on practitioners acquiring well-developed communication skills. What constitutes effective communication and what qualities or skills are required to be an effective communicator?

Communication involves both listening and responding to service users but the form this communication takes varies: for example, letters, case recordings and reports exemplify written forms of communication and home visits, office interviews and formal review meetings involve verbal communication. The biggest challenge of writing a chapter on communication skills is trying to identify which core skills to cover. We recognise that in deciding to concentrate in this chapter on the interpersonal, face-to-face communication skills, we are excluding important aspects of practice, in particular written communication skills. Useful texts that address these aspects of practice can be found in the Further Reading section at the end of the chapter. Our rationale for the decision to focus on interpersonal, face-to-face communication lies in our belief that there are some fundamental communication skills that underpin all forms of communication. These skills are an ability to demonstrate empathy, respect and authenticity. Without these fundamental skills in place, we would argue, all other forms of communication are impaired.

We start this chapter by focusing on how you can begin to develop empathic, respectful and authentic forms of communication. The second section builds on these qualities and considers the specific characteristics and skills involved in communicating with service users at the start, in the middle and at the end of a professional relationship, whether it is a one-off encounter or a sustained intervention. Three of the most common challenges of communicating with service users form the focus of the third section – dealing with aggression, dealing with pain and dealing with silence – before we move on to the fourth

and final section which looks at the specific communication skills required when working with different service-user groups.

Core characteristics of effective communication

Many social work students identify themselves as good listeners. However, when they come to undertake skills modules as part of their qualifying programmes, they discover that listening is a more demanding skill than they had first thought.

In order to listen and communicate effectively we need to make an individual feel they have been understood on two levels: first, intellectually or cognitively and secondly, emotionally or affectively. The first level of understanding requires attentive and accurate listening, with attention paid to the content of the communication, i.e. the factual information. At first glance it might appear to be relatively straightforward, except that it is invariably shaped and made more complicated by the emotional/affective level of listening. For this second level of listening to be undertaken effectively you need to be able to recognise and respond to what is being communicated, both verbally and non-verbally. It is estimated that approximately two-thirds of communication is non-verbal, i.e. something is communicated through 'body language': by a body movement, a posture, an inflection of the voice (Birdwhistell, 1970, cited in Trevithick, 2005). The work of the counsellor, Carl Rogers, has become influential within social work training and practice. Rogers developed the person-centred approaches that focus on empathic, respectful and authentic responses to emotionally charged situations (Rogers, 1951, 1961). By developing these skills practitioners can enhance their capacity to listen effectively at both levels of listening referred to above.

Reflect

Think about a recent conversation you have had where you have been discussing something that you are worried about or are having difficulty with, e.g. it may be a visit to your GP because of health concern, talking about a personal issue with a friend, discussing your worries about your academic progress with your tutor.

Which aspects of this encounter did you find helpful? Can you identify how the person who listened showed empathy towards you?

Empathy

A definition of empathy is that it

'involves attempting to put ourselves in another person's place, in the hope that we can feel and understand another person's emotions, thoughts, actions and motives. Empathy involves trying to understand, as carefully and sensitively as possible, the nature of another person's experience, their own unique point of view, and what meaning this conveys for that individual.'
(Trevithick, 2005: 81)

In order to develop empathic listening skills practitioners need to become attuned to the ways in which emotions are expressed. Another term for empathy is emotional attunement: the capacity of a professional to recognise what a service user is feeling (Koprowska, 2005). To become emotionally attuned involves paying close attention to the verbal and body language of the service user: how do they articulate/describe their situation, what specific words do they use, how did they come into the room or greet you, how are they sitting, do they look relaxed or strained, is their body language and their verbal language congruent, i.e. expressing the same message? It is not uncommon in a one-to-one situation, such as interviews with service users, for social workers to find their own body language mirroring that of the service user. For example, a worker talking with a depressed young man, who has recently attempted suicide and whose responses are subdued by medication, might find herself feeling very tired and lethargic in her responses to him and more slumped in the chair than would be normal for her. Alternatively the internalised anger that depressed people often experience can, unconsciously, be communicated and the worker can feel frustrated or angry but be surprised by their reaction as they are unable to make sense of these feelings in terms of their own experiences. Such responses arise from the unconscious dimension of the relationship between the service user and the practitioner and represent an unconscious form of communication (see Chapter 12 on interventions for psychodynamic approaches). A practitioner's acknowledgment to the service user of what they are feeling can be surprisingly effective as the service user feels accurately – empathically – understood. In his Progress Report (2009) following the death of the toddler Peter Connelly, Lord Laming underlined the importance of practitioners being able to express empathy by putting 'themselves in the place of the child or young person' and considering 'first and foremost how the situation must feel for them.' (p. 22) For children, Laming emphasised, non-verbal indicators such as bedwetting and headbanging can be their means of communicating distress.

There is a fine line to be trod, however, between being an empathic and emotionally attuned social worker and the role of a psychotherapist. The distinction is not an absolute one as all relationships have more or less explicit unconscious dimensions. It is not the role of the social worker, however, to engage in primarily therapeutic encounters, which explore and interpret the unconscious lives of service users. Attending exclusively to a service user's internal world, i.e. how they experience and make sense of and give meaning to their circumstances, and the role and impact of unconscious processes on professional relationships, puts the social worker in the role of a therapist and minimises the significance of the service user's social context. Conversely, by paying insufficient attention to the service user's internal world, practitioners run the risk of ignoring an important source of information that can enhance the quality of their involvement with the service user concerned. The challenge for social workers, as recognised in Chapter 12, is to balance the interplay between the internal and the external worlds of service users.

Accurate empathy, according to Egan (1994), requires the listener to respond to an individual in a way that accurately reflects the person's experience, behaviours and feelings. To begin to practise and develop empathic listening skills, you might like to try the following exercise devised by Gerard Egan.

Think ahead

Ask someone to tell you about a recent experience that had an emotional impact, positive or negative. Once they have described the event try in the first instance to use the following formula:

'You........... (describe experience)
'You........... (describe their response/action)
'You felt..... (describe their emotional reaction paying attention to its intensity, e.g. *extremely* angry, *slightly* upset, and as far as possible using their words)

Once you are familiar with the ingredients of empathic statements you can individualise them to suit your own style.

A closer look

Psychodynamic terms

Psychodynamic terms refer to psychological concepts that recognise the role that the unconscious plays in our behaviours. The unconscious refers to those aspects of our behaviour, thoughts and feelings that we are not consciously aware of. While the unconscious – 'the idea that a large part of our mental life is not accessible to us' (Trowell, 1995) – was not an entirely new concept at the turn of the nineteenth century, Sigmund Freud, the founder of psychoanalysis, brought it into the public domain and the individuals who followed him – Anna Freud (Sigmund Freud's daughter), Melanie Klein, Wilfred Bion and Donald Winnicott – developed his ideas further. Many psychodynamic concepts have become familiar terms, e.g. 'he's in denial' or 'she's being defensive', but they are not always fully understood. Listed below are the most relevant ones for social workers.

Defence mechanisms – these are behaviours which an individual resorts to when overwhelmed by anxiety, as a means of keeping the anxiety in the unconscious; the most commonly referred to are:

■ denial – refusing to accept something
■ repression – avoiding a difficult experience by forgetting it
■ regression – behaving as if at a younger developmental stage in response to a stressful event.

Transference – placing feelings and expectations linked to past significant relationships (the primary caregivers) into a current one, e.g. an adult behaving towards his/her female boss as if they were his/her mother and expecting similar responses to those characterising that earlier relationship.

Counter-transference – the feelings stirred up in the 'therapist' in response to the client's experiences, which may mirror those of the client or belong to the therapist themselves. Disentangling the two types of counter-transference is an important task.

Projection – the capacity to place into someone else's psyche unwanted aspects of one's own; splitting the 'good' and 'bad' aspects of the self and disowning the unacceptable 'bad' bits.

Reflect

Refer back to the case study of Marianne that opened the chapter. How do you think Jo could have been more empathic towards Marianne? Using the exercise above, what might she have said to Marianne?

Authenticity

Taken to the extreme, as the cartoon overleaf illustrates, there can be a danger when drawing on counselling skills in social work contexts to resort to depersonalised, caricatured responses to an individual's situation. Being empathic does not mean becoming robotic or mechanistic. It does mean being authentic. If you are to develop your empathic skills successfully you will also need to understand what it means to be authentic and how you put this into practice. It is not uncommon in undertaking interpersonal skills training workshops with social work students for them to report feeling that they are not being true to themselves when engaged in

the listening exercise they undertake. When asked to explain their feeling it transpires that they are seeking to behave in ways they think are expected of an effective listener, and adopt postures or behaviours they are not comfortable with. For some students, sitting in a 'counselling pose', i.e. legs uncrossed, hands on lap, still posture, feels uncomfortable and unfamiliar. While it is unhelpful to sit in a defensive position with arms and legs crossed or to fidget excessively, adopting a sitting position with which you feel comfortable and which is welcoming of the service user should guide how you position yourself. From this comfortable place you enhance the likelihood of attuning yourself and being empathic towards the service user you are meeting.

As the above example illustrates, accurate empathy and authenticity are inseparable. To be able to be empathic you need to be authentic. Authenticity is the congruence between what the worker says, what they feel and what they do; it is the ability to relate to others with integrity; to be able to engage with others 'person to person' while at the same time being aware of and

(Copyright Harry Venning 2000)

using their own feelings and values as well as the resources of their agency role and the other roles they occupy. If, as is the case with the students referred to above, you relate to a service user in a way with which you are not comfortable, it is highly unlikely you will be sufficiently attentive to the service user to be empathic. Your energy and attention are more likely to be absorbed in dealing with your own feelings of discomfort about how you are behaving. It can be helpful to think of authenticity as the conversation you are having in your head while engaging with the service user, the conversation that is not articulated at the time but which afterwards is often expressed to yourself or a colleague. It is not uncommon for social workers to find themselves after an interview commenting to a colleague how confused or frustrated, for example, they felt about an encounter. What they had not managed to do is to identify and acknowledge their feelings of confusion or frustration with the service user concerned. If these feelings can be articulated while you are with the service user, the second level of understanding is communicated and the service user has the opportunity to share their own feelings of confusion and frustration. From this example it is possible to see how authentic responses contribute to more effective communication.

Reflect

Thinking back to the case study of Marianne, how would you have demonstrated that you were authentic and empathic?

To prompt your response you might wish to consider the following:

- *Would you feel comfortable talking with Marianne's mother before and after speaking with Marianne? If you felt uncomfortable about this, how might it show itself and what might you do about it?*
- *What would you feel about conducting an interview in a bedroom? How might it affect what you do and say? How could you address this with Marianne if you are uncomfortable with this arrangement? How would you feel and respond to Marianne becoming tearful? How might you respond to Marianne's mother being the spokesperson for Marianne? What is the effect of your knowing Marianne has a speech impediment? Does it inhibit how you relate to her? How might you address this?*

If you can think about authenticity and congruence in your work it will contribute not only to your empathic capacity but also to the extent to which you show respect to service users, the third core communication skill that we will now turn to and consider.

Respect

In Chapter 5 you were introduced to 'respect for persons' as one of the fundamental cornerstones of social work practice, which is enshrined in the General Social Care Council's Code of Practice. 'Respect for persons' is the ability to communicate acceptance and valuation of people irrespective of their personal qualities and social or professional position. While you are unlikely to encounter a social worker who would dispute respect for persons as a core component of good social work practice, what you may discover is a limited ability to articulate how it is demonstrated in practice. As with empathy and authenticity, we would argue that respect is inseparable from these two core qualities. Empathic and authentic relationships engender respectful professional relationships. The consistent message of service users to social workers is their wish for honest, transparent relationships (Doel, 2010). This does not mean that you can always meet all the expectations of a service user but that you are clear from the outset about your role, remit and resources. Out of honesty and transparency come reciprocally respectful relationships: professional towards service user, and service user towards professional.

By referring back to the last 'reflect' question about the relationship Jo developed with Marianne, you can perhaps see how Jo's initial contact with Marianne did not appear to demonstrate respect for Marianne. Your answers to these questions might have shown how a more empathic and authentic approach, e.g. by going down to Marianne's level in her wheelchair, talking initially with Marianne, checking out how she wanted her mother involved and acknowledging Marianne's distress, communicates 'respect for persons' and contributes to establishing a relationship built on respect. Some of the skills and practical strategies for developing genuinely respectful relationships are explored in the following section where we consider the different stages of working with service users.

Contexts of communication

In this section we address issues arising from the context of communication. We are concentrating primarily on the communication skills associated with the beginning, middle and end phases of interventions with service users, whether they are the beginning, middle and end phases of a one-off encounter or of a sequence of meetings. Inevitably, all aspects of communication can come up at any stage of a professional encounter or intervention. For example, paraphrasing, discussed in relation to the middle phases of an intervention, is not a communication skill exclusive to this stage. Paraphrasing can be equally important in the early stages, particularly if you are deluged with information. It is important, therefore, when reading these sections to have a flexible mindset about where, when and how you might be required to communicate in a particular way. Developing such a flexible approach is an integral aspect of developing your reflective practitioner identity, discussed in Chapter 1.

Beginning the communication process

Reflect

Think about your first meeting with someone in a position of authority, e.g. a teacher, your practice educator, an employer. What made it 'work/not work'? How did you/they plan for it?

The significance of beginnings cannot be underestimated (see Chapter 10 on assessment). It is often apparent when reviewing social work involvement with an individual or family that what happened at the beginning reflects how you experienced your involvement throughout. For example, unclear, 'messy' beginnings with perhaps a missed appointment before you actually meet can be mirrored throughout the rest of your involvement in blurred time boundaries and unclear expectations of each other. Conversely, relationships that begin in a clear and straightforward way frequently continue in this manner. Social work students frequently comment on how evidence of their placement having been thoughtfully planned for, for example arriving to find a desk equipped with stationery and appropriate documents, contributes to their feeling welcome and valued by the team. In a similar way being well prepared for meetings with service users, whether an initial meeting or follow-up ones, is an important building block for a positive respectful working alliance.

Where to meet

Think ahead

You are planning a meeting to see a family comprising two parents and two school-aged children, a toddler and a baby, where there have been concerns raised by the school and health visitor about how the children are being cared for.

How would you decide on where to meet? What do you think might be the challenges of seeing the family in their own home, in the school/health clinic/children's services office?

Before you can begin to think about how you will communicate face to face with a service user it is important to give some thought to where the meeting will take place. Most social workers meet service users in their own homes. Other venues might include an office, clinic or other professional work base, e.g. a school, hospital or prison or public spaces such as cafés. The location of meetings is an important feature of social work practice and one which needs to be carefully thought about.

In many respects the principles of good practice apply regardless of setting. Service user feedback emphasises the value they place on social workers being:

- clear about the purpose and nature of their visit/ meeting, i.e. what will be discussed, how long it will last, who will be present, what will happen next;
- responsible in their use of the information that service users disclose, and responsive to their requests, even if they cannot meet them satisfactorily;
- reliable in carrying out what they say they will do, e.g. turning up on time, actioning tasks agreed on.

The main distinction between venues for meetings is the power differentials. Part of the challenge of doing home visits is that unlike in the office they are outside of your control. It is not uncommon, for example, to turn up to find different people present to those you had anticipated meeting with. The impact of interruptions, e.g. visitors, phone calls or the distractions of a television that might be on, on an interview require you as a social worker to be proactive in creating conditions that are conducive to an effective interview but which fully respect that you are in the family's home. One of the disadvantages of office/clinic-based work is that the power over the setting clearly resides with the professional, a situation which can leave a service user feeling quite disempowered. Recognising these power dynamics is fundamental to practising and communicating in an anti-oppressive and anti-discriminatory manner. By adopting a transparent approach that allows for the format and content of the meeting to be made clear from the outset, some of the power differentials can be minimised. In developing skills in home/office-based visiting it can be helpful to draw on the approach taken within therapeutic work, i.e. being clear about time boundaries and endeavouring to stick to them, and when arranging a home visit encouraging the family to try to ensure the time will be uninterrupted to maximise its usefulness. In this way the time set aside is valued and respectfully used and neither family nor professional needs to feel 'trapped' in an indefinitely long encounter or 'frustrated' by an unproductive meeting.

What to say and do

What makes for a 'good' communication in the early stages of professional involvement?

- **Verbal clarity:** as part of establishing a clear and respectful relationship it can be helpful to clarify with the service user how they would like you to refer to them, e.g. by formal title or their first name. It is important to have prepared yourself with the relevant background information and procedural knowledge so that you are equipped to address the issues raised. Being prepared to establish the nature of your involvement clearly from the outset is vital, but also being able to adapt your use of language to the circumstances you encounter is equally important. At all costs avoid using jargon, abbreviations or acronyms which can bewilder or intimidate service users and be experienced as excluding and disempowering. As part of being clear and transparent with service users it is essential that the issue of confidentiality is raised in the first meeting. When it is clear that your involvement will be more than one meeting, it can be helpful to draw up a written agreement with the individuals concerned to ensure a shared understanding of the purpose of the social work intervention. Included in the written agreement can be a confidentiality statement that clearly spells out the boundaries of confidentiality and how and when they would need to be breached. This level of clarity can be particularly important in situations where emotions are 'running high', for example when it is a statutory intervention where service users' involvement is not voluntary.
- **Physical contact:** it can be very helpful in establishing a relationship if some form of physical contact is established. A handshake, as Trevithick (2005) recognises, can be an appropriate and helpful professional gesture that can communicate important messages to service users of respect and acceptance, particularly for those with poor self-esteem. Cultural sensitivity is important, however, as handshakes may not always be meaningful or appropriate and professional discretion and intuition is required in all cases.
- **Non-verbal communication:** given that a large proportion of our communication is non-verbal, body language is another important way of communicating and understanding others' communications. It is important and informative to note how someone looks: do they have an anxious, disinterested or sad face, for example, and are they looking relaxed with open body posture or defensive with crossed arms and closed body position? Developing your observational skills as well as your conversational skills will enhance the effectiveness of your communication and contribute to your empathic understanding.

A closer look

Non-verbal communication

Trevithick (2005:121), in her book *Social Work Skills*, draws on the work of Kadushin and Kadushin (1997: 287–320) who identify seven types of non-verbal communication, of which body language is one.

- **Chronomics** (timekeeping, such as the likelihood of people being too early or too late, promptness)
- **Artificial communication** (the language of the physical setting, such as how the home is arranged and personal presentation, such as personal dress, state of clothes)
- **Smell** (emotional states communicated through subtle changes in body odour)
- **Touch** (handshaking, hugs; these tend to be defined according to situation and cultural norms)
- **Paralinguistics** (cues that depend on hearing and how words are said in terms of their tone, pitch, volume, speed, emphasis, intonation, articulation and intensity)
- **Proxemics** (communication through space and distance; the distance people need in order to feel comfortable)
- **Body language kinesics** (visual communication through the face, eyes, hands and arms, feet and legs).

- **Open questions:** in beginning to develop a relationship with a service user it is important that you seek to ensure that the information gathered:
    - incorporates the views of the person concerned;
    - minimises the professional assumptions that can be made about an individual's circumstances;
    - facilitates the development of anti-oppressive and empowering relationships with service users.

To develop the communication skills that contribute to such relationships the use of questions in professional encounters needs careful attention. It is all too easy to start an interview or meeting by bombarding the service user with a list of questions. Such professional behaviours usually are indicative of two factors: first, anxiety about completing the task satisfactorily and secondly, the bureaucratic expectations derived from the organisational context in which social workers operate that require

---

A closer look

Using closed and open questions

Examples of closed questions might be: '*Has your situation improved?*' or '*Are you feeling better today?*'

In contrast, open questions allow the service user to determine their own answer, rather than respond to your presumptions – '*How are you?*'

By becoming familiar with using open questions, social workers immediately demonstrate an interest in the service user that is not constrained to those aspects of their lives which fit certain eligibility criteria, but in the whole person. A more 'open' question is preferable particularly in the early stages of developing a relationship. It is not uncommon for referrals to social services, particularly if they are self-referrals, to have a 'presenting problem'. A 'presenting problem' (see Chapter 10 on assessment) is one which is usually easier for the service user to admit to experiencing,

e.g. having difficulties with benefits or another practical type of problem, in comparison with admitting to feeling out of control with their children. The presenting problem should never be dismissed as unimportant, nor should it be assumed that this is all the service user is having difficulty with. By asking open questions, such as '*How can I help?*' or '*Can you tell me about your current situation?*', opportunities are created for service users to say more about their circumstances should they wish to. Once a relationship has been established with a service user and the specifics of a particular difficulty need further exploration, it is at this point that closed questions can become useful to elicit more specific factual responses, e.g. '*Are you on medication?*', '*What sort?*', '*How long have you taken this?*' can be useful questions for getting more detailed information once the main areas to be covered have been mapped out.

information to be gathered in a prescriptive manner. As an effective, authentic and empathic practitioner you need to attend to the service user's anxious feelings and to resist bureaucratic drivers. With bureaucratic agenda to the fore of your mind it is all too easy to ask questions that elicit a 'yes' or 'no' answer for a narrowly defined purpose. These are known as closed questions. For some purposes closed questions can be helpful (see the Closer Look box above) but an important skill to develop is the ability to ask open questions that allow the respondent to determine their own answer.

In the following case study, you are asked to think about how you would manage your first meeting with a service user. What is important is that you consider not only what you will say but also how you will say it and how you, and the service user, will be communicating in more than just words.

Case study

Fran

Fran is a white, British woman in her mid-50s with a history of depression and self-harming. Fran has recently been discharged from hospital following a suicidal episode when she attempted to overdose. You are allocated to work with Fran in order to help her integrate back into the community and to help her access day-care services. Fran has had

periods when she has elected not to speak and finds communicating with others difficult. What she has told nursing staff is that she is 'at the end of her tether' and 'can't be bothered about anything, anymore.'

How would you prepare to meet with Fran for the first time? What would be your main concerns?

Gently shaking Fran's hand may be an appropriate way of establishing your acceptance of her, although this may be difficult if she cannot make eye contact with you initially because of her embarrassment and low self-esteem. You might like to think about taking written materials if Fran has difficulty talking with you. Being aware of the different levels of literacy that service users have is also important. For some people with learning difficulties pictorial information is greatly appreciated. In relaying written information it is always important to offer the service user the choice of reading the materials themselves or for you to go through it with them. When gathering information as part of an assessment, sharing official forms can be intimidating (although this should not be assumed and can be checked out with the service user(s) concerned). Alternative approaches involving visual representations of the relationships between family members, such as genograms or ecomaps, discussed in Chapter 10 on assessment and again in Chapter 16 on children and families, can be helpful in engaging new

A closer look

Finding the way and staying on track

The middle phases of involvement with service users can be characterised by a number of challenges. Two of the most common are:

'The Maze' – within an interview or over a number of sessions, social workers can find themselves confused by the direction in which the conversation has gone. For service users who are anxious about their circumstances, it is not uncommon for their anxiety to be exhibited in wide-ranging concerns, which may not always appear to be clearly connected. For the social worker the challenge is to help the service user manage their anxiety by focusing on the specific issues that the social worker can help them address. Skills such as summarising and paraphrasing, referred to above, are

necessary in order for the social worker to navigate the maze and may need to be quite forcefully introduced in order to avoid further confusion and to help the service user disentangle the different issues and sources of anxiety.

'The Desert' – in many respects this is the opposite of the maze, when a social worker is having difficulty enabling the service user to engage with the conversation. In such situations, as was the case with Fran, discussed earlier, it is important that the difficulties in engaging and discussing often painful or anxiety-provoking issues are acknowledged. In so doing it can 'free up' the service user to engage with the task in hand and not allow emotional barriers to block communications.

service users in the initial assessment process. Such approaches are designed to be engaging, non-threatening and informative. In some instances they are even experienced as enjoyable!

The beginning of a one-off encounter or the first session in a series of meetings is important as it sets the tone for what follows. Paying attention to what happens during the middle phase of an encounter is equally important, however, for ensuring the objectives of the intervention are achieved. It is all too easy in the middle stages of an interview or a sustained intervention to lose the focus and to jeopardise the effectiveness of your work. It is to communication during this middle phase of a professional encounter that we now turn.

Middle stages of the communication process

In the middle phase of a one-off interview or of a sustained intervention with a service user over several meetings/visits, it is important to remind yourself and the service user of the original reason for social work involvement. If an agreement was drawn up it can be useful to review it. In one-off encounters during the middle phase it is important to use clarifying techniques such as paraphrasing to demonstrate to the service user the understanding you have gained. This does not mean you have to agree with their comments but as the professional you need to be able to articulate how the service user experiences and makes sense of their experiences and circumstances. Accurate paraphrasing of the service user's account of their situation requires you to use the language of the service user and to make empathic statements. If we consider Fran, referred to in the case study earlier, who is experiencing mental health problems and is having difficulty communicating, it might be that, of the little that she says, you can summarise her situation by talking about her feeling 'at the end of her tether' and 'not bothered about anything'. An empathic comment that paraphrases what has already been said would be: 'Fran, you've talked about what happened when you were brought into hospital, that you didn't want to be admitted and were angry with the social worker involved. It seems to me you are feeling "at the end of your tether" and "can't be bothered" because you don't believe anyone understands how you feel.'

Repeating a service user's description of themselves back to them enables it to be heard differently, as it is voiced by an 'outsider'. Following these paraphrasing statements it is possible to explore further whether they are an accurate portrayal of their feelings and to demonstrate curiosity by asking 'wondering questions', such as 'I wonder what "being at the end of your tether" feels like for you?' Or 'I wonder what would need to happen for you to be bothered by something?' Questions of this nature indicate genuine interest in trying to work out what something is like and what would make it better. It enables a deeper exploration of the service user's circumstances to take place but ensures it is focused on the service user's definition of the problem and not professional assumptions. Research has shown (Mayer and Timms, 1970, cited in Koprowska, 2005) that service users are unhappy when questions are asked and routes of enquiry are followed that do not, from their perspective, relate to the problem that concerns them. It is particularly at this stage of the encounter where attending to your own responses can ensure you act authentically and in the interests of the service user. In Fran's case the social worker may feel that Fran's remark about 'not being bothered' does not appear congruent with the comments made by the nursing professionals caring for her or the concern Fran, herself, has exhibited about what will happen to her. The questions and confusion that this dissonant experience might generate for the social worker can be commented on to Fran and, in so doing, it reinforces a commitment to an authentic, empathic relationship. While navigating through the middle stages of work with a service user, it is vital to keep the end in sight and to inform the service user of when it will be. The importance of planned endings and the challenges of ending involvement effectively are addressed in the following section.

And finally . . . endings in the communication process

Endings need to be addressed from the beginning, whether they are the ending of one encounter or of a series of meetings. Paying attention to the ending of an encounter is as important as ensuring the beginning is handled well. In the case of a one-off encounter, if the beginning has been handled sensitively, the service user will be aware of the duration of the meeting or visit and will have an idea, therefore, of when it will end. If you do find you are running over the agreed timescales it is helpful to openly renegotiate with the service user when you will finish to allow them shared control over the duration of your involvement with them. If your involvement with a service user has been over an extended period of time, the final meeting should be anticipated in earlier meetings.

Professional tip

Key skills for developing relationships with service users

Below we have summarised the key skills you might use in developing empathic, authentic and respectful relationships with service users, with examples.

Verbal clarity:
'Hello, my name is Nadia Khan, I'm from the Community Mental Health team, you might hear it referred to as the CMHT. Before we start can I ask how you would like me to refer to you?'

Empathic comments:
'You seem to be feeling annoyed because you don't feel your family understand what pressure you have been under.'

Authentic comments:
'When you were talking about the difficulties you have with your mother I was aware that I felt quite confused. You looked and sounded quite sad but said you felt everything was better between you and her.'

Paraphrasing/summarising:
'We've spent some time discussing how you came to be admitted to hospital. You mentioned you felt "like giving up". It seems to me you are still feeling "like giving up" because your disability is getting worse and you would like someone to take seriously how worried you are and reassess your eligibility for services. Is that accurate?' 'While you were talking I noticed you were clenching your hands and appeared tense. It made me wonder if you were feeling anxious talking about your situation.'

Open questions:
'I wonder if you would mind telling me about what happened that led you to phone social services?'
    'Could you perhaps tell me why you think Social Services have got involved with your family?'
    'What do you think would be most helpful for you?'

Regardless of whether the relationship established has been positive or not it is important that you prepare service users for your withdrawal. This practice is crucial for people known to social services as so often their experience of endings has been damaging, as the endings might have been unannounced and unexpected, been abrupt and subsequently never been discussed. As a consequence service users can find it difficult to establish trusting personal and professional relationships. When meaningful professional relationships do develop they are often characterised by significant emotional attachments and, therefore, the need to handle the ending sensitively is heightened. The thoughtful ending of a professional encounter can provide an important opportunity to repair some of the damaging endings previously experienced. With children, whose timeframes are very different to those of adults, preparing them for the end of your involvement is essential. When ending meetings with service users it is always helpful for you to check back with them that they understand what has been discussed. Verbal summaries and a list of key decisions and action points clarify expectations and responsibilities. In some instances making brief notes for the service user to keep can help this process. For children or people with

learning difficulties with whom you have been involved for a lengthy period of time, age or developmentally appropriate methods of reviewing your involvement can include activities such as writing letters to them, reminding them of the happy as well as the more difficult aspects of your involvement along with the particular memories you would wish to highlight with them. Having a concrete, personalised (as opposed to the official records, reports and reviews) record of your involvement can be helpful and complements any special event you might organise to mark an ending. This process can affirm that a positive intervention has ended or, equally, acknowledge unresolvable differences of opinion. Either way, all parties are clear about the status of the intervention at its completion, which is important for any future professional involvement.

Challenges of communication

In this section we consider three of the most commonly identified challenges when engaging with service users: dealing with aggressive and violent behaviour, coping with pain and sadness and managing silence. While all three scenarios require different responses they have a common characteristic: all three types of behaviour provoke anxiety in the listener and frequently are generated by anxiety in the service user. By anxiety we are referring to an emotional state that makes it difficult for an individual to acknowledge their primitive emotional responses – fear, envy, hatred – to distressing experiences. In the case of Marianne, introduced at the beginning of the chapter, her tearfulness might be connected to her feeling anxious about going to a day centre, something she has not done before. A family being investigated because of concerns about their children's safety might behave aggressively towards the social workers undertaking the initial assessment because of their anxiety about their children being removed. It is useful then to always ask yourself the questions '*What is the service user anxious about and what is making me anxious?*'

'D'you want to take this outside?' – Aggressive and violent communication patterns

Anger is often construed as a negative and socially unacceptable emotion, one we should keep hidden. Allowing someone to 'vent their anger', however, can be a cathartic exercise and one that a social worker can facilitate without feeling threatened. Dealing with aggressive or violent behaviour is different and the harsh reality for social workers is that such behaviour is not uncommon in their daily work (Ferguson, 2005; Smith, 2005).

The bottom line when dealing with physically or verbally aggressive behaviour is that the safety of the worker is paramount. Often social work practitioners and students believe they ought to be able to manage aggressive behaviour and misconstrue failure to confront it as a sign of professional weakness. This places them in a double bind: they are anxious about dealing with aggressive individuals but equally anxious that their professional credibility will be marred if they fail to demonstrate they can. We strongly refute this position and assert that competent social workers are those who are able to remove themselves from a situation at the slightest hint of aggression or violence. In our view this is good practice. If you think about a situation in which you have felt anxious or afraid you will quickly recognise how these feelings make it difficult to think clearly, accurately and quickly. Should the situation involve a serious risk to a vulnerable individual and require further intervention it is then possible to return and undertake

it with appropriate levels of support – either a colleague or with police protection. In less dangerous situations where a service user is not at risk, responsibility lies with the individual who has behaved aggressively to recognise that if they require professional help they need to be able to conduct themselves in an acceptable manner.

Case study

Colin

You are taking a new referral through the duty system (the point of first contact for service users) on a Friday afternoon and involved in interviewing a young, white man, Colin, who has recently moved from a foster placement into a self-catering flat as part of an independent living scheme. Colin is asking for money to buy food to see him through the weekend until he receives his next weekly benefit payment. You are aware from his body language that Colin is agitated. When you return from having consulted the Duty manager and inform Colin you cannot provide him with money but can give him some food vouchers he gets extremely verbally aggressive towards you.

What might you say and do in response to Colin?

In situations such as Colin's one of the most important strategies for helping someone manage their angry feelings is to provide clear boundaries, i.e. stating their behaviour is unacceptable, refusing to stay in the room with them and only agreeing to continue the conversation once they have calmed down. Clear verbal boundaries reinforce the important non-verbal behaviours that are required in potentially or actually violent situations (Kowprowska, 2005). These would include:

- maintaining an appropriate distance from Colin and positioning yourself at a slight angle – turning away or standing 'square-on' could be interpreted as provocative;
- maintaining a neutral facial posture;
- avoiding intense eye contact but not averting gaze entirely;
- using a calm and low-register voice and not allowing your vocal intensity and intonation to mirror that of Colin.

At this stage of an aggressive outburst empathic comments are likely to be inflammatory rather than helpful.

Instead clear statements about what needs to happen for you to continue the meeting with Colin should be made. If a further conversation with Colin were to take place it would be appropriate to invite a colleague to join you to enable you to feel more protected and able to concentrate on Colin's concerns. Providing clear ground rules for continuing the conversation can run the risk of appearing to be patronising but in fact is often experienced as emotionally containing, i.e. by advising Colin what is acceptable and putting boundaries on his behaviour it helps him manage it. Once a degree of calm has been established it might be possible to explore with Colin his reactions. At this stage it may be possible to make empathic comments to Colin to help him reflect on and make sense of his anxiety-driven aggressive responses.

Case study

Colin cont . . .

While financial difficulties appear to be part of Colin's problem, you establish from talking with him that his anxiety-driven aggression is linked to his worries about spending the weekend on his own. A phone call to Colin's previous foster carers resolves both problems as they invite Colin to spend a day over the weekend with them.
Following the call, Colin leaves feeling calmer and somewhat relieved.

Koprowska (2005: 144), in her book on communication skills, provides helpful advice on factors contributing to aggressive and violent behaviours. Drawing on all the background information available it is possible for social workers to be vigilant and undertake comprehensive (although, it is important to emphasise, never absolute) risk assessments. Anticipating and preparing for potentially threatening situations is a further way of placing boundaries around a service user's behaviour and indicating to them how seriously antisocial behaviours are regarded. We feel it an important enough issue to reiterate, here, that ensuring they are safe is the social worker's first priority. If this principle of practice is adhered to, service users will be better protected.

We now turn our attention to a different but equally challenging aspect of interpersonal communication: responding to pain and distress.

Dealing with tears – painful and distressing communication patterns

Reflect

Think of an occasion when you were emotionally upset. Try to remember how your feelings were expressed non-verbally.

How did you react physically: did you, for example, lie down, slump or tense up? Did you cry?

Try to remember what you felt and describe it in words.

Do you think your verbal description of your distress and how you expressed your feelings non-verbally were congruent?

If someone was with you, how did they respond to you? What helped and what didn't?

Without doubt, at some point in your professional practice you will encounter a service user, or even a colleague, who is emotionally distressed and who expresses their distress in tears. Tears are the physical and visible demonstration of emotional distress but it is important not to make assumptions. Tears are not always a result of sadness or distress. They can be a sign of relief, for example, or in some cases anger or frustration. Nor should the absence of tears mislead you into believing that the level of distress a service user is experiencing is less than if they were crying. In such situations well-honed observational skills can help you pick up on other indicators that might inform your responses and contribute to your empathic understanding and communication.

In some cases, service users' difficult experiences have forced them to learn not to show emotional vulnerability. At this point you might like to revisit Chapter 7 in which we considered attachment theory. Children, for example, who exhibit insecure avoidant attachments rarely cry in circumstances which others might find very upsetting. While they are often very frightened, their early experiences and internal working models of adult responses have taught them to 'hide their feelings' and to act in pseudo-mature ways to manage the anxiety they feel. Adult attachment theory can also help you understand an adult's responses to painful and distressing experiences, particularly when they do not appear to 'make sense', e.g. a seemingly dismissive response to the death of a significant person in their life. The violent and aggressive behaviours referred to in the previous section are sometimes the direct result of emotional distress that cannot be tolerated or faced and so becomes displaced externally. A useful observational skill to develop to assist you in responding empathically, authentically and respectfully to a service user in distress is to note in the course of an interview, for example, if they begin to cry, *when* the tears began (the timing of the tears) and *what* triggered them. It is all too easy for us to assume we know why someone is crying but such assumptions need to be avoided at all costs. Of equal importance is your ability to allow someone to cry and not to feel the need to stop them. Often such responses reflect our own discomfort with tears but inhibiting someone else from crying can be disrespectful. While offering a tissue is respectful, if it is accompanied by a suggestion that they stop crying, it might serve to reinforce feelings of vulnerability or inadequacy that could be connected with the tears. Our instinctive responses to emotional distress make it imperative that while paying attention to the non-verbal communications emanating from the service user, we also attend to our own non-verbal responses and as far as possible prevent them from inhibiting the emotionally expressive behaviours of service users.

When tears are involved it can be helpful to think about your response in terms of 'less is more'. What we mean by this is that your response is likely to be more empathic and authentic if you allow the tears to speak for themselves. Tears often appear to have a cathartic effect, i.e. once released the person concerned can verbally express their feelings more accurately or does not feel the need to say anything further.

Reflect

Referring back to the 'Reflect' box that opened this subsection, which asked you to think of an emotionally upsetting experience, and thinking about what you have just read, identify an occasion when you were with someone, in a professional or personal capacity, who was distressed.

What did you find yourself doing? How did you respond both verbally and non-verbally? Can you remember what you felt?

In light of what you have read and reflected on, what would you endeavour to do differently when the situation next arises?

Less is more – the use of silence in communication

In the previous two sections we have considered the challenges of working in emotionally charged situations.

One way aggressive or painful experiences can be exhibited is by service users resorting to silence. Understanding and tolerating silence is an important skill for social workers to acquire.

The current cultural context in which we find ourselves located allows little opportunity for silence and appears to place little value on it. Our shopping centres, offices, cars and homes are full of sound, some might say 'noise', and the invention of email, mobile phones and iPods means people are constantly in communication with each other and are able, should they choose to, to talk or listen to someone or something all the time. Under these circumstances silence is an unfamiliar phenomenon and therefore when it is encountered it can be unnerving and potentially be perceived as threatening and deskilling. Yet, we would argue, it should not be and need not be.

To be genuinely empathic, authentic and respectful all relationships require moments of silence. How silence is used in professional contexts varies, however, according to the work context you find yourself in. Social workers located in clinical settings, such as in child and adolescent mental health teams, will discover that the more explicit therapeutic dimension of the work means silence is a key ingredient of the professional relationship and requires a skilled professional to maximise its effectiveness. In psychoanalytic psychotherapy, for example, it is not unheard of for a therapist and 'patient' to spend an entire session in silence, as it allows and encourages the 'patient' to tolerate their unvoiced thoughts and their feelings. For most social workers based in community contexts the use of silence is not so dramatic but no less important. Learning not to immediately respond to a service user's answer to your previous question with another question is a way of conveying respectful attention, reflection and thoughtfulness. Similarly, if a service user is unable to reply immediately to a question posed, it is important to resist answering it for them to avoid an awkward silence. It is all too easy to interpret silence as an absence of communication but this need not be the case. Silence, like words, is information. Why someone is silent at particular points in a meeting, or in response to a particular question, should be noted. Once again we need to hone our observational skills and attentiveness to non-verbal communication. Of equal importance is being attentive to the use of silence. In some cases it can be used by either party – social worker or service user – to manipulate a situation. Young people or service users with mental health problems may 'choose' to remain silent, and as a social worker you need to think carefully about how you respond to such behaviours and what your 'meta-communication' might be, i.e. your communication about a service user's communication.

Reflect

Think about how you cope with silence. Can you 'bear it' or do you find you tend to feel the need to fill it? Can you work out why you respond as you do?

Your answers to the above questions might shed some light on how you would communicate with and relate to Fran and her wish not to communicate openly with professionals. How do you think you would respond to periods of silence while meeting with Fran?

Perhaps one of the most important messages to take away from this subsection is that to hear silence you have to have experienced silence. It need not be intimidating and it can be releasing but in our noise-filled contemporary culture we need to develop, more now than we have had to ever before, our understanding and tolerance of silence.

We have explored, more generally, the core characteristics of communication skills, the skills that may be useful at different stages of engagement with service users and some specific common challenges in communicating. In the final four subsections of this chapter we look in more detail at the specific communication skills social workers need to acquire when working with different service-user groups.

COMMUNICATION WITH SPECIFIC SERVICE USERS

We begin this section of the chapter by considering some of the challenges involved in communicating with children and young people. The subsequent sections consider communication skills with people with disabilities, people with mental health difficulties and older people.

Communication with children

'The immediate purpose of communication . . . is to get in touch with the real self of the child, which is what he is feeling about himself and his life at the moment of the meeting. We want to help children remain in contact with themselves and maintain a sense of their own unique identity and worth in relation to other people.'   (Winnicott, 1964a)

The ability to communicate with children is a key skill for practitioners working with children and young people. In many ways, these skills are no different from those already described in this chapter, for the principles of good practice already discussed about communicating in a professional context apply in the same way to communicating with children. The quotation above from Clare Winnicott (a social worker who pioneered childcare practice in the middle decades of the last century) could equally be adapted to communication with other client groups. And accurate empathy, authenticity (sometimes called genuineness) and respect discussed earlier are also essential prerequisites for communicating

with children. However, as you probably instinctively or from experience realise, it does also require different skills. This is in part because of the ways in which children communicate (particularly their use of play and their developmental stage in language and understanding) and of differences in power and autonomy between adults and children. Moreover, as you may have learned already from your reading, social workers can sometimes experience difficulty in communicating effectively with children. Many of the early child abuse inquiries (e.g. London Borough of Brent, 1985; London Borough of Lambeth, 1987; London Borough of Greenwich, 1987) highlighted the failures of social workers to talk and listen to the children on their own, and social workers were again criticised in the Laming Report for failing to communicate properly with Victoria by herself (a specific example of this was when the social worker missed an opportunity by deciding not to see or speak to her when she was in hospital) (Laming 2003: 238). To balance this rather negative picture, you may be encouraged to hear of the findings of a small study exploring the characteristics of child-centred practice, which found social workers to be predominantly child rather than parent focused in their communications (Nice, 2005).

While it is right to remind ourselves of the difficulties, it is important also for you to acknowledge the experiences and skills which you can draw upon in developing your ability to communicate with children. One of the characteristics of reflective practice is to become aware of your own qualities and strengths, as well as being open to learning, understanding your own inner world, and the impact which listening to children's emotional pain may have on you.

Think ahead

(Ideally you would do this with a partner.)

Make an inventory of your skills and learning needs in communicating with children. Ask yourself: *what do I bring/what do I fear/ and what do I need to learn?*

Don't forget that even without much direct experience of being with children you will have absorbed more than you think.

So – how did you get on?

Here are some of the strengths which you might have identified:

- Feel quite close to age group myself – am not that long out of school! Have had contact with nephews and nieces, brothers and sisters, have my own children, etc.
- Have vivid memories of some childhood/adolescent experiences
- Have some skills to help me relate to children and young people – e.g. I can draw/paint/play card games/play football/am energetic/like joining in games/don't mind looking undignified

- Have some familiarity with music/games they like
- Watch TV programmes which children and young people watch – e.g. *Big Brother*, *Neighbours*, *Teletubbies*, *Bob the Builder*, *Blue Peter*, etc.
- Know or can find out what children's current crazes are
- Have close knowledge of particular community, culture, etc.
- Have direct experience of working with children.

And here are some of the things which people can worry about and may be blocks to effective communication:

- Fear of saying or doing the 'wrong' thing
- Not knowing what to do or whether you've properly understood some of the things the child is talking about
- Fear of feelings about your own past experiences, e.g. of separation and loss being triggered
- Managing the competing demands of other children/ adults
- Lack of time, management support
- Forgetting what it is like to be a child.

We hope that this exercise may have helped you to be aware of your existing knowledge and skills, as well as what you may need to learn about or practise. What follows is a brief guide to developing some of these skills, and to addressing some of the areas which can be stressful.

A closer look

The therapeutic value of talking to children

There are various ways in which it is possible to engage children in conversation about their situation. Often social workers find that significant conversations happen when they are driving a child somewhere. The confines of a car seem to create a safe space in which the child and social worker can talk directly to each other without needing to look at each other all the time.

One example of such a conversation happened with Paul, an 8-year-old boy who was being looked after by the local authority, and his social worker, who was driving him to and from a direct work session exploring Paul's feelings about his family. During the session the social worker noticed how difficult Paul found it to

concentrate, and whenever she broached a question about his family Paul moved away from what he was doing and engaged in another activity. When it came to the time for Paul to get back into the car to go back to his foster carer, Paul was reluctant to do so and tried to run off. Once the social worker had managed to get Paul into the car, on the journey home she brought up with him how difficult he found it talking and thinking about his family. Paul was then able to say, from the back seat of the car, 'It's really hard thinking about my mum because I'm not with her and it makes me sad. I don't want to forget her but I can't think about her when I'm with Karen because she wouldn't like it' (foster carer). With this information the social worker was able to suggest to Paul how they might talk to Karen about helping Paul think and talk about his mum in the foster home.

Communicating may involve a fleeting conversation with a child, a one-off interview, or it may involve a longer process of working with a child in order to build a relationship in which it becomes possible for the child to trust you, and you to begin to understand more about her or him. This is sometimes called 'direct work', clarifying the fact that it involves face-to-face communication. (We discuss the differences between this kind of exchange and therapy later in the book, in the chapter on working with children and families.)

Aldgate and Seden (2006) suggest that the rationale for working directly with children has its basis in three perspectives:

1. A rights perspective
2. A safeguarding and promoting-welfare perspective
3. A therapeutic perspective, grounded in developmental theory.

These approaches, which are not mutually exclusive, begin to suggest some of the reasons for the importance of communicating with children.

(a) It has therapeutic value. We know that children value the opportunity to talk through their anxieties with someone they can trust. So talking to a trusted adult can:
   – offer the opportunity to 'offload';
   – provide the chance for children to talk, make comparisons, express opinions, preferences, etc. without judgement or criticism;
   – help children make sense of what has happened/ is happening to them;
   – help remove feelings of self-blame;
   – help to lay some of the ghosts of the past;
   – help correct distortions, e.g. where the child holds themselves wholly responsible for the break-up of the family.

(b) It can prepare children living away from home for returning to their birth families by:
   – helping the child to understand what has happened within her/his family during separation;
   – helping the child re-negotiate her/his place within the family.

(c) It can prepare children for moving to new families, by:
   – helping the child to mourn for the loss of her/his birth family;
   – helping the child to understand what has happened;
   – helping the child to plan and build for the future.

The Closer Look box next summarises Vera Fahlberg's understanding of the different purposes of direct work. This list is helpful to bear in mind when you are preparing for working with a child, since you need to be clear what the reason for your work is, and also because it may help you to decide how to begin the work (and what materials, techniques, etc. to select).

A closer look

Fahlberg's purposes of direct work

- To help strengthen current relationships
- To understand the child's needs and perceptions
- To prepare the child for transitions
- To assess needs
- For disengagement work, i.e. from previous relationships
- To explain plans for the future
- To address areas of concern
- To facilitate identity formation by helping the child to know her/himself better
- To reintegrate early life experiences.

(Fahlberg, 1991: 326)

Thinking about possible purposes from this list, you might, for example, choose to do life-story work if you were wanting to help a child integrate early life experiences, or a life path for helping to prepare for transitions (e.g. to a new family).

Entering the world of the child

This discussion is necessarily selective and brief. We have tried to summarise the key issues which you need to think about, and also to introduce you to some of the wealth of techniques which have been developed, often very imaginatively by social workers and others for helping children and adults communicate with each other. Agencies sometimes produce packs of suggestions for play activities, and there are many commercially produced books and workpacks for helping children cope with separation and loss and for preparing children for moving to new families (see end of chapter but these should be seen as a starting or reference point to stimulate you to create your own ideas). The main focus is on work with the minimal material facilities usually available to practitioners, bearing in mind that, as Crompton points out, 'the most important constituents of communication are the individual people concerned, within time and space dedicated to the child' (2007: 397)

One way of attending closely is by being sensitive to the variety of possible meanings of what children are saying. Landreth illustrates this by suggesting a range of different underlying reasons for questions, which would lead, perhaps, to different responses. The following extract is from a longer detailed discussion which you might want to read for yourself:

'1. Do other children come here?
   David might be:
   (a) wanting reassurance he is special
   (b) establishing a sense of belonging in the playroom
   (c) wanting to feel secure in knowing the room is his for this time
   (d) wanting to know if there are going to be other children with him in the room
   (e) noticing something is different about the room this week.

2. Can I come back tomorrow? – or When can I come again?
   Dwight might be:
   (a) involved in a project which he wants to finish
   (b) enjoying what he has been doing – wanting the opportunity to do it again
   (c) saying – "this is an important place to me".
   (d) seeking reassurance of his time – that he does have a time in the playroom that belongs to him
   (e) unsure about trusting his world to be consistent and not disappointing him in this situation as it has in others, and/or
   (f) saying – I really like to come here – It is important to me that I can come again.'   (Landreth, 1991)

Using the 'third object'

Undertaking an activity with a child, sharing an experience and playing are all means of communicating with children using what has been called the 'third object'. Some children are able to talk without 'props' but children often feel more comfortable talking to adults in the context of a joint activity, and, for many, games and activities are essential to engaging, getting to know, and building a trusting relationship with them. (Lefevre, 2009) These activities essentially provide opportunities for interaction without being 'face to face' so that eye contact need not be sought or forced and verbal conversation may, especially with less articulate children, play only a minor part. So using a third object can:

■ Reduce some of the strain for the child, particularly on sensitive issues

■ Allow the child to proceed at her/his own pace
■ Allow the child to avoid eye contact if they wish
■ Afford the child the opportunity to express views/feelings which may be their own but which can be attributed to a 'teddy' or a doll – these views may be too threatening to own personally
■ Provide a concrete and other than verbal way of identifying and talking about feelings (see 'my happy face', in the Appendix to this chapter)

■ Help children to understand difficult experiences (see 'loving and caring liquid', in the Appendix to this chapter)
■ Help adults talk about and explain difficult or new experiences.

Principles of communication

As we stressed in the earlier section of this chapter, one way of showing respect for any user is by planning the work carefully. This will involve thinking through in advance how you intend to engage with the child, including such things as the setting, time of day, how you will introduce yourself and explain your role, what kinds of activities, materials and tools you will need, if any, and so on. Some of the key principles when embarking on direct work are as follows (some of these suggestions are developed more fully in Williamson, K. (see Further reading), Lefevre (2009), Crompton (2007), Romaine et al. (2007) and Aldgate and Seden (2006).

■ Choosing the right setting – preferably somewhere where the child feels safe and familiar, which is comfortable, and which will be free from interruptions (no phone calls!)
■ Observing, seeing, noticing and really listening to what the child says
■ Talking to children about topics, or doing activities with children, which interest them, in order to build a relationship
■ Being honest about roles and responsibilities
■ Being honest even if it means saying 'I don't know'
■ Being sensitive to the painfulness of a topic and not 'pressing the bruise'
■ Respecting the child's right not to say something or respond, and being sensitive to non-verbal clues of not wishing to pursue a particular topic
■ Being clear about the limits to confidentiality
■ Consulting the child as far as is possible
■ Checking the child's understanding from time to time

- Working at the child's pace as far as possible
- Taking account of how the child likes to communicate
- Being consistent and reliable and punctual
- Being imaginative in finding the means to communicate
- Adapting communications and activities to the child's level of understanding, age and capacity
- Thinking through how you will record the session in a way which is non-intrusive.

Getting started

This is often the tricky moment! Helping children to understand our role, why we are working with them, for how long and what will happen afterwards is important, and finding the right words can seem daunting to begin with.

Think ahead

To help you get started, it might be useful to imagine a child you are meeting for the first time and to list the kinds of things they may wish to know or may need to know.

Working if possible in pairs, spend time thinking about what you might say, and preparing a booklet or similar visual aid which could help you explain your role, etc. to a child.

Next, again if possible with others, practise introducing yourselves and explaining why you are here.

Remember, with young children especially, to use simple, short sentences.

How did you get on? You may have used drawings, but photographs of you, where you work, where the sessions will take place, your car and so on would be equally good. You may also have thought that what you said would depend on the age of the child – we would agree! For older children, you might want to put in how you can be contacted, times, etc. when you will be meeting, and something about confidentiality. Lefevre in a useful discussion (2009) about the skills involved in communicating with children, which she groups into 'knowing, being and doing', reminds us of the importance of this aspect of communicating for many children in the care system, who

'have complained about lax professional standards regarding this. They want to be able to fully confide in someone about their concerns but may become reluctant to share thoughts and feelings because it all gets written down in the file and shared with strangers.' (2009: 34)

For the latter, she suggests that the boundaries and limits to confidentiality should always be spelt out in advance, and argues that even young children are able to understand that social workers may need to pass on information about them. So you might want to explain that although total confidentiality cannot be guaranteed, perhaps because you are concerned that the child or other children are at risk, you *can* give an assurance that 'only people who are in a position to help either them or other children will be allowed to know what the child does or says in a session' (Doyle, 1997: 42). (See Wilson and Ryan, 2005b for a more detailed discussion of principles and complexities of confidentiality.)

Choosing the means of communication

After the introductions, the next task in communicating with children is (usually) to engage their attention (Brandon et al., 1998: 73). There are many techniques available to help practitioners communicate with children. K. Williamson groups these into methods which may be used for 'getting to know you', for 'developing the senses' (which may also evoke memories of the child's past), for 'giving and receiving information', for developing a sense of identity (often developed into a life-story book, which we discuss further in Chapter 16), for preparing children for moving to new families, for moving on and for helping children cope with separation and loss (see Appendix at end of chapter). It is useful to prepare a basic 'tool kit' of simple toys and play materials, which can be adapted for different age groups and is easily transportable. As well as coloured pencils, crayons or felt tips and paper, you might include play dough, farm animals, stickers and so on (see the Closer Look box below for suggestions), depending on the child's age. Adolescents may be content to draw or paint (but see Wilson and Ryan, 2001a, for an account of an adolescent who 'worked through' some of her traumatic experiences of sexual abuse using the medium of clay). Using music, creative writing and working with visual art and stories are discussed in more detail in Lefevre's chapter (2009) Children, like adults, have their preferences and it is important to allow them as much choice as you can.

Good-byes

This applies equally to those who care on a daily basis for the child or young person, and to you as a social worker, as you say good-bye. A common response of many adults to parting is to try to get it over as quickly as possible. But adults need to be sensitive to how important the parting is to the child – so prepare her or him carefully for the ending, and think about the parting message from you – whether it be a card or a small good-luck memento. And be prepared for how the child decides to end – Crompton (2007) and Wilson and Ryan (2005b) describe having to adapt their responses to unexpected ways of ending.

Difficulties which may arise in communicating with children

A closer look

A basic 'play kit'

The following might make up your basic 'play kit':

- Farm animals
- Play people (ideally small figures for school-age children)
- Soft toy
- Small ball
- Play dough
- Small doll, or action man or transformer type
- Coloured crayons, felt tips (for older children)
- Paper, stars, stickers (again for older children)
- Small cars
- Shoe box, cloth, etc. for making houses, putting animals in pen, figures to bed, etc.
- Paper plates (for drawing faces/masks)
- Magazines, scissors, pritt-stick for making collages (for adolescents)
- Post-its for messages.

In the third section of this chapter, we discussed three of the most commonly encountered challenges when engaging with service users. In thinking of these in relation to children, the same principles apply: the need to try to understand and respond empathically to what the child is communicating whether through aggressive behaviour or silence, and to be receptive to, and not block off, painful feelings which are being expressed. Child service users with whom you are working will almost invariably have been affected in some way by loss, and the framework of loss and grief can provide a useful frame of reference for responding sensitively and effectively to what the child is communicating. To do this will also require you to draw honestly on your own personal experiences of loss and to be scrupulous in reflecting on your own feelings and responses: for example, offering

quick reassurance or breaking a silence may be because your own experiences/feelings make you uncomfortable, helpless, uncertain or fearful of hearing painful emotions expressed. Many of the pointers which we give above are relevant here: for example, not 'pressing the bruise', being receptive to non-verbal indications that the child does not want a topic pursued and so on. With the caveat that with a really angry or out-of-control child 'reflection of feelings' will not be enough, perhaps the simplest guideline we can offer you, since space is short, is to reflect and acknowledge the feelings which are being communicated. For example, if a child has been silent for a while or has been recalling a painful memory, you might say, 'It's really hard for you to talk about this', or 'Perhaps you're not quite sure what you want to do next', or 'Thinking about x gives you some sad feelings inside'. The general principle, as with all communicating in a professional context, is to communicate acceptance, non-intrusiveness, and a genuine willingness and wish to understand.

Communication with people with mental health problems

Case study

Marie

Marie, a young, single woman of 25 was referred to a social worker attached to a GP surgery. The doctor said that she frequently consulted him about her 'anxiety' and that sometimes she came close to having a full-blown 'panic attack'. The GP was reluctant to prescribe drugs and thought that Marie would accept some simple counselling help. In the first two meetings the social worker explored with Marie exactly what her experiences of anxiety consisted of – what feelings and thoughts of events seemed to trigger episodes, what made her feel better, and so on. She described how she hated travelling on the underground, sometimes felt panicky on the motorway because she couldn't get off at exits, felt increased anxiety travelling by bus and on foot between home and work. After talking about this in supervision her social worker saw that the pattern of anxiety had something to do with 'safe places' (home, work) and the unsafe places where Marie felt 'trapped' or exposed (the underground, the motorway, the in-between places of her journey to and from work).

The social worker was now able to explore further with Marie how her anxieties were connected to feeling 'alone', out of contact with home and familiarity. They seemed to be a form of separation anxiety. Although Marie functioned perfectly well at work, had friends and got along reasonably well with her family, she did sometimes feel overwhelmed 'from inside' by these anxiety attacks. They limited her ability to do some 'normal things', worried her, and led to secondary anxieties – worrying about when she would have the next attack.

Do you think Marie had a mental illness or a mental health problem? Does it matter what we call it?

Do you think her condition might create any particular issues for the social worker in terms of communication, or the choice of setting in which she does her counselling?

In this section we concentrate on a few central principles about communicating with people who have mental health difficulties. There is a lot more that could be said, and some of this is covered in other parts of the book, for example, in Chapter 20 on working with people with mental health problems. Although we discuss some quite complex perspectives in this section, these are underpinned by some simple messages – there is no special or mysterious form of communication necessary in order to do mental health work, but in order to ensure the effectiveness of the ordinary principles of good communication already discussed in this chapter, you need to bear in mind a few key points:

- In mental health work it is especially important that you are able to think of communication as something that happens at many levels, not just verbally.
- Mental health difficulties involve the experience of 'mental pain' and this can operate at all sorts of complex levels. Social workers need to be 'emotionally available' to communications of mental pain from service users.
- Even when communicating verbally, people may talk about their most private and difficult states of mind in complex ways: for example, using metaphors and images, and you need to try to be sensitive to this.

- Often, what you say may be less important in building a relationship with a service user than your ability just to 'stick with them' over long periods of time. This *is* a kind communication: that you won't be frightened off, get bored with them, find them unacceptable, and so on. Service users themselves say that this is one of the aspects of social work they value most.

Use of self

One foundation for building good relationships with service users with mental health problems is your own self-knowledge. In this chapter you have already read about one of the basic principles of sound communication – empathy. If empathy really is about trying to 'think and feel yourself into someone else's situation', then it seems to follow that to be good at communicating with people who have a serious mental health problem, you must somehow draw upon personal experience of your own 'mental health difficulties'. This idea might be troubling or disturbing for many people and you might react by thinking, 'I don't have such experience, so I can't do this kind of work'. In this section we challenge this reaction, and in so doing seek to offer a perspective that is empowering for social workers and for service users.

However, it is difficult to think about the particular issues in communication with people with 'mental health problems', unless we are working with some agreed definition or understanding of what we mean by this phrase. This is a challenge in itself because the meanings of terms like 'mental illness' and 'mental health' have always been hotly contested. Here we propose a way of thinking about mental health that is certainly only part of the story, but it is a central part of the picture for thinking about questions of communication.

Each of us experiences and relates to the world around us, including other people, in terms of a sense of our own internal world and a sense of how and in what ways it meets and interacts with the external world. We all operate with a notion of the difference between our own minds and the minds of other people, a psychological boundary that provides us with some sense of a discrete self. We tend to be clear about what are our own thoughts, feelings and experiences, and what are those of other people: who communicate about these to us, as we do to them, all the time. Some, broadly less serious, kinds of mental health problems can be seen as primarily involving a 'disturbance' of ordinary feeling, thinking, and everyday emotional and social functioning within a basically 'intact' self. Others however, seem to involve a more radical or severe disruption to the very structure of the self or personality, so that the 'boundary' between inner and outer reality, between self and other people, blurs or 'breaks down'. The somewhat less serious difficulties include acute anxiety states and many forms of depression. The more serious ones include the 'psychoses' – schizophrenia, bi-polar disorder – and personality disorder.

In terms of communication, however, there is a single message that is important for any social worker to grasp: a person in the grip of the mental pain and confusion that mental health problems involve may be so dominated or burdened by their 'internal world' that it is very difficult for them to relate to or respond in an ordinary way to 'ordinary communications' from outside. This does not mean you should necessarily try to communicate differently: just that you should constantly bear in mind that it may be very hard for the service user to 'take in' and make use of what you do communicate. Think – perhaps there have been times when you have felt so worried and anxious you really could not 'hear' what anyone else had to say; or times when you felt so emotionally low that reassurance and encouragement just had no effect on you; or even times when you were so convinced that everyone disliked and hated you that you 'snapped their heads off' when they tried to come close. Now think again – suppose that such a state of mind were deeper and much more lasting than the experience you had. Perhaps that brings us closer to understanding part of what it is to 'have a mental health problem', and what the particular challenges are in terms of communication.

This view of what is at the core of mental health problems and mental health work is often absent from social work teaching and writing about these matters. People with mental health difficulties have been and still are systematically stigmatised in our society, and it is essential to understand mental health problems in their social and political context. Research tells us that, for example, Black Afro-Caribbean people in Britain are consistently treated more coercively than other ethnic groups by the mental health system, and are less often offered psychological help for their problems. But social constructionist views of mental health (see Chapter 20) can sometimes mislead us into thinking that mental health problems are 'constructions' attributed to particular people by others, and thus that they don't really exist. This is emphatically not the view taken by service user groups active in mental health, and is contrary to the direct subjective and interpersonal experience of all who have suffered with, or known someone who has suffered with, mental health problems. In the end, while inequalities in society mean that some social groups are more prone than others to mental health problems, and that some groups have been 'constructed' as prone to disturbance, we must be very careful to continue to treat mental health problems seriously whenever we encounter them.

Before going further, we want to go back to what we consider the foundation of good communication: the relationship between you and the service user, and your use of yourself to build this relationship.

A closer look

Mental health and communication

This is how a well-known psychiatrist and psychotherapist, who has spent many years working with people with mental health problems, thinks about the nature of mental illness and communication.

'When the earliest stages of mental development . . . have been sufficiently well negotiated, and the foundation of a secure sense of identity and a firm sense of reality has been achieved, the individual is unlikely to fall ill of a psychotic disorder later in life. Less severe or later developmental failures may result in *borderline* personality disturbances, in which brief episodic psychotic states of mind may occur under

stress, or in *neurotic* disordered, characterised by *inhibitions*, *symptoms* and *anxiety*.

In *psychotic* mental states, however, the individual has a very different experience from that of normal or neurotic people and is likely to have a different way of communicating, and, to a varying extent, a different use of language. This use of language is characteristically based on *primary process* thinking in which displacement, condensation, and symbolic expression figure predominantly, as is the case in the construction of the dream . . . In psychotic states, impairment of ego functions is particularly severe and is characterised by . . . impairment of the capacity to differentiate self from object and *inner reality* from *external reality*.' (Jackson, 2001: 280–1)

The social worker, the service user and mental health

First, everyone has had *some* personal experience that can help them understand what it is like to suffer with mental health problems. For example, almost everyone has suffered at least one loss in their lives that affected them deeply – perhaps a close relative, friend, partner or colleague, a loved home, school or country of origin; simply growing up and becoming an adult involves many losses. Loss nearly always involves mental or emotional pain, which we often call grief, or mourning. This experience involves more than just feeling 'low'; the writer C. S. Lewis, who described his experience of loss following the death of his wife in *A Grief Observed* (2001), noticed that his grief felt a lot like fear. The greater the impact of the loss, the more acute the mental pain is likely to be. In themselves, loss, grief, and mourning are not mental health problems, but interestingly many research studies have found a close connection between serious ('clinical') depression and multiple losses in the distant and recent past of people with this diagnosis (Brown and Harris, 1978). Looking back, you might recall a period of loss, and the sense of anxiety, sadness, low mood and so on that followed it; but also how things suddenly started to come right and seem better and brighter, often for no obvious reason. Perhaps then, serious depression can be a bit like getting 'stuck' in the state of mourning and unable to spontaneously recover, 'work it through' or let go of it. In fact this is how Freud thought of depression when he wrote his main paper on the subject, *Mourning and Melancholia* (1917).

Reflect

Maybe reading the above paragraph started you thinking about yourself and your experience of loss and emotional pain.

Are these periods of your life something you think you can make direct use of in social work, or do you really feel you want to keep them at bay, and put them behind you?

Secondly, and following from the discussion above, we suggest that *everyone* has a vulnerability or 'disposition' towards mental health problems. This is a way of saying that mental health problems are part of 'ordinary' life, but without minimising them; they always involve suffering, often involve fear, and frequently arouse fear and anxiety in other people, which is part of why they

can become a 'social stigma'. However, some people are afflicted by these sufferings in a way that makes it nearly impossible for them to live ordinary lives, for shorter or longer periods of time. Often people who have had 'chronic' mental health difficulties will have had contact with psychiatric services, have been diagnosed, and may have spent time in hospital. This does not make them 'a different kind of person' to whom you cannot relate; on the other hand it may tell you something about how acute and complicated their mental suffering is or has been. In Chapter 20 on working with adults with mental health difficulties we discuss in much more detail how social workers can think and act in a helpful way in relation to the psychiatric system and the various diagnoses of mental illness. Here we want to stress that one essential basis of good communication between social workers and service users with mental health difficulties is the *shared* capacity to 'be mentally unwell'. This perspective has always been central in one small but important part of the mental health service system, the therapeutic community movement (Kennedy et al., 1987). Many social workers have found inspiration in this way of working, because it emphasises the interpersonal and social side of what both mental health and mental ill health are, and says that in order to be able to help someone get better you've got to be prepared to get in contact with the 'unwell' part of yourself.

So, thirdly and perhaps restating the point of the paragraph above a little differently, one could say that in order to do mental health work properly you have got to be open to feeling 'disturbed' yourself. Otherwise, you are not really able to be in receipt of communications from *all* levels of the personalities of the people you are working with. There are serious issues at stake here, as the short case study below suggests.

Case study

Jim

Dave is an experienced mental health social worker in a Community Mental Health Team (CMHT). He has worked for two years with Jim, a very socially isolated man in his mid-50s who has had various diagnoses over the last two decades, and two hospital admissions in the last five years. Each admission was preceded by him becoming even more emotionally and socially withdrawn than usual, and developing delusional thoughts about his food being poisoned so that he stopped eating. Lately he seems quite trusting of Dave who spends at least an hour every fortnight with Jim at his flat, often sitting in silence for quite long periods. But last week, Dave had a disturbing experience. In the middle of his visit, he was suddenly overtaken by a strong conviction that Jim was suicidal. He tried to think what it might have been in the things Jim had said that day that gave rise to this, but it was very hard to pin down. The only thing he could think of was that near the start of the visit Jim had looked out of his window and said, 'Go on mate, jump', and then smiled at Dave, who had gone to the window and looked out. Jim had pointed across the road and said, 'See that old cat, on the wall there? He was trying to get down'. As Jim turned away from the window, Dave remembered that he thought he had looked very sad.

Dave sat out the rest of the visit feeling very anxious. Was he picking up something from Jim that he needed to pay attention to, or was he oversensitive and anxious himself? He really couldn't tell. But as he left the flat, he felt unbearably aware of Jim's loneliness and isolation. At the office he talked to a colleague, and eventually decided to phone Jim the next day and arrange to visit the following week, rather than in two weeks' time. He thought Jim sounded OK with this, though he was always hard to 'read'.

When he visited next, Jim seemed much the same. But early on Dave went to the window and looked out and said, 'Seen that old cat again?' 'Every day', Jim replied. 'I was thinking', said Dave, 'I wonder what keeps that old cat going day after day?' After a long silence Jim said, 'Hard to say, really'. 'Um, it's touch and go with him then?' Dave said. After a pause Jim said, 'He's got an owner like, lives across there. Comes out and calls for him sometimes. So he's OK. Basically'.

What do you think of the way Dave handled this episode? Did he react about right, or with too much or too little concern about the risk to Jim?

What do you think of his way of talking with Jim on the second visit? Do you think Dave has reason to be reassured at the end, or not? What other feelings and thoughts did the case study evoke in you?

This case study raises a number of questions and points for learning about communication:

- The use of silence: we have discussed this above, but in this example we can see how sitting quietly with a very withdrawn person might be the right thing to do in various ways. Such a person might not want to be 'crowded' with questions and talk. To be 'withdrawn' may be a way of saying *I easily feel intruded on – let me be in control of when talk happens*.

- Allowing silences may help Dave to 'pick up on' feelings and communications at other levels. These are hard to make sense of, and it could be that Dave is over-anxious; but equally it may be that after a long period of testing his trust, Jim feels able to let Dave know – at an emotional level – how close he is to feeling suicidal a lot of the time.

- Sticking with it: Dave has stuck with Jim over a long period of time, and this 'tells' Jim something important. On the surface not a lot seems to happen in their visits, but this may not matter that much. When Jim says he will do something he does it.

- Being sensitive to metaphors and latent meanings: Dave thinks there may have been a connection between what Jim said about the cat 'jumping', and his sudden concern for Jim's state of mind. He could ignore this altogether, or he could be very direct and ask Jim whether he has suicidal thoughts. Instead he decided to just let Jim know that he has heard this bit of communication and he opens up the conversation by using the metaphor. If Jim was conveying something significant through this, then it's clear Dave has heard it; if not then there is probably no harm done.

- Looking after yourself as well: at the office Dave has someone with whom he can communicate about his experience with Jim. This helps him think more clearly and decide how to act. You should always have someone *you* can communicate with in doing this kind of work, because there can be a lot of anxiety to bear at times. Organisations should provide regular reflective supervision for staff for just this reason.

Some key considerations . . .

In this section we have looked more deeply at what mental health difficulties are, in order to stress, not that there is a 'special' kind of communication needed in mental health work, but more that there are particular capacities needed in the social worker if 'good enough' ordinary communication is to be successful. In summary:

- Before you can communicate well in mental heath work, you must first listen well and make the effort to *understand* what state of mind a service user is in. Once you have understood something of their current experience, it will be easier to know how to communicate sensitively.

- Your own emotional availability is the key to good understanding. While you need to listen and empathise at the verbal level, the 'other 80 per cent' is especially important in terms of 'picking up' on a person's overall state of mind.

- Even if a service user is finding it difficult to take in or respond to ordinary communication, this does not mean that their right and need to be treated with respect, consideration, rationality, are any the less. The opposite is true, in fact: social workers have an important role to play as guardians of people's rights and dignity under these circumstances (cf. the case study of Marianne above).

- Communication in mental health work is often inherently uncomfortable. But this is unavoidable and you must be prepared to tolerate difficult, ambiguous, anxiety-making experiences and communications if you are to be a competent worker in this area.

- It is essential that you have your own professional support – someone whom you can communicate with – if you are doing mental health social work.

Communication with disabled adults and children

This section of the chapter considers the issue of communicating with disabled people. You will be asked to reflect on your own views and beliefs about communication, and think about how these might impact on your work as a social worker with someone who has a communication impairment. The section will describe different communication methods, consider the impact of communication on safeguarding children and give you basic guidelines for communicating with disabled people.

Ways of communicating

One of the most basic human rights is that of being communicated with and consulted about decisions affecting your life. This right is fully recognised in various pieces of legislation and government initiatives including *Valuing People* (DoH 2001e), Children Act 1989 and 2004 and *Every Child Matters* (DoH 2003e). In addition to this the *Framework for the Assessment of Children in Need* highlights the need to consult meaningfully with children in the assessment process and includes advice on how this can be done in the accompanying guidance. We all, including disabled children and adults, communicate in a variety of ways and, as noted earlier in the chapter, approximately two-thirds of communication is non-verbal. Communication can take place in many formats: for example, sound, movement, touch, play, pictures, signs and symbols, behaviour and body language; and a range of media can be used including speech, gestural signing, objects, visual helpers, social stories, use of third person and speaking through objects or characters. Social workers need to be creative in their thinking around the whole issue of communicating with disabled people.

Having a communication impairment can mean many things: a person might have a reduced or lost ability to communicate or their ability could be affected by the way they process language. Their impairment could result from physical, sensory or learning needs. For example, Marianne in our case study earlier may have impaired expressive communication as a result of cerebral palsy but cognitively understand all that is said to her, whereas a person with autism may use verbal language but experience difficulties with processing the language used by others.

Reflect

Think of a time where you were trying to communicate something to another person that they didn't understand. You might have been talking with someone who spoke another language or simply not getting yourself across.

How did this make you feel? What could have been done to improve the communication?

You might have felt frustrated, uncomfortable or anxious; you might also have picked up similar feelings from the person you were trying to communicate with. You might have felt like giving up or felt the other person wasn't really interested in what you were trying to say. These are all feelings which disabled people may experience. You may have thought of a number of things which can be done to aid communication, including asking for help from an interpreter or someone else who knows the person well. You will find a list of other suggestions that may help at the end of this section.

Communication and social work

As we know, communication is the absolute key to ensuring that views are known and needs properly assessed. It is unimaginable that a piece of work would be carried out or an assessment undertaken of a non-disabled adult or child without their views being sought and represented, yet this is something that often happens to disabled people who find that their way of communicating is not valued or respected. As was demonstrated in the case study of Marianne, it is often easier for non-disabled social workers to relate to the non-disabled parents or carers than to the disabled person (Middleton, 1992). Thinking back to Jo's response to meeting Marianne for the first time it is easy to see how this situation can arise if social workers do not have sufficient understanding or the appropriate skills, or indeed the confidence in their own abilities. Experience has shown that all too often social workers have written 'unable to communicate' in the section of assessments which should include the individual's views. One way of overcoming these difficulties is to plan ahead for a meeting or home visit. For example, find out as much as you can about the way in which the person communicates and think about what your response will be if a parent or carer talks for the service user, and remember their views are not always the same. As in any aspect of social work, the more prepared you are, the more confident you will feel in addressing any issues that arise. You could also discuss any concerns or fears you might have with more experienced colleagues or ask to shadow a colleague as a means of building your confidence.

There are many different situations that social workers might encounter in working with disabled people and each scenario will need to be planned for individually to ensure the person's communication needs are met, that they feel comfortable and their contribution is valued. You may, for example, work with a visually impaired person who is able to verbally articulate their feelings but needs information from the social worker about the setting in which the meeting is taking place and who else may be present; or with a person with a profound learning disability who needs someone with them who knows their communication system well. Local authorities have a legal duty to seek the wishes and feelings of all children and adults when undertaking assessments and providing services, and communication

needs should form an integral part of any assessment. We need to start from a point where we believe the person has something to say and then think creatively about how this can be achieved. By considering communication in line with the social model definition of disability (see Chapter 19 on working with disabled children and adults for an explanation of this), social workers can begin to reflect on the barriers in society which impact on communicating with disabled people.

Think ahead

You are a social work student on placement, about to undertake an assessment of need of a disabled person.

What barriers might there be to prevent you from communicating with the person you are assessing? Are these barriers linked to the disabled person or the way society views disabled people?

The barriers you might have considered could have included your own knowledge and skills in relation to different forms of communication or how much knowledge you have about the person you will be assessing. You will probably have also thought about other issues such as having the right environment or sufficient time. You might also have wanted to ask questions such as, 'Is the assessment form or other welfare service information available in Braille or other accessible formats?', 'Can a BSL interpreter be found at the time when needed?' or 'Is there a computer available with software compatible with that used by the disabled person?'

A lack of communication or understanding can lead to inappropriate or no services being offered. For example, the purpose of Jo's visit to Marianne was to assess her needs; Marianne was in tears after Jo arrived but this was not addressed and Jo did not speak directly with her to discover her wishes or needs. It is possible therefore that Marianne did not want to attend the day centre and was upset as a result of being referred or that she was simply frustrated at not being spoken to herself. These of course are both assumptions; Jo needed to communicate directly with Marianne to be clear about her wishes and needs and to avoid assumptions being made.

Valuing all forms of communication

The definition of communication used by social workers needs to be wide and open. Marchant and Page (2003) point out that, sadly, the biggest barrier to communicating with disabled children continues to be the attitudes and behaviour of professionals and the failure to follow guidance. They state: 'We see it as vital that communication is understood as more than the use of speech and language and that all professionals' working definition of communication includes the wide range of ways [disabled] children make their wishes and feelings known' (Marchant and Page 2003: 60). Morris (2002) points out that as the majority of people use spoken language to communicate, disabled children who use other means of communication often find their way is undervalued and unrecognised. This can apply equally to disabled adults. The onus is on the social worker to discover the disabled person's preferred method of communication. This can be done by asking the person themselves, using an interpreter or talking, with permission from the service user, to other people who know their communication method well. For example, a hearing social worker might think it appropriate to ask a Deaf British Sign Language (BSL) user to write down what it is they want to say but some deaf people would not find this acceptable. BSL as a language is not a direct translation of English and historically many deaf people were not taught English as a written language. By asking the person how they prefer to communicate, the social worker demonstrates that they value the service user's input and right to be communicated with in the way they choose.

Communication and safeguarding from harm

Communication is important of course in all aspects of social work but perhaps particularly so when considering work undertaken with disabled children and adults who may be at risk of harm. Marchant and Page (2003: 62) state: 'Ascertaining how and what a child communicates is key to safeguarding them, whatever their level of impairment. We know that it is possible to recognise signs of contentment or distress in the youngest of infants and we need to ensure that our definitions of communication are inclusive and not discriminatory'.

Research suggests that disabled children do not get a fair deal in the child protection or 'safeguarding' children process in comparison with their non-disabled peers and that indeed they are more vulnerable to abuse than their non-disabled peers (Cooke, 2000; Miller, 2003; Edwards and Richardson, 2003). There are numerous reasons for this including, for example, concerns not always being recognised as child protection issues, or behaviour/

physical symptoms being seen as the result of the child's impairment rather than an indicator of abuse. However, communication also plays a key role in this inequity. Research demonstrates that social workers may think the child can't communicate, or rely upon a parent or carer to talk for them; that the police or social worker may think that the child won't make a 'credible witness'; that Department of Health timescales for completing assessments often do not give disabled children enough time to make their views known and that disabled children who make a disclosure may not be believed (particularly children with a learning disability). In addition to this, fewer disabled children are given the opportunity to be interviewed as part of a criminal investigation than their non-disabled peers, and fewer cases get to court (Cooke, 2000; Love et al., 2003).

Case study

Billy

Billy is 15 years old; he has a moderate learning disability and some difficulties with expressing himself and making sense of what is said to him. Billy has told his mum and social worker that three days ago a man called John pulled down his trousers and tried to touch his penis. The police were informed; however, when they interviewed Billy he couldn't remember when the incident had taken place and the details he gave were different to those he had given the social worker. In addition to this it was known that local youths had been calling John a 'paedophile', thus leading the officer involved to state he thought Billy had been put up to making the allegation by the local youths and he would not be taking the allegation any further.

The police officer's ability to communicate with Billy will have impacted on the decision made. The officer may have thought that because Billy gave varying accounts of what happened he wasn't telling the truth or that he would not be able to give evidence should the case ever reach court. Billy does not have any concept of time and when asked questions he doesn't really understand he will say what he thinks the other person wants to hear. Had the police known this, Billy could have been interviewed in a way that was more enabling. Ways of doing this might have included interviewing him in a place he was familiar with, asking questions that he could understand and checking back that he had understood, and also checking that the interviewing officer understood Billy's answers.

The issue of communication in safeguarding disabled children has been receiving a higher profile over the past few years and is gaining a wider understanding both in policy and social work practice. For example, there is growing awareness of the need for child protection social workers to have a better understanding of disability and communication issues and for social workers working with disabled children to have more training in relation to safeguarding children. Examples of good practice have seen social workers practising in each area working more closely together in cases of abuse. In addition to this, recent government initiatives and legislation contain the grounding for improving protection structures and including disabled children in this process (for further information see *Every Child Matters*, *National Service Framework*, *Working Together* 2010, Safeguarding Disabled Children Practice Guidance 2009, Youth Justice and Criminal Evidence Act 1999 Special Measures).

Historically, many of the communication systems used by disabled people have not included the words, signs or symbols to describe private parts of the body or abusive acts. However, more recently, in line with the whole safeguarding disabled children issue gaining higher profile, the need for disabled children to access appropriate communication methods has been raised. This has led, for example, to Triangle, an independent voluntary organisation working with disabled children, and the NSPCC publishing 'how it is', a resource that will enable better communication with disabled children about their rights, needs and feelings. The pack includes images of body parts, sexual activity and physically abusive actions that disabled children can use to communicate their experiences, feelings and concerns. The pack should prove to be a valuable resource in helping social workers better understand what some disabled children are trying to tell them.

Communication systems

There are a wide range of communication systems used by people with a communication impairment; the type of system used will depend on the individual's own needs. For example, a deaf person may use British Sign Language which is the language of the Deaf community; Sign Supported English; lip reading and/or written text (although it must be remembered that some deaf people will not have had the opportunity to learn literacy in the same way as hearing people). It is important to have face-to-face and eye-to-eye contact with the person you are communicating with. Deaf people may also communicate using mobile phone text or a text phone. People with a visual impairment may use Braille and Moon, which are both methods of reading by touch or large text. Many also use computer aided packages to read, write and dictate information.

Those who have a dual sensory impairment (both impaired sight and speech may use the deafblind manual alphabet where words are spelt out onto the hand using handshapes. However, deafblind people may also communicate in a range of other ways depending on their level of hearing and sight loss: it is crucial to find out their preferred method of communication and not make assumptions.

Other methods of communication used by learning disabled and some physically disabled people include: Blisssymbolics which is a symbols system where the symbols can be accessed through a communication board or book or computer aided devices; Makaton, a language programme specifically designed for people with a learning disability, using signs from BSL and/or graphic symbols together with speech; Picture Exchange Communication System (PECS) which uses pictures rather than words or signs; lip-reading and finger spelling. Some disabled people use pieces of electronic equipment to access their chosen communication system, for example, using voice-output communication aids which involves personalised words being placed into the equipment (e.g. names, lessons at school, food etc.) that the individual can then choose by pressing a key.

The important thing to remember is that the key principles outlined in this chapter of empathy, respect and authenticity continue to apply to communicating with disabled people, whichever method is used. Basic guidelines for communicating are:

Do:
- Find out as much as possible about the person's preferred communication method before meeting them.
- Think carefully about how you will approach and plan for your first meeting.
- Give thought to where the meeting will take place; seating, comfort and lighting and so on will all impact on communication.
- Find a suitable place to speak, away from noise and distractions.
- Have an open view about what communication means and be flexible in your approach.

- Book an interpreter, if needed, in advance, where possible.
- With consent from the service user, involve others who know their communication system well.
- Have clear ground rules if a third person is to be present. For example, be clear about their role – to assist in communication rather than speak for the person.
- Speak directly to the disabled person and give them enough time to respond.
- Use clear and plain language and don't waffle. Say if you don't understand something.
- Develop a range of resources which you can use.

Do not:
- Make assumptions about whether or not a person can communicate.
- Make assumptions about how they communicate.
- Address a carer or third person instead of the disabled person.
- Put unrealistic time constraints on the meeting.
- Pretend to understand.
- Be frightened of asking questions or asking someone to repeat themselves.
- Hold a meeting in an inappropriate setting, e.g. consider lighting if lip-reading or a BSL interpreter is required.

Communication with older people

In this final section we focus on communicating with older people. Of course, the full range of communication skills and requirements that can be deployed with all service users are also relevant when working with older people. Social workers will need to demonstrate the same high levels of *empathy* for an individual's circumstances, *respect* for her/his wishes and desires and *authenticity* in responding to them that have been noted earlier in the chapter.

Communication in context

Although older people have the same sorts of need as other service users, both practical and emotional, the context of practice is such that the emotional needs of service users are often ignored, with particular emphasis being placed on practice that combines high volumes of work with low intensity in its nature (Lymbery, 2005).

The importance of context to social work with older people will be particularly emphasised in Chapter 22, but it is important that practitioners recognise that the nature of their communication with older people will be significantly affected by this. In thinking about the importance of communication with this group, it is important to be aware of a number of critical factors that affect the environment within which such communication takes place:

- *Ill-health*: Most older people who have contact with social workers have experienced a range of circumstances, often associated with ill-health, that have promoted this involvement. In the case of dementia, for example, the nature of the disease will fundamentally affect communication, such that it becomes increasingly difficult. In other circumstances – for example, following a stroke or the onset of Parkinson's disease – the illness itself creates an additional barrier to successful communication, beyond the problems that can occur in everyday situations. In addition, the physical ill health to which older people are particularly prone also means that the person is more likely to be living with a degree of physical pain.
- *History*: An obvious difference between older people and other service users is the simple fact that they have lived longer! This means that they are more likely to have had various experiences – social isolation, abuse, domestic violence, periods of mental ill health, etc. – that may affect their ability to communicate openly with others (Koprowska, 2007).
- *Loss*: In addition, the experience of loss is common among older people who need social work support (Thompson, 2002). This can assume different forms; older people are more likely to have experienced bereavement, often of a life-partner, as well as the losses that can derive from ill-health – loss of independence, reduced control over one's own life, housing, etc. A major consequence of this can be a high level of psychological pain and distress.

As a result of a combination of these circumstances, older people and their families are almost certain to be experiencing high levels of stress when they require assistance from social workers, owing in large measure to the other issues noted above; for practice to be successful, the tensions that this will provoke need to be sensitively addressed. Certainly, as indicated earlier in the chapter, the likelihood that communication will be marked by heightened emotions and tears is particularly marked. As a result of this, as a social worker you may be uncertain at the point of referral about what issues your first visit may bring up and what the implications of these may be for your communication. Typically, referral information will contain little about the emotional condition of an older person, and even the detail about her/his physical and mental capabilities may also be incomplete. As part of your preparation for an initial visit, it is essential to find out as much as you can about these issues. For example, although – as in other areas of social work practice with adults – there is likely to be a presumption that you will first see the older person on her/his own, the value of having a trusted person present at this point may be considerable. If you do not clarify this in advance, you may find the discussion doesn't achieve what you had hoped for it. Of course, if the older person does wish to have a trusted person present, it is vital to avoid the temptation to focus on what she/he has to say rather than the older person. (As noted earlier in this chapter, such a temptation is common to many different areas of social work practice.)

Verbal and non-verbal communication skills

Successful communication skills are, of course, central to good social work with older people, particularly if we accept the premise that the quality of relationship between social worker and service user is a key determinant of successful outcomes. Therefore, the messages from the rest of this chapter are transferable to this section. For example, it is inconceivable that good practice with older people could be carried out without effective communication skills, which, as Thompson (2003) reminds us, applies equally to verbal, non-verbal and written forms. Indeed, if only one aspect of communication (for example, the verbal) is addressed, there will be significant limitations in the quality of practice, particularly given the additional limitations noted above. Of course, much face-to-face communication with service users is carried out at the verbal level, and how a social worker *listens* to what is said to her/him is every bit as important as how she/he *speaks* to a service user. Such skills are vital in establishing a relationship with a person with dementia, for example (Killick and Allan, 2001). Here, aspects of communication that Thompson (2003) terms 'paralanguage' – tone of voice, speed of language, intonation and inflection, etc. – have a critical impact on the effectiveness of communication. Continuing to think about the needs of a person with dementia, verbal communication should be only part of a social worker's

repertoire. Various forms of non-verbal communication – facial expression, eye contact, distance and proximity, posture, etc. – can become more important than verbal communication, where a social worker must develop alternatives that communicate empathy and respect.

Communicating challenges

There are some general points about communicating with older people that you need to be aware of prior to your first visit. You can expect some level of hearing and sight loss, as such problems increase with age. However, it is obviously vital to know if they constitute significant impairments, and be prepared to act to alleviate some of the difficulties. For example, when working with people with a hearing impairment, it is important to speak slowly and clearly and not to obscure the face and mouth as there may be some lip-reading augmenting the impaired aural perceptions. If the hearing impairment is worse on one side or the other, it is important to position yourself so that the effect of your speech can be best heard. For people with a visual impairment, ensure that they know where you are located; recognise that the visual clues that we use to understand information fully are less likely to be in operation, which may require an increased level of compensation in other forms of communication – the 'paralanguage' noted above, or touch, for example.

In addition, if there is some dimension of cognitive impairment for the older person, then this will have to borne in mind. If there is doubt about whether or not the older person can fully comprehend what the social worker intends to communicate, then this will compromise the impact of the visit. Assessing the level of an older person's understanding is vital but can be difficult. For example, an individual may present as particularly clear in relation to past events, but have a poor short-term memory, presenting clear problems of comprehension. In addition, hearing impairments can often be interpreted to mean that an individual is losing their ability to comprehend what is happening around them; the difference between cognitive and hearing impairments can be difficult to ascertain, but are critical to effective relationship-building. The temptation to cut corners in such circumstances – communicating largely through another person, and hence denying the rights of the older person – is to be avoided. There is also much that will need to be learned about the individual with whom the social worker interacts. Many older people appear very polite and amenable to suggestion; in such circumstances, the social worker needs to be assured that any agreement is genuine and not formulaic. For example, a polite older person with some level of hearing impairment may not properly hear and understand the content of any discussion, but agree to what the social worker proposes despite this lack of comprehension. Conversely, a smaller number of older people present as awkward and querulous, presenting a different set of practice challenges. A social worker will need to explore what reasons might underpin the attitudes and behaviour of the older person, to which a variety of physical or psychological factors might potentially contribute. The important point is to find a way of engaging with the older person, and not to allow the difficulties of engaging with that person to deprive her/him of the services that are needed. In addition, because some older people are socially isolated, there may be a tendency for an older person to prolong the discussion because of the social contact it represents. Equally, some older people can be very talkative! This can ensure that visits take up considerable time; this does not sit well with the pressures on social workers who work with older people. The practitioner will need to balance the need to listen respectfully to the individual against the requirement to extract relevant information in a short space of time; obviously, these obligations can well be in conflict. To manage this, be clear about the nature of your involvement and what it is that you hope to achieve through it.

Communicating empathy, respect and authenticity

The following case study explores some of the dimensions of communicating with older people, focusing particularly on the issues caused by the factors of ill health, history and loss noted above. The commentary on each segment of the case study also focuses on the ways in which the values of *empathy*, *respect* and *authenticity* can be enhanced.

Case study

Della

Morag is a social worker employed in a busy local authority team providing social work services for older people. She is allocated the referral of Della Keen, a 77-year-old woman, who has been referred by her GP. The only information on the referral is that Della appeared to be struggling to cope on her own and that admission to a residential home may be indicated. On further investigation directly with Della's GP, Morag uncovers a pattern of generally good health until Della started to experience lapses of memory approximately three years ago. The GP says that she has made three referrals for Della to receive a more detailed specialist diagnosis, but that on each occasion Della has failed to attend for the appointment, despite apparently welcoming the opportunity to clarify her medical situation. The GP believes that Della is in the early stages of Alzheimer's disease, although he could not be certain of this, given her lack of cooperation. As far as her physical health is concerned, Della is reported as having few difficulties. When Morag first makes contact with Della, she seems confused and uncertain of who Morag is and what her role means. Once she grasps the idea that Morag has come from social services because of the GP's concerns about her ability to manage at home, Della is emphatic that she has no problems in managing her home and that she has no intention of ever leaving it. Morag is not convinced that these protestations represent a strong grasp of the realities of Della's situation.

The point at which a person's memory begins to fail heralds a profoundly difficult period for most people who experience the gradual onset of dementia. Denial of the existence of the problem is a particular feature of this stage, as an individual seeks to maintain a sense of normality under circumstances where that normality is threatened at every turn. The legal context for the issue of incapacity is complex, and the presumption for all adults is that they retain capacity unless it is demonstrated to be absent (Johns, 2007). There are potentially serious consequences for Della's future if steps are taken prematurely to deprive her of her right to take decisions that affect her own welfare. At the same time, Morag will recognise the considerable risks that can follow if Della remains living independently within the community, and her priority will be to ensure that Della has a clear grasp of what the consequences of taking such risks will be, and come to an understanding of the best way both to maintain and maximise her independence while ensuring that her safety and security are not compromised.

The most effective way of doing this will be to establish a relationship with Della, which in turn will depend upon the ability of the worker to establish an *empathic* bond with Della. Through this, she will have the opportunity to explore Della's feelings about her changed circumstances in some detail and where she is able to develop her trust and her ability to respond with sensitivity to the worker's (Morag's) concerns. The complexities of managing this with Della in the light of her cognitive impairments cannot be underestimated, requiring very well developed communication skills on the part of the social worker (Tibbs, 2001). In addition, the time that this will take to manage effectively should also be recognised (which has a direct impact on the contextual problems noted above). As Phillips et al. (2006) point out, the creation of a meaningful relationship should be seen as a prerequisite for practice in these circumstances, despite the time it will take, as this will make subsequently agreed actions more likely to be maintained by Della.

have an impact on her willingness even to consider moving out, even assuming that she had a full acceptance of the likely implications of her illness. Here, the difficult and traumatic experience that she witnessed in relation to her mother is likely to have an impact on her ability to accept the changes that are currently happening to her, particularly given the pain that she observed a similar process caused her mother. In both cases, the impact of key events in Della's life can be expected to have consequences as she embarks on this challenging period. In discovering detail about Della's early life, Morag will be reminded about the wealth of experience that she has packed into her 77 years. Given this, the need to approach her with *respect* is obvious; as we need to respect all human beings, perhaps there is an extra duty of respect due to those who have experienced more of the hardships, travails and traumas that characterise all of our lives.

Case study

Della cont . . .

In the process of working with Della, some detail about her personal history is uncovered that has a material impact on how she is responding to her current life changes. Apparently, Della originates from the East End of London. As she was 9 years old at the start of the Second World War she was evacuated into the countryside, where she remained for several years. She says that she 'hated' the time away from her family and her home, and 'loathed' living in an environment that she did not consider her own. Ever since, she has always thought of herself as somebody who took particular pride in her home. In addition, she talks about the slow and painful death of her own mother 11 ago, where her Alzheimer's disease had 'blighted' her final years.

Case study

Della cont . . .

As with many older people, Della has experienced numerous losses in her life. One of these was the protracted death of her mother, made worse by the fact that at the end she was unable to recognise Della or anybody else. More recently, Della nursed her husband through his final illness. (A life-long smoker, he succumbed to lung cancer four years ago.) Although Della feels that they received good support during this difficult time, she acknowledges that she has been feeling 'low' since then and that she misses him a lot. Her first experiences of significant memory loss occurred quite soon after his death. She has two children, but neither of them lives locally and therefore they do not play an active role in her life. She talks about how 'lovely' both of them were as small children, but how they became difficult as teenagers: apparently both left home before they were 20.

In both of these examples, Della's past experiences connect with two specific current issues. For example, her experience as a wartime evacuee appears to have made her particularly home-loving, a term that she accepts. She moved into the house she currently occupies when she and her husband were first married (in 1950) and has lived in it ever since. It can be predicted that this will

It is, of course, recognised that older people do tend to experience depressive periods, often associated with the losses to which they are increasingly subject (Stuart-Hamilton, 2006). What Della describes as her response to her husband's death is therefore consistent with this understanding. As we have previously noted, the nature

Professional tip

Good communication with older people

- Be aware of the impact that an older person's ill health is likely to have on both their level of need, and the appropriate response to that need.
- Try to understand as much as you an about the history and background of an older person.
- Be aware of the loss that an older person is likely to have experienced and its consequences in terms of the experiences of grief.
- Try to develop as full a picture as you can of the history, character and future desires of the older person.

- In talking to an older person, ensure that you speak clearly and that you position yourself in such a way as to maximise this aspect of communication.
- Use paralanguage to support and reinforce your verbal forms of communication.
- Ensure that any discussion with an older person proceeds at a pace with which they are comfortable.
- Never lose sight of, and never allow the older person to lose sight of, your reasons for being involved with that person.

of her mother's last illness might make it particularly difficult for Della to accept the reality of her own situation; we should also note that the effects of bereavement on older people can be long-lasting (Thompson, 2002) and hence represent a continuing difficulty in this case. In addition, there are elements of loss to be considered in relation to what appears to be a distant relationship between Della and her two children, both now in middle age. Certainly, Della has no expectation that either (or both) will provide the care and support that she gave to her mother. Given the expectations that exist about the nature of family caring responsibilities (Finch, 1989), it is quite possible that the absence of these children from her life constitutes another example of loss, albeit one that may be less recognised. This may have major consequences for the nature of the communication between the social worker and Della. The experience of loss is more likely to render Della highly emotional and prone to tears. This will present an enhanced challenge for Morag, who will need to respect Della's grief, empathise closely with what she may be feeling, while remaining capable of keeping the overall purposes of the discussion in mind. The *authenticity* of Morag's response here is critical; Della needs to feel that her loss and grief receive proper recognition, and that Morag is responding to her as a genuine human being, able to provide warmth, sympathy and understanding where indicated.

For Morag, therefore, establishing a productive working relationship with Della will be based on the exercise of creative skills of communication, where the various contextual issues that this section has noted could create practical difficulties. Certainly, the psychological pain that appears to beset Della could cause her to become highly emotional; this could potentially be a major obstacle to working positively to resolve the many problems that confront her. Similarly, the stress and distress that the process of seeking help can generate, both for the older person and for her/his family, can add to the difficulties confronted by the practitioner. If Morag does not manage these tensions well, the consequences for Della, and for what needs to be accomplished to support her properly, may be overwhelming.

Conclusion

Professional relationships with service users require you to have developed good communication skills. Interpersonal communication skills are numerous and in this chapter we have deliberately focused on only a small, but what we consider crucial, aspect of effective interpersonal communication: the capacity to communicate empathically, authentically and respectfully. With this firm foundation in place, we believe it is possible to develop communication skills pertinent to specific people, contexts and circumstances.

From reading the sections dedicated to communicating with specific service users you will have become aware of the common skills that are required for effective communication with any individual, regardless of their circumstances. On top of this foundational understanding, however, is the expectation that you will develop specific skills that will enable you to communicate with heightened sensitivity to the specific needs of each individual, whether they are a young child separated from their parents for the first time or an older person having to decide whether they can continue to live independently. Developing these general and specific communication skills takes time and cannot be rushed. You can start by reflecting on those positive encounters you have had where you felt genuinely understood and respected. As a practising student or qualified worker you can develop your skills by observing other more experienced colleagues at work and also by allowing them to observe and critique your practice. A good deal of social work practice is done on an individual basis in the privacy of people's homes, and once you are qualified opportunities to observe colleagues or be observed are rare. Allowing your practice to be transparent facilitates communication with colleagues about your practice, which will indirectly enable you to communicate in practice more effectively, empathically, respectfully and authentically. And this is what it is all about.

Key learning points

This chapter has covered the following learning points:

✔ Effective communication requires empathy, authenticity and respect.

✔ How you communicate will depend, in part, on the nature of the intervention.

✔ Learning to respond to difficult emotions is integral to effective communication.

✔ Communicating effectively with children requires similar skills to those needed in other professional contexts, but in addition social workers need to recognise the different ways in which children communicate (reflecting, for example, their use of play and their developmental stage).

✔ Communication which uses a 'third object' may be helpful for children in reducing anxiety and providing non-verbal means of expression and information-sharing.

✔ In mental health work it is especially important that you are able to think of communication as something that happens at many levels, not just verbally.

✔ Communicating with people with a disability requires you to ensure you do *not* make assumptions about an individual's capabilities.

✔ It is important to consider the contexts of ill health, the history of each individual and her/his experiences of loss, as these will affect your communication with older people.

Further reading

General

Egan, G. (2007) *The Skilled Helper*, 8th edn. Belmont, CA: Thomson Books/Cole. A book geared for counselling students and counsellors but with useful, relevant material and applied exercises for social workers.

Koprowska, J. (2005) *Communication and Inter-Personal Skills in Social Work*. Exeter: Learning Matters. An excellent, clearly written guide to basic communication skills with an emphasis on the emotional roots of effective communication.

Trevithick, P. (2005) *Social Work Skills: A Practice Handbook*, 2nd edn. Buckingham: Open University Press. A comprehensive guide to social work skills that pays particular attention to the theoretical underpinning of practical skills.

Children

Jones, D., Rose, W. and Jeffery, C. (2006) *The Developing World of the Child*. London: Jessica Kingsley. Chapters on direct work and detailed account of conducting interviews with children suspected of being abused.

Lefevre, M. (2010) *Communicating with Children and Young People*. Bristol: Policy Press. Combines an exploration of theoretical perspective on the dynamics of communication with children and young people with an introduction to key skills in such aspects of effective practice as forming relationships, understanding non-verbal communication, breaking bad news and so on.

Redgrave, K. (2000) *Child's Play: 'Direct Work' with the Deprived Child*. Cheadle: Boys and Girls Welfare Society. Gives numerous imaginative ideas, often with illustrations, for using 'the third object' in communicating with children.

Williamson, K. *Direct Work with Children and Life Story Work*. Unpublished workbook. Available from the author, Adoption and Fostering Team, North East Lincolnshire Council.

Wilson, K. and Ryan, V. (2005) *Play Therapy: A non-Directive Approach for Children and Adolescents*. London: Bailliere Tindall. Chapter 1 gives detailed guidance on core skills (reflection, empathy, genuineness, congruence) in working with children; Chapter 5 considers selecting play materials and setting up a playroom; Chapter 7 discusses reflection of feelings, limit setting and other practice issues such as responding to disclosures of abuse, confidentiality, involving carers, etc.

Mental health

Bateman, A. and Fonagy, P. (2006) *Mentalization-based Treatment for Borderline Personality Disorder: A Practical Guide*. Oxford: Oxford University Press.

Gabbard, G., Beck, J. and Holmes, J. (2007) *Oxford Textbook of Psychotherapy*. Oxford: Oxford University Press. Many chapters contain good sections on key practice principles, as well as thorough discussion of the nature and evidence base for particular conditions.

Prior, V. and Glaser, D. (2006) *Understanding Attachment and Attachment Disorders: Theory, Evidence and Practice.* London: Jessica Kingsley.

Older people

Killick, J. and Allan, K. (2001) *Communication and the Care of People with Dementia.* Buckingham: Open University Press. This book focuses helpfully on the uniqueness of every person with dementia and on the distinctive approaches to communication that are therefore needed to enable effective communication with each person.

Phillips, J., Ray, M. and Marshall, M. (2006) *Social Work with Older People.* Basingstoke: Palgrave Macmillan. The latest edition of this core text makes the case for a more person-focussed approach to social work with older people, and argues that the quality of communication determines the quality of outcome for each older person.

People with disabilities

Marchant, R. and Page, M. (2001) *Two Way Street* (handbook). NSPCC, Joseph Rowntree Foundation, Triangle. This handbook, published jointly by the NSPCC, Joseph Rowntree Foundation and Triangle, provides very useful information on different types of communication and issues relating to communicating with young people with a communication disorder.

Morris, J. (2002) *A Lot to Say! A guide for social workers, personal advisors and others working with disabled children and young people with communication disorders.* London: Scope. This is a very readable guide for professionals working with young people; it gives an insight into the thoughts of young people with communication impairments as to how they wish to be communicated with.

 **Useful websites**

www.ncb.org.uk/cwc
The National Children's Bureau website provides material to download, developed through a project set up to improve social workers' skills in communicating with children.

www.triangle.co.uk
Triangle is an independent organisation working with disabled children and young people. It provides training and consultancy throughout the United Kingdom focusing particularly on children's rights, communication and inclusion.

www.triangle-services.co.uk
Two Way Street: Communicating with Disabled Children and Young People. A video and handbook produced by Triangle and NSPCC 'how it is' resource pack. Further details available from **nspcc.org.uk**.

For additional cases and topic-organised, clickable links into additional media resources, including those produced by IRISS, visit **www.pearsoned.co.uk/wilsonruch**

Activity

Activity One

Imagine that you have been asked to do some work with one or more of the following children – working, if you can, in pairs:

a. Select two or three activities which you might use with them.
b. Say why you have chosen these.
c. Try them out with your partner, one of you taking the role of the child, and remembering the skills you were introduced to earlier – reflection of feelings, genuineness, careful listening – make it interesting and, where appropriate, fun.
d. Feed-back to each other – what was helpful, puzzling, difficult etc.

Sylvie is a white British 10-year-old whose parents have mental health problems and is often left in charge of her younger brothers. She has recently been subjected to a mild sexual assault (indecent exposure which she reported to her mother) and is due to give evidence in court.

Ashok is a 6-year-old mixed-race child, who recently moved to Scotland from England. He has told his teacher he doesn't want to live with his mother at the moment because she is drunk all the time; he has been placed in short-term foster care.

Three-year-old Alex is white British, and is being returned to live with his mother who has been in prison for six months. He was looked after by his grandmother while his mother was inside, then lived with another relative, then went into a short-term foster placement.

Twelve-year-old Kirsten is a black child, who came to England from Ghana when she was five. Her father has left home and she is now living with her mother. She is very attached to her father, who has a new partner, and wonders if she can live with him.

Activity Two

Have a go at devising an introductory leaflet explaining what your role as a social worker is for one of the following service user groups:

- Pre-school children
- Teenagers with limited literacy
- Adults with mild learning difficulties.

Activity Three

With a friend or another student, practise paraphrasing and experiencing what it is like to have your comments paraphrased. To do this the talker needs to tell the listener about a recent experience that has some emotional content. When talking about the incident the talker should keep on talking without stopping, which will require the listener to find a way of intervening in order to paraphrase and to check out what they have heard.

The listener has two key challenges:

- first, they need to find a way to interrupt the talker in order to paraphrase;
- secondly, they need to attempt as accurately as possible to paraphrase what they have heard and to check out with the talker the accuracy of their comments.
  When you have done this once, reverse roles.

Appendix to Chapter 11

Activities for getting to know you

Having a drink or snack together
Making things
Making models
Doing puzzles
Reading stories/magazines together
Casual play activities (e.g. ball games, board games, card games)
Drawing/painting
Visiting places
Taking photographs together, looking through photographs together

Work to develop the senses

'Smelling box' (different liquids etc. in unmarked boxes) 'Feeling book' (collection of different fabrics and materials)
Music and singing, with small trumpet, pipes, cassette recorder
Sand play
Dressing up

Ways of helping you and the child give and receive information

Drawing faces ('my happy face', 'my cross face', plus sentence completion e.g. 'My face has a big smile when . . .') Body
outline (draw on lining paper)
My jigsaw (see Figure 11.1)

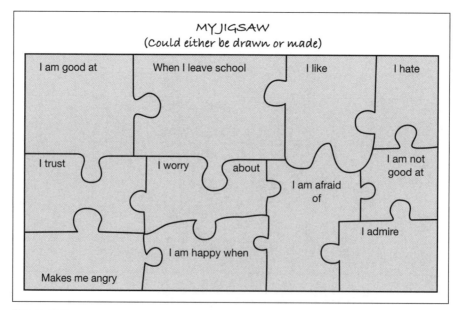

Figure 11.1

(*Source*: From a presentation by Keith Williamson)

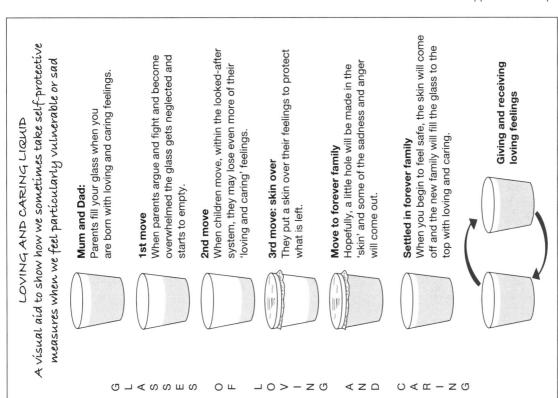

LOVING AND CARING LIQUID

A visual aid to show how we sometimes take self-protective measures when we feel particularly vulnerable or sad

Mum and Dad:
Parents fill your glass when you are born with loving and caring feelings.

1st move
When parents argue and fight and become overwhelmed the glass gets neglected and starts to empty.

2nd move
When children move, within the looked-after system, they may lose even more of their 'loving and caring' feelings.

3rd move: skin over
They put a skin over their feelings to protect what is left.

Move to forever family
Hopefully, a little hole will be made in the 'skin' and some of the sadness and anger will come out.

Settled in forever family
When you begin to feel safe, the skin will come off and the new family will fill the glass to the top with loving and caring.

Giving and receiving loving feelings

G L A S S E S   O F   L O V I N G   A N D   C A R I N G

Figure 11.3

[*Source*: Adapted from example developed by Marion Burch]

THE ECOMAP
For use e.g. as a barometer for feelings

I/Me _____ Today is _____

by _____ I am _____ years old

3. Social worker Why

4.

5.

6.

7. Brothers and sisters

2. Why am I here?

11. I worry about

12.

13. Dreams

8. I feel

9. Things that bug me

10. School

14. Friends

Things I like to do

My favourite colour _____ feels good

Least favourite colour _____ does not feel good

*** *** ***

1–10 scales

1 10

Figure 11.2

[*Source*: Adapted from Fahlberg, 1994: 331]

My shield

Feelings cards

Pretend interviews

Sentence completion (begin with safe areas, build up to more sensitive ones, leave the child with the last word, e.g. 'I wish . . .')

Write a letter (not for sending)

Interviews (use a toy microphone)

Ecomaps (see Figure 11.2)

Flow charts to illustrate moves (can be bus stops on a road, railway lines)

Family trees

'All about me' posters and books

Draw, write or talk about: if I had three wishes/a magic wand; how I see myself in five years' time; if I could choose to change one thing

Diagrams (e.g. of the Court)

Helping the child to cope with separation experiences

Thinking about feelings (e.g. brainstorm feelings, write them on separate postcards, draw illustrative faces)

Loving and caring liquid (see Figure 11.3)

Flow charts

Photographs/mementoes

Post box (to hold letters, cards or drawings about how children are feeling)

Preparing children for moving to new families

The life path

Family tree (one half of tree could contain apples/leaves representing birth family, the other half could symbolise new family)

Flash cards (a series of questions, written on separate cards, can help children identify questions which they would like answered, e.g. Will they have pets? Are they posh? Why do they want me? Will they hit me?)

Job descriptions

What kind of family for me (making a poster together which gives an overview of hopes/concerns/expectations about the new family).

Chapter 12
Planning and intervening

Chapter summary

In this chapter, we introduce you to some of the approaches to intervention which can help you practise in a systematic and thoughtful way. We begin by introducing you to the idea that there are five stages in any piece of social work practice, and that in this chapter, we shall be focusing on stages three and four – deciding what needs to be done and how to go about doing it, to put it at its simplest. We ask you to reflect on some of the key components of this aspect of your practice, and introduce you, at greater or lesser length, to some of the approaches most commonly drawn upon by social workers: psychodynamic and cognitive behavioural approaches, crisis intervention, task-centred practice and systems approaches in working with families and networks. We consider some of the evidence of the effectiveness of the different approaches, and the key aspects which need to be considered when applying them to your practice.

Learning objectives

This chapter covers topics that will enable you to achieve the following learning objectives:

- To explore the key principles which underpin all interventions in reflective practice
- To introduce you to methods of intervention most commonly used by social workers, bearing in mind the range of settings in which they are based and the variety of user groups with whom and problems with which they work
- To introduce you to some of the background and development of these approaches, and some of the research evidence of their effectiveness
- To help you identify where and in which situations you might choose to use the different approaches.

National Occupational Standards

The chapter will help you to meet the following National Occupational Standards:

Key Role 1: Prepare for, and work with individuals, families, carers, groups and communities to assess their needs and circumstances

Unit 1   Prepare for social work contact and involvement

Unit 2   Work with individuals, families, carers, groups and communities to help them make informed decisions

Unit 3   Assess needs and options to recommend a course of action for individuals, families, carers, groups and communities

Key Role 2: Plan, carry out, review and evaluate social work practice, with individuals, families, carers, groups, communities and other professionals

Unit 4   Respond to crisis situations

Unit 5   Interact with individuals, families, carers, groups and communities to achieve change and development and to improve life opportunities

Unit 6   Prepare, produce, implement and evaluate plans with individuals, families, carers, groups, communities and professional colleagues

Unit 7   Support the development of networks to meet assessed needs and planned outcomes

Unit 8   Work with groups to promote individual growth, development and independence

Unit 9   Address behaviour which presents a risk to individuals, families, carers, groups and communities

Key Role 3: Support individuals to represent their needs, views and circumstances

Unit 10   Advocate with, and on behalf of, individuals, families, carers, groups and communities

Unit 11   Prepare for, and participate in decision making forums

Key Role 4: Manage risk to individuals, families, carers, groups, communities, self and colleagues

Unit 12   Assess and manage risks to individuals, families, carers, groups and communities

Unit 13   Assess, minimise and manage risk to self and colleagues

Key Role 5: Manage and be accountable, with supervision and support, for your own social work practice within your organisation

Unit 14   Manage and be accountable for your own work

Unit 17   Work with multi-disciplinary and multi-organisational teams, networks and systems

Key Role 6: Demonstrate professional competence in social work practice

Unit 18   Research, analyse, evaluate, and use current knowledge of best social work practice

Unit 19   Work within agreed standards of social work practice and ensure own professional development

Unit 20   Manage complex ethical issues, dilemmas and conflicts

Unit 21   Contribute to the promotion of best social work practice

Case study

James

James is a 14-year-old white British boy who has been referred to a family consultation service run by the local children's services because he is having difficulties in attending school. James lives with his mother, Sue, aged 35, now working as a full-time agency carer and his sister, Isobel, aged 18 years, who works for their father as a secretary. Mother and father separated four years ago and are now divorced and father (Derek, a self-employed builder) lives with his new partner and 2-year-old daughter. The referred concerns were centred around the fact that James has a 'marked dislike of school and, recently, truancy'. Going to school had, according to his mother, been a problem since nursery school and had gradually got worse, with James 'making himself sick' in order to avoid having to go. The Education Welfare Officer has as a result of the truancy threatened prosecution under section 443(1) of the Education Act 1996. The GP makes some connection in the referral letter between the truancy and the separation of James's parents.

What do you think might be happening for James? (e.g. What of the many reasons for school attendance problems apply in James's case?)

What feelings do you have as you approach the family?

What is to be done? And how can James and his family be helped?

It is on these latter questions, i.e. the goals which you hope to achieve in working with James, and the feelings, methods and skills you might draw on for doing this, that this chapter focuses.

One simple way of thinking of any case or piece of practice in social work, such as that with James and his mother, Sue, is to think of it as a series of steps or stages, and that at each stage you need to address certain issues, or answer particular questions. So the earlier chapter in this section, that on assessment, may be said to consider the first two of these stages, answering the questions (a) what is the problem (and a series of what may be seen as a subset of questions such as – how long has it been a problem? Who is it a problem for? Is our organisation best placed to respond to this?) and (b) what is happening to create the problem, and why? – that is, you engage in a process of assessment, analysis or diagnosis of the situation which helps to make sense of what is going on. The third and fourth stages in the process involve (c) deciding what needs to be done (setting out goals and making a plan of action) and then (d) thinking about how to achieve these goals – what methods, techniques, skills and resources are needed to reach the desired outcome. Most textbooks quite properly introduce a fifth stage, that of evaluating the intervention, and whether you do this formally or informally it is clearly also an important step in the process. (Our Chapter 9 on research in the first section will have given you some ideas of how you might do this.) However, it is with these third and fourth stages – the *what* and *how* of the social work process, or in relation to our example of James, above, what goals would you have and how would you help him and his family in achieving them – that we are mostly concerned here.

Introduction

The chapter builds of course on earlier ones in our textbook. In particular, first, you will remember that in

Part One, we discussed the knowledge base of social work, and explored the range of theories which underpin practice. We introduced you to the idea of practice-related theories as 'middle range' theories (i.e. ones which combine influences of 'grand theoretical perspectives' with practice experience and include methods of intervention) and suggested that these embrace what are referred to as social work methods: e.g. task-centred practice and crisis intervention which have their roots in social learning theory, family therapy or systemic work associated with systems theory, and direct work with children, informed by psychoanalytic principles. These are generally seen as ways of organising the thinking and actions involved in trying to bring about change in the individual, family or group. We shall either explore these methods in more depth later in the chapter, or point you to where they are addressed in the chapters on working with specific user groups. Secondly, the chapter on communication in this section, with its exploration of the core skills and contexts for engaging with service users, sets out many of the principles or guidelines which form the essential basis for all the interventions which we discuss here.

We have already suggested that theories are useful because they help you to make sense of what is happening in a particular situation, and can guide you in what direction to take, so that you can approach your work systematically, rather than responding to events in a random or haphazard way. A small example of this might be the guidance you might give as a social worker to a parent struggling with a difficult toddler, where your advice might be informed by your theoretical understanding of what dynamics have produced the difficulty – perhaps reflecting learning theory, or psychodynamic understandings. However, one of the dilemmas in writing this chapter is to balance the need to give you enough specific guidance about particular methods to help you develop your practice in a systematic way, while at the same time managing to write about practice in a way which reflects both the messiness of the so-called 'real world' of practice and the complexity of the social work landscape, and which does not, in the process of identifying certain characteristics, make the intervention seem unrealistically neat and tidy.

Using methods of helping in social work practice

Sometimes social workers do move into settings where they follow a particular approach to intervention. For example, some social workers are based in Child and Adolescent Mental Health Services (CAMHS) which work almost exclusively with families, using an approach which is based on family systems theory; others may work in settings which specialise in helping users with particular problems – for example, eating disorders – and use certain specific approaches – such as a cognitive behavioural method – in working with the disorder. Others may work in settings which, while they do not necessarily work within a strict theoretical practice framework (although most do), nonetheless engage in what one might see as classically therapeutic intervention: a case in point might be marital counselling. But most social workers in their practice in fact rarely engage solely at this level, or follow one particular approach in their work. Most commonly they will need to be able to draw on different approaches to deal with different situations and circumstances, and need to be able to move flexibly in their practice between activity which may predominantly be concerned with practical resources and those which take account of feelings. So any one piece of work, or case, is likely to involve multi-dimensional activity – an awareness of different facets of every case. Thus for example, a social worker helping to plan the return home of an older person from hospital after a fall needs to be alert and responsive to the deeper feelings of, say, anger, fear and anxiety, as well as efficiently making arrangements for the necessary aids and adaptations, daily carers and so on to be put in place. Olive Stevenson (an eminent social work academic, who started her career as a childcare worker in the 1950s) makes this point, arguing that counselling skills are an essential component of social work practice. She adds:

'The difficulty for social workers is that the need for such practice skills has been minimised and sometimes denied. "Counselling" is being perceived as a separate activity. [But] . . . skills (and the associated knowledge) in understanding and relating to a person's feelings and taking these into account in her/his overall welfare are . . . an essential prerequisite of social work practice.'

(in Lymbery and Butler (eds), 2004: 243–4)

Because this point is so important, we shall pause here to reflect on what we consider to be some of the key aspects of helping in the contexts of social work practice.

Interventions in context

'Social work is a practical activity.' This was the pronouncement of a government minister responsible for social work in 2004. She was not wrong, but we strongly believe she was only capturing a part of the whole truth about actually 'doing' social work. In this chapter about different methods of intervening with service users, we emphasise two other dimensions apart from 'doing' which are (or should be) ever-present in how social workers conduct themselves. These are 'thinking' and 'being'.

The *thinking* component is partly about the importance of having a solid *theoretical* grasp of different social work methods, so that each step in your plan of activity is based on a clear understanding – a theoretically informed formulation – of the service user's situation to which you are responding in a particular way that reflects this formulation. The thinking component is also about *reflecting*, learning to step back both during and after each phase of activity or 'engagement' and look at how the *process* and the relationship you are both involved in has changed, developed, deepened, or become problematic, tense, anxious and so on. These reflections are all in the service of evaluating how you and the service user are getting on with the 'plans' you should have made on the basis of your assessment (we say service user for the sake of simplicity, but of course there may be several service users involved, and quite possibly other colleagues as well).

The *being* component may be less familiar to you in some ways, but it is no less important, and in fact once we have investigated it a little further it will probably seem obvious! Every time we meet, talk, engage, or develop even a superficial relationship with another person or a group, each of us has adopted a particular, emotionally invested way of 'being' in that relationship. We might compete with the other person or with the group members; we might be drawn to listen and

Frequently – far more frequently than we realise – what someone in a state of anxiety finds truly helpful is not to rush into action, but to have their anxious state listened to, understood, so that they can be helped to think more clearly. There is a word for this way of responding to anxiety in relationships – 'containment'.

empathise; sometimes we want to 'back off' at once; some encounters seem to make us passive or withdrawn; or we become caught up in a feeling of elation and mischief – the possibilities are endless. But, setting aside the fact that each of us has a more or less stable 'personality' (a fairly consistent tendency towards a range of ways of 'being'), the important point is that there is no neutral, emotionally uninvolved way to 'be' in a relationship. Something *particular* is always going on in terms of *feelings, emotional responses, patterns of interaction*, the ease or difficulty of the encounter; and over time there is always some kind of development, change, or evolution which is usually quite complex at the level of emotional engagement with other people. The *being* component of social work interventions is about reflecting on these processes, and coming to *know about them through thinking about them.*

So, even if a piece of work seems to be all 'doing' – for example, an emergency visit because a severely disabled person living alone hasn't been contactable for several days – these other levels of the engagement will be present; with the development of your skills, they become essential to carrying out the 'doing' in the most sensitive, thoughtful, attuned, and purposeful way. For example, often we can be impelled into action by other people's anxiety, when a better course of 'action' is to stop, think, reflect on the feelings that have already been

mobilised in us, and only then decide what, if anything, to do. Frequently – far more frequently than we often realise – what someone in a state of anxiety finds truly helpful is not to rush into action, but to have their anxious state listened to, understood, so that they can be helped to think more clearly, as our case example of work with a young mother, Michaela, illustrates. There is a word for this way of responding to anxiety in relationships – 'containment' – which is explored in more depth in the section below on psychodynamic ways of working.

Case study

Michaela

Michaela was a young single mother who came to England from Romania with her daughter to work. But she quickly found that it was hard to earn enough to pay rent, live and support her daughter. Christine was the duty social worker who saw her on her first visit to the office. Michaela poured out her distress, and Christine was able to sit and listen and empathise; but she also helped Michaela to understand some practical steps she could take to improve her financial situation, and she made a couple of initial phone calls on her behalf.

▶

When Michaela came to the office again she asked Christine to accompany her to the Housing Benefit Office. Christine thought about this for a moment, but said she didn't feel that would be so helpful and that maybe Michaela could tell her of her worries about going there herself. To her shock Michaela turned on Christine in fury, saying 'I thought you were going to be my friend', and stormed out of the office. Christine felt immediately overcome with distress herself, as well as guilty, and had to stop herself from rushing out of the office into the street to try to get Michaela to return.

Christine reflected on this episode, and began to see that maybe Michaela was even more vulnerable than she had appeared at the first meeting. She was a very competent person who spoke good English, but emotionally it seemed she had felt desperate, and developed an intense dependency on the idea of Christine as someone who could (and should) help her in the way she imagined. Christine also wondered if she felt guilty, possibly about the situation she had placed her daughter in as well as herself?

Christine decided to visit Michaela at home. Michaela seemed immensely relieved to see Christine, apologised for her outburst and explained that at that moment she had just felt quite panic-stricken and unable to cope. She had already been to the housing office and it had gone OK. Christine explored Michaela's feelings and situation further, and it did emerge that she felt hugely worried and guilty about her daughter's future as well as her own.

This case study illustrates how doing, reflecting and being in social work are intertwined, and how the value of not rushing into action can be empowering – Michaela's panic is intense but fleeting, and she recovers her *own* competence very quickly. Had Christine agreed to go to Housing Benefit, or rushed after Michaela, this might have been undermined rather than recovered. But this required a capacity in Christine to think on her feet about intense and complex feelings that arose in the encounter, and an ability not to get too 'drawn in' too quickly. Then she does 'act' by going to see Michaela, and this re-establishes a proper partnership in the work.

These interconnected components must, as we shall illustrate, inform whichever of the methods you select for working with a particular case or situation. However, in order to be able to think, do and be, you need also to have a strong theoretical grasp of the approaches; we shall introduce you to the essentials, and at the end of the chapter give you suggestions for reading to take your knowledge and understanding further.

Psychodynamic interventions

In the history of social work there are probably more myths about psychodynamic practice, and more strong opinions both for and against this method, than there are in relation to any other approach to practice, perhaps in part at least because it was seen by 'radical' social workers in the middle decades of the last century as ignoring societal inequalities and the impoverished circumstances of most service users. To some extent this merely reflects how our society and culture divides strongly for or against anything to do with psychoanalysis. The word 'psychodynamic' is an adjective meaning 'based on or deriving from psychoanalytic theory and practice', and we use this adjective in preference to talking about 'psychoanalytic' social work. In the earlier chapters about the history and development of social work, we saw how in Britain, in the 1970s and 1980s, there was almost a civil war in social work, with radical political social workers often taking psychodynamic social work as their main enemy (as we explored in Chapter 4 on history in Part One). But it has often been noted that key ideas based in psychoanalysis are now part of everyone's everyday thinking and language, as we illustrated in Chapter 7 (on human growth and development) in discussing the popular use of the term 'defence mechanism'. So, although psychoanalytic practice and theory is still hotly contested, in some respects it remains the most successful and influential psychological perspective of our times.

Because it has been influential and successful, there is a vast literature about psychoanalysis and its various related practices such as psychoanalytic psychotherapy and psychodynamic counselling. There is a more limited range of writing about psychodynamic social work, and we will refer to many of these texts as well as giving you pointers should you wish to look a bit deeper into psychoanalysis. However, our main aim will be to offer an accessible account of this approach that tries not to reproduce any of the myths and misconceptions which abound.

In this section we will cover the main concepts you need to understand in order to practise simply and effectively using psychodynamic principles. We then discuss the stages, or the process, which a typical psychodynamic piece of work entails and explore how to use yourself – your feelings, responses and observations of your own reactions – as a central tool in doing this kind of work. We conclude the section by reviewing some of the important current research into the effectiveness of psychodynamic work.

Getting started – thinking about emotional experience

The best way to begin thinking about psychodynamic practice is with your own experiences – on placement, at work, or in your own life. Psychodynamic theory proposes that people and relationships are made up of at least two 'layers' of experience and functioning: a conscious one and an unconscious one. The idea of the unconscious can seem mysterious and even frightening, but its manifestations are in fact ordinary and everyday. Some years ago one of us was teaching a group of qualifying social workers about psychodynamic work when a student said, 'You seem to be saying that these processes that relate to the unconscious are just *there* whether we like it or not. So we can't help encountering them in our work.' This seems exactly right, but in order to be convinced of the truth of such a statement, it is probably necessary to open yourself to examining your own experience.

Some social work training courses now require students to undertake a short, usually a 10 or 12 week observation of a baby or young child in an ordinary setting, either at home or in a day nursery. The observer is not asked to 'do' anything, but just sit and 'take in' what seems to be happening for the baby and then afterwards write up a detailed account of this. However, many observers find that this task stirs up very strong feelings and important memories and realisations in themselves. Watching a distressed baby who has been left alone by her caretaker for even three minutes – a perfectly normal everyday occurrence – *without* doing anything to intervene or comfort the baby can put anybody in touch with very powerful feelings of their own. For example, feelings of (and vivid thoughts about) our own emotional neediness, distress about times when we have been abandoned by a loved person whom we depended upon, anger with people we feel have mistreated us can suddenly come to the surface. This is unconscious experience becoming conscious. But it is not necessary to do a baby observation to access this kind of experience. An encounter with a service user who is stricken with grief

or guilt about the death of a loved one will almost certainly evoke powerful emotional reactions in us, and these reactions will not just be 'empathic' or 'altruistic'; we may find we become intensely emotionally preoccupied once again with experiences of loss that we *thought* were 'over and done with' when in fact they are still 'alive' in us, even if we aren't aware of this most of the time.

This then is the foundation of psychodynamic practice: openness to the emotional experience of other people, which leads on to the need to be open to our own emotional experience, which in turn leads on to the importance of us being able to hang on to the difference between our own experiences and those of other people. Most of us have no trouble with this most of the time; we come away from an encounter saying something like, 'She was dreadfully upset, and cried for a hour, and afterwards I burst into tears myself because I was thinking about my friend who died last year'. But there are important processes that go on between people, discussed below, which make it harder to know what is happening emotionally and whether it is 'us' or 'them' that feelings belong to.

Some psychodynamic processes and concepts

For now we will think back to the case study of Christine and Michaela in the opening sections of this chapter. This involved intense and rapid emotional exchanges that Christine somehow managed to handle to good effect. It is worth thinking, step by step, about what took place between them.

First, Michaela comes to the office and asks for help and it seems to Christine that Michaela is able to listen to the practical advice she offers despite being very distressed. Christine has listened and 'taken in' her distress, and for both of them this seemed a manageable if emotionally intense encounter. Consciously, all is going well and seems on course.

But secondly, Michaela returns to the office and makes a request that Christine gently refuses. This elicits an intense outburst of rage from Michaela that takes Christine completely by surprise. Emotionally she is almost 'knocked off her feet'. What has happened? In a way we can only reconstruct later what may have happened, when we learn that Michaela in fact went to the housing office straight afterwards and completed her tasks with them. Psychodynamic theory would suggest that two things have taken place. In the first place Michaela has projected an intense and unmanageable experience of frustration, despair, guilt and rage into Christine, who then becomes the one who feels incompetent, anxious, guilty and panicky. But importantly, she stops herself rushing after Michaela, and she succeeds in emotionally containing this experience. This gives her time to *think about and reflect upon her emotional experience.*

So, thirdly, it seems that perhaps Michaela has rid herself of a whole bundle of feelings which at that moment she found just unbearable. She was unable to 'contain' and think about them, and found a solution that we have all used in our lives, probably quite often: she forced them onto someone else. For the time being, this makes Michaela feel more able to cope. Later Michaela admits to Christine that as she left the office she was full of hate and anger towards her for refusing to do what she had asked. In some way she had gone in there feeling 'bad', but left feeling good (or at least better), but having turned Christine 'bad' in her own mind – and in fact Christine does actually now feel pretty 'bad' herself. In psychodynamic theory the process of projection is closely tied to another one called 'splitting' in which we project our bad thoughts and feelings onto someone else, leaving us good and them bad. In this way we often create a view of the world split rather rigidly between the good and the bad. Thus, projection and splitting are examples of psychological defences against mental pain. They are used to preserve a sense of the 'goodness' of the self; but as we can see, they also have a cost, for Christine certainly but perhaps also for Michaela.

Then, fourthly, as Christine begins to think about her emotional experience, she works on the idea that maybe the feelings 'put into her' by Michaela may give her information about Michaela's state of mind. In particular, she wonders whether the guilt she felt might be a clue to something Michaela is struggling with, but has not been able to communicate about explicitly or consciously. This is speculation on Christine's part, a kind of hypothesis that she must find a way to test. But if it is right, it is a very valuable clue she can follow up on. In psychodynamic language, this is Christine thinking about her counter-transference. You may be familiar with the psychodynamic concept of transference, a process in which one person 'transfers' feelings and images from their own inner life onto someone else, whom they then treat as if they were this 'figure' from their own internal mental life. When you are the object of someone else's transference, it is often difficult to spot this at first. The clue is often that you feel as though you have been systematically 'misrecognised' in some way – perhaps excessively loved and admired, or hated and despised by

the other person. Examining what this experience is all about is the process of thinking about your counter-transference. It was a big step in psychoanalysis when therapists began to realise that maybe transference was not just a 'nuisance', but in many ways the centre of the therapeutic process, the means by which the unconscious could be known about in an immediate, live way if the recipient of the transference could identify and make sense of what had 'got into them'.

So finally, when Christine visits Michaela again she finds her in a quite different state of mind. She is rather remorseful about how she treated Christine, and conveys that she knows she mistreated her although she couldn't help this at the time. She no longer sees Christine as bad, it seems. In effect, she has been able to 'take back' some of her projections onto Christine, and see these feelings and constructions about the other person as her own. Often in psychodynamic work, this part of the process takes a long time because people's defensive structures are much more entrenched than Michaela's seem to be. But working through such processes is a key aim of much psychodynamic work, whether with individuals, couples, families or groups. Psychodynamic work recognises that people need to be emotionally dependent on one another, but ideally also need to retain their 'separateness' from each other so they can be *both* individuals *and* fully participating members of couples, families and other groupings.

This is what psychodynamic thinking posits as 'good mental health', and contrasts this with relationships in which people are 'mixed up with one another' through the use of too much projection. In the latter state, individuals have 'lost' bits of themselves in other people and their capacity to function autonomously is diminished as a result. In the case study we saw how this might have happened at the point where Christine could have agreed to go to the housing office with Michaela, thereby unnecessarily increasing her dependence on Christine. She would temporarily at least have lost part of her competence by handing it over to Christine at a point of crisis. Of course, with a different service user it might be the right decision to accompany them in this way; it all depends on what kind of state of mind the person is in, and in crisis intervention work (which is psychodynamic in its approach) more of this kind of ego support – that is, direct support for the part of the personality that usually is capable of functioning well – may well be appropriate. Referring ahead to the discussion in that section, we might therefore assess Michaela to be someone in a state of great stress, but not in a state of crisis.

A final point to make about this case study concerns the social and political context in which the work takes place. As we have seen, this is often a point of contention about psychodynamic work, and we can only touch on the many complex debates and perspectives in this area. Michaela has come to this country from Romania. The case study suggests that she may have been seeking 'a better life' for herself and her daughter. She is what we sometimes call an 'economic migrant'. Her circumstances are therefore highly political in their nature and a consequence of social-structural forces acting on her, although her immediate predicament is very personal. Our impulse is likely to be to 'identify' strongly with the politically driven nature of a person's circumstances. We have immediate sympathy with the motives behind her seeking a life in Britain, and with the economic and social struggle that her life entails. But of course she remains a person in her own right, who has taken decisions for herself albeit in pressurised circumstances, and who feels an appropriate sense of responsibility and worry about her daughter and the consequences for her of the decisions she has taken.

Psychodynamic work and values

So, psychodynamic work does involve some central value principles as well as an account of how human beings develop and function psychologically. One such principle is respect for 'psychological truth' – for example, when Michaela turns out to feel guilty and anxious about her daughter, this can be taken as a sign of her being in touch with her sense of adult and parental responsibility, even though the experience of guilt is painful for her to bear. To attempt to reassure her, or excuse her from this pain, perhaps by reminding her of the difficult circumstances under which she decided to leave her country, is really to miss the point and would undermine her own sense of being a human agent who is capable of taking difficult decisions and working with the psychological consequences. Indeed, one could argue that her current social circumstances make it all the more important that she is respected and supported as a person in her own right who is experiencing pressure from external forces, and stress from internal psychic sources. One of the most influential original textbooks about psychodynamic casework used the idea that social workers are always working with a person-in-situation (not just one or the other), and that people in difficulties are usually experiencing a combination of 'stress and press'. The socio-political and the psychological are brought together in a useful way by these concepts (Hollis, 1981).

Thinking under fire: psychodynamic practice in ordinary social work contexts

Psychodynamic social work is not 'psychotherapy', although it will hopefully have 'therapeutic benefits' for service users, and draws heavily on the principles and theories informing psychotherapy. So, how exactly does psychodynamic social work differ from counselling or psychotherapy? The brief discussion above of the idea that psychodynamic casework entails working with the interaction between the person and their situation gives a first clue. Counsellors and therapists usually see individuals, couples or families for a programme of work that focuses almost exclusively on psychological and relationship issues. They will tend not to get involved in practical matters, although good therapy in public service settings will often involve working as part of a network (see below for an account of networking in social work) of other professionals who may be addressing these dimensions of the overall situation, with careful agreements about roles and boundaries: or, in other words, who is performing exactly what tasks. But psychodynamic casework will almost always involve attention to both sides of the equation.

Some of the most influential policy documents in the history of British social work have stressed this. For example, the Barclay Report (1982) conceived the key roles of social workers as a combination of counselling and social care planning. Perhaps the central skill in being a good caseworker is the ability to keep *both* these elements continually in mind as equally important parts of the task. In fact this is one main part of what makes social work as a job so interesting and challenging, but also so difficult. The brief case study below, as well as the story of Christine and Michaela, illustrates the need to maintain this 'binocular vision'.

Case study

Jamie and Tracey

Jamie and Tracey are both under five and were taken into care after they were discovered alone and unkempt in the family home. Their parents Kerry and Howard are both long-term drug users. John became the family's social worker after the

Emergency Protection Order was taken out. He arranged a package of 'kinship care' in which Kerry's parents (Jamie and Tracey's maternal grandparents) were key, although Howard's aunt was also able to offer important support taking the children to and from nursery.

Everyone in the office, including John's team leader, seemed to be relieved about these arrangements, and it seemed that a potentially difficult case involving contested care proceedings in court might be averted. At the case conference, there was a strong feeling of everyone being charmed by Kerry's parents. But over the next three weeks, John became more and more uneasy about the grandparents. Their actual care of the two small children did not seem that good, and he became suspicious that they were in fact involved in supporting Kerry's drug habit. When he voiced these worries to his supervisor, he did not feel heard, and came away feeling that he had been subtly rebuked for casting doubt on the care plan.

It now felt as though he was the 'bad guy' in the situation, and that everyone had a huge investment in maintaining the grandparents as the 'good' people who had 'rescued' the young 'victims' Jamie and Tracey. At first John had felt like the hero of the case, for finding a solution that looked like good practice and avoided painful and costly care proceedings, but now . . .

Clearly, John is responsible for the 'social care planning' dimension of his work with this family, but what about any 'counselling' dimension? To suggest immediately that he might embark on a programme of counselling with some or all of the many service users, carers and professionals involved in this case in order to address the complex feelings that are emerging would probably be to miss the point. At certain stages he might be able to make very good use of individual counselling skills – for example, he might decide that some sessions with the grandparents to explore more fully his worries about their relationship with Kerry and Howard would be helpful, or that some direct work with the children (see Chapter 16) would be beneficial – but for now the relevance of psychodynamic skills is to help him understand the overall dynamics of the case.

These dynamics seem to involve processes of splitting and projection (see above) and importantly also idealisa-

tion. Idealisation is often linked to splitting, because part of its function is to protect people from facing difficult, destructive, or 'bad' feelings and behaviour. In this case it seems almost everyone colludes to agree that 'It's not as dreadful as it seemed at first sight', and then to turn a blind eye to the evidence that the idealised solution may not be as perfect as people wish to believe. This process directly involves John. At first, when he proposes and implements the kinship care solution, he notices a slightly unusual sensation of near elation in himself, as his manager and colleagues congratulate and praise him. Actually, he remembers thinking to himself that it was not *that* difficult to make this plan, and in retrospect now he wonders if in fact it was not just a bit *too* easy. Later he has an even more uncomfortable sensation of being a 'spoiler' of the perfect solution everyone believed he had found. This case involves a lot of strong emotions for him. What underlies this turmoil and the rapidly shifting dynamics of the case? Perhaps the key will turn out to be the anxiety generated in everyone by the case, and the powerful defences against anxiety that are the surface or conscious manifestations of this underlying anxiety.

Common but difficult social work tasks such as removing children from their parents' care, helping a dependent person decide whether they will give up living at home, communicating with an angry and desperate young man who has run away from home, or listening to someone falling apart with grief, bring us into contact with states of great anxiety in service users, and mobilise great anxiety in us as workers. Much of the value of, and the skill involved in, psychodynamic work is about understanding how anxiety infects so much of the work and potentially distorts our capacity to do good work and make good decisions. After all, we have almost lost sight of the important question in the case study: what about the needs of the children? What is the best care solution for them? What does it mean for their future that their grandparents *may* be in collusion with their mother over her drug taking? Often, it is the powerful dynamics stemming from anxiety in those surrounding the vulnerable people we are supposed to be working with (including our colleagues and ourselves) that prevent us really working in their best interests.

The phases of psychodynamic work

Whether you are involved in doing psychodynamic work in everyday contexts, or in a more traditional piece of counselling work, many of the same principles apply when we come to consider the planning and the phases of the work over time. As we have seen, the central principles of this approach involve understanding the service user, or the system with which you are working, through the use of your emotional capacities.

Engaging

The need for identification or empathy with the service users' feelings, beliefs, experiences and conflicts comes first, and is achieved through careful listening and careful attention to what your own feeling responses tell you about this person and their situation. What kind of person does this service user seem to want, or need, me to be: an object of admiration, contempt, love, hate, or some mixture of these? How do they engage me in the process of getting help for themselves: as a true 'partner', or with hesitation, anxiety, fear? Do I feel kept in the dark, or invited to share their intimate secrets or something in between? These are the kinds of reflective questions that can lead you to understand at the outset 'who you are' to the service user, or what kind of 'transference object' you are to them.

However, at this stage the most important thing is just to allow the relationship to develop as the client wishes. They need to trust you, and see that you are capable of really turning your mind to understanding who they are and what is making them anxious, distressed, or conflicted. This is not always as easy as it sounds, as we saw in the case study of Christine. Strong feelings can suddenly erupt, and you are pitched into the middle of a powerful transference situation before you have had time to draw breath. In the case study of Jamie and Tracey and their family, the same is true in effect: the dynamics of the situation unfold, and make themselves known to John, because he is able to reflect on the *information* that his feelings and experiences give him. For Christine, the prospects of future psychodynamic work with Michaela seem good. On the one hand Michaela is capable of sudden, powerful changes of emotional state, but on the other she seems to be able to 'own' her part in these exchanges, even if this happens in retrospect. Through the attuned use of self Christine has begun to provide her with a helping relationship and has established a working or therapeutic alliance.

Working through

As the relationship with the service user develops, the main aim of psychodynamic work comes into focus, enabling some degree of change not just in their circumstances and practical affairs but in their personal capacity to function autonomously and interdependently.

Remember that psychoanalysis does not define good adult mental health in terms of 'independence', but in terms of capacity for good relationships which involve interdependence. This helps us understand the focus of a piece of psychodynamic counselling: which aspects of the relationship with us, as workers, seem to be difficult, problematic, not helpful to the service user's way of functioning? And can we use the experience we are both having of this here-and-now relationship to help them towards being a bit more 'in charge' and to take ownership of these problematic aspects?

For example, after you have had several meetings with the user, it may feel to you as though they have become something of an emotional burden to you. Nothing much seems to be happening now and they seem passive, leaving you to do all the work. Or, reviewing things after several weeks you find that they have missed half their appointments. Each time they do come, the service user seems to have forgotten everything that happened in the preceding sessions, so each meeting feels to you like starting at the beginning. Now, using your awareness of these emotional dynamics, the counter-transference, you are beginning to gain a deeper idea of the nature of the transference which the user has established with you. It is important to remember that they *are* engaged, and are attending sessions. So, something about what you are offering is important to them, but in other ways something seems to be problematic.

Case study

Michaela cont . . .

Everything went well for a time with Michaela. Christine was able to help her explore in some depth her anxieties about her daughter, and her grief over her husband who it turned out had left her suddenly not long before Michaela came to England. Michaela even arrived at the insight that perhaps part of the reason she had left Romania was to flee the painfulness of the situation. She suspected that her husband was having an affair with another woman in their town, and Michaela now realised that she had not been able to face the humiliation and pain of discovering that this might be true.

But suddenly Michaela starts making excuses and missing appointments with Christine. Christine is puzzled by this, and then she realises she feels hurt and rejected; she had felt the work was going so well, and she has grown to like and admire Michaela very much. She talks about this with her supervisor, who suggests to Christine that maybe Michaela has become scared of how much *she* likes and admires Christine; but knowing that this is a professional relationship Michaela might be protecting herself against the disappointment and anger that she knows she will feel when the relationship ends – as it must – so she has decided to take matters into her own hands and 'end it on her terms', not Christine's.

Christine writes to Michaela and to her relief she attends her next session. Christine wonders with her about the appointments she missed, saying that she had the feeling Michaela had got a lot out of these meetings but that perhaps this made her feel vulnerable again, and angry with Christine for still not 'being a friend' and available outside session times. Michaela is sad but also reflective. She recalls now that she always felt she was a 'clingy' child, anxious when she had to leave her mother and go to school, for example. She felt her mother had sometimes gone along with this anxiety, letting her stay at home when she perhaps should have helped her overcome her fears. Michaela thought she had 'got over' this, but now she sees that separations, and 'separateness', are still an issue for her.

In this phase of the work, Christine creates the possibility of something getting 'worked through' once more in Michaela's psychological life. She uses her ability to reflect on the emotional dynamics between them to engage directly with the developmental difficulty that Michaela still carries. From a psychodynamic perspective everything now depends on how Christine handles the ending phase of their work: will she get involved in a repetition of the dynamic that Michaela had with her mother, or will she hold to her boundaries in the face of the transference pressure this dynamic creates to avoid an appropriate ending? If she manages the latter, Michaela may actually have had an opportunity for psychological growth, by discovering that she can survive her fears about separation and loss in a new way. Hopefully, this may allow her to overcome her remaining unhelpful defences against loss and achieve deeper possibilities for intimate and supportive relationships, as well as to avoid repeating with her own young daughter the unhelpful aspect of her relationship with her own mother.

Ending

There are many ways of 'working through' emotional difficulties, similar to the one described above. But however successful or limited these have been in a piece of work, much of the progress can be undone if the ending phase of any piece of social work is not handled well. In her paper 'The end as a means to growth – in the social work relationship' Jean Nursten (1997: 75) says,

'The inability to handle termination may sabotage all that has gone before. When it is handled well it can become a growth experience for client and worker. This may be doubted by student social workers because a practice placement does not allow time for a follow-up and the results of handling and mishandling at this stage are not always seen during a student's training.'

Perhaps you have understood enough of the dynamics of the working through between Christine and Michaela to appreciate the importance of a well-handled ending in sustaining Michaela's 'growth'. But Nursten also refers to the benefits to the social worker of handling the ending well. What might she mean by this? Throughout this section we have stressed that psychodynamic social work is a process in which the workers are themselves emotionally involved: the 'self' of the worker is the most important resource brought to the work. We have also emphasised how the social worker has to know the difference between themselves and the service user, or in other words to be able to identify what feelings and experiences belong to whom. This is nowhere more important than at the ending phase.

Professional social workers make a clear and definite ending to a piece of work where at all possible, not because they are cruel, do not want to be friends, or because they feel themselves to be different from or superior to the service user, but significantly because not to do so perpetuates muddles about loss and separation, and perpetuates unnecessary dependency on services. Dependency on services is not of itself a bad thing, and some users just will need to be dependent on them for the long term. But if they do not, then poorly handled endings may leave everyone confused about who needs whom: does the social worker who does not end a piece of work cleanly 'need the service user' perhaps? Christine acknowledged to herself how much she had come to like Michaela, and maybe she would have liked to become friends with her. But her own ability to negotiate the loss of her client is the precondition of Michaela being able to negotiate the loss of her social worker, and perhaps complete the process of growth that the work has enabled. Because we are ordinary human beings, we all struggle with processes of loss and separation, and so each piece of work can evoke our internal conflicts about this. Managing it well may also help us grow a little more. Therapeutic social work is done in the service of the user, but there can be benefits for the social worker too, just as we might hope the whole project of doing good social work may be a part of the professional worker's growth process in their lifetime.

Does it work? Evidence-based practice, the user experience, and psychodynamic social work

In our era of evidence-based practice (discussed more fully in Chapter 9 on research), psychoanalytically based interventions have come under intense scrutiny to see whether they can hold their own in comparison to other forms of psychologically based treatment that make strong claims to be effective. There are those who would argue that such a discussion is in fact something of a red herring. However, reviewing the whole range of approaches to psychoanalytic research and social work, Briggs (a social work practitioner/academic working from a psychodynamic perspective) (2005) concludes that overall the contribution of research is to 'enrich the reflective psycho-social space in which social work takes place through bringing another perspective'. Those who are committed to the importance of scientific study of the outcomes of treatment would find this a weak position and point, for example, to the NHS National Institute for Clinical Excellence (NICE) guidelines on the most effective treatments for specific psychological disorders. On the whole, psychoanalytic approaches do not fare well in this context, but this is arguably because some varieties of psychotherapy such as cognitive behavioural therapy (CBT) have been better at playing the 'evidence based' political game than have their 'competitors'.

A dispassionate summary would perhaps conclude that the research evidence for the effectiveness of psychoanalytic psychotherapy is in fact quite good, but that so is the evidence for a number of other treatment 'modalities'. Kennedy (2004) has conducted a systematic review of a wide range of evidence for psychoanalytic child psychotherapy, and shows that there is strong, though not conclusive, support for the proposition that 'it works'. One study that combined psychotherapy for sexually abused girls with support for their parents and carers delivered by clinically trained social workers showed that the girls definitely improved; but in the absence of a proper 'control group', others have argued that this study does not prove anything conclusive one way or the other. Likewise, studies of the effectiveness of day hospital and therapeutic community interventions for people with personality disorders show strong support for its effectiveness, and in one case for a significant reduction in patients' subsequent use of mental health services – thus making a case on 'health economic' grounds as much as health grounds (Bateman, 2004; Warren and Norton, 2004).

In this section we have concentrated attention as much on the value of social workers having a 'general psychodynamic awareness' in relation to their total practice as on psychodynamic work as a form of 'treatment'. Few if any systematic studies have been conducted of the impact of such an approach on social work practice; equally no other methodological or ideological approach can really claim better 'scientific' support. Perhaps this takes us back to the heart of a question about what kind of activity social work really is, one which we have already explored in Chapter 4. Is it a science or an art, a question of intervening in 'causal chains' or of 'making meaning and sense' where little existed? Some of the case studies in this section could be interpreted in both ways, just to make matters more complicated! One thing is for sure: debates about the respective merits of the cultures of 'evidence' and 'meaning' will continue, and psychodynamic approaches will continue to be part of these, not least because a significant body of practitioners find them helpful, and a growing number of service users say they want 'relationship and talking' at the heart of their services.

We turn in our next section to an approach which is often contrasted, almost considered in opposition, to the one we have been considering, and which, as you will see, has been widely used and adapted to social work practice.

Cognitive behavioural approaches

Our second approach, as you can guess from its name, is aimed at changing behaviour, which can be both *covert* behaviour (thoughts and feelings, i.e. attributes which are not outwardly evident) and *overt* behaviour (observable actions), which are experienced as dysfunctional, by the individuals themselves, by their families and/or by the wider society. It is widely used as a method by those in the helping professions and has, as we pointed out earlier, been supported by NICE (National Institute for Clinical Excellence, the body set up to review the effectiveness of clinical treatments for the National Health Service) as *the* talking therapy method of choice within mental health settings. This is on the grounds that there is evidence for its effectiveness, that as a method it can be relatively easily learnt and conducted, and that it can be offered on a short-term basis and is therefore cost-effective. (See Joseph, 2001, Chapter 4.) Unlike the psychodynamic model, which emphasises the two 'layers', conscious and unconscious, of behaviour and functioning, this focuses on conscious and identifiable thoughts and behaviour. Like the task-centred approach which we come on to later, it has its roots in social learning theory. Unlike that approach, however, the method does not set out intervention necessarily as a complete model, but suggests certain principles or strategies, derived from learning theory, on which the intervention needs to be based. These have, however, themselves been developed into models of practice: for example, parenting programmes, social skills training, substance misuse programmes, anger-management training, can all be seen as offshoots of cognitive behavioural theory.

Many of the ideas contained in the approach will be familiar to you, and indeed have in recent years gained popular currency, for example, in some of the television parent-training programmes. Thus the importance of leading or showing by example (modelling) or encouraging good behaviour (positive reinforcement) while ignoring bad behaviour (extinction) – all concepts and techniques seen in cognitive behavioural approaches – have been ideas well known to teachers, health visitors and social workers, and indeed to many parents, in the context of child development and skill acquisition. What we aim to do here is to introduce you, as before, to some of the background to the approaches, outline the principle characteristics, identify those situations where it seems most useful, and then think about some of its strengths and limitations, particularly exploring the acknowledged disagreements between cognitive behavioural theorists and psychodynamic theorists to see if there can be common ground between the two.

Background

The cognitive behavioural approach has developed from two separate psychological theories and bodies of empir-

ical evidence, namely behavioural theories and cognitive theories. Historically, as Payne, a social work academic and author of a useful and widely read book on social work theories (Payne, 1997), suggests, learning theory came first, and then developed within clinical practice into interventions which are directed at changing people's behaviour. Behavioural theory argues (as you will have learnt from Chapter 7) that our behaviour is largely the product of learning. Genetic and other biological factors contribute to these interactions, but our behavioural responses are built up through a myriad of interactions with the physical and social environment from which we learn how to behave, what actions produce satisfactory responses, and so on. In theory then, we can learn new behaviour to meet our needs or replace existing behaviour if it is problematic. Cognitive theory, again as you will have read in earlier chapters, argues that, in addition to a focus on thinking and perceiving, behaviour is affected by perception and by how we interpret the environment in the process of learning. Thus how a person thinks about and construes what they experience, say, the origins of a difficulty, is seen to have an impact on how they respond to it. (For example, the offer of assistance in crossing the road may be seen by the recipient as helpful or humiliating; the response, brushing the helping hand away impatiently or accepting graciously will be at least in part a reflection of this perception.) Although some theorists are dubious about the amalgamation of the two psychological theories (e.g. Hudson and MacDonald (1986), two British exponents of behavioural models), on the whole, a pragmatic recognition of the realities of social work and clinical practice have meant that most practitioners currently practise a cognitive behavioural approach, and draw procedures from both bodies of knowledge.

The main originator of cognitive behavioural therapy (CBT) was an American, Aaron Beck, who qualified as a psychoanalyst in 1956, but over the ensuing decades became disillusioned with the psychoanalytic culture in which he was working, a culture which then as now was far more dominant in the United States than in the United Kingdom. In his clinical work, he began to develop a method of working with depressed or anxious patients, which emphasised the way in which symptoms were currently maintained and underpinned by 'negative cognitions', which in turn generated negative internal 'schemas' (the cognitive structures which organise experience and behaviour). Beck considered that discovering and challenging negative processes was a simpler and shorter path to change, and began to train patients to recognise and modify the conscious, maladaptive thinking which, he argued, maintained the problems and distress. Beck considered, however, a vital feature of the approach was that any change would only occur in the context of a sympathetic, collaborative relationship: a theme which you may recognise from the previous section and as running throughout our book!

Some cognitive behavioural principles, processes and concepts

Practitioners using a cognitive behavioural approach need to adapt their practice to the particular individual's circumstances or difficulty. For example, work with a child suffering from bed-wetting will involve a different technique from work with a child who is exhibiting a range of difficult behaviour, including skipping school, or a middle-aged woman with agoraphobic symptoms who is entirely reliant on her husband because of her inability to leave the house. It is therefore necessary to understand the different ideas underpinning the approach, so we introduce you here to some of the key concepts.

In **respondent** or **classical conditioning**, the key terms you need to know are stimulus and response, conditioning, extinction and counter-conditioning.

Many behavioural responses, such as withdrawing hands sharply from a hot surface, eyes watering on a windy day, coughing in a smoky room, are unconditioned, in that they happen naturally to stimuli. However, behaviours become *conditioned* when the individual comes to associate a response with a stimulus which does not naturally produce the particular response. You may have come across a reference to Pavlov's dogs in your reading. Ivan Pavlov (a Russian physiologist, 1849–1936), is credited with the discovery of this process of conditioning, sometimes called classical conditioning. He discovered that by ringing a bell before the dogs were going to be fed, the dogs began to salivate at the sound of the bell, whether or not it was accompanied by food, because they associated the bell with food. Thus, the bell-ringing in this situation is called a conditioned stimulus, and the salivating, a conditioned response. Extinction occurs when the association between the conditioned responses is not maintained. The conditioned response fades away and loses its connection with the stimulus.

Depending, however, on how firmly embedded the particular response to stimulus is, *counter-conditioning* may need to be used to remove the association, which seeks to bring desirable responses into competition with undesirable responses to particular stimuli. A common form of counter-conditioning is systematic desensitisation, which gradually introduces the unwanted stimulus in the context of alternative responses, so that the individual no longer responds to a difficult situation with, say, fear or anxiety. For example, a 14-year-old with an obsessive–compulsive disorder who could not tolerate others touching things in his room gradually practised different behaviours with his parents and therapist, and then as 'home work' allowed his mother to sit at his computer for a gradually increasing period of time, while he listened to music on his headphones. A common example of situations where this desensitising is used to good effect is helping children to stop wetting the bed by using a buzzer, which sounds when some urine reaches the mat and wakes the child, who can then go to the toilet. This process serves the dual function of conditioning the child to wake when their bladder is full, so ceasing to urinate while still asleep, as well as strengthening the bladder muscle. The normal reflex is to urinate when the bladder is full; the response of waking up, taught through this process, is a form of counter-conditioning, in that it is contrary to the reflex response.

Case study

The Browns

Mr and Mrs Brown were at their wits' end because of the behaviour of their 5-year-old son, Delroy, who was so disobedient and so badly behaved in public that they went out with him as little as possible. One example they gave on close questioning was what happened whenever Mrs Davies took him shopping to the supermarket. He would ask for sweets, which Mrs Davies might refuse because it was nearly teatime and he had already had crisps. He proceeded to cry, then scream and finally to start pulling items from the shelves on to the floor. In desperation, Mrs D. would buy the sweets, and Delroy immediately stopped screaming and behaved.

The effect, or *operation*, of Delroy's behaviour on the 'environment' is clearly to secure himself what he wanted, and receiving the sweets makes it very probable that he will behave in the same way again in the expectation, not of course conscious in this case, that he will get what he wants. Much social work attention focuses on operant behaviours of this kind, which are commonly described as a behavioural ABC. Something occurs – an Antecedent event – which produces Behaviour, which tries to deal with the event, and as a result of that behaviour, Consequences occur. The relationship between the behaviour and the consequences is strengthened or weakened by reinforcement, i.e. the response to the behaviour. So a diagram of Delroy's behaviour in the supermarket would look like this:

A	B	C
'No'	Tantrum	Receives sweets
Public place		
Mother		

The idea of **operant conditioning** proposes that behaviour is a function of its consequences, and focuses on strategies of changing the behaviour by interrupting the link between behaviour and result.

Operant conditioning is the way in which behaviour is changed by changes in the environment so that the behaviour becomes more and more likely to occur, in the anticipation that it will produce a given result. The antecedents of the behaviour are the setting in which it occurs, and quite literally the things which happen, often immediately, beforehand. Reinforcers are the things which are done in response to the behaviour which may serve to strengthen the behaviour and make it likely it will happen again. These techniques of reinforcing behaviour are called operant techniques. Reinforcing behaviours and operant techniques may be illustrated by the work of Allyon and Azrin (1968), two psychologists who pioneered the techniques' development (see our Closer Look box).

In the Closer Look box example, of course, the reinforcement (staff helping) in the original situation was benign (i.e. likely to be pleasant). It is important to remember, however, that reinforcers may also, on the face of it, be unpleasant. For example, a child's refusal to do homework may be reinforced by parents' repeated efforts to cajole them, say, with angry threats or punishment, into doing it. So it is worth remembering that no reinforcer is intrinsically good or bad, nice or unpleasant – the term 'reinforcement' simply refers to the effect the behaviour has in the particular individual's situation – 'one man's meat is another man's poison' as Katy Cigno, a social work practitioner and exponent of the approach, has described it (personal communication).

These basic principles of changing behaviour by altering the links between it and its consequences have been further refined and developed, mainly through identifying the kinds of reinforcements which are most successful. These include the following:

- **Positive reinforcement** is usually more effective – encouraging (rewarding) desired behaviour, while ignoring, rather than punishing or negatively reinforcing, undesired behaviour.
- **Continuous reinforcement** of every instance of desired behaviour is also said to work more quickly.
- **Shaping** can be used to change behaviour, by reinforcing small steps along the way. An adolescent who has been off school might be introduced to returning to school for very short periods, or someone fearful of leaving the house might be encouraged to do so gradually, by going first to the garden gate, then to the letter box down the road, and so on.

Encouraging desired behaviour is usually more effective.
(Kevin Smith (Kes): www.kescartoons.com)

A closer look

Changing behaviour through changing how it is encouraged (*reinforced*)

Allyon and Azrin observed eating problems among a group of psychotic patients on a mental hospital ward, and hypothesised that the responses of the staff to these patients were actually reinforcing (in this case, maintaining and making worse) the patients' maladaptive eating patterns. At mealtimes, those patients who had difficulty in eating were approached and helped by staff while the others received no attention. They hypothesised that this attention was rewarding to the patients. Other patients observed this (probably not consciously) and themselves began to display difficulties in eating. They therefore altered the reinforcement contingencies, so that staff attended to those eating in more socially desirable ways and ignored those having difficulty. Within days, it was reported that much of the problematic and undesirable behaviour had ceased or (to use behavioural terms) been extinguished.

- **Fading** is useful in ensuring that the behaviours which are wanted continue even without the positive reinforcers which have been used to produce it. This involves steadily reducing the level or type of reinforcement once the desired behaviour is on the way to being achieved. For example, the person fearful of leaving the house might have been reinforced by being accompanied in making her first small trips out. Later stages would see her doing so unaccompanied and with less and less back-up. The principle here is that we want the behaviour to continue, whatever the setting. Payne points out that without the removal of these reinforcers, we are 'likely to get a shift back into past behaviour patterns when we stop reinforcing.' He suggests, although of course there may be other reasons too, that 'this is why people in residential care often seem to do well, but fail when discharged' (1997: 125).

- **Modelling**. Another important way in which behaviours change is through modelling or, in everyday language, copying what someone else does: this can both reinforce existing responses and create the opportunities for developing new responses, through observing what others do. (We introduced you to these ideas in the context of thinking about how we build identities, particularly in adolescence but throughout our lives.) Sheldon, a social work academic who has been a powerful advocate for the use of cognitive behavioural approaches in social work practice, points out that much learning through modelling is cognitive: we think ourselves into the situation which we are observing, work out how we would act in such circumstances, and so on. This is similar to Bandura's proposition (to which you were introduced in Chapter 7 on human development) that how well we learn something is linked to our self-perception and how well such behaviour will serve our needs.

- **Negative schemas.** Drawing again on cognitive theories about how we learn, the individual is seen to be not a passive recipient of stimuli, but actively engaged in interpreting events in terms of their own unique set of values, thoughts, beliefs and assumptions. (We referred briefly to these ideas when describing Beck's contribution to CBT.) These cognitions shape the way in which individuals make sense of events. In turn, how individuals view experiences influences their affective state: for example, a depressed person may view the future bleakly, not because of the external reality, but because of the way in which they interpret it. A common focus in CBT is on modifying these negative thoughts of schemas, by teaching strategies such as focusing on positive thinking, relaxation, and so on. The negative messages are subverted and changed.

Reflect

Take a moment to think about the principles of changing behaviour we have just described.

Can you think of some examples in your own personal or professional life where you have witnessed or experienced any of them?

(You might have seen, for example, a teacher or parent encouraging a child's efforts, or showing a skill by example.)

Are you convinced that encouragement is a more effective strategy than negative reinforcement, as the theorists maintain?

The intervention process

Just as we found with psychodynamic approaches, you may become involved in using cognitive behavioural strategies in everyday contexts of social work practice, as one part, say, of an ongoing piece of work; or you may use them in a specific intervention based on cognitive behavioural principles: for example, a parent training programme, or one of the programmes referred to in Chapter 18 on youth offending, designed to change offending behaviour, or in Chapter 21 on substance abuse, to help substance abusers resolve their addictive behaviour. There are numerous detailed accounts of specific programmes based on these principles, which you may want to refer to (see end of chapter).

In any of these situations and contexts, however, you need to hold on to the three dimensions which we emphasised at the start of this chapter, namely thinking, feeling and doing. And perhaps because cognitive behavioural approaches are so 'up front' and 'doing' oriented, we should stress here the specifically reflective parts of

the process; as we discussed in introducing you to the ideas of Beck, cognitive behavioural approaches need to be used in the context of a sympathetic collaborative relationship. As soon as you as practitioner are engaged in helping, inevitably and properly your own feelings become engaged too. To take the case of Kerry and Howard in the previous section: as the work with the family progresses, the social worker John might decide to draw on cognitive behavioural techniques with Kerry in relation to her drug taking, or with the grandparents, to help them establish firmer boundaries between themselves, the grandchildren and their mother. Unless, however, he has fully understood, through the process of reflection discussed above, how his own feelings have switched back and forward, he will (a) be unlikely to assess accurately and (b) be unlikely to be able to model behaviours in a way which is helpful.

In our case example, we shall look at how you might use cognitive behavioural approaches as part of an ongoing intervention to show how they can be used alongside other approaches.

Case study

The Garretts

The Garretts, a second-generation family from southern Ireland, were referred to a family service unit (a voluntary organisation with centres in a number of deprived inner-city areas) by the local children's services, when one of their four children, Gerry, was put on the child protection register following over-chastisement by his mother, Siobhan. The central problems were identified as the younger children's, particularly their third child Gerry's, non-compliance and defiance towards their mother, who seemed lacking in child-management skills, and the lack of involvement and support by their father, Michael. As part of her assessment, the social worker, Rachel, as well as talking to Gerry's school, spent some time with the family, including observing times in the day which Siobhan had said she found especially difficult. Using an ABC analysis, Rachel noted the following:

Antecedents

- Background of poor, overcrowded housing and socio-economic disadvantage – Michael works intermittently as a roofer, and the seasonal nature of the work made it difficult to predict budgets, etc.

- Very active noisy children, constant low-level squabbling and fights between the two youngest
- Mother exhausted and overworked
- Gerry refuses to get dressed in the morning or eat breakfast
- Children's disobedience worse at home and with Siobhan
- Siobhan gives unclear instructions, then demands immediate compliance with the implicit or explicit threat of dire consequences, e.g. 'Pack it in! Stop that at once, or else.'

Behaviour

- Gerry fails to comply with requests/commands
- Flicks food, hits younger brother, runs round in pyjamas and refuses to get dressed.

Consequences

- Siobhan makes threats which she does not or cannot carry out – e.g. to send Gerry to his room, stop him playing out, no sweets, etc.
- If punishment is given – e.g. if Gerry is sent to his room, they are ineffective – he does not stay there
- Siobhan 'gives up', or 'goes over the top', yells and occasionally hits Gerry in an attempt to control him.

Having spent sessions with Gerry, his parents and the other children in the family, Rachel drew up an agreement for work which she, and a colleague at the FSU, would undertake with them. In it she specified the aims of the work, how it would be carried out, and the timescales. In accordance with the policies and procedures of the agency, the agreement also identified particular issues, such as, access to records, case notes and letters written on their behalf; timing of reviews (e.g. who would attend and how they would be conducted); dealing with the unexpected (e.g. Siobhan and Michael to do their best to contact FSU if unable to keep an appointment; Rachel to let family know at once if she is unable to see them, e.g. because of illness or a crisis with another family); action which would be taken if FSU receives a report that one of the children has been hurt or seems in some way distressed. The aims of the work were specified as improving the relationship between Gerry and Siobhan and the rest of the family, and improving the support which Michael gives to Siobhan in looking after the children. How these aims were to be achieved included:

- Rachel will spend two sessions with Siobhan, explaining principles of how you change behaviour most effectively and using role-play to enable her to practise how to reinforce Gerry's behaviour positively (stickers, hugs, praise) and will come to the house for a further three sessions to help her in doing this.
- Rachel will spend six sessions with Siobhan and Gerry after school, doing different enjoyable activities together, e.g. painting, playing board games.
- Michael will take the two youngest children out to a park, playground, etc. once a week to give Siobhan a break.
- Rachel will spend four sessions with Gerry on his own at the FSU looking at feelings: anger/sadness/happiness, using play as a means of communication. Rachel and Gerry will look at ways of expressing and managing temper which do not harm Gerry or other members of the family.
- Rachel, Michael, Siobhan and Gerry will make a chart of weekly activities done together alongside a chart of 'happy' days and 'sad' days. They will look at the connections between the two charts.

Of course, as we have commented from time to time throughout your text, such case accounts tend to present a very tidy snapshot of what is often a complex set of relationships – a pencilled outline rather than the coloured-in picture. We can see that behavioural principles come into this piece of work (modelling, positive reinforcement, and so on) but it is possible too that Rachel and Siobhan might need to spend time together talking about her family and early experiences, drawing on psychodynamic concepts such as 'working through' in doing so. In our example, however, we have tried to illustrate some of the key principles of this approach, particularly that it is:

- structured and directive in nature;
- problem and technique oriented;
- collaborative;
- reliant on dialogue and discussion, respect and trust;
- time limited – interventions are usually brief, between ten and at most twenty sessions;
- based on careful assessment.

Does it work?

Controversy, as Malcolm Payne suggests, has surrounded cognitive and behavioural models of treatment. In particular, there have also been fierce disagreements between cognitive behavioural and psychodynamic schools of thought, which you need to be aware of. Briefly, the behaviourists (to a lesser extent the cognitive theorists) have argued that psychodynamic models of social work are based on assumptions about psychological structures within the mind which we cannot examine empirically. The strong argument advanced for cognitive behavioural methods is that their approach has been empirically tested and found to be effective. Against this there have been objections on ethical grounds, in that practitioners may use methods which manipulate behaviour, against the wishes and agreement of the service user. It is argued that the techniques can be misused: for example, residential care homes have used reward and punishment strategies in oppressive or abusive ways. An instance of this was the 'pin-down' scandal in residential

A closer Look

How helpful responses can draw both on psychodynamic and also on cognitive behavioural principles

Wilson, Petrie and Sinclair analyse the quality of what they term 'responsive parenting' on the part of foster carers thus, as they describe the relationship between a foster carer and her 7-year-old foster child:

'To work successfully with such children, carers need to handle attachment sensitively; to reinforce socially acceptable self-esteem; and to handle difficult behaviour appropriately. James certainly had reasons to have difficulties in attachment and self-esteem, and certainly behaved in a very difficult way. How did Mrs Stanton [the foster carer] respond?

In analysing Mrs Stanton's . . . we simplify the picture. In particular we ignore the fact that the same behaviour on the part of the carer may serve multiple ends. For example, by speaking of the child as a "loved child" a carer may simultaneously reduce the child's fear of rejection, increase her/his self-esteem, and reduce the anger and anxiety that may lie behind the difficult behaviour. As we shall see, this ability to handle one area such as behaviour in such a way that other ends (for example, increasing attachment and self-esteem) are served is highly characteristic of Mrs Stanton . . . Her handling of his behaviour is based on attachment principles . . . but also involve[s] setting clear, achievable tasks for him to complete, "to the best of his ability". When he has experienced an upset, which they have talked about together, she repeats the experience in a safe way, soon after, to reinforce what he has learnt:

"So he took that on board, and I put it to the test a couple of days later, because I wasn't here when he came home from school . . . if I go through a situation like that with James [she had been out when he came back from a trip, and he had thrown a tantrum] I test it fairly soon afterwards, before he's forgot about it, so that I can acknowledge to him how proud I am if he's coped, and also work with him about that issue, if I need to, if it's failed . . . and I'd say, I'm so proud of you James, because it's been really hard, and you've done really well and I want to show you how proud I am of you. So I'd give him a little treat that way".'

(*Source*: Wilson et al., (2004) 'A kind of loving',
The British Journal of Social Work, 33: 995,
by permission of the British Association of Social Workers.)

homes for children in England, where children were locked up or physically held ('pinned down') in their night clothes for long periods, and this was justified as a method of training (Levy and Kahan, 1991). Behaviourists (e.g. Sheldon, 1995: 237–41) argue that service user consent is always required in an intervention; where the methods are misused, as they were here, it is in situations where the people concerned are already disposed to behave oppressively, and any approach, not just this one, is capable of being used coercively.

Reflect

Take a moment to think about the 'pin-down' scandal, and Sheldon's comments that all approaches are potentially open to abuse by practitioners.

Do you agree with him, or do you think that cognitive behavioural approaches could be more open to misuse? Why do you think as you do?

A further point, relevant to your own use of the ideas, is that some of the techniques specified may seem somewhat alien to practitioners, partly because they are directive in style, and partly perhaps because it may be difficult to switch from the exploratory, more psychodynamically based work to rather tightly specified interventions. One advantage of the method is that it does require you to do a detailed assessment and specification of what needs to change and this can give clarity and focus to intervention, which is helpful to both users and practitioners. There is, too, a sense in which the approaches can be used in conjunction to address the same problematic areas, as we show in our Closer Look box.

What the example of our foster carer and child in the box illustrates (and you may want to look at the article to see some of the other examples of the foster carer's responses to James's attachment and emotional as well as behavioural difficulties) is the way in which it is possible to draw both on psychodynamic and on cognitive behavioural concepts in a piece of practice. The foster carer's responses are in keeping with attachment theory and psychodynamic principles on the one hand, and cognitive behavioural principles on the other. Her warmth and refusal to respond to poor behaviour by rejection is in keeping with the ideas of psychodynamic theory. Her firmness and reinforcement of positive behaviour fit with ideas from learning theory and cognitive behavioural approaches.

Our next two methods are examples of brief, time-limited interventions which are probably the most widely known and practised models of short-term treatment used within social work practice. Together with cognitive behavioural approaches, they tend to focus on what Epstein (a clinician/researcher who discusses ten different models of brief intervention) describes as 'up-front' problems. So although it is arguably conceivable that you might choose a task-centred approach, say, with a couple where there have been child protection concerns identified by the agency but not acknowledged by the parents, usually this would not be the case. As its name suggests, crisis intervention is useful where individuals are experiencing some kind of situational or developmental stress; task-centred practice where individuals are capable of being helped to identify and work on a particular problem which they are facing.

Crisis theory draws on psychodynamic perspectives (e.g. defence mechanisms such as denial, displacement or projection) and focuses on emotional responses to critical experiences and helping people to resolve these successfully. Although the techniques of helping people in crisis can involve cognitive processes (such as breaking down problems into manageable 'chunks') and can include giving advice and guidance, much of the work may draw on person-centred counselling techniques such as accurate listening, reflection of feelings and congruence (see Chapter 4 on theories). Task-centred work, by contrast, focuses more on cognitive, problem-solving strategies, and emphasises a practical, rational approach to managing difficulties. In both, however, the ideas of reflection as well as action, encapsulated in the idea of *containment* on the part of the practitioner, provide the essential underpinnings.

Crisis intervention

Our next two case examples illustrate the way in which service users may experience crises.

Case study

Barbara

A white British woman, Barbara, had been separated for over a year from her husband, who had left her for another woman. He has recently petitioned for a divorce. After he had left, Barbara repeatedly approached doctors, psychiatrists and social workers to ask what could be done to treat what she considered to be the consequences of his mental illness, as she considered it to be. She refused to discuss his departure with their sons, saying that the only way of doing so was to acknowledge to them that their father was either bad or mad. She believed that he could not be held responsible for his actions, which she saw as the result of sickness, and wanted to know what could be done to cure him. When told that there might be nothing to be done but accept and come to terms with the end of her marriage, she became highly stressed. On receiving the divorce papers, she attempted suicide and had been admitted to hospital where she is being treated for severe depression.

Case study

Andrew

When Andrew, a mixed-race young man, was 16, social services removed him and his younger brother and sister from the care of their mother, who had been seriously neglecting their care and was using heroin regularly. Because of his age, Andrew was not accommodated. He was much older than his siblings, and had endured this most of his life although was apparently unknown to the local authority. He had very little basic skills and could not read and write. His self-esteem was low and his earlier experiences seemed to be weighing on him, resulting in his rejection of authority and his becoming very upset and aggressive when challenged about his behaviour. He turned up at a centre for homeless young people, designed to give them a 'roof over their heads' while they found employment and more permanent accommodation.

Many patients and service users seek or are referred for professional help because, like Barbara and Andrew in our case studies, they are in a state of crisis. In this section we shall introduce you to crisis theory and the method of intervention developed from it known as crisis intervention. Crisis *theory* provides practitioners with a theoretical model of the processes of adaptation that follow certain kinds of stressful, disquieting and seemingly unmanageable events in the lives of individuals. Its usefulness lies in its systematic organisation of events which appear random, unpredictable or overwhelming. Crisis *intervention* uses the concepts of crisis theory as a framework for understanding people's experiences and suggests steps to guide you in helping people who are in crisis.

You may wish, after reading this section, to question how often social workers encounter service users in acute states of crisis. However, many of us may be involved with people whose equilibrium has been upset by a previous crisis and who have made less than ideal adjustments. (For example, a woman and her ex-partner seek help in a child and adolescent unit with their 10-year-old son, who is showing extreme and prolonged distress at his parents' separation, which took place three years ago. In interview, the mother became tearful at the memory of her own parents' separation, and admitted that she had never got over it nor had the chance to talk it over when she was a child. It seemed highly possible that, because of this emotional legacy, she was unable to help her own child with his parents' divorce.) We may, however, work with users whose lives are punctuated by events which are described as crises in their lives, but which on closer examination are part of a long-standing pattern and therefore not appropriate for crisis intervention. Nonetheless, there are good reasons why you should be familiar with the principles of the crisis intervention model. Apart from a perhaps somewhat negative reason (to avoid misapplying the model to emergencies and dramas which might colloquially be described as crises but in fact are not), the model provides us with useful guidance for those infrequent but challenging situations when we are faced with real, acutely distressing crises in the lives of those seeking our help. And as social workers some of you may work in settings where this is a common occurrence (for example, a women's refuge, centres for the homeless such as Andrew attended, or Relate). To familiarise you with the theory, we shall first give you some brief background to its development; then discuss the concept of crisis, before moving on to some suggested steps in intervening.

Background

A catastrophic nightclub fire in Boston, USA in 1943 in which nearly 500 people died was the first officially acknowledged source of psychiatric interest in crisis theory. Psychiatrists and social workers observed the immediate and delayed reactions of survivors and their relatives. They argued that the duration of grief reactions was dependent on the success with which those affected did their mourning or 'grief work' and suggested that intervention over a limited period immediately after the onset of the crisis might enable them to avoid long-term psychiatric morbidity. This idea was taken further by Caplan, an American clinician, who suggested that, in addition to the occasional crises caused by unpredictable external events, we all have to overcome a number of developmental crises in our own lives. He argued (1964, 1961) that preventative work, offered at the time of such developmental crises, might be equally effective in reducing symptoms of psychiatric illness within the general population. These ideas, which originated in the field of adult mental health, were also taken up by American social work writers such as Rapoport (1970) and Golan (1978). Others (e.g. Parad and Caplan, 1960) developed the concept of family crisis from which a model of brief family therapy was developed. The concept of crisis seemed to become more and more widely drawn, to the point where it became almost synonymous with stress and transition (we come on to these distinctions in a minute). Subsequently, recognition of the syndrome of post-traumatic stress disorder has led to renewed interest in the possibility of prevention by prompt, proactive counselling.

What is a crisis?

A crisis is defined as any transitory situation in which a person's usual coping mechanisms are no longer adequate to deal with the experiences involved. Old habits are disturbed, and people's ordinary behaviour is no longer successful emotionally, intellectually and/or physically in responding to the changed circumstances in which they find themselves. Crisis theory proposes that the experience of crisis challenges the normal equilibrium (sometimes described as 'homeostasis' or a 'steady state') of a person's way of living, and that this very challenge generates energy which can provide the opportunity for developing more successful ways of dealing with experiences than before. In other words, a crisis provides an opportunity for personal growth and maturation. However, because of the stress involved and the felt threat to equilibrium, the person is also more vulnerable to regression, mental illness, feelings of hopelessness and inadequacy, or destructive action. So our definition needs to include the idea that the experiences pose the possibility of growth, but also the risk of spiralling downwards in the way we have just described.

In talking about crises, it is important to remember that we need to think about it as a process, rather than just an event, although the crisis can be triggered by a specific event (such as being a victim of crime), as we explain below. Encountering and resolving crises are, arguably, normal processes which each of us faces many times during our lives. The outcome, whether it is increased maturity and resilience, or a decreasing sense of competence and worth, will depend on how individuals respond to the crisis and the kinds of help and support which they receive.

Furthermore, in order fully to grasp the idea of crisis, we need to understand that it is the person's *perception* of and *emotional response* to the experience, rather than the experience itself, which constitutes the crisis, so that the concept includes recognising how the individual responds to the event in question. For one school child, for example, the opportunity to sing in the end-of-term concert provided an exciting and satisfying challenge. Her friend, who was also to sing a solo, was overcome with nerves, was barely able to sing, had nightmares afterwards and felt humiliated and inadequate for many months to come. This distinction means also that we have to differentiate between the notion of crisis and that of stress. During a stressful period, a person can use normal, coping techniques (such as talking, for example, or rehearsing an anticipated event), which the individual is accustomed to employ in resolving difficulties and discharging tension. In contrast, a person in crisis feels overwhelmed, despairing or helpless. Tension and anxiety are evoked, and unresolved problems from the past may be reawakened.

Reflect

Think of the last time you heard someone saying that they were feeling stressed, or felt this way yourself. Perhaps you have heard or used the phrase 'essay crisis' as a student to describe an anxious state of writing an assignment.

Do you think they, or you, on the basis of what you have read so far, were experiencing a crisis or stress?

Murgatroyd and Woolfe, two British practitioners and theorists, suggest that another way of distinguishing between stress and crisis, and of incorporating within the latter the essential notion of the person's perception of the event, is to use the idea of a threshold level. They comment that

'There is plenty of evidence to suggest that some life-events such as rape, redundancy, death of a spouse, divorce, separation, illness or injury, sexual or occupational problems, birth of a handicapped child and so on are frequently associated with stress in individuals and that, beyond a certain level, this may lead to a crisis. However, the threshold level is not the same for everybody, which implies that an adequate definition of crisis must incorporate a statement of how an individual comes to terms with the event in question.'

(1982: 9)

Situational and developmental crises

So far, we can see that the response to crisis, whether it is accomplished positively or not, is a way of adapting to new experiences. Such experiences of crises can be understood to arise either as part of development, or as situational events. You will probably more readily see the latter as likely to provide the kind of challenge which constitutes a crisis, so we shall begin with these, defining a *situational* crisis as one in which an external event or situation – which is often out of the range of normal everyday experiences and may be sudden, unexpected and distressing – occurs, and which threatens the person's normal ability to cope, and requires a change in behaviour. Situational crises involve natural disasters, illness, divorce or many of the examples given in the quotation above by Murgatroid and Wolfe. Not all crisis-laden events are unpredictable, in the sense that some of these circumstances can be foreseen, for example, when it is known that a baby will be born with a disability, or when someone is facing a partner's terminal illness. There are, too, different views about what might constitute a sufficiently hazardous event to justify regarding its victim as experiencing a state of crisis. An external catastrophe, such as a bomb explosion or an earthquake, would clearly fall into this category for most of the people directly affected. So would the onset of a sudden, serious illness or disabling condition, affecting oneself or someone close. Being assaulted by one's partner might be sufficiently stressful for some people to suffer a crisis reaction. So might the discovery that your partner had been sexually abusing your child, if you had had no previous suspicions.

It can also be possible to see some of the normal stages of development, such as starting at school, leaving home, going to university, getting married, childbirth, retirement and facing the death of others and oneself as crises, in that they are often periods when new challenges appear, and the individual may need to see themselves in different ways and act accordingly. For many, if not most people, these transitions, while commonly stressful, will not constitute a crisis. But some events, which would not constitute a crisis for most people, may trigger a crisis reaction for particular individuals. The death in old age of a grandparent, for example, after a long and fulfilling life, would not meet the criteria of a crisis for most of us; but for a person rejected or abandoned by their own parents, or who have experienced other acute losses, this loss may have a much more intense meaning and may resurrect more powerful feelings which had previously been suppressed.

Whether an event is experienced as a crisis may also depend on factors other than its 'objective' severity or painfulness. These might include the following:

■ whether you had any warning or suspicion;
■ whether you had undertaken the 'worry work' in relation to the hypothetical possibility of an event;
■ the support from your family and friendship network;
■ your own resilience;
■ your experience of dealing successfully or otherwise with previous crises.

For those who do experience one or more of these transitions as surpassing the stress levels which they can cope with using their normal strategies, it can be helpful to consider Spiegal's description of role theory. If we see roles as goal-directed patterns of behaviour which are carried out by a person in a particular situation or within a group because both the group and the individual expect this kind of behaviour, then it is possible to see that moving into a different developmental stage demands learning different roles. There are three main reasons for being unable to make the necessary role changes, an inability which may precipitate a crisis in development:

1. Lack of adequate role models for adapting to new requirements.
2. Lack of adequate intrapersonal resources to make the role changes – for example, social skills, inflexibility, mismatch between expectation and reality. A young person leaving home for the first time to go to college may be overwhelmed by the new social roles student life demands.

3. Refusal by others in the system to see the person in a different way (for example, a marital relationship where one partner resists the increasing independence of the other).

Finally in this section, before we move on to thinking about how this theory can guide you in helping people in crisis, you may find the work of Caplan, one of the key writers about crisis, useful. In addition to suggesting that individuals are motivated by a desire to maintain a sense of stability, so that crises occur when situations are perceived as being severely disruptive of this motive, he suggests that the individual in trying to cope will experience ever-increasing amounts of arousal. These two aspects of crisis theory – the motivation for stability and the frustration of this motive by arousal tension levels – are critical to an understanding of the crisis process as Caplan describes it. (He also describes different progressive phases in the crisis state, which you might want to look up.)

Reflect

Think about what you have read so far about crises.

Can you think of any period in your own life when you experienced a state of crisis?

What characterised your feelings and how did what you experienced 'fit' with what we have said about crises so far?

Principles of intervention

This framework for understanding the experiences and responses of people in crisis leads us to the principles of intervening. As we have seen, the salient characteristics proposed by crisis theory are, first, that people in crisis experience:

■ a period of psychological disequilibrium
■ which is the result of a hazardous event or situation
■ which cannot be remedied by familiar coping strategies and the use of customary habits
■ which creates an obstacle to important life goals.

(based on Roberts, 2000)

Individuals who have experienced a crisis can be expected to show a reaction soon after the hazardous event. This may consist of:

■ helplessness, confusion, anxiety, shock, disbelief, anger
■ low self-esteem and depression

- seeming incoherent, disorganised, agitated and volatile, OR being
- calm, subdued, withdrawn and apathetic.

The discovery of the inadequacy of normal coping patterns (whether or not consciously formulated as this) produces an openness and energy which can be harnessed to achieve change. Finally, the actual experience of being in crisis is time-limited, so that this emotionally availability does not endure (which is not to say that the actual pain, for example, of bereavement, does not continue). Building on these features, crisis intervention emphasises the following:

1. It is a short-term, time-limited intervention. Within a given period (which may be as long as nine months' duration, but is likely to be shorter), help is offered on an intensive basis, with flexibility as to the time made available in order to maximise the potential for change. The goal of crisis intervention is usually to try and resolve the most pressing problems within a period of one to twelve weeks.
2. It is designed to be highly supportive, with practitioners adapting their practice to meet the needs of the individual/family in crisis, for example, by visiting at home, being quickly responsive to expressed need.
3. A positive, concerned relationship is established, which offers a sense of hope, self-worth and lessened anxiety. The crisis offers the chance to establish this relationship of trust more quickly than may be achieved in other helping situations. During a crisis, however, you may be confronted by an angry, bitter or accusatory individual or family, who berate you for failings in how they have been treated. It can be helpful to bear in mind that what is being said may be accurate and justified, or it may be the only way in which they can cope with their own helplessness, frustration, guilt or fear. Try not to take it personally, or to get involved in verbal disputes. If it does concern something which you could or should have done, accept and acknowledge responsibility.
4. Listening and attending. These skills in communicating are vital, particularly in the early stages of establishing the relationship. One study, which evaluated a service of brief targeted support for families with a learning disabled child who were in crisis and at risk of break-up, underlined the importance of what they describe as 'wholly attentive' listening in making carers feel supported, commenting that: 'it was so emphasised and [so frequently] contrasted with previous lack of [attentive] listening that it demands inclusion [in the evaluation]' (Baldry et al., 2005).
5. Helping to confront the crisis by talking about present feelings of, say, anger, guilt or grief, and encouraging this to be done in small 'doses' which can be managed, being careful not to soften the impact of the event too much by, say, overreassurance. Fears and other feelings may be very valid. Show faith in the person's ability to manage, but do not reduce their motivation and the generation of new coping ability by saying that all will be fine. Explain the relationship between the crisis situation and present feelings – it can be helpful to understand that feelings are normal in the context of crisis.
6. Encourage, reinforce and support difficult decisions and understandings. The study cited above described how parents were helped to be realistic about their situations, and to develop understandings about what made things more difficult. One mother began to acknowledge how her feelings and the children's difficult behaviour were interlinked, saying: 'I feel better, and if I feel better then that's going to show with my kids, and if the kids are feeling better, then there's nothing to worry about.'
7. Explore past life occurrences only in relation to the existing crisis, and explore coping mechanisms which may help to identify alternative ways of coping, and in seeking and using new behaviours or alternate ways of satisfying needs.

Roberts sets out a seven-stage model (see Table 12.1) of crisis intervention, which practitioners are recommended to follow in their response to crisis situations.

1. *Immediate response and risk assessment.* The risk assessment should consider the following questions:
   - Does the person need immediate medical attention?
   - Are they considering suicide as a 'solution' to their problems?
   - Are they about to injure themselves?
   - If they have been a victim of violence, is the perpetrator still present or likely to return?
   - Do they have any children, and are they also at risk?
   - Does the victim need transport to a refuge or other place of safety?
   - (If possible) Has the person sought emergency help with similar problems before and, if so, how was the situation resolved?
2. *Establishing rapport.* In your first contact with someone experiencing an acute crisis reaction, it is essential that a degree of rapport and understanding

is established, in which reassurance is given about help being available, and genuine respect and acceptance of the person and their predicament are offered.

3. *Defining the major problems.* Once some rapport has been established, the practitioner needs to get a clear picture of the nature of the problems which have precipitated the crisis reaction. Those working in specialist settings where crisis reactions are common (for example, A and E units, paediatric clinics) will have established systems for ensuring they are kept informed about the situation. Those in emergency settings or staffing telephone helplines will have to work harder with the service user or caller to clarify what has precipitated the crisis reaction. The aim at this stage would be to get as clear a picture as possible of the current situation, and how things came to this point. More detailed explanations can wait until later.

4. *Encourage an exploration of feelings.* This is a key element of the model. Those experiencing crisis need to have space to ventilate and express their feelings in the context of a safe, understanding and empathic relationship, usually achieved by the technique referred to above of active listening. It is particularly important to give permission for the expression of any ambivalence about the event or the loss. This is a normal and understandable reaction to many crises, but often generates guilt in the survivor or victim.

5. *Consider alternative responses to the crisis.* Alongside the work of active listening, you will need to engage in cognitive work, thinking together about what turned this particular situation into a crisis, what alternative actions are open to them, what strengths and resources they can bring to this new and unexpected situation. This may involve discussion and evaluation of initial coping strategies. Any practicable options need to be considered and either rejected or identified as worth further explanation.

6. *Develop and implement an action plan.* The last stage of the model involves identifying a particular course of action, and supporting the client in its implementation. In order to move beyond the crisis successfully, the user needs to achieve three goals:
   - to acquire a full understanding of what happened, and why, and of the final outcome;
   - to understand the particular emotional and cognitive significance of the event for them;
   - to develop a plan for their future life, based on real beliefs and cognitions, rather than on irrational fears and distortions.

Table 12.1 Roberts's (2000) seven stages of working with crises

1	Assess risk and safety of service user
2	Establish rapport and appropriate communication
3	Identify and define major problems
4	Deal with feelings and provide support
5	Explore possible alternative responses
6	Formulate action plan
7	Provide follow-up support

7. *Follow-up plan and agreement.* At the end of the planned programme of work, both should agree whether and in what circumstances further help can be accessed if it is felt to be needed. Ideally, this should be freely available, but if this is not possible the offer of additional support at times of difficulty (for example, anniversary, or the beginning of a criminal trial) should be made.

Strengths of the crisis intervention approach

From the above, you can see that, in essence, crisis intervention calls on many of the skills of sensitive interviewing which you were introduced to earlier. What it also does, we think helpfully, is offer a coherent structure within which to operate for responding to many of those who are referred to, or seek, social work help in acute or severe distress, which otherwise might overwhelm you as well as the person in crisis. It emphasises the need to work with the emotional, felt experience (by attentive and supportive listening) using a set of personal and professional qualities which you will be developing, of warmth, genuineness and empathy; and the need to work also with cognitive processes (helping, for example, to 'divide up' the problem and think through how it can be dealt with). It reflects a positive and hopeful view of the human condition, in its premise that through the successful resolution of the crisis an individual can become stronger and more capable of dealing with subsequent threats, which can in turn foster new coping capacities and, as the theory suggests, new levels of maturity.

Limitations

The theory and model has been criticised on a number of counts, some of which (for example, the risk of diluting its value by the very wide range of events to which the term 'crisis' can be applied) we have already touched on. The more loosely we interpret the concept of crisis, the less likely that a specific set of directives will be appropriate for all the situations to which it is applied. (O'Hagan, 1986, a British social worker and writer, makes this point strongly, although he weakens his argument by caricature.) Other criticisms or limitations of the model include the following:

- Closer examination and observation suggests that individuals cope with severe, unexpected losses in very different ways, and at different speeds, without pathological outcomes. A model based originally on helping people maintain a specific route through the crisis does not cope very well with such findings. At the very least it will require adapting very flexibly to the particular individual's needs, and the more that is true, then the less useful the model may be in creating a safe, containing, structure.

- The model does not take into account the very different traditions in different cultures for coping with loss and acute distress. It has been criticised as being based on a very Western philosophy designed to patch people up as quickly as possible. Arguably, however, sensitive risk assessments will reflect these different ways of responding.

- On a practical level, many local authority social workers will not become involved in events early enough to implement a classic crisis intervention approach. Even agencies in the voluntary sector will not usually have the resources to provide a service within 72 hours, which may involve an ongoing commitment for up to three months. And the flexible model described in the study by Bawdry et al. is unlikely to be achievable unless the agency itself modifies its service delivery to enable you to work in this way.

Task-centred practice

The second time-limited model of practice which we consider has some features in common with that of crisis intervention. We shall end the discussion by exploring the similarities and differences, and the different situations where you might apply the model. But, as before, we first consider some of the background, then the theoretical framework and a step-by-step guide, concluding by suggesting how you might use this with one of the cases described in the book/chapter.

At the outset, we should stress that using the model of task-centred practice as an intervention does NOT just mean undertaking a series of tasks on behalf of or with a service user. Quite often, social work students say they are using a task-centred approach when it is quite clear (perhaps because it involves a one-off interview, or because the service user is an elderly person with dementia) that they cannot be implementing the model. We come back to this point in our discussion of the background (see quotation from Doel and Marsh below) and also ask you to reflect on it in relation to your own practice, at the end of the section.

Background

This model for practice originated in pioneer studies undertaken by Reid and Shyne in the United States in the middle of the last century, in which it was discovered that 'planned short term treatment' was, on the measures used, more effective than long-term treatment, and that a task-centred approach, in which user(s) and practitioner identified and agreed problems in the user's life to be worked on, was successful as a model of treatment. The method emerged as a reaction to the then dominant model of social work – an open-ended form of casework mainly with individuals, informed by a predominantly psychoanalytic perspective. Although the provision of material and practical help was not ignored by this model, it was delivered in the context of a therapeutic relationship with the client. There was also a 'hierarchy' of interventions, in which the psychotherapeutic form of casework was seen as the most skilled, requiring the highest level of qualification and training.

This challenge to the predominant mode of social work practice in the United States also reflected a theoretical tension, polarised as the struggle between the 'diagnostic' and 'functionalist' schools of social work. The former emphasised the treatment of dysfunctions in individuals' capacities to make and sustain relationships, which were treated through extensive counselling of a psychotherapeutic nature (Hollis, 1964). The latter argued that the transactions between worker and service user should be determined primarily by the agency's function: whatever was done should be demonstrably linked to the goals and purposes to which the agency was committed (Smalley, 1967). We mention this historic tension because it is still, in a slightly different form, present today, as our earlier quotation from the social services manager suggests. The 'Quality Protects' initiative (introduced by the 'new' Labour government in the

A closer look

Task-centred casework is born!

An experiment was carried out in New York with a social work agency which offered services and help to families experiencing relationship difficulties. The aim was to test out a number of different approaches and to evaluate the outcomes. The only factor associated with differences in outcome was that of the time boundary. Families who received 'planned short-term service' of no longer than 3 months seemed to do rather better than families receiving 'continuous service' lasting up to 18 months and on average 8 months (Reid and Shyne, 1969). The differences in outcome were small as were the numbers involved, and there were moreover serious methodological limitations in the study design. Nevertheless, one conclusion seemed indisputable: that with some families at least (the agency worked mainly with intact middle-income families), practitioners could achieve the same or improved results in 3 months as they could in 18. Social work managers around the western world seized on this finding with enthusiasm!

(*Source*: Corden, unpublished handout)

late 1990s to try to improve services for children and young people), with its emphasis on the achievement of measurable goals ('performance indicators'), may be represented as victory for managerialism. And the popularity of the task-centred approach (in the development of which Reid and Epstein acknowledge the specific influence of the functionalist school, referred to in the next section on systems) may be in part because of these current emphases in practice.

A third, unacknowledged source of influence must surely have been the growing interest in a cognitive behavioural approach to social work. Interestingly, Reid and Epstein make no reference to this (perhaps because the dominance of psychoanalytic ideas in the United States at the time would have made it so contentious?) but the model, as we shall see, clearly depends on a cognitive approach to problem-solving rather than on 'emotional therapy'.

The method seems to be one of the models of intervention most frequently cited by practitioners as informing their work, and may well be one which you have already come across on your training programme. It is worth bearing in mind, however, that although it does indeed seem to offer a useful and accessible framework, with its notion of an agreed set of steps, or actions, to be done, practising the approach requires more than *merely undertaking* a set of activities, whether these are carried out by the user, practitioner on their behalf, or both. As two writers who have contributed substantially to the development of the model in the United Kingdom warn:

'The absence of any selected problem, agreed goal or time-limit, let alone any shared record of the work, does not always shake a social worker's conviction that he or she is practising task-centred work. Too often, task-centred practice is loosely associated with a certain mood or style of practice – brisk and practical. At worst, it means telling the client what to do.' (Doel and Marsh, 1992: 95)

The activities or tasks, then, as we shall see, come out of a defined and planned period of engagement. Although the model focuses on performing tasks to resolve identified problems, the purpose of the intervention is to bring about longer-term changes in the individual's capacity to resolve problems of everyday living. Success in resolving one problem breeds success, and builds confidence and self-esteem. So the process of engaging together and agreeing what is to be worked on and how, with its attendant mutual engagement and self-recognition, is essential – and hence the model to be followed, and arguably to be effective, requires a framework for practice, and is more than just undertaking a sequence of actions on the part of either user or practitioner.

We shall first set out the key components of the approach, and then discuss how these can or may be adapted to meet the kinds of situations which you will encounter in your practice, bearing in mind that things never work out as neatly as the theory suggests.

1. The work is undertaken within an agreed time boundary. This is seen as essential in producing the kind of energy and commitment necessary for making progress.
2. The focus is on addressing problems
   – which the users acknowledge or agree; which can be clearly described;

– which are capable of being worked on outside the sessions between practitioner and user (although they can be addressed within these as well);

– and which reflect things which they want to change in their lives, rather than what others want them to change. This last point, about the user's 'ownership' of the problem, has been rather modified in the United Kingdom, with the dominance of statutory work (in contrast to the predominantly 'private' context in which the model was developed in the United States). It is possible to see a compatibility between the two positions, as long as one sees the process as one of dynamic engagement: for example, the courts might specify attendance at parenting classes, with or without the couple's agreement. Coming to understand and accept the usefulness of these can be a part of agreeing the task. Attending classes without accepting the need for them is unlikely to produce success in changing behaviour.

Reid and Epstein suggest that the kinds of problems which can be worked with effectively can be grouped into eight categories, as follows:

1. Interpersonal conflict
2. Dissatisfaction in social relationships
3. Problems with organisations
4. Difficulties in role performance
5. Problems in making decisions
6. Reactive emotional distress
7. Inadequate resources
8. Psychological and behavioural problems not otherwise categorised but meeting the general definition of problems in the model, including can be changed, specified and motivation to change.

Although Reid and Epstein would argue that only problems which fell within at least one of their categories would be susceptible to a task-centred approach, you may consider, as others have done, that almost any problem could be defined to fit their classification.

The intervention process

The model specifies a clear sequence of stages to be followed. The first stage involves a careful exploration of the difficulties being experienced (from the perspective of both users and others); then the focus moves to exploring, first, what is most wanted, and then what seems to be achievable; goals to be achieved, and how

these will be recognised, form the next stage; and the rest of the work is taken up with carrying out the tasks, which take them, step by step, towards their goals. Again drawing on Reid and Epstein and Doel and Marsh, the following specific stages are followed, to be undertaken within a timescale of two to four months, with a total of around 12 contacts between worker and service user:

- Problem exploration
- Identifying and agreeing the target, or selected, problem(s)
- Agreeing the goals ('the desired and agreed outcomes of the work', as Marsh and Doel (2005: 33) suggest)
- Drawing up an explicit agreement
- Identifying a task or tasks needed to address the problem
- Carrying out the task(s)
- Evaluation and termination.

We shall consider these stages in more detail below.

Problem exploration

This phase should be usually completed in the first session. The worker and service user together identify all the problems which are affecting the latter adversely, and which have led to their referral to the agency. These problems are defined by the service user not the practitioner, although the latter may help with clarifying and so on.

Identifying a target problem

1. Once all the relevant problems have been named, the service user is invited to place them in priority: which do they think is the most important to resolve from their point of view? Once the priorities have been decided, a decision is taken on whether only one, or more, can be addressed during the timescale of the intervention. This may depend on the scope of the problem as well as on the complexity of the service user's situation and predicament. Specify the range of problems which could be worked on.
2. Rank these in order of priority.
3. Define the desired goals or outcomes.

In their second book, Marsh and Doel have a useful section on the distinctions between problems and goals, concluding that 'Avoiding the verb "need" and beginning a statement with "I want" or "We want" guarantees a statement which is a goal' (p. 72). (So in our example from the Garrett family, in the case study below, the goal might be expressed as, 'We want a better marital relationship'.)

Making an explicit agreement

This is seen as an essential part of the model (and a significant departure from more traditional practice). The idea that the agreement should be written down was not part of the original model, but Doel and Marsh in their first book (1992) assign a whole chapter to written rather than verbal contracts (pp. 46–59).

Identifying a task or tasks

This is the central element of the model. A task or more often series of tasks is identified. Successful completion of this should eliminate or alleviate the selected, target problem. Choosing the right tasks is a crucial skill for the practitioner. They must be within the capacity of the service user to complete: they must make a difference to the situation; they may require resources which are provided by the worker or their agency; and successful completion should be a positive experience. So at this stage the key steps are to:

4. Design the first set of tasks.
5. Agree the length of time and pattern and number of contacts.

Task implementation

This will include both tasks to be accomplished by the user and also those to be undertaken by the practitioner. The latter may include the following:

1. Working with other people to help complete the task – e.g. negotiating with the school to smooth the way back where a child has been truanting.
2. Arranging for incentives and rewarding success.
3. Sharing tasks which may be difficult for the individual to manage on their own. Some of these will involve what Reid (1992) calls session tasks – i.e. they can be undertaken by practitioner and user in the session: for example, rehearsing for going to a job interview, planning and expressing feelings and dealing with anxieties (we give you an example of this in the Garrett case study, below).
4. Reviewing and, it is hoped, removing obstacles or things which are getting in the way of achieving tasks and goals.

The final ending phase

This involves both user and practitioner in describing what the problem was and how it now is, and the underlining of achievements and what has been learnt in the process; planning for the future, for example, how to use the skills learnt; possible new contracts for further work;

and agreements about how the intervention will end – for example, referral to another agency, or move to a different, long-term team within the same agency.

Case study

The Garretts cont . . .

Look back at the case study which we gave you in relation to cognitive behavioural approaches. Ask yourself how you might use a task-centred approach to work with Siobhan and Michael.

Do you think it would it have been helpful as a framework for working with them?

You might want to think about such things as whether they and you would have agreed on the targets and tasks, and how easily you could have included individual work with Sharon within a task-centred framework.

To start you off, let us suppose that in developing the list of problems, Siobhan and Michael identify the relationship between Sharon and Gerry as the one they most want to change. This would then be the target problem and the goal would be a positive relationship between them. Tasks might include Michael doing things with the other children to give Sharon and Gerry space, Sharon practising playing with Gerry (what Reid, as we describe above, calls 'sessional' tasks) and then doing so, and so on. One of the important things is to try not to focus on too many issues at once, the idea being that this can be confusing and a distraction, and make success less achievable and less identifiable when it has occurred.

Strengths of the task-centred approach

This approach reflects a trend within social work practice, as Payne comments, towards interventions which are based on more clearly specified procedures which are made explicit and are agreed with the users themselves. Its method is somewhat unusual in that the approach depends for its success explicitly on its acceptability to users and on their participation in the activities undertaken. So because, if followed properly, it depends on both sides being open about what is to be done, and articulating these clearly, it embodies at its core the social work values of anti-oppressive practice, partnership and empowerment. Sticking properly to the principles of developing a mutual, agreed understanding of the range of problems and giving over to the user the choice of which problem to work with does require practitioners to be open, and aware of what they are there for, with no 'hidden agendas'.

The model contributes to 'empowerment' in another way, if its advocates are correct. A crucial premise in the model is that the process is a sufficiently empowering experience to leave the satisfied user more capable of solving subsequent problems without help. The successful experience challenges 'learned helplessness' (a psychological response pattern graphically described by Seligman (1975), an American writer on depression). There is some empirical support for this claim, in that subjects involved in task-centred approaches were less likely to approach agencies for help again within a short period than other service users.

The model also requires the practitioner to make a commitment to a series of sessions of planned work, to adhere to an agreement, and to work on issues between sessions. One of the strengths of the approach is that it then promotes the kind of consistency and commitment which can provide the experience of containment seen to be key in reflective practice.

Further strengths of the approach are that it provides detailed guidance on the techniques to be followed in order to achieve success, which can be very helpful in guiding you through the process of thinking, reflecting and doing referred to in our earlier section.

Limitations

There are limitations with the method, some of which are inherent in it, and some which seem to arise more from its emphasis on learning and problem-solving behaviour, rather than being essentially incompatible with the approach. Payne (1997) suggests that it may not be effective in situations where there are constant debilitating difficulties, where long-term psychological problems are the main issue, or where users do not accept the right of the practitioner or the agency to be involved, although he points out that the method can be useful to achieve results with a specific problem, even in long-term work or child protection.

As Doel and Marsh suggest, the service user's ability to think and reason is a key ingredient of successful work. Like all work based on cognitive theory, the user has to be capable of cognition and rational thought:

'In those case where social work is appropriate, but where reasoning is seriously impaired, such as some forms of mental illness, people with considerable learning difficulties or a great degree of confusion, task-centred work is often not possible in direct work with that person.' (1992: 99)

Reid and Epstein make it clear that in their view, the 'voluntary client' seeking help should have complete responsibility for prioritising and selecting target problems to work on; in the case of individuals who are unwilling recipients of social work intervention, they envisage some form of negotiation, which may or may not have a successful outcome. However, other, later writers (e.g. Doel and Marsh, 1992; Marsh and Doel, 2005; Trotter, 1999) appear to argue that the user's right to decide which problems should be addressed is particularly useful in working with 'involuntary' users, since it begins the process of empowerment. Nonetheless, all proponents of task-centred work are agreed that where no target problems can be identified by the service user, or where they cannot or will not prioritise any problems which the agency can justify spending effort on (in the context of its particular remit), the task-centred approach has no further mandate.

A further limitation may be that where a wide range of problems is experienced, each of which interacts with and exacerbates other problems which threaten to overwhelm the family, the task-centred method seems a rather weak response. Unless one is able to deal with problems on several fronts, their combined influence will continue to undermine the functioning of family members: for example, one family member may have the capacity to reason, but if other family members are not prepared to engage in the same process and consistently undermine the efforts of the practitioner and user, the method may not achieve much. However, even where more serious and fundamental problems need to be worked with, the approach may appropriately be used in the initial phase of the work, to empower and give a sense of achievement, and to help develop greater trust in the practitioner.

One final question, which is not strictly a limitation but needs asking, is whether the success of the model depends on the task or the brevity. Most of the evaluative research compares the task-centred approaches with other approaches where there is neither a requirement to formulate tasks to be completed, nor a time limit. The alternative explanation for the apparent effectiveness of the model is that individuals have limited capacity to invest in any change effort, and that this will mostly be available in the initial stages. If this is the case, then whether or not tasks were used, work undertaken within a time limit would show better results. Quite probably, too, knowing in advance that work is limited by time constraints mobilises both practitioners and users to greater efforts. This may not imply a weakness in the model of course but may suggest that any planned short-term intervention is more likely to yield results. This much acknowledged, experience suggests that some service users do gain positive reinforcement from completing tasks and seeing some results flow from their own efforts. So, although the evidence may not yet distinguish between the relative impact of time or task, the reactions of service users suggest that both factors play a part (Gibbons et al., 1979).

Reflect

Think about the arguments suggested above for the success of the model, and decide which to you seems the most plausible: that it is effective because either (a) it is short-term, or (b) it focuses on particular actions which are manageable, or (c) that it works because the user identifies the problem to work on.

If you conclude that all are likely to be relevant, which do you think would be the most important?

Similarities and differences of the two approaches

To help you reflect on these two approaches, crisis intervention and task-centred practice, and to clarify where they may be appropriately used, we conclude this section by summarising briefly the features which the two models have in common, and some important differences:

Similarities:
- A time limit, usually not more than about three months to the intervention.
- An emphasis on cognitive restructuring as a key element.
- A recognition of the need to pay attention to the service user's feelings, both to maintain their involvement in the work, and also as a necessary preliminary to any cognitive work.
- A move from exploration of the problem, through a process of identifying alternative strategies to the development of a specific plan.

Differences:
- Crisis intervention can only be justified in specific circumstances: it is a reactive approach to an acute

problem, the origins of which are normally external to the individual or family, and usually involve loss or major change.
- Task-centred models can be applied to a broader range of social situations.
- The need to listen closely to and empathise with very painful emotions is an essential part of crisis intervention; it may not be required to such an extent in task-centred work.

We can only deal briefly, for reasons of space, with two other interventions, both based on systems thinking, which are important in social work practice.

Systems approaches

Systems thinking, as we discussed in Chapter 4 on theories, has been an important feature of social work practice since the 1970s. Systems theory was, as Payne points out, one of several strands of theoretical developments which came to the fore in the late 1960s, partly because of dissatisfaction with psychodynamic theory, arising from a sense that it failed to address adequately the 'social' component of social work: in other words, that it tended to ignore the way in which individuals are affected by, and in turn affect, others in their environment. Its emphasis on 'wholes', comments Payne, was 'an attractive contribution to social work' (Payne, 1997: 140).

If you refer back to our earlier Chapter 4, you will remember that systems theory was identified as a 'middle range' theory, with two practice theories seen as emerging from these. We are going to focus in this section and the next on two of these, and suggest that you look back at the earlier discussion for the basic foundations of systems thinking. Although we consider particular applications of systems thinking, it is also worth stressing that the ideas are in a sense as central to understanding yourself in practice as the psychodynamic principles explored earlier. Systems thinking does not just apply to the users of social work services and members of their family, friends and neighbourhood networks: it equally applies to the helping networks that you may be part of – that is, the agencies and professionals involved, and beyond that to the social environment which affects service users and helpers alike. (The nineteenth-century poet Tennyson was expressing this when he wrote in a well-known poem, 'I am a part of all that I have met'.) Systemic thinking encourages us to think as carefully about the systems (organisational, community, our own personal systems) of which we are part, as much as we consider those of the individuals and families with whom we work. As two commentators point out:

'Conflicting opinions and actions by the various professionals often affect the child and family and cause further disturbance. The family and professionals in turn are much affected by the social welfare system and fluctuations in child care policy.' (Schuff and Asen, 1996: 136–7)

Two perspectives based on systemic thinking became particularly influential from the 1970s onwards: the first saw its most influential expression in a widely used book by Pincus and Minahan (1973), which explicitly applied systems ideas to social work. They argued that people depend on systems, such as family, communities, work and schools, in their immediate social environment for a satisfactory life, and that social work needs to take account of these in any helping relationship. They define four basic systems in social work (the client system, change agent system, target system, action system), which can be helpful in clarifying which system the people you are dealing with are part of. Although they explore the kinds of interventions which are needed, the systems approach developed by Pincus and Minahan is particularly useful in providing a way of thinking clearly about the systems in which the people you as social workers are working with are placed. We are not going to explore their ideas in detail here, but introduce them partly to show you that systems thinking can be applied in a range of circumstances.

Family systems approaches

The second perspective based on systems thinking focuses on the family as a psychosocial system, and provides a way of understanding how all members of a family can affect and influence on another. From a systems perspective, the family is seen as developing characteristic patterns and core ways of being together and relating to each other. Working with families using a systems perspective may focus on the family as a unit (family therapy), or may work with different members of the family, but the latter will always involve 'holding in mind' the interactions between different family members. Systems thinking has resulted in a number of methods of treatment, the best-known of which is family therapy. We cannot do justice to the large literature on working with families here, but will introduce you to some of the main ideas, and point you in the direction of useful further reading.

Systems processes and concepts

Virtually all approaches to working with families see the family as an interactive system, consisting of a group of people which includes at least two generations who are related by biological and/or legal ties and expectations of loyalty and trust. All Western (and most worldwide) societies share the expectation that the family will perform certain tasks, for example, taking responsibility for the emotional, educational, social and physical development of children, and providing for the emotional well-being and personal growth of the adults. The tasks relating to the fulfilment of these responsibilities change depending on the life stage of the family. In a family with young children, for example, attention will probably centre on nurturing and ensuring their safety, while with adolescents, the focus will shift to helping them establish a secure sense of self and setting them on an educational, social and emotional path which will enable them to make a successful transition to adulthood. This developmental perspective means also that particular events, such as running away from home, out-of-the-ordinary eating patterns or continuing to live in the family home as an adult, will have different implications and be interpreted differently, depending on the family's life stage and the age of the child, young person or adult family member.

The way in which families carry out these tasks, functions and responsibilities varies according to the particular family's culture, ethnic group and religion, the balance of power within the family, and the values, attitudes, traditions and past experiences of the adult members in it. These functions are carried out in a social context, and are buttressed by other people and networks of extended family and friends, and a wider framework of educational, medical and statutory services. These can be experienced as helpful or hostile, the latter, for example, where family member(s) come into conflict with the law or officialdom.

All families have characteristics or properties which include the structure, boundaries and processes of communication of the particular family; the relationship between the different subsystems of the family (e.g. paternal grandmother and father; siblings) and between it and the wider world; and the family rules and the way in which individual members give meaning to their experiences. A variety of approaches are used by practitioners to stimulate family interaction – for example, setting them tasks and/or meeting with them together – to help them identify attributes of family functioning, which can then be used to act as a focus for therapeutic work.

Think ahead

Think of a family you know well, possibly your own or a friend's or a service user's. Imagine you had to describe them to a colleague.

What would you say? What do you see as the important things which characterise this family, and differentiate it, or makes it similar to, others you know?

How did you get on? You probably first mentioned composition (parents, children, any other family members), ages and genders, and then perhaps tried to describe how they seemed to you. Here are some of the characteristics which you might have thought of as important: how they care for the children/older family members; sense of family togetherness (perhaps you thought of their leisure pursuits, mealtimes together, shared activities such as sports, watching football); management of conflict and disagreements; discipline (perhaps here you thought about rules such as bedtimes, homework, doing chores round the house, punishments); quality of communication (listening, hearing, talking); alliances (perhaps one parent seems to favour one of the children, or to get on badly with another); how sociable they are (networks).

These underpinning characteristics are some of the aspects which practitioners trying to help families tend to focus on. However, family practitioners vary in the emphasis which they give in their work to the different characteristics of the family as a system. For example, while many family therapists focus their attention on working with current patterns of communication and relationships in the family (the 'here and now'), other approaches seek to unravel the influence of significant past events, experiences and relationships on current family relationships. These different approaches have tended to develop their own techniques and principles for practice, the main ones being structural family therapy, strategic family therapy and systemic family therapy.

As beginning practitioners you would be unlikely to need to explore these in detail, but useful summaries of the theoretical underpinning of the different approaches are contained in Bentovim (2001/2007), while Bell and Wilson (2003) give a range of examples of family approaches applied to different user groups or problems, such as couple difficulties, domestic violence.

You may also find it useful to read more about some of the insights and skills which family practitioners have developed to help families communicate better with each other, to enable them to consider how they relate to each other, and to reflect on and understand their experience of life together as a family. Many therapists make use of tasks and homework to be done between sessions, metaphor, storytelling or therapeutic narratives which

A closer look

Narrative approaches in systemic family therapy

White and Epston and others (e.g. Marner, 2000) have developed the use of narratives within systemic family therapy.

'The underlying principle is that people's lives are constituted by stories which they tell themselves, and which provide the frame of reference through which they interpret their lives. With troubled individuals, the varied stories often become one, problematic, story, or identity, which comes to dominate both their own view of themselves, and also how others see them, so that they and the problem become conflated. The aim of therapy is to separate the person from the problem, and externalise it so that it becomes something which

the individual can gain control over, rather than being subsumed by it. [For example] children suffering from a range of usually quite identifiable and specific problems, such as encopresis or school phobia, are encouraged to see them as things outside themselves, such as monsters or trolls, which are trying to take control. By in some way banishing them (perhaps by shutting them up in a box which is then thrown away) or outwitting them, the child ceases to be at the mercy of the problem, and can begin to construct an alternative and preferred personal story or way of being. The therapist relinquishes the role of expert to the child, but is influential in suggesting possible strategies, and may . . . write letters to the children between sessions to encourage them in their struggles.'

(Wilson and Ryan, 2005b: 9)

look for times the particular problem was beaten, and enlists the family in the battle to overcome the problem. Our Closer Look box discusses one such approach.

Most practitioners working with families have developed insights into common characteristics of the manner in which they behave towards each other, perhaps when talking together for the first time in the presence of the therapist. For example, very often as you begin to work with a family, you will encounter what are sometimes described as 'flight reactions' to what is being experienced as the new or threatening situation of sitting down together and reflecting on each other's experience. Flight defences may be expressed in the form of children running out of the room or climbing on the furniture and generally playing about. Or they can take the form of family members making negative or positive comments and predictions and sweeping statements, such as, 'this is going to be a complete waste of time' or, 'this is the best thing that has happened to this family'. They can also take the form of what are called 'mind reads', which are characterised by imputing thoughts and feelings to other people, for example, saying that another family member is feeling angry, or doesn't understand what is being said. (Perhaps you've had experience of this yourself, and felt irritated by it.) Or 'flight' may appear as focusing on one family member in order to manage the uncomfortable emotions around uncertainty, possibly by scapegoating the individual (when one member of the family is isolated and left on their own to carry the family problems).

It is important not to be thrown off course by reactions and comments such as these. McCluskey's chapter on theme-focused family therapy (a form of therapeutic intervention which addresses the emotional world of families by organising family sessions to focus on the feelings involved in these relationships) contains much useful detailed advice about how to deal with these, and helping the family to explore what they are experiencing in the here and now. Her suggestions include mind reads, negative and positive predictions, and interruptions and contradictions.

Mind reads need to be checked instantly because if one does not do this, a climate is promoted in the group [i.e. family] where what people think is going on inside people's heads is accepted as if it is true:

'Checking mind-reads is done by asking the person with the mind-read to put it in a form of a question that the other person can answer with a yes or a no. For example, "I think you have not understood what has been said, is that true?"

The person answers with a yes or no if they are old enough or in other ways if they are too young. One then asks the person who had the mind-read whether they believe the answer. What one does now is to encourage the person giving the answer to say what is true for them and make it clear that what is being imputed to them has much more to do with the other person than with them. Depending on the answer, i.e. whether they got a yes or no, one then asks the person who checked their mind-read what it is like to have one's assumptions about someone confirmed or disconfirmed in reality. In this way they bring their affect (their emotion) into the session to be worked with and attention is diverted away from their ideas about another person that are not based in reality.'   (McCluskey, 2003 pp. 115–16)

Negative and positive predictions commonly involve statements about what is going to come from the sessions and also need to be checked in terms of whether (a) the person with the prediction believes they can tell the future and (b) what is being predicted is actually happening this minute. We give an example of this below, in Martin's and Karen's family session.

It is natural for a family or any members of a group to join on similarity (i.e. to feel comfortable with what appears to be similar to themselves) and to separate on differences (to move away from, or to scapegoat what they perceive as different from themselves). When family members **interrupt** each other or **contradict** what is being discussed, the therapist might ask if they can find some similarity with what the other person is saying and build on it. At this point, it is important to notice the children's behaviour and non-verbal communication and to ensure that there is space for them when they have something to contribute. It is also important to point out to the rest of the family if any of the children's behaviour changes (including heightened colouring or changes in muscle tone) in response to painful or difficult subjects being talked about in the family. This could be an indication that the child is constricting their emotion (through tension) rather than expressing and exploring their affective experience (see McCluskey, 2003: 115–6, in Bell and Wilson).

Theme-focused family therapy, i.e. the approach developed by McCluskey and Bingley-Miller, is based on detailed interviews with the individual family members before the first family sessions take place, but the methods and techniques developed are particularly relevant and can be adapted for social workers in non-specialist settings. The aims of the method include promoting an open, attentive, empathic and reflective way of communicating which:

The Grey family

The Grey family first became known to social services when Martin, the father, presented himself at the office wanting help after physically assaulting his son, Ben. Ben was placed on the child protection register and the family separated for some time, with Karen, the mother, taking her two children, Ben and his sister Kayleigh, to live with her mother some miles away. However, four months later, they were back together again, living in a rented house elsewhere in the borough. Both Martin and Karen had received individual help in the past; Martin as a schedule one offender (he was charged and convicted of assault and placed on probation) was referred to and completed an anger-management course at a local clinic. Karen attended a childcare management group over the same period, and received a good deal of support from others in the group. Soon after they had completed their respective programmes, Karen became pregnant with a third child, Jasmine.

When Martin contacted one of the local family centres, he said that Ben, now nine, was having problems at school and had been excluded on several occasions. He also said he was worried about Karen's relationship with the two oldest children. He thought she was too hard on Kayleigh, and tended to favour and indulge Ben, who runs rings round her in consequence, and he was 'fed up' of having to control him himself.

Over the next few days, the social worker, Gemma, meets with Karen and Martin and two other professionals who have been involved with the family (see next section on networking), and begins to form an assessment and to lay down certain ground rules and boundaries for how she might work with the family. During these preliminary meetings, Gemma observes among other things the way in which Karen and Martin seem to communicate with each other. She also notices that the two professionals seem to mirror the ways in which Martin and Karen interact, with the clinic worker in particular responding over-sympathetically to Martin and taking a rather patronising attitude towards Karen. She wondered if this contributed towards the family's being stuck in their ways of handling things. She is keen to try to focus on the family as a unit, both because the parents have both already been the recipients of individual help, and

because one of the other professionals especially has indicated that he feels the problems are to do with the way family relationships are managed. She plans to work with the family for two to three months, this being the amount of time she has before leaving for another post.

During Gemma's work with the family, they agree to focus in particular on how Karen and Martin can become more physically and emotionally close, moving away from fixed ideas of blame and recognising how they adopt particular positions in relation to themselves and the children: for example, with Martin frequently adopting a position of superiority and Karen of inferiority. One instance of this is that in relation to Ben, Martin states repeatedly that he is 'the only one Ben listens to, and I'm fed up with it' while Karen says, 'I can't get him ever to do anything or listen to me.'

In the early sessions, Martin wanted it to be clear that he did not see why he needed to attend, but also drew attention to himself by interrupting or contradicting other family members, making comments such as, 'this isn't getting us anywhere', or burping when the topics became difficult. As well as using some of the ways of addressing communication (discussed above), Gemma also draws on a number of systems techniques and thinking, including:

- circular questioning (a technique which brings into the open what family members are thinking about each other, by asking, for example – what do you think Martin would say if I asked him why he is here?) and
- structural ideas such as recognising the way in which Martin maintains the power dynamics in the family by coercion and threats;
- scapegoating – the possibility that within the family a triadic relationship had developed which was leading to Ben being unduly 'picked on';
- boundaries between subsystems, e.g. with Karen at times allying herself with Ben against Martin and Kayleigh.

The work continued over eight weeks, and yielded considerable improvement in both Martin's and Karen's capacity for empathy, and in turn in their abilities to parent successfully, while Ben's behaviour in turn showed some modest improvement.

- enables family members to gain a greater understanding of each other's experience;
- validates individual experience and supports individuation;
- enables the voice of children to be heard so that their wishes and needs can be better understood and responded to;
- supports family members in making choices.

We give some suggestions for further reading for you to follow up on this approach and other systemic approaches to working with families at the end of the chapter.

In summary, systems thinking provides a coherent theoretical framework for working with families. The approach used by Gemma in our case study reflects the way in which systems thinking in family work is likely to be used in non-specialist settings – you are more likely to find certain techniques and ideas useful to you, than necessarily to follow one particular approach. Family systems approaches therefore are thus often about:

- engaging the whole family in understanding and working at things they are finding difficult;
- helping the family members to focus on and change particular difficulties, e.g. helping to find positive ways of communicating with each other (giving each other space to speak and listen, stopping 'mind reads', and so on);
- establishing proper boundaries between the generations – e.g. parents taking joint responsibility for managing children's behaviour.

Strengths of the system approach

As the above suggests, the approach is particularly helpful in situations where for a variety of reasons, the family seems unable to move forward in response to changed circumstances. It seems especially helpful at:

- improving interactions between people, with its emphasis on how one person is affecting another, rather than on internal thoughts and feelings;
- addressing power imbalances with families;
- helping those involved see problems and relationships 'in the round' rather than locating them in one individual;
- freeing up situations which have got stuck or entrenched;
- mobilising creative energies and resources of family (and in the case of networking, below, the community).

Limitations

There are a number of limitations which social workers may experience in working systemically. Some writers have expressed ideological doubts about systems theory, with a number of criticisms stemming from a structural–functional perspective on society (derived from e.g. the work of the sociologist, Talcott Parsons). From a more applied social work perspective, although the emphasis on being aware of the interdependence of different systems (or components of the situation) is a major contribution to understanding, social workers may find it harder to work systemically with families, because of difficulties, for example, in engaging key members of the family in family sessions. Other issues include a concern that in adopting a neutral stance which de-emphasises the cause of a problem (and by implication, blame and responsibility), the approach moves perilously close to denying culpability, and promotes injustice. A further limitation may be that although it emphasises the inclusion of all family members and their equal right to participate, it may inadvertently disempower less verbal family members (such as children) and either reinforce or ignore cultural and racial perspectives.

Systems thinking is also central to our final approach, the second which we have focused on involving systems thinking.

Networking

Networking is a vital but not very well conceptualised or researched aspect of social work practice. It is closely related to some varieties of 'systems'-based social work practice, and to 'ecological' theories and methods, but has its own repertoire of skills and challenges. As Trevithick (2000) notes, some key social policy documents have recognised the centrality of networks to social work practice. The Barclay Report (1982) identified the importance of 'local networks of formal and informal relationships' and their 'capacity to mobilize individual and collective responses to adversity' (p. xiii) while the NHS and Community Care Act 1990 referred to the importance of informal caring resources in its aim of promoting a new kind of relationship between professional services and 'the community'. Trevillion (1992) has produced the only general theory of networking as a social work method and his book is well worth reading. We cannot attempt to summarise his thinking in detail, but in his conclusion he writes:

'Networking is an attempt to self-consciously promote patterns of sharing by encouraging certain partnership processes to come to the fore. It is an enabling strategy which is concerned with:

1. Interpersonal relationships and in particular the way in which key individuals relate to one another.
2. Community as a source of self-identification and as a process of empowerment and mutual support.
3. Flexible and informal as opposed to bureaucratised and institutionalised ways of relating to other people.
4. Communication processes for sharing information and establishing a shared network culture.
5. Action sets and the strategies involved in mobilising them.

At any one time networkers may focus more on some of these processes than on others. But community partnership involves all of them.'   (Trevillion, 1992: 136)

In this short section we concentrate on the aspects of networking most likely to be of relevance to front-line social workers and their managers. This concerns the interplay between two levels of network, which we will call the 'case network' and the 'relevant organisational network'.

We need to identify why networking should be seen as a distinct method of intervention in social work, and why it so often not seen this way. Traditional social work practice concentrates attention on 'the case' or the 'service user' and her or his 'carers'. Of course, the case may be a family, or a complex kinship network (as in the case study of John and Kerry and Tracey which we looked at in the section on psychodynamic work), but it is rarer for social workers to step back and see the total system involving service users, carers and the whole involved group of professionals (including the social worker) *as the case system to be worked with*. But, this is what the principle of networking involves.

Case study

Mrs Atkins

Mrs Atkins (88 years old) was referred to an adult services team by three people in the space of two days. First the GP phoned up and conveyed rather abruptly that she was in need of an assessment for residential care since she was no longer coping on her own at home. Then a neighbour phoned to say that she was concerned because Mrs Atkins's flat was beginning to smell badly. Finally, Mrs Atkins's close friend Joan came into the office very distressed, and told the duty social worker that she could no longer cope with caring for her. She had been visiting every day for years now, working with the home help to organise shopping, cooking and cleaning. But Mrs Atkins was deteriorating now, she said, had become incontinent much more often, and Joan felt she could not cope with cleaning up after her as well as all the worry this now caused her.

From a networking perspective, the question facing the team at their allocation meeting in relation to this referral is: Who or what, is 'the case'? Is it Mrs Atkins, Mrs Atkins and her two main carers, or everyone they know to be involved (and quite likely more), including themselves? Is the case an individual, a system, or a network? From our point of view we need to ask: what difference does different answers to this question make to how we intervene?

Think ahead

On the basis of the information given in the above case study, how many different ways of defining the members of the 'case network' can you identify? What difference might different answers to this question make to the process and outcome of the case?

One good way to begin thinking about these questions is through family therapist Robin Skynner's (1991) concept of 'the minimum sufficient network'. Skynner was a psychiatrist as well as a family therapist, and so he thought of 'case networks' very much in psychological terms, as referring to ' a set of psychological structures which need to be connected to one another if the total system is to be autonomous, capable of intelligent response and adaptation' (1991: 6). Social workers may need to think of such networks as including a more directly practical component. Mrs Atkins seems to be housebound, and in need of practical care as well as psychological care which her key relationships provide her with – although we should not fail to notice that Joan, as her friend of long standing, probably gains from her relationship with Mrs Atkins as well. Nevertheless, the idea of the minimum sufficient network is still valuable as a way of asking ourselves whether the 'problem' really concerns just Mrs Atkins, or something that has become strained in the whole set of relationships that makes up this network. If we take this idea as our starting point, we need some way of establishing which relationships are essential to include in a viable approach to the case considered *as a network*.

Mrs Atkins cont . . .

David is interested in network approaches to work with vulnerable people in the community, so he takes on the case at allocation. He decides to visit Mrs Atkins, and he liaises with the home help in order to let her know of his wish to see Mrs Atkins, and to gain access to her flat. David finds Mrs Atkins in bed in the afternoon. She tells him that up till a few weeks ago she always got up in the late morning with the help of her friend and the home help, but now she can't manage this any more. However, in answer to his questions, it doesn't really seem that her physical capabilities are the problem. Eventually, David enquires gently about her incontinence – has it got worse? Mrs Atkins looks distressed, but says nothing, except that she is tired and thank you for the visit but would he mind leaving her to rest now? But David persists and muses out loud that perhaps if her incontinence has become worse, she might be finding this very embarrassing and difficult to talk about? Mrs Atkins nods very slightly, and tears start to fill her eyes.

Over the next few days, David talks to everyone in the network, including Mrs Atkins's sister who lives over 100 miles away but keeps in touch by phone. He begins to form an assessment: the problem which has put strain on the whole network is not just Mrs Atkins's incontinence, or even her difficulty in talking about it, but *everyone's difficulty in talking about it*. Even the GP, who knows about it from the community nurse, has not talked directly to Mrs Atkins, but seems instead to think of it as an inevitable development that leads directly to her needing residential care.

David goes back to visit Mrs Atkins, and establishes with her that she desperately wants to continue living in her own home. David puts it to her that he sees no reason why this shouldn't be possible, as long as a way can be found for everyone to help her manage her incontinence effectively. Mrs Atkins is fully aware that the flat has

been smelling badly, and feels very ashamed of this. David suggests that if only this embarrassing matter can be discussed, and plans made by everyone to deal with it, then there is every chance that the network of support can, with Mrs Atkins' cooperation, continue to sustain her life at home.

David has made contact with everyone important in the case system – the minimum sufficient network – from the point of view of the crisis that was developing. But there is another level to matters: the organisations in which the professionals involved are embedded. The GP is known to be rather reluctant to make 'home visits' unless there is an emergency involved, and the home help is a vital cog in the case system. As a community-based service, David's team has evolved a system of formal 'liaisons' with key organisations – the health centre, the home help service, community transport and so on – because they find that good relationships with the *organisational* network help to facilitate flexible and cooperative working with *case* networks. The two levels interact dynamically, because success at the individual case network level reinforces the value of organisational networking, and vice versa.

Mrs Atkins cont . . .

Respect for the service user and 'respect for the network' coincide for David. So, he organises, with Mrs Atkins' agreement, a network meeting at her home – round her bed in fact. The aim of the meeting is to agree a plan that will allow Mrs Atkins to remain at home. It might seem that doing things this way is likely to increase Mrs Atkins' embarrassment, but David has both gained her trust and also thinks that *everyone* in the network needs the support of everyone else – not just Mrs Atkins. If she is to remain at home, the 'difficult matter' needs to be talked about by everybody, and it seems everybody, for one reason or another, needs a bit of help in getting over their anxieties about this.

The meeting is also a good opportunity to review other aspects of her care and her overall situation, and it emerges that as a housebound person she is entitled to support for her telephone bills. But the main achievement of the meeting is to enable everyone to discuss and make clear plans about the delicate matter of how best to manage

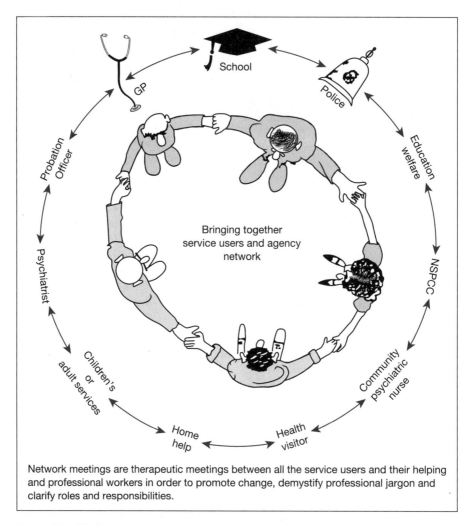

Figure 12.1 text inside the illustration:

School
GP
Police
Probation Officer
Education welfare
Psychiatrist
NSPCC
Children's or adult services
Community psychiatric nurse
Home help
Health visitor

Bringing together service users and agency network

Network meetings are therapeutic meetings between all the service users and their helping and professional workers in order to promote change, demystify professional jargon and clarify roles and responsibilities.

Figure 12.1 What are network meetings?

(*Source*: Adapted from *Doing Networks and Case Conferences*, undated.
© Rochdale Area Review Training Sub Committee)

Mrs Atkins's incontinence. The GP attends the meeting, encouraged by David's colleague who liaises with the health centre, and makes important and helpful contributions to the plans. David writes up the decisions of the meeting and circulates them to everyone. A date for a review network meeting is agreed.

Cooper (1990) has written about this style of networking from the perspective of a community social work team, emphasising the interconnection between systems of informal community support, social work and social care services, health provision and independent sector agencies. Networking of this kind both draws upon, and reinforces, the 'organic' or unpredictable character of communities and the complex systems that make up community relations. At one extreme this kind of practice shades over into community development work, which now sees communities as about networks of complex 'emergent' processes which require sensitive attuned responses by workers, rather than just as geographical localities that are more or less well resourced.

To sum up, networking in social work practice is thus often about 'reframing' elements of the work that are already present:

■ multi-agencies and multi-professionals are involved in complex cases;

- professionals need service users' and carers' cooperation as much as the other way round;
- case systems often grow to be messy, uncoordinated, and with their own dynamic;
- successful casework depends on the quality of inter-organisational relationships;
- problems and solution are 'systemic' and not individual, but the boundaries of the relevant 'systems' are often quite open-ended.

In so far as networking is about the practice of taking all the above into account, and taking up a 'meta' position with respect to the processes involved, it can be a highly creative aspect of social work practice, which surmounts obstacles to practice intentions and plans, and helps deliver good outcome for service users.

Conclusion

In this chapter, we introduced you to some of the different ways of thinking about how human beings function and relate to one another, and how these theories and concepts can be used to think about and organise the way in which you engage in work to help service users. We began by stressing that three components, thinking, being and doing, are essential in all methods of activity in social work. We considered ways in which you need to reflect on how you plan and engage in relationships with service users, which will include having a solid grasp of different social work methods and an awareness of feelings, emotional responses and patterns of interaction.

We then introduced you to the principles, concepts and methods of working in relationships with service users, first considering psychodynamic practice and next cognitive behavioural approaches and then briefly looking at how both can be drawn upon, and indeed may address the same kinds of behaviour. Two models, which draw on these principles and have been influential in social work practice, were then introduced.

Our final section looked at systems thinking and how social workers can apply these perspectives to family work and working with wider networks. Throughout the chapter, we have given you case examples to illustrate how these approaches shape or inform different social work interventions. Inevitably, in one chapter, it has not been possible to discuss the full range of methods which social workers draw on in their practice. One obvious omission is that of groupwork. This is currently less commonly taught on social work training programmes than it used to be, but it has a rich theoretical base, and for those of you moving into certain social work settings (for example, Youth Offending Teams, some mental health settings), it will be a useful method for you to learn about and use in your practice (as we suggest in three of our chapters on working with specific user groups).

Key learning points

This chapter has covered the following learning points:

- ✔ Any case or piece of social work practice can be thought of as a series of steps at each of which you need to focus on particular questions. At the third and fourth stages of the process you need to decide what needs to be done and what methods, techniques, skills and resources are needed to reach the desired outcome.

- ✔ In addition to 'doing', 'thinking' and 'being' should always be present in how social workers conduct themselves. The *thinking* component is partly about the importance of having a solid *theoretical* grasp of different social work methods.

- ✔ Social workers will usually need to draw on different approaches and methods to deal with different situations and circumstances; these include approaches based on psychodynamic and cognitive behavioural theory, systems thinking, and models of intervention such as crisis work and task-centred practice.

- ✔ Psychodynamic theory proposes that people and relationships are made up of at least two 'layers' of experience and functioning: a conscious one and an unconscious one; psychodynamic thinking and skills are particularly relevant in helping practitioners understand the overall dynamics of a case.

- ✔ Cognitive behavioural interventions are based on careful assessment, are structured and directive in nature, problem and technique oriented, collaborative and are usually brief, between ten and at most twenty sessions.

- ✔ Systems thinking provides a coherent theoretical framework for working with families and for engaging in users' networks. The latter is often about 'reframing' elements of the work that are already present.

- ✔ Crisis and task-centred practice are brief, time-limited interventions which are probably the most widely known and practised models of short-term treatment used within social work practice.

 **Further reading**

For those who are interested in a view of social work that combines psychodynamic, systemic and political perspectives, **Malcolm Payne** offers an excellent extended theoretical account. His book (1997) on modern social work theories gives useful summaries and critiques of the approaches we have discussed here, and identifies key texts in relation to each.

Stepney, P. and Ford, D. (2000) *Social Work Models, Methods and Theories: A Framework for Practice* (Lyme Regis: Russell House) is a useful general guide to the distinctions between the different methods, and also discusses the distinctions between models and methods and theories.

Trevithick, P. (2000) *Social Work Skills* (Buckingham: Open University Press) provides a useful all-round text on a range of skills for social work practice.

Psychodynamic approaches

There are many other concepts and ideas relevant to a deeper understanding of psychoanalytically informed work, and if you want to explore this further, then among the huge number of good introductions to psychoanalytic theory and practice is **J. Milton** et al. (2004) *A Short Introduction to Psychoanalysis* which stands out in recent years.

There are many excellent books and journal articles that explore the importance of psychodynamic practice in ordinary social work contexts. The *Journal of Social Work Practice* (Taylor & Francis) is the only British social work journal that concentrates on this type of work, and **Marion Bower's** (2005) *Psychoanalytic Theory for Social Work Practice: Thinking under Fire* (Oxfordshire: Routledge) contains many good examples of social work practitioners grappling with everyday practice situations using psychodynamic thinking.

Cognitive behavioural approaches

Brian Sheldon has written extensively on cognitive behavioural theory and practice, and his articles and books give a useful introduction to the approach for social workers. **Hudson and MacDonald's** short book (1986) on behavioural social work also gives a clear, basic introduction to the approach for practitioners.

Crisis intervention and task-centred practice

There are a number of useful books on crisis intervention and task-centred practice which are referred to in the chapter. Those by **Murgatroyd and Wolfe** and **Doel and Marsh** are particularly accessible. Marsh and Doel's updated and revised book on task-centred practice is full of case examples and they are enthusiastic and helpful guides to implementing the approach in practice settings.

Systems approaches

An edited book on working with families by **Margaret Bell and Kate Wilson** (2002, *The Practitioner's Guide to Working with Families*, Basingstoke: Palgrave Macmillan) gives individual chapters describing approaches to working with families with a range of problems. The chapter by McCluskey on theme-focused family therapy which we have cited extensively in our text is a useful accessible introduction to working systemically with families, albeit within a particular structured approach. The book also has useful chapters on working with a range of problems, such as domestic violence and difficulties arising in step-families and with couples, which our textbook has not, for reasons of space, specifically addressed.

Arnon Bentovim's chapter on 'Working with abusing families' in *The Child Protection Handbook* (2007: 451–78) 3rd edn (eds Wilson, K. and James, A., Edinburgh: Elsevier) gives a detailed account of different approaches to systemic working with families as well as practice guidance on working with abusing families.

Pincus, A. and Minahan, A. (1973) *Social Work Practice: Model and Method* (Illinois, USA: F.E. Peacock). The authors give a detailed discussion of their application of systems thinking.

Trevillion, S. (1992) *Caring in the Community: A Networking Approach to Community Partnership* (Harlow: Longman) provides the only general theory of networking as a social work method and his book is well worth reading.

 Useful websites

There are a number of websites which provide useful information on different approaches referred to in the chapter.

www.centreforsocialworkpractice
The Centre for Social Work Practice website is currently being developed as a discussion forum on relationship-based social work, with articles on the methods explored in this chapter and materials and articles to download.

www.instituteoffamilytherapy.org.uk
The Institute of Family Therapy website provides information on systemic work and other family-based problem interventions such as family mediation.

www.nch.org.uk/ourservices/index
The NCH website provides information on crisis interventions with children and families.

http://counsellingresource.com/types/cognitive-therapy
Extensive further reading on cognitive behavioural approaches and details of research.

www.psychnet-uk.com/psychotherapy/ psychotherapy_cognitive_behavioural_therapy.htm
Further information on cognitive behavioural approaches.

For additional cases and topic-organised, clickable links into additional media resources, including those produced by IRISS, visit **www.pearsoned.co.uk/wilsonruch**

Activity

Turn to the case study at the beginning of the chapter. On your own or with a fellow student or colleague, consider what alternative methods, discussed in the chapter, you might use in working with the family. For example, you might decide to spend time with Sue and James separately, or you might decide that an approach such as theme-focused family work (which involves individual interviews with the family members followed by family meetings) or task-centred work, would be appropriate. Or you might consider their networks and how these could be involved. Make a case for the alternatives. What additional 'aids' for working might you use? For example, you might use a genogram, a family tree, or life paths, or an ecomap; or you might set the family a task to be practised between sessions. Would some of the cognitive behavioural techniques suggested in the chapter (e.g. operant conditioning) 'work' for James, do you think?

Chapter 13
Inter-professional working

Chapter summary

This chapter will focus on social work practice from an inter-professional perspective, concentrating on the need for social workers to practise effectively with other professional groups. It stems from the recognition that, in many cases, it is impossible for an individual social worker to provide a sufficient and/or adequate response to the needs of a service user in isolation from other professionals.

Learning objectives

This chapter covers topics that will enable you to achieve the following learning objectives:

- To understand why emphasis is given to inter-professional working in government policy
- To discuss the particular contribution of social work to inter-professional activity
- To understand why inter-professional working is an integral part of social work practice
- To examine some of the obstacles that might obstruct effective inter-professional practice
- To identify the key components of successful inter-professional work
- To illustrate, through the medium of case studies, how inter-professional work can operate successfully in practice.

National Occupational Standards

This chapter will help you to meet the following National Occupational Standards:

Key Role 2: Plan, carry out, review and evaluate social work practice, with individuals, families, carers, groups, communities and other professionals

Unit 6   Prepare, produce, implement and evaluate plans with individuals, families, carers, groups, communities and professional colleagues

Key Role 3: Support individuals to represent their needs, views and circumstances

Unit 11   Prepare for, and participate in decision making forums

Key Role 5: Manage and be accountable, with supervision and support, for your own social work practice within your organisation

Unit 14   Manage and be accountable for your own work
Unit 17   Work within multi-disciplinary and multi-organisational teams, networks and systems

Key Role 6: Demonstrate professional competence in social work practice

Unit 18   Research, analyse, evaluate, and use current knowledge of best social work practice
Unit 19   Work within agreed standards of social work practice and ensure own professional development
Unit 20   Manage complex ethical issues, dilemmas and conflicts
Unit 21   Contribute to the promotion of best social work practice

Case study

Mr Rimmer

Yasmeen is a social worker located in a team responding primarily to the needs of older people. She receives the referral of Mr Rimmer, an 87-year-old man of Irish descent who has been referred from a hospital psycho-geriatrician. Apparently Mr Rimmer – whose wife died a year ago and who lives alone – has been diagnosed with Alzheimer's disease, and there are said to be a range of ongoing difficulties that relate to his physical health as well. When Yasmeen sees Mr Rimmer a number of issues concern her. He lives in privately rented accommodation; this flat has obviously had little maintenance in recent years: the only heating is an old one-bar electric fire, and there is only one ring on the equally old cooker that still works. Yasmeen is taken by how physically frail he is, and is concerned that his diet and nutrition may not be adequate. Because of his failing memory, Mr Rimmer acknowledges that he is experiencing considerable difficulty in managing his financial affairs. While seeking to resolve his financial and housing issues, concerns about his physical health also increase; having stumbled over a coffee table in his living room, a wound is opened that does not heal and becomes ulcerated. On investigation it emerges that Mr Rimmer is currently receiving no support from the Adult Social Care Department, even though his needs are clearly substantial. He struggles to fulfil even simple practical tasks, and accepts that his mobility has become increasingly reduced. At the same time, the flat lacks basic equipment that would assist him in the performance of various activities of daily living. In addition, Yasmeen believes that he would benefit hugely from the specialist home care support for people with dementia provided by a specialised service in the independent sector. Since Mr Rimmer seems to have very little social contact, Yasmeen is also concerned to ensure that he has enhanced opportunities to engage in various social activities. He indicates that he always loved gardening, and that he misses this part of his life – since he and his wife moved into this flat 10 years ago he has had no opportunity to do anything related to what used to be a passion of his. Over time, he also gives Yasmeen to understand that he misses his wife very much and still grieves for her; however, he says that he has never received any help with coming to terms with his loss, which still upsets him greatly.

What are the consequences likely to be if Mr Rimmer's needs are not addressed from an inter-professional perspective?

As you can see from this case study, it is obvious that a number of different agencies and professions can have a positive impact on Mr Rimmer's life. To help Mr Rimmer address the range of needs that Yasmeen can identify, there will need to be detailed work to resolve his housing and financial difficulties, the latter requiring the involvement of a solicitor. He has continuing needs in relation to his deteriorating Alzheimer's disease, will continue to see the consultant psycho-geriatrician on a regular basis and will also receive frequent visits from a community psychiatric nurse specialising in work with older people. His physical health means that he will have regular contact with his general practitioner and the involvement of a district nurse to dress his leg ulcer and to monitor his health will also be essential. To respond to his need for support in the community, the specialised home care service will be important, and Yasmeen will also consider whether or not a referral to a local horticultural club for older people would be beneficial to him. His reduced physical mobility calls for an assessment by a physiotherapist, while the condition of his accommodation also indicates that an occupational therapist's involvement would be indicated. A referral to a dietician is also indicated to review the appropriateness of his diet and to suggest nutritional improvements. Including Yasmeen, nine different professions could easily become involved in the provision of Mr Rimmer's care; in addition, Yasmeen will need to negotiate with numerous other agencies. As a result, she will be involved in considerable inter-professional and multi-agency work. The complexity of this is obvious: if Mr Rimmer is to receive the care and support he will require the coordinated input of numerous different sources of care and support. At the same time there is an obvious paradox: when his Alzheimer's disease is increasing in its effect Mr Rimmer also would benefit from stability in his personal life – an impossibility if the additional services are to be considered. Yasmeen must ensure that the potentially disruptive impact of numerous different people being involved in Mr Rimmer's care does not negate the benefits in providing specialised and appropriate forms of care.

A similar level of complexity could have been illustrated equally well in relation to children and families, adults with a disability or a mental health problem, etc.; the inter-professional dynamics that the case study highlights therefore can be said to typify the essence of social work practice, albeit with specific relevance to work with older people.

Think ahead

Think about any person who requires some form of social work support. Identify the scope of inter-professional working that could be required, and the numbers of different professional groups that could be involved.

Introduction

As the case study demonstrates, the skills and abilities of a social worker are not exercised in a vacuum; much effective practice can only be attained with full inter-professional cooperation. Of course, the dimensions of this will be different for different service users, but – as the chapter will argue – the principles of inter-professional working are common across all of the various settings within which social workers operate. And, as the welfare of a service user is likely to depend on the effectiveness of inter-professional working, social workers and other professionals have an ethical responsibility for ensuring that such working is as successful as can be managed (Irvine et al., 2002). Although the injunction to improve the quality of inter-professional working is not new – there has been literature on the subject for several decades (Leathard, 2003) – it has been given particular force by the importance of issues such as partnership in social policy (Clarke and Glendinning, 2002), the continued significance of such concepts as collaboration in the delivery of welfare (Loxley, 1997), and the recognition that effective practice for a range of service users will depend upon effective multidisciplinary working (for example, in relation to older people, Corley, 2000). Indeed, the premier academic journal in this area – the *Journal of Interprofessional Care* – celebrated its twentieth anniversary in 2007, as did the influential Centre for the Advancement of Interprofessional Education (CAIPE). All these developments indicate that there have been strong 'professional drivers' (Pollard et al., 2005) in support of inter-professional working in operation in recent years.

However, political pressures have also been particularly important in focusing attention on inter-professional working in recent years (Pollard et al., 2005). As a result, this chapter will open with a discussion of how political imperatives have shaped the professional agenda, concentrating particularly on the role that partnership and inter-professional working is envisaged as playing within health and social care; this necessarily means looking at the wider political dimensions that provide its context. Attention is then given to the unique contribution that social workers can make to inter-professional working, with several case studies indicating the scope of such practice in a number of varied social work settings. The following section focuses on the various reasons why the establishment of effective inter-professional working has often been problematic in the past. From this, the chapter will discuss the elements that enable inter-professional teams to work successfully together, illustrated with reference to the detail of the previous case studies.

It is important to be clear about the language that is used to describe inter-professional working. Already, in the relatively short duration of the chapter to date, several different terms – inter-professional, multidisciplinary, partnership, collaboration, etc. – have been used to describe what appear to be the same sorts of activity. The glossary at the end of this book will explain the differences between these terms, and the particular uses to which they are put within this chapter.

Why inter-professional?

There are a number of intersecting reasons that help to explain the emphasis that is given to the development of inter-professional practice. As we have noted already, it is important to understand that both political and professional pressures have created this (Pollard et al., 2005). It is equally vital to be aware of the connecting nature of the two sources of pressure: inter-professional working is less likely to come into being if either of these forces is absent.

If we take the political level first, the concept of 'partnership' was central to the social policy of the 'new' Labour government (Clarke and Glendinning, 2002). This stemmed from the government's recognition that many social problems cannot be effectively addressed by any given organisation acting in isolation from others. As a result, from the late 1990s onwards, there was a blizzard of official documents that promoted the importance of collaborative working as a means to improve the delivery of welfare. For example, the 1998 social services White Paper *Modernising Social Services* (DoH, 1998) had the development of improved patterns of partnership working as a key objective for services, devoting an entire chapter to the subject. A similar emphasis was evident in a policy document that focused

on the development of the health service, *The NHS Plan* (DoH, 2000), where again a whole chapter was focused on improving the relationship between health and social care. In relation to children's services, one of the main elements of the Green Paper *Every Child Matters* was in its recognition that improved multi-agency and inter-professional working was required if we were to avoid a repeat of the tragic events that characterised the Victoria Climbié case (DfES, 2003). Following the problems highlighted in the Peter Connelly case, the government has published detailed guidance for more effective collaborative working (HM Government, 2010). Although it is too early to determine the ways in which the policies and practices encouraged by the coalition government will differ from the legacy it inherited, it is most unlikely that the pressure towards enhanced levels of collaborative work will reduce.

Even though the pace of change towards inter-professional working has been accelerated since the late 1990s, it would of course be incorrect to suppose that the preceding decades had contained no indications of an interest in, and need for, improved systems of inter-professional working. For example, Ann Loxley (1997: 95–101) summarised the numerous health and social care legislative and policy documents that had promoted collaborative practice since 1970. From this it is clear that improving inter-professional working has been a preoccupation for much longer than the term of the 'new' Labour government. Of course, the lengthy period during which the benefits of inter-professional work have been promoted does imply a critical point: that is, despite the fact that professional groups have long been exhorted to work together more effectively, insufficient progress has been made, and much progress remains to be accomplished. (We will examine this further in a later section.) Part of the problem may well be that inter-professional working has been advanced at the 'common-sense' level (Cooper et al., 2004) without a proper appreciation of the difficulties that might obstruct its development.

Consequently, a presumption that underlies much policy informing inter-professional working is simply that the development of a 'seamless service' will do much to improve the lives of people in need. This principle is accepted by most of those people whose responsibility it is to provide such services, and is common in the academic and professional literature (see the various contributions to Leathard, 2003, which share an optimistic vision of the potential of inter-professional working). However, there is relatively little literature that attests robustly to the effectiveness of such practice

(Reeves et al., 2009). In addition, the failure of individual professions to work effectively with others that relate to their area of activity has been well documented. On occasions, such failures have exploded spectacularly into the public consciousness: for example, failures of inter-professional working were a critical finding of the Victoria Climbié inquiry (DfES, 2003b), contributing significantly to her death.

In many ways, the recommendations that the Climbié inquiry produced – including an emphasis on improved systems of sharing information and the development of a common assessment framework for children and their families – are typical of the sorts of thinking that have gripped the government in the early years of the twenty-first century. Although no single tragedy has defined policy in relation to services for older people in the same way as the Victoria Climbié case – and the later Peter Connelly case – has done for social work with children and families, there is an equivalent emphasis on ensuring improved working relationships, and the establishment of a single, common assessment framework is a major feature of such work (Lymbery, 2005). Indeed, it has been argued that inter-professional working has developed further in relation to older people than it has for children (Glendinning et al., 2003). By contrast, although inter-professional working has been accepted as a normal part of the organisation of services for many years in fields such as mental health and learning disability, governmental policies have provided fresh impetus in these areas as well. The important point to note is how professional and political pressures have combined to shape both policy and practice in the early years of the twenty-first century. Similarly, while much of the legislation and policy cited thus far specifically affects England and Wales, equivalent developments have impacted upon practice elsewhere in the United Kingdom (for example, see the analysis of the integration of health and social care in Northern Ireland by Heenan and Birrell, 2006).

The direction of public policy for the delivery of health and social care is therefore clear: inter-professional working is regarded as a key requirement of its delivery, a statement that holds good in relation to work with children, families and adults. The importance of social work in the context of inter-professional working should not be underestimated. It has been asserted that social work should be seen as 'the joined-up profession' (Frost et al., 2005: 195), providing a necessary link both between different professions within the system of welfare and between those professions and the users of services. This vision of social work indicates continuity with the thinking of Martin Davies, and his idea of social workers as maintenance mechanics oiling the wheels of the social welfare system within society, noted in Chapter 4 (Davies, 1981).

In recognition of this, the Department of Health's *Requirements for Social Work Training* (DoH, 2002) include a particular focus on inter-professional working, in the belief that social work students must be capable of functioning well in multidisciplinary environments. However, much research in the field of inter-professional working does point out the additional levels of complexity that attend this style of working (see, for example, Frost et al., 2005); as a consequence of this, a future section will identify some of the key obstacles that can obstruct such work.

Before this point, however, the chapter will address the critical issue of what social work can contribute to the inter-professional team, focusing on particular skills and attributes that characterise social workers as opposed to other practitioners. This will be illustrated through a number of circumstances that will necessarily require the exercise of inter-professional and inter-agency working.

Reflect

Does the requirement for effective inter-professional working typify all aspects of social work? Can you think of situations where social workers might, in complex cases, be the only professionals involved?

The social work role within inter-professional working

The purpose of this section is to provide some clarity about the specific role that social workers can provide within a multidisciplinary and inter-professional context. It could be argued that social work – and its practitioners – has never been sufficiently clear about what is unique and valuable about it; in addition, there is no accepted view about what constitute the most important role for social work. This section rests on a simple proposition, therefore: that if it is not possible to identify the specific roles and tasks that social workers fulfil, then it is not credible to insist that social workers have a unique and essential role within the inter-professional team.

Do you think that there are roles and functions that only social workers can fulfil? If so, what do you think these are?

Statutory obligations

In responding to these questions, it is reasonable to start with situations where social workers have a statutory duty to be involved. There are in fact relatively few aspects of social work where such a statutory requirement exists; more normally the requirement is on the social services agency to intervene, but there is seldom a parallel requirement for that intervention to be carried out by a qualified social worker. The exception to this was often cited – assessment and consent of an approved social worker (ASW) was required before an individual could be compulsorily admitted to a secure facility, under the terms of the Mental Health Act 1983. However, under the terms of the Mental Health Act 2007, this role – which could previously only be fulfilled by a social worker – was replaced by an equivalent role for an Approved Mental Health Professional. This can potentially be carried out by a number of professional groups within mental health, thereby removing one of social work's claims to a unique place in health and social care practice.

Even in child protection work, there is little that *requires* the intervention of a social worker. For example, decisions that children should be removed from families – and the powers to remove them – are based on the statutory authority of welfare agencies, rather than vested in the specific roles of qualified social workers. Similarly, the roles and functions that social work practitioners play in other areas of work – adoption and fostering, working with disabled people, assessing the needs of older people, etc. – are not statutorily limited to social workers. Indeed, in some areas of practice there is concern that tasks that have previously been the domain of qualified social workers may increasingly be delegated to other staff – either those from other disciplines, or those without qualifications at all (see, for example, in relation to older people, Lymbery et al., 2007). As a result, seeking to understand the social work role simply by relying on those statutory functions that require social work involvement is clearly inadequate.

Employer-led approaches

Another approach to the problem could be to define the social work role through aggregating the National Occupational Standards (TOPSS, 2002) for social work, which specify the required outcomes of qualifying training in relation to the performance of practitioners. Indeed, there have been many references to these throughout this text, as they set the standards against which social workers are assessed at the point of qualification. However, this would be to misunderstand the purpose of the standards, which specify in general terms the 6 key roles of social workers, the 21 units that comprise these roles and the 77 elements that constitute these units. At the point of qualification, a social worker has to be deemed to be competent in all of the roles and units; however, these do not immediately define a unique and distinctive role for social work. A number of occupations can legitimately claim that many of the roles and units are in fact part of their repertoire as well.

Educational approaches

Similarly, examining the knowledge that social workers are required to possess – for example, as specified in the Department of Health's *Requirements for Social Work Training* (DoH, 2002e) – does not conclusively differentiate social work from other occupations. As an example, while the requirements specify that social workers must demonstrate legal knowledge, similar obligations exist in relation to most other professions involved in health and social care – for example, community psychiatric nurses need to have a detailed knowledge and understanding of mental health law, while health visitors must also have a good working knowledge of childcare law. Social workers are also required to demonstrate their understanding of human growth and development, including disability. Again, numerous other professionals would claim a similar requirement – for example, specialist nurses working in learning disability must understand the developmental stages of people with a range of conditions, while medical doctors clearly also need to understand normal patterns of development. Also, social workers have to demonstrate the ability to undertake assessments, plan service responses, intervene appropriately and review the progress that has been made. It would be expected that other professionals – for example, occupational therapists or health visitors – demonstrate an equivalent ability within their fields.

Taken in isolation, therefore, neither the skills that social workers need to demonstrate nor the constituent elements of their knowledge base establish a unique repertoire of skills and knowledge in themselves.

Understanding what the specific contribution of social work is to a multidisciplinary team therefore has to start from another position. What we wish to suggest is that the uniqueness of a social worker's contribution to inter-professional activity rests upon a combination of skills, knowledge and values, particularly in relation to how these are then put into practice. It is worth remembering that what a social workers believes and understands has neither value nor purpose if s/he is unable to turn that knowledge into informed, capable, sensitive practice.

The international definition of social work and social work values

An alternative starting point for a consideration of the unique contribution of social work to society could also be found in the international definition of the social work task, originally formulated by the International Federation of Social Workers (IFSW) and the International Association of Schools of Social Work (IASSW), and subsequently adopted by the British Association of Social Workers (BASW):

'The social work profession promotes social change, problem solving in human relationships and the empowerment and liberation of people to enhance well-being. Utilising theories of human behaviour and social systems, social work intervenes at the points where people interact with their environments. Principles of human rights and social justice are fundamental to social work.'   (IFSW, 2001)

Think ahead

An international definition of social work should apply equally well in all countries. In the specifically British context, consider the following questions:

To what extent does social work actually promote social change?

How does social work contribute to the empowerment and liberation of people?

To what extent are the principles of social justice evident in the way in which social work is carried out?

When considering the above questions, we believe that the international definition of social work does present a number of problems when applied in a British context. However, it represents a general consensus of the sorts of activities that *ought* to be the substance of social work at the international level; as such, what it suggests about the social work task is worthy of consideration.

Richard Hugman (2007) has suggested that the international definition contains four elements that act as a global definition of social work:

1. social change
2. (social) well-being
3. human rights
4. social justice.

The uniqueness of social work does not lie in each individual aspect, but in the way in which they combine, reinforcing and supporting each other. In addition to this generally held set of principles, social workers will enter into any encounter with service users armed with their own set of beliefs and principles (as explored in Chapters 1 and 6) – as indeed will every service user. Practitioners must be capable of balancing the potential incompatibility of these professional and personal sets of values, in accordance with the overarching aims and principles of the social work profession. This has been termed as the development of moral fluency (Hugman, 2005), the ability to balance contesting perspectives in practice and the subsequent capacity to make informed judgements and decisions based on a consideration of this balance.

Another connected aspect of social work's occupational uniqueness lies in its commitment to anti-oppressive or anti-discriminatory practice (Dalrymple and Burke, 2006). The wellspring of this commitment in British social work derives from the recognition, dating back to the 1980s, that social work had not responded well to the needs of black people, women or disabled people (Taylor, 1993). Of course, on a global basis, this impulse can also be found in the commitment of social work to social justice; the essence of anti-oppressive practice can be located in the desire to ensure that all people – irrespective of race, gender, disability, sexual orientation, and so on – can be enabled to develop freely within each society.

It should not necessarily be assumed that this commitment to anti-oppressive practice is unique to social work, and therefore not shared by members of other professions: indeed, it would be arrogant to assume that social workers were the only people with an equivalent concern and commitment. However, there is evidence that social work's commitment to issues of social justice is both longer-standing and deeper than it is with other occupations (Beresford, 2000). Certainly, this was a major feature of the requirements for social work training in the Diploma of Social Work through the 1990s (CCETSW, 1995), and is a significant element of the Code of Practice for Social Workers which forms part of the current requirements (TOPSS, 2002). As such, it should affect both the social worker's orientation to practice as well as what that practitioner does in day-to-day work.

Balancing competing pressures

Another key aspect of a social worker's practice is the required ability to balance the needs of the individual as against the wider needs of society. (You will recall that Figure 1 in Chapter 1 highlighted this same issue.) Much of what a social worker does in practice – for example, in child protection, youth justice or mental health – has to be placed within the context of a wider set of responsibilities than simply to the individual. This is particularly true when considering the statutory role that social workers have to adopt in particular sets of circumstance, linked to the duty of the agencies within which they work. For example, in youth justice work, a social worker has to bear in mind what might be termed as the welfare needs of the individual, against other principles that relate more to society's need to punish those who break its laws, and yet more that focus on victims' rights and needs. In mental health work, this balance is well illustrated through the role of the Approved Mental Health Professional (AMHP), who will have to balance the expressed wishes of the individual with complex considerations of risk – both to the person directly, and to the wider society, while bearing in mind the statutory responsibility to come to a judgement that could result in the individual losing her/his liberty.

Linked to this is the social worker's orientation towards psychosocial modes of practice, focusing both on the internal dynamics of each individual as well as the external social pressures that might impact on her/his behaviour. (This was introduced in Chapter 1) If we reflect on the history and development of social work outlined in Chapter 4 we can identify that social workers have always tended to occupy precisely such a position – although a different emphasis has been followed at different points in social work's history. However, that social workers require a psychosocial orientation to their practice is both a key aspect of this text, and a significant element of the history and development of social work in the United Kingdom.

Therefore, we suggest that what makes a social worker unique within the inter-professional setting is not the nature of her/his knowledge and skills in themselves, but more the context within which they are understood and put into effect. A social worker deals with inherently complex interactions, working within the social dynamics of

families, seeking to balance issues of autonomy, risk and protection. In many cases, s/he will be working in circumstances of conflict, balancing different perspectives and priorities. This puts particular pressure on the ability of the social worker to establish and maintain productive relationships with service users, balancing competing demands and priorities. In addition, the social worker also has to maintain equally constructive working relationships within the multidisciplinary environment; the breadth and scope of her/his involvement provides a vital integrative function – with a social worker seen as the glue that binds such a team together (Herod and Lymbery, 2002), or as the occupation most able to integrate the workings of others (Frost et al., 2005).

A clear understanding of the general role of a social worker in inter-professional work is needed in order to clarify how social workers will carve out a unique role within such work, and to point to the specific forms of practice that will characterise her/him – although these will vary according to the specific setting within which the social worker is located. Of course, it is also essential to establish what the particular contributions of every other professional will be, and to accord them equal value. In seeking to establish the particular contribution of social workers we are not seeking to undervalue what other professionals can add; however, since effective inter-professional working does depend on the understanding of each person's role, alongside parity of esteem and respect, clarifying the social work role seems particularly significant here. In our view, this is also strongly affected by the sense that a social worker is characterised less by unique sets of knowledge and skills than the way in which these are put into effect.

Reflect

Where do you expect to experience most difficulty in maintaining the balance between these competing pressures?

Inter-professional working in practice

Having established a general sense of the social work role in an inter-professional context, the chapter will now move to a more detailed examination of a number of situations – through the medium of case studies – where the need for inter-professional working is apparent. These case studies will draw on both policy and practice dimensions. The focus on policy will establish the context within which the need for inter-professional working has been established, whereas the concentration on practice will enable a greater understanding of not just the role of social workers within the inter-professional context, but also the potential roles of other parties. In all of these case studies, a number of questions therefore present themselves:

- What is the precise policy context underpinning each case study?
- What is the specific role of the social worker in each?
- What are the dimensions of inter-professional work that you can identify?

Following all of the case studies, there is a general commentary on the issues raised: in all cases, leaving space for more detailed debate and discussion. (All of the case studies refer to contexts that are addressed in more detail in various chapters in Part Three of this book.) In a later section, we will use the case studies to illustrate our general points regarding the development of successful social work practice within the context of inter-professional working.

Case study

Carmel

Carmel is a 24-year-old single parent of dual African-Caribbean and white British heritage. She has a 6-year-old daughter, Alicia and a 3-year-old son, Kyle. She is expecting another child in three months' time and has no idea who the father of this child might be. Having been brought up in care, Carmel has been known to social services for many years. Although she has been previously described as a 'good mother', and the children have been felt to be both securely bonded with her and generally well looked after, in the last two years her personal life has been particularly stressful. She broke up with the children's father, Dwayne, who had been a part of her life for several years. He has moved to live in London, and has little contact with Carmel and his children, although he does contribute financially to their upbringing. Carmel has few contacts with family members who can assist her with childcare. While she has been a recreational user of marijuana for several years, in the past year she started to dabble in harder drugs and is now an addicted heroin user. Alicia's school have been in contact with the child protection team, concerned about her spasmodic pattern of attendance, her dishevelled appearance when she does attend, and the content of what she says about her home life. With some further exploration, it transpires that Carmel had been engaged in prostitution to earn money to feed her addiction – and that it is likely that one of her 'punters' is the father of the forthcoming baby. However, the progress of her pregnancy has meant that prostitution is no longer a viable option for her. As a result of the sexual contact, however, Carmel has been treated for a sexually transmitted disease. As an alternative means to raise money, Carmel has also been shoplifting on a regular basis for some months, and has been prosecuted for this, leading to her being sentenced to a community order with a condition of drug rehabilitation.

The above case study focuses on a common problem: the intersection of issues relating to child protection and substance use (separately considered in Chapters 16 and 21). In addition, there are complications deriving from Carmel's sexual activity – her prostitution and sexually transmitted infection – as well as her offending behaviour. Social workers in the field of child protection will be aware that there are many cases where children are considered to be at risk, and parental substance misuse is identified as a parallel problem (Forrester, 2000). In Carmel's case, there appears little doubt that her heroin use is having a negative impact on her ability to parent her children, and must also be taken into account in relation to her unborn child. The first priority of a social worker must be to protect the welfare of the children, but in this situation Carmel's drug use is a complicating factor and creates particular problems for the child protection practitioner (Kroll and Taylor, 2000). An apparently risk-free approach would be to remove the children, but the preferred option – in the majority of cases – would be to work with Carmel to enable her to manage her maternal role. In turn, this will require her to manage her substance misuse, and seek to reorder her life such that offending and prostitution are no longer part of it.

A clear problem in this case is that while many social workers feel that they do not have specialist knowledge about working with people who are substance users (see Chapter 21 on drug use), mothers in this position are unlikely to feel trusting towards child protection social workers (Hayden, 2004). As a result of this, it can often be difficult for workers to operate constructively with such mothers; the impact of this is much more likely to lead to removal of the children from Carmel's care. Carmel's ongoing involvement with the Probation Service also has to be taken into account as does her sexual health.

In reality, the best solution would necessarily be both inter-professional and inter-agency – with a child protection social worker focusing on the welfare of the children, a specialist drugs worker focusing on Carmel's addiction and a probation officer focusing on her offending. In addition, there is likely to be a need to involve medical and nursing staff in relation to Carmel's sexual health. If the heroin addiction remains unresolved, there may also be a need to engage with the sort of agency – often located in the voluntary sector – that responds to the needs of workers within the sex industry. To respond to any one issue in isolation from the others can only lead to a partial solution to Carmel's problems; however, it will be a challenge to ensure that work undertaken in any specific area is fully coordinated with the others.

Case study

Cal

Cal is a white British 15-year-old boy, who has been in and out of trouble ever since he entered his teenage years, accumulating a number of criminal convictions along the way. These started off with a string of shoplifting offences; more recently he has been in trouble for a series of motoring offences – stealing cars, driving without a licence or insurance, etc. He lives at home with his widowed father; his older brother, Jack, left home two years ago and set up house with his girlfriend. Jack has never been in any trouble with the police. Cal is said to have experienced a settled childhood, but this changed when his mother was diagnosed with breast cancer five years ago; the cancer proved resistant to treatment and she died two years later. This is reported to have unsettled Cal greatly. Previous to this he was doing well at school and was a promising junior footballer. Since her death, Cal's school attendance has been spasmodic and he has stopped playing football. His offending has all taken place in the company of a group of friends; his father has reported that he feels Cal is 'easily led' and that if he could move away from the influence of these friends he would settle down. In the recent past, he has disowned Cal, and refuses to have anything to do with him until he promises to offend no longer.

At Cal's most recent court appearance, the prospect of being sent to a Young Offenders Institution was a genuine possibility; in the end, he was sentenced to a supervision order with an accompanying requirement to attend an accredited groupwork programme to address his offending behaviour. The supervision would be carried out by the Youth Offending Team; a clear message was that if he did not stop committing crimes he would probably receive a custodial sentence.

Youth Offending Teams were created out of a desire to ensure that the responses to the needs of young offenders would be properly coordinated between the range of services that would be involved – as well as social work, also involving the police, the probation service, education and the voluntary sector (Home Office, 1997). (The broader context of work with young offenders is addressed in Chapter 18.) In many ways, therefore, the youth justice system can be seen to exemplify many of the priorities of the 'new' Labour government, particularly in relation to the need for improved levels of partnership and 'joined-up' working (Burnett and Appleton, 2004). In addition, their role and focus was also part of the highly interventionist and populist approach to young offenders that characterised the government's policies (Pitts, 2001).

Although it is easy to be sceptical of the direction of government policy (see Pitts, 2001), Youth Offending Teams do represent the reality of inter-professional practice in this area of activity. There is little doubt that, for many young offenders – including Cal – the range of problems that they encounter cannot sensibly be dealt with by one service in isolation. In this case, complex family circumstances underpin Cal's offending; these factors have also had a major effect on his education. To respond only to one element of this situation would potentially neglect others that are equally important. For example, an overly judicial response to his offending, failing to address the emotions that may have provoked it, is unlikely to resolve the problems that Cal is confronting. Similarly, it would be plainly impossible to respond only to his family pain, ignoring the fact that Cal's criminal behaviour appears to be worsening. In addition, his education – and hence his future life prospects – have been seriously affected by recent events.

It was in recognition of the complex needs of young people in trouble such as Cal that Youth Offending Teams were brought into being. Where such teams are working effectively they are able to maintain a balance between the competing demands of welfare and punishment; indeed, it has been suggested that the welfare ethic of Youth Offending Teams remains strong (Burnett and Appleton, 2004). For effective social work to take place, it is vital that the welfare ethic is maintained and enhanced. This could make it difficult for a Youth Offending Team to establish a unique identity that is separate from the occupational cultures of the preceding arrangements within youth justice (Souhami, 2007). However, it could be argued that the need to apply flexible responses to the complexity of young people's needs is an integral part of the role of work in such settings, and that such a response characterises social work more than the other professional disciplines involved in Youth Offending Teams (Eadie and Canton, 2002). Certainly, given that rehabilitation was the main purpose underpinning the sentence, securing Cal's consent to any of the prescribed activity is critical.

Case study

Claudette

Claudette is an African-Caribbean woman, aged 28 years, who has a son of mixed parentage (aged 13 years) presently living in a children's home. Claudette is divorced: her ex-husband, Colin, the father of the child, left the marital home five years ago. The boy, Darryl, has not seen his father for four years, and does not know where he is. Colin used to assault Claudette physically, would pull her by the hair, punch and kick her, and on one occasion he pushed her down a flight of stairs; on that occasion she sustained broken ribs and a dislocated shoulder. She never contacted the authorities about this violence. After Colin's

departure, Claudette became dependent on Darryl, and he was made the subject of a care order and removed from the home following concerns about his missed school and emotional abuse, with unproven allegations that she had also sexually abused him. She was also increasingly isolated, withdrawing from her family and other friends. Her neighbour contacted Claudette's GP because she said that she could hear Claudette shouting and screaming through the walls of the flat, and that since Claudette did not allow anybody into the flat, she thought that Claudette was having conversations with imaginary people. The GP visited Claudette, but could not gain access to the flat – with Claudette claiming that the GP was the devil come to torture her. The GP referred Claudette to a consultant psychiatrist and they did a joint visit. Although Claudette did allow access to her flat, she refused to be admitted informally to the psychiatric hospital because it was the house of the devil, and consequently the doctors recommended admission under the Section 2 of the Mental Health Act 1983. The Approved Mental Health Professional (AMHP) – a qualified social worker – obtained the medical recommendations from these doctors and made a home visit to conduct an assessment. The AMHP interviewed Claudette's neighbour, and ascertained that there was no 'nearest relative' (as defined under the Mental Health Act 1983, amended by the Mental Health Act 2007) who was contactable at this time. The AMHP agreed that Claudette should be compulsorily admitted to hospital; the police and ambulance were requested and Claudette was admitted. There was some uncertainty about her condition, with the consultant's initial diagnosis of schizophrenia subsequently challenged by the senior registrar who felt that Claudette was in fact clinically depressed. Following several months of treatment, involving copious medication and little opportunity for counselling or other 'talking therapies', Claudette was discharged, and was allocated to a social worker based in a Community Mental Health Team.

Claudette's circumstances are both complex and undoubtedly painful for her; the wider issues of social work and mental health are addressed in Chapter 20. In working with her, the social worker will need to understand the contested medical basis of her treatment. In community-based mental health work, there has been a long history of inter-professional working (Carpenter et al., 2003) – but this has also contained problems and difficulties due to the historical power dynamics and differences in perspective between medicine and social work (discussed in a later section). In addition, it has been suggested that there are significant differences in the ideologies and consequent practices that govern the work of the social worker and the community psychiatric nurse (CPN) (Hannigan, 1999). As a result, it has been suggested that – despite the lengthy history of collaborative working within the community mental health team – major structural, operation and professional barriers remain to be overcome (Hannigan, 1999). These will inevitably have an impact on the nature of practice that is undertaken with Claudette.

In an immediate sense, the contested nature of Claudette's diagnosis represents an obvious source of concern, as the treatment options for schizophrenia and clinical depression are very much at odds. It will be difficult to clarify an ongoing social work role with Claudette until there is more certainty about the nature of her illness and the appropriate form of treatment for it. A social worker is not a bystander in this situation, however, simply waiting for medical processes to run their course. S/he can also be a critical source of information about the nature of Claudette's illness and the extent to which different forms of treatment may be appropriate.

In this task, the continued support that will be provided to Claudette from the CPN is also critical. Taking responsibility for Claudette's day-to-day compliance with the medical regime that has been established, the CPN will also be a vital source of information about her progress; s/he will also be well placed to establish a productive working relationship with Claudette. Indeed, the quality of relationship will be a critical aspect of any subsequent work with Claudette; it would be surprising if she were not at the very least suspicious of any 'official' involvement in her life, a characteristic of people who have experienced the coercive aspect of health and social care interventions. Yet her capacity to improve may well depend on her willingness to use the support offered to her in a constructive way; the ability of all those professions who work with her to establish such a relationship will be critical, as will the quality of their communication within the multidisciplinary team.

Case study

Sarfraz

Sarfraz is a 28-year-old Muslim man, who is profoundly disabled, with both severe learning and physical disabilities. He was born in this country; his parents came here from what is now Bangladesh in the 1960s. He experienced severe trauma at birth which has caused multiple physical and learning disabilities. He never left hospital with his parents due to his intensive medical, nursing and care needs. His parents moved to another city several years ago and have since visited Sarfraz infrequently; there are three younger children, a girl aged 9, and two boys, aged 11 and 15, who have never met Sarfraz. Presently he lives in an NHS nursing home with his care being funded by the local health authority under continuing care arrangements. Although his case has been kept open to the adult social care department, he has had little contact with social workers – it has not been felt to have been a particularly high priority. However, the health service have informed the adult social care department that they no longer consider that he is eligible for continued health care funding – a decision which has implications for both the adult social care department and the family.

A broader perspective on social work with disabled children and adults can be found in Chapter 19. There are numerous dynamics of collaborative working in this case study, deriving particularly from the complexity of the national debate about continuing care. The problematic distinction between health and social care needs was the object of Lewis's critique (2001), outlined in more detail in the following section. This has caused an ongoing lack of clarity, charted in some detail by Mandelstam (2005), about the precise relationship between those needs that can be met by the health service and those that are defined as the joint responsibility of social care and families.

The outcome of this lack of clarity means that individual arrangements are increasingly negotiated by social workers operating in the uncertain ground between health and social care (Malin, 2000). Although the needs and wishes of Sarfraz would normally be the key determining factors in any decision about his future, in this set of circumstances they are outweighed by the rationing decisions taken by the health authority. He could be compelled to move from the nursing home where he currently lives as a result of the health authority's actions. This would be almost certain to disturb both Sarfraz and his family, and would be complicated by the relatively distant relationship between them.

The dispute that is at the centre of this case creates many pressures on the quality of inter-professional working that can be developed, as both health and social care agencies have clear financial interests in opposing solutions. Nonetheless, good quality inter-professional working is needed to establish detail about Sarfraz's medical condition and the prognosis for its development; the input of therapists is critical for an understanding of his likely capacity – if any – to improve his levels of functioning. At the same time, social workers will need to engage fully both with Sarfraz and his family. Although Sarfraz is seriously affected by his multiple disabilities, the social worker will need to ensure that he is as fully engaged as possible in the decisions that need to be made. As we have noted in Chapter 11, there is much that can be done to enhance the ability of even the most disabled people to communicate. Similarly, the fullest possible engagement of his family is also needed; apart from the additional financial responsibility that they may accrue, they clearly have the right to be involved in this process. In cases such as Sarfraz it is possible that no attractive solution may appear, with a range of health and social care professionals potentially vying to see who can have the most influence over where he is to live and how his care should be funded (Salter, 1998); however, the full engagement of all those involved in his care – the range of professionals, his family, his paid carers – will be needed to ensure that his future can be made as secure as possible. Moreover, as we have indicated in Chapters 14 and 15 a close engagement with Sarfraz and his family is the correct thing to do.

Reflect

In the context of the practice responses to the needs of the above four cases, what impact, if any, do you feel that their race and ethnic origins may have on how their problems are defined and any subsequent work that is undertaken with them?

Obstacles to effective inter-professional working

Think ahead

What do you think are the main obstacles to effective inter-professional working?

As we have indicated, it is both politically and professionally accepted that good inter-professional working is essential within health and social care. In addition, a substantial literature on the subject has developed over the past 30 years (Leathard, 2003). Given that a central tenet of much of this has been to emphasise the benefits that would follow from improved inter-professional working, the fact that it does not already exist requires some explanation. The purpose of this section is to examine some of the reasons why this goal has not been achieved, with reference to the numerous obstacles that have obstructed its development. The key issues that could affect the preceding case studies will also be noted.

Structural issues

This section will start by focusing on the impact of the structural separation between organisations. Although the negative impact of this has been recognised for many years (see, for example, Seebohm, 1968; Otton, 1974), effective policies to counteract this have yet to be developed. This failure at the policy level may serve to undercut the development of inter-professional responses to need, a point that is amply illustrated with reference to the findings of the inquiry that followed the tragic death of Victoria Climbié. (These are reported in more detail in Chapter 16.) Among many other aspects of the report *Every Child Matters* (Chief Secretary to the Treasury, 2003), the encouragement towards 'joined-up' services is particularly significant; the Green Paper on developments in social care for adults (DoH, 2005a) also emphasised the importance of this in formal and structural terms as well as in relation to patterns of professional working. It is recognised that this will create different practical expectations on staff, who would be expected to operate in much more integrated and collaborative ways. The expectation was that services should be governed by common sets of standard, with these unifying the performance of previously separate professional groups. As a result, numerous sections in the subsequent Children

Act 2004 required the development of collaborative working (Hudson, 2005). In the case of Carmel, these changed working conditions would have a significant impact on the response to the multiple problems with which she is confronted.

Every Child Matters therefore recommended a combination of structural change and an altered focus on professional practice. This was an ambitious agenda, particularly given the historical separation of the various functions – social care, health, aspects of early years learning – that were to be integrated. There was little hard evidence that the changes proposed – which were taken for largely political reasons in the wake of Victoria Climbié's death – would actually improve outcomes for children and their families, even though the changes apparently represented a 'common-sense' perspective on collaborative working (Cooper et al., 2004; Marsh, 2006). In addition, a lack of clarity about the nature of inter-professional working, and how it should best be promoted and developed, is also likely to obstruct developments.

Another potential barrier in the way of developing effective partnerships to respond to the needs of children and families is also due to the fact that more energy has been placed on the development of such arrangements in relation to the care of older people; as a result, it has been suggested that there is less successful history of joint working in the case of childcare (Glendinning et al., 2003). However, even in respect of services for older people a number of factors present problems for the development of effective inter-professional working – many of them structural in origin. For example, much has been made of the 'Berlin Wall' that is said to exist between health and social care organisations (see, for example, DoH, 1998; Glasby, 2003). One of the key difficulties with this concept lies in a misunderstanding of why divisions exist between health and social care (Lymbery, 2006). It seems to be assumed that these divisions are created by professional barriers and conflicts alone. As we shall discuss later in the chapter, the existence of such obstacles to joint working should not be denied; however, it would be incorrect to see them as the primary cause of such difficulties. This has been well illustrated in the case of older people by Jane Lewis (2001), an eminent academic and commentator on the development of social policy.

A closer look

Policy conflict between health and social care

Lewis takes issue with the perspective that informs much government policy on the provision of health and social care for older people, namely that these problems are primarily caused by professional rivalries. Taking a historical perspective, she argues that the origin of this conflict stemmed from a combination of the National Health Service Act 1946 and the National Assistance Act 1948. This created a division of organisational responsibilities for health and social care that rested on an apparently straightforward distinction: the newly established NHS would take responsibility for people's health needs whereas their social care needs would be addressed through the Welfare Departments established in local authorities. As Lewis points out, this has had immediate financial consequences for the organisations and for individuals. At the organisational level, this is significant because of two significant facts that were written into the legislation. As far as health services are concerned, the National Health Service Act 1946 enshrined the principle that those services should be free to those who needed them at the point of use. By contrast, the National Assistance Act 1948 created an entirely different practical reality for users of social care services, that they may be required to contribute towards the cost of whatever services were provided. In addition, the budgets to support health and social care services were separately managed – for health care by the NHS and for social care by local authorities.

In Lewis's analysis, the imprecise distinctions between health care and social care have been the source of much subsequent policy conflict in the above organisations. As the budgets of each have become increasingly stretched, both health and social care service providers have sought different ways of managing their budgets. For Lewis, one such mechanism – for the health services in general – has been to seek to redefine large numbers of older people for whom they previously accepted responsibility as no longer possessing the sorts of need that require the intervention of the health service. For Lewis, this has seen the gradual transfer of responsibility for many frail older people away from health to social care services, a move which social care has been relatively powerless to resist.

In Lewis's view, therefore, some of the key factors that helped to create the 'Berlin Wall' between health and social care were present in the very formation of the NHS in the 1940s; to see it as primarily the result of professional rivalries is therefore a considerable over-simplification. Of course the problems that this creates in relation to older people – the focus of her article – will also be replicated in relation to the numerous other service user groups where there is the need for collaborative working between health and social care. For example, issues equivalent to this underpin the case of Sarfraz.

Inter-professional issues

However, the sorts of structural problem cited here, and discussed in relation to the Victoria Climbié case, do not fully explain the problems of inter-professional working: for this we must also explore the rivalries that can exist between the various professions involved in the delivery of health and social care, accepting that these rivalries may affect the development of effective inter-professional working. Bob Hudson, a noted commentator on inter-professional working, has observed that they are a key aspect of the 'pessimistic' tradition of literature on the subject. He has suggested that this includes the following dimensions:

- relative status and power of professions;
- professional identity and territory;
- different patterns of discretion and accountability between professions (Hudson, 2002).

Inequalities of status and power have particularly bedevilled the establishment of good inter-professional working between medicine and social work; nonetheless, in Hudson's opinion there are more grounds for optimism than pessimism in relation to this (Hudson, 2007). However, it is important to understand both why these inequalities have developed and why they have had such an impact. To accomplish this, we need to understand something of the complex processes that brought professions into being. As the American sociologist, Magali Sarfatti Larson, has shown, all professions did not emerge fully formed, but struggled to establish a demand for their services, a process that she termed the 'professional project' (Larson, 1997). In this process, professions simultaneously organised a market for their services thereby becoming an indispensable part of ociety while also enhancing their collective status and prestige. While much early thinking and writing about professions emphasised their positive contribution to

society, taking their claims to altruistic endeavour at face value, from the 1970s several writers have taken a more critical perspective, focusing on some of their less welcome characteristics. For example, for the British writer, Terry Johnson, the defining feature of a profession was how it used its power and status for significantly self-interested ends (Johnson, 1972). It is generally accepted that medicine has been particularly successful in this respect, certainly in the area of health and social care.

Reflect

What is the impact of this difference in power in the case of Claudette (bearing in mind the status of social work in relation to the medical profession)?

By contrast, social work has never attained the same level of professional status. There are a number of reasons that have been advanced for this:

- Social work does not have a secure and unchallenged knowledge base, nor a set of skills that are unambiguously accepted as characteristic of high status occupations. As a result, the expertise of its practitioners has been downplayed – the notorious comment of the then Health Secretary Virginia Bottomley (herself a trained social worker!) that social workers should be like 'street-wise grannies' being a particularly graphic example.
- It has consequently struggled to establish itself as an enterprise for which specialist education is required; it was only as a result of the 2002 reforms of social work education that it became a graduate-entry occupation (DoH, 2002e), a position that had long been achieved by other equivalent occupations.
- If a profession is defined by its internal balance between elements of 'technicality' (the specific knowledge and skills that are applied) and 'indeterminacy' (the judgement about when and how they should be applied) (Jamous and Peloille, 1970), social work has struggled to gain acceptance on both counts.
- Social workers have often been located in settings where they were considered as subordinate to other more established professional groups, a point made explicitly by some critics of social work (Brewer and Lait, 1980).
- It has been suggested that the fact that social work is primarily a woman's occupation has confirmed its second-class professional status, in common with other similar occupations such as nursing (Witz, 1992).

An influential line of argument for many years defined social work as a semi-profession – having some but not all of the characteristics of a more established occupation such as medicine (see Etzioni, 1969). Certainly, social workers have never had the recognition and status bestowed on doctors, as an analysis of the working relationships between the two makes clear. For example, in the early years of collaborative working between the two, social work in hospitals, for example, existed only at the behest of the medical profession, and the practice of social workers was tightly circumscribed by what the doctors would allow them to undertake (Bell, 1961). The power of medicine over social work has always been apparent, therefore. And, as numerous commentators have emphasised, the differences in power and status have materially affected the establishment of good quality inter-professional working (see, for example, Baxter and Brumfitt, 2008).

Hudson's concern with the impact of professional identity and territory can also be interpreted as a concern with professional boundaries, the lines of demarcation between the responsibilities of different professional groups. The American sociologist, Andrew Abbott, has argued that the delineation of boundaries is an essential characteristic of professional formation, enabling the profession to determine what is and what is not part of its appropriate sphere of influence. (This is a critical issue in relation to inter-professional working, particularly where multidisciplinary teams have been established; issues relating to the boundaries between professions could be a key issue in relation to Cal, for example.) Further, in connection with the delivery of health and social care, he has suggested that medicine has been particularly effective in establishing its power in relation to a number of subordinate occupations – among which social work would feature, alongside nursing and numerous other 'professions allied to medicine' (Abbott, 1988). The occupational power of medicine is a significant element in its ability to maintain this dominant position, which presents significant problems in relation to effective inter-professional practice (Hall, 2005; Baxter and Brumfitt, 2008).

The issue of defining and maintaining the boundaries between different professions therefore becomes an important factor. In addition, a key area for debate within inter-professional work is the extent to which a clear distinction between different occupational groups is desirable (Miers, 2010). Certainly, one consequence of the changes to mental health law is the dilution of the unique role that social workers have played in relation to compulsory hospital admissions (the replacement of the

Approved Social Worker by the Approved Mental Health Professional). In addition, as the theorist, Etienne Wenger, has argued, there are inherent tendencies for people working in inter-professional teams – what he would define as 'communities of practice' (Wenger, 1998) – to develop a shared identity based on their common enterprise and mutual sense of loyalty to the 'community'. He suggests that such a development could constitute either a strength or a weakness – a passport to enhanced creativity or the creation of an environment resistant to, and mistrustful of, outside influences. Indeed, other writers have noted that each separate professional group necessarily embodies different cultural identities (Hall, 2005). Since the self-perception of all workers is a complex balance between individual and professional identities (Oliver and Keeping, 2010), managing their location within inter-professional settings requires careful consideration. If it is to be argued that the specific contributions of various professional disciplines should be maintained, a consequence of this needs to be clarity about the proper contributions of each, as we have previously suggested. In many cases, however, social workers are less able to define what their specific contribution to an inter-professional team might be, although other team members may be much clearer in this respect (see Herod and Lymbery, 2002).

The third obstacle identified by Hudson refers to the different systems of discretion and accountability of the various professions involved in the development of inter-professional working. Traditionally, social work has been a heavily managed occupation, with a consequent reduction on the levels of discretion and autonomy accorded to practitioners. Although it has been argued that the extent to which this has affected practice has been exaggerated (Evans and Harris, 2004), there are observable differences between social work and medicine in this respect. For example, in many local authorities social workers with adults are required to present any assessment to a panel which will in turn assess the extent to which resources can be committed. In addition, social workers' practice will be even more directly affected by the significant spending cuts having to be implemented under the coalition government. In general, therefore, social workers have become accustomed to operate in an environment where their discretion is more constrained than that of comparable occupations – not just doctors, but also nurses and therapists. While some analyses underestimate the significance of professionalism in relation to social workers' discretion (a point made by Evans, 2010), social workers are confronted by a range of issues that potentially restrict the extent of their professional discretion.

As Bob Hudson has recognised, it is difficult to construct viable patterns of inter-professional working that are built on such unequal foundations (see also Hall, 2005). However, he also suggests that it is important to find ways of developing such working. We would share the perception that this is firmly in the interests of those who need services; in addition, as much research makes clear, it can also provide a stimulating and challenging working environment for practice.

Reflect

Referring back to the case studies in the previous section, can you identify the various professional issues that might potentially obstruct the development of excellent inter-professional practice?

Differences in the forms of knowledge applied by social workers and other professions

Another key division between social workers and other professions lies in the forms of knowledge that social workers should apply as against the forms of knowledge that are central to other professions with whom social workers will operate. Within social work itself numerous debates have focused on the appropriate forms of knowledge for practice (Payne, 2001). (A flavour of this is given in Chapters 4 and 6.) Given that we consider the essence of social work to rest in the relationship formed with service users, our preference is for forms of knowledge that focus on social work's capacity to understand and respond effectively to a combination of complexity and uncertainty. We share with the noted American thinker, Donald Schön (1991), a sense that social work is best understood as occupying a central place in what he terms the 'swampy lowlands' of practice, where workers have to assist service users to negotiate through problems that are inherently complex and messy, and therefore resistant to straightforward technical solutions. Schön (1991) has suggested that a core characteristic of the increased bureaucratisation of professional work – discussed in Chapter 2 – is its attempt to transform such problems into ones that appear to be capable of being resolved by the rational application of technical expertise.

In somewhat reductive terms, this perception highlights alternative ways of seeing social work; following Schön we can conceive of social work as an 'art' – a vision that has been forcefully argued in the past (England, 1986), and which also informs more contemporary analyses (White, 1997; Parton, 2000; Taylor and White, 2001). Although each of these writers have a different perspective, they share the position that social work is characterised by ambiguity and uncertainty, and that consequently the act of professional judgement is necessarily at the heart of social work practice. The alternative conception is that social work should be considered as a 'science', where technical rationality is presumed to be the appropriate form of enquiry. This has been characterised as a clash between positivist and interpretivist visions of social work (White, 1997): it can also be interpreted with reference to Ife's (1997) conception – discussed in Chapter 4 – of the opposition between positivist and humanist forms of knowledge. Positivist knowledge derives from a scientific paradigm, whereas humanist knowledge focuses on the nature of the human encounter and the attempt to understand the other's subjective reality. It is important to reflect that this is an ongoing debate within social work; although we have placed ourselves on one side of this debate, we understand that others will locate themselves in a different position.

However, a humanist conception of knowledge is at variance with the positivist, scientific paradigm that operates in much of the medical world, and by which many health professionals operate (Murphy et al., 1998). For obvious reasons, a positivist approach to knowledge works effectively in relation to, for example, drugs trials; none of us would be happy with drugs being made available if there was no clarity either about their actual benefits or their potential consequences! However, there are many problems of human life where such a means of gathering evidence would either be inappropriate or ineffective. The development of an 'evidence-based' approach to the provision of health care has reinforced the point about the centrality of a positivist approach (Sackett et al., 1997; see Sheldon and Chilvers, 2002, for a social care equivalent); in summaries of what counts as evidence, positivist methodologies are generally preferred to softer, more qualitative approaches – the *National Service Framework for Older People* (DoH, 2001c) provides explicit evidence of this. There is a sense that a hierarchy of evidence quality is being pursued, and that this will automatically work against the insights to be drawn from a more humanist tradition – including the contributions of service users (see Glasby and Beresford, 2006; this issue is discussed further in Chapter 14).

Within an inter-professional setting – particularly those that are health-related – social workers are therefore likely to work alongside practitioners who do not share their primary orientations to knowledge. Indeed, since explicitly positivist approaches are held to produce the firmest quality of evidence (Sheldon and Chilvers, 2000), there is a real danger that the insights gained from a more humanist approach will be undervalued.

There is a close parallel between this analysis and the long-standing dispute concerning models of disability and the most appropriate form of response to them (see Chapter 19). Here, influenced particularly by disabled activists and theorists (Oliver and Sapey, 2006), social workers are more inclined to take a social model of disability, where the focus of intervention is on the way that society disables people rather than on the individual as an object of medical attention, pity and charity. An accurate flavour of the stance of the disability movement can be seen in the title of the book *Disabling Barriers – Enabling Environments* (Swain et al., 2004). It represents a significant divergence from the standard approach to disability, which has been labelled as the medical or individual model. It is this approach that doctors, nurses and therapists are more likely to follow, even though the dominance of the medical or individual model is unlikely to be absolute. It would be arrogant to suggest that only social workers will hold to the social model of disability, in addition. While the social and individual models can be brought together in a way that fuses insights related both to disability and the effects of impairment (see, for example, Thomas, 2004), relatively few practitioners in any discipline will possess the conceptual tools to enable them to undertake such work. If some form of fusion is not achieved, an adherent to the social model of disability can become isolated in numerous work settings.

What makes for successful inter-professional work?

Drawing on the analysis of the previous section, the purpose of this part of the chapter is to identify the features and characteristics of effective inter-professional working. We will also refer back to the case studies featured earlier in the chapter. It uses an adaptation of a set of explanatory classifications (Beattie, 1994) which provide a useful guide both to the sorts of obstacle that could be encountered and the ways in which action should be planned and organised to address the problem.

In examining the nature of inter-professional working within health promotion, Beattie identified three different types of problem that could be encountered, which are listed below, along with our interpretation of the levels at which they would be in operation:

1. 'Disparities in organisational arrangements', in which he includes issues such as autonomy, accountability, pay, management and planning. We have termed this the 'structural-organisational' level.
2. 'Competing professional rationales', which derives from the mixture of social and professional ideologies of the different groups. We have labelled this as the 'professional-cultural' level.
3. 'Psychodynamics of interpersonal relations', which examines the personal interaction of individuals. We have termed this the 'interpersonal' level.

The sorts of problems identified by Hudson (2002), noted earlier in this chapter, fit clearly within this analysis – although he gives less attention to the interpersonal level than we feel is appropriate, given the central concerns of this book.

The 'structural-organisational' level

Think ahead

Referring back to the section headed 'Obstacles to effective inter-professional working', can you identify the sorts of issue that will be considered in this subsection?

If we look first at the sorts of intervention that can be developed at the 'structural-organisational' level, it is important to recognise that these will not in themselves ensure a good quality of inter-professional working. They should, however, create the conditions wherein such working could flourish. It is interesting that the most likely indicator of successful inter-professional working is a history of projects that have worked well in the past (Cameron and Lart, 2003). This can instil confidence among those people who will have the primary responsibility for planning and organising such work, leading to a presumption of the benefits that this form of working can bring about. However, it is also possible – if perhaps more difficult – to establish successful inter-professional working where is no prior history of such work. For any inter-professional enterprise, whether or not it is located within an organisational context that features the prior success of such working, effective planning is an essential component of success. There are all sorts of ways in which this can become manifest – for example, clarity about the aims and objectives of the work are essential, as is their acceptance by all parties involved in the development of inter-professional working (Cameron and Lart, 2003).

Drawing on Cal's case study, in these 'structural-organisational' terms the creation of Youth Offending Teams was a significant development. From available research evidence, it has apparently not been a straightforward process (Souhami, 2007), with particular implications in relation to the 'professional-cultural' level, which will be explored later. The purpose of the teams was set through a sequence of government documents, all promoting the advantages of collaborative working in combating youth offending (Pitts, 2001). While some measure of collaborative working may have preceded the introduction of such teams, they were substantially new entities – therefore, the prior history of joint working is not necessarily evident. Similarly, while inter-professional teams such as this may have clearly stated aims and objectives, it is possible that support for these may be unevenly spread within the team, given the disparate nature of the occupational backgrounds of all staff. By contrast, the integrated community mental health team charged with the support of Claudette is much more likely to have been in existence for several years – many such teams were first established in the early 1980s (Carpenter et al., 2003). An established pattern of working relationships is therefore more likely; however, there may also be problems inherent within this structure which can materialise at the 'professional-cultural' level.

Similarly, it is vital to ensure that there are effective systems of information storage and retrieval. For example, it is particularly difficult to organise effective inter-professional assessment processes if each agency retains its own information systems, maintaining a level of incompatibility between them. This has been a continuing difficulty in the effort to establish single assessment processes for older people, undoubtedly compromising their efficacy (Lymbery, 2005). Correspondingly, any substantial structural change will have implications for the administrative function. If administrative arrangements are given insufficient attention, with the primary focus being on the inter-professional elements of the project, there are clear potential consequences for the overall effectiveness of the work. As we will discuss further in the following subsection, professional culture can also impact upon the quality of information-sharing, both in relation to the attitudes different professions have to information retrieval and the ways in which the professions interrelate (Richardson and Asthana, 2006).

In the context of the case studies, only two out of the four (Cal and Claudette) involve work within full multi-disciplinary teams. In the remaining two cases, inter-professional working will take place within the context of existing single-agency working. Both situations contain issues as far as administrative support and information systems are concerned. When formal multidisciplinary teams are established, it is more likely that they will share administrative systems and processes of information retrieval – indeed, integrated systems may well be part of the newly established structures for Youth Offending Teams, for example. As a result, it is possible that the absence of standardised administrative responses may highlight more fundamental differences in the priorities and values bases of contributing members, which can paradoxically contribute to a sense of fragmentation within the team (Souhami, 2007). By contrast, where inter-professional working takes place within the context of existing administrative arrangements (as in the cases of Carmel and Sarfraz), these have the potential disadvantage of being difficult – if not impossible – for other professional groups to access. As a result, the sharing of information will have to be a more conscious decision on the part of practitioners, involving some complex moral judgements around issues such as confidentiality. Many of these will be particularly difficult in the case of Carmel, given the complex pattern of inter-agency work that will be needed.

This will be one of the critical issues for which good quality planning will be needed. In general terms, one essential element of good planning is an effective preparation process for all staff, both those who are directly engaged in the work, and those whose practice will be affected by it. There are a number of aspects of this. For example, all parties need to be fully informed about what will be expected of them, provided with opportunities to discuss the philosophical and practical implications of change and given opportunities to discuss issues and concerns that they may have. For example, the creation of effective systems of inter-professional working may well serve to alter the normal working practices of staff members. Establishing new ways of interaction within the inter-professional environment will be a time-consuming process. The consequences of this not being managed effectively may be severe, and all the care and attention given to other aspects of preparation may come to naught as a result. For structural change to run ahead of the capabilities of those staff who will be required to ensure improved collaborative practice is a genuine risk, and indicates how the different levels noted at the start of this chapter can interact.

This becomes a particular issue when establishing new teams, such as in Cal's case; however, it is also germane when delegating key individuals to work in a specific liaison capacity. In Carmel's case, for example, many practitioners have stressed the need to have access to particular expertise around substance use within child protection arrangements (Hayden, 2004). While such a development could carry manifest advantages for the teams concerned, there would be potentially problematic issues for the worker to address – for example, familiarity with the requirements of child protection while maintaining a focus on the substance user. This would require detailed preparation, not just of the link-worker but also of social work colleagues within the child protection setting. Similarly, the social worker will need to ensure that there are effective links with the probation service, given the work that this service will be instigating in relation to Carmel's offending.

Perhaps the most critical element at this level in the development of effective systems of inter-professional working is a leadership process that can take staff through the changes, ensure support for both the aims of the new working arrangements and for the processes that will be required to make those a reality, and to ensure that all affected staff are fully involved with, and engaged by the work. This recognition reflects a growing understanding of the importance of leadership, as opposed to management, in the development of services (Lawler, 2007). This will help the new organisation to 'ride out' any tensions and difficulties that might develop, without the entire system of collaborative working being brought to the point of collapse. Allied to effective leadership there also needs to be effective systems of direct management, which can respond to two linked issues, implicit in Hudson's typology:

1. *Accountability*: this is a particular issue in inter-professional teams which may require the development of potentially incompatible principles, that of loyalty to the employer on the one hand, and to the inter-professional team on the other.
2. *Professional supervision and support*: in practice, social workers within multidisciplinary teams may often be located outside of normal managerial arrangements and will at the same time need to take relatively quick decisions regarding their work. In many cases, a revised form of professional supervision may be indicated, shifting the balance away from managerial dominance over the supervisory process.

It is important to maintain the distinction between management and leadership: this is often elided in practice (Lawler, 2007). The former is primarily connected to the promotion of organisational goals, while the latter aims to develop and empower individual practitioners. In the context of the case studies, effective leadership is obviously a point at issue when examining the establishment of new inter-professionally organised teams, such as in Cal's case. Equally, for multidisciplinary community mental health teams – as in Claudette's case – to have successful leadership is also a critical factor. However, we should not underestimate the impact of leadership even in more familiar and traditional sets of circumstance, particularly those that appertain in the case of Carmel. At the same time, the concept of leadership becomes particularly complicated when considering the dispute that it at the heart of Sarfraz's case. Leadership has become an increasingly important aspect within all social work practice – but is particularly important in the complex circumstances of effective inter-professional working.

The 'professional-cultural' level

Think ahead

Before reading this subsection, consider the stereotypes that exist of other professions, and the implications of such stereotypes for practice: for example, the images that spring to mind when you think of a doctor or nurse.

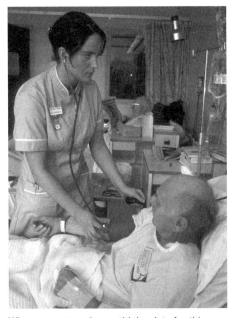

What stereotype do you think exists for this profession?

(*Source*: Photofusion Picture Library/Sam Tanner)

Moving to the professional/cultural level, there are a number of factors to consider. A particular point of principle that needs to be understood at an early stage is the extent to which the separate identities of various professional groups are to be maintained, or whether a form of hybrid professional identity is expected to emerge from the development of inter-professional working. We believe that there is considerable value in the maintenance and enhancement of the specific contribution of social workers to inter-professional working, although the maintenance of separate professional cultures may serve as barriers to the development of effective inter-professional teamwork. However, it is equally possible that there will be some alteration in the professional allegiances of staff when confronted with the realities of shared practice (Wenger, 1998). We also recognise that much of the literature on inter-professional working does raise fundamental concerns about the feasibility of effective collaboration (Hudson, 2002).

However, we believe that effective cooperation between different professional groups is possible, but that a range of differences between them – their professional goals, the nature and pace of their work, their essential orientations – need to be acknowledged and accepted as a prerequisite for such working. As we noted in the previous subsection, failure to accomplish such work will create issues even in apparently routine and straightforward matters such as the sharing of information (Richardson and Asthana, 2006). This implies not only clarity about the contribution of one's own professional voice, but also that of the other professions that make up the inter-professional team, alongside an awareness of the benefits that these perspectives can bring. It also implies a clear recognition of the cultural differences that exist between the various professional groups (Hall, 2005), alongside the impact of inequalities of status and power (Baxter and Brumfitt, 2008).

For example, reflecting on Claudette's case, it would be a foolhardy mental health social worker who did not acknowledge the importance and validity of a psychiatrist's contribution to debates concerning an individual's treatment, even where there is some dispute about the nature of the diagnosis on which the treatment depends, combined with different orientations to understanding mental ill health. Similarly, a social worker operating with older people must be clear that the combination of doctors' medical knowledge and the functional awareness of occupational therapists and physiotherapists is an essential part of any approach that seeks to meet the needs of an older person; this is clearly indicated in the example of Mr Rimmer that opened this chapter. In both cases, however, a social worker must ensure that s/he is not dominated by the higher status of the medical profession (Baxter and Brumfitt, 2008). If the different professionals are able to operate in an environment that is characterised by a parity of esteem, the tendency that they have to struggle for dominance and control over their particular areas of practice can be avoided, and can be balanced against the potential for individuals to develop a sense of collective identity that can cut across professional boundaries (Wenger, 1998).

At the level of teamworking, it will be important for members to share their perspectives regularly with their colleagues, developing understanding and deeper comprehension of their contributions along the way. In all of the above case studies, shared assessment is the basis for effective working (Wallace and Davies, 2009). This highlights the need for regular team meetings that can serve both as a forum for sharing, and as an opportunity to understand the precise contributions of other members. Through this a genuine sense of being engaged on a joint enterprise can emerge, which is turn can lead to the levels of informed and constructive criticism about ways forward that characterise the most effective forms of joint working. We believe that such conflict and potential disagreement should not be avoided, but welcomed as a helpful feature of collaborative working – not least because it can help to avoid the complacency that would be the antithesis of effective inter-professional work environments.

This is vital in relation to working with Carmel, to ensure that the worker whose priority is to focus on her substance misuse is given value in a team oriented towards child protection; in such circumstances it is possible that the specialist worker's knowledge of drugs would be considered to be of lesser value. Similarly, in the established multidisciplinary mental health team, the roles and relationships of team members is a critical issue, just as establishing an effective team process will have been a vital component of the establishment of a Youth Offending Team.

Reflect

Having considered how social workers might stereotype other professionals, consider the ways in which social workers might be similarly stereotyped, and think about the impact that this might have on inter-professional working.

The 'interpersonal' level

Our third category stems from the focus on interpersonal issues within inter-professional working, a perspective that has been theoretically less well developed, but which we consider to be equally important. We believe that the nature of relationship-based social work should not begin and end with the relationships that social workers are able to develop with service users, but also encompass the relationships that exist within the work environment. To achieve this, all practitioners not only need to possess a good range of inter-personal skills, but also need to be able to apply them in practice. They also need to consider the importance of such skills within the team, a neglected area of development. In addition, the development of *intrapersonal* skills is also important (Morison et al., 2010): the more that individuals are able to understand their own learning needs, preferences and behaviours, the more they will be enabled to engage in effective work with others.

For example, the conflict that underpins Sarfraz's case can potentially place a great burden on inter-personal communication, particularly between health and social care personnel. Without attention being paid to this dimension of inter-professional working, it would be quite easy for divisions to open up within the network of services, to the detriment of both Sarfraz and his family. Similarly, a disagreement over diagnosis underpins the case of Claudette, and this could also have ramifications within the multidisciplinary team. Nothing is more likely to disrupt inter-personal relationships than this sort of conflict; one of the critical challenges for a team is to disagree about specific issues while retaining the capacity to respond appropriately to each other as individuals. Examining the situation of a drugs advice worker in the case of Carmel also highlights the need for excellent interpersonal levels of communication. As noted in the previous subsection, it would be relatively easy for a person with this background to be considered as less central to the effective functioning of the child protection team. Good levels of communication between team members can help to ensure that this does not become a problem.

A high level of commitment to the wider aims and purposes of the team is another important requirement for effective working; an uninterested worker can easily become subversive in such a context, confounding not just her/his own goals and priorities, but also – and perhaps more significantly – those of the wider team. Understanding the purposes of the team and the ways in which those purposes are to be put into action become essential requirements for effective action. In addition, a certain level of personal humility is also important. Given that one of the supposed advantages of team working is the synergy that can be developed through the engagement of people with different beliefs, value positions and perspectives on a particular problem, disagreements can be expected to characterise its working. Operating from a position of personal humility can help to avoid the danger of positions becoming entrenched and practitioners consequently being unable to see the benefits of others' positions.

This is an issue that is likely to apply in the relatively early stages of the development of a team; at this point, uncertainty about the team's goals, aims and objectives can be at its peak, and team members may be more inclined to question these than later in its maturity. A contrast between the relatively new youth offending teams and the older-established community mental health teams may be instructive here: in the former case workers were developing new roles and relationships (Souhami, 2007) with a consequent impact on the nature of intra-team dynamics, where in the latter these had already been established, and new workers would consequently be joining a team where many of these issues had already been resolved.

Reflect

Having read the chapter, in what areas of inter-professional practice do you feel that you might need most support?

Conclusion

The development of inter-professional working has become accepted as both an integral part of the government's approach to partnership working within social policy, as well as a significant way of improving outcomes for people. As such, it is an unavoidable reality that underpins much practice; social workers – and other professionals who practise within the broad boundaries of health and social care – must demonstrate their capacity to operate in such a way. Consequently, social workers must accept the interlocking organisation, professional and personal dimensions of such practice (Hornby and Atkins, 2000).

In principle, at least, effective inter-professional working ought to provide a better and more appropriate response to the complex needs of the most vulnerable people. Whether or not improved practice will be the result is actually uncertain; the difficulties that can attend inter-professional practice are not always fully recognised in various policy formulations and numerous obstacles remain in the way of its final development. However, we have taken the starting position that effective practice within the inter-professional context is possible as well as desirable. In order to turn this principle into a reality, it is vital to be clear about what characteristics differentiate social work from other occupations. To this end, we have specified what we believe to be unique and particular about social work in this context, as follows:

- The orientation, values and ethical stance of social workers are attributes that are specific to them, in that we feel that there are key differences between social workers and other professionals in these respects. In particular, the fact that social workers ought to be able to see service users within a holistic context should provide a particular perspective to the inter-professional team.

- The quality of relationship that social workers should be able to establish with service users, carers and their families – as well as within the inter-professional team – should also be something that is particular to the occupation. While we would, of course, not argue that other professions do not also require such skills, the nature of what a social worker is required to accomplish, and the pace at which it should be carried out, should create opportunities for social workers to establish a better quality of inter-personal relationship with service users.

- In reality, most social workers will also have to demonstrate particularly strong skills in liaison, negotiation, and linking service users to resources. For example, the 'administrative' (Lymbery, 2005) role of the social worker in adult services is particularly evident in the central, coordinating position that they occupy in relation to the establishment and management of care packages. A similar position could be held in relation to children's services, where social work holds a long-established position of linking and coordinating the work of others (Frost et al., 2005).

If social workers are able to apply these unique characteristics to their practice in the various inter-professional settings within which they may be located, combined with a sense of the various 'structural-organisational', 'professional-cultural' and 'interpersonal'

barriers to successful inter-professional working, then there is every likelihood that their practice will lead to more successful outcomes for service users.

Key learning points

This chapter has introduced you to the following issues:

✔ Inter-professional working as an integral part of practice in health and social care, for all service user groups

✔ The particular attributes that social workers can contribute to multidisciplinary teams

✔ The benefits that effective inter-professional working can bring to service users and carers

✔ A number of obstacles that might obstruct effective inter-professional practice

✔ Identification of the key components of successful inter-professional work, illustrated through the medium of case studies.

Further reading

Barrett, G., Sellman, D. and Thomas, J. (eds) (2005) *Interprofessional Working in Health and Social Care*, Basingstoke: Palgrave Macmillan. A practical and accessible resource for a range of professional groups.

Carnwell, R. and Buchanan, J. (eds) (2009) *Effective Practice in Health, Social Care and Criminal Justice: A Partnership Approach*, Buckingham: Open University Press. This edited text focuses on the different dimensions of partnership working in a number of contexts and settings.

Cheminais, R. (2009) *Effective Multi-Agency Partnerships: Putting Every Child Matters into Practice*, London: Sage. This useful text provides a range of practical guidance on the provision of multi-agency partnerships in the context of caring for children.

Glasby, J. and Dickinson, H. (2008) *Partnership Working in Health and Social Care*, Bristol: Policy Press. This short book is one of a series, published in conjunction with *Community Care*, that explores the practical issues underpinning effective partnership working.

Hammick, M., Freeth, D. S., Goodsman, D. and Copperman, J. (2009) *Being Interprofessional*, Cambridge: Polity. This intriguing book explores the nature of working, collaboratively, establishing the concept of 'being' inter-professional.

Leathard, A. (ed.) (2003) *Interprofessional Collaboration: From Policy to Practice in Health and Social Care*, Hove:

Brunner-Routledge. This text contains a number of detailed analyses of policy and practice in relation to inter-professional collaboration and is essential reading.

Pollard, K., Thomas, J. and Miers, M. (eds) (2010) *Understanding Interprofessional Working in Health and Social Care*, Basingstoke: Palgrave Macmillan. This can best be seen as a companion volume to Barrett et al. (2005); it bases its analysis of inter-professional working on the individual experiences of students, practitioners and service users.

Whittington, C., Weinstein, J. and Leiba, T. (eds) (2003) *Collaboration in Social Work Practice*, London: Jessica Kingsley. This is another useful book, focusing on the various dimensions to be considered when establishing collaborative practice.

 Useful websites

www.caipe.org.uk/
Centre for the Advancement of Interprofessional Education (CAIPE) is an independent charity, founded in 1987. Its membership includes organisations and individuals across the UK statutory, voluntary and independent sectors and a growing international membership. It is a national and international resource for inter-professional education in both universities and the workplace across health and social care. CAIPE promotes and develops inter-professional education as a way of improving collaboration between practitioners and organisations, engaged in both statutory and non-statutory public services. It supports the integration of health and social care in local communities.

For additional cases and topic-organised, clickable links into additional media resources, including those produced by IRISS, visit **www.pearsoned.co.uk/wilsonruch**

Activity

Activity One

In the section 'Inter-professional working in practice', four case studies were included, all of which related to different locations and dynamics of inter-professional practice. Taking each of these in turn, identify what the policy issues are that affect each, and how these might affect the practice that is carried out.

Activity Two

(This activity should be undertaken following a placement experience.) Drawing on your experience on placement, identify the issues that derive from inter-professional working. (Be careful to focus on both positive and negative experiences.) Drawing on the material in this chapter, analyse the factors that caused these problems and identify ways in which they were resolved.

Chapter 14
User involvement

Chapter summary

This chapter will discuss a number of issues that need to be considered by social workers in their practice with people who use services. In pursuing the general theme of the book, it emphasises that the quality of relationship that social workers are able to promote with people is a key determinant of the success of any subsequent interactions. We start by focusing why this relationship is vital, drawing on a number of accounts including those from service users themselves. We discuss how the relationship can be made to work and move on to consider ways in which conflict between social workers and service users can be managed.

Learning objectives

This chapter covers topics that will enable you to achieve the following learning objectives:

■ To identify the importance of the nature of the relationship between social workers and service users

■ To understand what service users require from social workers, particularly in relation to how they perceive their treatment by professionals

■ To identify the components of successful relationships between social workers and service users

■ To understand how this could be played out in a variety of practice settings, focusing on those factors that might affect the sorts of relationship preferred by service users.

National Occupational Standards

This chapter will help you to meet the following National Occupational Standards:

Key role 1: Prepare for, and work with individuals, families, carers, groups and communities to assess their needs and circumstances

Unit 1   Prepare for social work contact and involvement

Key Role 2: Plan, carry out, review and evaluate social work practice, with individuals, families, carers, groups, communities and other professionals

Unit 8   Work with groups to promote individual growth, development and independence

Key Role 3: Support individuals to represent their needs, views and circumstances

Unit 10   Advocate with, and on behalf of, individuals, families, carers, groups and communities
Unit 11   Prepare for, and participate in decision making forums

Key Role 6: Demonstrate professional competence in social work practice

Unit 18   Research, analyse, evaluate, and use current knowledge of best social work practice
Unit 19   Work within agreed standards of social work practice and ensure own professional development
Unit 20   Manage complex ethical issues, dilemmas and conflicts
Unit 21   Contribute to the promotion of best social work practice

Case study

Gina

Gina is a white British 40-year-old woman, who has lived on the streets for the past eight years, following a traumatic sequence of domestic violence, during which her partner regularly beat her in front of their two children. Even when she moved out, he repeatedly tracked her down across the country, causing her to live an insecure and traumatic existence. When she turned to Social Services for assistance, the children were removed from her care, on the basis that she was unable to provide a secure environment for them. Traumatised by this event, she turned to drugs and became a street beggar in order to provide for her habit. She had been begging and using hard drugs for several years when she was befriended by Bernice, a community activist. Bernice helped Gina to resolve some outstanding fines she had accrued, and gradually reintroduced her to services that would help address her addictions. She acted as a liaison with the local housing department, eventually securing council accommodation for Gina, who is now trying to piece together the shattered fragments of her life.

Why was the role that Bernice was able to play with Gina not fulfilled by any of the professionally qualified social workers who had been involved in her life?

Although Gina had experienced social work involvement during her problems with domestic violence, this had ended in her losing her children – the very things that gave her life meaning. As a result, she is resistant to receiving any social work support, and highly mistrustful of the impact that social workers could have in her life. While it is accepted that the domestic violence that she experienced placed her children at extreme risk, the fact that they were removed from their mother's care (thereby provoking an ongoing crisis in her own life) is an imperfect

outcome from a number of different perspectives. However, when you think about the circumstances that provoked the removal of Gina's children, the complexities of the case become clear, as do the difficulties of negotiating a balance between the needs of different people within a family setting. In this case it is likely that the original social workers would have considered the needs of the children as having primacy over all other considerations – in line with the overriding principle of the Children Act 1989. This could easily have led to the action to remove them – if Gina was judged to be no longer capable of protecting them, such a decision would have been inevitable. However, there also appears to have been little consideration given to the impact of this action on Gina, nor any attempt to provide her with support. In addition, it was her husband's violence that actually created the crisis. As a result, there is little doubt that the desperate situation confronted by Gina has been caused by what happened to her and her children in the past. It will have been difficult for social workers both to have protected the children and given Gina adequate support; the fact that this support did not materialise leads directly to her deeply felt distrust of all social workers.

Introduction

If we follow the messages of earlier chapters, we can recognise that the nature of the relationship that a social worker is able to achieve with a service user is a critical element in the ability of the practitioner to undertake excellent work with that individual; in Gina's case, this clearly was ineffective such that she has subsequently resisted attempts to improve her life and circumstances. The purpose of this chapter is to indicate why the quality of relationship is vital to good practice, and to propose that there are particular ways in which social workers can act to promote this. We argue that social workers need to base their practice on what service users stress that they need from them, even if they are unable to provide the response that people desire. (This is not an uncommon outcome: after all, social workers are required to undertake work with a wide variety of people, and sometimes there are priorities that will override the wishes of a service user – the protection of children being a particularly clear example.)

This is one of the critical tasks of social work, and its achievement is not always straightforward; a number of potentially conflicting and contradictory issues will need to be addressed in the process. For example, as in Gina's case study above, there will often be different priorities to consider: in that example, her wishes were balanced against the needs of her children – the eventual decision that was taken prioritised her children's need for safety and security against her desire to maintain care for them. In other cases (for example regarding adults with a learning disability), balancing the interests of service users and their carers may become equally significant. Alternatively, there may be complex issues relating to individual capacity

that affect the balance between autonomy and protection that a practitioner has to maintain; there is a law in England (the Mental Capacity Act 2005) which aims to help in this process – see Chapter 17. There are obvious capacity issues where a service user has a cognitive impairment – for example, dementia – that affects their ability to make decisions that are in their best interests. The establishment of a productive working relationship with service users is therefore a complex task, and yet its importance is critical. Where possible, practice that is based on a clear agreement between a social worker and service user is much more likely to be successful, a point that we explore further when considering task-centred practice in Chapter 12. Of course, there will also be occasions when the practitioner is required to take action that is opposed to the expressed wishes of a service user; an example of this is where an Approved Mental Health Professional has to decide whether a person requires compulsory detention, as in the case of Kofi outlined below.

There are four key elements in this chapter:

1. An exploration of the reasons why the voice of the service user has become a central part of social work policy and practice.
2. A summary of service users' perceptions of social workers, drawing selectively on the available evidence. The primary purpose of this is to highlight what service users have specified as important characteristics in their social workers.
3. A focus on what social workers have to do in order to make the social worker/service user relationship effective, drawing on contemporary accounts from service users.
4. Consideration of how these principles can be put into effect, particularly given the problems that can be encountered when working with what Trotter (2006) has termed 'involuntary clients'. This will also include consideration of how the needs of different users, or of service users and their carers, can be held in balance.

We will argue that the greater involvement of service users and carers in the development of policy and practice for social work is appropriate, and also that it is consistent with our vision for social work. However, it will also be clear that this is complex territory: some of the dimensions of this will be explored in the final section. The main points of the discussion will be taken further in Chapters 15–20 with reference to specific groups of service user.

The central importance of the service user

In the early years of the twenty-first century, the active involvement of service users in the provision of social work has become a significant theme in British social work (Braye, 2000; Warren, 2007). There are a number of reasons for this. One the one hand, social work has increasingly recognised the impact of inequality and oppression within society. The internationally agreed statement about the nature of social work (cited in Chapter 4) emphasises the occupation's responsibility to combat such forces. This has been a key commitment of social work in Britain from the 1990s onwards (CCETSW, 1995). Critically, the government has also created legislative and policy requirements for the involvement of service users to be placed at the centre of policy and practice in health and social care (see, for example, DoH, 2000; DoH, 2006a; HM Government, 2007). A particularly striking example of this is the requirement for users and carers to be involved at every stage in qualifying social work education (DoH, 2002e).

The reasons for this development are worthy of note. On the one hand, the professional interest in the establishment of credible forms of anti-oppressive practice has undoubtedly influenced policy. The requirement for students to demonstrate competence in this area of activity resulted from strong pressure within social work, particularly from groups representing disadvantaged people (Taylor, 1993). Similar pressures were also present within the wider society, as groups of hitherto disadvantaged citizens sought collective ways to improve their life chances and opportunities (Crossley, 2002). In addition, the failures and limitations of many state agencies – most notably the police force, through the Macpherson Inquiry (1999) – were highlighted and criticised.

Another theme has become particularly significant in social work, however. This is the growing influence of service user voices: the strongest examples of this have come from the disability movement (see for example, Campbell and Oliver, 1996) or from mental health (Lindow, 1995). In relation to disability, these voices were first strongly heard in the 1970s, with the formation of the Union for the Physically Impaired against Segregation (UPIAS) (Campbell and Oliver, 1996). The critical approach that this organisation adopted was clear and has had enormous subsequent impact. It argued that there was a separation between the effects of physical impairment upon the individual and the problems that the organisation of society has upon the impaired individual. In the view of UPIAS, the cause of disability was not the impairment itself, but the fact that the wider society isolated impaired

The active involvement of service users is a significant theme in current social work practice.

(*Source*: Photofusion Picture Library/Bob Watkins)

individuals, excluding them from full participation and involvement. UPIAS suggested that social work – alongside medicine and nursing – was one of the key professions that helped to reinforce the disability experienced by impaired individuals (Oliver and Sapey, 2006). A similar development has been evident in respect of mental health, with the growth of the service user/survivor movement (Campbell, 1996). This movement has been simultaneously concerned both with self-help and mutual support and the reform of the wider service system. In this way, it has sought to move people from the condition of passive, and oppressed, patients within the psychiatric system to the fuller and more complete status of citizenship (Sayce, 2000). The mental health survivor movement has argued, in common with those people involved in the disability movement, that the forms of treatment that have routinely been made available make their conditions worse, rather than providing a substantial measure of relief from them (Glynn and Ansell, 2006).

One of the key features that characterised the formation of the disabled person's movement – as well as the mental health survivor's movement – was the rapidly acquired ability to speak out about their experiences, and to band together as like-minded individuals (Campbell and Oliver, 1996). It is important to recognise the *collective* basis of this movement; its power and authority was derived precisely from this, as opposed to the actions of isolated persons. Indeed, a consequence of this process has been the emergence of a number of organisations that are controlled by service users, and which seek to reclaim a measure of power and autonomy from the state. There is a direct parallel between the work of these organisations and the developing movement of disabled people, particularly in that they are based on people's '*direct experience of . . . policy and provision from the receiving end*' (Beresford, 2000: 493; emphasis in original). These organisations have focused on a number of different service user groups: seven examples of such organisations are cited in the following paragraphs (and information about their websites will be given at the end of this chapter).

■ *Advocacy in Action*: Advocacy in Action is a user-controlled organisation that has provided education and consultancy for over 16 years, with a particular focus on social work, housing and health care. Its members are from diverse backgrounds, all having direct involvement with services as either service users or carers. The organisation seeks to work across boundaries to promote social justice and welfare. (Unlike the other organisations cited here, it has no website.)

'Disability' is not the impairment itself, but rather seen as a social label enforced on to the individual which isolates impaired individuals from full participation in society.
(*Source*: Alamy Images/Photofusion)

■ *The Care Leavers' Association*: The Care Leavers' Association is a not-for-profit organisation, run by care leavers for care leavers. It aims to end the economic and social disadvantage of those who were in care by achieving significant, positive change, ensuring that care leavers are fully represented and participating at all levels of economic, social and public life.

■ *The Hearing Voices Network*: This is a network for people who hear voices. Its aims include raising awareness of voice hearing, visions, tactile sensations and other sensory experiences, giving men women and children who have these experiences an opportunity to talk freely about this together, and supporting anyone with these experiences seeking to understand, learn and grow from them in their own way.

■ *National Self Harm Network*: This is an organisation for people who self-harm. Its aims and objectives include supporting and empowering people who self-harm;

providing information, contacts and workshops on matters relating to self-harm; promoting survivor-written literature; challenging assumptions and demystifying common misconceptions surrounding self-harm; promoting and advocating for the interests, needs and aspirations of people who self-harm; influencing social and health care policies at a local and national level; raising awareness of the needs of people who self-harm.

- *People First*: People First is a self-advocacy organisation with a national membership, which starts from the standpoint that people with learning difficulties are the experts by experience. It works with service providers to ensure that people with learning difficulties are fully involved in policies and practice.
- *Shaping our Lives*: This is an independent organisation which undertakes user-controlled, emancipatory research and development work. It seeks to promote a society where all people have choice and control over the way they live and the support services they use. It supports the development of local user involvement at local and national levels, and aims to deliver better quality services and outcomes for service users.
- *Suresearch*: Suresearch is a network of service users in research and education. It welcomes as members users and survivors of mental health services and their allies who have experience and/or an interest in mental health research and education. It aims to influence the quality, ethics and values of mental health research by linking with other local, regional and national partnerships in the mental health arena.

All of these organisations are experientially based, and typical of many to have emerged in recent years. Collectively, they have helped to create a different form of knowledge for social work, based primarily on the testimonies of those people who have been on the receiving end of services. Although social work has some history of seeking to take account of the views of service users, there has been a tendency to discount this form of knowledge as less valid than what has been produced through seemingly 'objective' academic means (Beresford, 2000; Glasby and Beresford, 2006). However, in accepting the value of service user knowledge, we would not suggest that other forms of knowledge should be discounted in turn: in practice, social workers will have to balance what service users say about their experiences with information and levels of understanding derived from sources of knowledge that lie outside of their direct experiences. This will include information drawn from the following sources:

- Organisational knowledge, which derives from the framework of regulation, policy and governance in social work.
- Practitioner knowledge, which stems from the experience of those working in the field of social work.
- Research knowledge, which is based on empirical and scholarly material relating to social work.
- Policy knowledge, located in the community responsible for the formation and development of policy at governmental and professional levels.

(Pawson et al., 2003)

While we do not wish to create a hierarchy of importance given to particular forms of knowledge (Pawson et al., 2003), we would agree that service user knowledge has been historically given relatively little importance in social work. As a result, we strongly reject a form of tokenism that merely pretends to take account of the service user voice. This does not mean that such knowledge must override other considerations: given the breadth of a social worker's responsibilities, it is clearly not always possible for a practitioner to act in a way that a service user desires. The exercise of professional judgement is one of the core practice difficulties for social workers, deciding how best to understand events and hence act in response to them. Some examples of the difficulties that can attend such processes will be advanced in the final section of this chapter.

Reflect

Bearing this in mind, based on the information that has been given to you about the removal of Gina's children, what forms of knowledge appear not to have been deployed and how could understandings derived from them have changed the outcome?

It is important, therefore, that social workers do hear and respond appropriately to what service users have to say. In many respects, the messages that come from service users are not comforting for social work practitioners. Michael Oliver, who has a long history in writing about disability and social work, and who was one of the key thinkers in the development of a social model of disability, has protested that social work has failed to live up to its promise to focus attention more on changing society than on the impaired individual, and has taken little account of people's expressed needs and wishes (see Oliver and Sapey, 2006). As a result, he has suggested that social work has effectively become irrelevant to the lives of disabled people (Oliver, 2004). Certainly, many service users would agree that neither social work as an occupation nor individual social workers have responded well to the messages that they have sought to communicate. For example, these are voices of the service users who jointly edited a 'themed issue' of the journal *Social Work Education* on service users and carers in social work education:

'It is well recognised that despite its declared purposes, social work does not always operate with the interests of service users at its heart. Although in part social work springs from the human threads of citizenship, community and compassion, which support the least powerful, its development as a profession has involved a handing over of responsibility to dedicated workers, through voluntary services and statutory public agencies. In this process, citizen power and control has been lost. The professionalisation of social work has brought with it the colonisation of the life experience and value systems of citizens into expert territory, governed by the "trained helpers" and "custodians" of social care and control. In losing its caring focus social work has travelled far from what matters to service users.'

(Advocacy in Action/Suresearch Collective, 2006: 315)

How do you think service users view social workers?
(Kevin Smith (Kes): www.kescartoons.com)

Reflect

Do you agree with this summary of the relationship between social work and service users in the early twenty-first century? On what do you base your agreement/disagreement?

One of the main consequences of appearing to ignore the wishes of service users is that many people with lengthy experience of services have lost their trust in social workers. When this occurs, it will undoubtedly make it more difficult for practitioners to bridge the gap between themselves and those whom they are employed to serve. Unfortunately, as the following section will make clear, social workers have not always managed to provide responses that equated to the needs of services – the problems to which this chapter refers are not therefore of recent origin.

Service users' perceptions of social workers

In establishing the basis of service users' views of social workers, we draw particularly on two classic accounts.

That the messages of these accounts are relevant to the contemporary social world is made apparent by comparison with more recent reports. The first classic research study in the field was by Mayer and Timms (1970), who investigated the perceptions of 'clients' and workers of the Family Welfare Association, a voluntary organisation that had provided individual casework service for almost 100 years at that time. (In fact, this was the renamed Charity Organisation Society, which we identified in Chapter 4 as being instrumental in the establishment of social work.) As the authors note, the appraisals of those who use services would be of great benefit; the particular problem that they highlighted was the fact that 'clients are rarely asked to appraise the effectiveness of the services received' (Mayer and Timms, 1970: 3). As an illuminating point of contrast, Mayer and Timms also collected the evaluations of the social workers involved.

Perhaps the most interesting element of their findings is the mismatch that they uncovered between what each individual client believed was the nature of the problem, and the approach taken by workers. In a finding reminiscent of Wootton's (1959) critique of social work, explored in detail in Chapter 4, the purpose of the clients who presented for help was primarily to secure immediate assistance with either practical or emotional problems. The response of workers tended to focus more on enabling the client to gain insight into the nature and causes of the problem than it did in seeking to resolve it. For Mayer and Timms (1970: 77), this mismatch originated in the fact that social workers and clients had different understandings both about the essential nature of the problems at issue and the consequent ways of resolving them: '[T]he social workers were unaware that the clients entered the treatment situation with a different mode of problem-solving and that the clients' behaviour during treatment was in part traceable to this fact.'

These disparities emerged through the different sense held by workers and clients of the purpose of the organisation and the consequent roles of those social workers it employed. As far as those people who used the service were concerned, the consequences were significant. Even where the assistance sought was material, clients did not always receive a service that was consistent with their purposes in seeking help. Practitioners were consistently felt to underplay the impact of poverty upon people's lives, and tended to translate the material assistance sought into explorations about emotional matters. In one case, Mayer and Timms (1970: 121) note that a client had felt 'very degraded' by her treatment, and that she 'believed the worker was questioning her about her marriage because she (*the worker*) was unable to grasp the true nature of her difficulties'.

The lessons that can be learned from this are not as straightforward as the above account would indicate. Mayer and Timms (1970) do note the possibility that many people might seek material assistance when the genuine problem is emotional; however, they insist – and their research supports this contention – that a satisfied client is likely to be one whose initial reason for referral is met, even if the work subsequently undertaken focuses on other issues. In general terms, Mayer and Timms found that clients were more likely to be satisfied when they encountered workers who provided both emotional and material support when required, and adopted what Mayer and Timms termed a 'supportive–directive' approach. Those who were less satisfied often failed to have their material concerns addressed and were also treated by workers who, typically, had an 'insight-oriented' approach to the work, leading to misunderstandings about the nature and purpose of the contact. This may be translated into the need for social workers to be clear about how service users actually define their problems, and to ensure that these definitions form the basis of any subsequent work.

Mayer and Timms (1970: 140–1) are particularly critical of the difficulty many social workers of the time had in responding to the immediate, economic problems presented by many service users:

'To offer clients . . . psychological help – without satisfying, preferably at the start, their material needs – in our view utterly fails to come to grips with their problems . . . In their pre-occupation with psychological matters, social workers have tended to develop an occupational blindness to economic realities.'

This observation reflects the psychological bias within social work that was common at the time, as highlighted in Chapter 4. It suggests that social workers need to have a dual focus on both the external economic realities that confront service users as well as the internal workings of each individual. Consequently, they conclude by arguing that the essential task of the researcher – and also the social worker – is to discover the forms of treatment that are most appropriate for the particular circumstances that the client presents. They also specify that this is a problem that clients' opinions can help to resolve, noting the absence of such studies in the history and development of social work.

Reflect

Does the analysis offered by Mayer and Timms still apply to social work practice today?

Useful and trailblazing as this research was, it focused on the work of a specialist voluntary sector organisation, where the work of the social workers it employed was untypical of the day-to-day practice of social workers in statutory settings (see, for example, Rodgers and Dixon, 1960), and certainly not characteristic of what is required of contemporary practitioners. In addition, the predominantly psycho-dynamic frame of reference of the surveyed group of social workers was not then universally held, and is arguably even less common today.

You will note that Mayer and Timms refer to the 'client' of social workers, where the most commonly used terminology now is to refer to those who receive social services as 'service users'. The recent history of social work does feature an ongoing search for the most appropriate terms to use (McLaughlin, 2009). The use of the term 'client' derived from the standard usage, then as now, common in professions. The voluntaristic connotations of the expression were not helpful in social work, and many writers – particularly those within the more radical tradition (Simpkin, 1983) – were wary of the 'professional' ethos implicit in the term, believing that this was not the correct direction for social work. In counselling circles, the concept of 'helpee' was mooted (Truax and

Carkhuff, 1967) as a way of avoiding the connotations of the term 'client': however, 'client' remains the favoured term in the counselling word. By contrast, 'service user' is preferred in social work as a more neutral term that seeks to convey the related ideas of 'entitlement' and 'partnership'. Even here, the terminology remains controversial (McLaughlin, 2009): a 'user' has a different, less neutral, meaning in the context of drug and alcohol services, for example. In addition, each term has to be linked to the political philosophy that produces it, and therefore carries a weight of additional meanings. For example, it has been argued that the contemporary focus on 'service user involvement' derived from an essentially consumerist perspective, where 'progressive critiques of the Welfare State have become incorporated and used as the basis for advancing what was essentially a neo-liberal programme' (Cowden and Singh, 2007: 11); this insight has been further developed by Carey (2009). It is interesting that, after over 130 years of its history, there still is no accepted term for people who use social services. Indeed, it has been suggested that there are no good terms – each has both positive and negative elements and associations (McLaughlin, 2009). The contrast with health services is illuminating: here, the term 'patient' has become accepted in an uncontroversial way.

Reflect

Do you prefer the term 'service user' as one that conveys a sense of equality and respect? Can you think of a better, more appropriate one?

Approximately a decade on from Mayer and Timms' trailblazing work, Rees and Wallace (1982) sought to summarise the findings from a wide range of research that examined the responses of both clients and practitioners to social work intervention. Rather than primary research, therefore, this was a synthesis of a range of research, the majority of which was carried out in Britain or the USA. Interestingly, in view of the comments made a decade earlier by Mayer and Timms, Rees and Wallace drew on a large body of published material, testimony to the rapid growth of such studies.

While they express numerous caveats about the extent to which the responses from the studies are capable of further generalisation, they do identify a number of salient issues for consideration:

- The personal attributes and skills of social workers were held to be important; clients felt that it was important that the social worker was seen both as a 'person' and as a 'friend'.
- It was equally vital that the 'concerned, friendly approach' that was valued was matched by concrete action to change clients' circumstances.
- People most wanted help that was tangible and material; in Rees and Wallace's words (1982: 87): 'clients from all backgrounds seem generally oriented towards help that is concrete, directive and supportive'.
- Advocacy and negotiation skills were rated very highly by clients.
- It is not easy to generalise from individual experiences, as they are tied to both context and the nature of the problem.

Reflect

If these principles had held during social workers' involvement with Gina, outlined above, do you think that the outcomes would have been the same?

In a number of ways, there is a clear continuity between the findings of Rees and Wallace and the earlier study by Mayer and Timms. In both, the way in which the social worker manages the relationship with the service user is seen to be critical, emphasising the importance of the social worker's use of 'self'. Similarly, both publications focus on the importance of people being able to achieve their practical goals and the vital role of social workers in ensuring that this can take place. Naturally, there are also important differences between the two books. For example, Rees and Wallace brought an avowedly 'radical' perspective (see Chapter 4 for more on this) to their work, and castigated social workers for their limited and conservative aspirations, particularly in the light of the continuing poverty of the large numbers of people who required social work assistance. Although they acknowledge that there was little evidence that social workers had effectively addressed social and political inequalities in their practice, they argued that this should be no obstacle to their attempt to accomplish more. As is obvious from our earlier argument in Chapter 4, we do not believe that social work in Britain has been granted the political, legislative or professional authority to intervene at such levels. Indeed, particularly as demonstrated by Mayer and Timms (1970), were practitioners to act in such a way their practice could run directly counter to the expressed interests of people who need services.

When service users and carers were asked in the mid-1990s to specify what they valued and expected from social work and social care personnel, the answers given were very similar to what we have observed from the preceding accounts. Here, the key issues that concerned service users and carers were subdivided into three discrete elements, although it was recognised that there were overlaps between these:

1. the quality of relationships;
2. the quality of skills;
3. the quality of services.

(Harding and Beresford, 1995)

As far as the quality of relationships is concerned, the report states that the 'nature of the relationships between social services staff and people who use services is central to people's perception of what constitutes quality' (Harding and Beresford, 1995: 3), thus reinforcing a central tenet of this book. A number of aspects of this were identified, including credibility, respect, confidentiality, courtesy, empathy, honesty and reliability. Various tangible elements were valued in the relationship, but service users particularly cited the extent to which it could become empowering for the service user. In this respect, the report acknowledged the particular difficulties that could be experienced for people who are involuntary users of social work services; however, the quality of relationship that is developed could go some way towards allaying such concerns. They also were wary of social workers who imposed a prior theoretical perspective on them, strongly expressing dislike of an approach 'in which they and their circumstances are subordinated to theoretical interpretations, or in which predetermined or inappropriate theories are imposed' (Harding and Beresford, 1995: 10).

Within the context of good quality relationships, service users also pointed out the skills that they expected social workers to have, which included communication and listening, counselling, enabling and negotiating, knowledge about local services and the ability to judge risk. This final point is particularly important in the context of the various areas of conflict that will confront social workers. Service users and carers were in no doubt of the difficult judgements that social workers were required to make, but there was also a clear divergence of opinion about what people had experienced: some people reported social workers as being over-protective, others reported them as failing in their duty of protection. (The difficulty of the social work task is encapsulated in this apparent contradiction.)

As regards the quality of services, the picture is mixed. While some people received a service that reflected what they needed, others reported a combination of dissatisfaction with its quality with a sense of resignation that the quality of services would not improve. However, the organisations consulted were all committed to seeking such improvements; the two main elements that would embody such change being more effective and equitable partnerships (see Beresford et al., 2007) and the establishment of national performance standards. They were also particularly concerned about the potentially damaging centrality of clinical judgement in care services, where 'expert' judgement is imposed upon individuals without recognition of their perceptions about their own circumstances. The resolution of this danger lies in the fact that, as the service users reported, the quality of the relationship with practitioners represented the core of their satisfaction (or dissatisfaction) with services. If such relationships are developed on an equitable basis, respecting each user's individuality and treating them with dignity, the potential for abusive 'professional' judgement will be reduced.

In recent years there has been a spate of publications that focus on service user involvement in the delivery of social work and social care (see, for example, Doel and Best, 2008; Warren, 2007). One element of continuity has been provided in many of these by Peter Beresford, who has undoubtedly played a key role in ensuring that the position of service users continues to occupy an important place in debates about the development of social work. His position is unique, in that he is both a senior academic within the field of social policy and a long-term user of mental health services. He therefore straddles the often opposed worlds of academia and service users, and has represented a consistent, and sometimes isolated, voice for the interests of people (including practitioners) against organisations. In his combined role as Chair of the user-led organisation Shaping Our Lives (see below) and Professor of Social Policy at Brunel University, he occupies a pivotal position in relation to user involvement in social work, social care and more generally within social policy.

In recent years, he has reviewed the growing literature on user involvement in social work (Beresford, 2007). The conclusions reached in this paper echo those of his earlier work, cited above (Harding and Beresford, 1995). From his research he is able to state firmly that service users particularly value and hence welcome social work practice that:

- Is participatory in process and purpose
- Focused on supporting independent living and participation rather than dependence
- Offers continuity
- Is flexible and person-centred
- Is holistic and social model based
- Connects the personal with the social and political, offering personal/emotional and practical support
- Addresses rights, risks and their complex interrelations
- Is based on inclusive understanding of knowledge which includes the experiential knowledge of service users and the practice knowledge of face to face workers.

(Beresford, 2007: 6)

As a consequence, service users particularly value those social work practitioners who are able to:

- Support them to work out their own agendas with them
- Give them time to sort things out
- Are available and accessible
- Provide continuity of support
- Are reliable and deliver
- Are responsive
- Have a good level of knowledge and expertise
- Value the expertise of the service user.

(Beresford, 2007: 6)

It is interesting to compare these insights to those of Davis (2008), who suggests that the following characteristics of social workers are most welcomed by service users:

- **Being alongside** individuals and tuning into their lives and aspirations
- **Listening** to what service users say
- **Hearing** what service users say
- **Assessing** service users' needs holistically
- **Advocating** for service users in respect to their needs
- **Empowering** service users to actively engage with their difficulties
- **Helping** service users in practical ways to address the problems they face.

(Davis, 2008: 2)

There does seem to be a growing consensus about these issues. We can certainly conclude that the need for social workers to exercise good relational skills with service users is apparent, as is the need to respond with sensitivity and respect to the issues presented by each individual. This is a common theme within all the accounts; the fact that each was published within a separate decade testifies to the continuing and enduring nature of these concerns. This means that practitioners must retain awareness that people often have practical issues with which they require assistance, and have the ability to act to secure the resources which people lack. In addition, social workers will also need to balance the different aspects of their role, which may mean taking action that is not in accordance with the wishes of the individual. However, the essential characteristics of contemporary social work practice are not in step with these requirements: although service users emphasise the need for social workers to establish a productive working relationship with them, the roles that are expected of practitioners often make the establishment of such a rapport an impossibility for practitioners, who are provided with neither the time nor the support needed to undertake this form of practice (Tanner, 2009).

Nonetheless, as we will demonstrate in a later section, the personal attributes of a social worker are particularly important where there are differences in perspective – for example, between service users and their carers – or where the more controlling aspects of practice are required, as in child protection. It is also important for their employing organisations to recognise the value of such work and support those practitioners in carrying it out. In all of these circumstances, social workers need to pay particular attention to those aspects that are most likely to make a relationship work; it is to this aspect of practice that the chapter now turns.

Making the relationship work

In writing this section, we draw particularly on the words of service users themselves. It is perhaps too easy to establish precepts for how social workers should conduct themselves with service users without referring to what those people have to say about such involvement. It is important to recognise that, when asking service users about their experiences of social workers, there are a lot of factors that might obstruct a true and honest response, particularly the reality of the differences in power between worker and service user, deriving from the levels of inequality between the two. One particular service organisation, Shaping Our Lives, has been instrumental in developing a user-led response to the issues of power and inequality that dominate relations between service users and service providers, including professional social workers:

'There is a significant difference between partnerships with other service users and non-service user organisations and workers. This is because of the general inequality of power existing between the two. It is crucial to raise issues of power and powerlessness in relation to the idea of partnership with service users and their organisations. Historically, discussions and writings of service users have started with and focused on their powerlessness and disempowerment. That is, of course, why their empowerment (alongside participation, inclusion, integration and independence) has been a key concern of service users' movements. People included as service users have been routinely and institutionally devalued, discriminated against, pauperised and denied their human and civil rights. Their organisations have reflected this inequality, generally being under-resourced, fragile and insecure.'

(Beresford et al., 2007: 217)

Think ahead

What are the sources of the power held by social workers over service users? In what ways might these inequalities in power affect the communication between social worker and service user?

A closer look

Accounts from Shaping Our Lives

'Social workers wanted me to leave where I'm living now. I said to them don't be silly I can't live on my own, I don't want to live on my own. They asked me to live on my own and I can't live on my own in a flat. My family came here to say I had to live with people. I like living with people [rather] than living on my own. I like the social workers I have got now. They let me stay where I am. They let me feel settled. It's alright where I am now. People get on well with me where I live. I am pleased to stay where I am. Social workers ask me if I want to live there. I said, yes I will stay there. It's great that they understand what we want.'

(Man with learning difficulties)

'Social workers could have talked to me about why I went into a mental health home. They didn't give me a choice. I went to visit there and they said that's the only place available for you and I didn't have a mental health problem. I was low but I wasn't mentally ill. I didn't have to take tablets or anything. They should have asked me first where do you want to move to because I had nowhere to live. I had to move out of a place – a family. I wasn't happy in the mental health home. I went to visit a duty social worker and they found me a new social worker. His job was to help me move out of there, to see what kind of place I wanted to live in. He was very good because he didn't like me being in that home. He made me feel comfortable. He phoned up to put me on the waiting list and I went to visit a lady from Lifeways to talk to me if I wanted to live with a family, just to get on my two feet, to feel confident. I said that would be a good idea. I really enjoyed living there. It gave me more confidence because living in the home made me feel a bit unconfident.'

(A woman with learning difficulties)

'One of our lads with a learning difficulty had a social worker who used to visit him irregularly, always kept the appointment if he confirmed it, but whenever he turned up, without exception, every single time he took and made endless calls on his mobile phone when he was supposed to be with Daniel [not his real name]. Time and time again. It didn't matter what was going on, he never even said 'Oh excuse me' or turned it off – it was half a sentence to Daniel and then back to his mobile phone. So Daniel was never given any one-to-one private attention. He was never listened to. He is now, having got a new case worker, working at a local supermarket and says he is very, very happy.

He came to us and said he didn't want to complain but that he was fed up. So I made a phone call on his behalf and said that the social worker's behaviour was inappropriate . . . the person I was speaking to obviously didn't think this was too serious . . . but they looked into it and it was addressed. Apparently once Daniel had asked us to tell someone, other people got up the courage to complain as well and it had not only been Daniel who had been treated this way. So I think people have to be encouraged to speak up and try not to be afraid and I think that is the social worker's responsibility to listen to the service user and to hear what is being told them and to do something about it if it is not good. This was a good outcome for Daniel and for others who had had the same social worker.'

(A service user advocate)

(*Source*: all quotes are from Beresford et al., 2007: 218–19)

What are the key factors that made for good practice, as far as these witnesses are concerned? How could the negative impact of social workers' actions have been minimised?

If social workers are to build good working relationships with service users, these issues have to be recognised, as the experiences of service users – and the contact they have with figures of authority, including social workers – are mediated by these facts. If social workers do not recognise the experiences of service users, often including negative past contact with other practitioners, their practice will be based on insecure footings. And, as a result, it must be acknowledged that service users' experiences of professional social work intervention in their lives are often mixed, as exemplified by the recollections by members of Shaping Our Lives (see Closer Look box).

A key message from these narratives is the recognition of the importance of the way in which social workers responded to the needs of the service user. A positive reaction was more likely when a service user was listened to with respect, and when their wishes for the future were properly recognised, accepted and acted upon. This creates a sense of the genuineness of the social worker's response to the individual. The general message about the importance of the relationship between service users and social workers is reinforced in the following passage.

'The most important partnership for most service users between them and workers is the one that they have with individual practitioners. A helpful starting point for thinking about partnership is offered by the conventional idea of it being based on a contract between people engaged in business. Service users and social care workers need to negotiate how it will work for both of them. A set of rules or common values needs to underpin the partnership, which both sign up to.

We believe any partnership between service users and social care workers has to be built on a basis of mutual co-operation, openness and equality. This does not mean that either side has to agree with, or endorse all the other's choices, beliefs or opinions, but it should mean both sides respect the other's rights to make their own choices, decisions and beliefs.'

(Beresford et al., 2007: 223)

These sorts of idea are also evident in two research studies undertaken with service users on an international basis. On the one hand, work was undertaken with families who had experienced child protection services in Canada (De Boer and Coady, 2007). This is a particularly significant group of people, who have experienced some of the more powerful aspects of social work. The conclusions reported in the study were that good helping relationships were critical to the effectives of the intervention; it concluded that there were two characteristics of the practitioner that enabled such relationships to be established.

The first of these concerned the way in which the worker managed the power that was integral to the role, with service users valuing workers who used their power judiciously, held and maintained respect for the individual, conveyed a non-judgemental attitude and demonstrated the ability to understand the perspective of the service user and to support them through the child protection processes. The second related to the attitude and style of working, with service users particularly valuing a humanistic approach that made them feel appreciated and supported, and which went beyond the legal and technical mandates that governed the social worker's practice.

Similar reflections on the nature of the relationship between service user and social worker can be found in the conclusions of a study of young homeless people and the services they receive in the Netherlands (de Winter and Noom, 2003). From the words of the young people themselves, the authors define three ways in which the quality of relationship between homeless young people and social workers can be improved:

1. improved communication;
2. greater trust;
3. a greater say in what happens to them.

(de Winter and Noom, 2003: 333)

The priority given to improved communication and greater trust are similar to the priorities found in the Canadian research. The final point is particularly important; in seeking 'a greater say', the young people were not asking for a system whereby all decisions would be made by them alone, but rather suggesting that a shared approach will lead to much more successful outcomes. This refers back to the points made by British service users, noted above (Beresford, 2007). In practice, of course, the exercise of partnership between service users and social workers will be fraught with a range of practical difficulties, the nature of child protection practice representing a good example of this (De Boer and Coady, 2007). However, we believe that this is a position to which all social workers should aspire. In the following section we explore some more of these difficulties, illustrating our points by using case studies.

Managing conflict

It would be of no assistance to social workers in training, nor to the service users with whom they work, if we were to convey the notion that an ideal state of being between social workers and service users could be attained simply through following the precepts noted in the previous section. This would be to underplay, or even ignore, the fact that there are inherent conflicts in a social worker's role that necessarily affect their practice with service users. As we have seen in earlier chapters, the social worker has to mediate between a range of pressures on her/his practice, as exemplified in the potential clashes over the following points of principle:

- autonomy and protection;
- the needs of the service user as opposed to the needs of the carer;
- the needs of the individual as opposed to the requirements of society;
- balancing needs and resources.

A social worker cannot make blanket assumptions that s/he will act in a way that always favours one or other of these areas of potential conflict. Indeed, it would be wrong to do so; the essence of social work is the need to make judgements in a range of situations that critically depend on the context in order to understand them fully. We explore these through the medium of four case studies, each of which explores these issues more fully. We do not provide conclusive answers to the questions posed by these case studies: you might like to consider them as the basis for further debate and discussion, working out the possible range of response that can be considered, before identifying which has particular merit. In practice, social workers will have to negotiate within similar sorts of problem on a regular basis.

Case study

Autonomy and protection

Mary-Ann is a 16-year-old white British girl, who has recently left a residential care home to live independently within the community. She had been in residential care for the past two years, following the breakdown of her long-term foster care arrangement, following Mary-Ann's allegations of sexual abuse by her foster father (which led to a trial and his imprisonment). In general terms, Mary-Ann possesses good life skills – she cooks, cleans and manages her money well. She did not do well at school, but has recently gained a place at a local college to study health and

social care. She would like to go to university, and it is believed that she has the capability to study at that level. She has maintained informal contact with the residential care home since leaving. On one such contact, Mary-Ann seemed very excited about her independent life, talking animatedly about the exciting times she was having with her friends, particularly a new boyfriend. During the conversation, the identity of this boyfriend was revealed; he is rumoured to be a pimp and drug dealer. When you attempt to raise this subject with Mary-Ann, she clams up and quickly leaves the building.

As a residential social worker, what do you think is the most appropriate course of action, given Mary-Ann's age and vulnerability? How do you address the risks that can be observed in her current circumstances in ways that retain the trusting relationship you have developed with Mary-Ann?

In practical terms, your responsibility in this case will of course be dictated by Mary-Ann's legal status. However, underpinning this is a difficult area of judgement: the extent to which it is safe to allow Mary-Ann the opportunity to develop her own life and friendships. This is complicated by her age, history and vulnerability; action that is perceived by her as overly intrusive may only serve to alienate her from further support. By contrast, any failure to act now may leave her open to considerable risk of abuse.

All of these represent a serious dilemma for a social work practitioner, and it will be difficult to resolve these complex issues. The best opportunity to do so is within the context of a productive and respectful relationship between yourself and Mary-Ann. If trust and confidence is at the core of this, there is more likelihood of being able to discuss the issues and secure Mary-Ann's understanding that your concerns are genuine. It is important that she is able to recognise that there are serious issues to consider, and that your intervention is based on a genuine anxiety for her welfare, and not – as she seems to think at the outset – from a desire to curtail her chances for personal happiness. Although at 16 years of age Mary-Ann remains a child, and there is a need to ensure her protection (her life history may have rendered her more vulnerable to possible abuse than others of her age), she can also respond to reason and debate and has some legal capacity to make her own choices. (For example, she is over the age of consent for sexual activity.) Although it would be possible to move quickly into a potentially over-protective response, the first priority is to ensure that you are able to engage freely with her. In this way, you can start to assess the extent of the risk that the relationship may pose – remember, there is nothing of substance in the allegations about her boyfriend's activities, and it would be unwise to base all your practice on what currently rest as unsubstantiated rumours.

Of course, it may transpire that the suspicions are justified, and that he has a past history of establishing relationships with vulnerable young girls before using the trust that has been developed to introduce them to prostitution. If this is the case, of course the risk to Mary-Ann becomes hugely increased. Although it will be difficult to discuss the issues with Mary-Ann, the quality of relationship that has been developed with her may enable you to be more honest about this than a practitioner who does not have such a relationship. After all, you will be communicating information to Mary-Ann that will be very painful, and where a strongly emotional reaction can be predicted. If she has some understanding that you genuinely have her welfare at heart, there is more likelihood that she will be enabled to take decisions and subsequent actions that are in her own interests.

Case study

Users and carers

Lucy is a 53-year-old white woman with Down's Syndrome. She lives at home with her widowed mother, Martha, who is 87 and in failing health. Martha has always provided a protective and loving home for Lucy, who consequently has little experience of living independently and possesses few practical life skills. Martha has reluctantly acknowledged that plans have to be made for Lucy's future, and is insistent that she will need to be placed in a residential home so that she can continue to be 'looked after'. Lucy has expressed a wish to live more independently.

In planning for future arrangements for Lucy, you need to balance the competing wishes of her own and her mother. It is common within the field of learning disability for there to be conflict between parents and social workers over the future of children. Managing this conflict is a core task for social workers. In this set of circumstances, Lucy has well-established connections with social workers, having been known to the learning disability services for many years. However, Martha is now at an advanced age and may well soon develop needs that call for the provision of social care services in her own right. Clearly, this situation cannot be resolved without maximum discussion between the various parties, and the complex task facing the social worker is to resolve matters to the satisfaction of all.

At the core of this problem is the complex relationship between risk and independence. On the one hand, Martha's concern that Lucy needs to be cared for throughout the rest of her life indicates that she does not believe that Lucy can take care of herself, and also that such an action should not be risked. By contrast, Lucy has expressed a human wish to maximise her own autonomy, a characteristic shared by all service users. From the outside, as a social worker you could observe that part of the problem has been Martha's consistent refusal to allow Lucy to grow and develop. At this point in both their lives, it is late to begin a process of planning for life beyond Martha; in addition, it is possible that Lucy's situation will change as the onset of dementia is both more probable for adults with Down's Syndrome and more likely to occur at an early age. Perhaps the best way to seek to resolve the problems is not to take the concepts of 'care' and 'independence' as the ends of a continuum; in this way, a resolution could be found for Lucy that combines elements of care with a greater degree of independence. There are various forms of supported housing that could be considered, which could potentially meet the concerns of both Martha and Lucy.

One of the issues that social workers will confront is that not all problems are amenable to debate or discussion, where the opposed points of view are too far apart to be reconciled. It is possible that in this case, for example, the perspectives of Martha and Lucy may be so starkly opposed that a common middle ground could not be found. (This is perhaps unlikely, given the circumstances we have outlined.) If it should occur, however, as a social worker you need to be clear about the approach you are adopting to a problem and what that means in practice. Your goal is to enable the best possible quality of life for Lucy, and it is likely that this will involve some choices that her mother may feel are too 'risky' to be considered appropriate. Certainly, Martha's concerns have to be treated with respect, but cannot be allowed to take priority over all other considerations.

The individual and society

Kofi is a 27-year-old man of Ghanaian origin. He has been referred to you as an Approved Mental Health Professional (AMHP) for you to consider whether compulsory detention under mental health legislation is appropriate. He has apparently locked himself in his flat for several weeks, refusing to admit anyone who attempts to gain entry, and playing martial music at a very high volume 24 hours a day. When his GP tried to talk to Kofi through the letter box, he responded apparently rationally and calmly that he was preparing for the coming 'bloody conflict', that his actions are nobody's business other than his own and that he wants to be left alone.

Do you think that Kofi's wishes are paramount in this circumstance?

Here, there is a clear choice to be made: how to balance Kofi's rights to independence with the actions that you can authorise under the terms of the Mental Health Act 1983 and the Mental Health Act 2007 in England and Wales, or the Mental Health (Care & Treatment) (Scotland) Act 2003 in Scotland. There is no simple or straightforward course of action to be followed: as the AMHP you must judge whether Kofi's condition calls for compulsory detention. As in all of these case studies, the exercise of professional judgement is critical.

The nub of your responsibilities in this case is the decision whether Kofi should be compulsorily admitted to hospital. In the past, one of the few actions that could only be undertaken by a social worker relates to compulsory admission to hospital. It is still the case that an AMHP must give consent to this course of action; however, under the terms of the Mental Health Act 2007 this role is no longer restricted to social workers, and can be carried out by a range of 'approved professionals'. However, as yet few representatives from other professional groups have opted to become AMHPs (Rapaport and Manthorpe, 2008); consequently, it remains a role that is usually occupied by social workers. Here, the practitioner (who is required to undertake an extensive form of additional training in preparation for this role) must decide the extent to which Kofi's actions constitute a threat either to himself or to others. In

reality, therefore, the AMHP will be required to take decisions that are against a service user's immediate desires: this is inherently part of the role. In this case, Kofi's reported actions are certainly bizarre, and not immediately explicable to the outside world. There could be an apparently rational explanation underpinning them, but this is hard to determine. In addition, the fact that he is refusing to admit anybody makes it difficult to assess his condition and circumstances. A further complicating factor is your knowledge that African-Caribbean men are over-represented in the mental health system (Fernando, 2003).

The skills that a social worker in this case will need to develop are firstly to seek to gain access to Kofi's accommodation. (An assessment of safety must accompany this action – it is possible that Kofi may pose a direct threat to others including the social worker, although the context of his present behaviour would render that less probable. Practitioners must always be aware of the need to maintain their personal safety in carrying out their work.) Once the worker does gain access s/he needs to gain Kofi's confidence – the skills of communication (outlined in Chapter 10) will be of particular importance here. It is probable that Kofi will be unreceptive to many of the normal forms of communication, particularly if his behaviour is symptomatic of more serious mental ill health. If he is judged to be a threat to himself or others, this must be communicated clearly and the consequences of this made clear. The act of depriving an individual of her/his liberty is an immensely serious undertaking, which can create considerable anxiety for the practitioner. It is important that any such anxiety is not communicated to Kofi in this case, as it could easily further upset his equilibrium.

Needs and resources

Albert is a 92-year-old white man, who has been in hospital for several weeks following a series of strokes. He has been judged as medically fit for discharge. Under the terms of the Community Care (Delayed Discharges etc.) Act 2004, you have to facilitate his discharge within set timescales defined by the Act – failure to do so would leave the adult social care department facing a fine under the terms of the Act. He has been assessed as eligible for residential care, and has expressed

▶

a desire to enter a residential home near to his daughter. Unfortunately, the home caters largely for privately funded residents, and their weekly charge is more than the authority would normally expect to pay. There appears to be no third party available to make up the difference between this and the home's normal rate. Albert is adamant that if he cannot enter this home he will stay in hospital and die.

As a hospital-based social worker, how will you seek to resolve this position in such a way that Albert receives the service that he desires, the discharge is not delayed and the finances of the authority are not compromised?

In managing this situation, the social worker has to mediate between the (potentially conflicting) desires of the hospital, her/his own department, the service user and whatever the views and opinions might be of Albert's family. All of this will have to be concluded within very tight timescales. The legislative basis for action is clear and might point towards a particular outcome, but the wishes of the service user should override any financial and bureaucratic requirements. The critical question for a practitioner will be the process of holding all of these considerations in balance.

This is complicated by many of the characteristics of social work with older people, which has been dominated by financial considerations ever since the introduction of community care policies in the early 1990s (see Chapter 22 for more on this). In an attempt to make more efficient use of expensive resources, policy has been fixed on the more efficient use of existing resources – and expensive hospital beds are one such resource. The direction of policy is such that it affects the practice of social workers based in hospital settings in a fundamental way, sharpening the tensions between the needs of the service user and the resources available to meet those needs. The gap between the resources that would normally be made available to fund residential care and the charges of some residential care homes has been a long-standing cause of contention, with a local authority financially unable to fund care costed at high levels.

The social work task here is therefore complex: you are constrained by the policies of your employer, while also seeking to facilitate Albert's discharge within the time limitations of the Community Care (Delayed Discharges etc.) Act 2004. At the same time, your primary concern is to ensure that Albert's wishes are accommodated as far as possible. As far as the legislative requirement for discharge is concerned, the adult social care department has properly exercised its responsibilities if a viable option is offered to Albert: should he choose not to accept this, then the responsibility for any subsequent delay in discharge transfers from the local authority to the individual, and no fine can then be levied. However, this would be a limited and partial approach to practice, concerned only with discharging the statutory responsibilities of the social care department, without due consideration being given to Albert's needs and wishes.

There is a very real problem to overcome at this point, given the considerable gap between the fee that the local authority would normally expect to pay and the charge set by the home. Unless there is a third party willing and able to fund the difference – which can amount to significant sums even for somebody of Albert's advanced age – it will not be possible for him to enter his preferred home. A skilled social worker must be able to communicate the reasons that underpin this decision to Albert and to convince him that alternative possibilities could be explored. After all, very few older people actually *want* to end their days in hospital, and Albert's fixed view of his preference may have obstructed his ability to think through the affordable alternatives that exist. There are, for example, a number of less expensive residential homes within his daughter's community, and Albert would almost certainly be more comfortable within one of these rather than in hospital. If it is impossible to bridge the financial gap between the preferred home and the resources available to pay for it, the critical task for the social worker will be to persuade Albert to accept an alternative. Although this may be second best, it may still be preferable to his expressed intentions. The skills of relationship forming and communication are absolutely critical to this interaction. The practice can start from Albert's preferred position, and then move towards an outcome that is acceptable to all parties. In this case, as is typical for many older people, his wishes and desires have to be balanced against numerous other considerations.

Conclusion

As the preceding section makes clear, it is important to place great value on the knowledge and experience of service users and to incorporate this into policy, practice and education. The direct experience of service users does provide a source of knowledge that has long been undervalued in social work, even though the occupation has taken more steps in this direction than many others (Beresford, 2000). Indeed, it has been suggested that the subjective knowledge generated by focusing on the lived experience of service users is equally as valid as the apparent objectivity of 'evidence-based practice' (Glasby and Beresford, 2006). However, social workers have to balance knowledge derived directly from service users against other sources of knowledge that lie outside of their direct experience, as we have earlier noted (Pawson et al., 2003). As the case studies have demonstrated, there are also numerous practical difficulties that can complicate a social worker's intention to work alongside service users, acting as far as possible in accordance with their wishes.

There is no single way of managing service user engagement, a message that is made clear from a variety of different pieces of research. There is, however, an expectation that this should be accomplished effectively within social work education (see Branfield et al., 2007 for England; Ager et al., 2005 for Scotland) and beyond. Indeed, the involvement of service users has become an orthodox part of the social work world (Cowden and Singh, 2007; Carey, 2009). There is also substantial research that points to the successes of this approach. For example, an evaluation of children's views of family group conferences highlighted the potential benefits of their involvement, while also pointing to the key finding that this would in itself not be 'the panacea for all ills or necessarily the route to empowering practice for all children or all families' (Bell and Wilson, 2006: 679). There will be numerous sets of circumstance where the actions you take as a social worker will contradict an individual's expressed desires, or will balance the competing preferences of users and carers, or when the evidence from other forms of knowledge would strongly suggest a course of action that a service user does not welcome. In such circumstances, the challenge will be to reach a solution that respects the desires of each individual even if it does not equate with that person's wishes (Beresford et al., 2007). We do not underestimate the skill that this will require!

Key learning points

This chapter has covered the following learning points:

✔ It has identified why the perspective of service users is essential in the development of social work services.

✔ It has examined service users' perceptions of social workers, focusing on what they have found to be more and less useful; it has noted that the quality of relationship between social worker and service user is particularly important.

✔ It has explored ways in which the relationship between social workers and service users could be improved, drawing on the perceptions of service users themselves.

✔ Through the medium of four case studies, it has identified some of the tensions that social workers will need to address in working productively with service users, focusing on their need to balance different priorities and forms of knowledge.

Further reading

Doel, M. and Best, L. (2008) *Experiencing Social Work: Learning From Service Users*, London: Sage. This practical text seeks to explore the positive benefits of social work, by focusing on examples where people have been helped by social work interventions.

Kemshall, H. and Littlechild, R. (eds) (2000) *User Involvement and Participation in Social Care: Research informing Practice*, London: Jessica Kingsley. A useful text that focuses on the potential for the engagement of service users in the research process.

Mayer, J. E. and Timms, N. (1970) *The Client Speaks: Working Class Impressions of Casework*, London: Routledge & Kegan Paul. The first extended example of research that focused on service users' perception of the social workers with whom they are engaged: it remains a classic text.

Rees, S. and Wallace, A. (1982) *Verdicts on Social Work*, London. Edward Arnold. As a summary of a range of user-focused research, this also remains a classic text, and its conclusions are still pertinent.

Social Work Education (2006) Themed issue: 'Service users and carers in social work education', 25 (4). An important ground-breaking achievement for an academic journal in the social work field: it was guest-edited by a collective of service users and educators, and all contributions contained the direct involvement of service users.

Warren, J. (2007) *Service User and Carer Participation in Social Work*, Exeter: Learning Matters. This book aims to provide an overview of the knowledge, attitude and skills that are needed by qualifying social workers.

 Useful websites

www.careleavers.com
The Care Leavers' Association is a not-for-profit organisation, run by care leavers for care leavers. Its aim is to end the economic and social disadvantage of those who were in care by achieving significant, positive change. It seeks to ensure that care leavers are fully represented and participating at all levels of economic, social and public life.

www.hearing-voices.org
The Hearing Voices Network offers information, support and understanding to people who hear voices and those who support them. It aims to raise awareness of voice hearing and other sensory experiences, to give men women and children who have these experiences an opportunity to talk freely about this together and to support anyone with these experiences. It seeks to achieve these aims through promoting, developing and supporting self-help groups, organising and delivering training sessions for health workers and the general public and providing opportunities for people to talk about their experiences.

www.nshn.co.uk
The aims and objectives of the National Self-Harm Network include the following: to support and empower people who self-harm; to provide information on matters relating to self-harm; to promote survivor-written literature; to challenge assumptions and demystify common misconceptions surrounding self-harm; to promote and advocate for the interests, needs and aspirations of people who self-harm; to influence social and health care policies at a local and national level; and to raise awareness among the general public, health services, hospitals and their staff of the needs of people who self-harm.

www.peoplefirstltd.com
As a national organisation, People First aims to help people with learning difficulties speak up for themselves, with help and support if needed; to work towards doing away with labels which affect our lives in a bad way; to make sure that all people with learning difficulties are respected; to make sure that people with learning difficulties have the same rights as everybody else and can access these rights; to promote the needs and concerns of people with learning difficulties; to ensure that people with learning difficulties are fully involved, at all stages, in the planning and development of the services they receive; to encourage and support the growth of People First and Speaking Up for Yourself groups; and to make sure that people with learning difficulties have the chance to take risks like everyone else.

www.shapingourlives.org.uk
Shaping Our Lives has a vision of a society which is equal and fair where all people have the same opportunities, choices, rights and responsibilities. In such a society people have choice and control over the way they live and the support services they use.

www.suresearch.org.uk
Suresearch aims to influence the quality, ethics of values of research and education in mental health services. The organisation comprises people who are users and/or survivors of mental health services and their allies.

www.scie.org.uk
Social Care Institute for Excellence (SCIE) has been very active in the development of user-centred knowledge for social work in England, and has a major role in relating to a range of service user groups. It has also overseen a range of important publications relating to many areas of social work and social care. In Scotland the equivalent body is called the Institute for Research and Innovation in Social Services (IRISS).

www.iriss.org.uk/
The mission of IRISS is defined as being to promote positive outcomes for the people who use Scotland's social services by enhancing the capacity and capability of the social services workforce to access and make use of knowledge and research for service innovation and improvement.

For additional cases and topic-organised, clickable links into additional media resources, including those produced by IRISS, visit **www.pearsoned.co.uk/wilsonruch**

Activity

In small groups, work together to identify the obstacles that might obstruct the establishment of effective relationships with individual service users. In addition, think through how you might combat these problems in practice. Draw on the five service users – Gina, May-Ann, Lucy, Kofi and Albert – identified in the case studies earlier in this chapter. In addition you should consider the circumstances of:

Meena: A 3-year-old girl, left orphaned after her parents (both of whom were of Pakistani origin) drowned in a ferry disaster.

Ray: A 25-year-old homeless street drinker, who lived in children's homes from the age of 11, and who has also experienced several short periods of custody.

Gloria: A 63-year-old African-Caribbean woman with a degenerative eye condition (glaucoma) that is progressively restricting her vision.

Chapter 15
Informal family carers

Professor Saul Becker

Chapter summary

This chapter is about social work with informal family carers. There are 5.8 million adults and children in the United Kingdom who are providing unpaid care to relatives and friends who are sick, disabled, elderly or have another need for care, support or supervision. Informal carers now have legal rights to assessments of their own needs and to services, and social workers have a responsibility to *identify*, *assess* and *support* carers. The chapter discusses what is meant by 'informal' care and the nature of the 'caring relationship' and examines the number and characteristics of adults and children who are carers, as well as their needs and the outcomes of caring. The chapter identifies those carers who are most vulnerable to ill health, stress, social exclusion and other negative outcomes of caring, and who are thus in potential need of social work support and interventions. This analysis is placed within the context of policy initiatives that have relied heavily on family members taking on the main provision of care in the community. The chapter discusses the services and interventions that can assist carers and the key roles and responsibilities for social workers. It also provides a review of the legislative context for social work with informal carers and identifies models of good practice.

Learning objectives

This chapter covers topics that will enable you to achieve the following learning objectives:

- To understand what is meant by informal care, informal carers and the caring relationship
- To understand the characteristics, extent, nature and outcomes of informal caring among adults, young adults and children who are carers
- To be familiar with the policy and legal context for social work assessments of the needs of adult and young carers and for planning and delivering services and support to them
- To be able to identify research-informed strategies for good social work practice in assessing and working with informal carers.

National Occupational Standards

This chapter will help you to meet the following National Occupational Standards:

Key Role 1: Prepare for, and work with individuals, families, carers, groups and communities to assess their needs and circumstances

Unit 1   Prepare for social work contact and involvement
Unit 2   Work with individuals, families, carers, groups and communities to help them make informed decisions
Unit 3   Assess needs and options to recommend a course of action for individuals, families, carers, groups and communities

Key Role 2: Plan, carry out, review and evaluate social work practice, with individuals, families, carers, groups, communities and other professionals

Unit 4   Respond to crisis situations
Unit 5   Interact with individuals, families, carers, groups and communities to achieve change and development and to improve life opportunities
Unit 6   Prepare, produce, implement and evaluate plans with individuals, families, carers, groups, communities and professional colleagues
Unit 7   Support the development of networks to meet assessed needs and planned outcomes

Key Role 3: Support individuals to represent their needs, views and circumstances

Unit 10   Advocate with, and on behalf of, individuals, families, carers, groups and communities
Unit 11   Prepare for, and participate in decision making forums

Key Role 4: Manage risk to individuals, families, carers, groups, communities, self and colleagues

Unit 12   Assess and manage risks to individuals, families, carers, groups and communities

Key Role 6: Demonstrate professional competence in social work practice

Unit 18   Research, analyse, evaluate, and use current knowledge of best social work practice
Unit 19   Work within agreed standards of social work practice and ensure own professional development
Unit 20   Manage complex ethical issues, dilemmas and conflicts
Unit 21   Contribute to the promotion of best social work practice

Case study

Maggie

Sam, a newly qualified social worker, is visiting Maggie, aged 36. Maggie has been referred to Sam for a carer's assessment. During the assessment interview Sam learns that Maggie has lived with and cared for her mother, Julia, who has Alzheimer's disease, for almost four years. Julia had been assessed separately by another social worker a year earlier, but has become increasingly frail and vulnerable in recent times and now needs help with all physical and personal tasks. Maggie also ensures that her mother's medicine is taken and manages the household finances. Sam learns that Maggie provides '24 hour care' in that she needs to be available whenever her mum requires assistance and to 'keep an eye' on her, as well as doing all the household tasks and personal care. As such, Maggie reports that she often loses sleep because of anxiety and Julia waking up in the night and is finding the caring role to be increasingly tiring and stressful. Sam can see that Maggie's own health is not good – she looks very tired and is on the edge of crying throughout the assessment. Twenty minutes into the assessment a young boy enters the room. Maggie tells Sam that the boy is her son, Richard, aged 12, returning home from school. Maggie had said nothing beforehand about Richard but Sam now wonders whether Richard also has to provide care for Julia, and whether Richard may be drawn into caring for his mother, Maggie, if her own health and well-being continue to deteriorate.

Who is the carer in this household? Is it conceivable that Richard might be a carer for his grandmother and for his mother?

What should Sam do now?

If you were the social worker involved in the case study, your role would require you to undertake an assessment of Maggie's needs and her ability to continue to provide care. You would also need to consider whether Richard is a 'young carer' and whether he may also need support in his own right as a child and as a carer. To achieve these goals you would need to know about the legislative and policy framework for conducting carers' assessments, 'good practice' in this area, as well as have some knowledge and understanding about who carers are, what they do, and what the impacts and longer-term outcomes are of caring on carers themselves. Knowing about the research evidence on informal care and carers – including those carers who are most vulnerable to ill health, stress and social exclusion – will help you to *recognise* informal carers in their diverse forms and circumstances, and *sensitise* you to indicators of carer distress and those situations where social work interventions could be beneficial. This chapter introduces you to the research-informed knowledge base required for good social work practice with informal carers.

Introduction

Social work and social care practice with vulnerable families, particularly those where there is illness, disability, mental ill health, alcohol or substance misuse, and domestic violence, requires a professional social work engagement not just with the person with care needs (as other chapters in this volume show), but also with family members who take on unpaid caring roles – referred to in the United Kingdom as 'informal carers'. An official definition of informal carers is, 'people who look after a relative or friend who needs support because of age, physical or learning disability or illness, including mental illness' (Department of Health, 2005a). This 'looking after' (or 'special help' as it is sometimes referred to) can be in the forms of *active support, social interaction* or *supervision*. For example, many informal carers provide personal care and monitor medication, but they generally devote most time to practical care tasks including shopping and laundry. Large numbers can also provide company and keep an eye on the person with care needs (supervision).

In many families the informal carer is an adult, but in some families the carer will be a child or young person aged under 18 – a 'young carer' as they are now commonly referred to in the United Kingdom. Here we define young carers as

'children and young persons under 18 who provide or intend to provide care, assistance or support to another family member. They carry out, often on a regular basis, significant or substantial caring tasks and assume a level of responsibility that would usually be associated with an adult. The person receiving care is often a parent but can be a sibling, grandparent or other relative who is disabled, has some chronic illness, mental health problem or other condition connected with a need for care, support or supervision.'

(Becker, 2000a: 378)

As a social worker it is important that you are able to recognise and identify the needs of informal carers of any age, race, gender, sexuality, in any circumstances, especially 'heavily involved' and vulnerable carers, *alongside* the needs of the person who is receiving their care. Social workers need to understand what it is that carers do in the home and be able to identify the outcomes of caring on the carer's own health, well-being, social participation and opportunities. Social workers also need to be able to plan and deliver the services and support that will help carers the most.

Unfortunately, there is considerable research evidence to show that informal carers are often 'forgotten' or 'ignored' by social workers and other health and social care professionals, who can focus their attention, interventions and support on ill, disabled or elderly people and others with care needs, often neglecting the *needs* and *rights* of carers. As you can see in the Closer Look box, carers now have legal rights to assessments, information, services and support, and social workers have a responsibility under the law to inform carers of these rights and to conduct assessments and plan interventions. In other words, working with carers is not an optional 'extra' or 'luxury' for social workers.

Supporting carers is also a matter of social justice as well as sensible economics. Carers should be able to have a quality of life for themselves over and above their caring responsibilities (HM Government, 2008a). If they were to 'stop' caring, then the costs to the state of taking on their caring responsibilities would be enormous. It has been calculated by Carers UK that the annual cost of the 'hidden' contribution by the United Kingdom's adult carers is £87 billion, a similar cost to the NHS itself. Thus, social workers have a responsibility to help to identify and meet the needs of carers and to support them in their caring role. As well as being a matter of rights and social justice, this is also a sound investment.

The Closer Look box shows that carers have clear legal rights and that local authorities and social workers have responsibilities to meet carers' needs and promote

Carers' rights – the legal framework for social work practice

Carers can be jointly assessed alongside the person with care needs under the NHS and Community Care Act 1990 and the Carers (Recognition and Services) Act 1995.

The **NHS and Community Care Act 1990** establishes the legislative framework for the restructuring of both the NHS and the community care system. Section 47(1) places a duty on local authorities to carry out an assessment of an individual's needs for community care services and promotes the need for a carer's assessment as good practice.

The **Carers (Recognition and Services) Act 1995** gives carers of *any* age – including young carers – the right to an assessment of their 'ability to provide and to continue to provide care'. Social services are required (if so requested by a carer) to carry out this assessment of the carer at the same time as it assesses or reassesses the person for whom care is provided (the carers' assessment is therefore linked to the cared-for persons' assessment). The Act applies to carers who 'provide a substantial amount of care on a regular basis'. Circular LAC (96) 7 (DoH, 1996a) states: 'it is for local authorities to form their own judgement about what amounts to "regular" and "substantial" care'. Carers who do not provide substantial or regular care should also have their views and interests taken into account when an assessment is undertaken. 'Care' includes physical caring tasks as well as emotional care and general attendance to ensure the service user comes to no harm.

Under the 1995 Act, local authorities are legally obliged to take into account the results of this assessment when making decisions about any services to be provided for the person with care needs. However, the Act did not carry with it any additional resources for social care authorities in terms of implementation, or for meeting carers' needs or for providing services directly to carers.

The **Employment Relations Act 1999** gives employees (including those who are carers) the right to 'reasonable time off' to deal with emergencies.

The **Carers and Disabled Children Act 2000** gives family carers over the age of 16 (and caring for someone over the age of 18) specific rights:

- Carers may request an assessment of their own needs, even if the person receiving care does not wish to have an assessment

- Local authorities may provide services for carers in their own right
- Carers may receive vouchers for short-term breaks
- Carers may receive direct payments in lieu of services for which they have been assessed.

The Practice Guidance to the Act (DoH, 2001d) sets out to promote services and other provisions that are designed to sustain the caring relationship in a manner that is in the interests of all parties. Support for carers is essential to their own well-being and also to the well-being of their relatives with care needs. The Guidance (para. 70) advises adult social care departments to grade the 'extent of risk to the sustainability of the caring role' into one of four categories: critical, substantial, moderate or low. The grading system is a formal determination of the degree to which a carer's ability to sustain the role is compromised or threatened either in the present or in the foreseeable future by the absence of appropriate support. If the result of a carer's assessment indicate that the carer has needs which pose a risk to the sustainability of their caring role, the local authority has a duty to consider whether or not to provide services to the carer, without fettering its discretion. Carers should receive the support that they feel is most appropriate to their needs. In some cases, a cash payment in lieu of services ('direct payments') may be more appropriate so that carers can make their own arrangements and pay someone of their own choosing. Local authorities are able to charge for services that are provided directly to carers, subject to a test of means. Young carers under the age of 16 will need to access assessments and services through the 1995 Carers (Recognition and Services) Act or the 1989 Children Act (as children in need under Section 17).

The **Employment Act 2002** establishes the right to request flexible working arrangements for employed parents of disabled children under the age of 18.

In Scotland, the **Community Care and Health Scotland Act 2002** introduced new rights for carers. The Act made provision for the right to a carer's assessment which was independent of the person being cared for. It also placed a duty on local authorities and the NHS to inform carers of their rights. Local authorities are also required to recognise the care being provided by a carer and to take into account the views of a carer when deciding what services to offer to the person being cared for. Underpinning this legislation is the principle that informal unpaid family carers are to be treated as 'key partners' in providing care.

▶

The **Carers (Equal Opportunities) Act 2004** came into force on 1 April 2005. This Act made three main changes to the law with the objective of providing further support for carers and helping to ensure that they are not placed at a disadvantage because of the care they provide. First, the Act requires local authorities to inform carers, in certain circumstances, that they may be entitled to an assessment under the 1995 and 2000 Acts (see above). Secondly, when undertaking a carer's assessment, the local authority must consider whether the carer works, undertakes any form of education, training or leisure activity, or wishes to do any of those things. Thirdly, the Act provides for cooperation between local authorities and other bodies in relation to the planning and provision of services that are relevant to carers (HM Government, 2004, para. 10). This applies to adult and young carers.

The **Work and Families Act 2006** extends the right to request flexible working arrangements to all carers in paid employment.

The **Childcare Act 2006** places a duty on local authorities to provide sufficient childcare for working parents 'which includes provision suitable for disabled children'.

The **Pensions Act 2007** reduces the number of qualifying years carers need for a full basic state pension; introduces a new Carers Credit for those caring 20+ hours a week for someone who is severely disabled. The **Equality Act 2010** brings disability, sex, race and other grounds of discrimination (including discrimination by association, for example those with caring responsibilities) within one piece of legislation and also makes changes to the law.

those rights. However, you may be surprised to know that only a small proportion of carers (around 10 to 20 per cent) have ever had a social work or any other assessment of their needs. This is partly because professionals can fail to recognise and identify carers. You will see later in the chapter that carers are not a homogeneous group. Some carers, as we have said, are children or young adults. Others are very elderly and very frail themselves, often in poor health. Some carers are disabled people who care for other family members. Carers come in all shapes and sizes, and as a social worker you need to be sensitive to the diverse range of people who are informal carers and the diverse range of circumstances in which they live. For example, some people would find it hard to believe that Richard, in the case study above, could be a carer for both his mother *and* his grandmother when he is just 12 years of age. Many young carers complain that social workers fail to recognise their contribution, but many adult carers also report that they are offered no help or support in their caring role. The evidence presented in this chapter should make you alert to the experiences and needs of carers of *all* ages and circumstances so that you will be able to *recognise* and then *support* them.

The aim of the first half of the chapter is to give you as a social worker the knowledge base to help you to *recognise* informal carers and to be able to *identify* situations and circumstances where carers are experiencing negative outcomes which impact on their own health, well-being, development, social participation and opportunities. Thus, in this first part we provide an overview of what is meant by informal care and we report the best

available statistical and research evidence on the characteristics, nature, extent and outcomes of informal caregiving by adult and young carers. The second part of the chapter is concerned with social work practice, particularly *assessments* of carers and the identification of *outcomes* and *services* that carers want and need in order to promote their own health and well-being and to support their capacity to continue as a carer.

Reflect

Why should social workers support informal carers?

Do carers have rights? If so, what are these rights and what are social workers' responsibilities?

A mixed economy of community care

Think ahead

Think about your own family. What would happen if someone became seriously ill or disabled? Whose responsibility would it be to look after them? Why? How might this affect all members of your family?

In the Think Ahead feature, you may have started to think about the relationship between individuals,

Early days: how did we get here?

Griffiths and the recognition of family carers

Historically, carers have held an ambiguous and uncertain position within social and health-care systems. Up until relatively recently, carers had rarely been the focus of specific health or social work interventions; they had traditionally not been defined as the 'client', 'service user' or 'patient', and carers had seen their needs placed secondary (if ranked at all) to the needs of the specified client – the ill or disabled family member. However, since the mid-1980s the input of carers has been increasingly recognised as being a critical factor in maintaining vulnerable older and disabled people in the community, with or without formal (paid) professional support.

The implementation in 1993 of a new system for community care was the outcome of more than four decades of politics, debate and reformulation of policy responses to the health and social care needs of older people and those with physical and mental impairments. The belief that it is better to maintain people in their own home, rather than in institutions, had been the guiding principle of community care policy since the 1950s. A belief in the humanitarian value of home-based or community living had been coupled with a persuasive critique of the failings of institutions for people with physical impairments, those with mental health problems or learning difficulties, elderly people and the poor in general (Becker, 1997).

The Griffiths Report (Griffiths, 1988) was a catalyst in recognising the contribution of family carers, and it set the foundation for the system of community care that we have in place today. Having established where the prime responsibility for community care should rest, the report went on to highlight what relatively minor players statutory services actually were in the overall provision of community care:

'Publicly provided services constitute only a small part of the total care provided to people in need. Families, friends, neighbours and other local people provide the majority of care in response to needs which they are uniquely well placed to identify and respond to. This will be the primary means by which people are enabled to live normal lives in community settings'.

(Griffiths, 1988, para. 3.2)

In recognition of the major contribution made by informal carers, Griffiths proposed that the publicly funded services such as health and social care should operate in new ways:

'The proposals take as their major starting point that this is as it should be, and that the first task of publicly provided services is to support and where possible strengthen these networks of carers. Public services can help by identifying such actual and potential carers, consulting them about their needs and those of the people they are caring for and tailoring the provision of extra services (if required) accordingly'. (para. 3.2)

The ensuing White Paper, *Caring for People*, published in November 1989, continued the approach of the Griffiths Report. One of the key objectives of the White Paper was 'to ensure that service providers make practical support for carers a high priority' (HM Government, 1989, para. 1.1). It went on to say:

'While this White Paper focuses largely on the role of statutory and independent bodies in the provision of community care services, the reality is that most care is provided by family, friends and neighbours. The majority of carers take on these responsibilities willingly, but the government recognises that many need help to be able to manage what can become a heavy burden. Their lives could be made much easier if the right support is there at the right time, and a key responsibility of the statutory service providers should be to do all they can to assist and support carers. Helping carers to maintain their valuable contribution to the spectrum of care is both right and a sound investment. Help may take the form of providing advice and support as well as practical services such as day, domiciliary and respite care'. (para. 2.3)

Up until the Griffiths Report there was little public discussion of how best to support carers, and even less discussion about the tensions between the needs of carers and the person(s) for whom they care. The Griffiths Report, and the subsequent White Paper and guidance, confirmed family carers as the cornerstone of care in the community, but failed to give them any legal entitlements to assessments or to services in their own right. It took a few more years – till 1995 – for carers to get legal entitlement to an *assessment*, and then till the twenty-first century before they had any legal rights to *services* (see the Closer Look box on p. 429 for an overview of carers' legal rights).

families and the state, in terms of *whose* responsibility it is to provide care to ill or disabled people, or for those who are frail and elderly. The boundary between the state, the family and other sectors of care (such as voluntary or private sector providers of services) is a blurred one. There is no consensus where the contribution of the family ends and the responsibility of the state begins. Nor is there agreement where the contribution of the state ends and where the responsibility of the family begins. Between different countries the balance between the state, family and other sectors of care varies considerably (Becker et al., 1998: 78–103). In the United Kingdom there is a 'mixed economy of care' (Powell, 2007), with the state, family, voluntary organisations and private (for profit) agencies providing a 'patch-work quilt' of services to people with care needs (such as older people and those with physical impairments) and, more recently, to support informal family carers. It has been suggested that 'there is a need for increased clarity in overall policy on the role and responsibilities of the state, family and individuals (which affect the perceptions of potential carers)' (Wanless, 2006: 150).

Law and government policy has increasingly emphasised the intention that frail elderly people, disabled people, those with mental health problems and others with health and social care-related needs should stay in their own homes for as long as possible. 'Care in the community' (or 'community care' as it has often been called, rather than care within institutions or in residential settings) has been a central aim of social policy and social work for many decades, and health and social care agencies, and social workers, play a key role in trying to make this a reality. Care in the community, however, relies heavily on the contribution of informal carers. The Closer Look box outlines policy changes, most notably the 1988 Griffiths Report and subsequent White Paper, that have led to family carers being recognised as the *main* providers of 'care in the community'.

Informal care and the caring relationship

The Closer Look box shows how policy makers in the 1980s reconceptualised the relationship between family carers and professionals in health and social care. Informal carers were to be seen as the *primary* means by which vulnerable people would be enabled to live in the community, with professionals (including social workers) and publicly provided services taking on the role of *supporting* and *strengthening* networks of informal carers (Griffiths, 1988, para. 3.2). A clear distinction is being made in these policy documents between informal and formal (professional) caregiving: for example, the care provided by a social worker, nurse, care assistant or nursery worker. Informal care, unlike formal care, is founded on an *unpaid*, non-professional 'caring relationship' between a family carer and the person for whom they care. This care is personally directed and is given free of charge by virtue of an established relationship based on love, attachment, family obligation, duty or friendship. The caring relationship has both a *social* element (there is a bond or attachment of some sort) as well as a *physical* element (certain tasks or responsibilities are undertaken by one for or with the other). While some of these elements can be found in formal (professional, paid for) relationships, it is the unpaid nature of informal care and the 'caring relationship' that primarily distinguishes informal care and informal carers from other forms of caregiving or from other care providers. This is not to say that the unpaid caring relationship is always a happy one, free from tension or difficulties – indeed, far from it. There is considerable research evidence to show that the caring relationship can be difficult for both sides, and that the outcomes for carers can often include impaired health and well-being (including mental ill health), isolation, poverty and social exclusion. These outcomes are discussed later in the chapter.

It is important to acknowledge that many carers do not recognise themselves as 'carers': rather, they see themselves as sons, daughters, fathers, mothers, husbands, wives, partners, brothers, sisters or friends. The largest group of informal carers is 'filial' carers: that is, adult children and children-in-law caring for parents. As such, many carers view their actions as extensions of family or personal relations, based on an unwritten 'intergenerational contract', rather than as a distinct type of 'caregiving'. Because many carers do not identify themselves as 'carers', social workers may sometimes need to help carers to recognise themselves as carers and their own caring roles, and how these impact on the carers' well-being and health. If carers need or want support in their caring role then they need to first recognise that they are carers and to be aware that there is support available for them. Social workers have an important part to play here.

This ambivalence about the title of 'carer' is as much the case for many children who are carers as it is for adult carers. It has taken longer for children (under age 18) who are carers and for young adult carers aged 18–24 to be recognised in social policy, law and social work practice. The 1988 Griffiths Report and 1989 White Paper discussed in the Closer Look box had nothing to say about younger carers because at that time young carers were not seen or recognised by academics, researchers or policy makers. However, that position changed as the research evidence base grew and more studies were published about this 'hidden' group of carers. The Closer Look box below outlines how young carers and young adult carers became increasingly recognised in policy and law.

While there is a high degree of acceptance and legitimacy in older adults being involved in caring for other family members, where children are carers the situation is more challenging. Young carers, by being under the age of 18, are legally defined as children and young people and, as such, are not expected (or encouraged) to take on significant or substantial unpaid caring roles or responsibilities. When they do, and when these roles come to the attention of social workers, or social care,

health and education professionals, then they can become a cause for concern because, for example, of educational problems, child welfare concerns, children's poor health or safeguarding issues, etc. While adult carers can be seen to be conforming to individual, societal and familial norms in supporting family members, when children act as unpaid carers they can transgress, or certainly challenge, such norms in the United Kingdom and in other developed *and* developing countries (Becker, 2007). As the Closer Look box shows, the significant growth in dedicated young carers projects from just a handful in the early 1990s to around 350 today reflects the growing academic, political and social concern to identify and respond to the needs of children who take on caring roles within the family. The recognition of carers aged 18–24 has, however, been slower.

Reflect

Is it acceptable for adults to be carers? Why?

Is it acceptable for children to be carers? Why?

A closer look

The growing recognition of young carers under 18 and young adult carers aged 18–24

Across the United Kingdom, social policy, law and social work practice with young carers under the age of 18 have evolved and developed in a symbiotic relationship with the growing research evidence about the extent, nature and outcomes of children's caregiving. Prior to the 1990s, academics, researchers, policy makers and social welfare professionals had failed to recognise, account for and respond to children's informal caring within the family. The earliest studies of young carers can be traced back to the late 1980s (and these were very small-scale), although more academic and focused qualitative research examining the specific experiences of young carers started in the early 1990s. The dozens of studies and publications by the Young Carers Research Group at Loughborough University are especially important, as this work forms a body of qualitative and quantitative research evidence that spans more than a decade and

has informed academic thinking, policy and legal developments and social work practice in a number of countries (Becker, 2007).

Media interest in research outputs and the general experiences of young carers, particularly half a dozen television documentaries, helped to fuel public awareness and interest and further academic enquiry. But a critical role in developing the research agenda, and then the policy and practice agendas, was played by national non-governmental organisations, namely Carers UK (formerly Carers National Association), the Children's Society, The Princess Royal Trust for Carers, Barnardos and Crossroads Care, all of which funded research and helped to inform and influence the development of law and policy guidance, sometimes directly by drafting the documentation. Key individuals within these organisations, and a few Members of Parliament, all with an interest in and commitment towards young carers, also played an important part. Young carers themselves took a role in lobbying MPs and policy makers, politicised and helped by these carers and children's organisations.

▶

Between the early 1990s and today, young carers were 'well and truly placed on the map of child welfare services' (Newman, 2002: 614). From just a handful of young carers projects in the early 1990s, there are now over 350 dedicated projects across the United Kingdom in contact with around 30,000 young carers and employing hundreds of workers as well as many volunteers. Young carers have various legal rights secured over a number of years (see the Closer Look box, p. 429). Many young carers would also be considered as 'children in need' under children's legislation and they and their families would have rights to appropriate support. The Government's two National Carers Strategies (HM Government, 1999, 2008a) both have a chapter dedicated to young carers. The 2008 National Carers Strategy sets out the (then) Government's agenda and vision for supporting *all* carers, including more short breaks for carers; help towards supporting carers to enter or re-enter the labour market; and a package of programmes to support young carers. It also commits to more integrated and personalised support services for carers, although the new coalition government in 2010, and a period of austerity measures, may well threaten some of these commitments.

Additionally, young carers are referred to in much social care and health related guidance, in education circulars, in inter-professional guidance, and in various National Service Frameworks (see Aldridge and Becker, 2003: 175–98, and Bibby and Becker, 2000, for a review of relevant policy and law). However, despite these established rights and a relatively comprehensive legal and policy framework, there are still gaps and weaknesses. For example, most young carers have never had a formal assessment of their needs or ability to care and the vast majority are not in contact with any dedicated support provision. Moreover, the legal framework for young carers, by comprising carers and children's legislation and a wide range of guidance, is complex and confusing to many social work and social welfare professionals and can serve to exclude some young carers (for example, those under the age of 16 have no legal right to services in their own right *as carers*, only as children in need).

Until around 2008, however, there had not been a parallel development in terms of research, policy or practice for 'young adult carers'. These are carers aged 18–24. Essentially this group has remained 'hidden' until recently, too 'old' to be regarded as 'children' and 'too young' to be regarded as 'adult' carers.

Those providing services and interventions to young carers were increasingly concerned that support for young carers ceased when they turned 18 years because of the demarcation in the provision of children's and adult services, leaving young adult carers without appropriate support at a time when they faced major decisions and life challenges concerning their own futures. Furthermore, the evidence base in the UK and overseas concerning young adult carers was weak. In 2007/8 The Princess Royal Trust for Carers commissioned a study to explore the needs, experiences and service responses for young adult carers in Britain (Becker and Becker, 2009). The analysis identified that there are 290,000 carers aged 18–24 years in the UK with a quarter providing care for more than 20 hours per week. An active dissemination strategy of the research findings was devised and this enabled the research findings to become widely available to policy makers and practitioners within a very short timeframe. The launch of the research report in 2009 included national TV and radio interviews; coverage in professional journals and presentations at national conferences and seminars for policy makers and professionals. The report was made available to download from the website of the then Department for Children, Schools and Families (now Department for Education). The findings were also presented at an invited seminar to launch the National Young Carers Coalition in the Houses of Parliament in 2010 attended by members of both Houses, Ministers, senior policy makers, service providers and young adult carers themselves.

The research has had a very quick impact on policy-making and service development. In 2010, the Scottish Government was using the research to inform the development of their carers strategy. Meanwhile many English and Scottish local authorities have developed strategic plans to address the needs of this group of carers for the first time. Across the UK local service providers (e.g. local authorities, carers centres and third sector young carers projects) are citing the research as the basis for securing funding in order to develop new services for young adult carers. Several new services, albeit with short-term funding, are now in operation to deliver support and advice to young adult carers with the intention of improving outcomes for them and their families.

Reflect

What are the main factors and developments that helped to raise public, political and social awareness of young carers during the 1990s and young adult carers in the late 2000s?

Why should social workers be concerned about young carers and young adult carers?

Reciprocity and interdependence in the caring relationship

The Closer Look box shows the extent to which young carers and young adult carers have become recognised in law, policy and practice during the past two decades. However, the developments for young carers in particular have not been universally welcomed. Within the young carers literature, there has been a forceful critique arguing against the notion that children who are caring for disabled parents have become their 'parent's parent', and that disabled parents have become their children's dependants (Keith and Morris, 1995; Olsen, 1996; Olsen and Parker, 1997; Newman, 2002; Wates, 2002). The Social Model of Disability (see Chapter 19) has challenged the very language and ideology of 'care', arguing that notions of 'dependency' and 'caregiving' misrepresent and misunderstand both the needs of disabled people and their relationship with adult and young carers and with social workers and professional service providers (Morris, 1991, 1993; Keith and Morris, 1995). This is graphically illustrated in some families, for example, where disabled people are also carers themselves. The 2001 Census (ONS, 2003) shows that while there are nearly two million people aged 16–74 who are permanently sick or disabled in England and Wales, over a quarter of a million of these actually provide care to other relatives and 105,000 provide 50 or more hours of informal care per week. Similarly, 260,000 informal carers who are providing 50 or more hours of care per week state they are 'not in good health' themselves, and this group is likely to need health and social care support in their own right from professionals outside the family – the formal care sector. In other words, these carers can also be receivers of *formal* care support at the same time as they are providers of informal care.

This suggests that the traditional distinction between 'carer' and 'cared-for person' (and all the assumptions of dependency that can go along with this) are hard to sustain in theory and in practice when, as we have seen above, so many people both give and take help (from different sources, informal and formal) simultaneously. The relationship between those who receive care and those who provide it is also rarely or simply 'one-sided' (with one person 'giving' and the other 'receiving' care). There is often an element of *reciprocity* and *interdependence* involved, an 'intergenerational contract', whereby both sides 'give and take', including helping each other with household tasks, household finances, supervision of children, keeping an eye on each other, and so on (Becker and Silburn, 1999; Evans and Becker, 2009).

Social workers need to be alert to the fact that some ill or disabled people can also be informal carers and some informal carers can also be very young, very old, ill or disabled people themselves. People do not always 'fit' neatly into clearly defined categories, and as a social worker you will need to work out and understand the complex arrangements and circumstances that exist in families, rather than make assumptions about who is the 'carer' and who is the 'cared for' person. Think about the 'whole family', and how people's *needs* and *rights* interact. You may want to look again now at the case study at the start of this chapter in the light of the section above, and consider how the needs and rights of Julia, Maggie and Richard are interdependent and what Sam, the social worker, should do about this. Alternatively, look at the case study below, on Michael and Janine, to consider the elements of reciprocity and interdependence in the caring relationship and what social work support they might need.

Case study

Michael and Janine

Michael is French and aged 76 years old. He has lived in the United Kingdom for over 50 years. He cares for his wife, Janine, who is physically disabled and suffering from chronic illness. While Michael has provided substantial and regular care for his wife for over 10 years, the level and type of care he provides has recently altered greatly. Michael can no longer offer support in the same way because of his own deteriorating mental health and associated physical problems. Michael has become increasingly anxious and does not like to be left alone. A social work assessment was carried out as a result of Michael not being able to provide the same level of care. This assessment was triggered by a hospital admission and the necessary changes to Janine's care package when he was not there to care.

Janine is in her mid-60s. While she has been receiving substantial and regular care from Michael, she is now also his carer. Her husband's mental health has deteriorated over the past two years and he now needs considerable support and assistance in everyday tasks. Because of her own illness and impairments, Janine now relies on her husband to carry out physical tasks on her behalf, such as making drinks and helping her with her medication. While Janine is able to offer emotional support to her husband, this is dependent on support she in turn receives, including morning visits from outside agencies to help her out of bed.

What do you think are the elements of reciprocity and interdependence in this caring relationship?

Whom should social workers help, and why?

The knowledge base for recognising and identifying carers – what we know

Think ahead

As a social worker, why do you think it is important for you to know about the number of carers, their characteristics and the evidence about the outcomes of caring?

In the section above we have seen how the unpaid caring relationship is at the heart of what we understand by 'informal care', and that this relationship often involves elements of reciprocity and interdependence rather than simply being based on 'give or take'. We have also seen in the three Closer Look boxes above how adult carers (in the 1980s) and then young carers (in the 1990s) and young adult carers (in the late 2000s) have been recognised in policy, law and practice, and how informal carers of all ages now have legal rights to assessments and to services and support.

In the sections below we give an indication of how widespread informal care is among adults, young adults and young carers; we show what carers do in the home; and we outline the impacts and outcomes of caregiving

on carers' own development, health and well-being. The aim here is to give you as social workers the knowledge base to help you to *recognise* informal carers and to be able to *identify* situations and circumstances where carers are experiencing negative outcomes which impact on their own health, well-being, development and opportunities. This knowledge base is the foundation on which social workers will be alerted to the diversity of carers' experiences and will help you to make sound professional judgments about carers' needs and the interventions that will help them most, based on reliable research evidence.

Reliable sources of data

There are a range of sources of data on the extent of informal caring in the United Kingdom, including British Household Panel Surveys (Hirst, 1999), the 1985–2000 General Household Surveys of Carers (Maher and Green, 2002), the 2001 Census (ONS, 2003) and other sources from one-off large-scale surveys conducted by organisations such as Carers UK and The Princess Royal Trust for Carers. The 2001 Census included for the first time a question about whether people 'looked after or gave any help or support to family members, friends, neighbours or others because of long-term physical or mental ill-health or disability or problems related to old age'. An advantage of using the 2001 Census over and above other government sources such as the General Household Survey of Carers is that it provides data by every local authority on the number of adult *and* young carers, the amount of care that they provide (hours per week), and is based on a ten-yearly survey of *all* households in the United Kingdom. This is a source we use extensively in this chapter although we draw on other surveys and qualitative research findings where appropriate to illustrate the extent, nature and outcomes of unpaid caring.

Numbers

The overall picture from the 2001 Census shows that there are over 5.8 million carers (or around 10 per cent of the total population) who are carers in the United Kingdom (Table 15.1). Of these, around 5.7 million are carers aged 18 or over, and 175,000 are carers under the age of 18 (see Tables 15.2 and 15.4 for data specifically on young carers).

The peak age for caring is 50 to 59 years. Women are more likely to become a carer than men. Women have a fifty-fifty chance of providing care by the time they are 59, men by the time they reach the age of 74. Three in

Table 15.1 Number of carers (all ages) in the United Kingdom, as a percentage of total population, and number (and %) providing 50 hours or more care per week

Country	Number of carers	% of total population	Number of carers providing 50+ hours of care per week	% of all providing 50+ hours carers of care per week
England	4,877,060	10	998,732	20
Northern Ireland	185,086	11	46,912	25
Scotland	481,579	10	115,674	24
Wales	340,745	11	89,604	26
UK total	5,884,470	10	1,250,922	21

(*Source*: ONS (2003) Census 2001. Figures taken from separate country reports, compiled by Carers UK (2003))

Table 15.2 Number and proportion of children under 18 who are carers in the United Kingdom, by country and hours caring per week

Country	Number caring for 1–19 hours	Number caring for 20–49 hours	Number caring for 50+ hours	Total number caring	Proportion who provide informal care
England	116,823	12,284	10,092	139,199	1.7%
Wales	8,854	1,029	861	10,744	2.2%
Scotland	13,511	1,826	1,364	16,701	2.1%
Northern Ireland	6,666	974	712	8,352	2.5%
Total number of young carers in the United Kingdom	145,854	16,113	13,029	174,996	2.1% (UK average)
Total number as % of all young carers in the United Kingdom	83%	9%	8%	100%	

(*Source*: Calculated by the author from Office for National Statistics (2003) Census 2001 data, in Becker, 2007: 23–50)

five people will become a carer at some point in their lives (Parker et al., 2010).

The Census also shows that many carers are in paid employment: three million adult carers are in paid work and these carers account for one in eight of the total workforce. Two hundred thousand carers work full-time while providing 50 hours of care per week. As a social worker you will need to remember that many informal carers can also be trying to hold down a paid job at the same time as caring for someone. Indeed, you will need to consider the carer's wishes about paid work as part of any assessment under the Carers (Equal Opportunities) Act 2004 that is outlined in the Closer Look box above.

Table 15.1 also shows the number of carers who are providing the longest hours of informal care per week – 50 hours or more. There are just over 1.2 million carers (of whom 13,029 are children – see Table 15.2) who provide more than 50 hours of care each week. This represents about one-fifth of all adult carers and 8 per cent of young carers. In many families the full-time adult carer will be a parent (or parents) who are looking after their ill or disabled child(ren). Often this caring relationship will continue into, and throughout, the child's own adult life and well into the carer's (parent's) own old age. In other families the full-time carer will be a spouse or partner caring for another partner. Elsewhere,

Table 15.3 Number and proportion of young adult carers aged 18–24 in the United Kingdom, by country and hours caring per week

	Number caring for 1–19 hours	Number caring for 20–49 hours	Number caring for 50+ hours	Total number caring	Proportion of this age group who provide informal care
England	140,903	22,547	21,571	185,021	4.8%
Wales	9,675	1,697	1,690	13,062	5.7%
Scotland	15,417	3,203	2,495	21,115	5.0%
N Ireland	7,254	1,681	1,185	10,120	5.5%
Total number of young adult carers in UK	173,249	29,128	26,941	229,318	5.3% (UK average)
Total as % of all young adult carers in UK	75%	13%	12%	100%	

(*Source*: Calculated by the author from Office for National Statistics (2003) Census 2001 data, in Becker and Becker, 2008: 18)

the full-time carer will be an adult caring for their elderly parent(s).

Secondary analysis of Census 2001 data (Becker and Becker, 2008) shows the number of young adult carers aged 18–24 in the four nations of the UK (Table 15.3). In total, there are 229,318 young adult carers in the UK, and this is 5.3 per cent of all people in that age group. However, this varies between the four UK nations, with the highest levels of young adult caring being in Wales (where someone aged 18–24 has a 5.7 per cent probability of being a carer), compared to England (4.8 per cent). This regional variation is likely to reflect different levels of illness, disability, geography and need across the four UK nations, and also differences in the availability of local health and social care services and support for ill and disabled people, and for carers. Table 15.3 also shows that one-quarter of all young adult carers in the UK (56,069 people) are providing care for more than 20 hours per week and almost 27,000 of these (12 per cent of the total) are providing care for more than 50 hours each week.

Young carers under 18

In the United Kingdom there are almost three million children under the age of 16 (equivalent to 23 per cent of all children) who live in households where one family member is hampered in daily activities by a chronic physical or mental health problem, illness or disability. However, only a small proportion of these children and young people will become young carers to the extent or nature captured in the definition of a young carer given in the introduction to this chapter (Becker, 2000a: 378). Most children do not become young carers because there are other family members available to provide care, or because families receive social work or other professional support or services, thus reducing the need for children to take on caring roles.

The 2001 Census shows that 175,000 children provide some level of unpaid care to other family members. This is approximately 6 per cent of children who live in families with illness and disability. Table 15.2 above shows the number and proportion of children who provide unpaid care in the four countries that constitute the UK. So, for example, there are 29,142 children in the United Kingdom who provide more than 20 hours of care per week, and 13,029 of these provide more than 50 hours of unpaid care work per week. There are small variations between the four UK nations, with the highest concentration of children who are carers to be found in Northern Ireland, with 2.5 per cent of *all* children aged 5–17 being involved in caring. Overall, across the United Kingdom, 2.1 per cent of *all* children are young carers (Table 15.2). These figures and proportions are *minimums* rather than maximums because of limitations inherent within the Census questions and methodology. The Census figures rely on parents' self-reporting their children's caring roles, and thus the data are not likely to adequately identify or count children in some caring

Table 15.4 Number and proportion of children who are carers in the United Kingdom, by age and hours caring per week

Age	1–19 hours	20–49 hours	50+ hours	Total number	Total %
0–4	0	0	0	0	0
5–7	5,015	608	940	6,563	4
8–9	7,717	752	1,055	9,524	5
10–11	16,120	1,433	1,615	19,168	11
12–14	46,267	4,103	3,519	53,889	31
15	21,024	2,282	1,494	24,800	14
16–17	49,711	6,935	4,406	61,052	35
All	145,854	16,113	13,029	174,996	100
All as %	83%	9%	8%	100%	

(*Source*: Calculated by the author from Office for National Statistics (2003) Census 2001 data)

situations: for example, those who may be caring for parents who misuse alcohol or drugs or where there is enduring parental mental ill health or HIV/AIDS.

Table 15.4 shows the number of young carers in the United Kingdom by age and hours per week caring. This is an important table and deserves close inspection. Here you can see that 6,563 young carers are aged between 5 and 7, and that 940 of these provide at least 50 hours of care per week. Another 9,524 young carers are aged 8 or 9, and 1,055 of these are providing 50 hours of care or more each week. In total, around 35,000 young carers are of *primary school age* and nearly 4,000 of these are caring for more than 50 hours per week. These are alarming figures because they show that many children are drawn into a caring role from a very young age and that many of these children will have to care for very long hours each week, with one in six young carers having to care for more than 20 hours per week and almost one in ten caring for more than 50 hours each week. Remember again that these are minimums rather than maximums – the true *extent* of young caregiving is likely to be higher.

Reflect

Should social workers be concerned that so many carers are children?

As a social worker, which figures in Table 15.4 give you the most concern, and why?

Caring tasks and outcomes

Adult carers

Think ahead

Make a list of all the tasks and responsibilities that you think are undertaken by informal carers in the home.

In the previous section we examined the *extent* of caregiving among adults, young adults and children. In this section we look at the *nature* of caring – what carers actually do in the home, and the *outcomes* of caring on carers' own health, well-being and participation. As we discussed in the introduction and the section on informal care and the caring relationship at the start of this chapter, carers are involved in a wide range of unpaid caring tasks within the family. The 2000 General Household Survey of Carers provides a detailed statistical profile of what adult carers actually do and how long they have been doing it. Informal carers devote most time to practical care tasks such as shopping and laundry, although many are also involved in supervision and/or personal care. For example:

- Over two-thirds (71 per cent) of adult carers provide practical help, such as preparing a meal, shopping and doing laundry.

Many carers are elderly and infirm themselves and therefore vulnerable to the consequences of the demands of their role. Social workers need to be alert and sensitive to this in their assessments.

(*Source*: Alamy Images/Angela Hampton)

- About 60 per cent keep an eye on the person with care needs and 55 per cent provide company ('supervision').
- Just over a quarter of adult carers (26 per cent) give assistance with personal care, such as washing, 22 per cent administer medicines and 35 per cent provide physical help, for example, with walking (Maher and Green, 2002).

Many adult carers take on these kinds of responsibility for many years. Nearly half of all adult carers in the study above had been carers for five years or more while one in five carers had been caring for at least ten years.

As a social worker you need to be especially alert to the needs of carers who have been caring for many years and those who are caring for more than 20 hours per week – especially those caring 'full-time' for 50 hours or more per week. The Princess Royal Trust for Carers (PRTC) has published one of the few studies that focused exclusively on *full-time* adult carers (Warner and Wexler, 1998). The study shows that most of these carers are caring or are on call for 24 hours a day and, of these, 41 per cent had been caring for ten years or more (with 16 per cent caring for 20 years or more). Of those caring for 20 years or more, the majority were parents caring for a child with special needs. Some full-time

carers are themselves elderly and frail. Nine per cent of the PRTC sample were carers aged over 75 caring for others over 75. Almost three-quarters of those aged 75 to 84 were regularly washing and bathing the person they cared for. Full-time carers can find themselves in these roles for many years (a lifetime for some) and may well be frail and vulnerable themselves.

Another distinct group of adult carers that social workers need to be aware of is *older carers* over the age of 60. This is a group that can be very vulnerable but whose needs are often overlooked by health and social care agencies. Older people aged over 60 constitute one-third of the 5.7 million adult carers in the United Kingdom – almost 2 million carers (Milne et al., 2001). Analysis of the characteristics of this group of older carers shows that many are putting in long hours of intensive caring, on very low incomes, while suffering from serious health conditions themselves. One-third of carers aged 75 or over, many of whom are very frail, are providing at least 50 hours of care per week. Many older carers have already been caring for a long time, a quarter for 10 years or more.

It is carers who provide 20 hours or more care per week, especially full-time carers and those who are elderly, that are most likely to experience a range of negative outcomes relating to their own physical and mental health and well-being. Women who are carers are far more likely to report mental health problems than male carers (Singleton et al., 2002).

Becker and Silburn (1999) provide detailed case studies of families where adults in many different circumstances are in full-time caring relationships. They show how the onset of caring can be gradual or immediate, often traumatic, and always involving life changes for the carer *and* the person with care needs. Some examples of these real-life cases are contained in the Case Study box.

Reflect

Should social workers be concerned that so many carers are themselves elderly people? Why?

Case study

Adults who are carers

The case studies in this box are all real-life accounts given by adult carers and the persons for whom they care. Readers who are interested to know more about *these* and other adult carers should look at *We're in this Together: Conversations with Families in Caring Relationships* (Becker and Silburn, 1999).

Joy Shah is nine. Her birth was extremely premature, and for some months her continued survival was in doubt. She has cerebral palsy, with almost complete loss of mobility. She spends most of her time in a lying position, or sitting propped up. She is doubly incontinent. Her sight, hearing and speech are unimpaired, as are her mental faculties, so she is able to attend an integrated school. Both her parents care for her, although it is her mother who is the primary carer.

Frank Oates was diagnosed with multiple sclerosis in his twenties. He is now 52. The disease has progressed slowly but remorselessly. He was able to continue to work on his farm for many years, although he came to rely more and more upon mobility aids and adaptations to equipment, such as his tractor. But he had to stop work about 12 years ago, since when he has used a wheelchair. Now his paralysis is almost complete, and he has the use of only the lower part of his arm. He can move his head. He is mentally unimpaired, although he finds talking for any length of time very tiring. He is cared for by his wife, May.

Daniel Grant is now 44. From an early age his development and behaviour were such that it was suggested he had severe learning difficulties. It was many years later, and almost by accident, that the more accurate diagnosis of autism was made. Throughout his life he has been cared for by his parents. However, his father, David, suffered a stroke 13 years ago, since when his mother, Sarah, has had to care for both son and husband.

Emily Queen is 66 and just over two years ago suffered a stroke. This has affected her mobility (she now uses a wheelchair) and she has severe speech difficulties. Since she was discharged from hospital, she has been cared for by her only daughter, Fiona. Fiona was married only two years ago and until her mother's stroke was living with her husband a few miles away. But after the stroke she moved back to her mother's house to give her the care she needs. She wants to return to live with her husband when suitable alternative arrangements can be made for her mother.

What do these families have in common and how could social workers help?

Caring can also incur extra expenses for carers and their ill, disabled or older family members, not least in terms of economic, social, health and opportunity costs. Again, as a social worker you need to be aware that caring can incur these additional costs to families and that many carers find it difficult to meet these costs, especially when families are living on social security benefits.

These extra expenses include one-off capital costs (such as the costs of installing a downstairs toilet or shower), special aids and adaptations (making doors wider so that they are accessible to wheelchairs) and regular extra household expenditure (for example, on heating, laundry etc.). In a recent survey of almost 3,000 carers (Carers UK, 2007) 58 per cent of carers said that they were worse off because of the extra costs of disability and in a follow-up survey (Carers UK, 2008) 86 per cent of carers said that their financial position was worse than 12 months earlier.

Also, for many carers outside the full-time labour market, caring can lead to reduced or foregone earnings, lower future earning capacity because of interruptions to work, and financial insecurity in later life. The Carers UK (2007) survey of 3,000 carers found that on average carers retire eight years earlier in order to provide care, thus missing out on years of income and pensions contributions.

There is overwhelming evidence to show that there is a strong association between being a carer and the experience of poverty and social exclusion (Becker,

2000b; Howard, 2001; Carers UK, 2007, 2008). Carers UK (2007) found that one in three carers are, or have been, in debt as a result of caring, and 30 per cent struggle to pay their utility bills such as electricity, gas or telephone. Charging for social care services will often exacerbate poverty and social exclusion for many carers. A 2008 survey of 1,700 carers found that many carers continue to live under extreme financial pressure and many cut back on essentials to make ends meet (Carers UK, 2008). The Professional Tip box below outlines a number of factors that increase carers' vulnerability to social exclusion. As a social worker you should look out for these factors, especially when you are involved in conducting an assessment of a carer's needs and their ability to continue to care.

Professional tip

Identifying carers at risk of poverty and social exclusion

As we have seen in the section above, many carers experience poverty and social exclusion and this will have an impact on their own health and well-being, and on their ability to continue to provide care. It is important that social workers and other social and health-care workers can identify those carers who are most vulnerable to social exclusion, assess their needs and deliver services and support that will produce positive outcomes and reduce their risk of social exclusion.

An adequate income has been identified by carers as critical in supporting them to care and in meeting their own needs. Some carers are able to claim Carer's Allowance, although this is at a very low rate. Carers can also be eligible for income-related (means-tested) benefits and premiums or in-work financial benefits depending on their circumstances, although uptake can be low (Wanless, 2006: 145). The report by Carers UK (2007) contains a useful 2-page short guide to carers' benefits. The evidence overall suggests that many carers live in financial poverty as a result of low incomes and that the social security system does not adequately provide them with a standard of living that provides security or decency (Becker, 2000b, 2003; Howard, 2001; Carers UK, 2007).

In this box we identify the key factors that research tells us are likely to increase a carer's risk of social exclusion (Becker, 2000b; see also Becker, 2003). For example, carers who are themselves long-term

recipients of social security benefits and who are also full-time carers are more vulnerable to social exclusion than those who care for just a few hours per week or are in well-paid full-time employment. Carers who come from minority ethnic backgrounds, especially those of Pakistani and Bangladeshi origin, but also those of African origin, are also particularly vulnerable. By being aware of the factors that increase a carer's risk of social exclusion, a social worker can identify those carers who most need support to *prevent* them from becoming socially excluded, or help those who are showing signs (and outcomes) of social exclusion. A carer's assessment is a good time and place to identify the factors that restrict carers' lives and to identify the interventions and services that can help them achieve the desired outcomes – see later in this chapter.

Factors relating to the carer's personal circumstances:
- no source of independent income;
- long-term receipt of benefits;
- self-reporting difficulties in managing financially;
- own limiting, long-standing illness or disability;
- health over the last 12 months was reported as 'not good';
- working full or part-time in low-paid employment;
- aged under 18, 18–24, or over 60;
- minority ethnic origin (especially Pakistani and Bangladeshi origin).

Factors relating to caring:
- living in families with very high costs of disability and/or care;

- caring for person(s) who have conditions/illnesses which carry a high level of social stigma (e.g. AIDS, enduring mental health problems, drug misuse, etc.);
- caring full-time;
- co-resident caring;
- caring for more than one person;
- has been caring for three years or more in one episode of care;
- not had a break of two days since started caring;
- no help or support from health, social services or other agencies;

- no help or support from other family members or friends.

Factors relating to the family's circumstances:
- living in families reliant on means-tested benefits;
- living in households with below half average income;
- living in areas characterised by (multiple) disadvantage (e.g. low-income areas, areas of high unemployment, poor housing stock, few amenities, etc.).

Young carers

There are also profiles of what young carers do in the home, drawn from large samples of young carers in contact with dedicated support projects and from qualitative studies. Over half of the young carers in three national surveys (Dearden and Becker, 1995, 1998, 2004) are from lone-parent families and most are caring for ill or disabled mothers. In the 2003 survey of over 6,000 young carers (Dearden and Becker, 2004), 56 per cent were girls and 44 per cent were boys; 16 per cent were from minority ethnic communities (virtually no change since 1997). Half of the young carers in 2003 were caring for someone with a physical illness or disability, followed by mental health problems (29 per cent of young carers), learning difficulties (17 per cent) and sensory impairments (3 per cent). One in ten children were caring for more than one person.

As with adult carers, young carers can be involved in caregiving for many years. About 36 per cent of children had been caring for two years or less; 44 per cent for between three and five years; 18 per cent for six to ten years and 3 per cent for over ten years (Dearden and Becker, 2004). Given that the average age of these young carers is just 12, the findings suggest that informal caring can be a long-term commitment for many children and can start at a very early age. The 2001 Census figures confirm this, with children from the age of 5 being recorded as caregivers (see Table 15.3).

Children's caring roles are very similar to those of adult carers. It can be hard to believe that children can undertake the kinds of personal and nursing care and other responsibilities that adults perform, but the research evidence shows clearly that children's caregiving tasks range along a continuum from basic domestic duties to very intimate personal care – just like adults'. Most young carers (68 per cent) do some level of *domestic work* within the home. Forty-eight per cent of young carers are involved in *general and nursing care*, which includes organising and administering medication, injections, and lifting and moving parents. Eighty-two percent of children provide *emotional support and supervision*, particularly to parents with severe and enduring mental health problems (Dearden and Becker, 2004; see also Aldridge and Becker, 2003). One in five provide *personal and intimate care* including help with toileting and bathing tasks. A small proportion, about 11 per cent, also take on *childcare responsibilities* in addition to their caring roles for other family members. Around 7 per cent are involved in other *household responsibilities*, including translating (where English is not the first language), dealing with professionals, the family's money management and so on (Dearden and Becker, 2004). The Case Study box overleaf gives some examples – in their own words – of what young carers have to do within their families.

Case study

Children who are carers

The case studies in this box are all *verbatim* accounts given by young carers aged between 12 and 18. Readers who are interested to know more about these and other young carers should look at *Young Carers in Their Own Words* (Bibby and Becker, 2000). If you are interested in specific case studies of young adult carers aged 18–24 then please look at *Young Adult Carers in the UK* (Becker and Becker, 2008).

C, male, aged 16

'I empty her commode, do the kitchen, washing-up, most of the times I cook dinner . . . Collect her money from her social security, order her prescriptions, go down doctor's, get a prescription, then go down chemist – fetch tablets – bring them back, go down shop. Or if she's in the bath, just wash her hair or something when she can't do it herself. Stuff like that. Or at night time – because she has trouble getting out of a chair – so I have to lift her up and put her on the settee to go asleep, just stuff like that.'

Sarah, aged 14

'I have a twin sister and a younger sister who all have to care for our disabled dad. He had a major stroke just over a year ago and is still very disabled from it. It has changed all of our lives a lot. It has affected our schoolwork, our relationship with our dad and our daily lives. Instead of our dad looking after us, it has changed and now we have to look after him. We have to cook, wash, clean and do most of the household jobs for both him and ourselves. When we want to go out with our friends, our Granny has to look after him. She has moved in now to help us but she is nearly 80 and can't manage everything that she would like to help out with.'

C, male, aged 16

'He can't work. He lost his left side. So his left arm doesn't work, and he can't walk on his left leg. I wash him, bath him, put him in bed, dress him, go shopping, the little things like that. I'd just turned 11 when it happened. It was stomach ulcers that burst in his stomach. Two of them did. We went to hospital and they gave him too much anaesthetic and the doctor caused a blood clot in his brain which caused a stroke. He can walk a bit with his stick but he can't walk from there to here. He has to take his wheelchair.

He can't even move his hand at all. His hand is just lodged there. It's very hard for him to dress. I do all the cooking. I do all the shopping. Everything. For about five years now. I just got used to it. I won't go nowhere until my dad, like, passes away.'

D, female, aged 16

I would always go shopping for food and I used to cook. When my brothers used to come I used to cook for them. In the morning my mum used to do breakfasts and everything when she was sober. But when it got towards the day, through the day till evening she used to get drunk more, she used to drink more and more. I used to cook food when they used to come and for my mum every other day. If I didn't cook for myself I would have just starved.

S, female, aged 17

'Mum's got osteo- and that other arthritis. She's got both. Mainly in her hips and legs. She's had two hip replacements, but she's got it in her knees and stuff and sometimes in her hands. She can walk, but not very far, round the house she's okay. When she goes to church, she's okay, but if I actually wanted to go to the shops or anything, we have to take her in a wheelchair. I do most of the evening things, like cooking meals, cleaning round the house and make sure everything's tidy, because she's quite house-proud, and that makes it really hard for her really . . . She needs emotional support, a lot. She gets very upset because the fact that she can't go out, and she sees all her friends, or other people going out. They come and visit her – that's great – but they go out like other places, and they go on holiday, and it really upsets her that she can't. A lot of people would probably feel sorry for me. I don't want them to, because, you know, it's my mum that I'm looking after. That's sort of like one of my duties, and you know, because I love her that much, that's what I'm doing it for. Some people are like, "Oh, you look after your mum, you're so good", and it's like "yeah", but it's not like that. I do it because I love her, and not because I want any praise or any sympathy or anything like that.'

What do you think that the young carers have in common and how do they differ?

Think about the tasks and responsibilities that these young carers are performing. How could social workers help these families?

Research has shown that the caring responsibilities identified in the Case Study box above, especially when children are involved in caring for many hours each week and from an early age, are often associated with negative outcomes for young carers (and for young adult carers), which can include: restricted opportunities for social networking and for developing peer friendships; limited opportunities for taking part in leisure and other activities; poverty and social exclusion; health problems; impaired mental health; emotional difficulties; educational problems; limited horizons and aspirations for the future; a sense of 'stigma by association' (particularly where parents have mental health problems or misuse alcohol or drugs, or have HIV/AIDS); a lack of understanding from peers about their lives and circumstances; a fear of what professionals might do to the family if their circumstances are known; the keeping of 'silence' and secrets (again because of the fear of public hostility or punitive professional responses); and significant difficulties in making a successful transition from childhood to adulthood (Becker et al., 1998; Becker, 2005; Becker and Becker, 2008).

There is some limited evidence from research that young carers can experience *positive* outcomes associated with caring. Dearden and Becker (2000), for example, found that caring developed children's knowledge, understanding, sense of responsibility, maturity and a range of life, social and care related skills. Caring also helped to bring many children closer to their parents in terms of a loving, caring, relationship. However, while the authors noted that these positives were real outcomes for some children in their sample, they also observed that *all* the children experienced some negative consequences as well, and that these were often severe. These included: stress, depression, and restricted social, educational and career opportunities. The authors suggest that young people's choices were both influenced and restricted by caring. Career and job choices were sometimes influenced by the skills gained through caring but restricted by the lack of formal qualifications (because, for example, young carers had problems at school). This has a knock-on effect as young carers grow into young adulthood (Becker and Becker, 2008).

Other research (Aldridge and Becker, 2003; Becker and Becker, 2008; Evans and Becker, 2009) report some positive outcomes of caring. These studies show that caring can allay some of the fears, concerns and anxieties that children and young people have about their parent's conditions because it gives them some control and direct involvement in the provision and management of care and keeps family bonds close. The authors suggest that in some instances caring can actually help to enhance parent–child relationships and can make children feel *included* when often, outside the domain of the family, they are ignored or even excluded (not consulted, not recognised) by social workers, health, social care and other professionals.

As a social worker you need to look out for both the negative and the positive outcomes of caring on young and adult carers. Where the caring role is affecting carers' own health, well-being, development, opportunities and participation, then you will need to conduct a carer's assessment and identify an action plan that will help the carer in their caring role and meet their own needs. We discuss this later in the chapter.

Reflect

What are (a) the similarities and (b) the differences between what young carers and adult carers do in the home?

What are some of the outcomes of caring that can affect adult and young carers? What are the implications for social workers?

Demand and supply

Think ahead

What factors could influence the 'demand' for informal care?

What factors might influence the 'supply' of carers?

One might have thought that because so many carers are heavily involved in caregiving, *and* because the outcomes are often so negative for many carers, *and* because carers have legal rights to assessments and services, then carers would be identified by social workers and other professionals as in need of support. Unfortunately, this is not always, or generally, the case.

Research evidence shows that many heavily involved carers, including young carers, young adult carers, full-time carers, older carers and others in diverse situations, are not recognised by social workers and professionals and receive little if any help or support in their caring roles or with their own needs. For example, over one million *older carers* in the study reported in the section above (Milne et al., 2001) received no regular support from health, social services or home care agencies. Many *full-time carers, young carers* and *young adult carers* are also ignored by professionals (Warner and Wexler, 1998; Aldridge and Becker, 2003; Becker and Becker, 2008). Research shows that NHS staff often fail to provide information, advice or training to full-time carers; fail to consult carers about hospital discharge; and GPs are largely unaware of the needs of carers despite having the potential to be a significant source of support and for signposting (Warner and Wexler, 1998). A commonly voiced concern by all carers is what will happen to the person they care for if they are unable to continue caring, through death, ill health, old age or the growing demands of the caring role?

All of these carers are potentially people in need of social work, health and other support. Their vulnerability, through young or old age, or by virtue of their own ill health or frailty, suggests that social work interventions and services could provide them with the assistance and support that they require to meet their own needs and to help them in their caring role. *Early* social work interventions in these cases can also help to avert a breakdown in the informal caring relationship and sustain the carer as well as the person with care needs.

It is important that social workers try to maintain the informal caring relationship where the carer and the person with care needs both want this to continue. This may become increasingly important as an objective of social work if the 'demand' for informal care outweighs the 'supply' of carers. In the future there is evidence that there will be too few informal carers available to meet the 'demands' for care. Assuming current patterns of care, the demand for informal care is predicted to increase by about 45 per cent between 2003 and 2026 (Wanless, 2006). Various trends, however, have affected the 'supply' of informal care. There has been a decline in co-residence (living together) between adults and elderly parents and an increase in one-person households, both of which point to lower availability of informal care. Additionally, people who might currently be prepared to care for those in need may not be willing to do so in the future as bonds between family members become more fragile or expectations change over time (Wanless, 2006).

These figures and trends raise concerns about the demand for, and supply and sustainability of, informal care across the life cycle, given that so many carers are providing extensive hours of care per week, often to the detriment of their own health, well-being and participation (as we have seen above). With an ageing population, and community care policies that encourage and enable ill and disabled people to live in their own homes rather than in residential settings, there will be more pressure

on individuals, including young carers and young adult carers, to provide informal care. There are a number of strategies that can be adopted in response to this, including improving *services* for carers and social work support; giving potential carers *incentives* to supply informal care (for example, by making payments to carers and by compensating them for the costs of caregiving); and by increasing the provision of formal care services as an alternative to informal care.

The help that families can get from outside the family unit, in other words, from social workers and health and social care agencies, will be critical in determining the quality of life of carers and the person for whom they care, and whether carers can or will want to continue to provide care. As a social worker you will need to be able to recognise the positive and negative outcomes of caring among adult and young carers, and work with the family's strengths and weaknesses. In particular, you will need to be alert to the signs of fatigue and distress that many carers experience but which some will not admit to for fear of being judged or being seen as a 'bad' son, daughter, partner, parent or carer. Is the carer losing sleep? Are they eating properly? Do they ever get a break from caring? Have they any life outside caring? It is these carers that are likely to need social work interventions and support, and this is the focus of the next section.

Reflect

What, if anything, can social workers do to support the caring relationship and maintain the 'supply' of carers?

Social work practice with informal carers

We have seen in the sections above that social workers have an important role to play in recognising carers in their diverse forms and in identifying the situations and circumstances where carers are experiencing negative outcomes which impact on their own health, well-being, opportunities and participation. In this section we are concerned to outline in more detail 'good' social work practice with informal carers. The focus here is on assessments and identifying appropriate services to support carers.

First though, we need to know about the needs of carers. Research suggests that it is possible to classify the needs of both adult and young carers under a number of broad headings:

C CHOICE – the choice to care as well as a choice of services.

A ACCESS to information and services, which should be appropriate to culture, language, religion and age; and ASSESSMENTS of their capacity, ability and wishes as to whether or not to continue to care.

R RESPECT as an individual with his/her own needs, who may be entitled to a separate assessment of their needs and ability to care.

E EDUCATION by and for carers that recognises their skills, knowledge and aspirations for further training, education and paid work.

R RECOGNITION of their contribution to caregiving, and for this to be acknowledged and valued, particularly by professionals and society.

S SUPPORT relevant to their individual needs, encompassing someone to talk to; flexible respite care and time off from caring; flexible and sensitive services; complex support packages; counselling when the caring responsibility within the home ends or changes; and an adequate income so that carers do not live their lives in poverty and social exclusion.

In most instances these needs are modest and do not require very intensive (or very costly) social work interventions and services. However, each carer will have their own specific needs depending on family circumstances, the nature of the illness/disability and the need for care, family finances, who else can help provide care from within and outside the family, and so on.

It has been suggested that the best way to support adults and children who are informal carers is to improve the services and support offered to those who are currently recipients of their care – ill, disabled or elderly people themselves (Royal Commission on Long Term Care, 1999; Pickard, 2004). The Royal Commission, for example, proposed moving towards a 'carer-blind' situation where the presence of a carer did not impact on the likelihood of services being offered by the state to the person with care needs. Parker, Morris and others have argued that the best way to stop inappropriate caring by children and to support young carers is for their ill or disabled parents to receive services and support as disabled people and as disabled parents (Keith and Morris, 1995; Olsen and Parker, 1997; Wates, 2002). This position argues that formal services provided to those with care needs should *replace* informal care provision by children and adults who are carers.

An alternative approach, however, is to provide services and support to adult and young carers based on a social work assessment of need in order to support carers in their caring roles, to meet their own *needs* and to meet their *rights*. There has been growing recognition in recent years of the importance of supporting carers directly in their caring role and in their personal circumstances. Indeed, performance ratings for social services and social care authorities now include recognition of the amount and quality of local support provision for informal carers.

The impact of formal services on *carer outcomes* can be judged in at least two important ways:

1. in the way that services delay the need for people to go into care homes (because it delays a breakdown of the caring relationship at home)
2. in the way that services directly impact on measures of carer stress (Wanless, 2006).

The Department of Health (2010b) acknowledges that there is growing evidence that interventions can prevent or delay people entering social care thus producing better outcomes at a lower overall cost. There are a range of services now available to support carers to achieve one or both of the above outcomes, including respite care of various forms; information and advice services to enable informed choices; training; emergency planning schemes; advocacy; building capacity in carer and user-led organisations; social work and counselling. In 2000, it was estimated that 18 per cent of carers received therapeutic social work and counselling interventions (Pickard, 2004). Wanless (2006: 16) suggests that there is strong research evidence to show that social work and counselling support reduces 'subjective carer burden', relieves carer distress and can reduce psychological problems in carers. Thus, among the range of services and support currently available to carers, social work and counselling is one of the few with any reliable evidence on effectiveness. Improvements and increases in carer support should also impact directly on the quality of care provided by carers: 'A less stressed, overworked, unhealthy or tired carer will have an increased ability to care, and there is likely to be a generally improved atmosphere. In addition, training support should mean care of a higher quality' (Wanless, 2006: 148).

The approach taken in this chapter is that adults, young carers and young adult carers need services and support in their own right (as carers) *at the same time* as people with care needs require dedicated services and support (Aldridge and Becker, 1996, 2003; Becker and

Becker, 2008). It is not about supporting one *or* the other. Indeed, a 'whole family approach' would recognise the need for formal services to meet the needs of *all* family members rather than focusing on the carer or person with care needs in isolation. This is also a matter of rights – carers of all ages have legal rights to assessments and to services (see the Closer Look box on p. 429).

The Audit Commission's (2004b) review of what carers can 'reasonably expect' to receive suggests that carers across the United Kingdom should be able to expect the following:

- Identification of need (by primary care staff and councils)
- Provision of information in the form of literature, websites, call centres, verbal advice and training (from both local and national sources)
- Provision of support (including breaks from caring and help for those who are working or want to return to work)
- Assessments (of both the person with care needs and the carer).

Social workers have a role to play in all four of these areas. However, the Audit Commission report shows that there are issues around carer services and support with regard to not only the number of carers who receive services and assessments (which is usually very low) but also the consistency of coverage and monitoring (which is usually fragmented and partial). The large majority of carers do not receive any formal support from social work, health and social care agencies and most have not had a formal assessment of their own needs or their ability to continue to care (Wanless, 2006). More recently, the Department of Health (2010b) has reaffirmed what should be existing practice with regards to assessments: community care packages should not rely on the input of an inappropriate level of care from a child or young person; local authorities are required to assess people who are about to be discharged from hospital and their carers; councils should consider the sustainability of the caring role when deciding what community care services are necessary; councils should only decide eligibility after an appropriate assessment that involves the person seeking support and family/friends who may be assisting them; self assessment does not replace a council's duty to conduct a community care assessment. The Department of Health (2010b) reminds us that assessment is a process not a one-off event and that early assessments and early interventions and preventative support can improve carer and family outcomes.

Social work assessments of carers

As we have seen above, it is a key role of local authorities to plan for the general needs of its carer population and to assess the needs of individual carers (as well as assessing the needs of the persons for whom they care). This legal responsibility to assess individual carers relates to carers who provide 'substantial and regular care'. The Closer Look box at the start of this chapter outlines carers' legal rights in the United Kingdom. While the term 'substantial and regular' care is not defined in any legislation, the *Practitioner's Guide to Carers' Assessments Under the Carers and Disabled Children Act 2000* suggests that

'the test that a practitioner should apply will relate to the *impact* of the caring role on the individual carer. In particular the practitioner will need to address the following questions: Is the caring role sustainable? How great is the risk of the caring role becoming unsustainable?'

(DoH, 2001d, para. 14, emphasis added)

The Guidance lists 14 questions that can help social workers and other practitioners to identify levels of risk to the sustainability of the caring role, including: How long has the carer been caring? How often does the carer get a full night's sleep? How much emotional impact does the caring role have? How much does the carer gain of any sense of satisfaction/reward from caring? Throughout this chapter we have tried to sensitise you as a social worker to the need of recognising these indicators of carer distress, and to identify the negative (and positive) impacts and outcomes of caring.

The *Guidance to Carers' Assessments Under the Carers and Disabled Children Act 2000* also makes it very clear what the purpose of a carer's assessment is under this Act:

- To determine whether the carer is eligible for support
- To determine the support needs of the carer (i.e. what will help the carer in their caring role and help them to maintain their own health and well-being)
- To see if those needs can be met by social or other services.

(DoH, 2001d, para. 19)

It goes on to state that:

'Great sensitivity on the part of the assessors may be required. It is important that the assessment process does not assume that the carer wants to continue to provide care, or should be expected to. Nor should it be assumed that the cared for person necessarily wants to continue to receive care from this carer'. (DoH, 2001d, para. 20)

Carers UK summarises the purpose of a carer's assessment from the perspective of the carer:

'The purpose of a carer's assessment is for you [the carer] to discuss with social services what help you need with caring as well as any help that would maintain your own health and balance caring with other aspects of your life such as work and family commitments. Social Services use assessments to decide what help to provide'.   (Carers UK, 2004)

Assessments and the focus on outcomes

The Guidance also states clearly that:

'A carer's assessment should be focused on what the carer identifies as the best possible outcome. The best possible outcome will depend on the impact of caring on the particular carer. This impact is also the best test for 'regular and substantial' caring. While many carers may clearly be able to state from the beginning what it is they want to happen to make their lives easier, others may take time to identify their own needs . . . It is very important to make a clear distinction between 'outcomes' and services . . . The best service to provide the outcome will depend on the individual circumstances'.   (DoH, 2001d, paras. 22–4)

The assessment should also be 'carer-centred', in other words:

- The assessment is not a test for the carer. It should not be prescriptive but recognise the carer's knowledge and expertise.
- The assessment should listen to what carers are saying and offer an opportunity for private discussion so the carer can be candid.
- It should not be a bureaucratic process based on ticking boxes. It must focus on the outcomes the carer would want to see to help them in their caring role and maintain their health and well-being.
- It should be seen as part of a holistic assessment of the needs for support of the cared for person and the carer, identifying the outcomes desired by both and it should be reflected in the care plan (where it is appropriate for cared-for person and carer's issues to be dealt with together) or in a separately held carer's plan (where there is a need for confidentiality).
(DoH, 2001d, paras. 27–30)

This emphasis in the Guidance on outcomes is very important. The carer's assessment process is intended to determine the outcomes that carers want for themselves (and for the person with care needs) and the best ways in which these outcomes can be achieved through services

or other forms of support. As part of the assessment of need and a carer's ability to continue to care, a social worker or other person undertaking the assessment will need to identify and draw up a carer's action plan. This will be the plan of services and interventions that are required to meet the carer's needs, to deliver the specified outcomes and to help the carer maintain their own health, well-being, social inclusion and capacity to continue caring. This action plan should be agreed with the carer (as far as possible) and be communicated to the carer so that they have a record of what is proposed. As a social worker conducting a carer's assessment, you need to be aware of the purpose of an assessment (as outlined above), the legal framework (Closer Look box), the general needs of carers and the outcomes of caring (as described throughout this chapter), and the services and interventions that can deliver the desired outcomes. Before you undertake an assessment, make sure that you know about all the services that can help carers locally and nationally. When conducting the assessment, you need to relate the broad knowledge you have gained from this chapter to the *specific* case, age, needs and circumstances of the carer that you are now assessing.

Much of the approach perceived as 'good practice' in carers' assessments involves flexibility in fitting in with carer and service user preferences. In that sense both the process and the content of assessment are inextricably linked. Although some carers do report benefits from the assessment itself, even if no services are provided, the process is usually expected to result in a carer's action plan which will detail the support and assistance that is to be provided, together with some statement of intended outcomes (Qureshi et al., 2003: 79). The focus in assessments should not be on the type of services, but whether they are delivered in a way that enables people to achieve the things (outcomes) that are important to them. This is a very important message for social workers to learn. Do not go into an assessment simply thinking 'What services can I provide here?' Rather, identify *with* the carer: 'What outcomes do the carer and care receiver want for themselves and for each other, and what services and interventions can deliver these outcomes?'

Arksey et al. (2000) have identified a number of features of good practice in carers' assessments:

- The assessment process is made explicit and carers are given the time and information in preparation for the discussions.
- Consideration is given to the timing and arrangements for interviews, particularly when caring responsibilities

or work commitments make it difficult to fit in with the office hours of social services staff.

- Carers are given the opportunity for an informed choice over the matter of privacy and 'separate' assessment.
- Carers have face-to-face discussions, with self-assessment and other forms being an aid to this process rather than an alternative.
- Care is taken with the amount of written information, which some carers find difficult to absorb even if they find time to read it.
- Workers are prompt in responding to the carer assessment, and maintain contact even when no further direct support services result from the assessment.
- Written confirmation of the result of the assessment is backed by some, albeit limited, direct contact follow-up as a support and safeguard.

(Arksey et al., 2000, quoted in Qureshi et al., 2003: 78–9)

Unfortunately, most carers who provide substantial and regular care have not had a formal assessment of their needs and of their ability to continue to provide care. Further research shows that the quality of these assessments can also be very variable. Qureshi et al. (2003) have observed that nationally:

'Research with carers showed that their knowledge of the legislation was minimal, that many carers were not aware at the time of the event that they were being assessed, that the arrangements for the assessment – including the question of a separate discussion not in the presence of the care recipient – were not always a matter for negotiation and agreement and that written follow-up and/or further review was often not provided'.		(2003: 74)

In two separate studies of assessments of adult carers (Becker et al., 2005, 2007), it was found that in many instances the quality of the information collected about carers was not sufficiently high to enable a satisfactory carer's action plan to be devised. Social workers and other assessors often had little training on how to conduct an assessment and there was little attention on the need to focus on outcomes. In both studies the researchers also recommended changes to the assessment forms that were being used, to enable a more comprehensive and outcome-focused assessment to take place. Becker et al. (2007) also identify a number of issues for policy and practice arising out of their research on adult carers' assessments and these are outlined in the next Professional Tip box.

Young carers and young adult carers will also need a thorough assessment of their needs and of their ability to continue to provide care, and many of the suggestions about good practice above, and in the Professional Tip box apply to young carers and young adult carers as much as they do to older carers. When assessing young carers under the age of 18, however, it must be remembered that these are children and young people and that their needs (and rights) must be considered within a *children's* legislative and policy framework, not just under the law and policy that relates to adults and adult carers. Many young carers – especially those under the age of 16 – will need to be assessed as children in need under the 1989 Children Act (1995 Act in Scotland). Chapter 16 provides information about the assessment of children and children in need. This information should be referred to when assessing young carers. Dearden and Becker (2001) outline some of the issues to consider when assessing young carers using the *Framework for the Assessment of Children in Need and Their Families*. The *National Service Framework for Mental Health* (DoH, 1999c) urges caution when assessing young carers of parents with mental health problems. It states that

'Where the person with mental illness is a parent, health and local authorities should not assume that the child or children can undertake the necessary caring responsibilities. The parent should be supported in their parenting role and services provided so that the young carer is able to benefit from the same life chances as all other children, and have the opportunity for a full education, and leisure and social activities. The young carer's plan should take account of the adverse impact which mental health problems in a parent can have on the child'.		(DoH, 1999c: 72)

The Case Study (p. 453) shows some of the issues involved when working with a young person who is a carer of a parent with a mental illness.

It is important for social workers working with young carers (and adult carers) to know about the available services and resources that can help carers locally and nationally. So, in the context of children who are carers, you will need to think about 'what are the desired outcomes that need to be brought about by any interventions and services?', 'is there a local young carers project or other services that can provide support to the young carer to deliver the intended outcomes?', 'is there a contact at the young carer's school who has a responsibility for young carers issues (every school should have one)?', 'how can young carers, like any child, be helped to achieve the five *Every Child Matters* outcomes?' (Fox et al., 2007). New psychometric instruments (Joseph et al.,

Professional tip

Planning, conducting and reviewing carers' assessments

1. *Social workers and others need to inform carers of their legal right to an assessment.* Under the Community Care & Health (Scotland) Act 2002 and the Carers (Equal Opportunities) Act 2004 it is the duty of local authorities to inform adult and young carers of their right to an assessment. Many carers simply do not know of their right to an assessment even though assessments are the gateway to services and support for carers. Additionally, other organisations in contact with care receivers (and carers) should inform informal carers of their right to an independent assessment.

2. *Carers should be assessed or offered an assessment when the person receiving care is assessed or reassessed.* The process of meeting the needs of service users *and* their family carers would be streamlined considerably if the carer was informed of their right to an assessment, or assessed, as part of the same process that is used to assess the person with care needs. Whether both assessments should be done by the same person is a matter for social work and social care authorities, but devising clear and transparent institutional arrangements and processes that bring these two processes together would be a better use of resources, a more family-focused process, and deliver beneficial outcomes for carers and the person with care needs. Assessors should return to meet with carers after the formal assessment meeting to explain the carer's action plan that is intended. A written statement should be given to the carer as their record, with clear contact details so the carer can get in touch with the assessor if and when their needs and circumstances change.

3. *Carers need to be prepared for their assessment, as do assessors themselves.* Carers need some preparation about what a carer's assessment entails for them to be able to answer questions thoughtfully, fully and without anxiety, and for them to get the most out of the assessment process. A 'pre-assessment' form sent to them in advance can help prepare them for the assessment and is recommended by a number of organisations, including Carers UK.

Assessors too need to prepare adequately for the assessment, drawing on information that is known about the person with care needs and family circumstances. This 'case'-level preparation must also be based on good training of what the purpose is of a carer's assessment, and the relevant law and guidance. Assessors must also have a good knowledge of local (and national) services for carers and how these services can work to deliver particular and desired outcomes. Where assessors do not have this knowledge of services and resources, then the assessment process and the potential to meet outcomes in particular can be seriously compromised and limited.

Research also shows that assessors sometimes feel constrained by resources when conducting their assessments and are mindful not to raise carers' expectations in situations where they believe that there is little available for them. This is the opposite of an outcomes or carer-centred approach and needs to be discussed openly by assessors and policy makers and managers, and local guidance drafted for assessors on how to handle these tensions. This situation directly impacts on the quality of the assessment process (for carers and assessors) as well as the outcomes.

4. *Minimising the number and range of different assessments that carers and their families receive would be valued by families.* Wherever possible a carer's assessment should also draw on evidence from other assessments and information collected from other assessments (for example, of the service user), so as to minimise the number of questions asked and the repetitive or intrusive nature of the information collected by different sources.

5. *Multidisciplinary assessments can be valuable, perhaps involving a 'case conference'-type situation bringing together key professionals in contact with a care receiver and their family.* Assessments, particularly outcomes, can be improved where agencies and organisations in contact with carers and people with care needs work together and share information (within the limits of confidentiality and data protection).

6. *Carers' assessments must be sensitive to religious, ethnic and cultural needs (and for young carers, be age-sensitive) and services that are provided as part of a Carer's Action Plan must also be sensitive to these needs.* There is little evidence that assessments take account of 'identity' with regards to race, ethnicity or culture. Other 'identities' are similarly marginalised, including sexuality.

Carers' assessments must be sensitive to religious, ethnic and cultural needs.

(*Source:* Photofusion Picture Library/Paula Solloway)

7. *Carers' assessments and services need to be outcome focused.* The lack of focus on outcomes, despite the guidance, is a cause for national concern. Social workers and other assessors need information and training on how to make this a reality, and should know why it is important.

8. *A formal review of the carer's assessment, and the appropriateness of the Carer's Action Plan, need to be timetabled from the time of the original assessment.* In most authorities there is no systematic procedure for reviewing carers' assessments, despite guidance (for example, the *National Service Framework for Mental Health*, DoH, 1999c) which suggests an annual review of carers' needs and their ability to continue to care. Authorities need to devise a system whereby reviews of assessments, Carer's Action Plans, outcomes and services can take place as a matter of routine, with the ultimate results of reviews being informed in writing to carers.

9. *There is a need for regular training to ensure all assessors or potential assessors are up to date regarding the purpose of a carer's assessment, carers' rights, the law and guidance, the availability of local services and sources of information for carers.* Social workers and other assessors will need clear training input on *all* these aspects, with a 'booster session' (to update their knowledge and skills) probably at least once a year. This booster session might include local assessors being brought together to discuss issues and mutual concerns, good practice, services, etc.

10. *The carer's assessment form must be fit for purpose.* There is evidence that many authorities may be using assessment tools that do not allow assessors to collect the information that will enable them to deliver an outcomes-focused assessment in line with current legislation and guidance. Assessors should check that the form they are using is fit for purpose. If it is not, they should tell their managers and advocate for an improved form.

2009) to help social workers and other professionals to assess young carers have been produced by researchers at the University of Nottingham and are freely available from The Princess Royal Trust for Carers website. Perhaps the key issues to be considered when assessing young carers are 'what is "appropriate" and what is "not appropriate" for children to do at their age?', and 'what are the outcomes that we want to bring about by any interventions?' (HM Government, 2008a; see also Frank and McLarnon, 2008).

Case study

S (caring for parent with mental illness)

This is a verbatim account given by a young carer aged 17. Readers who are interested to know more about young carers' own accounts should look at *Young Carers in Their Own Words* (Bibby and Becker, 2000).

S, female, aged 17

'When you're younger you don't really understand what's happening. You know this person as your mum and you think, oh yeah I really love my mum. Then suddenly they turn into a totally different person and you can't understand. You're trying to relate what they're doing to the person that you've known all your life and you can't do it, and you get really confused.

I've started gradually being more understanding about what my mum does when she's ill. Last year she was really bad. She used to cry, she'd sit in a dark room and just cry and cry and I'd try and help her and when I used to say something to her she used to swear at me and tell me to get lost and I couldn't do anything and she'd just be crying. I could hear her upstairs and I didn't know what to do and then she'd just say really weird things as well, and I just had to keep telling myself that it wasn't her – if you know what I mean – it was her but I kept having to say "well this is the illness that's speaking, not herself", and it's really hard. It's really confusing because there's somebody saying really weird things and you can't relate to what they're saying and you're trying to communicate with them and you can't because you can't understand them and you're not on their level and it's really, really confusing.

You don't get any sympathy from anybody either because when you try to explain to your friends – say your friend will ring up and your mum will answer the phone and she'll be saying really weird things to them and then you'll get back to school and everybody will start picking on you saying "oh your mum's a nutter, she's a schizophrenic" – and that's a totally different illness anyway. And people never understand because a lot of people are really ignorant. You never get any of the support you would if your mum had got a physical illness because a lot of people, if your mum had cancer or something, they'd feel really sorry for you, but when it's a mental illness people react so differently and they just like slag you to the ground saying "oh your mum's a total nutter, she's a fruitcake", and it really upsets me. So, apart from having to deal with that, you're having to deal with everybody else's reactions as well and it's just really hard trying to explain to people. I mean my mum's not a nutter, she's just really depressed, she doesn't go out doing really silly things and stabbing people and talking to the television, she just gets really depressed and she talks to herself. I think that's because she hasn't got anybody else to talk to really so she talks to herself. It's just her way of channelling her anger and her bitterness out of what's happened in the past, but a lot of people won't try to understand and then I lose my temper sometimes when people are just so ignorant.

When she's ill she stops washing and everything so I was like washing the clothes. I know it's not much really, just washing the clothes and I didn't really mind . . . and like cooking and stuff, 'cause my mum just lets herself go, she doesn't even clean herself, she just loses . . . doesn't see herself as important and she just doesn't do anything. But I don't think that's very hard really, doing that, I mean I don't mind. It's when you're having to deal with all the psychological aspects of it, when you're having to sort of understand . . . and it's really hard, you know, when people say really strange things and you can't even try to understand it.

You don't fully sleep when she's up. You're always getting up and going into her bedroom to see if she's all right. Once she was really crying and she was talking into the mirror to herself and my sister's father – he's dead now because he took a drug overdose and he was a really depressed man – and she would talk to the mirror, into the mirror at him, saying, "Are you there?", and that was really weird as well and I kept having to get up in the middle of the night to see that she hadn't done anything to herself.'

What are the needs of this young carer? As a social worker who becomes aware of the family, what are your responsibilities in this case and what should you do?

Reflect

Try and identify the caring roles and responsibilities that you think are inappropriate for a child under 18 to be involved in. Now draw up a list of those roles which you think are appropriate.

How difficult was this? How does your list vary depending on age?

Conclusion

The 2006 Wanless review of social care has argued that

'Informal care will continue to provide a very significant input to social care, even if increases in availability fall short of future demand. Greater carer support is needed to relieve some of the pressure of care, as the costs of increasing formal care to meet a significant reduction in informal care would be prohibitively high'. (Wanless, 2006: 138)

Social work, health and social care agencies have a legal responsibility to ensure that carers are recognised and that their needs and ability to continue to care are assessed alongside the needs of the person with care needs. A carer's action plan should identify the outcomes that are to be achieved through a range of services and interventions. The gateway to services and support for carers is often the carer's assessment, which can be carried out by a social worker or other key worker in contact with families. The purpose of an assessment needs to be clearly understood by the assessor and carer, and should identify the support needs of carers – to enable them (if they wish) to continue caring and to help them with their own needs and circumstances. Carers of all ages have identified that time off from caring, flexible and reliable support from social care and health services, information and advice, emergency planning schemes and recognition of their caring role, all help them to maintain their caring capacity. Social workers need to think creatively about what services are available, or need to be established, to produce the desired outcomes in each case. Social work practice and services with informal carers will play a critical role in determining the impact and outcomes of caring and the quality of life of carers, be they adults, young adults or young carers.

Key learning points

✔ Working with carers is not an 'optional extra' for social workers. Social workers have ethical and legal responsibilities to identify, assess and support family carers of any age, race, gender, sexual orientation or background.

✔ Good social work practice requires social workers to recognise informal carers in their many forms, and identify the diverse situations and circumstances where carers are experiencing negative outcomes which impact on their own health, well-being, development, opportunities and capacity to continue caring.

✔ To work effectively with carers of all ages social workers need to be familiar with the legislative and policy contexts and published guidance, which must inform their practice.

✔ Ascertaining the views, feelings, needs and aspirations of family carers of all ages must be a priority, including finding out about, and respecting the outcomes that carers want for themselves and their family members.

✔ Social workers need to think about and respond to the interrelated and interdependent needs of all family members. When conducting an assessment, think 'whole family', and provide a package of relevant services and support which will meet the needs and outcomes that carers have identified for themselves.

Further reading

Becker, F. and Becker, S. (2008) *Young Adult Carers in the UK: Experiences, Needs and Services for Carers aged 16–24.* London: The Princess Royal Trust for Carers. The first detailed study of this 'hidden' group of carers with reference also to young carers aged 16–17 in transition.

Clements, L. (2009) *Carers and Their Rights: The Law Relating to Carers* (3rd edn). London: Carers UK. A very useful guide to carer's legislation and rights.

HM Government (2008) *Carers at the Heart of the 21st-Century Families and Communities.* London: Department of Health. The second National Carers Strategy with a ten-year vision.

Joseph, S., Becker, F. and Becker, S. (2009) *Manual for Measures of Caring Activities and Outcomes for Children and Young People.* London: The Princess Royal Trust for Carers. Very useful instruments for assessment and evaluation with young carers.

Wanless, D. (2006) *Securing Good Care for Older People: Taking A Long-Term View*. London: King's Fund. An excellent review of social and informal care, including dedicated chapters on informal care and background papers.

 ## Useful websites

www.carers.gov.uk
A website aimed at professionals who work with carers.

www.direct.gov.uk/carers
An extensive website for informal carers themselves.

www.statistics.gov.uk
Website to access National Statistics Office figures (search by typing in carers or informal care).

www.youngcarer.com
A website provided by the Children's Society for young carers, their families and professionals.

www.youngcarers.net
A UK-wide online service from the Princess Royal Trust for Carers for young carers and professionals.

www.saulbecker.co.uk
A website with multiple free downloads of Becker's research and publications on young and adult carers.

For additional cases and topic-organised, clickable links into additional media resources, including those produced by IRISS, visit **www.pearsoned.co.uk/wilsonruch**

Activity

Refer back to the case study at the start of this chapter, on Sam, Maggie, Julia and Richard.

Working, if you can, in pairs:

(a) Write down the key questions that Sam needs to ask to be able to adequately assess Maggie's needs and her ability to continue to provide care.
(b) Write down what questions Sam needs to ask Richard to be able to adequately assess him as a (potential or current) young carer.
(c) Identify the 'outcomes' that you think Maggie and Richard would want for themselves and for their family. Had you included questions about outcomes in (a) and (b) above?
(d) Investigate what services and support are available locally (in your city or county) for adult and young carers and make separate lists of them. Which of these might be of potential benefit to Maggie and to Richard? Why?
(e) What lessons have you learnt from doing this activity?

Part Three
SOCIAL WORK IN RELATIONSHIP-BASED PRACTICE WITH USER GROUPS

Chapter 16
Social work with children and families

Chapter summary

The chapter will help you engage in the absorbing and challenging task of working with children and families. In it, we provide you with theoretical and practical guidance on social work in this important area of practice, with the aim of giving you an introduction to what we see as the key debates and dilemmas. We begin by exploring four fundamental principles which underpin sound childcare social work practice. We then consider some of the key ways in which social work with children has developed over the last century, outlining the legal and policy context of social work with children and families and highlighting ways in which the emphasis on protection and rescue or support and prevention has changed over time and will undoubtedly continue to do so in response to significant events. The current frameworks for assessment and intervention are explored and attention focuses on practice issues which arise when supporting families in bringing up their children in their homes and also on those arising when children cannot live with their birth families. Although it is an important area of practice for those working with children and families, the chapter does not specifically consider issues facing disabled children and their families, since these are considered in detail in Chapter 19.

Learning objectives

This chapter covers topics that will enable you to achieve the following learning objectives:

- To familiarise you with some fundamental principles informing effective and ethical social work with children and families
- To outline historical trends in child welfare policy and the current policy and practice context
- To help you understand key dilemmas, challenges, achievements and debates in current child welfare policy and practice
- To examine the Common Assessment Framework, its relationship to the Framework of Assessment and its application in practice
- To explore support services for children in need and the child protection procedures for children at risk
- To explore the different types of placement for children unable to live with their birth families and the practice decisions and skills involved in achieving successful placements.

National Occupational Standards

This chapter will help you to meet the following National Occupational Standards:

Key Role 1: Prepare for, and work with individuals, families, carers, groups and communities to assess their needs and circumstances

Unit 1   Prepare for social work contact and involvement
Unit 2   Work with individuals, families, carers, groups and communities to help them make informed decisions
Unit 3   Assess needs and options to recommend a course of action for individuals, families, carers, groups and communities

Key Role 2: Plan, carry out, review and evaluate social work practice with individuals, families, carers, communities and other professionals

Unit 4   Respond to crisis situations
Unit 5   Interact with individuals, families, carers, groups and communities to achieve change and development and to improve life opportunities
Unit 6   Prepare, produce, implement and evaluate plans with individuals, families, carers, groups, communities and professional colleagues
Unit 7   Support the development of networks to meet assessed needs and planned outcomes
Unit 8   Work with groups to promote individual growth, development and independence
Unit 9   Address behaviour which presents a risk to individuals, families, carers, groups and communities

Key Role 4: Manage risk to individuals, families, carers, groups, communities, self and colleagues

Unit 12   Assess and manage risks to individuals, families, carers, groups and communities
Unit 13   Assess, minimise and manage risk to self and colleagues

Key Role 5: Manage and be accountable, with supervision and support, for your own social work practice within your organisation

Unit 14   Manage and be accountable for your own work
Unit 17   Work with multidisciplinary and multi-organisational teams, networks and systems

Key Role 6: Demonstrate professional competence in social work practice

Unit 18   Research, analyse, evaluate, and use current knowledge of best social work practice
Unit 19   Work within agreed standards of social work practice and ensure own professional development
Unit 20   Manage complex ethical issues, dilemmas and conflicts
Unit 21   Contribute to the promotion of best social work practice

Case study

Rosie

Rosie Ashton was born prematurely, but by the time she was a year old, she was, according to the health visitor's contemporary notes, progressing satisfactorily and both she and her younger sister, born eighteen months later, seemed happy, healthy children. She and her sister live with her parents in a council house on an estate in the West Midlands. Her parents, a white British couple, married in their teens; her father worked as a lorry driver while her mother was at home caring for the children.

When Rosie was 4 years old Mr Ashton suffered a stroke, for which he was hospitalised, and has been unemployed since then.

At the age of 6, Rosie is referred to the local authority children's services because of her neglected appearance and difficult behaviour at school.

What do you think has happened to Rosie to bring about these changes? What, as a child care professional, might you do to try to help?

Introduction

Social work with children and families is one of the most changing and challenging areas of practice; it is also, as we hope you will find out too, one of the most absorbing, fascinating and, potentially at least, satisfying. However, despite the major shifts in legal provision, policies and how services to children and families are delivered which have occurred in the past decade or so, and which we explore later, there are certain 'constants' at the heart of good practice with children and families which we begin the chapter by addressing.

Principles of relationship-based practice in working with children and families

There are four fundamental principles which we believe you need to understand in order to undertake sound childcare social work practice:

1. recognising the 'child within'
2. listening to the voice of the child
3. working with children *and* families
4. acknowledging power and purpose.

Recognising the 'child within'

Reflect

Close your eyes and remember a time as a child when you experienced something sad or something you could not understand. Try to recall how old you were, how big you were, who else was around, what you felt.

Who would you have liked to talk to about your feelings? Who did you talk to?

Describe one thing that helped you. Describe one thing you would have liked to happen.

What do you remember about the adults around you at that time?

How might your experiences inform your professional perspectives and development?

It is impossible for you to come to this chapter without your own experiences of being a child informing and influencing what you read and how you respond to it. Unlike other aspects of social work practice – e.g. work-

ing with older people or people with a physical disability, where you may or may not draw on personal experience – working with children and their families always resonates in some way with our own experiences, since we have all been children. In addition to your personal experiences 'colouring' your understanding of the chapter, the public portrayal and media coverage of childcare social work will undoubtedly have contributed to your ideas of what social work with children and families is like. Unless the experiences, assumptions and prejudices that determine our values, beliefs and behaviours are made explicit, we are in danger of practising in potentially misguided and less effective ways. Chapter 1 on reflective and relationship-based practice develops these ideas more fully and it is worth referring back to this chapter to remind yourself of how reflective practice needs to underpin your professional activities. This is particularly the case when considering social work with children and families. More than in any other area of social work, working with children and families evokes strong reactions from the general public, associated with notions of children as innocent and defenceless members of society, although you need also to be aware of society's apparently equal readiness to blame and condemn children for their behaviour. When thinking about working with children and families, it is important that you make connections between your own experiences of childhood and their significance for your professional practice.

Listening to the voice of the child

As social workers you have a responsibility to engage with children in ways that respect their views and promote their best interests. The most effective ways of achieving these objectives are:

- to develop enhanced self-awareness, as outlined above, and understand how your own experiences of childhood influence your approach to children;
- to develop professional skills in relating to and communicating with children (see later in chapter and the chapter on communication skills).

How we listen to children is influenced by how we perceive them. Remembering only a sad or confusing occasion, which can evoke feelings of vulnerability and powerlessness, does not do justice to the capabilities, strengths and resilience of children. In her research exploring children's experiences of living with a parent with a terminal illness, Chowns (2006) introduced the idea of the able-child citizen, a child who, unlike the vulnerable, needy and dependent children portrayed by many perspectives on children, has innate strengths and is capable of participating in decision-making processes. Through her research Chowns was able to explore sensitively a profoundly sad life event with a group of children but simultaneously avoided reducing the children to a category – i.e. children with a terminally ill parent. Instead she related to them as children first and foremost, children coping with everyday preoccupations and having fun, who go on living everyday lives, while simultaneously recognising their competence to cope with a difficult and sad situation. And perhaps that is the most important message to convey in the opening section of this chapter – that children, above all else, are children and should not be reduced to depersonalised labels, e.g. an 'abused child', a 'looked-after child', a 'child in need', a 'child at risk'. Later in the chapter you will be introduced to the legal and procedural contexts from which these labels are derived. The priority is to consider how we respond to children as children and to ensure our responses acknowledge the unique social circumstances of each child and the vulnerability and resilience (concepts we introduced you to in our chapter on development through the lifespan) which children exhibit within their specific contexts.

In addition to our own perceptions of children, it is important to be aware of how children perceive us as social workers and what they say counts in terms of effective social work relationships and interventions. Several pieces of research referred to in the Social Care Institute for Excellence's (SCIE) knowledge review on communicating with children (Luckock et al., 2006) along with the UK government *Every Child Matters* (DfES, 2003a) document which has shaped the Children Act 2004, have sought out children's views on what they want for their lives and how social workers can help them. The overwhelming message is that children want to be respected. Children want social workers to be available, reliable and straightforward. In terms of how children want to be treated by and included in society, the findings of research conducted for the government's *Every Child Matters* report (DfES, 2003a) identified five key themes. Children want:

1. to be healthy;
2. to be safe;
3. to enjoy and achieve;
4. to make a positive contribution;
5. to experience economic well-being.

These five key objectives are also an example of how *collectively* children have been given a voice to influence government policy. Government appointments of independent Children's Commissioners is another indication of the increasing seriousness with which children's views are being taken.

Listening to children on an *individual* basis is of equal importance. As we discussed in Chapter 11 (on communication), as a social worker you will need to ensure when you become involved with families that you create opportunities for children to express their views, wishes and feelings as freely as possible and that you become attuned to both their verbal and non-verbal communications. Later in the chapter we consider some of the challenges of 'ascertaining the wishes and feelings of the child' as required under the Children Act 1989, the Children (Scotland) Act 1995 and the Children (Northern Ireland) Order 1995.

Children *and* families, not children *or* families – a difficult dilemma

As soon as we begin to think about children, however, we are confronted with a dilemma – how can we focus on the needs of a child while attending simultaneously to the family circumstances in which they are located? This dilemma has been a feature of numerous inquiries into the deaths of children known to Social Services (London Borough of Greenwich, 1987; London Borough of Brent, 1985; DfES, 2003b). A recurrent finding of these inquiries has been the difficulty social workers have had 'holding the child in mind' and not having their attention diverted to the child's parents/carers.

It is not a solution, either, to focus simply on the child and overlook other family members. All children are located in social systems and promoting their best interests involves working with their social networks as well as with them. The ecological model (Bronfenbrenner, 1979), referred to later in this chapter and in Chapter 7, encourages such perspectives and underpins the Framework for Assessment also discussed later in this chapter. Children come to the attention of social workers because of deprived, disadvantaged, dysfunctional or abusive family circumstances and often their parents have grown up in similar situations. The 'cycle of abuse' (see Hanks and Stratton, 2007 for a thoughtful account of this), as it has been framed, is a well-recognised feature of some families. This is not to suggest that it is a foregone conclusion that deprived, disadvantaged or abused children become disadvantaged or abusive parents but as Chapter 7 illustrated, early experiences play an important part in an individual's emotional and cognitive development.

Working with children and their families requires social workers to address the needs of the parents as well as the child, as often both require attention. Parents with impaired emotional development can find it difficult to manage feelings of jealousy and envy, for example, when children receive individual attention from a social worker. To avoid parents undermining the work with a child, it can be helpful to provide individual sessions for them too. One way of ensuring no one is excluded or overlooked is to co-work with families, with different workers being responsible for the adults and children concerned. This is an important principle in effective work with children and families and it should be a fundamental feature of good practice in childcare teams.

A further justification for co-working cases relates to the intensity of feelings aroused by social work involvement in families where there are concerns about the well-being and safety of the children. Co-working relationships by their very nature require practitioners to talk to each other about their shared work, thereby creating opportunities for concerns to be raised or anxieties acknowledged that have arisen from involvement with a particular family/individual. All too often the risks and challenges of working with families are underestimated. Ferguson (2005) in his research into child protection work explored social workers' experiences of violent responses to their interventions and discovered that such risks are all too common. While not wishing to scaremonger, it is vital that you have a realistic understanding of the strength of feelings this area of work evokes for everyone involved – parents and other adults, children and practitioners. We do families a disservice if we do not acknowledge the emotionally charged and challenging nature of social work involvement with them.

Reflect

The dilemma of holding both the needs of the child(ren) and their family in mind simultaneously may well resonate for you with an experience in your own childhood where you felt your opinions, feelings and what you wanted to happen were not heard.

What needed to happen for you to feel your voice was heard?

What systems could be put in place to ensure the needs of children and their families are equally attended to?

Power and purpose

The fourth fundamental principle informing effective relationship-based social work with children and families relates to the power social workers have vested in them. One of the main reasons emotions run so high in social work with children and families relates to the statutory responsibilities of childcare social workers, which allow them under certain circumstances to remove children from their families. There are specific and rigorous legal grounds that need to be met in order for such action to be taken (see Chapter 8). The strength of family ties and vehement nature of reactions to social workers, which are often compounded by inaccurate and distorted media representations of social workers' interventions, however, can make it difficult for both parents and children to manage their emotions appropriately. For this very reason it is essential that social workers understand the powers they have and exercise them thoughtfully and respectfully. Difficulties arise when heightened emotional responses from parents and carers obstruct clear thinking on the part of social workers, whose interventions as a result may be more reactive than reflective. Social workers are expected to work in partnership with families; to facilitate this working relationship, it is vital that from the outset families understand the purpose of social work involvement and the remit of the social worker. You might like to refer back at this point to the article by de Boer and Coady (2007) mentioned in the introductory chapter, which highlighted the qualities of 'good' professional partnerships in child protection cases.

With these principles – maintaining self-awareness, listening to the child, balancing the needs of children and of their carers and establishing transparent, honest relationships with families – informing your practice, there is every reason to be confident that the challenges of this area of social work can be effectively addressed in the interests of the children and families concerned. Their compatibility with the core values underpinning social work as discussed in Chapter 5 – respect for persons, non-judgemental attitude, acceptance, balance of rights and responsibilities – also ensures that practice is not only effective but ethical as well.

Childcare practice with children over the last century

We now look at the way in which social work with children has developed over the last century. Our reasons for wanting you to familiarise yourselves with earlier policies and practice are:

- An historical perspective is helpful in understanding current dilemmas and concerns, such as the emergence of children's rights.
- History can help us see that the way in which we think about and treat children is fundamentally shaped by when and in which society we are living.
- It can alert us to the danger of complacency, of thinking either that the ways we do things now are how they've always been done (and are therefore unchangeable) or that how we do things now is much better than what happened before (and therefore cannot be improved/changed).

The social construction of childhood

Although the basic biological facts of childhood have not changed much over the centuries, how we think about children and how society responds to these biological differences have changed a good deal, and vary considerably between societies as well. Every society has different rules and laws about what children are allowed and expected to do, what their families' and the state's responsibilities towards them are, and how much children themselves should be involved in decisions which are taken about them. These different understandings (or 'constructions') about childhood are commonly referred to as 'the social construction of childhood', which is a way of saying that how we think about children and childhood, what we expect of their behaviour and how we expect society and families to look after them are neither fixed nor static, but are fundamentally shaped by the perspectives which we bring as members of particular societies at a particular time. Thus James and Prout (1991: 7) suggest that 'The immaturity of children is a biological fact of life but the ways in which this immaturity is understood and made meaningful is a fact of culture.'

Think ahead

Think about your own personal views about how children should be cared for while they are growing up. Make a list of those you feel are most significant.

How many of these would you think would have been thought appropriate in a different era, or might even be considered inappropriate for the present era?

Children have across the centuries had diverse experiences of childhood, varying from the loving and affectionate to the cruel and neglected, and heavily influenced by class, custom and culture. Contrasting and often contradictory attitudes towards children can be discerned in our own culture, with its depiction of children either as little angels in need of protection, or as little devils in need of discipline and constraint. The changing meanings of childhood can also be seen in the development of childcare legislation and policy, which has at times both created and reflected different versions of childhood. One interesting illustration of this is the Children and Young Persons Act 1969, which was enacted at a time of political

A closer look

The Children Act 1948

The Act reflects the contemporary construction of childhood which Hendrick (1997) has entitled that of 'the child of the welfare state'. Within this, he discerns two identities: that of the family child and that of the child as a public responsibility. Although this awareness (of the importance of the attachment of children to their mother figure) was not new, the Curtis committee (from whose recommendations the 1948 Children Act emerged) expressed its concern with particular force, finding it shocking that

'the child in these Homes was not regarded as an individual with his rights and possessions, his own life to live, and his own contribution to offer . . . Still more important, he was without feeling that there was anyone to whom he could turn who was vitally interested in his welfare or who cared about him as a person'. (Curtis Committee 1946: 450)

Thus the publicly cared-for child was not only a citizen whom the state had a duty to treat as an individual with rights and possessions, but also one who wherever possible was to be returned to his or her natural parents, or if this was not possible, cared for in a replacement family which would provide the necessary environment 'for the proper development of his character and abilities' (Children Act 1948, section 12(1), Wilson and Petrie, 1998: 185).

and social liberalism, and emphasised the perception that a young delinquent was in need of help rather than punishment. This part of the Act, which would have taken large numbers of children and young people out of the criminal courts by raising the age of criminal responsibility, was, however, never implemented. By the early 1970s, it seems public opinion had moved on, and the criminal justice system, reflecting this, judged it no longer acceptable to see children who had committed offences as being in need of help rather than restraint and/or punishment. (See Harris, 1969: 247–63.)

Some key trends in the UK over the past century include:

- The late nineteenth and early twentieth centuries saw a range of protective measures being taken which, by curtailing child labour and introducing universal education, effectively made children more dependent on their parents and removed children from the adult world of work. In a number of respects, this period laid the foundations for many of the structures and policies which are still current today.
- In 1886, for the first time, English law placed the welfare of the child over and above that of the parents (see Chapter 8). Although not always agreeing among themselves, social psychologists and psychologists, such as Melanie Klein, Anna Freud, Susan Isaacs, Donald Winnicott and John Bowlby (whose work you were introduced to in the chapter on human development), played a significant role in the underlying thinking which shaped an important law enacted soon after the Second World War, namely the 1948 Children Act. This significant piece of legislation was also heavily influenced by the experiences of evacuated children, which provided ample confirmation of the harmful effects of separation from family and, in particular, mother or mother figure.
- The public inquiry (1946) into the death of Dennis O'Neill at the hands of his foster parents also raised public awareness about the plight of children separated from their families and placed in state care. (See Closer Look box opposite for further discussion.)
- The concept of 'prevention', in contrast to the earlier curative, 'rescue' practices of the nineteenth century and pre-war years, began to develop during the 1950s, with the idea that, through 'casework', families could be helped to improve their care for their children, an approach enshrined in the Children and Young Persons Act 1963 and the Social Work (Scotland) Act 1968. (Before this, children's departments' social workers could technically only work with children who were actually in care, or, as we would now say, 'looked after'.)

- By the 1960s, services were given an almost limitless brief of promoting children's welfare through working with their families as a whole. The era was one of considerable optimism both about the strength and formative power of families, and, where families were deficient, about the ability of judicious professional interventions to effect improvements in the lives of children and families. The 1960s also saw, however, the 'discovery' of non-accidental injuries, and childcare social workers began to incorporate recognition of the dangers inherent in families and this potential risk into their practice. In response, the Children and Young Persons Act 1969 emphasised the protection of children through such measures as 'place of safety' orders which involved the compulsory removal of children from their families.
- The death in 1974 of Maria Colwell (who had been returned to her parents from her foster home) at the hands of her stepfather, led to child abuse being placed high on professional agendas and the inauguration of a system of child abuse management, with social workers holding the statutory responsibility. (See Parton, 2001, and for a detailed analysis of the impact of the case, Parton 1985.) One of the key themes of the Maria Colwell Inquiry was the failure of the relevant agencies to communicate and work together (themes which are still central today and are highlighted in the report by Lord Laming, DfES 2003b. See Chapter 13 for full discussion).
- In 1975, the child protection register (then called the 'at risk' register) was established as a national requirement for all local authorities in order to improve communication between social workers, the medical profession and the police.
- The late 1970s saw a shift in emphasis, with increasing importance attached to the legal mandate to protect children, and the need to improve the recognition of signs and symptoms of abuse and skills in interdisciplinary working.
- A series of childcare tragedies in the 1980s saw the direction of much childcare practice set firmly away from preventative work with families in the direction of securing 'psychological' parents elsewhere (see section on looked-after children), in the context of a much more proceduralised and rigorous practice framework.

In 1987, however, another shift in emphasis arose following from the events in Cleveland where 121 children were taken into care on emergency orders over a period of six months on grounds of suspected sexual abuse. The ensuing Cleveland Inquiry led to social workers being accused of interfering 'too much' as opposed to 'too little' (as they had been criticised for in the Jasmine Beckford, Kimberley Carlile and Tyra Henry inquiries) and challenged the right of the state to intervene in family life.

A closer look

Changing emphases in childcare policy and practice

19th to early 20th century
Child and family social work starts in the United Kingdom as a service for helping children who were orphaned, maltreated or unable to live with their own families by placing them elsewhere, in residential care or alternative families.

1960s
Emphasis shifts to preventative work, directed towards helping families so that alternative care was unnecessary, and towards the prevention of delinquency.

1970s–80s
Focus of work changes to protection from physical and then sexual abuse. With the recognition that children could be harmed both by their carers and by the care system, a 'child rescue' philosophy predominates, with emphasis on finding permanent alternative families for maltreated children. The emphasis shifts firmly from residential to family care.

Reflect

The Children Act 1989 Part 1 Section 1 (3)a requires the court to establish the 'ascertainable wishes and feelings of the child concerned (considered in the light of his [sic] age and understanding) before making or discharging any order'.

In the light of the discussion above, what does this requirement suggest to you about how children and young people are currently perceived by society?

The Children Act 1989 and beyond

The 1989 Children Act was recognised to be a landmark piece of legislation designed to respond to the historical backdrop of Cleveland and earlier inquiry reports. The Act brought together public and private law to ensure that children's welfare is paramount and that all children's needs are recognised in the same way. A number of fundamental principles underpin the Act:

- **The paramouncy principle and child-centred practice.** The child's well-being is the most important consideration and children should be consulted and their religion, culture, ethnicity and language given due attention.
- **Family-focused.** Children are best looked after by their families. Parents are seen as having continuing responsibility for the care of their children, and the aim is, wherever possible, to maintain their care at home.
- **Minimal intervention and partnership.** Compulsory proceedings (i.e. care proceedings and emergency protection orders) should be avoided and parents should be involved in all decision-making processes, such as reviews and child protection conferences, and involved as partners in any intervention within their families.
- **Corporate responsibilities.** Healthy development is key to a child's welfare and local authorities are required to take a corporate and collaborative approach to providing services (Working Together, 1991 and Children Act 1989 section 27).

Thus the emphasis of the Act reflects a shift in philosophy away from 'child rescue' back to prevention, now reframed as 'family support'. Despite the focus on children's welfare needs, mainstream social work with children in the early part of the 1990s was dominated not by focusing on children in need (s. 17 Children Act 1989, s. 22 Children (Scotland) Act and **Article 18 of the Children Order**), as one might have anticipated, but by s. 47 (ch. 3 Children (Scotland) Act) enquiries relating to concerns about protecting children from harm. Social workers were still central to the process, not as social caseworkers or counsellors, but as key workers, with responsibility for coordinating, assessing risk, monitoring and evaluating progress in a context of formalised procedures and accountable policies and practice. By the mid-1990s, therefore, much childcare practice could be characterised as taking place 'in a context where notions of working together were set out in increasingly complex yet specific procedural guidelines and where the work was framed by a narrow emphasis on legalism and the need for forensic evidence'.

(Parton, 2001: 20)

The 'refocusing' of children's services

The changes which took place from the mid-1990s on in government thinking, and leading to a broad range of efforts to improve services for children and their families, have been frequently referred to as the 'refocusing' of children's services. The underlying theme of this is that social workers need to move away from an almost exclusive emphasis on child protection towards family support. The publication of the Audit Commission's 1994 report and *Child Protection: Messages from research* (DoH, 1995) focused on the perception that the preoccupation with significant harm meant resources were poorly targeted and that large numbers of children in need were not being offered help. The Audit Commission's Report, which was informed by and in part reflected findings from *Messages from Research*, recommended that:

- local authorities and health authorities produce strategic children's services to target resources more effectively;
- services should focus on identifying and assessing need and producing flexible and non-stigmatising services;
- more emphasis should be placed on prevention and less on reactive intervention.

In 1997 the Labour Government added their momentum to a broad policy shift to family support and early intervention in people's lives to prevent the downward spirals seen to be the result of disadvantage. One feature of its family policy was the recognition of the important role of poverty in family dysfunction, and accordingly a number of attempts were made to eradicate child poverty by, for example, the Children's Tax Credit and by measures to encourage employment (including of lone mothers). Another was a preoccupation with promoting stable (married) families through good parenting and community regeneration. Attempts to address social exclusion especially of young people disaffected by school were increasingly accorded high priority as problems in schools escalated. The number and range of initiatives, legislation and guidance, reproduced below, give an idea of the extent and scope of the changes.

- Children's Services Planning Order (1996) urged local authorities to reconsider their use of scarce resources. The ensuing debate resulted in a sharper focus on s. 17 (10) of the Children Act (i.e. on children 'in need').
- *Quality Protects* 1998 (*Children First* in Wales) – a programme designed to raise the standards of care for children who are vulnerable and/or looked after children by specifying eight objectives for local authorities to meet. These objectives include ensuring that children are securely attached to their caregivers, gain maximum life chance benefits from educational opportunities, and that they enter adulthood adequately prepared.
- Sure Start – an initiative targeted on areas of deprivation, bringing together early education, health and family support in the community.
- *Framework for the Assessment of Children in Need and their Families* 2000. The Framework offers detailed guidance on maintaining a focus on the child, through a systematic way of recording and analysing developmental needs and carer responses and the impact on these of the wider family and community (see next section).
- Children (Leaving Care) Act 2000 – an Act which focuses on the needs of young people after the age of 16 who are looked after by local authorities, and aims to improve the support offered to these young people (see Chapter 8 on law and social work).
- *A Review of the Safeguards for Children Living Away from Home* (Utting, 1997) was commissioned to assess the adequacy of child protection measures, particularly for children in residential care.
- Connexions Service – set up to provide young people with focused one-to-one support in making the transition to adulthood.
- Carers and Disabled Children Act 2000. This gives disabled children through their parents/carers the opportunity to commission services through direct payments (see Chapter 19).
- *National Services Framework* 2004 – long-term strategies, designed to set national standards and identify key interventions for children's health and social services, and the integration of those services with education.
- The Adoption and Children Act 2002.

Similar legislative and policy developments have taken place in Scotland, e.g. policy initiatives such as

Getting It Right For Every Child (2006) and the Protection of Children (Scotland) Act 2003.

Every Child Matters

The Laming inquiry (2003) into the death of eight-year-old Victoria Climbié at the hands of her great-aunt and the latter's partner had a profound effect on government policies. The inquiry identified multiple failures of child protection management and practice in the agencies involved, and made 108 recommendations aimed at improving practice. This report, together with the Safeguarding Children's Report 2006, were key drivers for major policy changes, identified in the government paper, *Every Child Matters* (DfES, 2003a), and incorporated into the Children Act 2004 (England and Wales).

However, arguably, despite the dramatic visual strategy adopted by Lord Laming (see A Closer Look) in order to make us face the appalling experiences which led to her death, the Report largely fails to help us make sense of *why* the various professionals and their organisations failed to exercise their responsibilities, and ends 'once again in a list of organisational and procedural recommendations for enforcing agency and professional responsibility' (Luckock, 2007: 266).

The emotional impact of child protection work

One explanation for the recurrent shortcomings in childcare social work practice may lie in the emotional impact which child protection work can have on those undertaking it. Individual professionals need to reflect on their own responses to anxiety-provoking and distressing situations such as that of Victoria Climbié. Fear and anxiety are common but under-acknowledged feelings associated with childcare social work (Ferguson, 2005; Smith, M., 2005; Smith and Nursten, 2004). Cooper (2005) in a paper exploring the Climbié Inquiry suggests that the Laming Report fails to consider this aspect of practice. He emphasises the importance of professionals being able to address the emotional impact on them of child protection work and having access to appropriate support systems. As we highlighted at the outset of this chapter, attending to distressing events in one's own childhood and in those of other children are integral components of relationship-based practice, and the events surrounding Victoria Climbié's death and that of Peter Connelly, which when it was announced in 2008 was greeted by a similar media furore, reinforce this point.

Think ahead

Think back to the opening section of this chapter and the subsection headed 'Children *and* families, not children *or* families – a difficult dilemma'.

From what you know of the circumstances surrounding Victoria Climbié and Peter Connelly's deaths, how would you explain the professional errors that arose?

What made it difficult for the professionals to keep their attention on Victoria and Peter?

What part might professionals' fears and anxieties have played?

Rather than focusing (as we think it should) on the underlying dynamics of the work, what the Laming Report *does* focus on are the failings of individuals, and their organisations, to communicate and work effectively together. Many of the changes in childcare policy arising from the Laming Inquiry, proposed in the *Every Child Matters* Green Paper and incorporated into the Children Act 2004 (England and Wales), reflect this emphasis and were designed to improve inter-professional communication and practice (as indeed earlier inquiries also repeatedly sought to do). The key policy changes included:

■ The appointment of children's commissioners throughout the countries of the UK to ensure a voice for children and young people, and to monitor how effective services are in improving services for children and young people.

■ The appointment of directors of children's services who are responsible at a minimum for local authority social services for children and young people, and education functions in relation to them.

■ The establishment of children's services separate from local authority provision of adult services.

■ The creation of Children's Trusts (England and Wales), which integrate the provision of social care, health and education services.

■ The establishment of local safeguarding-children boards (England and Wales) to replace the existing non-statutory Area Child Protection Committees.

■ A Common Assessment Framework and shared databases.

The Children Act 2004 confirmed the lead role of the local authority in planning and coordinating integrated services for children, and extended requirements on partner and other agencies to cooperate with these plans and provide their own services in ways that would safeguard and promote child welfare. A new duty required

A closer look

Victoria Climbié and Peter Connelly

At the front of his Inquiry Report into the death of Victoria Climbié, Lord Laming (2003) has had reproduced a colour photograph of Victoria Climbié. It is a striking snapshot. Presumably taken a year or more before her murder, it presents Victoria brightly dressed as she is in a yellow, red and black outfit and posh new trainers. Below the photograph is a quotation from Antoine de Saint-Exupéry's *The Little Prince* and a statement of dedication to Victoria. The quote had been selected to convey Lord Laming's sentiments in presenting his Report. 'I have suffered too much grief in setting down these heartrending memories', it says. 'If I try to describe him, it is to make sure that I shall not forget him.'

The intention is apparent. By placing Victoria within our direct gaze, readers are required to hold her in mind rather more effectively than had those professionals and managers who were supposed to support and protect her. This reinforces a central finding of the inquiry. For although she 'was not hidden away' (DfES, 2003b: 3), during the 10 months she spent in England before her death, Victoria had still been 'abandoned, unheard and unnoticed' (p. 2) by the people responsible for her support and protection.

In this period no fewer than three housing authorities, four social service departments, two police child-protection teams, the NSPCC and two NHS hospitals had contact with Victoria. In each case, as Health Secretary Alan Milburn told the House of Commons on the day the Laming Report was published, 'the authorities and the agencies empowered by Parliament to protect children . . . did nothing to help her' (Hansard 28 January 2003, column 738; Luckock, 2007: 266).

'Baby Peter', as Peter Connelly was referred to in the press, died following serious and sustained abusive and neglectful care at the hands of his mother and her partner. Similar to the circumstances surrounding Victoria's death, numerous agencies and professionals were involved with the families but no one managed to 'see' the extent of the harm Peter was experiencing before it was too late. Although not subject to a public inquiry, the engaging picture of a blue-eyed blond-haired toddler alongside the florid details surrounding his death caught public attention and generated a powerful response in the public at large and in the intense professional scrutiny which the social work profession in particular has been subjected to as a result of the shortcomings in practice identified.

Picture of Victoria Climbié, prefacing the Laming Inquiry Report
(*Source*: PA Photos)

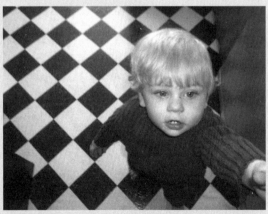

Peter Connelly
(*Source*: ITV News)

the English and Welsh local children's services authorities to set up local safeguarding-children boards to put the local arrangements for coordinating the work of key agencies in relation to child protection on to a statutory footing. Taken together, these duties and powers have created a legislative context within which arrangements to cooperate can be used to facilitate integrated planning, commissioning and delivery of services.

The Children Act 1989 functions of social services remained unchanged under these new developments, but how services are delivered locally changed dramatically through the establishment of multi-agency Children's Trusts to include health, education, voluntary and independent partnerships. The policy of integration was intended to reconnect specific arrangements for protecting children from harm with broader policies to improve child well-being as a whole and to ensure that child safety and well-being becomes a 'shared responsibility' (DfES, 2003a: 64).

These changes in part reflected yet another attempt to address difficulties arising between different groups of professionals which had been seen to lead to failures to protect children adequately. Since strategies for interprofessional working based on guidance are ineffective, then services must be brought together.

By embedding routine procedures to protect a small number of children at risk of harm within an integrated system of services for all children, the reforms aimed to build in communication and coordination both earlier and later in the process of safeguarding children's welfare. Integrated practice was demanded for reasons of *prevention of harm*, enabling the effective identification of a wide range of 'additional needs' in children and the provision of appropriate support. For those children who had been identified as in need of protection, as well as in need of support, it was also required for the *promotion of well-being*, once children had been made safe through the formal child protection process.

We return to explore some of the dilemmas created by this shift in policy towards a new inclusive and preventative ethos in more depth at the end of this first part of the chapter (see 'Where are we now?').

The Social Work Task Force

Despite the apparent confidence in the 'transformed' landscape associated with the agendas of *Every Child Matters* and *Getting It Right For Every Child*, it is well documented in the history of childcare social work that structural changes in their own right are inadequate

responses to the difficulties they are intended to address (Parton, 2004; Reder and Duncan, 2004a). In many ways, therefore, the public announcement in 2008 of the death of Baby Peter Connelly (see the Closer Look Box), came as no surprise.

Equally unsurprising and all too familiar was the official response – the announcement of a comprehensive review and overhaul of the social work profession and the setting-up of a task force to undertake this. An encouraging aspect of this most recent development, however, has been the thoughtful manner in which the task force has been constructed and conducted, evident in its efforts to incorporate a wide range of stakeholder perspectives and its efforts to find out what it is really like for practitioners 'on the ground'. The fifteen recommendations of the Task Force Report (set out in Chapter 3) have been broadly welcomed by the profession but will require ongoing government support in order for them to be realised. A positive development following the recent change of government has been its commitment to follow through on the task force recommendations, although at the same time it has instigated a more specific review into front-line child protection services.

Serious Case reviews

An important policy shift in recent years has been the greater prominence given to the role of Serious Case Reviews (SCRs). This has occurred in the light of the recent high profile deaths of children known to Children's Services (see A Closer Look which sets out the policy background to these).

The guidance for these Reviews is explicit at various points that the main purpose of an SCR is to assist organisational and child protection system learning, and not to assign blame. (see DCSF, 2010, 8.6, p. 234)

SCRs in a 'blame, name and shame' culture

However, in the climate of public and political controversy surrounding child protection work, and the Baby Peter case in particular, SCRs, their authors, the agencies and professionals on whom they report and Ofsted (the national body with responsibility for assessing the quality of SCRs) have become embroiled in the dynamics of blame for alleged errors, oversights and 'missed opportunities' associated with the deaths of particular children. Current guidance requires that LCSBs publish only the executive summary of an SCR, but in the wake of the Baby Peter crisis political pressure mounted in favour of

A closer look

The policy background

Local Children Safeguarding Boards (LCSBs) are required to carry out Serious Case Reviews (in Scotland, Child Protection Committees conduct Significant Case Reviews) under a range of defined circumstances, including when:

(a) abuse or neglect of a child is known or suspected; and

(b) either –
   (i) the child has died; or
   (ii) the child has been seriously harmed and there is cause for concern as to the way in which the authority, their Board partners or other relevant persons have worked together to safeguard the child.   (DCSF, 2010, 8.4, pp. 233–4)

Working Together to Safeguard Children: A Guide to Inter-Agency Working to Safeguard and Promote the Welfare of Children (DCSF, 2010) is the most up-to-date version at the time of writing of the guidance for the requirements of SCRS. This states that the purposes of SCRs are to:

■ establish what lessons are to be learned from the case about the way in which local professionals and organisations work individually and together to safeguard and promote the welfare of children;

■ identify clearly what those lessons are both within and between agencies, how and within what timescales they will be acted on, and what is expected to change as a result; and

■ improve intra- and inter-agency working and better safeguard and promote the welfare of children.
    (DCSF, 2010, 8.5, p. 234)

publication of the full report. SCRs became a focus of conflict between their original and stated purpose of contributing to 'system learning' and the principles of transparency and accountability for publicly funded bodies with respect to their 'performance'.

Accountability or learning – the dilemma

The dilemma is that in a climate favouring public accountability, 'telling the truth' or 'accepting responsibility' for mistakes in relations to events surrounding something as sensitive as the death of a child can have *or will be feared to have* drastic consequences for individuals. Under these conditions 'truth' is the first casualty. Pressure for SCRs to be part of a system of public accountability, and the identification of individuals who are then held to account, detracts from the goals of 'organisational learning' in several ways:

■ It moves the focus away from systems and systems analysis towards individuals and their 'accountability for their actions'.

■ It moves the focus away from learning in the direction of blaming and scapegoating.

■ As a result, it becomes less likely that we can learn from experience and thus better protect vulnerable children.

On the other hand, there is no shortage of evidence to support the argument that unless public bodies are required to operate transparently they may not learn

from experience. Instead, they may cover up their mistakes, and over time degenerate into corrupted and fearful organisations harbouring 'skeletons in the cupboard'.

Alternative models

Some have argued that the model on which SCRs are conducted is not well adapted for systems learning under any circumstances, and have set about developing and piloting alternative approaches. The Social Care Institute for Excellence (SCIE) has taken this work furthest. *Learning Together to Safeguard Children: Developing a multi-agency systems approach for case reviews* (SCIE, 2008) sets out its case like this:

'The goal of a systems case review is not limited to understanding why specific cases developed in the way they did, for better or for worse. Instead, a case is made to act "as a 'window' on the system" (Vincent, 2004, p. 242). It provides the opportunity to study the whole system, learning not just of flaws but also about what is working well. The cornerstone of the approach is that individuals are not totally free to choose between good and problematic practice. The standard of their performance is influenced by the nature of
– the tasks they perform
– the available tools designed to support them
– the environment in which they operate.
The approach, therefore, looks at *why* particular routines of thought and action take root in multi-agency professional practice. It does this by taking account of the many factors that

interact and influence individual worker's practice. Ideas can then be generated about ways of re-designing the system at all levels to make it safer. The aim is to "make it harder for people to do something wrong and easier for them to do it right".' p. viii

Reflect

One experienced SCR author summarised the dilemmas and questions that the process raised for her as follows:

'I'm still puzzling over: The difference between 'blame' and assigning responsibility when things have gone wrong. The requirement to treat the SCR as an opportunity for learning should not be seen as a means of evading responsibility for what went wrong. In addition to this, the question remains about how far up the managerial chain should responsibility go.'

How far do you think contextual issues can absolve individuals from blame? How can the tensions between assigning responsibility, learning from mistakes, and blaming individuals for them be reconciled?

Where are we now?

Children and families social work – the 'Hot Zone'

How then in the face of the significant changes and shifts in policy and practice that have taken place over the past 30 years can we collectively make sense of the constantly changing landscape of children and families social work? Child protection work is difficult, sensitive and uncertain work, and we come to the core skills and knowledge required in the next section of the chapter. But first, it is important to summarise our thinking on how the situation outlined above arose, and to set the record straight about the achievements of the child protection system in recent decades.

Periodically during this time social work's role in a few child protection cases has attracted such intense media, government and public attention that anyone could be forgiven for thinking that social work is nothing but child protection work – and that child protection work is carried out only by social workers. This is a terrible distortion of the truth, which has damaged both the profession of social work as a whole as well as what is, in fact, the multidisciplinary task of child safeguarding. As a result, social workers themselves often speak in metaphors and images that give the impression of child protection work as a 'war zone' (Beckett 2003). Sadly, this emotional and political climate has become part of the reality of this area of work.

Many newly qualified practitioners and students are openly afraid of venturing into this 'firing line', although they often nevertheless do so out of genuine interest and dedication.

Social work under pressure

The story of social work in Britain from the mid-1980s onwards is, as we have seen from the preceding chronological account of events, punctuated by a series of high profile 'crises' involving the non-accidental deaths of children in care, the revelation of widespread intra-familial sexual abuse of children as a result of the 'Cleveland affair' in 1987, the uncovering of regimes of systematic physical and sexual abuse in children's homes, claims (never substantiated) of 'Satanic abuse' rings in various parts of the country, and intense debates about whether adults and children could 'recover' reliable memories of earlier abuse. Most of these episodes involved the whole system of child protection, which was already a multi-agency, multi-professional task. But repeatedly, it was social work, including particular social workers in particular cases, who were singled out as most responsible and blameworthy for perceived 'failures' to protect children – or it was social work which was accused of intervening too quickly, too zealously and with insufficient evidence to protect children suspected of suffering abuse. This was the 'double bind' the profession then found itself in: 'damned if it did intervene, and damned when it didn't'.

Every Child Matters *and child protection*

Every Child Matters (DoE, 2003) which we introduced you to earlier, together with *Getting It Right For Every Child* in Scotland, reflected a major turning point in British childcare policy, the arrival of a new kind of 'universalism' in government intervention in the public sphere. The previous 20 years had seen various efforts to 'refocus' child care services away from an over-preoccupation with investigating child abuse in favour of more preventative services. These were largely unsuccessful, and the system remained imbalanced in many people's eyes, with too much resource and attention focused on the small number of seriously at risk children, and too little on the much larger population of children who are vulnerable or in need.

ECM attempted to turn this situation on its head. In this era child welfare policy is about *all* children, with those in most need or at most risk as just one part of this much more inclusive policy strategy. Important principles shaping *Every Child Matters* include:

- Bringing services nearer to where children spend most of their time, especially school. 'Co-location' of social work, child health and child mental health services in educational settings, and the development of 'extended schools' with a much wider remit than just educational provision, have been important developments.

- The introduction of a duty to cooperate for all services of relevance to children, whether vulnerable/at risk or not. This led to the notion of an integrated children's service 'sector' with an integrated inspection process to match.

- The lowering of the threshold for a requirement to notify children to services from 'significant harm' to 'concern'. Some have argued that this effectively introduced the principle of 'mandatory reporting' into British child welfare policy for the first time (Munro and Parton, 2007).

- These principles were intended to support the development of much more widespread 'early intervention' in the lives of vulnerable or at risk children and their families. So also, the wider concept of 'safeguarding', first introduced in the 1989 Children Act, supplants the concept of child 'protection'.

- This new terminology is reflected in the introduction of Local Child Safeguarding Boards (LCSBs) (see page 471 earlier in the chapter).

Nigel Parton (2006) has discussed *Every Child Matters* in terms of the wider emergence under 'new' Labour governments of a 'preventative state'. This idea has wider application than just child and family policy, and can be seen, for example, in adult mental health (See Chapter 20). At its simplest it involves two elements. First, an emphasis on early intervention in the lives of vulnerable people, rather than just detecting and responding to crisis; and, second, measures to place restraints on the liberty of dangerous individuals such as 'paedophiles'.

In many respects, children's policy in the last decade of the twentieth century and the early years of the twenty-first century was shaped as much by concern about children as actual or potential 'villains' than as potential victims (Parton 2006). Policies supporting interventions in the psychosocial circumstances of families identifiable as at risk of generating antisocial behaviour in their children dovetailed with continuing public and professional anxiety about child abuse and neglect. Research played an important role in this new vision. Drawing together studies from many sources, new

Labour policy consistently took the view that we now had sufficient evidence to design services that would 'work', if they were well targeted on those children, families and communities whom multiple 'risk factors' rendered most vulnerable to future difficulties.

Thus, the world that ECM brought into being was defined by the following key characteristics:

- A grand structure of universal, targeted and specialist services, respectively directed at *all* children, children in targeted *areas* or groups of children with identifiable *needs*, and children with *complex needs* or at *high risk*.

- The introduction of a wide range of 'evidence based' initiatives aimed at supporting and developing *parenting capacity*, including as a last resort compulsory 'parenting orders'.

- A massive increase in systems of *information sharing* and electronic surveillance, alongside new standardised systems for undertaking, recording, and sharing *assessments* at different levels of need or concern. (See Chapter 2.)

- The emergence of new local structures – Children's Trusts and Safeguarding Boards, as well as Children's Services designed to bring together all relevant agencies and professionals into a coordinated children's 'sector'.

In this new world of 'safeguarding' and 'concern' what happened to 'child protection' and social work with high risk cases? As we describe in the remainder of this section, child protection work continued to be an unfortunate focus of episodic explosions of social anxiety, and consolidated an unwelcome status as the riskiest specialism in a risky profession doing its work in a risk-averse world. As we have just described, policy makers did not intend this – in fact they intended something like the opposite – but policy makers do not control everything.

ECM tried to introduce a much stronger focus on family support principles, emphasising strengths-based approaches, flexible and culturally sensitive services, and some service user empowerment through involvement in planning services, including more consultation with children themselves. However, as Parton (2006: 171) notes, 'it is not straightforward to integrate such an approach with one which is explicitly suspicious of parents and carers, emphasises centralisation, accountability and the sharing of information between professionals, particularly where professionals are encouraged/required to flag up any "causes for concern" they might have to a database.'

A closer Look

Reforming child protection systems

In 2004 one of the authors of this book was consulted about the development of ECM by a member of the then Prime Minister's policy unit. On the basis of our research into the nature of child protection systems and practices in Europe and its implications for England and Wales, we were arguing for reform to the child protection system on something like 'family support' principles, with much more emphasis on 'space' for negotiation, flexibility, trust in parents and carers, and confidence and authority to be invested in social workers. On the one hand this was completely consistent with the principles of ECM, on the other hand it was clear that child protection work with high risk cases sat very uneasily within the inclusive, preventative, universalist ethos of the new policy framework – which seemed to pay little attention to the contradiction. Our impression was that Tony Blair's policy maker did not quite know which way to turn.

Good child protection work need not be incompatible with family support principles. It is a tiny minority of cases that eventually require statutory intervention or the removal of children from their homes. But this minority, and the even smaller number of children who die or are seriously harmed by carers and parents, have disproportionately influenced child protection *practice*, as well as the image and confidence of social work. As Parton says:

'The current situation is full of paradox, for while most agree that certainty in child welfare is not possible, the political and organisational climate demands it. Professionals, not just social workers as previously, have been found wanting and are no longer trusted.'   (2006: 177)

Child protection: a balance sheet of achievement

It is difficult to summarise the overall long-term impact of this turbulent decade, but there were clearly many positive consequences for society as a whole of which social work can be proud, and some very negative ones with which the whole child protection system still struggles today.

On the positive side of the balance sheet:

■ As child abuse became a matter of prominent and repeated media and political concern in our society, so public awareness of its prevalence and damaging consequences for mental well-being increased. Public

awareness campaigns such as the NSPCC's 'Full Stop' initiative played an important role here, although some of these campaigns have been criticised for creating unrealistic expectations about our capacity to prevent abuse.

■ After the Cleveland crisis of 1987, child sexual abuse, especially within families, was accepted to be a far more common occurrence than it was previously believed to be. This new understanding and acceptance spread throughout much of the world. Adults who have been sexually abused as children, a high proportion of whom are women, became more able to disclose these experiences and seek help. It became clear that sexual abuse plays an important antecedent role in the development of later mental health difficulties in adolescence and adulthood.

■ Although no evidence was found to confirm suspicions and allegations of 'Satanic abuse' in Britain or other European countries, investigations into this phenomenon helped to establish that organised abuse rings, and abuse involving ritualised practices do exist. The detection and prevention of organised abuse became much more sophisticated, although the rapid expansion of the World Wide Web has facilitated new opportunities for systematic abuse, and created new challenges for child protection services.

■ Cases of serious and systematic abuse of children in the care system were uncovered, and it was accepted that this continues to be a risk. 'Care' settings should not automatically be assumed to be safe. As recently as 2009, the disclosure of entrenched, organised abuse of children within institutions managed by the Catholic Church in Ireland revealed that the police and the state itself were complicit in maintaining systems of abuse and covering up knowledge of these.

■ Child protection work was established as a multi-agency, multi-professional responsibility, undertaken within a clear framework of legislation and guidance. However, the 'blame culture' that evolved in connection with high profile 'failures' to protect some children undermined the potential for a more equal sharing of responsibility among the professions. No one is eager to step into the firing line, and help relieve social work of its role as a convenient scapegoat when things 'go wrong'.

■ In the better local authorities, statutory child protection work became a high status, well-managed, effective service for responding to referrals involving immediate risk to children. But services of this quality are almost certainly a significant minority.

- The *Every Child Matters* and *Getting It Right For Every Child* policy initiatives have led to significant efforts to locate social work and child protection services closer to where children actually are most of the time – in schools and day-care settings. 'Co-location' of child welfare professionals alongside teachers, with the latter taking a more active and informed role in responding to children's communications about possible abuse and emotional distress, is a sound move.

- A vast amount of high quality research has been undertaken into the nature and causes of child maltreatment, better and worse ways in which services and organisations can be designed, the potential for the therapeutic care and treatment of abused children and adults, and how best to understand the social and psychological 'meaning' of different kinds of abuse. But the impact of this research has been more limited as each wave of child abuse 'moral panic' has overtaken our society, leading to panic-stricken responses by successive governments. The resources to meet the level and complexity of need revealed by the research have not been made available.

- The 'Baby Peter Connelly' crisis led to the establishment of a Social Work Task Force charged with producing a plan to radically strengthen the status, confidence, professional identity, and public image of social work. A national College of Social Work is being formed, intended to be an independent body representing the interests of social work and social workers.

Then, on the negative side of the balance sheet:

- From about 1984 onwards child protection policy in Britain was driven along by political, media and public reactions to 'single cases' of alleged 'system failure'. There was never a wholehearted attempt to stand back and understand the complexity, difficulty and sensitivity of the child protection task in our society, and then design and resource a service that responds to our new level of understanding about child maltreatment. International comparative studies of child protection work showed that Britain is unusual in its degree of political sensitivity to 'failures' of the system, and that there are child protection systems in nearby countries that operate on completely different assumptions about how best to understand and respond to child abuse.

- The series of public inquiries into child deaths starting with Jasmine Beckford in 1984 through to the Victoria Climbié Inquiry in 2003, and the 'Baby P' crisis of 2008–9 (see Closer Look boxes) resulted in successive waves of new guidance, procedures, risk assessment instruments, information-sharing protocols and systems, performance criteria, and inspection processes that were well-meaning but led to child protection work becoming, at worst, a 'bureaucratic prison'. Practitioners' time and mental space for face-to-face work with children and parents contracted.

- Media and public inquiry scapegoating of individual social workers, and occasionally other professionals such as doctors, contributed to high staff vacancy rates and turnover in many front-line services, and a reluctance to consider child protection work as a long-term career choice. Some high-profile paediatricians were challenged in court proceedings and found to have made errors of medical judgement in child abuse cases. Some were struck off their professional register. Consequently there is a serious shortage of these specialists willing to become involved in child protection work. Media vilification of named social workers reached its peak in late 2008 in a *Sun* newspaper campaign pressurising the then Secretary of State, Ed Balls, to step in and sack workers and managers in the London Borough of Haringey.

- The statutory system for reviewing individual 'serious cases' of child maltreatment or child death, which was originally intended as a way of learning from mistakes and improving practice, became caught up in the conflicted political climate surrounding child protection work. The question of whether the full text of each Serious Case Review (SCR) should be made public, rather than just the executive summary, became a political football in the lead up to the May 2010 general election in Britain (See Closer Look box). Most professionals believed that if it became policy to publish the full text, all likelihood of meaningful 'learning' would dissolve. Fear of public blame would cause everyone involved in these cases to 'cover their backs' rather than tell the truth to SCR authors.

Child protection: what could have happened but did not

The increase over the past 30 years in political and media attention to the realities of child abuse has had mixed consequences for everyone – the child protection system, social work, children and families, and our wider society. Arguably, where child abuse is concerned we are all now much more *aware* but also much more *anxious*, more *responsive* but also more *risk averse*, more *open* to the thought that abuse might be occurring but still in collective *denial* about its extent.

When child abuse hits the headlines, it is always in a context of alleged 'failure', and never one of success. From one point of view this is just the way of the world. Good news, or even just 'less' bad news, does not make the news. As someone once pointed out 'Small Earthquake in Peru – Not many Dead' is an unlikely candidate for the front page. So it is important to be aware of some hard facts that contradict the pessimistic picture often painted by the media. Researchers who have studied the changing pattern of deaths as a result of abuse, and compared these to the patterns of change in deaths of children from all causes, are cautiously optimistic about the contribution of child protection services to the improvement recorded:

'England and Wales were only one of four major developed countries whose child abuse related deaths, primarily the responsibility of the children protection services (CPS), fell significantly more than "All Causes of Death", the primary responsibility of medicine. Though there is an overlap of services, the greater improvement in the CPS-related deaths than those primarily related to child health reflect well on the CPS. This should help to offset something of the media stereotypes and be a boost for the morale of front line staff of the CPS and the families with whom they serve.'

(Pritchard and Williams, 2010)

In the light of all this, what could have happened, but so far has not, might be summarised as follows:

- Our society has tended to be reactive, blaming, and encouraged defensive organisational solutions to problems that hit the headlines in an unpredictable and arbitrary way. What has been missing is really positive, evidence-based leadership.
- Public awareness and sensitivity about child maltreatment although it has undoubtedly grown could have been much better developed. Encouraged by irresponsible media reporting, people often rush to deny feelings of fear and memories of cruelty which they have either experienced or themselves perpetrated, and locate blame with the 'messengers' – who all too often are social workers.
- Social work became progressively caught in a spiral of demoralisation, negative publicity and damaged self-confidence – a receptacle for profound social anxieties and conflicts. Of course, good and even excellent

practice survived and still does, but despite rather than because of the public and political climate surrounding child protection work.

For social work, for children and families and for society as a whole there could have been an alternative script. In future there needs to be, if we can bring it about. Social work lost confidence in itself, and needs to find an ability to fight for its self-esteem and for much greater recognition of the prevalence and destructive significance of child abuse. The Social Work Task Force and the proposed College of Social Work is placing much emphasis on building the confidence of profession. This is surely the right strategy, but it is important to remember that much of the damage done to social work over the years has had its source in the complex dynamics of child protection work in our society.

Reflect

In our previous section, we summarised the key themes and challenges In child welfare over the past decades and gave you a kind of 'balance sheet' of gains and losses. We concluded that while there have been some achievements, much more could have been achieved.

Thinking about what you have read and learned so far, and about what you have read about social work and child protection in the press, do you agree with our analysis of what has happened in this area over the past decade or so?

What In your view have been the main achievements? What have been the main barriers In the UK to achieving more? Do you feel that there are grounds for optimism/ pessimism for child welfare social work In the years ahead? What are your reasons for thinking this?

Before we move on to our next sections, we suggest that you undertake some further reading and reflection for yourself on these debates. (See the end of the chapter for some suggestions.)

Childcare practice with children

We now come to the practice and knowledge base on which social workers who are engaged in supporting and protecting children must draw. We have discussed above the change in emphasis in child protection policies and practice. The aim of these recent ones broadly has been to direct more resources towards supporting children 'in need' and their families in the community and away from resource-intensive procedural and legal interventions which offered little to children and did not ameliorate the damaging consequences of material deprivation for the children concerned.

However, this 'refocusing', which recognises the impact of socio-economic pressures on families, must not occur, as we said above, at the expense of abandoning knowledge gained, not least through the tragic lives and deaths of a, albeit small, number of children who are subject to cruel and abusive behaviour and are in need of protection. Working with families where there are child protection concerns demands highly competent practitioners. You will need to manage a highly complex environment, keep yourselves informed about legislative, policy and practice developments, while establishing and maintaining helping relationships with individual children and adults. In a short section, we can only begin to give you a brief outline of key issues and guide you to other sources of information. Throughout your involvement, you will need to base your work on the principles for good practice to which we introduced you at the beginning of the chapter.

In the following sections we begin by describing the first stages of contact between children and social workers. We go on to look at working with families where the child has been identified as in need, and working with children in need of protection, before considering the place of children who for a range of reasons are unable to live with their birth families.

Inevitably, we have to set this out as a linear process but as Chapter 10 on assessment highlighted, the process of assessing and intervening in a situation is never entirely linear. However, some of the discussion, e.g. on skills and principles, clearly forms the *framework* within which practice is conducted. It is also important to remember that children in need of protection may often also need to receive the kinds of supportive services which we describe in the section on family support. Equally, families where there are child protection concerns may be dealt with entirely through section 17 of the Children Act or section 22 of the Scottish Children Act or Article 66 Children (N.Ireland) Order 1995, rather than through section 47 investigations. The key, of course, is that a child may at any time cease to be a child 'in need of services' and either become a child 'in need of protection' or be assessed as needing no further help from services.

The referral process

In the early stages of social work involvement with a family, the social worker will most likely come from a children and families team within the children's services sector of the local authority. These teams, which have been created in line with the requirement of the Children Act 2004, will be working inter-professionally with a range of childcare professionals from social care, education and health in the best interests of the children and families in the locality they cover.

Case study

Rosie cont . . .

Below are more details about Rosie to whom you were introduced at the beginning of the chapter.

Rosie is a 6-year-old white girl who lives with her parents Carol and Mike Ashton and her younger sister Samantha, aged 3^1/$_2$. When Samantha was born, the Health Visitor records note that the family seemed to be flourishing, and that the Ashtons had good supports from friends and relatives in the neighbourhood. Mrs Ashton is now five months' pregnant. The family live on benefits in local authority housing, since Mr Ashton is currently unable to work. The house is sparsely furnished, untidy and often unhygienic. Shortly after the birth of Rosie's younger sister Samantha, Mr Ashton was admitted to hospital having had a stroke, and on his discharge he required considerable nursing care from his wife, which is ongoing.

During the last three years of Rosie's life there have been several brief social work interventions, mainly owing to concerns about Rosie's development that were identified by the Health Visitor and the pre-school playgroup that Rosie attended. Since starting school the teachers have been concerned about Rosie's unkempt appearance and her behaviour at school which was described as disruptive, volatile and attention-seeking. They are worried that her behaviour might mean that she was being abused or neglected. She was thought to have stolen food from the other children in her class, and had been seen taking discarded food from the waste bin in her classroom. She was scruffily dressed, seemed generally listless, her hair was lank and unwashed, and she was difficult to stimulate in class. Her teacher had tried to talk to her mother, but had been rebuffed. A referral was made to the Children's Team when Rosie appeared in school inappropriately dressed for a cold winter's day with bruise marks on her upper arms.

Children and young people, such as Rosie, first come to the notice of children's services in a variety of ways. Parents and children may refer themselves directly seeking help. The local authority Children's Services may be contacted by members of the public, members of the extended family or other professionals:

- a neighbour may report disturbances and children screaming all times of the day and night;
- a grandmother may be concerned about her 5-year-old granddaughter's sexualised behaviour on visits to her;
- a health visitor may raise concerns about how a teenage mother is caring for her newborn baby;
- a teacher may express concern about bruises and changes in the behaviour of a young person in their class.

The causes for concern vary enormously:

- children may be living with parents who are not able to care for them adequately, where the problems are long-standing or have arisen in the face of some temporary crisis or family problem such as divorce or separation;
- a young person may be showing a range of emotional and behavioural problems which make it difficult for parents and teachers to control them;
- some children are disabled and need specific support;
- some children are unaccompanied asylum seekers, newly arrived in the United Kingdom and unfamiliar with our systems; and finally
- some children are at risk of harm and in need of protection. This may be because of maltreatment or neglect by a parent or carer, or because the parent or carer is seemingly unable to protect them from accidental or deliberate harm by a relative or neighbour or stranger. While much less numerous, this group of

children consume a considerable proportion of social work time and resources.

Once an approach is made or a referral is received a social worker must assess whether any child in the household is *in need* (of protection S.47 or in need of support S.17) under the terms of the legislation. At this stage the social worker is required to gather basic information about the child and family:

- the nature of the concerns;
- how and why they have arisen;
- what appear to be the needs of the child and the family.

Following a referral, there are specific timescales in which referrals have to be explored and decisions reached about further action, or no action (see Framework for Assessment section below). One of the main reasons for setting down timeframes is the need to avoid the kinds of damaging delays experienced by children, when months and sometimes years might go by without a clear decision. Recognising that a year's delay, for example, could represent a third of the life of a 3-year-old, and the impact which delays may have on children's capacity to form relationships, the government guidance on assessments attempts to place a greater sense of urgency into interventions.

If it does appear that there are problems with which the family needs help, then in consultation with family members, the social worker must work out how best any identified need can be met. In most cases, the social worker will, with the permission of the family and any older child – unless to seek this would put the child at risk – consult with other agencies, for example, teachers, health visitors and general practitioners, who may have relevant information or who are already working with the family.

If a referral concerns a matter which suggests that a criminal offence has been committed, then the police must automatically be informed. Where there are offences against a child, children's services and the police will work together (according to Achieving Best Evidence in Criminal Proceedings guidelines which replaced Memorandum of Good Practice) during the initial inquiries. In less serious cases, it is usually agreed that it is in the best interests of the child for the intervention to be led by the social workers, but where a more serious offence is suspected, it is the responsibility of the police to instigate criminal proceedings. All these issues are explored further in the section below on the Framework for Assessment.

Reflect

Thinking about Rosie's circumstances, what would be your initial response? Would you consider Rosie as 'in need' or 'at risk', remembering that these need not be mutually exclusive categories?

In either case, whether the child is deemed to be 'in need' or 'at risk', the Framework for Assessment informs the early stages of intervention.

The Common Assessment Framework and the Framework for Assessment

The assessment process – principles, potential and pitfalls

Think ahead

Principles of Framework for Assessment

- It is a multi-agency approach model
- Assessment is seen as a process not an event
- It is grounded in knowledge
- It is derived from theory, research, policy and practice
- It is based on ensuring equality of opportunity for all children and their families
- It builds on strengths
- It takes an ecological approach that considers the wider social systems in which the family lives
- It is rooted in child development
- It is based on working in partnership with families and young people
- It is child-centred
- Actions and services should be provided in parallel with assessment.

(based on Calder, 2003)

In order to help you get to grips with the thinking underpinning the Framework for Assessment, place in order of priority the principles outlined above and give a reason for your decision.

The Framework for Assessment (DoH, 2000c), introduced in 2000 in England and Wales and the Integrated Assessment Framework (the 'My World Triangle', *Getting It Right for every Child*: The Guide, November 2008), replaced existing assessment frameworks that had fallen into disrepute for two main reasons. First, they failed to adopt a sufficiently holistic, proactive or inclusive approach by focusing too narrowly on who was included in the assessment process and on what was assessed. Only immediate family members were involved in the assessment process, and risk and protection issues were addressed at the expense of support needs and preventative measures. Secondly, their format and structure – primarily lists of questions – were overly prescriptive and restrictive and inhibited any creative application of the guidance in practice. As a consequence the guidance was used increasingly by social workers in a mechanistic, checklist manner. The new framework sought to redress these shortcomings (Calder, 2003) and was designed around a number of fundamental principles (see Closer Look box above). These principles in turn were informed by research (Cleaver et al., 1998), which had highlighted the pitfalls of undertaking assessments. According to Colton et al.'s (2001) summary of this research, the pitfalls include:

- Insufficient attention being given to children's views and their presentation and behaviour
- Underestimating importance of information provided by family, friends and neighbours
- Failing to ascertain family's understanding of situation
- Premature decision-making and action-taking, based on assumptions and prejudgements
- Concentrating too heavily on the presenting problem and not looking beyond it
- Failing to redirect families to other services
- Failure of social workers to seek support in anxiety-provoking or risky situations
- Inadequate recording.

The principles and pitfalls of the assessment task referred to above highlight the complex and challenging nature of the assessment process. This is particularly so in childcare social work situations where emotions 'run high' because the welfare of a child is of concern and in some instances the child's place in their family might be at risk. As the earlier chapter on assessment highlighted, however, it is all too easy to restrict understandings of assessment to procedural ones, which simply require a one-off meeting and the completion of paperwork. It is worth reiterating here as a reminder of what constitutes good practice – that assessments are a process, not an event. To be completed effectively, assessments need to involve working in partnership with the families concerned and in ways that incorporate the fundamental principles of working with children and families identified at the beginning of this chapter.

A closer look

Reform of assessment processes in Northern Ireland

In N. Ireland, concerns about the timeliness and appropriateness of childcare assessments coupled with systematic failures in safeguarding procedures (Overview Child Protection Report 2006) led to the reform of assessment processes and the introduction of the UNOCINI (Understanding the Needs of Children in Northern Ireland) Assessment Model. This model was developed to enhance greater consistency in approach, to improve the standards of assessment which would underpin decision-making and ultimately contribute to better outcomes for children.

This reform also resulted in the development of Gateway Teams within each Health and Social Care Trust which are responsible for dealing with referrals and initial assessments. (Guidance for Northern Ireland Health and Social Care Trusts April 2008). There is a clear expectation that the initial assessment will be completed within a maximum 10-working-day period with a view to automatic transfer to children's services known as Family Intervention Services (FIS) or Looked After Services. Gateway Teams also have responsibility for dealing with applications for adoption and fostering, early years registrations and enquiries, Article 4 court work applications and referrals relating to children with disabilities.

The Common Assessment Framework was introduced as a requirement of the Children Act 2004. This builds on the existing Assessment Framework and is a shared assessment tool for all practitioners working with children across all Children's Services and all local areas in England. It aims to ensure the early identification of need for children requiring additional help to achieve the 5 ECM outcomes.

The Assessment Triangle figure has become a familiar visual aid for the Framework for Assessment in England and Wales, with each side of the triangle referred to as a domain – the child's domain, the parents' domain and the family/environment domain. Each domain has a number of dimensions and it is expected that as a social worker you will explore each of the domains and dimensions with the child and family. Rose (2001) and Ward (2001) provide more detailed analysis of each domain and its components and you are encouraged to read *The Child's World* (Horwath, 2001) as it is an excellent companion reader for the Framework for Assessment itself.

On receipt of a referral you will have to decide whether further action is required, in which case an initial assessment will be initiated. If on completion of the initial assessment, within ten working days of the referral (increased in Working Together guidelines, DCSF 2010, from seven days) concerns remain, a core assessment will be instigated. So to summarise, the purpose of an initial assessment (which must be completed in 7 days) is to decide what if any further action needs to be taken. A core assessment is a fuller and more detailed process, and involves systematically collecting and analysing information in order to enable professional judge-

ments to be made as to the nature and causation of the problems, and how these can be addressed in the best interests of the child. The following factors need to be included: a risk assessment in relation to the child's developmental needs; the parents' capacity to respond to these; and the impact which the wider family and environmental factors have on the child and her/his parents.

Conducting the assessment – why, with whom, about what and how?

Why assess?

Commencing an initial or a core assessment can be distressing for all concerned – children, families and practitioners. For children it can be unsettling, even frightening, as it will mean talking to professional people with whom they may be unfamiliar. For parents it can be experienced as persecutory, involving a process of what might feel like an interrogation, with blame attached for not being 'good enough parents'. Strong feelings of confusion, anger, frustration and fear are mixed in. For practitioners, meeting with families where child welfare and protection issues have been raised can generate considerable nervousness and anxiety about how the family will respond and what actions might need to be taken. In such an emotionally charged context it is vital that all concerned have a clear understanding of why the assessment is being completed. This is particularly the case for younger children who, without clear and accurate information, can easily misunderstand professional involvement, and blame themselves for what is happening in their family (see Chapter 7).

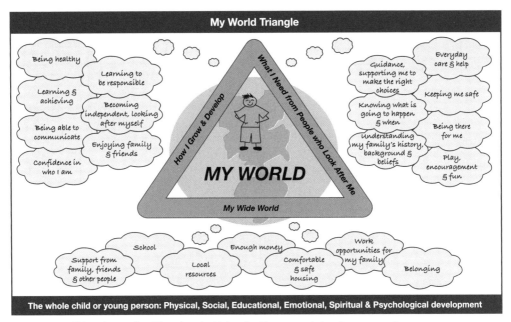

Assessment Triangle – a familiar visual aid for the Framework for Assessment

(*Source: The Framework of the Assessment of Children in Need and their Families*, Dept. of Health ISBN 0113223102.
© Crown copyright material is reproduced with the permission of the Controller of HMSO and the Queen's Printer for Scotland.)

For younger children it can be helpful to devise a child-friendly explanation, perhaps using a leaflet that describes in words and pictures your role and what will happen. With older children and adults it is helpful to draw up together a written agreement of what the assessment process comprises. Adopting such practices sets the tone, from the outset, for a shared and transparent understanding of professional involvement – the first phase of the relationship-based assessment model referred to in Chapter 1. By developing such approaches to the assessment process, you will be establishing an approach which is in keeping with several of the key principles underpinning the Framework for Assessment – child-centred, developmentally appropriate and partnership-based.

With whom?

Once a family has been referred to Social Services it may seem to you immediately apparent who will need to be consulted in the course of the assessment process. As a social worker, however, it is important that you invite the family to identify the key people who should contribute to the assessment process. Relying on your own assumptions of who are 'key players' in this family runs the risk of excluding important individuals in the family's wider social network. By consulting with the family in the early stages of the assessment process, you will be promoting the strengths-based and ecological perspectives that are embedded in the Framework for Assessment. These perspectives recognise the family as experts on their own situation and the family's wider social networks as significant for their functioning. This can be experienced as empowering to the family in a situation that often makes families feel powerless. This is particularly the case if anonymous referrals have been made about a family or when other professionals have referred a family without informing them of their intention to do so. Empowering approaches early on in the assessment process contribute to building an authentic partnership with families.

A useful way of establishing who are the important members in a family and its social networks is to invite the family to complete a genogram or ecomap, tools used in individual and family work discussed later in this chapter and in Chapter 10. Put simply, genograms and ecomaps are visual depictions of family relationships. They are particularly useful with families for whom verbal or written forms of communication are difficult to use.

Genograms and ecomaps can be a rich source of information particularly when the family do them collectively, as they highlight the different perspectives on family relationships held by individual family

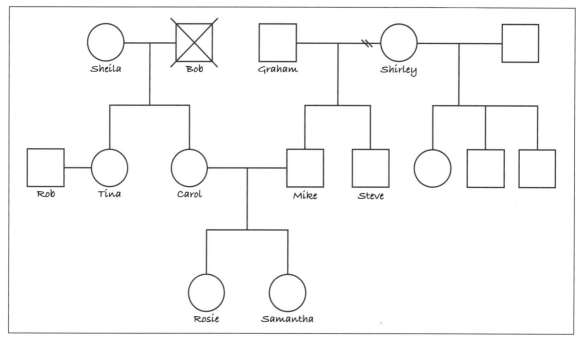

Figure 16.1 The Ashton family genogram

members. In Rosie's case, completing the ecomap highlighted the important relationship Carol has with her sister and the informal source of support she offers the Ashton family (Figure 16.1). The completed ecomap can then be used when meeting with individuals to develop conversations and to explore the different perceptions encountered. Genograms and ecomaps can be extended to include professionals involved with the family, or a separate genogram or ecomap of these professionals can be created. These visual aids illuminate how the family relates to the different people concerned about them and their children. It is important for you as the social worker to make clear who you will be talking to and how inter-professional communication is vital to the wellbeing and safety of children.

In conjunction with the negotiations about who should be involved in the assessment, there are important conversations to be had about the combination of people who might be seen together/individually and where and when the meetings take place. The time constraints of core assessments referred to earlier in the chapter make it imperative that the meetings are well organised. In families with babies, arrangements need to be put in place to observe different key carers with the baby. Where young children are involved, seeing them individually is important to ensure they have the

opportunity to voice their views and to fulfil the legal requirement of 'ascertaining the wishes and feelings of the child'. A repeated criticism of social work practice reported in childcare inquiries is the failure of practitioners to see the child alone (DfES, 2003b). Finding a private space in the home can be difficult to achieve and, if appropriate, arranging to meet in another venue (with parents on site but separate for younger children) can be helpful. While the individuality of children means it is essential each child in a family is engaged with separately, observing and interviewing sibling groups together can be informative, as children experience their circumstances differently and their interactions and relationships can contribute to a more comprehensive assessment. In the same way, it is important that at some point the *whole* family meets with the social worker(s) concerned, both to ensure common understandings exist about what is happening and to enable the social worker(s) to observe the whole family interacting together. Various permutations and combinations of the whole family, sub-groupings and individual meetings will contribute to a more holistic assessment and it is your responsibility to devise with the family the right pattern of meetings for them.

In addition to the family and friends who are included in the assessment process, consideration must also be given to the professionals who are approached. Inter-professional collaboration is a central thrust of the new CAF. It should not be seen, however, as the exclusive domain of the professionals who consult with each other to the exclusion of the family. Wherever possible the views of other professionals should be shared through meetings that include the family. Such strategies promote transparent working relationships and are key to sound partnership approaches. Once again the relevant professionals should be identified by both the family and the social worker as they will not necessarily be the same group of people. Families may, for example, have involvement with a religious group and choose to include the group's leader in the assessment process as someone who understands their beliefs and culture. You may not be aware of this affiliation.

Reflect

Consider the Ashton family genogram in Figure 16.1.

In beginning the assessment process who would you want to meet? In what combination? In what order?

Where would you think is most appropriate to meet with the people you identified above?

You might find it helpful to meet with the key family members – Carol, Mike, Rosie and Samantha – together first of all to get a 'feel' for the family. It is probably important early on to meet with Carol and Mike, who can explain how they see their situation. Meeting with Rosie initially with her parents would be appropriate, given her age, but a separate meeting with Rosie is vital too. As these suggestions indicate, however, there is no

right or wrong order and you will need to judge how best to organise the meetings in ways that enable you to effectively complete the assessment task but simultaneously promote partnership.

About what and how?

Once it is clearly established why an assessment is being conducted and who is involved, it should be possible to move into the second, third and fourth phases of the assessment model outlined in Chapter 10 on assessment, which involve developing:

- a collaborative construction of the concerns;
- a mutually determined analysis;
- a collaborative intervention strategy.

Within the Framework for Assessment guidance and the associated *Working Together to Safeguard Children* (DoH, 2006c) publication, clear expectations are given about what should be addressed in the course of an assessment (see the Closer Look box below).

It is unlikely you would dispute the appropriateness of these guidelines. However, what they fail fully to recognise is the emotionally charged nature of the assessment task. In thinking about conducting an assessment, you need to consider not only *what* information to gather but also *how* to gather it. All of the phases of the assessment process rely on the concerns raised being discussed in a transparent, reflective and cyclical manner. What this means in practice is adopting an approach that moves beyond a checklist and invites the child and family to tell their story. This may require going back over information or understandings as they emerge over the course of time. As the social worker, it is your

---

A closer look

Guidance for conducting assessments

- There must be clarity of purpose about the questions to be answered by the assessment process.
- Evidence, and not unsubstantiated opinion, of what is seen, heard and read must be carefully collected and recorded.
- Attaching meanings to information collected must distinguish the child's and family's understanding from that of professionals'.
- There must be clarity about the sources of knowledge which inform professional judgement.

- Severity, immediacy and complexity of the child's situation will have important influences on the pace, scope and procedural formality of assessment.
- Coordinated and holistic assessments must be followed by judgement, leading to clear decisions and coordinated and holistic planning and intervention/action.
- There has to be clarity about what has to change, how it will be achieved, in what timescale and how it will be measured and reviewed.

Framework for the Assessment of Children in Need (DoH, 2000c) and Working Together to Safeguard Children (1999a), cited in Rose (2001))

responsibility to explore the information given and to address areas that the child and family may not have touched on. Acknowledging and making explicit the heightened sensitivities that develop when children's services become involved with a family can help to diffuse some of the initial tension that can characterise early assessment meetings. By adopting a 'position of curiosity', a term used in systemic work (see Chapter 12 and Cecchin, 1987), it is possible to undertake assessments which are respectful of the family, even in situations of hostility, and in ways which minimise what can be experienced as the accusatory or inquisitorial dimensions of the assessment process. Being curious involves asking when comments surprise you, checking out with the individual/family when something does not make sense, commenting when different family members' contributions contradict each other. It is also about observing the process of gathering information, i.e. what it feels like 'in the room' and afterwards, and how you experience the encounter with an individual, sub-group of the family/family network, or whole family. Working in this way reduces the sense of you as the professional 'sitting in judgement' over a family and emphasises your wish to understand more openly, honestly and accurately what happens in this unique family context.

Reflect

Bearing in mind the guidance for conducting assessments, what are the questions in your mind from the little that you know of the Ashton family's circumstances? How would you think about phrasing them?

How would you structure your meeting with the family?

What would you say about your role?

You might want to think about asking each member of the family how they think another member perceives the problem, for example, as this can open up different perspectives on the situation and encourage dialogue between family members. (We explore this approach, sometimes called 'circular questioning', in the section on systems approaches in Chapter 12). While it might take time, inviting the family to 'tell their story' can provide more information than by simply adhering to the structured format of assessment guidance.

As highlighted in Chapter 10, an important principle when undertaking an assessment is to remember that everything that occurs is informative. For example, missed appointments and chaotic or seemingly unproductive sessions need to be thought about and reflected back to

the family. How do they understand what is going on? The challenge for the social worker is to ensure they balance the risks to the child(ren), the needs of the child(ren) and the family and their strengths. You might find it useful at the end of each session to invite the family to comment on how they have found the session, what they found helpful or less helpful. Clearly when a session has been tense and difficult it is important that you acknowledge this. Once again using pictorial techniques, particularly with children, can facilitate this aspect of the work. It is well recognised in counselling contexts that the most significant comments are often made as the person is leaving the room. In a similar vein, incorporating an evaluation component into each assessment session should be seen as integral to the session and a point at which important information may be gathered. You might, for example, think about asking each person to tell you:

- something they discovered in talking about their circumstances;
- how they are feeling now the meeting has finished;
- what they think they could do differently to help the situation.

An integral part of the assessment framework and process is ensuring the information gathered is fully analysed by all concerned before a decision is reached. This is not to say that there will not be any disagreement or discord during the assessment process. It is inevitable that you as a social worker may see a situation differently to parents whose parenting capabilities are being questioned. Partnership-based approaches, however, encourage the instances of discord and disagreement to be openly and honestly acknowledged. Any recordings made, decisions reached or actions taken need to reflect the differences of opinion, and how the negotiated 'next steps' reflect these differing positions. The final step in the process, and one which is often omitted, is formulating the information into an assessment, which identifies key concerns and attempts to explain (develop a hypothesis about) the causes and, through this, the target problems for change.

Case study

Rosie cont . . .

A detailed history identified that Rosie's behaviour had begun to deteriorate when she was 2½, triggered by her introduction to playgroup for which she was emotionally unready (see page 150 onwards in Chapter 7 on human development through the lifespan as to why, in attachment and development terms, this might have been a critical time for her) and her mother's preoccupation with the new baby. Her worsening behaviour coincided with Mr Ashton's illness, and Mrs Ashton lacked the spare emotional resources to reassure her and had resorted to punishment and the withholding of love. Neither parent really understood that their behaviour could have an effect on Rosie, but their embarrassment about it had led to their withdrawing from potentially supportive contact with their extended family. This assessment suggested that with support and help in addressing the above issues, Rosie's place in her family could be secured.

Children in need and the role of support services

We now consider the kinds of services which might be provided to a child and their family if the assessment has concluded that the child is in need (under the terms of the Children Acts of 1989 and 1995 – see Chapter 8). Thus in the case of Rosie, the social workers might have concluded that she was unlikely to reach a reasonable standard of development unless her parents were given some help and guidance in caring for her, or help in managing other issues within the family and so on, and might have wondered what additional resources, perhaps from the wider family, could be brought in to provide support.

As you have learnt earlier in the chapter, the emphasis in recent years has been towards ensuring one route is not focused on to the exclusion of others, i.e. that the welfare needs of children are not overlooked by too narrow a focus on risk and child protection interventions. Children in need of social work support and children in need of protection can unhelpfully be separated into two categories – children in need and children at risk. This false distinction overlooks the inevitable fact that if a child is at risk s/he is in need, and that children in need are more likely to become children at risk than children not identified as 'in need'. *Messages from Research* (DoH, 1995), the Children's Acts and Frameworks for Assessment all underline the importance of the welfare needs of children referred to Social Services being identified and responded to at the earliest opportunity, regardless of whether child protection concerns have been raised. Core assessments for children in need will focus on family support services as defined under Section 17 of the Children Act 1989 and also in Schedule 2 para. 9 (Section 22 of the Scottish Children Act). The primary emphasis of these sections of the Acts, in keeping with their overarching principle, is on helping families stay together. You may wish to refer to Chapter 8 to remind yourself of this aspect of childcare law.

The idea behind support services for families is two-fold:

- First, as a preventative measure – to prevent a deterioration in a family's circumstances that could place the child(ren) at risk
- Secondly, to support a family in which the child(ren) is/are deemed to be at risk.

A closer look

The Children Act 1989 (England and Wales)

The support services identified in the Children Act include the following:

- Providing day care for pre-school children
- Advice, guidance and counselling – for child or family member to promote their functioning
- Occupational, social, cultural or recreational activities – this can include such services as after-school or holiday clubs for children, parenting or other activity-based groups

- Home help – to support parents caring for children, particularly younger children or those with complex needs/disabilities
- Travel costs to enable families to benefit from any services provided
- Holidays
- Family centre provision – which could encompass any of the above services
- Accommodation – short-term breaks for children to stay with foster carers, providing parents with a 'breather'. This can be particularly useful and appropriate when there are limited family/social networks that could offer similar support.

In a chapter looking at prevention and family support, Colton et al. (2001) explore in more detail what these different types of services might look like. An interesting aspect of their approach is the distinction between social networking – i.e. strategies for helping families to identify within their own social context the sources of support – and neighbourhood-based and family centre services – i.e. those services provided by professional bodies.

An important characteristic of support services in the Children Act is the emphasis on their being understood as a positive resource for families which are designed to support them, rather than being conceived of as stigmatising and as a sign of parents having failed. This is an important distinction, particularly for families who already feel vulnerable and 'judged', but unfortunately this distinction is one that is not always clearly made. In our Closer Look box, and below, we consider some of the formal sources of support that might be offered to families, before exploring how these were used to help Rosie and her family.

Intervening, supporting and sustaining families

Think ahead

Refer back to the support services identified above. Which of the services identified in the Children Act 1989 do you think would be most helpful and supportive for Rosie and her family's current circumstances?

Can you think of any different services/interventions that the family might find helpful?

The Ashtons might well find it helpful if Rosie attended an after-school club, or if a home help was provided to support the family when the third baby arrives. Such small but significant informal offers of support can make all the difference to a family struggling to cope. It sometimes requires, however, the social worker to help mobilise the family's own resources and strengths. Being able to develop effective relationships with families that maximise the families' strengths and draw on the resources located in their informal networks is a vital skill to develop.

Alongside a family's resources and support networks, there are a number of well-established professional interventions that come under the umbrella of support services. Four of the most important of these, and ones which might be considered in supporting the Ashtons are:

- Family group conferences
- Family work
- Family centres
- Parenting programmes.

Family group conferences

Family group conferences (FGCs) originate from the Maori communities of New Zealand (Marsh and Crow, 1998). FGCs are a means of drawing on the strengths of families and their ability to devise their own solutions to family difficulties. A neutral facilitator convenes the conference with invitations extended to people identified by the family as important in their lives. The end result is a mutually agreed plan of action that ensures that the well-being and safety of the children in the

A closer look

Help which family group conferences may provide

The researchers concluded that part of the success of family group conferences in their study lay in the fact that the process was seen as separate from the statutory one, and that the convenor was independent of social services, someone with her feet on the ground – 'she's lovely – she's sound as a pound – she's really lived life – she was like me, really', as Kirstie's mother commented. The preparation time, with the convenor making two or three visits to the house, had helped set the scene, as a chance for the family to get together and see what they themselves could come up with. In their case, this had

worked – one 15-year-old who had been in and out of care was asked, *what made it different?* 'Being given the choice. I had the decision whether or not I wanted to [go on a rehab scheme] and all the family decided whether it was a good idea, and whether it was good for me. I think it was me that made the decisions really. So that's good, because I've never been able to do that before, I've just had social workers making decisions for me, without even consulting me, so that was really brilliant, because you get to decide for yourself.'

(*Source*: Bell and Wilson 'Children's views of family group conferences', *The British Journal of Social Work*, 2006, 36(4): 671–81, by permission of the British Association of Social Workers)

family are promoted. While not without their difficulties, particularly when different 'sides' of families do not 'see eye to eye', they do empower families to resolve their problems without too much professional 'intrusion'/ intervention (see our Closer Look box, above).

Case study

Rosie cont . . .

You may have noticed in the earlier account of Rosie's family that there was a wide extended family scattered through the town. The assessment found that over the years the Ashtons had lost touch with their wider family, as they struggled with ill health, financial difficulties, and as Mrs Ashton became more depressed. With the Ashtons' agreement, it was decided to arrange a family group conference, which Mrs Ashton's sister Tina, her husband Rob and two other of her relatives attended. It emerged that Tina had been concerned about the family, and particularly about Rosie for some time but had not wanted 'to be nosey'. Tina offered to look after Samantha two afternoons a week to enable Mrs Ashton to spend more time with Rosie after school. Rob also agreed to help out by driving Mrs Ashton to the supermarket once a week for the 'family shop' as Mr Ashton was not well enough to drive.

Family work

Family work, discussed more fully under systemic working in Chapter 12, is an opportunity to involve the whole family in thinking about their current position. Many of the techniques used with children, such as ecomaps and life maps, are equally suited to family work and can be an interesting way of helping the family cooperate on a task. For many adults the opportunity to get down on the floor and engage in creative activities is surprisingly enjoyable and empowering as it enables them to express themselves in ways that more formal verbally based approaches prohibit.

Family centres

Family centres are a significant support system for families as they are specifically referred to in the Children Act 1989 and provide a wide range of diverse services to support families. Family centres come in all shapes and sizes (Warren-Adamson, 2006; McMahon and Ward, 2001). They range from statutory provision which supplements

the work of Local Authority children and family teams, for example by undertaking assessments, through to centres run by voluntary organisations such as Barnardo's and the NSPCC, which provide more community-based services such as play schemes, activity groups and parenting programmes. As a means of providing support for both the children and parents in families, family centres have an important role to play in family support (see our Closer Look box, below).

Case study

Rosie cont . . .

As part of the core assessment process, it was arranged for the Ashton family to attend a family centre where they met with social workers to discuss their circumstances. One of the recommendations of the assessment was for Mr and Mrs Ashton to attend a parenting group to help them develop their parenting skills and think about Mrs Ashton's poor relationship with Rosie.

Parenting programmes

Many family centres now offer a variety of parenting programmes in order to support and help parents. Some examples of parenting programmes which you may have heard of are the Webster-Stratton Parenting Programmes, the Mellow Parenting Programmes and Family Links. Parenting programmes vary in the way in which they are organised and delivered, for example, some are fairly informal and run by volunteers, others such as the Webster-Stratton programmes follow a strictly delineated schedule delivered by professionals, who must be trained in the method in order to be permitted to use the materials. The training is delivered to parents drawn from the same community; parents undertake 'homework' between sessions with the help of a mentor or 'buddy', and parallel groups for their children are usually run at the same time. The training in all programmes is based on the principles that parents can be helped to learn new and more effective ways of interacting with their children, and that usually working in groups with other parents is experienced as non-stigmatising and therefore facilitates parents' engagement.

A review of the effectiveness of these programmes, carried out by the Policy Research Bureau (Moran et al., 2004), showed that parenting support benefits families, especially where efforts were made to 'normalise' access

A closer look

Family centres

Many family centres provide a range of services within an existing social and geographical community, identifying individual and group needs for information, support, advocacy, play and so on. Since family centres are generally sited where they are particularly accessible to vulnerable families, they are often working to help families with the highest need (and this is their *raison d'être*). The social work model of targeted intervention of family support services may become incorporated into the community work model of these 'integrated' family centres (Gill, 1988), helpful in offering the flexible and non-stigmatising service recommended by the Audit Commission Report (1994). Other family centres have different specialisms and some may concentrate on assessment or more avowedly therapeutic work while others take on a more educational role in teaching parenting skills. On the whole, family centres are the friendly acceptable face of social services. They are able to engage families who would avoid a child guidance clinic or fear a child-protection social worker.

What families find most supportive and helpful from family centres are: working in partnership, having time to build trusting relationships with staff in a safe and secure environment, feeling empowered, having strengths as well as weaknesses identified, working openly and honestly – with effective communication and having their needs met as well as their children's.

(McMahon and Ward, 2001: 16)

---

to support. Better outcomes were evidenced where interventions were early, where they had a strong theoretical base and clearly articulated model of mechanisms for change, and where close attention was paid to engaging parents. However, many parents find the prospect of attending groups daunting, and those who lack confidence or have few social skills may be difficult to engage. One study of play therapy with individual children reported improvements on the part of their carers, and argued that sometimes individual work with children, provided that it fully involves carers in the therapy, may at least initially be more acceptable and effective (Wilson and Ryan, 2001b).

Think ahead

Louise Casey, coordinator of the UK government's Respect Programme, reports that the government has been working with a group of experts to assemble standard-format parent classes, and will soon start integrating parenting classes in the handout of Asbos. She argues that 'these parenting courses are needed and wanted and the evidence . . . shows that they work.' Casey is open that some parents – with children on the edge – may have to be forced on to parenting classes as part of parenting orders.   (*Guardian Society*, 1 August 2006)

How successful do you think these measures will be?

Given that programmes are found to be more successful when they are non-stigmatising (as the study cited above about 'normalising' support indicates), what drawbacks might there be in such compulsory attendance?

Working with children in need of protection – the framework for safeguarding children*

Case study

Rosie cont . . .

The school's referral of Rosie resulted in a section 47 Child Protection investigation being undertaken alongside the initial assessment, because of concerns about the bruising, Rosie's evident hunger and lack of appropriate clothing. Given the history of low-grade concerns about Rosie, the lack of an acceptable explanation for the bruising, and the pressures on the family with Mrs Ashton being heavily pregnant and Mr Ashton in poor health, it was decided to call a Child Protection conference.

---

*For ease of flow and comprehension this section uses the English framework. The Scottish framework for child protection is under review and updates can be found at www.scotland.gov.uk/Topics/People/Young-People/children-families/17834/GuidanceReview. Similarly Northern Ireland's child protection framework 'Co-Operating to Safeguard Children' (DHSSPSS 2003) is due for review as part of the DHSSPSS 'Reform Implementation Strategy' 2008.

Section 47: inquiries and initial discussions

As Figure 16.2 outlines, there are various stages which must be gone through in response to a possible child protection inquiry under section 47 of the Children Act 1989. Following a referral, an immediate strategy discussion will take place, initiated by the social worker and involving other professionals as appropriate. A decision will then be made as to whether or not to undertake further investigations. These inquiries must all be conducted within a specified timetable (see Closer Look box following).

Children who are thought to be suffering or likely to suffer significant harm and their families may find themselves entering the child protection system as a result of an inquiry under section 47 of the Children Act 1989. These inquiries enable the local authority to decide if they need to take action to protect the child from harm or to promote her or his welfare, or if the child is likely to suffer significant harm. It will often be the context (i.e. circumstantial evidence, history, etc.) in which the harm has occurred which will influence whether or not it is seen as significant harm.

Timescales for statutory interventions

Within a maximum of one day, a decision is required to determine if an initial assessment is needed:
– Either initial assessment planning and intervention
– Or no further action.

A maximum timescale of seven working days:
– Strategy meeting
– Decision to undertake a core assessment.

A maximum of 35 working days:
– Core and specialist assessment/planning interventions
– Initial child protection conference
– Outline of child protection plan.

Decision that child is experiencing significant harm
Detailed child protection plan
Analysis of needs of child and parenting capacity
Core group meeting.

Further assessments if necessary/planning/intervention

Review plan
Further review conference(s)
Deregister

It is clear therefore that minor shortcomings in the health care provided, or minor deficits in physical, psychological or social development, should not give rise to compulsory intervention unless they are likely to have or are having serious and lasting effects on the child.

Forms of abuse

As we shall see, sadly, most children who are considered to be in need of protection have been abused (or as it is sometimes called, maltreated) by family members, friends or acquaintances. 'Stranger abuse' is much less common. It may nonetheless cause serious emotional upset to the child and support to the child and the family in helping her/him, together may be required.

How do we judge 'significant harm?'

Guidance from the Department of Health (1999a) states that

'there are no absolute criteria on which to rely when judging what constitutes significant harm. Consideration of the severity of ill-treatment may include the degree and the extent of physical harm, the duration and frequency of abuse and neglect, and the extent of premeditation. More often, significant harm is a compilation of significant events, both acute and long-standing, which interrupt, change or damage the child's physical, social and psychological development. Some children live in family and social circumstances where their health and development are neglected . . . In each case it is necessary to consider any ill-treatment alongside the families' strength and support.'

Child maltreatment is often identified in categories which are used to define abuse, and which were until recently used when placing a child on the child protection register. This national system for the annual collation of child abuse statistics was introduced in the 1970s, and continued until April 2008, when it was abolished for England, although there is now provision for a child to be designated as the subject of a child protection plan. (Registration is still used in Scotland, Wales and Northern Ireland.)

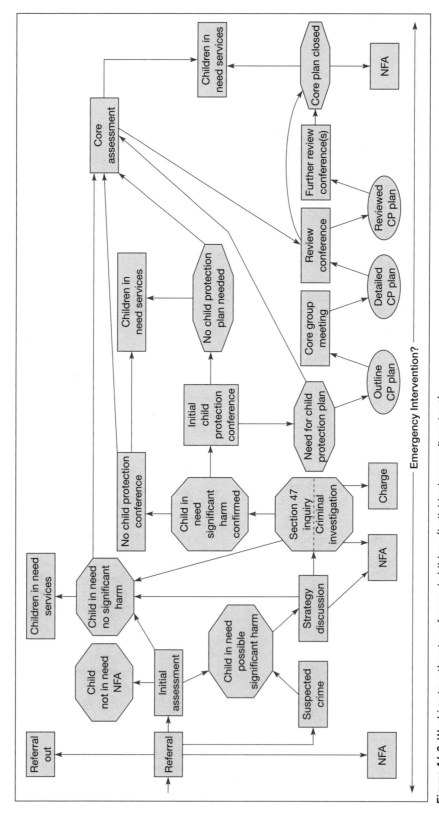

Figure 16.2 Working together to safeguard children (individual cases flowchart)

(*Source*: Based on Department of Health (2000) *The Framework for the Assessment of Children in Need and their Families*)

Think ahead

The abolition of child protection registers in England from April 2008

These were abolished without any research evidence to justify this change, following the recommendation by Lord Laming (2003, 17.10). We may ask why, since the register provided an effective alert system to hospitals, police and other professionals in facilitating the identification of vulnerable children. And evidence that registration provided some protection is demonstrated in studies of serious case reviews which show that few children died who had been on the register. (Brandon et al. (2008) reviewed 161 SCRs over a two-year period, two-thirds of which involved a fatality: only 12 per cent were on the register – although this may be evidence of 'hidden maltreatment', it may also show that registration offered some protection.)

Do you think that the provisions to identify children subject to a child protection plan within the children's database will provide adequate safeguards in the future? How easily will social workers be able to manage and access the systems and identify those vulnerable children who are most at risk?

It is important to remember that many maltreated children suffer different forms of abuse, and their experiences cannot be neatly pigeon-holed into one form or another. For example, children who are sexually abused may be subject to physical injuries, and are often threatened or coerced into concealing or denying the abuse. (Multiple categories which are used in Wales and Northern Ireland to some extent address this.) Moreover, all forms of abuse have a strong emotional component, and for most children it is the whole experience which is abusive and there are no dividing lines between the different kinds of abusive acts. Although the categories may be useful in helping us understand abuse, therefore, and are important for those planning child welfare services (Kirton, 2009) they should be treated with caution, since they may distance you from understanding the actual, complex experience of the individual child.

Since the abolition of the child protection registers, it has proved harder to establish up to date incidence or prevalence figures. However, you will see from the figures for registrations or of children with a child protection plan up to 2009 that neglect forms by far the largest category for which children were registered. Registrations of children under the categories of sexual abuse and physical abuse have shown a marked proportional decline since the mid-1990s.

Think ahead

The frequency of child abuse in a country is usually derived from prevalence or incidence studies:

- **Prevalence** *of child abuse refers to the proportion of the defined population who have been abused during a specified time period – usually childhood (i.e. 0–18)*
- **Incidence** *refers to the number of new cases identified as occurring in a defined child population over a year. There are four key types of maltreatment: physical abuse, sexual abuse, emotional abuse and neglect.*

In the light of this, and our discussion above about public awareness of abuse but also some of the barriers to disclosure, how likely do you think that the figures of child maltreatment in the UK shown in the following tables are an accurate representation of its occurrence?

What follows are the definitions of child abuse which were customarily used as criteria for registration.

Neglect

'The persistent or severe neglect of a child or the failure to protect a child from exposure to any kind of danger, including cold and starvation or extreme failure to carry out important aspects of care, resulting in the significant impairment of the child's health and development, including non-organic failure to thrive.'   (DoH, 1991a: 48)

Child neglect can arise from:

- Inadequate or inappropriate clothing
- Inadequate or inappropriate food
- Denying or failing to provide the child with adequate warmth or shelter
- Failing to wash or bathe the child
- Failing to provide the child with clean clothing and a hygienic environment.

Children who have been neglected are likely to show symptoms which are very similar to those of emotional abuse, to which it is closely linked. The consequences of neglect, as with physical abuse, can range from death in extreme cases (from starvation, cold, lack of medical care or daily care) to physical neglect (poor hygiene and nutrition, dangerous physical surroundings), understimulation, and lack of monitoring of children's whereabouts. Indeed, the effects of serious neglect have more serious, generalised developmental effects that are often less amenable to intervention than other forms of maltreatment. These children, if their neglect occurs over a

A closer look

UK child abuse registration figures showing national trends in registration for different forms of abuse, 2005–9

Children and young people subject of a Child Protection Plan (CPP) – England 2005–2009, at 31 March, by category of abuse

Category of abuse	2005	2006	2007	2008	2009
Neglect	11,400	11,800	12,500	13,400	15,800
Physical abuse	3,900	3,600	3,500	3,400	4,400
Sexual abuse	2,400	2,300	2,000	2,000	2,000
Emotional abuse	5,200	6,000	7,100	7,900	9,100
Mixed/not recommended by 'Working Together'	3,000	2,700	2,700	2,500	2,900
Total	25,900	26,400	27,900	29,200	34,100

Source: www.nspcc.org.uk/inform

Number of registrations following a case conference – Scotland 2005–2008/09, at 31 March, by category of abuse/risk identified by conference

Category of abuse	2005	2006	2007	2008	2009
Physical injury	628	781	778	715	876
Sexual abuse	226	303	270	189	229
Emotional abuse	376	438	550	615	877
Physical neglect	1,035	1,261	1,520	1,255	1,625
Failure to thrive	11	6	7	8	14
Unknown	18	22	23	32	7
Total	2,294	2,811	3,148	2,814	3,628

Note: Figures prior to 2005/06 may not be comparable due to a definitional change made in counting child protection referrals in 2005/06 (see background notes).

Source: www.nspcc.org.uk/inform

Children and young people on the Child Protection Register – Wales 2005–2009, at 31 March, by category of abuse

Category of abuse	2005	2006	2007	2008	2009
Neglect, physical abuse and sexual abuse	15	10	10	0	5
Neglect and physical abuse	120	140	170	125	130
Neglect and sexual abuse	65	40	25	30	45
Physical abuse and sexual abuse	25	20	20	15	10
Neglect (only)	975	1,055	1,125	1,095	1,120
Physical abuse (only)	425	345	350	315	385
Sexual abuse (only)	175	145	160	160	175
Emotional abuse (only)	470	410	470	580	645
Total of all abuse categories	2,270	2,165	2,325	2,320	2,510

Source: www.nspcc.org.uk/inform

Children on the Child Protection Register – Northern Ireland 2005–2009, at 31 March, by category of abuse

Category of abuse	2005	2006	2007	2008	2009
Neglect, physical and sexual abuse	15	18	40	42	72
Neglect and physical abuse	153	142	245	223	367
Neglect and sexual abuse	49	46	59	80	89
Physical and sexual abuse	30	39	84	63	74
Neglect (only)	554	582	569	665	706
Physical abuse (only)	316	323	357	488	618
Sexual abuse (only)	234	226	225	244	242
Emotional abuse (only)	242	263	226	266	320
All categories of abuse	1,593	1,639	1,805	2,071	2,488

Source: www.nspcc.org.uk/inform

Note: The compilation methods of the statistics can change from year to year and from region to region, and so the figures are not always comparable.

period of time, are likely to experience significant developmental delay, often with poor speech and learning ability. Hanks and Stratton (2007) list additional possible outcomes, suggesting that neglected children often exhibit the following symptoms:

- very passive in infancy;
- are sometimes very active, but totally unfocused when older;
- have limited ability to attend to the behaviour of others;
- are accident prone, because they are not properly protected;
- may have stunted growth.

Case study

Rosie cont . . .

Given the history of concerns about Rosie's development and well-being and the recent more acute concerns, there is reason to believe that Rosie may be experiencing neglectful parenting as a number of the symptoms of neglect below apply to her.

Professional tip

Possible signs of neglect

- Constant hunger
- Poor personal hygiene
- Constant tiredness
- Poor state of clothing
- Frequent lateness or non-school attendance
- Untreated medical problems
- Destructive tendencies
- Low self-esteem
- No social relationships
- Compulsive stealing, especially food or clothes
- Neurotic behaviour (e.g. rocking, thumb-sucking)

It is all too easy to focus on and respond to the signs of physical abuse which are more often (but not always) immediately visible (as in Rosie's case) and may seem to present more of an 'emergency', and to underestimate the implications of long-term neglectful parenting. As a social worker, it is important that you are attentive to the less visible, but no less significant, signs of neglect.

Physical injury

This is defined as actual or likely physical injury to a child, or failure to prevent physical injury (or suffering) to a child, including deliberate poisoning, suffocation, and Munchausen's syndrome by proxy (DoH, 1999e).

There have been a number of child death inquiries since the late 1970s which have highlighted the fact that between 150 and 200 children die every year at the hands of their parents. Most of these inquiries have involved cases of physical abuse where the professional child protection services have been involved with the child who has died, and are set up to try to establish the ways in which the services failed to protect the child, and to make future recommendations for changes in working practices or the relevant legislation.

Physical abuse may involve any of the following:

- Hitting, kicking, punching or beating the child
- Burning and scalding
- Smothering or suffocating
- Shaking or throwing the child violently against something
- Poisoning
- Scratching, squeezing, grabbing or twisting child's body violently
- Stabbing or cutting.

It is generally recognised that children, if they are to survive in a physically abusive atmosphere, need to make emotional adaptations to their damaging environments. In addition, physical abuse, whatever form it takes, will incorporate elements of emotional abuse. As with other forms of abuse, it will be experienced very differently by individual children, and a full assessment is essential in order to explore not just the nature of the physical harm, but also the context in which it has occurred, for example:

- whether or not children are basically loved, but over-chastised on a one-off or occasional basis;
- whether one child, rather than all the children in the family, is singled out for punishment, perhaps being seen as difficult or unappealing;
- whether or not the physical abuse is the only physical contact in an otherwise highly neglectful emotional environment.

Emotional abuse

'Actual or severe adverse effects on the emotional and behavioural development of a child caused by persistent or severe emotional ill-treatment or rejection'.

(DoH, 1999e)

All abuse as we have said involves some emotional ill-treatment. This category is used where it is the main or sole form of abuse. Emotional abuse can include:

- Verbal abuse
- Rejection and withdrawal of affection
- Lack of warmth
- Constant criticism
- Holding the child in low regard
- Telling the child that they are unwanted, unloved and unacceptable
- Criticising the child to other people.

Professional tip

Possible signs of physical abuse

- Unexplained injuries or burns, particularly if recurrent
- Improbable explanations for injuries
- Refusal to discuss injuries
- Untreated injuries
- Fear of parents being contacted
- Fear of medical help
- Flinching at sudden movements
- Arms and legs covered in hot weather
- Injuries in unusual places and unusual types of injuries
- Aggression towards others
- Fear of returning home
- Self-destructive tendencies
- Chronic running away

Children who have experienced emotional abuse may be particularly vulnerable to psychological harm. Garbarino et al. (1986) classify different types of emotional abuse, and suggest that parents may impair their children's healthy development by responses which reject, isolate, terrorise, ignore and/or corrupt them (i.e. mis-socialise) them. Children may have had their natural drive for exploration punished, their attachment needs rejected, may have been penalised for any signs of positive self-esteem, and been discouraged from social relationships with peers. Their parents' failure to respond to their children's experiences of feeling distressed, anxious or happy will have affected the children's ability to recognise and accept their thoughts and feelings. With others, the repeated experience of being ridiculed or discouraged may impair the healthy development of broader cognitive skills and affect their confidence in

learning and exploration. Garbarino et al. (1986: 12) suggest that practitioners need to be particularly aware of the destructive patterns of emotions which are projected on to children:

'what most children typically cannot handle is a pervasive pattern of destructive emotions or extreme outbursts that threaten their world. In most cases, isolated trauma is not nearly so threatening as repeated emotional assault.'

Professional tip

Possible signs of emotional abuse

- Physical, mental and emotional developmental delay or disturbance
- Overreaction to mistakes
- Sudden speech disorders
- Fear of new situations
- Inappropriate emotional responses to stressful situations
- Neurotic behaviour
- Self-mutilation
- Extremes of passivity or aggression
- Substance misuse
- Absconding
- Enuresis/encopresis

Sexual abuse

'Actual or likely exploitation of a child or adolescent. The child may be dependent and/or developmentally immature.' Sexual exploitation is defined (by Kempe and Kempe, 1978) as ' the involvement of dependent, developmentally immature children and adolescents in sexual activities they do not truly comprehend, to which they are unable to give informed consent or that violate social taboos of family roles.' Sexual abuse has been described in its effect as most akin to severe emotional abuse. Glaser and Frosh state that 'in general, and except in instances of associated physical injury or rape by strangers, child sexual abuse is best classed alongside severe emotional abuse in terms of its structure and effects' (Glaser and Frosh, 1993: 9). One such emotional accompaniment is the abusers' intentional distortions of children's everyday realities. Because abusers usually try constantly to present sexually abusive relationships as 'normal', enormous conflicts and confusions are created for children who must endeavour to integrate their inner experiences of sexual abuse with their abusers' presentations of reality. Abusers may describe their relationships

A closer look

The Cleveland Report

The inquiry into events in Cleveland (Butler-Sloss, 1988) resulted from complaints by a group of parents, supported by a local MP, whose children had been taken into care because of suspected child sexual abuse. At the heart of the controversy was the anal reflex dilation test, which had been developed through use with gay men, as a method of ascertaining whether sexual abuse had occurred. Children were deemed to have been sexually abused on the basis of this disputed evidence alone. The situation was worsened by the ever-increasing number of suspected cases of children who were brought into hospital on emergency protection orders (then Place of Safety orders), despite the fact that sexual abuse is not usually life-threatening. Parents were not allowed to see their children or told what was happening to them, and there were strong disagreements between the paediatricians and the police surgeons. Although inter-agency procedures existed, they were not always adhered to, and there were disagreements among some of the professionals involved, including the child protection coordinator, a social worker, who was also at the centre of the controversy. Over 120 children were assessed as being sexually abused over a five-month period, with the result that the child protection systems were overloaded.

The report made a range of recommendations, including that for better inter-agency coordination, proper assessment of the child, the importance of listening to children's accounts and avoiding repeated examinations and interviews, and the importance of informing parents of their rights and involving them in any interventions and investigations.

in terms of 'special and loving' and the experience of sexual abuse as something children should find pleasurable and good, which is often different from children's inner experiences (Frosh and Fyson, 2007). Other emotional dimensions that are characteristic of sexual abuse are an emphasis on secrecy and the often compulsive nature of the abuse. The additional, heightened emphasis on secrecy, while also present in some physically abusive episodes, seems an essential component of sexual abuse if it is to continue. It is crucial that abusers maintain children's silence throughout their abusive experiences, which may continue for many years.

The effects of sexual abuse can be evident in a number of ways:

- The compulsive nature of sexual behaviour that characterises sexual offenders (Giaretto, 1982; Wyre, 1996) is often mirrored in the compulsive sexualised behaviour of children who have been subject to sexual abuse.
- The repeated sexual arousal and resulting tension created by the abuse may lead children to find relief through their own sexual stimulation, either alone or with the involvement of others.
- Sexual abuse also distorts children's views of other significant relationships and of themselves, and the sexual abuse interrupts and damages their subsequent emotional development from the onset of the abuse.

- Sexual abuse may have been used as a punishment for, say, behaviour such as wetting or soiling and consequently children's feelings of shame and self-consciousness can be greatly heightened by sexual abuse.

Professional tip

Possible signs of sexual abuse

- Child depressed or suicidal
- Substance misuse
- Self-harming behaviour
- Unexplained pregnancy
- Memory loss
- Anorexia/bulimia
- Running away
- Inappropriately seductive, sexualised behaviour
- Fearful of certain people
- Anger or irritability
- Not being allowed to have friends or go out
- Soreness/bleeding of genitals, anus or mouth
- Nightmares or sleep problems
- Disclosure about 'a friend'
- Changes in behaviour or habits
- Withdrawn, excessively worried

Perhaps the most well-known and controversial inquiry involving sexual abuse is that by Butler-Sloss (1988), whose report followed an investigation into the way in which a large number of suspected child sexual abuse cases were handled in the Cleveland area (see the Closer Look box). Unlike earlier inquiries, in this case the professionals involved were not criticised for failing to act, but for being overzealous in their intervention, and acting on the basis of evidence which was considered controversial. Although the agencies involved, and especially the medical professionals, were criticised in the report, again especially for failures in inter-agency cooperation, but also for failures properly to inform and involve the parents, it is important to remember that the terms of the inquiry did not include examining evidence to establish whether or not the children were in fact experiencing sexual abuse.

To conclude this overview of forms of abuse there is an extensive amount of research and practice knowledge concerning child maltreatment, which you need to familiarise yourself with as you develop your specialist knowledge.

Strategy discussions and initial case conferences

As a section 47 inquiry is being undertaken, the process of collecting information, consulting with different professionals, and talking to the family and child continues, in order to decide whether or not further action is necessary. This work is guided by the procedural document, *Working Together to Safeguard Children* (DoH, 2006c), which sets out the stages to be followed. This supports the earlier guidance in recommending that the professionals and the family members involved should first have 'a strategy discussion' to decide on the need for emergency action, further inquiries and/or the provision of interim services and support. Where it does indeed seem that children were at risk, but where their safety can be assured – for example, where the perpetrator has left the household, or where the incident seemed to be an isolated occurrence – the professionals are encouraged to undertake different interventions rather than proceeding to an initial child protection conference. Family group conferences (discussed earlier) or other meetings are seen as providing possible alternatives.

However, where there seems to be sound evidence for continuing to be concerned about a child's safety, an initial child protection conference needs to be held within 15 working days of the strategy discussion. The initial conference has a twofold purpose:

- to consider whether the child is at continuing risk of significant harm and, if so,
- to consider whether safeguarding the child requires inter-agency help and intervention delivered through a formal, detailed child protection plan.

Local Safeguarding Children Boards (set up under the Children Act 2004, s. 14 (1) to replace Area Child Protection Committees) must provide protocols specifying a required quorum for attendance, a list of who should attend and must also set out the method of decision-making. The local authority social worker has to provide an Initial Child Protection Conference Report on each child being considered by the conference, and other professionals should also contribute information, preferably in writing. In the Closer Look box, we give a checklist for professionals preparing for a case conference, which can be adapted to the particular role undertaken.

If the case conference does decide that both of the criteria for holding the conference are met, and that the child is at risk and also needs inter-agency help and intervention, then the case conference has to determine which category (or categories) of abuse or neglect the child has suffered, and set out a child protection plan, which should identify the risk factors, establish short- and long-term aims and objectives and identify which professionals are responsible for what, and within specified timescales (DoH, 2006c). In addition, it has to make sure that the following are carried out:

- The plan is recorded on a social care IT system (which local authorities are required to set up, and which will have an electronic care record for every known child). All 'legitimate' agencies and professional can thus, in theory at least, obtain the relevant information.
- The plan must nominate an experienced social worker to have a key role in managing the intervention.
- A 'core group' meeting takes place 10 days later which will operationalise a more detailed plan; written agreements are made and timescales appropriate to the child/ren established.
- Within 35 working days a comprehensive assessment consistent with guidance in the *Framework for Assessing Children in Need and their Families* (DoH, 2000c) is to be undertaken.

A closer look

Preparing for a child protection conference: checklist

1. Describe the nature of your involvement with the child, e.g. as a worker in the child's playgroup, including how long you have known her/him and how frequently you have contact.
2. Detail any specific work or role you have undertaken, e.g. monitoring her/his physical health.
3. Give any details you can about past or present causes for concern, including dates, what you were worried about, and any further details.
4. Offer relevant information about the child and family circumstances, including any information about other family members.
5. Detail any changes you may have noticed in the child's behaviour or appearance or any other relevant information.
6. Describe any attempts you have made to discuss your concerns with the child's carer(s) and their reactions.
7. Make it clear when you are speaking from your own knowledge or observations, and when you are passing information from a third party.

(Kay, 1999: 87)

Case study

Rosie cont . . .

A child protection conference is held on Rosie and various key professionals attend it – the social worker, the teacher, the GP, the school nurse and the police. Mrs Ashton attends with her sister Tina, Mr Ashton being too unwell to attend. At the earlier strategy meeting it was concluded there was insufficient evidence to initiate criminal proceedings, but the bruises on Rosie are suspected to be non-accidental. Neither Rosie nor her parents have been able to offer an explanation for how she got them. From talking to Rosie on her own, the social worker recognises that Rosie wants to be at home, but is concerned at the strains on the family and the limited attention that is paid to Rosie's needs. The social worker has witnessed Rosie displaying difficult behaviour and Mrs Ashton becoming very worked up about it.

The conference decided, in the light of the bruising and the concerns about Rosie's appearance, presentation and behaviour at school, that there is a strong likelihood that she has been physically harmed and neglected and that the family should receive ongoing social work help. It was agreed under the Children Act 2004 that Rosie should be made the subject of a child protection plan, which would:

- identify the risk factors;
- establish short- and long-term aims and objectives;
- identify which professionals are responsible for what;
- specify the timescales for the plan.

In addition, the support services for the family discussed earlier in the chapter were also identified as being necessary for this family, to address the difficulties they are currently experiencing.

Within three months, and every six months thereafter, a review conference should be held to consider the child's developmental progress against the intended outcomes. The Integrated Children's System (ICS) provides a number of electronic records (exemplars) for each stage of the process where all this information will be recorded. Throughout this process you will need to keep partnership practice to the fore of your mind while ensuring the child's needs remain paramount. Recent research (Pithouse et al., 2009) has highlighted how the requirements of ICS have encroached on the time practitioners have available to spend directly in face-to-face contact with children and families. This limitation of the computerisation of welfare practice is a central characteristic of contemporary practice and one practitioners need to continually be aware of and wherever possible resist being compromised by.

Case study

Rosie cont . . .

Following the child protection conference on Rosie, the support services are put in place and the social worker monitors progress. Despite the support offered, the situation in the family deteriorates further, with Rosie's behaviour at school becoming more problematic. A crisis point is reached when Mrs Ashton turns up at the social work office with Rosie, saying she is unable to cope following the birth of her third baby. As an underlying principle of partnership practice and in the spirit of the Children Act, the social worker explored with Mrs Ashton if anyone in the family or wider network could look after Rosie. Although Mrs Ashton's sister has been supportive, she feels unable to look after Rosie full time. Having exhausted potential informal carers for Rosie, the social worker agrees to explore accommodating Rosie under section 20 of the 1989 Children Act, and following further discussions with the family and Rosie's school and GP, it is agreed that she be accommodated on a short-term basis.

Removal from home is always a distressing experience for a child. Even if it provides relief from living in fear of physical injury, many children will actively resist being removed from home because it is an emotionally painful experience. If removal is not required, it is essential that families are provided with the appropriate support services and interventions outlined earlier in relation to children in need.

Think ahead

See if you can remember your own experience as a child of first being away from home. Although it may have been exciting and fun – perhaps it was a sleepover, for example – you may also recall finding things strange and possibly uncomfortable, with a different bedroom to wake up in, different food and family customs. You can imagine how much harder being away from home would be if you didn't fully understand why you were away, and perhaps felt that your parents were upset about it.

In Rosie's case, too, any actual relief may have been less marked because, from what we know so far, her experiences were of parenting which was, apart from the bruises, not actively cruel, but chronically neglectful. And she would be likely to miss – and possibly feel resentful of – her sister and the baby who were still at home. Sinclair et al. (2005) in their study of foster care, for example, found that fostered children with siblings still at home did less well.

An important principle of social work practice, therefore, is that the additional trauma of intervention should be kept to the minimum so that the child does not experience that intervention as further abuse. When children

leave home this raises many issues and problems, and it is important to give them as much information as possible. Where will Rosie go to school? How will she see her friends and family members? Which toys, clothes and possessions does she want to take with her? Who will know about her routines and her likes and dislikes? Who will understand her language for different needs? How will she explain to school friends what has happened to her? As the social worker, you may not know the answer to all the questions (e.g. how long she is going to be in the foster home), but you can say what you do and don't know, and what you will try to find out. A notebook which sets out this information (in pictures for younger children) is a good idea, since children cannot always remember details and dates. And it does underline the importance of getting as much information as possible from Rosie's parents to enable her foster carers to help her settle.

Of all the outcomes of a section 47 investigation the most far-reaching for children and their families is the decision to remove a child. Our following sections examine what is involved in working with children who are unable to live at home and who are 'looked after' by the local authority in foster families or residential settings or are given a new, permanent family through adoption.

Caring for looked-after children who cannot live at home

The research which we shall refer to below about the outcomes of a range of placements for children who cannot be cared for at home shows that, sadly, as for Graham in our next brief case example, 'love may not be enough'. Many of the children who are placed with new carers or adoptive parents will continue to need additional services if they are to overcome the damaging effects of their earlier emotional experiences, and a proportion of these will never totally resolve these and will remain vulnerable to adversity once they leave their birth families.

Case study

Graham

Graham, now aged 36, first came into care at the age of 5, following the discovery of an incestuous relationship between his mother and grandfather. Together with his younger brother, he was placed in a succession of foster homes. At 9, when it was discovered that he was being physically and possibly sexually abused by his foster mother and her son, he was moved to a children's home, from where he was placed at the age of 13 in an adoptive placement. He found it difficult to settle to family life, and as he grew older, suffered a number of breakdowns and has never held down a job for longer than a few weeks. He met and married a woman, also from a damaging background, by whom he has one daughter. The couple split up after a short time, as a result of his violent behaviour, but Graham remained in contact with his daughter, persisting with this despite difficulties put in his way by his ex-wife. Now he is suspected of attempting to sexually abuse his daughter, and all contact has been terminated. His adoptive parents have remained in close touch with him, helping and supporting him, but no longer feel able freely to have him to stay in their own home, because they are visited frequently by their granddaughters and their friends. Lonely and isolated, it is difficult to see what the future holds for him.

A closer look

Is the State a 'bad parent'?

You may often have heard it said that the 'State is a bad parent'. However, there is much evidence of good practice undertaken by foster carers, social workers and others working with and caring for looked-after children and the majority of looked-after children speak highly of their experiences particularly in foster care.

It is indeed arguable that the frequently poor outcomes for these children are 'not the State's fault'. Unfortunately, it seems that earlier damaging experiences have a lasting impact which it is difficult to overcome. And the ongoing problematic circumstances of the birth families to which so many looked-after children return make it difficult for foster care and other placement settings, however positive in themselves, to achieve a greater measure of change in the outcomes for these children. (You can follow up these debates, which touch on the tensions between state and family care, in an article by a group of distinguished UK researchers (Bullock et al., 2006).)

Graham's case, culminating in his being placed for adoption (rather unusually, since in the UK adoption for children over the age of six is in practice relatively rare) in his early teens, illustrates too the way in which practice and policies in the provision for children cared for away from home mirror more general developments in child welfare policies, which we discussed earlier in this chapter (see page 463). As June Thoburn, a social work academic who has conducted extensive research into fostering and adoption, writes:

'A substantial minority of children placed with loving and dedicated new parents will still need additional services if they are to overcome the harmful effects of their early experiences, and . . . a proportion will not totally recover and will remain emotionally vulnerable.'   (2007: 495)

However, to set against this rather gloomy observation it is also important to note the heartening evidence both in Gillian Schofield's retrospective study of adults who had been fostered, that long-term foster care *could* provide a 'family for life', and also the 'impressive successes' which were to be found in a large sample of foster children, alongside many less positive outcomes (Sinclair and Wilson, 2009: 132). (See Closer Look box for further discussion.)

The social work context for looked-after children

Social workers are likely to become involved with children in the looked-after system in a variety of ways. Most local authorities have specialist teams consisting of experienced social workers (variously called family placement workers or 'link social workers') who are responsible for recruiting, training and supporting foster carers. Approval of adopters and the matching and placement of children who are to be adopted are undertaken either by the same team, or by another allied team. As a qualified social worker at the outset of your career, you are more likely to be involved as key worker for a child who is coming into the looked-after system, when you normally retain responsibility for the child, supervising her or his care plan, overseeing the placement and return home or moves into an adoptive placement. Finally, social workers may undertake discreet pieces of work with looked-after children or provide them with therapeutic help (but see below for Simmonds's reservations about the frequency with which social workers actually undertake such work (Simmonds, 2008)).

Social work with children looked after by the local authority draws on skills and values shared with other areas of social work with children which we highlighted at the beginning of this chapter. However, there are some important areas of knowledge and practice for you to develop which we shall introduce you to in this section. There is now an extensive literature on the placement of children in residential care, adoption and fostering, and in a short section we can only give you a brief overview of the issues. SCIE has produced some helpful summaries of the research with a range of placements and a useful practice guide to foster care, all of which are available to download from their website. The British Association for Adoption and Fostering (BAAF) is another authoritative source of information on looked-after children and young people, and has an excellent record in promoting research and policy and practice guidance and advocacy in this field.

We start by explaining the legislative and statutory framework for looked-after children, then consider the various placement options available for children. Using a framework developed by June Thoburn (Thoburn, 2007), we discuss the key tasks in making plans for a child who cannot remain at home and then summarise some of the key practice activities and skills involved.

The legal and statutory framework

- Children who are accommodated. (s. 20, Children Act 1989 England and Wales and s. 17 of the Children (Scotland) Act 1995) and Article 21 of the Children (N. Ireland) Order 1995) These are either children whose parents are unable to care for them (which may include children who arrive here from abroad alone) or children whose parents have agreed with the local authority that it would safeguard or promote the children's welfare to be looked after by the local authority. Parents must agree to accommodation unless children are over 16 when they can agree on their own behalf.

- Children who are subject to an interim or full Care Order (s. 30). When a Care Order is made, the local authority is given parental responsibility shared with the parents, for a child until s/he reaches the age of 18. There are also duties concerning the welfare of people leaving care which continue until they are 21.

The legal basis for caring for looked-after children in England and Wales is laid down in the Children Act 1989. A number of other government publications inform practice with looked after children:

- Department of Health publications which accompanied the Children Act 1989 are still important sources, especially Guidance volumes 2 and 3 on family support and foster care placements, and volume 4 on residential care.

- *Principles and Practice in Regulations and Guidance* (DoH, 1989b) summarises the principles which should underlie all family social work, including the placement of children away from their families of origin.

- The Utting (1997) Report, which raised the issue of the safety of children living away from home, the Government's response (DoH, 1998) and the Quality Protects performance indicators (DoH, 1998; National Statistics and DfES, 2004) provide guidance for policy and practice to safeguard the welfare of children looked after away from their families.

- Further key policy and legislative developments include the Quality Protects Initiative, the Government Objectives for Social Services and the publication of the National Minimum Standards for Foster Care (DoH, 1998a) and the National Adoption Standards for England (DoH, 2001).

- Significant changes in placement practice followed the implementation of the Adoption and Children Act 2002 and the Children Act 2004, including the introduction of Special Guardianship as a placement option, which required the development of new procedures and practice at local level.

- Standards are buttressed by guidance, regulation and the Looked After Children Assessment and Action records, developed with funding from the Department of Health which are intended to measure whether children's day-to-day needs (on five dimensions of health, education, identity, family relationships and social presentation) are being met.

- Most recently, the Children and Young Persons Act 2008 aims significantly to improve outcomes for children in public care. This forms part of a comprehensive programme ensuing from the White Papers *Care Matters: time for change* and *Time to deliver for children in care* (DCSF, 2007; 2008.)

- Part of the Legislative Competence Order for Wales focuses on all vulnerable children.

- The Scottish Government policy initiative *Getting It Right For Every Child* (2005b) mirrors these developments. The Adoption and Children (Scotland) Act (2007) and revised policies for kinship and foster care further reflect the concern to improve outcomes for children and young people temporarily or permanently separated from their birth families.

Types and purposes of placements for looked-after children

The main kinds of placements available for children which you need to know about are foster care, residential care and adoption, with a small number of placements in locations such as secure units and hostels. As can be seen from the table, numerically fostering is the most important option in the 'care system'. On the most recent figures around 64,000 children are looked after by English local authorities at any one time, with around 15,000 in Scotland, 5,000 in Wales and 2,500 in Northern Ireland, making a total of roughly 86,500. (However, figures are collated somewhat differently by the four countries, making close comparison difficult: for example in Scotland, children at home under supervision orders are included in the overall looked after figures and in Northern Ireland, children placed for adoption are omitted from them. For this reason, Table 16.1 gives figures for England and Wales alone). Well over two-thirds of looked after children live in foster families, a proportion that has been growing steadily since the 1970s, although their actual numbers have remained fairly constant as has the estimated number of carers (around 20,000 for England). Fostering dominates provision for younger children but offers a service for children of all ages. Around sixty per cent of all foster children are aged ten or over. Some children who are the subject of full and interim care orders are living with parents but because of the orders they are still part of the looked-after system. It is now mandatory to collect data on the ethnic origins of looked-after children, although differences in definitions of ethnicity make existing proportions of children from minority groups difficult to establish. UK research, however, suggests that minority ethnic children make up approximately 23 per cent of the looked-after population in England, a figure which conceals wide variations between authorities and across regions and cultures. The situation in Scotland and Wales is different, in that, as Selwyn and Wijedesa point out: 'their populations are less ethnically diverse' (2009: 367) and minority ethnic children account for 2 per cent and 5 per cent of their respective LAC populations respectively. Age and gender clearly have an impact on the provision: for example, the likelihood of adoption drops sharply with age – in Sinclair et al.'s study (2005), for example, only one child over the age of eight was adopted (2005a: 96).

Foster care

There are a wide variety of different kinds of foster care and although local authorities classify foster care in different ways (one study found 47 different names were in use: Waterhouse, 1997), some understanding of the classifications may be helpful in thinking out the purpose of the placement you are arranging for a particular child. Broadly it can be classified by provider (placements may be offered by relatives or friends of the family, by local authorities and by the independent sector, length of stay (e.g. short term) or purpose (e.g. a placement to provide a permanent substitute family and 'upbringing'). Private fostering placements, i.e. informal arrangements between families for providing care, which legally have to be notified to the local authority, have recently also, post-Climbié, attracted more attention (Luckock and Lefevre, 2008).

These different classifications overlap. For example, different providers may care for all age groups for a variety of purposes. Some short-stay care may simply be to provide a break, say, for a mother admitted to hospital, while other short-stay care may be a 'remand' placement (where a young person is awaiting trial for a criminal

Table 16.1 Children looked after in England and Wales by placement at 31 March 2010

	England		Wales	
	No.	%	No.	%
Foster placements	47,200	74	4,049	77
Children's homes (incl. secure units and hostels)	6,200	10	230	4
Placed with parents, friends or family[1]	4,200	7	482	9
Placed for adoption	2,300	4	204	4
Other e.g. lodgings, living independently, schools, and hostels[2]	3,930	6	269	5
Totals	63,830		5,234	

[1] In England, Wales and N. Ireland these figures refer to children placed on a care order with adults who have parental responsibility for them. In Scotland they include children on supervision orders.

[2] Includes Youth Treatment Centres, Young Offenders Institutions and various other categories.

Percentages may not equal 100 due to rounding. 'Absent' not included.

Sources: www.education.gov.uk; www.statswales.wales.gov.uk; www.baaf.org.uk

offence). One general classification adapted from Rowe (1989) – who, with her colleagues, did one of the important early studies into foster care – which still appears useable, distinguishes between

- Short-term – emergency, assessment, roof over head, remand
- Shared care – regular short breaks
- Medium-term (task centred) – treatment, bridging placements preparation for independence
- Long-term – upbringing

Short-stay foster care (short term) caters for a greater number of children than any other. Social workers see such placements as serving a variety of ends – to cool an inflamed situation, to support parents at the end of their tether, to manage a temporary crisis, or to allow a risky situation to be managed and assessed (Packman and Hall, 1998).

In *shared care*, respite or relief foster carers can work with birth parents in a variety of ways. They can offer a series of short-breaks, most commonly but not exclusively to disabled children. They can foster parent and child together. They can offer support to parents while the child is with them and subsequently after he or she returns home. (Aldgate and Bradley, 1999). *Support foster care* has been developed as a model of family preservation in some parts of the UK where, for example, lone parents and their adolescent offspring are experiencing severe relationship problems (Howard, 2000).

Specialised, therapeutic or treatment foster care (medium term) is likely to be provided by special schemes (Walker et al., 2002). These are marked out by a number of features, not all of which are necessarily present in each scheme. The features include:

- An above average level of support, training and remuneration for carers
- A theoretical model of the aims and approach needed in the scheme
- A difficult (often teenage) clientele
- A restricted length of stay.

In Rowe's classification such foster care is part of a wider set of fostering activities designed to achieve particular ends, for example to prepare a child for adoption.

The phrase '*long-term foster care*' is widely used but the way it is defined is not always very clear. In general, long-stay foster children are those who are not seen as returning home in the near future but who are not going to be adopted (Schofield et al., 2000, Lowe and Murch, 2002). In Rowe's terms they are there for 'upbringing'.

Much of the policy and research on foster care focuses on this group.

Adoption

The likelihood of adoption drops rapidly with age, for reasons which include the frequent reluctance of older children to be adopted, their greater emotional and behavioural difficulties and the fact that they are less likely to be wanted by adopters (Rushton, 2003). Of the 3,700 children in England who left care through adoption in 2003/4, 230 were aged 10 or upwards (DfES, 2004). There has been a slight increase over the past few years in the numbers of children who have been adopted and, in contrast to the age profile of fostered children, the great majority are in the 1–9 age group (3,300 out of the total).

A closer look

Outcomes in adoption

Three relatively recent UK studies (Rushton and Dance 2006; Selwyn et al., 2006 and Steele et al., 2008) underline how as practitioners you need to be aware of the complexity of the adoption experience. These studies found that although some children achieved good developmental outcomes, for some there were serious ongoing struggles for them and their parents, and for others the placement broke down altogether. John Simmonds concludes his discussion of these issues by saying that while there are many which are important, one in particular stands out: it is this message which we want to highlight here:

Adoption works best the younger the child is, and the quicker it is arranged. (2009: 237)

The general evidence on the effects of adoption is favourable (but see the Closer Look Box, above, for studies highlighting a range of outcomes). An overview review of the research conducted by an experienced researcher in the field of out-of-home care, John Triseliotis, concluded that, other things being equal, adoption was to be preferred to long-term fostering since it offers adopted children greater emotional security, sense of well-being and belonging (Triseliotis, 2002). As you might expect, the outcomes for children adopted at a young age are better than for older children and young people.

- Those adopted as infants (less than six months) are as successful as any members of the community and perform decidedly better than comparison groups such as those living with lone parents or fostered (Bohmann, 1966, 1971; Maugham et al., 1998; Maugham and Pickles, 1990; St Claire and Osborne, 1987; Tizard and Rees, 1975; Triseliotis and Russell, 1984).

- Later adoptions (i.e. those age 10 and above) are more problematic (Rushton, 2003; Rushton and Dance, 2006). Most studies confirm that older age is one of the factors associated with disrupted placements. Below the age of 11, the younger the child at placement, the more likely the placement is to be successful on all measures, with a breakdown rate for 'stranger adoptions' of around 20 per cent for those placed at 8, arising to around 50 per cent for those placed around 10 or 11 (Department of Health, 1999).

Reflect

Why do you think that adoption for older children and young people is less common, and on the whole less likely to be successful than for younger children?

There is a wide variation in the use made of adoption by different authorities. However, despite government encouragement for adoption, such English evidence as exists suggests that the scope for increasing adoption is limited (Schofield et al., 2000; Sinclair et al., 2005). The latter study suggested that its use might be slightly increased through greater decisiveness when the child was very young or by greater encouragement of the use of foster carer adoptions among older children. Nonetheless, the UK is already high in any international league table for the number of adoptions: in most of the countries in Europe, by comparison, long-term foster care and/or residential care are the placements of choice, as Selman (2009) points out. Then, too, older children are often implacably opposed to adoption and the adoption of younger children may be limited by consideration of family rights (See Rushton, 2004, and Simmonds, 2009 for a fuller discussion.)

Residential care

Residential care refers to placements in institutional settings, often referred to as children's homes. Policy changes over the past decade or so have meant that children are generally placed in some form of residential care only when other forms of placement have been tried and failed. Therefore it is likely that the children it caters for are among the most difficult in the looked-after system, and hence, if you are trying to choose between placements by comparing their relative success rates you may not be comparing like with like – on this basis you would expect children from residential care to do worse. There are also a wide range of residential homes, including local authority children's homes, independently run therapeutic homes and some evidence of variation in the success rates of different types of provision (e.g. the head of the establishment may influence outcomes).

- Observations of the two forms of care suggest that foster care is, on the face of it, a more positive form of provision (Colton, 1988; Triseliotis, 1995; Roy et al., 2000). Residential care is also rated as a less safe and adequate environment by social workers (Sinclair et al., 2005, 2005a).

- Foster children almost universally prefer to be fostered (Colton, 1989). However some formerly fostered residents in children's homes say that they prefer residential care (Sinclair and Gibbs, 1998).

- One piece of research (MacDonald et al., 1996) found those who have been in residential care have worse outcomes as young adults than their formerly fostered peers. However, this may only reflect the fact that the children and young people being placed in residential care were more difficult and had more problems than children in foster care – so these apparently poor outcomes of residential care may not 'be its fault'.

- Benefits which may occur while children are in residential care rarely seem to carry over or are much reduced on leaving the home, and the long-term effects of residential care have proved difficult to quantify (Fonagy, 2002; Bullock, 2009).

Now that you are familiar with the different types of placement which looked-after children may live in, and have been introduced to some of the positives and hazards of these, we turn to your role in managing and planning the care of children who are looked after.

Care planning: the social worker's roles and tasks

When a child is being looked after by the local authority, a care plan has to be made, in consultation with the child and her/his parents, which must be reviewed on a regular basis. Under the Review of Children's Cases (Amendment) (England) Regulations 2004 an Independent Reviewing Officer is required to monitor care plans and take an active problem-solving role on behalf of the child, particularly to ensure that children do not get lost in the system through lack of planning and drift.

In drawing up this plan, you will need, together with other professionals and the child's family to consider the following questions:

- What sort of placement
- For how long
- What will be the appropriate legal status for the placement
- What sort of contact will be appropriate, where and with whom
- What services, support or therapy will be needed by all those involved in the placement – the child, the carers, and members of their families, the child's family and other relatives
- What financial help and practical support will be needed to maintain the placement.

What sort of placement?

The above discussion suggests the range of options which need to be considered. Perhaps the most crucial underlying question here is whether what is needed is a placement where the birth parent(s) will remain the psychological parents, by which we mean the adult(s) who will be responsible for bringing up and parenting the child, or whether new psychological parents are likely to be needed in cases when long-term or permanent separation from birth parents is likely to be the outcome. In the latter case, while adoption may seem to offer the best hope of permanence for the child, the latter's own feelings, and particularly links with birth family will need to be carefully considered. As Thoburn suggests, if it appears that the child will be unlikely to return home , at least in the near future, but there is a good attachment between birth parent and child, then what is needed is a placement where the carer will supplement the care of the parent, or indeed, either by helping the child's sense of self-esteem and behaviour or, through supporting the parents themselves, work on improving the relationship between them.

When the essential purpose of the placement has been identified, you will need to find a placement which most closely 'matches' the needs of the child. Often because of the inevitable shortage of placements (however desirable, it is unrealistic for authorities to keep a sufficiently large 'bank' of placements to meet all the criteria which placements need to meet), this will involve making a judgement of what the most critical features are – e.g. the location may be important if contact with

school and parents is maintained; the ability of carers to work sensitively with parents may be crucial if a return home is planned, and so on. Although there has been a search for some core 'rules' or principles for practice – for example, that children should be placed with siblings, or where there are no children of the foster carers close in age, or with relatives, or in placements of the same ethnicity – in fact the evidence on these 'rules' is not at all clear. In most cases there is a moral presumption in favour of the 'rules' (for example, that children should be placed with siblings or in 'same race' placements). However, this has to be backed by careful attention to what the children want and to particular factors in the situation, e.g. a child's extreme jealousy of a sibling (Sinclair and Wilson, 2003). See SCIE's guides for further discussion on choosing adoptive parents and 'matching' in foster care.

Reflect

In the light of the developments in the Ashton family, culminating in Mrs Ashton's request for Rosie to be accommodated, what kind of placement would the social worker be looking for?

We assume you would look for a foster placement! Think through some of the features which you would want the placement to offer.

Now imagine that the assessment considers that Rosie cannot safely return home in the short term. What kind of placement would you be looking for, using the above classification?

For how long?

Although the situation may be unclear, it is usually possible to give an approximate idea of how long the placement will be needed for, and it is usually preferable to overestimate the time needed to carers, and thus avoid a change of placement.

What legal status?

You will recall that Rosie was first accommodated on a voluntary basis and, as a general principle, the first option is for voluntary arrangements. Very often, however, greater legal security is required in order to ensure the child's safety and, sometimes, to give them a sense of security.

What sort of contact and with whom?

This has proved to be one of the more complex areas in out-of-home care. There has been an increase in what are called 'open adoptions' (where some form of continued contact is agreed between adopters and birth parents, whether to face, which is more common for older adoptees, or ongoing letter-box contact, more usual for younger children.) Young and Neil, in their chapter on contact in *The Child Placement Handbook* (2009) provide a useful overview of the research, describe the wide variations in the use and success of different forms of contact, and have helpful suggestions for issues to be considered in planning contact.

In situations such as that of Rosie and her family, when the plan (or at least hope) is that the child will return home, then, clearly, continued contact needs to be arranged. It is important too that contact embraces everyone the child considers important, for example in Rosie's case this is likely to include her aunt Tina and her family who have supported the family throughout and might include her grandmother too. In other situations, although contact would generally undoubtedly be the preferred option, research suggests that a careful judgement needs to be made, which includes the wishes of the children concerned, assesses the likely risks as well as benefits to the child, and ensures that proper support is given to carers and birth parents alike (see the Closer Look box for some contraindications).

What sort of help?

A range of services, some of them discussed in the previous section, may be needed to support foster placements, and recent practice has highlighted the need for support after adoption. As some researchers have shown, lack of support from young people's social workers was related to poorer placement outcomes, and the opposite can also be true: there were significantly more successful placements when social work support was good (Farmer et al., 2004).

Children in the looked-after system have similar needs to other children in need who remain at home. But being away from home can, as we showed earlier, be very stressful, and social workers need to be alert to helping children with the experience of change and loss. Vera Fahlberg's books on children separated from their parents provide an excellent source of understanding. For example, she explains that children may make sense of separation in a number of ways, and that each explanation has consequences for how they view their situation and their emotional reaction to it:

- Belief that they have been taken away or kidnapped
- Belief that they have been given away by their parents
- Belief that they have caused the loss of their parents by something they have done.

A closer look

Research evidence about contact

One study of foster care (Sinclair, Wilson and Gibbs, 2005) found that:

- Most children want more contact than they get and most parents want to provide it.
- There is a need to distinguish between different kinds of contact – contact with some members of the family may be desired and that with other members not; similarly some children may want supervised contact or telephone contact only, while others want unsupervised contact.
- Contact is commonly (not invariably) distressing to parents, children and foster carers.
- In certain circumstances contact may be associated with abuse and placement breakdown. Where (a) there was strong evidence of prior abuse and (b) contact was unrestricted (i.e. no family member was forbidden contact), breakdown was three times more likely and the chance of re-abuse was increased.

A closer look

The impact of good social work practice on foster care

Sinclair and his colleagues conclude that the key to successful foster care lies in recruiting, training and supporting good foster carers. Social workers need skills in managing contact with birth families, in discussing with children what they really want, and in intervening when the foster carer and the child start to get the worst out of each other (Wilson et al., 2000; Fisher et al., 2000). They should treat disrupted placements seriously and caringly, engage with carers who are struggling to manage challenging behaviour or difficult birth families and resist the tendency towards 'splitting' when allegations are made – that is, not treat the 'accused' as if he or she were automatically guilty.

Think about these possible reactions, and the way in which they would make the child feel (e.g. self-blame, magical thinking, feeling responsible, depressed).

Now think about Rosie, and ask yourself if she might feel any of these worries.

Another key difference for looked-after children, especially those who are placed permanently away from home, is that it may be much harder for them to build up a picture for themselves which explains who they are, where they come from and how they came to be away from home. If you think about your own experiences, you may realise that sharing early memories is a part of ordinary family life, and that (though you may not always have been conscious of it!) as a young child you will have had opportunities for talking with adults who have been through these experiences with you and can help you retrieve and process early memories. Shared memories also help you to see that events are not random, that life has patterns which can be understood and explained. For looked-after children, especially those who remain in long-term foster care or are adopted as older children, this process has been interrupted and they will have a range of non-shared experiences from their earlier lives which they may not be able to retrieve from memory or understand by themselves. It is therefore necessary to construct what is, in a way, an artificial means of helping children to hang on to their own history (Brandon et al., 1998: 156).

Focused therapeutic play with children

Focused therapeutic work has up until recently been more commonly known as 'direct work with children'. However, paradoxically, 'work' for children is play, and 'direct' work is more accurately understood as 'indirect' as it involves using a variety of different mediums – drawing, toys, role-plays – to help a child make sense of their circumstances and express their feelings about it. Focused therapeutic play, therefore, is a more accurate term to describe work undertaken with children. Referring to it as 'focused' therapeutic play ensures it does not get confused with the more conventional forms of therapy, e.g. child psychotherapy and play therapy, where the intervention is sustained and the purpose is to bring about some change in children's emotional and social functioning and in their primary relationships, which have been distorted or impaired during development (Wilson and Ryan, 2005b).

Focused therapeutic play is an appropriate intervention at all stages of social work with children as it draws on a fundamental means of communicating with and relating to children. It is an important way of ensuring that the voice of the child, referred to as a fundamental principle of work with children at the opening of the chapter, is not overlooked. For example, at the assessment stage it can be used when you are ascertaining a child's wishes and feelings. Following an assessment, it is appropriate as a support mechanism as it allows a child space to explore their current circumstances and it is a crucial form of intervention following major life events for a child, e.g. removal from home, loss of a family member, parental separation. At all of these stages the effectiveness of focused therapeutic play depends on the social worker clearly explaining the reasons for the intervention. Some of these reasons are set out in the Closer Look box.

There are a number of well-established focused therapeutic play techniques. Ken Redgrave's (2000) book on working with children is full of helpful ideas that you can adapt to fit the specific child and circumstances you are working with. Wilson and Ryan discuss the use of structured exercises, role-plays and painting and drawing, set these within a framework of child development and show how they can be incorporated into a non-intrusive and enabling approach to working with children and adolescents (2005b: 214 following). For Rosie, four well-known techniques could be productively used with her. Both are in essence quite simple, requiring only pens and paper.

Life maps

Life maps are a means of helping a child make sense of what has happened to them in their lives (you were introduced to them in Chapter 7). Invite the child to think about their life and to draw it as a road map. Think with the child about what they can remember or know about since they were born and use the different features of roads to represent these, e.g. crossroads for when decisions were made about where they would live or when they moved house; potholes for bumpy difficult events, such as problems at school; straight sections for calm periods; steep hills or bendy sections for hard times.

Ecomaps

Another helpful technique – ecomaps – helps children think about the relationships in their lives – who do they include (don't forget pets!), who are they close to, who

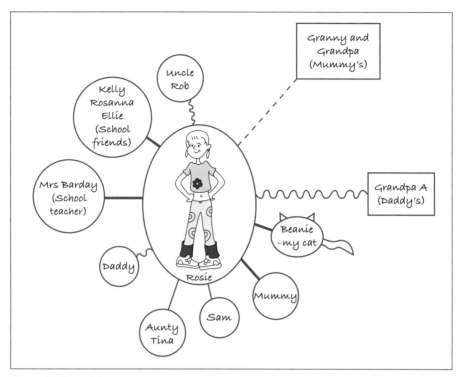

Figure 16.3 Rosie's ecomap

do they have more difficult relationships with? The thickness of the lines between people represent the strength of relationships, and how different people are positioned indicates the closeness/distance of relationships (Figure 16.3). Ecomaps represent a 'point in time' and it can be helpful for a child to revisit ecomaps some time after they were drawn to see how relationships have changed.

All these therapeutic play techniques can appear deceptively simple but, as you may have discovered

drawing your own life map, they can be very powerful and unearth forgotten memories or touch on sensitive issues. What you need to remember is that these approaches are only as good as the relationship you have established with the child. They depend on children trusting you enough to explore their experiences and feelings. When using such approaches it is important you ensure you take enough time to prepare and debrief from the sessions, and to seek out good supervision to help you think about the work.

A closer look

Reasons for undertaking 'focused' therapeutic work

There are many reasons why therapeutic work with 'looked-after' children is necessary and appropriate:

- to 'make up for' some early lost experiences, especially missed opportunities to play
- to make sense of confusing events in the past, understand and come to terms with feelings about those who may have abused them

- to prepare for life in a new family
- to enable the child to understand and leave behind the emotional baggage associated with destructive early life experiences
- to enable the child to experience the full range of emotions, pleasurable as well as painful
- to enable the child to modify antisocial behaviour
- to improve the child's self-esteem.

(Carroll, 1998; Brandon et al., 1998 and Wilson and Ryan, 2005b)

Life-story books

One way of helping a child make sense of and hold on to their history is by creating a life-story book, which provides a detailed account of significant events in the child's life. But it is more than a factual record of events: as well as containing copies of important documents (e.g. birth certificate, health check as a baby), photographs and other objects (one child carefully stuck in stitches taken from a cut, and three teeth he had recently lost), it can involve drawings of family trees, collages and so on, and activities which give children the chance to talk about feelings and experiences. There are useful guides to preparing these, with Walker and Ryan's guide probably being the most widely used by UK practitioners (see suggestions for further reading). They stress that it is 'the process rather than just the product' of the discussion and understanding resulting from the activity that should be defined as the 'life-story work' (Ryan and Walker, 2007: 4).

The feelings and views of children who have undertaken life-story work are described in a rare if small empirical study of their experiences by Willis and Holland (2009) which is worth reading to get an idea of the impact, strengths and pitfalls of the approach. Brandon et al. (1998) have a particularly useful section and the SCIE website has a number of abstracts and materials about doing this work (SCIE: Artistic licence for children in care. CC 29/4/2010.) Here are the key factors which you should remember in preparing a life-story book:

- Although they are especially useful for children separated for some time or permanently from their birth parents, they can also be useful as a means of reflecting on experiences for children who do go home.
- Timing and planning are very important. You will need to adapt things like detail and language to the individual child's developmental age and understanding.
- Remember that preparing a life-story book requires regular time over a period of weeks (it cannot be a one-off), and that
- You *must* take responsibility for ensuring that the book is completed.
- Life-story work requires careful preparation and research – e.g. tracking down personal records – as well as providing enjoyable opportunities for joint work together – e.g. going together to take photographs of the hospital ward in which the child was born.
- Work at children's pace – be sensitive to when they are distracted, have had enough for one day, and respect their timetable rather than insisting on your own.

- Encourage children to own the work – e.g. by being involved in the planning process, deciding what to include, how to design the book, and so on. This will also include clarifying whose book it is: the book should not be part of a formal assessment, but seen as theirs, for their emotional benefit – nonetheless, you need to clarify with them who will look after it when it is complete, especially for a child who may be facing moves within foster care.
- Help children's carers or adopters to keep the book accessible – it can be an invaluable tool in enabling the child to talk about feelings, to put them into words, rather than suppressing them – for example, the birth of a new cousin, or a visit from an official, may trigger anxieties which a quiet half hour together, going through the life-story book, and perhaps recalling from photographs happy recent experiences, can assuage.

Solution-focused approaches

A solution-focused approach to safety-building and responsibility-taking may be particularly helpful for carers looking after children who are exhibiting difficult and challenging, often sexualised, behaviour. Judith Milner in a useful discussion, explains that the approach involves helping to develop children's potential for controlling their own behaviour rather than depending solely on carers to manage risks. For example, the approach might involve the carer taking a 'signs of safety approach'

A closer look

'Direct work' with children

Since 'direct work' with children is so evidently valuable and valued by them, it is worth asking yourself how much time the child social workers you know actually are able to spend undertaking this. John Simmonds, in a persuasive if rather pessimistic preface to a recent book on direct work with looked-after children, asks whether it is the case that

'despite repeated messages from research, from inspections and from serious case reviews [that] social workers need to focus their attention on children and engage directly with them and their parents in sustained, thoughtful and detailed work, . . . the movement has been in the opposite direction, and . . . it has now become "exceptional" for social workers to do this work themselves'.

(Simmonds, 2008, pp xvii–xviii)

by looking with the child at times when s/he could have exhibited sexualised behaviour or acted violently and didn't (Milner, 2008: 42–50).

What financial support?

Financial support can be available, when appropriate, through adoption allowances, payments as well as allowances to foster carers, grants made under section 17 of the Children Act (s. 22 of the Children (Scotland) Act 1995), settling-in grants and one-off grants, for example, to send a child on a trip or pay for repairs if the child is very destructive. There is some evidence that retention (i.e. foster carers not leaving the service) is better in authorities who offer higher rates of pay.

We conclude the section, and indeed the chapter, by returning to Rosie and her family, and show how in her case a relatively brief period way from home in foster care helped her and her family to get back on to a better footing and began an 'upward spiral', particularly in the relationship between Rosie and her mother, which led eventually to a successful return home.

Case study

Rosie cont . . .

The social worker reported that on first arriving in her foster home, Rosie ate voraciously, as if she did not know how to stop. She wet the bed, and her behaviour especially in public places was difficult. However, after a few weeks, significant positive changes had occurred. She had begun to gain weight, her enuresis had largely ceased, and her behaviour in the foster home and at school was improving, albeit slowly. Twice-weekly contact between Rosie and her parents was arranged at a family centre.

Reflect

Rosie's desperate need for food and initial difficult behaviour, followed by improvements, does seem to confirm that she had suffered significant harm.

As the social worker, would you at this stage be considering permanent long-term foster care as an option, or would you still hope that she could be reunited with her family? Another factor in your thinking will be the extent to which her parents seem to cooperate in the work.

Despite Rosie's difficult behaviour, and her tiredness at the end of the day, Mrs Ashton, rather against expectations, nonetheless attended every contact session and gradually, with some prompting from the social worker and on occasion the foster carer, began to take more responsibility for controlling Rosie's behaviour and to initiate play and other activities with Rosie, while Mr Ashton, with Tina's help, looked after her sister and the baby at home.

Rosie's passionate wish to return home had been clearly identified in the focused therapeutic work undertaken with her. Mrs Ashton had faithfully kept in touch with her and seemed to be more in harmony with her, and Rosie's behaviour, appearance and eating habits as a result of her time in foster care had improved markedly. She was less clingy and, as her teachers reported, more communicative and cooperative and less solitary in school, so it was hoped that she would be easier too to look after at home. Her father was now on the road to full recovery, and both parents expressed their readiness to resume attendance at parenting classes. After four months in foster care, she was successfully returned home to her family.

Conclusion

We started this chapter asking you to think about your own childhood and how childhood is understood and children are perceived. In so doing you will have identified what influences your practice as a social worker working with children and their families. As we emphasised at the outset, this level of self-awareness is vital in an area of social work that is charged with emotion and heavily influenced by societal and, particularly, media pressures. Given the need for social workers involved with children and families to simultaneously be reflective practitioners, who are alert to the influences on their practice and familiar with the complex legal and procedural requirements of children in need and at risk, it is self-evident that regular and sound supervision and support is essential for effective and ethical practice (see Chapter 1). If social workers are expected to care for vulnerable children, it is only right they receive the professional care needed to do their job:

'The more that workers are cared for, nurtured and protected the more they will be able to provide this for the children they serve.'   (Ferguson, 2005: 794)

Key learning points

This chapter has covered the following learning points:

✔ Working with children and families is complex and challenging and involves being self-aware and balancing the needs of children and the rights of families.

✔ Effective and ethical practice with children and families is built on open and honest relationships that are based on the principles of partnership-working.

✔ Childhood is a social construct that changes over time in responses to different understandings of children, families and the role of the state.

✔ International comparative studies of child protection work show Britain to be unusual in its degree of political sensitivity to 'failures of the system'. Child protection systems in nearby countries operate on very different assumptions about how best to understand and respond to child abuse.

✔ To work effectively and ethically with children and families, social workers need to be familiar with the legislative contexts and procedural requirements which guide their practice.

✔ Ascertaining the wishes and feelings of children must be a priority at all stages of involvement with children, wherever they are living.

✔ The heightened emotional content involved in working with children and families makes it imperative that social workers have good supervision on a regular basis.

Further reading

The third edition of *The Child Protection Handbook* (**Wilson and James**, 2007) is divided into three sections on Understanding, Managing and Intervening in child protection and provides useful, up-to-date information on all areas of work with children in need, and children in need of protection, and their families.

Richard Barker's (2009) edited book *Making Sense of Every Child Matters* provides an overview of child protection practice from different professional perspectives and is a useful basic text in this regard.

More detailed analysis of the social work role in child protection settings is included in **Parton, N. and Frost, N.**

(2009) *Understanding Children's Social Care: Politics, Policy and Practice*.

Vera Fahlberg's three books collected into one are classic texts on children's experiences and feelings of being in the looked-after system which are still an invaluable guide for social workers today.

Ken Redgrave's book on focused therapeutic play with children is full of suggestions for techniques, games etc. to be used with children and young people and is a revised version of his earlier book on the same subject.

Gillian Schofield and Mary Beek and social work colleagues from the University of East Anglia have written a number of books on foster care, attachment and adoption which are full of helpful suggestions as well as being rooted in research evidence.

There have, as you will by now have identified from your reading, been a succession of public inquiries following (other than the Cleveland Inquiry) deaths of children either in care or known to social services. Possibly the ones which (for a variety of reasons) caused most public outcry are those involving Maria Colwell, Jasmine Beckford, Tyra Henry, Kimberley Carlile, Victoria Climbié and most recently Peter Connelly in addition to the Cleveland Inquiry (which had far-reaching consequences, particularly in speeding up the long-awaited introduction of new legislation to address and reform the existing legal child-welfare frameworks). However, it is worth looking at some of the less publicised inquiries, such as that of Lucie Gates, which highlighted the risks of social workers over-identifying with needy parents, or Sukina, which highlighted significant inter-professional dynamics, such as the way in which the comments from the better-informed but lower-status participants at the case conference tended to be overlooked.

A number of useful books on working with children and families are suggested in other chapters in the book (communicating with children, human development through the lifespan, and planning and intervening). That by **Marion Brandon, Gillian Schofield, and Liz Trinder,** (1998) *Social Work with Children*, is an excellent and accessible introduction.

A book on non-directive play therapy by one of the present authors, **Kate Wilson**, and a colleague, **Virginia Ryan**, gives an introduction to the therapeutic method derived from Carl Rogers, and contains detailed discussion of techniques of working non-directively with children in statutory settings, including court work, as well as giving an overview of different therapeutic methods. (Wilson, K. and Ryan, V., 2005, *Play therapy: A Non-directive Approach for Children and Adolescents*, 2nd edn, London: Bailliere Tindall.)

Two books on unaccompanied asylum-seeking children provide very useful and sensitively written accounts of policy and practice issues involving a group of children with complex needs whom we have not, for reasons of space, been able to discuss in the chapter. One is an edited book which explores the legal and policy frameworks, assessment and therapeutic support, and includes an excellent chapter by John Simmonds on the relevance of the narratives of unaccompanied asylum seekers. The other presents research findings from a study by the author:

Kohli, R. and Mitchell, F. (2007) *Working with Unaccompanied Asylum Seeking Children*, Basingstoke: Palgrave Macmillan.

Kohli, R. (2007) *Social Work with Unaccompanied Asylum Seeking Children*, Basingstoke: Palgrave Macmillan.

A useful collection, edited by two academics at the University of Sussex, on direct social work with children in the looked-after system contains a range of chapters on communicating and working with children 'in care' (Luckock, B. and Lefevre, M. (2008) *Direct Work: Social work with children and young people in care*, London: BAAF).

 Useful websites

www.baaf.org.uk
The website of the British Association for Adoption and Fostering is a useful source of information on looked-after children, and includes summaries of recent statistical information.

www.dfes.org.uk and **www.doh.org.uk**
The relevant government websites for policies relating to children and young people.

www.surestart.gov.uk/surestart
More information on SureStart centres.

www.fostering.net
A useful source of information on foster care.

www.youngminds.org.uk
www.jrf.co.uk
The Joseph Rowntree Foundation website includes summaries of research projects, and is particularly useful on children with disabilities and issues of poverty.

www.everychildmatters.gov.uk
The key website for keeping abreast of the range of documents which are informing the various changes currently taking place in the wake of the Children Act 2004 is the official government website *Every Child Matters: Change for Children*.

www.scotland.gov.uk/Topics/People/Young-People/childrensservices/girfec
Similarly to the Every Child Matters website, the key site for overview of the initiative, guidance and practice materials.

www.incredibleyears.com
The Webster-Stratton Parenting Programme website gives further information on these programmes.

www.fathersdirect.com
Fathers Direct as the title suggests is a source of information on fathers.

www.parenting-forum.org.uk
Parenting Education and Support forum.

www.scie.org.uk
Useful reviews of research on fostering and adoption (nos 2 and 5), and a guide on fostering, are available to download.

For additional cases and topic-organised, clickable links into additional media resources, including those produced by IRISS, visit **www.pearsoned.co.uk/wilsonruch**

Activity

Think back over the past decade or so, and see what you can remember that you have read in the media about child protection and child abuse. Read one or more of the inquiry reports we have suggested in Further Reading, which give a careful account of events when a child has died, sometimes when under the supervision of social services. Then answer the following questions, working on your own or with a colleague.

How do you think the media accounts, or those in the inquiries themselves, reflect some of the difficulties for professionals in intervening unnecessarily or not enough?

What are the key difficulties and errors which the inquiries identify? Make a note of the main recommendations for improving services.

How successful do you think these will be in addressing the problems which gave rise to the inquiry?

As you have been reading you may have begun yourself to see that legislation and policies over the years seem to be attempting to address common themes. One social policy writer, Lorraine Fox Harding, has suggested that four themes

Table 16.2 Perspectives on childcare social work practice

State paternalism and child protection	Laissez-faire and patriarchy perspective	Children's rights and children's liberation	Parental rights and defence of the birth family perspective
Reflecting extensive state intervention to protect children from what professionals judge to be poor parental care	Reflecting the importance of family privacy and minimal state intervention	Emphasising children's autonomy, and their rights to be consulted and to 'have a voice' in decisions made about them	Valuing the integrity of the family and opposing interference in family life

(*Source*: Based on Fox Harding, 1991)

may be discerned in child welfare practice, and that each 'age' is dominated by one of them. Although there is a danger of oversimplification, they may interest you as one way, among others, of understanding how policies, philosophies about children (i.e. the 'construction of childhood'), child-rearing practices and the role of state involvement in family life interlink and affect social work practice (see Table 16.2).

Preferably working with a colleague or fellow student, consider whether or not any of these perspectives seem accurately to describe the past decade. If they don't, can you think of a description which might better summarise it? You may want to return to the discussion at the end of the first part of the chapter to help you.

Chapter 17
Social work with adults: policy and practice

Chapter summary

This chapter will focus on the policy context that underpins social work with adults. We demonstrate that an understanding of policy debates is critical to understanding how social work practice with adults will develop in response to those policy changes. This is particularly important given the heightened profile of social care in the context of significant reductions in public expenditure, which inevitably affect the context of social work practice. We summarise policy in three distinct ways: its historical basis, the dimensions of community care introduced in the 1990s, and the so-called 'transformation' of social care. We also comment on a number of the general questions that remain to be resolved in future. Finally, we discuss some key policy issues in relation to specific areas of practice – safeguarding, capacity and domestic violence.

Learning objectives

This chapter covers topics that will enable you to achieve the following learning objectives:

- To clarify the importance of understanding the dynamics of social care policy
- To identify the key historical trends that have affected the development of policy
- To understand how the establishment of personalisation derives from these movements
- To isolate the key issues that suffuse specific developments in policy, notably mental capacity, safeguarding and domestic violence
- To introduce some of the key practice dilemmas in relation to working with adults.

The publishers gratefully acknowledge the contribution of Dr Margaret Bell to this chapter with her section on domestic violence.

National Occupational Standards

This chapter contributes towards the following National Occupational Standards:

Key Role 1: Prepare for, and work with individuals, families, carers, groups and communities to assess their needs and circumstances

Unit 1   Prepare for social work contact and involvement

Unit 2   Work with individuals, families, carers, groups and communities to help them make informed decisions

Unit 3   Assess needs and options to recommend a course of action for individuals, families, carers, groups and communities

Key Role 2: Plan, carry out, review and evaluate social work practice, with individuals, families, carers, groups, communities and other professionals

Unit 5   Interact with individuals, families, carers, groups and communities to achieve change and development and to improve life opportunities

Unit 9   Address behaviour which presents a risk to individuals, families, carers, groups and communities

Key Role 3: Support individuals to represent their needs, views and circumstances

Unit 10   Advocate with, and on behalf of, individuals, families, carers, groups and communities

Key Role 4: Manage risk to individuals, families, carers, groups, communities, self and colleagues

Unit 12   Assess and manage risks to individuals, families, carers, groups and communities

Unit 13   Assess, minimise and manage risk to self and colleagues

Key Role 5: Manage and be accountable, with supervision and support, for your own social work practice within your organisation

Unit 14   Manage and be accountable for your own work

Key Role 6: Demonstrate professional competence in social work practice

Unit 18   Research, analyse, evaluate, and use current knowledge of best social work practice

Unit 19   Work within agreed standards of social work practice and ensure own professional development

Unit 20   Manage complex ethical issues, dilemmas and conflicts

Unit 21   Contribute to the promotion of best social work practice

Case study

Salma, Derek and Robert

Salma is a 38-year-old woman with cerebral palsy. She was one of the first people to take advantage of the opportunity to receive direct payments, which she has always managed directly. She has ongoing and relatively stable needs for care and support, and her personal assistants have worked with her for a number of years.

Derek is a 45-year-old man with fluctuating levels of mental ill health, which have led to compulsory admission to psychiatric hospital on three occasions over the past 6 years. These admissions all appear to be connected to his failure to comply with his extensive regime of medication. When this is managed effectively, Derek is described as a gentle and easy-going man. However, when he fails to comply with his medication he becomes paranoid and prone to violence. Currently, he does receive a stable care package but is casting doubt on the efficacy of his medication. He has little contact with his family, but one brother has a peripatetic involvement in his circumstances; the adult social care department is very suspicious about his motives.

Robert is a 75-year-old man with advanced vascular dementia. He is currently maintained at home with the support of his 79-year-old wife Grace. His behaviour is described as increasingly disinhibited, and places considerable pressure on Grace; at times he has been violent towards her. Although Grace is willing to accept this additional pressure, her physical health is not strong. She needs to enter hospital for a hip replacement operation in the near future: although she has suggested that this should be postponed, this would not be in her interests. Robert has consistently refused to accept care from people other than Grace.

Think ahead

Why is it essential for social workers to understand the basic elements of policy development in adult social care?

Introduction

In the changed world of adult social care all the above cases should be considered for what is defined as personalised support. However, different levels of complexity govern each of the above examples. Salma represents people who are very experienced in resolving their own needs, and has been an early adopter of direct payments. As such she appears to be an example of the sort of service user for whom the various elements of personalisation ought to work well. Derek's situation is less certain; his needs fluctuate as does his ability to manage them. The situation is further complicated by the presence of his brother and the shadowy possibility of abuse that has been identified. Robert's case is more complex again, with his dementia clearly affecting his cognitive abilities and Grace's ability to maintain a caring role under question. In both Derek's and Robert's cases there are clear obstacles to be overcome before the principles of personalisation can easily be put into effect.

This chapter engages with some key policy dimensions in adult services. It will explore what is meant by the 'transformation agenda', placing the change into a historical context. For the sake of clarity the chapter will focus on three distinct policy periods:

1. The years before the passage of the National Health Service and Community Care Act 1990, and its full implementation in 1993.
2. The purpose and meaning of community care policy in the 1990s.
3. Developments in policy that have been current in the early part of the twenty-first century, with particular emphasis on personalisation and the transformation of social care.

The chapter will conclude by identifying a number of themes to emerge from particular areas of policy development: mental capacity, safeguarding and domestic violence. Throughout we will focus on the role that social workers occupy within the various elements of policy.

The historical summary necessarily represents an abbreviated version of events, which are addressed in more detail in a number of other texts (see, for example, Lewis and Glennerster, 1996; Means and Smith, 1998; Means et al., 2003; McDonald, 2006). Our main purpose is to identify the elements of the historical development of social care that impinge on contemporary concerns. Although the policy applies to all adult service user groups, they have a particular impact on vulnerable older people as the largest group in both numbers and cost (see Chapter 22).

It is important that a key recommendation of the Social Work Task Force report was that social work should remain a generically based profession (SWTF, 2009: 19); however, there is little doubt that the primary focus of their discussions was the perceived problem of social work with children and families, notably issues around safeguarding and protection. Nonetheless, the context of social work practice with adults has also changed markedly in recent years: the Labour government's adoption of personalisation as a governing framework led to what they term as a transformation of social care (DoH, 2008). After some uncertainty about the precise role of social work in this new policy world (Scourfield, 2010; Lymbery and Postle, 2010), a number of organisations have collaborated to produce what they suggest is a definitive statement of the social work role in adult social care. This document argues that social work can have a vital role to play in all dimensions of *Putting People First* (HM Government, 2007). Indeed, it suggests that:

'Social work and its values could be important in shaping the responses of all the workforce. Listening, empowering individuals, being alert to conflict, safeguard needs and the capacity of individuals, being sensitive to diversity and putting people in control should be part of the behaviours of all staff and services, from the very first contact. Social workers could have a leadership role here, particularly in the career structure envisaged by the Social Work Task Force, with advanced practitioners and consultant social workers.'
(ADASS/DH/SFC/BASW/SCA, 2010: 3)

In a parallel statement the Association of Directors of Adult Social Services (ADASS) have identified that social workers could have a greater involvement in direct psychosocial intervention and interpersonal support, aspects of service where there are currently gaps (ADASS, 2010). However, the language of both extracts highlights a strong element of conditionality: it is argued that social work *could* have an impact, not that it *will*. Where it is recommended that social workers will play a specific role in the new frameworks of adult social care, it is clear that issues around mental health assessments, safeguarding and abuse take precedence over these sorts of intervention (ADASS, 2010). Consequently, it is vital for social workers to understand the nature of policy in order to understand how social work is perceived and to develop the breadth of its impact on service users and carers.

The historical basis of social care policy

Relatively little specific attention was given to social care policy until the period following the Second World War. This led to the inauguration of a Labour government under the leadership of Clement Attlee (a former social worker!), which can legitimately claim to have founded the modern welfare state. Prior to this, the social care needs of adults were met under legislation derived from the Poor Law, which had been in place, in varying forms, from the sixteenth century (Digby, 1978). The workhouse had been a central feature of the services that were available; indeed, there was a very strong focus on the establishment of institutional care for those in need, whether they were old, experienced mental ill health, or had either a physical or learning disability (Jack, 1999).

The National Health Act 1946, when combined with the National Assistance Act 1948, helped to create a different world for health and social care. However, the focus on residential care inherited from the Poor Law still remained (Reed et al., 2004). Alongside a range of formal statutory duties and powers relating to people's health and welfare, these two Acts also constructed a distinction between health and social care (Means and Smith, 1998). In Chapter 13 we suggested that this has been the basis of many subsequent problems, including (a) the difficulty in distinguishing clearly between health and welfare needs, and (b) the organisational and budgetary separation between the two. At this time, different services were rarely effectively coordinated, often functioning in isolation from each other; in addition, the fact that there were separate financial imperatives for each organisation created further practical obstacles (Lewis, 2001). As we discussed in Chapter 13, the emphasis on partnership and collaboration is partly in response to this organisational separation and confusion.

The development of social work with adults was also slow, with the majority of time given to the development of a response to the needs of children and families. There were different dynamics in play for the various user groups. For example, for people with learning disabilities their

needs were medicalised and hence most forms of treatment were developed in long-stay hospitals (Malin et al., 1980); many of these hospitals remained open until wholesale policies of hospital closure were effected in the 1970s and 1980s (Jack, 1999). For many older people, models of institutional care – often first developed under the poor law – dominated; the expansion of alternatives to residential care (particularly forms of support for older people in their own homes: home help, laundry services, meals, etc.) was gradual in nature (Means and Smith, 1998). The lack of movement in these areas is indicative of the low priority given to them as aspects of policy; the slow pace of social work development also speaks to its relatively low professional priority.

The formal policy for community care that was adopted with the passage of *Caring for People* in 1989 (DoH, 1989a) took 40 years to arrive following the creation of the National Health Service and the passage of the National Assistance Act 1948. The main single issue which compelled a policy shift came as a result of the changes to supplementary benefit regulations in 1980. For social care, the purpose of these changes is less important than their (unintended) consequences, which ensured that all people requiring state support who wished to enter residential care were enabled to do so, with no cap on the numbers that could be admitted and no process by which a judgement was made that an individual 'needed' such care (Lewis and Glennerster, 1996). The resultant cost is startling: in 1979/80 £10m was spent from the income support budget for people in independent sector residential care, which rose to £744m in 1987/88 as a consequence of the change in supplementary benefit regulations (DoH, 1989a). By the time community care was fully implemented in 1993 it was estimated that this had mushroomed to over £2bn (Lewis and Glennerster, 1996). It is unlikely that community care policy would have been established were it not for these budgetary problems, although other occurrences in the 1980s did also provide a strong motivation for the community care reforms.

In this regard the Audit Commission report *Making a Reality of Community Care* (1986) was particularly significant. This report highlighted the numerous obstacles in the way of developing a coherent policy, which can be summarised as follows:

- The organisational and budgetary complexity that characterised health and social welfare for adults, including the range of organisations, funding sources and priorities within the health and social care system.

- The lack of priority given to transferring from a hospital-based to a community-focused service.
- The fact that the social security system created a 'perverse incentive' in favour of residential care, which worked in opposition to the desire to create more community-based alternatives.
- Major operational and organisational problems that contributed to policy failures in community care.

As a result of these problems the critical conclusion of the report was that care arrangements for groups and individuals were neither organised nor coordinated, and that the overall funding of policy was equally confused.

Recognising the reality of these problems the government of the day commissioned a review of community care, which reported in 1988 (Griffiths, 1988). This report proposed a number of changes to the system, including that community care policy needed to be taken more seriously by government, and that coordination between health and social care agencies should be improved. To resolve this, it recommended that:

- Local authority social services departments (SSDs) should function as the lead agency for all community care.
- These organisations should have the responsibility for assessing the care needs of any individual who may be in need of care services.
- SSDs should develop as enablers and purchasers of care, and hence move away from seeing themselves as monopolistic providers of services, to ensure the continuation of a vibrant independent sector.

Although the government perceived a number of difficulties with specific recommendations, one central fact underscored their eventual reaction: doing nothing was not an option, due to the impact of the spiralling social security budget (Lymbery, 2005). Although a number of difficulties had to be resolved before policy could be agreed (Lewis and Glennerster, 1996), the community care White Paper emerged in 1989. The following subsection will focus on its main implications.

Caring for people: the outline of community care policy

The foundations of contemporary policy and practice were laid in the community care White Paper, *Caring for People* (DoH, 1989a). This established the basis of policy;

the groundwork for its implementation was laid out in subsequent guidance documents (for example, DoH, 1990a; DH/SSI, 1991). It contained six key objectives for service delivery, which are as follows:

1. to promote the development of domiciliary, day and respite services to enable people to live in their own homes wherever feasible and sensible
2. to ensure that service providers make practical support for carers a high priority
3. to make proper assessment of need and good case management the cornerstone of high quality care
4. to promote the development of a flourishing independent sector alongside good quality public services
5. to clarify the responsibilities of agencies and so make it easier to hold them to account for their performance
6. to secure better value for taxpayers' money by introducing a new funding structure for social care.

(DoH, 1989a: 5)

These objectives are different in their nature and scope. The first two reflect the ways in which the policy was sold to service users and carers as well as to professionals; that there was little argument over the core principles of the White Paper at the time (but see Hudson, 1990) testifies to the success of this strategy. Given that financial priorities have been argued as the core priorities of community care (Lewis and Glennerster, 1996), there is little doubt that the success of community care policy depended on being able to reduce the reliance on long-stay institutional care; in turn, it was recognised that high levels of support for carers would be needed in order to turn this aspiration into a reality. For social workers, the third of these objectives is particularly significant, highlighting the centrality of needs-based assessment and also specifying the intention to develop case management systems; both of these issues are further explored in the following section.

From the fourth objective onwards, the government's political motivation becomes easier to discern. The requirement to develop a 'flourishing independent sector' was supported by the terms of the subsequent financial settlement, with 85 per cent of it needing to be spent in the independent sector (Lewis and Glennerster, 1996). In turn, this objective also required SSDs to act in accordance with the Griffiths report, as enablers and purchasers of care services rather than as the major providers. This represented a belief in the benefits that the independent sector could bring to the provision of care, notably in its presumed flexibility and efficiency, which is profoundly ideological in its nature. The fifth objective reflects back to the concern with the coordination of community care, highlighted as a problem both by the Audit Commission and the Griffiths Report.

However, the essence of the reforms is contained in the final objective. As we have noted, the government had to find a new funding structure for community care that would remove the existing financial incentive in favour of institutional care and control the financial pressure on the social security budget. The policy's intention was to introduce a system that could manage this; what is not specified here, but became clear in later guidance issued by the Department of Health (DoH, 1990a), is that a simple control mechanism would be introduced. This was the provision of a cash-limited budget to local authorities, making it impossible for SSDs to perpetuate the expansion of residential and nursing homes – for no other reason than that they could not pay for such an increase.

The critical balance between needs and resources reappears throughout considerations of policy for adult social care. For example, the proposal that there should be free personal care contained in the Royal Commission Report on long-term care (Sutherland, 1999) was rejected in England due to concerns about the overall cost that would result from such a measure. This recommendation was, however, fully implemented in Scotland (see further discussion on p. 652); in recent times the concerns about its affordability have resurfaced (Christie, 2009).

Although the National Health Service and Community Care Act was passed in 1990, it was not fully implemented until 1993; this was because the local authorities needed this time to put the complex policies into place to bring about the changes required. The concept of becoming an 'enabling authority' was a major shift for SSDs, and a vast amount of increased work was generated by the requirement to assess the needs of each person who required state support with their care. In conjunction with the simultaneous revolution in child care services following the implementation of the Children Act 1989 (discussed in Chapter 16) changes were in train that would radically alter the landscape of social work and social care.

Financially, community care policy has been a marked success – but since the financial imperatives of the policy were not overt this success has never been loudly acclaimed. Despite some regional difficulties, the escalation in costs of independent sector residential and nursing home care was immediately halted. The establishment of a market within social care has been

difficult; most resources within the independent sector were tied up in residential facilities, while SSDs had little experience of market management and development. If we examine social work practice, the creation of systems of assessment and care management is a good example of the sorts of problem that have emerged. While there was a belief that care management could make a positive contribution to the lives of vulnerable people in the 1980s (Challis and Davies, 1986), this optimism has not been borne out by subsequent experience; indeed, a critical sense of history suffuses official documents that argue for the need to 'transform' social care (HM Government, 2007; DoH, 2008). The social work components of care management have reduced in importance, with the economic purpose of rationing scarce resources being brought to the fore. This has made it particularly difficult to maintain the relational focus of social work that is central to this book, and has contributed to a number of practice dilemmas for social workers, which will be discussed in subsequent chapters.

Although the independent sector has certainly flourished under community care, with a vast increase in both the volume and proportion of care provided outside the statutory sector, market conditions have become increasingly tough as the tight financial limitations within which SSDs had to operate took effect. Although the 'mixed economy of welfare' that the government wished to develop has come into being, alternatives to residential care were slow to develop. There has also been a relative lack of investment in prevention and rehabilitation (Bauld et al., 2000). In addition, successive governments have failed to make practical support for carers a sufficiently high priority. There has also been an ongoing concern with quality in the delivery of services, magnified by that fact that a large proportion of such services is provided under contract by independent sector organisations.

The organisational problems that were held to exist between social care, health and other agencies have also been apparently intractable, and relatively slow progress has been made towards the 'seamless service' that was emphasised in the community care policy guidance (DoH, 1990a). The exhortations to improve collaboration and develop stronger working partnerships were manifold, but proved insufficient to bring about major policy changes. As a result, concepts of partnership re-emerged as a key feature of the social policy of the 'new' Labour government, particularly in relation to health and social care.

Social care and 'new' Labour: continuity or change?

The change of political administration in 1997 came after community care had been in place for only four years; the majority of time since then has featured developments associated with the 'new' Labour administration. In reality, there was considerable continuity between the original conception of community care and the modifications that were made to it by successive governments. This subsection will identify the key aspects of these developments, focusing on the needs of all adults requiring social care support.

An understanding of the priorities that governed the social policy of the 'new' Labour government created a general background for this (see, for example, Lister, 2001), as this gives a sense of what might be considered to be distinctive about its approach. In the early years, much was made of the way in which its policies represented a 'third way' for welfare, supposedly positioned between the ideological excesses of both left and right (Powell, 2000). As the years have progressed the sense that this policy possessed a distinctive approach has diminished, although there is now more certainty about its core characteristics. These can be identified as follows:

- *Populism:* as the government sought to avoid being constrained by ideological baggage, it became increasingly timid in its consideration of policies that may prove to be unpopular – the increasingly hard-line approach to criminal justice policy being a case in point (Lister, 2001), with the failure to grasp the nettle of climate change another example. This was clearly manifested in its inability to resolve the ongoing problems about funding long-term care, with a White Paper only appearing in the dying days of government in 2010 (DoH, 2010a): there was never a realistic likelihood that the proposed National Care Service could proceed into law, leaving the question of how this 'wicked issue' (Clarke and Stewart, 2003) will be resolved. One key option that was ruled out of court would be an increase to general taxation – the reasons for this critically included a desire not to alienate an electorate for whom low levels of taxation are perceived as a given. As with policies around climate change, there was a clear avoidance of long-term policy changes, with a preference for short-term electoral gain.

- *Pragmatism:* a closely related tendency in policy is the focus on an eclectic mixture of responses, governed by a concern with 'what works' (Powell, 2000). In health and social care the evidence-based movement is a reflection of this (Sheldon, 2001; see also Chapter 8 of this text), despite the limitations that have been identified within this (Webb, 2001). The *National Service Framework for Older People* (DoH, 2001c) contained a clear example of the way in which the pursuit of 'evidence' potentially privileges some forms (typically those derived from quantitative forms of analysis) over others (in this case, qualitative forms of enquiry, the testimonies of service users and practitioners, etc.).

- *Modernisation:* the government sought to 'modernise' numerous aspects of social policy, with social services one of the early recipients of this label (DoH, 1998). Strange as it has been to see a term primarily associated with home improvements used in relation to public policy, its use has been ubiquitous. Its precise meaning is often less hard to determine (Newman et al., 2008); certainly, it carries a symbolic message that services have been shackled to the past, and that a process of 'modernisation' is needed in order to make them 'fit for purpose' (to borrow another early twenty-first century phrase). For some commentators (Finlayson, 2003) the term also functions at a rhetorical level, making proposed changes appear to be beyond serious debate. The consumer-driven notion of 'choice' suffuses many of these policies (see DoH, 2005b); this is also a key aspect of personalisation and the key to transforming social care (DoH, 2008).

- *Performance:* although a preoccupation with performance is part of the 'modernisation agenda' (Lymbery, 2007; Harris and Unwin, 2009), it has developed a particular force of its own. The original intentions were to create objective measurements against which improvement of performance could be judged (Sanderson, 2001); in social care, the introduction of the Performance Assessment Framework (PAF) was the device used for this purpose, combined with a regular process of inspections and reviews. The focus on performance carries particular implications for the practice of social workers in adult social care, notably in the requirement for speed in responding to assessments. It confirms the difficulty of maintaining a relationship-based approach to practice, noted earlier in this chapter.

- *Safeguarding:* the 1998 White Paper carried an entire chapter that focused on protection (DoH, 1998), with a particular focus on vulnerable children. However, the protection of vulnerable adults has also become a more prominent aspect of policy, particularly following the publication of *No Secrets* (DoH, 2000f). As we will discuss in a later section, there are particular contradictions between the focus on safeguarding and steps that the government is taking to maximise the level of independence of service users.

- *Independence:* Much of the development of health and social care policy has the goal of enhanced independence at its core. There is a clear continuity between this goal and community care policies introduced in the 1990s (see above). The Green Paper of 2005 (DoH, 2005b) and the subsequent White Paper of 2006 (DoH, 2006b) focus particularly on this concept. However, the interaction of the themes of dependence, independence and interdependence are not fully worked out, leading to problems in the detail of policy. Put briefly, a level of dependence is a normal feature of life for all of us (Lloyd, 2006), and hence not necessarily problematic. In addition, most of us live in an interdependent way, rather than entirely independently. A recognition of these factors is scarcely present in government documents: this suggests a lack of reality in relation to this policy aim (Lymbery, 2010).

- *Prevention:* The development of this concept was particularly evident in the Green Paper for adult social care (DoH, 2005b), and has been prominent in numerous policy statements since (see HM Government, 2007; DoH, 2008). The effectiveness and popularity of this sort of approach has long been demonstrated (Clark et al., 1998), but there are unexamined conflicts between such priorities and the nature of much social care, which since the 1989 White Paper has been targeted specifically towards those most in need. The Fair Access to Care Services (FACS) guidance (DoH, 2002b) created obligations for local authorities that work directly *against* the idea of increased levels of preventive services. With this in mind, the government undertook a review of these eligibility criteria, publishing the result of this in early 2010; the intention was to ensure that there is a greater fit between them and the priorities of personalisation:

'Public funding for social care will always be limited in the face of demand and such resources as are available should therefore be allocated according to individual need in a way that is as fair and transparent as possible . . . To broaden their focus beyond those with the highest needs, councils should ensure that the application of

eligibility criteria is firmly situated in the wider context of personalisation, including a strong emphasis on prevention, early intervention and support for carers.'

(DoH, 2010b: 6–7)

There remains a tension between the aims of prevention and the efficient use of scarce resources, as the above quotation indicates. This will be explored further in a future section

- *Partnership:* As we discussed in Chapter 13, the development of enhanced levels of inter-professional working has been an article of faith for the 'new' Labour government in all aspects of service delivery, including social care.

These elements have interacted to create a new wave of policy in relation to social care, referred to within government documents as the 'transformation agenda' (DoH, 2008). It unites numerous of the themes noted above, particularly in relation to independence and prevention. It is also consistent with the principle of modernisation. However, the basis of criticism can also be discerned in the above themes. The issue of prevention highlights the problem of inadequate resources, which forced eligibility criteria to be deployed increasingly restrictively (Carvel, 2007). Even with the redrafting of the criteria the problems of inadequate resources do represent a major problem. In addition, the focus on safeguarding highlights another potential issue: the lack of fit between policies that promote independence and the need to ensure effective safeguarding of vulnerable people (Fyson and Kitson, 2007). While it is too early in the life of the coalition government to detect its core approach, it is unlikely that they will deviate greatly from the emphasis on personalisation that characterised the last years of the 'new' Labour government. The main problem that may be encountered is the overwhelming desire to curb public expenditure, which is strikingly at odds with the demographic reality of social care (Lymbery, 2010). Consequently, the following section will outline the key elements of the transformation of social care, and will introduce some critical problems with the policy that urgently need to be addressed and resolved.

The transformation of social care

The core principle that underpins this transformation is the concept of 'personalisation' (Glasby and Littlechild, 2009). It draws strongly on influential work carried out by Charles Leadbeater, which was first pursued as a general principle that should inform all public services. The explicit intention of this is for people to have more control over the services they receive and more choice regarding their provision (Leadbeater, 2004); subsequently Leadbeater and colleagues have written specifically about how the principle can best be applied to social care (Leadbeater et al., 2008). This latter document makes bold claims for the potential of personalised services both to provide a more satisfactory response to people's care needs, and to do so at lower cost. (It is possible that the latter claim may come to be the most significant for policy.)

Choice and control have become key terms in official discourse. For example, the Green Paper specified that 'social care should be about helping people maintain their independence, leaving them with control over their lives, and giving them real choice over those lives' (DoH, 2005b: 8). (It is important to note that a Green Paper is essentially a consultative document expressing the government's broad principles for the development of services. A White Paper expresses the firm policy intention for an area of activity, which may later be turned into legislative form. Whereas a Green Paper seeks to establish the overall direction of policy, a White Paper should contain more concrete proposals.)

This sort of theme was echoed in subsequent documents, particularly in the *Putting People First* concordat (HM Government, 2007), which outlined an intergovernmental approach to social care. This clearly established the overarching vision for social care: 'The time has now come to build on best practice and replace paternalistic, reactive care of variable quality with a mainstream system focused on prevention, early intervention, enablement and high quality personally tailored services' (HM Government, 2007: 2).

Subsequently, £522 million was made available to English local authorities to facilitate this change from 2008 to 2011 (DoH, 2008). It is expected that this will enable councils to have made measurable steps in the direction the government has indicated by March 2011 (DoH, 2008). It also appears to promise the sorts of social work engagement that fit well with the focus of this text. However, there are more critical perceptions of the change that should be noted. For example, Ferguson (2007) challenged an uncritical acceptance of the tenets of personalisation, noting the connection that it had with a continued marketisation of social work. Houston (2010) has extended this analysis, disparaging personalisation as a 'fad' and emphasising its dependence upon

what he sees as fundamentally flawed: 'the view of the actor as rational, individualistic, utilitarian, calculative and instrumental' (Houston, 2010: 842). Fundamentally, he regards the inherent individualisation of policy in adult social care to be flawed, and believes that greater emphasis should be placed on numerous interactive characteristics of services. In addition, Scourfield (2007) has indicated that the policy may be in danger of forgetting that the very reason why the public sector first emerged was to ensure that those people who required support could have it provided in a secure and dignified manner, both potentially outside the confines of the family or the dictates of the market. In establishing the welfare state, it was recognised that there were many people who would be unable to act as the autonomous and enterprising individuals envisaged by the transformation of social care.

However, despite these core criticisms, it is clear that throughout the United Kingdom social care policy is being conceptualised on precisely this individualistic basis. Even on these terms, there are inherent problems that have to be resolved: for example, there are obvious and crucial resource implications to settle. The unresolved tension in policy between limited resources – insisted upon as a given in all government documents (see, for example, HM Government 2008; DoH, 2010a: DoH, 2010b) – and the desire for early intervention (Henwood and Hudson, 2008) is a critical indicator of this. The official answer to this is to amend the way in which resources are allocated and administered, combining the advantages of improved cost-effectiveness with better quality care services which are also more appropriate to people's needs (Glasby and Littlechild, 2009). Consequently, the government has identified two types of development to support personalisation. The first of these is the principle of direct payments, an extension of the radical policy first developed in the 1990s (Glasby and Littlechild, 2009). The second is the notion that each individual should have a personal budget to indicate clearly and transparently the resources that are available to them. Underpinning this is the requirement to establish a new resource allocation system to ensure that people receive resources at the appropriate level to support their needs (Duffy, 2005).

In principle, the development of direct payments is a means to increase people's direct control over the way in which they want to live their lives (DoH, 2005b). They were introduced as a result of the Community Care (Direct Payments) Act 1996; the radical aspect of their introduction was that they represented the first opportunity for

'Direct payments and social work practice'

Research was carried out in a single English local authority aiming to explore social workers' actions in relation to direct payments, in the light of the mandatory direction that direct payments should be offered to all eligible individuals (Ellis, 2007). The resulting paper notes that, although the principle of direct payments is in accordance with both the professional training of social workers and consistent with the principles of the disability rights movement, there has been a limited uptake of direct payments for specific service user groups, including older people. In particular, it is suggested that social workers operate without clear policy or operational guidance, within a climate of stringent eligibility criteria; as a result, rationing decisions are pressed upon practitioners at every stage of the assessment process. As a result, social workers have been placed in an untenable position, seeking to balance the wishes and demands of service users against their rationing roles. They have therefore practised in ways that enable them to manage the inherent tensions, using the ambiguity of policies and procedures to exercise discretion in the assessment process. Practitioners framed a number of justifications for their actions, including concerns about principles of equity between different service users, and that service users managing direct payments may experience forms of financial abuse. In the case of older people, these 'justifications' also connected to some more stereotyping assumptions about older people: their perceived vulnerability, their low expectations of services, their desire not to take the responsibility for managing the payments or the people, and so on. The paper observes that it was interesting that practitioners were able to exercise so much discretion in their practice, given the extent to which assessment practice had been constrained by the requirements of the community care reforms. It also reports that assumptions about who might constitute the 'right sort of person' to receive direct payments specifically excluded older people in many cases, as they 'were assumed not to want the bother of direct payments or to lack the gumption to manage them' (Ellis, 2007: 418). In conclusion, the paper notes the contradiction between encouraging the uptake of direct payments and the continuing need to ration services tightly, and argues that this tension underpins social workers' actions during assessment.

service users to be provided with money to purchase their own care, thereby increasing their level of control over the expenditure. They have long been popular with service users (Leece, 2008), particularly adults with physical disabilities (Glasby and Littlechild, 2009). However, they have become less widely used than intended, despite the requirement that local authorities offer direct payments to all people in receipt of community care services (DoH, 2003b). There has been a particularly slow take-up of direct payments for older people (Glasby and Littlechild, 2009); the findings of one research study underline some of the dilemmas practitioners have experienced (see above).

There are a number of issues that Ellis's paper highlights, which we believe are central to the development of direct payments for vulnerable service user groups:

- There is an apparent conflict between the rationing function of local authorities, largely carried out through qualified social workers' assessments, and the extension of direct payments to a wider range of service users. As this is a central principle of the transformation agenda, this represents a particular problem for the implementation of policy.

- A way of managing this appears to be the application of stereotyped perceptions of service users, in this case older people. Social workers in the study have perceptions of who would be the 'right sort of person' to receive direct payments, which may not include some of the particularly troubled and vulnerable people in receipt of social care services.

- Social workers have retained considerable discretion over their practice; although the research found that this discretion was used to limit the numbers of people for whom direct payments was found to be appropriate, the opposite could also be true: relatively wide levels of discretion have the potential to enable practitioners to become more flexible in their practice rather than less.

The development of personal budgets represents the other key element of personalisation (Glasby and Littlechild, 2009); however, the evidence base for their success is distinctly ambiguous (Glendinning et al., 2008). The principle underpinning this is that individuals should have an allocation of resources that they manage, ideally through direct payments, as an individual budget. This changes the core role of local authorities, which will no longer be expected to manage resources on people's behalf; rather, the money will be disbursed for people to manage themselves. For this to operate successfully two things need to happen.

1. A system has to be established to govern the allocation of resources according to need, in order to ensure essential elements of transparency and clarity.

2. Service users need to be supported to maximise their control over these resources, either personally, through carers or through an independent agency (Glasby and Littlechild, 2009).

Consequently, to be effective this requires a change to the entire structure of social care resource allocation. As we have noted, local authorities have previously been required to respond to those people with the highest

A closer look

'A whole system approach to eligibility for social case'

This guidance was published in February 2010 and took effect as from April 2010, replacing the previous FACS system. The core argument for its existence is in the message that many councils were using FACS to shift their focus towards people and groups with the highest levels of need. This has the effect of ruling many people as ineligible to receive state support for their care needs, despite evidence that limiting access has only a 'modest and short-term effect on expenditure' (DoH, 2010b: 6). It is recognised that this interpretation runs counter to the principles of personalisation and may therefore counteract the ideals underpinning the transformation of social care.

Four principles are set out as a governing framework for the policy, which is aimed to improve support in each of these areas:

■ universal services
■ early intervention and prevention
■ choice and control
■ social capital.

(DoH, 2010b: 7)

It encourages local authorities to think about social care in a way that recognises the limitations of their care resources, and therefore places eligibility criteria within the context of wider responsibilities, encompassing housing, health care, new technology, greater benefits take-up and enhanced levels of community support. It also recognises the continuing need for support for carers.

At the practical level, many of the elements of FACS are retained. Councils keep the four tier categorisation – low, moderate, substantial and critical, in relation to the 'seriousness of the risk to independence and well-being or other consequences if needs are not addressed' (DoH, 2010b: 21) – but the guidance insists

that they 'should consider the needs of their wider population and put into place support strategies to reduce the number of people entering the social care system in the first place' (DoH, 2010b: 18).

However, the problems that a new system has to overcome are made apparent in the early pages:

'Public funding for social care will always be limited in the face of demand and such resources as are available should therefore be allocated according to individual need in a way that is as fair and transparent as possible . . . . To broaden their focus beyond those with the highest needs, councils should ensure that the application of eligibility criteria is firmly situated in the wider context of personalisation, including a strong emphasis on prevention, early intervention and support for carers.'

(DoH, 2010b: 6–7)

It is therefore acknowledged that councils will need to draw in alternative resources to enable this problem to be resolved (DoH, 2010b): as there is little evidence that this has so far been effective (Glendinning et al., 2008), this represents a substantial leap of faith. Indeed, the government appears to be aware – albeit perhaps rather dimly! – of the tenuous basis of this approach to social care:

'At a time when resources are tight it is recognised that it will not be possible for councils to invest large amounts in prevention and early intervention schemes. Rather *it is hoped* that that (*sic*) councils and those applying this eligibility guidance *will be prompted to think about* prevention and early intervention beyond just adult social services.'

(DoH, 2010b: 7 emphasis added)

The italicised elements sound an almost apologetic note: given the problems of public finances it is hard to think that councils will in fact be able to act in this way. Indeed, if this does happen, the revisions will make little or no practical difference to the experiences of either service users or local authorities.

levels of need first and only respond to people with lower levels of need once the higher levels have been met (DoH, 2002a). However, this approach is to be overturned and replaced by a different system, where the intention is for the service user to be in direct control of resources and the way in which they are to be used (DoH, 2010b).

What is unproven in this reform process is the extent to which the wholesale adoption of the principles of transformation will enable the uncomfortable balance between needs and resources to be managed. Implicit in the change is the belief that direct payments and individual budgets may save money, enabling the same amount of resource to serve a wider population (Leadbeater et al., 2008). We should point out that this is little more than a belief: robust evidence that will support such a claim is hard to come by (Carr and Robbins, 2009).

In a text focusing on social work, it is particularly important to identify ongoing concerns about precisely what their contribution is to be within the revised framework of adult social care. In early documents there was little that indicated what social workers might do, other than to specify that they will be expected to spend less time on assessment and more on support, brokerage and advocacy (HM Government, 2007). This lack of detail continued in subsequent documents (DoH, 2008) leading commentators to interrogate more closely how social workers might be enabled to contribute effectively to policy. ADASS (2009) has warned councils that sufficient numbers of qualified social workers will be needed to enable them to fulfil their duties of care, but only general issues on which social workers could work are identified. Indeed, there has been little agreement about the role that social workers might play in the new arrangements, although some of the difficulties and contradictions have been clearly identified (Scourfield, 2010; Lymbery and Postle, 2010). It has been suggested that social work has a potential role to play in all dimensions of social care policy, and may feature in a number of different ways:

- building professional relationships and empowering people
- working through conflict, including supporting people to manage their own risks
- knowing and applying legislation
- accessing practical support and services
- inter-professional working

(ADASS/DH/SFC/BASW/SCA, 2010)

The first of these clearly has a particular link with the themes of this text. This general understanding has been narrowed down to three specific areas of activity:

1. supporting people in the assessment of their needs, circumstances and option
2. working with families to improve well-being and safeguard vulnerable family members
3. contribute to early intervention and preventative services.

(ADASS/DH/SFC/BASW/SCA, 2010)

The first of these represents what could be identified as a traditional role for social work, and is addressed in Chapter 10 of this volume. Part of the second area of activity – work focused on safeguarding – is common in childcare, and has come to assume a greater level of prominence in adult social care over recent years, particularly since the publication of *No Secrets* (DoH, 2000f). (It also features in a subsequent section.) However, the way in which social work could help to enhance people's well being, and contribute towards early intervention and preventative services is less clear-cut, and little in the way that social work has been constructed in recent years (see Chapter 4 for a summary of this) suggests that this role could strongly be considered to be part of its role in recent times.

We would suggest that social work's role in assessment will remain the cornerstone of practice. Without a degree of professional involvement in the assessment process it is hard to imagine how issues such as safeguarding could be identified, let alone resolved (Lymbery and Postle, 2010). Similarly, the importance of ensuring that there is a good fit between the outcomes of assessment and the provision of services – a core aspect of social work practice under community care – does not decline, although it may appear in different ways. However, practitioners have long been concerned that assessment has dominated and circumscribed social work practice with adults (Postle, 2002), a corollary of which is the sense that more traditional social work skills have disappeared (Postle, 2001). The impact of this undeniably affects the injunction to reconstruct social work in more preventative ways, reconnecting with more traditional forms of practice, many of which are celebrated in this text. However, there has also been a strong emphasis on different possible directions of practice, all of which have the potential to involve social work. In the following sections, therefore, we examine issues in relation to, in sequences: capacity, safeguarding adults and domestic violence.

In the light of the various contextual factors that affect the provision of services, and the changes implied by the transformation of social care, can you argue for a continued role for social work?

Capacity

Case study

Ruby

Ruby is an 87-year-old woman. She was diagnosed with Alzheimer's Disease six years ago; following this she moved into sheltered accommodation. However, she has experienced increasing problems in managing her day-to-day existence: managing her finances, maintaining the upkeep of the flat, etc. She has been in receipt of an extensive package of care, and the manager of the sheltered housing complex has recently contacted social services owing to the number of problems that Ruby has caused. Before a revised assessment could be completed, Ruby caused a fire in her kitchen; although the damage to the flat was not serious, Ruby did suffer burns that required in-patient treatment in hospital. Her behaviour on the ward to which she was first admitted was categorised as bizarre and Ruby was moved to a specialist ward for older people with dementia. At this point, the warden of the sheltered housing complex indicated that she did not wish for Ruby to return owing to the risk that she posed to other residents. A decision was therefore needed to enable Ruby to be discharged safely and securely, but hospital staff were concerned that she seemed to be largely unaware of her surroundings and were not sure that she had the capability of contributing to such a decision.

Ruby's situation is by no means unique; there are many thousands of people who do not possess the capacity to make decisions that affect their own welfare. The concern of the warden for the well-being of other residents is clearly not ill-placed, and Ruby has no close living relatives who can assist in the decision-making process either.

It is for situations such as this that the Mental Capacity Act 2005 was created. Its passage was the culmination of a lengthy process of deliberation, and represented an attempt to codify the issues around decision-making in relation to health and social care for people such as Ruby without the capacity to make their own decisions. Previously, there had been no statute law that affected this area of practice; past judicial precedents had been established in common law as opposed to statute (Laird, 2010). That this is a critical area for social work with adults is important to recognise: many people in need of social care services have limited or impaired cognition, and potentially need assistance to exercise their rights.

As Leslie and Pritchard (2009) have indicated, there are four elements that combine to determine the capacity of a person to make decisions:

1. that s/he understands the information needed to make a decision
2. that s/he is able to retain this while making a decision
3. that s/he is able to use and weigh it when coming to a decision
4. that s/he is able to communicate what the decision actually is.

These elements are often difficult to determine for adults in receipt of social care or health services, particularly if their levels of cognition are compromised by organic diseases such as dementia; this situation applies in relation to Ruby. It is therefore apparent that capacity judgments will be required for numerous people in a variety of different sets of circumstance. It is important to be mindful, in addition, that such judgments are both decision-specific and time-specific (Stanley and Manthorpe, 2008). In other words, decisions regarding capacity may be required in a number of different situations: the determination of a lack of capacity in particular situations cannot mean that a person lacks capacity to make decisions in other areas. In addition, the fact that these are time-specific decisions means that the levels of capacity may have to be reassessed at different points during the provision of care.

There are clearly numerous complexities that govern this process; indeed Johns (2010) has suggested that the Mental Capacity Act 2005 engages centrally with issues of service user autonomy and vulnerability, core issues in the future development of practice. Consequently, it is important for social workers to be familiar with the five principles that underpin the Act, as they all link to actions that may subsequently be required:

1. It is assumed that each person has capacity unless it is demonstrated that s/he doesn't.
2. An individual cannot be treated as lacking capacity unless it can be shown that all practicable steps have been taken that would allow her/him to demonstrate this without any success.
3. A person should not be treated as lacking capacity because s/he has chosen to make what is considered to be an unwise decision.
4. An action taken under the requirements of the Act in relation to an individual who lacks capacity must be taken in her/his best interests.
5. Any decision taken must as little restrictive of the person's rights and freedom of action as possible.

> (Mental Capacity Act 2005: s1(2–6);
> see Stanley and Manthorpe, 2008; Hewitt, 2009)

There are apparent links and connections between these principles and social work (Johns, 2007; 2010). For example, the first principle enshrines the idea that all people should be presumed to have capacity: it is for services to take all reasonable steps to determine whether or not capacity exists in reality (principle 2). In other words, there should be the maximum effort to recognise and respond to an individual's autonomy; decisions should not be taken out of her/his hands for the sake of convenience. This overarching aim is reinforced by the third principle, which allows people the right to make unwise decisions. If we return to the case study, were it decided that Ruby did have the capacity to make decisions, her choice to return to live independently would be critical. However, the extent of the risk posed to other people as a consequence of Ruby's decision would also need to be considered.

The fourth and fifth principles have particular moment in relation to social work, the idea that decisions must be in an individual's best interests and that they should be as little restrictive as possible. It is particularly difficult to determine best interests in cases such as Ruby, where there appear to be no family or friends who can attest to her personality and preferences prior to the onset of dementia (Manthorpe et al., 2009a). However, the centrality of the concept of 'best interests' does highlight the principle that the Act should be applied in such a way as to ensure that the outcome of the decision-making process must be judged by the extent to which an individual's interests and overall welfare are maximised (Dunn et al., 2007). The principle of less restriction will particularly apply in certain settings: it has often been practice within various forms of institutional care to secure an individual's 'safety'

by restricting her/his freedom of movement. While this may generally be allowable in some circumstances, the key change if that there has to be broad discussion of each case and the principle will have to be meshed with that of 'best interests'. Consequently, there has been considerable discussion about what safeguards need to be in place to constrain the deprivations of individuals' liberty.

In this sort of case, the role of the Independent Mental Capacity Advocate (IMCA) becomes critical, linking the core elements of advocacy to the specific circumstances of supporting people at risk. In this respect it is important to remind ourselves of common themes and principles that characterise advocacy, including the independence of the advocacy provider from case decisions, and that the purpose of advocacy should be to ensure that the user of advocacy services can be assured of maximum right and representation, with the process leading to her/his empowerment (Harris, 2009). Under the Mental Capacity Act 2005 the IMCA role has statutory force, and must be commissioned by local authorities and primary care trusts. This has led to the development of systems and structures that can ensure it is properly fulfilled.

In this, it is particularly important to be clear about the nature of the IMCA, and what this role contains that is different from the roles of friends, families or professionals. An IMCA does not exist to supplant the contribution of family and friends, who are more likely to have extensive knowledge of an individual's life and preferences, but rather to ensure that the rights of the individual are upheld. This is critical, and what may be in the best interests of family members may not coincide with the best interests of the service user. In addition, as in Ruby's case, there may be no people with the extensive knowledge that family members may bring. There are requirements that IMCAs are trained to perform their role, but the extent and duration of such training is often fairly minimal. Although there are overlaps between the IMCA role and social work, it is vital that an IMCA must be independent from the care team (Manthorpe et al., 2008a); in addition, the training requirements for an IMCA are much less extensive than for a social worker (Harris 2009). There is also considerable resistance within the advocacy world to its potential professionalisation (Scourfield, 2010). Consequently, it appears unlikely to be a role that social workers would fulfil.

The links between determinations of capacity and safeguarding issues are clear and beginning to be addressed in the literature (Manthorpe et al., 2009b). Certainly, there is an increased likelihood that people lacking capacity may be more vulnerable to exploitation and abuse of varying sorts. Indeed, '[c]apacity to take risks, consent to a sexual relationship, decisions about where to live, managing financial affairs and choosing what action to take, were cited as examples at the heart of safeguarding deliberations when abuses in these areas were suspected.'

(Manthorpe et al., 2009b: 16–17)

As a result, it is vital for practitioners to be simultaneously aware of the principles underpinning both capacity and safeguarding; in addition, there is little doubt that the social work role in relation to safeguarding is growing in importance.

Reflect

Thinking about your own practice or placement experience, consider the times when issues of capacity have been a factor – acknowledged or otherwise – in the care provided. Remember that this does not simply relate to the major decisions, but can also refer to 'small acts of care' (Stanley and Manthorpe, 2008).

Safeguarding

Case study

Leah

Leah is a 22-year-old woman. She has spent much time in the care of the local authority, owing to the impact of her volatile and often aggressive behaviour. She has a complex personality and a range of needs that touch on numerous issues: she is lesbian, and involved in an often abusive relationship with an older woman. She is a periodic user of both drugs and alcohol: she appears to have difficulty slowing down or stopping when she uses either. She has moderate learning disabilities, but has learned to cover these up, and presents as higher functioning than is in fact the case. She has a fierce desire to maximise her independence from statutory services. She is registered to attend a local college, but her actual attendance has been spasmodic. In addition, she has a history of both self-harming and fire-starting. Her mother has retained contact with Leah over the years, but there have been numerous unsubstantiated allegations that she has misused financial resources and benefits intended for Leah's use.

This case illustrates the overlaps between personalisation, safeguarding and capacity. A social worker will operate in the awareness of all three of these principles:

1. That the way in which services are organised in relation to Leah should maximise her autonomy and independence.
2. That statutory services retain a duty to ensure that Leah is safeguarded from exploitation and abuse as much as possible.
3. That her capacity to make decisions affecting her welfare is kept in mind, particularly in the light of her apparent desire to make choices that would be considered to be unwise.

The complexity and volatility of her circumstances is clear. There is no necessary fit between these three principles, and yet services must be delivered in the awareness of all of them. Certainly, if the principle of autonomy and independence is foregrounded, then there are concerns that Leah may be placed at insupportable risk (Fyson and Kitson, 20007). As yet, there is inadequate research that analyses the connections between personalisation and safeguarding, with only some relatively small studies that investigate the issue (see, Manthorpe et al., 2008). However, if practice is governed predominantly by issues around safeguarding, her ability to act independently may also be unacceptably compromised, an event that has occurred for many disabled people over years (Lymbery and Postle, 2010). In relation to capacity, it is likely to be determined that Leah does possess the capacity to make decisions, many of which will appear unwise. As a consequence, work must focus around the need to ensure that the effect of her unwise decision-making is not critical in relation to her future life and well-being.

It is well recognised that the statutory framework for Adult Social Care in England is characterised by a confusing patchwork of legislation (Law Commission, 2010), which is regarded as particularly problematic in relation to the law relating to safeguarding adults in England (Fitzgerald, 2008; Spencer-Lane, 2010). *No Secrets* (DoH, 2000f) represents the government's formal guidance to support the protection of vulnerable adults and represents the clearest attempt in England to establish clear definitions of abuse and what constitutes a vulnerable adult, alongside a set of policies and procedures requiring agencies to work together to combat abuse. This was followed by a statement of good practice from the Association of Directors of Social Services (ADSS, 2005); although this was intended to establish a framework of good practice in relation to safeguarding adults, its publication was attended with some confusion over the status of the document (it had no statutory force) (Fitzgerald, 2008). Indeed, there is some evidence to suggest that the implementation of *No Secrets* has been patchy, with marked differences between areas in relation to their understanding and implementation of policy (Mansell et al., 2009). It is interesting to note that, by comparison, Scotland has a very clearly defined legal framework, with three statutes – Adult with Incapacity (Scotland) Act (2000), Mental Health (Care and Treatment) (Scotland) Act (2003), Adult Support and Protection (Scotland) Act (2007) – that interact to safeguard adults at risk of harm (Mackay, 2008). Among other developments, this carries a duty to investigate the possible abuse of an adult at risk; as Brammer (2009) notes, this creates a much clearer requirement for local authorities to act than is the case under *No Secrets*.

The Law Commission (2010) has proposed that a duty should be placed on English local authorities to identify when there are adult safeguarding issues and to take appropriate action, thus paralleling what already exists in Scotland. It has been suggested that the current lack of clarity significantly reduces the level of protection that people at risk can expect and can potentially compromise a local authority's ability to act in accordance with *No Secrets* (Spencer-Lane, 2010). In part, this contributed to the need to review the processes for safeguarding adults (DoH, 2009b), reflecting a lack of satisfaction with the existing framework. One area of practice which has been felt to be particularly unsatisfactory relates to prevention. Within *No Secrets* the prevention of abuse was defined as being a core aim of policy (DoH, 2000), yet this preventive orientation has come under threat, given the restrictive nature of eligibility criteria (Brammer, 2009). In addition, the capability of different bodies in relation to safeguarding adults has been criticised: in some areas there has been little movement in respect of the essential partnership working that would characterise effective safeguarding policies. This has led to the suggestion that a 'duty to cooperate' should be imposed upon all agencies engaged in safeguarding adults and that the work of Safeguarding Adults Boards should be placed on a statutory footing (DoH, 2009b).

The growth of safeguarding adults as a vital aspect of policy and practice lends support to the need to review the policies and procedures that govern it in England. As Mansell et al. (2009) discovered, the number of referrals has increased over time; while there has been relative stability in relation to older people, there has been a marked increase in referrals of younger service users. However, it was accepted that there may be significant under-reporting of incidents of abuse, particularly that which was located in people's own homes. Certainly, as we have observed, the social work role in relation to safeguarding is regarded as highly significant in the new world (ADASS, 2010). Mansell et al. (2009) believe that this holds true both strategically and operationally. At the strategic level there are apparent issues to resolve concerning the numbers of qualified social workers required and their disposition and management; operationally, any given social worker in this field of activity can expect safeguarding issues to be a significant element of her/his caseload. In this context, the apparent failure of practitioners to manage the process of risk assessment effectively, particularly given that this is central to the entire safeguarding approach, represents a problem that needs urgently to be addressed (Pritchard, 2008).

Returning to the case study at the head of this section, it is essential that all the different agencies involved in the provision of services to Leah are able to identify risk factors and accommodate these into a proactive support plan. The complexity of her fluctuating circumstances makes a consistent plan hard to create and arguably even harder to monitor effectively. As we noted in Chapter 13, effective inter-professional working will be needed to ensure that all agencies act in full awareness of the risk factors that exist, but also that they act in such a way as to respect Leah's desire to maximise her levels of autonomy. There are a number of complexities that characterise Leah's case, notably the apparently malign presence of her mother. In addition, she presents a periodic risk to herself through self-harming behaviour which has led to several periods of hospital care. Her fire-starting has led to several calls on the Fire Service's time; while there has as yet been no serious damage to property or to people, it is suspected that this may just be a matter of time. Effective practice in this case must certainly derive from accurate and appropriate forms of risk assessment (Pritchard, 2008). There are numerous agencies that have a role in maintaining both Leah's autonomy and her safety, and consequently it is vital that they both share a general understanding of the circumstances that apply and more specifically can agree on the precise meaning of terminology to be applied (Pritchard, 2008). It is particularly important for practitioners to be aware of the hazards that Leah may encounter, alongside the dangers that she may encounter. In Jacki Pritchard's view, a danger can be seen as representing a feared negative

A closer look

Safeguarding adults in Northern Ireland

In Northern Ireland the Safeguarding Vulnerable Adults policy was introduced in September 2006. The policy initiative stemmed from work undertaken by a Regional Adult Protection Forum which had sought to introduce a coordinated and standardised policy and procedural guidance to safeguard vulnerable adults. The policy has identified requirements for inter-agency working and established core stages for the adult protection procedures and reporting mechanisms. The policy's reform (DHSSPSNI, 2010) led to the introduction of current guidance relating to adult protection infrastructures. The emphasis is now placed on the formation of a Regional Safeguarding Partnership (NIASP) working alongside the five Health and Social Care Trusts to form Local Adult Safeguarding Partnerships (LASPs). These arrangements will replace the existing Regional Adult Protection Forum. In addition, the Reform places service users and carers at the heart of its policy with a specific requirement to establish a system of formal user participation by 2012. The ultimate aim of the policy is to secure improved outcomes for vulnerable adults. It can be seen, therefore, that similar approaches to the same problem are in train across all four countries within the United Kingdom.

outcome for the services user, as opposed to the more neutral concept of hazard, which can either stop people from securing a benefit or develop into a more critical danger (Pritchard, 2008).

We should not seek to create an environment where an individual is discouraged from any risk: at some level, risk-taking is an essential part of every individual's life, and we should not seek to legislate this away from existence. However, every practitioner needs to understand that there are some elements of risk that are unacceptable, and which an individual should not be expected to face. In general terms, therefore, the balance between the principles of autonomy and safeguarding is critical: the role of a social worker in helping to manage this tension is potentially critical.

Domestic violence

Case study

Norman and Marie

Norman is 70 years old and is small and frail. He has difficulty walking and therefore has a motability car; his income is £247 a week. He lives alone in a downstairs flat in a disadvantaged area of an inner-city housing estate. A district nurse had been asked by the GP to visit him to dress ulcers on his leg and to look at some unexplained bruising to his face. She was appalled by the conditions in which he was living. The central heating was broken in the flat so it was freezing, wires were exposed, the bed was soaked with urine and there was little food in the fridge. The walls and windows appeared damaged through violence. Her concerns about his living conditions, safety and depressed state prompted her to refer him to the Adult Social Care team for assessment and support. Norman's initial response to the social worker, Mrs Walton, was that he was fine. However, she assessed that he was in danger. In addition to the poor living conditions and his depressed state, there was evidence from the damage to the property and the location that the flat was being used as a drinking den and that he had been assaulted. After four visits Norman began to gain trust in Mrs Walton and disclosed that his son had taken his car and all his money.

(adapted from *Community Care*, 30.10.03)

Marie had a serious car accident ten years ago, aged 30 years old, which left her with paralysis of the left leg, urinary incontinence and some brain damage. Walking proved to be painful and difficult. She was registered as disabled and allocated the higher rate disability living allowance. She rarely went outside, and, when she did, used a wheelchair. She lives at home with her husband, Geoff, an accountant, and their 15-year-old daughter, Florence. Prior to the accident Marie had led an active social life and worked as a solicitor's clerk. As a result of her disability she was unable to return to her job and needs considerable help with personal care and household tasks. Geoff has had difficulty in accepting his wife's disability and, in particular, coping with the changes from her outgoing and independent personality to a person with substantial physical and emotional needs. As time went on Marie became increasingly dependent and socially isolated, and Florence undertook much of her mother's physical care. Geoff has spent more and more time away from home. When he does return, often late in the evening, he becomes increasingly angry with Marie, saying she is hopeless, a drain on him and needs to try harder and to cheer up. He has told Florence that she was doing too much and should 'get a life'. On occasions he has hit Marie hard: however, he has always been repentant the next morning.

Like Leah, these two cases also illustrate the difficulty for their social workers of holding together and managing the dictates of personalisation, safeguarding and capacity – in this case in situations of domestic violence. The Home Office (2008) estimates that domestic violence has more repeat victims than any other crime and will affect one in four women and one in six men in their lifetime. While violence in the home is now more commonly documented where children are concerned, there is increasing recognition of its occurrence between adults and older people – and it is most commonly carried out by men. Disabled women are particularly vulnerable to such abuse: Magowan (2004) reports that more than 50 per cent of disabled women in the UK have experienced domestic violence, although this does not take into account that domestic abuse is chronically under-reported. Research by Chenoweth (1997) in Australia suggests that disabled women are 'invisibilised' and perceived as asexual, exposing them to risk of a range of emotional, physical and sexual abuses. Similarly, elder abuse both in the community and in institutions often remains hidden and undisclosed and is promulgated most commonly by carers or by family (Hague et al., 2010).

Another feature of adult abuse concerns context and typology. The Home Office (2004) defines domestic violence as 'any incident of threatening behaviour, violence or abuse between adults who are or have been

in a relationship together, or between family members, regardless of gender or sexuality'. Women's Aid adds to this by specifying violent acts which are 'physical, sexual, psychological or financial' – and they broaden it to include 'a range of abusive behaviours, not all of which are themselves inherently violent' (Women's Aid, 2009). Institutional cultures have also often been described as abusive, incorporating such features as management distance and intimidation (Cambridge, 1999).

The legislative framework for the protection of vulnerable adults, unlike that for child protection, derives from a number of Acts relating to care and mental health. *No Secrets* (DoH, 2000f) was a key document providing guidance on the protection of vulnerable adults, mainly by inter-agency collaboration and through investigative action (Penhale and Parker, 2008). The Domestic Violence, Crime and Victims Act 2004 was followed by the National Report on Domestic Violence in 2005, which recommended that there needed to be early identification, prevention and improved responses.

In a parallel development, a strategy to address domestic violence was published in Northern Ireland (DHSSPSNI, 2005). Amongst its many recommendations was the commitment to developing 'a more effective system of communication and collaborative working between departments and agencies' (DHSSPSNI, 2005: 7) to ensure the needs of victims were not marginalised and more specifically that perpetrators were held accountable for their behaviours and actions. Regional structures were established to build effective multi-agency commitment to implementing the five-year strategy under the auspices of a Regional Steering Group on Domestic Violence, and Regional Good Practice Guidelines and Standards were introduced to enhance a consistent, regional approach to tackling domestic violence. Again, this indicates that similar interdisciplinary approaches to the problem are common across all four home countries.

The case studies

Norman's case provides a good example, both of the specifics of physical, psychological and financial abuse, but also of abuse which could be reframed as 'inherently violent'. And, while Marie's case clearly involves physical violence, her treatment by Geoff is also suggestive of emotional abuse and possibly sexual abuse. Jansson et al. (2007) found that that where the main carer is the abuser, intimate violence and sexual abuse may co-occur.

Because of the presence of violence in their homes, ensuring their safety is paramount. Removal from home might seem the only sure means of doing this, if necessary to a refuge. However, although both Norman and Marie were suffering and wanted things to change, neither wanted to escape or move. In addition, why *should* those people who experience domestic violence always be the ones expected to move? Marie's case is both easier and more difficult in this respect because of the presence of Florence. While Florence helped to safeguard and look after her mother the violence continued, and Florence became complicit in it. The potentially negative effects on Florence are twofold, firstly arising from her role as a young carer (see Aldridge and Becker, 2003), and secondly as a child witness of domestic violence (see Humphreys, 2006).

In Norman's case ensuring his physical safety could mean rehousing him in warden-controlled accommodation in a safer area, but he does not want to leave his home. Further, such a move would not necessarily mean the neglect and the financial abuse by his son has been addressed. Questions of capacity and personalisation are critical here. In relation to capacity, is he mentally capable of making informed decisions and, if he is, what should happen if he will not accept any change? Secondly, given the policy of personalisation (discussed earlier in the chapter), what are the continued implications for Norman?

In fact, Norman's present state of self-neglect, impotence and openness to abuse has to imply some loss of control and self-care suggesting depression. His capacity to make decisions meets some if not all four of the elements of the Mental Capacity Act 2005. At the same time, some optimism in relation to improvement – and so self-determination – seems realistic, given what we know of the present situation. Norman's reactive depression should be time-limited. There is evidence that, when fit and well, he has the capacity for safe, independent living, and this is what he wants.

As we have seen, a key objective of personalisation is to increase the levels of choice and control over your own life. To achieve those objectives in Norman's case, the social worker would need time to establish a relationship of trust within which Norman was helped to assert control over who came into his house, and to understand that accepting help with cleaning and shopping would increase not decrease his independence. Consequently, after some months, new locks were fitted and curtains hung. In addition day care once a week and a volunteer visitor were set up to provide him with some continuing social engagement and support. Contact with his daughter was re-established and she agreed to set up meetings with

her brother to discuss and deal with the financial abuse. However, this would need careful monitoring. Hague et al. (2010) found that social workers often failed to understand the nature of abuse perpetrated by trusted helpers, such as family or paid carers, whose control was often pervasive. Continuing social work help would need to address possible collusion between Norman and his family to ensure that financial abuse had, in fact, ceased, meaning close contact with Norman should be maintained over time.

Turning to Marie, the safeguarding, capacity and personalisation aspects of her care were both similar to and different from Norman's. Both had suffered physical violence and emotional humiliation from close family, and in both cases their mental capacity was reduced. However, Marie's disabilities added different dimensions. Firstly, her mental capacity was not time-limited and would therefore require a different approach. Secondly, her physical disabilities meant that she could not get out at all without help, and her personal care needs were complex. Additionally, we know from users' reports that abusers often make use of the disability as part of the abuse, to control and dehumanise; also Florence has substantial needs.

Marie, like many disabled women, is reluctant to seek outside help. To date, Marie's experiences of health care had been negative and she had not sought social work help (see Radford et al., 2006), in common with many disabled women. A systematic review of adult victims' experiences of accessing health services (Robinson and Spilsbury, 2008) describes inappropriate responses, discomfort and lack of confidence in the outcomes which set up barriers to disclosure. However, following a visit from her GP, and in line with the personalisation agenda, a thorough multi-agency assessment of both her mental and physical capacities was carried out, the outcome of which was that significant potential for improvement was identified. Physiotherapy resulted in improved mobility; the occupational therapist had rails fixed in the bathroom and in the hall, and the psychologist provided cognitive behavioural therapy to increase her coping and assertiveness strategies.

Eventually Marie gained confidence sufficiently to tell her social worker about her husband's violent outbursts. The first consideration was the safety of Marie and Florence, and whether to treat the abuse as a criminal offence rather than a welfare issue and whether to appoint an Independent Mental Capacity Advocate. Recent Crown Prosecution policy (2009) in relation to cases of domestic violence states that prosecutions will be based on the seriousness of the offence and the victim's injuries. They would also take into account 'if the offence was committed in the presence of, or near, a child or young person, and the chances of the defendant offending again'. In this case some of these criteria do appertain; others are less clear-cut.

In undertaking the carer assessment, the social worker was struck by Geoff's stressed state (see Bennett and Kingston, 1995). He said he drank heavily before getting home in order to cope. He did not realise how much he was hurting Marie and was unaware of the effects on Florence. He wanted them both to stay at home, the marriage to continue and things to improve. The social worker talked to the family together about the best way forward and all were in agreement that things needed to change, and the violence to stop. Marie felt stronger and Geoff agreed to attend an anger management programme, a group-work method used to enable men to think differently about dealing with situations that make them angry, while at the same time suggesting new ways of communicating feelings and reducing stress (Bell, 2003).

Both of these cases illustrate not only the dilemmas to be managed in holding the balance between risk (safeguarding) and self-determination (personalisation), but also the skills, time and resources required by the professionals involved to work towards what Norman and Marie and her family wanted. But does existing policy and practice support what best social work practice would prescribe and what these families want? Unfortunately research (see Williamson, 2000) suggests that many social workers and other professionals lack the understanding and skills necessary for working with violence. Critics of the recent bureaucratic management culture in social work (Munro, 2008; Shaw et al., 2009) argue that social workers no longer have the time to undertake the longer-term family work necessary. In addition, Gregory et al. (2010) found that doctors and nurses were unaware of appropriate interventions and had seldom received any training. Linked to this, provision of resources by the statutory and voluntary sector is poor. However, the Home Office has estimated that the costs of domestic violence exceed £23 billion a year. Despite the apparent intention to address the problems and improve services, campaigners say that a national

strategy with funding is needed. As things stand, 80 per cent of the disabled women in the study by Hague et al. (2010) reported adult services as being the least helpful, and only 17 per cent found disability organisations helpful. As a result, there is substantial improvement to be made, which must stem from a thorough understanding of both the impact of domestic violence and the policy framework within which it is located.

Conclusion

The purpose of this chapter has been to chart the overall development of social care policy. It has also paid particular attention to specific issues in a number of areas that have a direct impact on the practice of social workers. It has been developed on the basis that a greater understanding of these issues will assist in the establishment of innovative social work that can respond to the different interests of each individual. It is particularly important to make the case for sustained social work engagement in these issues, as this has been significantly downplayed in many official documents. It is only more recent publications that promote a more sophisticated understanding of the potential for social work to be actively involved (ADASS/DH/SFC/BASW/SCA, 2010); even here there is a tendency to limit the social work contribution to matters of safeguarding.

One area of particular interest in charting the policy changes that are underway is that there is a level agenda in coherence between the social work practice that we are seeking to promote – individually focused, relational work – and the imperatives of the personalisation agenda in social care. In times of economic plenty, it would be a relatively straightforward task to argue that the social work role merely needs to be actively promoted to find a niche within new systems of social care. However, the terms of the financial debate for local authorities – with substantial budgetary cuts over the next few years – will inevitably reduce the potentially beneficial, emancipatory potential of social work. Indeed, it is hard to see how the grander expectations of personalised services can survive the austerity of coming years (Dunning, 2010).

Key learning points

This chapter has introduced you to the following issues:

✔ The historical basis within which changes to social care can best be understood.

✔ The core dimensions of community care, the key policy dynamic that has driven social care over the past two decades.

✔ The development of social care policy, with particular emphasis on the policy developments associated with the 'new' Labour government.

✔ The key aspects of the transformation of social care, put in place by this government and looking to be perpetuated by the ruling coalition from 2010.

✔ The core dilemmas and tensions that characterise policy developments in three areas: capacity, safeguarding and domestic violence.

 ## Further reading

British Journal of Social Work, 37 (3), Special Issue on Adult Social Care. This volume is the first special issue of the leading academic British social work journal to focus on adult social care in recent years, and contains a number of articles that focus on issues that are relevant to this chapter, both nationally and globally.

Glasby, J. and Littlechild, R. (2009) *Direct payments and personal budgets: Putting personalisation into practice* (2nd edn), Bristol, Policy Press. This is the most comprehensive textbook to engage with the changes in the delivery of adult social care.

Leadbeater, C., Bartlett, J. and Gallagher, N. (2008) *Making it Personal*, London, Demos. This relatively short document applied Leadbeater's precepts about personalisation to adult social care, arguing that the changes can deliver a better quality of care for reduced costs.

Leece, J. and Bornat, J. eds (2006) *Developments in Direct Payments*, Bristol, Policy Press. This is an accessible collection exploring how direct payments have grown and developed since their inception.

McDonald, A. (2006) *Understanding Community Care: A Guide for Social Workers* (2nd edn), Basingstoke: Palgrave. This is the second edition of an excellent summary text that addresses the changes to social care policy.

Useful websites

www.elderabuse.org.uk/
Action on Elder Abuse (AEA) works to protect, and prevent the abuse of, vulnerable older adults. It was the first charity to address these problems and is the only charity in the UK and in Ireland working exclusively on the issue today. It works in accordance with a desire to create a society which values older people and one in which they and other adults can live free from abuse perpetrated by those in whom they have an expectation of trust.

www.dh.gov.uk
The Department of Health issues a range of policy documents covering health and social care. Because it is responsible for establishing the direction of social care policy this is an essential website for British, and particularly English, readers.

www.in-control.org.uk/
In control is the website of the organisation which has been particularly influential in the development of self-directed support since its inception; it contains highly useful material relating to the development of all forms of personalised services.

www.scie-socialcareonline.org.uk/
Social Care Institute for Excellence, social care online is the information database which contains huge detail about changes to policy and practice. While it is more general than adult social care, there is considerable detail pertaining to this aspect of work; for example, at the time of writing (June 2010) there were 283 references to personalisation and 693 references to mental capacity!

www.womensaid.org.uk
This is the website for Women's Aid, which has had over 30 years experience in the field of responding to domestic violence. Their philosophy is best summarised by the statement that '[w]e believe that everyone has a right to live in safety and to have a future without fear'. The organisation takes the view that domestic violence is primarily an abuse of power and control, and consequently affects those with least power in society – women and children.

For additional cases and topic-organised, clickable links into additional media resources, including those produced by IRISS, visit **www.pearsoned.co.uk/wilsonruch**

Activity

Activity One

Personalisation is reliant on the capacity of service users to assume more control over their lives. Thinking about the adults you know, who may or may not be service users, what are the factors that might promote or obstruct this?

Activity Two

Using the material in this chapter as a starting point, think through the issues and problems that may attend the introduction of personalisation within adult social care. The following questions may be helpful.

How do questions of mental capacity affect the individual's ability to manage her/his own care services?

To what extent is there a conflict between the principles of autonomy and safeguarding?

Where an individual is being subjected to domestic violence, but appears willing to accept its continuance, what are the ways that a social work might seek to address this within the context of personalisation?

Chapter 18
Social work with young offenders

Professor Brian Littlechild and Professor Roger Smith

Chapter summary

Social work with young offenders has changed considerably in terms of approaches and methods during the final years of the twentieth century and in the first decade of the twenty-first. This chapter explores the ways in which policy and legislative change have affected our views about why young people offend, and what to do about it when they do. These changes have had a significant effect on the contexts and practices of social work with this group of service users. Following this, we will set out the key roles and responsibilities of social workers in the contemporary youth justice system. Key issues for social work practice are identified, such as the specific challenges associated with multi-agency settings such as Youth Offending Teams, and the nature of the relationship between social workers and young people in trouble. The chapter subsequently moves on to examine particular areas of practice, and areas of particular consideration for social workers within youth justice. Practice contexts will be considered in detail, including work with young people who are arrested and detained by the police; work with young people subject to community orders; and work with young people who experience custody.

The chapter will examine, within historical and contemporary policy frameworks, how social workers can best respond to the issues raised by their work within the youth justice system. Key areas for social workers are the relationship of professional values and the GSCC Codes of Practice to the expectations placed upon them in complex settings such as multi-agency youth justice teams, concerning assessment of risk and need, anti-discriminatory practice and addressing specific issues such as mental health concerns. We will use case examples and exercises to highlight 'best practice' requirements in this very complex area, of young people caught up in the justice system.

Learning objectives

This chapter covers topics that will enable the reader to achieve the following learning objectives:

- To understand the historical and contemporary development of key areas of social policy and legislation relevant to social work within the youth justice system

- To be able to identify how the General Social Care Council's (GSCC) Codes of Practice can be applied in social work with young offenders

- To appreciate the social work role within multi-agency and multi-professional environments such as the justice system

- To be aware of the methods and programmes which social workers can utilise in this area of work

- To be familiar with specific knowledge sets, for example acting in the role of the appropriate adult, the preparation of pre-sentence reports, custody and post-release work, and addressing the mental health needs of young offenders.

National Occupational Standards

This chapter will prepare you to be able to meet the following National Occupational Standards:

Key Role 1: Prepare for, and work with individuals, families, carers, groups and communities to assess their needs and circumstances

Unit 1   Prepare for social work contact and involvement
Unit 2   Work with individuals, families, carers, groups and communities to help them make informed decisions
Unit 3   Assess needs and options to recommend a course of action

Key Role 2: Plan, carry out, review and evaluate social work practice, with individuals, families, carers, groups, communities and other professionals

Unit 5   Interact with individuals, families, carers, groups and communities to achieve change and development and to improve life opportunities
Unit 6   Prepare, produce, implement and evaluate plans with individuals, families, carers, groups, communities and professional colleagues
Unit 7   Support the development of networks to meet assessed needs and planned outcomes
Unit 9   Address behaviour which presents a risk to individuals, families, carers, groups and communities

Key Role 3: Support individuals to represent their needs, views and circumstances

Unit 10   Advocate with, and on behalf of, individuals, families, carers, groups and communities

Key Role 4: Manage risk to individuals, families, carers, groups, communities, self and colleagues

Unit 12   Assess and manage risks to individuals, families, carers, groups and communities

Key role 5: Manage and be accountable, with supervision and support, for your own social work practice within your organisation

Unit 16   Manage and be accountable, with supervision and support, for your own social work practice within your organisation
Unit 17   Work within multi-disciplinary and multi-organisational teams, networks and systems

Key Role 6: Demonstrate professional competence in social work practice

Unit 18   Research, analyse, evaluate, and use current knowledge of best social work practice
Unit 19   Work within agreed standards of social work practice and ensure own professional development
Unit 20   Manage complex ethical issues, dilemmas and conflicts
Unit 21   Contribute to the promotion of best social work practice

John

John is 15 years of age, and is white British. He is staying with a friend, who is aged 17, at a hostel for young people who are homeless. He has lived alternately with both his mother and his father, who are separated, and his father has a new partner, as does his mother, both of whom have other children within the relationship. John had become involved with a group of young people who are involved in the regular and extensive use of alcohol and soft and hard drugs, and has been given a final warning for possession of cannabis. He is subject to a one-year Referral Order (which involves a contract concerning John's behaviour, supervised by a social worker in this instance; see later section on referral orders in this chapter) from the Youth Court, as he was involved in (a) an assault on another young person, he says due partly to other young people making very hurtful remarks about his sister's sexuality, and (b) stealing alcohol while under the influence of drink in a large supermarket late at night, assaulting an assistant manager who challenged him.

During the course of the work, it becomes clear to the social worker that John is feeling rejection from his mother, whom he has been to live with on two occasions, but she found his presence difficult and telephoned his father on both occasions to say he must have John back. While John's father is fairly sanguine about the situation, he is very concerned about the pressure John's behaviour and attitude is putting on his new partner and his younger children with her.

In the Referral Panel meeting these areas are discussed with John's father. In addition, regular meetings with the social worker are part of the contract, following through themes of how John's behaviour may affect those he is living with, and their attitudes towards him. Discussions of how he might act differently with his carers and react to peer group pressure are also pursued as part of the contract.

The Panel also identified that John has difficulty controlling his anger, so will be attending several sessions on anger management, both individually with the social worker, and also in a group set up specifically for this purpose.

The area of risk identified in relation to alcohol and other types of drug is addressed with a drugs worker in the YOT.

What do you believe are the important aspects of the social worker's role in supervising these areas aimed at supporting John with his current problems, and in developing changes in his behaviour?

What are the key issues for a social worker to consider in building a relationship with John? (See Chapter 1.)

The case study above concerning John highlights a number of areas which are issues for young offenders themselves, and for the agencies and professionals working with young people. In considering approaches to effective work with such young people, it is important first of all to set the current context of work with young offenders within a history of the major policy and practice developments, since youth offending came to be seen as a different field of work from that with adult offenders in the nineteenth century, which created the initial impetus towards policies and legislation under which social workers now work.

Such developments and their effects become particularly important for social work, within the values and ethics which qualified and registered social workers now have to adhere to, as set out in the General Social Care Council's Code of Practice (2002). This has an impact on the work with young people such as John, in relation to the approaches which social workers take, the nature of their relationship with their clients, and the multi-agency and multi-professional contexts within which their work is carried out.

Introduction

This chapter considers these points within an examination of the legal and policy structure – determined to a great extent by central government (Crawford, 2006) – which has affected social workers' inputs to, and relationships with, young people who offend, currently operationalised through Youth Offending Teams. These teams were set up by the UK government, with an executive body, the Youth Justice Board, being influential in directing policy at local levels, and in setting the National Standards by which youth justice services within local areas have to set out their plans, oversee implementation and review progress.

Think ahead

There is evidence in the youth justice system that the assumptions about, and treatment of, young people from Black and Minority Ethnic (BME) groups may be different from that accorded to white British groups (see section on ethnic and faith sensitive work with young offenders later in this chapter).

What preconceptions/prejudices might the different groups of professionals involved in youth justice work – e.g. police, judiciary, social workers, teachers, other professional groups – have about John if he were from a BME group?

What might be the effects of these on John, and his progress through the youth justice system?

What might you be able to do in your role as a social worker to (a) diminish the risk of your own preconceptions/prejudices affecting your relationship with John, and your work with him; (b) try to avert the preconceptions/prejudices of others in the system from adversely affecting John's progress through the youth justice system?

Social work and youth justice: uneasy bedfellows?

There is a long tradition of interventions with young offenders which seek to provide support, control and guidance, and which are informed by principles of reform and rehabilitation rather than retribution or punishment. However, it has been argued that in the past 20 years policies have been very much based on punitive approaches

(Smith, 2010). As a result, those engaged in social work with young offenders have continually felt under pressure to justify their role and activities, especially where these appear to be beneficial to the young people concerned. For instance, in recent memory, the provision of a 'safari holiday' by a local authority for a young person subject to a supervision order attracted significant adverse publicity (*BBC News*, 23 July 1998).

There are clearly powerful moral and ideological influences which continue to affect people's – including social workers' – views on young offenders and their treatment. Social workers need to be clear about their own views of young people who offend, in order to adopt suitable approaches in their work, which require acknowledging the effects on victims of offending, but which also have a considered view on how to provide interventions for the young person who has offended and promote her/his social and emotional development.

'Juvenile delinquency' has been a feature of criminological discourse for a considerable period of time. The early to mid-nineteenth century saw the emergence of a strand of thinking which acknowledged the distinctive 'concept of the young offender' (King, 1998), probably in response to a growing sense of alarm about increasing disorder and the corruption of 'childhood'. Thus, even from this early stage in the development of methods of dealing with youth crime, the demand for punishment and discipline was moderated by a concern to reform wayward children in their formative years. Debates at that time, and now, have centred on 'the child's "incapacity" to distinguish between right and wrong and to what extent "his age, the neglect or vice of his parents, and the depraving circumstances of his childhood should be taken into account"' (Magarey, 2002: 108).

The search for how best to deal with youthful perpetrators of crime began to be mediated by a belief that the crimes of children might be seen differently from those of responsible adults. Thus, it is reported, 'for the first time' legislation was brought into effect which identified 'juvenile delinquency' as a specific 'social phenomenon', in the form of the Youthful Offenders Act 1854 (Hendrick, 2006: 6). The Children Act 1908 sought to 'reconcile welfare and justice imperatives' (Hendrick, 2006: 8) by combining responsibility for meeting the needs of ill-treated children by way of positive activities and relationship-building and applying criminal sanctions to offending children in one body, the juvenile court. Subsequent developments could be seen largely to rework rather than resolve this tension between 'welfare' and 'justice' perspectives. Thus, according to Hendrick (2006: 9), welfare perspectives were in the ascendancy during the inter-war period (1918–39), as the link between juvenile delinquency and the offender's 'social and personal condition' became more readily accepted. The influential Moloney Inquiry into the treatment of young offenders (Home Office, 1927) concluded that:

'There is little or no difference in character and needs between the neglected and the delinquent child. It is often a mere accident whether he is brought before the court because he is wandering or beyond control or because he has committed some offence. Neglect leads to delinquency and delinquency is often the direct outcome of neglect'.

(Home Office, 1927)

The Children and Young Persons Act 1933 went some way towards creating a legislative basis for bridging the gap between welfare and penal interventions. It effectively bought together three groups of children (Hendrick, 2003: 118): offenders; neglected children; and children against whom offences were committed. Although the responses to children's errant behaviour or welfare needs were still primarily institutional (in 'approved schools', for example), interventions were assumed to meet a common purpose, to promote the 'welfare of the child'.

This changing legislative and policy climate was associated with a growing sense of certainty that offending could be linked with social and psychological problems, and that the provision of the right form of 'treatment' would enhance children's well-being and creating suitable opportunities for social and personal development, while also reducing their propensity for further offending.

Set against the emergence, and strengthening, of the 'welfare' discourse in youth justice, punitive approaches were still evident as well; the 'short, sharp' shock was explicitly advocated by the Home Office in 1938 (Muncie, 2002: 333), and subsequently the detention centre order was introduced by the Criminal Justice Act 1948.

Welfare versus justice?

United Kingdom countries have some of the lowest age of criminal responsibility in the European Union, and some of the highest rates of custody for young offenders. Ages of criminal responsibility are 7 in Ireland, 8 in Scotland, and 10 in England and Wales. In Denmark Finland and Sweden it is 15, and it is 18 in Luxembourg and Belgium. This raises questions about the way the youth justice system tries to find a way between competing approaches in how to deal with young people who offend, and the consequences of this.

Think ahead

The welfare versus justice debate has been a feature of policy affecting social work practice for over a century.

The key question here is whether young people who offend are viewed as developing towards adulthood, and therefore allowed to make some mistakes, and 'helped' by social workers and welfare services, or are they to be seen as young adults, fully responsible for their actions, and therefore to be judged as such in courts of law, and face due punishment?

The issues contained in the Think Ahead box, combined with policies concerning how families are responsible for the offending of their children, have been key influences on developing policy and legislation. By the end of the 'liberal' 1960s, the most prominent voices were those of the family-oriented left. This trend culminated in the Children and Young Persons Act 1969.[1] Under this legislation, there was to be a dismantling of the remaining barriers between welfare and justice processes for children and young people. Decriminalisation of offending was the intention, with the provision instead of social work interventions and care proceedings to address delinquent behaviour. This was, as Rose (1999: 179) puts it: 'the high point of therapeutic familialism as a strategy for government through the family'. Social workers were believed to have the answers to many social problems, including youth offending. Children should be treated solely in terms of their welfare and developmental needs, and there should be no expectation of holding them responsible for their actions or punishing them accordingly.

Considered from a contemporary perspective, it may be difficult to imagine that this position could have been reached in the second half of the twentieth century. However, the growing influence of social work and the welfare perspective in the context of youth crime raises a number of important questions which remain relevant to social workers today. In particular, it seems that the approach taken to this point (the late 1960s) effectively drew on welfare discourses to minimise the young person's responsibility for her/his actions. It is important, however, to consider the extent to which this is either desirable or realistic. If assessments and interventions come to be based on pathologising prescriptions of 'good

---

[1] This legislation covered England and Wales, while parallel developments led to even more radical outcomes in Scotland with the establishment of the Children's Hearings system under the Social Work (Scotland) Act 1968. See later in this chapter.

parenting', for example, children and their families might find themselves subject to coercive and prescriptive interventions 'for their own good'. Thorpe et al. (1980) in their study of young offenders sent to large institutionalised residential units found very poor outcomes for these young people on nearly all measures. 'Welfare' principles do not necessarily lead to good practice, it seems.

Welfare and autonomy

Think ahead

Does a 'welfare' based intervention necessarily involve denying the young person concerned the autonomy to make their own decisions and be accountable for their actions?

Social workers face a challenge concerning how they view their primary work with young people who offend, bringing us back to the issue of how responsible should a young person be seen to be for her/his actions?

In addition, the absence of concern about the offence which triggers social work involvement begs the question of whether or not the social worker should be involved in addressing the young person's behaviour and its consequences. This, again, has contemporary resonance, in that the role of social work practitioners in working with offence victims and engaging in restorative processes may

appear to be problematic, although it has been argued that restorative approaches have the potential to provide a new way of working in youth justice which cuts through the tensions between justice and welfare approaches (Gelsthorpe and Morris, 2002). If social worker's concerns are primarily with the well-being and development of the young person, what part should they play in offence resolution processes, and addressing concerns for the well-being of victims? (For further exploration of this issue, see the section on referral orders and restorative justice later in this chapter). These are key issues when we come to consider the place of welfare approaches in the contemporary youth justice system.

System 'creep' – the parallel expansion of welfare and justice interventions

Having achieved its political 'high point' in 1969, the place of welfare in youth justice became problematic in the ensuing years. Firstly, a change in the political climate had significant consequences (Thorpe et al., 1980). The more radical elements of the 1969 Children and Young Persons Act were never implemented. The age of criminal responsibility in England and Wales was not raised from 10 to 14 as intended, and the sentencing powers of the courts were virtually unchanged. Courts' fears that social workers would undermine care orders by allowing

Young people may be seen as a threat, but this is not the whole story.
(*Source:* Alamy Images/Arclight)

A closer look

'Net widening'

The term 'net widening' has come to be used to define the process by which the entry points of an institutional system are varied to include a greater number of cases within its remit. This can be done by 'widening' the scope of the system (including pre-criminal behaviour as a trigger for intervention, for example); 'strengthening' the existing measures in place (more rigorous application of breach procedures, possibly), and using 'finer mesh' (fewer cases may be dealt with informally by criminal justice agencies, for instance. The cumulative result is that more young people are drawn into the formal justice system, and are then subjected to increasingly intensive forms of intervention, as occurred in the 1970s and again in the 1990s/2000s (see Austin and Krisberg, 2002). In turn, this is likely to intensify other problems, such as the disproportionate representation of young black males in the youth justice system (see section on ethnically sensitive work with young offenders later in this chapter).

---

children to return home appeared to lead to a greater, rather than reduced, reliance on custody.

At the same time, the contemporaneous structural reforms to social services[2] also saw an expansion in the range and number of social work interventions with young people. If anything, the 1970s saw a parallel expansion in welfare and justice disposals. Muncie (2002: 337) reports that between 1965 and 1981 there was a fivefold increase in the number of juveniles sentenced to a detention centre or borstal, the latter being of another prison-based institution. At the same time, the proportion of younger offenders (aged 10–13) made subject to care orders by the courts remained relatively high (Thorpe et al., 1980: 12). The parallel growth of both welfare and justice provision became the subject of substantial criticism (Morris and McIsaac, 1978; Morris et al., 1980; Thorpe et al., 1980).

The dual expansion of welfare and justice interventions during the 1970s has become seen as a quintessential example of the problem of net widening. The subsequent accession of a radical right-wing government in 1979 and the associated sense that the welfare state had gone into decline led to a growing sense of pessimism and self-doubt among those involved in social work with young offenders. The result was a period of reflection and refocusing on the part of those involved in this area of practice. If welfare interventions were not perceptibly helping young offenders, diverting them from crime or preventing them from being incarcerated (Haines and Drakeford, 1998: 42), then alternative strategies must be sought. Indeed, the view became established that, at the very least, youth justice practitioners should avoid 'doing harm', and that this might mean doing less, rather than

intervening in ways which might draw young people into the justice system unnecessarily, or involve them in inappropriate services. It was at this point that the understanding of the role of social work practitioners in youth justice underwent a significant change. It was no longer possible to justify unevidenced programmes and approaches; monitoring of programmes and outcomes (usually in terms of reoffending rates) became prime agency drivers, at the expense of less easily measurable relationship-based social work interventions. The aims of practice were therefore refocused to concentrate on a much narrower range of objectives:

- offence confrontation work – reinforcing the unacceptability of offending;
- developing a victim perspective – educating young people into the impact of their behaviour on victims;
- the offending curriculum – teaching young people how to avoid situations where offending can occur.

(Haines and Drakeford, 1998: 66)

These preoccupations were reflected in the refocused Intermediate Treatment schemes of the 1980s. Approaches based on 'prevention' and addressing the welfare needs of young people had become much less evident than previously, and the primary focus was on providing behaviourally focused 'alternatives to custody' (Haines and Drakeford, 1998: 53).

These articulations of principle and strategy had a number of implications for the organisation and conduct of social work with young offenders which continue to resonate at the present time. Firstly, the orientation of practice around offence resolution and behavioural change gave rise to a quite distinctive professional ethos which began to establish a clear separation between practitioners in this area and other strands of social work

---

[2] Under the Local Authority Social Services Act 1970.

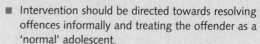

A closer look

Diversion and minimum intervention

The kinds of approaches set out in the previous paragraphs infused the spectrum of youth justice activities, and at the entry point to the system, rigorous diversionary strategies were also put in place. These were based on a set of clear principles:

- The reasons for intervention must be clear, explicit and have positive consequences for the offender or injured party.

- Intervention should be directed towards resolving offences informally and treating the offender as a 'normal' adolescent.
- Minimum appropriate intervention should be used.
- Intervention should aim to increase the amount of community involvement and create a greater tolerance and understanding of the problem of youth crime.
- Concern should be shown for the injured party as well as the offender. (Bell et al., 1999 cited in Smith, 2003: 13)

---

with children and families. A new range of intervention techniques was developed and the scope of practice shifted noticeably: for example, to include work with offence victims and 'systems' intervention with community organisations and other statutory agencies. These forms of practice took those involved into new areas, and appeared to require the development of new skills. Despite fears about the loss of a focus on welfare needs and a relative downplaying of the value of the social work relationship, there was an overwhelming sense that the achievements of the 1980s were positive. Largely through the efforts of dedicated youth justice practitioners, a very substantial change occurred in the shape of practice and outcomes for young offenders. It has been suggested, for example, that the methods of intervention developed were 'successful', both in terms of reducing reoffending and limiting the use of custody. The emphasis on tackling offending behaviour and diverting young people into constructive activities seemed to bear fruit, not without a degree of irony, as one commentator has observed:

Youth justice workers in the 1980s developed methods of face-to-face work with young people in trouble which were broadly in line with what subsequent research and analysis have suggested is likely to be most effective in reducing offending. This is in a sense paradoxical, since many of these practitioners were strongly influenced by the view that had prevailed since the mid-1970s that 'nothing worked'.

(Smith, 1999: 153)

So, it seemed that structured, intensive, community-based interventions which promoted personal and social development promised benefits in terms of the future behaviour of young people.

Between 1981 and 1991, there was a 34 per cent reduction across England and Wales in the number of

14–16-year-olds formally processed, for example, while the number from the same group sent to custody fell from 7,700 to 1,400. Although 'systems' interventions and behavioural programmes are accepted methods within the social work repertoire, there is clearly a much wider range of approaches which have effectively been marginalised in this particular practice context. In addition, the specialisation of social work in this area arguably paved the way for the emergence of a widening split between youth (and other criminal) justice work and the broader range of social work activities, an issue examined in later sections of this chapter. Thus, the development of distinctive training routes and the establishment of discrete vehicles for the delivery of practice (Youth Justice Services and Youth Offending Teams) represent the further development of the logic of specialisation which has its roots in the 1980s. The big question emerging from this, to which we shall return, is how these changes in structure and practice are likely to impact on the emerging agenda of integrated working following the *Every Child Matters* (ECM) reforms.

Contemporary policy and practice

The diversionary systems management approach to youth justice probably reached its high point in the early 1990s, when the strategy appeared to be gaining government support, and an end to the use of penal custody for children was fleetingly viewed as a realistic objective (The Children's Society, 1988). However, the climate changed rapidly (Smith, 2003: 30), and by the end of the decade, a new mode of 'punitiveness' had set in. The election of a Labour government in 1997 led to the Crime and

Disorder Act 1998 which, along with subsequent legislation[3] reshaped the structure and processes of youth justice. Social work became less central as the youth justice system became explicitly organised around principles of joint working and inter-agency collaboration.

Think ahead

Social workers can have good intentions in developing young people to their full potential. However, at times, welfare approaches based on certain theories – for example, deficits in parenting, leading to treating young people in residential units – have not always been productive.

In what ways their do social workers need to use knowledge from research and their Codes of Practice in order to provide a just and fair welfare approach, not only in their direct practice, but also in trying to influence other important agencies?

As the new structures have developed and matured (since their inception in 2000), this has had a noticeable effect in terms of establishing a new professional identity, that of the youth justice practitioner, with a specialist body of skills and knowledge associated with it. Increasingly, then, youth justice practice attains a distinctive character, both as a form of professional practice and as a separate organisational form, which stands apart from the contributing agencies, rather than operating as a collaborative arrangement between them.

The tensions between the welfare orientations of social workers and the more punitive characteristics of the criminal justice system can be seen clearly reflected in the development of the *Every Child Matters* initiative. The origins of ECM lay in a renewed recognition that many children were being failed by the absence of collaboration between agencies to meet their needs; this was epitomised by the circumstances surrounding the death of Victoria Climbié. Children would be better served, it was suggested, by the development of a universal service framework. Children should:

- Be healthy
- Stay safe
- Enjoy and achieve
- Make a positive contribution
- Achieve economic well-being.

(HM Government, 2004: 9)

It is suggested that securing these broad but specific aims requires wide-ranging cooperation and integrated practice. The Children Act 2004 gave substance to these objectives by establishing a framework for the collaborative organisation of children's services. Within this framework, inter-professional collaboration is expected to be the norm, supported by shared and common responsibilities and more effective processes, such as common information-sharing systems. Social work might be thought to be particularly suited to this way of working, given the networking and advocacy skills integral to the profession, and considering its holistic and empowering approach to meeting children's needs.

Against this background, the Commissioner for Human Rights recently stated that 'there is a disturbing trend in Europe today to lock up more children at an earlier age. The age of criminal responsibility is already very low in some countries, such as the United Kingdom', although 'it is imperative that young persons are taught to take responsibility for their actions'. The Commissioner at the same time emphasised that 'Young offenders are children first and foremost and should be protected by all the agreed human rights standards for children.'[4]

At the same time, the nature of direct work with young offenders can be said to have changed relatively little. For example, the Intensive Supervision and Surveillance Programme (ISSP) was introduced to provide more structured and concentrated input with persistent and serious young offenders. Contemporary programmes appear to comprise many of the same components as their predecessors, such as work to address offending behaviour, constructive activities, anger management and education courses. The ISSP was targeted at young people at risk of custodial sentences and focused heavily on changing behaviour rather than other intervention techniques. Unlike the experience of the 1980s, however, the programme also includes a 'surveillance' element, sometimes using electronic means, and emphasises compliance and enforcement. This then raises the question for social workers as to how much of an authoritarian role should be adopted by social workers, and how more traditional skills and methods can be adapted to provide an effective base for practice in such programmes. In view of this, it is perhaps ironic that ISSP has so far failed to achieve the kind of outcomes demonstrated by the IT programmes of the 1980s, based on relationship-based approaches between workers and young people (Smith, 2007).

---

[3] Further legislation can now be anticipated with a change of government in 2010.

[4] European Commissioner on Human Rights, *Human Rights in Europe: time to honour our pledges*, 2 February 2009.

A closer look

Community-based programmes for young offenders

Since the 1980s there have been repeated attempts by practitioners and agencies in youth justice to establish genuine 'alternatives to custody', which maintain the confidence of the courts, but manage also to divert young people into community sentences and away from custody. An early successful example of this strategy was the Woodlands Centre in Basingstoke (Rutherford, 1992).

However, problems have been encountered in maintaining a balance between the 'rigour' and usefulness of the programmes while also ensuring that they are used in place of, rather than as an adjunct to, custody. The early experience of ISSPs in this respect was not encouraging.

By contrast, the All Wales Youth Offending Strategy is significant to the extent that it takes a 'children first' as opposed to an 'offender first' approach (Muncie and Goldson, 2006: 44). Consistent with this, the Welsh Assembly government has located responsibility for youth justice with Health and Social Services rather than treating it primarily as a matter of crime prevention. Again, unlike England, the Welsh approach does seem to be based on a genuine attempt to pursue an integrated approach, based on principles of 'primary prevention' (Williamson, 2005), and 'extending entitlement' in order to address need. The framework for intervention thus provides a different rationale for practice, and enables social work once again to prioritise the welfare needs of children who offend.

If we look again at the case study of John, set out at the beginning of this chapter, it is clear that while there is work be done on John's understanding of the effects on others of his actions, there are also issues concerning his living situation, and relationships with others, including his parents, which need to be taken into account to deal with the factors which may be affecting not only his well-being, but also his offending.

Reconciling practice tensions

What are we to conclude, then, about the current relationship between social work and youth justice, and the prospects for future developments? As we noted initially,

the discourse of 'welfare' began to exert an influence on ideas and practice in the treatment of young offenders at least as early as the mid-nineteenth century. Indeed, over the following 150 years, for the most part, continuing debates and reform measures were based on the goal of achieving the most appropriate balance between the needs of children and the requirements of the criminal justice system. The legitimacy of welfare-led interventions in the youth justice sphere was not in question during this time. However, the period from 1980 onwards has seen a fundamental change in the climate of opinion on this subject, and an emerging consensus incorporating both liberal reformers and authoritarian populists has sanctioned the erosion of social work ideas and practice from the repertoire of interventions with young people who offend.

Think ahead

Effective social work practice in the youth justice sphere requires the adoption of a number of operating principles, which should ensure the delivery of both welfare and justice for young people in trouble. These include:

- *Minimum intervention* – we know that more extreme forms of punishment, especially custody, are harmful, and their use should be avoided, wherever possible.
- *Empowerment* – the commission of an offence does not, of itself, obviate the importance of seeking to negotiate and engage with young people in seeking solutions.
- A *'needs-based' approach* – the social work task is to address the needs of the young person in context, of which the offence is just one element.
- *Responsibility* – intervene in ways which promote and encourage a sense of personal responsibility rather than imposing solutions which undermine this.
- *Problem-solving* – social work principles require that all the issues surrounding the offence are addressed constructively.

As we have been reminded by *Every Child Matters*, an integrated response to the problems faced by children and young people is required, and this includes applying social work values and practices to young people in trouble, irrespective of their behaviour.

Such integrated responses now must find a space within multi-agency and multi-professional settings in the youth justice field: namely, Youth Offending Teams, a development explored in detail in later sections of this chapter.

The Youth Offending Teams are locally organised, multi-professional, multi-agency teams which provide one of the first examples of an increasingly common feature of the social welfare landscape in the United Kingdom. These teams include representatives from local authority children's social care services, police, probation, health workers and, depending upon local arrangements, mental health workers, drug and alcohol workers, victims' workers, as well as Connexions workers, who provide education, training, careers and work advice and support, and youth workers.

One key development in the youth justice system in recent years are Referral Panels, operated by Youth Offending Teams, within which social workers often provide the central service in relation to a large proportion – about 40 per cent – of young offenders who appear in the youth courts. One element of such panels was meant to incorporate another major development in the justice system, Restorative Justice (RJ); both these initiatives, and the relationship between them, are discussed in detail later.

Having examined the key elements of policy, legislation and societal influences on young people who offend, the rest of this chapter draws on these themes in discussion of key areas of professional social work practice with young offenders. The issues raised in the first part of this chapter relate to how far professional social work practice is determined by policy, legislation, and how working in multidisciplinary environments has had significant implications for the type of work social workers do. These factors need to be borne in mind when considering how professional social work practice can best apply its own values and objectives effectively in a working context which may not always prioritise the well-being of children in trouble.

Social work practice in Youth Offending Teams

There are a number of key practice issues for social workers in Youth Offending Teams, and these are now explored through consideration of the types of interventions and approaches available to them.

One of the most important elements of the social work approach is its holistic view of the needs of young people, and its commitment to enhancing as far as possible their capacity to draw on, participate in, and contribute to, society. Social work has a strong and respected history of working with young people to access resources in order to support these aims, so that they are able to develop to

their fullest capacity in relation to education, employment, and relationships, whatever their circumstances – including, for example, offering continuing support and guidance to them while in custody. Custodial sentences, and transition to living in the community again post-custody, are thus important areas of social work intervention in youth justice work.

At the same time, social work's traditional role has been modified as new expectations and responsibilities have been placed on practitioners. For example, risk assessment and risk management has become particularly a feature of work with young offenders in the Youth Offending Teams.

All of these areas are examined here with a consideration of key skills, methods, approaches and values which social workers need to bring to work with young people who offend or are held accountable for antisocial behaviour.

Role, skills and approaches

Think ahead

The role of social workers in collaborative practice

What are the key skills, methods and approaches which social workers bring to youth justice work?

In your work with young people who have offended, how important would you rate:

- *networking;*
- *communicating with other agencies/professionals; and*
- *use of authority?*

What are the reasons for your answers?

Social work may focus on work with families and their children or with young people who are 'looked after', where a young person is believed to be at risk of offending, where s/he is reported to be involved in antisocial behaviour, where a young person has been in trouble with the police, or where s/he has formally entered the youth justice system.

The activities of social workers include working with young people to address antisocial behaviour, developing prevention programmes, participating in diversion schemes (NACRO, 2006), liaising with police and other agencies, presenting pre-sentence reports to the youth courts, and devising and supervising community programmes for young offenders, as well as working with and advocating for those who are sentenced to custody, before and after release.

Much the same skills are needed when working with young people who offend as with other social work clients, although it is important to recognise that their application is often circumscribed by the specific context of youth justice. Skills such as listening carefully to the person and communicating with her/him effectively, including appropriate responses to issues of language or communication difficulties, ensuring that the clients know what the social worker's role is, and her/his powers and duties within that role, valuing the person as an individual while not endorsing unacceptable behaviour, recognising the young person's rights, and ensuring that no one is discriminated against unfairly are all important elements of the task. Key findings from research confirm that social work approaches which value a person for whom they are, while not necessarily condoning what they have done, is an important element of what young people value in the worker: for example, in relation to young people from BME groups (Lovell, 2006). Empathetic relationships with young people, incorporating approaches that engender trust and respect from workers who are perceived to be concerned about their welfare, are particularly important not only for a developing the self-worth of the young person, but also other positive outcomes for them (see e.g. Williamson, 2001).

What is different in the social work role within the youth justice system is the clarity with which the control and power elements are set out. Social workers need to examine this area carefully, in order to feel confident in their role within this setting, and ensure that their clients also understand this. The Crime and Disorder Act 1998 makes the primary duty of workers in the youth justice system the prevention of offending. In addition, the social worker works under the National Standards issued by the Youth Justice Board, according to orders made by the court, and in line with their own agency policies and procedures. Courts will make orders which include certain attendance requirements, under which youth justice workers have only a small amount of discretion to make allowances where young people miss appointments without good reason.

If the young person fails to abide by the terms of an order, as may be set out in formal contracts with them, the practitioner needs to be clear that, while s/he will seek to carry out the practice role in accordance with their professional skills and values, s/he also has a responsibility to abide by the control functions which are implicit in formal requirements of the justice system. Even applying

principles of minimum intervention does not absolve the practitioner from acting in accordance with these, and it is important to be open and honest with young people about the obligation to return the young person to court in the event of serious non-compliance.

The values and ethics base for practice

Think ahead

The BASW *Code of Ethics for Social Work* state that social work is committed to five basic values:

1. Human dignity and worth
2. Social justice
3. Service to humanity
4. Integrity
5. Competence.

The Codes state that 'they [social workers] do not act out of prejudice against any person or group, on any grounds, including origin, ethnicity, class, status, sex, sexual orientation, age, disability, beliefs or contribution to society?' The Codes also require that they 'Recognise and respect ethnic and cultural identity and diversity, and the further diversity within ethnic and cultural groups, and promote policies, procedures and practices consistent with this objective', and 'Seek to ensure that services are offered and delivered in a culturally appropriate manner'. The Codes state that 'integrity comprises honesty, reliability, openness and impartiality, and is an essential value in the practice of social work'.

Consider how these values might affect your work with young people who offend.

The *Code of Practice for Social Workers* (General Social Care Council (GSCC) 2002), which all qualified social workers in England and Wales have to abide by, features a number of elements of importance to social work with young offenders. In addition, members of the British Association of Social Workers (BASW) are obliged to abide by the BASW Code of Ethics.

We would pick out several elements of the GSCC Codes which we believe are particularly important and relevant to youth justice. Section 1 states:

'As a social care worker, you must protect the rights and promote the interests of service users and carers. This includes:

– treating each person as an individual;
– respecting and, where appropriate, promoting the individual views and wishes of both service users and carers;

- supporting service users' rights to control their lives and make informed choices about the services they receive;
- respecting and maintaining the dignity and privacy of service users;
- promoting equal opportunities for service users and carers; and
- respecting diversity and different cultures and values.'

(General Social Care Council, 2007)

This section emphasises the social work value and tradition that we treat each individual with whom we work with respect. According to the BASW Codes: 'Every human being has intrinsic value. All persons have a right to well-being, to self fulfilment and as much control over their lives as is consistent with the rights of others', and 'service in the interests of human well being and social justice is a primary objective of social work. Its fundamental goals are to meet personal and social needs; to enable people to develop their potential; to contribute to the creation of a fairer society.'

However, these principles, and item 1.3 in the GSCC Codes, create some difficulties for social workers because the main statutory aim of the criminal justice system, including work with young offenders, is purely to prevent offending. This means that social workers working with young offenders have to take into account the needs of victims and the wider community, as set out in section 4 of the GSSC Codes:

'As a social care worker, you must respect the rights of service users while seeking to ensure that their behaviour does not harm themselves or other people',

and in the BASW Codes:

'Ensure the protection of service users, which may include setting appropriate limits and exercising authority, with the objective of safeguarding them and others.'

This approach is also emphasised in legislation and policies (see Angus (2005) for relevant research on victims, including young victims) in the light of the wider needs of the community to be protected from offending by young people. This means that social workers intervening with young offenders (similarly to other areas of work where they combine a care and control function, such as certain forms of mental health work), have to take into account the power which they wield within such systems, and how they apply this in their work with young people, while maintaining a clear focus on working respectfully with young offenders both to realise their potential and to promote a sense of responsibility.

Section 2.3 of the GSCC Codes emphasises the importance of '[r]especting confidential information and clearly explaining agency policies about confidentiality to service users and carers'. This is important not only in direct work with young offenders, but also for taking into account in inter-agency settings such as Youth Offending Teams, where joint records are kept, and information is passed from one set of professionals to another, including the police. In order to ensure that social workers are clear about the limits of confidentiality and information-sharing, when going into a practice learning situation, or in a multi-agency, multi-professional setting such as the YOT, they should be familiar with policies about information-sharing, and they should make the implications known to their clients. Such issues of openness and honesty (section 2.1 in the Codes) are important in building up trust in the relationship with the young person.

The dual role mentioned above has implications arising from other relevant sections of the GSCC Codes, as in section 3:

'As a social care worker, you must promote the independence of service users while protecting them as far as possible from danger or harm. This includes promoting the independence of service users and assisting them to understand and exercise their rights.'

These contradictory aspirations have particular consequences for practice within the youth justice arena. Young people with whom social workers engage may simultaneously be seen as posing a risk of harm to the community, while also being at risk of harm or in need themselves according to the definitions of the Children Act 1989. The social worker should always prioritise concern for the young person according to her/his needs as determined under the relevant children's legislation, even though this may lead to possible disagreements with other professional colleagues, such as police or education workers. It is not necessary to agree on every aspect of practice in a multi-agency setting, and indeed representing different perspectives may be a necessary and legitimate aspect of the social work task.

Think ahead

How do you think you will manage disagreements with colleagues from other disciplines, say, over the question of whether a young person's needs should modify the demands of the justice system for punitive measures?

Would it be better to establish a prior understanding that differences may arise and should be aired openly and freely, rather than responding to these problems as they arise?

The Codes of Practice emphasise the importance of anti-oppressive practice. These particular elements social workers have to take account of are referred to again later in this chapter, in relation to BME groups. These are set out in section 5:

'You must not:
- Discriminate unlawfully or unjustifiably against service users, carers or colleagues; or
- Condone any unlawful or unjustifiable discrimination by service users, carers or colleagues'.

In addition, the Codes (section 6) expect social workers to show that they are:

- Working openly and co-operatively with colleagues and treating them with respect;
- Recognising and respecting the roles and expertise of workers from other agencies and working in partnership with them.'

Areas of work for social workers in the youth justice system

Think ahead

Within a multi-professional YOT, social workers will share many of the tasks of the team with other professional groups. Therefore, an understanding of inter-professional and inter-agency working, and building up relationships with those other professionals, including an awareness of the differences in professional focus (for example, with the police, counsellors, Connexions workers) of each group which may cause tensions and misunderstandings between them, is a key area in approaching such work.

What are the strategies which social workers should use in order to ensure good working relationships with other professional groups in their YOT?

Which of the following roles do you think social work are particularly suited to, and why?

1. Acting as an Appropriate Adult
2. Addressing antisocial behaviour
3. Carrying out risk assessments
4. Key worker responsibility for young people on orders, for example, Youth Rehabilitation Orders, Referral Panel Orders
5. Through and after care for young people in custody.

We can now go on to consider some of the ways in which social workers are likely to be called upon to carry out these functions.

The social worker acting as appropriate adult (AA)

Social workers are frequently called upon to act as the AA where young people have been detained by police. This can be in relation to families and children work in general, or where social workers are operating within a YOT, where a young person over the age of 10 is detained by the police and the parent/s are unwilling or unable to attend. In addition, social workers may be called upon to act in this role for a young person who is looked after by the local authority.

The role was formally instituted by the Police and Criminal Evidence Act 1984 Codes of Practice in Code C of the Codes, the latest version of which was published in 2008 (www.homeoffice.gov.uk/publications/police/operational-policing/pace-codes/pace-code-c), which set out the role of the AA as follows:

'If an appropriate adult is present at interview, they shall be informed they are not expected to act simply as an observer; and the purpose of their presence is to: advise the person being interviewed; observe whether the interview is being conducted properly and fairly; facilitate communication with the person being interviewed'.

(Home Office, Code C, paragraph 11.17)

When it is considered how the role was debated in the development of the Codes, and in subsequent case law, it is clear that the role is meant to be an active one, and not a passive one, although there are indications from the available research that AAs who are social workers often do not intervene, or do not intervene effectively, when they have the right, and duty, so to do in protecting the rights of young people who are detained (Robertson et al., 1995; Littlechild, 2001; Evans, 1993). It is expected by the courts that Appropriate Adults will intervene if they believe procedures are not being carried out correctly, or the questioning is such that it can be seen as 'oppressive' (Home Office, 2008, paragraph 11.5).

One very important element to be aware of in the Appropriate Adults' role and duties is that if the young person has not asked for legal representation, the AA can, and where appropriate, should request free legal representation, for the young person (paragraph 6.5) Some Youth Offending Teams have a policy that they will always call a solicitor when they are called up as an

The different stages of work in the youth justice system

The following points set out the different stages at which a social worker may become involved in work with young offenders, from the beginning of preventive processes, through to where young people are released from custody.

- Representation on behalf of Youth Offending Teams in local Crime Reduction Partnerships
- Preventive work with children and young people 'in need' under s.17 of the Children Act 1989 who are also at risk of offending
- Assessment and supervision of Acceptable Behaviour Contracts, Parenting Orders and Individual Support Orders under antisocial behaviour legislation
- Involvement in Youth Inclusion and Support Panels (YISPs) which work with families and young people

where there is a risk of social exclusion and offending
- Appropriate Adult work with young people who are detained by the police, having been suspected of having committed an offence
- Preparing Pre Sentence Reports for the Youth Courts, and reports for Youth Offender Panels
- Devising, implementing and supervising programmes for young people on various requirements under orders of the court, for example Referral Orders, Youth Rehabilitation Orders
- Visiting young people in custody, monitoring those who are deemed 'vulnerable', and preparing for their release
- Post-custody work with young people, supervising additional requirements and addressing their resettlement needs.

AA, although it is not a requirement for the AA to do so under the Codes. If at any point during the young person's detention the AA believes the presence of a solicitor is necessary, they can request that the interview be stopped until a solicitor arrives (paragraph 6.5A).

Who may act as an appropriate adult?

In order of preference, these can be any of the following, unless s/he is suspected of being involved in the offence, is a victim, a witness, or has received an admission about the offence prior to attending as the AA, or is an estranged parent to whom the young person objects (Note of Guidance1B):

1. the parent, guardian or, if the juvenile is in local authority or voluntary organisation care, or is otherwise being looked after under the Children Act 1989, a person representing that authority or organisation;
2. a social worker of a local authority;
3. failing these, some other responsible adult aged 18 or over who is not a police officer or employed by the police. (para. 1.7a).

At the police station

If it is safe to do so, the social worker acting as Appropriate Adult should see the young person alone to explain her/his role. However, be aware that this does not confer 'legal privilege', which the solicitor has, which means

that the worker cannot promise confidentiality to the young person. So in the preparatory individual meeting with him/her, the social worker should emphasise s/he is there for the young person's welfare, and to facilitate communication, so that if, for example, there is any uncertainty about questions and answers, the practitioner can be included in the discussion with the police.

What does the social worker need to be aware of in the AA role?

The social worker needs to be aware of the following points:

- Before going to the police station check whether a solicitor has been called, and ensure the police call one if it is believed necessary.
- Where it is safe to do so, meet privately with a young person before the interview starts, to explain the process.
- Explain that s/he is there to safeguard the young person's welfare.
- Discuss with the solicitor any issues that s/he needs to be aware of for them to represent their client effectively: for example, any specific communication requirements.
- If there are concerns about the physical or mental health of the young person, representations can be made to the custody officer for an assessment by the 'appropriate health professional'.

In the interview itself, issues might arise if the social worker believes that the nature of the questioning is oppressive or not clearly understood, or there are problems in communication with the young person. The role of the AA includes facilitating communication, and s/he is expected to intervene to ensure that the young person understands what is being spoken about. While the AA is expected to intervene to check that the detainee understands questions and answers, s/he is not able to put questions directly to the young person, except about their experience of the process, rather than the content of the interview.

There may be problems where the complexity of language used by officers is too great; where there are multiple and confusing questions; leading questions, or where the behaviour of the interviewing officers in terms of raised voices or confrontational behaviour possibly amount to oppression, which is expressly forbidden; if concerns arise about the style or content of the questioning, the right to bring in the solicitor continues to apply.

Case study

Jody

Jody is 15 years old, is white British and has been arrested and detained by the police as they suspect her of having assaulted another young woman outside a bar in a town centre. Jody lives with her mother and her younger brother. You are called by the police to act as an Appropriate Adult for her as her mother is very angry with Jody, as she has felt frustrated in recent months about Jodys 'out of control' behaviour. Jody, you are told via the custody officer responsible for her detention, has been swearing at the police and being generally uncooperative.

What do you think you need to take into account when deciding how to approach Jody and explain your role when you arrive at the police station?

Consider how you will explain your role in the interview to Jody.

What are the issues of inter-professional working with the police which you would need to take into account to deal with this situation in the best way possible?

What preconceptions/prejudices might the different groups of professionals involved in youth justice work – e.g. police, social workers, teachers, other

professional groups – have about Jody if she were from a BME group?

What might be the effects of these on Jody, and her treatment at this stage, and then possibly later, through the youth justice system?

What might you be able to do in your role as a social worker to diminish the risk of your own preconceptions/prejudices affecting your relationship with Jody, and your work with her; or try to avert the preconceptions/prejudices of others in the system from adversely affecting Jody's progress through the youth justice system?

New developments in pre-court and court-based legislation and procedures

The Criminal Justice and Immigration Act 2008, most of the provisions of which were implemented in 2009, introduced new provisions which develop themes already present in previous policy and legislation, with no dramatic changes in philosophy or procedures. The disposals now include (for full details see the YJB website):

- **Pre-court measures:** Reprimands and Final Warnings
- **Anti-social behaviour measures:** Acceptable Behaviour Contracts and Anti-Social Behaviour Orders (NB the coalition Government in Whitehall announced in 2010 it is intending to abolish these)
- **Other pre-court measures** include: Local Child Curfews; Youth Restorative Disposal and Youth Conditional Caution (both piloted in some areas only)
- **Child Safety Orders** for under-10-year-olds
- **Court ordered Community Sentences** (which may in addition have Parenting Orders, Curfew Orders and Drug Treatment and Testing Orders attached to them – orders which were available prior to the Criminal Justice and Immigration Act 2008 implementation in 2009): Youth Rehabilitation Orders; Referral Orders; Reparation Orders; Fine; Conditional Discharges; Absolute Discharges. The following sentences are now replaced by Youth Rehabilitation Orders: Supervision Orders; Supervision Order and conditions; Curfew Orders; Community Rehabilitation Orders; Exclusion Order; Community Rehabilitation Order and conditions; Community Punishment Orders; Drug Treatment and Testing Order; Community Rehabilitation and Punishment Orders; Action Plan Orders; and Attendance Centre Orders.

The main orders social workers are likely to work with are the Youth Rehabilitation Order and Referral Order. The Youth Rehabilitation Order (YRO) is a generic community sentence for young people who offend and combines a number of existing sentences into one generic sentence. Its aim was to simplify sentencing for young people and allow greater flexibility of interventions, and the following long list of attachments may be inserted into such orders:

- Activity Requirement
- Curfew Requirement
- Exclusion Requirement
- Local Authority Residence Requirement
- Education Requirement
- Mental Health Treatment Requirement
- Unpaid Work Requirement (16/17 years)
- Drug Testing Requirement
- Intoxicating Substance Treatment Requirement
- Supervision Requirement
- Electronic Monitoring Requirement
- Prohibited Activity Requirement
- Drug Treatment Requirement
- Residence Requirement
- Programme Requirement
- Attendance Centre Requirement
- Intensive Supervision and Surveillance (based on the current ISSP)
- Intensive Fostering

One possible consequence of this array of attachments is that young people may be sentenced to onerous requirements because of their youth status, which would not be commensurate with interventions for an adult convicted of similar crimes. In PSRs, social workers should be aware of this possibility, and try to ensure their recommendations are commensurate with the requirements of the order, and the rights and needs of the young person. However, the other side of this is that the YJB sees the YRO as a 'robust' community sentence providing a menu of interventions which can be used on multiple occasions to help minimise the use of custody, which the UK makes greater use of than any other Western European country, the problems with which are examined in a special section of this chapter which looks specifically at them. There are no restrictions on the number of times an offender can be sentenced to an YRO. Courts are expected to use the YRO on multiple occasions, adapting the menu as appropriate to deal with the offending behaviour.

Referral Orders under the new 2008 Act are more wide-ranging than previously, reflecting confidence in their use by the government, and these are examined in more detail in the section of this chapter which looks specifically at them.

Alongside these changes, the Scaled Approach is a new required process, and reflects the same approach which has been developed in adult criminal justice agencies. It introduces a tiered approach to assessment which then bases the intensity and nature of interventions on that completed assessment which informs the increased responsibility given to the YOT workers to recommend programmes to the courts in their PSRs, demonstrating a small shift in power from the courts to YOT professionals. The main aim of the Scaled Approach is to put in place interventions the YJB consider most likely to reduce likelihood of reoffending and risk of serious harm. This is part of a new sentencing framework, within revised *National Standards for Youth Justice Services*, new *Key Elements of Effective Practice*, and new *Case Management Guidance*, all published on the YJB website.

The Youth Justice Board has also instigated a *Directory of Emerging Practice* which contains details of programmes and other information across a range of practice themes. They are meant to provide a starting point for youth justice services' development of their programmes. Elements include:

- **Accommodation**
- **Assessment, planning interventions and Supervision**
- Behaviour management
- Diversity (including young women who offend)
- **Education, training and employment**
- **Engaging young people who offend**
- Intensive supervision
- **Mental health**
- Mentoring
- **Offending behaviour programmes**
- **Parenting**
- Resettlement
- **Restorative justice**
- Risk management
- Safeguarding
- Serious youth violence (including PVE, gangs and weapons)
- Social and life skills programmes
- **Substance misuse**
- Working with partners
- **Young people who sexually abuse**

(see http://www.yjb.gov.uk/en-gb/)

Pre-sentence reports and the youth court

One key element of work for social workers in the youth justice system is to prepare pre-sentence reports (PSRs) for the Youth Court. The PSR sets out the circumstances leading up to the offence, brief background concerning the young person, and a discussion of possible disposals for the court. In preparation for this task, an ASSET assessment will be carried out, as specified by the National Standards for Youth Justice, which is designed to assess risk factors for the young person, including why the young person offended, their attitudes to the offence, their family and lifestyle circumstances, and whether they have specific mental health or drug and alcohol related problems, in addition to issues in relation to education training and, if appropriate, employment (see below). ASSET has a dual purpose, in order to assess risks that young offenders might pose to themselves, or others, as well as more general areas to consider concerning risk of reoffending. Goldson, a leading researcher and commentator on policy with young offenders, sets out how there are different forms for different phases of the process, so for pre-court bail assessments, there is a shortened form for example (Goldson, 2002). For details of the ASSET assessment, and pre-sentence report preparation, see the Youth Justice Board website and the National Standards for Youth Justice. ASSET is used across England and Wales in Youth Offending Teams, with the purpose of standardising the risk assessment process, in conjunction with the new Scaled Approach discussed previously. The approach embedded in this form of assessment contrasts dramatically with the holistic, needs-led principles underpinning the *Framework for Assessment of Children in Need and Their Families* (Department of Health, 2000c), with which social workers may be much more familiar, and more comfortable. The new array of attachments in the YRO under the Criminal Justice and Immigration Act 2008 has the possibility of onerous requirements being attached to a YRO, an issue we have examined earlier in this chapter, and social workers need to be considering the balance of the rights and needs the young person against pressure to provide recommendations for over-restrictive attachments.

A pre-sentence report will normally be obtained before the court makes any community sentence, so that it can be satisfied that the restriction of liberty imposed is commensurate with the seriousness of the offending and the requirements in the order, suitable for the offender. The purpose of the report is to provide information to the court concerning the suitability of the offender for one or more of the community sentences the court could make. The report must comply with the requirements set out in the National Standards for the Supervision of Offenders in the Community, requiring an introduction, offence analysis, relevant information about the offender, the risk to the public of reoffending and an evaluation of the options available to the court.

Think ahead

What would you consider to be the main factors for a young person which might put her/him at risk of offending?

What are some of the most effective elements you might recommend to the court in putting a programme into place to deal with these for an individual young person, while not breaching their rights and best interests?

Risk assessment in youth justice

This section sets out to consider the question posed in the above Think Ahead box. ASSET is the key tool used in youth justice risk assessment at all its different stages, so is important to be fully aware of its content and processes.

Risk assessment is a key feature in government policy in England and Wales, and the wider UK countries. ASSET is the key tool, developed by the Youth Justice Board, used in youth justice risk assessment at all its different stages, in all Youth Offending teams across England and Wales.

Some of the factors which evidence suggests are associated with youth offending are incorporated into the ASSET framework, and attempt to provide risk predictive factors which have relevance for both early prevention as well as for reoffending for young people at that stage. A specialist tool for early prediction, the Onset referral and assessment framework was recently introduced by the YJB (www.yjb.gov.uk/publications/Scripts/prodView.asp?idproduct=303&eP=).

Onset aims to identify risk factors to be reduced and protective factors to be enhanced with identified children and young people, and to provide information which aids in selecting appropriate interventions for young people so identified. The YJB requires all the prevention programmes they fund to use Onset as the basis for their referral and assessment recording and monitoring.

A review of the research literature for the Youth Justice Board (2001) indicated that intervention programmes can be effective in reducing the risk of youth offending if targeted at high-risk children and young people, at the appropriate stage, and, we would contend, if they take into account the specific needs of different economic, racial and cultural groups which, while being integrated into a comprehensive prevention package, should include issues of family, community and personal and individual factors. The research also acknowledged that such factors are clustered together in lives of the most disadvantaged children. It claimed that the chances of such young people becoming antisocial and criminally active increases exponentially as the number of risk factors increase. The research review also indicated that the wide variety of risk factors identified meant that preventing crime requires the active involvement of agencies outside the justice system, including education and health services. The review found evidence from the UK (and the United States of America) that the interventions most likely to reduce reoffending programmes are those that are designed to improve personal social skills, and also focus on changing behaviour, combining a number of different approaches. The issues for assessment and intervention on the basis of such risk approaches are in using such approaches, while acknowledging and taking account of other issues of disadvantage such as poverty, unfair discrimination because of ethnicity, culture, gender, and disability, which have an effect on the individual person's potential for greater social inclusion.

One of the key issues for social workers in this process is for young people to have an awareness of their risk assessments, and being able to comment upon them, in terms of sharing of information, and their knowledge of what professionals are saying about them in order to be able to discuss any differences in opinion. This would appear to be required by the UNCRC's article 12, which states that States Parties shall ensure to the child who is capable of forming his or her own views the right to express those views freely in all matters affecting the child, and the views of the child being given due weight in accordance with the age and maturity of the child.

Indeed, in a wider sense, young people engaged in criminal activity are 'experts by experience' and research illuminating their first-hand experience is fruitful in gaining knowledge to tackle the antecedents of crime and formulating more meaningful and effective policy responses. It is important that research raises awareness of what impacts on young people's lives in disadvantaged, high-risk communities, and young people from ethnic minority groups and disaffected groups, to feed into knowledge about the problems and solutions in local areas, alongside others' interests, such as adult residents in particular areas. Another key area of participation can also be by way of young people's involvement in young people's panels in local areas, to gain their views on their situation and possible solutions to their perceived problems. While young people's involvement by way of 'school councils', e.g., is already a feature in some European countries, the involvement of disaffected young people and young people who offend tends not to be. Social workers need to be at the forefront of attempting to get individual and collective views into the different levels of the system they work within.

Early interventions

In youth justice jurisdictions, a key issue is to what extent the welfare and best interests of the child/young person – as a developing, learning being, and still open to positive socialising influences – are incorporated. A substantial number of young people in the UK and Europe lack the means to participate fully in the economic, social, cultural and political life or are prevented from doing so by economic disadvantage, lack of skills and knowledge, discrimination or personal attitudes.

Young offenders often come from among the most disadvantaged groups in society and have complex needs. Many have histories of educational disadvantage and/or disaffection, substance misuse, mental health problems, and disrupted and/or abusive family backgrounds. Systematic processes of social exclusion in terms of lack of formal education and training and ensuing low earning capacity often result in barriers for young people earning money within the legal economy – a phenomenon likely to be exacerbated by the current economic downturn. Many young people depend upon state benefits and find it increasingly difficult to gain access to jobs that allow them greater legitimate integration into the social and economic fabric of society.

Early intervention programmes, such as the YISPs mentioned previously, include consideration of the areas of possible risk as set out in the above sections, the level of risk, and therefore if an intervention will be offered, and in what ways. Some of the criticisms of claims that such young children can be predicted for their future antisocial behaviour are that while scientific methods demand replicability and experimental evidence as the basis of knowledge and action, usually examining only very few factors (and often only one), in the area of social work services, this is much more problematic. It can be argued that there is a multitude of possible influences which can vary over time, within different contexts, at any one particular point in time which can affect the service user's actions and decisions, and thus the professional assessment – and therefore prediction – of risk. This means it is very difficult to attempt to have a high level of certainty and predictability in the personal social services (Morgan, 2007; Titterton, 2005; Webb, 2007).

One key area for social workers to be wary of is that such targeting of young people at a very early age – often through schools, or as embedded on antisocial behaviour orders – does not unfairly label and disadvantage the child/family further.

Early prevention: geographical and demographic issues

Evidence is increasingly showing high concentrations of young and adult offenders in localised geographical areas who are known to the criminal justice system and who are disaffected from education, training and work (Metropolitan Police Authority, 2009; Metropolitan Police Service, 2005). This suggests the need for detailed mapping work on demographics, educational attainment and crime rates, and then the exploration of alternative ways of deploying resources and offering family and youth support services and activities in those areas.

It is therefore important to examine the overlaps and commonalities between social groupings within discreet geographical areas that are socially excluded in order to facilitate effective multi-agency intervention across a range of policy areas.

According to a House of Commons Select Committee Report in 2004, '*Providing high quality youth services*' (clubs, activities, enhanced schooling, restorative justice/mediation services, training and work opportunities) '*is a fundamental requirement for addressing social cohesion*'. Alongside this primary-based approach, services at the secondary level can be targeted at those children and their families who come to the attention of the authorities – potentially for all families in identified areas – where there are high indices of disadvantage, such as poor housing, low incomes, poor job opportunities, interpersonal and inter-ethnic conflict, and high crime rates.

Local multi-agency groups can identify such areas and groups of young people for interventions, and formulate and review action plans for community and restorative programmes, and also formulate action plans for young

people who are clearly exhibiting offending and disaffected behaviours. For example, one programme in England has used a system to provide professional and mentoring services, by inviting families and young people to partake in a support programme if they became known to the triumvirate of social services, school, and police agencies. Wider use of functional family support programmes is also found in Sweden and anti-bullying programmes in Norway.

Ideally, these programmes should be presented positively, as fostering safe and healthy communities by strengthening protective factors, rather than as a negatively framed labelling process. This is in accordance with the UN guidelines for the prevention of juvenile delinquency which say that '*Formal agencies of social control should only be utilized as a means of last resort*'.

Some of the factors which evidence suggests are associated with youth offending, and thus are incorporated into the ASSET framework (see Farrington, 1996, for example), are:

- *Parenting* – too strict/too lenient/inconsistent; this has been associated with the development of parenting groups, either ordered by the court, or undertaken voluntarily by the parents.
- *Peer pressure* – this tends to be dealt with by programmes based on cognitive behavioural approaches, which have gained great credence in the criminal and youth justice system in recent decades. Such programmes concentrate on the cognitive processes of young people who offend, taking into account the antecedents of what they were thinking and doing in the build-up to a scenario, what happened within their thought processes during the commission of the offence, and what the consequences of the offending were. Anger Management is a common type of programme used to deal with such problems for some young people which uses such an approach.

Different types of programmes can take into account different worksheets for the young person and worker to be able to identify and work on these, cartooning of the situations where drawings are done to help illustrate, for example, the effects of illegal and dangerous driving, on themselves and others. Such cognitive behavioural approaches can be used in many areas of the risks identified for further offending. For description and analyses of these widely used approaches, see the work of two psychologists, Hollin and Palmer (2006), who have carried out extensive research on young offending.

- *Substance misuse*, involving drug and alcohol – this has been an increasing feature of risk for offending behaviour in recent years, and is associated not only with offences carried out while a young person is abusing substances, and in relation to crimes committed to gain the money to buy intoxicating substances but also with violence between young people involved in dealing in such substance abuse. This involves assessment, and liaising with local drug and alcohol agencies, or, in some local areas, workers who are specifically employed for this within the YOT.

- *Educational disaffection*, and lack of opportunity – relating to issues of social disaffection and exclusion, and financial disadvantage, where work will concentrate on identifying the problems with educational engagement and attendance, and working with, for example, schools, specialist educational units, and educational psychologists, or participation in training and employment, in order to improve life chances for the young person. This can include work with the local Connexions service, sometimes with workers seconded to YOTs, which provides wide-ranging services for young people in relation to careers, training and employment. Mentoring, using volunteers who befriend the young person, and provide concern and emotional support, and sometimes a role model, is also used to help increase social inclusion and feelings of connection with the wider community.

- *Self image* – which may include issues of poor self-image, and also, potentially, the effects of abuse and violence on the young person.

- *Mental health problems* – which would involve assessment, and liaising with other workers, such as those in the Child and Adolescent Mental Health Service provided by the local health trusts, or, in some local areas with Youth Offending Teams, specialist mental health workers who are employed within the team.

Restorative justice (RJ)

RJ has been discussed earlier in this chapter, and while presenting some dilemmas for its incorporation within a primarily adversarial based system, social workers' knowledge and skills in interpersonal relationships, and in how individuals relate to their immediate, and wider social systems, are important in order to achieve understanding and change for both the individual, and the social networks in which they are developing and learning. Ashover and Caldwell (2006) discuss, and give examples, of schemes which have been put into place for young people based on the RJ approach.

Restorative justice has been an area of great interest within the youth and wider criminal justice systems for some 30 years, although the approach has been present within various social systems for centuries. RJ is put forward as a way to move beyond the binary divide of welfare and justice-based approaches, and to compensate for areas they do not deal with. Restorative approaches have the potential to provide a new approach to youth justice which cuts through the tensions between justice and welfare approaches discussed earlier in this chapter, and may provide for a partial return to welfare approaches (Gelsthorpe and Morris, 2002). They encourage pro-social behaviour, and learning about and respecting the needs of others. Such approaches are used within the youth offender referral orders, which account for some 40 per cent of all disposals from youth courts in England and Wales.

In addition, restorative justice is seen as a cost-effective and accountable way of dealing with crime (Shaw and Jane, 1999). These approaches concentrate on the idea of repairing the harm done, allowing the victim to have an apology and/or reparation. They encourage and require the offender to feel some shame and sorrow for what they have done, to learn to appreciate the effects of their behaviour and attitudes on others and be part of changing this. They have been successfully used for all types of disputes, e.g. conflicts between different ethnic and religious groups, and specifically in the Northern Ireland Belfast Agreement to end such violence. They also have been used most extensively in the Scandinavian countries, worked in with their welfare-based models. This model has struggled to make headway in punitive-based countries, partly because the adversarial approach militates against offenders admitting to what they have done, and the effects of it, as this could negatively affect the outcome for them in such a system. However, the idea of restorative justice contains other problems in relation to the justice model. One of the criticisms of the new youth offender referral panels which administer the referral orders relates to the fact that legal representation is not present. A counter-argument to this concerns the fact that if solicitors take part in these processes, the young person can have the solicitor argue their case for them, and the young person does not have to engage with the members of the Panel who set and administer the details of the contract under the order, and discuss the young person's responsibilities within any offences, and the risk factors which can be dealt with in the elements of such a referral order.

Case study

Ann

Ann is a young woman, 15 years of age, and from a BME group who had experienced difficulties with others in her school concerning interpersonal conflict. There had been a build-up of issues where a group of other female school pupils had denigrated her, and excluded her from certain social processes at the school. There had been no previous history of problematic behaviour, or of offences. One evening when school had finished, and they were leaving school, she felt again denigrated by these girls, and attacked one of them quite seriously, leaving her with injuries which needed treatment at hospital. In a consequent meeting arranged by the YOT social worker at her school, there were discussions about the incident, following police and court involvement, which led to an apology from her, but also an acknowledgement of the issues which were taking place which led up to the incident. In subsequent meetings, it was reported that there had been no further incidents between her and the other girl, who was reportedly satisfied with the outcome.

Reflect

Consider your views about the causation of offending by young people, and whether you believe that young people are fully responsible for their own actions, and should be punished in some way for wrongdoing; or whether you take the view that young people themselves are victims of circumstances, and therefore deserve help and support to address their problems, including those associated with their offending.

Think about where you are on such a spectrum, and where other colleagues from different disciplines might stand. Will this invariably affect how you approach the young people with whom you are working?

Would your preconceptions/responses to Ann possibly have been different if she were white British? Why?

Case study

Andrew

Andrew Jones (14 yrs) lives with his mother and stepfather, Susan and John Black and older brother Mike (18 yrs) in a pleasant suburb of a large Scottish city. The family members are all white Scottish in origin. Susan's husband and the boys' father died in an accident 12 years ago. Susan and John Black both work full-time and John is often away from home on business for lengthy periods of time. Andrew and Mike attend the local comprehensive school, which draws upon a broad catchment area taking children from socially deprived and more advantaged communities. Mike is academically successful and very popular in school; he also captains the football team. Andrew struggles with his academic work; he is small for his age and has always found it difficult to make close friends. He and Mike do not get on and although both boys appear to have a good relationship with John, there has recently been some friction between himself and Andrew.

A short time ago Andrew became friendly with a group of boys at school who are seen as 'trouble makers' and uninterested in school or education. Andrew has been involved in truanting from school, and one day Mike found him smoking cannabis and drinking alcohol. He was grounded for one week. More recently, the police caught Andrew shoplifting with two friends. All three boys were suspected of being under the influence of drugs. Andrew was charged with theft (as were his friends). A police report was sent to the Reporter to the Children's Hearings and the Reporter has decided to arrange a Hearing.

Referral orders

The Scottish Hearing system in part provided the model for the referral order in England and Wales, but with a number of significant differences, as set out below.

Referral orders of between three months and one year were introduced under the Youth Justice and Criminal Evidence Act 1999, and were made more wide-ranging than previously under extension to them in the Criminal Justice and Immigration Act 2008.

The Act extended the circumstances in which a court can make a referral order, making changes to the discretionary conditions applying to referral orders, allowing the court to make a referral order where the offender has had one previous conviction but has not previously received a referral order, or to make a second referral order, in exceptional circumstances, on the recommendation of the YOT. The court can also now revoke a referral order early for good behaviour, or extend the term of a referral order for up to three months on the recommendation of the youth offender panel (for example where non-compliance occurs through circumstances beyond the control of the offender, i.e. illness).

Young people who are experiencing their first appearance in the youth court should normally be given a referral order of between three months and one year, unless it is a particularly serious offence.

Social workers frequently play a leading part in referral orders, which are made by the youth court in most cases involving a young person's first appearance (and admission of guilt). They are carried out by YOTs, and while others might be allocated such work with a young person, it is normally the social workers in these inter-agency teams who are allocated these cases. They therefore have the responsibilities for preparing the reports for the Youth Offender Panels which oversee the operation of the order. This involves assessing the factors which may have contributed to the young person's offences, and the types of approaches in a referral order which could reduce the possibility of reoffending, taking into account risk factors as set out in this chapter previously.

The determination of the work to be undertaken on such an order is decided by way of a contract agreed with the young person at a panel meeting which takes place as soon as possible after the making of the referral order. Panels consist of two community members, and a named worker from the YOT.

Panels should be timetabled to fit with the young person's and her/his family's commitments. At the first meeting of the Panel, there will be discussion with the young person, their parents, and others present (which could also include teachers, Connexions workers, and victims), about the situation which led up to the offence/offences, the factors which might be impacting upon the young person and their offending, including issues of family conflict, conflict with others, issues in education or work/training, accommodation, drug use, mental health problems, etc. The young person is invited to actively participate in these discussions, as are the parents/carers, and the victims, if present. Further meetings are then arranged to review the development of the young person, and the requirements of the contract.

Custody and post-release work

Custody can arise from remands, where young people are held while awaiting court appearances, or while completing a custodial sentence.

Custody for young offenders in remand centres and Young Offender Institutions poses particular risks for young people. While young people might also be detained in secure accommodation, this is unusual – for a discussion of secure units see Goldson (2002). In this section, we will concentrate on the risks for those held in penal settings, as it is far more likely that young people will be held in such institutions, rather than other secure settings, despite many concerns by government's own bodies, and other observers, over many years (Goldson, 2002).

'prisons collect [children] who find it difficult to cope, they collect excessive numbers of [children] with mental disorder, they collect [children] with weak social supports, they collect [children] [children] who, by any objective test, do not have rosy prospects. This collection of [children] is humiliated and stigmatised by the process of arrest, police inquiry in court appearance ... Above all, they are by the process separated from everything familiar, including all the social support and loved ones, however unsatisfactory.'

(Gunn, cited in Her Majesty's Chief Inspector of Prisons, 1999: 25)

John Pitts, a sociologist and criminologist who has carried out extensive research into youth offending, and published widely in this area, considers that while the media often represents young people who offend as morally reprehensible and fully responsible for their actions and therefore deservedly punished (Pitts, 2000), most young people sent to custody have a history of a range of disadvantages, suffering from poverty, family conflict and abuse; of being looked after by local authorities; of drug and alcohol misuse; mental disorder and distress; ill health; emotional, physical and sexual abuse; self-harm and suicide; homelessness; isolation; educational, skills, training and unemployment disadvantage – all areas associated also with social and educational disengagement and poor attainment. All these areas

A closer look

The Scottish Children's Hearings system

The Children's Hearings system is unique to Scotland and was established in 1971 to replace the former juvenile court system. The Hearings deal with children who commit crimes and all other children and young people who face serious problems in their lives. One of the system's basic principles is that of 'addressing deeds, meeting needs', i.e. the needs of the child must be a priority in any consideration of their offending behaviour. The system is not concerned with guilt or innocence but the welfare principle: what is in the child's best interests. In other words, the same system that deals with juvenile criminal justice also promotes children's welfare.

The purpose of the Children's Hearings system is to determine the main problems a child has and to decide what has to be done to solve them. The system has a number of distinctive characteristics. These include:

- a unified, welfare-based system for children who have offended or are in need of care and protection;
- diversion from the courts with cases referred to a local official, the Children's Reporter, to consider whether there is sufficient evidence to support the grounds of referral and whether there is a prima-facie need for compulsory measures of supervision (i.e. when voluntary measures are not regarded as sufficient to ensure the child receives the care and support required);
- an emphasis on family participation and relative informality;
- the separation of adjudication from disposal, with the establishment of any disputed facts remaining the responsibility of the courts but responsibility for decisions on treatment being transferred to Children's Hearings.

A Children's Hearing will consider a case where the child and the child's parents, or other relevant person with parental responsibilities and rights, accept the grounds for referral stated by the Reporter (who acts in some ways like a clerk to the Hearing), or where they accept them in part and the Hearing considers it proper to proceed. After acceptance or establishment of the grounds, the Hearing discusses the grounds and any reports on the child received from the social work department of the local authority and other reports where appropriate: for example, from the child's school or a psychological report. This discussion includes the three specially recruited lay members (the children's panel), the child and the child's parents (or other relevant persons) – and the Reporter to the Hearing. The aim is to reach consensus about what should happen, in the best interests of the child. Other people who are likely to be present at a Hearing include any social workers involved with the child, a representative from the child's school and any other person the Hearing thinks would assist. However, it is considered important to minimise the number of people attending a Hearing and to ensure that the surroundings do not intimidate the child.

Where a Hearing decides that compulsory measures of supervision – measures taken for the protection, guidance, treatment or control of children – are appropriate, the child is placed under the supervision of the local authority by way of a supervision requirement. A supervision requirement is a programme of work, support and services to assist the child, and section 71 of the Children (Scotland) Act 1995 compels local authorities to give effect to the supervision requirement. The supervision requirement may be renewed annually, at a Review Hearing, until the child is 18. The child may continue to live at home under the supervision of a social worker.

Further information can be found on the Hearings' website www.scra.gov.uk in Lockyer and Stone (1998) and McGhee, Mellon and Whyte (2004).

---

should be examined by social workers, as suggested earlier in this chapter at an early stage for families and young people in order to combat social exclusion and reduce criminality among young people. Custody and punitive-based measures as found in a number of European countries can only very rarely, if ever, achieve this. In their

peer groups, custody leads to expectations (labelling) by peers, professionals and families on them to be criminal and antisocial, leading to further social exclusion from positive peer groups and family support.

Young people in custody need special measures to deal with their vulnerability, including issues of abuse,

Young people in custody can often be at risk of self-harm, suicide, abuse, and mental health problems.

(*Source*: Alamy Images/Photofusion)

monitoring of the mental health state, protection from abuse and well-being of the young person while incarcerated, and an action plan with detailed measures for their support for each young person recognised as being at risk; access to support and counselling within the institution; and liaison with Youth Offending Teams and their associated health professionals to meet their needs on release.

While not condoning the effects of the behaviour on others, social workers need to take into account the stresses, disadvantages and problems they are experiencing, in assessing their problems and developing plans and strategies to help them develop beyond disadvantage and criminality.

Custody is a very depersonalising and risk-laden enterprise, with many young people receiving such sentences having a history of:

- suffering from poverty, family conflict
- being looked after by local authorities
- drug and alcohol misuse
- mental disorder and distress
- ill-health; emotional, physical and sexual abuse
- self-harm and suicide
- homelessness
- isolation
- educational, skill, training and unemployment disadvantage, and they are often profoundly vulnerable.

(Goldson, 2002)

race hate and bullying.[5] These factors have contributed to murders and many suicides of young people and exacerbated drug and mental health problems. Prison-based institutions have failed to deal with educational disadvantage and social inclusion, as the smaller custodial residential institutions based upon welfare and treatment models in Scandinavian countries can do. Where custody is so required, this should be in small units, with psychiatric/psychological/social work input, and near to their families and communities. A particular feature of these services should be mental health services in secure units, owing to the high levels of abuse and suicide. Social workers need to be at the forefront of arguing for such provision for individual young people, and on a policy level.

One key issue in relation to the rights of such young people relates to proper screening by professionals prior to and/or entry into the custodial institution, regular

The extensive and serious criticisms of the welfare of young people in prison-department custody can be argued to run contrary to young people's human rights under Article 3 of the European Convention on Human Rights, which provides that no one shall be subject to inhuman or degrading treatment. The bullying, intimidation and high number of incidents of abuse – physical violence and racist, for example – self-harm and suicide also can be argued to contravene several articles of the United Nations Convention on the Rights of the Child (UNCRC), including: Article 3 – '*it shall be the duty of governments to consider the best interests of a child*'; Article 19 – '*the right of children to protection from all forms of violence, abuse and neglect*'; and Article 24, that provides for the highest attainable standards of health for children and young people, which also includes mental health and emotional health. Until 2006, Children's Safeguarding procedures (HM Government, 2006), intended to protect children and young people from abuse as required under

---

[5] As acknowledged by a number of recent reports from the England and Wales Government's Prison Inspectorate.

legislation, were held by government not to apply to such young people in custody, until a challenge in the courts from a pressure group led to a change in policy on this (Howard League, 2002: www.howardleague.org/legalachievements00/).

Social workers have a duty to be aware of the psychosocial and structural issues which can affect young people in custody, and use their interpersonal skills to allow them to talk about their fears and concerns, to see beyond the bravado many feel they must demonstrate while often feeling vulnerable and scared underneath. They should help them think about the options concerning complaints procedures, safeguarding procedures, and to help support them to make use of them, and/or advocate with their agreement from an awareness of the risk of young people self-harming or committing suicide, and means to deal with such issues. This includes situations where there might be issues of abuse and where children and young people may be deemed 'vulnerable' (as defined by the National Standards for Youth Justice), and need safeguarding, including from bullying towards a young person in custody (HM Government, 2006, paras. 2.112–2.117; see also, Hill et al., 2006).

In addition, social workers have a duty to advise police and courts on disposals which meet the needs of the young person without, if at all possible, making use of custody. From this understanding, they need to gain the young person's trust to discuss post-release planning, and support, particularly concerning social and family contacts, education, training and employment, and the other areas highlighted above.

Case study

John

Assume that John has received a custodial sentence for eight months. In your first visit as his social worker to him, he appears distracted, and unable to concentrate on his discussions with you. He appears very 'flat', and cannot think (or is avoiding) engaging with you in your discussions about his contact with his family, how he is relating to the prison staff and other young people detained in the institution with him. He does not seem concerned about anything very much at all, and is distracted and listless.

What further strategies would you use to find out more about any problems John may be suffering? With whom?

What skills and methods are key in working with John to enable him to trust you in your role, given the points we have covered in this section? How would you agree with John/reassure him about any actions in relation to any vulnerability/concerns you may uncover with him?

From your knowledge of problems that young people might suffer while in custody, what types of problems do you think John might be experiencing at this point, and what actions might you take to try to deal with these?

What additional areas would you need to consider in your work with John if he were from a BME group?

A closer look

Risk assessments in custodial establishments

Goldson (2002) notes how there has been an absence of systematic assessment of young offenders, a deficiency also acknowledged by the Youth Justice Board, which sees ASSET as an important tool in assessing the risks for young people on secure remand or serving custodial sentences. However, Goldson (2002: 72) points out that it is not used effectively in this respect.

This risk assessment needs to be carefully judged and the young person followed through the different elements of the custodial process, to ensure that relevant staff are all aware of any risks of harm identified and that these are managed properly. The risk assessment system does not work well within England and Wales at the point in the system where we know that young people are at greatest risk of self-harm, suicide, and abuse.

This is a particularly key area for social workers in light of their responsibilities under the Children Act 1989, and involves networking with other agencies, and sharing of information, emphasised in the Codes of Practice, and in the National Standards.

Leaving custody

The Youth Justice Board has clearly set out standards for support for young people while in custody for social workers to work to (YJB, 2004c).

Mental health needs of young people who offend

Mental health issues have been mentioned previously in this chapter as being important in consideration of many young people's needs. The Prison Reform Trust (2001) states that many young people with mental health problems are sent to prison owing to the inadequacy of existing support services for children and young people with mental health problems. It is estimated that 10 per cent of young people in custody have mental health problems. The Director of the Prison Reform Trust stated, 'Troubled children and young people need secure care and treatment, not punishment and neglect'. It stated that the Department of Health and the Home Office must act to respond to the largely unmet mental health needs of disturbed young people in Young Offenders' Institutions and transfer mentally disturbed young people from prison settings.

A Mental Health Foundation report, *The mental health needs of young people with emotional and behavioural difficulties: Bright futures: Working with vulnerable young people* (2002) found that young offenders in custody have three times the rate of mental health problems as their counterparts. As is argued in relation to suicide prevention, the report argues that systems of assessment of the troubled young people must be greatly improved to prevent so many from being present in the prison system. Social workers are well placed with their knowledge and skills of services for other client groups, particularly in relation to mental health social work and services. They have a responsibility to assess whether young people may have mental health problems, and to work with those young people to access – and advocate for – appropriate services for them. This is the case at any point in the youth justice process, including pre-prosecution as well as while the young person is on any form of community order, in custody, and post-release.

Ethnic and faith based sensitive work with young offenders

Children and young people from certain ethnic minority and faith communities continue to be disproportionately over-represented throughout the youth justice system. In the police and prison systems in the UK, official reports have determined that there are forms of discrimination which act against the rights and interests of young Black and Minority Ethnic (BME) groups (MacPherson, 1999; Keith, 2006; *The Guardian*, 2006). There is clear evidence from a number of research studies and official statistics that young people from Black and Minority Ethnic (BME groups), especially of African-Caribbean origin and mixed heritage, have different and worse experiences of the youth justice system from their white counterparts (Sender, Littlechild and Smith, 2006).

As discussed previously in this chapter, several sections of the Codes of Practice (1.6, 5.2 and 5.5) and BASW's Code of Ethics (2003) emphasise social workers' duties in this area, and Smith (2003: 120): states that: 'the evidence of overrepresentation of young black people each stage of the youth justice system . . .

produces an overall picture of progressively intensified discriminatory practices'. Section 95 the Criminal Justice Act 1991 includes a 'duty to avoid discrimination against any person on the grounds of race or sex or any other improper grounds'.

The MacPherson report concerning the murder of a young black man, Stephen Lawrence, found the police inquiry was hampered by their racist prejudices, leading them to doubt whether Stephen was the innocent victim that he was. The report concluded that the police were institutionally racist, and heavily criticised their investigation into his death. The report defined institutional racism as:

'the collective failure of an organisation to provide an appropriate and professional service to people because of their colour, culture, or ethnic origin. It can be seen or detected in processes, attitudes and behaviour which amount to discrimination through unwitting prejudice, ignorance, thoughtlessness and racist stereotyping which disadvantage minority ethnic people'.

(MacPherson, 1999, para. 6.34).

This has been found to be an issue not only for the police, but also in custodial settings. Goldson refers to 'endemic racism' in prisons (2002: 55) as noted by Her Majesty's Chief Inspector of Prisons (2001: 16).

The Youth Justice Board has also carried out a study examining the treatment of BME groups in the youth justice system, which found that young black men were considerably over-represented on the caseloads of the Youth Offending Teams studied, and similar problems were encountered for both males and females from mixed heritage backgrounds. The study also found that the YOTs failed to record ethnicity in ways which allowed effective ethnic monitoring to occur (Youth Justice Board, 2004b). The YJB has acknowledged that public authorities need to become more active in preventing discrimination, including monitoring the impact of policies and practice on race equality both internally and in relation to the services delivered (Youth Justice Board, 2004a). The Youth Justice Board's Race audit and action planning toolkit for Youth Offending Teams (YOTs) stated that BME 'children and young people continue to be disproportionately represented throughout the youth justice system. In some respects, the gap has increased in recent years' (YJB, 2004b: 4).

Social workers need to be aware of such issues, and to take these into account alongside an appreciation of how young BME groups might be experiencing the police and prison systems, and working to challenge any discriminatory behaviours and practices, by supporting complaints and ensuring that they are dealt with appropriately, while ensuring that the young person feels safe within such processes.

A study carried out by the University of Central England, Just Justice, on behalf of the Children's Society, explored young black people's experience of the youth justice system in various parts of England (Lovell, 2006). The report highlighted the experiences of racism that young people believed that they had suffered. These types of racism ranged from name-calling to physical attack. However, as noted in the Zahid Mubarek Report (Keith, 2006), where a young Asian man was murdered by his white racist cellmate, the inquiry found many experiences of lack of response from professionals, where racism from other professionals, young people and community members was known of, but ignored. These included race-hate graffiti in custodial settings and the police speaking differently to young black people than their white friends. Most young people affected were reluctant to use official complaints procedures either because they did not know about them, or because they did not trust them.

A study conducted by Wilson and Moore (2003) on the experiences of young black men in custody found that few people who had made a complaint regarding racism had experienced a positive response, or were aware of any resulting action. Social workers need to be part of finding ways – both personally in their relationships with young people and in structural ways – to make young people feel safer to make use of procedures, for them to make complaints against racist or faith based discrimination. One young person in a research study reported discrimination on the basis of being Moslem, not because of her ethnicity (Sender, Littlechild and Smith, 2006).

In addition to structural issues, and working within systems to try to ensure that unfair discrimination is dealt with as effectively as possible, social workers should acknowledge their own possible prejudices, using training opportunities, reflection, and supervision. They should ensure that these are addressed. There is evidence within the youth justice system, both from the USA and the UK, that individual workers' attributions and constructs concerning young people from minority ethnic groups affected their decision-making and assessments, which need to be recognised and dealt with by the individual practitioner for her/his own professional development, and for fair treatment of their clients (Sender, Littlechild and Smith, 2006).

The importance of professional judgement in such decision-making was first highlighted in England by Thorpe et al. (1980), who found that social workers judged young offenders according to what we would now term a 'deficit' model of family functioning, such that young people who had offended to a very minor extent were subjected to placement away from home far in excess of any disposal based on the seriousness of the offence. Given the evidence set out previously about the over-representation of young people from BME groups on the public care system, it can be surmised that such a deficit model is a key feature in decision-making processes for these groups, alongside prejudices about the perceived 'dangerousness' of such young people.

Think ahead

Based on the preceding discussion:

- Consider your own attitudes and possible prejudices to those from different ethnic groups and cultures. *How might this impact upon your approach to such young people and their families, and your assessment and decision-making in relation to how you present issues in pre-sentence reports?*
- *How can you ensure that you address these concerns in your day-to-day practice?*
- Consider how you can work within your agency to ensure that monitoring of issues such as ethnicity, and possibly gender, is properly implemented and reviewed in order to ensure that all action possible is being taken to ensure that no groups are discriminated against unfairly (a legal requirement under s.95 of the Criminal Justice Act 1991, and the Race Relations Amendment Act 2000 (see www.legislation.hmso.gov.uk/legislation/htm).

Case study

A young man from an ethnic minority group has been sentenced to custody; when you visit him in the Young Offender Institution, he informs you that he is being bullied, and subjected to racist abuse by other young people detained there.

How would you deal with this? How would you take it further within your own Youth Offending Team? What monitoring should you put in place?

Conclusion

This chapter has examined the historical and contemporary framework of policy and legislation which frames the work of Youth Offending Teams, which are now the main means of delivery of services to young people who offend. It has drawn out the particular features of a system which contains within it a variety of identifiable perspectives on the causes of youth offending, and the appropriate means to deal with the problems which the young people themselves face, and problems which they may present to others. This dual role of social work within work with young offenders is examined in light of a consideration of the values, ethics, skills and methods which are fundamental to practice. We have sought to demonstrate how key elements of the social worker's role might best be approached in the multi-agency settings which are now the norm within the field of youth justice.

Key learning points

This chapter has covered the following learning points:

- ✔ The development of key areas of social policy and legislation relevant to social work within the youth justice system from historical and contemporary perspectives.
- ✔ The ways in which the GSCC Codes of Practice can be applied in social work with young offenders.
- ✔ The social work role within multi-agency and multi-professional environments.
- ✔ The methods and programmes which social workers utilise in this area of work.
- ✔ Specific knowledge sets – for example, acting in the role of the Appropriate Adult, the preparation of pre-sentence reports, custody and post-release, and the mental health needs of young offenders.

Further reading

Arthur, R. (2010) *Young Offenders and the Law: How the Law Responds to Youth Offending.* This book concentrates on youth offending as a legal problem, while also discussing a blend of issues related to law, policy and practice. It examines to what extent the law protects and promotes the rights of young people in conflict with the law.

Bateman, T. and Pitts, J. (2005) *The Russell House Companion to Youth Justice*. Lyme Regis: Russell House. A thorough and wide-ranging account of the different elements of the youth justice system, with an emphasis on understanding different approaches to intervention and direct practice.

Case, S. and Haines, K. (2009) *Understanding Youth Offending: Risk Factor Research, Policy and Practice*. Cullompton: Willan. This is a book written by two very experienced academics and researchers in this field, providing a comprehensive account and analysis of one of the key areas in social work practice in working with young people.

Muncie, J. and Goldson, B. (eds) (2006) *Comparative Youth Justice*. London: Sage. With its companion volume, *Youth Crime and Justice*, this offers a thorough up-to-date review of international developments in youth justice practices. Importantly, it helps to demonstrate that different models are both imaginable and feasible.

Smith, R. (2007) *Youth Justice: Ideas, Policy, Practice*. Cullompton: Willan. A comprehensive analysis of the reformed youth justice system, providing a critical assessment of its achievements, and suggesting some alternative and more progressive models of intervention.

Youth Justice. This journal provides up-to-date articles on a wide variety of issues in the youth offending arena, covering law, policy and practice.

Useful websites

www.youth-justice-board.gov.uk
The most comprehensive source of information and practice guidance available, although it does tend to make excessive claims for the efficacy of its own policies and initiatives. NB: Subject to change with the board's abolition.

www.childrenssociety.org.uk
Independent site hosted by a national voluntary organisation which has been an innovator in practice, and reliable critical commentator on current policy and practice developments.

www.nacro.org.uk
A good source of current policy analysis, and advice on the practice implications of legislative changes.

Key organisations

www.childrenslegalcentre.com
Children's Legal Centre: the website provides valuable information concerning children in trouble with the law, but also in relation to all aspects of young people's legal rights in relation to services given to them across areas of social care, education, etc.

www.howardleague.org
The Howard League: An organisation which provides information about, and lobbying on behalf of, offenders of all ages, including young offenders. It took an important initiative in recent years to make legal challenges to issues of child protection of young people within custodial institutions, which eventually led to changes to include young people in custody to make them subject to such procedures.

www.dfes.gov.uk/aboutus
Department for Education and Skills: provides governmental policy and guidance on all areas relevant to the well-being of children and young people, including young people who offend: for example, *Every Child Matters*, which has its own important website.

www.dh.gov.uk
Department of Health: responsible for mental health issues for young people and other health issues for young people.

www.ncb.org.uk
National Children's Bureau: provides publications and information about young people, particularly in relation to looked-after children. Such children go on to make up something like 25 per cent of the population in custody.

www.justice.gov.uk
Department for Justice: since 2007, the government department responsible for all issues of the criminal justice system relating to orders of the court, custody, etc.

www.yjb.gov.uk
Youth Justice Board: government sponsored quango working to the Department for Justice, which provides the National Standards for work in the Youth Offending Teams.

For additional cases and topic-organised, clickable links into additional media resources, including those produced by IRISS, visit **www.pearsoned.co.uk/wilsonruch**

Activity

Activity One

Using available sources, such as the Prison Reform Trust and Howard League websites, as well as 'official' government sites, can you identify key characteristics of the young offender population. And, can you say why this information is important for social work practitioners?

Activity Two

When it came into office in 2010, the government began to talk about a 'rehabilitation revolution'. In light of this, and reflecting on this chapter, what do you think should be the relationship between justice, welfare and rights when working with young people who are 'at risk' of getting involved in crime?

Chapter 19
Social work with disabled children and adults

Rachael Clawson

Chapter summary

This chapter will discuss a number of key aspects of social work with disabled adults and children. There will be particular focus on both our own understanding of disability and its political nature and how this impacts on policy and practice. You will learn about some of the issues facing you as social workers working with disabled adults and children. It would not be possible to outline all theories, models and practice issues relating to both adults and children in one chapter but you will be provided with a basic knowledge which you can then build upon by reading the suggested additional material or referring to the websites listed. The chapter begins by considering where our views of disability and impairment come from and what our understanding of both terms are. How we think about, speak about and view disability has a big impact on the way in which legislation and policies are shaped; it also impacts on the way we work as social workers with disabled adults and children. Next the concept of disability being socially constructed will be considered and the chapter will then move on to outline different 'models' and definitions of disability and will explain how these impact on social work practice. The legislative framework for working with children and adults will then be outlined with particular reference made to current changes in the way services will be delivered in future. Finally, the chapter will finish by looking at some of the practice issues and dilemmas that social workers might encounter in practice with disabled adults and children.

Learning objectives

This chapter covers topics that will enable you to achieve the following learning objectives:

■ To understand where your own views of disability come from and how these might impact on your work

■ To understand the meaning of the social construction of disability and how this impacts on policy and social work practice

■ To understand the different models of disability and their impact on social work policy and practice

■ To understand the legislative framework for working with disabled adults and children

■ To understand some of the social work practice issues and dilemmas in working with disabled people.

National Occupational Standards

This chapter will help you to meet the following National Occupational Standards:

Key Role 1: Prepare for, and work with individuals, families, carers, groups and communities to assess their needs and circumstances

Unit 1   Prepare for social work contact and involvement
Unit 2   Work with individuals, families, carers, groups and communities to help them make informed decisions
Unit 3   Assess needs and options to recommend a course of action

Key Role 2: Plan, carry out, review and evaluate social work practice, with individuals, families, carers, groups, communities and other professionals

Unit 5   Interact with individuals, families, carers, groups and communities to achieve change and development and to improve life opportunities
Unit 6   Prepare, produce, implement and evaluate plans with individuals, families, carers, groups, communities and professional colleagues
Unit 7   Support the development of networks to meet assessed needs and planned outcomes
Unit 9   Address behaviour which presents a risk to individuals, families, carers, groups and communities

Key Role 3: Support individuals to represent their needs, views and circumstances

Unit 10   Advocate with, and on behalf of, individuals, families, carers, groups and communities

Key Role 6: Demonstrate professional competence in social work practice

Unit 18   Research, analyse, evaluate, and use current knowledge of best social work practice
Unit 19   Work within agreed standards of social work practice and ensure own professional development
Unit 20   Manage complex ethical issues, dilemmas and conflicts
Unit 21   Contribute to the promotion of best social work practice

Case study

Ben

Ben is 12 years old; he lives at home with his mum and dad, his twin brother Tom and younger brother Charlie who is 3. Ben has autism; he has a communication impairment and a learning disability. He is able to communicate his needs to those who know him well but can easily become very frustrated with people who don't know him or understand him. Ben is able to read some words and uses symbols. Charlie is also thought to have autism and is currently being assessed: he is behaving in a similar way to Ben at the same age and also gets very frustrated with other people. Tom is not disabled; he sometimes feels left out as his mum and dad focus their attention on Ben and Charlie. He has to share a bedroom with Ben, which neither of them likes. Ben and his brothers often don't get on very well and the situation at home can become stressful.

(*Source*: Photofusion Picture Library/ Paul Doyle)

Until he was 9, Ben attended a local mainstream primary school with Tom. However, the school felt increasingly that they could not meet his needs so he moved to a special school which is 10 miles away from home. Ben was really unhappy about this and wanted to stay at school with his brother and friends. He demonstrated his unhappiness through his behaviour which his parents found difficult to manage.

Ben's parents have recently referred him to social care services requesting support for him to access social opportunities.

What do you think are the issues for Ben and his family? Can social care services play a role in supporting them?

You might have considered that both Ben and his parents have their own needs, as indeed do Charlie (as a child who possibly has autism) and Tom as the sibling of a disabled child. Ben and his family could be supported by social care services to meet their needs. Ben has a right to an assessment of his needs by a social worker, as do his parents as carers.

To enable you to link what you will be reading throughout the chapter to social work policy and practice, we will be using Ben and other case studies to provide examples of practice and opportunities for you to reflect on or think about particular issues.

Think ahead

To get you started in your thinking, write your own definition of disability. Revisit this definition when you have read the chapter and then consider whether you would or would not change what you have written down.

Introduction

To be prepared for and effective in your work with disabled adults and children you need to have an understanding of disability and be prepared to question your own views and assumptions. On the surface this may seem like an obvious point: however, the politics of disability can be complex and contentious, as can the many different views you will come across in your work.

The academic writer Sally French makes the point that 'Most people have a rather simplistic and superficial understanding of disability' (1994: 8). Many people are employed in the statutory, voluntary and private sectors to devise policies and services, assess need and provide care and support. It could follow then that many of those employed in 'disability services', including social work, may also have a simplistic and superficial understanding of disability and the issues facing the very people they are employed to work with. The reasons for this will vary but could include a lack of interest or knowledge in relation to disability issues and politics or a lack of experience in professional or personal terms of disability. One of the ways in which you can begin to address this situation as a social worker is to question your own views and assumptions and understand how these and your knowledge can impact upon your practice.

Different forms of social work practice derive from particular ways of seeing people. On a very simple level,

the way in which you see things will influence the way in which you practise as a social worker with disabled adults and children. The effects of your practice, however, can be far-reaching and should not be underestimated.

The way you were bought up, where you lived and went to school, the way you socialise and where you work will all impact on the way you think about impairment and disability. For example, if you were bought up in a family where no member had an impairment and had no friends with impairments or you went to mainstream school with few or no disabled pupils, it is likely that the thought of disability did not cross your mind as you were growing up. You may, on the other hand, have personal experience of disability yourself or with a family member or friend and so have a different perspective. Whatever your experience, it will impact on your thinking about disability and how you perceive disabled people.

Reflect

Thinking back to the case study at the start of the chapter, write down three words or short phrases that you feel sum up the experience of being disabled for Ben.

How might what you have written impact on your practice as a social worker with him?

You might have used words or phrases such as *frustrated*, *lonely*, *unable to communicate* or *unhappy*, or alternatively you may have written more positive phrases. Whatever you did write will illustrate your thoughts and these will impact on your practice, for example in terms of how you assess Ben's strengths and needs and any support services required. We will now move on to look at how our understanding of disability can be described as socially constructed.

Disability as a social construct

How do we as members of society build and make sense of the world we live in? Where do we get our understanding of disability from and how is it perpetuated? What impact does this have on us as social workers? In answer to these questions, social constructionists would argue that people in any given society construct knowledge between them: the way of understanding the world comes not from objective reality but from other people. For further discussion of this concept, please see Chapter 6; Social work knowledge and practice. One general example of a social construct might be the use of the colour red as a sign of danger: the colour in itself is not dangerous but in our society we as individuals have a common shared understanding that, for example, a red flag on beach means it is dangerous to swim. This concept can also be seen to have a direct impact on the way we communicate and think about disability and disabled people: our views of ourselves and others are shaped and constructed through what we have learned socially; the way we view the world is culturally and historically specific (Burr, 1995).

It has been argued by many disabled academics (e.g. M. Oliver, C. Barnes, S. French, J. Morris, L. Crow) that 'disability' can be seen as a social construct rather than something which is an inherent fact. A distinction is made by the Disabled Peoples Movement between the terms 'impairment' and 'disability' based on the definition put forward by the Union of Physically Impaired Against Segregation in 1976:

- Impairment – lacking all or part of a limb, or having a defective limb, organ or mechanism of the body
- Disability – the disadvantage or restriction of activity caused by a contemporary social organisation which takes no or little account of people who have physical impairments and thus excludes them from the mainstream of social activities.　　　　　(UPIAS, 1976)

Crow states, 'Impairment is about our bodies' ways of working and any implications these hold for our lives. Disability is about the reaction and impact of the outside world on our particular bodies' (1996: 218).

Disability is constructed by the way society is shaped rather than it being an inherent physical state. This line of thought means disability is not about the individuals' impairment, rather it is about social oppression and discrimination. Society disables people through the barriers in place to their obtaining full citizenship rights (for example barriers to education, employment, housing, social life, physical environment, etc.).

The language we use also plays a key role in these social processes and directly impacts on disabled people. Social workers have a responsibility to construct a positive image of disabled people through the use of accurate language; Barnes et al. state, 'there is little doubt that if impairment is defined in negative terms this reinforces disparaging attitudes towards disabled people' (2005: 6).

We will now move on to consider the question of language in more detail.

What's in a name?

The issue of language has been hugely important in thinking about ways to address the discrimination and oppression of disabled people. Neil Thompson, a social work academic, writer and former practitioner states, 'The language we use either reinforces discrimination through constructing it as normal or contributes in some small way at least to undermining the continuance of a discriminatory discourse' (2007: 39). The debate on language is ongoing, for example, in changing terms used to describe people who are in receipt of welfare services from 'clients' to 'service users' or 'customers' and more recently in the move to discuss 'safeguarding' children rather than 'child protection'. In terms of disability, using 'person first' terminology has been one cause for debate. Some disabled adults endorse person first terminology (e.g. people with disabilities) stating that the person comes before the disability (Datillo and Smith, 1990; Kailes, 1985; Millington and Leierer, 1996). Others argue that a person's disability is part of their identity in much the same way as their ethnicity or gender is. Many disabled writers (e.g. M. Oliver, V. Finkelstein, J. Morris, S. French) advocate use of the term 'disabled people', as disability is not a secondary feature of their identity.

Reflect

A number of local authorities have changed the names of teams working with disabled children from 'Children with Disabilities Team' to 'Disabled Children's Team' to reflect the thinking described above. The change, however, has attracted mixed reactions from staff and parents, some of whom prefer the 'child first' approach.

Why do you think this is? Why might it be important?

Many staff and parents still prefer a 'child first' approach to the language used as they believe it is demeaning not to see the child first and foremost and that the child should not be labelled disabled, although as we have seen above many disabled writers would argue to the contrary and say that impairment is part of a person's identity. We will now move on to consider the impact labelling can have on disabled people.

Labels

Labels are often attached to disabled people; the term 'disabled person' is a label in itself, constructing specific images in the mind of the person who is labelling and the person being labelled. The term 'handicapped' is argued by some to have historical associations of being 'cap in hand' and begging (Barnes, 1991; Kailes, 1985). Labelling theory states that by referring to an individual by means of a specific word or term (e.g. 'handicapped' or 'victim') their identity is constructed as such and their place in the world defined by the label; the labelled person can then also expect certain responses from others and behave in such a way to get that response. By the same logic then, there is a belief that naming a person differently could have a different impact. Some people argue that language simply works like a mirror to reflect a true meaning that already exists, so using words such as 'handicapped' or 'invalid' simply reflects or communicates the person's position as being someone with an impairment. However, if you consider, as social constructionists do, that language actually moulds meaning rather than simply reflecting it, the word 'handicapped' or 'invalid' can be used to construct a meaning about the person; it is not neutral and carries value judgements with it. Things do not just 'mean': we as individuals construct the meaning. This could have implications for the way disabled people perceive themselves and are perceived by others in social work practice and policy.

Case study

Sophie

Sophie is 31 years old; she lives in an independent annex to her parent's house, has cerebral palsy and is deaf. Sophie communicates using a mixture of lip-reading and some British Sign Language signs and uses a wheelchair.

When she was younger Sophie attended a residential school for deaf children and came home in the holidays. It was always her wish to return to live at home when she had finished school and college. Her parents are supportive of her but Sophie is clear that she doesn't want them involved in her day-to-day support or care; she feels this is her own business. Sophie requires support with getting up, personal care and preparing and eating meals. Sophie is not working at the moment but would like to; she has very few social contacts outside of home.

What impact might labels have on Sophie? The label 'spastic' (the historical term for cerebral palsy) has

negative connotations and may lead people to assume that Sophie cannot have any control over her life or make her own decisions. Those people will then treat her as if this is true and Sophie herself may begin to think it is true. If the label is removed and Sophie is seen as an individual person with rights, this situation will change. However, this is not the same as saying that, if labels and language changed, discrimination would simply disappear or attitudes would change.

Reflect

'The person you are, your experience, your identity, your "personality" are all the effects of language' (Burr, 1995: 39).

You are a social work student on placement in a disabled children's team. You hear a colleague discussing Ben from the case study at the start of the chapter using derogatory language.

What do you do? What impact might your colleague's behaviour and views have on their work with Ben and his family?

As a social work student you may or may not feel in a position to raise any concerns with your colleague: you might instead want to discuss your views in supervision. Your views might include concerns about assumptions being made about Ben's abilities and needs or perhaps discriminatory or oppressive practice.

Definitions and models of disability

Definitions play a powerful role both in the construction of disability and in the way in which disabled people are perceived by wider society and professionals. French points out that 'It is very important to explore the ways in which disability is defined, as well as who defines it, for attitudes and behaviour towards disabled people, professional practice and the running of institutions . . . are based, at least in part, on those definitions' (1994: 3).

Reflect

Think back to the definition you wrote at the start of the chapter. Do you think what you wrote would have any impact on the things mentioned by French?

One of the difficulties posed to social workers is that there is actually no simple way to define disability: it can be viewed from many different perspectives. Thinking back to the first exercise in this chapter, if you were to discuss what you had written down with a friend or family member, their definition would probably differ from yours, depending on their experience and understanding of disability.

A wide range of models of disability have been put forward by different individuals and groups: for example, policy makers, the medical profession, charities and disabled people themselves. Again, each model differs depending on the understanding of disability underpinning it. Historically, the models that have tended to dominate are those put forward by the most powerful groups in society, such as the government and the medical profession, rather than disabled people themselves (French, 1994). Since the 1960s, disabled people have been campaigning for the right to define their own situations, determine their own needs and how these should be met by social welfare and medical practice. As noted previously, the Disabled Peoples Movement makes a distinction between 'disability' and 'impairment'.

Models of disability help us understand the context in which disability is viewed by different groups and individuals in society. The most commonly known models are the social model and the individual model (sometimes called the medical model) of disability and many people on a very basic level draw the conclusion that the social model is 'good' as it looks to break down the barriers in society and the individual/medical model is not, as it has its basis in 'curing' the person or viewing disability as a personal tragedy. However, the debates relating to the models are complex and, as social workers, it is crucial to have an understanding of the issues, as elements of all models will impact upon your own thinking and practice.

Individual model of disability

This model stems from the view that the difficulties disabled people face are a direct consequence of their impairment. For example, this model would see the difficulties Sophie in the case study might face on public transport or accessing public buildings or in communicating with people as a result of her having cerebral palsy and using a wheelchair or being deaf, rather than as a result of transport or buildings being inaccessible for wheelchair users or BSL not being used by many people. The model has its basis in the view that disability is a

personal tragedy and it is up to health and welfare services to help the disabled person overcome the tragedy caused by physical, sensory or intellectual impairment and 'fit into' mainstream society by providing rehabilitation or services to help disabled people cope with their disability.

Many disabled academics (e.g. M. Oliver, C. Barnes, V. Finkelstein, J. Morris, S. French) have argued that health and welfare services, including social work, are based on an individualistic model of disability. Oliver states, 'social policies in respect of disability have been influenced, albeit unknowingly, by the core ideology of individualism' (1990: 94). There has been criticism levelled at local authorities to say that social work with disabled people is a Cinderella service with little funding and little 'kudos' attached to it (Sapey and Hewitt, 1993; Oliver and Sapey, 2006).

The individual model is argued to be entrenched in society and focusing on body abnormality and functional incapacity, for example, the ability to wash, dress, use the toilet, etc. These 'incapacities' are then used as a basis to classify the person as invalid. The 'victim' is seen as in need of care and dependent upon help from the welfare state to live in society (or indeed out of it if living in an institution). Disabled people have argued that the individual model makes them dependent as they have to rely on professionals to provide therapeutic and social support (Barnes et al., 2005). For example, in relation to this model Sophie would be classified as a person in need of care and support because she needs help with dressing, feeding and washing, etc. as her needs make her dependent on welfare services for support to live at home. Sophie is seen as being someone who is 'done to' rather than being in control.

It can also be argued that viewing themselves in the same way that wider society views them may internally oppress disabled people as they behave and think in a way that is expected of them. For example, an adult living in a residential home may not feed or dress themselves even though they are physically able because they have always been used to someone else feeding or dressing them. We then have a self-fulfilling prophecy where society has 'proof' that the attitudes towards disabled people are correct and this in turn justifies the treatment they receive.

The individual model sees children as being particularly vulnerable to being socialised into accepting disability as an individual problem by their parents, whose views are shaped largely by professionals and wider society (French, 1994). So using Ben from the case study as an example, Ben's parents may have believed that he was not capable of attending mainstream school because this is what they were told by teachers, educational psychologists, etc. and Ben in turn would believe this himself; this sets a pattern for Ben's belief system about himself throughout his life. In addition to this, the individual model would say disabled children are taught to accept that medical appointments for physiotherapy etc. will take priority in their lives: for example, appointments often interrupt their school life and although they may be necessary they take precedence over a child's opportunity for learning. Oliver (1990) argues these points remain ignored as teachers do not have an understanding of the history and politics of disability and so do not challenge what is seen as the norm. It can be argued that tackling discrimination and prejudice needs to begin in schools, where children who are educated together learn about each other. However, it can also be argued that disabled children currently may not get the educational or social support they need in mainstream schools.

Reflect

As Ben's social worker how would you have worked with him in the transition between schools? Does special education contribute to the exclusion of disabled children from society? Does it empower them?

You might have felt it would have been appropriate to ask the school to consider whether any other forms of educational, emotional or behavioural support could have been put in place for Ben to enable him to stay at the school, or you might, on the other hand, believe a special school could offer him what he needs in a more consistent way. There are a number of perspectives in relation to special schools, with some people believing they contribute to disabled children being excluded from their own communities and peer groups, while others hold that because the children are not having to contend with other aspects of mainstream schools, such as bullying or being made to be the 'odd one out', they have the opportunity to flourish.

The individual model is often viewed by students and social welfare practitioners alike as being synonymous with the medical model of disability. The two are not the same: it is perhaps more helpful for social workers to think of the medical model as being one component that goes to make up the individual model which covers a range of individualistic perspectives. Other components include the philanthropic model which is characterised by charities portraying disabled people as sad, courageous and in need of care and protection: these images make money but also do a lot of harm as they perpetuate stereotypes (French, 1994; Oliver, 1990) and the language model which has already been outlined earlier on in the chapter.

The individual model sees the solution to disability to be in medical cure and rehabilitation, where the expert defines the disabled person's need and how to meet it, the object being to overcome and minimise disability: this is where the term 'medical model' fits in. Medical terminology has played a great part in pathologising disability. Finkelstein (1993) links the medicalisation of disability back to the nineteenth-century Poor Law, when it became necessary to separate the unemployed into the infirm and the indolent. This need for classification enabled doctors to secure a role in relation to the infirm and marked the beginning of classifying and interpreting disability in medical terms. The power to change things for disabled people is seen to lie in the hands of medical and allied professions, normalisation and science.

The medical model is heavily criticised by many disabled people, although one of the impacts of this has been that many people believe that disabled people think all medical intervention is wrong or that people wanting intervention (for example, for a cochlear ear implant) are experiencing a false consciousness which tells them they want to be 'normal'. However, more recently some disabled writers have clarified the issue – medical intervention is not always wrong, what is wrong is the imbalance of power and control medical professionals have over the lives of disabled people:

'Disabled people define their situation not in terms of individual impairment but in terms of social oppression. By doing so they are not implying that medical intervention is wrong, or that it cannot be sensible, helpful or vital. What disabled people are demanding of professional workers is a broadening of their perspective on disability and a relinquishing of their power.'   (French, 1994: 15)

Social model of disability

The model of disability put forward by disabled people is the social model of disability. Mike Oliver, himself a disabled person, first coined this phrase in the early 1980s to help social work students he was teaching better understand the position of disabled people in society. The social model involves moving away from focusing on the individual's physical limitations to looking at the way physical and social environments create barriers to disabled people becoming full members of society and having all the benefits associated with this. Disabled people have long called for a self-definition of disability to be used rather than a definition made up from the views of non-disabled people.

Liz Crow, a writer and film producer/director who is herself disabled, states the social model helped her make sense of her own situation: 'I was being disabled – my capabilities and opportunities were being restricted – by prejudice, discrimination, inaccessible environments and inadequate support. Even more important, if all the problems had been created by society, then surely society could un-create them. Revolutionary!' (1996: 206). The social model sees the solution to disability as lying within the restructuring of society and removal of social, physical, environmental and institutional barriers. This would actually benefit all members of society, as no one would be excluded. So, for example, within this model, instead of the Education Departmart agreeing that Ben's needs could only be met in a special school, all main-stream schools would meet the needs of all children; there would not be barriers in place to prevent children being educated together. Within this model, assumptions would not be made about what people can or cannot do and welfare services would not be a uniform 'one style fits all': 'The message for social workers . . . is not to make assumptions about how different individuals might respond to similar situations but to work with people from their own perception of the reality of their lives' (Oliver and Sapey, 2006: 118).

The social model has, however, been criticised by some disabled people for not including the experiences of all disabled people. Disabled people are not one homogenous group; people have very different experiences, beliefs and views. If the model is imposed in such a way that it denies the experience of individuals it could be seen as oppressive (Morris, 1991, cited in Oliver and Sapey, 2006). Crow argues that the social model works well on a large scale in tackling discrimination and oppression but it lets disabled people down on a personal level as it does not have the capacity to represent all disabled people. There has also been a tendency to focus on disability and to play down the impact of impairment on the individual. Pain, fatigue, depression and chronic illness are facts of life for many people and these will still remain when disabling barriers no longer exist. Many will still not be in a position to participate fully in society because of pain etc., hence '[r]emoval of disability does not necessarily mean the removal of restricted opportunities' (Crow, 1996: 219). Silence about impairment has made it taboo

to discuss worries and fears, including seeking medical intervention. Many people do experience pain and may wish to seek treatment and perhaps see more resources going into funding research relating to pain relief or other forms of medical treatment. Tom Shakespeare, a disabled academic, argues there is a need for a new approach to understanding disability that rejects the current understanding of the social model and looks instead to something that neither reduces disability to an individual medical problem nor neglects body limita-tion and difference (Shakespeare 2006).

We will now move on to consider some of the differ-ing issues relating to working with people with physical disabilities, learning disabilities and sensory impairment.

Working with people with a physical disability, learning disability and/or a sensory impairment

Disabled people are not one homogeneous group; all people are unique with their own individual views, needs and wants. People may be born with an impairment or may acquire disability, for example, through illness or injury at any point throughout their lifetime. Acquired disability may involve having a physical disability, sensory impairment or a cognitive impairment. Some people have a 'hidden' impairment which is not obvious to others. People can have one or a combination of im-pairments (i.e. physical and learning disability/physical, learning and sensory impairment).

Each person will have their own identity which may or may not include an understanding or agreement about 'being disabled'. For example, many deaf people who use British Sign Language as a means of commun-ication do not consider themselves disabled, but instead view themselves as a linguistic minority.

It is important that social workers understand the individual's own perception of identity and how this has been formed and also how the impairment impacts upon the person; a lack of knowledge in this area could lead to assumptions wrongly being made. For example, Sophie has a physical and sensory disability, she does not have a learning disability – it may be easy for a social worker who does not know her to assume that her cognitive ability is also impaired and that she does not have the capacity to make certain decisions about her life. It may equally be possible for a social worker to assume that a person with a learning disability has more or less cognitive ability than they have. Issues relating to the ability or capacity to make decisions may arise in working with people who have a learning disability or communication impairment. Social workers need to avoid making assumptions about a person's capacity to make decisions for themselves and must also accept that people with capacity to understand a given situation can make 'unwise decisions', (for example, in deciding to smoke cigarettes or enter a relationship with someone whom might be considered an unsuitable person). The Mental Capacity Act 2005 provides a framework for assessing a person's capacity to make decisions; the Act relates to specific decisions at any given time rather than assessing whether or not a person has capacity per se. More information about the Act itself is provided later in this chapter in the legal and policy section while a discussion of its use is provided in Chapter 17 on social care policy for adults.

Following an assessment of need local authorities provide services to those with physical, sensory or learning disabilities who meet the eligibility criteria. Support can be provided to children and adults with physical disabilities to develop skills to become as independent as possible. A range of services can be provided: for example, aids and equipment to help with daily living tasks, supported accommodation, residential services, short breaks, housing adaptations, disabled parking badges, homecare, meals at home, occupational therapy, provision of day service opportunities/education, supported employment and information on welfare rights and support to parents, carers and siblings. Support is also given to people with learning disabilities to help make decisions relating to services, such as choosing where to live, education, employment, accessing community activities and support with daily living.

People with a hearing, sight or dual sensory impairment (combined hearing and sight loss) can be provided with equipment, rehabilitation support and advice and information and many local authorities also employ staff who are proficient in the use of British Sign Language. We will now move on to consider the policy and legislative framework underpinning the provision of services.

Legal and policy framework relating to children

This section of the chapter will address the legal and policy framework within which social work with disabled children and adults is undertaken. The provision of social welfare including social care services is governed by law which is made up of Acts of Parliament and Rules and Regulations. The framework relating to children will be addressed first.

The Children Act 1989

This Act sets out the underlying principle that disabled children should be seen as children first, and brought them into mainstream legislation for the first time. The Act has been criticised by some for being geared towards meeting the needs of non-disabled children: however, it was an important step forward in the recognition of disabled children's needs and represented a new approach to the provision of services. A number of recent policy and legislative initiatives designed to address the needs of all children: for example, the Assessment Framework, *Every Child Matters* and the *National Service Framework* have all included the needs of disabled children, specifically in their published material which also represents a commitment to bringing disabled children into the main arena of childcare policy.

Within the Children Act 1989 the local authority has two main responsibilities to all children. First, within section 17 it is the general duty of every local authority to safeguard and promote the welfare of children within their area who are 'in need' (s. 17(1)). Secondly, where a local authority is informed or has cause to suspect that a child is suffering harm or likely to suffer significant harm, section 47 of the Act places a duty to make enquiries necessary to decide whether they should take action to safeguard or promote the child's welfare.

Disabled children are deemed 'children in need' by virtue of having a disability (s. 17(10)(c)) and are therefore entitled to an assessment of need. The Act also contains specific provisions for disabled children, which includes requiring that the local authority:

- ensures accommodation for a looked-after disabled children is not unsuitable (s. 23(8)). This means, for example, that a foster home should be adequately equipped to meet the child's needs.
- opens and maintains a register of disabled children within their area (schedule 2, para. 2). The main aim of this requirement is to enable local authorities to know how many disabled children live in their area and plan properly for services needed. Registration is voluntary (parents decide whether they want their child's name to go on).
- provide services to minimise the effect of disability and to provide the opportunity to lead lives which are as normal as possible (schedule 2, para. 9).

Services provided to disabled children under the Children Act 1989 might include:

- short breaks (respite care)
- holiday play schemes
- care at home – for example, help with personal care, bathing, feeding, etc.
- some aids and adaptations
- a befriender.

The Act also provides under schedule 2 para. 5 that a local authority can assess a child's needs for the purpose of the Children Act at the same time as any other assessment under certain other Acts: for example, the Education Act 1981, the Disabled Person's Act 1986 and the Chronically Sick and Disabled Person's Act 1970. These situations might occur, for example, if a young person under 18 was in the transition process (the process of being transferred from children to adult services); the 1986 Act requires that social services assess the needs of young disabled people at the time they leave school for services they may need as an adult. In Scotland, section 23 of the Children (Scotland) Act closely mirrors the preceding provisions.

As a social worker working with children, including disabled children, you need to have a good understanding of this legislation as it underpins most of the work you would undertake.

Framework for the Assessment of Children in Need and their Families 2000

The Assessment Framework is designed to be inclusive of all children in need and to provide a framework for multi-agency assessment. A more in-depth focus of the Assessment Framework is included in Chapter 16 on working with children and families. In the past many standard assessment frameworks were developed with only non-disabled children in mind, with disabled children needing to 'fit in'. The Framework was developed as a multi-agency assessment tool, meaning there should be one comprehensive assessment of a child that incorporates the views of all agencies working with the child. However, in practice, the extent to which the Framework is used to aid multi-agency assessment is not clear, and many disabled children continue to undergo a variety of assessments from different professionals and agencies in order to ensure that a holistic view of their needs is obtained.

The Assessment Practice Guidance for practitioners, issued as an aid to completing the assessment, contains a specific chapter on assessing the needs of disabled children and their families. It gives a clear foundation and practical advice for assessing the needs of disabled children, including their need to be safeguarded from harm. Possible indicators of abuse or significant harm of disabled children may be difficult to separate out from the effects of their impairment, particularly if the child has multiple impairments (Westcott, 1994). A multidisciplinary approach to assessment, which avoids assumptions about the child and involves all the professionals and carers (if appropriate) who know the child best, is essential if disabled children are to be adequately safeguarded.

As a social worker working with disabled children you need to familiarise yourself with the chapter discussed above in order to ensure your assessments are holistic, child-centred and focused on strengths as well as needs.

Carers and Disabled Children Act 2000

In 1999 The Carers National Strategy document *Caring about Carers* was published and highlighted the need for legislation to enable local authorities to provide services directly to carers. Assessment of carers' needs could be made under the 1995 Carers and Recognition Act but this was of the carer's ability to provide and sustain the care being provided, and local authorities did not have to offer services to support carers in their caring role. The 2000 Act changed this, giving local authorities the power to provide certain services to carers. The Act also empowered local authorities to make direct payments to carers, to people with parental responsibility for disabled children and to 16- and 17-year-old disabled children for services that meet their assessed needs. The provision of payments to parents of disabled children and disabled 16- and 17-year-olds enables them to have more choice over how, when and by whom services are delivered. For instance, payments can be used to employ a befriender to accompany the child or young person to social or recreational activities or to purchase personal care support at home. An example of how this can work in practice might be supporting Ben to go to the local youth club. He wants to go to the youth club with his brother and friends; he needs support to do this but does not want to go with his mum. The social worker assesses his need for social activities and identifies the need for a befriender to accompany him. Ben and his parents identify a friend of the family whom they all know well to take on this role and employ him using direct payments.

The equivalent legislation that applies in Scotland is the Community Care and Health (Scotland) Act 2002.

For social workers working with disabled children and their families the introduction of direct payments led to a key shift in the thinking of how services are, or can be, provided. Care packages can be put together in a much more creative way, sometimes using people familiar to the child.

Every Child Matters 2004 and the Children Act 2004 (England and Wales)

Every Child Matters is the Green Paper produced following the Laming Inquiry into Victoria Climbié's death. It sets out an agenda for proposed changes in reshaping English and Welsh services to all children. The agenda is discussed in more depth in Chapter 16. The Green Paper was given legal force in the Children Act 2004. The duties and functions of English and Welsh Local Authorities arising from the Children Act 1989 remain unchanged but the way services are delivered will change as they become integrated around the child and family. Listening to and involving children are at the heart of the way services are to be delivered and the focus is very much on local change (DoH, 2004). The challenge will be how disabled children are included in this process. As social workers, good practice would include ensuring disabled children's views are obtained and included. The Children Act 2004 also places a duty on local authorities to obtain the wishes and feelings of all children who may have an assessment or provision of services under s. 17 of the 1989 Children Act, or be subject to child protection inquiries under s. 47 as far as is reasonably practicable and consistent with the child's welfare.

National Service Framework for Children, Young People and Maternity Services 2004

The Children Act 2004 gives a clear focus for changes to the way in which children's services will be delivered, but in itself is not enough to implement the changes needed at a local level. *The National Service Framework (NSF) for Children, Young People and Maternity Services* 2004 is a 10-year programme which sets out standards for the planning, commissioning and delivery of children's services in England and Wales. It aims to ensure high-quality and integrated health and social care and will play a key role in helping children to achieve the five outcomes outlined in *Every Child Matters*.

The NSF is set out in three parts and has eleven standards. Part one has five standards which apply to all children, part two has five standards which apply specifically to children and young people with specific needs arising from health or impairment and part three has one standard which addresses the needs of women and babies throughout pregnancy and the first three months of parenthood (DoH, 2004). Arguably, it builds a framework from which disabled children can clearly benefit and in which there will be a framework for their views to be heard.

(The standards can be found in the *Every Child Matters*: Change for Children Executive Summary produced by the Department for Education and Skills and the Department of Health in the *National Service Framework for Children, Young People and Maternity Services 2004* or accessed via: www.everychildmatters.gov.uk.)

One example of a standard relating specifically to disabled children is standard 8 which is:

'Children and young people who are disabled or who have complex health needs, receive co-ordinated, high quality child and family-centred services which are based on assessed needs, which promote social inclusion and, where possible, enable them and their families to live ordinary lives.'

For you as social workers this standard sets out clear expectations for how services should be assessed for and provided. For example, services should promote social inclusion; there is a need for an integrated diagnosis and assessment process, for early intervention and support to parents and for multi-agency planning.

Reflect

As a social worker working with disabled children, what would your priority be in meeting the child's needs?

In answering the above question you might have considered what the term 'ordinary lives' (see standard 8) means and thought about issues including how to best assess the needs of the child and who might be included in this process (for example, occupational therapist, physiotherapist, educational psychologist, clinical psychologist, paediatrician, specialist teachers, early years workers, etc.). You might also have thought about how you would go about planning resources to meet the child's needs and how you could work in conjunction with other professionals to provide a holistic service to meet the whole family's needs.

Early Support Programme

This programme was set up in 2004 to achieve better coordinated, family-focused services for young disabled children and their families in England and Wales. It also fits in with changes to the way children's services are to be delivered as set out in *Every Child Matters* and the *National Service Framework*. The programme focuses on children aged 0–3 years and brings together the different services available to disabled children. It aims to build on existing good practice of all those involved in working with disabled children and improve multidisciplinary working.

The Early Support programme has also developed a range of materials for professionals and families to use, including a family file to keep all relevant information together; this also provides information to all professionals who work with the child and prevents the parents having to repeat their child's story time and again. The programme provides a range of information to parents including specific booklets on:

- sensory impairments
- autism
- rare conditions
- speech and language difficulties.

Through the programme a keyworker is appointed to work with the child and family and act as a liaison point between the family and professionals involved. The programme is accessed through social care services. Further information relating to the programme can be accessed via: www.earlysupport.org.uk.

As you can see, the legislative and policy framework for working with disabled children is complex and varied. The new policies all have a common theme in that the child should be at the centre of assessing and planning for services and a holistic, multi-agency approach is needed which listens to and takes account of children's views. As social workers you will need to have a sound understanding of legislation and policy in order to perform your role and duties. This section has provided you with a basic outline and we suggest that you also refer to Chapter 8 on legislation and undertake further reading and research using the books and websites listed at the end of the chapter.

Children and Young Persons Act 2008

In 2007 the Government published a White Paper *Care Matters: Time for Change* which set out plans to improve outcomes for children looked after by the local authority and care leavers. The 2008 Act implemented proposals from the White Paper, its purpose being to reform the statutory framework for the care system in England and Wales. The Act covers a range of issues which includes

short breaks for disabled children. Disabled children and their families very often say that regular and reliable short breaks from caring are what they most benefit from. S. 25 of the Act imposes a duty on local authorities to provide short breaks to assist parents/carers to enable them to continue caring for a disabled child or to do so more effectively. The Act states that short breaks should not only be provided to those struggling to care for their disabled child but also to parents/carers for whom a break from caring would improve the quality of the care they are able to provide.

Safeguarding Disabled Children Practice Guidance 2009

This practice guidance makes it absolutely clear that disabled children have the same human rights to be protected from harm as their non-disabled peers. The document provides practice guidance to Local Safeguarding Children Boards and to professionals. It documents why disabled children are both more vulnerable to being abused and less likely to be protected from harm than non-disabled children. The practice guidance also contains useful information relating to research on the abuse of disabled children. The issue of safeguarding disabled children is discussed in detail in the section on p. 585.

A closer look

More vunerable to abuse

Research demonstrates that disabled children are both more vulnerable to abuse and less likely to be protected from harm than non-disabled children (Sullivan and Knutson 2000, Cooke and Standen 2002, NSPCC 2003). There are a wide range of reasons for this which are outlined more fully in the section on safeguarding disabled children further on in this chapter.

Signs and symptoms of abuse of disabled children are sometimes masked by their disability, that is to say behaviours or injuries are attributed to their disability rather than a broader view being taken on a range of possibilities for the injury or behaviour. Sometimes injuries are missed or wrongly thought to be a result of the impairment – an example of this could be a broken bone in a child who has frail bones and is not independently mobile; the fracture may or may not be a result of having frail bones so it is crucial to have an open mind.

Another example may be of a young person exhibiting 'challenging behaviour' – they may actually be demonstrating emotional distress.

We can learn from the findings of Serious Care Reviews which are held when a child dies or is seriously injured and neglect or abuse is suspected. The findings and recommendations from a 2010 serious case review into the death of an 8-year-old child with a learning disability who had been neglected by her parents highlight some of the complexities involved in recognising abuse and keeping disabled children safe. The review found:

- Many agencies tried to deliver a good service to improve the child's developmental progress and maximise potential; however, services were not provided in such a way that safeguarding issues could be clearly identified.
- Agencies need to have an open mind as to the possible range of reasons for a particular behaviour and not just attribute behaviours to the child's disability.
- Professionals still do not always recognise signs and symptoms of abuse, particularly if the focus of their intervention is on supporting the child and family.
- Services should be coordinated to ensure agencies can work together and share information effectively.

The serious case review highlighted lessons to be learned, including:

- Disabled children have the right to receive a comprehensive, child-centred assessment of their needs to ensure safeguarding concerns are not masked by their support needs.
- The views and experiences of children must be central to any work undertaken; disabled children must be communicated with directly.
- Practitioners should be offered the opportunity to 'stand back' and reflect on what they are seeing; any 'mind set' about a particular case should be challenged.

Working Together to Safeguard Children 2010

Working Together is the document that sets out the government's expectations for how agencies – for example, social care services, health, education and voluntary organisations – and individuals in England and Wales should work together to safeguard children. The 2010 edition updates the 2006 edition, it provides a national framework within which agencies and professionals at a local level draw up and agree on their own ways of work-

ing together to safeguard and promote the welfare of children. The new guidance provides specific advice in relation to the abuse of disabled children, paying particular attention to recognising why disabled children are more vulnerable than their non-disabled peers and to listening to disabled children and finding ways of communicating with them; it also makes clear that safeguards for disabled children are essentially the same as for non-disabled children, (HM Government, 2010: 211–13). *Getting It Right For Every Child* (Scottish Executive, 2005b, section 3: 10) sets out the Scottish Parliament's expectations and guidance and *Changing Childhoods?: The Same As You?* is a set of policy statements that embed disability provision and practice within mainstream equality initiatives.

Social workers and other professionals working with children, for example, health visitors, teachers, physiotherapists, occupational therapists, etc. all need to have a good understanding of this document to aid the process of working together. As social workers you need to be clear about your own role and that of others in the safeguarding process in order that children are adequately protected from harm.

We will now move on to look at legislation and policy in relation to working with disabled adults.

Legislation and policy relating to adults

Legislation relating to disabled people can be traced as far back as the Poor Laws and beyond and includes some interesting historical perspectives on disability and the way in which disabled people have been viewed and treated by society. It would not be within the scope of this chapter to list all legislation and policy currently in use in relation to assessment for and provision of services to disabled adults, therefore an overview will be provided. Chapter 17 on social care policy for adults provides a more in-depth view of policy and legislation.

The National Assistance Act 1948

This Act laid the foundation for the welfare state as we know it and placed some duties on local authorities to make provision to support the welfare of disabled adults: for example, in providing residential accommodation. It also gave local authorities the power to provide certain services for some disabled people who were 'aged 18 or over who are blind, deaf, or dumb, or who suffer from mental disorder of any description, and other persons aged 18 or over who are substantially and permanently handicapped by illness, injury, congenital deformity or such other disabilities as may be prescribed by the Minister'.

(sec. 29)

The Chronically Sick and Disabled Persons Act 1970

This Act placed a duty on local authorities to assess the needs of everyone who falls within section 29 of the National Assistance Act 1948; it also imposed a duty on local authorities to inform themselves of the number and needs of disabled people in their area and to publicise information relating to available services (section 1). Although it has been said that this Act raised public awareness of disability and laid down the statutory framework for services to which disabled people were entitled, there have been concerns raised that it actually promised more than it delivered, and services were based on locality rather than need (Oliver and Sapey, 2006: 146; Davis, 1994).

As social workers you will need to have an understanding of this Act as it underpins many of the services provided to disabled people. The Act sought to enable people to live in their own communities, by providing appropriate support services to those assessed as having a need. Section 2 of the Act lists services which can be provided, including:

- practical assistance in the home;
- help to travel to services arranged by the local authority;
- meals;
- adaptations and equipment;
- recreational facilities;
- holidays.

Disabled Persons (Services, Consultation and Representation) Act 1986

This Act imposes a duty to consult with disabled people and to decide whether the provision of any services in accordance with section 2 of the Chronically Sick and Disabled Persons Act 1970 need to be provided. Whether working with disabled adults or children, social workers need to understand this Act as it also introduced formal procedures which oblige social service departments to communicate with the education authority to identify and assess needs of disabled school leavers.

National Health Service and Community Care Act 1990

Part III of this Act places a duty on local authorities to assess people who may be in need of community care services and to decide whether a service is required to be provided to meet the need. This Act introduced the concept of needs-led assessments as opposed to resource-led assessments and the drawing-up of written care plans. The social work role became defined as that of a 'care manager' as a result of this Act. The care manager's job is to assess the individual's need, plan packages of care, commission the package of care from perhaps a range of sources and then review it. As social workers working with disabled adults, you would need to have sound understanding of this Act as it provides the basis for most of the policy which is currently in use today in working with disabled adults.

The Community Care and Health Act 2002 (Scotland)

This piece of legislation has broken new ground in the United Kingdom in that it requires local authorities in Scotland to provide for free personal care for people over 65, many of whom may have disabilities.

Eligibility criteria

Following the completion of a community care assessment, local authorities have to decide whether they have a duty to provide support to the person being assessed. The *Fair Access to Care Services* policy on eligibility criteria was in place until March 2010: it provided local authorities with a framework to help them decide eligibility criteria for the services they supply. One of the aims of FACS was to have greater consistency in terms of service provision across the country. The framework was based on the person's needs and any associated risks there might be to their independence; it includes four eligibility bands – critical, substantial, moderate and low. The guidance for FACS asked local authorities to identify immediate needs and needs that would worsen if support was not provided. The intention of the replacement eligibility policy – *A Whole System Approach to Eligibility for Social Care* (DoH, 2010b) (discussed in more detail in Chapter 17) – is to provide a better fit with the principles of personalisation. However, the core problem of balancing needs and limited resources (which bedevilled FACS) still remains: arguably given the troubled economic climate, it is now much more problematic than before.

For more information on eligibility criteria for adult social care, go to the publications and statistics section of the Department of Health website at www.dh.gov.uk. Many local authority websites also contain information on FACS relating to their own particular area.

Think ahead

Are there any links between policy and legislation and the different models of disability?

In answering the above question you will probably have thought about the impact of the social and individual models of disability on disabled people. There have been many criticisms of welfare state policy and legislation by disabled people themselves, which link into the view that welfare systems are based on an individualistic model of disability. Legislation and policy is argued to be paternalistic, prescriptive, inflexible and maintaining the dependency of disabled people. Disabled people have argued for services as of right and determined by a self-assessment of need, rather than services created and delivered by professionals whose understanding of disability is underpinned by the 'personal tragedy theory' (e.g. Oliver and Sapey, 2006; Davis, 1994). In addition to this, it has been argued that provision is provider-led not consumer-led, with disabled people relying on a menu of services, with policies and services both framed in terms of people's deficits (French, 1994).

Community Care (Direct Payments) Act 1996

The purpose of this Act was to go some way to changing the above situation. The Act made it possible for a local authority to make payments in cash to the disabled person (not to relatives) to purchase their own care, following an assessed and identified need for services. The decision to make payments was discretionary, however; the Community Care Services for Carers and Children's Services (Direct Payments) (England) Regulations 2003 which came into force in April 2003 made it mandatory for local authorities to offer direct payments in particular circumstances (under the Health and Social Care Act 2001).

The impact of this Act could be far-reaching in changing the way services are delivered to disabled people. Disabled people can employ their own support and to a

Direct payments can increase a disabled person's control over their own lives.

(*Source*: Photofusion Picture Library/Paula Solloway)

larger extent take more control over how, when and by whom the service is delivered. Take-up of direct payments has varied across the country, as local authorities have worked in different ways to set up the schemes and support disabled people wishing to employ their own carers. Local authorities must be satisfied that the disabled person can manage the payments, although an advocate can be appointed to take on this role if need be.

As noted above, the Direct Payments scheme was extended to disabled children under the Carers and Disabled Children Act 2000. (The Community Care (Direct Payments) (Scotland) Regulations 2003 and the Community Care (Direct Payment) (Scotland) Amendment Regulations 2005 in Scotland.)

Case study

Sophie cont . . .

Sophie is receiving meals at home and assistance with personal care. She would like to get up at 7.00 a.m. and have breakfast but the support worker does not start work until 9.30 a.m.

How might this impact on Sophie? As the social worker, what might you do about this? Could the provision of direct payments do anything to change this situation?

Sophie is not able to get out of bed when she would like to because of the way in which her home care is organised. You might have considered that this could affect her in a number of ways: she might feel physically uncomfortable because of being in bed too long or because she needs assistance with personal care; she might also be hungry. Sophie might not be able to plan morning activities outside the home as she is not up in time: this could also impact on her opportunities for employment. You might have thought that as her social worker you could support Sophie to access direct payments if she so wished and assist her to employ her own support staff who will work at the times she wants them to.

Valuing People 2001/Valuing People Now 2009

This White Paper published in 2001 set out a strategy for working with adults and children with a learning disability. *Valuing People* was born out of concern that people with learning disabilities were among the most vulnerable and socially excluded in society. It was recognised that problems included poorly coordinated services for families with a disabled child, poor planning for the transition of young people to adult services, insufficient support for carers, limited choice in the areas of housing, health and employment and that people had little control over many parts of their lives. The four key principles of Rights, Independence, Choice and Inclusion lie at heart of the concept of *Valuing People*. A significant emphasis is placed on the views of service users and their parents or carers and on multi-agency working.

The principles of *Valuing People* apply to working with disabled children and adults alike. In 2000 the Scottish Executive published a policy document that incorporated disability as part of mainstream equality concerns (*Equality Strategy: Working Together for Equality*). Social workers need to have a good grasp of the principles that underpin these documents and adhere to the values they represent.

In 2009 the government published a new three-year strategy *Valuing People Now*, the key priorities of which are housing, employment and health.

As was the case with disabled children, there are a range of pieces of legislation and government policy that as social workers you will need a thorough understanding of in order to do your job. We will now move on to look briefly at some of the areas in which social workers working with disabled people might be employed and

then consider some of the practice issues and dilemmas that might be encountered.

Organisational structure

Think ahead

Try to think of all the organisational structures you know for working with disabled people.

Social workers working with disabled children and adults can be employed in a variety of agencies, for example, in social services, voluntary organisations, health or private organisations and in a range of settings, such as residential homes, independent living schemes, hospitals, local authority statutory childcare or adult care teams, child development centres, hospices or projects with a specific remit for working with people who have a specific impairment or health condition. For example, you could be employed by a voluntary organisation in a project where your role would be to support parents whose child has only just received a diagnosis or with an organisation that works specifically with autistic people. Workers undertaking statutory social work tasks – for example, assessing the need for services, arranging services to meet need, devising care plans, reviewing case and safeguarding work – will usually be employed by the local authority.

Social workers working with disabled adults tend to be employed in Community Learning Disability Teams which may or may not be multi-agency, Physical Disability Teams and Community Care Teams. Transitions social workers (those working with young people in the transition from children's to adult services) are usually employed by adult services although some local authorities have discussed whether they would be better placed in children's services to avoid young people falling through the net. Some local authorities have also recently set up Vulnerable Adult teams or have specific social work posts dedicated to working with vulnerable adults who may not reach the eligibility criteria for a service from a disability team. An example of this could be an 18-year-old young person with Asperger's syndrome who may need support to move out of the family home but does not fit the criteria for other adult services teams.

Until recently in many parts of the country, disabled children were allocated social workers who worked with a range of children referred to social care services.

Unfortunately this meant their needs were often competing with those of other children who might be seen as a higher priority: for example, children in need of protection from harm or those who were subject to court proceedings. Disabled children often had to wait for an assessment of their needs to take place. In addition to this, many social workers had not received adequate training relating to working with disabled children and so did not have the skills or knowledge to provide a good enough service. This had an impact on the quality of service offered in terms of:

- having the skills to communicate with disabled children;
- understanding specific issues relating to safeguarding disabled children;
- appropriate services being offered;
- practice not being child-centred (as support needs of carers dominated);
- menu of services being offered rather than packages tailored to individual need.

However, more recently in an attempt to address some of these difficulties many local authorities have set up teams of social workers and social work assistants to work specifically with disabled children. Some teams also include workers seconded by other agencies: for example, community nurses with experience in working with children who have a learning disability. Many social services teams also have very good links with other professionals working with disabled children: for example, education early support staff, teachers, school nurses, physiotherapists, occupational therapists and psychologists. As noted previously, *Every Child Matters* sets out a model for whole-system change: this will involve new ways of English and Welsh agencies working together with integrated front-line delivery, processes and strategies to be delivered by Children's Trusts which should be of benefit to disabled children.

Practice issues in working with disabled children

Think ahead

What do you think the needs of a disabled child and their family are? Do the needs of the disabled child differ from those of the parents and siblings?

In answering the above you may have thought about a range of practice issues and dilemmas that you will encounter in working with disabled children and their families. Some of the issues most commonly raised centre around the need for parents to be supported in their caring role, particularly in the form of short breaks, balancing the needs of the child with those of the parent/carer and safeguarding disabled children. Issues relating to communication are also frequently raised: however, these are explored in Chapter 11 on communication and so will not be revisited here. As with other areas of practice you will need to be aware of your own values and assumptions, for example, in terms of what it means to be disabled and a child and what it means to be a parent of a disabled child and what it means to have social workers in your life.

The Every Child Matters: Change for Children website includes the following facts and figures regarding disabled children:

- About 29 per cent of disabled children live in poverty.
- The educational attainment of disabled children is unacceptably lower than that of non-disabled children.
- Disabled young people aged 16–24 are less satisfied with their lives than their peers and there is a tendency for support to fall away at key transition points as young people move from child to adult services.
- Families with disabled children report particularly high levels of unmet needs, isolation and stress.
- Only 4 per cent of disabled children are supported by social services. A report by the Audit Commission in 2003 found that there was a lottery of provision, inadequate strategic planning, confusing eligibility criteria, and that families were subject to long waits and had to jump through hoops to get support.
- The prevalence of severe disability is increasing.

(*ECM: Change for Children* website)

The above points help to illustrate a picture of the issues many disabled children and their families encounter in their everyday lives. These issues will impact on the work you do as social workers and will also impact on outcomes for young people in terms of what they are expected to achieve and their own self-esteem and self-belief.

Think ahead

The fourth point above states 'families with disabled children report particularly high levels of unmet needs, isolation and stress'.

Why do you think this might be? Thinking back to the circumstances in Ben's family how might this point relate to them? What could the impact on Ben's family be?

In response to the questions above you might have thought about issues, such as Ben needing support to go out or support with daily living skills or his parents needing support to have a break from caring, feeling tired or not getting the chance to go out by themselves or as a whole family. The family may be isolated because of difficulty in getting out and about or by the attitudes of others living nearby. All family members might need a break from each other; a lack of opportunity for this could lead to stress levels at home rising. Very often parents state that the service they most value is that of short breaks – a service designed to give the parents a break from caring and the child, an opportunity they might not otherwise have. Research has demonstrated that families with chronically ill or disabled children have a wide range of support needs but these needs are often not met. Parents often report feeling unsupported or needing to 'battle' to get support. At the same time reports from researchers, practitioners working with disabled children and parents themselves show that there are services which families really value (Mitchell and Sloper, 2002).

Over the years disabled children and their parents/carers have made clear their views on what they think makes a 'good' service: their points (adapted from Mitchell and Sloper, 2002; DoH, 2002d) have included:

- *Having a 'keyworker'.*
  One person who knows the child well to act as a link between all those involved. The keyworking role can be undertaken by any person who knows the child well and has the skills to negotiate and liaise between all involved parties. This system benefits parents and carers as they do not need to spend a lot of time explaining their situation to a number of people. In some areas this is known as the 'team around the child' approach. This approach sees the child at the centre and then includes all the people who play a role in the child's life, creating a team around the child. People move in and out of the team at different times in the child's life. Any person within the team can take on the keyworker role.

- *Having a holistic assessment and all the child's information in one central place.*
  Parents and carers frequently state that one of the most difficult and frustrating situations they face is telling different professionals the same story and updating it. Having a holistic multi-agency assessment can help a parent and child avoid the need to retell their story to each new professional that becomes involved. As we saw in the legislation section, this point has been picked up on in standard 8 of the *National Service Framework*.

- *Having community-based services local to home, particularly in rural areas.*
  Very often children who live in rural areas have to travel a number of miles to school and also travel to attend any leisure-based services. This reduces opportunities to make friends or meet up with friends outside of school. Community-based services help maintain those links and enable children to socialise with friends outside of school hours.

- *Agencies and professionals working together.*
  Where this is achieved, parents and carers often feel they are listened to and that more appropriate services are offered. As social workers you will be aware that the various professionals involved in working with disabled people have different value bases (think back to the section earlier on in the chapter about the social and individual models of disability). How do you think this might impact on working together?

- *Trained staff who have the ability to communicate and listen.*
  Parents, carers and children all want to have confidence in the staff who work with them. Being able to communicate and demonstrate you have listened are core skills for a social worker.

- *Accessible information provided at the right time.*
  Many parents and carers say that having the right information at the right time makes a huge difference in their ability to manage and understand difficult situations. Particular key times are at the time of diagnosis, when a child starts nursery or school, when the child moves to secondary school, becoming a teenager and then finally transferring to adult services at 18 years of age.

- *Integrated appointments to prevent numerous trips to hospital or the Child Development Centre.*
  Parents and carers can find the numerous visits to hospital difficult, particularly if the hospital is a

number of miles away, they do not have transport, have a low income or indeed they have to juggle other childcare or work commitments. Having a number of appointments arranged at the same hospital on the same day is enormously helpful to the child and parent.

- *Disabled children say they would like to make choices, and for professionals to take notice of them and listen to what they have to say.*

  As you have already read in the legislation section of this chapter, all children, including disabled children, have a right to be asked their opinions and wishes. Finding out a child's preferred method of communication is absolutely key to any work you will undertake as a social worker.

- *Having short breaks available.*

  As noted in the policy and legislation section the Children and Young Person's Act 2008 places a duty on local authorities to provide short breaks. The issue of short breaks warrants further exploration as it is this need that is most frequently reported as being unmet by parents of disabled children The government agenda *Aiming High for Disabled Children: better support for families* (DfES, 2007) set out plans for improving service provision for disabled children and their families, including short break services. It focuses on three main areas:

  1. Access and empowerment – disabled children will be engaged in shaping services at a local level and there will be increased transparency about services available and entitlements to those services.
  2. Responsive services and timely support – disabled children and their families should benefit from responsive, flexible services at times when they need them.
  3. Improving quality and capacity – a specific grant of £280 million has been made available by the government to deliver a change in the provision of short breaks.

The meaning of short-term break is wide-ranging although often mistakenly thought of as only being 'respite' or overnight stays out of the child's home. Short-term breaks can be provided through a befriender or 'sitting service', where the worker either takes the child out or looks after them at home; a place at a playscheme, out-of-school club or nursery; or through overnight care which can be provided at a residential unit, with a foster family (local authority or voluntary/private organisation), at the home

of a person employed through direct payments or at the child's own home. Any short break provided needs to also promote the welfare of the child and provide positive experiences, including, for example, social activities which offer the opportunity to make friendships and have new experiences. Many parents report that having short breaks helps them to continue with the caring role and many teenagers enjoy spending time away from the family doing different things. However, difficulties for social workers can occur if the needs or wants of the parents differ from those of the child.

Case study

Ben cont . . .

Ben's parents have asked for his needs to be reassessed. He still has his befriender funded through direct payments but they feel he needs to spend more time with his peers and possibly have overnight short breaks to enable them to go out. Ben has said he would like to go to The Orchard, a short break residential unit, as that's where his friends from school go. The social worker assesses that Ben does need overnight short breaks and arranges for him to go to The Orchard but his parents request direct payments for overnight care so they can pay the befriender to look after Ben instead. Ben doesn't want this.

What are your thoughts on this situation?

Whose needs will be met?

As Ben's social worker what would you do?

One dilemma often faced by social workers is that of balancing the child's needs with those of the parents or carers for support. In answering the above questions, you might have considered that it can be a struggle to maintain child-centred practice when assessing the needs of a child if carers or parents are requesting services to meet their own needs. You also might have asked yourself questions such as, 'Who is the service user, the child, the carer or both?', 'Whose needs will the service meet?' and 'What does the child want to happen?'. The answers are not always clear-cut but asking this kind of question will help you remember that the child is at the centre of your assessment. In addition to this, it is good practice to offer a carer's assessment alongside an assessment of the child's needs (although carers can of course request an assessment of their own needs without the child's needs being assessed).

While it is widely accepted that carers and parents of disabled children do need support in their caring role and a break from that role in order to continue caring, that view must be balanced with the child's right to be a part of family life, particularly with very young children or those whose views we do not really know. Very often the solution to 'the problem' (i.e. support needs of the child) is seen in removing the child from home to another place for overnight or day care rather than seeking other ways to solve the difficulties. For example, if Ben does not sleep very well, his parents may become extremely tired and feel unable to cope. The solution could be seen in Ben going somewhere else for one or two overnight stays per month to give his parents a good night's sleep. However, another solution could possibly be for a sleep assessment to be undertaken to discover the reasons for Ben not sleeping and work done with him and his family to resolve the difficulty. This is not to say that there will always be another solution for the family as a whole, but there is a need to be open-minded and creative to ensure children's needs are met in the most appropriate way. In addition to this, families need to be supported to stay together: disabled children are over-represented in the population of children living in a residential setting. Research demonstrates that children living away from home have an increased vulnerability to being abused, which leads us to the issue of safeguarding disabled children.

Safeguarding disabled children

The issue of safeguarding disabled children often raises concerns and dilemmas for social workers. There is a wealth of research to demonstrate that disabled children are more vulnerable to abuse and neglect than their non-disabled peers (Kelly, 1992; Miller, 2003). In addition to this, research also demonstrates that disabled children are not protected from harm to same extent as their non-disabled peers (Edwards and Richardson, 2003; Marchant and Page, 2003; Cooke, 2000). Historically the focus of child protection services has been on non-disabled children, with policies and procedures being drawn up with only them in mind. However, since the late 1990s, the level of awareness of the increased risk of abuse for disabled children has risen significantly and the situation has started to change both in front-line services and politically: for example, principles of good practice are included in government guidance such as *Working Together*

2010, the Assessment Framework guidance, *Changing Childhoods* and the *Every Child Matters* and *National Service Framework* documentation.

Despite what is said above, there are still many reasons as to why disabled children may not be safeguarded from harm to the same extent as non-disabled children (for more information on this read Cooke, 2000 and '*It Doesn't Happen to Disabled Children*', the Report of the National Working Group on Child Protection and Disability published by NSPCC). In working with disabled children, social workers can easily collude in failing to act on evidence that could be of concern, or accepting standards of care that would not be accepted for non-disabled children. This might happen for a number of reasons, for example:

- Behaviour or physical symptoms are sometimes seen as the result of the child's impairment rather than an indicator of abuse.
- There may be a reluctance to challenge carers.
- There may be a reliance on carers to speak for the child or explain behaviour or symptoms and a ready acceptance of explanations given.
- The emphasis can be placed on support for the carers rather than the child's welfare.
- It can be difficult for the social worker to remain confident in their own expertise when challenged by a carer who knows the child well.
- Social workers' attitudes and assumptions have an impact – they may doubt abuse has occurred or find it difficult to obtain evidence and so may be more willing to take the risk of not taking any action.
- Support services might not have the necessary 'expertise' to work with disabled children.
- There may be a lack of appropriate foster or residential placements if a child needs alternative care.

(Adapted from Edwards and Richardson, 2003: 31–44. This material was produced by in Control, www.in-control.org.uk)

Case study

Ben cont . . .

Ben is now having short breaks at The Orchard residential unit. He arrives there by taxi after school and at teatime one of the staff notices that he has two bruises, one on either side of his neck. She asks Ben how he got the bruises and he says he doesn't know. The staff member happens to

▶

mention this to you (as Ben's social worker) the following week and says she thinks the bruises must have been caused by the seat belt in the taxi.

What do you think of this explanation?

What would you do? Should this have been reported earlier?

As Ben's social worker you might have been concerned that the staff member waited a week to inform you of the bruises as they would no longer be visible. You might also have questioned how a seat belt could cause such bruising and whether any other explanations could be offered. In this situation you would be expected to discuss what had happened with your line manager so the two of you together could decide what action might be necessary.

The provision of direct payments for services for disabled children has further opened up debate relating to safeguarding disabled children and created new dilemmas both for social workers and for parents. It is known that some abusers of children are drawn to jobs which involve care of children, for example, in schools or residential units. The provision of direct payments opens a whole new sphere of working with disabled children in their own homes. The Protection of Children Act 1999 enables people who are considering employing someone to care for their child to request a criminal background (CRB) check; the local authority has a duty to undertake such a check when employing people to work with children. However, legislation does not require this to be the case for people employed by direct payments. Most local authorities would consider it good practice to have a check in place and payments should only be made if the local authority is satisfied that the child will be safe.

The difficulty lies in deciding what measures will be used by the local authority to satisfy themselves: the onus will be on the social worker undertaking the assessment to make that decision with their line manager. A range of issues can be considered when trying to decide whether the individual is a safe person, for example, whether the person already has a CRB check in place, whether they are employed already to work with children and whether they are personally known to the family or employed through advertising (there is support available from organisations helping people to advertise, interview and employ carers through direct payments).

There is a need to balance what is seen as the right of the carer to make choices in whom they employ with the right of the child to be safe.

Case study

Ben cont . . .

Ben's befriender has moved out of the area, his parents have not been able to identify another and so decide to advertise. They have recruited a male carer not known to them. They have been told that it could take up to five weeks for the CRB check to be undertaken and as they are eager for him to start as soon as possible have decided not to have a check done. The carer has a reference from a school he used to work at, stating a check was done two years ago.

As Ben's social worker you might be considering questions such as, '*Am I satisfied that Ben will be safe?*' or '*What is known about this carer?*' You would most likely want to advise Ben's parents to wait for a new CRB check as the previous one has not been seen, is now two years out of date and the carer is not someone they know personally. You would want to advise them to check the employer's reference by speaking personally to the referee and to also obtain a second reference.

Where safeguarding concerns are known, there has been much debate relating to who is best placed to investigate. Social workers working in Disabled Children's Teams have the knowledge and skills to communicate with disabled children and understand issues linked to their impairment and its impact but might not have a great deal of experience of child protection; the reverse may be true of social workers working in child protection teams. One way of addressing this difficulty is for more co-working and skill-sharing between disability and child protection teams, a point which was borne out in research by the Ann Craft Trust (Cook, 2000).

Policy and guidance also clearly plays an important role in how services, including those that safeguard disabled children, will be delivered and it is essential for good practice that you familiarise yourself with these. *Every Child Matters* provides markers of good practice for working with disabled children (see website) and the *National Service Framework* gives very clear guidance on safeguarding which stipulates that Local Safeguarding Children's Boards in England and Wales should ensure the specific needs of disabled children are addressed in comprehensive, inter-agency protocols (*Every Child Matters: Change for Children* – DfES, 2003a; DoH, 2003e, 2004a). *Working Together* 2010 also has specific guidance for safeguarding disabled children as of course does the Safeguarding Disabled Children Practice Guidance.

Professional tip

Good practice in safeguarding disabled children

- A really useful question to keep in mind when undertaking an assessment of a disabled child is: Would I consider that option if the child were not disabled? (DoH, 2000b: 80).
- Find out the child's preferred method of communication.
- Be aware of your employer's safeguarding children policy and procedures.
- Good practice would involve being open-minded about the picture you are presented with and not making assumptions about what may or may not have happened.
- Good practice also involves questioning decisions you may not be happy with or clear about and considering all evidence from all relevant parties.
- Discuss issues of concern with your line manager.

This section has addressed some practice issues you might encounter in working with disabled children. We will now move on to consider some of the issues relating to working with disabled adults. Safeguarding vulnerable adults will not be included here as it is discussed in Chapter 17 on social care policy for adults.

Practice issues in working with disabled adults

There are number of issues and dilemmas that you will come across as a social worker working with disabled adults. Again, it would not be within the remit of this chapter to include them all, but some of the key issues impacting on practice relate to the way in which adults are assessed for services and the way services are then delivered. Chapter 17 on social care policy for adults looks in more detail at a range of issues impacting on

vulnerable adults including mental capacity, safeguarding, personalisation and the modernisation agenda. In this chapter we will look at principles for independent living, person-centred planning and balancing risk and protection. It is advised that you read this alongside Chapter 17 in order to obtain a fuller view of the political context underpinning these practice issues.

In many ways some of the issues and dilemmas raised are similar to those cited in working with children. For example, many disabled adults refer to their needs not being met because their rights to be heard, be understood and to make choices are not being adhered to. Likewise carers of adult relatives may feel the same frustrations as parents of disabled children in relation to the way some services are delivered, a lack of short-breaks provision or being in contact with social workers who do not appear to listen to or understand them. We will look first at the concept of person-centred planning.

Person-centred planning

Think ahead

When you hear about the concept of person-centred planning, what springs to mind? How would you go about working in this way? What challenges do you think you might encounter?

For a number of years, disabled people have been calling for more control over their lives and the way their needs are assessed and services provided. In the past the emphasis has been on professionals deciding what the disabled person needs or what support they can have. This way of working would fit in with the individual model of disability, which sees the person as the problem and needing professionals to help them adapt or come to terms with their situation. One of the key themes of *Valuing People* (see the legislation and policy section above) is the importance of person-centred planning: the concept of this is that services will be based on what the disabled person wants, giving them more choice and control over their lives. The premise is that services should be geared to meet the needs of the person rather than the person fitting in with services available. Person-centred planning is based on inclusion and the social model of disability and the four principles – of rights, independence, choice and inclusion – outlined in *Valuing People*.

Valuing People identifies five key features of person-centred planning which are:

1. The person is at the centre.
2. Family members and friends are full partners.
3. Person-centred planning reflects a person's capabilities, what is important to that person, and specifies the support they require to make a valued contribution to the community.
4. Person-centred planning builds a shared commitment to action that will uphold a person's rights.
5. Person-centred planning leads to continual listening, learning and action, and helps a person to get what they want out of life.

(SCIE, 2005)

So, what does this mean for social work practice? To take Sophie as an example, person-centred planning would mean that planning would start with Sophie herself and not with services available in her area. It would take account of her wishes, hopes and goals in life and make her central to the process of assessment and planning for services. This is in contrast with 'service-led' assessments which would look at what services are available in Sophie's area and 'fit her in'. However, dilemmas might occur for social workers where the wishes of the disabled person are not the same as the wishes of the parent/carer or where the views of the disabled person are not clearly known. For example, if Sophie decided that she would like to move away from home to live on her own, her parents might be against the idea and tell you as her social worker that she will not cope on her own. They might also state that they think you are being irresponsible by even listening to Sophie regarding this issue. How would you manage this situation? You might feel in conflict with Sophie's parents or you might think they have a point. In terms of person-centred planning, Sophie must be central to any planning regarding her life; however, as we have seen, another principle of person-centred planning sees family and friends as full partners. You might want to support Sophie's parents in exploring their concerns and fears and find ways to alleviate these, while recognising that Sophie's wishes must take priority. We now move on to consider issues relating to independent living.

Independent living

Over the years disabled activists have called for disabled people's right to independence to be recognised formally as a civil right and for support to be made available to achieve independent living. Independent living in itself is a complex and controversial area of discussion and practice and you will again need to be aware of your own values and assumptions of what it means to be disabled. This chapter can only give a basic outline of the issues: you can get more information from the National Centre for Independent Living website (www.ncil.org.uk) and links from this site. Independent living means ensuring that disabled people have the same freedom, choice, dignity and control as other people in society at home, at work, and in the community. It also means having the right to practical assistance and support to participate in society and live an ordinary life (Disability Rights Commission, 2006).

There is general agreement among disabled activists that the concept of independent living is founded on four basic principles, which are:

1. That all human life, regardless of the nature, complexity and/or severity of impairment is of equal worth.
2. That anyone, whatever the nature, complexity and/or severity of their impairment has the capacity to make choices and should be enabled to make those choices.
3. That people who are disabled by societal responses to any form of accredited impairment – physical, sensory or cognitive – have the right to exercise control over their lives.
4. That people with perceived impairments and labelled 'disabled' have the right to participate fully in all areas – economic, political and cultural – of mainstream community living on a par with non-disabled peers.

(*Source*: SCIE, 2004)

This concept fits in with the social model of disability, where independence is established as a civil right. However, there have been criticisms levelled at local authorities, saying that independent living is not a reality for many disabled people as it is subject to tight financial restrictions, strict means-testing and that design and delivery focuses on 'managing "vulnerability", "risk" and "dependency", rather than supporting choice, control, and participation' (Disability Rights Commission, 2006: 2).

Funding independent living can be complex and is done by a range of means, for example, through social services and health funding, welfare benefits, the Independent Living Fund and direct payments. The Independent Living Fund was set up as a resource for severely disabled people who meet its eligibility criteria; the fund gives financial support to enable people to choose to live in the community rather than in residential care. (See www.ilf.org.uk for more information.) As noted previously, direct payments are a different way of providing certain social care services for disabled adults who have been assessed as needing services. The aim of direct payments is to help people who want to manage their own support packages, and to promote choice, independence and inclusion by enabling people to purchase care that will allow them to live in their own homes and participate in family and community life. Disabled people can be supported to manage the payments and other aspects of employing carers by organisations set up to provide such support. People can also have mixed packages of care so that some services are commissioned directly by the local authority and others are funded through direct payments. So, for example, Sophie could have personal care provided by the local authority and use direct payments to fund a support worker for leisure activities.

There is currently a call for all disabled people to manage their own finances and support; this is very much seen as the way forward in service delivery. 'in Control' is about self-directed support for adults with learning disabilities and being in charge even if the person needs help to do this. The organisation began work in 2003 to change the social care system in England, as the arrangements in place did not put people in control of their own support or finances. Consequently, in Control designed a new system – Self-Directed Support. The government now wants all local authorities to change their approach to be in accordance with the principles of Self-Directed Support. In Control Partnerships is now a social enterprise – a charity and an independent company. It is a unique partnership between individuals, local authorities, services, families and many other organisations working together to define best practice in self-directed support. It states there are seven ethical principles that underpin self-directed support:

'1. Right to Independent Living – if someone has an impairment which means they need help to fulfil their role as a citizen, then they should get the help they need.
2. Right to an Individual Budget – if someone needs on-going paid help as part of their life they should be able to decide how the money that pays for that help is used.
3. Right to Self-Determination – if someone needs help to make decisions then decision-making should be made as close to the person as possible, reflecting the person's own interests and preferences.
4. Right to Accessibility – the system of rules within which people have to work must be clear and open in order to maximise the ability of the disabled person to take control of their own support.
5. Right to Flexible Funding – when someone is using their Individual Budget they should be free to spend their funds in the way that makes best sense to them, without unnecessary restrictions.

6. Accountability Principle – the disabled person and the government both have a responsibility to each other to explain their decisions and to share what they have learnt.
7. Capacity Principle – disabled people, their families and their communities must not be assumed to be incapable of managing their own support, learning skills and making a contribution.'

(This material was produced by in Control, www.in-control.org.uk. See website for further information.)

So what does this mean for the social work or care management role? Potentially the commissioning role of the care manager could change considerably if the move is towards individuals commissioning their own support packages. If care management has been about providing individualised services, 'in Control' could be seen as being about providing individualised budgets. The future of this movement remains to be seen but could perhaps redefine the social work role again.

Reflect

What do you think the benefits and challenges of independent living principles will be for both disabled people and social workers?

In answering the above question, you may have considered the benefits to disabled people as being in terms of the right to manage one's own life and finances and the right to make decisions; the benefits for social workers may be in terms of enabling or supporting people to live life the way they want to. Challenges will present themselves, however, for social workers putting together packages of support. The financial climate will have an impact on the budgets available for paying for self-directed support as social care and other organisations are forced to save money and/or cut service provision. Challenges may also arise, as we saw with Sophie at the end of the person-centred planning section above, if what the disabled person wants differs from what their parents want or indeed what other people working with them consider to be safe. This thought leads us now into the next section which considers issues relating to the risk and protection of disabled people.

Risk and protection

Balancing risk and protection is an issue in all areas of social work. Managing risk is a feature of everyday life for everyone, for example, negotiating a busy road or making decisions regarding education, employment, personal relationships, etc. Dilemmas can occur for social workers in trying to balance supporting disabled people to make their own decisions and take risks with protecting people from harm or other hazards.

The social work academic, Paul Williams (2006), states that there are two kinds of risk relevant to working with people with learning disabilities:

- the risk of unnecessary exposure to undesirable events or experiences;
- the risk of negative consequences when possible benefits and desirable experiences are pursued.

He argues that for the first the key is prevention so that the person is not exposed to these events, and for the second it is management so that risk and benefit are balanced. In addition to this, there are risks to the person themselves, for example, hazards such as fire, dangerous substances or road traffic, ill health, abuse and abandonment (for example, in having no contact with family or friends) and possibly risks from the person (for example, to carers or the public from violent, destructive or upsetting behaviour) (Williams 2006: 99–109).

Part of your role as a social worker will be managing risk or helping other people to manage it, while promoting independence and choice for the people you work with. You might work with staff or family in putting together a risk-management plan for someone who is known to be violent towards staff or family, or for someone who often disappears from home or is at risk from making themselves vulnerable to exploitation. You will also be managing the risk of abuse: research demonstrates that people with learning disabilities are at risk of abuse from a range of sources including staff, family, friends and strangers (for more information see the Ann Craft Trust website).

Another social work academic, Rachel Fyson (2007), argues that there is a tension between calls for better adult protection systems and the desire to promote choice and independence and that this is reflected in recent government policy. Fyson states that, since the late 1990s, there have been a range of laws and policy guidelines issued which aim to protect vulnerable adults from abuse; however, running alongside this there has also been, as we can see from the previous section of this chapter, a range of policies developed which promote greater choice and independence for service users. One of the difficulties, however, is that there are few connections between the two: 'The problem is that those

policies which seek to promote choice and independence pay little or no attention to issues of abuse prevention' (Fyson, 2007: 21).

In 2000 the UK government produced a report called *No Secrets – Guidance on Developing Multi-Agency Policies and Procedures to Protect Vulnerable Adults from Abuse* (this document is currently under review). The aim of the document is to help create a framework for action within which all agencies work together to ensure a consistent and effective response to concerns. The emphasis is on preventing abuse but also having procedures in place for dealing with incidents of abuse. The types of abuse covered include physical, sexual, psychological, financial, neglect and discriminatory abuse. All local authorities now have procedures in place for protecting vulnerable adults from abuse and will have a nominated person employed to make decisions in relation to the procedures. However, managing the risk to vulnerable people of being abused can be fraught with difficulties. Vulnerable adults do not have same level of protection as is given to children, as adults are free to make their own decisions and, as we have seen, there is a conflict between respecting the rights of adults to make their own decisions and protecting people from risky situations. Unlike in England and Wales, Scotland has legislation that provides a framework to protect vulnerable adults from abuse (Protection from Abuse (Scotland) Act, 2001).

Case study

Ben cont . . .

Ben is now 22 years old; he is supported to live in his own house. Ben's carers raise an issue with you regarding a friendship he has with a 50-year-old man who lives close by. The carers have no evidence but feel sure the man is taking money from Ben. You ask Ben about this: he says he gives the man money because he is his friend.

What are the issues of risk? How could these be addressed?

You might have considered Ben's vulnerability in thinking about the issues of risk: he could be easily persuaded to give his money away or might be threatened into parting with it. However, you might also have considered that there is a need to balance this with Ben's right to make friendships and make his own decisions about how he spends his money. This would reflect the tension described above by Fyson between the need for rigorous adult protection policies and the desire to promote equality and independence. The risks could be addressed by working with the staff who work with Ben and Ben himself by exploring his capacity to make his own decisions: this could be done by involving a psychologist. The Mental Capacity Act 2005 has recently been implemented: this provides a framework to help protect people who are not able to make their own decisions; it also makes clear who can make decisions and in what circumstances (see Chapter 8 for further discussion).

There a number of routes which could be taken, including supporting Ben to make other friendships or stopping him from giving his away his money or, if it was felt he was being exploited or abused, using the adult protection procedures.

Conclusion

This chapter has introduced you to some of the key concepts and practice issues you will encounter in working with disabled adults and children. We have seen how our own views and beliefs are influenced by our life experiences and dominant views of disability in society. We have considered how language and labelling and the social and individual models of disability can play a role both in social work policy and practice and in wider societal views of disability. The impact of all these issues on social work practice, policy and legislation has also been examined as has the potential impact on service users themselves. Following on from this, we considered a range of issues and dilemmas that social workers come across in social work practice, including safeguarding disabled children and vulnerable adults, balancing the needs and views of disabled children and adults with those of the parent or carer and looking at what families say makes a good service. We also looked at the tensions that can arise between choice and independence and the protection of vulnerable adults. The chapter has, we hope, given you a taster on which you can build: the suggested additional reading material and website links will help you to develop your thinking and knowledge in the areas covered.

Key learning points

This chapter has covered the following learning points:

✔ Our own life histories, values and views of disability impact upon social work policy and practice.

✔ Disability can be viewed as a social construct and there are a range of different understandings and models of disability, all of which impact on social work policy and practice.

✔ To work in an effective and equitable way with disabled children and adults, social workers must have a good understanding of the relevant legislation, policy and agency procedures which underpin their practice.

✔ Social work often involves balancing the rights and wishes of the disabled child or adult with the parents' or carer's need for support.

✔ Social work with disabled children and adults can be complex and raises many ethical and moral dilemmas.

 Further reading

NSPCC (2003) *It Doesn't Happen to Disabled Children.* This is the Report of the National Working Group on Child Protection and Disabled Children. The report contains a number of articles written by researchers and practitioners who are experienced in the field of safeguarding disabled children.

Oliver, M. and Sapey, B. (2006) *Social Work with Disabled People* (3rd edn). Basingstoke: Palgrave Macmillan. Key text covering a range of issues relating to social work practice with disabled people; has its basis in the social model of disability.

Williams, P. (2006) *Social Work with People with Learning Disabilities*, Exeter: Learning Matters Ltd. A book from the *Transforming Social Work Practice Series*, highly readable and practice-based, covering a wide range of issues relating to working with people with learning disabilities.

Useful websites

www.scotland.gov.uk/Publications/2005/07/25112327/23294

For more information on *Getting It Right For Every Child.*

www.scotland.gov.uk/Publications/2006/04/24104745/13

For more information on *Changing Childhoods.*

www.anncrafttrust.org

A national charity working with professionals, parents and carers to protect children and adults with learning disabilities from abuse.

www.disability.gov.uk

Government disability website – contains official documents relating to disability and links to other sites.

www.everychildmatters.gov.uk

More information can be found about *Every Child Matters* at this very useful website: it has a wide range of information relating to delivery of services, strategies and governance.

www.everychildmatters.gov.uk/workingtogether

For more information on *Working Together to Safeguard Children* 2006.

For additional cases and topic-organised, clickable links into additional media resources, including those produced by IRISS, visit **www.pearsoned.co.uk/wilsonruch**

Activity

Activity One

Reread the definition of disability you wrote at the start of the chapter. *Would you like to change it? If so, why?*

Activity Two

Read the Executive Summary of *Valuing People* and *Valuing People Now.*

How do the principles laid out in this paper fit in with (a) your own views on disability and (b) the models and definitions your have read about in this chapter?

How do you think they will impact on your practice?

Chapter 20
Social work with adults with mental health problems

Chapter summary

In this chapter you will be introduced to some of the many complicated and long-standing debates about the nature of mental ill health and mental well-being as a basis for exploring the core roles and tasks of mental health social work. Mental health work has always been a multidisciplinary undertaking, but the different professions involved in the work – psychiatrists, social workers, nurses, psychotherapists, occupational therapists, advocates, therapeutic community workers – have all traditionally had slightly different perspectives on the question 'What is mental health or ill health?'

In recent years, the principal agency responsibility for mental health work has shifted decisively towards the health sector, and this has had a big impact on social workers. As with some other specialist areas of social work, for many decades important statutory and legal responsibilities assigned to social workers helped to define the social work role in mental health and give it 'legitimacy' and importance. In particular, the role of Approved Social Worker (previously Mental Welfare Officer), which confers the power and the duty to contribute to decisions about people's compulsory detention under the Mental Health Act, seemed to be a foundation stone of social work authority. But this is about to change, even as this book is being written. Perhaps more than in any other arena, mental health social work is in a period of change and renegotiation about its core roles and tasks. Nevertheless, it remains a very important, challenging, rewarding and exciting specialism.

Ideally, this chapter should be read in conjunction with Chapter 12 which is about different models of social work intervention, and the section on communication with people who have mental health problems in Chapter 11. All of the models discussed in the former chapter are directly relevant to adult mental health work, and many of them are referred to below. The sections on networking, crisis intervention, cognitive behavioural therapy, and psychodynamic approaches are especially relevant.

Learning objectives

This chapter covers topics that will enable you to achieve the following learning objectives:

■ To provide a basic introduction to a variety of perspectives on the nature of mental health and well-being

■ To introduce you to the contemporary policy developments affecting the roles, tasks and responsibilities of mental health social workers

■ To introduce some recent innovations in mental health practice, such as assertive outreach and crisis intervention

■ To explore some of the challenges, benefits and tensions of multidisciplinary working in mental health work

■ To provide a clear idea of what relationship-based mental health social work means

■ To introduce you to some critical and alternative perspectives on mental health practice.

National Occupational Standards

The chapter will help you to meet the following National Occupational Standards:

Key Role 1: Prepare for, and work with individuals, families, carers, groups and communities to assess their needs and circumstances

Unit 1   Prepare for social work contact and involvement
Unit 2   Work with individuals, families, carers, groups and communities to help them make informed decisions
Unit 3   Assess needs and options to recommend a course of action

Key Role 2: Plan, carry out, review and evaluate social work practice, with individuals, families, carers, groups, communities and other professionals

Unit 4   Respond to crisis situations
Unit 5   Interact with individuals, families, carers, groups and communities to achieve change and development and to improve life opportunities
Unit 7   Support the development of networks to meet assessed needs and planned outcomes
Unit 9   Address behaviour which presents a risk to individuals, families, carers, groups and communities

Key Role 4: Manage risk to individuals, families, carers, groups, communities, self and colleagues

Unit 12   Assess and manage risks to individuals, families, carers, groups and communities
Unit 13   Assess, minimise and manage risk to self and colleagues

Case study

Mohammed

Mohammed (Mo) was referred to the Community Mental Health Team (CMHT) by his GP after he became very depressed and started talking of suicide. He is a refugee with permanent leave to remain, who came to Britain from Bosnia during the war in the Balkans during which he was in the army for a time. He was injured when the armoured vehicle he was driving crashed. He was discharged from the army, and came to England with his wife and young daughter.

While the family settled well and Mo started his own business as a plumber, his wife says he was never quite the same person after the accident. He has had periods of depression for which he has been prescribed antidepressants and is often touchy and irritable. Nine months ago his wife miscarried quite late in her pregnancy, and Mo seems to have reacted very badly to this. The couple had been hoping very much for another child, but now they have been told it is unlikely that they will be able to have more children.

In recent weeks Mo has become very withdrawn. He sleeps badly, usually waking in the early hours, doesn't eat much and often gives up work in the middle of the day. When you go to see him at home, he seems to want to talk but sometimes he lapses into silence and appears to be preoccupied with his own thoughts. He speaks mostly about his mother, saying he feels terribly guilty because she is ill and perhaps dying, and there is nothing he can do to help. Mo says he has been thinking about returning to Bosnia so that he can be nearer her and offer some support. Afterwards you reflect that he seemed so preoccupied with this, that you didn't manage to gain any sense of what he thought about his current situation in the UK.

What do you think are some of the possible origins or causes of Mo's depression?

How does his story make you feel? If you were to see him again, is there anything you would consider offering him, or saying to him?

Mental health problems are intensely personal experiences for both the person who is directly affected, but also for those close to them. However, the causes of mental health difficulties are not just personal but also social and political, or as is sometimes said, 'psychosocial'. In the case study above, Mo's experience of being a refugee from a war-torn region may be as important in understanding him and responding to his situation as is an appreciation of his personality and individual psychological vulnerabilities. In fact, these are all intertwined in complex ways, and this chapter aims to introduce you to a perspective on mental health work that integrates psychological, psychiatric and social perspectives. From the point of view of relationship-based social work practice, the context of service provision is also part of the overall picture because people have relationships with services, and different types of service facilitate different relationship possibilities. In the first part of this chapter we discuss the modern mental health service provision context, before moving on to look at different kinds of mental health problems as well as a range of more specialised perspectives on mental health work.

Introduction

It is now rare to see adult mental health social work identified as a specific area of service delivery. But this is a fairly recent development, reflecting big changes in how services are thought about at the organisational and policy level, and how they are 'configured' and delivered at local level. Just as social work with children and families has been mostly reorganised within the broad multi-agency and multi-professional sweep of 'children's

services', adult mental health social work is now usually a part of 'adult services' which will include older people, people with learning difficulties, and so on.

Similarly, as principal responsibility for children's services has shifted towards Education, responsibility for mental health services, including social work, now rests, in England and Wales, with Health. This has had a major impact on the identity of adult mental health social work, not least because its political, organisational and policy base has moved out of the local government sector, while that of child and family social work is still rooted there alongside education. Thus, while many mental health social workers may be formally employed by a local authority, they are often permanently 'seconded' to health, and work in the overarching context of the new mental health and social care trusts which are usually 'partnerships' between health and local authority employers.

Care in the community

Think ahead

Care in the community is one of those ideas that it is very hard to be against. On the other hand, the 'community' sometimes has the NIMBY (Not in my back yard!) response when hostels for psychiatric patients are established.

Think honestly – how would you react if the house next door to you were to be converted into residential accommodation for former long-stay patients? What might your reactions tell you about some of the real world dilemmas of community care?

These changes are part of a long-term trend, which was given major impetus in Britain by the 1990 NHS and Community Care Act and the introduction of the Care Programme Approach (CPA) which aimed to standardise and improve community care and establish duties for English health authorities. This legislation not only led the way in establishing the new 'internal market' system in health and social care, dividing the organisation of care into 'purchasers' (or 'commissioners') of care on the one hand, and 'providers' of care on the other, it also signalled a major policy development – the commitment to 'care in the community' as opposed to 'institutional care'. In mental health this was associated with a policy of closing and running down the huge Victorian psychiatric hospitals (or asylums) which were often located in rural settings outside major urban centres, and wherever possible relocating, or maintaining, long-term psychiatric patients in community settings. Many of these old psychiatric hospitals are still standing, but they have often been sold off and redeveloped into privately owned housing estates or have even become university campuses. If you train as a social worker at the University of the West of England, you will be based at a campus that was once a psychiatric hospital. Of course, in-patient facilities are still needed for people with severe mental health difficulties at certain points in their lives, but these are now usually provided in smaller, more local psychiatric facilities.

Implementing community care is challenging, partly because processes of care that were once rather invisible – locked away from public view in psychiatric hospitals, as were the patients themselves – have become more visible. In 1998 Frank Dobson, who was then Secretary of State for Health, declared 'Community Care has failed'. Perhaps this was a plea for increased funding and resources, but at any rate it did not deter governments from progressing policy. In 1999 the National Service Framework (NSF) for mental health was introduced, organised around seven minimum standards for mental health services. Policy now developed towards a focus on combating social exclusion arising from mental health problems, improving access to services, creating effective services for people with severe and enduring mental health conditions, supporting carers and reducing suicide rates. One of the most important and exciting overarching principles to emerge from this policy drive was an emphasis on early intervention (EI), which to some extent has replaced the more traditional idea of 'prevention'. The development and evaluation of EI is discussed more fully below.

For many decades, up until about 1980, 'psychiatric social work' was a large and thriving specialist area of practice with its own training courses, professional associations and a strong sense of professional identity. A few such posts still survive, but the big traditional division between community and hospital-based mental health social work services has now largely disappeared as a result of the policy initiatives outlined above. In their place a series of new styles of service have evolved, the most important of which are:

- Community Mental Health Teams (CMHTs)
- Assertive Outreach Teams
- Crisis resolution/ home treatment services.

All these services share some common characteristics:

- They are multidisciplinary
- They are community-based and focused
- They continue to rely heavily on psychiatric *clinical* leadership
- They promote 'early intervention' for mental health problems where at all possible.

In addition, in line with the overall trend towards a 'primary care' led health service, there have been more recent moves to train and develop 'primary mental health care workers' (for both adult and child mental health) who work in health centres, GP practices and so on.

A Victorian psychiatric hospital
(*Source*: Corbis/Robert Sciarrino/Star Ledger)

Community care – integration or threat to identity?

'When CMHTs are formed, staff come not only with their own personal culture and history, but with their professional culture and history. Staff used to working within hospitals are familiar with a culture of benign patriarchy with doctors at the top . . . Within social service departments, where fieldwork in the community was the major preoccupation, workers were "held" by statutory obligations and by supervision and management systems that monitored this.

The formation of CMHTs places all these people (some willingly, others unwillingly) in the community where, it can be argued, the dominant defence against the anxiety of working with disturbed clients in this setting is fight or flight. There is no shortage of opportunities for staff in CMHTs to fight each other as the team included workers from different professional disciplines who would previously have worked in separate agencies with different cultures and different defences. We can all recognise a tendency in ourselves to preserve the goodness of our discipline or team by projecting the conflict and having arguments with people who are outside this. However, when we acknowledge those people who might conveniently have been "our enemies" in the past as "part of us", we have to struggle with the discomfort this produces.'

(Foster and Roberts, 1998: 136–7)

In 2007 The NHS Confederation published *Time and Trouble: Towards Proper and Compassionate Mental Healthcare* (NHS Confederation, 2007*)*, a short and accessible review of progress in the new mental health system. With respect to early intervention this report says: 'There is a strong relationship between delay in treating psychosis and poorer outcomes, and EI cost effectiveness is clear' (2007: 15). In one audit of an EI service, 77 patients were assessed. 'Hospital admissions were dramatically reduced, as were compulsory treatment under the Mental Health Act, suicide rates, and cannabis use. No users were lost to follow up . . . and employment/occupation were markedly improved' (2007: 5). However, in another part of Britain, a first audit of EI in 2005 showed that a third of the population had no local EI service, found marked variations in service delivery standards and that a third of services were not covering the full age range. So although there is further work to do, the report quotes a GP whose daughter has schizophrenia: 'EI has been a story of alignment between what service users and their families have been asking for, what has been increasingly shown to be clinically effective, and what has now been shown to be cost effective' (2007: 13).

Assertive outreach (AO) is a proactive way of working to help people in their own homes 'when relationships between services and user are complex, where managing daily life may be difficult, and problems exacerbated by repeated hospital admissions', while crisis resolution and home treatment services (CRHT) offer rapid assessment, support, treatment and alternatives to hospital admission (2007: 16–17). The report quotes a vice-president of the Royal College of Psychiatrists: 'When done properly, CRHT reduces admissions by 25–50 per cent and halves compulsory admissions, improves wards by eliminating or reducing overcrowding, and is hence the single best quality and efficiency improvement in mental health in the last 30 years' (2007: 17).

There are very few 'gold standard' randomised controlled trial (RCT) research studies of these new interventions but one, which examined the impact of a Crisis Resolution Team in London, found that the service did reduce the number of hospital admissions, although the effect was mostly in relation to voluntary rather than compulsory admissions. There was some evidence that patient satisfaction was improved in comparison to ordinary acute services (Johnson et al., 2005).

New Horizons – beyond care in the community to mental health is 'everybody's business'

In 2009 the Labour government published its *New Horizons* (DoH 2009a) consultation document outlining a fresh strategy for mental health in Britain. The vision informing this approach goes beyond 'care in the community' and has parallels with the 'preventative state' policy vision for childhood represented in *Every Child Matters* (DoE 2003a and see Chapter 16). *New Horizons* proposes that mental health is 'everybody's business' and this is one aspect of locating mental health within a broad public health policy framework. In turn this connects to an emphasis on prevention and early intervention as the key to improving mental health outcomes in our society.

'Early intervention' has more than one meaning or application. At one level it refers to the need to respond and intervene as quickly as possible when an individual shows signs of deteriorating mental health. For example, it is quite well evidenced that accurate diagnosis and carefully planned intervention in a first episode of psychosis can prevent relapse or recurrence later on. But there is another meaning, which is more to do with social strategies for prevention, based on the best available scientific evidence about the social origins of mental well-being and mental health problems. You can get a flavour of this thinking from the following short extracts from one of the vast range of publications generated by the Government Office for Science 'Foresight' project:

'Learning difficulties are a particular problem, affecting up to 10 per cent of children. Yet too often they remain unidentified, or are treated only when advanced. The result can be underachievement in school and disengagement by the child, sometimes leading to a long-term cycle of anti-social behaviour, exclusion and even criminality. Improvements in early detection combined with focused interventions could prevent problems developing and create broad and lasting benefits for the child and society.'

'Interventions to promote the best possible mental development need to start as early as possible – mental development starts in the womb.'

(Foresight Mental Capital and Well-being
Project, Executive Summary, 2008,
www.foresight.gov.uk)

The ambition of this vision and its basis in 'science' can also be gauged from the Figure below which attempts to represent the whole life course in terms of biological, social, and other factors affecting mental health.

At the time of writing it seems that the new coalition government in Britain will be committed to implementing the New Horizons agenda. A cynical view of this commitment would point to those aspects of the programme

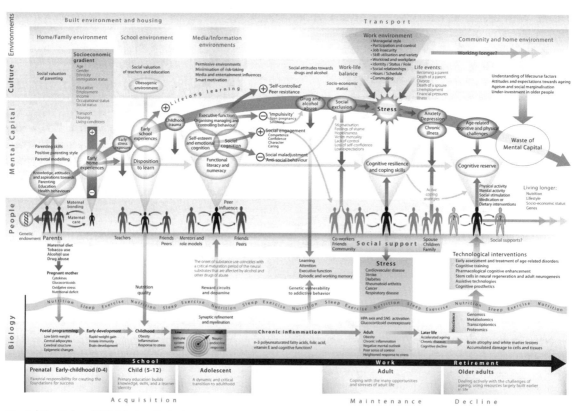

Mental Capital and Well-being Project

A closer look

Mental Health Services in Scotland

The Mental Health (Care and Treatment) (Scotland) Act 2003 provides the legislative framework for Scottish mental health services for adults. The Act has a greater focus on advocacy and the rights of the individual. There is also a greater focus on recovery, which involves supporting people to be active in managing their own health care and to carry out everyday activities even with ongoing symptoms.

There have been significant developments in mental health policy since the publication of the *Framework for Mental Health Services in Scotland* in 1997 (Edinburgh: Scottish Executive, 1997). The Framework was written to assist staff in health, social work and housing agencies to develop a joint approach to the planning, commissioning and provision of integrated mental health services and to also help others who use the services, care for them, and staff in other agencies. *Delivering for Mental Health* (Edinburgh: Scottish Government, 2006) is the current national plan for improving mental health services and covers the prevention and treatment of mental health problems. It sets out

the key services that should be available across Scotland.

There is now a greater focus on recovery within Scottish mental health services. This involves supporting people to be active in managing their own health care and to carry out everyday activities, even with ongoing symptoms. The Scottish Recovery Network, with Scottish Government support, is developing a tool, known as the Scottish Recovery Indicator, to help service providers to develop their services in a way that supports people to recover from long-term mental health problems. The Scottish Recovery Indicator was piloted in five NHS boards during 2007. An evaluation of the tool showed it could help services make changes to strengthen their approach to recovery (*Evaluation of the Scottish Recovery Indicator Pilot in Five Health Board Areas in Scotland*, Edinburgh: Scottish Government Social Research, 2008). The tool is currently being further developed.

In keeping with New Horizons (see above) the emphasis in Scotland is on mental health being 'everyone's business'.

For further information see www.scotland.gov.uk/Topics/Health/health/mental-health/servicespolicy/Framework/intro

---

that seem consistent with the 'low cost' priorities of the new political administration. 'Personalisation', for example, is a key feature of the New Horizons vision for mental health services of the future – but personalisation is not a 'service' with identifiable costs. Might it then transpire to mean something more like 'organised informal care' in the context of depleted professional services? Equally, public health' strategies can range from intensive, high-cost programmes of universal intervention based on scientific analysis to low-cost, educational 'life-style' campaigns.

IAPT – A win–win formula?

An important development from the last years of New Labour's period of office, which looks set to remain, is the Improving Access to Psychological Therapies (IAPT) initiative. Consistent in many ways with the public health orientation of *New Horizons*, this was the brainchild of Lord Richard Layard, an economist with an interest in social well-being (Layard 2005). Layard worked out an

apparently simple 'win–win' formula for improving the nation's mental health at no cost, and turned it into a policy programme. In short, he found evidence that many people on long-term incapacity benefit were diagnosed with depression. Trials of short-term cognitive behavioural therapy (CBT) for mild to moderate depression seem to show impressive results in helping people improve sufficiently to return to work. Layard reasoned that increased government investment in community-based psychological therapy services would yield an equivalent financial return from savings in incapacity benefit, as well as improved mental health for significant numbers of people. Pilot IAPT centres were established and then the programme was 'rolled out' on a much wider front.

Like most apparently simple solutions to complex problems, the project was both inspired and flawed. On the one hand, it promoted the role of 'talking therapies' in mental health work, and took these closer to ordinary people, something which mental health service users and many therapeutically minded professionals have long been agitating for. On the other hand, it took a naive view of the evidence for CBT which was weaker than its proponents tended to proclaim, and ignored the fact that a high proportion of people diagnosed with depression have a number of other complicating conditions which mean that a short course of CBT was unlikely to have the immediate results anticipated by Layard. On the ground, IAPT services and local policy makers quickly realised that the situation was more complicated, and that while many people referred into therapy could benefit in the short term, the value of the exercise lay in having engaged them in a manner which could allow for more subtle assessment of their longer-term needs. CBT-trained psychologists rather than social workers or even nurses and psychiatrists predominate in IAPT services, but gradually multidisciplinary teams have re-formed in response to this complex new field of primary care intervention.

IAPT thus presents a mixed picture. Some critics would argue that it merely represents an extension of the 'medicalisation' or 'psychologisation' of everyday distress, since CBT tends to view mental health difficulties in a rather mechanical way, as the product of 'faulty thinking' which can be put right through learning new 'cognitive strategies'. This is an oversimplification, and many CBT therapists take a more nuanced and subtle view of their work. Darian Leader is a trenchant critic of the way our society and our health services respond to depression, and his book *The New Black– Mourning, melancholia and depression* (2009) is a subtle and insightful account of how a socially engaged psychoanalytic practitioner sees this phenomena. He writes:

'CBT, however, is almost the only psychological therapy on offer through healthcare trusts. This is for a simple reason: it works. But not in the sense we might wish for. As a superficial treatment, it cannot access unconscious complexes and drives. What it can do is provide results on paper that keep NHS managers happy.'   (2008: 19)

Reflect

Have you ever been severely depressed (many people have been, even if for short periods)? What do you think triggered it, or do you think of depression as something that people have in their 'genes' or 'brains'?

If you were in acute distress as a result of depression, might you accept a course of drugs – or would you prefer to engage in some therapy? Why?

Mental health in society – some different perspectives

The entire trend towards care in the community is not unique to Britain, and most Western European countries, as well as the USA, Canada, etc. have been developing in the same direction. However, the underlying political and policy motivation has not always been the same in all countries. Indeed, there are quite complex debates about the underlying forces driving this global trend; overall, there does seem to be a basic humanitarian element informing the movement towards 'community care'. The asylums (or psychiatric 'bins' as they were often known) often functioned as a way of keeping people with mental health problems 'out of sight, out of mind' in relation to the rest of society. In the 1960s and 1970s many scandals emerged concerning the ill treatment and neglect of long-term patients, while radical political and sociological critiques of how the system perpetuated itself through the 'institutionalisation' of people into a passive, dependent, patient 'role' added immense weight to the impetus for change (Goffman, 1961). An entire alternative 'anti-psychiatry' movement developed in this period, which argued vociferously that conventional psychiatry and the associated 'psy' professions (including mainstream social work) were in effect little more than a method of controlling a particular 'problem population' who were more 'disturbing than disturbed', and were thus the object of a massive programme of social 'scapegoating' (Laing, 1967; Sedgwick, 1982). However, others (Scull, 1984) have argued that while the movement towards care in the community *seemed* to be a largely politically and ethically led trend, in fact it was only made possible by the discovery in the 1950s and 1960s of new kinds of 'psychotropic drugs' that allowed the worst symptoms of psychotic conditions to be better managed, enabling people to live in the community. These developments opened the door to a more politically progressive stance towards mental health difficulties in society, but in Scull's view the latter was taking a piggyback ride on the former.

Meanwhile in some countries, there definitely was a much more self-conscious, organised political radicalism informing the move out of the old hospitals. In 1978 in Italy the celebrated Law 180 was enacted to oblige regional authorities to set up community treatment centres, and relocating psychiatric patients as a productive part of the local community and economy. In some areas, worker's cooperatives were set up to enable patients not just to do productive work, but to gain a genuine sense of ownership and control of their lives and work, while the old hospitals were not sold off but refurbished as hostels for visitors to the region, for example. These radical initiatives can still inspire professionals in other countries, and quite recently *Community Care* magazine carried an article about one mental health service manager's study trip to Italy to learn from how services work in Trieste (Hayes, 2007).

A closer look

Recent developments in Northern Ireland: The Bamford Report

The key legislative framework for the delivery of Mental Health services in Northern Ireland has been the Mental Health (Northern Ireland) Order 1986. In 2002 the DHSSPSS established the Northern Ireland Review of Mental Health and Learning Disability chaired by Professor Roy McClelland and the late Professor Bamford. The primary focus of the work involved four core aspects:

1. Reforming and modernising services
2. Improving community mental health and well-being
3. Preventing mental ill health and reducing suicide
4. Developing a vision of services underpinned with rights to full citizenship, equality and social inclusion.

The subsequent report became known as the 'Bamford Report' and it was the most comprehensive review of mental health and learning disability services undertaken in Northern Ireland. Over a six-year period the review led to the publication of 11 reports and established the strategic direction for service delivery. However, the associated financial and resource implications associated with over 600 recommendations have hampered and delayed its implementation.

The survival of 'alternatives'

While the intensity of the 'politics of mental health' that underlay some of these trends has largely quietened, something of its spirit lives on in contemporary mental health service user movements and in some voluntary-sector organisations such as MIND that provide a more 'grass roots', supportive, participatory style of service in local communities while also actively campaigning at national policy levels on mental health issues. Helen Morgan (1998) has written about an important and interesting project led by service users, but with full involvement from mental health commissioners and providers to enable a meaningful dialogue with the statutory and independent sectors. Service users, with consultative help, designed and led the various meetings and interventions. Something of both the realism but also the radicalism of this initiative is captured in a remark made by a service user who said at one meeting, 'We may be ill, but we're not stupid'. Very often, as in other service areas, an unhelpful 'split' can develop between mental health service user organisations and professionals in which the latter come to feel devalued, passive and unable to give voice to their perspective, while service users may feel temporarily 'empowered'; but in the mental health system as a whole, nothing changes. Cooper and Lousada (2005) comment on this dynamic in terms of how the service user as a 'citizen' with rights gets pushed to the fore, while the service user as a patient with needs becomes suddenly invisible, which results in the professionals feeling as though they have no role. This enacts a kind of 'reversal' of an 'oppressor/victim' dynamic which, like all such simple, 'binary' formulations, misses many other dimensions of the situation. In fact, all the evidence is that service users *want* professionals to be active, competent, engaged and to get on with their jobs, *but also* to be respectful, to consult properly, to be realistic and to stand up for patients in the face of the more 'mindless' aspects of the 'system of care'.

An important but now threatened tradition of treatment and care for people with serious mental health problems that has always acknowledged the complexity of relationships between service users and professionals is the therapeutic community movement. Therapeutic communities are sometimes residential, and sometimes based on day care, although elements of their philosophy and practice can be found incorporated into mental health settings that are not fully modelled on community lines. One founding principle of this tradition is that 'everyone has ill or disturbed parts to them, and everyone has well parts to them'. However, the *role* of 'staff' in a therapeutic community is distinct from that of residents, and this is what underpins the *work* of the community. In line with the principles and practices informing psychoanalysis and psychotherapy, staff will usually have had a good deal of therapy themselves, and will be engaged in regular and intense (individual and group) reflective supervision in the course of the work. Staff continue to explore and *value* contact with their 'disturbed' aspects because it is through understanding of these processes in themselves that they can be of help to others.

A central idea of this tradition is that mental disturbance is not only something that is 'inside' individuals. Because of their family or community histories some individuals may be more vulnerable or susceptible to 'breakdown', to becoming 'ill', or manifesting disturbance at particular points in their lives; but the line dividing the patients from the staff is always assumed to be a thin one, and a dynamic one, because the forces that 'make people mad' are assumed to be interpersonal, group, and also societal, as much as individual. Thus, a principle of 'democracy' lies at the core of therapeutic practice, not in a populist sense of 'we are all equal in all respects' but more one of 'we are all in this together'. Daily community meetings of all staff and residents, at which events, feelings, interactions, and changes in the life of the community are aired, are an essential part of putting this philosophy into practice. In 'pure' forms of therapeutic community, the major decisions, such as whether to admit a new patient, or exclude one who has become too disruptive, are taken by the whole 'community'.

A few therapeutic communities survive in the NHS, offering help to people with personality disorders (Bateman, 2004), to families in which there has been abuse or neglect of children, and to adults with mental health difficulties. More are still to be found in the independent sector, especially for children and young people, but also for adults (Kennedy et al., 1987). In the short term this is an expensive and labour-intensive method of intervention, but there is good research evidence to show that subsequent dependence on health and social care services is significantly reduced (Warren and Norton, 2004).

Summary: modern mental health social work

Mental health has frequently been seen as a 'Cinderella service' of the NHS in Britain. It wins few votes and for politicians, policy makers and the general population may be more an object of fear and anxiety than curiosity and commitment. Recent governments have tried to rectify this and the National Service Framework (NSF) for mental health was one of the first to be introduced by the Blair government. However, as in all health and welfare sectors, cost pressures and the search for 'what works' (as fast and cheaply as possible) has distorted the development of mental health services. Recent initiatives around Improving Access to Psychological Therapies (2007) have aroused huge controversy because of policy

arguments linking adult depression, inconclusive evidence for the effectiveness of (cheap and quick) cognitive behavioural therapy, and the assumption that treatment on this model will enable large numbers of people to come off state benefits and return to work, thus cancelling out the additional investment in expanding CBT services nationally. The 2007 Mental Health Bill broadened the range of professions, beyond social workers, eligible to perform key statutory mental health functions.

Below we examine in more detail the key roles and tasks of mental health social workers, but in contexts such as those outlined above, modern mental health social work is struggling somewhat to define and promote its identity successfully. Many workers feel that the statutory sector is still where the most challenging work is done, while others feel that the independent sector provides more professional 'space' for creativity, autonomy and a questioning approach to this always controversial area of practice.

Naming and classifying

Think ahead

'Schizophrenic' and 'Bipolar' are the names of common but serious mental disorders. They are also highly emotive words that are misused by people, sometimes to evoke anxiety and fear.

What does the word 'schizophrenic' conjure up for you?

Are your immediate reactions rational and well grounded, or do they stem from some of the more 'tabloid' uses of the term that evoke unfounded anxieties?

Mental health problems make themselves known to the sufferer, and to those around them, in particular ways. On the one hand it is important to have a language for naming and classifying these different 'presentations' of mental ill health, while on the other hand we should avoid the traps of 'labelling' people. When a name becomes a label, then it means we have stopped thinking about the person and their living experience. Yet to understand what is happening in their experience and relationships we need to retain respect for the work that others have done to try to make sense of the different varieties of mental health difficulty. Mainstream psychiatry has evolved highly systematic procedures for classifying and diagnosing mental health conditions, which are contained in two current manuals to which you will hear reference in mental health settings. These are known as ICD-10 (WHO, 2003) and DSM-IV-TR (American Psychiatric Association, 1994).

Typically in our society, mental health problems have been divided into two major categories: the psychoses, sometimes called the 'major' mental illnesses, and the neuroses. A mistaken implication of this division is that the psychoses are always to be understood as more serious than neuroses. As we shall see and as with most things in mental health work, it is not that simple.

The psychoses

Within the psychoses, the following sub-classification is important:

- The organic psychoses which have a definite physical basis, perhaps as a result of epilepsy or brain injury
- The functional psychoses which include the range of conditions known as the schizophrenias, and the range of conditions known as affective psychoses which include psychotic depression, manic depression (bipolar disorder as it is now often known) and mania.

Functional psychoses are called this because the primary disturbance is to mental 'functions'. Thus, for example, hallucinations are disturbances of perception, and delusions are disturbances in thinking, while disturbances of mood and feeling affect emotional functioning. In psychotic states, hallucinations may be found in one or several of the 'senses': for example, auditory hallucinations ('hearing voices'), hallucinations of smell (olfactory) and of taste (gustatory). Disturbances of thought include the more familiar idea of delusions (e.g. the absolute conviction that your neighbour is plotting to murder you), but also experiences such as 'thought broadcast' (the belief that your thoughts can be heard by others) or thought insertion (the conviction that someone else is inserting thoughts into your mind). Affective psychoses are called by this name because the primary area of difficulty is in the area of emotional functioning. 'Affect' is just another word for emotion or feeling. A tendency towards very extreme elation in which a person's mood overrides all else and may convince them that they are all-powerful, hugely rich and so on, is characteristic of the condition known as mania. When a person swings between the two 'poles' of mania and acute depression or low mood, then 'bipolar' affective disorder might be diagnosed.

These kinds of extreme and rather dramatic symptoms can distract attention from the fact that people suffering from a psychotic condition are often also profoundly affected in their capacity to relate to others in an ordinary, realistic way. A central experience of someone afflicted by psychotic symptoms is of being under attack *by someone else*, or being subject to profound intrusion of their mind *by someone else*. The delusion will usually centre on a particular person, or perhaps an organisation, but if you spend time and build a relationship with someone suffering from a continuing psychotic state, you are likely to realise that their intense vulnerability with respect to their 'persecutors' extends to most if not all people. Building trusting relationships with people who suffer from a psychotic condition is thus very important, but difficult and testing for the professional.

The category of affective psychoses includes depression, if assessment shows that particular patterns of symptoms are present. Very profoundly depressed people may often be afflicted by delusions of guilt – that they have caused a major disaster, for example. So the line between functional and affective psychotic states is not always so clear. Depression in general is often represented in the psychiatric literature as a spectrum with psychotic or 'endogenous' depression at the severe end, and neurotic or 'reactive' depression at the mild or less severe end. These terms imply that the causes of psychotic depression are somehow located inside the person (this is what 'endogenous' means), while neurotic depression is a reaction to external events, such as a bereavement. While there is some meaning in this distinction, it also quickly becomes problematic. Because of 'internal' factors in their history, a person may be more or less vulnerable to depression (as opposed to an ordinary grief reaction) following a loss; equally it is obviously the case that external factors play a significant part (in the present and the past) in accounting for the emergence of a psychotic depression.

The neuroses

According to psychiatric systems of classification, 'neurotic' mental health difficulties include anxiety states, phobias, obsessive–compulsive disorders, panic disorders, and, as we have seen, reactive depression. While fewer of us might think we have any direct experience of the more extreme symptoms of functional psychoses, all of us can probably identify to some extent with the experience of some of the common neuroses. The difference between being 'a bit neurotic' and having a diagnosable mental health condition becomes quite difficult to define. Is a fear of spiders (arachnophobia in the jargon) a 'disorder' or 'condition'? Is fear of flying a mental health problem? When does being a 'perfectionist' or habitually checking very carefully that all the lights are turned off before leaving the house shade over into an obsessional neurosis?

The answer is indeed largely one of degree, and of the extent to which the condition affects the capacity for ordinary living and relating to people. At one end of the spectrum 'neurotic' difficulties do shade into ordinary personality traits, while at the other end the distinction between major and minor mental illnesses starts to look a bit shaky. Severe obsessive–compulsive disorder can completely ruin a person's life; a genuine phobia about flying might severely affect a modern business person's career potential. Chronic depression that does not respond to drugs or CBT affects large numbers of people, many of whom have long-term difficulties in forming relationships and finding satisfying work.

In community mental health settings, a social worker may well work with service users who suffer from one or more 'neurotic' disorders, as well as people with diagnoses of schizophrenia or other psychotic conditions. One reason why classifications are no more than a useful starting point for practitioners is that many service users are diagnosed as afflicted by more than one condition; this is known as 'co-morbidity'. A further complication is the prevalence of what is now known as 'dual diagnosis', which refers to alcohol and drug dependence alongside a mental health condition.

Personality disorder

'No longer a diagnosis of exclusion' was the catchphrase used for a recent policy initiative in England to develop and promote new services for people with personality disorder (Department of Health, 2003). The 1983 Mental Health Act was partly responsible for 'excluding' people with this diagnosis, because it specifies that in order to be eligible for compulsory admission to a psychiatric hospital a person must be both suffering from a recognised mental disorder and be 'treatable'. Personality disorder (PD) has, until recently, mostly not been regarded as a 'mental disorder' under the meaning of the Act and/or as untreatable. However, there is a double edge to this question because it is possible that many of the people who will become the focus of new powers of detention under the Mental Incapacity Bill in Britain will have this diagnosis. This controversial legislation allows the

detention of people on the grounds of an assessed risk that they *could* harm others, rather than evidence that they have done so, even though they do not have a recognised mental disorder.

People with a diagnosis of personality disorder or Borderline Personality Disorder (BPD) are sometimes violent towards other people. But they are much more likely to harm themselves. 'BPD is common, affecting about 1 per cent of the general population and up to 20 per cent of psychiatric inpatients. Approximately 9 per cent of BPD patients eventually kill themselves', writes one of the leading psychiatrists and psychotherapists in this field (Bateman, 2004). However, the same author's research studies are part of a growing body of evidence that personality disorder can be treated, particularly through intensive day hospital or therapeutic community methods (see also Warren and Norton, 2004).

People suffering with PD are often not easy to be with. Perhaps part of the reason why they have become an 'excluded' group within the mental health system is that they may often be experienced as aggressive, manipulative and very self-centred. Because they do not appear to 'suffer' much, but rather make others suffer, they can be readily rejected or misrecognised as just 'nasty people'. But sophisticated research, drawing on attachment theory and psychoanalysis, has started to reveal the developmental roots of PD. Fonagy and his colleagues have shown how the absence of what they call 'reflective function' or difficulties in 'mentalisation' underlie the personality-disordered individual's extreme difficulty in taking account of other people or their feelings, wishes, and autonomy. (Bateman and Fonagy, 2006). Because they often move around in a no-man's land between ordinary society and the mental health system, people with these difficulties often come to the attention of social care services by default. Cooper and Trevillion's (1985) paper on 'Social work with angry men' is an account of trying to work with a number of such people in a front-line social work setting.

Summary

This section has provided a very brief introduction to some of the main ways of classifying mental health difficulties. But a glance at one of the diagnostic manuals mentioned at the opening of the section will show you that this is a vast and complex topic in itself. Do mental health social workers need to have thorough specialised knowledge of this kind in order to practise? Yes, and no

A closer look

A campaigner speaks

Paul Jenkins, the chief executive of *Rethink*, one of Britain's largest mental health charities, was interviewed in a national newspaper just after he took up his post. Here is an extract from the article that focuses on the new mental health bill that was passing through parliament at the time:

'As with many in the mental health sector, he is convinced that some measures – including detaining people who are not proven to be a danger to themselves or others, and Community Treatment Orders, which are designed to force discharged patients to take medication – will not enhance public safety, which was a key argument put forward by ministers for their inclusion in the bill.

"The facts and figures just don't support the level of concern," Jenkins says. "We're sceptical that what's

being proposed has any evidence behind it as being an effective solution."

It is a view bolstered last week by the publication of a review of 72 international studies into the effectiveness of CTOs by the Institute of Psychiatry [which] concludes: "There is no robust evidence about the effects of CTOs on key outcomes."

The government should, he suggests, take a leaf out of the Scottish executive's legislative book. "I think some of the things that are in the Scottish legislation would be very powerful steps in the right direction to saying this isn't a one way street. For example, the automatic right to assessment. The other thing is the right to independent advocacy".'

(*Source*: Mary O'Hara, *The Guardian*, Society p. 5, 14 March 2007. Copyright Guardian News and Media Ltd. 2007)

would be our response! Twenty years ago, many social work trainings offered extensive teaching on psychiatry, in a way that almost none now do. This is a loss, because while the social work role in mental health work is not primarily one of providing 'treatment', practitioners need to be confident in understanding how their psychiatric and nursing colleagues think about the work. In a thorough and thoughtful book about mental health social work Colin Pritchard (2006: 109) writes: 'Social workers in this field are confronted with a range of theories, data and approaches, often with an overlap with the medico-psychiatric . . . How therefore can the social worker maintain their core psychosocial attributes, yet incorporate the necessary psychiatric information, without losing the essential individual client focus?' This is a good statement of the core challenge for adult mental health social workers, and it helps explain the range and complexity of the material you are engaged with in this chapter.

As we said at the start, classifications and names can become labels that hinder our thinking, but equally they do aim to capture something 'real'. It is not enough for social workers in this field to define their role as just advocates or as guardians of anti-oppressive practice for people with mental health problems. The helping relationship also requires an ability to engage with the

complex and difficult emotional and psychological realities that service users and carers are struggling with in themselves and their families.

Case study

Mohammed cont . . .

After his referral to the CMHT, Mohammed began a course of CBT treatment, but he failed several appointments. Then his wife contacted the social worker to say she feared he was deteriorating. He can't get up in the mornings, complaining that he is often awake through much of the night. That afternoon she found him crying uncontrollably, and saying he had no right to live. He made references to 'terrible things' he had done during the war, and also to how God will never forgive him if he is not with his mother when she dies. She has become frightened about what Mohammed 'might do'.

How do these developments make you feel?

Are there any particular courses of action you think you should now consider?

What is mental health and ill health?

Even in the apparently innocent act of choosing to give this section the above title, we have pitched ourselves (and you!) right into the middle of controversy. Some people would claim that there is no such thing as mental *ill health*. Others would fiercely contest this, but as we shall see not always for the same reasons. In Western societies there are several main frameworks of explanation for mental health problems that we will explore in more depth in a moment. But before moving on to this, we want to introduce you to the particular perspective on mental health that we will gradually develop in this section of the book.

The beginnings of a relationship-based perspective

The whole field of mental health is overrun with obscure jargon, scientific and pseudo-scientific terminology, contradictory research evidence, and competing viewpoints about how to understand mental health problems. Some of this undoubtedly derives from the dominance of the so-called 'medical model' of mental health. Non-medical professionals often worry about the predominance of experimental and epidemiological research associated with the psychiatric tradition, and the continuing prevalence of what is often called the 'disease model' of mental health, which implies that mental health and illness should be understood on the same principles as physical health and illness. The place of psychoactive drugs in mental health is intimately bound up with this worldview, and can be another factor that makes social workers feel disempowered, since even (!) nurses have training and expertise in dispensing them. Social workers, whose training and personal inclinations are often in tension with such views, can find all this overwhelming. One response, which in our view never works, can be to decide that if we cannot beat them, then we had better join them. The result is social workers spouting psychiatric jargon and posing as something they are not, which helps nobody. Another, which works equally badly, is to take up an 'oppositional' stance, refusing what the psychiatric tradition has to offer while being unclear about what to offer in exchange.

What is often lost in this complicated tussle is the perspective from 'lived experience', which we advocate as

the best starting point for developing a relationship-based approach to the work. Donald Winnicott, a child psychiatrist and psychoanalyst who greatly valued the contribution of social workers to the whole field of mental health work and often wrote with them in mind, once quoted a colleague as saying 'Mental illness consists in not being able to find anyone who can stand to be with you' (Winnicott, 1965). This remark was not intended as a definition, but as a way of reminding us that mental ill health almost always involves periods of intense *suffering* or *mental pain*; in turn those who are suffering usually find it impossible not to transmit a good deal of their suffering to those around them. People in extreme or prolonged (sometimes called 'acute' and chronic') states of mental distress can be emotionally very difficult to tolerate being with over extended periods of time. In turn this may increase their sense of isolation which is already acute because of the sense that their 'inner torment' is not really understandable or accessible to anyone else. Already, taking this viewpoint, we can see that *relationships* are at the heart of doing mental health work – whether as a professional, or as a carer.

Here we would ask you to reflect on your own life experience for a moment, because many distressing, troubling and difficult aspects of everyday relationships are on a 'continuum' with mental health problems as defined more technically. Most of us have been depressed or very 'low' in spirits for a considerable period of time at some point, or we have been close to someone who has; many of you will have suffered the intense grief reaction that inevitably follows the death or loss of someone loved and important; many of us have known people who despite surface appearances to the contrary, turn out to be profoundly and unshakeably self-centred, to the extent that we come to realise they actually *cannot* see things from anyone else's point of view; perhaps you have known someone whom you decided was quite paranoid – always 'touchy', always inclined to believe that others are conspiring or deliberately excluding them (which can often be a kind of self-fulfilling prophecy); maybe the everyday task of staying in continual emotional contact with a very young baby's acute and seemingly boundless distress has felt completely overwhelming and frightening; very possibly you are, or know adults who are, intensely and inexplicably anxious or panic-stricken at times and just cannot be reassured; or maybe all of us can recognise that some of these descriptions apply to ourselves at least some of the time.

If so, we believe that an honest assessment of these experiences involves the recognition that the person is usually suffering. But to the extent that they are rather helpless – unaware, self-preoccupied, lacking any emotional resources to help themselves – while in the grip of such states of mind, those around them tend to suffer in their turn. The possible exception to this is the very self-centred person. At worst, people like this can inflict their extreme self-centredness on others and also dominate and control others' reactions to this behaviour, so that everyone becomes caught in a vicious 'system' from which it is hard to extricate themselves. Sometimes, the problem with people who display this kind of pattern is that they *do not* seem to suffer, or be aware of how they make others suffer. People diagnosed with 'personality disorders' are often extreme cases of this.

If the above vignettes seem a bit stark or depressing, then we would make two comments. On the one hand, few people are permanently in the grip of such experiences and patterns of relating; there are more hopeful, more engaged and realistic aspects to them as well, and it is terribly important not to lose sight of this. On the other hand, if mental suffering is to be taken seriously, then we must be emotionally capable of engaging with such states of mind – it is the suffering, helpless aspect of themselves that people in mental pain want to be recognised and understood, and we suggest that no amount of 'reassurance' or 'positive thinking' will, by itself, do much good. So, this leads to a kind of principle – in order to do mental health work well, we must be prepared to feel disturbed and distressed ourselves, at least some of the time. If we do not or cannot, then surely we are not in true emotional contact with the very aspect of matters that needs our emotional attention?

We will develop this stance on mental health social work as the chapter progresses. But first, it is helpful to delve a little more deeply into some of the surrounding theories and perspectives that actively inform the world of modern multi-professional mental health work.

Three perspectives on mental health

As we noted above there are a number of frameworks for understanding mental ill health and well-being in Western societies. The three we will focus on are:

- A cluster of explanations that argue for a biological basis to most mental illnesses, especially the more serious ones
- A range of theories that locate the origins of mental health (or well-being) primarily with psychological or developmental factors in the history of the individual

and/or his or her family or circumstances of childhood care
- A set of theories that emphasise the social causation of mental health problems.

Today, there is quite a high degree of consensus about the value of an integrated 'bio-psychosocial' model of explanation for mental health problems, although this level of theory is very general and often cannot tell us much, if anything, about either particular varieties of mental health problem, or particular individuals. The bio-psychosocial model will often seek to integrate the three above perspectives. It has less to say on a fourth perspective – social constructivism. On this view, ideas about what count as mental health and ill health are 'constructed' or produced by the 'discourses' that predominate in our social life (see Chapter 6 for further discussion of social constructivist ideas).

Biological explanations

Within the first set of theories or explanations which concern the underlying importance of biological factors in producing mental ill health, we find a whole number of sub-specialities, reflecting different traditions of research and clinical psychiatric practice. Important among these are genetic explanations, and neuroscientific and biochemical explanations. In turn, each of these comes in 'stronger' and 'weaker' forms; the former tends to insist on biological causes as a kind of ultimate, underlying reality that independently produces particular effects on mental life, or at least a disposition or vulnerability to such effects; the 'weaker' versions place greater emphasis on the importance of *interaction* between genetic or biochemical processes and the influence of the 'environment', which is to say the psychological and social developmental context of the individual. Strong causal theorists see the influence of genes, brain chemistry and so on as a 'one way street', while weak causal theorists see it more as a 'two way' one.

There is not space here to enter into detailed discussion of these 'models of the mind', but it is important to know that in recent years there have been huge, technologically enabled, advances in our capacity to study the relationship between brain activity and everyday emotional and cognitive functioning. These advances have not completely settled the 'one way or two way street' debate, but perhaps they have tended to favour the second. This is because it is now known that the human brain has two very important characteristics: first that it is 'plastic', in the sense that it does not automatically develop towards 'maturity' in the early years of life, but is shaped, modified, inhibited, and encouraged in its growth by a wide range of physical and other environmental factors in the first two-and-a-half years of life; secondly, even if the right physical environment (diet, physical care of the growing child, appropriate physical stimuli, etc.) is present, the brain also requires the right emotional and interpersonal conditions in order to develop fully, so that sometimes writers refer to the 'social brain'. There used to be debate about the relative contributions of nature (i.e. biology) and 'nurture' (i.e. the emotional and social environment) in shaping human development and character, but this has now largely been exposed as a 'false dichotomy'. Nature and nurture demonstrably interact in such complex and indissoluble ways that they are often, but not always, impossible to disentangle (Damasio, 1995; Wheeler, 2006).

However, the brain and its development is a separate process from the influence of genetic inheritance on our bodies and minds. Genetic inheritance can be thought of as a deeper form of biological 'encoding'. For many decades some psychiatrists and researchers have held that most of the 'major' mental illnesses have a strong genetic component to their causation. This position is strongly, though not conclusively, supported by research studies involving identical and non-identical twins who

have been separated at birth (thus disentangling the impact of environment from the impact of genes) and whose later mental health histories have then been charted. Such studies tend to converge around a set of common findings that suggest there is a powerful contribution from genetic inheritance in rendering an individual *susceptible* to specific later mental ill health. The main criticism of these studies is first of all that the numbers of research subjects are very small; secondly that they only provide us with evidence of 'risk', or statistical likelihood of developing a condition, and cannot predict anything about individuals; thirdly, that we still understand very little about what 'makes the difference' between those who do and those who do not develop a mental disorder in later life. Are the differentiating factors ones that could be the object of positive, preventative interventions, or is the nature of genetic 'susceptibility' such that the underlying disposition will always manifest itself in a defined but not individually predictable proportion of those with an inheritance of risk?

In many respects therefore this evidence is of little use to the practitioner who is almost always working with the individual and his or her family and network in circumstances where either a condition has already manifested, or where it has not and we have no way of predicting whether it will or will not. But, and this is

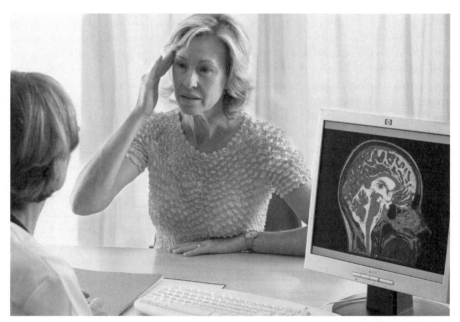

Brain scanning technology now provides hard evidence for many of the assumptions of developmental psychology and counselling about how the mind works
(*Source*: Corbis/Imane/Image Point FR)

an important point, this dilemma holds for the practitioner's relationship to *most* scientific and experimental research – at best it fills in the background picture, but rarely offers clear indications about what to do *in this particular case*.

Developmental and psychological explanations

The idea that childhood experiences influence our later development as people and shape our personalities is now part of 'common sense'. But this was not always the case. The emergence of psychoanalysis in the second half of the nineteenth century was probably the turning point in this view of the origins of mental health becoming established. Today, psychoanalysis and psychotherapy generally play only a small part in modern statutory mental health services in Britain. The situation is a bit different in other countries, such as the USA or France, but it is safe to say that the biological perspective on mental health problems is the dominant one. Nevertheless, many mental health workers, including many psychiatrists, continue to be heavily influenced by a 'developmental' perspective, and to combine a range of views about the causes of mental health difficulties in their thinking.

Whatever your view about causes, it is important to realise that the question of *causation* (or 'aetiology' in the jargon) is often treated separately from the question of *intervention* with people suffering a mental health problem. This is true in different ways. If a person is actively suicidal, or dangerously psychotic in their behaviour, questions about causes have to give way, at least temporarily, to questions about intervention or case 'management'. Today, this is often framed in terms of 'risk assessment' and 'risk management'. However, psychological therapies (sometimes known as 'talking therapies') are quite often selected as the 'treatment of choice' for people with mild or moderately severe diffi-

culties. But even here, depending on what variety of psychological therapy is on offer, the link between causes or early development and the therapy itself will be stronger or weaker.

The most common psychological therapy on offer today for adults is cognitive behavioural therapy (CBT), but CBT pays very little attention to the causes of the difficulties it aims to address (see Chapter 12 for a more extended discussion of CBT). Rather, it focuses on the individual's habits and patterns of thinking, and how these may be associated with a person's unrealistically 'negative' view of themselves and their life. The treatment then focuses on identifying and systematically changing these habits of thought. But how or why the patterns arose in the first place is not considered especially relevant. CBT does not really tell a story about psychological development. On the other hand, psychodynamic therapy does make a strong connection between childhood experience and adult mental health. The trained psychodynamic worker will be very interested in the service user's psychological, developmental and relationship history, and knowledge of this will inform the therapy process itself.

Statue of Sigmund Freud, the founder of psychoanalysis, at the Tavistock Clinic, London

There are two main developmental perspectives in adult mental health that social workers might make use of in their practice. One of these is the psychodynamic, and the other is attachment theory. Both of these are discussed in other chapters of this book (see Chapters 12 and 16) and so we concentrate here on just some of the features of these ways of thinking.

Attachment theory

Attachment theory was first developed by the psychiatrist and psychoanalyst John Bowlby and his work has generated a powerful tradition of further research and clinical practice with adults as well as children and young people. Bowlby (1973) held that 'The young child's hunger for his mother's love is as great as is hunger for food . . . Attachment is a "primary motivational system" with its own workings and interface with other motivational systems'. You may often see infant attachment to a parent or primary caretaker described as an 'instinctual' matter. But this is not quite what Bowlby meant. Rather, he thought that attachment was a psychological bond in its own right, although because the infant is so utterly dependent on their caretaker for survival it inevitably involves physical dimensions. This is immediately evident once an infant or young child is *separated* from his or her primary attachment figure. It was through observing how infants responded to separations that Bowlby and later researchers established the range of attachment 'categories' that now organise how we think when we use attachment theory. Initially, researchers thought that there were three main categories of attachment:

1. Secure attachment
2. Insecure attachment (avoidant)
3. Insecure attachment (resistant/ambivalent).

Although children classified as insecure have an anxious relationship to their caregiver, their 'strategy' for dealing with this is a reasonably consistent or 'organised' one. But later researchers (Main and Solomon, 1986) showed that there was a group of children who seemed not to fit within the threefold classification, and eventually they developed a fourth classification:

4. Disorganised/disoriented attachment.

Infants or young children who show a disorganised response to separations and reunions with their mother or caregiver can be seen to manifest contradictory behaviours or apparently inexplicable movements and postures such as stumbling for no apparent reason. We now understand that these children are often those who we think of

as 'abused', or whose parenting has involved hostility towards them, placing them in a kind of 'double bind' in which they are dependent on a person of whom they may be afraid.

Reflect

Attachment theory is in part all about our reactions to loss. Think back on your life.

How did you react to an important loss? What helped you cope? Do you think you have 'got over' the loss for good?

Attachment patterns established in childhood have been shown to 'endure into adulthood, although their expression and measurement change with age. Any changes in the patterns follow "lawful discontinuity", which can be brought about by a change in caregiving, caregiver, significantly traumatic events in the child's life or following therapy in adulthood' (Prior and Glaser, 2006). Experienced adult mental health workers may draw upon their knowledge of attachment theory in understanding adults with mental health difficulties, but on the whole this does not yet translate into many set methods for intervention.

However, here are some important exceptions to this statement. First, therapists and researchers working with people diagnosed with borderline personality disorder (BPD) have developed a method of treatment which is based on a combination of attachment theory, psychoanalysis, and clinical experience in helping people with such difficulties. Bateman and Fonagy (2006) describe how people with BPD often seem to suffer from the adult equivalent of disorganised attachment, usually referred to as an 'unresolved state of mind' with respect to the trauma they have suffered in childhood. The authors describe how, when faced with the emotional 'arousal' of a close or intense relationship, these people's capacity to think (or to 'mentalise') starts to disintegrate. In particular, this means that their ability to think about their own mind and behaviours and those of other people almost disappears. In other words, adult 'relationships' involving any closeness are very threatening to them, since they re-evoke in a very concrete form the traumatising relationships of childhood. This difficulty in taking account of the fact that other people have minds, intentions, needs, and so on is what characterises 'personality disorder'. Nevertheless, through carefully conducted research, Bateman and Fonagy have shown that a properly planned and implemented therapy and treatment programme produces good results. This is a good example of evidence-based mental health work with therapeutic relationships at its core.

Another important application of attachment theory in general mental health work concerns our reactions to loss and bereavement. The 'separation anxiety' that underlies different childhood responses to the loss of a primary attachment figure is echoed in adulthood when we experience the loss of important people in our lives through death or permanent separation. Bowlby saw grief as a special case of separation anxiety, since bereavement is an irreversible form of separation (Holmes, 1993). Despite temporary difficulties in accepting loss, such as that described in the Closer Look box, most people eventually 'work through' loss and recover the capacity and trust to make close relationships. But the 'working through' of mourning can be lengthy, intense and painful. Sometimes people need counselling or relationship-based help to resolve their grief, and this is work that mental health social workers should be able to offer. There is much evidence that unresolved grief contributes to the onset of depression in adults, so bereavement counselling can be seen as an important form of preventative work.

Attachment-based studies of children's reactions to loss helped us to understand the phases of normal mourning and grief in both children and adults. There are a number of slightly varying ways of describing these phases but the following (based on Holmes, 1993) is typical:

Emotional 'numbing' and denial is a common first response until it feels safe enough to tolerate the intense feelings following news of a loss (see the example in the Closer Look box).

Yearning, searching, anger – a bereaved person may continually scan their environment, hoping that the lost person will reappear. In the inner world, a process of continual exploration of the events leading up to the loss is common, perhaps involving a kind of wish that some 'mistake' has occurred and things will turn out differently. Similarly, the bereaved person may experience intense feelings of yearning, or pining for the lost figure. Anger towards anyone and everyone associated with the loss, including the dead or departed person, is also typical (and healthy) as the bereaved comes to terms with the irrevocable facts of the situation.

Disorganisation and despair, not least because loss of an intimate or loved one means that the 'secure base' to whom one would usually turn in times of distress is the very person who is lost. Where can hope or comfort be found? All the assumptions of security and predictability associated with an important relationship are thrown into question, and the mind is in turmoil.

Reorganisation and 'resolution' – at some level perhaps we never completely 'get over' important bereavements, as we discover each time we experience another loss and old internal 'wounds' seem to be opened up. But most people will achieve a good enough resolution of their grief so that they can envisage forming new attachments and intimate relationships.

Social work is often described as about working with people 'in transition'. Perhaps this expression tends to disguise the reality that 'transitions' often entail losses. Social workers need to be alert to the possible involvement of grief reactions, and responses to loss of many kinds, in their work. In effect, people may be profoundly 'attached' to all kinds of aspects of their lives apart from just loved ones – their home, their country, their job, their neighbourhood – and the loss of any of these can induce something akin to mourning.

A closer look

An initial reaction to loss

'A young scaffolder was brought into the casualty department dead, having fallen from a tall building. There were no external signs of injury. When his wife arrived she was completely and chillingly calm, expressing no emotion, simply saying: "Oh, but he's not dead, he's asleep, doesn't he look beautiful and peaceful." It was only when, several hours later, her mother arrived that she began to sob and wail uncontrollably.'
(Holmes, 1993: 90)

Psychoanalytic and psychodynamic theory
By contrast with attachment theory, psychoanalytic theory has been less successful so far in validating its concepts and models of development in a systematic 'scientific' fashion. However, researchers who combine psychoanalytic theory with models from the more traditionally scientific perspective of developmental psychology are making a lot of headway in validating psychoanalytic theory (Hobson, 2002), and there are an increasing number of attempts to bring attachment theory and psychoanalysis into a proper scientific

relationship (Bateman and Fonagy, 2006). For the practising social worker, it is the value of the applied skill in using psychodynamic understanding of people and their psychological development that should be emphasised. Here, there is a rich tradition of research and writing upon which to draw, which we link to the section above in which we presented the outline classifications of mental health problems.

We have already mentioned the work of D. W. Winnicott above. As a psychoanalyst, his thinking is of particular interest to social workers because he always kept in mind the interaction between the developmental potential of the infant, child or adult and what he called the 'environment'. 'Environment' for Winnicott could mean the quality of emotional caregiving in the first weeks of life, or it could mean the quality of response provided by a mental health agency to an adult in acute mental distress. In this, he was pointing out something about the connection between the two. Winnicott thought that particular adult mental health difficulties had their roots in particular forms of failure in the facilitating environment of infancy and childhood. Very young infants are *absolutely dependent* on their caregivers, but if all goes well they develop towards a stage of *relative dependence* and then *towards independence*. Psychosis in Winnicott's view has its origins in a failure of the very early emotional caretaking environment, when the infant has almost no internal resources of its own. Exposed to an extreme lack of emotional care, or to very poorly attuned emotional care at this stage, the infant in effect suffers a mental breakdown which manifests itself in later life as a serious mental illness in which, as we have noted above, the very core of the self is experienced as under terrible threat. The symptoms of psychosis are actually the manifestation of 'defences' against complete psychic disintegration.

Neurotic conditions in adulthood concern difficulties encountered at the stage of relative dependence, when the infant is capable of interpersonal relationships but may have developed defences against anxiety that are too rigid. The adult neurotic symptoms are once again the emergence of these defences in an organised form. The anxieties (for example, of loss of control over other people) are hidden 'behind' the defensive organisation that cause the adult problems (such as obsessive–compulsive behaviour).

Winnicott was also interested in another variety of adult difficulty, perhaps more closely associated with personality disorder. If individual development has proceeded well because of 'good enough' environmental

provision, but this caretaking is then withdrawn or lost for some reason, he thought this often resulted in the emergence of an 'antisocial tendency' in children and adolescents. In effect, antisocial behaviour for Winnicott is a kind of effort to make the environment recognise that something has been *lost*. Stealing would be the classic instance of this, if the act is seen as *symbolic* of the individual's experience that something was once 'stolen' from them.

How is this relevant to everyday mental health social work? In effect Winnicott thought that the mental health agency (or team) should think of itself, and its responses to the service user, in terms of the degree of dependence that is 'called forth' by the service user's distress and symptoms. A service user who suffers from anxiety attacks is unlikely to need hospital admission or residential care, and they can be helped through a well-structured programme of individual or group therapy. Their degree of 'dependence' on services reflects something about their basic degree of personality integration. An acutely mentally distressed person may be 'held' psychologically and practically through the provision of a reliable network of professional and family support, so that admission to hospital or another kind of residential facility is avoided; or matters may become so acute that a hospital admission is needed. If so, Winnicott does not consider this to be a failure, but an expression of the degree of psychological dependency required by the person at that point in time. The original meaning of 'asylum' becomes relevant here – a place of psychological as well as physical safety.

Although his writing can now seem rather dated in language and tone, some of the papers Winnicott wrote for social workers remain classics. Interested readers could start with 'The mentally ill in your caseload' (1965) which develops the point of view discussed above. A more contemporary resource that draws on the Kleinian developmental and psychoanalytic perspective, as well as some systemic thinking, is *Psychoanalytic Theory for Social Work Practice* (Bower, 2005). This book is subtitled *Thinking under Fire*, reflecting the fact that social work with people in distressed or disturbed states of mind is often emotionally charged and demanding by its nature. Some of the central developmental concepts from this tradition are used in the section on psychodynamic interventions in social work in Chapter 12. In the case study in that section, we noted how the worker found herself the object of sudden and extreme 'splitting' and 'projection' by a fragile service user. These defensive processes are held to be both features of early childhood development, and of everyday adult functioning. This is typical of the way developmental perspectives in mental health function, in that adult states of mind are always seen as continuous to one degree or another with the states of mind we traversed, more or less successfully, as children and adolescents. On this view, we never completely outgrow our psychological origins, however mentally 'healthy' or 'unhealthy' we believe ourselves to be.

Social origins of mental health problems

Mental health problems are not evenly distributed through the population of this country, or any country. How do we account for the variations that exist with respect to gender, social class, and ethnicity? This is a topic of heated and unending debate and research, and in this short section we introduce you to a few key perspectives on these questions.

The contemporary social policy perspective on these issues has been outlined in Chapter 2 of this book where we looked at 'social exclusion', but many would argue that this 'official' perspective is a less than adequate account of how and why inequalities in mental health arise and persist. Government policy has now situated mental health problems and services as part of the wider dynamic of 'social exclusion', and thus sees the persistence of inequalities in the distribution of these problems in broadly the same terms as other aspects of social exclusion – poverty, disability, poor housing and so on. The thrust of modern policy is very much 'solution focused' rather than 'problem focused', and concentrates on the idea that removing barriers to 'opportunity' is the key to unlocking the problem of inequalities of all kinds in our society. But are mental health problems the same kind of thing as 'housing problems', child poverty, or gender inequalities? There may be good evidence for saying that each of these other forms of exclusion *contributes* to increased levels of mental health difficulty in certain communities or sectors of society, but that is not the same as all of them being identical kinds of problem. There is an oversimplification at the heart of modern policy that is connected perhaps to an overemphasis on 'solutions' rather than a more detailed understanding of the nature and origins of different kinds of 'problem'.

Income inequalities

An important perspective that explains why different countries have such different patterns of inequality is the work of Richard Wilkinson (1996) who has shown that

a key to explaining these differences is underlying patterns of income inequality. Above a certain rather basic level, it is not 'poverty' that accounts for the presence or absence of 'well being' as measured on all sorts of indices, but whether people live in a country with large or small income differentials separating the richest from the poorest. Countries with small overall income differentials consistently score well in terms of the population 'well being', while those with large differentials score badly. These measures of well-being include measures of prevalence of various common mental health problems. However, the explanation for these 'between country' variations do not, as far as we know, account for the patterns of inequality within nations, and it is to these that we now want to give some attention.

Social class

In the mid-1970s, researchers began to publish the results of a major study into the social origins of depression, based on a large-scale study of women living in Camberwell, south London. The comprehensive account of this work by Brown and Harris (1978) has in many respects not been surpassed in sophistication, although many other important studies flowed from the methodologies and findings of this original work (e.g. Bifulco and Moran, 1998). Brown and Harris studied only women in their research because they already knew that a much higher proportion of women than men are diagnosed with clinical depression, so they would be able to 'capture' more depressed research subjects from a community sample of women than a sample of men. Thus, their research tells us less about this particular gender-based 'inequality' of mental health outcome than it might otherwise do. But the research did reveal an important relationship between social class and the risk of developing clinical depression for a woman.

Brown and Harris found that working-class women with three or more children under the age of 14 were four times more likely to be diagnosed depressed than were middle-class women with children in the same age range. The explanation for this finding can only be understood in terms of the complex model they developed to account for the origins of depression. Women became depressed if (a) they had experienced a 'provoking agent' – a major 'life event', such as a bereavement, material loss, a forced change of residence, or a long-term 'difficulty', such as living in overcrowded accommodation *and* (b) if they also had one or more of a number of 'vulnerability factors' in their lives. Vulnerability factors turned out to include absence of a confiding relationship, loss of mother before the age of 11, no employment outside the home, and having three or more children under 14 living at home. However, neither provoking agents nor vulnerability factors by themselves were sufficient to cause the onset of depression – a woman needed to have one or more vulnerability factors present *and* have suffered an event or major difficulty. Broadly, the more vulnerability factors she had, the greater the risk of becoming depressed if she did experience a provoking agent. So why are working-class women with children so much more at risk of becoming depressed than their middle-class counterparts? The former group do experience more 'events' and 'difficulties' than the latter, but in fact this did not explain the social-class difference. It was the fact that working-class women tended to be much more likely to have vulnerability factors (and more of them) in their lives that really made the difference.

This study shows that social class and risk of developing mental health difficulties are likely to be strongly related – but not in a simple manner. As Wilkinson's work also shows, we should be cautious about generalised 'political' statements linking adverse social conditions and mental health difficulties. Good research shows that the connections are rather specific. Nevertheless both these studies, and many more, definitely support the view that there *is* a 'politics of mental health' to which we should attend if we are serious about prevention, and about interventions that are sensitive to the social circumstances of people who suffer mental health problems.

Race and ethnicity

In Britain today people of different racial and ethnic origins are not diagnosed with mental health difficulties on an even pattern, and nor do they receive services on an even pattern. The effort to understand these inequalities in health outcome and in service delivery has been an important aspect of research, policy and service user activity since the late 1970s. This activity will continue because there is plenty of evidence that these patterns of inequality are persistent.

Roland Littlewood and Maurice Lipsedge, two psychiatrists with an interest in anthropology, were the first people to put the issue of racism and mental health on the wider professional and public agenda when they first published their book *Aliens and Alienists* in the early 1980s (Littlewood and Lipsedge, 1997). However, some ethnic minority communities themselves had been acutely aware of a pattern of discrimination, differential treatment responses, and consequently fear and suspicion of mainstream mental health services, for some

decades before this. Much of the work on racism and the mental health system has focused on the experiences of the black African and Caribbean communities in Britain because they seem to have suffered most. *Breaking the Circles of Fear* (The Sainsbury Centre for Mental Health, 2002) is an excellent, balanced, although perturbing review of the state of research, policy, and contemporary experience of black people's relationships with the mental health system. As yet, there is no proper consensus about the explanation for different patterns of diagnosis of major mental disorders among black British people. Formal psychiatric studies are helpful in identifying the patterns and trends, but usually lack any psychosocial or socio-political dimension to their interpretation of events. There tends to be something of a divide between those studies that emphasise the impact of institutional racism and those that seek for a more traditional biopsychosocial explanation.

Reflect

Whatever your own ethnicity, you may have unexamined prejudices and stereotypical beliefs about mental health in other racial groups. Think for a moment – what might these be? What evidence do you have for these beliefs?

What do we actually know? Most studies seem to confirm that black Afro-Caribbean people are more often diagnosed with schizophrenia than other ethnic groups, are more likely to be subject to compulsory detention under mental health legislation (Mental Health Act Commission, 1997; Morgan et al., 2005), are much less often diagnosed as depressed if they have a psychosis (McKenzie et al., 2001); thus they are also prescribed antidepressants less often, and less likely to be treated with psychotherapy whatever their diagnosis. Black people are perceived as more 'dangerous' by staff despite having lower scores for aggressive behaviour than white patients (Bhui, 2001). These kinds of factors are often cited to explain the disproportionate use of police powers to compulsorily detain patients (Turner et al., 1992). Overall then there is a strong basis for the perception within the black community that contact with mental health services is much more 'adversarial' than it is for white patients. However, the wider picture is also complicated, since there is evidence that, for example, white Irish people are over-represented in some but not all of the same ways.

Some commentators have emphasised 'cultural' misunderstanding as the root problem. For example, Littlewood and Lipsedge (1997) speak of a pattern of misdiagnosis of schizophrenia among black people because of a failure on the part of psychiatrists to understand short-term manifestations of mental distress in this community. Others stress the role of prejudice, institutional racism, and in effect a culture of 'fear' among *white* professionals that is systematically projected on to black people, with resulting distortions of perception, diagnosis, treatment and care. Here then 'relationship-based social work' becomes a complex and subtle matter, since, before they even begin, relationships can be imbued with suspicion, anxiety and fear deriving from a difficult history of contact between communities and mental health staff.

Social workers need to acquaint themselves thoroughly with the literature on these matters, get to know about their own prejudices and fears and take careful, account of the different pressures they may experience when working with service users from communities that have been part of the 'circle of fear'.

Case study

Mohammed cont . . .

Mohammed was assessed at home by a psychiatrist and an Approved Social Worker from the CMHT. The psychiatrist thought he was now suffering from a severe depression with some psychotic features, and both professionals agreed there was a risk of suicide. However, Mo seemed to be quite relieved to talk about his state of mind, and to have some insight. With some prompting from the social worker, he began to speak about his complicated thoughts about his wife's miscarriage. Mo felt guilty about his wife, as though he believed he might have been responsible for the loss of the baby, and this idea was mixed up with feelings of excessive responsibility for the family coming to England in the first place. He believed his wife secretly blamed him for not being 'strong enough' to have stuck it out in Bosnia.

Still, both professionals felt concerned enough about him to advise that he should be admitted to hospital so that he could be assessed more

thoroughly, and after some discussion Mo agreed to a voluntary admission.

In considering the case study, do you think this was a good course of action?

What factors can you identify for or against an admission?

How would you feel if you were to be involved in such a decision at some point?

Could Mo's ethnic background be influencing how people are responding to him?

The social work role

As Colin Pritchard (2006) notes, social workers in adult mental health are confronted with a dilemma – they are part of a multidisciplinary system of care but working alongside colleagues who seem to have a much stronger knowledge base to help them locate their role in the team. Social workers are not psychiatrists, or (usually) trained therapists, and they do not have the paramedical identity or training that helps psychiatric nurses define their contribution. Clinical psychologists are usually trained in formal, systematic and quantitative (psychometric) methods of assessment, and are often skilled in providing cognitive behavioural therapy treatment programmes. So what is the key contribution social workers can make?

We propose that it is ideally found in a combination of systemic, psychodynamic and broadly relationship-based skills and perspectives. However, to provide this effectively, social workers will also need a confident understanding of the psychiatric and clinical perspectives which their colleagues carry. This understanding can only be acquired through working experience in the field, allied to training as part of continuing professional development. This is not to dissuade anyone from entering mental health work as a specialism, or preparing to do so while in qualifying training. But it is useful to recognise that mental health work really is a specialism.

Assessment and intervention: a systems psychodynamics approach

Pritchard (2006) includes a valuable framework for helping a practitioner organise the many dimensions of the social work assessment task in mental health work. One can imagine the social worker involved in Mohammed's case study making use of this. The BASIC IDDS framework originates in clinical psychology but has been adapted to social work. As Pritchard says, it helps the worker explore 'the modalities of people's lives ranging from their interpersonal relationships, their feelings, their social situation and crucially any "biophysical" aspect of their situation' (2006: 109). Thus it helps social workers to *integrate* their thinking about the large number of dimensions of the service user's situation. BASIC IDDS is a 'mnemonic', an aid to remembering the main categories of the framework: Behaviour, Affect, Sensory, Imagery, Cognition, Interpersonal relationships, Drugs, Defences and Social factors.

Below we set out Pritchard's use of this framework in relation to assessment of someone with a mood disorder, which is another name for what we have called 'affective disorders'. Many of the detailed elements of the table should be familiar from your reading of this chapter so far. While our own list of 'possible bio-psychosocial responses' might be slightly different to Pritchard's, and would include more attention to the dynamics and process of the whole service user–family–professional system, it is still a valuable tool and one that you can adapt and extend using your own experience. For example, you might think that ethnicity, culture and gender should play a more prominent part in the table since there is no doubt that in various ways these factors can play a significant part in both how we understand the origins of mental health problems, and in how services do or do not respond.

In an age when risk management and a performance culture help give rise to excessive lengthy assessment and case record protocols, a common criticism of social work assessment practices is that they collate vast amounts of information which is never properly synthesised. Information collation is not assessment (see Chapter 10 on assessment in social work). Other members of the multidisciplinary team may contribute to the assessment process of which you are a part, but this does not mean that you should not consider all the dimensions included in the table (Table 20.1) when interviewing a service user. You are entitled to your own view about matters that may be more the central expertise of a medical colleague, for example. This is about confidence, but also about knowing the limits to your knowledge and training, and is one step towards establishing social work as an appropriate and solid contribution to the overall effort.

The key contributions social workers can make to assessment – considered as a process of synthesising and evaluating information into a *whole picture that informs the development of an intervention plan* – are similar to those we consider below with respect to the intervention process itself. They concern:

- A perspective that sees the *whole system* as more than the sum of its parts
- An approach that tries to bring the various *elements of the assessment into dynamic relationship* with one another in forming the 'whole picture'
- A stance that accepts there may be *tensions or conflicts* within the whole picture – among members of the team, or between the team and the service user and/or carers, for example, but *which is not afraid* of these tensions and conflicts
- A skill in naming and describing the whole picture, including any tensions, and helping everyone think about their role and their contribution to the dynamic process of forming the assessment
- A stance in which the evolution of the assessment through time is respected as a dynamic, changing *process*
- A capacity to absorb but also stay 'separate' from the strong feelings that may be engendered in everyone (service user, carers, family, professionals) as part of the process. Emotions are 'intelligence' (i.e. information) not 'disturbance' that tell you about the state of the whole system.

The role of the Approved Mental Health Professional (formerly the Approved Social Worker or ASW), or Mental Health Officer in Scotland, in assessing people for possible compulsory admission to hospital, as well as a range of other responsibilities, is about keeping the above perspectives in mind. It is the job of the psychiatrist to determine whether the person being assessed is suffering from a recognised and treatable mental disorder, but both parties must agree to an admission before it can happen, which means that there is always a psychosocial as well as a medical or psychiatric aspect to these crucial decisions.

This characterisation of the social work contribution to assessment is consistent with the more general picture of social work skills and roles drawn by Preston-Shoot and Agass (1990) in their valuable book *Making Sense of Social Work: Psychodynamics and Systems in Practice*. Feelings and the flow of feelings are part of what makes up the system, whether the 'system' is being thought of as the team, the team plus the service users and carers, or

Table 20.1 Use of BASIC IDDS assessment in mood disorder

Area	Expressed problem	Possible bio-psychosocial responses
Behaviour	Avoids people Takes time off work	Counselling – possibly 'assertive' Techniques – explore realistic expectations CBT and reframe Determine any activities with children
Affect	Low mood Constant misery, especially in the mornings Feels worthless Unaccountable guilt	Create therapeutic relationship Consider CBT Start appropriate antidepressants via referral to psychiatrist/GP
Sensory	Feels tired Loss of appetite Loss of weight Tense headaches Fall in libido	Via relationship, highlight support available Monitor analgesics Teach relaxation techniques and biofeedback
Imagery	Often imagine themselves in self-defeating situations	Counselling, rehearsal techniques If images intrusive, teach thought-stopping techniques
Cognition	Finds thinking difficult Slow Feels worthless and a personal failure Guilty because they feel inadequate Suicidal ideas – 'there is no alternative – no hope'	CBT in conjunction with antidepressants Explore and identify areas for reframing 'Educate' person and family as to nature and process of unipolar disorder Consider consultation or referral to psychiatrist to deal with suicidal thinking
Interpersonal relations	Prior to problem – good circle of friends, good marital relationship and good parent Now finds children unmanageable 'Gone beyond rows' with partner Painful silences between patient and partner (you need to discover partner's views)	Counselling – consider family therapy/conjoint counselling with significant others if client agreeable Teach social skills if necessary Explore and check out relationships with children, especially if vulnerable
Drugs (treatment effect)	Has taken analgesics Increased use of alcohol First time sought psychological help	Liaise with doctors/nurse/psychiatrists Check out any source of prescribed and/or illegal drug Where necessary, liaise with permission with any other appropriate agency
Defences	Previously appeared a well-balanced and flexible person Now withdraws, some denial, tendency to self-blame and head off criticism	Counselling Remember defences are not to be confronted – explore extension and more flexible approach to dealing with psychic 'threats'/distress
Social	Graduate, middle class Situation threatens marriage, which could have major implications for accommodation	Check out financial and housing situation Are there potential stressors here? Check out, where necessary, benefit entitlements Liaise/advocate with other agencies

(*Source*: Pritchard, 2006: 112–13)

all of these plus the network of agencies involved. Assessment in mental health social work is almost always a process that involves being 'network-minded' (see the section in Chapter 12 on networking methods).

The idea of keeping the 'whole picture' in mind needs to be followed through in the intervention phases of social work with people with mental health problems. Sometimes, people with chronic difficulties can become very socially isolated, but practice experience tells us that there is always *someone* who is concerned, anxious or troubled about the service user. More often there are a number of people who form a 'network of concern' – relatives, neighbours, friends or others in the community. These people can be considered as the *service user system*. When mental health services become involved there is also a *professional system* to think about. And then there is the interaction between the two systems which creates the *case system*. As one of the professionals working within the second system, you are also part of the whole case system. From this vantage point, you are in a position to observe, monitor and attempt to influence the *state* of the whole system as it unfolds, develops and changes. There are some key questions which help you to do this on a continual basis:

- How resilient is the service user system at this point in time? How much worry and anxiety does it seem to be capable of managing? What are its strengths and weaknesses? Are key figures at the end of their tether or capable of continuing to support the user, perhaps with additional support from you or other colleagues?
- How 'contained' or 'held' by the systems at any point in time does the service user feel themselves to be? Can the system be augmented or strengthened by the introduction of additional services?
- Are there difficult feelings that cannot be acknowledged within the systems? For example, carers may be at the end of their tether but also feeling guilty at the prospect of 'colluding' with a hospital admission. Some professionals may be very 'identified' with the service user, and unable to see the carers' point of view, or vice versa, and so people may be afraid of the argument or conflict that this implies.

These questions imply that feelings, perceptions, actions and interactions are closely linked. Assessing and monitoring these is like continually 'scanning' the state of the system. In the last phase of the case study of Mo (see above) it makes a lot of difference to the 'outcome' of the assessment that Mo was able to talk about what he felt were some of the roots of his depression. If he had

been more withdrawn, family members and professionals might have become more anxious about the risks involved, and felt more inclined to think about a compulsory admission. So engaging, talking and *using a relationship-based approach* can be crucial in affecting outcomes, and achieving a less 'adversarial' and more negotiated, cooperative course of action. It is possible that this kind of factor underlies the partial success of the crisis resolution team work that was researched in S. Johnson et al. (2005) in which the work of the service seemed to help avoid voluntary admissions to hospital.

Conclusion

Modern mental health social work is all about multi-professional, multi-agency teamwork. There are important and exciting developments in mental health services of which social work is a crucial part, and the emphasis on early intervention and prevention is central to these. But it is also true that social workers can tend to feel 'deskilled' by comparison with their medically trained colleagues. Confident mental health social work depends upon a good grasp of the nature of mental health problems, an ability to be realistic and empathic about the suffering people endure, but also upon a capacity to acknowledge and respond to risk.

The central role of social work is to maintain a whole-systems perspective, and this means the network of people around the patient (carers are especially important), and the professional system that interacts with the patient and his or her network. The 'systems' approach concerns how powerful feelings of anxiety, helplessness, fear and anger may become 'lodged' in different people in the system (some of whom have more power and control than others). Helping colleagues, service users and carers stay in touch with the emotional realities of a case, and understanding how the dynamics of a case can become stuck, are important roles for social workers. Hope and optimism can be in short supply where chronic mental health problems are concerned, but a capacity to maintain respect for the *person* as well as the 'illness', and to stick with service users over long periods of time is central. Relationship-based skills are crucial, because other people may have 'given up' in various ways especially if a service user has had repeated admissions to hospital or shows little sign of 'getting better' over the years. Good social workers do not give up, even if they feel they want to sometimes!

Key learning points

This chapter has covered the following learning points:

✔ Mental health services in Britain have evolved rapidly in recent years, and now emphasise multidisciplinary working, early intervention, community care and the idea that mental health is a public health issue that concerns 'everybody' as well as being important to our economic and social 'well being'. Social workers have found it hard to sustain their professional identity in this new context and tend to see other professions as having all the 'expertise'.

✔ There are a variety of 'models' for understanding and explaining mental health problems and the chapter examined three in some detail: biological models, developmental accounts, and explanations in terms of social factors. Some of these, for example attachment theory, provide a promising basis for evidence-based relationship oriented interventions.

✔ Social workers need a good working knowledge of psychiatric classifications of mental distress, but also need to retain their distinctive perspective on mental health work which is about the total *system* care, and how to work effectively with this.

✔ The accepted diagnostic classifications have often been dismissed as 'social constructs', but we need to respect the reality of patterns of mental distress while remaining sceptical and cautious about psychiatric diagnosis when it is used too concretely.

Further reading

Foster, A. and Roberts, V. Z. (1998) *Managing Mental Health in the Community: Chaos and Containment*, London: Routledge. This is a very valuable collection of writing about the 'systems-psychodynamics' approach to mental health work, written by practitioners many of whom also consult to mental health organisations. The book stresses the importance of understanding the dynamics and tensions that can arise among users, professionals, carers and 'the community'. How do we keep all of these 'stakeholders' in mind while attending to risk, potential for change, and the suffering of service users and carers?

Newton, J. (1994) *Preventing Mental Illness in Practice*, London: Routledge. This is a very useful text for linking theory and research to preventative practice. Jennifer Newton describes real-life examples of good practice in preventative mental health. Five areas covering the lifespan are identified and promising strategies are described in detail: what is provided, how the target group is engaged, resources required, management problems and the evidence of effectiveness. Interviews with both clients and providers help to bring to life the descriptions, and demonstrate how the support came to be needed and what benefits clients themselves feel have been reaped.

Pritchard, C. (2006) *Mental Health Social Work: Evidence Based Practice*, Abingdon: Routledge. This is a thorough and accessible text which integrates everyday practice perspectives with up-to-the-minute evidence for 'what works', and useful guides to thinking about assessment and intervention.

The Sainsbury Centre for Mental Health (2002) *Breaking the Circles of Fear: A Review of the Relationship between Mental Health Services and African and Caribbean Communities*, London: The Sainsbury Centre for Mental Health. This text is discussed above, but it offers an excellent perspective on current practice, policy, and research on this difficult topic. The report pulls no punches, but remains balanced and informative.

Useful websites

www.nhsconfed.org/mental-health
For a useful and incisive perspective on contemporary NHS and social care mental health policy, go to the Mental Health Network website.

www.mentalhealth.org.uk/information/
organisations-and-websites/
The Mental Health Foundation is the leading British charity trying to influence policy and practice through research, practice development and political influence. Their website also has a very useful gateway to a huge range of other web addresses relevant to mental health work.

www.iop.kcl.ac.uk
For information about recent cutting-edge research into mental health work, go to the Health Service and Population Research Department's site at the Institute of Psychiatry, London.

www.tavi-port.org
For information about relationship-based mental health social work training and links to other psychotherapy websites, try the Tavistock Clinic's website. The Tavistock Clinic is one of the leading centres for therapeutic social work training in the country.

For additional cases and topic-organised, clickable links into additional media resources, including those produced by IRISS, visit **www.pearsoned.co.uk/wilsonruch**

Activity

Activity One

The 2007 Mental Health Bill introduced important changes into mental health practice.

Find two or three experienced practitioners or team managers and ask them what difference they think the bill has made to everyday practice.

If possible talk to an approved social worker and find out how the introduction of the broader Approved Mental Health Professional role has impacted on the sense of status that ASWs used to carry.

Activity Two

Visit some of the new services and teams that have probably grown up around your agency in recent years – assertive outreach, crisis resolution, and so on.

Learn about their view of their role and their experience of working with each other.

Activity Three

Is there a nearby independent sector agency providing services to a particular ethnic minority community? Ask if you can visit and talk to some of the staff.

Why do they think they are needed? What shortcomings of mainstream mental health services do they identify?

Are there particular issues which their service user group has to contend with?

Chapter 21
Social work and drug use

Dr Ian Paylor

Chapter summary

In the specific context of social work with drug users, there are particular issues which social work encounters and which practitioners must address in order to intervene effectively; social workers need some indications of the factors to consider, for example, when dealing with parents who use alcohol problematically and who also have the responsibility for the care of young children. Drug users and their behaviour are seen as fundamentally problematic, not least because using drugs covered by the Misuse of Drugs Act 1971 is illegal, and this is accentuated by the specific impact of wider causes such as 'marginalisation'; this can perhaps be summarised in terms of the processes of stigmatising to which drug users are peculiarly susceptible. For social work practitioners, these tensions are intensified by the requirement to 'see both sides', and to respond equally to concerns about problematic behaviour, and drug users' rights and occasional sense of injustice. In order for social workers to understand and address these challenges, and develop creative and empowering interventions, there is a need to locate the specifics of practice within a broad analysis of the complex interplay between differing perspectives, interests and cultural and structural influences. The aim of this chapter will be to explore these problematic issues by highlighting four specific areas: coercion, parental drug use, service user involvement and blood-borne viruses.

Learning objectives

This chapter covers topics that will enable you to achieve the following learning objectives:

- To understand the importance of attitudes and beliefs in determining how drug use is conceptualised
- To consider the recurrent dilemmas for social workers involved with drug users
- To be knowledgeable about contemporary debates over drug use and the effects of drug use.

National Occupational Standards

This chapter will help you to meet the following National Occupational Standards:

Key Role 1: Prepare for, and work with individuals, families, carers, groups and communities to assess their needs and circumstances

Unit 1   Prepare for social work contact and involvement
Unit 2   Work with individuals, families, carers, groups and communities to help them make informed decisions
Unit 3   Assess needs and options to recommend a course of action for individuals, families, carers, groups and communities

Key Role 2: Plan, carry out, review and evaluate social work practice, with individuals, families, carers, groups, communities and other professionals

Unit 4   Respond to crisis situations
Unit 5   Interact with individuals, families, carers, groups and communities to achieve change and development and to improve life opportunities
Unit 6   Prepare, produce, implement and evaluate plans with individuals, families, carers, groups, communities and professional colleagues
Unit 7   Support the development of networks to meet assessed needs and planned outcomes
Unit 8   Work with groups to promote individual growth, development and independence
Unit 9   Address behaviour which presents a risk to individuals, families, carers, groups and communities

Key Role 3: Support individuals to represent their needs, views and circumstances

Unit 10   Advocate with, and on behalf of, individuals, families, carers, groups and communities
Unit 11   Prepare for, and participate in decision making forums

Key Role 4: Manage risk to individuals, families, carers, groups, communities, self and colleagues

Unit 12   Assess and manage risks to individuals, families, carers, groups and communities
Unit 13   Assess, minimise and manage risk to self and colleagues

Key Role 5: Manage and be accountable, with supervision and support, for your own social work practice within your organisation

Unit 14   Manage and be accountable for your own work
Unit 15   Contribute to the management of resources and services
Unit 16   Manage, present and share records and reports
Unit 17   Work within multi-disciplinary and multi-organisational teams, networks and systems

Key Role 6: Demonstrate professional competence in social work practice

Unit 18   Research, analyse, evaluate, and use current knowledge of best social work practice
Unit 19   Work within agreed standards of social work practice and ensure own professional development
Unit 20   Manage complex ethical issues, dilemmas and conflicts
Unit 21   Contribute to the promotion of best social work practice

In addition to the GSCC National Occupational Standards for Social Work, readers may find it useful to access the Drugs and Alcohol National Occupational Standards (DANOS). Website: **www.skillsforhealth.org.uk/danos/**

Case study

Trevor and Barbara, Fiona and Michael and Karl and Sue

Trevor is 34 years old and works for a large public relations company. He has worked for the same organisation for eight years and was recently made a director of the company. The nature of his work means he regularly entertains clients at lunchtime and in the evening. 'Hospitality' in these cases invariably involves the consumption of alcohol. PR is a notoriously competitive business and Trevor feels he needs to be available to maintain the 'edge'. Although married to **Barbara** (38 years old) with two teenage children 'his work is his life' and his social life revolves around clients' parties and events. On an average day Trevor may consume the equivalent of three or four bottles of strong lager, a bottle of wine and two or three gin and tonics. On the rare occasions when not 'working' he allows himself to get drunk with his friends.

Fiona is 28 years old and has been using heroin for twelve years, injecting the drug for the last eight. For the last two years she has been taking methadone (heroin substitute) on prescription. She does occasionally use 'street' heroin when she can afford it. She lives with her partner (**Michael**, also 28 years old) who is also on a methadone prescription. They both smoke cannabis on a regular basis. Both are on benefit and have a 2-year-old girl and another child on the way. Fiona prides herself on being a good mother and works hard to ensure that her daughter is well dressed and their flat is tidy and clean. She knows about the risk of drug use in pregnancy but is also well aware of the harmful effects of withdrawal on the foetus. Fiona feels she may need some help when the baby is born but is wary of approaching social services for help in case their children are 'taken away'.

Karl and **Sue** are both 26 years old, married and have two girls, both at primary school. Karl is a local builder and Sue works part-time at a local clothes shop. Karl works long hours during the week, especially during the summer months, while Sue works mainly afternoons, Tuesday–Saturday. They have a mortgage but it is manageable and financially feel things are OK. Both smoke cigarettes. They rarely go out during the week but at weekends they will do some amphetamine (and occasionally cocaine), several bottles of wine and beer and 'hit' the local pubs and clubs. Most weekends are somewhat of a blur – their 'lost weekends' have become something of a family joke. Karl has got himself in a few fights but nothing serious. Sue has fallen while drunk and suffered some bumps and bruises and has missed work on a couple of Saturdays which has resulted in her getting a warning about her attendance. Monday morning invariably means Karl drives to work 'hung-over' from the weekend.

How do you think the particular individuals perceive their drug use? What is the nature of the risks involved in each example? To what extent do these people have control over their drug use?

The families in the case studies illustrate the complexity of the issues surrounding social work and drug use. Drug use can embrace illegal as well as legal activity, including the problematic use of drugs prescribed by some of your fellow professionals. People use drugs, certainly initially, as part and parcel of an enjoyable experience. For example, alcohol plays a large part in our social lives – it is associated with celebration, achievement, relaxation and pleasure. The 'policing' of pleasure, which your social work involvement with these families may necessitate, can be fraught with problems which will draw on most aspects of social work practice.

Introduction

Since the early days of the profession, social workers have been confronted with personal and social problems caused by their clients' use of drugs. Substance misuse is a key feature in social work with children and families. In particular, parental alcohol misuse is the most important contributory factor in the reception of children into local authority care. Handling parental misuse of drugs and alcohol and drug use is perhaps the most important challenge facing social workers today (Forrester and

A closer look

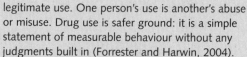

Terminology (1)

There are complicated debates about what exactly a drug is, and terms – such as, addiction, dependency, drug abuse and misuse – are widely used but rarely defined. The choice of terminology relates to different models for understanding drug and alcohol use, and it is essential to have an appreciation of this. Drug abuse is an implied judgement about the wrongness of drug use. It is a label used by some people to describe other people's drug use. There is no objective definition of drug abuse which avoids this judgement trap. Drug misuse is also a value-laden term. It contains the assumption of easily definable, legitimate drug use. The problem is that there is no agreed definition of

legitimate use. One person's use is another's abuse or misuse. Drug use is safer ground: it is a simple statement of measurable behaviour without any judgments built in (Forrester and Harwin, 2004).

The non-medical use of drugs is not a single activity but can involve a range of behaviours. These can best be understood as falling into three main forms – experimental, recreational and dependent. However, the three forms of drug use are not absolute states. Users may move between the different forms. The recreational form is a broad band of activity which ranges from occasional use at one end and heavy, regular but not necessarily dependent, use at the other. Problems can occur with any of the three forms of use but the problems (and solutions) may be very different.

Harwin 2009). Yet, as various authors (Deehan et al., 1998; Heather and Mason, 1999; Harbin and Murphy, 2000; Phillips, 2004; Galvani and Hughes 2008) repeatedly point out, there is still a lack of training in basic skills such as in making the links between a child's difficulties and the nature and severity of parental substance misuse. Despite this we still have a situation where new social work degree courses are not required to teach about substance misuse when the evidence presented makes a strong case for it being compulsory (Paylor 2008).

Indeed, as the British social work academics Collins and Keene (2000) argue, social workers are 'ideally placed' to deal with substance use problems because of their education, training and experience. They describe how social workers have expertise in social care, housing liaison work, welfare rights, assisting with financial problems and in linking clients with a wide range of other agencies. This point also sits comfortably with the ethical standpoint of social work in which a holistic approach is emphasised (Clark, 2000a). What is more, social workers are trained in assessment skills (Axford 2010; Seddon et al. 2010), which are identified by service users as essential to the development of an effective and needs-led aftercare package (Drainey et al., 2005). Many social workers will also have experience of working with clients under stress and at periods of crisis in their lives (Collins 2008; Tham and Meagher 2009). This is obviously extremely beneficial when working with drug users.

Problem drug use is an issue that cuts across many boundaries and impacts on a wide range of agencies. The treatment depends upon the philosophical perspectives

of the individual and indeed the agency providing the assistance. Some suggest that problem drug use is a disease with a genetic disposition. Those agencies that subscribe to the disease model of addiction suggest the best time to work with people is when they have 'hit rock bottom'. In-patient and out-patient detox, residential rehabilitation units and Alcoholics Anonymous are key services to assist people to become and stay drug and alcohol free. Interventions based upon the disease model (i.e. abstinence) have had a remarkable and positive impact on a number of people. However, this approach is sometimes criticised for pathologising the individual, failing to pay enough attention to environmental factors as well as removing personal responsibility by blaming sickness or genetics.

Spot the difference competition

 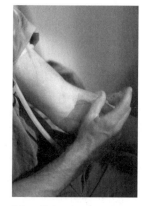

Client injecting insulin   Client injecting heroin
(*Source:* PunchStock/Photodisc)

The current debate

In the late 1980s an alternative school of thought developed that worked from the premise that problem drug users are people who have lost control over their behaviour, not because of a biological disposition, but because they had developed patterns of habitual behaviour that have become dysfunctional. Promoted by Miller (1983), the distinguished professor of psychology and psychiatry at the University of New Mexico (UNM) and co-director of UNM's Centre on Alcoholism, Substance Abuse, and Addictions (see also Scott, 1989), they suggest that controlled drug taking is a possibility. Drug problems are seen as essentially socially and psychologically based issues. This approach seeks to educate and empower the problem drinker by concentrating on the identification of triggers, insight into high-risk situations, the development of relapse prevention strategies and positive self talk. They suggest that five key stages exist (Prochaska and DiClemente 2009), though not necessarily in any order (these are Precontemplation, Contemplation, Preparation, Action and Maintenance), and believe that it is possible to intervene at any stage, provided the stage has been properly identified. In short, it describes the process of change as a series of motivational stages and is often depicted as a 'revolving wheel' (Miller and Rollnick, 2002).

This approach emphasises client choice and client responsibility. It is up to the problem user whether they intend tackling their drug problem; *they* must take responsibility not the worker. Analysis of the concept of 'motivation' highlights that motivating factors can be either intrinsic or extrinsic (López Viets et al., 2002, Battjes, 1999, McMurran, 2002), internal or external. Internal motivating factors can include: perceived health implications; achieving valued goals; and escape from or avoidance of negative emotions such as shame or guilt; while external factors would include: gaining social acceptance or avoiding sanctions or disapproval (McMurran, 2002) – see below, the discussion on 'coercion'.

Motivation plays an important role in all therapeutic interventions, and perhaps more so in drug treatment, as the competing influences of desire to change and positive reinforcement of the drugs themselves may create greater ambivalence about the change process. The 'failure' of individuals to enter, continue in, comply with and succeed in treatment is often attributed to a lack of proper motivation (Simpson and Joe, 1993, Miller, 1985). The use of language such as 'resistant' and 'denial' suggests that the problem and the blame lies with the individual (López Viets et al., 2002, Miller and Rollnick, 2002). This 'trait concept' can lead to confrontational approaches based on the idea that if you can make someone feel bad enough, they will change, or that readiness can be forced on someone (López Viets et al., 2002). Miller and Rollnick (2002) suggest that rather than perceiving motivation as a trait, it should be thought of as a state of readiness which can be influenced and is modifiable. As López Viets et al. (2002) propose, the question is not whether clients are motivated, but rather how best to enhance their motivation, and in this way social workers increasingly perceive client engagement and motivation as a part of their job and recognise that it is not effective to passively wait for clients to 'get motivated'.

A closer look

The 'cycle of change'

Starting with the *precontemplation* stage, we see individuals typified as being unaware of the extent of their problems, with a definite ignorance about or unwillingness to change their problem behaviour (Collins and Keene, 2000). Once the individual begins to recognise that their substance use constitutes a problem, they are said to move on to the *contemplation* stage. Characterised by serious thought about the nature of their problems, individuals may begin to consider the pros and cons of changing their behaviour. The *action* stage represents a period in which definite change is made and is closely followed by the *maintenance* stage in which behavioural change is integrated into the person's lifestyle. However, as dependent drug use is a relapsing condition (Hearnden, 2000), in reality many individuals attempting to alter their behaviour slip back into using substances. For some this could be a temporary 'blip' but others will return to 'the addicted life of the precontemplator' (Barber, 2002).

Motivational interviewing techniques have been widely used with much success in this area (Easton et al. 2000; Wahab 2005; Forrester et al. 2008). Rather than working with a small percentage of 'rock bottom' clients, motivational interviewing and the cycle of change model enables services to work constructively with a much wider clientele, i.e. those with a drug problem, but not at 'rock bottom'. The approach is sometimes criticised for encouraging people to consider controlled drinking when they may not have the personal resources (e.g. the 'willpower' to stop before complete intoxication) to cope with controlled drinking.

To briefly illustrate, for precontemplators (i.e. those at the first stage) the aim is to raise doubts and increase awareness of the risks and problems of using drugs (Casselman, 2002). The Australian social work academic, Barber (1995), recommends this be achieved by facilitating the flow of feedback about the negative consequences of drug consumption. Feedback should be individualised and provided in an empathetic and non-judgmental manner in direct accordance with social work values. An in-depth understanding and familiarity with the cycle of change and its varying tenets will enhance practice. General social work methods and skills can be utilised at different times in the helping process.

The cycle of change model is useful in providing guidelines for the most appropriate kinds of interventions to use at each stage (Miller and Rollnick, 2002) and with increasing measures to coerce drug users into treatment (see below), it is likely that more precontemplators will find themselves in treatment.

Treatment for drug and alcohol problems

Treatment for drug and alcohol problems in the United Kingdom can be roughly divided into two classes of activity: general and specialist responses. While adequate provision must be made for the totality of care, the particular needs of problem drinkers and illicit drug users could be met with a combined service (Heather and McCarthy, 1999). However, as Sen (2006), the (then) Chief Executive of Alcohol Concern, has pointed out, the misuse of illicit drugs has dominated the political agenda and there is a risk that combined services may become overwhelmed with illicit drug users.

The UK government's latest illicit drugs strategy echoes previous ones in aiming to restrict the supply of illegal drugs and reduce the demand for them. Its two overarching aims are to reduce illicit and other harmful drug use and increase the numbers recovering from their dependence. Within the strategy are three main and interlinked themes: reducing demand, restricting supply and building recovery in communities (HM Government 2010). The aspiration for treatment and recovery is to be applauded, but the challenge will be ensuring that high level ambition is delivered and sustained locally, not least at a time of policy change, uncertainty and spending cuts.

As with previous strategies the main element of the treatment theme is to increase the number of problem drug users entering structured treatment programmes; in addition the length of time people stay in treatment is also monitored and is used to indicate the effectiveness of the interventions, as there is evidence that the longer people are retained in treatment then the more effective it will be (Dundon et al. 2008).

Findings Reports from the National Treatment Agency for Substance Misuse (NTA) Effectiveness Review suggest that the relationship between social worker and client is a key feature in retaining clients in treatment (Murray, 2005) and that this leads to increases in positive treatment outcomes (Gossop, 2006, Wanigaratne et al., 2005). Engagement and retention in the drug treatment process predicts positive treatment outcomes over and above any other factors (Meier et al., 2005).

Drug Intervention Programme

Central to the government's strategy for tackling drugs in England and Wales is the Drug Intervention Programme (DIP). The delivery of the DIP at a local level is through Drug Action Teams (DATs) using criminal justice integrated teams (CJITs) (Home Office, 2009). Social workers will occupy key worker roles within CJITs, with responsibility for agreeing care plans, motivational engagement, referring to other agencies and linking with other services (NTA, 2005). Within the treatment sector, social workers are invariably employed within Community Drug Teams (CDTs), residential rehabilitation units and in a range of private and voluntary drug services. In Scotland, Drug Action Teams have also been established and the Scottish Government has accompanied this with its Knowthescore campaign (www.knowthescore.info) and new national drugs strategy that focuses on recovery but also looks at prevention, treatment and rehabilitation, education, enforcement and protection of children (*The Road to Recovery: A New Approach to Tackling Scotland's Drug Problem*, 2008).

Think ahead

Tyuse and Linhorst (2005) call for social work students to receive specific training in working with coerced clients and their family members to ensure they are 'competent to use their authority comfortably and appropriately'.

How do you feel about that?

What are the implications for social work?

It is a continuing issue whether treatment entered through either pressure or compulsion from the criminal justice system can, in fact, be successful, given, in particular, the common assumption that individuals must be motivated for treatment in order to get the best results.

Bean (2002: 61) suggests that coercion is a fundamental and *sine qua non* feature of the criminal justice system; however, a conceptual weakness is the notion that coercion into treatment can be inferred from the referral source (Wild et al., 1998). Coercion is more complicated than merely route of entry into treatment (Stevens et al., 2006), and within clients groups sharing the same referral source there is considerable heterogeneity in terms of perceived levels of coercion (Wild et al., 1998), in drugs used, and in physical, psychological and social factors (Klag et al., 2005). Additionally, there is a lack of consensus about what constitutes coercion (Klag et al., 2005; Farabee et al., 1998; Prendergast et al., 2002), though mere involvement with the criminal justice system is commonly seen as sufficient (Farabee

et al., 1998; Klag et al., 2005; van Ooyen-Houben, 2008; Stevens, 2008), but it is typically defined in contrast with 'voluntary' treatment (Seddon, 2007).

According to Seddon (2007) the notion of coerced treatment can be broken into three component parts: *persuading someone to do something; which they are unwilling to do; by using force or threats*. The first component, the act of persuasion, therefore involves choosing between two or more options, and as Seddon (2007) notes, this notion of choice marks the distinction between *coerced* and *compulsory* treatment.

There is a close link between the concept of coercion as external pressure and motivation as internal pressure (Seddon, 2007) and an understanding of the relationship between the two is critical. Those with low external pressures and high internal pressures may be perceived as being the most 'voluntary' clients, as external pressures are lowest, and as such may be seen as being the most likely to make the most positive treatment outcomes. However, several studies have found that a combination of strong external coercion and strong internal motivation may lead to the best outcomes (Longshore et al., 2004, Simpson and Joe, 1993).

In reality, coercion is both a multidimensional and a continuous variable (Longshore et al., 2004). Varying degrees of coercion may be applied to individuals referred to treatment from the criminal justice system and the extent of this coercion may vary over time. Entering treatment under compulsion does not necessarily imply that the individual cannot become an essentially

A closer look

Involuntary clients

With the spotlight firmly focused on a criminal justice agenda, attention is appropriately drawn to the issues of working with 'involuntary clients' (Trotter, 2006). Clearly, with their emphasis on positive therapeutic approaches (Maguraz, 1994) and concern for the enhancement of well-being (Clark, 2000a), working with such resistant, hard to reach, hostile and unmotivated clients is likely to compromise the fundamental ethos of the social work profession (O'Hare, 1996). When the idea of change is forced on an unwilling recipient, it is not uncommon for the individual to further engage in the problem behaviour in 'an attempt to assert his or her freedom'. If these are an accurate reflection of reality, such scenarios pose a significant threat to the rudiments of social work

(Ginsburg et al., 2002). Trotter identifies a range of applicable questions such as:

- How do you help someone who has no interest in being helped?
- What can you do with clients who are not motivated to change?
- How can you help someone with their problems and at the same time exercise authority over them?

In their day-to-day work, social workers will be confronted with the dilemma of 'welfare versus social control' (Trotter, 2006). For instance, are they agents of the criminal justice system focused on enforcement and supervision, or do they cling protectively on to their traditional concern for welfare? This, according to Trotter (2006), is one of the greatest challenges in working with involuntary clients.

A closer Look

Terminology (2)

As Prendergast et al. (2002) highlighted, terms – such as, coerced, compulsory, involuntary, legal pressure and criminal justice referral – are often used interchangeably when they actually describe different phenomena. Similarly, De Leon (1988) emphasises a common failure to distinguish between 'legal referral', 'legal status' and 'legal pressure' although these represent, in reality, very different things. As a result of oversimplifying the concept, researchers have had a tendency to divide study participants into 'coerced' and 'non-coerced' or 'voluntary' and 'involuntary'.

There are problems with oversimplifying the concept of coercion. Coercion represents a range of degrees of force used across various stages of the treatment and criminal justice process (Prendergast et al., 2002). It is essential to distinguish between those who have entered via a criminal justice route under relatively little pressure, those who are under a significant degree of compulsion (for example, if treatment participation forms part of a criminal sentence) and those who fall somewhere in between. The tendency to dichotomise 'coercion' is not only a simplification but also represents a failure to address the complexity of the concept of legal coercion (Marlowe et al., 1996; Longshore et al., 2004).

'voluntary' participant at some later stage. Similarly it is possible for an initially 'voluntary' patient to become 'coerced' at some stage in the treatment process (Longshore et al., 2004). This is one reason why it is essential not to confuse the experience of coercion with the source of the referral into treatment, although this is commonly done (Marlowe et al., 1996). This is particularly important given the huge variation in the nature and application of legal treatment mandates between time and place (Anglin, 1988; Stevens et al., 2005). A failure to identify the extent and nature of the 'coercion' applied makes it impossible to generalise from research conclusions.

Case study

Trevor . . . Fiona . . . Sue cont . . .

Trevor is told by his employers to attend a private clinic to address what they describe as his problematic drinking behaviour.

Fiona is coming under increasing pressure from her family to enter into treatment and come off the methadone.

Sue is beginning to worry about her general health and her capacity to look after the children. Her GP has advised her to contact her local Community Drug Team.

All three are being coerced into seeking help.

What do you think are the differences between the pressures being exerted on Trevor, Fiona and Sue?

Will the differing forces being placed on Trevor, Fiona or Sue impact on your work with them?

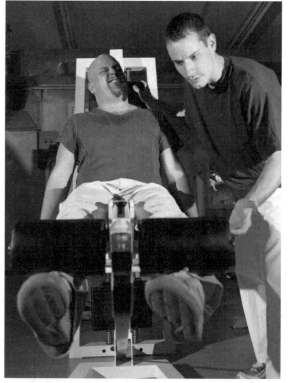

'I know what is good for you. Trust me I'm a social worker.'
(*Source:* Corbis/Image Source)

A second issue with the oversimplification of 'coercion' in much of the literature is the assumption that 'coerced' clients are under greater pressure and are less motivated or ready for treatment than voluntary clients. Yet, it is by no means clear that there is a direct relationship between a criminal justice referral into treatment and the client's experience of 'coercion'. In reality, there is a divergence between the way 'coercion' is applied and the perception of it by the individual drug user. This has led recent research to emphasise the importance of the individual drug user's perceptions. If coercion is experienced differently by different people, examining 'coerced' treatment solely by referral source is not very helpful. Wild et al.'s (1998) study of perceived coercion among drug users in treatment revealed that 35 per cent of those who had entered treatment under legal mandates did not perceive any coercion. Other studies have shown that even those who are subject to legal coercion may rate other coercive factors, such as family pressure, as more relevant to the treatment experience (Marlowe et al. 1996). Furthermore, it is incorrect to assume that users who have been 'coerced' into treatment are not motivated or 'ready' for treatment. Farabee et al. (1998) found no statistically significant correlation between perceived coercion and perceived need for treatment.

Arguably, it is inaccurate to assume that those entering treatment through the criminal justice system are under greater coercion than others (Longshore et al., 2004). Even voluntary treatment participants often enter under some form of social or pharmacological pressure (Maddux, 1988). Those who have entered treatment under legal pressure do not necessarily perceive a greater level of coercion than those who have not (Wild et al. 1998). Wild (2006) points out that social pressures are commonly an integral part of the process of seeking treatment and outlines a typology of coercion: legal social controls, such as court-ordered treatment; formal social controls, such as mandatory referrals to employee assistance programmes through work, and informal social controls, such as pressures from family and friends. Each of these, he argues, may play a significant role in accessing and remaining in treatment. Thus it may be incorrect to assume that criminal justice clients have been coerced while 'voluntary' clients have not.

Hence there is no clear division between 'voluntary' and 'involuntary' treatment participants. The use of the term 'coercion' as a proxy for 'criminal justice referral' is insufficient. Rather, the exact level of compulsion, the effect on the subject and its interplay with other factors is highly relevant (Welsh and McGrain 2008).

Case study

Trevor and Barbara, Fiona and Michael and Karl and Sue cont . . .

Provisions in the Criminal Justice Act 2003, including the new Community Order, were brought into force on 4 April 2005. The new order consists of a 'menu' of requirements, including the Drug Rehabilitation Requirement for different types and levels of drug treatment.

Karl was arrested at the weekend and charged with assault. He was drug-tested at the police station. He tested positive for cocaine which led to an interview with an arrest referral worker; the test result was given to the courts to inform bail decisions and sentencing. In court Karl received a Community Order with a Drug Rehabilitation Requirement. In his first meeting with you he denies that there is a problem and states he was 'sent here' by the court.

Michael has decided that he wants to 'turn his life around', stop using drugs and work towards getting a job. He has applied for a place in a Structured Day Programme (SDP). Most SDPs provide interventions based on a five- or three-day week basis. A holistic approach to rehabilitation is adopted, promoting: life skills and vocational training; sessions on building and restoring confidence; practical workshops to improve an individual's chances of either gaining employment or going into further or higher education. In his first meeting with you he states that he is aware that he has a significant problem but is motivated to change.

The complexity of the treatment experience is well understood, and it is essential to apply this to our understanding of the concept of 'coerced' treatment. The significance of the user's internal and external motivation has been described above and illustrated in the case studies. Is your attitude and approach going to be different with regard to Karl and Michael?

It is often argued that motivated clients often have little or no need of treatment clinics or rehabilitation centres. The real challenge for social workers is to meet the needs of the unmotivated client. Thus 'coercion' must be understood with reference to its role in this wider process, as opposed to a variable in its own right. The relevant question is not whether 'coerced' treatment can be successful but what role 'coercion' can play in creating, sustaining or potentially destroying a user's motivation to engage in treatment (Prendergast et al., 2002).

Childcare and parental drug use

As more drug users are brought into treatment, practitioners within the DIP are likely to be faced with a wide range of issues, many of which will include childcare and parenting. In 2003, it was estimated that there were 200,000 to 300,000 children in England and Wales who had one or both parents with a serious drug problem (ACMD, 2003). In Scotland, which has a tenth of the population of England and Wales, the estimate is as many as 60,000 children who have a parent or parents who misuse drugs (Scottish Executive, 2004). Parental drug use can and often does compromise children's health and development (ACMD, 2003); nevertheless only a minority of cases overall result in children being placed on 'at risk' registers: indeed, the majority of drug-using parents provide adequate care for their children (Buchanan and Young, 2002).

Think ahead

Think about your own views regarding how children should be cared for.

Are there factors that are important in judging unacceptable parenting?

Why should this be so? Is it based on your attitudes and values or is there some objective test that can be applied?

Consider the three families in the case studies above:

Have you any concerns over the parenting displayed?

How would you feel about criticisms of your parenting?

(Think about the earlier comments about coercion – what about those parents ordered to undertake parenting classes under the Crime and Disorder Act 1998?)

Legally, the Children Acts (1989 and 2004 in England and Wales; 1995 in Scotland) place a duty on agencies engaging with problem drug users who have dependent children to assess the needs of children if their health and well-being may be at risk (ACMD, 2003). When such instances occur, it would be reasonable to presume that because of their background, social workers within

CJITs will be allocated this task. However, this does not arrive without problems. In repeated studies of social workers' attitudes and knowledge, it is found that workers feel ill-prepared to work with parents who use drugs and they have significant gaps in their knowledge (Galvani and Hughes, 2008; Loughran et al., 2010).

Substance use fails to reach the mainstream social work agenda, yet practitioners regularly face such issues in their daily work (Hayden, 2004). It is essential that social workers as a whole, including those within CJITs, advocate and lobby for increased training and guidance on working with substance-using parents. It is possible that childcare social workers may lack training in substance-use issues and vice versa (Forrester and Harwin, 2004). Without a commitment to providing training, social workers within all settings will continue to be 'set up to fail'.

Parental drug use

Parental substance misuse is a common factor in social work (Fraser et al., 2009) especially in the more serious cases, for example, where children are on the child protection register and/or are involved in court proceedings (Taylor et al., 2008; Forrester and Harwin, 2009).

This is not to suggest that substance misusing parents are a homogeneous group (Kroll and Taylor, 2000) or that that all parents who suffer from problem alcohol or drug use present a danger to their children (Cleaver et al., 1999). Indeed, in isolation, the problem drug use of a parent presents little risk of significant harm. To fully understand the effect of parental drug use the social worker must 'enter the world of substance misusing families' (Aldridge, 1999) and look beyond the actual drug use and more towards how the use of drugs actually impacts on parenting ability and the welfare of the child. Approach and assess each case individually (Barnard, 2007), irrespective of the negative stereotypes that society and other professionals alike may have of drug-using parents.

Invariably the drug use is not an isolated issue but usually a feature among many, such as mental health, accommodation and finances (Kroll and Taylor, 2003). The multi-layered nature of the problems experienced make decisions about both how to intervene and where to intervene very problematic and can lead to workers choosing either to 'condemn or condone' as opposed to sitting on the fence somewhere (Kroll and Taylor, 2000). In addition social workers have to be able to separate recreational drug use from problem drug use without over-reacting to the former and under-reacting to the latter (Measham and Paylor, 2009). As mentioned previously, this means it is important to treat each case individually and without preconceived notions of the quality of care drug users can provide. If this is not the case there is the danger of either making baseless assumptions about chaotic substance use and parenting or of under-reacting and failing to identify the mistreatment that a minority of children experience (Taylor and Kroll, 2004).

Additionally, we see further challenges for social workers with the 'fear factor' of coming into contact with services – the commonly articulated concern expressed by some drug users that their children will be 'taken away' (Buchanan and Young, 2002). Women in particular fear contacting services because of the possible initiation of child protection proceedings (ACMD, 2003). In light of the social work commitment to anti-discriminatory and anti-oppressive practice, it is surprising that this is still so (Buchanan and Young, 2002). Social workers are therefore confronted with the task of dispelling and working with such attitudes in a bid to engage and retain drug users, and, in particular, female drug users.

Women's illicit drug use has been increasing rapidly since the late 1980s in the United Kingdom and elsewhere in the developed world. Lifetime prevalence rates show that gender is no longer a significant predictor of, or protector from, illicit drug use (Measham, 2002). Also in the period between 1988 and 2002 the number of women drinking beyond the medically recommended alcohol limit increased by 70 per cent and in 2005 stood at 13 per cent of the female population (Alcohol Concern, 2008). While women have made significant inroads to achieve equality in many areas, sexism, inequality and gender stereotypes still pervade their daily lives. The female alcohol/drug user can be portrayed as a morally inadequate person failing to fulfill their duty as a 'decent woman'. The same judgments rarely apply to equivalent men. Services need to be gender-sensitive and ensure that sexism does not hinder women coming forward for help. Services tend to be geared for male clients. Services need to consider providing crèche facilities, ensuring that they are accessible for people with pushchairs; have nappy changing facilities; children's toys, etc. This omission tends to exclude women, who are generally the main carers of children. Detox, rehabs,

Professional tip

For social workers coming into contact with adults (or their children) who use drugs

The advice includes the following:

- **Do not ignore drug (including alcohol) use** – but do not over-react.
- **What are your own feeling and views about drug use?** Do not let these 'colour' your judgements but make sure your assessment is based upon evidence not optimism.
- **Get details about the drugs used.** 'Drug use' is not a single phenomenon but can encompass a wide range of behaviours. You will need information about the drugs used, and the implications of such use, in order to assess the impact on parenting. Is the drug use 'stable' or 'chaotic'? Does it swing between states of severe intoxification and periods of withdrawal and/or poly-drug use including alcohol? Where are the drugs kept?
- **What are the parents' perceptions of the problem?** Do the parents place their own needs before those of their children? If the drug use is at the centre of

their life, then it will adversely affect their relationship with others, including children. If household resources (money, emotional and practical) are invested in drug use, there will be deficits for the children.

- **Drug users can be good parents.** Do not assume that stopping using will improve their parenting skills. Parents may find it hard to cope with a drug-free lifestyle. Withdrawal from drugs can impair capacity to tolerate stress or worry. Be realistic about your expectations. Rather than abstinence, stability in treatment may be a more realistic option. The arrival of a new baby is a time of great change. Coping with a demanding new baby is perhaps not the best time to be changing your drug use!
- **Do not forget partners and other social networks and support systems.** Assessment can sometimes focus on the mother; others may have an impact on parenting capacity. Is there a drug-free parent or supportive parent? Will parents accept help from relatives and other professional/voluntary agencies?

(*Source*: Adapted and abridged from SCODA guidelines)

drop-ins and group-work programmes need to ensure that women are not isolated and whenever possible women-only groups should be offered.

Service user involvement

Over the years a number of government publications concerned with health and social care, and some specific to substance-misuse services, have identified the importance of 'user involvement' at all levels, including policy and planning, and in treatment decisions (Scottish Government, 2008; NTA, 2005; Audit Commission, 2004a; Hunt, 2002; see also Chapter 14 in this volume).

Being involved in treatment decisions means different things to different people. Clients equate user involvement with being able to communicate effectively with staff; referrers tend to associate it with informed consent; community drug workers see it reflected in clients having some choice within treatment programmes and staff from drug residential services tend to focus on prioritised participation in group treatment processes and in the general running of the residential community (Fischer et al., 2007). The foundation of effective drug user involvement is a willingness on the part of both professionals and clients to listen, communicate and negotiate with each other.

However, it appears that good intentions do not always translate effectively into practice (Neale, 2006). The path of true user involvement rarely runs smooth: a lack of resources, knowledge base, skills, understanding and support from the field are common stumbling blocks to user involvement (Efthimiou-Mordaunt, 2002). McDermott (2002) characterises the relationship between drug services and service users as one of 'mutual antagonism' and user involvement as often a mere 'tick-box gesture'.

It might be suggested then, that the low retention rates for services are down to the fact that service users' views are not central to decisions made about their treatment package. As a consequence, it is possible that service users lose interest in treatment because they are excluded from the decision-making and management of their future. Thus, the issue of control is exclusive rather than inclusive of the service user.

Perhaps from the service provider's point of view, the lack of user input would be challenged if research evidence suggested retention rates for treatment could increase with greater service user participation. Only then would the issue of service users' views become paramount to the survival of key treatment services in the future. Claims are made that involvement is good for drug users' well-being (Hunt, 2002), is central to the development of services (Audit Commission, 2004a), and increases feelings of satisfaction, with treatment thereby improving retention (Neale, 2006). Therefore, if user involvement brings about such hailed benefits, there is surely an urgent need for it to be incorporated into all drug services.

Social work and service users

Social workers are probably at the 'leading edge' in involving the perspectives of service users (a point

A closer look

User involvement

The guidance for the implementation of the NHS and Community Care Act (1990) in England and Wales (Community Care and Health (Scotland) Act 2002 in Scotland) encouraged services to involve service users in their planning: a requirement that was further clarified in the publication *Negotiating Care in the Community*. This says that planning should be a 'product of negotiation between providers, users and carers [and] that planning at whatever level, should be conducted through a process of negotiated collaboration between all the relevant "stakeholders"'. The drug service user's charter lacks statutory status but was developed by the Standing Conference on the Misuse of Drugs (SCODA – now Drugscope) in consultation with its members. The charter was developed in line with the NHS and Community Care Act (1990) and the Patient's Charter (1991) and, by embracing its principles, agencies can develop services that properly attend to the rights of their clients. The drug service user's charter includes a balance of rights and responsibilities and endorses self-help and advocacy groups through the right to 'information about self-help groups and drug user advocacy groups' and by referring to the 'right to the development of advocacy'. The AIDS and drug misuse update by the Advisory Council on the Misuse of Drugs (ACMD) also discussed the role of 'drug user groups'.

further emphasised in Chapter 14). Indeed, within social work theory, new significance has been given to the involvement of service users in recent years (Beresford, 2000). Considering their commitment to social change, empowerment, enhancing well-being and advocacy, it seems social workers cannot escape rallying for increasing the scope of user involvement within the DIP. Good practice indicates that social workers must 'recognise the expertise of users and carers about their own situation and have regard for their wishes . . . involving users and carers when setting goals and developing care plans' (Topss England, 2004). Social workers should concentrate on involving individuals in their treatment decisions, and identify barriers to user participation. Indeed, of direct relevance to the DIP, individuals who took part in the consultation by Addaction (a leading UK charity working in the field of drug and alcohol treatment) identified that they should play a key part in the development of release/aftercare plans to ensure their needs and goals are identified (Drainey et al., 2005).

Research evidence on user involvement is now starting to accumulate (Neale, 2006): this comes alongside renewed government interest and a growth in user self-organisations (McDermott, 2002). However, the real challenge is to transform these good intentions into effective practice at national and grass-roots levels.

(Kevin Smith (Kes): www.kescartoons.com)

Reflect

While there has been a significant growth in interest in the participation of users, especially in policy and research, it is less clear that this aspiration has been consistently achieved in practice (Shapiro, 2005).

What is the challenge of involving drug users directly in service arrangements?

What about the 'small and significant pool' of drug users who are also in frequent contact with the criminal justice system (Eley et al., 2005: 401). Should their views on participation in services be taken into account?

Since the early 2000s, there has been significant growth in drug user self-organisations: a number of new groups have started up across the United Kingdom. They now have a national umbrella organisation, the National Association of Drug User Groups (to assist groups through networking), and a development agency, the National Drug Users Development Agency (to assist with organisation and community development).

The formation of the National Treatment Agency (NTA) launched in April 2001 (subsequently moved into the new Public Health Service in 2012) has seen an increase in momentum and a commitment to engage drug users. One of the NTA's eight key areas is 'Service User Consultation' under which it states that the NTA will 'involve service users in planning and monitoring drugs service provision [and] ensure that users views contribute to the development of its policy and practice'.

Despite this movement the government has been unable to establish a meaningful funding relationship with drug user self-organisations, concerned as they are that they would end up funding organisations that would campaign against their own Drug Strategy. It also remains clear that that there is a degree of ambivalence among professionals about moving to a new relationship with drug users, and concerns still exist about the legitimacy of the drug user movement. At the moment most user groups are not currently able to make a meaningful contribution. Even the most developed user-run projects are still in their infancy. The process has begun but there is a long way to go.

Drug users have been so forced to the sidelines of society that the drug users in Allman et al.'s (2007) study stated that they did not feel able to talk to 'straight people' (people who do not use drugs), despite the fact that interaction between the two is precisely what is necessary to reduce this marginalisation and to reduce further public health threats and encourage service user involvement.

This is not aided by the fact that UK government (and governments in the US, Canada and Asia (Crofts and Deany 1999; Rolles 2009) responses to drugs have continued to reinforce (and perhaps encouraged) such marginalisation. There is evidence to suggest that these marginalising terminologies continue to dominate within treatment services: statements that sections of the population are 'hard to reach' reinforces such labels and actually represents the failings of treatment and support services to meet service users' needs (Sampson, 2008). Hunt (2002) draws attention to the wide spread usage of terms such as 'difficult client' or the 'chaotic' or 'problematic' user who has 'unrealistic demands' (Fischer et al., 2007) in treatment (echoed also by Brooks, 2007).

In light of this, it is unsurprising that drug users are demanding a visible stake and an audible and credible voice in the services that are designed to support them and are integral to their lives (Shapiro, 2005, Allman et al., 2007). The beginnings of change in such official attitudes to drug users can be detected in the most recent strategy document which talks of 'building recovery in communities' involving three overarching principles – wellbeing, citizenship, and freedom from dependence. More explicitly is the Scottish Government strategy (*The Road to Recovery: A New Approach to Tackling Scotland's Drug Problem*, 2008) which indicates aspirations for partnership with service users and has as a key principle: the view that 'recovery is most effective when service users' needs and aspirations are placed at the centre of their care and treatment.' (p. 23).

If drug workers and users are to see changes in the way services are run and in the ethos of the therapeutic relationship, they will have to be approximately equal partners in the project. To accomplish this the user movement has to be assisted through its present period of embryonic development. Organisations need to develop through a programme of research to identify what works. This information must be disseminated throughout the drugs field.

To date, drug services continue to carry a degree of social stigma because of a lack of public information about drug use and service provision that is still largely a mystery to the rest of the community. Many treatment services, particularly those forced by community expectations and social stigma, therefore feel under pressure to achieve rapid results from treatment intervention. As a consequence, decisions around treatment can often be prescriptive, with little involvement from the service user.

Blood-borne viruses and social work

An area where the involvement of service users has been most noticeable has been in the vital role they can play in the reduction of isolation and stigma associated with a Hepatitis C (HCV) diagnosis.

 ### A closer look

Terminology (3)

The term 'hepatitis' means inflammation of the liver. This can be caused by alcohol, autoimmune disease (when your body's own defences attack healthy body tissues), specific liver diseases or viruses. HCV is a blood-borne virus which was discovered in 1989 but a blood test to diagnose it was not developed until 1991. About 10 per cent of those infected will go on to develop serious liver damage after 20–30 years. The virus infects the liver; the body's immune system tries to fight off the infection and causes inflammation in the liver as a result. This inflammation can lead to fibrosis (scarring) of the liver tissue and in some cases may cause the development of cirrhosis. Those who develop cirrhosis are at risk of developing liver cancer and/or liver failure.

Weapon of mass destruction. Hep C: Britain's best kept secret.
(Kevin Smith (Kes): www.kescartoons.com)

Services users have formed a peer advisory service (DoH, 2006b) run by individuals who have themselves been diagnosed or treated for HCV; acting as a source of information and support and assisting those people who are recently diagnosed or whose condition is beginning to deteriorate to take control of their condition and improve the quality of their life. For individuals who are still using drugs this might mean providing support to access harm reduction materials, or clean injecting equipment, or recommending a particular drug treatment agency, particularly as injecting drug users (IDUs) have traditionally been deeply suspicious of formal treatment services (Paylor and Orgel, 2004), and peer groups often have much more credibility than a professional. Peer advisers, as current, ex or potential service users, are also in a prime position to suggest how services might be improved (DoH, 2006b, NTA, 2006) in order to ensure all groups who might be at risk of contracting or transmitting HCV are reached.

One of the many consequences of injecting drug use is the potential risk of exposure to infectious blood-borne viruses (BBV), the most obvious being HIV. However, more recently there is evidence (Bird et al., 2001; Pybus et al., 2004; Danta et al., 2007; Levin, 2009) that risk of exposure to HCV is more of a 'threat' especially for IDUs, with 80 per cent of IDUs estimated to be infected (ACMD 2009).

Case study

Trevor and Barbara, Fiona and Michael and Karl and Sue cont . . .

Following a routine health check and subsequent precautionary blood tests Barbara was told by her GP that she had the blood-borne virus Hepatitis C (HCV), that she had a good chance of being cured, but that it could cause cirrhosis and cancer of the liver. Barbara dabbled with injecting heroin in her late teens but those days were a distant memory. The brief experimentation involved sharing injecting equipment with her then boyfriend.

Following complications during the pregnancy Fiona lost her baby. Devastated by her loss Fiona has relapsed and is using crack cocaine. This is putting considerable strain on her relationship with Michael, not least because of the financial strain this is putting on the household income. Michael has got a place on a structured day programme and has reduced his daily methadone intake.

Just over a year ago Sue had unprotected intercourse during a drunken 'one night stand' with a guy she met in a club. More recently, after complaining of genital soreness Sue was persuaded by her friend to attend a Genitourinary (GU) clinic for a sexual health check. Tests revealed that she is HIV positive. She received pre- and post-test counselling but is still in a state of shock. She has not told Karl, but since learning of the result she has not had sexual intercourse with Karl which has been the source of numerous rows.

More than a decade of harm reduction initiatives in the UK did have a significant impact on the transmission of HIV and did contribute to a low prevalence rate among IDUs in the past. The UK is able to show levels of HIV in injecting drug users lower than most of the rest of Europe (UKDPC, 2007). The success can be pinpointed to, amongst other things, the expansion of needle exchange services and methadone programmes (Reuters and Stevens, 2007).

Current estimates of HCV infection prevalence in the UK vary from 250,000 (DoH, 2002) to 600,000 (RCGP, 2007). This wide differentiate in estimate is due to the fact that the majority of people experience no or vague symptoms at the time of infection (DoH, 2002). HCV is slow to proliferate in the body (Dolan, 1998) and an individual can therefore take between 10 and 40 years to develop serious liver disease (Foster, 2008). This means that symptoms, if and when they do appear, can be 'chronic and debilitating' (Dolan, 1998) and difficult to recognise until the HCV has significantly advanced (RCGP, 2007).

Continuing IDUs have historically been denied treatment, despite being the most at risk for transmission and contraction of HCV (Hopwood and Treloar, 2003; NTA, 2008; Foster, 2008; Mack, 2009) and being likely to have the biggest impact on the NHS when the disease becomes too serious to ignore (Paylor and Orgel, 2004). Reasons for refusal of treatment include perceived inability to adhere to regime, chaotic contact with services and risk of reinfection if injection continues (Stein et al., 2002).

However, as those on substitution treatments are considered eligible (Paylor and Orgel, 2004) and the National Institute for Clinical Excellence (NICE is the independent organisation responsible for providing national guidance on the promotion of good health and the prevention and treatment of ill health) states that accepting treatment is the mutual decision of the clinician and patient, even those who continue to inject could be eligible. IDUs who began HCV treatment in detox and continued into the community setting successfully but injected intermittently had no incidence of reinfection despite relapse into injecting (Schafer et al., 2004).

Refusing to treat IDUs may be connected with a perception of moral failure by those who inject drugs, deeming them undeserving of treatment (Rehm et al., 2003). To combat this, it is necessary to raise awareness among professionals of harm reduction principles emphasising pragmatism and non-judgementalism (UKHRA, 2005).

Disability Discrimination Act

From December 2005, HIV was included under the Disability Discrimination Act 1995 (DDA) from the point of diagnosis as an impairment which will have substantial and long-term effects on an individual's ability to undertake day-to-day activities.

Many individuals with HCV experience a similar reduced day-to-day functioning and with HCV's prevalence in the population becoming impossible to ignore (Paylor and Orgel, 2004), it is likely that HCV will also be included under the DDA in future. This places duties on local authorities (particularly social work teams) to assess those individuals who appear in need of community care services under the NHS and Community Care Act 1990 and a duty to provide these services under section 3 of the National Assistance Act 1948 (Brayne and Carr, 2005).

As HCV advances throughout the population, it is likely that we will need specialised Hepatitis C social work teams who are able to provide information for those at risk as well as post-diagnosis support. This might include appropriate welfare rights advice, access to advocacy, conducting community care assessments, commissioning Direct Payments or Individual Budgets (DoH, 2003b) and to act as sources of information to a wider network of allied professionals.

The vital role of social care in provision of emotional support should not be overlooked, as the isolation and anxiety in being diagnosed with HCV and the support of a social worker can be central to treatment engagement and adherence (Rhodes et al., 2004). This is particularly important, given that strong social support networks have been shown to have a positive effect on HCV treatment adherence (Treloar et al., 2002).

As HCV diagnoses in future affect those who no longer use drugs and who may have been drug-free for

some years, there is an urgent need for knowledge of Hepatitis C to expand beyond drug teams and agencies and into mainstream society and social care (APPGH, 2008): social care workers (particularly those working with physically disabled adults or older adults (Paylor and Orgel, 2004)) will find themselves with vastly increased caseloads as HCV diagnoses increase. This will necessitate their being able to adequately support families in a non-judgmental and non-stigmatising manner (Fraser and Treloar, 2006), which will mean a significant expansion of training and awareness-raising among professionals, in addition to strong inter-agency links and a transparent integrated care pathway (Paylor and Mack, 2009).

Conclusion

Social work with drug users is significantly influenced by many of the wider tensions and challenges encapsulated within the relationship between the wider society and its drug-using members. That this is the case for many, if not most, drug users only generates a more acute sense of challenge and discontinuity for drug users who are marginalised in one or more senses: that is, the population with whom social work is most likely to engage.

Social work practice has a role to play in achieving social justice for drug users, especially those who are excluded in some way. In contrast to widely held concerns about the 'threat' represented by drug users, the aim of social work should be to restate the importance of listening to them, taking their concerns seriously, and challenging the discrimination they encounter. A necessary feature of social work practice with drug users is, indeed, a commitment to social justice.

Key learning points

This chapter has covered the following learning points:

✔ Attention was drawn to the importance of attitudes and beliefs in determining how drug use is conceptualised and how the problems represented by drug users are defined. Consideration was given to a range of discourses which have typically 'problematised' drug users in general, and specific groups in particular.

✔ The consideration of recurrent dilemmas for social workers involved with drug users, particularly around the need to find a balance between 'care' and 'control'. Social workers are expected to represent authority at the same time as addressing the welfare needs of their service users, and this is a particularly challenging task in the light of the overarching social tensions described previously. Practitioners are responsible for balancing the needs of drug users against the risks posed by their behaviour. At the same time, social work values stress the importance of promoting individual rights and autonomy, while protecting service users (and others) from harm. This means trying to negotiate accommodations between the interests and wishes of drug users and other people, including family members, the 'community', and their peers.

✔ The challenge of involving drug users directly in service arrangements was addressed. While there has been a significant growth in interests in the participation of users, especially in policy and research, it is less clear that this aspiration has been consistently achieved in practice. This chapter sought to explore in more detail some of the methods which have been adopted, and evaluated the extent to which a 'rights' approach might be both practical and realistic in the complex circumstances in which interventions are carried out.

Further reading

Harris, P. (2007) *Empathy for the Devil: How to Help People Overcome Drugs and Alcohol Problems.* Lyme Regis: Russell House Publishing. Examining the core skills necessary for effecting change in problematic substance users, this book explores practical ways of establishing or improving your practice. It steps beyond clinical, theoretical and moral undertones to the reality of working with substance misuse. It suggests ways ahead to workers stuck in seemingly perennial impasses, as they strive with their colleagues to address multifaceted and entrenched problems.

Phillips, R. (ed.) (2004) *Children Exposed to Parental Substance Misuse: Implications for Family Placement.* London: British Association for Adoption and Fostering. This wide-ranging collection tackles the variety of issues that confront social workers when considering placement for the children of drug users, but it also operates as a very good introduction to the issues social workers face generally in the drugs field.

Useful websites

www.nta.nhs.uk
The National Treatment Agency for Substance Misuse (NTA) is a special health authority established by the UK government to increase the availability, capacity and effectiveness of treatment for drug misuse in England.

www.drugs.gov.uk
This is a cross-government website to support the National Drug Strategy and the work of Drug Action Teams. It contains information for Drug Action Teams and interested individuals to find out about the government's Drug Strategy. It includes links to reports, publications and research that are relevant to the National Drugs Strategy.

www.dh.gov.uk
The Department of Health issues a range of policy documents covering health and social care. While this is obviously a much broader field than for older people alone, there has been a particular flurry of policy documents that affect older people in recent years, and as such this is an essential website.

www.hda-online.org.uk
The Health Development Agency (HDA) identifies the evidence of what works to improve people's health and reduce health inequalities. In partnership with professionals, policy makers and practitioners, it develops guidance and works across sectors to get evidence into practice.

www.sdf.org.uk
The Scottish Drugs Forum (SDF) is the national non-government drugs policy and information agency working in partnership with others to coordinate effective responses to drug use in Scotland. The SDF aims to support and represent, at both local and national levels, a wide range of interests, promoting collaborative, evidence-based responses to drug use.

www.drugscope.org.uk
Drugscope is an independent UK charity concerned with drug information and policy. The charity is a merger between the Institute for the Study of Drug Dependence (ISDD) and the Standing Conference on Drug Abuse (SCODA). The website contains information on UK trends and updates; an events calendar; information on European drug laws and access to drug prevention and education resources. There is also a drug-search facility; a searchable drug encyclopaedia giving information on drug news, history, law, effects and risks. There is also free search-access to their database, which contains over 80,000 records.

www.alcoholconcern.org.uk
Alcohol Concern is the leading national organisation with issues surrounding alcohol use. The Alcohol Concern website contains a wealth of information about related issues and useful links to many other alcohol-related websites.

For additional cases and topic-organised, clickable links into additional media resources, including those produced by IRISS, visit **www.pearsoned.co.uk/wilsonruch**

Activity

Activity One

In relation to Hepatitis C (HCV), social work has been described as 'sleepwalking through an epidemic' (Paylor and Orgel, 2004). Why do you think this is? What are the implications for social work?

(Find out more about HCV – a good place to start would be The British Liver Trust which provides excellent information and advice on hepatitis and liver disease connected to drug and alcohol use. A very useful site for those who want to know more about Hep C and B: **www.britishlivertrust.org.uk**.)

Activity Two

The key piece of legislation governing psychoactive drugs is the 1971 Misuse of Drugs Act which came into force in 1973. This legislation created a structure whereby psychoactive substances were classified from Class A to C according to the specified drugs' perceived potential for dependency and relative harmfulness (for individuals and society), and their medicinal usage was governed by their segregation into Schedules One through to Four, according to their perceived clinical value and consequent availability for use. Classification of individual drugs also determines severity of penalties for offenders convicted under the 1971 Misuse of Drugs Act. On 17 December 1999, Ruth Wyner, the Director of Wintercomfort for the homeless in Cambridge, England, and John Brock, the charity's Day Centre Manager, were sent to prison for five and four years respectively because some of the people they were helping were secretly exchanging drugs on the premises. Ruth and John were arrested, under Section 8 of the 1971 Misuse of Drugs Act, because they were running the premises. They were charged with knowingly permitting or suffering the supply of a Class A drug (heroin) on the premises. In almost every setting, illicit drugs will provoke management problems. Management problems will be your problems as social workers.

What is the legal position of social workers working with drug users? (An excellent resource regarding all the legislation in this area is published by the British Medical Association at **www.bma.org.uk**.)

Activity Three

Certain groups have special service needs, notably young people (e.g. Roberts 2010), the homeless (e.g. Bonner and Luscombe 2009) and those with coexisting psychiatric disturbances (e.g. Crome et al., 2009).

What are the particular challenges that these groups present? In relation *to drug use, find out* what wet-houses and drug consumption rooms are. *How do you* **feel** *about such places*?

Chapter 22
Social work with vulnerable older people

Chapter summary

This chapter will focus on the important but often neglected area of social work with vulnerable older people. In it, we show you why establishing and maintaining productive working relationships with older people is an essential part of achieving high-quality service outcomes which are in accordance with their wishes. We summarise the recent literature relevant to the development of social work with older people, and then go on to identify the limitations and dilemmas of current practice. We finally suggest more creative approaches which you can use in helping people with the problems which many may encounter in later life.

Learning objectives

This chapter covers topics that will enable you to achieve the following learning objectives:

- To clarify the importance of social work with older people, in the context of ongoing demographic changes
- To review the development of social and health care policy for older people
- To identify the key factors within this policy that will affect the practice of social workers, both now and in the future
- To outline the elements of a form of practice that can help older people respond more positively to the challenges posed by old age
- To illustrate, through the medium of case studies, how this practice can be brought into reality by committed, aware social workers.

National Occupational Standards

This chapter will help you to meet the following National Occupational Standards:

Key role 1: Prepare for, and work with individuals, families, carers, groups and communities to assess their needs and circumstances

Unit 1   Prepare for social work contact and involvement
Unit 2   Work with individuals, families, carers, groups and communities to help them make informed decisions
Unit 3   Assess needs and options to recommend a course of action for individuals, families, carers, groups and communities

Key Role 2: Plan, carry out, review and evaluate social work practice, with individuals, families, carers, groups, communities and other professionals

Unit 4   Respond to crisis situations
Unit 5   Interact with individuals, families, carers, groups and communities to achieve change and development and to improve life opportunities
Unit 6   Prepare, produce, implement and evaluate plans with individuals, families, carers, groups, communities and professional colleagues
Unit 7   Support the development of networks to meet assessed needs and planned outcomes
Unit 8   Work with groups to promote individual growth, development and independence
Unit 9   Address behaviour which presents a risk to individuals, families carers, groups and communities

Key Role 3: Support individuals to represent their needs, views and circumstances

Unit 10   Advocate with, and on behalf of, individuals, families, carers, groups and communities
Unit 11   Prepare for, and participate in decision making forums

Key Role 4: Manage risk to individuals, families, carers, groups, communities, self and colleagues

Unit 12   Assess and manage risks to individuals, families, carers, groups and communities
Unit 13   Assess, minimise and manage risk to self and colleagues

Key Role 5: Manage and be accountable, with supervision and support, for your own social work practice within your organisation

Unit 14   Manage and be accountable for your own work
Unit 15   Contribute to the management of resources and services
Unit 16   Manage, present and share records and reports
Unit 17   Work within multi-disciplinary and multi-organisational teams, networks and systems

Key Role 6: Demonstrate professional competence in social work practice

Unit 18   Research, analyse, evaluate, and use current knowledge of best social work practice
Unit 19   Work within agreed standards of social work practice and ensure own professional development
Unit 20   Manage complex ethical issues, dilemmas and conflicts
Unit 21   Contribute to the promotion of best social work practice

Case study

Alistair and Jean

Alistair is a married man of 74 who lives with his wife Jean (who is the same age) in an owner-occupied house in a former mining village. He has been referred to the Adult Social Care Department by his GP, who describes the situation at home as 'insupportable'. Apparently, Alistair has been diagnosed as having Alzheimer's disease for the past four years, and Jean has been his sole carer; during that time his behaviour has come to present an increasing problem to his wife. In the early stages, Alistair had difficulty recollecting friends and family and appeared to be generally forgetful. He then started to lose his sense of direction when out of the house, and was found wandering near the local shops in a state of disorientation on a few occasions. More recently, Alistair has become more restless, finding it difficult to sleep at night, and is subject to severe mood swings. In addition, his behaviour has become significantly disinhibited, such that he behaves inappropriately when out in public, embarrassing Jean with his lewd and aggressive behaviour. In the home, Alistair is reported as creating another type of problem, following Jean all over the house, and refusing to settle to anything if she is out of his sight. Attempts have been made in the past to provide Jean with some respite, but this has always foundered on Alistair's refusal to accept care from anybody other than her. Alistair and Jean are reported as having been a 'devoted couple', who have been married for 51 years. They have no children and no other members of either family live locally – Alistair and Jean came down to England from Scotland in order that he could secure work in 1960, and their relatives still live in Scotland. Alistair wants to continue to live with Jean in their house, and becomes quite upset and emotional if any other possibilities are mentioned. Jean also wants him to remain, but does not believe that she can continue as she has – the responsibility is adversely affecting her own health, and her GP has strongly suggested that she cannot continue acting as Alistair's sole carer.

What do you think the effect of these changes is likely to be on Alistair's sense of self? In addition, what is the probable impact of Alistair's gradual deterioration on Jean, his wife and companion for over 50 years? How will you seek to encompass these issues within any care plan?

This is a typical case within older people's services. A number of issues of importance for a social worker are highlighted in the above case study: others are implicit. Among the obvious issues for consideration are the following:

- the effect of dementia (in this case Alzheimer's disease) on both the person who is subjected to it, and the carer(s) of that person;
- identifying the range and scope of the needs that both Alistair and Jean have;
- balancing a service user's needs and wishes against those of a carer.

The more implicit issues are equally important for a successful outcome, however, and include the following:

- The lengthy, and reportedly loving, relationship between Alistair and Jean. A couple who have lived closely for such a long time build up a very close bond between them, which is implied in the narrative. Even forms of action that may be in the best interests of both can also impair, even fracture, such bonds, with a consequently huge emotional impact. Certainly, it is probable that Jean is experiencing a deeply felt sense of loss, akin to bereavement, due to the enormous, irreversible change that Alistair is undergoing.

- The fact that it is very likely that needs will be identified that require both health and social care support. As we discussed in Chapter 13, detailed inter-professional and partnership working will be needed to turn this into an effective piece of practice.
- Often, the most effective support for carers of people with dementia is provided by people and organisations that are not directly part of the state welfare system: the Alzheimer's Society, Age Concern, Help the Aged, the Carers' Federation, etc. Knowledge of the operations of these organisations will help a social worker bring them into Alistair's care network.
- The financial circumstances of Alistair and Jean. Given that most forms of social care attract a charge, a social worker will need to be aware of the financial implications of any decision that is made.

Taken together, there are a number of interpersonal, administrative and collective types of response to Alistair and Jean's circumstances (discussed in more length in an increasing number of texts: see, for example, Lymbery, 2005; Phillips et al., 2006; Hughes and Heycox, 2010; McDonald, 2010). A social worker's role will involve ensuring that all of these are properly considered.

Introduction

Social work with older people has consistently been an unpopular area with prospective practitioners, with proportionately fewer students on qualifying courses expressing interest and enthusiasm in this aspect of practice (Jack and Mosley, 1997; Quinn, 1999) than in other areas of social work, particularly with children and families. This profile is not unique to Britain, as similar findings are seen in reports from other countries (from Israel see Litwin, 1994; from Australia see Hughes and Heycox, 2006). There are a number of reasons that have been advanced for this position:

- that it reflects the low status of older people in society;
- that practice with older people is seen as being of low status, reflecting both the position of older people and the lack of complexity that is perceived to characterise much of social workers' practice with them;
- that there are emotional demands that affect students' career choices, particularly in the fact that it forces practitioners to confront their own mortality.

(Quinn, 2000)

All of these factors will be discussed in the course of this chapter: indeed, one of its key purposes is to pose a fundamental challenge to such a limited and negative perception of social work with older people. Indeed, in taking this approach, we must acknowledge the remarkable growth of high-quality academic texts that focus on social work with older people, in – both a British (Lymbery, 2005; Phillips et al., 2006; Harris and Tanner, 2007; Ray et al., 2009; McDonald, 2010) and an international context (for example, in Australia, Hughes and Heycox, 2010). Drawing on the reality of contemporary British practice, we acknowledge that there are serious problems afflicting social work with older people, which has been dominated for too long by administratively oriented concerns. However, we suggest that these do not represent an automatic limitation to the potential and value of social work interventions with older people.

In order to justify this contention, we need to establish a number of lines of argument, which will form the main sections within this chapter. The first of these is to explain the high priority that we argue should be given to social work with older people. There are two elements of this:

1. the nature of demographic change is such that there will be an increasing number of older people in society, with a consequent growth in the demands on health and social care services;

2. that older people have the same rights as other groups to an excellent service, whether from health or social care.

The chapter will start by discussing these issues, reflecting how they affect older people and the ways in which they are perceived within society. It will then briefly examine the policy context for social care with older people; this was charted in general terms in Chapter 00 Particular reference is made to the impact of particular policy changes to older people, which have created a number of dilemmas in practice – many deriving directly from the financially dominated elements of community care, identified in an earlier chapter – which will be identified and expanded upon. These will then be illustrated though three case studies, which draw upon the themes that have been identified through the chapter.

Ageing and older people

Think ahead

What are the first words that come to your mind if asked to describe what being 'old' means to you? What is the balance of these between broadly positive and negative terms? If they tend to the negative, what does this say about the way in which you (a) think about getting old yourself, and (b) think about those people who are old?

In order to practise successfully with older people, social workers must understand a number of connected factors:

- The demographic profile of Britain, especially the numbers and proportions of older people within the population as a whole.
- The nature of ageing, which implies an understanding of the physical, biological and psychological manifestations of the ageing process.
- The political, social and cultural status of older people in contemporary society.
- The subjective experiences of older people.

This section will address these issues in turn, focusing on a broad understanding of the experiences that people have as they age, combined with the ways in which society responds to those issues.

Table 22.1 Predicted population changes during the twenty-first century

Year	Total population (millions)	Older people of pensionable age (millions)	Older people of pensionable age (as % of total)
2006	60.254	11.366	18.95
2011	61.401	12.182	20.04
2021	63.835	12.703	21.65
2031	64.700	15.271	23.60

(based on Shaw, 2004b)

Table 22.2 Predicted increase in the numbers of people over 75 years of age

Year	People over 75 (millions)	People over 75 (as % of total)	People over 75 (as % of older people)
2006	4.651	7.72	40.92
2011	4.930	8.03	40.46
2021	6.075	9.51	47.82
2031	7.675	11.86	50.26

(based on Shaw, 2004a and 2004b)

Demographic changes

If we start first with the demographic changes that can be anticipated in the population of Britain, by the middle years of this century the balance in the population will be significantly altered, as the figures in Table 22.1 make clear.

It is important to be clear about the likely accuracy of these figures. While population projections will inevitably have some measure of inaccuracy – for example, it is uncertain what the 'normal' lifespan will be in future – a reasonably precise prediction can be made of the numbers of people currently alive who will live into old age. This, of course, is aided by the fact that all people who will be characterised as being of pensionable age in the middle years of the twenty-first century have already been born! The only exceptions to this are the relatively small numbers of people who will migrate to this country in the future as adults, which are calculated in relation to the numbers of people who emigrate. These have a small impact on the overall figures; it is therefore possible to make informed judgements about the size of the population of older people to 2050 and beyond, assuming that mortality rates remain stable. Regarding the balance of older people within the population, the birth rate needs also to be taken into account. The fact that birth rates increased in the early part of the twenty-first century

(ONS, 2007) does not change the essential balance of the future population, as a birth rate of 2.1 children per adult woman is required to maintain the population; the present rate remains short of this figure, despite its increase. At present, it is believed that both men and women can expect to live longer, in better health than ever before. As the above figures suggest, when examined in crude terms, there is set to be a considerable increase in both the overall numbers of older people and the proportion of older people within society. This general impression has been confirmed by later analysis (Blake, 2009), and appears to be even more of an issue when the increase in the numbers of people over the age of 75 is considered; these figures are outlined in Table 22.2.

As we can see, there will be an increase in the absolute numbers of people over 75, as well as a sharp increase in the percentage of this group both in terms of the overall population and those people of pensionable age. On the face of it, therefore, the increase in the numbers of over-75s will constitute a major potential problem for the provision of services: for example, this group uses the highest proportion of health and social care services. If we focus particularly on the very oldest in society, these issues become even more stark. All local authorities in the entire United Kingdom (except two – Newham and Lewisham) are expected to see increases in the

Table 22.3 Changes in the dependency support ratio

Year	Total population (millions)	Children under 16 (millions)	People of pensionable age (millions)	Dependents (as % of overall population)
2006	60.254	11.496	11.366	37.94
2011	61.401	11.181	12.182	37.95
2021	63.835	11.149	12.703	37.37
2031	64.700	11.242	15.271	40.98

(based on Shaw, 2004b)

population of those over 85. The largest single increase is estimated as being in Carrickfergus, Northern Ireland, which is primed for an increase of 85 per cent in this population group (Blake, 2009). The government has also suggested that the current structure of old age pensions is no longer affordable, with proposals both to increase the age of retirement and to require individuals to undertake a more active role in preparing for their retirement. Although this has been framed as an impending 'demographic time bomb' that will fracture the fabric of society, many contemporary references are now rather more measured in their tone. However, the almost apocalyptic nature of the rhetoric that has surrounded this concept has had a major impact, not only on public policy in relation to ageing, but also in the way in which ageing is thought about. This appeared to confirm the negativity that pervaded much of the debate. A recurrent concern for health and social care policy in respect of older people, evidenced at least partly through a number of developments in the early years of the twenty-first century, is how to produce services that simultaneously respond better to the needs of older people while being affordable. Arguably, the emphasis on personalisation, outlined in Chapter 00, is primarily an attempt to address both concerns.

Returning to the issue of demographics, an important further consideration is the balance within the population between those of working age and those – who are in general either children, old or disabled – who are defined as not economically active. It is of course much more difficult to be certain about the numbers of children in the population in the future, as this substantially depends upon unknown factors such as birth rates. Current estimates indicate that the increase in the numbers of older people will be balanced to some extent by the projected decline in birth rates. Once the dependency of children is taken into account, the overall 'dependency support

ratio' (that is, the ratio of people who are categorised as dependent as against the population of working age) will not alter greatly until 2031 and beyond. The projections for the future are shown in Table 22.3.

As Tinker (1997) has observed, this means that the accepted dependency support ratio – which for all of the twentieth century was between 37 and 40 per cent – will remain within these bands in the early part of the twenty-first century, although it is projected to increase, particularly between 2021 and 2041 (Shaw, 2004b). The main change is that the balance between 'dependent' older people and younger people changes markedly, continuing a process that has been in train for some while. However, a note of caution has been injected into these calculations:

'It should be emphasised, however, that demographically defined support ratios . . . whatever age boundaries are used, take no account of workforce participation rates and therefore do not represent real levels of economic dependence'.
(Shaw, 2004b: 13)

In addition, some influential thinking has maintained the distinction between the support ratio in relation to older people and for children. On this basis, for example, Blake (2009) has suggested that there will be a sharp decline in what she terms the Old Age Support Ratio, with most localities featuring a shift in this balance as proportionately more older people remain alive. Once again, it is particularly interesting that the 'problem' of older people is highlighted here, rather than the more neutral notions of dependency, which crossed generations.

In this context, the fact that more people living for longer is not always treated as 'one of the great successes of modern times' (Wilson, 2001: 1) presents a fascinating insight into the nature of debate that has surrounded this topic. By contrast, the focus has tended to be more on the problems that this could create in terms of the increased burden on the rest of society, particularly health and social care services. The subtleties of demographic change appear not to be properly understood: for example, little account appears to be taken of the positive contributions that older people make to society in a range of different ways, not least the amount of informal care that older people provide (Wilson, 2001). However, on the basis of current knowledge, it is reasonable to assume that social work services for older people will be even more required in the future than they are at present, even if it remains uncertain how such services can be funded. It is therefore important that we understand the effects of ageing: this is the focus of the following sub-section.

The nature of ageing

This subsection will briefly summarise the physical, biological and psychological effects of the ageing process. As you read it, you should bear in mind that we do not wish to suggest that older people should only be perceived in relation to what happens to them physically as they age. Such an approach could lead to what Simon Biggs, a noted social gerontologist, has called 'biological reductionism' (Biggs, 1993), reducing the complexity of an individual's life and experiences to what will inevitably occur to the physical body. Our point is more to note that there *are* many observable physical and biological changes when one ages; if social workers disregard these and their potential impact, this can also reduce the effectiveness of their practice.

It is important to be clear at the outset that while particular diseases may be associated with the process of ageing, ageing is not in itself a disease. Not all of the changes that people experience will necessarily require the response of health and social care agencies, although some aspects of biological ageing (the onset of dementia, for example) will almost certainly require this form of assistance. An important distinction to draw, therefore, is between those elements of ageing that are part of 'normal' processes, and those which are indicative of 'abnormal' developments. For society in general an understanding of the ageing process is essential so that we can seek both to live longer and to maintain better health; this can help to avoid one of the major problems associated with increased life expectancy: that a large proportion of this is taken up by serious physical ailments (Westendorp and Kirkwood, 2007).

For example, if we examine sensory functioning – vision and hearing – many older people will experience some measure of sight or hearing loss as they age. While these impairments can create practical and psychological problems, the difficulties can be managed relatively easily in most circumstances. However, a proportion of older people develop problems that the use of spectacles or hearing aids alone cannot resolve. A similar point can be made if we examine the ways in which our physical appearance changes as we age. For example, owing to a gradual degeneration in the skin's elastic tissues, older people develop a wrinkled appearance; in addition, for many the skin and (most noticeably) the hair tend to lose their pigment with age – i.e. most of us go grey! Neither of these common experiences of ageing are problematic in themselves, although they can lead to psychological difficulties; in a youth-obsessed culture, not every individual is comfortable with the physical signs of their own ageing and hence their mortality. A decline in muscle power is also associated with ageing, although this can be compensated to some extent by maintaining physical activity. Indeed, weight-bearing exercise can also help to preserve bone density, the extreme thinning of which, known as osteoporosis, can affect many women following the menopause, potentially rendering them more prone to fractures and to serious skeletal and postural problems. Many people also experience a form of arthritis as they age: most commonly osteoarthritis, which is usually caused by wear and tear on the major weight-bearing joints such as hips and knees. In the worst cases these problems can be relieved by joint replacement operations. Less frequently, people may be affected by rheumatoid arthritis, which is often experienced as more painful and which tends to affect the smaller joints in the hands and wrists.

In addition, there are a number of changes to the internal workings of the body. For example, the effectiveness of the kidneys generally starts to deteriorate from the age of about 30 years, although this does not necessarily create a problem in later life. A general weakening of the bladder function is directly associated with ageing, with more serious and potentially irreversible bladder problems created by a range of diseases: for example, incontinence is strongly associated with recovery from a stroke and also with dementia. The operation of the heart and lungs also changes during the ageing process. For example, heart muscles degenerate with age; in more serious cases this can lead to heart failure, where the heart is no longer sufficiently effective to pump blood around the body. Similarly, the lungs become less efficient with age, creating problems with breathing. A combination of these occurrences make it difficult to maintain the level of exercise that can help to ameliorate reduced muscle tone and bone density, noted above. Circulatory problems can be exacerbated by the 'furring up' of arteries, known as atherosclerosis, which is particularly prevalent in developed societies; this is a direct cause of coronary heart disease, a major cause of death in industrialised Western societies.

Forms of hormonal imbalance, such as diabetes and disorders of the thyroid gland, are also more commonly found in older people, as are a number of physiological effects that can derive from disorders to the brain and nervous system. For example, the process of atherosclerosis can limit the supply of blood to the brain, potentially leading to a stroke – another major cause of death and illness among older people. It can also promote the vascular form of dementia; a more common form of dementia is Alzheimer's disease, a degenerative condition of the brain's nerve cells. This is probably the most feared form of disease in old age, disproportionately affecting people over the age of 80, and almost inevitably involving extended contact with health and social care services. Given the projected increase in the numbers of people with dementia – from an estimated 700,00 in 2006, to approximately 1.2m in 2031, and over 1.7m in 2051 (Alzheimer's Society, 2007) – the needs of people with dementia and their carers will become of increasing significance. Other sorts of disease can affect the brain's ability to function, and affect the lives of older people. For example, Parkinson's disease causes selective degeneration in the nerve cells that release the chemical transmitter 'dopamine', leading to increasing problems with muscle control; although this disease can affect people in their middle years, it is particularly associated with old age.

Consideration of the psychological changes that occur for older people presents a more varied set of outcomes, which are not necessarily negative in their impact. The effect of these on each individual is a shifting balance between various different factors (Marcoen et al., 2007); there are gains as well as losses in the ageing process, with these often balancing each other out. However, the popular belief is often that the decline noted in people's physical capabilities is necessarily mirrored in the psychological sense. This is borne out in the common conviction that older people experience a considerable decline in their intellectual ability. In fact there is minimal decline up to 70 years, although there is an increased likelihood of some decline in intellectual functioning in very old age. Memory loss is popularly believed to be the other key aspect of decline in psychological functioning in old age. While there are changes in memory function, their impact is not always indicative of deterioration and decline. While problems may emerge in respect of short-term memory, an older person's long-term memory is less likely to be affected. Often, perceptions about memory loss are derived from more general concerns about dementia; as noted above, this relates more to 'abnormal' processes of ageing, rather than indicating that serious decline is part of 'normal' ageing processes.

Older people are also capable of learning to perform unfamiliar tasks, and adopt new skills, although many older people may lose interest in extending their repertoire of skills and abilities. In fact, many tend to underestimate their abilities in this respect, perhaps reflecting the negative views current within society. Older people may be very skilled in making sense of a wide range of information, applying experience and good judgement to issues at hand; this links to a more positive belief in the wisdom of older people, a perspective that is more common in societies that particularly value age and experience (Slater, 1995). On balance, therefore, during the course of 'normal' ageing, older people retain much of the capacity for learning and memory that they possessed as younger adults. The age-related changes that do occur in the 'normal' process of ageing do not necessarily constitute a major obstacle to the ability to function effectively in later life.

Whether or not people's personalities alter as they age is an important question. For many people the personality characteristics developed as an adult endure into old age (Stuart-Hamilton, 2006), although a number of older people do change some facets of their behaviour and interests as they age. Certainly, older people are more likely to experience depression than younger people; while there is little evidence to suggest that older people are more likely to become seriously clinically depressed, there is more likelihood that older people will experience reactive forms of depression (Slater, 1995). Given that the probability of significant losses and other negative life events increases with age, this should perhaps not surprise us; however, given this, the resilience of many older people is notable.

This subsection has indicated the main physical and psychological changes that older people are likely to experience. Although some of these are inevitable – in particular, the range of physical change will almost inevitably create difficulties in people's daily lives – their cumulative impact is less dramatic than might be popularly believed; indeed, how we live can affect the ageing process to a significant degree (Westendorp and Kirkwood, 2007). For example, there is nothing about the process of ageing that leaves older people inherently less able to cope with the psychological demands of life. However, there are factors beyond the individual that materially affect how older people experience their lives – notably the place of older people in the political and economic context of society, and the ways in which the experience of ageing is socially constructed. There are certainly some aspects of ageing that are more likely to impact upon people from lower classes: for example, increases in mortality are unevenly spread within society and survival into healthy old age is more likely to be compromised for people from poorer communities (Victor, 2005). Both of these issues will affect the practice of social workers, who tend to work with people from the more deprived parts of the community often denied the advantages that have accumulated elsewhere.

Reflect

Much of our direct experience of old age is gathered from observation of people within our own families.

How many of the affects of ageing have you observed in your relatives? Are there other indications of ageing that you have observed?

The political, social and cultural status of older people

One of the limitations of traditional thinking about the needs of older people is that it has focused on people's experiences of ageing as a more or less exclusively individualised problem. By contrast some authors (see, for example, Estes et al., 2001) have argued that the ageing process in Western societies cannot properly be understood unless the relationship between older people and capitalism is explored, as this represents a major source of the problems that older people encounter. (Indeed, this is evident if one examines the differences in life expectancy, health outcomes, etc. between different sectors of society, to which reference was made in the previous section; it is also implied in a more general critique of the impact of inequality on people lives – see Wilkinson and Pickett, 2009.) With specific reference to older people, the argument is that in a capitalist system they are seen as inherently problematic primarily because they represent a drain on resources, to which they no longer contribute actively either as workers/taxpayers or as parents raising the next generation of workers/taxpayers. In addition, unlike children – another group of people

defined as dependent – older people will not be workers/taxpayers in the future.

In practical terms, this perspective focuses on the relationship between the social policies that impact specifically on older people and the wider political context within which they were produced (Estes et al., 2001). For example, social policies that focus on retirement and pensions have to be viewed in relation to concerns about the effects of demographic change, noted above, and their consequent affordability. It is also suggested that the social gains that older people have made have arisen more as the outcome of struggle and challenge than from the beneficence of government; proponents of a critical perspective on ageing are critical of those theories that do not take these factors into account (Estes et al., 2001). In respect of health and social care, the policies that treat old age as a 'disease' and older people as primarily a medical problem are held to be symptomatic of this, as they ignore the social and political position of older people. The particular value of this approach to ageing is that it forcibly reminds us of the marginal status of many older people in society, especially those who become known to social care services. It is held that we cannot understand the nature of ageing today unless we are also able to appreciate the systems of inequality that have affected people throughout the life course (Phillipson, 2005).

There are a number of policies that approach population ageing as a 'problem' to be resolved. The 'harmonisation' of retirement ages for men and women, to take place between 2010 and 2020 (Shaw, 2004a), is a good example of this; similarly the heavily trailed proposals following the recession of 2008/2009 to raise the overall retirement age can also be seen in this light. Another similar policy option has been discussed, that people should be allowed to work beyond the statutory retirement age should they and their employers desire. Although there are obvious merits in these three approaches – the first is more equitable, the second is responsive to significant problems that afflict public finances, while the third accords with the desires of many older people themselves – it is important to analyse all of these proposals in relation to their financial impact. In this respect each of them would result in reduced expenditure on pensions and would therefore allay the concerns about older people being 'unproductive' members of society. Given the financial problems that affect the global economy, it is to be expected that other apparently 'rational' plans to address the perceived problem will be produced in the near future.

One proposed policy is for older people to work past the retirement age.

(*Source:* Alamy Images/Adrian Sherratt)

Many of the elements that make up our understandings of old age are socially constructed, as much as they are innate products of the ageing process. Indeed, while the physical signs of ageing are slow to accumulate, the social constructions of ageing are suddenly applied and are experienced as particularly problematic as a result (Biggs, 1993). For example, the notion of 'retirement' from work is a socially constructed concept; this is applied at an arbitrary stage of life, and yet has become central to the experience of older people, not least because it defines the point at which one officially becomes an 'older person'.

Other forms of social construction significantly affect the experience of old age, particularly 'class', 'gender' and 'race'. It is important to remember that the experience of older people from the 'working class' is qualitatively different from older people from the middle and upper classes. The effects of prior disadvantage and inequality are magnified by getting older; one only has to examine the huge differences in mortality between different parts of the country to understand this (Davey Smith et al., 2002), as well as the enormous inequalities in health between the poor and the rest of society (Townsend et al., 1992). Another point of inequality concerns housing quality which is significantly worse for the poorest people in society. Such older people are also more likely to experience significant financial hardship, which will

have an impact on their diet as well as their leisure activities. The combination of all of these factors means that older people from poorer backgrounds are far more likely to come to the attention of social services than others.

As far as 'gender' is concerned, there are consequences in two ways. First, older women typically live longer than men (Shaw, 2004b) and therefore greatly outnumber them among older people, particularly beyond 75 years of age. Secondly, women are more likely than men to have caring responsibilities that will continue into old age (Arber and Ginn, 1991). Although increasing numbers of men identify themselves as carers, it remains a highly gendered form of activity; social work and social care services are also staffed by larger numbers of women than men – the effect of gender cannot be ignored, therefore. 'Race' is a third important social construction that will have a major impact on the development of services for older people. Although the majority of post-war immigrants were predominantly adults of working age, these first generations constitute an ageing population (Blakemore and Boneham, 1994). There are also large numbers of 'invisible' minorities – particularly with an Irish ancestry, but also from eastern European backgrounds – who also have needs that are particular to their group, which may not be adequately met.

It is impossible to consider the place of older people within society without considering the impact of 'ageism', which has been simply defined as the unwarranted application of stereotypes to older people (Bytheway, 1995). In this analysis, the distinctive quality of ageism is that it identifies a process whereby older people are systematically disadvantaged by the place that they occupy within society. It can be argued that this disadvantage is made apparent in a number of ways, spanning both policy and practice. The following points indicate some of the more common ways in which ageism is made manifest in health and social care:

- *In a range of government policies.* These policies span both national and local levels, including pensions and retirement noted above. In relation to community care, the fact that a primary motivation was to control the social security budget (Lewis and Glennerster, 1996) ensures that this can be seen as a policy constructed on the ageist basis that cost considerations have precedence over the quality of lives of older people, the majority of people affected by the policy.
- *In the organisation and staffing of services for older people.* The fact that health and social care policy for older people has traditionally been poorly organised

and developed (Means and Smith, 1998) implies that ageist considerations have affected its development. The limited development of social work for older people, and its relative lack of popularity as an area of practice, noted earlier in this chapter, is another indicator of ageist assumptions (Lymbery, 2005). It is probable that, given the impending cuts to public expenditure, that older people may experience the strongest impact (AgeUK, 2010).

- *In the differential development of similar sorts of service.* While child protection has become a pre-occupation within social services, adult protection has seldom had the same level of priority. Although the publication of *No Secrets* (DH, 2000f) has put adult protection more firmly on the policy agenda, the impact of the abuse of older people is rarely the same as for children.
- *In the language used to describe older people.* This ranges from casual stereotyping in everyday language to more insidious and dehumanising references to older people by professionals.

As students and social work practitioners you will need to understand the ways in which older people's lives are affected by these factors. Given that social workers tend to focus primarily on the individual, a perspective that we promote within this text, it is relatively easy for them to ignore policy-related issues. However, when linked to the issues of 'class', 'gender' and 'race', noted above,

What are your feelings towards this person?
(*Source:* Photofusion Picture Library/David Hoffman)

they can combine to create even more difficulties for the older person.

Reflecting on the use of language to define and stereotype older people also causes us to consider other culturally bound images of ageing (Gilleard and Higgs, 2005). For example, when older people make the news it is often through their vulnerability, thus conferring a 'victim' status upon them. It is partly for that reason that the official terms to describe older people who may be abused are moving from the concept of 'vulnerability' to the more neutral 'at risk' (DoH, 2009b). The images of older people in popular culture tend to reflect commonly accepted perceptions, and rarely therefore pose a challenge to these. The relationship between older people and society is therefore complex. At one level it is normal and relatively mundane: we all draw our images of ageing from the family, the community as well as the local and national forms of media. At the same time it contains a number of apparently paradoxical elements. Although the ageing process is accepted as 'normal', it is simultaneously feared by many. Similarly, the extent of the 'normality' is bounded, with the range of experience that is seen as appropriate for younger people somehow less so for the older generation.

As a result of these factors, the ways in which older people experience their later years are much more complex than a focus on the 'inevitable' consequences of physical ageing, thereby directly challenging the 'biological reductionism' referred to earlier. However, a critical aspect of older people's lives has so far been absent from our considerations: that is how people subjectively experience ageing. Given that much social work takes place with individuals, it is vital for you as practitioners to get a clear sense of this in respect of each individual. It is a reality that older people of the same age, from similar economic and social circumstances, will experience ageing in different ways. It is to an examination of the development of the individual identity in older age that we now turn.

Identity and older people

Think ahead

How can we best understand how people are experiencing the ageing process? What are the potential pitfalls of the approaches that we might consider?

As we have shown in the previous subsections, the ways in which people experience their older age cannot be fully explained by considering physical and psychological changes, even with the added consideration of the political, social and cultural aspects of ageing. The reality is that in order to appreciate each person's subjective experience of ageing, and to practise creative forms of social work, we must be capable of understanding her/his inner life (Biggs, 1993). Naturally, physical changes will have a substantial effect on the developing older person, and we can recognise that these will be mediated by a number of external factors, as we have considered. However, for social workers this represents necessary but insufficient knowledge on which to found practice, as it takes little account of the individuality of each older person. For the development of sound social work practice more is required: particularly, this must include understanding how each older person experiences her/his personal encounter with old age. It has been suggested that the increased frailty of extreme old age creates an 'existential challenge' for older people (Nolan et al., 2001); as a result, social workers need to establish ways of interacting with each older person that can help them to understand what these challenges might be.

The following are some critical factors to take into account in assessing the way in which the process of ageing may affect the individual person's sense of identity:

- The awareness that ageing takes place in an environment which emphasises competitiveness, productivity and consumption to the exclusion of cooperation and mutuality, aspects of life that are necessary for older people (as they are for others).
- Many of the rapid changes within society have a major impact on the lives and hence the identity of older people: for example, the growth of personal computing which has fostered a growing assumption that business and pleasure can be found online may be experienced as threatening rather than liberating.
- That for most older people the core of an 'inner self' will persist, despite all the changes to which an ageing person is subject.

(Biggs, 1999)

This final point is critical: if it is accepted, a vital role for a social worker will be to work towards the maintenance of an older person's sense of identity. In addition, it also suggests that the individual identity is not pre-determined by social and economic factors; each older person will therefore respond differently to similar sets of occurrence.

The notion of the 'life course' (Hockey and James, 2003) is a way of connecting individual to more structural experiences of ageing. The basis of the theory is that a more complete understanding of the ageing process can be reached by connecting the elements that combine to construct each individual's experience. For example, to refer back to the case study that started this chapter, Alistair and Jean share similar experiences to others of their generation simply because of their shared age; this is made more specific by their shared cultural background. They are both Scottish, having lived most of their adult lives in an English community; this highlights potential sources of difference between them and the bulk of that community. On a more individual level, they have been married for a very long time, and the identity of each is likely to be bound up in the other as a result. Added to this is an even more personal dimension: the specific nature of Alistair's dementia and its impact on their relationship, the caring role that Jean has adopted, etc. An understanding of Alistair and Jean's unique experiences of ageing is generated from an understanding of the complex interweaving of all of these influences.

The policy context

Think ahead

Why is it essential for social workers to understand the basic elements of policy development in relation to older people?

This section will focus on the specific policy issues that affect the delivery of social work and social care services in relation to older people, building on the general analysis contained in Chapter 17. As this is being written only a matter of months into the life of the coalition government, it is not always clear about what will be distinctive about the way in which it intends to develop social policy. Consequently, much of the chapter will focus on what is known and understood about the legacy of the 'new' Labour government, which had many years to embed its response to social needs into policy. As we have seen, there are particular themes that have consistently affected the provision of services, which can be briefly summarised as follows:

- *Modernisation:* as noted earlier, the 'new' Labour government between 1997 and 2010 sought to 'modernise' numerous aspects of social policy, and focused particularly on social care social services within this. Certainly, the emphasis on 'personalisation' can easily be seen to fit within this overarching framework.

- *Performance:* this has been a particular feature of practice within local authorities, as noted in an earlier chapter. In this respect it has affected all adult social care: however, owing to the numbers of older people, it has a particular impact on practice with this group as a future section will explore in more detail.

- *Independence:* As noted earlier, this has been a core theme of policy; its particular significance for older people rests in the large numbers of people who are affected by this policy.

- *Prevention:* The general importance of the concept of prevention within adult social care was particularly evident in the Green Paper (DoH, 2005b, and has suffused subsequent policy documents (see, for example, DoH, 2005b). The effectiveness and popularity of this sort of approach for older people has been demonstrated in the past (Clark et al., 1998) and more recently (Windle et al., 2010) but, as this chapter will explore, there are unexamined conflicts between these priorities and the nature of much social care provision, which since the 1989 White Paper has been targeted specifically towards those most in need.

- *Partnership:* As we discussed in Chapters 13 and 17, the development of enhanced levels of inter-professional working has suffused thinking across all social policy. However, particular inroads have been made in relation to work with older people (Glendinning et al., 2003), and active levels of collaborative working characterise numerous policy developments: intermediate care and delayed discharge being two such examples (these will be further discussed later in this chapter).

These characteristics have affected the detail of many policy developments in health and social care for older people. For example, relatively early in the tenure of the 'new' Labour government a Royal Commission was established to examine the funding of long-term care for older people. The Commission's remit was to 'examine the short- and long-term options for a sustainable system of long-term care for elderly people, both in their own homes and in other settings . . . and to recommend how, and in what circumstances, the cost of such care should be apportioned between public funds and individuals' (Sutherland Report, 1999: ix).

Although the Royal Commission insisted that change was imperative and urged the government to act rapidly, it actually failed to act for an extended period following the publication of the report. When it finally did respond, the government in England did not accept the proposal that all personal care should be provided free of charge, because of the unacceptable financial burden that it would represent. However, under its devolved powers, the Scottish Assembly agreed to implement the recommendations in full; this created a situation where different, incompatible policies were put into effect across Britain (see Dickinson et al., 2007 for a review of the impact of this development in Scotland). It is hard to avoid the conclusion that the English government avoided the longer-term concerns of the impact of an ageing population for short-term political gain, highlighting the populist underpinnings of its response. This conclusion carries even more weight, given the approach of the coalition government in 2010. Rather than take specific action to address a known problem, it has replicated the actions of the incoming Labour government in 1997; it has set up a commission to investigate the issue, and will decide upon a course of action once this commission reports. This will mean that over a decade will have elapsed since the publication of the Sutherland

A closer look

The Royal Commission on Long-Term Care

There were two main recommendations:

- That the costs of long-term care should be split between living costs, housing costs and personal care, and that personal care should be provided free of charge to the individual.
- That the government should establish a National Care Commission to monitor trends, including demography and spending, ensure transparency and accountability in the system, represent the

interests of consumers and set national benchmarks.

The first recommendation caused the most controversy, and two members of the Commission would only sign the document if their objections, and alternatives, were noted. They claimed that the proposal for free personal care would add an extra burden to the public purse without actually providing any more care than was currently available, and that it would benefit the better-off – who could afford to pay care fees – at the expense of the worst-off, for whom it would have been effectively free anyway.

A closer look

Social care for older people in Scotland

Free personal and nursing care is an important and unique policy for older people in Scotland which has increased the well-being of many (Bowes and Bell, 2007). As regards social work with older people, there is a variety of legislation governing policy, practice and services, e.g. the Community Care and Health (Scotland) Act 2002. In 2007 The Scottish government published a long-term strategy aimed to engage the entire country in a consideration of how best to manage the changing nature of the country's population (Scottish Executive, 2007). This outlines the opportunities and choices available to people as they get older, addressing the issues of an ageing

population, an issue that confronts all countries within the United Kingdom. It aims to transform the perception of older people, moving away from seeing them as a burden towards a greater recognition of the value that they bring to the overall community. However, despite its popularity, the Scottish government must also grapple with the financial implication of continuing this policy, which is particularly problematic in a period of massive fiscal restraint. The fact that there has long been concern about shifting the costs of care on to the public purse (Bowes and Bell, 2007) provides the context within which the effectiveness of this policy will be evaluated.

(For further information on this issue see www. scotland.gov.uk/Resource/Doc/169342/0047172.pdf.)

Report, with no specific action having been taken anywhere in the United Kingdom except Scotland. Even here, there is concern about the affordability of its policies (Christie, 2009); however, as the Closer Look box indicates, policy on social care for older people has developed further and faster than elsewhere in the United Kingdom.

The *National Service Framework for Older People* (NSF) (DH, 2001c) represented another significant policy development in the life of the previous government. The particular emphasis on independence and autonomy that is apparent within the NSF is consistent with global policies on the care of older people (Nolan et al., 2001),

A closer look

The National Service Framework For Older People

The purpose of the NSF was to set the parameters for the care of older people; it is one of a sequence that have been produced in the early years of the twenty-first century relating to different areas of care. It contains four general themes, with eight standards being linked to these themes. The first broad theme is 'Respecting the individual', and the two standards attached to it are both central to social work concerns. Standard 1 is 'Rooting out age discrimination', and applies equally to health and social care services, where it has been a significant theme for many years (Thompson, 2007). Standard 2 is 'Person-centred care', stressing that people should be treated as individuals and proposing a pattern of integrated service delivery, including single assessments, etc. (This has had particular consequences for social work practice with older people, as the following subsection will identify.) The second general theme of the NSF is 'Intermediate care', which is also the title of standard 3. It requires

the development of services to prevent unnecessary hospital admission, enable avoidance of long-term care, and aid early discharge from hospitals; in all respects these have been significant issues for social work.

The NSF also contains some themes and standards that are less directly relevant to social care and social work. For example, the third general theme is 'Providing evidence-based specialist care' – reflecting the priority that we addressed above – with four separate standards attached to this theme, three of which are not central to social work practice: standard 4 on 'general hospital care', standard 5 on 'stroke' care, and standard 6 on 'falls'. However, standard 7 focuses on 'mental health and older people' and is also defined as a joint health and social care responsibility; this points to the increased level of acceptance of the impact of dementia on both older people and their carers. The fourth general theme is 'promoting an active, healthy life'; standard 8 relates to this, and is 'the promotion of health and active life in older age'. The significance given to the concept of 'well-being' (DoH, 2005b) in subsequent policy development is testimony to the importance of this.

as well as subsequent policy developments. In relation to the particular characteristics of 'new' Labour governance, the framework is also typical in its numerous exhortations towards improved partnership. Its key elements are identified in the Closer Look box.

The development of intermediate care was initially outlined in the *NHS Plan* (DoH, 2000e) as a way both to meet the needs of older people for increased levels of independence and to reduce the number of days older people spent in hospital care – an expensive and often wanted form of treatment. The concept of intermediate care developed from a narrower focus on rehabilitation that had dominated the latter years of the twentieth century (Lymbery, 2005), and encompassed a bewildering array of local developments that had grown in the latter years of the twentieth century (Wilson, 2003). In essence, these were of three different types, which together have come to be seen as the basis of intermediate care policy:

1. schemes based in hospitals;
2. projects located within residential or nursing care homes;
3. developments based in the community, including hospital-at-home schemes.

While numerous benefits have been identified from a number of intermediate care projects, it has also been suggested that there are a number of problems that have impeded its effective development. These include lack of capacity, problems of access, and failure to promote the benefits of intermediate care sufficiently among medics and other referrers (Regen et al., 2008). The difficulties of creating effective structures of intermediate care will undoubtedly be made more difficult by budgetary problems, which are likely to exacerbate the tension between investing to achieve excellent outcomes as opposed to saving money.

Indeed, one of the particular areas of interest regarding the policy of intermediate care has been its combination of financial necessity and innovative professionally driven approaches. Similar imperatives have underpinned policy that has sought to avoid delays in discharges of people from hospital settings, following the passage of the Community Care (Delayed Discharges etc.) Act 2003, guidance for which was published later the same year (DoH, 2003a). The basis of the policy was that a social services organisation could be fined if an individual who is assessed as being safe for discharge is delayed as a result of its lack of action, which was presumed to be the primary cause of such delays. As

has been pointed out by a number of commentators (see, for example, Glasby, 2003; Lymbery, 2005), this represents a considerable oversimplification of a complex problem. As far as service users' interests were concerned, most older people would wish to be discharged from hospital as quickly and safely as possible; as a result, the legislation was clearly in their interests. While there is some uncertainty about the impact of the policy – delayed discharges were reduced even before it took effect – it has been concluded that, at the very least, 'the downward trend in the number of hospital discharge delays has been accelerated' (CSCI, 2004a: 4). However, as in the case of intermediate care the financial imperative was critical: maintaining people in hospital beyond the time when they need that level of medical care is financially wasteful, a grave concern for successive governments. The connection between the two policies is therefore that they serve both user-related and organisational goals; arguably, neither would have come into being had financial imperatives not been in existence.

The title of the 2005 Green Paper – *Independence, Well-being and Choice* – gives a clear indication of its focus and content (DoH, 2005b). It is also typical of the 'modernisation' project in a number of ways: for example, it insists that it represents a fresh vision for adult social care in seeking to increase service users' independence by enhancing their control over the services provided, and favours the concepts of independence and choice. As noted in Chapter 17 it discusses widening access to direct payments while also floating the possibility of individual budgets being directly made available to service users. It also seeks to rebalance the nature of services by focusing on a more community-oriented preventative approach, to counter the reliance on services being made available only to people with high levels of need.

Comprehensive recent research into the Partnership for Older People Projects (POPP) (Windle et al., 2010) has indicated that a preventive approach can produce what may be considered to be the ideal for any social care policy: improved outcomes at reduced cost. However, the evaluation also revealed problems in moving budgets between health and social care services as well as more general problems in relation to partnerships between health and social care services. In particular, it was argued that the gains to be found from early intervention and prevention could only be realised if savings could be reinvested into new projects. This is problematic on two counts:

1. The scale of savings from POPP was often only marginal.
2. The level of cuts proposed by the coalition government is substantially beyond what could be achieved through the implementation of these approaches alone.

Where the evaluation of POPP does highlight potential in relation to both costs and outcomes, it remains to be seen whether or not these can be fully realised in policy. In the following section we will discuss the tensions that direct conflict – to which reference is made in the Green Paper – between prevention and the requirements of eligibility criteria (DoH, 2002a; DoH, 2010b).

When a White Paper finally emerged (DoH, 2006a) it was significant that it encompassed community-based health care as well as social care: indeed, the concerns of social care are subordinate to those of health care. As a result, the new vision for social care that had been relatively clear in the Green Paper became somewhat blurred. Given the delay in stating a clear policy direction for the social care of older people by the coalition government, there is no certain direction for the future. However, two issues are apparent at this stage:

1. any choices that are made will pay particular attention to their financial consequences;
2. partly as a result of the notion that it can help to resolve budgetary problems, the concept of personalisation will continue to drive policy.

Reflect

As a result of reading the above, what do you believe that governments should do to improve the lives of older people?

Dilemmas in practice

Think ahead

Before reading the following section, think about the sorts of issue that you would expect to see addressed.

Why do you think that these sorts of issue are likely to present dilemmas for social workers?

Once you have read this section, check the extent to which the issues you identified accord with the ones we have raised.

As the preceding sections indicate, we believe that a number of dilemmas are faced by social workers working with older people, particularly when they are employed within statutory settings. These are caused by a number of different factors, some of which stem back to the original intentions of community care legislation, while others are more directly related to more recent policy choices. Unless practitioners understand the scope of these dilemmas, what causes them and how they could be overcome, there is little prospect of their being able to develop sensitive and appropriate forms of practice. Underpinning all of these dilemmas is the belief that services for older people can be improved if social workers are enabled to carry out the full range of professional abilities that they possess, in particular the establishment of productive working relationships with older people.

Rationing

As we have seen, one of the key purposes of the community care reforms was the reduction in social security expenditure (Lewis and Glennerster, 1996). As a means of achieving this, local authorities were transferred a fixed amount of money that they had to manage on an annual basis. While the settlement that was fixed on local authorities was reasonably generous, the reality was that those authorities had to ensure that they managed all need in their localities within the money that was made available. From the earliest days of community care, therefore, the management of budgets was an important concern: indeed, at certain times and within certain authorities, this became an overriding issue.

The Green Paper criticised the fact that a key result of this has been that social work 'has been perceived as a gatekeeper or rationer of services' (DoH, 2005b: 28), implicitly therefore unable to devote sufficient time and attention to the development of more creative, preventive forms of practice. This orientation was confirmed with the introduction of the FACS guidance (DoH, 2002a) as its basis was to regularise the eligibility criteria deployed by local authorities. Four eligibility bands were broadcast: within these, local authorities were to ensure that they responded to needs defined as 'critical' before 'substantial', 'substantial' before 'moderate', and 'moderate' before 'low', emphasising eligibility criteria's role as a rationing device, to be adjusted as the budgetary situation in each local authority indicated. However, this has generated consequences that are out of step with the government's intention to enhance its preventative services, clearly expressed in the Green Paper:

'In future, greater focus should be placed on preventative services through the wider well-being agenda and through better targeted, early interventions that prevent or defer the need for more costly intensive support. *Current eligibility criteria allow for early intervention and support.*'

(DoH, 2005b: 39, emphasis added)

While this statement about eligibility criteria is technically accurate, the guidance that indicated how such criteria should be used (DoH, 2002b) does not support it. For example, in some local authorities the only needs now met are those defined as 'critical', leading even government-established bodies to question the impact of policy (Commission for Social Care Inspection, 2006). If a need can only be met at the point it becomes 'critical', the scope for early intervention has been curtailed. One of the consultation questions in the Green Paper invited responses that related to this dilemma. Because there was no specific reaction to this problem in the subsequent White Paper (DoH, 2006a) the issue of rationing was substantially unresolved. In fact, even the review of eligibility criteria published in 2010 (DoH, 2010b) (discussed in Chapter 17) failed to address this problem. The core problem remains: if there are inadequate levels of resource to meet the needs of all people, what money that is available is likely to be directed more towards those with more pressing concerns. There is a clear gap between the rhetoric of national policy and the reality that governs practice at local levels, therefore.

Reflect

In principle, do you feel that social services should seek to intervene early to resolve people's problems? What are the sorts of issue that influence your judgement?

Assessment

The centrality of the rationing function of social workers has had a major impact on practice, with social workers seeking to balance the potentially incompatible pressures between needs and resources (Parry-Jones and Soulsby, 2001). The assessment process is the point at which these issues come to a head, with social workers necessarily at the forefront of any problems that subsequently emerge. In respect of social work with older people, this position has been a major element of practice from the implementation of community care. The particular focus on performance measurement has aggravated this difficulty, with practitioners under pressure to complete large numbers of assessments within tight timescales. This has also tended to confirm the tendency for social workers to focus more on the functional elements of assessment – for example, an individual's level of physical functioning – rather than, for example, on social, spiritual and emotional factors (Phillips and Waterson, 2002). It also encourages a focus on what an individual cannot do, as opposed to their strengths, contributing to the prevalence of what are

A closer look

The Northern Ireland single assessment tool

Across the different countries in the United Kingdom, there has been an increasing expectation that assessment will be undertaken on a joint basis between health and social care. In England, this principle was established in the *National Service Framework for Older People* (DoH, 2001c), followed up by detailed sets of guidance (DoH, 2002c). Other countries have also instigated a similar approach, which it suggested significantly extends the nature of such joint activity. For example, the Northern Ireland Single Assessment Tool was launched in February 2009 (DHSSPSNI, 2009). This is a validated and fully tested assessment tool designed specifically for health and social care

professionals. Its introduction is intended to standardise and streamline assessment and care planning processes resulting in simplifying the access to community care services. As is the case in England, the principles underpinning the tool are based on holistic, strengths perspectives focusing on abilities rather than disabilities and promoting person-centred, multidisciplinary assessment of individual needs. As a result, it is intended to break down professional barriers and ensuring care packages in either home, residential care or nursing homes are tailored to meet needs. Although similar assessment processes are in operation in other areas of the UK, the unique feature of this tool is its specific design for the health and social care system in Northern Ireland and its ability to promote consistency across professional assessments through offering a single approach.

sometimes called deficit models of assessment. By deficit model, we mean a focus on what people cannot do, as opposed to what they can achieve. It is argued that this confirms individuals' weaknesses rather than helping to promote their strengths, which should be a key goal of social work intervention.

In practice, a combination of limited resources and the disciplines of performance measurement have served to confirm the problems of securing these benefits for practitioners, however. In England, this is compounded by three other relevant factors:

1. the requirement to offer direct payments to service users;
2. the balance between autonomy and protection;
3. the potential development of self-assessment mechanisms.

(DoH, 2005b)

Issues related to direct payments have been previously discussed, and represent perhaps the most significant developments in social care for adults in the early years of the twenty-first century. The balance between risk management and the enhancement of service users' autonomy is a critical issue for consideration, as the Green Paper recognises:

'There is a balance to be struck between enabling people to have control over their lives and ensuring they are free from harm, exploitation and mistreatment, particularly if they have the capacity to make informed choices. . . . The greater appetite for people to retain more responsibility for their own life may at times conflict with the view of wider society and the media about the need to adopt a more protective stance.' (DoH, 2005b: 28–9)

Since the enactment of community care policies in the early 1990s, the pressing issue of risk assessment and management has dominated other considerations (Lymbery, 2005), – in children's services as much as adults (see Chapter 16). According to the Green Paper, the apparent lack of tolerance of risk within the wider society has a major influence on this. As the distinguished social work academic Olive Stevenson has indicated (see Stevenson, 1989) the balance between autonomy and protection has long been a characteristic of social work. One of the key distinguishing factors in working with older people is the presumption that, as adults, they have the capability to judge what is or is not in their best interests; indeed, as we have earlier discussed, this principle underpins the Mental Capacity Act 2005. This can be complicated by the increased likelihood that an older person's capacity will become affected by cognitive disorders such as dementia (Alzheimer's Society, 2007). Social workers have therefore to manage, in their assessment practice, the balance between acting in accordance with the wishes of the individual, and in accordance with their best interests, a matter of great complexity when individual capacity is impaired.

As yet, the establishment of self-assessment mechanisms is far from the norm, but the Green Paper is clear that self-assessment would enable people to have quicker access to relatively small adaptations or minor items of equipment, while freeing up the time of skilled practitioners – social workers and particularly occupational therapists – to undertake more complex assessments (DoH, 2005b). (However, it has been recognised that implementing this policy to the fullest degree may have complex legal ramifications – ADASS, 2009.) Even in the more complex forms of assessment, it is still intended that the views and wishes of people, directly expressed through self-assessment, would remain at their heart. The Green Paper recognises two elements that combine to create a single complex dilemma that will be at the heart of future assessment processes:

1. the course of action to be followed if the services user's assessments of needs conflicts with that of a professional assessor;
2. what happens if there are inadequate resources to supply what the individual believes to be necessary.

(DoH, 2005b: 32)

For example, it is both relatively straightforward and inexpensive to install some adaptations – for example, bath rails or raised toilet seats – into an older person's house to assist their ability to move around the house, or to undertake daily functions safely. By contrast, in the case of Alistair and Jean identified at the start of the chapter, their life circumstances are much more complex, and there are significant differences of view between the user and carer. In addition, some options that might be considered – night sitting services, for example – are highly costly. The fact that these dilemmas are recognised is important, but likely to be experienced as insufficient by practitioners, who will retain concerns about how to reconcile them so that appropriate action can be taken. As with much else, the Green Paper is unclear about the precise forms of action that will help to resolve the problems that are likely to emerge. In addition, subsequent policy has failed to clarify these issues (Lymbery and Postle, 2010), leaving the future social work role in the assessment of adults as an uncertain and unresolved issue.

In summary, therefore, the difficulties in the assessment process that have characterised community care are likely to continue, with the added levels of complexity that ongoing policy changes will bring about. As noted in Chapter 17, systems of personalisation and the more active use of direct payments and individual budgets are the critical additional factors to consider. Consequently, social workers will continue to be involved in skilled assessment work with older people in future: however, the extent and scope of this are quite uncertain.

Care management

Since the inception of community care, there has been considerable literature on the development of care management. Some of this (for example, Carey, 2003) has been critical in its nature; while other contributions (Lloyd, 2002) maintain a critical stance, they are perhaps more optimistic about its potential for affecting change. Critics have argued that the administrative nature of much care management means that there is a disjunction between it and more traditionally defined social work. While this trend has been accepted by other commentators, they have contended that the range of skills required by care managers are much more varied than the procedural and bureaucratic elements that have dominated other accounts (Gorman, 2003). There perhaps should be little surprise about the nature of this debate, as care management practice has to be seen in the light of intersecting issues relating to the history of social work, the detail of the community care reforms and the organisational structure of social services departments (Lloyd, 2002). In the light of this, it was perhaps inevitable that care management would focus on a particularly 'administrative' approach to the problem of resolving burgeoning levels of need with inadequate resources (Lymbery, 2005).

The administratively ordered priorities of care management sit uncomfortably alongside the requirements of personalisation, as noted in Chapter 17. In addition, these priorities do not accord to the imperatives of relationship-based social work practice, the focus of this book. Despite this, it has been contended that the range of skills required by a care manager would be greater than those normally used by a social worker (Challis et al., 1995). More recent research has argued that relationship-based skills remain central to the care management role, although these skills do need to be augmented by another, more administratively focused set of capabilities (Gorman, 2003; Dustin, 2006). It is vital that practitioners are able to identify how the relational basis of care management can be enhanced; recognition of the importance of this to social workers was implied in the Green Paper (DoH, 2005b), which specified that care management may be particularly useful for people with more complex levels of need. However, the potential of social workers to maintain this sort of ongoing relationship has been downplayed in subsequent official documents (see, for example, DoH, 2008). Indeed, although the potential for social workers to continue with complex long-term work has been argued (ADASS/DH/SFC/BASW/SCA, 2010), there are other policy documents that seem to suggest a merely residual role of qualified social workers in this form of ongoing work (Lymbery and Postle, 2010).

One of the problems that has most troubled practitioners has derived from the insistence in community care policy that a care management approach should be instituted in relation to all service users, rather than being reserved for those with more complex needs (McDonald, 2006). If a broad definition is adopted, there is less of an obvious role for social work, or any other comparable occupation, within it. In the Green Paper, there is an attempt to clarify the different roles that may be needed, and to distinguish between them (DoH, 2005b). However, there has been relatively little focus on this in subsequent policy documents (Lymbery and Postle, 2010).

A key component of care management as originally proposed for community care was the circularity of the process: assessment, planning, implementation, monitoring and review (DH/SSI, 1991). One of the elements that has most hamstrung its successful development has been the lack of effective monitoring and review; the recognition of this led to a key element of the FACS policy, the requirement that there be regular reviews of care plans leading to a reassessment of individuals' needs (DoH, 2002b). The weaknesses of monitoring and review had long been recognised as a serious problem within community care; certainly, large numbers of older people admitted to long-stay institutional care have typically been provided with less care management support than others (Lymbery, 2005). It has also contributed to what many have seen as the central reality of much care-managed practice with older people – that it has been short-term, focusing particularly on the assessment stage; even where they have occurred, reviews have been significantly less detailed than assessments. Given financial constraints, there seems little indication that policy will substantially change in future.

The roles that were identified as appropriate for social workers within care management – within the full cycle from assessment to review – remain central to the effective support of older people, but there continues to be debate about the appropriate role for qualified social workers to occupy within longer-term work (Lymbery et al., 2007). In particular, there is concern about the extent to which the social work task with older people has become mechanistic, and does not fulfil the core task of enabling older people to secure the best possible quality of care services. In addition, it confirms the low priority of this activity, thus confirming some of the more critical perceptions that we noted at the start of the chapter. All of these issues represent significant problems to be overcome by social workers in their practice.

Partnership

Chapter 13 contained our general perceptions about partnership and inter-professional working, and much of this is of clear applicability to social work with older people. The following represent the major reasons why improved partnership working is required in relation to older people:

- *Assessment:* The needs of older people are often complex and cannot easily be broken down into health or social care in isolation from each other. In addition, older people are also likely to have other types of need that require specialised intervention: housing, welfare benefits and other financial issues, etc. Proper detail about an older person's needs cannot be gathered in isolation; effective inter-professional and collaborative working will be required at this point.
- *Care management:* Just as social workers require effective partnership working at the point of assessment, if older people have a need for ongoing care management – particularly if their needs are particularly complex as suggested in the Green Paper (DoH, 2005b) – there will also have to be effective systems of inter-professional working, as it is probable that they will require the support of a number of professionals. This becomes particularly apparent when looking at the work of social workers and community matrons; the particular focus of each may differ, but their work is clearly closely connected.
- *Intermediate care:* When intermediate care was first introduced in the late 1990s it was dominated by the concept of rehabilitation, and therapists and nurses have been professionally dominant in well-established

intermediate care systems. However, there is a clear, if relatively neglected, role for social workers within the context of intermediate care; in reality, it is an aspect of practice that calls for a fully coordinated inter-professional approach, as the recovery of an individual's skills of daily living encompasses a number of issues that are the special areas of different professions.

- *Hospital discharge:* Effective hospital discharges depend upon the collective skills of a number of professionals and agencies. Without a good quality of partnership working, it is unlikely that discharges will be either safe or speedy.

There are a number of ways in which inter-professional working could be improved in all the above areas of practice. Close collaboration is likely to be enhanced by co-located workers (Lymbery, 2005); this already is the norm within hospitals, and there are increasing numbers of co-located workers within primary health care settings. In addition, there needs to be an improved recognition of the qualities of the professional working practices of different occupations. This will start during educational programmes, but will need to be an ongoing requirement for practitioners. Certainly, there are now requirements in social work, alongside other professional educational process, for practitioners to have a clear understanding not just of their own roles but also the roles of others (Pollard et al., 2010). Consequently, there are clear expectations that partnership working will be managed both as a routine element of practice and to demonstrate its effectiveness as a form of intervention.

Balancing the needs of users and carers

Repeated promises of additional support for carers have been a consistent theme of British policy since the community care reforms of the early 1990s. However, this rhetorical commitment has not always been transformed into concrete policies. In actuality, the system of social care would be unsustainable were it not for the contributions of unpaid, informal carers – usually members of service users' direct families, and often women. (We discuss the role of carers more fully in Chapter 15.) There are complex reasons why people provide extensive levels of care to other family members, often encompassing a combination of altruism and reciprocity: in other words, when a person has been cared for well as a child, s/he feels a sense of obligation to do the same when the parent requires assistance (Nolan et al., 1996). However, the quality of care experienced in the first

It's important to balance the needs of the cared-for and the carer.

(*Source*: Photofusion Picture Library/Paula Solloway)

stage of this arrangement may well have an impact on the way in which this reciprocity is perceived (Victor, 2005); understanding something of the family dynamics may then assist in recognising the nature of caring relationships that occur later in people's lives.

For a social worker there are clear dilemmas to be addressed when thinking about the balance between formal and informal care in the provision of services. Working within tight budgetary constraints may encourage over-reliance on unpaid carers, whereas the government wishes policy and practice to develop so as to enhance carers' lives and to support them in their tasks more effectively (DoH, 2006a). While many people who act as carers require relatively little in the way of support, with periodic respite from their responsibilities being one of the key issues that is cited, a social worker has a clear responsibility to examine the individual circumstances of families, balancing the wishes and needs of both service users and carers, and, where possible, finding ways to ensure that these are met. Of course, this might not always be possible. There are many occasions, particularly involving older people, often with dementia, when a carer becomes unable to continue with the support that had previously been provided. Even where there is a close bond between service user and carer, on some occasions it is not possible to meet the needs of both. If you refer back to the case study of Alistair and

Jean Macpherson the practical problems are clear: to what extent can Alistair's desire to remain at home be met if Jean is actually no longer able to provide the care and support that he needs?

As a result, the social work task here is one of considerable sensitivity, dealing with often painful emotional responses and reactions. It is certain that the requirements of personalisation will not change this, but rather relocate potential areas of conflict; social workers will continue to engage is sets of circumstance where there is no necessary conjunction of interest between user and carer. Consequently, it has to be recognised that a practitioner will not always be able to secure outcomes that are the most desired for both service users and carers. As a way of responding to the problems that will be encountered, it cannot simply be stated that a social worker must focus on the user and not the carer: both are important, and both need their concerns to be heard and acknowledged. Another aspect of sensitivity that a social worker requires is when there is a clear divergence between the interests of the two, or where there are more problematic issues to be confronted. The general issue of safeguarding is one such theme.

Safeguarding

As the balance between autonomy and protection is further shifted in the direction of user choice, as strongly indicated in policy documents relating to personalisation (see, for example, DoH, 2008), issues relating to the safeguarding become particularly significant. The abuse of older people has only relatively recently been accepted as a social problem in this country; much of the literature that first identified the problem stemmed from the United States (see, for example, Pillemer and Wolf, 1986). However, in the twenty-first century, there has been an increased recognition of the importance of adult protection in the United Kingdom, particularly fostered in England by the publication of *No Secrets* (DoH, 2000f), followed by the document *Safeguarding Adults* (ADSS, 2005). As this understanding has increased, it has been accepted that it represents a major social problem to which a coordinated response by statutory agencies is indicated. Gradually, the research base concerned with adult protection has expanded (Cambridge and Parkes, 2006; Mansell et al., 2009), and the organisational structures to respond to it have become more sophisticated. In the United Kingdom as a whole, substantial time is devoted to the investigation of abuse and in providing support to those people who have been the victims of it.

While these developments clearly indicate an increase in the profile of abuse and a commitment to seeking to respond to it, numerous problems remain to be addressed. Although it has reached the national policy stage, the framework for responding to instances of abuse is less well developed than in the case of childcare, as is the legislative basis for such work (discussed in Chapter 8). There are tensions about whether it is best to establish specialist posts of adult protection coordinators, or whether ordinary social workers are better placed to pick up adult protection work alongside their normal social work responsibilities (Cambridge and Parkes, 2006). Patterns of implementation have been patchy and different localities have widely disparate sets of procedure. There appear to be consistent difficulties both in identifying the signs of abuse and then responding effectively to the abuse once it has been identified. Practitioners often deploy tools of risk assessment and management in forms that are unreflectively and inadequately constructed (Pritchard, 2008). Similarly, there are unresolved tensions concerning how best to accommodate principles of safeguarding within the overall drive towards personalisation (Manthorpe et al., 2008; there appears to have been relatively little work that has systematically explored the extent to which notions of personalisation are consistent with the need to ensure that adults are adequately safeguarded (Fyson and Kitson, 2007)).

Whether a specialist worker is identified as an adult protection coordinator or not, there are additional responsibilities for social workers, even if these may not extend beyond the ready identification of abuse. Here, the pressures of the high volume/low intensity work that social workers are expected to carry out with older people become particularly significant. A critical balance for a social worker will be the ability to respond appropriately to the needs of vulnerable older people at risk of abuse and exploitation, while also carrying out a heavy workload of assessments, driven by the exigencies of reduced budgets and performance assessment.

Capacity

Closely linked to considerations of safeguarding are judgements with which social workers will need to be involved regarding individuals' capacity to make decisions. There are many people who will be affected by this at any given time, where their cognition means that they are unable to take some or all decisions regarding their futures (Laird, 2010). While these will not exclusively be older people – indeed, mental capacity judgements all relate to adults

with disabilities – the largest single group who will be affected by the act are older people, particularly given the increasing numbers affected by dementia.

It is important that any decisions that are required under the Mental Capacity Act are both decision- and time-specific: having determined that an individual lacks capacity in one aspect of decision-making it does not follow that s/he will lack capacity for ever, or can be so affected in each aspect of decision-making. However, there are numerous areas of day-to-day practice where decisions about capacity will be needed for older people; two of the most significant areas of judgement are as follows:

1. Decisions about where a person might live: for example, when considering entry to residential or nursing home care;
2. Decisions about the sorts of care that an individual might receive at home.

Because these issues are inherently contentious, the need for a social worker to engage with them in a balanced way is critical. In addition, of course, the Mental Capacity Act contains further safeguards that further protect the individual service user. The potential involvement of an IMCA is critical, as are the safeguards that exist to ensure that there is no unjustified deprivation of an individual's liberty when issues of capacity are decided.

Dementia

A similar balance also applies when considering work with people with dementia and their carers. Much of what we understand about the impact of dementia stresses the difficulty of managing dementia successfully in community settings, yet this is both the preferred policy option and the preferred choice of those who have dementia and their carers. One of the clearest effects of the cognitive impairment that accompanies dementia is that relatively simple tasks take longer to execute; as a result, in order to work effectively assessments and other forms of social work need to be carried out at a slower pace than would be possible in other sets of circumstance. In addition, the issues of capacity and the legal framework of the Mental Capacity Act 2005 (previously discussed) also have to be considered in cases involving an individual's dementia, which places social workers in a potentially pivotal position.

This is particularly difficult in practice, given the insights generated by the work of the distinguished academic, Tom Kitwood – expressed in most detail in his book *Dementia Reconsidered* (1997) – which have had a striking effect on the development of care services for people with dementia. Essentially, the radical nature of Kitwood's perspective is that he highlighted the subjective experience of people with dementia, arguing that the dominant biomedical paradigm for understanding dementia was inadequate, leading to processes of depersonalisation. He considered that people's identity and 'personhood' was under attack when experiencing dementia, both in relation to the impact of the disease itself and the ways in which society responded to those people. As a result of these perceptions, before his untimely death Kitwood started to argue that a different form of care and support should be provided for people with dementia, focusing on their individuality and seeking to contribute towards the maintenance of their 'personhood', rather than contributing to its fragmentation (Kitwood, 1993).

The fact that this thinking highlights the sorts of response that social workers are capable of providing should provide fertile ground for social work practitioners (Adams and Bartlett, 2003). The advantages of relationship-based practice for people with dementia are clear, and there are measurable benefits to be gained through following a counselling approach (Bartlett and Cheston, 2003). Of course, there are difficulties in this process, and the lack of time that social workers typically have available to work with people with dementia and their carers is not conducive to more flexible and creative forms of practice. These practical difficulties are unlikely to alter in the foreseeable future.

As the Alzheimer's Society (2007) has indicated, the numbers of people with dementia will rise substantially in the foreseeable future. This will create a number of policy challenges: decisions which are taken now will materially affect people with dementia both now and in the future, and could potentially create the context for more effective social work practice. This is hampered by the considerable variations in the extent and quality of dementia care available across the UK. However, one fact remains consistent: the bulk of care and support provided for people with dementia comes from family carers, who are themselves not provided with sufficient levels of assistance. In many cases, much of what a social worker actually does in practice is currently focused on carer support, although with little financial or other practical measures to reinforce this. The dilemma for social workers is to recognise the developments that would be most effective with older people with dementia and their carers and to put these into effect within the present context.

Loss and bereavement

An understanding of theories of loss and bereavement are of vital importance in work with older people. Because older people have necessarily lived longer than many of their contemporaries, it is common for them to have experienced multiple forms of loss. This can manifest itself in a range of different ways: for example, older people are likely to have experienced the loss of individuals – life partners, some of their friends and relatives, even children in some cases. However, as these individual experiences are also likely to be compounded by others, the impact on the individual may be misunderstood. For example, older people experience numerous more diffuse forms of loss: for example, their capacity to live independently, often requiring moving from a much-loved home to another that is less familiar and beloved to them.

Theoretical sources that might assist social workers to understand these processes are numerous: for example, Elizabeth Kübler-Ross's work on the stages of bereavement has become an acknowledged classic, a fact recognised by its remarkable fortieth anniversary publication (Kübler-Ross, 2009). However, there have been criticisms of the apparently schematic approach to bereavement that her model of stages appears to imply. For example, Tony Walter (1999) has suggested that bereavement is best approached from a biographical perspective: that it is inextricably related to the past experiences of the individual concerned, and her/his relationship to that which has been lost. Consequently, he argues for caution in constructing a more schematic approach to loss and bereavement.

One thing that all writers on the subject can agree upon is the profound impact of these issues on individuals. Indeed, this creates an obvious dilemma for social workers. Simply put, social workers commonly encounter older people experiencing the pain of loss and bereavement: it has also been suggested that they have the capacity, through their sensitive engagement, to enable service users to combat the worst outcomes of their troubles (Beresford et al., 2007). The core problem that they encounter, however, is simply managing to secure sufficient time and space to undertake this work. In this respect it was interesting that the research by Beresford et al., on which their book was based, investigated the specific contributions of social workers deployed in palliative care settings. However, there is a clear need for all social workers to be able to practise with the tact, empathic engagement and sensitivity that characterised the best of these practitioners. However, the extent to which social workers are enabled to practise in this way is uncertain. Indeed, pressures of time may also affect their capacity even to identify the more detailed concerns of service users. After all, it is a human characteristic for social workers, as with any individual, only to identify needs to which they can respond. Consequently, this requires social workers to adopt a clear two stage process:

1. They must robustly identify a range of needs and issues that may include a more therapeutic engagement with issues of loss and bereavement.
2. They should clarify what an effective response to these needs would entail: this may entail referring an individual on to other services – a hospice, for example, if the service user is terminally ill – or to identifying how s/he can respond effectively to the therapeutic needs that are identified.

While we have identified issues of loss and bereavement as creating a focus for this need, the problem revealed for social workers has more general applicability. Owing to the focus on rationing, already identified, social workers are likely to struggle to encompass a more therapeutic dimension of their work with older people. The harsh cuts to public services, emblematic of the coalition's approach to social policy, create even more of a problem in this respect than previously. Even though there has been a long-standing inability to define older people's problem as requiring social work or a more general therapeutic intervention (Curtis and Davies, 2005), the impending financial crisis can only make matters worse. It is hard to see, for example, how the desirability to accommodate issues of spirituality (Holloway and Moss, 2010) into practice can be met under these reduced circumstances for social workers and other related practitioners. The ongoing balance between needs, resources and time will continue in a sharpened form, therefore.

Having outlined nine dilemmas which affect social work practice with older people, we shall help you think through some of the implications they have for your own practice, using some illustrative case studies.

Contemporary social work practice with older people

In what follows, we use the dilemmas identified in the previous section as a guide to the sorts of issue that you

will have to face as a practitioner, grounding the discussion as far as possible in the realities of practice. We also assume that the majority of social work practice takes place within the context of the statutory duties carried out by Adult Social Care Departments in England and Social Work Departments in Scotland. This is not to suggest that social work is impossible in other contexts (we believe that, if anything, the reverse is true) but rather to reflect the reality that the majority of social work support for older people does take place within this context and will continue to do so for the foreseeable future. Underpinning all of our case studies is the belief that social workers have to find ways of relating to each individual person, and that the more effectively this is managed the better the quality of work undertaken.

Case study

Joyce

Kalpna is a social worker employed in a busy local authority team providing social work services for older people. She is allocated the referral of Joyce Heller, an 87-year-old woman, who has been referred by her GP. The only information on the referral is that Joyce appeared to be struggling to cope on her own and that admission to a residential home may be indicated. There were numerous referrals discussed in the team meeting, and Kalpna's manager expressed concern that all assessment work needed to be completed as swiftly as possible to accord to the timescales within which local authorities are required to operate.

Many referrals of older people unfortunately contain little useful information, leaving much to be uncovered by the social worker. In particular, referrals from medical doctors containing little other than the expressed 'need' for residential care are common. In this case, the priority for a quick assessment reinforced by a defined care plan has been made clear by Kalpna's manager. In addition, Kalpna herself is only too aware of the unremitting pressure of cases. There is no easy way for a social worker to manage the complexities that this may generate, particularly balancing the need to work with older people at a depth and pace that responds appropriately to their needs with the agency priorities for work to be completed within tight timescales.

For many social workers operating within the statutory sector, these pressures represent the normality of their working experiences. Successful practice with older people must first acknowledge and work within the constraints that the agency context provides. The factor that gives social workers the single most effective mechanism to combat managerial and organisational constraints is simply that of quality (Lymbery, 2004). The better the quality of work undertaken – in other words, the more thorough, detailed and accurate it is, with the case for the particular intervention convincingly and plausibly argued – the more it will be possible for social workers to argue for the sorts of service that the person requires. This is particularly significant in that within the context of rationing it is simply impossible for all service users to secure the range and quality of services that they desire. This is an uncomfortable reality for social workers, but there is little indication that the financial parameters within which social workers operate will change at any time in the near future.

Case study

Joyce cont . . .

When Kalpna begins the process of working with Joyce, she discovers a number of salient issues. Joyce is 87 years of age, and has lived independently since the sudden death of her husband following a heart attack 33 years previously. She has no children. He had been a jeweller – a family tradition – and left his wife well provided for; among other things, she has a large number of shares in a range of companies, and is an owner-occupier. As a result, she has never experienced financial difficulties, although her health has gradually deteriorated over the years. For example, in her late 60s Joyce was diagnosed with breast cancer, as a result of which she underwent a double mastectomy. From her mid-70s onwards she has been increasingly afflicted by osteoporosis, which has contributed to a number of chronic problems, notably congestive heart failure. In addition, she has severe osteoarthritis, which is causing her difficulties in relation to various activities of daily living. It transpires that the referral was caused by a bout of bronchitis, from which Joyce has been slow to recover. This has also affected her previously very active social

life. Her GP, who has known her for almost 30 years, is very concerned that she may not be able to manage living independently any longer, an opinion he has shared with Joyce. However, Kalpna finds that she is a very strong-minded woman, who has no intention of (as she puts it) 'going into a home', as she has seen a number of her friends go into such places and 'lose the will to live'.

Kalpna's first actions are concerned with the assessment: does Joyce have needs that are located in an eligibility band that the council would normally expect to meet? Because this decision is subject to available resources, it is uncertain precisely where any given local authority would locate Joyce's needs. Good assessment practice (as you will have learned in Chapter 10 on assessment) will ensure that the activity is carried out in close partnership between Kalpna and Joyce, with the judgements that Kalpna makes informed directly by what Joyce says about her circumstances, needs and their impact on her life. Similarly, the assessment must be carried out in line with the requirements of the single assessment process (DoH, 2002c). This was first introduced in the *National Service Framework for Older People* (DoH, 2001c), which defined four broad types of assessment: contact, overview, specialist and comprehensive. While a specialist assessment is required where there are specific sorts of issue (for example, cognitive impairment or mobility problems), comprehensive assessments are indicated where the needs of older people are problematic, or where any support/treatment that is needed is likely to be intensive or prolonged. A comprehensive assessment will necessarily involve the full participation of a range of different professional groups and should be used where admission to long-term care is a possibility (DoH, 2002c).

Reflect

Given the range of needs that we have identified, within which eligibility band do you feel that Joyce would be located?

What sort of assessment is indicated under the Single Assessment Process? On what do you base your judgement?

Having done this task (and for the sake of argument we have located Joyce's needs within a band that the local authority would normally expect to meet), Kalpna next has to undertake two related activities. She has to explain to Joyce what the implications of her judgement are for the sorts of service that can be made available, while simultaneously explaining about how any services will be funded; as with many other areas of policy, there is detailed guidance from the Department of Health which outlines how this should be managed (DoH, 2003c). This is particularly significant for Joyce in that her savings, shares and the value of her house mean that she is placed within the band of people who are expected to fund large amounts of their care. Indeed, were she to enter residential or nursing home care – which she could decide to do at any time, although this is unlikely given her antipathy to such an action – she would be expected to fund the costs of such care in full. In addition, Joyce is not obliged to accept any advice or guidance that Kalpna may offer; should she disagree with what is proposed she can then make her own arrangements. While this is of course the case for all people who have the capacity to make such judgements, the fact of her relative financial independence makes a substantial difference to the range of options that are available to her.

The assessment process is significant for older people, as for other service users, as through this the relationship between the person and the care services that could be available is made explicit. The act of assessment is therefore an essential task for the social worker, and represents a form of action with which all social workers must therefore be proficient. In a system that is, as we have seen, heavily bound up with financial requirements, the issue of eligibility is critical: if Joyce were to be placed in a band that was outside the needs that the local authority will meet, Kalpna's obligations would change markedly, offering advice and guidance about how Joyce might be able to access support that is outside the adult social care department's range of responsibilities.

There are a number of issues that should weigh heavily on Kalpna's judgement about the nature and extent of Joyce's needs. These can be summarised as follows:

- *Health:* There are a number of issues that derive directly from Joyce's state of health, and which appear to be having a particular effect on her functioning. The two which are most apparent are her osteoporosis and her osteoarthritis, both of which affect her mobility and ability to function within the home. In respect of both of these issues, Kalpna will need to secure detailed information about the nature of the illness and its likely progress. In addition, she will need further

information about the impact of both on Joyce's ability to function and the resources that might be available to help her with her daily tasks. In the course of a 'comprehensive' assessment under the Single Assessment Process the close involvement of Joyce's GP, community nursing and occupational therapy staff will be critical.

- *Social functioning:* The limited information that Kalpna has secured so far indicates that Joyce has had a very active social life; she has lived in the same small village for all of her married and widowed life, and has been a very active part of the local community. In this case, managing to restore Joyce's links to community support can potentially assist both in relation to her daily care needs and to the maintenance of her social networks.

- *Maintaining independence:* Joyce has already lived a long life, and has managed to maintain both an active and a meaningful role for herself into old age. She has never before come to the attention of social workers, and wishes no part of long-term care at this stage. As such, she is among the most obvious people to be considered for the option of direct payments, should the extent of her needs fit within the appropriate eligibility criteria. As we have previously outlined, it is a statutory responsibility for social workers to offer the opportunity to Joyce to manage direct payments, which could be an appropriate option to help maintain her independence. In addition, there may be resources within the village that she could access using the direct payments that would strengthen the place she has within the village community. Ironically, because it is the middle class that are more frequently offered the option of direct payments (Ellis, 2007), Joyce's class location may be a significant factor: indeed, it may offset the tendency, previous noted, for older people not to be considered. (However, given her financial situation, direct payments are not relevant here.)

- *Prevention:* Although talk of prevention is interesting when considering the inexorable ageing process, there is an opportunity here to intervene in such a way as to boost Joyce's independence and to seek to ensure that she does not decline rapidly from this point onwards. It has been suggested that social work skills are particularly suited to this aspect of practice, drawing on the social worker's commitment to the strengths of the individual and ability to engage with that person productively (Tanner, 2003). In addition, the social worker can usefully devote time exploring with Joyce her feelings, given the likely additional stress that her growing dependence will cause. These are skills that closely connect to the relational basis of social work.

■ *Loss and bereavement:* What Joyce has experienced can certainly be understood through this lens: many of her recent life experiences can be seen as having been acutely psychologically painful for her. It is likely that she will need additional support to enable her to engage with these effects: it is therefore important for Kalpna to identify their extent and the most effective ways of resolving them.

Underpinning all of the detailed work that Kalpna must undertake is the simple imperative that she needs to establish a close working relationship with Joyce. The success of work will be tightly bound up with the quality of her interaction with Joyce.

Case study

Velma

Terry is a social worker based in a local health centre; he receives a referral of an 81-year-old woman, Velma Fields, from Maureen, a District Nurse who is based in the same health centre. Velma lives alone in a council flat in a tower block. She came to the UK with her husband Tyrone from Jamaica in 1958; she worked as a nurse, while Tyrone worked as a bus conductor. Tyrone died in 1986, not long after retiring from his job. Velma has three grown-up children, all of whom live in the locality. Velma receives home care which is arranged by the local authority; she contributes toward its costs, the bulk of which are met by the local authority. Maureen informs Terry that Velma has a history of ill health, which goes back over more than 10 years. She has chronic respiratory problems, which often deteriorate markedly in the winter; she has had angina for a number of years, which contributes to her respiratory problems and makes it difficult for her to undertake any form of physical exercise. Velma had a hip replacement operation 12 years ago, but is now once again complaining of considerable hip pain. Although Velma used to have an active social life, much of it centred around her local church, her various

ailments have tended to keep her housebound. The flat is reported as being warm, but rather spartan; the block within which Velma lives is notorious for problems with vandalism, and the lifts are inoperative for much of the time. The District Nurse, Maureen, states that Velma's children appear not to be much in evidence, and expresses a view that there has been 'bad blood' within the family. The reason for the present referral is that Maureen is concerned about Velma on three counts. The first is that she appears to be depressed. The second is that her poor physical health means that Velma periodically struggles to carry out tasks of daily living, even with home care support. The third is that Velma appears to be socially isolated. Velma also complains a lot about the flat and the poor locality within which it is found. She also has expressed concern about the risk posed by 'gangs' in the neighbourhood, which is another reason why she rarely goes out.

As Velma is already known to the adult social care department Terry will be able to secure information from her original assessment, and also any data that relates to the ongoing receipt of home care. This puts him into an advantageous position, in that much information about Velma and her circumstances will already be recorded. Of course, this is potentially a double-edged sword: if he does not subject this data to some questioning there is a danger of simply replicating any errors, inaccuracies or value judgements that might have crept into the earlier documentation. However, this is outweighed by the fact that there will be a record of the original assessment and subsequent reviews. (One of the other elements of the FACS guidance was to ensure that all people in receipt of a service should have their circumstances reviewed on at least an annual basis.)

Another benefit, created by Terry's location alongside primary health care colleagues, is that there will be ready contact between Terry and Maureen, who is also in regular contact with Velma. This is important in that her worsening health appears to be creating some of the problems that she is currently encountering, and it may well be appropriate for Terry and Maureen to undertake a joint visit to discuss the various aspects of her care and health. As occupational therapists are also based in the same health centre, and there is ready access to

Velma's GP, it will be practically much easier to develop systems of inter-professional working. This is particularly important in relation to the range of needs that Velma appears to have; as defined through the information imparted to Terry these are as follows:

- *Depression*: Velma is said to be depressed, a condition that is frequently overlooked or misdiagnosed in relation to older people (Fiske and Jones, 2005). As a result, it may neither be recognised nor treated for many older people.
- *Physical health*: As Maureen has suggested, Velma has a combination of medical problems, any of which would be serious in themselves, but when taken together pose a considerable threat to her ability to maintain her independence.
- *Social isolation*: In accordance with Maureen's account, Velma leads a much more isolated existence than she used to do, and appears to have less social contact than she would ideally desire. Her physical health is almost certain to have contributed to this in some measure; her depression may be related to this isolation.
- *Housing*: Although Maureen did not consider this to be a particular problem, Terry is concerned that Velma's anxiety about the locality within which she lives is having a material impact on her state of mind and that some consideration of housing options is at least indicated.

Of these four issues, the first two are concerns that are beyond Terry's particular area of professional expertise, and effective inter-professional working is therefore particularly important. The later two are themes that Terry will be able to address directly, drawing on the 'administratively' oriented skills that social workers possess (Lymbery, 2005). However, the relational nature of the work that is required will apply across all of the four areas of activity, and Terry will have a key part to play in this. For example, individuals who are prone to experiencing depression are not necessarily receptive to this form of diagnosis; in addition, it is likely that Velma's lack of social support is a contributory factor to the depression that she may be experiencing. Both of these issues could potentially be addressed through a focus on her housing, particularly if there are age-appropriate supported housing options available for her to consider (Peace et al., 2007). In this respect, Velma's race is a particular element to consider. Terry will have to think very carefully about a possible change of housing location for Velma if the only supported housing options that are available are in localities that are a distance from the community support networks that Terry would wish to enhance, or if the population of such settings is not racially diverse. In addition, however much Velma may be anxious about her current housing, particularly its location, she may baulk at the major upheaval of a move. Ascertaining precisely what Velma wants to do, and helping her to recognise what may be in her best interests, represents a skilled task for the social worker.

There are a number of complex emotional issues for Velma to consider, requiring considerable tact, sensitivity and time for the practitioner to manage effectively. This puts a premium on Terry's ability to form and sustain a positive, therapeutic relationship with Velma – drawing on the communication skills identified in Chapter 11 – and directly relates to the balance between needs, resources and time, noted above. It also will require Terry to be able to manage communication within the organisation effectively; if he is to argue for intensive, short-term involvement with Velma, he must be willing and able to make a case for this in the terms that the adult social care department will both understand and accept. There are two strands of such work. Firstly, Terry must carry out his practice proficiently, making clear professional arguments for extended work with Velma; he can draw on the governmental priority to maintain people's independence for as long as possible to achieve this. Secondly, he also has to find a way to couch this in financial terms: will there be a longer-term financial benefit if, through his action, Velma's well-being is enhanced? It is of course difficult to be certain about what the future holds for anybody who is 81 years of age; however, he can mount an effective argument that if Velma's health is supported, her depression addressed, her housing put on to a more secure footing and her social support network enhanced, there is much less likely to be extensive long-term funding required for Velma, whether that be from health or social care.

Case study

Alf

The referral of 75-year-old Alf Hitchens is picked up by the hospital social work team, relatively soon after his admission to a ward for older people, and assigned to Kirstie, a newly qualified social worker.

Alf was admitted to hospital following a fall at his home, and the hospital ward has alerted the adult social care department of his likely need for community care services under section 2 of the Community Care (Delayed Discharges etc.) Act 2003. In accordance with the terms of the Act, Kirstic understands that it is likely that her team will receive a notice of his date of discharge under section 5 of the Act within a few days; she knows that this could come after a minimum of three days, with a subsequent minimum requirement for discharge of only one further day. When Kirstie visits Alf on the ward, she also finds his daughter Barbara in attendance; she is able to make little contact with Alf directly, Barbara repeatedly answering for him, and claiming that she can sort all of his needs out at home when he is discharged. Kirstie is struck by how quiet Alf appears, and how little he seems to be engaged in what is happening; at the same time she notices how little engagement there appears to be between Alf and Barbara. She succeeds in getting permission to approach Alf's GP for information about his ongoing health, and arranges to discuss his condition with nursing staff at the hospital.

Case study

Alf cont . . .

The next time Kirstie comes to see Alf on the ward she has discovered more information about his circumstances. From his GP she gathers some worrying information about his life and character; apparently, Alf was a miner for 40 years, made redundant when his pit closed in the late 1980s. He lives in council housing and is described as being an 'old sod' by the GP, referring to his drinking and casual violence – with strong hints that he may have assaulted his wife (Edith, who died 10 years ago) and children throughout the marriage. Apart from Barbara, there are two younger sons, who moved away from the area over 20 years ago and have had no contact with their father after Edith's death. The GP also expresses concern over the relationship between Alf and Barbara, wondering whether she actually has his best interests at heart. From the nursing staff at the hospital, the picture Kirstie receives of Alf is of a man who is surly, rude and verbally aggressive to the nursing staff, but very polite to the doctors. Alf is reported as having 'very poor' short-term memory.

At this stage, Kirstie is placed in a typical situation for a hospital-based social worker: she is expected to carry out a full assessment of Alf's needs, negotiate with family and carers to find a safe and secure place to which he can be discharged, while being aware that this all has to be concluded with some urgency, owing to the timescales indicated by the Community Care (Delayed Discharges etc.) Act 2003. From the limited information that she has at this point, there seems to be little that is problematic about the nature of Alf's circumstances. Barbara is presenting as a caring relative willing and able to accept much of the responsibility for Alf's care. Although the lack of communication between the two should provide some cause for concern, at this stage circumstances do not appear complex or troubling. Had there been any obvious concerns or areas of complexity, it is likely that a more experienced worker than Kirstie would have been allocated.

The situation is rather more complex than it had initially appeared. Kirstie does now have concerns that Alf's situation may not be all that it appeared to be at first sight. However, her suspicions alone do not provide sufficient evidence on which she can act. As a result of this, Kirstie believes that further action is needed; she also recognises her limited experience, and is careful to talk over the detail of the case with her line manager. Whenever there are complex issues in a case, or when an individual staff member is uncertain about the appropriate course of action to follow, consultation with more experienced colleagues, and specifically the line manager, is an essential element of a practitioner's repertoire.

As a result of this process, the following issues and courses of action are decided:

■ Rather than taking Barbara's protestations at face value, Kirstie should investigate Alf's home circumstances in some more detail. This will encompass a visit to his home to see what the conditions are that he has come from and the extent to which these are sustainable. If there are problems in this respect, Kirstie should seek to admit Alf to an interim care bed, taking steps to return his home to a fit condition.

- In respect of Alf's poor short-term memory, it has agreed that Kirstie should seek permission to refer Alf for an assessment of his cognitive functioning; it may be that a form of dementia is present: if so, this may well also have implications for Alf's capacity to make decisions, and care for himself on a daily basis.

- In addition, judgements will need to be made concerning Alf's capacity, relating to the requirements of the Mental Capacity Act 2005.

Kirstie first has a conversation with Alf to enquire about his home circumstances and to test out Barbara's assertion that she does everything for him. He is not particularly communicative with Kirstie, replying in monosyllables when he can't avoid talking to her, and trying to ignore her as much as possible. When she presses him about his home circumstances he suddenly snaps at her to 'f*** off, you c***'. Following this he refuses to have any more communication with her. Alf's behaviour creates a difficulty for Kirstie: she is seeking to act in his best interests, but finds it hard to establish precisely what he desires. His failure to engage with her and his verbal aggression are both complicating factors in resolving his circumstances effectively.

As a result, her subsequent discussion with Barbara (held in a meeting room in the social work office) is an important opportunity for Kirstie to clarify Alf's situation. However, when she raises the possibility of visiting Alf's home, Barbara voices a number of objections, crossly questioning both Kirstie's need to be involved as well as her right to do so. Kirstie indicates that she is concerned about the conditions that Alf will be living in, and that she has a duty to ensure that his discharge from hospital is as safe as can be assured. She also indicates that she believes that Alf needs an assessment of his cognitive functioning before discharge could be managed safely and effectively; at this point Barbara becomes very agitated and verbally aggressive towards Kirstie, stating that there is nothing wrong with Alf other than that he 'forgets things', and that this is only to be expected at his age. When Kirstie tries to calm her down, claiming that she only has Alf's best interests at heart, Barbara suddenly becomes physically aggressive towards her, pushing

her and shouting 'where have you f***ing social workers been whenever I needed you?' Although feeling increasingly anxious about her safety, Kirstie tries to stay calm and not inflame the situation by arguing with Barbara; rather, she says that she cannot continue to discuss matters with her while Barbara is acting in such a threatening manner and terminates the discussion.

At this point Kirstie is confronted with two people who are rude, aggressive and uncooperative – a difficult situation for an experienced worker, let alone one who is newly qualified and relatively inexperienced. Once more, she needs further guidance from her supervisor about possible courses of action. This is particularly true because of the need to ensure that Alf's discharge is not delayed. In the absence of any clarity about his home circumstances and with the ongoing assessment of his cognitive functioning, Kirstie's manager suggests that it may be appropriate to consider discharge to an interim care bed, to allow more time to assess Alf's needs and to allow for further investigation into his home circumstances. In relation to the Mental Capacity Act 2005 this action can be interpreted as being in his best interests. Kirstie and her manager both want to understand what lies behind Barbara's comment about social workers. In addition, they agree that there are serious concerns about the nature of their relationship; Kirstie is urged to make further contact with Barbara and try to explore a little of the background to their current situation.

In planning for such a meeting, Kirstie has to consider both the acrimonious ending of their previous discussion and her own personal safety. As a result, she rules out seeking to visit Barbara in her home, as this would increase her vulnerability; also, conducting an interview while in a state of considerable anxiety is not a good way to address potentially delicate and emotional subject material. As a result, she and her manager decide to invite Barbara to meet Kirstie in the social work offices in the hospital, on the basis that she can combine a visit to Alf with this meeting. Although they accept that taking Barbara out of her own environment may make her more defensive and hence uncooperative, this is counter-balanced by the issue of Kirstie's own safety. They also discuss strategies that Kirstie can deploy to repair the relationship between them, aware that an approach that initially focuses on the unacceptability of Barbara's past behaviour is likely to confirm her lack of cooperation. As a result, it is agreed that when Kirstie telephones Barbara she will adopt a conciliatory tone, seeking more clearly to understand Barbara's point of view. From her defensive reactions it is possible that she has been abusing Alf, but Kirstie and her manager accept that they need to understand more fully the context of their relationship. It is accepted that, if effective, this may well set off a process which will not be concluded before Alf's discharge; this also contributes to their belief that Alf should be discharged to an interim care bed.

When Kirstie does telephone Barbara, she finds her much more reasonable than before; Barbara apologises for 'flying off the handle', explaining that she has strong feelings about Alf, and that not all of these are positive. Kirstie explains that the hospital is pressing to discharge Alf as the medical staff do not believe that he requires further immediate medical assistance: in their terms, he is judged to be 'fit' for discharge. She suggests that the best way of ensuring that this is managed safely would be to discharge Alf temporarily to an interim care place in a residential care home, to give time to resolve the various issues that would be needed to maintain him independently in the community. Although she expects Barbara to be resistant to this idea, Kirstie is surprised by her ready acceptance of this temporary solution. They arrange to meet in the social work office the following day to talk further about matters.

When this meeting does take place Kirstie is taken aback by its nature. Whereas she had expected Barbara to be prickly and defensive, she finds her in a very different frame of mind – resigned and rather sad. At first, Kirstie assumes that this relates to Alf's admission to a residential care home, if only on a temporary basis. When she seeks to empathise with Barbara on this, the response is quite different from what she had anticipated. Barbara states that she is actually pleased not to have any responsibility for Alf for the time being, and that getting away from him is a good thing for her. When asked why that might be, Barbara states that she thinks that Alf is 'a horrible man, no better now than when he was younger'. When Kirstie asks Barbara what she means by this, she starts to cry and explains that he has always drunk heavily, and used to beat his wife and children when under the influence. She says that these are her earliest and strongest memories. She also knows that this violence was the direct cause of her brothers leaving the area in their late teens, and she claims that it forced her mother into an early grave (Edith was only 60 years old when she died, apparently).

Although these revelations do not cause Kirstie any surprise, she does find it significant that Barbara has opened up about this history without any significant prodding. As a result, Kirstie asks Barbara why she has revealed this information at this point; in response, Barbara says that she hasn't been very good to Alf in return, and that she feels guilty about it. Kirstie presses her on this point to explain what she means by this. In reply, Barbara says that she has been 'paying him back' – not looking after him when she has been pretending to do so, keeping him short of money, and generally making his life as unpleasant as possible. Apparently, Alf 'never lifted a finger' in the house when he was younger, and had no idea about how to prepare food even before his problem with short-term memory. As she recounts all this, she becomes increasingly distraught, and says that her husband Carl had advised her to be honest about all that had happened to her, which is why she is confessing to all of this. She says that Carl has been her rock; before meeting him she thought that all men were rotten, and that violence was all that could be expected from them. He was the only reason why Barbara still lives in the area; he was a work colleague of Alf's, and they met on a works outing. Alf tried to keep them apart, but Carl put him straight on that, and said that Alf would have him to answer to if there were any more drunken assaults on Edith. Apparently, he has recently been encouraging Barbara to seek help, but Barbara was focused on what she has thought of as revenge on Alf. When she told Carl about how she acted when last she saw Kirstie, he had apparently been very cross and pointed out that she shouldn't be focused on getting her own back on Alf; by contrast, Carl says that it would be better if she simply had nothing to do with him. Barbara says that her reaction to Kirstie was caused by a combination of anger and guilt: anger at Alf for how he had treated her for all those years, and guilt because she knew that how she treated him was also wrong. She sobs that she knows that what she has done was wrong, and that she deserves to be punished for it. Kirstie tells her that there will need to be further discussions about what has occurred and that she must refer all the information to the Adult Protection Co-ordinator. Barbara understands this, and says that she is relieved to have been able to rid herself of the burden. Following discussion with Kirstie's team manager, the issue is referred for an Adult Protection investigation; in Kirstie's authority, there is a specific social worker who undertakes this work and it is not kept as part of the responsibilities of every practitioner in adult care.

These revelations are followed in a couple of days by the information that Alf does have a rare form of dementia, Korsakoff's Syndrome, caused by long-term alcohol abuse. It is irreversible and Alf will therefore never be able to recreate his short-term memory. When combined with the issues revealed by Barbara, it raises genuine concerns about whether or not Alf will be able to manage to live independently. His capabilities in relation to self-care are weak, and his dementia means that he will not be able to make good use of a programme of intermediate care. Arguably he could manage on an extensive package of home care support, although the fact that he is able to do little for himself means that this is less likely to be successful. Reportedly, he has been treating the staff in the residential care home like servants, routinely swearing at them for every real and imagined lapse. When Kirstie visits him to see how he has settled, and to try to secure a sense of whats he wants to happen next, she can make little headway. Again, he barely responds to her questions, showing no interest in the reasons for her visit. He is asked directly whether he wants to move back home, but provides no coherent answer.

It is an open question whether Alf retains the ability to make decisions affecting his own welfare under the terms of the Mental Capacity Act 2005. At this stage, his failure to engage with Kirstie does appear to be affected by his lack of understanding of events, although his natural truculence is also a significant element in this. Essentially, a judgement must be made whether Alf has the capacity to make each specific decision with which he may be confronted (Johns, 2007; 2010). If it is decided, for example, that Alf is incapable of judging where he should live, this doesn't necessarily mean that he would be deemed to be incapable of managing his financial affairs. The Mental Capacity Act 2005 does not specify who would be responsible for this assessment; it does, however, indicate that it is for the professionals involved to demonstrate that an individual lacks capacity: in other words, a person is assumed to have capacity unless it can be proved that this capacity is lacking. If a person is deemed to lack capacity, then those taking decisions on her/his behalf must act in her/his best interests.

In working with Alf, there are obviously issues of capacity to consider; in the light of the adult protection issues that have been highlighted by Barbara's confes-

sion, these are complicated by uncertainty about who would be best placed to take decisions on Alf's behalf. In addition, it is important to focus on Alf's specific needs, and not allow these to be obscured by the other factors that have influenced his treatment. Irrespective of his past history and current unpleasant attitude and behaviour, he is a vulnerable older person, who is likely to be experiencing all the anxiety and uncertainty that accompanies dementia. As a result, maintaining a focus on him as an individual is critical, although by no means easy to accomplish.

Reflect

What are the possible outcomes to Alf's case, given what you have read? What do you think is most likely to occur? Would your belief change if he was a different sort of a person – polite and charming, say – even if his capabilities were at the same level?

This case study illustrates a number of the dilemmas that we noted earlier in the chapter:

- *Abuse and protection*: There is a clear admission of abuse from Barbara, which will automatically trigger the Department's procedures. A complicating factor in the case study is the prior abuse that she appears to have experienced herself, and the generally abusive nature of her upbringing.
- *Dementia and capacity*: There are clear issues about dementia and the consequent judgement that will need to be made concerning Alf's capacity to make decisions affecting his life.
- *Balancing the needs of users and carers*: Although a consideration of this balance will have been superseded by other considerations, at the outset it will have been a fundamental part of Kirstie's thinking.

In addition, the case study highlights an important point: that whatever the myths that might be perpetuated about older people, individual older people can also be truculent and uncooperative. This can require a high level of skill in the social worker as well as test her/his resilience – an important concept when applied to practising social workers as it is when considering the stages of human development!

Conclusion

If we return to some of the points made during this chapter, a number of the reasons for the compromised position of social work with older people become clear. In all of the case studies, successful outcomes are much more likely if there is sufficient time for the practitioner to establish a productive working relationship, in which the process of the work is perceived as equally important as the specific outcomes. In this respect, the way in which a social worker practises with an older person becomes particularly important. However, assumptions about the nature of older people's problems, and the most appropriate way of responding to them, has led to circumscribed forms of practice, characterised by high volume and a presumed low intensity.

As the case studies have indicated, there is no lack of complexity in older people's circumstances; as could be expected, they are likely to have the same range of issues and problems that would characterise any person. Indeed, one factor that might be associated with their advanced age is the increased period during which complexities could have been nurtured. If the social work that is undertaken with older people is to be consistent with what is normal with other groups, this recognition must come at an early stage.

In addition, as we have seen, this gives the lie to the denigration of such practice, and the fact that relatively few social workers in training consider that this would be their preferred career destination. We would contend that what has made such work perceived as less interesting is little to do with its inherent nature and much more connected to the limitations imposed upon practitioners by their work settings. In addition, this is work that can be emotionally challenging, as the case study of Alf Hitchens indicated. It can also be emotionally demanding in other ways: for example, it is certainly the case that social workers with older people will be confronted by more death in their professional lives than would be the case for other groups, and this could have implications for their emotional welfare and stability. The same points that have underpinned the text of the entire book apply here; older people need social workers who are emotionally mature, sensitive and empathic to their needs, with the capacity to help them to identify what resources would be more effective in improving their situation, and having the confidence and organisational skills to argue for the allocation of these.

Key learning points

This chapter has covered the following learning points:

✔ The impact of ongoing demographic changes within British society, and their implications for social work.

✔ Different ways of understanding the ageing process, including biological, psychological and sociological considerations.

✔ How social and health care policy has developed for older people.

✔ The key aspects of these developments that will affect the practice of social workers.

✔ The core practice dilemmas that exist for social workers with older people.

✔ Practical ways of addressing these dilemmas, through the medium of case studies.

 Further reading

Bond, J., Peace, S., Dittmann-Kohli, F. and Westerhof, G. (eds) (2007) *Ageing in Society* (3rd edn), London: Sage/Open University. This is the third edition of a standard text on social gerontology, containing a number of highly useful and readable chapters.

Hughes, M. and Heycox, K. (2010) *Older People, Ageing and Social Work: Knowledge for Practice*, Crows Nest, NSW: Allen and Unwin. This is the first text of this nature published for the Australian market: however, the authors demonstrate the global nature of the problems encountered by both society and older people.

Johnson, M., Bengtson, V., Coleman, P.G. and Kirkwood, T.B.L. (eds) (2005) *The Cambridge Handbook of Age and Ageing*, Cambridge: Cambridge University Press. This is the most thorough and detailed contemporary text focusing on issues related to age and ageing. It benefits particularly from the breadth of its coverage, with chapters written from a wide range of perspectives.

Lymbery, M. (2005) *Social Work with Older People: Context, Policy and Practice*, London: Sage. This book is particularly strong on the relationship of policy to practice in relation to social work with older people.

McDonald, A. (2010) *Social Work with Older People*, Cambridge: Polity. This is the most recent addition to the literature: it is informed by detailed legislative knowledge and practical wisdom.

Phillips, J., Ajrouch, K. and Hillcoat-Nallétamby, S. (2010) *Key Concepts on Social Gerontology*, London: Sage. This book provides brief, accessible and authoritative explanations of the core concepts underpinning social gerontology, which are essential for social workers operating in this field of endeavour.

Phillips, J., Ray M. and Marshall, M. (2006) *Social Work with Older People* (4th edn), Basingstoke: Palgrave Macmillan. This is the most recent, substantially updated and revised version of the standard social work text in the area.

Ray, M., Bernard, C. and Phillips, J. (2009) *Critical Issues in Social Work with Older People*, Basingstoke: Palgrave Macmillan. This is a sister volume to the above text, more profoundly influenced by social gerontology but with an equivalent insistence that the needs of older people require both proper conceptualisation and response.

http://www. Useful websites

www.elderabuse.org.uk

Action on Elder Abuse (AEA) works to protect, and prevent the abuse of, vulnerable older adults. AEA provides advice and guidance to older people and others; provides training to care staff and others, either as standard packages or specially designed programmes; work to raise general awareness and stimulate debate; interact with, challenge and support regulators, care providers and government; and undertake special projects.

http://ageUK.org.uk

Age UK is the new organisation created by the recent merger of Age Concern and Help the Aged. By combining the two separate large charities that focused on the welfare of older people, Age UK aims to become more effective both in providing services for older people and in political lobbying for change.

www.alzheimers.org.uk

The vision of the Alzheimer's Society is of a radically improved world for people with dementia, where their rights are recognised, their needs – and those of their carers – are fully met, where they can fully contribute to family and community life and where they can live with dignity, free from discrimination. The Alzheimer's Society exists to champion the rights of everyone with dementia and those who care for them.

www.carersfederation.co.uk/

From the starting point that carers are often isolated and can find themselves in situations where their wishes and needs take second place to the person they care for, the Carers Federation was established in 1992. From its roots in the Nottingham area the organisation has steadily grown and now works across the East Midlands, the North East, North West and Yorkshire and Humberside.

www.carersuk.org/

Carers UK is an organisation of carers fighting to end the injustice experienced by carers within society. It is fighting for recognition of the true value of carers' contribution to society and to ensure that carers get the practical, financial and emotional support they need.

For additional cases and topic-organised, clickable links into additional media resources, including those produced by IRISS, visit **www.pearsoned.co.uk/wilsonruch**

Activity

Activity One

Discuss the following question: why are comparatively few older people the subjects of fictional coverage in television drama? (As guidance for this you might like to consider the points made in this chapter about ageism, with particular reference to forms of popular entertainment.)

Activity Two

Policy has given much attention to the development of informal sources of care and support. Working through the four case studies that feature in the chapter, identify the possible sorts of response that can be developed, focusing on families and communities.

Bibliography

Abbott, A. (1988) *The System of Professions*, Chicago: University of Chicago Press

ACMD *see* Advisory Council on the Misuse of Drugs

ACMD (2003) *Hidden Harm: Responding to the Needs of Children of Problem Drug Users*, Report of an Inquiry by the Advisory Council on the Misuse of Drugs, London: Home Office

Adams, R. (1998) 'Social work processes', in R. Adams, L. Dominelli and M. Payne (eds) *Social Work Themes, Issues and Critical Debates*, pp. 253–72, Basingstoke: Macmillan

Adams, T. and Bartlett, R. (2003) 'Constructing dementia', in T. Adams and J. Manthorpe (eds), *Dementia Care*, London: Arnold

ADASS *see* Association of Directors of Adult Social Services

Adler, A. (1948) *Studies in Analytical Psychology*, New York: Norton

ADSS *see* Association of Directors of Social Services

Advisory Council on the Misuse of Drugs (2009) *Primary Prevention of Hepatitis C Among Injecting Drug Users*. [Online]. Available at: http://drugs.homeoffice.gov.uk/publicationsearch/acmd/acmdhepcreport22835.pdf?view=Binary (accessed 21 January 2010)

Advocacy in Action/Suresearch Collective (2006) 'Editorial', *Social Work Education*, 25 (4): 315–18

Ager, W., Dow, J., Ferguson, I., Gee, M., McPhail, M. and McSloy, N. (2005) *Service User and Carer Involvement in Social Work Education: Good Practice Guidelines* June 2005, Scottish Institute for Excellence in Social Work Education (accessed on 20 July 2010 at http://www.iriss.org.uk/files/IA33GoodPracticeGuidelines.pdf)

AgeUK (2010) 'Protect care from budget cuts', accessed on 9 July 2010 at http://www.ageuk.org.uk/latest-press/emergency-budget-protect-social-care/

Ainsworth, M., Blehar, M., Walters, E. and Walls, S. (1978) *Patterns of Attachment*, Hillsdale, NJ: Erlbaum

Alcock, P. (2004) 'Social policy and professional practice', in S. Becker and A. Bryman (eds) *Understanding Research for Social Policy and Practice*, Bristol: The Policy Press

Alcohol Concern (2008) *Women and Alcohol: A Cause for concern?* London: Alcohol Concern

Aldgate, J. (1988) 'Working with children experiencing separation and loss', pp. 36–48 in J. Aldgate and J. Simmonds (eds) *Direct Work with Children*, London: BAAF

Aldgate, J. (1993) 'Attachment theory and its application to child care social work: an introduction', pp. 11–35, in J. Lishman (ed.) *Handbook of Theory for Practice Teachers in Social Work*, London: Jessica Kingsley

Aldgate, J. (2001) 'Safeguarding and Promoting the Welfare of Children in Need Living with their Families', in L. Cull and J. Roche (eds) *The Law and Social Work: Contemporary Issues for Practice*, Basingstoke: Palgrave

Aldgate, J. and Bradley, M. (1999) *Supporting Families Through Short-Term Fostering*, London: The Stationery Office

Aldgate, J. and Seden, J. (2006) 'Direct work with children', in D. Jones, W. Rose and C. Jeffery (eds) *The Developing World of the Child*, pp. 229–72, London: Jessica Kingsley

Aldgate, J., Jones, D., Rose, W. and Jeffery, C. (eds) (2006) *The Developing World of the Child*, London: Jessica Kingsley

Aldridge, J. and Becker, S. (1993) *Children Who Care: Inside the World of Young Carers*, Loughborough: Young Carers Research Group

Aldridge, J. and Becker, S. (1996) 'Disability rights and the denial of young carers: the dangers of zero-sum arguments', *Critical Social Policy*, 16 (3) issue 48: 55–76

Aldridge, J. and Becker, S. (2003) *Children Caring for Parents with Mental Illness: Perspectives of Young Carers, Parents and Professionals*, Bristol: The Policy Press

Aldridge, M. and Eadie, T. (1997) 'Manufacturing an issue: the case of probation officer training', *Critical Social Policy*, 17: 111–24

Aldridge, T. (1999) 'Family values: rethinking children's needs living with drug-using parents', *Druglink*, 14 (2): 8–11

All Party Parliamentary Group on Hepatology (2008) 'Divided nations: tackling the hepatitis C challenge across the UK'. http://www.hepctrust.org.uk/Resources/HepC/HCV%20Reports/APPHG%20Report%20-%20Divided%20Nations.pdf (accessed 5 August 2009)

Allman, D. M. T., Schellenberg, J., Strike, C., Cockerill, R. and Cavalieri, W. (2007) 'Improving health and social care relationships for harm reduction', *International Journal of Drug Policy* 18: 194–203

Allyon, T. and Azrin, N. (1968) *The Token Economy: A Motivational System for Therapy and Rehabilitation*, New York: Appleton Century Crofts

Alzheimer's Society (2007) *Dementia UK*, London: Alzheimer's Society

American Psychiatric Association (1994) *Diagnostic and Statistical Manual of Mental Disorders (DSM IV)*, 4th edn, Washington, DC: American Psychiatric Association

Andersen, T. (1987) The reflecting team: dialogue and meta-dialogue', *Family Process*, 26 (4) (Dec): 425–8

Bibliography

Anglin, M. D. (1988) 'The efficacy of civil commitment in treating narcotic addiction', in C. Leukefeld and F. Tims (eds) *Compulsory Treatment of Drug Abuse: Research and Clinical Practice*, NIDA Research Monograph 86, DHHS Publication Number ADM 89–1578, Washington, DC: US Government Press

APPGH *see* All Party Parliamentary Group on Hepatology

Arber, S. and Ginn, J. (1991) *Gender and Later Life*, London: Sage

Arksey, H., Hepworth, D. and Qureshi, H. (2000) *Carers' Needs and the Carers Act: An Evaluation of the Process and Outcomes of Assessment*, York: Social Policy Research Unit

Arthur, R. (2010) *Young Offenders and the Law: How the Law Responds to Youth Offending,* Routledge: London

Asendorpf, J. (1993) 'Abnormal shyness in children', *Journal of Child Psychology and Psychiatry*, 34: 1069–83

Ash, E. (1992) 'The personal–professional interface in learning: towards reflective education', *Journal of Interprofessional Care*, 6 (3): 61–71

Ash, E. (1995) 'Taking account of feelings', in J. Pritchard (ed.) *Good Practice in Supervision*, pp. 20–30, London: Jessica Kingsley

Ashover, V. and Caldwell, K. (2006) 'An act of restoration', *Professional Social Work*, December, 2006

Association of Directors of Social Services (ADSS) (2005) *Safeguarding Adults*, London: ADSS

Association of Directors of Adult Social Services (ADASS) (2009) *Personalisation and the law: Implementing Putting People First in the Current Legal Framework*, London: ADASS

Association of Directors of Adult Social Services (ADASS) (2010) *Ensuring the Adequacy of Social Work in Adult Social Services* Advice Note 1, London: ADASS

Association of Directors of Adult Social Services/Department of Health/Skills for Care/British Association of Social Workers/Social Care Association (ADASS/DH/SFC/BASW/SCA) (2010) *The Future of Social Work in Adult Social Services*, London: ADASS/DH/SFC/BASW/SCA

Attlee, C. (1920) *The Social Worker*, London: Bell

Audit Commission (1986) *Making a Reality of Community Care*, London: HMSO

Audit Commission (1994) *Seen but not Heard: Coordinating Child Health and Social Services for Children*, London: HMSO

Audit Commission (2004a) *Drug Misuse 2004: Reducing the Local Impact*, London: Audit Commission

Audit Commission (2004b) *Support For Carers of Older People: Independence and Well-being*, London: Audit Commission

Austin, J. and Krisberg, B. (2002) 'Wider, stronger and different nets: the dialectics of criminal justice reform', in J. Muncie, G. Hughes and E. McLaughlin (eds) *Youth Justice: Critical Readings*, pp. 258–74, London: Sage

Avis, J. and Harris, P. (1991) 'Belief-desire reasoning among the Baka children: evidence for a universal conception of mind', *Child Development*, 62: 460–7

Axford, N. (2010) 'Conducting needs assessment in children's services' *British Journal of Social Work*, 40 (1): 4–25

Aymer, C. (2002) 'The dilemmas for black social work professionals: therapeutic implications', *Journal of Social Work Practice*, 16 (1): 15–21

Aymer, C. and Bryan, A. (1996) 'Black students' experience on social work courses: accentuating the positives', *British Journal of Social Work*, 26 (1): 1–16

Aymer, C. and Okitikpi, T. (2000) 'Epistemology, ontology and methodology: what's that got to do with social work?', *Social Work Education*, 19 (1): 67–75

Badham, B. and Eadie, T. (2004) 'Social work in the voluntary sector: moving forward while holding on', in M. Lymbery and S. Butler (eds) *Social Work Ideals and Practice Realities*, Basingstoke: Palgrave Macmillan

Bailey, R. and Brake, M. (eds) (1975a) *Radical Social Work*, London: Edward Arnold

Bailey, R. and Brake, M. (1975b) 'Introduction: social work in the welfare state', in R. Bailey and M. Brake (eds) *Radical Social Work*, London: Edward Arnold

Baldry, E., Bratel, J., Dunsire, M. and Durrant, M. (eds) (2005) 'Keeping children with a disability safely in their families', *Practice*, 17 (3): 143–56

Baldwin, N. and Walker, L. (2005) 'Assessment', in R. Adams, L. Dominelli and M. Payne (eds), *Social Work Futures: Crossing Boundaries, Transforming Practice*, pp. 36–53, Basingstoke: Palgrave Macmillan

Bamford, T. (1990) *The Future of Social Work*, Basingstoke: Macmillan

Bandura, A. (1969) *Principles of Behaviour Modification*, New York: Holt, Rinehhart and Winston

Bandura, A. (1973) *Aggression: a Social Learning Analysis*, Englewood Cliffs, NJ: Prentice Hall

Barber, J. (1995) 'Working with resistant drug abusers', *Social Work*, 40 (1): 17–23

Barber, J. G. (2002) *Social Work with Addictions*, 2nd edn, Basingstoke: BASW/Palgrave

Barclay Report (1982) *Social Workers: Their Role and Tasks*, London: Bedford Square Press/NISW

Barker, P. (1990) *Clinical Interviews with children and Adolescents*, New York: W Norton and Co.

Barker, R. (ed.) (2009) *Making Sense of Every Child Matters*, Bristol: Policy Press

Barnard, M. (2007) *Drug Addiction and Families*, London: Jessica Kingsley

Barnes, C. (1991) *Disabled People in Britain and Discrimination*, London: Hurst & Co.

Barnes, C., Mercer, G., Shakespeare, T. (2005) *Exploring Disability: A Sociological Introduction*, Oxford: Polity Press

Barnett, Canon S. A. and Barnett, Mrs S. A. (1915) *Practicable Socialism*, London: Longman Green & Co.

Barrett, G. and Keeping, C. (2005) 'The processes required for interprofessional working', in G. Barrett, D. Sellman and J. Thomas (eds) *Interprofessional Working in Health and Social Care*, Basingstoke: Palgrave Macmillan

Barrett, G., Sellman, D. and Thomas, J. (eds) (2005) *Interprofessional Working in Health and Social Care*, Basingstoke: Palgrave Macmillan

Bartlett, E. and Cheston, R. (2003) 'Counselling people with dementia', in T. Adams and J. Manthorpe (eds) *Dementia Care*, London: Arnold

Bartlett, H. M. (1970) *The Common Base of Social Work*, New York: National Association of Social Workers

Bartlett, W., Roberts, J. and Le Grand, J. (1998) *Revolution in Social Policy: Quasi-Market Reforms in the 1990s*, Bristol: Policy Press

BASW *see* British Association of Social Workers

Bateman, A. (2004) 'Psychoanalytically orientated day-hospital treatment for borderline personality disorder: theory, problems, and practice', in P. Richardson, H. Kachele and C. Renlund (eds) *Research on Psychoanalytic Psychotherapy with Adults*, pp. 109–32, London: Karnac

Bateman, A. and Fonagy, P. (2006) *Mentalization-Based Treatment for Borderline Personality Disorder: A Practical Guide*, Oxford: Oxford University Press

Bateman, T. and Pitts, J. (2005) *The Russell House Companion to Youth Justice*, Lyme Regis: Russell House

Bateson, G., Jackson, D. and Haley, J. (1956) 'Towards a theory of schizophrenia', *Behavioural Science*, 1: 251–64

Battjes, R. J., Onken, L. S., Delany, P. J. (1999) 'Drug abuse treatment entry and engagement: report of a meeting on treatment readiness, *Journal of Clinical Psychology*, 55: 643–57

Bauld, L., Chesterman, J., Davies, B., Judge, K. and Mangalore, R. (2000) *Caring for Older People: An Assessment of Community Care in the 1990s*, Aldershot: Ashgate

Baumrind, D. (1971) 'Current patterns of parental authority', *Developmental Psychology Monographs*, 9: 239–76

Baumrind, D. (1989) 'Rearing competent children', in W. Damon (ed.) *Child Development Today and Tomorrow*, pp. 349–78, San Francisco: Jossey-Bass

Baxter, S. K. and Brumfitt, S. M. (2008) 'Professional differences in interprofessional working', *Journal of Interprofessional Care*, 22 (3): 239–51

Bean, P. (2002) *Drugs and Crime*, Cullompton: Willan

Beattie, A. (1994) 'Healthy alliances or dangerous liaisons? The challenge of working together in health promotion', in A. Leathard (ed.) *Going Inter-Professional: Working Together for Health and Welfare*, London: Routledge

Becker, F. and Becker, S. (2008) *Young Adult Carers in the UK: Experiences, Needs and Services for Carers aged 16–24*, London: The Princess Royal Trust for Carers

Becker, S. (1997) *Responding to Poverty: The Politics of Cash and Care*, London: Longman

Becker, S. (2000a) 'Young carers', in M. Davies (ed.) *The Blackwell Encyclopedia of Social Work*, p. 378, Oxford: Blackwell

Becker, S. (2000b) 'Carers and indicators of vulnerability to social exclusion', *Benefits*, 28, April/May: 1–4

Becker, S. (2003) ' "Security for those who cannot": Labour's neglected welfare principle', in Millar, J. (ed.) *Understanding Social Security: Issues for Policy and Practice*, pp. 103–22, Bristol: The Policy Press

Becker, S. (2004) 'Carers', *Research Matters*, Special 2004 issue (August): 5–10

Becker, S. (2005) 'Children's hidden care work within the family: a labour of love or a matter of necessity?', invited paper presented at 'Cash and Care: Understanding the Evidence Base for Policy and Practice' – A Conference in Memory of Sally Baldwin, University of York, 12 April

Becker, S. (2007) 'Global perspectives on children as caregivers: research and policy on "young carers" in the UK, Australia, the United States and sub-Saharan Africa', *Global Social Policy*, 7 (1): 23–50

Becker, S. and Bryman, A. (eds) (2004) *Understanding Research for Social Policy and Practice*, Bristol: The Policy Press

Becker, S. and Silburn, R. (1999) *We're In This Together: Conversations with Families in Caring Relationships*, London: Carers National Association

Becker, S., Aldridge, J. and Dearden, C. (1998) *Young Carers and Their Families*. Oxford: Blackwell Science

Becker, S., Bryman, A. and Sempik, J. (2006) *Defining Quality in Social Policy Research*, Social Policy Association

Becker, S., Becker, F., Silburn, R., Silburn, P. and Sempik, J. (2005) *Carers' Assessments in Nottinghamshire: Content, Process and Outcomes*, Nottingham: Nottinghamshire County Council

Becker, S., Bryman, A. and Sempik, J. (2006) 'Defining Quality in Social Policy Research', Social Policy Association

Brammer (2010), *Social Work Law*, third edition, Pearson: UK

Becker, S., Hughes, N. and Beirens, H. (2007) *Carers' Assessments in Coventry: Content, Process and Outcomes*, Nottingham: University of Nottingham

Beckett, C. (2002) *Human Growth and Development*, London: Sage

Beckett, C. (2003) 'The Language of Siege: military metaphors in the spoken language of social work', *British Journal of Social Work*, 33 (5): 625–39.

Bee, H. (1994) *Lifespan Development*, New York: Harper Collins

Bee, H. (1995) *The Developing Child*, New York: Harper Collins

Bell, A., Hodgson, M. and Pragnell, S. (1999) 'Diverting children and young people from crime and the criminal justice system', in B. Goldson (ed.) *Youth Justice: Contemporary Policy and Practice*, London: Ashgate

Bell, E. M. (1961) *The Story of Hospital Almoners*, London: Faber and Faber

Bibliography

Bell, M. (1996) 'An account of the experiences of 51 families involved in an initial child protection conference', *Child and Family Social Work*, 1 (1): 43–57

Bell, M. (2002) 'Promoting children's rights through the use of relationship', *Child and Family Social Work*, 7 (1): 1–11

Bell, M. (2003) 'Working with families where there is domestic violence', in M. Bell and K. Wilson (eds) *The Practitioners Guide to Working with Families*, Basingstoke: Palgrave Macmillan

Bell, M. and Wilson, K. (eds) (2003) *Working with Families: The Practitioners' Handbook*, London: Palgrave Macmillan

Bell, M. and Wilson, K. (2006) 'Research note: children's views of family group conferences', *British Journal of Social Work*, 36 (4): 671–81

Bennett, G. and Kingston, P. (1995) *Elder Abuse: Concepts, Theories and Intervention*, London: Chapman and Hall

Bentovim, A. (2001) 'Working with abusing families', in K. Wilson and A. James (eds) (2007) *The Child Protection Handbook*, Edinburgh: Elsevier

Beresford, P. (2000) 'Service users' knowledge and social work theory: conflict or collaboration?', *British Journal of Social Work*, 30 (4): 489–503

Beresford, P. (2007) *The Changing Roles and Tasks Of Social Work From Service Users' Perspectives: A literature informed discussion paper*, London, Shaping Our Lives National User Network

Beresford, P. and Croft, S. (2000) 'Empowerment', in Davies, M. (ed.) *The Blackwell Encyclopaedia of Social Work*, pp. 116–18, Oxford: Blackwell

Beresford, P., Branfield, F., Lalani, M., Maslen, B., Sartori, A., Jenny, Maggie and Manny (2007) 'Partnership working: service users and social workers learning and working together', in M. Lymbery and K. Postle (eds) *Social Work: A Companion for Learning*, London: Sage

Beresford, P., Croft, S. and Adshead, L. (2007) *Palliative Care, Social Work and Services Users*, London: Jessica Kingsley

Bhui, K. (2001) 'Over-representation of black people in secure psychiatric facilities', *British Journal of Psychiatry*, 178 (6): 575

Bibby, A. and Becker, S. (2000) *Young Carers in Their Own Words*, London: Calouste Gulbenkian Foundation

Bifulco, A. and Moran, P. (1998) *Wednesday's Child*, London: Routledge

Biggs, S. (1993) *Understanding Ageing*, Buckingham: Open University Press

Biggs, S. (1999) *The Mature Imagination*, Buckingham: Open University Press

Bird, S. M., Goldberg, D. M., and Hutchinson, S. J. (2001) Projecting severe sequelae of injecting-related hepatitis C virus epidemic in the UK – Part 1. *Journal of Epidemiology and Biostatistics*, 6 (3): 243–65

Birdwhistell, R. (1970) *Kinesics and Context*, Philadelphia, PA: University of Pennsylvania

Blake, S. (2009) 'Subnational patterns of population ageing', *Population Trends*, 136: 42–57

Blakemore, K. and Boneham, M. (1994) *Age, Race and Ethnicity*, Buckingham: Open University Press

Blaug, R. (1995) 'Distortion of the face-to-face: communication, reason and social work practice', *British Journal of Social Work*, 25: 424–39

Blom Cooper *see* London Borough of Greenwich

Bobbitt, P. (2003) *The Shield of Achilles: War, Peace and the Course of History*, London: Penguin

Bohmann, M. (1966) 'Predisposition to criminality: Swedish adoption studies in retrospect', in S. Mednick, W. Gabriella and B. Hutchings (eds) *Ciba Foundation Symposium: Genetics of Criminal and Antisocial Behaviour*, Chichester: John Wiley and Sons

Bohmann, M. (1971) 'A comparative study of adopted children, foster children and children in their biological environment born after undesired pregnancies', *Scandinavica: Acta Psychiatrica*, 47 (221): 1–38

Bond, J., Peace, S., Dittmann-Kohli, F. and Westerhof, G. (eds) (2007) *Ageing in Society: European Perspectives on Gerontology*, 3rd edn, London: Sage/Open University

Bonner, A. and Luscombe, C. (2009) '*The seeds of exclusion 2009*' The Salvation Army with the University of Kent and Cardiff University [Online] Available from: http://www1.salvationarmy.org.uk/seeds (accessed 24th March 2010)

Bosanquet, H. (1914) *Social Work in London*, London: John Murray

Bostock, L., Bairstow, S., Fish, S. and Macleod, F. (2006) *Managing Risks and Minimising Mistakes in Services to Children and Families*, SCIE Report 6, London: SCIE

Boud, D., Keogh, R. and Walker, D. (1985) *Reflection: Turning Experience into Learning*, London: Kogan Paul

Bower, M. (2003) 'Broken and twisted', *Journal of Social Work Practice*, 17 (2): 143–52

Bower, M. (ed.) (2005) *Psychoanalytic Theory for Social Work Practice: Thinking Under Fire*, London: Routledge

Bowes, A. and Bell, D. (2007) 'Free personal care for older people in Scotland: issues and implications', *Social Policy and Society*, 6 (3): 435–45

Bowlby, J. (1973) *Separation: Anxiety and Anger*, London: Hogarth Press

Bowlby, J. (1979) *The Making and Breaking of Affectional Bonds*, London: Tavistock

Bowlby, J. (1991) *Attachment and Loss Vol. 3: Loss, Sadness and Depression*, London: Penguin Books

Bowlby, J. (1997) *Attachment and Loss Vol. 1: Attachment*, (2nd edn), London: Pimlico

Bowlby, J. (1998) *Attachment and Loss Vol. 2: Separation: Anxiety and Anger*, London: Pimlico

Bowpitt, G. (1998) 'Evangelical Christianity, Secular Humanism and the Genesis of British Social Work', *British Journal of Social Work*, 28 (5): 675–93

Boydell, L. (2007) 'A psychosocial perspective on multisectoral collaboration for improving public health', unpublished PhD thesis, Bristol: University of the West of England

Brammer, A. (2006) *Social Work Law*, 2nd edn, Harlow: Pearson Education

Brammer, A. (2009) 'Legal developments since *No Secrets*', *Journal of Adult Protection*, 11 (4): 43–53

Brandon, M., Schofield, G. and Trinder, L. (with Stone, N.) (1998) *Social Work with Children*, Basingstoke: Macmillan

Brandon, M., Belderson, P., Warren, C., Howe, D., Gardner, R., Dodsworth, J. and Black, J. (2008) *Analysing Child Deaths and Serious Injury through Abuse or Neglect: What can we learn?* London: Department for Children, Schools and Families

Branfield, F., Beresford, P. and Levin, E. (2007) *Common Aims: A Strategy to Support Service User Involvement in Social Work Education*, SCIE Position Paper 7, London: Social Care Institute for Excellence

Braye, S. (2000) 'Participation and involvement in social care', in H. Kempshall and H. Littlechild (eds) *Participation in Social Care: Researching for Practice*, London: Jessica Kingsley

Braye, S. and Preston-Shoot, M. (2006) 'Teaching, learning and assessment of law in social work education', Resource Guide 06, London: Social Care Institute for Excellence

Braye, S. and Preston-Shoot, M. (2010) *Practising Social Work Law*, 3rd edn, Basingstoke: Palgrave Macmillan

Brayne, H. and Carr, H. (2005) *Law for Social Workers*, 9th edn, Oxford: Oxford University Press

Breger, L. (2000) *Darkness in the Midst of Vision*, New York: Wiley

Brewer, C. and Lait, J. (1980) *Can Social Work Survive?* London: Temple Smith

Briggs, S. (2005) in Bower, M. (ed.) (2005) *Psychoanalytic Theory for Social Work Practice: Thinking Under Fire*, London: Routledge

Briggs, S. (1992) 'Child observation and social work training', *Journal of Social Work Practice*, 6 (1): 49–61

British Association of Social Workers (2003) *Code of Ethics for Social Work* (www.basw.co.uk)

Broadhurst, K. et al. (2010) 'Performing "initial assessment": identifying the latent conditions for error at the front door of local authority children's services', *British Journal of Social Work*, 40: 352–70

Bronfenbrenner, U. (1979) *The Ecology of Human Development: Experiments by Nature and Design*, Cambridge, MA: Harvard University Press

Brooks, F. (2007) 'Nursing and public information in health: an ethnographic study of a patient council', *International Journal of Nursing Studies* 45: 3–13

Brown, G. and Harris, T. (1978) *Social Origins of Depression: A Study of Psychiatric Disorder in Women*, London: Tavistock Publications

Bryman, A. (2004) 'Research for social policy and practice', in S. Becker and A. Bryman (eds), *Understanding Research for Social Policy and Practice*, Bristol: The Policy Press

Buchanan, J. and Young, J. (2002) 'Child protection: social worker's views', in H. Klee, M. Jackson and S. Lewis (eds) *Drug Misuse and Motherhood*, London: Routledge

Bullock, R. (2009) 'Residential care', in G. Schofield and J. Simmonds (eds) *The Child Placement Handbook* London: BAAF

Bullock, R., Courtney, M., Sinclair, I. and Thoburn, J. (2006) 'Can the corporate state parent?' *Adoption and Fostering* 30 (4): 6–19

Bumpus, M., Crouter, A. and McHale, S. (2001) 'Parenting autonomy granting during adolescence: exploring gender differences in context', *Developmental Psychology*, 37: 163–73

Burnett, R. and Appleton, C. (2004) 'Joined-up services to tackle youth crime: a case study in England', *British Journal of Criminology*, 44 (1): 34–54

Burr, V. (1995) *An Introduction to Social Constructionism*, London: Routledge

Burton, L. and Bengston, V. (1985) 'Black grandmothers: issues of timing and continuity of roles', in V. Bengston and J. Robertson (eds) *Grandparenthood*, Beverly Hills, CA: Sage

Butler, I. and Drakeford, M. (2001) 'Which Blair Project? Communitarianism, social authoritarianism and social work', *Journal of Social Work*, 1 (1): 7–19

Butler, I. and Drakeford, M. (2005) 'Trusting in social work', *British Journal of Social Work*, 35 (5): 639–53

Butler-Sloss, B. (1988) *Report of the Inquiry into Child Abuse in Cleveland, 1987*, Cm 412. London: HMSO

Butrym, Z. (1976) *The Nature of Social Work*, London: Macmillan

Bytheway, B. (1995) *Ageism*, Buckingham: Open University Press

Cabinet Office (2006) *Reaching Out: An Action Plan on Social Exclusion*, London: Social Exclusion Task Force

Cabinet Office/Social Exclusion Task Force (2009) *Understanding the Risks of Social Exclusion Across the Lifecycle* London Cabinet Office Available from www.cabinetoffice.gov.uk

Calder, M. (2003) 'The Assessment Framework: critique and reformulation', in M. C. Calder and S. Hackett *Assessment in Child Care: Using and Developing Frameworks for Practice*, pp. 3–60, Lyme Regis: Russell House

Cambridge, P. (1999) 'The first hit: a case study of the physical abuse of people with learning disabilities and challenging behaviour in residential service', *Disability and Society*, 12 (3): 427–53

Cambridge, P. and Parkes, T. (2006) 'The tension between mainstream competence and specialization in adult protection: an evaluation of the role of the adult protection co-ordinator', *British Journal of Social Work*, 36 (2): 299–321

Cameron, A. and Lart, R. (2003) 'Factors promoting and obstacles hindering joint working: a systematic review of the research evidence', *Journal of Integrated Care*, 11 (2): 9–17

Cameron, C. (2004) 'Social pedagogy and care: Danish and German practice in young people's residential care', *Journal of Social Work*, 4 (2): 133–51

Cameron, D. (2010) 'Big Society Speech', accessed on 23 August 2010 at: www.number10.gov.uk/news/speeches-and-transcripts/2010/07/big-society-speech-53572

Campbell, J. and Davidson, G. (2007) 'An examination of the use of coercion by community based mental health teams', *British Journal of Social Work*, 37 (3): 537–55

Campbell, J. and Oliver, M. (1996) *Disability Politics: Understanding our Past, Changing our Future*, London: Routledge

Campbell, P. (1996) 'The history of the user movement in the United Kingdom', in T. Heller, J. Reynolds, R. Gomm, R. Muston, and S. Pattison (eds) *Mental Health Matters: A Reader*, Basingstoke: Macmillan

Caplan, G. (1961) *A Community Approach to Mental Health*, London: Tavistock

Caplan, G. (1964) *Principles of Preventative Psychiatry*, New York: Basic Books

Carers UK (2003) 'Census 2001 and carers: results from around the UK', Policy Briefing, July 2003, London: Carers UK

Carers UK (2004) 'Your guide to a carer's assessment', Carers UK website (accessed 7 October 2004)

Carers UK (2007) *Real Change, Not Short Change: Time to Deliver for Carers*, London: Carers UK

Carers UK (2008) *Carers in Crisis: A Survey of Carers' Finances in 2008*, London: Carers UK

Carey, M. (2003) 'Anatomy of a care manager', *Work, Employment and Society*, 17 (1): 121–35

Carey, M. (2009) 'Critical commentary: happy shopper? The problem with service user and carer participation', *British Journal of Social Work*, 39 (1): 179–88.

Carpenter, J., Schneider, J., Brandon, T. and Wooff, D. (2003) 'Working in multidisciplinary community mental health teams: the impact on social workers and health professionals of integrated mental health care', *British Journal of Social Work*, 33 (7): 1081–103

Carr, S. (2004) *Has Service User Participation Made a Difference to Social Care Services?* Position Paper 3, London: Social Care Institute for Excellence (SCIE)/Policy Press

Carr, S. and Robbins, D. (2009) *The Implementation of Individual Budget Schemes in Adult Social Care*, Research Briefing 20, London: Social Care Institute for Excellence

Carroll, J. (1998) *Introduction to Therapeutic Play*, Oxford: Blackwell Science

Carvel, J. (2007) 'Councils turn backs on care for older people', *Guardian Unlimited*, http://www.guardian.co.uk/society/2007/nov/22/longtermcare.socialcare (accessed 29 April 2010)

Case Con Manifesto (1975), in R. Bailey and M. Brake (eds) *Radical Social Work*, pp. 144–7, London: Edward Arnold

Casselman, J. (2002) 'Motivation enhancement in clients referred from the criminal justice system', in P. Bean and T. Nemitz (eds) (2004) *Drug Treatment: What Works?* London: Routledge

Castells, M. (2000) *The Information Age. Vol. 1: The Rise of the Network Society*, Oxford: Blackwell

CCETSW *see* Central Council for Education and Training in Social Work

Cecchin, C. (1987) 'Hypothesising, circularity and neutrality revisited: an invitation to curiousity', *Family Process*, 26: 405–13

Central Council for Education and Training in Social Work (CCETSW) (1995) *Assuring Quality in the Diploma of Social Work*, London: CCETSW

Challis, D. and Davies, B. (1986) *Case Management in Community Care*, Aldershot: Gower

Challis, D., Darton, R., Johnson, L., Stone, M. and Traske, D. (1995) *Care Management and Health Care of Older People*, Aldershot: Arena

Chapman, J. (2002) *System Failure: Why Governments Must Learn to Think Differently*, 2nd edn, London: Demos

Cheetham, J. (2002) 'The research perspective', in M. Davies (ed.) *The Blackwell Companion to Social Work*, Oxford: Blackwell Publishing

Chenoweth, L. (1997) 'Violence and women with disabilities: silence and paradox', in S. Cook and J. Bessant (eds) *Women's Encounters with Violence: Australian Experiences*. Thousand Oaks, CA: Sage

Chief Secretary to the Treasury (2003) *Every Child Matters* Cm 5860, London: The Stationery Office

Chowns, G. (2006) 'No, you don't know how we feel'. Researching the experience of children facing the life-threatening illness of the parent: a collaborative inquiry. Unpublished PhD thesis, University of Southampton

Christie, B. (2009) 'Free personal care in Scotland may have to end, amid public spending pressure', *British Medical Journal*, 339: 4639

Clare, B. (2000) 'Becoming a social worker: learning, being and doing', in J. Harris, L. Froggett and I. Paylor (eds) *Reclaiming Social Work: The Southport Papers*, pp. 37–50, Birmingham: Venture Press

Clark, C. (2000a) *Social Work Ethics: Politics, Principles and Practice*, Basingstoke: Macmillan

Clark, C. (2000b) 'Values in social work', in Davies, M. (ed.) *The Blackwell Encyclopaedia of Social Work*, Oxford: Blackwell

Clark, H., Dyer, S. and Horwood, J. (1998) *'That Bit of Help': The High Value of Low Level Preventative Services for Older People*, Bristol: Policy Press/Community Care

Clarke, J. and Glendinning, C. (2002) 'Partnership and the remaking of welfare provision', in C. Glendinning, M. Powell and K. Rummery (eds) *Partnerships, New Labour and the Governance of Welfare*, Bristol: Policy Press

Clarke, J., Cochrane, A., and Mclaughlin, E. (eds) (1994) *Managing Social Policy*, London: Sage

Clarke, M. and Stewart, J. (2003) 'Handling the wicked issues', in J. Reynolds, J. Henderson, J. Seden, J. Charlesworth and A. Bullman (eds) *The Managing Care Reader*, London: Routledge.

Cleaver, H., Unell, I. and Aldgate, J. (1999) *Children's Needs – Parenting Capacity: The Impact of Parental Mental Illness, Problem Alcohol and Drug Use and Domestic Violence on Children's Development*, London: The Stationery Office

Cleaver, H., Wattam, C. and Cawson, P. (1998) *Assessing Risk in Child Protection*, London: NSPCC

Clifford, D. (1998) *Social Work Assessment Theory and Practice: A Multi-Disciplinary Framework*, Aldershot: Ashgate

Cohen, S. (1975) 'It's all right for you to talk: political and sociological manifestos for social work action', in R. Bailey and M. Brake (eds) *Radical Social Work*, London: Edward Arnold

Collins, S. (2008) 'Statutory social workers: stress, job satisfaction, coping, social support and individual differences', *British Journal of Social Work*, 38 (6): 1173–93

Collins, S. and Keene, J. (2000) *Alcohol, Social Work and Community Care*, Birmingham: Venture Press

Collins, W., Laursen, B., Mortensen, N., Luebker, C. and Ferreira, M. (1997) 'Conflict processes and transitions in parent and peer relationships: implications for autonomy and regulation', *Journal of Adolescent Research*, 12: 178–98

Colton, M. (1988) *Dimensions of Substitute Care: A Comparative Study of Foster Care and Residential Care*. Aldershot: Arena

Colton, M., Sanders, R. and Williams, M. (2001) *An Introduction to Working with Children: A Guide for Social Workers*, Basingstoke: Palgrave

Commission for Social Care Inspection (CSCI) (2004a) *Leaving Hospital: The Price of Delays*, London: Commission for Social Care Inspection

Commission for Social Care Inspection (CSCI) (2004b) *Direct Payments: What are the Barriers?* London: Commission for Social Care Inspection

Commission for Social Care Inspection (CSCI) (2006) *The State of Social Care in England 2005–06*, London: Commission for Social Care Inspection

Connor, A. and Tibbit, J. (1988) *Social Workers and Health Care in Hospitals*, London: HMSO

Cooke, P. (2000) *Final Report on Disabled Children and Abuse – Research Project Funded by Children-in-Need Oct 1996 – December 1999* Ann Craft Trust

Cooke, P. and Standen, P. J. (2002). 'Abuse and disabled children: hidden needs?' *Child Abuse Review*, 11: 1–18

Cooper, A. (1990) 'Neighbourhood and network: a model from practice', in G. Darvill and G. Smale (eds), *Partners in Empowerment: Networks of Innovation in Social Work*, London: National Institute for Social Work

Cooper, A. (2005) 'Surface and depth in the Victoria Climbié Inquiry Report', *Child and Family Social Work*, 10 (1): 1–11

Cooper, A. (2009) 'Hearing the grass grow: emotional and epistemological challenges of practice-near research' *Journal of Social Work Practice*, 23 (4) December: 429–42

Cooper A. (2010a) 'How to (Almost) Murder a Profession: The unsolved mystery of British social work', unpublished paper given to the International Association for Forensic Psychotherapy, conference 'Brutal Cultures', May 2010.

Cooper, A. and Dartington, T. (2004) 'The vanishing organization: organizational containment in a networked world', in Huffington, C. et al. (eds) *Working Below the Surface: The Emotional Life of Contemporary Organizations*, pp. 127–50, London: Karnac

Cooper, A., Hetherington, R., Katz, I. (2003) *The Risk Factor: Making the child protection system work for children*, London: DEMOS

Cooper, A. and Lousada, J. (2005) *Borderline Welfare: Feeling and Fear of Feeling in Modern Welfare*, London: Karnac Books

Cooper, A. and Trevillion, S. (1985) 'Survival and change: social work with angry men', *Journal of Social Work Practice*, 2 (1): 41–51

Cooper, A., Hetherington, R., Pitts, J., Baistow, K. and Spriggs, A. (1995) *Positive Child Protection: A View from Abroad*, Lyme Regis: Russell House Press

Cooper, C. (1985) *Good Enough Parenting*, London: BAAF

Cooper, H., Braye, S. and Geyer, R. (2004) 'Complexity and interprofessional edcuation' *Learning in Health and Social Care*, 3 (4): 179–89

Cooper, J. (1983) *The Creation of the British Social Services 1962–1974*, London: Heinemann Educational Books

Copley, B. and Corryan, B. (1997) *Therapeutic Work with Children and Young People*, London: Robert Royce

Corley, G. (ed.) (2000) *Older People and their Needs: A Multidisciplinary Perspective*, Oxford: Whurr Publishers

Coulshed, V. and Orme, J. (1998) *Social Work Practice: An Introduction*, Basingstoke: Macmillan

Cousins, J. (2009) 'Placing Disabled children with permanent new families: linking and matching', in Schofield, G. and Simmonds, J. (eds) *The Child Placement Handbook*, pp. 345–62, London: BAAF

Cowden, S. and Singh, G. (2007) 'The "User": Friend, foe or fetish? A critical exploration of user involvement in health and social care', *Critical Social Policy*, 27 (1): 5–23

Crawford, A. (2006) 'Networked governance and the post-regulatory state?', *Theoretical Criminology*, 10 (4): 449–79

Crawford, K. and Walker, J. (2003) *Social Work and Human Development*, Exeter: Learning Matters

Create Foundation (2000) *Consultation and Participation Models for Children and Young People in Care* at: www. create.net.au//create_world/ctw_html/pubs.html

Cree, V. (2003) 'Becoming and being a social worker', in Cree, V. (ed.) *Becoming a Social Worker*, pp. 155–70, Abingdon: Routledge

Cree, V. and Davis, A. (2007) *Social Work: Voices from the Inside*, Abingdon: Routledge

Crerar, L. (2007) *The Crerar Review: Report of the Independent Review of Regulation, Audit, Inspection and Complaints*

Handling in Public Services in Scotland, Edinburgh: Scottish Government

Criminal Justice Act 1991 (2000) at: www.hmso.gov.uk/legislation/uk.htm (last accessed 7/7/07)

Crisp, B., Anderson, M., Orme, J. and Green Lister, P. (2005) *Learning and Teaching in Social Work Education: Textbooks and Frameworks on Assessment*, London: SCIE

Crofts, N. and Deany, P. (1999) 'A global voice for harm reduction: the establishment of regional harm reduction networks' *Drug and Alcohol Review*, 18 (2): 221–9

Crome, I., Chambers, P. with Frisher, M., Bloor, R. and Roberts, D. (2009) 'The relationship between dual diagnosis: substance misuse and dealing with mental health issues' SCIE Briefing No 30 [Online] available from: http://www.scie.org.uk/publications/briefings/files/briefing30.pdf (accessed 24 March 2010)

Crompton, M. (2007) 'Individual work with children', in K. Wilson and A. James (eds) *The Child Protection Handbook*, 3rd edn, pp. 391–413, Edinburgh: Elsevier

Crossley, N. (2002) *Making Sense of Social Movements*, Maidenhead: Open University Press

Crow, L. (1996) 'Including all of our lives: renewing the social model of disability', in J. Morris (ed.) *Encounters with Strangers Feminism and Disability*, London: The Women's Press

CSCI *see* Commission for Social Care Inspection

Cumming, E. (1975) 'Engagement with an old theory', *International Journal of Ageing and Human Development*, 6: 186–91

Cumming, E. and Henry, W. (1961) *Growing Old: The Process of Disengagement*, New York: Basic Books

Curtis, E. A. and Davies, M. S. (2005) 'Family therapy and systemic practice with older people: where are we now?' *Journal of Family Therapy*, 27 (1): 43–64

Dallos, R. and Draper, R. (2000) *Introduction to Family Therapy: Systemic Theory and Practice*, Buckingham: Open University

Dalrymple, J. and Burke, B. (2006) *Anti-Discriminatory Practice*, 2nd edn, Buckingham: Open University Press

Damasio, A. (1995) *Descartes' Error: Emotion, Reason and the Human Brain*, London: Picador

Daniel, B., Wassell, S. and Gilligan, R. (1999) *Child Development for Child Care and Protection Workers*, London: Jessica Kingsley

Danta, M., Brown, D., Bhagani, S., Pybus, O. G., Sabin, C. A., Nelson, M., Fisher, M., Johnson, A. M., and Dusheiko, G. M. (2007) 'Recent epidemic of acute hepatitis C virus in HIV-positive men who have sex with men linked to high-risk sexual behaviours', *AIDS*, 21 (8): 983–91

Dartington, T. (2010) *Managing Vulnerability*. London: Karnac Books

Datillo, J. and Smith, R. (1990) 'Communicating positive attitudes towards people with disabilities through sensitive terminology', *Therapeutic Recreational Journal*, 24 (1): 8–17

Davey Smith, G., Dorling, D., Mitchell, R. and Shaw, M. (2002) 'Health inequalities in Britain: continuing increases up to the end of the 20th century', *Journal of Epidemiology and Community Health*, 56: 434–45

Davidson, R. (2002) 'Cycle of change: ideas, issues and implications', *Drugs: Education, Prevention and Policy*, 9 (1): 7–14

Davies, H., Nutley, S. and Smith, P. (2000) 'Introducing evidence-based policy and practice in public services', in Davies, H., Nutley, S. and Smith, P. (eds) *What Works? Evidence-Based Policy and Practice in Public Services*, pp. 1–11, Bristol: The Policy Press

Davies, M. (1981) *The Essential Social Worker*, London: Heinemann Education Books

Davies, M. (ed.) (2002) *The Blackwell Companion to Social Work*, Oxford: Blackwell Publishing

Davies, M. and Sinclair, I. (1971) 'Families, hostels and delinquents: an attempt to assess cause and effect', *British Journal of Criminology*, 11 (3): 213–19

Davis, A. (2008) *What Service Users Expect from Social Work*, Presentation to the International Conference on Social Work Education, Profession and Practice, Tblisi State University, Georgia, accessed on 20 July 2010 at http://www.ceimh.bham.ac.uk/documents/Ann_Georgia_presentation.pdf

Davis, K. (1994) 'Disability and legislation', in S. French (ed.) *On Equal Terms: Working with Disabled People*, Oxford: Butterworth-Heinemann

Dawson, S. and Dargie, C. (2002) 'New public management: discussion with special reference to UK health', in K. Mclaughlin, S. Osborne and E. Ferlie (eds) *New Public Management: Current Trends and Future Prospects*, pp. 34–56, London: Routledge

Deacon, J. (2009) 'From perversion to policy', unpublished doctoral thesis, University of East London and Tavistock and Portman NHS Trust

de Boer, C. and Coady, N. (2007) 'Good helping relationships in child welfare: learning from stories of success', *Child and Family Social Work*, 12: 32–42

de Bruin, H. (2002) *Managing Performance in the Public Sector*, London: Routledge

DCSF (Department of Children, Schools and Families) (2009) *Safeguarding Disabled Children: Practice Guidance*

De Leon, G. (1988) 'Legal pressure in therapeutic communities', in C. Leukefeld and F. Tims (eds) *Compulsory Treatment of Drug Abuse: Research and Clinical Practice*, NIDA Research Monograph 86, DHHS Publication Number ADM 89–1578, Washington, DC: US Government Press

De Winter, M. and Noom, M. (2003) 'Someone who treats you as an ordinary human being . . . homeless youth examine the quality of professional care', *British Journal of Social Work*, 33 (3): 325–37

Dearden, C. and Becker, S. (1995) *Young Carers: The Facts*, Sutton: Reed Business Publishing

Dearden, C. and Becker, S. (1998) *Young Carers in the United Kingdom: A Profile*, London: Carers National Association

Dearden, C. and Becker, S. (2000) *Growing Up Caring: Vulnerability and Transition to Adulthood: Young Carers' Experiences*, Leicester: Youth Work Press for the Joseph Rowntree Foundation

Dearden, C. and Becker, S. (2001) 'Young carers: needs, rights and assessments', in J. Horwath (ed.) *The Child's World: Assessing Children in Need*, pp. 221–33, London: Jessica Kingsley

Dearden, C. and Becker, S. (2004) *Young Carers in the UK: The 2004 Report*, London: Carers UK

Deehan, A., Templeton, L., Taylor, C., Drummond, C. and Strang, J. (1998) 'How do GPs manage alcohol misusing patients? Results from a national survey of GPs in England and Wales', *Drug and Alcohol Review*, 17: 259–66

DeHart, G., Stroufe, A. and Cooper, R. (2004) *Child Development: Its Nature and Course*, New York: McGraw-Hill

Denscombe, M. (2002) *Ground Rules for Good Research: A 10 Point Guide for Social Researchers*, Buckingham: Open University Press

Department for Education and Skills (DfES) (2003a) *Every Child Matters*, London: The Stationery Office

DfES (2003b) *The Victoria Climbié Inquiry: Report of an Inquiry by Lord Laming*, London: DfES

Department of Education and Skills (2004) *Every Child Matters: Change for Children*, TSO: London.

DfES (2007) *Aiming High for Disabled Children: Better support for families*, May, London: DfES

DfES (2007a) *Care Matters: Transforming the Lives of Children and Young People in Care*, London: Department for Education and Skills

Department of Children, Schools and Families (2009) *The Social Work Task Force Report*, TSO: London.

Department of Children, Schools and Families (2010) 'Working Together to Safeguard Children: A guide to inter-agency working to safeguard and promote the welfare of children', HM Government

Department of Health (DoH) (1989a) *Caring for People: Community Care in the Next Decade and Beyond*, Cm 849, London: HMSO

Department of Health (1989b) *The Children Act 1989*, London: HMSO

Department of Health (DoH) (1990a) *Community Care in the Next Decade and Beyond: Policy Guidance*, London: HMSO

Department of Health (1990b) *National Health Service and Community Care Act 1990*, London: HMSO

Department of Health (1991a) *Child Abuse: A study of Inquiry Reports 1980–1989*, London: HMSO

Department of Health (1991b) *Working Together under the Children Act 1989: A Guide to Arrangements for Inter-Agency Co-operation for the Protection of Children Against Abuse*, London: HMSO

Department of Health (1995) *Child Protection: Messages from Research*, London: HMSO

Department of Health (DoH) (1996a) *Carers (Recognition and Services) Act 1995: Policy Guidance and Practice Guide* (LAC(96)7), London: DoH

Department of Health (1996b) *Community Care (Direct Payments) Act 1996*, London: TSO

Department of Health (DoH) (1998) *Modernising Social Services*, Cm 4149, London: The Stationery Office

Department of Health (1998a) *Quality Protects: Transforming Children's Services (LAC(98)28)* London: DH

Department of Health (1999) *Adoption Now: Messages from Research*. Chichester: Wiley

Department of Health (1999a) *Care Plans and Care Proceedings under the Children Act 1989*, London: DH

Department of Health (1999b) *Caring about Carers: A National Strategy for Carers*, London: HMSO

Department of Health (1999c) *National Service Framework for Mental Health*, London: The Stationery Office

Department of Health (1999d) *The Protection of Children Act*, London: HMSO

Department of Health (1999e) *Working Together to Safeguard Children: A Guide to Inter-agency Working to Safeguard and Promote the Welfare of Children*, London: HMSO

Department of Health (2000a) *Assessing Children in Need and their Families: Practice Guidance*, London: HMSO

Department of Health (2000b) *Carers and Disabled Children Act 2000*, London: TSO

Department of Health (DoH) (2000c) *Framework for the Assessment of Children in Need and Their Families*, London: HMSO

Department of Health (2000d) *Lost in Care: Report of the Tribunal of Inquiry into the Abuse of Children in Care in the Former County Council of Gwynedd and Clwyd since 1974*, London: HMSO

Department of Health (DoH) (2000e) *The NHS Plan*, London: HMSO

Department of Health (DoH) (2000f) *No Secrets: Guidance on Developing and Implementing Multi-Agency Policies and Procedures to Protect Vulnerable Adults*, London: HMSO

Department of Health (DoH) (2000g) *A Quality Strategy for Social Care*, London: Department of Health

Department of Health (2000h) *Prime Minister's Review: Adoption: Issues for Consultation*. A Performance and Innovation Unit Report

Department of Health (2001) *National Adoption Standards for England*

Department of Health (2001a) *Health and Social Care Act 2001*, London: TSO

Department of Health (DoH) (2001b) *Hepatitis C: Guidance for Those Working with Drug Users*

Department of Health (DoH) (2001c) *The National Service Framework for Older People*, London: HMSO

Department of Health (2001d) *A Practitioner's Guide to Carers' Assessments Under the Carers and Disabled Children Act 2000*, London: DoH

Department of Health (2001e), *Valuing People: A New Strategy for Learning Disability for the 21st Century*, London: TSO

Department of Health (2002) 'Hepatitis C Strategy for England', London: Department of Health

Department of Health (DoH) (2002a) *Fair Access to Care Services: Guidance on Eligibility Criteria for Adult Social Care*, LAC(2002)13, London: Department of Health

Department of Health (DoH) (2002b) *Fair Access to Care Services: Policy Guidance*, London: Department of Health

Department of Health (DoH) (2002c) *Guidance on the Single Assessment Process for Older People*, HSC2002/001: LAC(2002)1, London: Department of Health

Department of Health (2002d) *Meeting the Needs of Disabled Children*, Research in Practice, London: TSO

Department of Health (DoH) (2002e) *Requirements for Social Work Training*, London: Department of Health

Department of Health (2003) *Personality Disorder: No Longer A Diagnosis of Exclusion*, London: Department of Health

Department of Health (DoH) (2003a) *The Community Care (Delayed Discharges etc.) Act 2003: Guidance for Implementation*, HSC 2003/009: LAC(2003)21, London: Department of Health

Department of Health (DoH) (2003b) *Direct Payments Guidance: Community Care Services for Carers and Children's Services (Direct Payments) Guidance England 2003*, London: Department of Health

Department of Health (DoH) (2003c) *Fairer Charging Policies for Home Care and other Non-Residential Social Services*, London: Department of Health

Department of Health (2003d) *The Victoria Climbié Inquiry: Report of An Inquiry*, London: HMSO

Department of Health (DoH) (2003e) *Every Child Matters* Cm 5860, London: The Stationery Office

Department of Health (DoH) (2004a) *The Children Act 2004*, London: TSO

Department of Health (DoH) (2004b) *Improving Chronic Disease Management*, London: Department of Health

Department of Health (DoH) (2005) *Independence, Well-Being and Choice*, London: The Stationery Office

DoH (2005a) 'Caring about carers: government information for carers'. Available online at: www.carers.gov.uk/ (accessed on 14 November 2005)

Department of Health (DoH) (2005b) *Independence, Well-Being and Choice*, London: The Stationery Office

Department of Health (DoH) (2006a) *Our Health, Our Care, Our Say: A New Direction for Community Services*, Cm 6737, London: HMSO

Department of Health (DoH) (2006b) *A Stronger Local Voice: A Framework for Creating a Stronger Local Voice in the Development of Health and Social Care Services*

Department of Health (2006c) *Working Together to Safeguard Children: A Guide to Inter-agency Working to Safeguard and Promote the Welfare of Children*, London: HMSO

Department of Health (DH) (2008) *Transforming Social Care* LAC (DH) (2008) 1, London, Department of Health.

Department of Health (2009) *Valuing People Now*. London: Department of Health

Department of Health (2009a) *New Horizons: Towards a Shared Vision for MentalHhealth*. London: DH

Department of Health (DH) (2009b) *Safeguarding Adults: A Consultation on the Review of the 'No Secrets' Guidance*, London: Department of Health

Department of Health (DH) (2010a) *Building the National Care Service*, London: Department of Health

Department of Health (DH) (2010b) *Prioritising Need in the Context of Putting People First: A whole system approach to eligibility for social care*, Guidance on Eligibility Criteria for Adult Social Care, England, London: Department of Health

Department of Health and Social Security (1970) *Chronically Sick and Disabled Persons Act 1970*, London: HMSO

Department of Health and Social Security (1985) *Social Work Decisions in Child Care: Recent Research Findings and their Implications*, London: HMSO

Department of Health and Social Security (1986) *Disabled Persons (Services, Consultation and Representation) Act 1986*, London: HMSO

Department of Health, Social Services and Public Safety Northern Ireland (DHSSPSNI) (2005) *Tackling Violence at Home: A Strategy for Addressing Domestic Violence and Abuse in Northern Ireland*, Belfast: Northern Ireland Office

Department of Health/Department for Education and Skills (2004), *National Service Framework for Children, Young People and Maternity Services*, London: HMSO

Department of Health/Social Services Inspectorate (DH/SSI) (1991) *Care Management and Assessment: Practitioners' Guide*, London: HMSO

DfES *see* Department for Education and Skills

DH/SSI *see* Department of Health/Social Services Inspectorate

DHSS *see* Department of Health and Social Security

DHSSPSS (2003) *Co-Operating to Safeguard Children*

DHSSPSS (2003) *Northern Ireland Framework Specification for the Degree in Social Work*

DHSSPSS (2004) *Northern Ireland Child Care Law 'The Rough Guide'*

DHSSPSS (2005) *Tackling Violence at Home. A Strategy for Addressing Domestic Violence and Abuse in Northern Ireland*

DHSSPSS (2006) *The Bamford Review of Mental Health and Learning Disability (Northern Ireland)*

DHSSPSS (2006) *Our Children and Young People – Our Shared Responsibilities' Overview Report*

DHSSPSS (2006) *Safeguarding Vulnerable Adults. Regional Adult Protection Policy and Procedural Guidance. Safeguarding Vulnerable Adults* can be accessed at: http://

www.nhssb.n-i.nhs.uk/publications/social_services/Safeguarding_Vulnerable_Adults.pdf

DHSSPSS (2006) *Thresholds of Needs Model*

DHSSPSS (2007) *Our Children and Young People – Our Shared Responsibility*

DHSSPSS (2008) *Gateway Service – Processes. Guidance for Northern Ireland Health and Social Care Trusts*

DHSSPSS (2008) *Independent Review Report of Agency Involvement* with Mr Arthur McElhill, Ms Lorraine McGovern and their children (Toner Report)

DHSSPSS (2008) *Understanding the Needs of Children in Northern Ireland (UNOCINI) Guidance*

DHSSPSS (2009) *Reforming Northern Ireland's Adult Protection Infrastructure*

DHSSPS (2010) *Adult Safeguarding in Northern Ireland – Regional and Local Partnership Arrangements*

Dickens, J. (2004) 'Risks and responsibilities: the role of the local authority lawyer in child care cases', *Child and Family Law Quarterly*, 16 (1): 17

Dickinson, H., Glasby, J., Forder, J. and Beesely, L. (2007) 'Free personal care in Scotland: a narrative review', *British Journal of Social Work*, 37 (3): 459–74

Digby, A. (1978) *Pauper Palaces*, London: Routledge and Kegan Paul

Disability Rights Commission Briefing on Lord Ashley's Disabled Persons (Independent Living) Bill 8 June 2006 at: www.drc-gb.org/Docs/DRCBriefingIndependentLivingBillJune06.doc

Dittmann-Kohli, F. (2005) 'Self and identity', in M. Johnson, V. Bengtson, P. G. Coleman. and T. B. L. Kirkwood (eds) *The Cambridge Handbook of Age and Ageing*, Cambridge: Cambridge University Press

Dockar-Drysdale, B. (1968) *Therapy in Child Care*, London: Longmans

Doel, M. (2010) 'Service-user perspectives on relationships', in Ruch, G., Turney, D. and Ward, A. (eds) *Relationship-based Practice: Getting to the Heart of Social Work*, London: Jessica Kingsley

Doel, M. and Best, L. (2008) *Experiencing Social Work: Learning from Service Users*, London: Sage

Doel, M. and Marsh, P. (1992) *Task-Centred Social Work*, Aldershot: Ashgate

DoH *see* Department of Health

Dolan, M. (1998) *The Hepatitis C Handbook: revised edition*, London: Catalyst Press

Dominelli, L. (2004) *Social Work Theory and Practice for a Changing Profession*, Bristol: Polity Press

Donzelot, J. (1979) *The Policing of Families*, Baltimore: Johns Hopkins University Press

Doyle, C. (1997) *Working with Abused Children*, 2nd edn, Basingstoke: BASW/Macmillan

Drainey, S., Rooney, J., Wood, N., and Stephenson, M. (2005) *Aftercare Consultation 2005: The Service User Perspective*, London: Addaction

Drury-Hudson, J. (1999) 'Decision making in child protection', *British Journal of Social Work*, 29 (1): 142–69

Dube, E. and Savin-Williams, R. (1999) 'Sexual identity development among ethnic minority male youth', *Developmental Psychology*, 35: 1389–98

Duffy, S. (2005) 'Individual budgets: transforming the allocation of resources for care', *Journal of Integrated Care*, 13 (1): 8–16

Duffy, F. (2010) 'Can Self-Directed support Transfirm the Welfare State?', in Gregg P. and Cooke C. *Liberation Welfare*, 93–103, London: DEMOS

Dumaret, A.-C., Coppel-Batsch, M. and Couraud, S. (1997) 'Adult outcome of children cared for long-term periods in foster families', *Child Abuse and Neglect*, 21: 911–27

Dundon, W. D., Pettinati, H. M., Lynch, K. G., Xie, H., Varillo, K. M., Makadon, C. and Oslin, D. W. (2008) 'The therapeutic alliance in medical-based interventions impacts outcome in treating alcohol dependence', *Drug and Alcohol Dependence*, 95: 230–236

Dunn, J. and McGuire, S. (1994) 'Young children's non-shared experiences: a summary of studies in Cambridge and Colorado', in E. Hetherington, D. Reiss and R. Plomin (eds) *Separate Social Worlds of Siblings: The Impact of Nonshared Environment on Development*, pp. 111–28, Hillsdale, NJ: Erlbaum

Dunn, M. C., Clare, I. C. H., Holland, A. J. and Gunn, M. J. (2007) 'Constructing and reconstructing 'best interests': an interpretive examination of substitute decision-making under the Mental Capacity Act 2005', *Journal of Social Welfare and Family Law*, 29 (2): 117–33

Dunning, J. (2010) 'Cuts threaten transformation agenda', *Community Care*, 20 (5): 14–15

Dustin, D. (2006) 'Skills and knowledge needed to practice as a care manager', *Journal of Social Work*, 6 (3): 293–313

Eadie, T. and Canton, R. (2002) 'Practising in a context of ambivalence: the challenge for youth justice workers', *Youth Justice*, 2 (1): 14–26

Easton, C., Swan, S. and Sinha, R. (2000) 'Motivation to change substance use among offenders of domestic violence', *Journal of Substance Abuse Treatment*, 19: 1–5

Edwards, A., Daniels, H., Gallagher, T., Leadbetter, J. and Warmington, P. (2009) *Improving Inter-Professional Collaborations: Learning to do Multi-agency Work*, Abingdon: Routledge

Edwards, H. and Richardson, K. (2003) 'The child protection system and disabled children', in *It Doesn't Happen to Disabled Children*, London: NSPCC

Efthimiou-Mourdant, A. (2002) 'Spanner in the works', *Druglink*, 17 (1): 12–13

Egan, G. (1994) *The Skilled Helper: A Problem management Approach to helping*, 5th edn, Pacific Grove, CA: Brooks Cole

Eichenbaum, L. and Orbach, S. (1982) *Outside In . . . Inside Out*, London: Penguin

Eichenbaum, L. and Orbach, S. (1985) *Understanding Women*, London: Penguin

Eley, S., Beaton, K. and McIvor, G. (2005) 'Co-operation in drug treatment services: views of offenders on court orders in Scotland', *The Howard Journal*, 44 (4): 400–10

Elkind, D. (1967) 'Ego-centrism in adolescence', *Child Development*, 38: 1025–34

Ellis, K. (2007) 'Direct payments and social work practice: the significance of "street-level bureaucracy" in determining eligibility', *British Journal of Social Work*, 37 (3): 405–22

England, H. (1986) *Social Work as Art: Making Sense of Good Practice*, London: Allen Unwin

Erikson, E. (1959) *Identity and the Lifecycle*, New York: International Universities Press

Erikson, E. (1982) *The Lifecycle Completed: A review*, London: Norton

Erikson, E. (1995) *Childhood and Society*, London: Vintage

Estes, C. and Associates (2001) *Social Policy and Aging*, New York: Sage

Etzioni, A. (ed.) (1969) *The Semi-Professions and their Organization*, New York: Free Press

Evans, R. (1993) *The Conduct of Police Interviews with Young People*, Royal Commission on Criminal Justice Research Study No. 8, London: HMSO

Evans, R. and Becker, S. (2009) *Children Caring for Parents with HIV and AIDS: Global Issues and Policy Responses*, Bristol: The Policy Press

Evans, T. (2010) 'Professionals, managers and discretion: critiquing street-level bureaucracy', *British Journal of Social Work*, Advance Access published 10 June 2010 at doi:10.1093/bjsw/bcq074.

Evans, T. and Harris, J. (2004) 'Street-level bureaucracy, social work and the (exaggerated) death of discretion', *British Journal of Social Work*, 34 (6): 871–95

Eysenck, H. (1952) 'The effects of psychotherapy: an evaluation', *Journal of Consulting Psychology*, 16: 314–19

Fahlberg, V. (1991 and 1994) *A Child's Journey Through Placement*, London: BAAF

Farabee, D., Prendergast, M. and Anglin, M. (1998) 'The effectiveness of coerced treatment for drug-abusing offenders', *Federal Probation*, 62 (1): 3–12

Farmer, E., Moyers, S. and Lipscombe, J. (2004) *Fostering Adolescents*, London: Jessica Kingsley

Feilzer, M. and Hood, R. (2004) *Differences or Discrimination*, London: Youth Justice Board

Ferguson, H. (2001) 'Social work, individualization and life politics', *British Journal of Social Work*, 31 (1): 41–56

Ferguson, H. (2003) 'In defence (and celebration) of individualization and life politics for social work', *British Journal of Social Work*, 33 (5): 699–707

Ferguson, H. (2005) 'Working with violence, the emotions and the psycho-social dimensions of child protection: reflections on the Victoria Climbié Case', *Social Work Education*, 24 (7): 781–95

Ferguson, I. (2007) 'Increasing user choice or privatizing risk? The antinomies of personalization', *British Journal of Social Work*, 37 (3): 387–403

Ferguson, I. (2008) *Reclaiming social work: challenging neo-liberalism and promoting social justice*, London: Sage

Ferguson, I. and Woodward, R. (2009) *Radical Social Work in Practice: Making a Difference*, Bristol: Policy Press

Fernando, S. (2003) *Cultural Diversity, Mental Health and Psychiatry: The Struggle against Racism*, Hove: Brunner-Routledge

Finch, J. (1989) *Family Obligations and Social Change*, Oxford: Polity Press

Finkelstein, V. (1993) 'The commonality of disability', in J. Swain, V. Finkelstein, S. French and M. Oliver (eds) *Disabling Barriers: Enabling Environments*, London: Sage

Finlayson, A. (2003) *Making Sense of New Labour*, London: Lawrence and Wishart

Fiorentine, R., Nakashima, J. and Anglin, D. (1999) 'Client engagement in drug treatment', *Journal of Substance Abuse Treatment*, 17 (3): 199–206

Fischer, J., Jenkins, N., Bloor, M., Neale, J. and Berney, L. (2007) *Drug User Involvement in Treatment Decisions*, Joseph Rowntree Foundation

Fish, S., Munro, E. and Bairstow, S. (2008) *Learning Together to Safeguard Children: developing a multi-agency systems approach for case reviews*, SCIE Report 19. London: SCIE

Fisher, T. and Somerton, J. (2000) 'Reflection on action: the process of helping social work students to develop their use of theory in practice', *Social Work, Education*, 19 (3): 387–401

Fisher, T., Sinclair, I., Gibbs, I. and Wilson, K. (2000) 'Sharing the care: the qualities sought of social workers by foster carers', *Child and Family Social Work*, 5 (3): 234–5

Fiske, A. and Jones, R. S. (2005) 'Depression', in M. Johnson, V. Bengtson, P. G. Coleman and T. B. L. Kirkwood (eds) *The Cambridge Handbook of Age and Ageing*, Cambridge: Cambridge University Press

Fitzgerald, G. (2008) 'No Secrets, Safeguarding Adults and adult protection', in J. Pritchard (ed.) *Good Practice in Safeguarding Adults: Working Effectively in Adult Protection*, London: Jessica Kingsley

Fonagy, P. *What Works for Whom? A critical view of treatment for children and adolescents*, New York: Guilford Press

Fonagy, P., Steele, M., Steele, H. and Target, M. (1994) 'The theory and practice of resilience', *Journal of Child Psychology and Psychiatry*, 35: 231–57

Fook, J. (2002) *Social Work: Critical Theory and Practice*, London: Sage

Ford, D. and Ford, P. (2000) 'Theorising social work assessment', unpublished article

Forrester, D. (2000) 'Parental substance misuse and child protection in a British sample. A survey of children on the child protection register in an inner London district office', *Child Abuse Review*, 9 (4): 235–46

Forrester, D. (2004) 'Social work assessments with parents who misuse drugs and alcohol', in R. Phillips (ed.) *Children Exposed to Parental Substance Misuse: Implications for Family Placement*, London: British Association for Adoption and Fostering

Forrester, D. and Harwin, J. (2004) 'Social work and parental substance misuse', in R. Phillips (ed.) *Children Exposed to Parental Substance Misuse: Implications for Family Placement*, London: British Association for Adoption and Fostering

Forrester, D. and Harwin, J. (2009) *Parents who Misuse Drugs and Alcohol. Effective interventions in social work and child protection*, Chichester: Wiley

Forrester, D., McCambridge, J., Waissbein, C., Emlyn-Jones, R. and Rollnick, S. (2008) 'Child risk and parental resistance: can motivational interviewing improve the practice of child and family social workers in working with parental alcohol misuse?' *British Journal of Social Work*, 38 (7): 1302–19

Foster, A. and Roberts, V. Z. (1998) *Managing Mental Health in the Community: Chaos and Containment*, London: Routledge

Foster, G. (2008) 'Injecting drug users with chronic Hepatitis C: should they be offered antiviral therapy', *Addiction*, 103: 1412–13

Foster J. (2009) 'Thinking on the Front Line: Why some social work teams struggle and others thrive.' Unpublished Doctoral thesis. London: Tavistock & Portman NHS Trust and University of East London

Fox, A., Becker, F. and Becker, S. (2007) 'Does every young carer matter? What *Every Child Matters* means for young carers', *Childright*, 235: 16–19

Fox Harding, L. (1991) *Perspectives in Child Care Policy*, Harlow: Longman

Fraiberg, S. (1977) *Insights from the Blind*, London: Souvenir Press

Frank, J. (2002) *Making It Work: Good Practice with Young Carers and Their Families*, London: The Children's Society and The Princess Royal Trust for Carers

Frank, J. and McLarnon, J. (2008) *Young Carers, Parents and their Families: Key Principles of Practice*, London: The Children's Society

Fraser, C. McIntyre, A. and Manby, M. (2009) 'Exploring the impact of parental drug/alcohol problems on children and parents in a Midlands county 2005/06', *British Journal of Social Work*, 39 (5): 846–66

Fraser, S., and Treloar, C. (2006). '"Spoiled identity" in hepatitis C infection: the binary logic of despair', *Critical Public Health*, 16: 99–110

Fratter, J., Rowe, J., Sapsford, D., Thoburn, J. (1991) *Permanent Family Placement: A Decade of Experience*, London: BAAF

French, S. (1994) 'What is disability?', in French, S. (ed.) *On Equal Terms: Working with Disabled People*, Oxford: Butterworth-Heinemann

Freud, S. (1917) *Mourning and Melancholia*, Standard Edition of the Works of Sigmund Freud, Vol. XIV, London

Freud, S. (1923) *The Ego and the Id*, Vol. 19, London: Hogarth Press

Freud, S. (1949) *An Outline of Psychoanalysis*, London: Norton

Froggett, L. (2002) *Love, Hate and Welfare: Psychosocial Approaches to Policy and Practice*, Bristol: Policy Press

Frosh, S. and Fyson, R. (2007) 'Child sexual abuse: who are the perpetrators?', in K. Wilson and A. James (eds) *The Child Protection Handbook*, 3rd edn, pp. 69–89, Edinburgh: Elsevier/Bailliere Tindall

Frost, N., Robinson, M. and Anning, A. (2005) 'Social workers in multidisciplinary teams: issues and dilemmas for professional practice', *Child and Family Social Work*, 10: 187–96

Furniss, T. (1991) *The Multi-Professional Handbook of Child Sexual Abuse: Integrated Management, Therapy, and Legal Intervention*, London: Routledge

Fyson, R. (2007) 'A fine line: balancing protection, choice and independence', *Ann Craft Trust Bulletin*, Issue 59

Fyson, R. and Kitson, D. (2007) 'Independence or protection – does it have to be a choice? Reflections on the abuse of people with learning disabilities in Cornwall', *Critical Social Policy*, 27 (3): 426–36

Galvani, S. and Hughes, N. (2008) 'Working with alcohol and drug use: exploring the knowledge and attitudes of social work students', *British Journal of Social Work*, Advance Access published on 20 October 2008; doi:doi:10.1093/bjsw/bcn137

Garbarino, I., Guttman, E. and Wilson Seeley, J. (1986) *The Psychologically Battered Child*, San Francisco: Jossey Bass

Garrett, P. M. (2003) 'The trouble with Harry: why the "new agenda of life politics" fails to convince', *British Journal of Social Work*, 33 (3): 381–97

Garrett, P. M. (2004) 'More trouble with Harry: a rejoinder in the "life politics" debate', *British Journal of Social Work*, 34 (5): 577–89

Gelsthorpe, L. and Morris, A. (2002) 'Restorative justice: the last vestiges of welfare?', in J. Muncie, G. Hughes and E. McLaughlin (eds) *Youth Justice: Critical Readings*, pp. 228–37, London: Sage

General Social Care Council (GSCC) (2002) *Code of Practice for Social Care Workers and Employers*, London: GSCC

General Social Care Council (GSCC) (2005) *Post-Qualifying Framework for Social Work Education and Training*, London: GSCC

General Social Care Council (GSCC) (2008) *Social Work at its Best: A Statement of Social Work Roles and Tasks for the 21st Century*, London: GSCC

George, M. (2001) *It Could Be You: A Report on the Chances of Becoming a Carer*, London: Carers UK

Gershon, P. (2004) *Releasing Resources to the Front-Line: Independent Review of Public Sector Efficiency*, London: HM Treasury

Gibbons, J., Conroy, S. and Bell, C. (1995) *Operating the Child Protection System: A Study of Child Protection Practices in English Local Authorities*, London: HMSO

Gibbons, J., Bow, I., Butler, J. and Powell, J. (1979) 'Clients' reactions to task-centred casework: a follow-up study', *British Journal of Social Work*, 10 (2): 203–15

Gibbons, J., Gallagher, B., Bell, C. and Gordon, D. (1995) *Development After Physical Abuse in Early Childhood: A Follow-Up Study of Children on Child Protection Registers*, Norwich: University of East Anglia

Gibbons Wood L. (2008) *Social Work Law in Scotland*, 2nd edn, Edinburgh: Sweet and Maxwell

Gibbs, G. (1988) *Learning by Doing: A Guide to Teaching and Learning Methods*, Oxford: Further Education Unit, Oxford University

Gibbs, I. and Sinclair, I. (1998) 'Residential care for elderly people: the correlates of quality', *Ageing and Society*, 12 (4): 463–82

Giddens, A. (1990) *The Consequences of Modernity*, Cambridge: Polity Press

Gill, O. (1988) 'Integrated work in a neighbourhood family centre', *Practice*, 2 (3): 243–55

Gilleard, C. and Higgs, P. (2005) *Contexts of Ageing: Class, Cohort and Community*, Oxford: Polity

Ginsburg, J., Mann, R., Rotgers, F. and Weekes, J. (2002) 'Motivational interviewing with criminal justice populations', in W. Miller and S. Rollnick (eds) *Motivational Interviewing: Preparing People for Change*, 2nd edn, London: The Guilford Press

Glasby, J. (2003) *Hospital Discharge: Integrating Health and Social Care*, Oxford: Radcliffe Medical Press

Glasby, J. (2005) 'The future of adult social care: lessons from previous reforms', *Research, Policy and Planning*, 23 (2): 61–70

Glasby, J. and Beresford, P. (2006) 'Commentary and issues: who knows best? Evidence-based practice and the service user contribution', *Critical Social Policy*, 26 (1): 268–84.

Glasby, J. and Littlechild, R. (2003) *Social Work and Direct Payments*, Bristol: Policy Press

Glasby, J. and Littlechild, R. (2009) *Direct Payments and Personal Budgets: Putting Personalisation into Practice*, 2nd edn, Bristol: Policy Press

Glaser, D. (2000) 'Child abuse and neglect and the brain: a review', *Journal of Child Psychology and Psychiatry*, 41: 97–116

Glaser, D. and Frosh, S. (1993) *Child Sexual Abuse*, London: Macmillan

Glendinning, C., Coleman, A. and Rummery, K. (2003) 'Looking outwards: primary care organisations and local partnerships', in B. Dowling and C. Glendinning (eds) *The New Primary Care*, Buckingham: Open University Press

Glendinning, C., Powell, M. and Rummery, K. (eds) (2002) *Partnerships, New Labour and the Governance of Welfare*, Bristol: Policy Press

Glendinning, C., Challis, D., Fernandez, J-L., Jacobs, S., Jones, K., Knapp, M., Manthorpe, J., Moran, N., Netten, A., Stevens, M., and Wilberforce, M. (2008) *Evaluation of the Individual Budgets Pilot Programme: Final Report*, York: Social Policy Research Unit, University of York

Glynn, T. and Ansell, J. (2006) 'Survival and abuse: what we can learn from it', *Social Work Education*, 25 (4): 418–28

Goffman, E. (1961) *Asylums: Essays on the Social Situation of Mental Patients and Other Inmates*, New York: Anchor Books

Golan, N. (1978) 'Crisis theory', in F. Yurner (ed.) *Social Work Treatment: Interlocking Theoretical Approaches*, London: Free Press

Goldsmith, M. (1996) *Hearing the Voice of People with Dementia*, London: Jessica Kingsley

Goldson, B. (2002) *Vulnerable Inside: Children in Secure and Penal Settings*, London: The Children's Society

Gorin, S. (2004) *Understanding What Children Say: Children's Experiences of Domestic Violence, Parental Substance Misuse and Parental Health Problems*, London: National Children's Bureau for the Joseph Rowntree Foundation

Gorman, H. (2003) 'Which skills do care managers need? A research project on skills, competency and continuing professional development', *Social Work Education*, 22 (3): 245–59

Gossop, M. (2006) Treating drug misuse problems: evidence of effectiveness. London: NTA

Gould, N. and Baldwin, M. (eds) (2004) *Social Work, Critical Reflection and the Learning Organisation*, Ashgate: Aldershot

Government Office for Science (2008) *Mental Capital and Well Being: Making the most of ourselves in the 21st century*, London: GOS

Gregory, A., Ramsay, J., Agnew-Davies, R., Baird, K., Devine, A., Dunne, D., Eldridge, S., Howell, A., Johnson, M., Rutterford, C., Sharp, D. and Feder, G. (2010) 'Primary care Identification and Referral to Improve Safety of women experiencing domestic violence (IRIS): protocol for a pragmatic cluster randomised controlled trial', *BMC Public Health*, 10 (54), doi:10.1186/1471-2458-10-54, accessed 11 August 2010 at: www.Biomedcentral.com/1471-2458/10/54

Griffiths, R. (1988) *Community Care: Agenda for Action*, London: HMSO

GSCC *see* General Social Care Council

Guardian (2006) 'Mubarek inquiry calls for urgent jail reform', 30/6/2006

Gunn, J. (1994) 'Suicide in Scottish prisons', unpublished report cited in HM Chief Inspector of Prisons (1999)

Gupta, A. and Blewitt, J. (2007) 'Challenges and opportunities for the social work workforce', *Child and Family Social Work*, 12: 172–81

Hafford-Letchfield, T. (2006) *Management and Organisations in Social Work*, Exeter: Learning Matters

Hagestad, G. (1986) 'Dimensions of time and the family', *American Behavioral Scientist*, 29: 679–94

Hague, G., Thiara, R. and Mullender, A. (2010) 'Disabled women, domestic violence and social care: the risk of isolation, vulnerability and neglect', *British Journal of Social Work* Advance Access published online on 7 July 2010, doi:10.1093/bjsw/bcq057.

Haines, K. and Drakeford, M. (1998) *Young People and Youth Justice*, Basingstoke: Palgrave

Haines, K. and O'Mahony, D. (2006) 'Restorative approaches: young people and youth justice', in B. Goldson and J. Muncie (eds) *Youth Crime and Justice*, pp. 110–24, London: Sage

Hall, P. (2005) 'Interprofessional teamwork: professional cultures as barriers', *Journal of Interprofessional Care*, 19 (2): 188–96

Hanks, H. and Stratton, P. (2007) 'Consequences and indicators of child abuse', in K. Wilson and A. James (eds) *The Child Protection Handbook*, 3rd edn, Edinburgh: Elsevier

Hannigan, B. (1999) 'Joint working in community mental health: prospects and challenges', *Health and Social Care in the Community*, 7 (1): 25–31

Harbin, F. and Murphy, M. (2000) 'Background and current context of substance misuse and child care', in F. Harbin and M. Murphy (eds) *Substance Misuse and Child Care: How to Understand, Assist and Intervene When Drugs Affect Parenting*, Lyme Regis: Russell House

Harding, T. and Beresford, P. (1995) *What Service Users and Carers Value and Expect from Social Services Staff: A Report to the Department of Health*, London: Department of Health

Harlow, E. (2003) 'New managerialism, social services departments and social work practice today', *Practice*, 15 (2): 29–44

Harris, J. (2008) 'State social work: constructing the present from moments in the past', *British Journal of Social Work*, 38 (4): 662–79

Harris, J. and Tanner, D. (2007) *Working with Older People*, London: Routledge

Harris, J. and Unwin, P. (2009) 'Performance management in modernised social work', in J. Harris and V. White (eds) *Modernising Social Work: Critical Considerations*, Bristol: Policy Press.

Harris, J. and White, V. (eds) (2009) *Modernising Social Work: Critical Considerations*, Bristol: Policy Press

Harris, R. (1969) 'Institutionalized ambivalence: social work and the Children and Young Persons Act 1969', *BJSW*, 12 (1): 247–63

Harris, R. (2009) 'The role of advocacy and the Independent Mental Capacity Advocate (IMCA) in adult protection', in J. Pritchard (ed.) *Good Practice in the Law and Safeguarding Adults*, London: Jessica Kingsley

Harrison, K. and Ruch, G. (2007) 'Social work and the use of self: on becoming and being a social worker', in M. Lymbery and K. Postle (eds) *Social Work: A Companion to Learning*, pp. 40–50, London: Sage

Harter, S. (1999) *The Construction of Self: A Developmental Perspective*, New York: Guilford Press

Hayden, C. (2004) 'Parental substance misuse and child care social work: research in a city social work department in England', *Child Abuse Review*, 13 (1): 18–30

Hayes, D. (2007) 'Wooed by an Italian model', *Community Care*, 34–5

Hazan, C. and Shaver, P. (1987) 'Romantic love conceptualised as an attachment process', *Journal of Personality and Social Psychology*, 52: 511–24

Hazan, C. and Shaver, P. (1990) 'Love and work: an attachment-theoretical perspective', *Journal of Personality and Social Psychology*, 59: 270–80

Hazan, C., Hutt, M., Sturgeon, J. and Bricker, T. (1991) 'The process of relinquishing parents as attachment figures'. Paper presented at the biennial meeting of the Society for Research in Child Development, Seattle, USA

Hearnden, I. (2000) 'Problem drug use and probation in London: an evaluation', *Drugs: Education, Prevention and Policy*, 7 (4): 367–80

Heather, N. and Mason, P. (1999) 'Generalist treatment and minimal interventions', in D. Rastrick, R. Hodgson and B. Ritson (eds) *Tackling Alcohol Together*, London: Free Association Books

Heather, N. and McCarthy, S. (1999) 'Specialist treatment', in D. Rastrick, R. Hodgson and B. Ritson (eds) *Tackling Alcohol Together*, London: Free Association Books

Hedges, F. (2005) *An Introduction to Systemic Therapy with Families*, Basingstoke: Palgrave Macmillan

Heenan, D. and Birrell, D. (2006) 'The integration of health and social care: the lessons from Northern Ireland', *Social Policy and Administration*, 40 (1): 47–66

Helfer, R. (1990) 'The neglect of our children in child abuse', *Paediatrics Clinics of North America*, 37 (4): 923–42

Hendrick, H. (1997) 'Constructions and reconstructions of British childhood: an interpretative survey, 1800 to the present', in A. James and A. Prout (eds) *Constructing and Reconstructing Childhood*, pp. 34–62, London: Falmer Press

Hendrick, H. (2003) *Child Welfare*, Bristol: Policy Press

Hendrick, H. (2006) 'Histories of youth crime and justice', in Goldson, B. and Muncie, J. (eds) *Youth Crime and Justice*, pp. 3–16, London: Sage

Henwood, M. and Hudson, B. (2008) *Lost In the System? The Impact of Fair Access to Care*, London: Commission for Social Care Inspection

Herod, J. and Lymbery, M. (2002) 'The social work role in multi-disciplinary teams', *Practice*, 14 (4): 17–27

Hesse, E. (1999) 'The adult attachment interview: historical and current perspectives', in J. Cassidy and P. Shaver (eds) *Handbook of Attachment: Theory, Research and Clinical Applications*, pp. 395–432, New York: Guilford Press

Hetherington, R., Cooper, A., Smith, P. and Wilford, G. (1997) *Protecting Children: Messages from Europe*, Lyme Regis: Russell House

Hewitt, D. (2009) 'The vulnerable adult and the Mental Capacity Act 2005', in J. Pritchard (ed.) *Good Practice in the Law and Safeguarding Adults*, London: Jessica Kingsley

Hill, J. (2006) '"Dreaming out of despair": a retrospective post-custody study', in D. Wilson and G. Rees (eds) *Just Justice*, pp. 22–36, London: The Children's Society

Hill, M. (2009) 'The place of child placement research in policy and practice', in G. Schofield and J. Simmonds (eds) *The Child Placement Handbook*, London: BAAF

Hill, M. (1993) *The Welfare State in Britain*, Aldershot: Edward Elgar

Hill, M., Lockyer, A. and Stone, F. (eds) (2007) *Youth Justice and Child Protection*, London: Jessica Kingsley

Hillman, J. and Mackenzie, M. (1993) *Understanding Field Social Work*, Birmingham: Venture Press

Hirst, M. (1999) *Informal Care-giving in the Lifecourse*, York: SPRU

HM Chief Inspector of Prisons (1999) *Suicide is Everyone's Concern*, London: The Stationery Office

HM Chief Inspector of Prisons (2001) *Annual Report 1999–2000*, London: The Stationery Office

HM Government *see under individual Government departments for publications after 1997*

HM Government (1989) *Caring For People*, London: HMSO

HM Government (1999) *Caring About Carers: A National Strategy for Carers*, London: Department of Health

HM Government (2004) *Every Child Matters: Change for Children*, London: The Stationery Office

HM Government (2004) *Explanatory Notes to Carers (Equal Opportunities) Act 2004*, London: The Stationery Office

HM Government (2006) *Working Together to Safeguard Children: A Guide to Inter-Agency Working to Safeguard and Promote the Welfare of Children*, London: The Stationery Office

HM Government (2007) *Putting People First*, London, HM Government

HM Government (2008a) *Carers at the Heart of the 21st-Century Families and Communities*, London: Department of Health

HM Government (2008b) *The Case for Change – Why England needs a new care and support system*, London: Department of Health

HM Government (2010) Reducing demand, restricting supply, building recovery: supporting people to live a drug free life London: The Stationary Office

HM Government (2010) *Working Together to Safeguard Children: A guide to inter-agency working to safeguard and promote the welfare of children*, London: The Stationery Office

HMSO *see under individual Government departments for publications after 1997*

HMSO (1974) *Report of the Committee of Enquiry into the Care and Supervision Provided in Relation to Maria Colwell*, London: HMSO

HMSO (1988) *Report of the Enquiry into Child Abuse in Cleveland 1987*, London: HMSO

Hobbes, C., Hanks, H. and Wynne, J. (1993) *The Clinician's Handbook*, Edinburgh: Churchill Livingstone

Hobson, P. (2002) *The Cradle of Thought: Exploring the Origins of Thinking*, London: Macmillan

Hockey, J. and James, A. (2003) *Social Identities across the Life Course*, Basingstoke: Palgrave

Hoggett, P. (2006) 'Conflict, ambivalence, and the contested purpose of public organisations', *Human Relations*, 59 (2): 175–94

Hollin, C. and Palmer, E. J. (eds) (2006) *Offending Behaviour Programmes: Development, Application, and Controversies*, Chichester: Wiley

Hollis, F. (1964) *A Psycho-Social Therapy*, New York: Random House

Hollis, F. (1981) *Casework: A Psychosocial Therapy*, 3rd edn, New York: Random House

Holloway, M. and Lymbery, M. (2007) 'Editorial – Caring for people: social work with adults in the next decade and beyond', *British Journal of Social Work*, 37 (3): 375–86

Holloway, M. and Moss, B. (2010) *Spirituality and Social Work*, Basingstoke, Palgrave Macmillan

Holmes, J. (1993) *John Bowlby and Attachment Theory*, London: Routledge

Holzhausen, E. (2002) *Without Us . . . ? Calculating the Value of Carers' Support*, London: Carers UK

Home Office (1927) *Report of the Departmental Committee on the Treatment of Young Offenders* (Molony Committee), London: HMSO

Home Office (1960) *Report of the Committee on Children and Young Persons* (Ingleby Committee), London: HMSO

Home Office (1997) *No More Excuses: A New Approach to Tackling Youth Crime in England and Wales*, Cm 3809, London: HMSO

Home Office (2004) *Guidance on Investigating Domestic Violence*, Association of Chief Police Officers, by National Centre for Policing Excellence, www.acpo.police/uk/asp/policies (accessed 10 August 2010)

Home Office (2006) *Police and Criminal Evidence Act 1984 (66 (1)): Code of Practice C and Code of Practice H*, London: Home Office

Home Office (2008) *Government Statistics on Domestic Violence*. Estimating the number of incidents 1995–2006/7, www.dewar4reserach.org (accessed 10 August 2010)

Home Office (2008) 'The Police and Criminal Evidence Act 1984 (s.60 (1)(a) and s.66) Code of Practice C', Revised edition, London: The Stationery Office.

Home Office (2009) *Moving up a Gear-the Next Steps for DIP: Executive Summary*. [Online]. Available from: http://drugs.homeoffice.gov.uk/publication-search/dip/moving-up-a-gear?view=Binary (accessed 15 October 2009)

Honey, P. and Mumford, A. (1987) *The Manual of Learning Styles*, Maidenhead: Peter Honey

Hood, C. (1991) 'A public management for all seasons?', *Public Administration*, 61 (1): 3–19

Hopwood, M. and Treloar, C. (2003) *The 3D Project: Diagnosis, Disclosure and Discrimination – Living with Hepatitis C*, Sydney: University of New South Wales

Hornby, S. and Atkins, J. (2000) *Collaborative Care: Interprofessional, Interagency and Interpersonal*, Oxford: Blackwell

Horwath, J. (ed.) (2001) *The Child's World: Assessing Children in Need*, London: Jessica Kingsley

Hothersall, S., Maas-Lowit, M., Golightley, M. (2008) *Social Work and Mental Health in Scotland*, Exeter: Learning Matters

Houston, S. (2010) 'Beyond *Homo Economicus*: recognition and self-realization and social work', *British Journal of Social Work*, 40 (3): 841–57

Howard, J. (2000) 'Support care: a new role for foster carers', in A. Wheal (ed.) *Working with Parents*, Lyme Regis: Russell House

Howard, M. (2001) *Paying The Price: Carers, Poverty and Social Exclusion*, London: CPAG

Howe, D. (1987) *An Introduction to Social Work Theory*, Aldershot: Ashgate

Howe, D. (1994) 'Modernity, postmodernity and social work', *British Journal of Social Work*, 24 (5): 513–32

Howe, D. (1995) *Attachment Theory for Social Work Practice*, Houndsmill, Basingstoke and London: Macmillan Press

Howe, D. (1996) 'Surface and depth in social work practice', in N. Parton (ed.) *Social Theory, Social Work and Social Change*, London: Macmillan

Howe, D., Brandon, M., Hinings, D. and Schofield, G. (1999) *Attachment Theory, Child Maltreatment and Family Support: A Practice and Assessment Model*, Basingstoke: Macmillan

Hudson, B. (1990) 'Social policy and the new right – the strange case of the community care White Paper', *Local Government Studies*, 16 (6): 15–34

Hudson, B. (2002) 'Interprofessionality in health and social care: the Achilles' heel of partnership', *Journal of Interprofessional Care*, 16 (1): 7–17

Hudson, B. (2005) 'User outcomes and children's services reform', *Social Policy and Society*, 5 (2): 227–35

Hudson, B. (2007) 'Pessimism and optimism in interprofessional working: The Sedgefield Integrated Team', *Journal of Interprofessional Care*, 21 (1): 3–15

Hudson, B. and MacDonald, G. (1986) *Behavioural Social Work*, London: Macmillan

Hughes, L. and Pengelly, P. (1997) *Staff Supervision in a Turbulent Environment: Managing Process and Task in Frontline Services*, London: Jessica Kingsley

Hughes, M. and Heycox, K. (2006) 'Knowledge and interest in ageing: a study of final-year social work students', *Australasian Journal on Ageing*, 25 (2): 94–6

Hughes, M. and Heycox, K. (2010) *Older People, Ageing and Social Work: Knowledge for Practice*, Crows Nest NSW: Allen and Unwin

Hugman, R. (1998) *Social Welfare and Social Value*, Basingstoke: Macmillan

Hugman, R. (2005) *New Approaches in Ethics for the Caring Professions*, Basingstoke: Palgrave

Hugman, R. (2007) 'The place of values in social work education', in M. Lymbery and K. Postle (eds) *Social Work: A Companion to Learning*, London: Sage

Humphreys, C. (2006) *Domestic Violence and Child Abuse*, Making Research Count Briefing Paper, London: Department of Education and Science

Humphries, B. (2004) 'An unacceptable role for social work: implementing immigration policy', *British Journal of Social Work*, 34 (1): 93–107

Hunt, N. (2002) 'Involvement and empowerment: why bother?', *Druglink*, 17 (1): 14–16

Huxley, P. (1993) 'Case management and care management in community care', *British Journal of Social Work*, 23 (4): 365–81

Ife, J. (1997) *Rethinking Social Work*, Melbourne: Addison Wesley Longman

IFSW *see* International Federation of Social Workers

Independent Living: 'SCIE's helping to turn hope into reality', press release 23 November 2004

Ingelby, E. (2010) *Applied Psychology for Social Work*, 2nd edn, Exeter: Learning Matters

Inskip, F. and Proctor, B. (1995) *Becoming a Supervisor*, Twickenham: Cascade

International Federation of Social Workers (IFSW) (2001) *The Definition of Social Work*, Berne, IFSW, retrieved on 1 August 2006, at: http://www.ifsw.org/en/p38000208.html

Irvine, Lord of Lairg, The Lord Chancellor (1997) *Who Decides? Making Decisions on Behalf of Mentally Incapacitated Adults*, The Lord Chancellor's Dept

Irvine, R., Kerridge, I., McPhee, J. and Freeman, S. (2002) 'Interprofessionalism and ethics: consensus or clash of cultures?', *Journal of Interprofessional Care*, 16: 199–210

Ixer, G. (1999) 'There's no such thing as reflection', *British Journal of Social Work*, 29: 513–27

Ixer, G. (2000) 'Assumptions about reflective practice', in J. Harris, L. Froggett and I. Paylor (eds) *Reclaiming Social Work: The Southport Papers Volume One*, 79–92, Birmingham: Venture Press

Jack, R. (1999) 'Institutions in community care' in R. Jack (ed.) *Residential versus Community Care*, Basingstoke: Macmillan.

Jack, R. and Mosley, S. (1997) 'The client group preferences of diploma of social work students: what are they, do they change during programmes and what variables affect them', *British Journal of Social Work*, 27 (6): 893–911

Jackson, M. (2001) *Weathering the Storms: Psychotherapy for Psychosis*, London: Karnac

James, A. and Prout, A. (eds) (1991) *Constructing and Reconstructing Childhood*, London: Falmer Press

Jamous, H. and Peloille, B. (1970) 'Professions or self perpetuating systems? Changes in the French University Hospital system', in J. A. Jackson (ed.) *Professions and Professionalization*, Cambridge: Cambridge University Press

Jansson, K., Coleman, K., Reed, E. and Kaiza, P. (2007) *Home Office statistical bulletin 02/07*, London: Home Office

Jardine, C. (2004) 'Children are taken away: but the system can't admit it's wrong', *Daily Telegraph*, 3 August 2004

Johns, C. (2004) *Becoming a Reflective Practitioner*, 2nd edn, Oxford: Blackwell

Johns, R. (2007) 'Who decides now? Protecting and empowering vulnerable adults who lose the capacity to make decisions for themselves', *British Journal of Social Work*, 37 (3): 557–64

Johns, R. (2010) 'Vulnerability, autonomy, capacity and consent', in Long, L-A., Roche, J. and Stringer, D. (eds) *The Law and Social Work: Contemporary Issues for Practice*, 2nd edn, Basingstoke: Palgrave Macmillan/Open University.

Johnson, B., Shulman, S. and Collins, W. (1991) 'Systemic patterns of parenting as reported by adolescents: developmental differences and implications for psychosocial outcomes', *Journal of Adolescent Research*, 6: 235–52

Johnson, M., Bengtson, V., Coleman, P. G. and Kirkwood, T. B. L. (eds) (2005) *The Cambridge Handbook of Age and Ageing*, Cambridge: Cambridge University Press

Johnson, S., Nolan, F., Pilling, S., Sandor, A., Hoult, J., McKenzie, N., White, I., Thompson, M. and Bebbington, P. (2005) 'Randomized controlled trial of acute mental health care by a crisis resolution team: the North Islington Crisis Study, *BMJ* (published 15 August 2005)

Johnson, T. (1972) *Professions and Power*, Basingstoke: Macmillan Education

Jones, C. (2001) 'Voices from the front line: state social workers and New Labour', *British Journal of Social Work*, 31 (4): 547–62

Jones, C. and Novak, T. (1993) 'Social work today', *British Journal of Social Work*, 23 (3): 195–212

Jones, C., Ferguson, I., Lavalette, M. and Penketh, L. (2004) 'Social work and social justice: a manifesto for a new engaged practice', retrieved on 1 August 2006 at: http://www.liv.ac.uk/sspsw/Social_Work_Manifesto.html

Jones, D., Rose, W. and Jeffery, C. (2006) *The Developing World of the Child*, London: Jessica Kingsley

Jordan, B. (1978) 'A comment on "Theory and practice in social work"', *British Journal of Social Work*, 8 (1): 23–5

Jordan, B. (1984) *Invitation to Social Work*, Oxford: Martin Robertson

Jordan, B. and Jordan, C. (2000) *Social Work and the Third Way*, London: Sage

Joseph, S. (2001) 'Behavioural and cognitive approaches', in *Psychopathology and Therapeutic Approaches: An Introduction*, Basingstoke: Palgrave

Joseph, S., Becker, F. and Becker, S. (2009) *Manual for Measures of Caring Activities and Outcomes for Children and Young People*, London: The Princess Royal Trust for Carers

Kadushin, A. (1976) *Supervision in Social Work*, New York: Columbia University Press

Kadushin, A. and Kadushin, G. (1997) *The Social Work Interview*, 4th edn, New York: Columbia University Press

Kahn, S., Zimmerman, G., Csikszentmihalyi, M. and Getzels, J. (1985) 'Relations between identity in young adulthood and intimacy at mid-life', *Journal of Personality and Social Psychology*, 9: 117–26

Kailes, J. (1985) 'Watch your language, please!', *Journal of Rehabilitation*, 51 (1): 68–9

Kanter, J. (ed.) (2004) *Face to Face with Children: The Life and Work of Claire Winnicott*, London: Karnac

Kaplowitz, P., Slora, E., Wasserman, R., Pedlow, S. and Herman-Giddens, M. (2001) 'Earlier onset of puberty in girls: relation to increased body mass index and race', *Pediatrics*, 108: 347–53

Kay, J. (1999) *Protecting Children: A Practical Guide*, London: Cassell

Keith, L. (2006) *Inquiry into the Death of Zahid Mubarak*, London: The Stationery Office

Keith, L. and Morris, J. (1995) 'Easy targets: a disability rights perspective on the "children as carers" debate', *Critical Social Policy*, 44/45: 36–57

Kelly, L. (1992) 'The connections between disability and child abuse: a review of the research evidence', *Child Abuse Review*, 1: 157–67

Kempe, T. and Kempe, C. (1978) *Child Abuse*, London: Fontana Books

Kennedy, E. (2004) *Child and Adolescent Psychotherapy: A Systematic Review of Psychoanalytic Approaches*, London: North Central Strategic Health Authority

Kennedy, R., Heymans, A. and Tischler, L. (1987) *The Family as In-Patient: Families and Adolescents at the Cassel Hospital*, London: Free Association Books

Kilbrandon Report (1964) *Children and Young Persons: Scotland*, Edinburgh: HMSO

Killick, J. and Allan, K. (2001) *Communication and the Care of People with Dementia*, Buckingham: Open University Press

King, P. (1998) 'The rise of juvenile delinquency in England, 1780–1840: changing patterns of perception and prosecution', *Past and Present*, 166: 116–66

Kirton, D. (2009) *Child Social Work Policy and Practice*. London: Sage

Kitwood, T. (1993) 'Towards a theory of dementia care: the interpersonal process', *Ageing and Society*, 13 (1): 51–67

Kitwood, T. (1997) *Dementia Reconsidered*, Buckingham: Open University Press

Klag, S., O'Callaghan, F. and Creed, P. (2005) The use of legal coercion in the treatment of substance abusers: an overview and critical analysis of thirty years of research', *Substance Use & Misuse*, 40: 1777–95

Knott, C. and Scragg, T. (2101) *Reflective Practice in Social Work*, 2nd edn, Exeter: Learning Matters

Kohlberg, L. (1969) 'Moral stages and moralisation', in Linkons, T. (ed.) *Moral Development and Behaviour*, New York: Holt, Rinehart and Winston

Kolb, D. A. (1984) *Experiential Learning: Experience as the Source of Learning and Development*, Englewood Cliffs, NJ: Prentice Hall

Koprowska, J. (2005) *Communication and Inter-personal Skills in Social Work*, Exeter: Learning Matters

Koprowska, J. (2007) 'Communication skills in social work', in M. Lymbery and K. Postle (eds) *Social Work: A Companion for Learning*, pp. 123–33, London: Sage

Kroger, J. (2000) *Identity Development: Adolescence Through Adulthood*, London: Sage

Kroll, B. and Taylor, A. (2000) 'Invisible children? Parental substance abuse and child protection: dilemmas for practice', *Probation Journal*, 47 (2): 91–100

Kroll, B. and Taylor, A. (2003) *Parental Substance Abuse and Child Welfare*, London: Jessica Kingsley

Kübler-Ross, E. (2009) *On Death and Dying: What the dying have to teach doctors, nurses, clergy and their own families* (40th anniversary publication – first published 1969), Abingdon, Routledge

Laing, R. D. (1967) *The Politics of Experience and the Bird of Paradise*, Harmondsworth: Penguin

Laird, S. E. (2010) *Practical Social Work Law*, Harlow: Pearson.

Laming Report (2003) *The Victoria Climbié Inquiry: Report of an Inquiry by Lord Laming*. Cmnd 5730, London: TSO. Available online at: www.victoira-climbie-inquiry.org.uk/finreporthtm

Laming, Lord, (2009) *The Protection of Children in England: A Progress Report*, London: TSO

Landreth, G. (1991) *Play Therapy: The Art of the Relationship*, Muncie, IN: Accelerated Development

Larson, M. S. (1977) *The Rise of Professionalism: A Sociological Analysis*, Berkeley, CA: University of California Press

Law Commission (2010) *Adult Social Care: A Consultation Paper*, London: Law Commission.

Lawler, J. (2007) 'Leadership in social work: a case of caveat emptor?', *British Journal of Social Work*, 37 (1): 123–41

Layard, R. (2006) *Happiness – Lessons from a New Science*, London: Penguin

Le Riche, P. and Tanner, K. (1998) (eds) *Observation and its Application to Social Work: Rather Like Breathing*, London: Jessica Kingsley

Leadbeater, C. (2004) *Personalisation Through Participation: A New Script for Public Services*, London: Demos

Leadbeater, C., Bartlett, J. and Gallagher, N. (2008) *Making it Personal*, London: Demos

Leader, D. (2009) *The New Black – Mourning, Melancholia and Depression*, London: Penguin

Leathard, A. (ed.) (2003) *Interprofessional Collaboration: From Policy to Practice in Health and Social Care*, Hove: Brunner-Routledge

Leece, D. and Leece, J. (2006) 'Direct payments: creating a two-tiered system in social care?', *British Journal of Social Work*, 36 (8): 1379–93

Leece, J. (2008) 'Paying the piper and calling the tune: power and the direct payment relationship', *British Journal of Social Work* Advance Access published 17 June 2008, doi:10.1093/bjsw/bcn085

Leece, J. and Bornat, J. (eds) (2006) *Developments in Direct Payments*, Bristol: Policy Press

Lefevre, M. (2008) *Direct Work: Social work with children and young people in care*. London: BAAF

Lefevre, M. (2009a) 'Knowing, being and doing: core qualities and skills for working with children and young people in care', in Luckock, B. and Lefevre, M. (eds) *Direct Work: Social Work with Children and Young People in Care*, pp. 21–36, London: BAAF

Lefevre, M. (2009b) 'Communicating and engaging with children and young people in care through play and the creative arts', in Luckock, B. and Lefevre, M. (eds) *Direct Work: Social Work with Children and Young People in Care*, pp. 130–150, London: BAAF

Leslie, S. and Pritchard, J. (2009) 'A review of relevant legislation in adult protection', in J. Pritchard (ed.) *Good Practice in the Law and Safeguarding Adults*, London, Jessica Kingsley

Levin, J. (2009). *Epidemic of Acute HCV Among MSM in Europe and New York City. Conference on Retroviruses and Opportunistic Infections Montreal, Canada*. [Online]. Available at: http://www.natap.org/2009/CROI/croi_62.htm (accessed 21 January 2010)

Levinson, D. (1978) *The Seasons of a Man's Life*, New York: Knopf

Levinson, D. and Levinson, J. (1996) *The Seasons of a Woman's Life*, New York: Knopf

Levy, A. and Kahan, B. (1991) *The Pindown Experience and the Protection of Children: Report of the Staffordshire Child Care Inquiry*, Stafford: Staffordshire County Council

Lewis, C. S. (2001) *A Grief Observed*, New York: Harper

Lewis, J. (1995) *The Voluntary Sector, the State and Social Work in Britain*, Aldershot: Edward Elgar

Lewis, J. (2001) 'Older people and the health-social care boundary in the UK: half a century of hidden policy conflict', *Social Policy and Administration* 35 (4): 343–59

Lewis, J. (2004) 'Documents in qualitative research', in S. Becker and A. Bryman (eds) *Understanding Research for Social Policy and Practice*, pp. 290–4, Bristol: The Policy Press

Lewis, J. and Glennerster, H. (1996) *Implementing the New Community Care*, Buckingham: Open University Press

Lindeman, E. (1944) 'Symptomatology and management of acute grief', *American Journal of Psychiatry*, 101

Lindon, J. (2010) *Understanding Child Development: Linking theory and practice*. London: Hodder Arnold

Lindow, V. (1995) 'Power and rights: the psychiatric system survivor movement', in R. Jack (ed.) *Empowerment in Community Care*, London: Chapman & Hall

Lipsky, M. (1979) *Street Level Bureaucracy*, New York: Russell Sage Foundation

Lister, R. (2001) 'New Labour: a study in ambiguity from a position of ambivalence', *Critical Social Policy*, 21 (4): 425–47

Littlechild, B. (ed.) (2001) *Appropriate Adults and Appropriate Adult Schemes: Service user, Provider and police perspectives,* Venture Press: Birmingham

Littlechild, B. (1995) 'The role of the social worker as appropriate adult under the Police and Criminal Evidence Act 1984: problems, possibilities, and the development of best practice', *Practice*, 7 (2): 35–44

Littlewood, R. and Lipsedge, M. (1997) *Aliens and Alienists*, London: Routledge

Litwin, H. (1994) 'The professional standing of social work with elderly persons among social work trainees', *British Journal of Social Work*, 24 (1): 53–69

Lloyd, L. (2006) 'A caring profession? The ethics of care and social work with older people', *British Journal of Social Work*, 36 (7): 1171–86

Lloyd, M. (2002) 'Care management', in R. Adams, L. Dominelli and M. Payne (eds) *Critical Practice in Social Work*, Basingstoke: Palgrave

Lloyd, M. and Taylor, C. (1995) 'From Hollis to the Orange Book: developing an holistic model of social work assessment in the 1990s', in *British Journal of Social Work*, 25: 691–710

London Borough of Bexley (1982) *Report of the Panel of Inquiry into the Death of Lucie Gates*, London: London Borough of Bexley

London Borough of Brent (1985) *A Child in Trust: The Report of the Panel of Enquiry into the Circumstances Surrounding the Death of Jasmine Beckford*, London: London Borough of Brent

London Borough of Greenwich (1987) *A Child in Mind: Protection of Children in a Responsible Society. The Report of the Commission of Enquiry into the Circumstances Surrounding the Death of Kimberley Carlile*, London: London Borough of Greenwich

London Borough of Lambeth (1987) *Whose Child? The Report of the Public Enquiry into the Death of Tyra Henry*, London: London Borough of Lambeth

Long, L. A., Roche, J. and Stringer, D. (eds) (2010) *The Law and Social Work: Contemporary Issues for Practice*, 2nd edn, Basingstoke: Palgrave Macmillan

Longshore, D., Prendergast, M. and Farabee, D. (2004) 'Coerced treatment for drug-using criminal offenders', in P. Bean and T. Nemitz (eds) (2004) *Drug Treatment: What Works?* London: Routledge

López Viets, V., Walker, D. D. and Miller, W. R. (eds) (2002) *What is Motivation to Change? A Scientific Analysis*, Chichester: John Wiley & Sons.

Loughran, H., Hohman, M. and Finnegan, D. (2010) 'Predictors of role adequacy of social workers working with substance-using clients', *British Journal of Social Work*, 40 (1): 239–56

Love, A., Cooke, P. and Taylor, P. (2003) 'The criminal justice system and disabled children', in *It Doesn't Happen to Disabled Children*, London: NSPCC

Lovell, E. (2006) 'Just justice: a study into young black people's experience of the youth justice system', *Childright*, 227: 20–23

Lovell, E. and Wilson, D. (2006) 'Conclusions and discussion', in D. Wilson and G. Rees (eds) *Just Justice*, pp. 46–61, London: The Children's Society

Lowe, M. and Murch, M. (2002) *The Plan for the Child: Adoption and Long-Term Fostering*, London: BAAF

Loxley, A. (1997) *Collaboration in Health and Welfare*, London: Jessica Kingsley

Luckock, B. (2007) 'Safeguarding children and integrated children's services', in K. Wilson and A. James (eds) *The Child Protection Handbook*, 3rd edn, Edinburgh: Elsevier/Bailliere

Luckock, B., Lefevre, M., Orr, D., Jones, M. and Tanner, K. (2006) *Teaching, Learning and Assessing Communication Skills with Children and Young People in Social Work Education*, London: SCIE

Luckock, B. and Lefrevre, M. (eds) (2008) *Direct Work: Social Work with Children and Young People in Care*, London: BAAF

Lymbery, M. (2001) 'Social work at the crossroads', *British Journal of Social Work*, 31 (3): 369–84

Lymbery, M. (2004) 'Managerialism and care management practice', in M. Lymbery and S. Butler (eds) *Social Work Ideals and Practice Realities*, Basingstoke: Palgrave

Lymbery, M. (2005) *Social Work with Older People: Context, Policy and Practice*, London: Sage

Lymbery, M. (2006) 'United we stand? Partnership working in health and social care and the role of social work in services for older people', *British Journal of Social Work*, 37 (7): 1119–34

Lymbery, M. (2007) 'Social work in its organisational context', in M. Lymbery and K. Postle (eds) *Social Work: A Companion to Learning*, London: Sage

Lymbery, M. (2010) 'A new vision for adult social care? Continuities and change in the care of older people', *Critical Social Policy*, 30 (1): 5–26

Lymbery, M. and Butler, S. (2004) Social work ideals and practice realities: an introduction', in M. Lymbery and S. Butler (eds) *Social Work Ideals and Practice Realities*, Basingstoke: Macmillan

Lymbery M. and Millward, A. (2009) 'Partnership working', in R. Adams, L. Dominelli and M. Payne (eds) (2009) *Practising Social Work in a Complex World*, Basingstoke: Palgrave Macmillan

Lymbery, M. and Postle, K. (2010) 'Social work in the context of adult social care in England and the resultant implications for social work education', *British Journal of Social Work* Advance Access published online 9 April 2010, doi:10.1093/bjsw/bcq045

Lymbery, M., Lawson, J., MacCallum, H., McCoy, P., Pidgeon, J. and Ward, K. (2007) 'The social work role with older people', *Practice*, 19 (2): 97–113

Maccoby, E. (1990) 'Gender and relationships', *American Psychologist*, 45: 513–20

Maccoby, E. and Martin, J. (1983) 'Socialization in the context of the family: parent–child interaction', in Hetherington, E. (ed.) *Handbook of Child Psychology: Socialisation, Personality and Social Development*, Vol. 4, pp. 1–102, New York: Wiley

Macdonald, G. (2002) 'The evidence-based perspective', in M. Davies (ed.) *The Blackwell Companion to Social Work*, pp. 424–30, Oxford: Blackwell Publishing

Mack, H. (2009) 'Exploring the responses of health and social care professionals to people living with Hepatitis C', Undertaking a PhD in Substance Misuse Symposium, Oxford Brookes University, 8 July 2009

Mackay, K. (2008) 'The Scottish adult support and protection legal framework', *Journal of Adult Protection*, 10 (4): 25–36

MacPherson, Sir William of Cluny (1999) *The Stephen Lawrence Inquiry*, London: HMSO

Maddux, J. F. (1988) 'Clinical experience with civil commitment', in C. Leukefeld and F. Tims (eds) *Compulsory Treatment of Drug Abuse: Research and Clinical Practice*, NIDA Research Monograph 86, DHHS Publication Number ADM 89-1578, Washington, DC: US Government Press

Magarey, S. (2002) 'The invention of juvenile delinquency in early nineteenth century England', in J. Muncie, G. Hughes and E. McLaughlin (eds) *Youth Justice: Critical Readings*, pp. 115–22, London: Sage

Magowan, P. (2004) 'The impact of disability on women's experiences of domestic abuse: an empirical study into disabled women's experiences of, and responses to domestic abuse', ESRC/PhD research, University of Nottingham

Maguraz, S. (1994) 'Social workers should be more involved in substance abuse treatment', *Health and Social Work* 19 (1): 3–5

Maher, J. and Green, H. (2002) *Carers 2000*, London: The Stationery Office

Main, M. (1995) 'Attachment: overview with implications for clinical work', in S. Goldberg, R. Muir and J. Kerr (eds) *Attachment Theory: Social, Developmental and Clinical Perspectives*, pp. 407–74, Hillsdale, NJ: Analytic Press

Main, M. and Solomon, J. (1986) 'Discovery of an insecure disorganized/disoriented attachment pattern: procedures, findings and implications for the classification of behaviour', in T. Braselton and M. Yogman (eds) *Affective Development in Infancy*, Norwood, NJ: Ablex

Malin, N., Race, D. and Jones, G. (1980) *Services for the Mentally Handicapped*, London: Croom Helm

Malin, V. (2000) 'From continuous to continuing long-term care', in G. Bradley and J. Manthorpe (eds) *Working on the Fault Line: Social Work and Health Services*, Birmingham: Venture Press/Social Work Research Association

Mandelstam, M. (2005) *Community Care Practice and the Law*, 3rd edn, London: Jessica Kingsley

Manktelow, R. and Lewis, C. (2005) 'A study of the personality attributes of applicants for postgraduate social work training', *Social Work Education*, 24 (3): 297–309

Mansell, Beadle-Brown, J., Cambridge, P., Milne, A. And Whelton, B. (2009) 'Adult protection: incidence of referrals, nature and risk factors in two English local authorities', *Journal of Social Work*, 9 (1): 21–38

Manthorpe, J., Rapaport, J. and Stanley, N. (2008) 'The Mental Capacity Act and its influence on social work practice: debate and synthesis', *Practice*, 20 (3): 151–62

Manthorpe, J., Rapaport, J. and Stanley, N. (2009a) 'Expertise and experience: people with experiences of using services and carers' views of the Mental Capacity Act 2005', *British Journal of Social Work*, 39 (5): 884–90

Manthorpe, J., Rapaport, J., Harris, J. and Samsi, K. (2009b) 'Realising the safeguarding potential of the Mental Capacity Act 2005: early reports from adult safeguarding staff', *Journal of Adult Protection*, 11 (2): 13–24

Manthorpe, J., Stevens, M., Rapaport., J., Harris, J., Jacobs, S., Challis, D., Netten, A., Knapp, M., Wilberforce, M. and Glendinning, C. (2008) 'Safeguarding and system change: early perceptions of the implications for adult protection services of the English individual budgets pilot – a qualitative study', *British Journal of Social Work* Advance Access published online on 26 March 2008, doi:10.1093/bjsw/bcn028

Marchant, R. and Page, M. (2003) 'Child protection practice with disabled children', in *It Doesn't Happen to Disabled Children*, London: NSPCC

Marcia, J. (1980) 'Identity in adolescence', in J. Adelson, (ed.) *Handbook of Adolescent Psychology*, pp. 159–87, New York: Wiley

Marcia, J., Waterman, A., Matteson, D., Archer, S. and Orlofsky, J. (1993) *Ego Identity: A Handbook for Psychosocial Research*, New York: Springer-Verlag

Marcoen, A., Coleman, P. G. and O'Hanlon, A. (2007) 'Psychological ageing', in J. Bond, S. Peace, F. Dittmann-Kohli and G. Westerhof (eds) *Ageing in Society: European Perspectives on Gerontology*, 3rd edn, London: Sage/Open University

Marlowe, D. B., Kirby, K. C., Bonieskie, L. M., Glass, D. J., Dodd, L. D., Husband, S. D., Platt, J. J. and Festinger, D. S. (1996) 'Assessment of coercive and noncoercive pressures to enter drug abuse treatment', *Drug and Alcohol Dependence*, 42 (2): 77–84

Marner, T. (2000) *Letters to Children in Family Therapy*, London: Jessica Kingsley

Marsh, I. and Keating, K. (2006) *Sociology: Making Sense of Society*, Harlow: Pearson Education

Marsh, P. (2006) 'Promoting children's welfare by interprofessional practice and learning in social work and primary care', *Social Work Education*, 25 (2): 148–60

Marsh, P. and Crow, G. (1998) *Family Group Conferences in Child Welfare*, Oxford: Blackwell

Marsh, P. and Doel, M. (2005) *The Task-Centred Book*, London: Routledge

Marsh, P. and Triseliotis, J. (1996) *Ready for Practice?* Aldershot: Avebury

Bibliography

Martinson, R. (1974) 'What works? Questions and answers about prison reform', in *The Public Interest*, 35

Martyn, H. (2000) 'Introduction', in H. Martyn (ed.) *Developing Reflective Practice: Making Sense of Social Work in a World of Change*, pp. 2–9, Bristol: Polity Press

Mattinson, J. (1992) *The Reflective Process in Social Work Supervision*, 2nd edn, London: Tavistock Institute of Marital Studies

Mattinson, J. and Sinclair, I. (1979) *Mate and Stalemate*, Oxford: Basil Blackwell

Maugham, B. and Pickles, A. (1990) 'Adopted and illegitimate children grown up', in L. Robins and M. Rutter (eds) *Straight and Devious Pathways from Childhood to Adulthood*, Cambridge: Cambridge University Press

Maugham, B., Collishaw, S. and Pickles, A. (1998) 'School achievement and adult qualifications among adoptees: a longitudinal study', *Journal of Child Psychiatry and Psychology*, 39: 669–85

Mayer, J. E. and Timms, N. (1970) *The Client Speaks: Working Class Impressions of Casework*, London: Routledge & Kegan Paul

McCluskey, U. (2003) 'Theme focussed family therapy', in M. Bell and K. Wilson (eds) *Working with Families: The Practitioners' Handbook*, London: Palgrave Macmillan

McCluskey, U. (2005) *To be Met as a Person: The Dynamics of Attachment in Professional Encounters*, London: Karnac

McCullers, C. (1952) 'The member of the wedding', in *The Ballad of the Sad Café*, London: Cresset Press

McDermott, P. (2002) 'Flavour of the month: users in service provision', *Druglink* 17 (1): 18–21

McDonald, A. (2006) *Understanding Community Care*, 2nd edn, Basingstoke: Palgrave

McDonald, A. (2010) *Social Work with Older People*, Cambridge: Polity

McDonald, T., Allen, R., Westerfelt, A. and Piliavin, I. (1996) *Assessing the Long-Term Effects of Foster Care*, Washington, DC: Child Welfare League of America

McKenzie K., Samele, C., Van Horn, E., Tattan, T., Van Os, J. and Murray, R. (2001) 'Comparison of the outcome and treatment of psychosis in people of Caribbean origin living in the UK and British whites', *British Journal of Psychiatry*, 178: 160–5

McLaughlin, H. (2009) 'What's in a Name: "Client", "Patient", "Customer", "Consumer", "Expert by Experience", "Service User" – What's Next?' *British Journal of Social Work*, 39 (6): 1101–17

McLaughlin, K. (2008) *Social Work, Politics and Society: From radicalism to orthodoxy*, Bristol: Policy Press

McMahon, L. and Ward, A. (1998) 'Helping and the personal response: intuition is not enough', in A. Ward and L. McMahon (eds) *Intuition is not Enough: Matching Learning with Practice in Therapeutic Child Care*, pp. 28–39, London: Routledge

McMahon, L. and Ward, A. (eds) (2001) *Helping Families in Family Centres: Working at Therapeutic Practice*, London: Jessica Kingsley

Mcmurran, M. (ed.) (2002) *Motivating Offenders to Change: Selection Criterion or Treatment Need?*, Chichester: John Wiley & Sons

McNeish, D., Newman, T. and Roberts, H. (eds) (2002) *What Works for Children?*, Buckingham: Open University Press

Meadows, S. (1986) *Understanding Child Development*, London: Routledge

Means, R. and Smith, R. (1998) *From Poor Law to Community Care*, 2nd edn, Bristol: Policy Press

Means, R., Richards, S. and Smith, R. (2003) *Community Care: Policy and Practice*, 3rd edn, Basingstoke: Palgrave.

Measham, F. (2002) '"Doing gender" – "doing drugs": conceptualising the gendering of drugs cultures', *Contemporary Drug Problems*, 29 (2): 1–44

Measham, F. and Paylor, I. (2009) 'Legal and illicit drugs', in Adams, R., Dominelli, L., and Payne, M. (eds) *Practising Social Work in a Complex World*, Basingstoke: Palgrave

Meier, P. S., Donmall, M. C., Barrowclough, C., Mcelduff, P. and Heller, R. F. (2005) 'Predicting the early therapeutic alliance in the treatment of drug misuse', *Addiction*, 100: 500–11

Mental Health Act Commission (1997) *Seventh Biennial Report*, London: The Stationery Office

Mental Health Foundation (2002) *The Mental Health Needs of Young People with Emotional and Behavioural Difficulties: Bright Futures: Working with vulnerable young people*, London: Mental Health Foundation

Menzies-Lyth, I. (1988a) *Containing Anxiety in Institutions: Selected Essays Volume One*, London: Free Association Books

Menzies-Lyth, I. (1988b) 'The functioning of social systems as a defence against anxiety', in *Containing Anxiety in Institutions, Vol. 1, Selected Essays*, pp. 43–88, London: Free Association Books

Metropolitan Police Authority (2009) *MPA response to the London Safeguarding Children's Board's 'Safeguarding children affected by gang activity and/or serious youth violence' draft consultation paper*, Report 13, 5 February 2009, available at http://www.mpa.gov.uk/committees/sop/2009/090205/13/#fn003-back

Metropolitan Police Service (2005) MPS recorded crime 12 months October 2005, available at http://www.london.gov.uk/gangs/docs/guns-weapons-report.pdf

Middleton, L. (1992) 'Children first: working with children and disability', Birmingham: Venture Press

Middleton, L. (1997) *The Art of Assessment*, Birmingham: Venture Press

Miers, M. (2010) 'Professional boundaries and interprofessional working', in K. Pollard, J. Thomas and M. Miers (eds) *Understanding Interprofessional Working in Health and Social Care*, Basingstoke: Palgrave Macmillan

Miles, G. (2002) 'Commentary (12 years on) on "The contribution of child observation training to professional development in social work" by Judith Trowell and Gillian Miles', *Journal of Social Work Practice*, 18 (1): 61–4

Millan, B. (2001), *New Directions: Report of the Review of the Mental Health (Scotland) Act 1984*, Edinburgh: Scottish Executive

Miller, D. (2003) 'Disabled children and abuse', in *It Doesn't Happen to Disabled Children*', London: NSPCC

Miller, W. (1983) 'Motivational interviewing with problem drinkers', *Behavioural Psychotherapy*, 11: 441–8

Miller, W. R. (1985) 'Motivation for treatment: A review with special emphasis on alcoholism', *Psychological Bulletin*, 98: 84–107

Miller, W. R. and Rollnick, S. (2002) *Motivational Interviewing: Preparing People to Change Addictive Behaviour*, London: Guilford Press

Millington, M. and Leierer, S. (1996) 'A socially desirable response to the politically incorrect use of disability labels', in *Rehabilitation Counselling Bulletin* 39 (4): 276–82

Milne, A., Hatzidimitriadou, E., Chryssanthopoulou, C. and Owen, T. (2001) *Caring in Later Life: Reviewing the Role of Older Carers*, London: Help the Aged

Milner, J. (2008) 'Solution-focused approaches to caring for children whose behaviour is sexually harmful', *Adoption and Fostering* 32 (4): 42–50

Milner, J. and O'Byrne, P. (2000) *Assessment in Social Work*, 2nd edn, Basingstoke: Macmillan

Milner, J. and O'Byrne, P. (2002) 'Assessment and planning', in R. Adams, L. Dominelli and M. Payne (eds) *Critical Practice in Social Work*, pp. 261–68, Basingstoke: Palgrave Macmillan

Minhas, A. (2009) 'On the receiving end: reflections from a service user', in R. Carnwell and J. Buchanan (eds) (2009) *Effective Practice in Health, Social Care and Criminal Justice: A Partnership Approach*, Buckingham: Open University Press

Mitchell, W. and Sloper, P. (2002) *Quality Services for Disabled Children*, Research Works no. 2002-02, Research Findings from the Social Policy Research Unit, University of York

Moore, M. (1994) 'Common characteristics in the drawings of ritually abused children and adults', in V. Sinason (ed.) *Treating Survivors of Satanist Abuse*, London: Routledge

Moore, T. and Wilkinson, T. (2005) *Youth Court Guide*, Haywards Heath: Tottel Publishing

Moran, P., Ghate, D., van de Merwe, A. (2004) *What Works in Parenting Support? A Review of the International Evidence*, Policy Research Bureau, Nottingham: DfES

Morgan, C., Mallett, R., Hutchison, G., Bagalkote, H., Morgan, K., Fearon, P., Dazzan, P., Boydell, J., McKenzie, K., Harrison, G., Murray, R., Jones, P., Craig, T. and Leff, J. (2005) 'Pathways to care and ethnicity. 1: Sample characteristics and compulsory admission', *British Journal of Psychiatry*, 186: 281–9

Morgan, H. (1998) 'A potential for partnership? Consulting with users of mental health services', in A. Foster and V. Z. Roberts (eds) *Managing Mental Health in the Community: Chaos and Containment*, pp. 177–87, London: Routledge

Morgan, J. (2007) 'Giving up the culture of blame': Risk assessment and risk management in psychiatric practice-briefing document to Royal College of Psychiatrists', London: Royal College of Psychiatrists

Morison, S., Johnston, J. and Stevenson, M. (2010) 'Preparing students for interprofessional practice: exploring the intra-personal dimension', *Journal of Interprofessional Care* 24 (4): 412–21

Morris, A. and McIsaac, M. (1978) *Juvenile Justice?* London: Heinemann

Morris, A., Giller, H., Szwed, E. and Geach, H. (1980) *Justice for Children*, London: Macmillan

Morris, J. (1991) *Pride Against Prejudice*, London: Women's Press

Morris, J. (1993) *Independent Lives*, Basingstoke: Macmillan

Morris, J. (2002) *A Lot to Say! A Guide for Social Workers, Personal Advisors and Others Working with Disabled Children and Young People with Communication Impairments*, London: Scope

Morrison, T. (1997) 'Learning, training and change in child protection work: towards reflective organisations', *Social Work Education*, 16 (2): 20–43

Morrison, T. (2007) 'Emotional intelligence, emotion and social work: context, characteristics, complications and contribution', *British Journal of Social Work*, 37: 245–63

Mowat, C. L. (1961) *The Charity Organisation Society*, London: Methuen

Mullaly, R. (1993) *Structural Social Work: Ideology, Theory, and Practice*, Toronto: McClelland & Stewart

Muncie, J. (2002) 'Failure never matters: detention centres and the politics of deterrence', in Muncie, J., Hughes, G. and McLaughlin, E. (eds) *Youth Justice: Critical Readings*, pp. 332–44, London: Sage

Muncie, J. and Goldson, B. (2006) 'England and Wales: The new correctionalism', in Muncie, J. and Goldson, B. (eds) *Comparative Youth Justice*, pp. 34–47, London: Sage

Munro, E. (1996) 'Avoidable and unavoidable mistakes in child protection social work', *British Journal of Social Work* 26: 793–808

Munro, E. (2000) 'Defending professional social work practice', in J. Harris, L. Froggett and I. Paylor (eds) *Reclaiming Social Work: The Southport Papers Volume One*, pp. 1–10, Birmingham: Venture Press

Munro, E. (2001) 'Empowering looked after children', in *Child and Family Social Work*, 6 (1): 129–37

Munro, E. (2002) *Effective Child Protection*, London: Sage

Munro E. (2004) 'The impact of audit on social work practice', *British Journal of Social Work*, 34 (8): 1075–95

Munro, E. and Parton, N. (2007) 'How far is England in the process of introducing a mandatory reporting system?', *Child Abuse Review*, 16 (1): 5–16

Munro, E. (2008) *Effective Child Protection*, London, Sage.

Murgatroyd, S. and Woolfe, R. (1982) *Coping with Crisis: Understanding and Helping Children in Need*, London: Harper and Rowe

Murphy, E., Dingwall, R., Greatbatch, D., Parker, S. and Watson, P. (1998) 'Qualitative research methods in health technology assessment: a review of the literature', *Health Technology Assessment*, 2: 4

Murray, T. (2005) *Retaining Clients in Drug Treatment*, London: NTA

NACRO (2006) *Youth Crime Briefing, September 2006. Effective practice with children and young people who offend – Part 1*, London: NACRO

Nash, C. (2000) 'Applying reflective practice', in C. Davies, L. Finlay and A. Bullman (eds) *Changing Practice in Health and Social Care*, pp. 73–80, London: Sage

Nathan, J. (2002) 'The advanced practitioner: beyond reflective practice', *The Journal of Practice Teaching*, 4 (2): 59–83

National Statistics and DfES (2004) *Children Looked After by Local Authorities, Year Ending March 31st*, London: DfES

National Treatment Agency (2005) *Retaining Clients in Drug Treatment*, London: NTA

National Treatment Agency (2006) *NTA Guidance for Local Partnerships on User and Carer Involvement*, London: NTA

National Treatment Agency for Substance Misuse (2008) *Good Practice in Harm Reduction*, http://www.nta.nhs.uk/publications/documents/nta_good_practice_in_harm_reduction_1108.pdf (accessed 28.02.09)

National Working Group on Child Protection and Disability (2003) *It doesn't happen to disabled children: child protection and disabled children*, London: NSPCC

Neale, J. (2006) 'Feel good factor', *Druglink* 21 (1): 20–21

Neil, E., Beek, M. and Schofield, G. (2003) 'Thinking about and managing contact in permanent placements: the differences and similarities between adoptive parents and foster carers', *Clinical Child Psychology and Psychiatry*, 8 (3): 401–18

Network for Psycho-Social Policy and Practice (2002) *Network for Psycho-Social Policy and Practice: Mission Statement*, unpublished

Neugarten, B. (1975) 'The future of the young-old', *The Gerontologist*, 15: 4–9

Newman, J. (2001) *Modernising Governance: New Labour, Policy and Society*, London: Sage

Newman, J., Glendinning, C. and Hughes, M. (2008) 'Beyond modernisation? Social care and the transformation of welfare governance', *Journal of Social Policy*, 37 (4): 531–57

Newman, T. (2002) ' "Young carers" and disabled parents: time for a change of direction?', *Disability and Society*, 17 (6): 613–25

NHS Confederation (2007) *Time and Trouble: Towards Proper and Compassionate Mental Healthcare*, London: NHS Confederation

Nice, V. (2005) 'Child-centred practice', unpublished doctoral thesis, University of East Anglia

Nolan, M., Davies, S. and Grant, G. (2001) 'Quality of life, quality of care', in M. Nolan, S. Davies and G. Grant (eds) *Working with Older People and their Carers*, Buckingham: Open University Press

Nolan, M., Grant, G. and Keady, M. (1996) *Understanding Family Care*, Buckingham: Open University Press

NSPCC (2003) *It Doesn't Happen to Disabled Children: Child protection and disabled children*, National Working Group on Child Protection and Disability, London: NSPCC

NTA *see* National Treatment Agency

Nursten, J. (1997) 'The end as a means to growth – in the social work relationship', *Journal of Social Work Practice*, 11 (2): 73–80

O'Brian, C. and Lau, L. S. W. (1995) 'Defining child abuse in Hong Kong', *Child Abuse Review*, 4: 38–46

O'Hagan, K. (1986) *Crisis Intervention in Social Services*, Basingstoke: Macmillan

O'Hagan, K. (1994) 'Crisis intervention: changing perspectives', in C. Harvey and T. Philpott (eds) *Practising Social Work*, pp. 138–56, London: Routledge

O'Hare, T. (1996) 'Court-ordered versus voluntary clients: problems differences and readiness for change', *Social Work* 41 (4): 417–22

Office for National Statistics (ONS) (2003) *Census 2001 Data* [Tables SO25], London: ONS

Office for National Statistics (ONS) (2007) *Regional Trends 39: Population & Migration Highlights*, accessed on 11 September 2007 at: http://www.statistics.gov.uk/cci/nugget.asp?id=1433

Office for National Statistics (ONS) (2009) *Statistical Bulletin 2008* accessed on 9 July 2010 at http://www.statistics.gov.uk/pdfdir/births1209.pdf

Oliver, B. And Keeping, C. (2010) 'Individual and professional identity', in K. Pollard, J. Thomas and M. Miers (eds) *Understanding Interprofessional Working in Health and Social Care*, Basingstoke: Palgrave Macmillan

Oliver, M. (1990) *The Politics of Disablement*, London: Macmillan Press

Oliver, M. (1996) *Understanding Disability: From Theory to Practice*, London: Macmillan Press

Oliver, M. (2004) 'If I had a hammer: the social model in action', in J. Swain, S. French, C. Barnes and C. Thomas (eds) *Disabling Barriers: Enabling Environments*, 2nd edn, London: Sage

Oliver, M. and Sapey, B. (2006) *Social Work with Disabled People*, 3rd edn, Basingstoke: Palgrave Macmillan

Olsen, R. (1996) 'Young carers: challenging the facts and politics of research into children and caring', *Disability and Society*, 11 (1): 41–5

Olsen, R. and Parker, G. (1997) 'A response to Aldridge and Becker: "Disability rights and the denial of young carers: the dangers of zero-sum arguments"', *Critical Social Policy*, 50: 125–33

ONS *see* Office of National Statistics

Otton Report (1974) *Report of the Working Party on Social Work Support for the Health Service*, London: HMSO

Packman, J. (1981) *The Child's Generation*, Oxford: Basil Blackwell/Martin Robertson

Packman, J. and Hall, C. (1998) *From Care to Accommodation: Support, Protection and Control in Child Care Services*, London: The Stationery Office

Parad, H. (ed.) *Crisis Intervention: Selected Readings*, New York: Columbia University Press

Parad, H. and Caplan, G. (1960) 'A framework for studying families in crisis', *Social Casework*, 5: 3–15

Parker, G., Arksey, H. and Harden, M. (2010) *Scoping Review on Carers Research*, York: Social Policy Research Unit

Parker, J. (2004) *Effective Practice Learning in Social Work*, Exeter: Learning Matters

Parker, J. (2007) 'The process of social work: assessment, planning, intervention and review', in M. Lymbery and K. Postle (eds) *Social Work: A Companion to Learning*, pp. 111–22, London: Sage

Parker, J. and Bradley, G. (2003) *Social Work Practice: Assessment, Planning, Intervention and Review*, Exeter: Learning Matters

Parry-Jones, B. and Soulsby, J. (2001) 'Needs-led assessment: the challenges and the reality', *Health and Social Care in the Community*, 9 (6): 414–28

Partington, M. (20063) *Introduction to the English Legal System*, 3rd edn, Oxford: Oxford University Press

Parton, N. (1985) *The Politics of Child Abuse*, Basingstoke: Palgrave Macmillan

Parton, N. (1991) *Governing the Family: Child Care, Child Protection and the State*, London: Macmillan

Parton, N. (1994a) 'The nature of social work under conditions of postmodernity', *Social Work and Social Sciences Review*, 5 (2): 93–112

Parton, N. (1994b) 'Problematics of government, (post) modernity and social work', *British Journal of Social Work* 24: 9–32

Parton, N. (1998a) 'Child protection and family support: possible future directions for social work', 18th Annual Lecture, Department of Social Work Studies, University of Southampton

Parton, N. (1998b) 'Risk, advanced liberalism and child welfare: the need to rediscover uncertainty and ambiguity', *British Journal of Social Work*, 30 (4): 449–64

Parton, N. (2000) 'Some thoughts on the relationship between theory and practice in and for social work', *British Journal of Social Work*, 30 (4): 449–63

Parton, N. (2001) 'Risk and professional judgement', in L-A. Cull and J. Roche (eds), *The Law and Social Work*, Basingstoke: Palgrave Macmillan

Parton, N. (2004) 'From Maria Colwell to Victoria Climbié: reflections on public inquiries into child abuse a generation apart', *Child Abuse Review*, 13 (2): 80–94.

Parton, N. (2006) *Safeguarding Childhood: Early Intervention and Surveillance in a Late Modern Society*, Basingstoke: Palgrave Macmillan

Parton, N. (2007) 'Safeguarding children: a sociohistorical analysis', in K. Wilson and A. James *The Child Protection Handbook*, 3rd edn, Edinburgh: Elsevier/Balliere Tindall

Parton, N. and Frost, N. (2009) *Understanding Children's Social Care: Politics, Policy and Practic*, London, Sage

Parton, N. and O'Byrne, P. (2000) *Constructive Social Work: Towards a New Practice*, Basingstoke: Macmillan

Parton, N. (2005) *Safeguarding Childhood: early intervention and surveillance in a late modern society*, Basingstoke: Palgrave

Pawson, R., Boaz, A., Grayson, L., Long, A. and Barnes, C. (2003) *Types and Quality of Knowledge in Social Care: A Knowledge Review*, London: Social Care Institute for Excellence

Paylor, I. (2008) 'Degrees of substance', Letter *Druglink* 22 (7): 28, January/February

Paylor, I. and Mack, H. (2009) 'Gazing into the scarlet crystal ball. Social work and hepatitis C', *British Journal of Social Work* Advance Access published on 20 November 2009; doi:10.1093/bjsw/bcp136

Paylor, I. and Orgel, M. (2004) 'Sleepwalking through an epidemic: why social work should wake up to the threat of hepatitis C', *British Journal of Social Work*, 34 (6): 897–906

Payne, M. (1997) *Modern Social Work Theory*, 2nd edn, Basingstoke: Palgrave Macmillan

Payne, M. (1998) 'Social work theories and reflective practice', in R. Adams et al. (eds) *Social Work Themes, Issues and Critical Debates*, pp. 253–72, Basingstoke: Macmillan

Payne, M. (2000) 'The politics of case management and social work', *International Journal of Social Welfare*, 9 (2): 82–91

Payne, M. (2001) 'Knowledge bases and knowledge biases in social work', *Journal of Social Work*, 1 (2): 133–46

Payne, M. (2005) *The Origins of Social Work*, Basingstoke: Palgrave

Peace, S., Wahl, H-W., Mollenkopf, H. and Oswald, F. (2007) 'Environment and ageing', in J. Bond, S. Peace, F. Dittmann-Kohli and G. Westerhof (eds) *Ageing in Society: European Perspectives on Gerontology*, 3rd edn, London: Sage/Open University

Penhale, B. and Parker, J. (2008) *Working with Vulnerable Adults*, London, Routledge

Perrott, S. (2002) 'Gender, professions and management in the public sector', *Public Money and Management*, 22 (1): 21–5

Petitto, L. (1988) '"Language" in the pre-linguistic child', in Kessell, F. (ed.) *The Development of Language and Language Researchers*, pp. 187–222, Hillsdale, NJ: Erlbaum

Phillips, J. and Waterson, J. (2002) 'Care management and *social* work: a case study of the role of *social* work in hospital discharge to residential or nursing home care', *European Journal of Social Work*, 5 (2): 171–86

Phillips, J., Ray, M. and Marshall, M. (2006) *Social Work with Older People*, 4th edn, Basingstoke: Palgrave

Phillips, R. (ed.) (2004) *Children Exposed to Parental Substance Misuse: Implications for Family Placement*, London: British Association for Adoption and Fostering

Phillipson, C. (2005) 'The political economy of old age', in M. Johnson, V. Bengtson, P. G. Coleman and T. B. L. Kirkwood (eds) *The Cambridge Handbook of Age and Ageing*, Cambridge: Cambridge University Press

Phinney, J. (1989) 'Stages of ethnic identity in minority group adolescents', in *Journal of Early Adolescence*, 9: 34–49

Piaget, J. (1932) *The Moral Judgement of the Child*, New York: Macmillan

Piaget, J. (1936) *The Origins of Intelligence in the Child*, London: Routledge and Kegan Paul

Piaget, J. and Inhelder, B. (1969) *The Psychology of the Child*, New York: Basic Books

Pickard, L. (2004) *The Effectiveness and Cost-effectiveness of Support and Services to Informal Carers of Older People*, London: Audit Commission and PSSRU

Pierpoint, H. (2006) 'Reconstructing the role of the appropriate adult in England and Wales', *Criminology and Criminal Justice*, 6 (2): 219–37

Pietroni, M. (1995) 'The nature and aims of professional education', in M. Yelloly and M. Henkel (eds), *Learning and Teaching in Social Work: Towards Reflective Practice*, pp. 34–50, London: Jessica Kingsley

Pillemer, K. A. and Wolf, R. S. (1986) *Elder Abuse: Conflict in the Family*, Dover, MA: Auburn House

Pincus, A. and Minahan, A. (1973) *Social Work Practice: Model and Method*, Illinois, USA: F. E. Peacock

Pinker, R. (1982) in Barclay Report *Social Workers: Their Role and Tasks*, London: Bedford Square Press/NISW

Pithouse, A., Hill-Tout, J. and Lowe, K. (2002) 'Training foster carers in challenging behaviour: a case study in disappointment', *Child and Family Social Work*, 7 (3): 203–15

Pithouse, A., Hall, C., Peckover, S. and White, S. (2009) 'A Tale of Two CAFS: The Impact of the Electronic Common Assessment Framework', *British Journal of Social Work*, 39, pp. 599–612.

Pitts, J. (2000) 'The new youth justice and the politics of electoral anxiety', in B. Goldson (ed.) *The New Youth Justice*, Lyme Regis: Russell House

Pitts, J. (2001) *The New Politics of Youth Crime*, Basingstoke: Macmillan

Pollard, K., Sellman, D. and Senior, B. (2005) 'The need for interprofessional working', in G. Barrett, D. Sellman and J. Thomas (eds) *Interprofessional Working in Health and Social Care*, Basingstoke: Palgrave Macmillan

Pollard, K. C., Thomas, J. and Miers, M. (eds) (2010) *Understanding Interprofessional Working in Health and Social Care*, Basingstoke: Palgrave Macmillan

Postle, K. (2001) 'The social work side is disappearing. I guess it started with us being called care managers', *Practice*, 13 (1): 13–26

Postle, K. (2002) 'Working "between the idea and the reality": ambiguities and tensions in care managers' work', *British Journal of Social Work*, 32 (3): 335–51

Powell, M. (2000) 'New Labour and the third way in the British welfare state: a new and distinctive approach', *Critical Social Policy*, 20 (1): 39–60

Powell, M. (ed.) (2007) *Understanding the Mixed Economy of Welfare*, Bristol: The Policy Press

Power, M. (1994) *The Audit Explosion*, London: Demos

Prendergast, M. L., Farabee, D., Cartier, J. and Henkin, S. (2002) 'Involuntary treatment within a prison setting: impact on psychosocial change during treatment', *Criminal Justice and Behaviour*, 29 (1): 5–27

Preston-Shoot, M. and Agass, D. (1990) *Making Sense of Social Work: Psychodynamics and Systems in Practice*, London: MacMillan

Prior, V. and Glaser, D. (2006) *Understanding Attachment and Attachment Disorders: Theory, Evidence and Practice*, London: Jessica Kingsley

Prior, V., Lynch, M. and Glaser, D. (1999) 'Responding to child sexual abuse: an evaluation of social work by children and their carers', *Child and Family Social Work*, 4 (2): 131–43

Prison Reform Trust (2001) 'Troubled inside: responding to the mental health needs of children and young people in prison', PRT, London at: (http://www.prisonreformtrust.org.uk/subsection.asp?id=314. Last accessed 4/11/06)

Pritchard, C. (2006) *Mental Health Social Work: Evidence Based Practice*, Abingdon: Routledge

Pritchard, C. and Williams, R. (2010) 'Comparing possible "child-abuse-related-deaths" in England and Wales with the major developed countries 1974–2006: signs of progress?', *British Journal of Social Work* 40 (6) 1700–18

Pritchard, J. (2008) 'Doing risk asessment properly in adult protection work', in J. Pritchard (ed.) *Good Practice in Safeguarding Adults: Working Effectively in Adult Protection*, London: Jessica Kingsley

Prochaska, J. O. and DiClemente, C. C. (2009) 'Towards a comprehensive model of change', in Miller, W. R. and Heather, N. (eds) *Treating Addicitve Behaviours: Processes of Change*, 2nd edn, New York: Plenum.

Pybus, O. G., Cochrane, A., Holmes, E. C., and Simmonds, P. (2004). 'The hepatitis C virus epidemic among injecting drug users', *Infection, Genetics and Evolution*, 5 (2): 131–9

Quality Assurance Agency for Higher Education (QAA) (2000) *Social Policy and Administration and Social Work: Subject Benchmark Statements*, Gloucester: QAA

Quinn, A. (1999) 'The use of experiential learning to help social work students assess their attitudes towards practice with older people', *Social Work Education*, 18 (2): 171–82

Quinn, A. (2000) 'Reluctant learners: social work students and work with older people', *Research in Post-Compulsory Education*, 5 (2): 223–37

Quinn, F. M. (2000) 'Reflection and reflective practice', in C. Davies, L. Finlay and A. Bullman (eds) *Changing Practice in Health and Social Care*, London: Sage

Quinton, D. (2004) *Supporting Parents: Messages from Research*, London: Jessica Kingsley

Quinton, D., Rushton, A., Dance, C. and Mayes, D. (1997) 'Contact between children placed away from home and their birth parents: research issues and evidence', *Clinical Child Psychology and Psychiatry*, 2 (3): 393–413

Quinton, D., Selwyn, J., Rushton, A. and Dance, C. (1999) 'Contact between children placed away from home and their birth parents: Ryburn's "Reanalysis" analysed', *Clinical Child Psychology and Psychiatry*, 4 (4): 519–31

Qureshi, H., Arksey, H. and Nicholas, E. (2003) 'Carers and assessment', in K. Stalker (ed.) *Reconceptualing Work with 'Carers': New Directions for Policy and Practice*, pp. 72–95, London: Jessica Kingsley

Race Relations Amendment Act 2000 at: www.hmso.gov.uk/legislation/uk.htm (last accessed 7/7/07)

Radford, J., Harne, L., Trotter, J. (2006) 'Disabled women and domestic violence as violent crime in practice', *Practice*, 18 (4): 223–46

Ramsey, M. and Partridge, S. (1998) *Drug Misuse Declared in 1998: Results of the British Crime Survey*, London: The Home Office

Rapaport, J. and Manthorpe, J. (2008) 'Putting it into practice: will the new Mental Health Act slow down or accelerate integrated working?' *Journal of Integrated Care*, 16 (4): 22–9

Rapoport, L. (1970) 'Crisis intervention as a mode of brief treatment', in R. Roberts and R. Nee (eds) *Theories of Social Casework*, Chicago: University of Chicago Press

Ray, M., Bernard, C. and Phillips, J. (2009) *Critical Issues in Social Work with Older People*, Basingstoke: Palgrave Macmillan

RCGP *see* Royal College of General Practitioners

Reder, P. and Duncan, S. (2004a) 'From Colwell to Climbié: inquiring into fatal child abuse', in N. Stanley and J. Manthorpe (eds) *The Age of the Enquiry: Learning and Blaming in Health and Social Care*, pp. 92–115, London: Routledge

Reder, P. and Duncan, S. (2004b) 'Making the most of the Victoria Climbié Inquiry', *Child Abuse Review*, 13: 95–114

Redgrave, K. (2000a) *Care-Therapy with Children*, London: Continuum

Redgrave, K. (2000b) *Child's Play: 'Direct Work' with the Deprived Child*, Cheadle: Boys and Girls Welfare Society

Reed, J., Stanley, D. and Clarke, C. (2004) *Health, Well-being and Older People*, Bristol: Policy Press

Rees, S. and Wallace, A. (1982) *Verdicts on Social Work*, London: Edward Arnold

Reeves, S., Zwarebstein, M., Goldman, J., Barr, H., Freeth, D., Hammick, M. and Koppel, I. (2009) 'Interprofessional education: effects on professional practice and health care outcomes', *Cochrane Database of Systematic Reviews*, Issue 1. Art. No. CD002213. DOI: 10.1002/14651858.CD002213.pub2

Regen, E., Martin, G., Glasby, J., Hewitt, G., Nancarrow, S. and Parker, H. (2008) 'Challenges, benefits and weaknesses of intermediate care: results from five UK case study sites', *Health and Social Care in the Community*, 16 (6): 629–37

Rehm, J. Fischer, B. and Hayden, E. (2003) 'Abstinence ideology and somatic treatment for addicts: ethical considerations', *Addiction Research and Theory*, 11 (5): 287–93

Reid, W. (1992) *Task Strategies: An Empirical Approach to Clinical Social Work*, New York: Columbia University Press

Reid, W. and Shyne, A. (1969) *Brief and Extended Casework*, New York: Columbia Univeristy Press

Reuters, P., and Stevens, A. (2007) *An Analysis of UK Drug Policy*. [Online]. Available at: http://www.ukdpc.org.uk/docs/UKDPC%20drug%20policy%20review%20exec%20summary.pdf (accessed 23 November 2009)

Rhodes, T., Judd, A., Mikhailova, L., Sarang, A., Khutorskoy, M. and Platt, L. (2004) 'Injecting equipment sharing among injecting drug users in Togliatti City, Russian Federation: maximizing the protective effects of syringe distribution', *Journal of Acquired Immune Deficiency Syndromes* 35: 293–300

Richardson, S. and Asthana, S. (2006) 'Inter-agency information sharing in health and social care services: the role of professional culture', *British Journal of Social Work*, 36 (4): 657–69

Richmond, M. (1917) *Social Diagnosis*, New York: Russell Sage Foundation

Rierdan, J. and Koff, E. (1991), 'Depressive symptomology among very early maturing girls', *Journal of Youth and Adolescence*, 20: 415–25

Ritchie, J., Dick, D. and Lingham, R. (1994) *The Report of the Inquiry into the Care and Treatment of Christopher Clunis*, London: HMSO

Roberts, M. (2010) *Young People's Drug and Alcohol Treatment at the Crossroads*, London: DrugScope

Roberts, R. (2000) *Crisis Intervention Handbook: Assessment, Treatment and Research*, 2nd edn, Oxford: Oxford University Press

Robertson, G., Pearson, R. and Gibb, R. (1995) 'The Entry of Mentally Disordered People to the Criminal Justice System', Home Office Research and Statistics Department: Research Findings No.21, London: Home Office

Robinson, L. (1995) *Psychology for Social Workers: Black Perpectives*, London: Routledge

Robinson, L. and Spilsbury, L. (2008) 'Systematic review of the perceptions and experiences of accessing health services by adult victims of domestic violence', *Health and Social Care in the Community*, 16 (1): 16–30

Rodgers, B. N. and Dixon, J. (1960) *A Portrait of Social Work*, Oxford: Oxford University Press

Rogers, C. (1951) *Client-Centred Therapy*. Boston, MA: Houghton Mifflin

Rogers, C. (1961) *On Becoming a Person*, Boston, MA: Houghton Mifflin

Rolfe, G., Freshwater, D. and Jasper, M. (2001) *Critical Reflection for Nursing and the Helping Professions: A Users Guide*, Basingstoke: Palgrave

Rolles, S. (2009) *After the War on Drugs: Blueprint for Regulation*, Bristol: Transform Drug Policy Foundation

Romaine, M. with Turley, T. and Tuckey, N. (2007) *Preparing Children for Permanence*, London: BAAF

Rooff, M. (1969) *A Hundred Years of Family Welfare*, London: Michael Joseph

Rooney, R. (2009) *Strategies for Work with Involuntary Clients*, 2nd edn, Columbia University Press

Rose, N. (1999) *Governing the Soul*, 2nd edn, London: Free Association Books

Rose, W. (2001) 'Assessing children in need and their families: an overview of the framework', in J. Horwath (ed.) *The Child's World: Assessing Children in Need*, pp. 35–50, London: Jessica Kingsley

Rowe, J., Cain, H., Hundleby, M., Garnett, L. (1989) *Child Care Now: A Decade of Experience*, London: BAAF

Roy, P., Rutter, M. and Pickles, A. (2000) 'Institutional care: risk from family background or pattern of rearing?', *Journal of Child Psychology and Psychiatry*, 41: 139–50

Royal College of General Practitioners (2007) *Guidance on the prevention testing treatment and management of Hepatitis C in primary care*

Royal Commission on Long-term Care (1999) *With Respect to Old Age: Long term Care – Rights and Responsibilities*, London: The Stationery Office

Ruble, D. (1987) 'The acquisition of self-knowledge: a self-socialisation perspective', in N. Eisenberg (ed.) *Contemporary Topics in Developmental Psychology*, New York: Wiley-International

Ruch, G. (2001) 'Self in social work: towards an integrated model of learning', *Journal of Social Work Practice*, 14: 99–112

Ruch, G. (2002) 'From triangle to spiral: reflective practice in social work education, practice and research', *Social Work Education*, 21 (2): 199–216

Ruch, G. (2004) 'Reflective practice in contemporary child care social work', unpublished PhD thesis, university of Southampton

Ruch, G. (2005) 'Relationship-based and reflective practice in contemporary child care social work', *Child and Family Social Work*, 4 (2): 111–24

Ruch, G. (2007) 'Reflective practice in child care social work: the role of containment', *British Journal of Social Work*, 37: 659–80

Ruch, G. (2010) 'The contemporary context of relationship-based practice', in Ruch, G., Turney, D. and Ward, A. (eds) *Relationship-based practice: getting to the heart of social work*, London: Jessica Kingsley

Ruch, G., Turney, D. and Ward, A. (eds) *Relationship-based Social Work: Getting to the Heart of Practice*, London: Jessica Kingsley.

Rummery, K. (2002) 'Towards a theory of welfare partnerships', in C. Glendinning, M. Powell and K. Rummery (eds) *Partnerships, New Labour and the Governance of Welfare*, pp. 229–46, Bristol: Policy Press

Rushton, A. (2003) 'The adoption of looked after children: a scoping review of research', *SCIE Knowledge Review 4*, Bristol: Policy Press

Rushton, A (2004) A scooping and scanning review of research on the adoption of children placed from public care' *Clinical Child Psychology and Psychiatry*, 9 (1): 89–106

Rushton, A. and Dance, C. (2006) 'The adoption of children from public care: a prospective study of outcome in adolescence', *Journal of the American Academy of child and Adolescent Psychiatry*, 45: 877–83

Rushton, A., Dance, C. and Quinton, D. (2000) 'Findings from a UK based study of late permanent placements', *Adoption Quarterly*, 3 (3): 51–71

Rustin, M. (2004) 'Learning from the Victoria Climbié Enquiry', *Journal of Social Work Practice*, 18 (1): 9–18

Rustin, M. (2005) 'Conceptual analysis of critical moments in Victoria Climbié's life', *Journal of Social Work Practice*, 10: 11–19

Rutherford, A. (1992) *Growing Out of Crime: The New Era*, Winchester: Waterside Press

Rutter, M. and Rutter, M. (1993) *Developing Minds: Challenge and Continuity Across the Lifespan*, Harmondsworth: Penguin Books

Ryan, T. and Walker, R. (2007) *Life Story Books*, London: BAAF

Ryan, V. and Wilson, K. (2000) *Case Studies in Non-Directive Play Therapy*, London: Jessica Kingsley

Ryburn, M. (1999) 'Contact between children placed away from home and their birth parents: a reanalysis of the evidence in relation to permanent placements,' *Clinical Child Psychology and Psychiatry*, 4 (4): 505–18

Sackett, D. L., Richardson, W. S., Rosenberg, W. M. C. and Haynes, R. B. (1997) *Evidence-Based Medicine: How to Practice and Teach EBM*, London: Churchill Livingstone

Safeguarding Vulnerable Adults, accessed on 16 September 2010 at: www.dhsspsni.gov.uk/index/hss/safeguarding_vulnerable_adults.htm

Salter, B. (1998) *The Politics of Change in the Health Service*, Basingstoke: Macmillan

Sampson, R. and Laub, J. (1994) 'Urban poverty and the family context of delinquency: a new look at structure and process in a classic study', *Child Development*, 65: 523–40

Sampson, S. (2008) 'Access all areas' *Druglink* (November/December): 12–15

Sanderson, I. (2001) 'Performance management, evaluation and learning in "modern" local government', *Public Administration*, 79 (2): 297–313

Sapey, B. and Hewitt, N. (1993) 'The changing context of social work practice', in M. Oliver (ed.) *Social Work: Disabled People and Disabling Environments*, London: Jessica Kingsley

Sapey, B. (1997) 'Social Work tomorrow: Towards a critical understanding of social work in technology in social work', *British Journal of Social Work* 27, (6), pp. 803–14

Satyamurti, C. (1981) *Occupational Survival*, Oxford: Blackwell

Sayce, L. (2000) *From Psychiatric Patient to Citizen: Overcoming Discrimination and Exclusion*, Basingstoke: Macmillan

Scarman, Lord (1981) *The Brixton Disorders, 10–12 April, 1981*, London: Pelican

Schaefer, M., Heinz, A. and Backmund, M. (2004) 'Treatment of chronic hepatitis C in patients with drug dependence; time to change the rules?' *Addiction*, 99: 1167–75

Schofield, G. (1998) 'Inner and outer worlds: a psychosocial framework for child and family social work,' *Child and Family Social Work*, 3: 57–67

Schofield, G. (2003) *Part of the Family: Pathways Through Foster Care*, London: BAAF

Schofield, G. and Beek, M. (2006) *The Adoption Handbook*, London: BAAF

Schofield, G., Beek, M., Sargent, K. and Thoburn, J. (2000) *Growing up in Foster Care*, London: BAAF

Schön, D. (1987) *Educating the Reflective Practitioner*, San Francisco: Jossey Bass

Schön, D. A. (1991) *The Reflective Practitioner*, Aldershot: Arena

Schuff, H. and Asen, E. (1996) 'The disturbed parent and the disturbed family', in M. Gopfert, J. Webster and M. Seeman (eds) *Parental Psychiatric Disorder*, pp. 136–7, Cambridge: Cambridge University Press

SCIE (2004) 'Improving the use of research in social care', *Knowledge Review* 7, Bristol: The Policy Press

SCIE (2005) 'Practice Guide 4: Adult placements and person-centred approaches', Guide 8

SCIE (2008) '*Learning Together to Safeguard Children: Deleveloping a multi-agency systems approach for case reviews*', Report 19

Scott, M. (1989) *A Cognitive Behavioural Approach to Clients' Problems*, London: Routledge

Scottish Executive (2002) *Youth Justice Strategy*, Edinburgh: Scottish Executive

Scottish Executive (2004) *Hidden Harm: Scottish Executive Response to the Report of the Inquiry by the Advisory Council on the Misuse of Drugs*, Edinburgh: Scottish Executive

Scottish Executive (2005a) *Better Outcomes for Older People: Framework for Joint Services*, Edinburgh: Scottish Executive

Scottish Executive (2005b) *Getting it Right for Every Child*, Edinburgh: Scottish Executive

Scottish Executive (2007) *All Our Futures: Planning for a Scotland with an Ageing Population*, Edinburgh: Scottish Executive

Scottish Government (2008) *The Road to Recovery: A New Approach to Tackling Scotland's Drug Problem*

Scottish Government (2009) *Children Looked After Statistics, 2008–9*. Edinburgh: Scottish Government

Scourfield, P. (2007) 'Social care and the modern citizen: client, consumer, service user, manager and entrepreneur', *British Journal of Social Work*, 37 (1): 107–22

Scourfield, P. (2010) 'Going for brokerage: a task of independent support or social work?' *British Journal of Social Work*, 40 (3): 858–77

Scraton, P. and Haydon, D. (2002) 'Challenging the criminalization of children and young people: securing a rights-based agenda', in Muncie, J., Hughes, G. and McLaughlin, E. (eds) *Youth Justice: Critical Readings*, pp. 311–328, London: Sage

Scull, A. (1984) *Decarceration: Community Treatment and the Deviant: A Radical View*, 2nd edn, London: Basil Blackwell

Seddon, T. (2007) 'Coerced drug treatment in the criminal justice system: conceptual, ethical and criminological issues', *Journal of Criminology and Criminal Justice*, 7: 269–86

Seddon, D. Robinson, C. and Perry, J. (2010) 'Unified assessment: policy, implementation and practice', *British Journal of Social Work*, 40 (1): 207–25

Sedgwick, P. (1982) *Psychopolitics*, London: Pluto Press

Seebohm Report (1968) *Report of the Committee on Local Authority and Allied Personal Social Services*, Cmnd. 3703, London: HMSO

Seed, P. (1973) *The Expansion of Social Work in Britain*, London: Routledge and Kegan Paul

Seligman, M. (1975) *Helplessness: on Depression, Development and Death*, San Franciso: Freeman

Selwyn, J. and Wijedesa, D.(2009) 'The placement of looked after minority ethnic children', in Schofield, G. and Simmonds, J. (2009) (eds) *The Child Placement Handbook*, London: BAAF

Selwyn, J., Sturgess, W., Quinton, D. and Baxter, C. (2006) *Costs and Outcomes of Non-infant Adoptions*, London: BAAF

Sen, S. (2006) 'Bottling it: Britain's booze bugbear', *Druglink*, 22 (4): 12–13

Sender, H., Littlechild, B. and Smith, N. (2006) 'Black and minority ethnic groups and youth offending', *Youth and Policy*, 93: 61–76

Shakespeare, T. (1993) 'Disabled people self-organisation: a new social movement?' *Disability, Handicap and Society*, 8 (3): 256–7

Shakespeare, T. (2006) *Disability Rights and Wrongs*, Oxon: Routledge

Sharipo, H. (2005) 'Nothing about us, without us: user involvement, past, present and future', *Druglink* 20 (3): 10–11

Shardlow, S. and Nelson, P. (2005) *Introduction to Social Work*, Lyme Regis: Russell House Publishing

Shardlow, S. M. (2007) 'Social work in an international context', in M. Lymbery and K. Postle (eds) *Social Work: A Companion to Learning*, London: Sage

Shaw, C. (1998) *Remember My messages . . . The Experiences and Views of 2,000 children in Public Care in the UK*, London: Who Cares? Trust

Shaw, C. (2004a) '2002-based national population projections for the United Kingdom and constituent countries', *Population Trends*, 115: 6–15

Shaw, C. (2004b) 'Interim 2003-based national population projections for the United Kingdom and constituent countries', *Population Trends*, 118: 6–16

Shaw, I., Bell, M., Sinclair, I., Sloper, P., Rafferty, J. and Mitchell, W. (2009) 'An exemplary scheme? An evaluation of the integrated children's system', *British Journal of Social Work*, Advance Access published online on 8 April, 2009, doi:10.1093/bjsw/bcp040

Shaw, M. and Jane, F. (1999) 'Family Group Conferencing with Children Under Twelve: A Discussion Paper', Canada: Department of Justice

Sheldon, B. (1978) 'Theory and practice in social work: a re-examination of a tenuous relationship', *British Journal of Social Work*, 8 (1): 1–22

Sheldon, B. (1995) *Cognitive-Behavioural Therapy: Research, Practice and Philosophy*, London: Routledge

Sheldon, B. (2001) 'Research note. The validity of evidence-based practice in social work: a Reply to Stephen Webb', *British Journal of Social Work*, 31 (5): 801–9

Sheldon, B. and Chilvers, R. (2000) *Evidence-Based Social Care*, Lyme Regis: Russell House

Shemmings, Y. and Shemmings, D. (2000) 'Empowering children and family members to participate in the assessment process', in V. Horwath (ed.) *The Child's World: Assessing Children in Need*, London: Jessica Kingsley

Sheridan, M., Frost, M. and Sharma, A. (1997) *From Birth to Five Years*, London: Routledge

Siegler, R., DeLoache, J. and Eisenberg, N. (2003) *How Children Develop*, Basingstoke: Palgrave Macmillan

Simmonds, J. (2008) 'Foreword: Direct work with children: delusion or reality' in Luckock, B. and Lefrevre, M. (eds) *Direct Work: Social Work with Children and Young People in Care*, London: BAAF

Simmons, R., Carlton-Ford, S. and Blyth, D. (1987) 'Predicting how a child will cope with the transition to junior high school', in R. Lerner and T. Foch (eds) *Biological-Psychosocial Interactions in Early Adolescence*, pp. 325–75, New Jersey: Erlbaum

Simpkin, M. (1983) *Trapped within Welfare*, 2nd edn, London: Macmillan

Simpson, D. D. and Joe, G. W. (1993) 'Motivation as a predictor of early dropout from drug abuse treatment', *Psychotherapy: Theory, Research, Practice, Training*, 30: 357–68

Sinclair, I. (1992) 'Social work research: its relevance to social work and social work education', *Issues in Social Work Education*, 11 (2): 64–80

Sinclair, I. (2002) 'A quality-control perspective', in M. Davies (ed.) *The Blackwell Companion to Social Work*, pp. 431–7, Oxford: Blackwell Publishing

Sinclair, I. and Gibbs, I. (1998) 'Children's homes: a study in diversity', in DoH *Caring for Children away from Home: Messages from Research*, Chichester: Wiley

Sinclair, I. and Wilson, K. (2003) 'Matches and mismatches: the contribution of carers and children to the success of foster placements', *BJSW* 33 (7): 871–84

Sinclair, I and Wilson, K. (2009) 'Foster care in England', in Schofield, G. and Simmonds, J. (eds) (2009) *The Child Placement Handbook*, London: BAAF

Sinclair, I., Gibbs, I. and Wilson, K. (2004) *Foster Carers: Why They Stay and Why They Leave*, London: Jessica Kingsley

Sinclair, I., Wilson, K. and Gibbs, I. (2005) *Foster Placements: Why Some Succeed and Some Fail*, London: Jessica Kingsley

Sinclair, I., Baker, C., Wilson, K. and Gibbs, I. (2005a), *Foster Children: Where They Go and How They Get On*, London: Jessica Kingsley

Singleton, N., Maung, N., Cowie, A., Sparks, J., Bumpstead, R. and Meltzer, H. (2002) *Mental Health of Carers*, London: The Stationery Office

Skynner, R. (1991) *Institutes and How to Survive Them: Mental Health Training and Consultation*, London: Routledge

Slater, R. (1995) *The Psychology of Growing Old: Looking Forward*, Buckingham: Open University Press

Smale, G., Tuson, G. and Statham, D. (2000) *Social Work and Social Problems: Working Towards Social Inclusion and Social Change*, Basingstoke: Macmillan

Smalley, R. (1967) *Theory for Social Work Practice*, New York: Columbia University Press

Smith, D. (1999) 'Social work with young people in trouble: memory and prospect', in B. Goldson (ed.) *Youth Justice: Contemporary Policy and Practice*, pp. 148–69, Aldershot: Ashgate

Smith, D. (2005) 'Probation and social work', *British Journal of Social Work*, 35 (5): 621–37

Smith, M. (2005) *Surviving Fears in Health and Social Care: The Terrors of the Night and Arrows of the Day*, London: Jessica Kingsley

Smith, M. and Nursten, J. (2004) 'Social workers' responses to experiences of fear', *British Journal of Social Work*, 34: 541–59

Smith, R. (2003) *Youth Justice: Ideas, Policy, Practice*, Cullompton: Willan

Smith, R. (2007) 'Youth Justice – Ideas, policy, practice', 2nd edn, Dorset: Willan Publishing

Smith, R. (2010) 'Children's rights and youth justice: 20 years of no progress', *Child Care in Practice*, 16 (1): 3–17

Social Work Task Force (2009) *Building a Safe, Confident Future: The final report of the Social Work Task Force*, London: Department of Health/Department for Children, Schools and Families.

Souhami, A. (2007) *Transforming Youth Justice: Occupational Identity and Cultural Change*, Cullompton: Willan

Spencer-Lane, T. (2010) 'A statutory framework for safeguarding adults? The Law Commission's consultation paper on adult social care', *Journal of Adult Protection* 12 (1): 43–9

St. Claire, L. and Osborne, A. (1987) 'The ability and behaviour of children who have been "in care" or separated from their parents', *Early Development and Care*, 28, Special Issue

Stake, R. (1995) *The Art of Case Study Research*, Thousand Oaks, CA: Sage

Stanley, N. and Manthorpe, J. (2004) *The Age of Inquiry: Learning and Blaming in Health and Social Care*, London: Routledge

Stanley, N. and Manthorpe, J. (2008) 'Small acts of care: exploring the potential impact of the Mental Capacity Act 2005 on day-to-day support', *Social Policy and Society*, 8 (1): 37–48

Statham, D. and Kearney, P. (2007) 'Models of assessment', in Lishman, J. (ed.) *Handbook for Practice Learning in Social Work and Social care: Knowledge and Theory*, London: Jessica Kingsley

Stattin, H. and Magnusson, D. (1990) *Pubertal Maturation in Female Development*, Hillsdale, NJ: Erlbaum

Steele, M., Hodges, J., Kanuik, J., Steele, H., Hillman, S. and Asquith, K. (2008) 'Forecasting outcomes in previously maltreated children: the use of the AAI in a longitudinal adoption study', in Steele, H. and Steele, M. (eds) *Clinical Applications of the Adult Attachment Interview*, New York: The Guilford Press

Stein, M. (2004) *What works for young people learning care?*, Barkingside: Barnado's

Stein, M. D., Anderson, B., Charuvastra, A., Maksad, J. and Freidmann, P. D. (2002) 'A brief intervention for hazardous drinkers in a needle exchange program', *Journal of Substance Abuse Treatment*, 22: 23–31

Steinberg, L. (1988) 'Reciprocal relation between parent–child distance and pubertal maturation', *Developmental Psychology*, 22: 433–9

Steinberg, L. and Levine, A. (1990) *You and your Adolescent: A Parent's Guide for Ages 10 to 20*, New York: Harper and Row

Stepney, P. (2000) 'The theory to practice debate revisited', in P. Stepney and D. Ford (eds) *Social Work Models, Methods and Theories*, pp. 20–24, Lyme Regis: Russell House

Stevens, A. (2008) *Quasi-compulsory Treatment in Europe: An evidence-based response to drug-related crime*, Brighton: Pavilion

Stevens, A., Berto, D., Frick, U., Hunt, N., Kerschl, V., Mcsweeney, T., Oeuvray, K., Puppo, I., Maria, A. S., Schaaf, S., Trinkl, B., Uchtenhagen, A. and Werdenich, W. (2006) 'The relationship between legal status, perceived pressure and motivation in treatment for drug dependence: results from a European study of quasi-compulsory treatment', *European Addiction Research*, 12: 197–209

Stevens, A., Berto, D., Heckmann, W., Kerschl, V., Oeuvray, K., Van Ooyan, M., Steffan, E. and Uchtenhagen, A. (2005) 'Quasi-compulsory treatment of drug dependent offenders: an international literature review', *Substance Use and Misuse*, 40: 269–83

Stevenson, O. (1981) *Specialisation in Social Services Teams*, London: Allen and Unwin

Stevenson, O. (1989) *Age and Vulnerability*, London: Edward Arnold

Stevenson, O. (2005) 'Genericism and specialization: the story since 1970', *British Journal of Social Work*, 35 (5): 569–86

Stuart-Hamilton, I. (2006) *The Psychology of Ageing*, 4th edn, London: Jessica Kingsley

Sugarman, L. (1986) *Lifespan Development: Concepts, Theories and Interventions*, London: Routledge

Sullivan, P. M. and Knutson, J. F. (2000). 'Maltreatment and disabilities: a population-based epidemiological study', *Child Abuse & Neglect*, 24: 1257–74

Sullivan, S. (1953) *The Interpersonal Theory of Psychiatry*, New York: Norton

Sutherland Report (1999) *With Respect to Old Age: Long Term Care – Rights and Responsibilities: A Report by the Royal Commission on Long Term Care*, London: The Stationery Office

Suzman, R., Harris, T., Hadley, E., Kovar, M. and Weindruch, R. (1992) 'The robust oldest old: optimistic perspectives for increasing life expectancy', in R. Suzman, D. Willis and K. Munton (eds) (1992) *The Oldest Child*, pp. 341–58, New York: Oxford University Press

Swain, J., French, S., Barnes, C. and Thomas, C. (eds) (2004) *Disabling Barriers: Enabling Environments*, 2nd edn, London: Sage

Sykes, J., Sinclair, I., Gibbs, I. and Wilson, K. (2002) 'Kinship care versus stranger foster care: how do they compare?' *Adoption and Fostering*, 26 (2): 38–48

Tanner, D. (2003) 'Older people and access to care', *British Journal of Social Work*, 33 (4): 499–515

Tanner, D. (2009) 'Modernisation and the delivery of user-centred services', in J. Harris and V. White (eds) *Modernising Social Work: Critical Considerations*, Bristol: Policy Press

Taylor, A. and Kroll, B. (2004) 'Working with parental misuse: dilemmas for practice', *British Journal of Social Work*, 34 (8): 1115–32

Taylor, A., Toner, P., Templeton, L. and Velleman, R. (2008) 'Parental alcohol misuse in complex families: the implications for engagement', *British Journal of Social Work*, 38 (5): 843–65

Taylor, C. (2004) 'Underpinning knowledge for child care practice: reconsidering child development theory', *Child and Family Social Work*, 9: 225–35

Taylor, C. and White, S. (2001) 'Knowledge, truth and reflexivity: the problem of judgement in social work', *Journal of Social Work*, 1 (1): 37–59

Taylor, G. (1993) 'Challenges from the margins', in J. Clarke (ed.) *A Crisis in Care: Challenges to Social Work*, London: Sage/Open University

Taylor, H., Beckett, C. and McKeigue, B. (2008) 'Judgements of Solomon: anxieties and defences of social workers involved in care proceedings', *Child and Family Social Work* 13: 23–31

Taylor, I. (1996) 'Facilitating reflective learning', in N. Gould and I. Taylor (eds) *Reflective Learning for Social Work*, Aldershot: Arena

Terr, L. (1988) 'What happens to early memories of trauma? A study of 20 children at the time of documented traumatic events', *Journal of the American Academy of Child and Adolescent Psychiatry*, 27: 96–104

Tham, P. and Meagher, G. (2009) 'Working in human services: how do experiences and working conditions in child welfare social work compare?', *British Journal of Social Work* 39 (5): 807–27

The Children's Society (1988) *The Line of Least Resistance*, London: The Children's Society

Long, L., Roche, J. and Stringer, D. (eds) (2010) *The Law and Social Work: Contemporary Issues for Practice*, 2nd edn, Basingstoke: Palgrave Macmillan/Open University.

The Sainsbury Centre for Mental Health (2002), *Breaking the Circles of Fear: A Review of the Relationship Between Mental Health Services and African and Caribbean Communities*, London: The Sainsbury Centre for Mental Health

The Stationery Office (1998) *Modernising Social Services: Promoting Independence, Improving Protection, Raising Standards*, Cmd 4169, London: The Stationery Office

The Stationery Office (1999) *The Stephen Lawrence Inquiry: Report of an Enquiry by Sir William Macpherson of Cluny*, London: The Stationery Office

The Stationery Office *see also under individual Government departments for publications after 1997*

The Toner report is available at: http://www.dhsspsni.gov.uk/independentreview2008.pdf

Thoburn, J. (2007) 'Out of home care for the abused or neglected child', in K. Wilson and A. James (eds), *The Child Protection Handbook*, 3rd edn, Edinburgh: Elsevier

Thomas, C. (2004) 'Disability and impairment', in J. Swain, S. French, C. Barnes and C. Thomas (eds) *Disabling Barriers: Enabling Environments*, 2nd edn, London: Sage

Thompson, N. (1995) *Theory and Practice in Social Welfare*, Buckingham: Open University Press

Thompson, N. (2001) *Anti-Discriminatory Practice*, 3rd edn, Basingstoke: Palgrave

Thompson, N. (2003) *Communication and Language*, Basingstoke: Palgrave Macmillan

Thompson, N. (2007) *Anti-Discriminatory Practice*, 4th edn, Basingstoke: Palgrave Macmillan

Thompson, S. (2002) 'Older people', in N. Thompson (ed.) *Loss and Grief: A Guide for Human Services Practitioners*, Basingstoke: Palgrave

Thorpe, D., Smith, D., Green, C. J. and Paley, J. H. (1980) *Out of Care: The Community Support of Juvenile Offenders*, London: George Allen and Unwin

Tibbs, M. A. (2001) *Social Work and Dementia: Good Practice and Care Management*, London: Jessica Kingsley

Tinker, A. (1997) *Older People in Modern Society*, 4th edn, Harlow: Addison Wesley Longman

Titterton, M. (2005) *Risk and risk taking in health and social welfare*, London: Jessica Kingsley

Tizard, B. and Rees, J. (1975) 'Effects of early institutional rearing on the behaviour problems and affectional relationships of four-year-old children', *Journal of Child Psychology and Psychiatry*, 16: 61–73

Tobin-Richards, M., Boxer, A. and Petersen, A. (1983) 'The psychological significance of pubertal change: sex differences in perceptions of self during early adolescence', in J. Brooks-Gunn and A. Petersen (eds) *Girls at Puberty: Biological and Psychological Perspectives*, pp. 125–54, 137, New York: Springer

TOPSS *see* Training Organisation for the Personal Social Services

Townsend, P. (1962) *The Last Refuge*, London: Routledge and Kegan Paul

Townsend, P., Davidson, N. and Whitehead, M. (eds) (1992) *Inequalities in Health*, Harmondsworth: Penguin

Training Organisation for the Personal Social Services (TOPSS) (2002) *The National Occupational Standards for Social Work*, Leeds: TOPSS

Training Organisation for the Personal Social Services (TOPSS) (2004) *Analysing the 'Redrawn and Redesigned': A Halfway Report on Topss England's New Roles Project*, Leeds: TOPSS

Treloar, C. J., Hopwood, M. N. and Loveday, S. K. (2002) 'Hepatitis C-related discrimination in healthcare', *Medical Journal of Australia*, 177 (5): 233–4

Trevillion, S. (1992) *Caring in the Community: A Networking Approach to Community Partnership*, Harlow: Longman

Trevillion, S. (2000) 'Social work research: what kind of knowledge/knowledges? An introduction to the papers', *Br J Soc Work*, 30: 429–32

Trevithick, P. (2005) *Social Work Skills: A Practice Handbook*, 2nd edn, Buckingham: Open University Press

Triseliotis, J. (1989) 'Foster care outcomes: a review of key research findings', *Adoption and Fostering*, 13: 5–17

Triseliotis, J. and Russell, J. (1984) *Hard to Place: The Outcomes of Adoption and Residential Care*, London: Heinemann and Gower

Triseliotis, J., Sellick, C. and Short, R. (1995) *Foster Care: Theory and Practice*, London: B. T. Batsford

Troll, E. (1985) 'The contingencies of grandparenting', in V. Bengtson and J. Robertson (eds) *Grandparenthood*, Beverly Hills, CA: Sage

Trotter, C. (2006) *Working with Involuntary Clients*, 2nd edn, Basingstoke: Palgrave

Trowell, J. (1995) 'Key psychoanalytic concepts', in J. Trowell and M. Bower (eds) *The Emotional Needs of Young Children and their Families: Using Psychoanalytic Ideas in the Community*, London: Routledge.

Truax, C. B. and Carkhuff, R. R. (1967) *Toward Effective Counseling and Psychotherapy: Training and Practice*, Chicago, IL: Aldine Publishers

Tunnard, J. (2004) *Parental Mental Health Problems: Messages from Research, Policy and Practice*, Dartington: Research into Practice

Turner, T. H., Ness, M. N. and Imison, C. T. (1992) 'Mentally disordered persons found in public places: diagnostic and social aspects of police referrals (section 136)', *Psychological Medicine*, 22 (3): 765–74

Turney, D. (2009) *Analysis and Critical Thinking in Assessment* Dartington: Research in Practice (available at www.rip.org/publications)

Tyuse, S. W. and Linhorst, D. M. (2005) 'Drug courts and mental health courts: implications for social work', *Health and Social Work*, 30 (3): 233–40

UKDPC (2007). *An Analysis of UK Drug Policy (April 2007)*. [Online]. Available at: http://www.ukdpc.org.uk/publications.shtml (accessed 25 November 2009)

UKHRA (2005) *UK Harm Reduction Alliance: Definition of harm reduction* at: http://www.ukhra.org/harm_reduction_definition.html

UPIAS/Union of Physically Impaired Against Segregation (1976) *Fundamental Principles of Disability*, London: UPIAS

Utting, W. (1997) *Children in the Public Care: A Review of Residential Care*, Social Services Inspectorate study, London: HMSO

Utting, W., Rose, N. and Pugh, G. (2001) *Better Results for Children and Families*, London: NCVVO

van Ooyen-Houben, M. (2008) *Quasi-compulsory Treatment in the Netherlands: Promising Theory, Problems in Practice*, Brighton: Pavillion

Victor, C. (2005) *The Social Context of Ageing*, Abingdon: Routledge

Vincent, A. W. (1999) 'The Poor Law Reports of 1909 and the social theory of the Charity Organisation Society', in D. Gladstone (ed.) *Before Beveridge: Welfare before the Welfare State*, London: Institute for Economic Affairs

Vincent, C. (2004) 'Analysis of clinical incidents: a window on the system not a search for root causes', *Quality and Safety in Health Care*, 13: 242–3

Vostanis, P. and Anderson, L. 'Evaluation of a family support service: short-term outcome', *Clinical Child Psychology and Psychiatry*, 11 (4): 513–28

Vygotsky, L. (1962) *Thought and Language*, New York: Wiley

Waddell, M. (1998) *Inside Lives.* London: Duckworth (Tavistock Clinic Series)

Wahab, S. (2005) 'Motivational interviewing and social work practice', *Journal of Social Work*, 5 (1): 45–60

Walaskay, M., Whitbourne, S. and Nehkre, M. (1983) 'Construction and validation of an ego integrity status interview', *International Journal of Ageing and Human Development*, 18: 61–72

Walker, J. and Crawford, K. (2010) *Social Work and Human Development*, 3rd edn, Exeter: Learning Matters Ltd.

Walker, L. (1989) 'A longitudinal study of moral reasoning', *Child Development*, 62: 264–83

Walker, M., Hill, M. and Triseliotis, J. (2002) *Testing the Limits of Foster Care: Fostering as an Alternative to Secure Accommodation*, London: BAAF

Walker, S. and Beckett, C. (2003) *Social Work Assessment and Intervention*, Lyme Regis: Russell House

Wallace, C. and Davies, M. (2009) *Sharing Assessment in Health and Social Care*, London: Sage

Walter, T. (1999) *On Bereavement: The Culture of Grief*, Buckingham: Open University Press

Wanigaratne, S., Davis, P., Pryce, K. and Brotchie, J. (2005) *The Effectiveness of Psychological Therapies on Drug Misusing Clients*. Research Briefing: 11, London: NTA

Wanless, D. (2006) *Securing Good Care for Older People: Taking a Long-Term View*, London: King's Fund

Ward, A. (1998) 'Helping together', in A. Ward and L. McMahon (eds) *Intuition is Not Enough: Matching Learning with Practice in Therapeutic Child Care*, pp. 40–54, London: Routledge

Ward, A. (2010) 'Use of self in relationship-based practice', in Ruch, G., Turney, D. and Ward, A. (eds) *Relationship-based Practice: Getting to the Heart of Social Work*, London: Jessica Kingsley

Ward, A. and McMahon, L. (eds) (1998) *Intuition is Not Enough: Matching Learning with Practice in Therapeutic Child Care*, London: Routledge

Ward, H. (2001) 'The developmental needs of children: implications for assessment', in J. Horwath (ed.) *The Child's World: Assessing Children in Need*, London: Jessica Kingsley

Ward, M. and Applin, C. (1998) *The Unlearned Lesson*, London: Wynne Howard Books

Wark, G. and Krebs, D. (1996) 'Gender and developmental differences in real-life moral judgements', *Developmental Psychology*, 32: 220–30

Warner, L. and Wexler, S. (1998) *Eight Hours a Day and Taken for Granted?* London: The Princess Royal Trust for Carers

Warren, F. and Norton, K. (2004) 'Henderson Hospital democratic therapeutic community: outcome studies and methodological issues', in P. Richardson, H. Kachele and C. Renlund (eds) *Research on Psychoanalytic Psychotherapy with Adults*, pp. 133–53, London: Karnac

Warren, J. (2005) 'Carers', *Research Matters*, 19, April–October issue: 5–10

Warren, J. (2007) *Service User and Carer Participation in Social Work*, Exeter: Learning Matters

Warren-Adamson, C. (2006) 'Research review: family centres: a review of the literature', *Child and Family Social Work*, 11 (2): 171–82

Waterhouse, L. and McGhee, J. (2009) Anxiety and child protection-implications for practitioner–parent relations, *Child and Family Social Work*, 14: 481–90

Waterhouse, S. (1997) *The Organisation of Fostering Services*, London: NFCA

Wates, M. (2002) *Supporting Disabled Adults in their Parenting Role*, York: York Publishing Services

Watson, F. and Burrows, H. (2002) *Integrating Theory and Practice in Social Work Education*, London: Jessica Kingsley

Webb, B. (1971, first published 1926) *My Apprenticeship*, Harmondsworth: Penguin

Webb, S. A. (2001) 'Some considerations on the validity of evidence-based practice in social work', *British Journal of Social Work*, 31 (1): 57–79

Webb, S. A. (2006) *Social Work in a Risk Society: Social & Political Perspectives*, Basingstoke: Palgrave

Webb, S. A. (2007) 'The comfort of strangers: social work, modernity and late Victorian England – Part I', *European Journal of Social Work*, 10 (1): 39–54

Weiss, R. (1991) 'The attachment bond in childhood and adulthood', Chapter 4 in C. Murray Parkes, J. Stevenson-Hinde and P. Marris (eds) *Attachment Across the Lifecycle*, London: Routledge

Welsh, W. N. and Mcgrain, P. N. (2008) 'Predictors of therapeutic engagement in prison-based drug treatment', *Drug and Alcohol Dependence*, 96: 271–80

Wenger, E. (1998) *Communities of Practice: Learning, Meaning and Identity*, Cambridge: Cambridge University Press

Werner, E. (1990) 'Protective factors and individual resilience', in S. Meisels and J. Shonkoff (eds) *Handbook of Early Childhood Intervention*, Cambridge: Cambridge University Press

Westcott, H. (1994) 'Abuse of children and adults who are disabled', in S. French (ed.) *On Equal Terms: Working with Disabled People*, Oxford: Heinemann

Westcott, H. (1998) 'Disabled children and child protection', in C. Robinson and K. Stalker (eds) *Growing Up with Disability*, London: Jessica Kingsley

Westendorp, R. G. J. and Kirkwood, T. B. L. (2007) 'The biology of aging', in J. Bond, S. Peace, F. Dittmann-Kohli and G. Westerhof (eds) *Ageing in Society: European Perspectives on Gerontology*, 3rd edn, London: Sage/Open University

Wheeler, W. (2006) *The Whole Creature: Complexity, Biosemiotics and the Evolution of Culture*, London: Lawrence & Wishart

White, S. (1997) 'Beyond retroduction: hermeneutics, reflexivity and social work practice', *British Journal of Social Work*, 27 (5): 739–53

White, S. Broadhurst, K. Wastell, D. Peckover, S. Hall, C. and Pithouse, A. (2009) 'Whither practice-near research in the modernization programme? Policy blunders in children's services', *Journal of Social Work Practice*, 23 (4) December: 401–12

Whittaker, A. (2009) *Research Skills for Social Work*, Exeter: Learning Matters

Whittington, C. (2003) 'Collaboration and partnership in context', in C. Whittington, J. Weinstein and T. Leiba (eds) *Collaboration in Social Work Practice*, London: Jessica Kingsley

WHO (2003) *International Classification of Diseases*, 10th edn, Geneva: World Health Organisation

WHSSB and EHSSB (2008) Report of the Independent Inquiry Panel to the Western and Eastern Health and Social Services Boards: Madeline and Lauren O'Neill. May 2007

Wild, T. C. (2006) 'Social control and coercion in addiction treatment: towards evidence-based policy and practice', *Addiction*, 101 (1): 40–9

Wild, T. C., Newton-Taylor, B. and Alletto, R. (1998) 'Perceived coercion among clients entering substance abuse treatment: structural and psychological determinants', *Addictive Behaviors*, 23: 81–95

Wilding, P. (1982) *Professional Power and Social Welfare*, London: Routledge and Kegan Paul

Wilkinson, R. (1996) *Unhealthy Societies: The Affliction of Inequality*, London: Routledge

Wilkinson, R. and Pickett, K. (2009) *The Spirit Level: Why More Equal Societies Almost Always Do Better*, London: Penguin

Wilkinson, R. G. (2005) *The Impact of Inequality: How to Make Sick Societies Healthier*, New York: New Press and London: Routledge

Williams, F. (1989) *Social Policy: A Critical Introduction*, Cambridge: Polity Press

Williams, P. (2006) *Social Work with People with Learning Disabilities*, Exeter: Learning Matters

Williamson, E. (2000) *Domestic Violence and Health: The Response of the Medical Profession*, Bristol: Policy Press

Williamson, H. (2001) *Supporting Young People in Europe: Principles, Policy and Practice*, Strasbourg: Council of Europe

Williamson, H. (2005) 'Preventive work in youth justice', in Bateman, T. and Pitts, J. (eds) *The RHP Companion to Youth Justice*, pp. 205–9, Lyme Regis: Russell House Publishing

Williamson, K., 'Direct work with children/Life story work', available from the author, Adoption and Fostering Team, North East Lincolnshire Council

Willis, R. and Holland, S. (2009) 'Life story work: reflections on the experience by looked after young people', *Adoption and Fostering*, 33 (4): 44–52

Wilson, A. and Beresford, P. (2000) 'Anti-oppressive practice: emancipation or appropriation', *British Journal of Social Work*, 30 (5): 553–73

Wilson, D. and Moore, S. (2003) 'Playing the Game: The Experiences of Young Black Men in Custody', London: Children's Society

Wilson, G. (2001) *Understanding Old Age*, London: Sage

Wilson, K. (2006) 'Foster family care in the UK', in C. McCauley, P. Pecora and W. Rose (eds) *Enhancing the Well-Being of Children and Families*, London: Jessica Kingsley

Wilson, K. and James, A. (2007) *The Child Protection Handbook*, 3rd edn, Edinburgh: Elsevier/Bailliere Tindall

Wilson, K. and Petrie, S. (1998) 'No place like home: lessons learned and lessons forgotten: the Children Act 1948', *Child and Family Social Work*, 3: 183–8

Wilson, K. and Ryan, V. (2001) 'Helping children by working with their parents in indivdual child therapy', *Child and Family Social Work*, 16 (3)

Wilson, K. and Ryan, V. (2005a) 'Helping parents parent by working with their children in non-directive play therapy', *Child and Family Social Work*

Wilson, K. and Ryan, V. (2005b) *Play Therapy: A Non-Directive Approach for Children and Adolescents*, London: Bailliere Tindall

Wilson, K., Petrie, S. and Sinclair, I. (2003) 'A kind of loving: a model of effective foster care', *British Journal of Social Work*, 33: 991–1003

Wilson, K., Sinclair, I. and Gibbs, I. (2000) 'The trouble with foster care: the impact of stressful events on foster carers', *BJSW* 30: 191–209

Wilson, K., Sinclair, I., Taylor, C., Pithouse, A. and Sellick, C. (2004) *Fostering Success: Conceptualising and Effecting Good Outcomes in Foster Carer: An Exploration of the Research Literature*, SCIE, Bristol: The Policy Press

Wilson, K. V. (2003) 'Intermediate care: from innovation to . . . post mortem?' *Journal of Intermediate Care*, 11 (6): 4–6

Windle, K., Wagland, R., Forder, J., D'Amico, F., Janssen, D. and Wistow, G. (2010) *National Evaluation of Partnership for Older People Projects; Final Report*, University of Kent/London School of Economics/University of Manchester, Personal Social Services Research Unit, accessed on 9 July 2010 at http://www.dh.gov.uk/en/Publicationsandstatistics/PublicationsPolicyAndGuidance/DH_111240

Winnicott, C. (1964a) 'Communicating with children', *Child Care Quarterly Review*, 18 (3): 84–97

Winnicott, C. (1964b) 'The development of self awareness', in J. Kanter (ed.), *Face to Face with Children: The Life and Work of Clare Winnicott*, London: Karnac

Winnicott, D. W. (1965) 'The mentally ill in your caseload', in *The Maturational Processes and the Facilitating Environment*, pp. 217–29, London: The Hogarth Press

Winston, J. and Pakes, F. (2005) *Community Justice: Issues for Probation and Criminal Justice*, Cullompton: Willan

Witz, A. (1992) *Professions and Patriarchy*, London: Routledge

Women's Aid (2009) *About Domestic Violence*, accessed August 11 2010, at www.womensaid.org.uk

Woodhouse, D. and Pengelly, P. (1991) *Anxiety and the Dynamics of Collaboration*, Aberdeen: Aberdeen University Press

Woodroofe, K. (1962) *From Charity to Social Work*, London: Routledge and Kegan Paul

Wootton, B. (1959) *Social Science and Social Pathology*, London: George Allen and Unwin

Wright-Mills, C. (1959) *The Sociological Imagination*. London: Oxford University Press

Wyre, R. (1996) 'The mind of the paedophile', in P. Bibby (ed.) *Organised Abuse: The Current Debate*, Aldershot: Arena/Ashgate

Yang, S. (2005) 'Approaches to child rearing in South Korea', unpublished PhD thesis, University of Nottingham

Yelloly, M. and Henkel, M. (eds) (1995) 'Introduction', in *Learning and Teaching in Social Work: Towards Reflective Practice*, London: Jessica Kingsley

YJB *see* Youth Justice Board

Young, J. and Neil, E. (2009) 'Contact after adoption' in Schofield, G. and Simmonds, J. (2009) (eds) *The Child Placement Handbook*. London: BAAF

Younghusband, E. (1955) 'Conclusion', in C. Morris (ed.) *Social Case-work in Great Britain*, 2nd edn, London: Faber and Faber

Younghusband, E. (1978) *Social Work in Britain: 1950–1975 (Volume 1)*, London: George Allen and Unwin

Youth Justice Board (2001) *Risk and Protective Factors Associated with Youth Crime and Effective Interventions to Prevent it*, London: Youth Justice Board for England and Wales

Youth Justice Board (2004a) 'Race audit and action planning toolkit for youth offending teams' at: www.yjb.gov.uk/en-gb/ (last accessed: 20/09/05)

Youth Justice Board (2004b) *National Standards for Youth Justice*, London: Youth Justice Board for England and Wales at: www.yjb.gov.uk/en-gb/ (last accessed: 20/10/06)

Zirkel, S. and Cantor, N. (1990) 'Personal construal of life tasks: those who struggle for independence', *Journal of Personality and Social Psychology*, 58: 172–85

Glossary

Accountability A recent but now central principle of professional and organisational life in which the decisions, actions, and performance of individuals and teams are considered 'accountable'. Usually, a person's job description describes who in the organisational hierarchy they are accountable to, but often accountability is assumed ultimately to rest with the most senior manager in an organisation or political hierarchy. Arguably, accountability has replaced the concept of professional responsibility, and tends to be used in a rather negative way when things go wrong, and somebody needs to be 'held accountable'.

Action research This is usually held to be an orientation to inquiry rather than strictly a method. It emphasises the collaboration between all those involved in the research project (the researchers *and* those engaged in whatever phenomenon is being examined) so that participants engage in a cycle of action followed by critical reflection. Cooperative inquiry is a means, involving a group of people who share a common concern to develop understanding about a particular phenomenon, through which action research may be carried out.

Analytic deduction This refers to the process of scientific inquiry which assumes that research considers examples of phenomenon which need to be explained (for example, the outcomes of a particular intervention) and develops explanatory hypotheses which then need to be tested against other examples. To begin with, a hypothesis will usually fail to fit all the cases studied and this will lead either to the hypothesis being refined until it does fit them, or to its being abandoned and a new formulation developed.

Anti-discriminatory practice/Anti-oppressive practice Important central principles of modern social work which stress the need to engage with service users on the basis of their position in personal and political power dynamics that may disadvantage, marginalise or oppress them. The dynamics of class, race and racism, disability, and sexual identity in relation to mainstream attitudes and behaviours in society are all relevant to ADP or AOP. Therapeutic or relationship-based work and anti-discriminatory practice should be seen as complementary, but sometimes these perspectives of social work have come into tension.

Approved Mental Health Professional Under the terms of the Mental Health Act 2007 the judgement of an Approved Mental Health Professional (AMHP) is required before an individual can be compulsorily admitted to hospital for treatment. (Under the Mental Health Act 1983 this role as previously restricted to social workers; it can now be filled by members of a number of different professions.) An extended and specialised form of post-qualifying training is required before this role can be fulfilled.

Approved social worker Under the terms of the Mental Health Act 1983 the judgement of an Approved Social Worker (ASW) is required before an individual can be compulsorily admitted to hospital for treatment. An extended and specialised form of post-qualifying training is required before social workers can fulfil this role.

Assessment The process for identifying the needs of individuals and families and reaching decisions on how to intervene.

ASSET The tool developed by the Youth Justice Board which is used by all Youth Offending Teams to assess the risk of further offending by young people.

Attachment An emotional tie developed between a child and a preferred adult (usually a parent who has the main caregiving responsibility) which endures over time, whether or not the caregiver is present. It is distinguished from attachment *behaviour*, which is the outward manifestation of this tie, i.e. 'seeking and maintaining proximity to another individual'.

Authenticity The ability to behave in ways which are true to oneself and one's professional identity.

Autonomy The capacity of individuals to make informed decisions concerning their lives.

Care management A form of practice, popularised in community care policy, where the range of services that are provided to an individual are managed by an individual, the 'care manager'. Many care managers are qualified social workers, although there is debate about the extent to which care management is a continuation of social work.

Carer's assessment A social work assessment of the carer's own needs, the impact of being a carer, their ability to continue to care and what services and interventions can deliver agreed outcomes.

Case study A case study usually consists of a single individual, family or group, or particular events or a specific organisation considered over a given period of time. It can be defined as a phenomenon which can be described and analysed, in order to illustrate experiences and develop principles for policy and/or practice.

Child abuse Harmful acts or behaviours to which children and/or young people, other than accidentally, are subjected by someone inside or outside the home (i.e. intrafamilial or extrafamilial abuse). The four categories of child abuse (maltreatment) currently used in the UK are: physical abuse, emotional abuse, sexual abuse and neglect, including non-organic failure to thrive.

Child protection register (previously known as child abuse/'at risk' registers). A system of identifying in each local authority those children who were officially recorded as requiring protection from child maltreatment and for whom services are provided. In the UK, these registers have been in existence for over 30 years and provided an annual measure of the incidence of child abuse, but are now being replaced by a new electronic record, the Integrated Child System, on which one or more categories of physical or emotional abuse or neglect may be recorded.

Code of ethics A formal set of guidelines designed to set out ways in which researchers should behave in conducting the research, in accordance with ethically acceptable practice.

Cognitive–behavioural approach A way of understanding and working with problems derived from cognitive and behavioural theories.

Cognitive psychology An approach which emphasises internal, mental processes such as thinking, mental representations, language, reasoning, etc.

Collaboration This term refers to two activities – the process of working together to establish a *partnership* and the process of working together to achieve the desired outcomes of a *partnership*. The development of

collaborative working will necessarily entail close *inter-professional* working.

Common Assessment Framework An assessment tool developed by the Department for Education and Skills in 2004 for use by all agencies with responsibilities for children, with the aim of recording concerns at an early stage and having children with 'additional needs' for support referred to the appropriate specialist or targeted service.

Community care This has two meanings; (a) used generally, it refers to a policy whereby preference is given to the maintenance of people in the community rather than in institutional care; (b) used more specifically, it refers to the range of policies brought about in England, Wales and Scotland following the passage of the National Health Service and Community Care Act 1990.

Community development An orientation to social work that focuses on the development of the ability of communities to respond to the problems that they encounter. In the history of social work it is usually contrasted with individually-oriented practice.

Community Safety Partnerships (CSPs) *see* **Crime and Disorder Reduction Partnerships**

Consumer research *see* **Service user or consumer research**

Cooperative inquiry *see* **Action research**

Counter transference The feelings and reactions stirred up in someone about their own past experiences by the feelings directed on to them by another person (*see* **Transference**).

Crime and Disorder Reduction Partnerships (CDRPs) or Community Safety Partnerships (CSPs) in Wales are statutory partnerships which ensure that key agencies come together to work in partnership in a CDRP/CSP, and carry out an audit of local crime, disorder and misuse of drugs every three years. Using the information arising from this audit and based on consultation with local communities, they then formulate a strategy for combating crime, disorder and the misuse of drugs in the local area.

Crisis Any transitory situation in which a person's usual coping mechanisms are no longer adequate to deal with the experiences involved; an 'upset in a steady state'.

Crisis theory Derives from the view that the experience of crisis challenges a person's normal equilibrium (sometimes described as 'homeostasis' or a 'steady state') and that this very challenge generates energy which can provide the opportunity for developing more successful ways of dealing with experiences than before.

Data These are the raw material, i.e. the information, which has been collected and which can be stored and analysed using one or more techniques, in order to produce research findings or outputs.

Defence mechanism A term used in psychodynamic theory to denote the psychological process whereby individuals maintain a sense of their own self-worth and protect themselves from painful feelings. Defence mechanisms include denial, projection, idealisation, displacement, splitting and passive–aggressive behaviours.

Dementia Dementia is the progressive decline in cognitive function due to damage or disease in the brain beyond what might be expected from normal ageing. Although not exclusively so, it is a disease closely linked to ageing.

Developmental milestones Significant behaviours which are used to mark, and which signal, the progress of development, e.g. walking is a milestone in locomotor development.

Developmental psychology The field of psychology which is concerned with the lifelong process of change, i.e. any qualitative or quantitative change which involves alterations in structure and function.

Direct payments The essential basis of direct payments is that money is given directly to service users, enabling them to organise their own care services rather than those services being mediated by a local authority.

Direct work A way of working with children that involves face-to-face sessions and uses play-based activities and exercises to help a child explore and understand her/his circumstances.

Drug Action Teams/Drug and Alcohol Action Teams Drug action teams (**DATs**) or Drug and Alcohol Action Teams (**DAATs**) are the multi-agency partnerships working to implement the National Drug Strategy at a local level, taking strategic decisions on expenditure and service delivery within the four aims of the National Drugs Strategy: treatment, young people, communities and supply. The DATs/DAATs ensure that the work of local agencies is brought together effectively and that cross-agency projects are coordinated successfully.

Early Intervention A principle now widely informing service delivery in health and social care that emphasises the importance of intervening positively at an early point in the development of social, psychological, interpersonal or social difficulties. Early intervention services in adult mental health have been a particular focus of recent policy development. Early intervention has to some extent replaced the concept of 'prevention'.

Ecomap A tool used with children to help them identify and understand their network of relationships.

Empathy The ability to understand how someone else is feeling; to be able 'to stand in someone else's shoes'.

Enabling authority Under community care policy local authorities were expected to move away from their position of near-monopolistic service provision to act as enabling authorities, increasingly stimulating the independent sector to provide the services. It is argued that this step helped to ensure that services are most responsive to the needs of people and are provided in a more competitive and hence cost-effective manner.

Essentialism A way of thinking that reduces complex social and psychological factors to a hidden 'essence' that is held to explain the way people are. Essentialist positions tend to be used conservatively, in order to assert that a characteristic of a person or group is beyond change because it resides in their essence. Progressive social theory, and social work theory, is always 'anti-essentialist'.

Evidence-based/evidence-informed policy and practice The development and implementation of policy and practice based on the best evidence available, including that from research and other sources such as the views of service users, professionals and other stakeholders.

Exchange model A way of working with service users that recognises and respects the different expertise professionals and service users can contribute to a problem.

Family systems approaches Approaches to working with troubled families, derived from systems theory, which see the family as an interactive system, and which focus predominantly on working with the interactions between family members.

Framework for the Assessment of Children in Need and their Families The standard tool, established by the Department of Health in 2000, for identifying need and informing decisions about services and support.

Genericism The principle that there is a common foundation to all social work practice; from this principle can develop a preference for social workers to respond to all types of social difficulty. In Britain, the peak period for generic social work was the 1970s.

Genogram A technical word for a family tree and used as a means of helping families identify significant family members and how they relate to one another.

Governance This may be seen as the system of principles and practices to guarantee purposeful and cooperative working among diverse organisations all of whom are pursuing a common aim or agenda. On this model, governance may be the means by which an inter-organisational and multi-professional system releases all the creativity and potential it contains. An alternative understanding argues that governance is used by traditional government organisations to control policy and practice in the new, more complex and devolved systems of cooperation that now deliver social work and other public services.

Harm reduction Harm reduction approaches prioritise reducing the negative effects of drug use over eliminating drug use or helping people stop their drug use. A focus on reducing harm rather than drug use, although harm reduction approaches retain the ultimate goal of helping people become drug free (because no drug use usually means no drug-related harm); responses are based on the idea that where this is not practicable, the priority is to reduce risks to the individual and society.

Independent living (disabled children and adults) Reflects the principle that disabled people have control and choice over their own lives and are able to enjoy the same civil rights as non-disabled people.

Individual model of disability A model which stems from the view that the difficulties disabled people face are a direct consequence of their impairment. The solution to this lies in medical and social welfare services helping people to 'fit into' society.

Informal care Care that is personally directed and is given free of charge by virtue of a relationship based on love, attachment, family obligation, duty or friendship.

Informal family carer People who provide care, support or supervision, on an unpaid basis, to relatives or friends who need help because of age, physical or learning disability or illness, including mental illness or substance misuse.

Interim care Interim care is the period of care between leaving hospital and an individual taking up a more permanent option. This can either be due to the need for some rehabilitative work, or because an individual's preferred assessed option is not yet available.

Inter-professional We use this term to describe the working together of two or more professionals, implying that there is some level of *collaboration* between them. Therefore, we would characterise the work that was required in our introductory case study as needing some level of inter-professional activity, for example, between the social worker, district nurse and community psychiatric nurse.

Justice approaches In contrast to **welfare approaches**, justice approaches have included the view that young people should be subject to formal judicial processes, where their rights before the law can be maintained, but can also lead to punishment-based outcomes.

Learning disability/difficulty People with an intellectual impairment (formerly called mental handicap, which is now seen as a derogatory label).

Learning theory A theory of development which emphasises the role of learning, including modelling and conditioned responses to stimuli, in development.

Literature review is a compilation which summarises the existing literature (such as research studies, government documents, etc.) in order to give a kind of 'state of the art' view of a particular topic, i.e. it provides an assessment of what is known about the issue through a description and analysis of the existing literature on it.

Local Safeguarding Children Boards Boards which local authority children's services are required by statute to establish, with responsibility for coordinating the work of key agencies in relation to child protection.

Looked-after children Children who cannot for a variety of reasons remain safely at home and are placed, on either a voluntary ('accommodated') or statutory basis, in the care of their local authority. Children may variously be described as being placed 'in care' or in 'out-of-home' care.

Managerialism This refers to an ideology – prevalent within the New Public Management – that more effective and powerful forms of management will resolve a wide range of social and economic problems.

Marketisation The process via which public services are increasingly delivered in the context of competitive market conditions, or 'quasi-markets'. The relationship between commissioning and providing reflects the structure of such markets, and the requirement to tender competitively for the delivery of services shows how no organisation is completely secure about its position within the local economy of welfare: a service provided today may be lost tomorrow in a competitive tender as a result of failure to achieve.

Mixed economy of welfare Under community care policy, a mixed economy of welfare is presumed to feature a combination of public services, private services and services provided by not-for-profit agencies. The variety of types of welfare provision is what makes it a 'mixed economy'.

Modernism Understanding of society as being characterised by belief in a single objective and scientific truth, informed by large-scale theoretical frameworks.

Multi-agency This term describes the involvement of two or more agencies in work that bears on the welfare of service users. As the term implies, *multi-agency* working focuses on the work of the organisations rather than on the practice of individual workers.

Multi-disciplinary This term is used when representatives of different disciplines and agencies are brought together, for example in community mental health or learning disability teams. A *multi-disciplinary* approach should foster *inter-professional* working, but cannot guarantee it. In the earlier case study, multi-disciplinary working was indicated between representatives of various agencies – social services, health, housing, the independent sector, etc.

Networking An approach to intervention, derived from systems thinking which sees the total system (service users, carers, professionals and community) potentially as the case system to be worked with.

Neurosis Mental health difficulties characterised by psychological conflict, anxiety, panic or obsessional behaviour but normally within a more intact personality or sense of self than in the psychoses.

New Public Management The New Public Management is a disparate set of practices through which the transformation of management within the public domain was to be transformed from the administrative-bureaucratic model that had prevailed into the 1980s (see Hood, 1991).

Non-verbal communication All forms of communication that do not rely on words, most commonly referred to as body language.

Normative or typical development General changes and reorganisations in behaviour which virtually all children share as they grow older.

Open questions Asking questions in such a way that it allows the respondent to decide what to include in their reply, e.g. 'How are you?' as opposed to a closed question which would ask 'Are you well?'

Operant conditioning A term used in cognitive–behavioural interventions to describe the way in which behaviour is changed by changes in the environment so that the behaviour becomes more and more likely to occur.

Outcome A visible or practical product, effect or result. The desired end result and intended improvement after a specified period. The impact, effect or consequence of a particular service intervention.

Outcome (for carers) The changes or benefits for carers and their families resulting from social work or other interventions or services.

Paraphrasing Providing a response to someone in such a way that it restates to the speaker what they have said in a simpler and shorter format.

Parenting orders/classes Introduced in the Crime and Disorder Act 1998, Parenting Orders can be made in respect of the parent(s) or guardian(s) of children who are (a) under 10 and subject to a child safety order; (b) between 10 and 17 and subject to an antisocial behaviour order or a sex offender order; (c) convicted of a criminal offence. A parenting order may also be imposed where a person fails to comply with a school attendance order or fails to secure regular attendance at school of a registered pupil. The effect of a parenting order is that the parent or guardian will be expected to comply with the requirements specified in it for a maximum of 12 months and may also be required to attend weekly classes for counselling or guidance sessions for a maximum of three months.

Partnership This term is deployed when two or more agencies have established formal arrangements that enable them to work together. Therefore, a *partnership* is an outcome of collaborative processes, and could not be developed without close *collaboration*. For organisations involved in *inter-professional* working, the development of a partnership may be a desired end. However, successful *inter-professional* working can develop without the requirement of formal partnership arrangements, although they are encouraged in both legislation and policy.

Personalisation The principle underpinning contemporary social care policy, where it is framed in accordance with the wishes and preferences of each individual.

Person-centred planning The process of life planning for individuals, based on the principles of rights, choice and inclusion.

Positivism An approach to understanding knowledge that believes it is an objective phenomenon, governed by universal laws and discovered through empirical research.

Post-modernism An influential form of social theory, arguing that there have been profound changes in the organisation of society such that many of the 'truths' that have characterised our lives are no longer applicable. In social work terms this has led to a questioning of the essential nature and purpose of the occupation, and a renewed sense of the plurality of meanings that can be attributed to every encounter, according to perspective (see Howe, 1994).

Power In social work, particularly concerns *inequalities* of power, especially the limited capacity of service users to make decisions concerning their own lives, in contrast to the considerable capacity of others – specifically social workers – to make such decisions.

Practical moral knowledge Knowledge that is relative and subjective, understood to be constructed in response to specific situations.

Pre-Sentence Report Reports prepared by the Youth Offending Teams to provide background information on the young person, and importantly, on their attitudes towards the offence, and the effects on victims, at the end of which the report writer makes suggestions for possible orders to be made by the court.

Professional There is a distinction between two uses of the term; the sociological use of the term focuses on the extent to which an occupation can be defined as a profession, and hence that its members can in turn be defined as professionals. In this analysis, professions are usually self-regulating, and require a high level of educational attainment (usually at least to undergraduate level) to enter them. It is presumed that the professional has a distinct knowledge base, and is the possessor of unique sets of skill. A more common usage focuses on the skill of professionals, or on the fact that they carry out tasks for financial reward – the distinction between professional and amateur footballers, for example. It is the sociological perspective that is deployed here.

Professionalisation The process by which an occupation seeks to become accepted as a profession, by establishing a legally restricted title, extended forms of qualifying and post-qualification education at least at graduate level, a professional association, etc. Within social work there has been clear steps in this direction in recent years, yet the process has also been historically controversial.

Psychoanalysis (a) A theory of human behaviour, typically used to refer to the theories propounded by Sigmund Freud, although it may also be used to refer to related dynamic theories such as that of Carl Jung. (b) A set of techniques for exploring the underlying components of human behaviour, and a method of treating various mental disorders.

Psychologising Closely associated with 'structural' critiques and perspectives in social work, psychologising is the reduction of complex social, political or psychosocial explanations for people's difficulties to factors located entirely in their individual psychology or mental functioning.

Psychosis One of the major categories of mental health difficulty, in which there are disturbances to core mental functions: perception, feeling, thinking. Psychotic conditions are often contrasted with neurotic conditions and personality disorders.

Psychosocial The interface between an individual's internal psychological world and their external social world.

Psychosocial perspectives Psychosocial perspectives in social work and related disciplines emphasise the importance of bringing together sociological and psychological ways of understanding people, relationships, and trends in society. Psychosocial theorists are always 'interdisciplinary' in their approach, often combining traditions of thinking and research in unusual and surprising ways in order to open up new and creative spaces for thinking about people, and solutions to social, personal and interpersonal problems.

Qualitative research A research method which focuses on meanings and experiences, through which the research attempts to understand the lives of those being studied, their behaviour, values, beliefs and so on, from the perspectives of the people themselves. Typically, the approach of the investigation is relatively unstructured so that the research is more likely to reveal the individuals' meanings and experiences rather than impose the researchers' perspectives. Types of data collected include: semi-structured interviews, observational recordings, focus groups and illustrative vignettes.

Quantitative research A research method which emphasises the measurement of prior concepts and uses indicators to act as measures which can stand for or point towards underlying concepts. The method typically uses variables (attributes on which people or things may be distinguished) as a means of measuring the dimensions on which people differ from or resemble one another in order to demonstrate causal relationships between variables. (i.e. what factors influence people's behaviour, attitudes and beliefs.)

Questionnaire A research instrument (tool) used to collect information from a respondent.

Radical social work A form of social work that developed in opposition to the psychologically-oriented individual casework that predominated at the time (the late 1960s/ early 1970s). It adopted a more political focus and explicitly sought to change the fundamental nature of society more than affect the lives of isolated individuals.

Randomised controlled trial Research in which subjects are allocated randomly between treatment and comparison groups.

Reference manager Computer applications designed to hold and manipulate details of references and the bibliography.

Reflective practice The ability to draw on a diverse range of knowledge, from both formal and informal sources, to inform professional practice.

Reflexivity Generally associated with research practice, reflexivity refers to the ability to be critically self-reflective and to identify personal biases that influence the research process.

Reinforcers A term used in cognitive-behavioural interventions to describe the things done in response to behaviour which may serve to strengthen the behaviour and make it likely it will happen again.

Relationship-based practice An approach that ensures the professional relationship is at the centre of all interventions and that attention is paid to the interpersonal dynamics of professional encounters.

Respect The ability to convey to someone that they are unique and valued.

Restorative justice This is a means of making victims' interests central to ways of dealing with crimes and their effects, which the formal criminal justice process, with its emphasis on due process, cannot do. It aims to provide a safe forum for victims where they can set out how they have been affected by the offender's crime, and confronts the latter with the effects of his/her actions. The process attempts to give the victim the opportunity to receive an apology or other form of reparation which is more personal and meaningful than is possible in the courts. At the same time, the offender is able to appreciate the impact of her/his actions and take responsibility for them.

Role A goal-directed pattern of behaviour carried out by a person in a particular societal situation or within a group because both the group and the individual expect this kind of behaviour.

Schizophrenia A mental disorder which can involve various cognitive, emotional and behavioural features, such as hallucinations, thought disorders or delusions. Literally the term means 'splitting in the mind'.

Schizophrenogenic Pertains to any factor (such as a cold but dominating parent) hypothesised to be causally related to the development of schizophrenia.

Service user The term currently deployed for those people who use social services, or are eligible for such services.

Service user or consumer research Research which gathers the views of the users of services and is designed to provide information about the needs of individuals and communities and feedback about how a particular service or intervention is experienced by its recipients.

Short breaks service A service that provides a break for disabled children and adults and their parents or carers. The services can range from befriending or sitting, through to overnight stays and can be provided either in the person's own home or another place.

Single case designs A form of qualitative research which seeks to identify critical features in a particular case by close scrutiny of it and by understanding these, to collect data which can then be tested with other cases in order to build a picture of processes and outcomes.

Social action A type of practice recommended by the radical social work movement, often associated with community development. It shares similar characteristics in that it is collectively rather than individually-oriented; as the name implies, it takes a more positive and oppositional stance in relation to the basic structures of society. (However, note that the term 'social action' has been co-opted by the coalition government in relation to the development of the Big Society.)

Social anxieties Collective states of anxiety about social trends or events. Anxieties may be 'reality based' or significantly rooted in collective fantasies. Research into crime rates in the community often show that actual levels of crime and fears about crime are inconsistent with one another. Thus, social anxieties may drive or shape policy development in a matter that is more irrational than rational.

Social construction Associated with post-modern thinking, socially constructed phenomenon, social constructs and social constructionism reflect the fragmented, partial and multiple nature of reality.

Social construction of childhood The way in which views of childhood are shaped by the perspectives and concerns of the particular societies in which people live.

Social model of disability A model that sees the person as being disabled by the way in which physical and social environments create barriers to participating as full members of society and enjoying all the benefits this brings.

Social pedagogue A social pedagogue operates in an area of the welfare state to increase personal responsibility and self-dependent handling of common circumstances of life. In addition, a social pedagogue seeks to minimise the impact of all forms of discrimination and to promote the social skills that enable people to take part in society.

Social theory A means of explaining the nature of society and the consequent approach to responding to social problems. In the early days of social work, both the COS and the Settlement Movement had a clear social theory, and the different form of practice they espoused derived directly from this.

Socio-cultural theory A theory of development which emphasises the part played by social interaction and cultural practices on cognitive development.

Specialisation The principle that social workers should specialise in a single area of activity rather than become expert in a wide range. There are gradations of specialisation; for example, within the specialist area of child care

social work a practitioner may further specialise in adoption and fostering or child protection.

Structural factors in society Patterns of social life such as persistent inequality affecting particular groups or communities that significantly impact upon or determine the 'life chances' of individuals within those groups. Structural social work tends to be critical of social work practices and strategies that focus too much upon the individual and their responsibility for their circumstances, when their difficulties are explicable as a consequence of membership of a community or group that is affected by structural factors in society.

Structured day programmes Following the introduction of the NHS and Community Care Act in 1993 which had major consequences for the provision of residential care for drug users, many services reacted by developing structured day programmes **(SDPs)**. A holistic approach to rehabilitation is adopted, promoting: life skills and vocational training; sessions on building and restoring independence and responsibility; and helping maintain drug users' links with their families and social support networks. Some SDPs also employ a rolling programme of activities which allow individual clients to negotiate a customised timetable for their rehabilitation. Some programmes also accommodate drug free and current problem drug users.

Task-centred practice A planned, short-term time-limited intervention in which service users and practitioners agree on the specific problems to be worked on.

Technical rational knowledge Knowledge which is absolute and objective in nature, and explicable in terms of clear cause-and-effect relationships.

Theory of mind An understanding, which begins to develop in a rudimentary way between the ages of two or three, that others see and experience the world differently.

Tiered models of care Services for drug and alcohol users have been arranged into four tiers following publication, by the NTA, of Models of Care 2002 – updated in 2006. Tier 1 interventions include provision of drug-related information and advice, screening and referral to specialised drug treatment, and are provided in the context of general health-care settings, where the main focus is not drug treatment. Tier 2 interventions include provision of drug-related information and advice, triage assessment, referral to structured drug treatment, brief psychosocial interventions, harm reduction interventions (including needle exchange) and aftercare. Tier 2 interventions may be delivered separately from Tier 3 but will often also be delivered in the same setting and by the same staff as Tier 3 interventions. Tier 3 interventions include provision of community-based specialised drug assessment and coordinated care-planned treatment and drug specialist liaison. Tier 3 interventions are normally delivered in specialised drug treatment services with their own premises in the community or on hospital sites. Other delivery may be by outreach (peripatetic work in generic services or other agencies or domiciliary or home visits). Tier 4 interventions include provision of residential specialised drug treatment, which is care-planned and care-coordinated to ensure continuity of care and aftercare.

Transference The capacity of past experiences of significant relationships to be transferred into current relationships with other people. A psychodynamic concept referring to the process in which one person 'transfers' feelings and images from their own inner life onto someone else, who they then treat as if they were this 'figure' from their own internal mental life.

Unconscious mind That area of the mind which is not conscious but which acts as a kind of reservoir of experiences, and is involved in our decision-making, activities and choices.

Universalism The principle that services should be available to all. The NHS was established on universalist principles, whereas social services in Britain have always been selective.

Vignette A brief story illustrating an experience or event (for example, a parent's chastisement of a disobedient child) which respondents are then asked to discuss and reflect on. They are a means of helping elicit more consistent information about respondents' feelings or attitudes, or helping them explore something which might be difficult for them to consider spontaneously or to discuss if they were asked to recall a personal experience.

Vulnerable older people In order to be considered to be vulnerable, older people must be at risk of some harm – whether physical, emotional, psychological or financial – due to their advanced age and the heath and social circumstances that characterise that age.

Welfare approaches: young offenders Assessment and intervention strategies designed to respond to young people who commit crimes, derived to a large extent from psychodynamic approaches and family systems based approaches. There have been various formulations of welfare approaches, including at times, a concentration on what were viewed (and by some still are) as supposed deficits in parents' socialisation of their children. Such views led to intervention strategies which looked at treatment both within and outside of the family to rectify such identified deficits. This approach often took the view that interventions should happen outside the judicial system, for example by cautioning young people, residential treatment, etc.

Whole-systems approaches A perspective on social work intervention and analysis of complex situations that emphasises the need for the practitioner to maintain a focus on the interaction between all members of the 'system' that constitutes the case or problem situation. The identified service user, extended family, carers, and the variety of professional systems which may be involved all combine to produce a whole system.

Young carer Children and young persons under 18 who provide care, assistance or support to another family member. They carry out, often on a regular basis, significant or substantial caring tasks and assume a level of responsibility that would usually be associated with an adult.

Young offender Within England and Wales, a young person is held to be criminally liable for their actions at the age of 10 upwards. At one time services under legislation and policy were closely aligned between children in need and young offenders, but in recent years legislation and policy have made these areas very different.

Youth justice system The different agencies and professionals that can become involved with the young person who offends: for example, the different courts, prisons, youth offending institutions, secure training centres, and the professional groups such as social workers, probation officers, police, magistrates and judges.

Youth offending team A multidisciplinary team typically comprising social workers, probation officers, Connexions workers, police, and possibly mental health counsellors, educational staff and professional assistants. The government requires that such teams are the direct responsibility of the chief executive of the local authority in whose area they reside, although they are often managed by someone within the equivalent of the social services department. The prime duty of such teams is to prevent offending, and they are responsible for services to courts, young people on court orders, and young people in custody, as well as preventive work for young people who are subject, for example, to Youth Inclusion and Support Programmes.

Index

MORE KEY TEXTBOOKS FROM PEARSON EDUCATION

2011
ISBN: 9781408224434

UNDERSTANDING
SOCIAL WORK
ETHICS

Annie Pullen &
Stephen Cowden

2010
ISBN: 9781405847391

SIOBHAN E. LAIRD

PRACTICAL
SOCIALWORK
LAW

ANALYSING COURT CASES AND INQUIRIES

'One of the best social work law books I have come across'

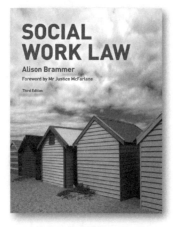

2009
ISBN: 9781405873376

SOCIAL
WORK LAW

Alison Brammer

Foreword by Mr Justice McFarlane

Third Edition

2010
ISBN: 9781405858502

Bob Matthews and Liz Ross

RESEARCH METHODS

A practical guide for the
social sciences

"A welcome and invaluable
addition to the literature."
Professor Saul Becker,
University of Nottingham

2009
ISBN: 9781405858366

Second Edition

Social Policy
Themes, Issues and Debates

Hugh Bochel
Catherine Bochel
Robert Page
Robert Sykes

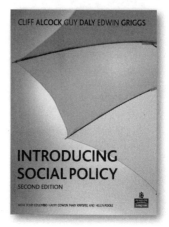

2008
ISBN: 9781405858489

CLIFF ALCOCK GUY DALY EDWIN GRIGGS

INTRODUCING
SOCIAL POLICY

SECOND EDITION

WITH TONY COLOMBO HARRY COWEN PARIY KNYSPEL HELEN POOLE

For further information or to order these books, please visit:
www.pearsoned.co.uk

SOCIAL WOR~

Endorsements for the first edition:

'This is a ground breaking, exciting new textbook for students of social work and their teachers . . . The authors have achieved a beautifully written, thorough exploration of contemporary social work practice . . . As a social worker educator working with students across the spectrum, from qualifying to professional doctorate level, I wholeheartedly welcome this invigorating new social work text. I have no doubt that this completed work represents a crucial milestone in social work education . . . The level is suitable for qualifying courses at undergraduate and Master's level and for those registered for post qualifying social work awards.'   **Clare Parkinson, Senior Lecturer in Social Work, University of East London**

'This is an ambitious and very impressive book which will make a valuable and significant contribution. Kate Wilson and her colleagues have produced an exhaustive introduction for any student studying social work and preparing to become a social worker. However, it is more than this, in that we are provided with a detailed and serious book which is explicitly located in an increasingly important orientation – relationship-based reflective approaches. This is not simply an introductory summary and tour of the field, but provides students with a clear framework and foundation for locating their practice through the rest of their studies, future training and professional careers.'

Nigel Parton, NSPCC Professor in Applied Childhood Studies, University of Huddersfield

'I am enthusiastic about this book and very much welcome its appearance. Relationship-based social work, if not exactly out-of-fashion, has been greatly undervalued in recent years. These authors put relationships at "the heart" of practice and make a compelling case for a relationship-based approach to social work, an approach that includes developing reflective practice. The approach is then applied with great skill and expertise to the full range of social work's interests and concerns – values, assessment, communication, planning, intervention, and work with children, families, disabled children and adults, adults with mental health problems, and vulnerable older people. A key text, an excellent read, and highly recommended.'   **Professor David Howe, University of East Anglia, Norwich**

'Recent concerns about risk and accountability in social work have resulted in increasingly managerial and mechanistic practice, dominated by a proliferation of targets, tick-boxes, and assessment frameworks. In the process, the relationship between service-user and social worker has been devalued and marginalised. This book, written by a team of leading social work academics, therefore comes as a breath of fresh air – by placing relationships once more at the heart of social work practice, it provides a much-needed antidote to such reductionist trends whilst also meeting the needs of students in the context of modern social work education.'

Professor Adrian James, Department of Sociological Studies, University of Sheffield

'I found this text interesting and user friendly. It clearly explains the theoretical context and usefully links it to practice in a way that will enable students and newly qualified social workers to integrate theory and research to their own practice. The use of case studies and thought provokers engages the reader and helps make the topic relevant to their own experience. I will certainly use this text with social work students on placement and newly qualified social workers.'   **Dawn Maxwell, Children's Services and Learning Directorate, Southampton City Council**

'*Social Work: An Introduction to Contemporary Practice* is an important and immediately useful text for social work practitioners and learners at both pre and post qualifying stages. This book provides clear explanation and illustration of a comprehensive range of social work themes and areas of practice and is informed by a wealth of contemporary social work research and literature. Any social work learner with a limited book budget should view this text as an extremely worthwhile investment.'   **Teresa de Villiers, Social Work Tutor, Cardiff University**

'This is a useful introductory text which provides opportunity for beginning social work students to consider a range of issues that have influenced, and impact, on contemporary professional practice.'

Judy Kerr, Teaching Fellow in Social Work, University of Stirling

Visit the *Social Work: An introduction to contemporary practice*, companion website at **www.pearsoned.co.uk/wilsonruch** to find valuable learning material, including:

- Links to interactive and virtual learning materials including those produced for the Learning Exchange of the Institute of Research and Innovation in Social Services (IRISS), and further developed by Neil Ballantyne.